FEDERAL INCOME TAXATION OF CORPORATIONS AND PARTNERSHIPS

Aspen Casebook Series

FEDERAL INCOME TAXATION OF CORPORATIONS AND PARTNERSHIPS

Fifth Edition

RICHARD L. DOERNBERG
K. H. Gyr Professor of Law Emeritus
Emory University School of Law

HOWARD E. ABRAMS
William K Jacobs, Jr. Visiting Professor
Harvard Law School
Warren Distinguished Professor
University of San Diego School of Law

DON A. LEATHERMAN
W. Allen Separk Distinguished Professor of Law
University of Tennessee College of Law

Wolters Kluwer
Law & Business

Published by Wolters Kluwer Law & Business in New York.

Wolters Kluwer Law & Business serves customers worldwide with CCH, Aspen Publishers, and Kluwer Law International products. (www.wolterskluwerlb.com)

To contact Customer Service, e-mail customer.service@wolterskluwer.com, call 1-800-234-1660, fax 1-800-901-9075, or mail correspondence to:

Wolters Kluwer Law & Business
Attn: Order Department
PO Box 990
Frederick, MD 21705

Printed in the United States of America.

1 2 3 4 5 6 7 8 9 0

ISBN 978-1-4548-2480-0

Library of Congress Cataloging-in-Publication Data

Doernberg, Richard L., author.
Federal income taxation of corporations and partnerships / Richard L. Doernberg, K. H. Gyr Professor of Law Emeritus, Emory University School of Law, Howard E. Abrams, William K Jacobs, Jr. Visiting Professor, Harvard Law School, Warren Distinguished Professor, University of San Diego School of Law, Don A. Leatherman, W. Allen Separk Distinguished Professor of Law, University of Tennessee, College of Law. — Fifth edition.
pages cm. — (Aspen casebook series)
Includes bibliographical references and index.
ISBN 978-1-4548-2480-0 (casebound : alk. paper)
1. Corporations — Taxation — Law and legislation — United States — Cases. 2. Partnership — Taxation — United States — Cases. I. Abrams, Howard E., 1955- author. II. Leatherman, Don A., 1953- author. III. Title.
KF6464.D64 2013
343.7305′267—dc23

2013038664

About Wolters Kluwer Law & Business

Wolters Kluwer Law & Business is a leading global provider of intelligent information and digital solutions for legal and business professionals in key specialty areas, and respected educational resources for professors and law students. Wolters Kluwer Law & Business connects legal and business professionals as well as those in the education market with timely, specialized authoritative content and information-enabled solutions to support success through productivity, accuracy and mobility.

Serving customers worldwide, Wolters Kluwer Law & Business products include those under the Aspen Publishers, CCH, Kluwer Law International, Loislaw, ftwilliam.com and MediRegs family of products.

CCH products have been a trusted resource since 1913, and are highly regarded resources for legal, securities, antitrust and trade regulation, government contracting, banking, pension, payroll, employment and labor, and healthcare reimbursement and compliance professionals.

Aspen Publishers products provide essential information to attorneys, business professionals and law students. Written by preeminent authorities, the product line offers analytical and practical information in a range of specialty practice areas from securities law and intellectual property to mergers and acquisitions and pension/benefits. Aspen's trusted legal education resources provide professors and students with high-quality, up-to-date and effective resources for successful instruction and study in all areas of the law.

Kluwer Law International products provide the global business community with reliable international legal information in English. Legal practitioners, corporate counsel and business executives around the world rely on Kluwer Law journals, looseleafs, books, and electronic products for comprehensive information in many areas of international legal practice.

Loislaw is a comprehensive online legal research product providing legal content to law firm practitioners of various specializations. Loislaw provides attorneys with the ability to quickly and efficiently find the necessary legal information they need, when and where they need it, by facilitating access to primary law as well as state-specific law, records, forms and treatises.

ftwilliam.com offers employee benefits professionals the highest quality plan documents (retirement, welfare and non-qualified) and government forms (5500/PBGC, 1099 and IRS) software at highly competitive prices.

MediRegs products provide integrated health care compliance content and software solutions for professionals in healthcare, higher education and life sciences, including professionals in accounting, law and consulting.

Wolters Kluwer Law & Business, a division of Wolters Kluwer, is headquartered in New York. Wolters Kluwer is a market-leading global information services company focused on professionals.

To Dania and Elizabeth

DAL

SUMMARY OF CONTENTS

CONTENTS

21
A Partner's Outside Basis 653

22
Nonliquidating Distributions 681

PREFACE

This book traces its ancestry back to Professor Bittker's one-volume Federal Income Taxation casebook, published in 1955. Over the years, Congress has amended virtually every section of the Internal Revenue Code, almost always in the direction of greater complexity. Professor Bittker's original work has split three-for-one into separate volumes on individual, transfer, and corporate taxation. With the increasing importance of partnership taxation in the world of commerce, the third edition combined both corporate and partnership taxation in a single volume and this fifth edition continues that combination. The fifth edition includes substantial revisions to account for recent changes in the law. It can be used to teach corporate taxation, partnership taxation, or a course that combines both areas.

Ironically, the increasing complexity demands a more principled and straightforward treatment of teaching materials than ever before. It is neither possible nor desirable in an introductory course on business taxation to tame the sea of minutiae that now comprise subchapters C, K, and S. Instead, we hope to offer a thoughtful and orderly presentation of the themes that permeate the taxation of business entities, allowing readers to develop the sophistication necessary to confront new challenges in the practice of law.

We have updated every chapter of the book, interspersing new examples and problems throughout and substantially reworking some of the chapters. Recent legislative and administrative developments have been integrated into the discussion. New cases and rulings have been added where helpful, and outdated cases and rulings removed. We have tried to choose illustrative cases that not only describe typical commercial transactions but also emphasize major themes that run through the provisions dealing with entity taxation. We believe that the book can be covered in a three- or four-hour integrated course, or can be used for separate two- or three-hour courses on corporate or partnership taxation.

The taxation of business entities is a difficult subject even under the best of circumstances, and we have tried not to "hide the ball." In most chapters, we begin with a broad overview, and each chapter makes liberal use of examples. We have no doubt that, notwithstanding our approach, students will be left with plenty to ponder. We have tried to clear away some of the underbrush so that students can contemplate the forest. In addition to the cases and note materials, the book features problems in almost every chapter. They can be used to lead students through the fundamentals of the tax provisions and can form a centerpiece for discussion of the cases and notes.

In exploring the tax consequences of business entities, the fifth edition is divided into three parts. Part I deals with the classical double tax system: tax at the corporate level, and tax at the shareholder level, embodied in subchapter C. Bridging Parts I and III is Part II's discussion of subchapter S, which contains elements of both subchapters C and K. Part III addresses the pass-through paradigm of partnership taxation laid out in subchapter K, where partners are taxed directly as the partnership earns income.

Each part unfolds in a manner calculated to help students master the concepts within. Part I uses a "cradle-to-grave" approach to reveal the mysteries of subchapter C. Starting with the formation of a corporation, including the capital structure, this part discusses the tax implications of corporate operation at the corporate level. Next, nonliquidating distributions are considered, followed by liquidating distributions. This part also considers the world of taxable and nontaxable corporate acquisitions and other reorganizations. It concludes with several chapters on important aspects of corporate operation, including a section on consolidated returns.

Part II first looks at the operation of S corporations with no subchapter C history. It then turns to the treatment of S corporations that had previously been or subsequently become C corporations, considering issues that arise because of that change in status.

Part III explains the taxation of partnerships. Starting with the structure of partnership taxation, this part turns to the seminal issue in partnership taxation — determining distributive shares. It then discusses the treatment of distributions, outside basis, a partner's transactions with the partnership, acquisition and disposition of partnership interests, and a variety of partnership-level issues.

Students of taxation must possess an eye-hand coordination not required of other students. Not only must they read and study the casebook, but at the same time they must closely examine the Internal Revenue Code and corresponding regulations. The ability to digest two or more things at the same time is a residual benefit one receives from the study of taxation. The book refers to the Code constantly, and we rely on students to study the Code as they study the book.

A few ministerial comments are in order at this point. First, the book makes ample use of cross-references because tax provisions do not operate in a vacuum. As students learn more and more pieces of the tax puzzle, the pieces will begin to interrelate and form a pattern. Second, the cases have been edited to feature the salient points. We indicate the omissions, but readers should be aware that citations and footnotes in the cases have often been omitted or abridged. Third, we have tried to incorporate some of the themes developed in the individual tax course. Assignment of income, the value of deferral, the interplay of the original issue discount rules with the installment sales rules, and the concepts of recapture are often invoked in the context of corporate transactions. Fourth, while we hope the book has a certain timeless quality to it, we would be remiss if we failed to note that it is current only through September of 2013.

While our friend and colleague Richard Doernberg did not participate in this revision, we hope that his detailed knowledge of corporate taxation and his clarity of presentation remains intact. The authors are greatly indebted to Professor Bernard Wolfman of the Harvard Law School who taught generations of corporate tax professionals and whose pedagogy is apparent throughout. We also would like to thank the American Law Institute for permission to reprint an excerpt from the Reporter's Study of Corporate Tax Integration (Federal Income Tax Project 1993). Copyright © 1993 by the American Law Institute. Reprinted by permission.

Howard E. Abrams
Don A. Leatherman

September 2013

I

SUBCHAPTER C CORPORATIONS

1

Introduction to the Corporate Income Tax

In 1895, the Supreme Court struck down the 1894 federal individual income tax as a direct tax requiring apportionment pursuant to article I, §9, clause 4, of the Constitution. Pollack v. Farmers' Loan & Trust Co., 158 U.S. 601 (1895). In *Pollack*, the Court also invalidated a corporate income tax too intertwined with the individual income tax to stand on its own. In a 1909 act, Congress enacted a stand-alone corporate income tax, which the Supreme Court upheld as an indirect or "excise" tax imposed on corporations exercising the privilege of engaging in business as a corporation. Flint v. Stone Tracy Co., 220 U.S. 107 (1911). Congress has taxed corporate profit continuously since 1909, and with the enactment of the sixteenth amendment in 1913, the constitutional validity of the federal corporate income tax was made doubly secure.

The 1909 act imposed a tax of 1 percent on corporate net income in excess of $5,000. Some 262,500 corporations filed returns for 1909, paying an aggregate tax of about $21 million. As of 1993, the highest corporate tax rate became 35 percent, see §11(b), and as of 2009, the number of annual corporate returns exceeded 5.8 million.[1] These 5.8 million returns reported taxable income of about $894.9 billion and produced about $205 billion in revenue. For comparison, in 2009, more than 140 million individual returns were filed, generating almost $965.4 billion in revenue. Thus, the corporate income tax produces about 21 percent of the revenue generated by the individual income tax. Combined, the corporate and individual income taxes account for more than half of all federal revenues and represent about 8.4 percent of the gross national product (GNP).

The United States imposes an income tax on every citizen and resident alien. Dividends received, as well as most other accessions to wealth, form the base of that tax. Together, the corporate and individual income taxes form what is often called a double tax on corporate income. It is called a double tax because under this system the earnings of a corporation are taxed once when earned by the corporation and a second time when distributed to its shareholders as dividends.

For example, suppose corporate earnings are taxed at a flat rate of 35 percent while dividends are taxed to shareholders at a flat rate of 20 percent. See §11(h)(11)

1. These figures are taken from the Statistics of Income reports published quarterly by the Internal Revenue Service and made available on the Service's web page at www.irs.gov/uac/Tax-Stats-2.

(providing a preferential rate for qualified dividend income). The combined tax burden imposed by the corporate double tax is 48 percent, computed as follows. If the corporation earns $100, it must remit $35 in taxes, given the rates assumed in this example. That leaves $65 available for distribution, and if that entire amount is distributed, the shareholder receiving this $65 will in turn owe $13 in taxes. Thus, the shareholder will have only $52 ($65–$13) to spend, and that means $48 of the $100 in earnings were paid in taxes. If dividends are taxed at, say, 40 percent, then the total tax burden will increase from 48 percent to 61 percent.

Because a double tax is imposed on corporate earnings while only a single tax is imposed on unincorporated profits, you might suspect that businesses would eschew the corporate form in favor of some less heavily taxed enterprise such as a partnership. There are several non-tax reasons why taxpayers might prefer the corporate form even at the cost of higher taxes. Traditionally, limited liability is one obvious reason for preferring a corporation to a partnership. However as noted at pages 499-501, taxpayers can now elect to have a limited liability company treated for tax purposes as if it were a partnership, thereby resulting in a single level of taxation while retaining limited liability. This development has changed the calculus for deciding whether to incorporate or to "check the box" to have a limited liability company treated as a partnership.

Nevertheless, the corporation is the most common form of business organization, and using such a familiar form may result in significant economies. Surprisingly, use of the corporate form also can be tax advantageous, depending on the relative rates of the individual and corporate taxes. For example, assume that the individual tax is imposed at a 50-percent rate while the corporate tax is imposed at a 10-percent effective rate (the low rate may result from available deductions). If $100 of corporate earnings are distributed in the year earned, they will be subject to a combined tax of $55, $10 at the corporate level and an additional $45 (50 percent of the remaining $90) at the shareholder level. This of course compares unfavorably with profits earned directly by a shareholder, taxed (under our assumptions) at a flat rate of 50 percent.

But now suppose that the corporation delays for three years distributing its after-tax $90 of earnings. The shareholder-level tax remains $45, but because the distribution has been delayed for three years, the present value of that tax burden as of the year in which it was earned is only about $38, assuming a 6-percent annual discount rate.[2] Thus, the total effective tax burden is only about $48 (the $10 corporate-level tax plus the present value of the shareholder-level tax), which compares favorably with a single, immediate tax of $50. In other words, if the shareholder-level income tax can be deferred and the corporate-level income tax is sufficiently low, the combined burden of the double tax on corporate earnings can be less than the single tax imposed on unincorporated profits. Similarly, if distributed corporate earnings are taxed to the shareholders at a preferential rate as compared with unincorporated profits, the combined burden of the corporate double tax may be less than the burden of the single, individual income tax.

Historically, the highest corporate tax rate was well below that of the highest individual tax rate. Accordingly, taxpayers often structured their transactions to deflect income away from themselves and their family members and to their

2. That is, $38 invested for three years at 6-percent annual interest will grow to about $45.

controlled and family corporations. Between 1986 and 1992, however, the highest corporate tax rate exceeded the highest individual income tax rate. During this period, taxpayers shifted their strategy, trying instead to deflect income away from corporations and to individual taxpayers. As a result, some existing businesses were disincorporated, some new businesses were started in unincorporated form, and presumably many transactions were structured to minimize or wholly avoid the corporate income tax.

Starting in 1993, the highest marginal corporate tax rate became 35 percent while the highest individual rate became 39.6 percent (where both currently reside).[3] Thus, we returned to where we began, with taxpayers once again able to reduce their tax liabilities by sheltering taxable income within the corporate form. To be sure, a second tax might be due if corporate earnings are eventually distributed as dividends, but that second tax often can be postponed, minimized, or avoided by astute tax planners.

A major change then arrived in 2003, with a reduction in the rate of tax imposed on most dividend distributions to the net capital gain rate (currently typically at no more than 20 percent).[4] The effect of this change cannot be overstated: Not only are most corporate distributions significantly tax-advantaged (as compared with other accessions to wealth) but the incentive to convert dividend distributions into capital gain largely has disappeared. Many provisions within subchapter C are devoted to preventing this precise type of conversion, and while these provisions remain, their role has been diminished substantially.

If a corporation could deduct the dividends it pays, the corporate double tax would be eliminated because the shareholder-level taxation would always be accompanied by a corporate-level deduction. Although corporations cannot, in general, deduct their dividends, they can, like other taxpayers, deduct interest paid or accrued. §163. Interest and dividends are to some extent substitutes for each other because each is the price paid by a corporation to its investors for the use of their funds. For example, a corporation using debt to finance a continuing or new project will be entitled to deduct interest payments made to its lenders for the use of their money. On the other hand, if equity is used instead of debt, what would have been deductible interest payments becomes nondeductible dividends. It should come as no surprise that the use of corporate debt is widespread, due in part to the deductibility of payments on debt (interest) versus the nondeductibility of payments on equity (dividends).

For most of the income and deduction provisions with which you are already familiar, a corporation is a taxpayer like any other. Subchapter C addresses those issues peculiar to corporate taxpayers: In particular, it addresses corporate formations, corporate terminations (called *liquidations* in tax parlance), corporate rearrangements (*reorganizations*), and the complex set of problems incidental to corporate distributions made to shareholders as part of a corporation's ongoing operations. Subchapter C is divided into seven parts, the first three of which form

3. Although 39.6 percent is the highest nominal tax rate, the effective tax rate for a high-bracket individual may be higher to the extent that his personal exemptions as well as itemized deductions are phased out. See generally §§68 and 151(d)(3) (providing the phase-outs).

4. In addition, an unearned income Medicare contribution tax of 3.8 percent is imposed on investment income of higher-income individuals. §1411. For individuals subject to this additional tax, the effective tax rate on capital gain is almost 24 percent.

the primary concern of this course. Take a moment to examine subchapter C, particularly part I, §§301-318 (distributions by corporations); part II, §§331-346 (corporate liquidations); and part III, §§351-368 (corporate organizations and reorganizations). Examination of these and other provisions of the Code begins in Chapter 2.

2

Corporate Formation

A. INTRODUCTION

1. *The §351 Philosophy*

If a taxpayer sells or exchanges property, the taxpayer realizes gain or loss, measured by the difference between the value of the property received (i.e., the amount realized) and the adjusted basis of the property surrendered. §1001(a) and (b). The taxpayer recognizes that realized gain or loss, except as the Code provides. §1001(c).

One Code exception to nonrecognition is found in §1031, illustrated by the following example:

T, an individual, holds an office building as an investment with a $30,000 adjusted basis and $100,000 value. *T* exchanges the building for another office building worth $100,000, also to be held as an investment. Under §1031(a), *T* does not recognize his $70,000 gain realized on the exchange, and under §1031(d), he takes a $30,000 "exchanged" or "substituted" basis in the new building. Thus, §1031 preserves *T*'s unrecognized gain, deferring it until a later disposition.

Section 1031 reflects a Congressional belief that taxation may be inappropriate when the taxpayer, in substance, continues its investment after the exchange. Note as well that the exchange may provide no ready medium for the taxpayer to pay tax.

How far does the Code extend that "continuity of investment" principle? For example, should *T* also qualify for nonrecognition if he transfers the office building to a newly created *X* Corp. in exchange for all *X* stock? Although §1031 does not apply to this exchange, *T* has hardly altered the substance of his original investment even though its form has changed: *X* Corp. owns the building, and *T* owns *X* Corp. In fact, since 1921, Congress has provided that this type of transaction is a nonrecognition exchange.

At the same time, not all transfers of property to a corporation are tax free. For instance, a taxpayer who sells appreciated property to a corporation for cash recognizes the realized gain, and properly so.

How then does the Code differentiate between transfers to a corporation that are taxable and tax free, in whole or in part? Section 351 provides the answer.

It allows a person to defer tax on an exchange with a corporation if the following three requirements are met:

1. The person transfers property to the corporation;
2. The person receives stock of the corporation in exchange; and
3. Along with other members of the transferor group, if any, the person controls the corporation immediately after the exchange.

These three requirements may be met either when a new corporation is formed or when property is transferred to an existing corporation (in a so-called midstream contribution).

Each requirement contemplates a transfer to a corporation in which the transferor's investment remains substantially the same. First, §351 requires a transfer of property, not the provision of services. For example, if *T* provides services to *X* Corp. and receives *X* stock, *T* has compensation income equal to the value of the *X* stock received. See §351(d)(1) (providing that §351 does not apply to stock issued for services). *T* converts human capital to corporate capital, a significant change in "investment" justifying immediate tax.

Second, for §351 to apply, the transferor must receive stock of the transferee corporation. Suppose *T* transfers an office building to *X* Corp. for cash. *T* has simply made a sale, retaining no direct or indirect interest in the building, and recognition is appropriate. The result is the same even if *T* receives a long-term debt instrument (i.e., a security) from *X* Corp. instead of cash. In contrast, if *T* receives *X* stock, he maintains a continuing, albeit indirect, investment in the building, and §351 may apply.

Finally, for §351 to apply, the transferor (and others who transfer property in the same transaction) must control the transferee corporation immediately after the exchange. By way of illustration, compare the following two transactions:

1. *T* transfers a building to *X* Corp., a newly formed corporation, for all *X* stock.
2. *T* transfers a building to Microsoft for a very small percentage of Microsoft stock.

In the first case, *T* retains a substantial, indirect interest in the building. In the second, his continuing interest is almost non-existent, almost like an all-cash transaction. In the first case, but not the second, *T* controls the transferee corporation and qualifies for nonrecognition.

Section 351 may also apply to a transaction in which more than one taxpayer transfers property to a corporation, a transaction that falls between the two cases considered in the previous paragraph. Suppose that *T*, *A*, and *B* transfer a building, machinery, and a truck, respectively, to *X* Corp., together receiving all *X* stock in exchange. Now *T* has a stock interest in more than his original asset, having exchanged part of the building for indirect interests in the machinery and truck. At the same time, *A* and *B* acquire indirect interests in the building. Is the continuity sufficient in this type of transfer? Section 351 generally answers that question in the affirmative. However, when the transferred assets are passive assets or a transfer has a tax-avoidance purpose, §351 may not apply. See the discussion of "swap funds" at page 10 infra, and of accommodation transfers at pages 19-23 infra.

2. *The Statutory Terrain*

When a corporation is formed, we are concerned with the tax consequences of both the transferors and the transferee corporation:

Transferors

§351 and §357 determine whether any gain or loss realized on the exchange is recognized;

§358 and §362(e) determine the transferor's basis in stock and property received from the corporation; and

§1223(1) may determine the holding period of stock received from the corporation.

Transferee Corporation

§351(f) treats a corporation that distributes appreciated, nonqualified property as if it sold that property for its fair market value;

§1032 provides nonrecognition for the corporation issuing its stock in exchange for money or other property;

§362(a) and (e) determine the corporation's basis in property received; and

§1223(2) determines the holding period of the property received.

To illustrate: *B* owns undeveloped real estate that she transfers to *X* Corp., a newly created corporation, solely in exchange for all *X* stock. Assume that *B* is an individual U.S. citizen and resident who held the real estate as a capital asset.

B realizes any gain or loss on the exchange, none of which is recognized. §1001(a); §351(a). Her holding period for the stock received includes her holding period for the real estate. §1223(1). Stated colloquially, the holding period for the real estate is "tacked" on to the holding period for the *X* stock received. With the "tacked" holding period, *B* may be able to sell the *X* stock shortly after she receives it and recognize long-term capital gain, taxed at a preferential rate. See §1(h) (for the preferential rates); §1222(3) (providing that long-term capital gain results from the sale of a capital asset held for more than one year).

X Corp. recognizes no gain or loss when it acquires the real estate for its own stock. §1032. Its holding period for the real estate includes *B*'s holding period for that asset. §1223(2).

B and *X* Corp.'s bases in the assets each receives in the exchange depend on the real estate's basis and value before the exchange. Assume first that the real estate has a $30,000 basis and a $75,000 value. Then, *B* takes a $30,000 basis in her *X* stock, preserving her realized but unrecognized $45,000 gain. §358(a). In addition, *X* Corp. takes a $30,000 basis in the real estate, also preserving that gain. §362(a). Consequently, if *B* immediately sells her *X* stock and *X* Corp. immediately sells the real estate, each for $75,000, each will recognize a $45,000 gain, duplicating *B*'s realized but unrecognized gain on the §351 exchange.

Can this gain duplication be justified? Consider what would happen if the gain were preserved in either the *X* stock or real estate, but the other asset took a fair market value basis. If *X* Corp. took a fair market value basis in the real estate, it could immediately sell the real estate at no gain. If *B* took a fair market value basis in the stock, she could immediately sell the stock at no gain. Under either alternative, then, with proper planning, *B* could indefinitely defer her gain. To avoid that result, §358 and §362(a) duplicate the gain at the shareholder and corporate levels.

In sharp contrast, §358 and §362 do not necessarily duplicate loss. Suppose, in the example above, that *B*'s basis in the real estate was $110,000, rather than $30,000. If no §362(e)(2)(C) election is made, *B* takes a $110,000 basis in her *X* stock, and *X* Corp. takes a $75,000 basis in the real estate. §358(a); §362(e)(2)(A). If the election is made, *B* takes a $75,000 basis in the *X* stock, while *X* Corp. takes a $110,000 basis in the real estate. §362(a) and (e)(2)(C)(i). Thus, because of §362(e)(2), if *B* immediately sells her stock and *X* Corp. immediately sells the undeveloped real estate, each for $75,000, one will recognize a $35,000 loss, but the other will recognize no gain or loss. In other words, §362(e)(2) prevents *B* and *X* Corp. from duplicating *B*'s built-in loss in the real estate through the §351 transfer.

Can the disparate treatment of gain and loss be justified? Perhaps Congress was concerned that the shareholder and corporation would recognize duplicate losses more often than duplicate gains. Cf. §1014(a) and (b)(1) (providing that the basis of property acquired from a decedent generally is its date-of-death value); §1367(a)(1) (providing that a shareholder's basis in *S* corporation stock is increased [or decreased] for her share of the corporation's gain [or loss]); Treas. Regs. §1.1502-32 (for members of a consolidated group, providing that a shareholder member's basis in a subsidiary member's stock is increased [or decreased] for its share of the subsidiary's gain [or loss]). Whether or not disparate treatment can be justified, however, it is the rule.

Finally, suppose that a dozen independent business people transfer their separate businesses to a newly organized corporation, each receiving stock equal to the value of the assets given up. Does §351 apply even though the nature of each transferor's investment has changed, or must there be a showing (although no statutory provision explicitly requires it) that the transferors have not drastically altered their economic status? The cases and the rulings do not require any such showing in general, but Congress has focused on this issue in one specific area.

Section 351(e)(1) deals with so-called swap funds. These were investment pools organized by stockbrokers to enable investors holding appreciated securities (ordinarily in a single company or in a few companies) to transfer these undiversified investments to a holding company in exchange for stock in a newly organized company that would obtain a wide range of investments (because the transferors as a group held a variety of securities, even though each individual might not). Note how such an exchange would satisfy the three requirements of §351 set out at page 8 supra. The result was diversification on a tax-free basis, assuming the applicability of §351. After a few favorable rulings, the Service announced that it would no longer accede to §351 treatment for swap-fund exchanges. See Treas. Regs. §1.351-1(c)(1). Congress thereafter enacted §351(e) to settle the question.

With these general principles in mind, we turn to the specific requirements of §351, first considering qualification under §351, next discussing tax consequences, and finally considering other issues.

B. QUALIFICATION UNDER §351

For §351 to apply to a person's transfer, the following three requirements must be met:

1. The person must transfer property to the corporation;
2. The person must receive stock of the corporation in exchange; and
3. Along with other members of the transferor group, if any, the person must control the corporation immediately after the exchange.

1. *Property*

First, for §351 to apply to a person, the person must transfer property to a corporation. For this purpose, "persons" include not only individuals but also trusts, estates, partnerships, associations, companies, and corporations. §7701(a)(1) (defining "person"); Treas. Regs. §1.351-1(a)(1) (repeating that definition).

Surprisingly, neither the Code nor regulations define the term "property" for purposes of §351, leading to two types of disputes. First, a taxpayer may create an asset through her own effort, and the taxpayer and Service sometimes argue about whether the taxpayer has created the asset on behalf of the corporation and therefore provided services to the corporation. If the person has just provided services in exchange for stock, she does not fall under §351 and typically will recognize compensation income equal to the value of the stock received, taking a basis in that stock equal to its value.

Second, the taxpayer may transfer less than all of the taxpayer's interest in an asset to a corporation. The Service may argue that the taxpayer has not transferred "property," so that §351 cannot apply to the transfer.

The following case deals with the first issue. The second issue is considered in notes following the case.

James v. Commissioner

53 T.C. 63 (1969)

SIMPSON, Judge. . . .

The issue for decision is whether the transaction by which Mr. James and Mr. Talbot acquired stock in a corporation was taxable or whether such transaction was tax free under section 351 of the Internal Revenue Code of 1954. The answer to the question thus posed with respect to each person depends on the determination of whether Mr. James received his stock in exchange for a transfer of property or as compensation for services.

FINDINGS OF FACT

For many years, Mr. James was a builder, real estate promoter, and developer with offices in Myrtle Beach, S.C. He has held the office of vice president of the National Association of Home Builders and was chairman of the association's Senior Citizens

Housing Committee. During 1963, the James Construction Co. was licensed by the State of South Carolina to engage in the business of general contracting.

On January 12, 1963, Mr. and Mrs. Talbot entered into an agreement with Mr. James for the promotion and construction of a rental apartment project, consisting of not less than 50 apartments, the project to conform to Federal Housing Administration (FHA) standards. The agreement provided that on completion of the project the parties would form a corporation to take title to the project. The voting stock in such corporation was to be distributed one-half to the Talbots and one-half to Mr. James, and nonvoting stock was to be issued to the parties "as the equity of each party in the corporation shall be," with the proviso that Mr. James should have the right to purchase up to 50 percent of such stock over a period of years. The Talbots agreed to transfer to the corporation the land on which the apartment project was to be built, such land to be the only asset contributed by the Talbots to the venture. Mr. James agreed "to promote the project . . . and . . . [to] be responsible for the planning, architectural work, construction, landscaping, legal fees, and loan processing of the entire project." . . .

After the execution of the January 12 agreement, Mr. James began negotiations to fulfill his part of the contract. He made arrangements with an attorney and an architectural firm to perform the work necessary to meet FHA requirements— development of legal documents, preparation of architectural plans, and the like; and he obtained from United Mortgagee Service Corp. (United Mortgagee), a lender, its agreement to finance the project and a commitment by FHA to insure the financing. Mr. James personally met with the FHA only twice — once in connection with the amount of the commitment and again at the final closing of the loan, after construction of the project was completed in the late summer of 1964. Most of the arrangements necessary to the securing of the loan and the FHA commitment were handled by the attorney, the architectural firm, and United Mortgagee. The attorney's and architect's fees were not paid by Mr. James but were paid out of the proceeds of the construction loan by the corporation subsequently established.

On August 8, 1963, the FHA issued to United Mortgagee a commitment for the insurance of advances in the amount of $850,700 to Chicora Apartments, Inc., for the apartment project sponsored by Mr. James and the Talbots. On August 27, 1963, United Mortgagee sent Mr. James a draft of a proposed agreement to make a first mortgage loan of $850,700 on the Chicora Apartment project in accordance with Mr. James' application for such loan. . . .

On November 5, 1963, Chicora Apartments, Inc. (Chicora), was granted, upon application of Messrs. Talbot and James, a corporate charter, stating its authorized capital stock to consist of 20 no-par common shares. On the same date, the land on which the apartment project was to be constructed was conveyed to Chicora by Mrs. Talbot in consideration for 10 shares of stock. Nine of these shares were issued to Mrs. Talbot, and one share was issued to Mr. Talbot. . . . Also on November 5, 1963, 10 shares of stock were issued to Mr. James. The minutes of a meeting of Chicora's board of directors held on that date state that those 10 shares were issued to Mr. James in consideration of his "transfer" to the corporation of the "following described property":

> 1. FHA Commitment issued pursuant to Title 2, Section 207 of the National Housing Act, whereby the FHA agrees to insure a mortgage loan in the amount of $850,700.00, on a parcel of land in Myrtle Beach, South Carolina. . . .

2. Commitment from United Mortgagee Servicing Corp., agreeing to make a mortgage loan on said property in the amount of $850,700.00 and also commitment from said mortgagee to make an interim construction loan in an identical amount.
3. Certain contracts and agreement which W. A. James over the past two years have [sic] worked out and developed in connection with the architectural and construction services required for said project.
4. The use of the finances and credit of W. A. James during the past two years (and including the construction period) in order to make it possible to proceed with the project.

Thus, as a result of these transactions, Chicora had outstanding all 20 of its authorized shares of stock. . . .

Both Mr. and Mrs. James and Mr. and Mrs. Talbot deemed their receipt of Chicora common stock to be in return for a transfer of property to a controlled corporation under section 351. Accordingly, neither family reported any income from such receipt on their respective income tax returns for 1963. In his statutory notice of deficiency, the respondent determined that Mr. James received such stock, with a value of $22,000, for services rendered and not in exchange for property, and thus received taxable income in that amount. He further determined that the Talbot's [sic] transfer of property to Chicora did not meet the requirements of section 351, with the result that they should have recognized a long-term capital gain of $14,675 — the difference between $7,325, the basis of the land transferred, and $22,000, the value of the stock received.

Opinion

The first, and critical, issue for our determination is whether Mr. James received his Chicora stock in exchange for the transfer of property or as compensation for services. The petitioners argue that he received such stock in consideration of his transfer to Chicora of the FHA and United Mortgagee commitments and that such commitments constituted "property" within the meaning of section 351. . . . The respondent does not appear to challenge the petitioners' implicit assertion that Mr. James was not expected to render future services to the corporation in exchange for the issuance of stock to him. Although the accuracy of this assertion is subject to some question, the state of the record is such that we must decide the issues as the parties have presented them. Thus, the sole question on this issue is whether Mr. James' personal services, which the petitioners freely admit were rendered, resulted in the development of a property right which was transferred to Chicora, within the meaning of section 351. . . .

[The predecessor to §351(d)(1)] was first included in the statute as a part of the 1954 Code, although it is said merely to restate the case law. See Bittker & Eustice, Federal Income Taxation of Corporations and Shareholders 70 (2d ed. 1966). In explaining the [provision], the House Ways and Means Committee stated:

> In accordance with this provision, such stock or securities received by a person who has rendered or will render services to the transferee corporation would be fully taxable as compensation upon receipt. Your committee does not intend, however, to vitiate the remaining portion of the transaction, through application of this provision.

(H. Rept. No. 1337, to accompany H.R. 8300 (Pub. L. 591), 83d Cong., 2d Sess., p. A117 (1954).)

According to the petitioners' argument, Mr. James, as a result of the services performed by him, acquired certain contract rights which constituted property and which he transferred to Chicora. The fact that such rights resulted from the performance of personal services does not, in their view, disqualify them from being treated as property for purposes of section 351. In support of this position, the petitioners refer to situations involving the transfer of patents and secret processes. . . .

It is altogether clear that for purposes of section 351, not every right is to be treated as property. . . . [Section 351(d)(1)] indicates that, whatever may be considered as property for purposes of local law, the performance of services, or the agreement to perform services, is not to be treated as a transfer of property for purposes of section 351. Thus, if in this case we have merely an agreement to perform services in exchange for stock of the corporation to be created, the performance of such services does not constitute the transfer of property within the meaning of section 351.

Although patents and secret processes — the product of services — are treated as property for purposes of section 351, we have carefully analyzed the arrangement in this case and have concluded that Mr. James did not transfer any property essentially like a patent or secret process; he merely performed services for Chicora. In January of 1963, he entered into an agreement to perform services for the corporation to be created. He was to secure the necessary legal and architectural work and to arrange for the financing of the project, and these were the services performed by him. Although he secured the services of the lawyer and the architect, they were paid for by the corporation. He put in motion the wheels that led to the FHA commitment, but it was not a commitment to him — it was a commitment to United Mortgagee to insure a loan to Chicora, a project sponsored by Mr. James. It was stipulated that under the FHA regulations, a commitment would not be issued to an individual, but only to a corporation. Throughout these arrangements, it was contemplated that a corporation would be created and that the commitment would run to the corporation. The petitioners rely heavily on the claim that Mr. James had a right to the commitment, that such right constituted property, and that such right was transferred to the corporation in return for his stock. However, the commitment was not his to transfer; he never acquired ownership of the commitment — he could not and did not undertake to acquire such ownership. The evidence as to the commitment by United Mortgagee to make a loan for the construction of the project is somewhat incomplete, but since all the parties knew that a corporation was to be formed and that the FHA commitment would be made to that corporation, it seems clear that there was no commitment to loan to Mr. James the funds necessary for the construction of the project. Thus, throughout these arrangements, Mr. James never undertook to acquire anything for himself; he was, in accordance with his agreement with the Talbots, making the preliminary arrangements for the construction of the apartment project. The enterprise would be operated, once the initial steps were completed, by a corporation, Chicora, and everything that was done by him was done on behalf of the contemplated corporation. In these circumstances, it seems clear that Mr. James received his share of the stock in the corporation in return for the services performed by him and that he did not transfer any property, within the meaning of section 351, to the corporation. . . .

The facts of this case are substantially similar to those in United States v. Frazell, 335 F.2d 487 (C.A.5, 1964), . . . certiorari denied 380 U.S. 961 (1964). In that case, the taxpayer, a geologist, investigated certain oil and gas properties to be acquired by a joint venture, and he was to receive an interest in the joint venture. However, before any transfer was made to him, a corporation was formed to take over the assets of the joint venture, and part of the stock was transferred to the taxpayer. It was not clear whether the taxpayer acquired an interest in the joint venture which was then exchanged for his share of the stock or whether he acquired the stock directly in exchange for the services performed by him. The court found that, in either event, the taxpayer received compensation for his services. If he received the stock in return for the services performed by him, such stock was taxable as compensation; and he did not transfer any property to the corporation within the meaning of section 351. See also Mailloux v. Commissioner, 320 F.2d 60 (C.A.5, 1963), affirming on this issue a Memorandum Opinion of this Court.

Decisions will be entered for the respondent.

NOTES

1. *The statutory framework.* Section 351 provides a statutory exception to recognition under §1001. Is income from the provision of services a "gain" within the meaning of §1001? Would James have transferred property if the FHA had committed to insure a loan to James or his assignee? If so, why should the result be different? Compare §61(a)(1) with §61(a)(3).

2. *Services.* Services provided to a corporation do not qualify as property transferred for purposes of §351. §351(d)(1). One reason for this restriction is to prevent the conversion of ordinary income from services into capital gains when the worker sells the stock received. Note the inconsistency between the treatment of services that do not qualify as property under §351 and inventory that does qualify even though its sale would produce ordinary income. If a transferor of appreciated inventory receives stock in a §351 transaction, does the sale of stock produce a capital gain? If the sale occurs within one year of the transfer, is any capital gain long-term or short-term capital gain? See §1223(1). At what rate is an individual's net short-term capital gain taxed?

Note that the Talbots and James had some tax counseling before forming the corporation. The Chicora corporate minutes stated that the transfer of stock to James was in exchange for property. What property? The line between services and property is fuzzy at best. In United States v. Frazell, discussed in *James,* the taxpayer-geologist was to locate certain properties for a group of unincorporated investors in return for an interest in the properties. When the taxpayer received stock in a corporation organized to hold the acquired properties, he did not report the fair market value of the stock as income, arguing instead that he had transferred a partnership interest to the corporation. The Fifth Circuit ruled against the taxpayer without having to decide whether the taxpayer transferred a property interest. Either the taxpayer received stock for services, in which case §351 would be inapplicable, or if property (that is, a partnership interest) was transferred, the taxpayer was taxable on the receipt of the partnership interest for services rendered. In the latter case, the transfer of the partnership interest would qualify under §351. For a collection of cases on the property versus services question, see Stafford v. United States, 727 F.2d 1043 (11th Cir. 1984).

3. *Intellectual property. James* and *Frazell* illustrate the tension between services and service-flavored property. Nowhere is the line more blurred than in cases involving industrial "know how," secret processes and formulas, etc. In Rev. Rul. 64-56, 1964-1 C.B. (pt. 1) 133, and Rev. Rul. 71-564, 1971-2 C.B. 179, amplifying it, the Service set forth guidelines for distinguishing between industrial know-how and services. Did the court in *James* adequately address this issue?

Section 351 requires that property be "transferred." What constitutes a transfer? The issue arises most often when intangibles are assigned to corporations. The Service has asserted that there must be a sale or exchange within the meaning of the capital gains provisions of §1222 to qualify under §351, or else the transaction will be considered a license resulting in income to the licensor in the amount of the stock or securities received. The Service's requirement means that an exclusive, unqualified right in perpetuity must be given to the transferee. See Rev. Rul. 71-564, 1971-2 C.B. 179; Rev. Rul. 69-156, 1969-1 C.B. 101; Rev. Rul. 64-56, 1964-1 C.B. (pt. 1) 133. In E.I. DuPont de Nemours & Co. v. United States, 471 F.2d 1211 (Ct. Cl. 1973), however, the court held that the sale or exchange requirement of §1222 is not embodied in §351. The court determined that a nonexclusive, royalty-free license in exchange for stock was a sufficient transfer to qualify under §351.

4. *Accounts receivable.* Suppose a cash basis transferor has performed services for a third party prior to incorporation in exchange for an account receivable. What treatment is appropriate if the receivable is transferred to a newly formed corporation as part of a §351 transaction? In Hempt Bros., Inc. v. United States, 490 F.2d 1172 (3d Cir. 1974), the court held that accounts receivable constituted property for purposes of §351. Does the assignment of income doctrine render the transferor or the corporation taxable when the receivable is paid? See page 73 infra.

Suppose a cash basis taxpayer performs services for the transferee corporation in exchange for an account receivable. If the taxpayer exchanges the receivable for stock of the corporation, does the receivable constitute property? Is this more or less what happened in *James*? How does this hypothetical differ from the facts in *Hempt Bros.*?

5. *Miscellaneous property interests.* Money constitutes property for purposes of §351. See Rev. Rul. 69-357, 1969-1 C.B. 101. An equitable interest in property constitutes property for purposes of §351. In Roberts Co. v. Commissioner, 5 T.C. 1 (1945), attorneys who transferred a contingent fee interest in the proceeds from an eventual sale of land were considered transferors of property.

6. *Debt of the transferee corporation.* Stock is not considered issued for property if issued for debt of the transferee corporation not evidenced by a security. §351(d)(2). Presumably, this exclusion allows the creditor to claim a bad debt deduction under §166 if the debt is only partially satisfied with the transferee's stock, but the creditor must recognize gain to the extent that the fair market value of the stock exceeds the debt's basis. For the treatment of the debtor corporation, see §108(e)(10).

Further, stock is not considered issued for property to the extent received for interest on indebtedness of the transferee corporation accrued after the transferor's holding period for the debt began. §351(d)(3).

2. *Stock*

For §351 to apply to a property transferor, the transferor must also receive stock in the exchange. Like the term "property," the term "stock" is defined in neither the Code nor the regulations. Stock includes common or preferred stock and voting or nonvoting stock but excludes stock rights, options, warrants, or other rights to purchase stock at a fixed price. Treas. Regs. §1.351-1(a)(1); compare Helvering v. Southwest Consolidated Corp., 315 U.S. 194 (1942) (concluding that warrants issued as part of a reorganization are not voting stock). Stock also includes contingent stock interests, interests distinguished from stock rights because no additional payment is required from the transferor. See Carlberg v. United States, 281 F.2d 507, 517-518 (8th Cir. 1960), and Hamrick v. Commissioner, 43 T.C. 21, 32-33 (1964). Is this a distinction without a difference? Why should stock rights and warrants not be treated in the same manner as contingent stock interests?

Suppose a person transfers property to a wholly owned corporation but receives no stock in the exchange. Is stock "deemed" issued to the person, so that §351 applies to the transfer? The answer is yes. Under the "meaningless gesture" doctrine, stock is deemed issued if, with or without the issuance, the rights of the corporation's shareholders would be the same. See Peracchi v. Commissioner, 143 F.3d 487 (9th Cir. 1998) (page 43 infra). Could this doctrine also apply if someone else received common stock as part of the same transaction? How about if, instead, that person received a new class of nonvoting preferred stock?

To answer the last question, you must examine the characteristics of the issued stock and understand the differences between common and preferred stock. A corporation's common stock is a residual interest in the entity, which means that its holders are paid last but in a potentially unlimited amount. In contrast, holders of preferred stock are typically paid both dividends and liquidating distributions before holders of common stock. Further, their return is often limited to a fixed dividend rate and fixed amount on liquidation, regardless of the success of the venture.[1] Thus, common shareholders take a larger risk (because they are paid last) for a bigger potential gain (because their return is unlimited).

Note that under §351(g), certain "nonqualified preferred stock" is treated as property other than stock (i.e., "boot") if received in a §351 transaction. Nonqualified preferred stock must be both preferred *and* limited. §351(g)(3)(A). Thus, stock is not nonqualified preferred stock if it can share in future growth of the corporation by being converted into common stock. This definition of "preferred" stock is much more restrictive than that used in the context of §305 and §306.

Further, nonqualified preferred stock must have certain features that make it more like straight debt than common stock on a debt/equity spectrum. It must either have (a) a dividend rate tied to interest rates, commodity prices, or the like or (b) one of the following three redemption features:

1. The stockholder may require the issuer to redeem the stock;
2. The issuer must be required to redeem the stock; or

1. A corporation's bonds and debentures also represent an investment that is both preferred and limited. Debt holders, however, enjoy a preference over any equity holders and are therefore paid before any common or preferred stock holders. Further, their interests typically are limited, because they receive a specified interest rate (even if it varies over time) and a fixed return of their principal regardless of the success of the venture.

3. The issuer may redeem the stock, and the redemption is, as of the issue date, more likely than not to occur.

Section 351(g)(2)(A) (also adding corresponding rules for purchases by persons related to the issuer). However, these redemption provisions are relevant only if they can be exercised within 20 years of the stock's issuance and the redemption is not subject to a contingency that makes the likelihood of redemption remote. §351(g)(2)(B). In addition, there are special rules for redemptions related to death, disability, or change of employment status. §351(g)(2)(C).

3. Control

Finally, for §351 to apply, the transferor, together with any others who transfer property in the same exchange, must control the corporation immediately after the exchange. This requirement raises several questions:

1. What is control?
2. Which persons transfer property in the same exchange?
3. Who owns stock "immediately after the exchange"?

a. Definition of Control

Section 368(c) defines control as "stock possessing at least 80 percent of the total combined voting power of [the corporation's voting stock] and at least 80 percent of the total number of shares of all other classes of stock of the corporation." Rev. Rul. 59-259, 1959-2 C.B. 115, "clarifies" §368(c), concluding that the second 80-percent test applies separately to *each* class of nonvoting stock. With this clarification, a person or persons control a corporation if they own stock of the corporation possessing at least 80 percent of its total voting power plus at least 80 percent of *each* class of nonvoting stock.

Does the clarification make sense? In answering that question, consider how §351 applies to the following facts both under the literal language of §368(c) and as clarified:

A owns all voting stock of a corporation, *X* Corp., and *B* owns all 10 shares of its only class of nonvoting preferred stock. *A* transfers property to *X* Corp. in exchange for either 10 or 90 shares of a new class of nonvoting preferred *X* stock. Note that §351 applies to *A*'s transfer if he controls *X* Corp. after the exchange. How freely could *X* Corp. alter the number of shares it issues to *A* in the exchange? If §368(c) applied literally, could *X* Corp. and *A* effectively elect the application of §351?

b. The Transferor Group

Section 351 may apply to property transfers by several persons, and it may apply even if those persons do not make simultaneous exchanges. The regulations state that persons are considered together (i.e., as a transferor group) in applying §351 if their rights "have been previously defined and the execution of the agreement proceeds with an expedition consistent with orderly procedure." Treas. Regs. §1.351-1(a)(1).

What if a person makes a relatively small transfer to qualify others under §351? The following case considers a regulatory exception to the transferor group definition that may apply to such a transfer.

Kamborian v. Commissioner

56 T.C. 847 (1971)

... **Findings of Fact**

1. International Shoe Machine Corp. (International) was incorporated in Massachusetts in 1938 and at the time of the trial herein was engaged in the business of manufacturing and leasing shoe machinery and the sale of related supplies. . . .

On September 1, 1965, prior to the transaction here in question, International's capital stock was held as follows:

	Shares of International	
Name	*Class A common*	*Class B [nonvoting] common*
Jacob Kamborian Revocable Trust	20,324	182,916
Jacob Kamborian, Jr.	4,220	37,980
Lisabeth (Kamborian) Godley	3,620	32,580
Michael Becka	60	540
Elizabeth Kamborian Trust	5,000	45,000
Others	3,916	35,244
Total	37,140	334,260

Jacob S. Kamborian (Jacob) founded International and served as its president at all times relevant herein. Jacob S. Kamborian, Jr., and Lisabeth Kamborian Godley are the children of Jacob and his wife, Elizabeth. Michael Becka (Becka) is not related to the members of the Kamborian family. At the time of the trial herein he had been employed by International or an affiliate since at least 1943 and had served as International's executive vice president and general manager since approximately 1960. . . .

The Elizabeth Kamborian Trust (Elizabeth's trust) was established by Jacob in 1949. At about that time Jacob and Elizabeth experienced domestic difficulties; they separated for a time; and the trust was established on their reconciliation in order to provide financial security for Mrs. Kamborian. . . .

As of September 1, 1965, Becka and Lisabeth K. Godley were the trustees. Jacob had appointed them as successor trustees in 1963 and 1964, respectively. At all times relevant herein, Becka served as the managing trustee; Mrs. Godley did not live in Boston during this period; and periodically Becka informed her of the trust's activities. As of September 1, 1965, the only assets of the trust were 5,000 shares of International's class A common stock and 45,000 shares of its class B common stock.

On September 1, 1965, and prior to the transaction here in question, the outstanding stock of Campex was held as follows:

Name	*Shares of Campex*
Jacob Kamborian Revocable Trust	39
Jacob Kamborian, Jr.	4
Lisabeth (Kamborian) Godley	4
Michael Becka	3

[The Campex shareholders proposed exchanging their Campex stock for International stock.]

As part of the transaction it was contemplated that the Elizabeth Kamborian Trust would purchase additional shares of theretofore unissued International stock for about $5,000, so that the former owners of the Campex stock and the Elizabeth Kamborian Trust, when considered collectively and treated as transferors under section 351(a) . . . would own at least 80 percent of International's stock immediately after the transaction in an attempt to comply with the requirements of section 368(c). . . . If the Elizabeth Kamborian Trust were not taken into account, the International stock held by the former owners of Campex immediately after the transaction amounted to 77.3 percent of each class of outstanding stock of International — an amount that was insufficient to satisfy the requirements of section 368(c). . . .

As trustee of Elizabeth's trust, Becka borrowed approximately $5,000 at an interest rate of 6 percent in order to finance the trust's purchase of the total of 418 shares of International stock on September 1, 1965. The corpus of the trust consisted exclusively of International stock, and Becka anticipated that the loan would be repaid out of dividends paid on the stock. In deciding to acquire additional International stock, Becka also anticipated that International would make a public offering which might enhance the value of the stock. Prior to the purchase of the International stock on behalf of the trust, Becka discussed his plans with both Jacob and Elizabeth. Jacob, personally and as grantor of the Jacob S. Kamborian Revocable Trust, held a sufficient number of International shares to control the corporation and thus to determine whether it would issue additional shares. In his discussions with Elizabeth, Becka explained that because the $5,000 loan would have to be repaid out of dividends paid on the International stock held by the trust, her income from the trust would be diminished until the loan was repaid. Elizabeth told Becka to go ahead with the transaction. . . .

On their respective Federal income tax returns for 1965, petitioners reported no gain or loss stemming from the exchange of their Campex stock for International stock. . . .

Opinion

Raum, Judge.

1. Exchange of Campex Stock for International Stock

Petitioners contend that the gain they realized on their transfer of Campex stock to International in return for International's common stock qualifies for nonrecognition under section 351(a). . . . That section provides for nonrecognition of gain or loss on the transfer of property to a corporation in exchange for the corporation's stock or securities—if immediately after the exchange the transferor or transferors are "in control" of the corporation. . . .

Immediately after the exchange here in issue the stock of International was held as follows:

	Shares of—		
Name	*Class A (voting common)*	*Class B (nonvoting common)*	*Percent of total of each class*
Jacob S. Kamborian Revocable Trust	22,108	198,971	56.01
Jacob S. Kamborian, Jr.	4,403	39,627	11.16
Lisabeth (Kamborian) Godley	3,803	34,227	9.64
Michael Becka	197	1,775	.50
Elizabeth Kamborian Trust	5,042	45,376	12.77
Others	3,916	35,244	9.92
Total	39,469	355,220	

Petitioners contend that the transferors of property for purposes of section 351(a) were the five named stockholders listed above and that their percentage stockholdings after the transfer satisfy the 80-percent-control requirement imposed by sections 351(a) and 368(c).

The Commissioner's position is that only the first four stockholders listed above—i.e., the former owners of Campex—may be considered as transferors of property here, that the fifth (the Elizabeth Kamborian Trust) may not be taken into account in this connection, and that since there would thus be a failure to satisfy the control requirement, all gain realized on the exchange must be recognized. In particular, he urges that International stock issued to the Elizabeth Kamborian Trust in return for $5,016 does not qualify as stock issued for property within the meaning of section 351(a) and that consequently the persons making qualified transfers of property to International in return for its stock held only 77.3 percent of its stock after the exchange. The Commissioner relies on regulations section 1.351-1(a)(1)(ii). . . .

The Commissioner contends that since the Elizabeth Kamborian Trust purchased only 42 shares of class A common and 376 shares of class B common, the securities issued were "of relatively small value" in relation to the 5,000 shares of class A common and 45,000 shares of class B common which is already held and that the primary purpose of the transfer was to qualify the exchange of Campex stock by the other stockholders for nonrecognition treatment under section 351(a).

Petitioners attack the Commissioner's position on a variety of grounds. They urge (a) that regulations section 1.351-1(a)(1)(ii) is invalid; (b) that even if valid it is inapplicable to the transaction in issue. . . .

(a) *Validity of the regulation.* Initially we note the well-settled principle that "Treasury regulations must be sustained unless unreasonable and plainly inconsistent with the revenue statutes and that they constitute contemporaneous constructions by those charged with administration of these statutes which should not be overruled except for weighty reasons." Commissioner v. South Texas Lumber Co., 333 U.S. 496, 501. . . .

Petitioners . . . contend that the regulation's reference to "property which is [of] relatively small value in comparison to the value of stock . . . already owned" and its reliance upon the taxpayer's motive find support nowhere in the language of section 351 and that the regulation is for that reason invalid as beyond the scope of the statute. Again, we must disagree. By disqualifying certain token exchanges, the regulation is reasonably designed to exclude from the scope of section 351 transactions which comply with its requirements in form but not in substance. Far from being unreasonable or inconsistent with the statute, the regulation promotes its purpose by helping to ensure substantial compliance with the control requirement before the nonrecognition provisions become operative. In this light the absence of direct support for the regulation in the language of the statute is of minimal significance. . . . We conclude that the regulation is valid.

(b) *Applicability of the regulation.* Petitioners contend that even if it is valid, the regulation is inapplicable to the transaction here in issue. They argue first that even if Elizabeth's trust had not purchased shares of International stock, the control requirement would have been satisfied, that therefore the purchase was not necessary to meet the control requirement, and that consequently the regulation is by its own terms inapplicable. Petitioners reach this conclusion by asserting that the shares held by Becka and Lisabeth Godley as trustees of Elizabeth's trust should be attributed to them as individuals . . . and added to the shares they held personally in nonfiduciary capacities. On the basis of this premise, petitioners conclude that the 80-percent-control requirement would have been satisfied even if Elizabeth's trust had not participated in the September 1, 1965, transaction. . . . Petitioners' argument is ingenious but unacceptable, for it falters on petitioners' premise that the trust's shares may be attributed to the individual trustees. While legal title to the shares may have been in the names of the trustees, they had no beneficial interest in such shares. The distinction is not one of form but of plain economic reality. . . . In these circumstances we think the trustees' interests in the trust's shares were far too remote to justify attributing the shares to them for purposes of section 351. . . .

Petitioners also contend that the primary purpose for the trust's acquisition of International's stock was not to qualify the other stockholders' exchanges under section 351 and that for this reason the regulation is inapplicable. We note at the outset that the regulation does not make it entirely clear whose purpose is to be taken into account. However, both parties have assumed that the purpose of the transferor of property is critical. The language of the regulation (which appears to distinguish between a "transfer" of property and the issuance of stock) supports their assumption, and we shall therefore proceed on this basis. Although Elizabeth's trust was technically the transferor herein, the parties have also assumed that Becka's purpose is critical in this respect—apparently on the ground that as the managing trustee he was primarily responsible for the decision to make the purchase of International stock. We shall proceed on the basis of this assumption as well.

The question of Becka's primary purpose is one of fact, compare Malat v. Riddell, 383 U.S. 569, and after a review of all the evidence we conclude that his primary purpose was to qualify the other stockholders' exchanges under section 351. We note in particular that at about the time of the transaction, Jacob was ill and Becka was in charge of International's affairs, that in planning the acquisition Becka participated in lengthy discussions with regard to planning the transaction as a tax-free exchange, and that both the vote of International's board of directors and the agreement of September 1, 1965, treated the purchase by Elizabeth's trust and the exchange of Campex stock by the other stockholders as component parts of an integrated transaction avowedly designed to meet the 80-percent-control requirement and thereby qualify for nonrecognition treatment under section 351.

At the trial herein, Becka testified that if the trust had not participated in the transaction, the issue of International stock to the other major stockholders would have diluted the trust's percentage interest in International and that he authorized the purchase of International stock in order to minimize such dilution. In particular he testified that the total percentage stock interest held by the trust and the two Kamborian children exceeded 33 1/3 percent and that preservation of that interest protected Mrs. Kamborian against the making of certain corporate decisions (requiring a two-thirds majority) without her consent. . . . We do not give his testimony very much weight, however. The record does not establish whether or why the children were regarded as allies of Mrs. Kamborian rather than as allies of her husband. Moreover, the trust's participation in the transaction left them with an aggregate stock interest of 33.57 percent—only 0.08 of 1 percent more than they would have held if the trust had not purchased any additional shares.

Becka also testified that he authorized the purchase of the stock because it was a "good investment." While he may well have taken this into account in making his decision, the record leaves us convinced that the purchase was made primarily to qualify the exchanges by the other stockholders (one of whom was Becka himself) . . . under section 351. We conclude that section 1.351-1(a)(1)(ii) is applicable. . . .

Decisions will be entered under Rule 50.

NOTES

1. *Who is in the transferor group?* As *Kamborian* indicates, an exchange can qualify under §351 even though the transferors do not *acquire* control in the exchange itself. Rather, the transferors can include their previously owned stock in satisfying the 80-percent requirement. The problem in *Kamborian* was the amount being transferred by the Elizabeth Kamborian Trust relative to its existing holdings. The trust transferred $5,000 for new stock while it owned almost $600,000 in preexisting stock. If the receipt of stock in an amount of about 0.84 percent of the value of existing stock is not enough, what *is* the magical amount?

In Rev. Proc. 77-37, 1977-2 C.B. 568, the Service stated that for advance ruling purposes, property will not be considered "of relatively small value" within the meaning of Treas. Regs. §1.351-1(a)(1)(ii) if it equals at least 10 percent of the value of stock or securities already owned by the transferor, or to be received for services by the transferor. Note that this advanced ruling standard acts as a safe harbor; it does not establish the minimum amount necessary for property not to be considered "of relatively small value." In *Kamborian,* if the Elizabeth Kamborian Trust had purchased $60,000 of additional stock, could the transferor group have included all the trust's stock in the 80-percent calculations?

2. *Unbalanced exchanges.* In *Kamborian* the taxpayer also argued that Treas. Regs. §1.351-1(a)(1)(ii) was invalid because it supposedly adopted a "proportionate

interest" test repudiated by Congress in 1954. Section 351 dropped the requirement contained in its predecessor, §112(b)(5) of the 1939 Code, that "in the case of an exchange by two or more persons this paragraph shall apply only if the amount of the stock . . . received by each is substantially in proportion to his interest in the property prior to the exchange." This clause gave rise to difficult questions of valuation as well as to conflicting opinions on how the proportion of change was to be calculated and on what constituted a "substantial" change. Moreover, the purpose of the requirement was obscure.

Though abandoning the proportionate interest requirement, the Code points out that an exchange may have the effect of a gift or of the payment of compensation. §351(h)(3) and (h)(4); Treas. Regs. §1.351-1(b). See also Rev. Rul. 76-454, 1976-2 C.B. 102, in which *T* and his wholly owned subsidiary, *X* Corp., formed *Y* Corp. with *T* receiving a disproportionate amount of stock for the property transferred; held, recharacterized to give *T* and *X* each a proportionate number of shares, followed by a taxable dividend by *X* of the "excess" *Y* stock. What would the result be if *X* had received and retained more than its share of the *Y* stock?

3. *Alternative structures.* How could the Campex shareholders have structured a transaction to qualify under §351 and still achieve their business goals?

c. Immediately after the Exchange

Control is determined by comparing the stock owned by the transferor group with all outstanding stock, with both being measured "immediately after the exchange." The outstanding stock includes not only stock issued to members of the transferor group in the exchange but also any stock issued to a person providing services to the corporation as part of the same transaction.

Consider *James*, a case we studied earlier (page 11 supra). In that case, the Talbots transferred land to a corporation (Chicora), and James provided services to Chicora, but the Talbots and James each received half of Chicora's only class of stock. Their rights in Chicora were defined by agreement before the corporation was formed. Section 351 did not apply to the Talbots' exchange because they did not control Chicora immediately after the exchange. The court reasoned as follows:

> The next question is whether the Talbots are taxable on the gain realized from the exchange of their land for Chicora stock. Section 351(a) applies only if immediately after the transfer those who transferred property in exchange for stock owned at least 80 percent of Chicora's stock. Sec. 368(c). Since Mr. James is not to be treated as a transferor of property, he cannot be included among those in control for purposes of this test. Fahs v. Florida Machine & Foundry Co., 168 F.2d 957 (C.A.5, 1948); . . . Bittker & Eustice, supra. The transferors of property, the Talbots, did not have the required 80-percent control of Chicora immediately after the transfer, and therefore, their gain must be recognized.

Thus, the Talbots were taxed on the difference between the adjusted basis of their land and the fair market value of the stock received. Given §351's purpose, is this an appropriate outcome? Note that recognition may be welcome to property transferors who recognize loss on the exchange or who recognize gain but have available offsetting losses from other transactions.

Would the outcome to the Talbots have been different if James had been issued his Chicora stock sometime after the Talbots but as part of the same transaction? How about if the Talbots and James had received different classes of Chicora voting stock, and the stock received by both was of equal value, but the Talbots' stock possessed 80 percent of the total voting power?

Suppose, instead, that James had transferred $10,000 of property as well as services in exchange for $22,000 of Chicora stock. Would he have income or gain on the transaction? Would the Talbots? In answering these questions, consider that one who transfers both property and services may be treated as a property transferor for purposes of satisfying control. If so treated, the person does not recognize gain or loss attributable to the property transferred for stock under §351, and *all* stock received (whether for property or services) can be counted toward the 80-percent-control test. Treas. Regs. §1.351-1(a)(2) (example 3).

What if James had transferred $1 of cash and $21,999 of services in exchange for his $22,000 stock interest? See Treas. Regs. §1.351-1(a)(1)(ii) and *Kamborian.*

Finally, is a person always treated as owning stock received in a §351 exchange if the person later transfers that stock? The following case considered that issue.

Intermountain Lumber Co. v. Commissioner

65 T.C. 1025 (1976)

WILES, Judge. . . .

The only issue for decision is whether a certain corporate formation was nontaxable under section 351(a). . . . This depends solely upon whether the primary incorporator had "control" of the requisite percentage of stock immediately after the exchange within the meaning of section 368(c).

FINDINGS OF FACT

From 1948 until March of 1964, Mr. Dee Shook (hereinafter Shook) individually owned a sawmill at Conner, Mont. During that time Mr. Milo Wilson (hereinafter Wilson) had logs processed there into rough lumber for a fee. Shook owned the remaining logs processed at the sawmill, which constituted about half of all the logs processed there.

From 1954 until March of 1964, rough lumber from the sawmill was processed into finished lumber at a separate finishing plant which Shook and Wilson owned as equal shareholders.

In March of 1964, fire damaged the sawmill. Shook and Wilson wanted to replace it with a larger one so that the finishing plant could operate at full capacity. Shook was financially unable, however, to do so. He accordingly induced Wilson to personally coguarantee a $200,000 loan to provide financing. In return, Wilson insisted upon an equal voice in rebuilding the sawmill and upon an opportunity to become an equal shareholder with Shook in the new sawmill.

On May 28, 1964, Shook, Wilson, and two other individuals, all acting as incorporators, executed articles of incorporation for S&W Sawmill, Inc. (hereinafter S&W). . . .

Minutes of the first stockholders meeting on July 7, 1964, stated in part that "Mr. Shook informed the meeting that a separate agreement was being prepared between he [sic] and Mr. Wilson providing for the sale of one-half of his stock to Mr. Wilson." Also on that date, 1 share was issued to each of the other two incorporators.

Shook executed a bill of sale for his sawmill equipment and deeded his sawmill site to S&W on July 15 and 16, 1964, respectively. In exchange, Shook received 364 S&W shares on July 15, 1964. Shook and Wilson also received 1 share each as incorporators. The 364 shares and the 4 incorporation shares constituted all outstanding capital stock of S&W on July 15, 1964.

Also on that date, minutes of a special meeting stated in part that "The President, Dee Shook, announced that he and Milo E. Wilson had entered into an agreement whereby Mr. Wilson was to purchase 182 shares of Mr. Shook's stock." That agreement, dated July 15, 1964, and entitled "Agreement for Sale and Purchase of Stock" (hereinafter agreement for sale) provided in part as follows:

> [I]t is the intention of all the incorporators that Shook and Wilson are to be the owners of the majority of the stock of said corporation;
>
> AND WHEREAS, it is the desire and plan of both parties hereto that a sufficient number of shares of stock be sold by Shook to Wilson so that eventually the stock ownership would be equal;
>
> AND WHEREAS, the purchase of said shares of stock by Wilson from Shook is to be financed by a series of payments;
>
> IT IS THEREFORE AGREED, that for and in consideration of the covenants to be performed and the payments to be made as hereinafter set forth, the sale and purchase of said stock is to be as follows:
>
> 1. Dee Shook is to sell to Milo E. Wilson 182 shares of stock in S&W SAWMILL, INC. for the agreed price of $500.00 per share.
> 2. Wilson is to pay Shook for said stock as follows:
>   Interest on unpaid balance due is to be paid annually at 3% per annum from August 1, 1964 to July 31, 1968.
>   Interest on unpaid balance due is to be paid annually at 4% per annum from August 1, 1968, to July 31, 1970.
>   Interest on unpaid balance due is to be paid annually at 5% per annum from August 1, 1970, until entire balance is paid in full.
>   In addition to interest $6,000.00 on the principal is due November 1, 1969.
>   In addition to interest, $15,000.00 on the principal is due annually, beginning Nov. 1, 1970, and continuing until the entire purchase price is paid. The payments may be made in advance at any time and in any amount.
> 3. As each principal payment is made the proportionate number of shares of stock are to be transferred on the corporate records and delivered to Wilson.
> 4. In the event any payment of principal is not made on the due date, or within 90 days thereafter, Wilson thereby forfeits and loses his right to purchase that proportionate number of shares of stock; PROVIDED HOWEVER, that nevertheless any subsequent, or later payment of principal may be made according to the above payment schedule, and thereupon Wilson will be entitled to the proportionate number of shares of stock as represented by such payment. Interest payment must always be kept current before any delivery of stock is to be made resulting from a payment of principal.

> 5. For the period of one year from the date hereof Wilson is to have the full power to vote all of the stock herein agreed to be sold to him by Shook. Thereafter the voting rights of the stock is [sic] to be determined by the stock ownership records of the corporation.

On July 15, 1964, Shook also executed an irrevocable proxy granting to Wilson voting rights in 182 shares until September 10, 1965. Two other documents also executed on that date related to share ownership between Shook and Wilson. One, entitled "S&W Sawmill, Inc. Stockholders' Restrictive Agreement," provided in part as follows:

> [S]uch provisions (against stock transferability) do not apply to the presently existing Agreement for Sale and Purchase of Stock entered into between Dee Shook and Milo E. Wilson, dated the 15th day of July, 1964, and providing for the purchase by Milo E. Wilson of 182 shares of stock in the company.
>
> IT IS THE INTENTION AND PURPOSE of the incorporators that the majority of the ownership of the corporation is to be held by Dee Shook and Milo E. Wilson on an equal share basis when Milo E. Wilson completes the purchase of the stock certificates which are the subject of said purchase agreement. The other, entitled "Option to Buy Stock Forming Part Of Stockholders' Restrictive Agreement," provided in part that "the ownership of shares in S&W Sawmill, Inc., as the same now stands, to-wit: Dee Shook 365 shares, Milo E. Wilson 1 shares [sic] . . . shall continue."

In connection with the agreement for sale, Shook deposited stock certificates representing 182 shares with an escrow agent on July 17, 1964.

On August 19, 1964, S&W borrowed $200,000, in part upon the personal guarantees of Shook, Wilson, and their wives. The loan agreement referred to Shook and Wilson as "the principal officers and stockholders" of S&W. S&W agreed therein to insure the lives of Shook and Wilson for $100,000 each.

On March 19, 1965, Shook and Wilson agreed to purchase additional shares from S&W in an agreement which provided in part as follows:

> **Witnesseth**
>
> THAT WHEREAS, Prior to this date stock in the Corporation had been purchased by the Stockholders and a number of said shares are subject to an escrow agreement at Citizens State Bank, Hamilton, Montana, providing for the purchase by Milo E. Wilson of a certain number of shares of such stock from Dee Shook; that the purpose of said escrow arrangement is to provide for an equal ownership of the stock of said Corporation by Milo E. Wilson and Dee Shook;
>
> THAT WHEREAS, it is the desire of all parties at this time that each of the Stockholders purchase an additional One Hundred Shares of Stock at Five Hundred Dollars ($500.00) per share, and payment for the same having been made to the Corporation;
>
> NOW, THEREFORE, for and in consideration of the mutual benefits to be derived by all parties hereto, IT IS HEREBY AGREED AS FOLLOWS:
>
> That each of the Stockholders are to purchase One Hundred Shares of stock of the Corporation at Five Hundred Dollars ($500.00) per share;
>
> That, as well as with other stock purchases, it is the desire of the Stockholders that stock ownership held by Dee Shook and Milo E. Wilson are [sic] to remain equal; that any stock purchased or issued as a result of this agreement is to be regulated accordingly. . . .

Wilson made all payments in 1965 and 1966 specified in the agreement for sale and accordingly claimed interest deductions on his Federal income tax returns for those years.

On July 1, 1967, before principal payments were required by the agreement for sale, petitioner purchased all outstanding S&W stock. In anticipation of this purchase, a letter to petitioner dated May 3, 1967, and signed by Shook and Wilson stated as follows:

> To have it in the record, Milo E. Wilson owes Dee Shook $91,000 for 182 shares of S&W Sawmill Inc. stock in escrow at Citizens State Bank Hamilton Montana. On the purchase contract, Intermountain Lumber Co. would pay Dee Shook $91,000.00 more over the 14 yrs. than Milo E. Wilson.

Opinion . . .

In this case, respondent is in the unusual posture of arguing that a transfer to a corporation in return for stock was nontaxable under section 351, and Intermountain is in the equally unusual posture of arguing that the transfer was taxable because section 351 was inapplicable. The explanation is simply that Intermountain purchased all stock of the corporation, S&W, from its incorporators, and that Intermountain and S&W have filed consolidated income tax returns for years in issue. Accordingly, if section 351 was applicable to the incorporators when S&W was formed, S&W and Intermountain must depreciate the assets of S&W on their consolidated returns on the incorporators' basis. Sec. 362(a). If section 351 was inapplicable, and the transfer of assets to S&W was accordingly to be treated as a sale, S&W and Intermountain could base depreciation on those returns on the fair market value of those assets at the time of incorporation, which was higher than the incorporators' cost and which would accordingly provide larger depreciation deductions. . . .

Petitioner thus maintains that the transfer to S&W of all of S&W's property at the time of incorporation by the primary incorporator, one Dee Shook, was a taxable sale. It asserts that section 351 was inapplicable because an agreement for sale required Shook, as part of the incorporation transaction, to sell almost half of the S&W shares outstanding to one Milo Wilson over a period of time, thereby depriving Shook of the requisite percentage of stock necessary for "control" of S&W immediately after the exchange.

Respondent, on the other hand, maintains that the agreement between Shook and Wilson did not deprive Shook of ownership of the shares immediately after the exchange, as the stock purchase agreement merely gave Wilson an option to purchase the shares. Shook accordingly was in "control" of the corporation and the exchange was thus nontaxable under section 351.

Respondent has abandoned on brief his contention that Wilson was a transferor of property and therefore a person to also be counted for purposes of control under section 351. Respondent is correct in doing so, since Wilson did not transfer any property to S&W upon its initial formation in July of 1964. Wilson's agreement to transfer cash for corporate stock in March of 1965 cannot be considered part of the same transaction.

Since Wilson was not a transferor of property and therefore cannot be counted for control under section 351, William A. James, 53 T.C. 63, 69 (1969), we must determine if Shook alone owned the requisite percentage of shares for control. This determination depends upon whether, under all facts and circumstances surrounding the agreement for sale of 182 shares between Shook and Wilson, ownership of those shares was in Shook or Wilson.

A determination of "ownership," as that term is used in section 368(c) and for purposes of control under section 351, depends upon the obligations and freedom of action of the transferee with respect to the stock when he acquired it from the corporation. Such traditional ownership attributes as legal title, voting rights, and possession of stock certificates are not conclusive. If the transferee, as part of the transaction by which the shares were acquired, has irrevocably foregone or relinquished at that time the legal right to determine whether to keep the shares, ownership in such shares is lacking for purposes of section 351. By contrast, if there are no restrictions upon freedom of action at the time he acquired the shares, it is immaterial how soon thereafter the transferee elects to dispose of his stock or whether such disposition is in accord with a preconceived plan not amounting to a binding obligation. Stephens, Inc. v. United States, 464 F.2d 53, 66-67 (8th Cir. 1972), cert. denied 409 U.S. 1118 (1973). . . . After considering the entire record, we have concluded that Shook and Wilson intended to consummate a sale of the S&W stock, that they never doubted that the sale would be completed, that the sale was an integral part of the incorporation transaction, and that they considered themselves to be co-owners of S&W upon execution of the stock purchase agreement in 1964. These conclusions are supported by minutes of the first stockholders meeting on July 7, 1964, at which Shook characterized the agreement for sale as a "sale"; minutes of a special meeting on July 15, 1964, at which Shook stated Wilson was to "purchase" half of Shook's stock; the "Agreement for Sale and Purchase of Stock" itself, dated July 15, 1964, which is drawn as an installment sale and which provides for payment of interest on unpaid principal; Wilson's deduction of interest expenses in connection with the agreement for sale, which would be inconsistent with an option; the S&W loan agreement, in which Shook and Wilson held themselves out as the "principal stockholders" of S&W and in which S&W covenanted to equally insure Shook and Wilson for $100,000; the March 1965 stock purchase agreement with S&W, which indicated that Shook and Wilson "are to remain equal" shareholders in S&W; the letter of May 1967 from Shook and Wilson to Intermountain, which indicated that Wilson owed Shook the principal balance due on the shares as an unpaid obligation; and all surrounding facts and circumstances leading to corporate formation and execution of the above documents. Inconsistent and self-serving testimony of Shook and Wilson regarding their intent and understanding of the documents in evidence is unpersuasive in view of the record as a whole to alter interpretation of the transaction as a sale of stock by Shook to Wilson.

We accordingly cannot accept respondent's contention that the substance varied from the form of this transaction, which was, of course, labeled a "sale." The parties executed an "option" agreement on the same day that the "agreement for sale" was executed, and we have no doubt that they could and indeed did correctly distinguish between a sale and an option.

The agreement for sale's forfeiture clause, which provided that Wilson forfeited the right to purchase a proportionate number of shares for which timely principal payments were not made, did not convert it into an option agreement. Furthermore, the agreement for sale made no provision for forgiving interest payments on the remaining principal due should principal payments not be made on earlier dates; indeed, it specifically provided that "Interest payment must always be kept current before any delivery of stock is to be made resulting from a payment of principal."

We thus believe that Shook, as part of the same transaction by which the shares were acquired (indeed, the agreement for sale was executed before the sawmill was deeded to S&W), had relinquished when he acquired those shares the legal right to determine whether to keep them. Shook was under an obligation, upon receipt of the shares, to transfer the stock as he received Wilson's principal payments. Cf. S. Klein on the Square, Inc., 14 T.C. 786, 790 (1950), aff'd 188 F.2d 127 (2d Cir. 1951), cert. denied 342 U.S. 824 (1951). We note also that the agreement for sale gave Wilson the right to prepay principal and receive all 182 shares at any time in advance. Shook therefore did not own, within the meaning of section 368(c), the requisite percentage of stock immediately after the exchange to control the corporation as required for nontaxable treatment under section 351.

We note also that the basic premise of section 351 is to avoid recognition of gain or loss resulting from transfer of property to a corporation which works a change of form only. . . . Accordingly, if the transferor sells his stock as part of the same transaction, the transaction is taxable because there has been more than a mere change in form. In this case, the transferor agreed to sell and did sell 50 percent of the stock to be received, placed the certificates in the possession of an escrow agent, and granted a binding proxy to the purchaser to vote the stock being sold. Far more than a mere change in form was effected.

We accordingly hold for petitioner. Because of concessions of other issues, decisions will be entered under Rule 155.

NOTES

1. *Debt satisfaction?* Was Wilson's $91,000 debt to Shook satisfied when Shook and Wilson sold their stock to Intermountain Lumber and the sales agreement provided that Shook would receive $91,000 more than Wilson?

2. *Litigation posture.* The taxpayer argued that §351 did not apply, while the Service argued that the nonrecognition provision did apply, a reversal of the typical litigation posture. What is the reason for the reversal? If §351 were inapplicable, then Shook should have been taxed on the formation of the corporation. (Presumably, he already had paid a tax on the gain associated with his sale of stock to Wilson.) Can the Service send him a notice of deficiency for the tax on the gain associated with the stock not sold to Wilson? If not, why not?

3. *Immediately after.* Section 351 requires that the transferors be in control of the corporation "immediately after the exchange." See Treas. Regs. §1.351-1(a)(1). *Intermountain* typifies much of the litigation over this term. Most of the cases involve situations in which the transferors are momentarily in control of the transferee but thereafter dispose of enough shares to bring the transferor group below the 80-percent threshold.

The court ruled in favor of the taxpayer because of the preconceived plan for Shook to sell stock to Wilson. In essence, it concluded that Shook and Wilson each owned half of the S&W stock "immediately after the exchange," measuring stock ownership for this purpose immediately after the stock sale. Although Shook and Wilson together controlled S&W, Wilson and Shook were not members of a transferor group, because Wilson transferred no property to S&W as part of S&W's incorporation. Thus, Shook's exchange with S&W could qualify under §351 only if he alone controlled S&W. Because he owned only half of the S&W stock after the stock sale, he did not control S&W, and §351 did not apply to Shook's exchange.

4. *Wilson as transferor?* Could §351 have applied to Shook (and Wilson) if Wilson had also transferred property to S&W in exchange for S&W stock? Suppose that, as part of S&W's incorporation, Wilson had transferred property to S&W for 20 percent of its stock and had then purchased the remainder of his half interest from Shook? Would Shook and Wilson be members of a transferor group? What if Wilson had received only 1 percent of the S&W stock on his property exchange with S&W?

Similar issues were considered in Rev. Rul. 79-194, 1979-1 C.B. 145, a ruling that examined two situations in which *B* and *C* formed a corporation, Newco, each transferring property to Newco in exchange for Newco stock. In the first situation, *B* and *C* received 80 percent and 20 percent of the Newco stock, respectively. In the second situation, *B* and *C* instead received 99 percent and 1 percent of the Newco stock, respectively. In each situation, as part of a prearranged plan, *B* sold Newco stock to *C*, leaving *B* with 49 percent and *C* with 51 percent of the Newco stock.

In the first situation, the Service ruled that *C* was a transferor and that *B* and *C* were members of a transferor group that controlled Newco "immediately after the exchange" (i.e., immediately after *B*'s sale to *C*). Thus, §351 applied to *B*'s and *C*'s transfers of property to Newco for Newco stock.

In the second situation, however, the Service ruled that *C* was not a transferor, citing to (and arguably expanding) Treas. Regs. §1.351-1(a)(1)(ii), the "accommodation transferor" provision. The Service concluded that *C* was not a transferor, reasoning that the amount of Newco stock *C* received from Newco was relatively small in value compared to the Newco stock *C* "received . . . in the transaction." Because *B* alone did not control Newco immediately after the sale, §351 did not apply to *B*'s exchange with Newco.

5. *The step transaction doctrine.*

a. *In general.* The "immediately after" problem arises in the context of the pervasive step transaction doctrine, examined in more detail at page 276 infra. That doctrine will sometimes be applied to integrate more than one transaction into a single, unified transaction, and a person's receipt of control in a purported §351 exchange will sometimes be integrated with a post-acquisition sale of stock to spoil nonrecognition treatment. The test most often applied to integrate two transactions is the "mutual interdependence" test. (*Query*: Can there be nonmutual interdependence?) One court stated the test as follows: "Were the steps so interdependent that the legal relations created by one transaction would have been fruitless without a completion of the series?" American Bantam Car Co. v. Commissioner, 11 T.C. 397, 405 (1948), aff'd, 177 F.2d 513 (3d Cir. 1949). The Tax Court, though articulating the mutual interdependence test, refused to integrate steps in the absence of a preexisting binding commitment by the transferors to sell the stock received in McDonald's of Zion, Ill., Inc. v. Commissioner, 76 T.C.

972 (1981), rev'd sub nom. McDonald's Restaurants of Ill., Inc. v. Commissioner, 688 F.2d 520 (7th Cir. 1982).

In ascertaining whether steps are interdependent, the amount of time between transactions can be important. If the steps are contemporaneous or separated by short time intervals, courts are more likely to integrate the steps. See American Bantam Car v. Commissioner, supra. But compare Commissioner v. Ashland Oil & Refining Co., 99 F.2d 588 (6th Cir. 1938), cert. denied, 306 U.S. 661 (1939) (steps that occurred six years apart integrated), with Henricksen v. Braicks, 137 F.2d 632 (9th Cir. 1943) (transactions one half-hour apart treated as separate).

b. *Distributions by corporate shareholders.* In one circumstance, Congress has determined that fleeting control is insignificant. Section 351(c) specifically allows corporate transferors to distribute the stock received to their shareholders without violating the control requirement. See Martin Ice Cream Co. v. Commissioner, 110 T.C. 189 (1998). Does this restricted exception suggest that fleeting control is insufficient where the special rule is inapplicable?

c. *Post-exchange gift.* Consider a transfer followed by a gift of stock received in the exchange. Wilgard Realty Co. v. Commissioner, 127 F.2d 514 (2d Cir. 1942), involved a transfer of appreciated property by an individual to a corporation in exchange for all of its stock. Immediately after the stock was issued to him, he transferred more than 20 percent of it by gift to members of his family. On a later sale of the transferred property, the corporation claimed a stepped-up basis on the ground that the incorporation failed the control test and therefore that §351 was inapplicable. The court held that §351 was applicable because the transferor was not legally bound to make a gift. In contrast, the court in Fahs v. Florida Machine & Foundry Co., 168 F.2d 957 (5th Cir. 1948), ruled that §351 did not apply when more than 20 percent of the shares were issued directly to the transferor's son, even though the transferor may have been under no obligation to make the gift. See also Mojonnier & Sons v. Commissioner, 12 T.C. 837 (1949). But see Stanton v. United States, 512 F.2d 13 (3d Cir. 1975), and D'Angelo Associates v. Commissioner, 70 T.C. 121 (1978), rejecting a distinction in gift cases based on whether the donee receives stock directly from the transferee or from the transferor.

d. *Stock issuance.* The "immediately after" issue also arises when, soon after the exchange, the transferee corporation issues additional stock. In American Bantam Car Co. v. Commissioner, supra, the transferors transferred assets to the corporation in exchange for common stock. The plan also called for a sale of preferred shares to the public through underwriters who were to get more than 20 percent of the common shares if they sold the preferred. Four months later, the underwriters sold the preferred and received the common shares. The court held §351 applicable, concluding that control existed after the exchange and that a later loss of control was not an integral part of the transaction because the exchange itself would have taken place even if the plan for the public sale of the preferred had failed.

e. *Underwriting.* If a person buys stock from an underwriter for cash in a "qualified underwriting transaction," the person is treated as buying the stock directly from the corporation for purposes of §351. Treas. Regs. §1.351-1(a)(3). A qualified underwriting transaction is one where the corporation issues stock for cash in an underwriting in which the underwriter is the corporation's agent or its ownership of the stock is transitory.

PROBLEM

2-1. In the following, Alex and Bertha form *X* Corp. Alex begins with a parcel of land held for investment worth $1,000 with an adjusted basis of $300 and ends up with a 50-percent interest in *X* Corp. stock plus $500. Bertha begins with $500 and ends up with a 50-percent interest in *X* Corp. stock. *X* Corp. ends up with the land. Are the following transactions described in section 351?

a. Alex transfers the property to *X* Corp. for all of *X*'s stock. Shortly thereafter, Alex sells half of his *X* stock to Bertha for $500.
b. Prior to the incorporation, Alex sells a half interest in the land to Bertha for $500, and then both Alex and Bertha form *X* Corp.

C. TAX CONSEQUENCES OF A §351 EXCHANGE

In surveying the tax consequences of a §351 exchange, this section first examines transactions where no boot is paid or liabilities are assumed by the controlled corporation. It next studies the effect of the receipt of boot in a §351 exchange. It then explores the various ways that the assumption of liabilities may affect the tax consequences to the shareholders and controlled corporation before concluding with a study of some special basis and holding period rules that may apply to a §351 exchange.

1. A "Solely for Stock" Exchange

Under §1001(a), a person realizes gain or loss on her exchange of property, in whole or in part, for stock of a corporation. Under §1001(c), the person recognizes that gain or loss, except as the Code provides. Section 351 provides one exception.

If §351 applies to a person's exchange of property for stock of the transferee corporation and the *sole* consideration that she receives is transferee stock, the person recognizes none of her realized gain or loss on the exchange. §351(a). She takes a basis in the stock received equal to the aggregate basis of the property surrendered in exchange. §358(a). Finally, because she takes an exchanged basis in the stock received, her holding period for that stock includes the holding period of the property surrendered for that stock, but only if she held that property surrendered as a capital asset or §1231 asset at the time of the exchange. §1223(1).

Under §1032(a), a corporation recognizes no gain or loss when it acquires property for its stock (whether or not §351 applies to the transferor on the exchange). Thus, the transferee corporation recognizes no gain or loss on its acquisition of property for its stock. If the transferor recognizes no gain on the exchange, the transferee corporation's basis in the transferred property generally equals the transferor's basis in that property. §362(a). But cf. §362(e). Finally, because the transferee corporation takes a "transferred" or "carryover" basis in the property received from the transferor shareholder, the corporation includes or "tacks" the transferor's holding period in the property received. §1223(2).

PROBLEMS

2-2. John, an individual and cash basis, calendar year taxpayer, operates a retail store. On January 15 of year 1, he purchased land and a building for $500,000, and $420,000 of the purchase price properly was allocable to the building. He used the property in his trade or business, and for year 1 properly took a $20,000 depreciation deduction on the building. On January 1 of year 2, he contributed the land (worth $80,000) and building (worth $420,000) to a newly formed, wholly owned corporation, *C* Inc., in exchange for all of its stock. *C* Inc. uses the land and building in its trade or business. For the sake of simplicity, assume that John took no depreciation deductions on the building for year 2.

a. Does the transaction qualify under §351(a)? Why? What are the federal income tax consequences of the transfer and exchange to John and to *C* Inc.?
b. John sells the *C* stock on December 1 of year 2 for $550,000. What are the federal income tax consequences of the sale to John and *C* Inc.?
c. *C* sells the land and building on January 14 of year 2 for $500,000. (Assume that the land and building have the same values as when John bought them.) What are the federal income tax consequences of the sale to John and to *C* Inc.? How do the answers change, if at all, if the sale occurs on January 16 of year 2? Do the differences, if any, make sense?
d. Assume that instead of transferring the land and building, John transferred inventory described in §1221(a)(1) with a $120,000 basis and $500,000 value to *C* Inc. on January 1 of year 2. How does that affect your answers to (a) and (b) above?
e. Would the answers to (a)-(d) be affected if *C* Inc. was an existing corporation wholly owned by John? How about if *C* Inc. issued no stock to John in exchange for the property? How about if John, Inc., rather than John, made the transfers to *C* Inc.?

2-3. Assume that the facts are the same as in problem 2-2, except that later in the day on January 1 of year 2, Mary contributes property to *C* Inc. and receives in exchange 30 percent of the only class of *C* stock.

a. Are Mary and John part of a transferor group? How would you assure that they are members of a transferor group?
b. How would your analysis change if Mary's contribution occurred on January 20 of year 2, rather than on January 1?

2. Boot

a. Shareholders — Gain or Loss

If a person transfers property to a transferee corporation in a §351 exchange and receives other property ("boot") in addition to transferee stock, she still cannot recognize a loss but must recognize any realized gain up to the boot's fair market value. §351(b). Thus, if §351 applies to a person's exchange, the person recognizes no loss and recognizes gain equal to the smaller of (i) any realized gain and (ii) the fair market value of any boot received in the exchange.

For example, suppose that *T* transfers an asset with a \$10 basis and a \$50 fair market value to *X* Corp. in exchange for \$20 of *X* Corp. stock and \$30 cash in a transaction that would otherwise qualify under §351. Under §1001(a), *T* realizes a \$40 gain, but under §351(b)(1), *T* recognizes only \$30 of that gain, the smaller of his realized gain (\$40) and the value of the boot received (\$30). If, however, *T*'s basis in the surrendered asset had been \$70, not \$10, *T* would have realized a \$20 loss, but under §351(b)(2), he would have recognized none of that loss.

The recognized gain may be capital gain or ordinary income, and its character depends on the nature of the property transferred. For example, any taxable gain is treated as ordinary income to the extent the transferred property is subject to depreciation recapture. Note that in the absence of boot, depreciable property transferred in a §351 exchange is not subject to recapture. §1245(b)(3) and §1250(d)(3).

If a person transfers more than one asset to a transferee corporation in a §351 exchange, gain or loss must be computed separately for each asset, raising at least two questions: (1) If boot is received in the exchange, how is it allocated among those assets; and (2) can the person offset realized gain on one asset with realized loss on another asset in computing her overall recognized gain?

Rev. Rul. 68-55

1968-1 C.B. 140

In determining the amount of gain recognized under section 351(b) . . . where several assets were transferred to a corporation, each asset must be considered transferred separately in exchange for a portion of each category of consideration received. The fair market value of each category of consideration received is separately allocated to the transferred assets in proportion to the relative fair market values of the transferred assets. Where as a result of such allocation there is a realized loss with respect to any asset, such loss is not recognized under section 351(b)(2) of the Code.

Advice has been requested as to the correct method of determining the amount and character of the gain to be recognized by Corporation *X* under section 351(b) . . . under the circumstances described below.

Corporation *Y* was organized by *X* and *A*, an individual who owned no stock in *X*. *A* transferred 20*x* dollars to *Y* in exchange for stock of *Y* having a fair market value of 20*x* dollars and *X* transferred to *Y* three separate assets and received in exchange stock of *Y* having a fair market value of 100*x* dollars plus cash of 10*x* dollars.

In accordance with the facts set forth in the table below if *X* had sold at fair market value each of the three assets it transferred to *Y*, the result would have been as follows:

	Asset I	*Asset II*	*Asset III*
Character of asset	Capital asset held more than [one year]	Capital asset held not more than [one year]	Section 1245 property.
Fair market value	$22*x*	$33*x*	$55*x*
Adjusted basis	40*x*	20*x*	25*x*
Gain (loss)	($18*x*)	$13*x*	$30*x*
Character of gain or loss	Long-term capital loss.	Short-term capital gain.	Ordinary income.

The facts in the instant case disclose that with respect to the section 1245 property the depreciation subject to recapture exceeds the amount of gain that would be recognized on a sale at fair market value. Therefore, all of such gain would be treated as ordinary income under section 1245(a)(1) of the Code.

Under section 351(a) of the Code, no gain or loss is recognized if property is transferred to a corporation solely in exchange for its stock and immediately after the exchange the transferor is in control of the corporation. If section 351(a) of the Code would apply to an exchange but for the fact that there is received, in addition to the property permitted to be received without recognition of gain, other property or money, then under section 351(b) of the Code gain (if any) to the recipient will be recognized, but in an amount not in excess of the sum of such money and the fair market value of such other property received, and no loss to the recipient will be recognized.

The first question presented is how to determine the amount of gain to be recognized under section 351(b) of the Code. The general rule is that each asset transferred must be considered to have been separately exchanged. See the authorities cited in Revenue Ruling 67-192, C.B. 1967-2, 140, and in Revenue Ruling 68-23, [1968-1 C.B. 144], which hold that there is no netting of gains and losses for purposes of applying sections 367 and 356(c) of the Code. Thus, for purposes of making computations under section 351(b) of the Code, it is not proper to total the bases of the various assets transferred and to subtract this total from the fair market value of the total consideration received in the exchange. Moreover, any treatment other than an asset-by-asset approach would have the effect of allowing losses that are specifically disallowed by section 351(b)(2) of the Code.

The second question presented is how, for purposes of making computations under section 351(b) of the Code, to allocate the cash and stock received to the amount realized as to each asset transferred in the exchange. The asset-by-asset approach for computing the amount of gain realized in the exchange requires that for this purpose the fair market value of each category of consideration received must be separately allocated to the transferred assets in proportion to the relative fair market values of the transferred assets. See section 1.1245-4(c)(1) of the Income Tax Regulations which, for the same reasons, requires that for purposes of computing the amount of gain to which section 1245 of the Code applies each category of consideration received must be allocated to the properties transferred in proportion to their relative fair market values.

Accordingly, the amount and character of the gain recognized in the exchange should be computed as follows:

	Total	*Asset I*	*Asset II*	*Asset III*
Fair market value of asset transferred	\$110*x*	\$22*x*	\$33*x*	\$55*x*
Percent of total fair market value		20%	30%	50%
Fair market value of *Y* stock received in exchange	\$100*x*	\$20*x*	\$30*x*	\$50*x*
Cash received in exchange	10*x*	2*x*	3*x*	5*x*
Amount realized	\$110*x*	\$22*x*	\$33*x*	\$55*x*
Adjusted basis		40*x*	20*x*	25*x*
Gain (loss) realized		(\$18*x*)	\$13*x*	\$30*x*

Under section 351(b)(2) of the Code the loss of 18*x* dollars realized on the exchange of Asset Number I is not recognized. Such loss may not be used to offset the gains realized on the exchanges of the other assets. Under section 351(b)(1) of the Code, the gain of 13*x* dollars realized on the exchange of Asset Number II will be recognized as short-term capital gain in the amount of 3*x* dollars, the amount of cash received. Under sections 351(b)(1) and 1245(b)(3) of the Code, the gain of 30*x* dollars realized on the exchange of Asset Number III will be recognized as ordinary income in the amount of 5*x* dollars, the amount of cash received.

b. Shareholders — Basis and Holding Period

As a general rule under §358(a)(1), the shareholder takes an aggregate basis in the transferee stock received in the exchange equal to the following:

1. The aggregate basis of the property transferred, plus
2. Any gain recognized by the shareholder on the exchange, minus
3. The value of any boot received.[2]

See also §358(b) and Treas. Regs. §1.358-2(b) (providing that if a transferor receives more than one class of transferee stock, basis is allocated among the classes based on the fair market values of the stock received in each class). This basis rule preserves the shareholder's realized but unrecognized gain or loss in the basis in the transferee stock received in the exchange.

2. Section 358(h) and §362(e)(2)(C) provide possible exceptions to this general rule. Section 358(h) is discussed at page 54 infra, and §362(e)(2)(C) is discussed at page 58 infra.

The shareholder takes a basis in any boot received equal to its fair market value. §358(a)(2).

Because the shareholder takes an exchanged basis in the stock received, her holding period for that stock includes the holding period of the property surrendered for the stock, but only if she held the property surrendered as a capital asset or §1231 asset at the time of the exchange. §1223(1).[3]

c. Transferee Corporation — Gain or Loss

When a corporation acquires property for its stock, it recognizes no gain or loss. §1032. By regulation, a corporation also recognizes no gain or loss when it acquires services for its stock. See Treas. Regs. §1.1032-1(a). Can the corporation take a deduction, if appropriate? See Rev. Rul. 62-217, 1962-2 C.B. 59, modified by Rev. Rul. 74-503, 1974-2 C.B. 117 (deduction allowed, if appropriate).

If the transferee corporation transfers boot in the §351 exchange, it may recognize gain but not loss. §351(f) (adopting the principles of §311). It recognizes gain on its use of appreciated non-cash property, equal to the excess of the property's fair market value over its adjusted basis. Of course, the corporation recognizes no gain or loss on its use of cash.

d. Transferee Corporation — Basis and Holding Period

When the transferee corporation receives property in exchange for stock in a §351 transaction, §362(a) generally provides that the transferor's basis for the transferred property "carries over" to the corporation. If the corporation receives multiple assets, the transferor's basis in each transferred asset "carries over" to the corporation. See P.A. Birren & Son v. Commissioner, 116 F.2d 718 (7th Cir. 1940).

More precisely, the transferee corporation generally takes a basis in the property transferred equal to the transferor's basis plus any gain recognized by the transferor. §362(a).[4] If more than one asset is transferred, it is not altogether clear how this gain is allocated among the transferred assets. Consistent with Rev. Rul. 68-55, page 35 supra and (under the only approach that really makes sense), any gain recognized by a transferor on an asset should be allocated to that asset under §362. See Priv. Ltr. Rul. 200842038 (Oct. 17, 2008) (implying that this approach is used).

Because the transferee corporation takes a basis in a transferred asset determined by reference to the transferor's adjusted basis in that asset, the corporation's holding period for the asset includes the transferee's holding period. §1223(2).

3. If a shareholder transfers multiple properties, her basis and holding period for each share may be split. For a discussion of that issue, see page 55 infra.

4. This basis increase may be limited if the transferor recognizes gain as the result of the transferee assuming a liability. See §362(d), discussed at page 55 infra. See also §362(e), discussed at page 58 infra, which may limit the basis that the transferee corporation takes in transferred property.

PROBLEMS

2-4. Sally and George form *W* Inc. As part of one plan and on one day, Sally transfers land worth $100,000 in exchange for 100 shares of *W* stock, and George transfers equipment worth $140,000 in exchange for 100 shares of *W* stock and $40,000 cash. Sally held the land for investment and purchased it several years ago. George used the equipment in his trade or business, purchasing it five years ago. Does §351 apply to the exchange? Assuming that it does, describe the gain or loss that Sally, George, and *W* Inc. recognize, the basis each takes in the property received in the exchange, and the holding period for the property. In this analysis, assume that Sally's basis in the land is $60,000, and George's basis in the equipment is—

a. $20,000; or
b. $130,000.

What issues (in addition to tax issues) would you have to discuss with Sally and George if they asked you to represent both of them on the exchange?

2-5. How would your answers to problem 2-4 differ if, instead of transferring cash to George, *W* Inc. transferred an asset with a $35,000 basis and $40,000 value? What if that asset had a $55,000 basis?

3. *Assumption of Liabilities*

a. In General

When a buyer assumes a seller's liability, the seller's amount realized includes the amount of the assumed liability. See §1001(b). In effect, the seller is treated as receiving property with a dollar value equal to the liability amount.

If the transferee corporation assumes a transferor's liability in a §351 exchange, could the transferor be treated as receiving boot equal to the liability amount? In United States v. Hendler, 303 U.S. 564 (1938), the court concluded that an assumption of the transferor's liability was boot under somewhat parallel reorganization sections. The Service quickly recognized that its "victory" threatened the federal coffers by encouraging transferee corporations to claim a stepped-up basis under §362(a) for gain that should have been recognized by the transferors under *Hendler*—even if tax on that gain was unreachable because of the statute of limitations. The Treasury hastened to relinquish its victory, culminating in the enactment of §357.

Under the general rule of §357(a), the assumption of a liability by the transferee corporation is not treated as the payment of boot in a §351 exchange. Thus, the transferor generally does not recognize gain in a §351 exchange merely because the transferee corporation assumes the transferor's liability. That result makes sense, for example, if the transferor incurs the liability to acquire the transferred property. Then, the transferor does not cash out any gain on the transferred property through the transferee's liability assumption.

The result seems troubling, however, if a transferor's assumed liabilities exceed the aggregate basis of the transferred property, because the transferor has then either cashed out a portion of the gain (e.g., by borrowing against appreciation) or enjoyed a tax benefit (e.g., depreciation deduction) that should be recaptured on the transfer. Section 357(c)(1) responds to that concern, providing that a transferor recognizes gain to the extent that the assumed liabilities exceed the aggregate adjusted basis of *all* property transferred by the transferor.

Sometimes, though, §357(c)(1) seems either too generous or too harsh. It seems too generous, for example, if, instead of the transferor's receiving cash in a §351 exchange, she incurs a liability in anticipation of the exchange that the transferee corporation assumes. If §357(c)(1) applies, the transferor recognizes gain only to the extent, if at all, that the assumed liabilities exceed the aggregate basis of the transferred assets. If the transferor had instead received boot, she would have recognized realized gain up to the boot's value.

The concern raised by that example may be addressed by §357(b). Under §357(b), a transferor treats the assumption of *all* liabilities by the corporate transferee as the payment of boot for purposes of §351(b) if the transferor's principal purpose for the assumption of *any* liability was not a "bona fide business purpose" or was to avoid federal income tax on the exchange. See Thompson v. Campbell, 353 F.2d 787 (5th Cir. 1965) (considering a mortgage placed on property on the eve of incorporation). See also §357(c)(2)(A) (providing that §357(c)(1) does not apply to the assumption of §357(b) liabilities).

On the other hand, §357(c)(1) seems too harsh if a transferor recognized gain merely because the corporate transferee assumed a liability that, if paid by the transferor, would have resulted in a deduction or added basis. A deductible liability may include, for example, an accounts payable of a cash basis taxpayer.

Congress addressed deductible liabilities in §357(c)(3). Under that provision, a liability is disregarded in applying §357(c)(1) if it would have given rise to a deduction if paid by the transferor.[5] In Rev. Rul. 95-74, 1975-2 C.B. 36, the Service expanded §357(c)(3) to include liabilities that would have created or increased basis *if paid* by the transferor. Cf. §357(c)(3)(B) (providing that §357(c)(3) liabilities do not include any liability that *when incurred* resulted in the creation of, or increase in, basis).

A transferor's basis in the transferee corporation stock received in the exchange generally equals (i) the aggregate basis of the property transferred, plus (ii) any gain recognized by the shareholder on the exchange under §351(b) and §357(c)(1), minus (iii) the value of any boot received. §358(a)(1). But see §358(h) (for a special basis rule, discussed at page 54 infra). For this purpose, an assumed liability, other than a §357(c)(3) liability, is treated as money received on the exchange. §358(d).

The transferee corporation's basis in property received in the §351 exchange generally equals the transferor's adjusted basis in the property, plus any gain recognized by the transferor. §362(a). But see §362(d) and (e) (for special basis rules,

5. Somewhat surprisingly, the Service has ruled that a transferee corporation generally may deduct a deductible liability when paid, even though it was incurred by the transferor. Rev. Rul. 80-198, 1980-2 C.B. 113 (warning that the transferee may not be entitled to a deduction for the liability payment if the §351 exchange improperly separated income from related expenses).

If the transferee corporation may deduct assumed account payables, is it then also taxable on transferred account receivables, contrary to the assignment of income rules? See Hempt Bros. v. United States, 490 F.2d 1172 (3d Cir. 1974) (assignment of income doctrine not applicable). See also page 73 infra.

discussed at page 55 infra and page 58 infra). Note that the transferor's adjusted basis in the transferred property is increased by gain recognized under either §351(b) or §357(c)(1).

To illustrate these rules, suppose that *T* transfers an asset with a $1,000 basis and a $15,000 fair market value to *X* Corp. in a transaction that qualifies under §351. In exchange, *T* receives $12,000 of *X* Corp. stock, and *X* Corp. assumes *T*'s $3,000 liability.

Assume first that the assumed liability is neither a §357(b) nor a §357(c)(3) liability. Then, *T* treats *X*'s assumption of the liability as the payment of boot for purposes of §358, but not for purposes of §351, and the liability is taken into account in applying §357(c)(1). Under §357(c)(1), *T* recognizes a $2,000 gain, the amount by which the assumed indebtedness ($3,000) exceeds the adjusted basis of the transferred asset ($1,000).[6] *T*'s basis in the *X* stock equals $0, the basis of the transferred property ($1,000), plus the gain *T* recognized on the exchange ($2,000), minus value of the boot considered received on the exchange ($3,000 for the assumed liability). §358(a)(1) and (d)(1). *X*'s basis in the transferred asset equals $3,000, *T*'s adjusted basis in the asset ($1,000), plus *T*'s recognized gain ($2,000). §362(a).

Assume instead that the assumed liability is a §357(b) liability. Then, *T* treats *X*'s assumption of the liability as the payment of boot for purposes of both §351 and §358, but the liability is not taken into account in applying §357(c)(1). Under §351(b), *T* recognizes a $3,000 gain, the smaller of *T*'s $14,000 realized gain and the $3,000 boot received. *T*'s basis in the *X* stock equals $1,000, the basis of the transferred property ($1,000), plus the gain *T* recognized on the exchange ($3,000), minus value of the boot considered received on the exchange ($3,000 for the assumed liability). §358(a)(1) and (d)(1). *X*'s basis in the transferred asset equals $4,000, *T*'s adjusted basis in the asset ($1,000), plus *T*'s recognized gain ($3,000). §362(a).

Finally assume that the assumed liability is a §357(c)(3) liability. Then, the liability is not taken into account as boot under §351(b) or §358 and is disregarded in applying §357(c)(1). Thus, *T* is treated as receiving solely *X* stock in the exchange and recognizes no gain. §351(a). *T*'s basis in the *X* stock equals $1,000, the basis of the transferred property ($1,000), plus the gain *T* recognized on the exchange ($0), minus value of the boot considered received on the exchange ($0). §358(a)(1) and (d)(2). *X*'s basis in the transferred asset also equals $1,000, *T*'s adjusted basis in the asset ($1,000), plus *T*'s recognized gain ($0).

b. Assuming a Liability

A corporate transferee is treated as assuming a recourse liability if, based on the facts and circumstances, "it has agreed to, and is expected to satisfy" the liability. §357(d)(1)(A). The transferee may assume a liability even if the transferor remains

6. For purposes of §1001(b), *T*'s amount realized equals the sum of the value of the stock ($12,000) plus the amount of the assumed liability ($3,000). Treas. Regs. §1.1001-2(a)(1) and (4). Thus, *T*'s realized gain equals $14,000, the excess of the amount realized ($15,000) over the basis of the transferred asset ($1,000).

legally responsible for the liability. *Id.* See also Owen v. Commissioner, 881 F.2d 832 (9th Cir. 1989).

However, if the transferee does not agree to or is not expected to satisfy a recourse liability, the liability is ignored for purposes of §357 and §358. §357(d)(1)(A). For example, assume that a person transfers property to a corporation in a §351 exchange, and the property has a $40 basis and a $100 fair market value and is secured by a $70 recourse loan. The transferee is not treated as assuming the loan if it is clear that the transferor rather than the transferee will satisfy the $70 loan. Then, the transferor recognizes no gain.[7] If, however, the corporate transferee is treated as assuming the loan, the transferor recognizes a $30 gain under §357(c)(1) (assuming that the liability is not described in §357(b) or (c)(3)).

In general, if a transferee receives an asset subject to a nonrecourse liability, the transferee is treated as assuming that liability. §357(d)(1)(B). However, the amount of the liability treated as assumed is reduced by the smaller of the following two amounts:

1. The amount that an owner of nontransferred assets subject to the liability has agreed with the transferee to, and is expected to, satisfy; or
2. The fair market value of those nontransferred assets.

§357(d)(2) (also determining the fair market value of the assets without regard to §7701(g)).

c. Avoiding §357(c)(1) Gain

Disregarding §357(b) and §357(c)(3) liabilities, a transferor recognizes gain under §357(c)(1) to the extent that the transferee corporation assumes liabilities of the transferor that exceed the aggregate basis of the property transferred by the transferor in the §351 exchange. A transferor can avoid this gain in two ways—by transferring additional assets with sufficient basis or by limiting the liabilities that the transferee corporation assumes.

Suppose *T* owns a building with a $60,000 basis and $100,000 value that secures a $75,000 recourse liability. Assume that the liability is neither a §357(b) nor §357(c)(3) liability. If *T* transfers the building to newly formed *X* Corp. in a transaction qualifying under §351 and *X* assumes the liability, *T* recognizes a $15,000 gain under §357(c)(1), the excess of the amount of the liability assumed ($75,000) over the building's basis ($60,000).

T could avoid that gain by limiting the amount of the liability that *X* assumed in the exchange to $60,000. She could also avoid the gain by transferring additional assets in the exchange. For example, suppose *T* transfers not only the building but also equipment with a $15,000 basis to *X* Corp. in the exchange, and *X* assumes the $75,000 liability. Even though the liability secures only the building, *T* applies §357(c)(1) by looking to her $75,000 aggregate basis in the building and equipment. Because that aggregate basis equals the $75,000 amount of the assumed

7. Note, however, that if the transferee corporation later pays all or a portion of the liability, the transferor will be treated as receiving a constructive distribution taxed under §301. See page 126 infra.

liability, *T* recognizes no gain under §357(c)(1). See Treas. Regs. §1.357-2(a). Note that if *B* had transferred the equipment and *T* had transferred the building, *T* could not use the basis of *B*'s asset to avoid §357(c) gain. Rev. Rul. 66-142, 1966-2 C.B. 66 (applying §357(c)(1) using a person-by-person approach).

The result in the previous example is the same if *T* transfers $15,000 of her own money rather than transferring the equipment. Would the result also be the same if *T* instead transferred a promise (i.e., *T*'s own note) to pay $15,000 to *X* Corp. in five years, bearing appropriate interest? *T* arguably avoids §357(c)(1) gain on the transfer of the note only if the note is "property" for purposes of §351 and *T* has a $15,000 basis in the note, issues considered in the following case.

Peracchi v. Commissioner

143 F.3d 487 (9th Cir. 1998)

Kozinski, Circuit Judge:

We must unscramble a Rubik's Cube of corporate tax law to determine the basis of a note contributed by a taxpayer to his wholly-owned corporation.

The Transaction

The taxpayer, Donald Peracchi, needed to contribute additional capital to his closely-held corporation (NAC) to comply with Nevada's minimum premium-to-asset ratio for insurance companies. Peracchi contributed two parcels of real estate. The parcels were encumbered with liabilities which together exceeded Peracchi's total basis in the properties by more than half a million dollars. As we discuss in detail below, under section 357(c), contributing property with liabilities in excess of basis can trigger immediate recognition of gain in the amount of the excess. In an effort to avoid this, Peracchi also executed a promissory note, promising to pay NAC $1,060,000 over a term of ten years at 11% interest. Peracchi maintains that the note has a basis equal to its face amount, there by making his total basis in the property contributed greater than the total liabilities. If this is so, he will have extracted himself from the quicksand of section 357(c) and owe no immediate tax on the transfer of property to NAC. The IRS, though, maintains that (1) the note is not genuine indebtedness and should be treated as an unenforceable gift; and (2) even if the note is genuine, it does not increase Peracchi's basis in the property contributed.

The parties are not splitting hairs: Peracchi claims the basis of the note is $1,060,000, its face value, while the IRS argues that the note has a basis of zero. If Peracchi is right, he pays no immediate tax on the half a million dollars by which the debts on the land he contributed exceed his basis in the land; if the IRS is right, the note becomes irrelevant for tax purposes and Peracchi must recognize an immediate gain on the half million. The fact that the IRS and Peracchi are so far apart suggests they are looking at the transaction through different colored lenses. To figure out whether Peracchi's lens is rose-tinted or clear, it is useful to take a guided tour of sections 351 and 357 and the tax law principles undergirding them.

Into the Lobster Pot: Section 351

The Code tries to make organizing a corporation pain-free from a tax point of view. A capital contribution is, in tax lingo, a "nonrecognition" event: A shareholder can generally contribute capital without recognizing gain on the exchange. It's merely a change in the form of ownership, like moving a billfold from one pocket to another. See I.R.C. section 351. So long as the shareholders contributing the property remain in control of the corporation after the exchange, section 351 applies: It doesn't matter if the capital contribution occurs at the creation of the corporation or if — as here — the company is already up and running. The baseline is that Peracchi may contribute property to NAC without recognizing gain on the exchange.

Gain Deferral: Section 358(a)

Peracchi contributed capital to NAC in the form of real property and a promissory note. Corporations may be funded with any kind of asset, such as equipment, real estate, intellectual property, contracts, leaseholds, securities or letters of credit. The tax consequences can get a little complicated because a shareholder's basis in the property contributed often differs from its fair market value. The general rule is that an asset's basis is equal to its "cost." See I.R.C. section 1012. But when a shareholder like Peracchi contributes property to a corporation in a nonrecognition transaction, a cost basis does not preserve the unrecognized gain. Rather than take a basis equal to the fair market value of the property exchanged, the shareholder must substitute the basis of that property for what would otherwise be the cost basis of the stock. This preserves the gain for recognition at a later day: The gain is built into the shareholder's new basis in the stock, and he will recognize income when he disposes of the stock.

The fact that gain is deferred rather than extinguished doesn't diminish the importance of questions relating to basis and the timing of recognition. In tax, as in comedy, timing matters. Most taxpayers would much prefer to pay tax on contributed property years later — when they sell their stock — rather than when they contribute the property.[7] Thus what Peracchi is seeking here is gain deferral: He wants the gain to be recognized only when he disposes of some or all of this stock.

Continuity of Investment: Boot and Section 351(b)

Continuity of investment is the cornerstone of nonrecognition under section 351. Nonrecognition assumes that a capital contribution amounts to nothing more than a nominal change in the form of ownership; in substance the shareholder's investment in the property continues. But a capital contribution can sometimes allow a shareholder to partially terminate his investment in an asset or group of assets. For example, when a shareholder receives cash or other property in addition to stock, receipt of that property reflects a partial termination of investment in the

7. Of course, should the taxpayers be lucky enough to die before disposing of the stock, their heirs would take a stepped-up basis in the stock equal to its fair market value as of the date of death. See I.R.C. section 1014.

business. The shareholder may invest that money in a wholly unrelated business, or spend it just like any other form of personal income. To the extent a section 351 transaction resembles an ordinary sale, the nonrecognition rationale falls apart.

Thus the central exception to nonrecognition for section 351 transactions comes into play when the taxpayer receives "boot"—money or property other than stock in the corporation—in exchange for the property contributed. See I.R.C. section 351(b). Boot is recognized as taxable income because it represents a partial cashing out. It's as if the taxpayer contributed part of the property to the corporation in exchange for stock, and sold part of the property for cash. Only the part exchanged for stock represents a continuation of investment; the part sold for cash is properly recognized as yielding income, just as if the taxpayer had sold the property to a third party.

Peracchi did not receive boot in return for the property he contributed. But that doesn't end the inquiry: We must consider whether Peracchi has cashed out in some other way which would warrant treating part of the transaction as taxable boot.

Assumption of Liabilities: Section 357(a)

The property Peracchi contributed to NAC was encumbered by liabilities. Contribution of leveraged property makes things trickier from a tax perspective. When a shareholder contributes property encumbered by debt, the corporation usually assumes the debt. And the Code normally treats discharging a liability the same as receiving money: The taxpayer improves his economic position by the same amount either way. See I.R.C. section 61(a)(12). NAC's assumption of the liabilities attached to Peracchi's property therefore could theoretically be viewed as the receipt of money, which would be taxable boot. See United States v. Hendler, 303 U.S. 564 (1938).

The Code takes a different tack. Requiring shareholders like Peracchi to recognize gain any time a corporation assumes a liability in connection with a capital contribution would greatly diminish the nonrecognition benefit section 351 is meant to confer. Section 357(a) thus takes a lenient view of the assumption of liability: A shareholder engaging in a section 351 transaction does not have to treat the assumption of liability as boot, even if the corporation assumes his obligation to pay. See I.R.C. section 357(a).

This nonrecognition does not mean that the potential gain disappears. Once again, the basis provisions kick in to reflect the transfer of gain from the shareholder to the corporation: The shareholder's substitute basis in the stock received is decreased by the amount of the liability assumed by the corporation. See I.R.C. section 358(d), (a). The adjustment preserves the gain for recognition when the shareholder sells his stock in the company, since his taxable gain will be the difference between the (new lower) basis and the sale price of the stock.

Sasquatch and the Negative Basis Problem: Section 357(c)

Highly leveraged property presents a peculiar problem in the section 351 context. Suppose a shareholder organizes a corporation and contributes as its only asset a building with a basis of $50, a fair market value of $100, and mortgage debt of $90. Section 351 says that the shareholder does not recognize any gain on the transaction. Under section 358, the shareholder takes a substitute basis of $50 in the stock, then adjusts it downward under section 357 by $90 to reflect the assumption of liability. This leaves him with a basis of minus $40. A negative basis properly preserves the gain built into the property: If the shareholder turns around and sells the stock the next day for $10 (the difference between the fair market value and the debt), he would face $50 in gain, the same amount as if he sold the property without first encasing it in a corporate shell.[8]

But skeptics say that negative basis, like Bigfoot, doesn't exist. Compare Easson v. Commissioner, 33 T.C. 963, 970 (1960) (there's no such thing as a negative basis) with Easson v. Commissioner, 294 F.2d 653, 657-58 (9th Cir. 1961) (yes, Virginia, there is a negative basis). Basis normally operates as a cost recovery system: Depreciation deductions reduce basis, and when basis hits zero, the property cannot be depreciated farther. At a more basic level, it seems incongruous to attribute a negative value to a figure that normally represents one's investment in an asset. Some commentators nevertheless argue that when basis operates merely to measure potential gain (as it does here), allowing negative basis may be perfectly appropriate and consistent with the tax policy underlying nonrecognition transactions. See, e.g., J. Clifton Fleming, Jr., The Highly Avoidable Section 357(c): A Case Study in Traps for the Unwary and Some Positive Thoughts About Negative Basis, 16 J. Corp. L. 1, 27-30 (1990). Whatever the merits of this debate, it seems that section 357(c) was enacted to eliminate the possibility of negative basis. See George Cooper, Negative Basis, 75 Harv. L. Rev. 1352, 1360 (1962).

Section 357(c) prevents negative basis by forcing a shareholder to recognize gain to the extent liabilities exceed basis. Thus, if a shareholder contributes a building with a basis of $50 and liabilities of $90, he does not receive stock with a basis of minus $40. Instead, he takes a basis of zero and must recognize a $40 gain.

Peracchi sought to contribute two parcels of real property to NAC in a section 351 transaction. Standing alone the contribution would have run afoul of section 357(c): The property he wanted to contribute had liabilities in excess of basis, and Peracchi would have had to recognize gain to the extent of the excess, or $566,807:[10]

	Liabilities	*Basis*
Property #1	1,386,655	349,774
Property #2	161,558	631,632
	1,548,213	981,406
Liabilities	1,548,213	
Basis	981,406	
Excess (357(c))	566,807	

8. If the taxpayer sells the property outright, his amount realized includes the full amount of the mortgage debt, see Crane v. Commissioner, 331 U.S. 1, 14 (1947), and the result is as follows: Amount realized ($10 cash + $90 debt) – $50 Basis = $50 gain.

10. Peracchi remained personally liable on the debts encumbering the property transferred to NAC. NAC took the property subject to the debts, however, which is enough to trigger gain under the plain language of section 357(c). See Owen v. Commissioner, 881 F.2d 832, 835-36 (9th Cir. 1989).

THE GRIFT: BOOSTING BASIS WITH A PROMISSORY NOTE

Peracchi tried to dig himself out of this tax hole by contributing a personal note with a face amount of $1,060,000 along with the real property. Peracchi maintains that the note has a basis in his hands equal to its face value. If he's right, we must add the basis of the note to the basis of the real property. Taken together, the aggregate basis in the property contributed would exceed the aggregate liabilities:

	Liabilities	*Basis*
Property #1	1,386,655	349,774
Property #2	161,558	631,632
Note	0	1,060,000
	1,548,213	2,041,406

Under Peracchi's theory, then, the aggregate liabilities no longer exceed the aggregate basis, and section 357(c) no longer triggers any gain. The government argues, however, that the note has a zero basis. If so, the note would not affect the tax consequences of the transaction, and Peracchi's $566,807 in gain would be taxable immediately.

ARE PROMISES TRULY FREE?

Which brings us (phew!) to the issue before us: Does Peracchi's note have a basis in Peracchi's hands for purposes of section 357(c)?[12] The language of the Code gives us little to work with. The logical place to start is with the definition of basis. Section 1012 provides that "[t]he basis of property shall be the cost of such property. . . ." But "cost" is nowhere defined. What does it cost Peracchi to write the note and contribute it to his corporation? The IRS argues tersely that the "taxpayers in the instant case incurred no cost in issuing their own note to NAC, so their basis in the note was zero." Brief for Appellee at 41. See Alderman v. Commissioner, 55 T.C. 662, 665 (1971); Rev. Rul. 68-629, 1968-2 C.B. 154, 155.[13] Building on this premise, the IRS makes Peracchi out to be a grifter: He holds an unenforceable promise to pay himself money, since the corporation will not collect on it unless he says so.

12. Peracchi owned all the voting stock of NAC both before and after the exchange, so the control requirement of section 351 is satisfied. Peracchi received no boot (such as cash or securities) which would qualify as "money or other property" and trigger recognition under 351(b) alone. Peracchi did not receive any stock in return for the property contributed, so it could be argued that the exchange was not "solely in exchange for stock" as required by section 351. Courts have consistently recognized, however, that issuing stock in this situation would be a meaningless gesture: Because Peracchi is the sole shareholder of NAC, issuing additional stock would not affect his economic position relative to other shareholders. See, e.g., Jackson v. Commissioner, 708 F.2d 1402, 1405 (9th Cir. 1983).

13. We would face a different case had the Treasury promulgated a regulation interpreting section 357(c). A revenue ruling is entitled to some deference as the stated litigating position of the agency which enforces the tax code, but not nearly as much as a regulation. Ruling 68-629 offers no rationale, let alone a reasonable one, for its holding that it costs a taxpayer nothing to write a promissory note, and thus deserves little weight.

It's true that all Peracchi did was make out a promise to pay on a piece of paper, mark it in the corporate minutes and enter it on the corporate books. It is also true that nothing will cause the corporation to enforce the note against Peracchi so long as Peracchi remains in control. But the IRS ignores the possibility that NAC may go bankrupt, an event that would suddenly make the note highly significant. Peracchi and NAC are separated by the corporate form, and this gossamer curtain makes a difference in the shell game of C Corp organization and reorganization. Contributing the note puts a million dollar nut within the corporate shell, exposing Peracchi to the cruel nutcracker of corporate creditors in the event NAC goes bankrupt. And it does so to the tune of $1,060,000, the full face amount of the note. Without the note, no matter how deeply the corporation went into debt, creditors could not reach Peracchi's personal assets. With the note on the books, however, creditors can reach into Peracchi's pocket by enforcing the note as an unliquidated asset of the corporation.

The key to solving this puzzle, then, is to ask whether bankruptcy is significant enough a contingency to confer substantial economic effect on this transaction. If the risk of bankruptcy is important enough to be recognized, Peracchi should get basis in the note: He will have increased his exposure to the risks of the business — and thus his economic investment in NAC — by $1,060,000. If bankruptcy is so remote that there is no realistic possibility it will ever occur, we can ignore the potential economic effect of the note as speculative and treat it as merely an unenforceable promise to contribute capital in the future.

When the question is posed this way, the answer is clear. Peracchi's obligation on the note was not conditioned on NAC's remaining solvent. It represents a new and substantial increase in Peracchi's investment in the corporation.[14] The Code seems to recognize that economic exposure of the shareholder is the ultimate measuring rod of a shareholder's investment. Cf. I.R.C. section 465 (at-risk rules for partnership investments). Peracchi therefore is entitled to a step-up in basis to the extent he will be subjected to economic loss if the underlying investment turns unprofitable. Compare HGA Cinema Trust v. Commissioner, 950 F.2d 1357, 1363 (7th Cir. 1991) (examining effect of bankruptcy to determine whether long-term note contributed by partner could be included in basis). See also Treas. [Regs.] §1.704-1(b)(2)(ii)(c)(1) (recognizing economic effect of promissory note contributed by partner for purposes of partner's obligation to restore deficit capital account).

The economics of the transaction also support Peracchi's view of the matter. The transaction here does not differ substantively from others that would certainly give Peracchi a boost in basis. For example, Peracchi could have borrowed $1 million from a bank and contributed the cash to NAC along with the properties. Because cash has a basis equal to face value, Peracchi would not have faced any section 357(c) gain. NAC could then have purchased the note from the bank for $1 million which, assuming the bank's original assessment of Peracchi's creditworthiness was accurate, would be the fair market value of the note. In the end the corporation would

14. We confine our holding to a case such as this where the note is contributed to an operating business which is subject to a non-trivial risk of bankruptcy or receivership. NAC is not, for example, a shell corporation or a passive investment company; Peracchi got into this mess in the first place because NAC was in financial trouble and needed more assets to meet Nevada's minimum premium-to-asset ratio for insurance companies.

hold a million dollar note from Peracchi—just like it does now—and Peracchi would face no section 357(c) gain.[15]

The only economic difference between the transaction just described and the transaction Peracchi actually engaged in is the additional costs that would accompany getting a loan from the bank. Peracchi incurs a "cost" of $1 million when he promises to pay the note to the bank; the cost is not diminished here by the fact that the transferor controls the initial transferee. The experts seem to agree: "Section 357(c) can be avoided by a transfer of enough cash to eliminate any excess of liabilities over basis; and since a note given by a solvent obligor in purchasing property is routinely treated as the equivalent of cash in determining the basis of the property, it seems reasonable to give it the same treatment in determining the basis of the property transferred in a section 351 exchange." Bittker & Eustice paragraph 3.06[4][b].

We are aware of the mischief that can result when taxpayers are permitted to calculate basis in excess of their true economic investment. See Commissioner v. Tufts, 461 U.S. 300 (1983). For two reasons, however, we do not believe our holding will have such pernicious effects. First, and most significantly, by increasing the taxpayer's personal exposure, the contribution of a valid, unconditional promissory note has substantial economic effects which reflect his true economic investment in the enterprise. The main problem with attributing basis to nonrecourse debt financing is that the tax benefits enjoyed as a result of increased basis do not reflect the true economic risk. Here Peracchi will have to pay the full amount of the note with after-tax dollars if NAC's economic situation heads south. Second, the tax treatment of nonrecourse debt primarily creates problems in the partnership context, where the entity's loss deductions (resulting from depreciation based on basis inflated above and beyond the taxpayer's true economic investment) can be passed through to the taxpayer. It is the pass-through of losses that makes artificial increases in equity interests of particular concern. See, e.g., Levy v. Commissioner, 732 F.2d 1435, 1437 (9th Cir. 1984). We don't have to tread quite so lightly in the C Corp context, since a C Corp doesn't funnel losses to the shareholder.[16]

We find further support for Peracchi's view by looking at the alternative: What would happen if the note had a zero basis? The IRS points out that the basis of the note in the hands of the corporation is the same as it was in the hands of the taxpayer. Accordingly, if the note has a zero basis for Peracchi, so too for NAC. See I.R.C. section 362(a).[17] But what happens if NAC—perhaps facing the threat of

15. In a similar vein, Peracchi could have first swapped promissory notes with a third party. Assuming the bona fides of each note, Peracchi would take a cost basis in the third party note equal to the face value of the note he gave up. Peracchi could then contribute the third party note to NAC, and (thanks to the added basis) avoid any section 357(c) gain. NAC could then close the circle by giving the third party note back to the third party in exchange for Peracchi's note, leaving Peracchi and NAC in exactly the same position they occupy now.

16. Our holding therefore does not extend to the partnership or S Corp context.

17. But see Lessinger v. Commissioner, 872 F.2d 519 (2d Cir. 1989). In *Lessinger*, the Second Circuit analyzed a similar transaction. It agreed with the IRS's (faulty) premise that the note had a zero basis in the taxpayer's hands. But then, brushing aside the language of section 362(a), the court concluded that the note had a basis in the *corporation's* hands equal to its face value. The court held that this was enough to dispel any section 357(c) gain to the taxpayer, proving that two wrongs sometimes do add up to a right.

We agree with the IRS that *Lessinger*'s approach is untenable. Section 357(c) contemplates measuring basis of the property contributed in the hands of the taxpayer, not the corporation. Section 357 appears in the midst of the Code sections dealing with the effect of capital contributions on the shareholder; sections 361 et seq., on the other hand, deal with the effect on a corporation, and section 362

an involuntary petition for bankruptcy — turns around and sells Peracchi's note to a third party for its fair market value? According to the IRS's theory, NAC would take a carryover basis of zero in the note and would have to recognize $1,060,000 in phantom gain on the subsequent exchange, even though the note did not appreciate in value one bit. That can't be the right result.

Accordingly, we hold that Peracchi has a basis of $1,060,000 in the note he wrote to NAC. The aggregate basis exceeds the liabilities of the properties transferred to NAC under section 351, and Peracchi need not recognize any section 357(c) gain.

Genuine Indebtedness or Sham?

The Tax Court never reached the issue of Peracchi's basis in the note. Instead, it ruled for the Commissioner on the ground that the note is not genuine indebtedness. The court emphasized two facts which it believed supported the view that the note is a sham: (1) NAC's decision whether to collect on the note is wholly controlled by Peracchi and (2) Peracchi missed the first two years of payments, yet NAC did not accelerate the debt. These facts certainly do suggest that Peracchi paid imperfect attention to his obligations under the note, as frequently happens when debtor and creditor are under common control. But we believe the proper way to approach the genuine indebtedness question is to look at the face of the note and consider whether Peracchi's legal obligation is illusory. And it is not. First, the note's bona fides are adequate: The IRS has stipulated that Peracchi is creditworthy and likely to have the funds to pay the note; the note bears a market rate of interest commensurate with his creditworthiness; the note has a fixed term. Second, the IRS does not argue that the value of the note is anything other than its face value; nothing in the record suggests NAC couldn't borrow against the note to raise cash. Lastly, the note is fully transferable and enforceable by third parties, such as hostile creditors. On the basis of these facts we hold that the note is an ordinary, negotiable, recourse obligation which must be treated as genuine debt for tax purposes. See Sacks v. Commissioner, 69 F.3d 982, 989 (9th Cir. 1995).

The IRS argues that the note is nevertheless a sham because it was executed simply to avoid tax. Tax avoidance is a valid concern in this context; section 357(a) does provide the opportunity for a bailout transaction of sorts. For example, a taxpayer with an unencumbered building he wants to sell could take out a nonrecourse mortgage, pocket the proceeds, and contribute the property to a newly organized corporation. Although the gain would be preserved for later recognition, the taxpayer would have partially cashed out his economic investment in the property: By taking out a nonrecourse mortgage, the economic risk of loss would be transferred to the lender. Section 357(b) addresses this sort of bailout by requiring the recognition of gain if the transaction lacks a business purpose.

Peracchi's capital contribution is not a bailout. Peracchi contributed the buildings to NAC because the company needed additional capital, and the contribution of the note was part of that transaction. The IRS, in fact, stipulated that the

---

defines the basis of property contributed in the hands of the corporation. Because we hold that the note has a face value basis to the shareholder for purposes of section 357(c), however, we reach the same result as *Lessinger*.

contribution had a business purpose. Bailout potential exists regardless of whether the taxpayer contributes a note along with the property; section 357(b), not 357(c), is the sword the Service must use to attack bailout transactions.

Is the Note a Gift?

The IRS also offers a more refined version of the sham transaction argument: The note was really a gift to NAC because Peracchi did not receive any consideration from the exchange. The IRS admits that the tax deferral resulting from avoiding section 357(c) gain is a benefit to Peracchi. It argues, nonetheless, that this is not enough to make the bargain enforceable because it works no detriment to NAC. This argument would classify all contributions of capital as gifts. A corporation never gives up anything explicitly when it accepts a capital contribution. Instead, the corporation implicitly promises to put the money to good use, and its directors and officers undertake the fiduciary duty to generate the highest possible return on the investment. The contribution of the note was no more a gift than the contribution of $1 million in cash to the corporation would have been; it does not reflect the "detached and disinterested generosity" which characterizes a gift for purposes of federal income taxation. See Commissioner v. Duberstein, 363 U.S. 278, 285 (1960).

The Aftermath

We take a final look at the result to make sure we have not placed our stamp of approval on some sort of exotic tax shelter. We hold that Peracchi is entitled to a step up in basis for the face value of the note, just as if he contributed cash to the corporation. See I.R.C. section 358. If Peracchi does in fact keep his promise and pay off the note with after tax dollars, the tax result is perfectly appropriate: NAC receives cash, and the increase in basis Peracchi took for the original contribution is justified. Peracchi has less potential gain, but he paid for it in real dollars.

But what if, as the IRS fears, NAC never does enforce the note? If NAC goes bankrupt, the note will be an asset of the estate enforceable for the benefit of creditors, and Peracchi will eventually be forced to pay in after tax dollars. Peracchi will undoubtedly have worked the deferral mechanism of section 351 to his advantage, but this is not inappropriate where the taxpayer is on the hook in both form and substance for enough cash to offset the excess of liabilities over basis. By increasing his personal exposure to the creditors of NAC, Peracchi has increased his economic investment in the corporation, and a corresponding increase in basis is wholly justified.[20]

20. What happens if NAC does not go bankrupt, but merely writes off the note instead? Peracchi would then face discharge of indebtedness income to the tune of $1,060,000. This would put Peracchi in a worse position than when he started, since discharge of indebtedness is normally treated as ordinary income. Peracchi, having increased his basis in the stock of the corporation by $1,060,000 would receive a capital loss (or less capital gain) to that extent. But the shift in character of the income will normally work to the disadvantage of a taxpayer in Peracchi's situation.

Conclusion

We hold that Peracchi has a basis of $1,060,000 in the note, its face value. As such, the aggregate liabilities of the property contributed to NAC do not exceed its basis, and Peracchi does not recognize any section 357(c) gain. The decision of the Tax Court is REVERSED. The case is remanded for entry of judgment in favor of Peracchi.

FERNANDEZ, Circuit Judge, Dissenting:

Is there something that a taxpayer, who has borrowed hundreds of thousands of dollars more than his basis in his property, can do to avoid taxation when he transfers the property? Yes, says Peracchi, because by using a very clever argument he can avoid the strictures of 26 U.S.C. section 357(c). He need only make a promise to pay by giving a "good," though unsecured, promissory note to his corporation when he transfers the property to it. That is true even though the property remains subject to the encumbrances. How can that be? Well, by preparing a promissory note the taxpayer simply creates basis without cost to himself. But see 26 U.S.C. section 1012; Rev. Rul. 68-629, 1968-2 C.B. 154; Alderman v. Commissioner, 55 T.C. 662, 665 (1971). Thus he can extract a large part of the value of the property, pocket the funds, use them, divest himself of the property, and pay the tax another day, if ever at all.

But as with all magical solutions, the taxpayer must know the proper incantations and make the correct movements. He cannot just transfer the property to the corporation and promise, or be obligated, to pay off the encumbrances. That would not change the fact that the property was still subject to those encumbrances. According to Peracchi, the thaumaturgy that will save him from taxes proceeds in two simple steps. He must first prepare a ritualistic writing — an unsecured promissory note in an amount equal to or more than the excess of the encumbrances over the basis. He must then give that writing to his corporation. That is all. But is not that just a "promise to pay," which "does not represent the paying out or reduction of assets?" Don E. Williams Co. v. Commissioner, 429 U.S. 569, 583, 97 S. Ct. 850, 858, 51 L. Ed. 2d 48 (1977). Never mind, he says. He has nonetheless increased the total basis of the property transferred and avoided the tax. I understand the temptation to embrace that argument, but I see no real support for it in the law.

Peracchi says a lot about economic realities. I see nothing real about that maneuver. I see, rather, a bit of sortilege that would have made Merlin envious. The taxpayer has created something — basis — out of nothing.

Thus, I respectfully dissent.

NOTES

1. *Basis in a taxpayer's own note — in general.* Basis in an asset under federal income tax law is the amount that can be received tax free on a sale of that asset. Suppose that a taxpayer buys property from a third person, paying $5,000 down and giving the seller a $10,000 note, due next year (together with adequate interest). The taxpayer takes a $15,000 cost basis in the purchased property and recognizes no gain on the note. In effect, a taxpayer has a $10,000 basis in his own note.

The tax system assumes that the taxpayer will satisfy the note. When the assumption proves wrong and a portion of the note is cancelled, the taxpayer has cancellation of indebtedness income, included in gross income except to the extent provided in §108.

2. *Basis in a taxpayer's note—issued to wholly owned corporation.* Should the tax system also assume that the taxpayer will satisfy a note issued to her wholly owned corporation? That was the central, but unstated question in *Peracchi.* The Ninth Circuit answered the question in the affirmative, but its decision is contrary to the result in Alderman v. Commissioner, 55 T.C. 662 (1971). If *Alderman* was correctly decided (i.e., a taxpayer has no basis in his own note), then what basis does the transferee corporation take in the note following a §351 transaction?

Suppose *T* transfers her own $5,000 note bearing a market rate of interest to *X* Corp. in exchange for $5,000 of *X* Corp. stock in a §351 transaction. If *T* has a basis of $0 in her own note, then under §362, *X* Corp. would take a $0 basis in *T*'s note. What happens when *T* pays off the note? Should *X* Corp. have $5,000 of income? That would be an odd result. If *T* had originally transferred $5,000 in cash to *X* Corp., then *X* Corp. would have had no income; there is no reason why a different result should occur if the $5,000 is paid at a later date. *X* Corp. should have no income when *T* pays off the note. To achieve that result, *X* Corp. must have a $5,000 basis in the note. Because *X* Corp.'s basis derives from *T*'s basis under §362, *T* must have a $5,000 basis in her own note.

Suppose, instead, that *T* does not pay off the note, and *X* Corp. cancels the note. If form is followed, *T* would be treated as receiving income when the note is cancelled. If *T* controls *X* Corp., she may be able to time when the cancellation occurs. Why should *T* be able to time that income event? Is it more appropriate to treat the note as having a $0 basis and require *T* to recognize gain, as appropriate, under §357(c)(1) in the §351 transaction?

The preceding two examples illustrate the underlying tension in *Peracchi* and perhaps reveal why the Service has litigated the issue. Note, however, that the Service did not argue that the shareholder debt should be disregarded because the shareholder likely controlled when (or whether) the debt was repaid. Instead, it argued that the debt had a zero-dollar basis. See also Rev. Rul. 68-629, 1968-2 C.B. 154 (reaching this conclusion). Would a better approach have been to argue that the debt, in form and substance, should not have been respected as bona fide debt? If the Service were to adopt this approach, should it presume that a shareholder's debt to a corporation is bona fide (and creates basis) if the corporation has another, unrelated shareholder?

In any case, resolution of the issue presented in *Peracchi* is clear in two circuits—the Ninth Circuit, where *Peracchi* was decided, and the Second Circuit, which decided Lessinger v. Commissioner, 872 F.2d 519 (2d Cir. 1989), a case discussed in *Peracchi* that reached the same result but with different reasoning. In other circuits, the result is less clear. In those other circuits, what steps could a taxpayer take to avoid the issue?

PROBLEMS

2-6. In the following, Alex and Bertha form *X* Corp. Alex begins with a parcel of land held for investment worth $1,000 with an adjusted basis of $300 and ends up with a 50-percent interest in *X* Corp. stock plus $500. Bertha begins with $500 and ends up with a 50-percent interest in *X* Corp. stock. *X* Corp. ends up with the land and, depending on the facts, $500. Determine the tax consequences to all the parties of the following:

a. Alex and Bertha together form *X* Corp., with Alex contributing his land in exchange for $500 cash (borrowed by *X* Corp.) and a 50-percent stock interest and Bertha receiving a 50-percent stock interest for her cash.
b. Alex borrows $500 from a lender, using his property as security. Alex then transfers the property (subject to the debt) to *X* Corp. in exchange for a 50-percent stock interest, while Bertha receives a 50-percent interest in return for her $500 cash.

2-7. Suppose in 2-6(a) that Alex transfers two parcels, one with a basis of $200 and a value of $700 and the other with a basis of $800 and a value of $300. What are the tax consequences?

2-8. Suppose in 2-6(a) that *X* also issued $100 of nonvoting preferred stock to Charles, *X* Corp.'s lawyer, for organizing the corporation. What are the tax consequences?

2-9. When is a liability described in §357(c)(3)? Would the following liabilities be §357(c)(3) liabilities?

a. *T* incurred a liability to purchase the equipment;
b. *T* owed the $40,000 to his employee as reasonable compensation for services already performed and *T* was (i) a cash basis taxpayer or (ii) an accrual basis taxpayer; or
c. *T* had a contingent liability to build a water treatment plant to deal with environmental waste.

d. Some Anti-Abuse Rules

Section 358(h) targets duplicate loss at the shareholder and corporate levels. Under §358(h)(1), a transferor's basis in transferee stock received in a §351 exchange is reduced (but not below its fair market value) by the amount of any "non-§358(d)(1)" liabilities assumed by the transferee in the exchange. §358(h)(1). A non-§358(d)(1) liability is one not described in §358(d)(1) (i.e., generally, a §357(c)(3) or contingent liability). §358(h)(3). Note that this reduction does not occur if the trade or business with which the liability is associated is transferred to the transferee in the exchange. §358(h)(2). See also Treas. Regs. §1.358-5 and §1.358-5T (together providing that §358(h)(2)(B) does not apply to an exchange occurring after June 24, 2003).

For example, suppose that *T*, a cash method taxpayer, forms *X* Corp., transferring property with a $1,000 basis and $1,000 fair market value in a §351 exchange for all *X* stock, worth $100, and *X* Corp.'s agreement to pay *T*'s $900 deductible liability. Later, *X* Corp. pays the liability and deducts $900. But see Rev. Rul. 80-198, 1980-2 C.B. 113 (noting that the corporation may not be entitled to a deduction where the §351 exchange separates income and related expenses). Without §358(h), *T* would take a $1,000 basis in her *X* stock, see §358(a) and (d)(2), and could sell that stock for $100, recognizing a duplicate $900 loss. Under §358(h), however, *T* takes a $100 basis in her *X* stock, eliminating the potential duplicate loss.

Another provision, §362(d), targets "inflated" basis at the corporate level. Under §362(d)(1), the corporation's basis in any property cannot be increased above its fair market value because of gain recognized to the transferor on a liability assumption. This rule is consistent with how some courts have computed the buyer's basis in an asset acquired subject to a nonrecourse liability, where the liability exceeded the asset's fair market value. See Pleasant Summit Land Corp. v. Commissioner, 863 F.2d 263 (3d Cir. 1988).

For example, suppose that *T* transfers property to *X* Corp. in a §351 exchange, and the property has a $50 basis and a $100 fair market value and secures a $120 nonrecourse loan. Section 362(d)(1) clarifies that *X* Corp.'s basis in the transferred property cannot exceed $100, the property's fair market value. Presumably, if *X* Corp. later satisfies the entire $120 liability, it will increase its basis in the property by $20.

Further, §362(d)(2) limits the corporate transferee's basis in transferred assets if—

1. The transferor recognizes gain on the assumption of a nonrecourse liability by the transferee;
2. The liability is secured by assets not transferred to the transferee; and
3. No person is subject to federal income tax on that gain.

Then, in applying §362(a) or (b), the transferor's gain deemed recognized on the liability assumption under §357(c)(1) is computed using the transferee's ratable portion of the liability, instead of the full liability. The ratable portion is determined based on the relative fair market values of all assets subject to the liability. §362(d)(2) (determining asset values without regard to §7701(g)).

For example, suppose that *T* transfers property to *X* Corp. in a §351 exchange, and the property has a $50 basis and a $100 fair market value and secures a $120 nonrecourse loan. Other property with a $100 fair market value also secures the liability but is not transferred to *X* Corp. Further, no person is subject to federal income tax on any gain *T* recognizes on the transfer. Under §362(a) and (d)(2), *X* Corp.'s basis in the transferred property equals $60, *T*'s $50 basis in the property plus *T*'s $10 deemed gain on the liability assumption.

That gain is computed by allocating the $120 liability ratably between properties that secure the liability and computing the deemed gain based on the allocation. Because the $120 liability is secured by two properties of equal value, $60 of the $120 liability is allocated to each one. Thus, for purposes of §362(a), the transferred property is deemed subject to just a $60 liability, resulting in a $10 deemed gain on the liability assumption under §357(c)(1).

4. *Additional Basis Rules*

a. Multiple Asset Transfers

Generally, if a person transfers several properties to a transferee corporation in a §351 exchange, the person determines her basis in the transferee stock received by considering the aggregate basis of the property transferred. Are there circumstances, however, where the person could trace the basis and holding period of stock received to particular assets surrendered in the exchange? If not, are there circumstances where the basis and holding period of a share of stock received must be split?

Rev. Rul. 85-164

1985-2 C.B. 117

Issue

May a transferor determine the bases and holding periods of stock . . . received in a transfer under section 351 of the Internal Revenue Code by designating the specific property to be exchanged for particular stock. . . ?

Facts

A, an individual, was engaged in a business as a sole proprietor. The assets of the sole proprietorship consisted of trade accounts receivable with an adjusted basis of zero and a fair market value of 60x dollars, machinery with an adjusted basis of 5x dollars and a fair market value of 10x dollars, and real estate (land and building) with an adjusted basis of 25x dollars and a fair market value of 30x dollars. *A* had held the real estate and machinery for over one year. Both the real estate and machinery were property described in section 1231 of the Code.

In order to limit personal liability, *A* transferred all of the assets associated with the sole proprietorship to a new corporation, *Y*, in exchange for all of *Y*'s stock. . . . *A* transferred the accounts receivable to *Y* in exchange for 100 shares of common stock, the fair market value of which was 60x dollars. *A* transferred the machinery and real estate to *Y* in exchange for [100 shares of preferred stock],* which had . . . a fair market value of 40x dollars. The selection of specific items for exchange was made to allocate assets with a high basis and long-term holding period to the [preferred stock].

Law and Analysis

Section 351(a) of the Code provides that no gain or loss will be recognized if property is transferred to a corporation by a person solely in exchange for stock . . . in such corporation and immediately after the exchange such person is in control (as defined in section 368(c)) of the corporation.

* In the ruling, *A* receives common stock and securities that under the law then in effect were qualifying property under §351. Although securities are no longer qualifying property under §351, the principles of the ruling apply to allocate basis among multiple classes of stock received (e.g., common and preferred stock) and the ruling has been modified to illustrate such an allocation. — Eds.

Section 358(a)(1) of the Code and section 1.358-1 of the Income Tax Regulations provide that in the case of an exchange to which section 351 applies in which only nonrecognition property is received, the basis of all of the stock . . . received in the exchange shall be the same as the basis of all property exchanged therefor. Section 358(b)(1) directs that, under regulations prescribed by the Secretary, the basis determined under subsection (a)(1) shall be allocated among the properties permitted to be received without the recognition of gain or loss.

Section 1.358-2(a) of the regulations prescribes rules for the allocation of basis among nonrecognition property received in corporate reorganization exchanges governed by sections 354, 355, 356. . . . In general, these rules allow limited tracing of the basis of old stock . . . into new only with respect to (i) persons who owned stock . . . of more than one class . . . before the exchange and (ii) corporate recapitalizations under section 368(a)(1)(E). In all other cases, including exchanges under section 351, section 1.358-2(b)(2) provides that the basis of property transferred shall be allocated among all the stock . . . received in proportion to the fair market values of the stock of each class. . . .

Section 1223(1) and section 1.1223-1(a) of the regulations require that, in determining the period for which a taxpayer has held property received in an exchange, there shall be included the period for which he held the property exchanged if (i) in the taxpayer's hands the property received has the same basis in whole or in part as the property exchanged and (ii) for exchanges after March 1, 1954, the property exchanged was at the time of exchange a capital asset as defined in section 1221 or property used in a trade or business as described in section 1231.

Rev. Rul. 62-140, 1962-2 C.B. 181, holds that a share of stock received in exchange for a debenture and a cash payment had a split holding period. The portion of each share received attributable to ownership of the debenture was treated as including the period for which the taxpayer held the debenture and the portion of each share received attributable to the cash payment was treated as held beginning with the date following the date of acquisition.

Rev. Rul. 68-55, 1968-1 C.B. 140, holds that when property is transferred to a corporation under section 351(a) of the Code each asset must be considered transferred separately in exchange for a proportionate share of each of the various categories of the total consideration received.

In the instant case, *A* formed *Y* by transferring all of the business assets of the sole proprietorship to *Y* in exchange solely for all of *Y*'s stock. . . . *Y* will continue to carry on the business that *A* conducted, and *A* will remain in control of *Y*. The transfer, therefore, is subject to section 351 of the Code, with the bases and holding periods of the *Y* stock . . . in the hands of *A* determined under sections 358 and 1223 of the Code respectively.

A may not determine the bases and holding periods of the *Y* stock . . . received by designating specific property to be exchanged for particular stock. . . . Under sections 1.358-1 and 1.358-2(b)(2) of the regulations, the aggregate basis of the property transferred is allocated among the stock . . . received in proportion to the fair market values of each class. The holding period of the *Y* stock . . . received by *A* is determined by referring to the assets deemed exchanged for each portion of the stock. . . . The aggregate basis of the property transferred was 30x dollars. Since the [common and preferred] stock . . . *A* received had fair market values of 60x dollars and 40x dollars, respectively, a basis of 18x dollars (60x/100x × 30x) is allocated to the *Y* [common] stock received by *A*, and a basis of 12x dollars

(40x/100x × 30x) is allocated to the *Y* [preferred stock] received. In addition, each share of *Y* stock . . . received by *A* has a split holding period and a split basis for purposes of determining long-term or short-term capital gain or loss. That fraction of each share of *Y* stock . . . attributable to the real estate and machinery (40x/100x) is treated as including the period (over one year) for which *A* held the real estate and machinery and has a basis solely attributable to the real estate and machinery (e.g., the 40x/100x of each share of stock attributable to the real estate and machinery will have a basis of .18x dollars (18x/100 shares) [for the common stock and .12x dollars (12x/100x) for the preferred stock]). The fraction of each share of *Y* stock . . . attributable to the accounts receivable (60x/100x) has a holding period beginning on the day after the exchange and has a zero basis. If part or all of the stock . . . received in the exchange is disposed of at a time when the split holding period is relevant in determining tax liability, the same fractions will be applied to apportion the amount realized among the above components of the stock. . . .

This holding would be unaffected if *A* were to make a transfer in exchange for stock at separate times, and the transfers were part of a single integrated transaction.

b. Section 362(e)

The general basis rule under §362(a) is limited by §362(e)(2), which prevents the duplication of loss in a §351 exchange. Under §362(e)(2), a corporate transferee cannot take an aggregate basis in property contributed by a transferor in excess of the property's aggregate fair market value. This provision applies on a transferor-by-transferor basis to all §351 transactions, including those in which the transferor is subject to U.S. taxation, but it disregards any transferred property to which §362(e)(1) applies.[8]

Section 362(e)(2) applies if the transferee's aggregate basis in the applicable property received from a transferor under §362(a) would exceed the property's aggregate value. §362(e)(2)(A). Under §362(e)(2)(B), that aggregate basis is reduced to the property's aggregate value, and this basis reduction is allocated among the transferred built-in loss property in proportion to their built-in losses. For this purpose, property has a built-in loss to the extent its adjusted basis exceeds its value immediately before the transfer.

Instead of reducing the corporate transferee's basis in the transferred property, the transferor can instead apply the basis reduction to decrease her basis in the corporation's stock received in the exchange. *Id.* at (e)(2)(C)(i). Both the transferor and transferee corporation must elect to have this alternative rule apply. *Id.* at (e)(2)(C)(ii). Thus, the effect of §362(e)(2) is to preserve the aggregate built-in loss at the shareholder or corporate level, but not at both.

8. For §362(e)(1) to apply to transferred property, the following two requirements must be met. First, any gain or loss on the transferred property cannot be subject to tax in the transferor's hands immediately before the transfer but must be subject to tax in the transferee's hands immediately after the transfer. §362(e)(1)(B). Second, without taking into account §362(e), the transferee would take an aggregate basis under §362 in all such property received from transferors in the transaction exceeding that property's value. *Id.* at (e)(1)(C). If those two requirements are met, the transferee takes a fair market value basis in each piece of that property. *Id.* at (e)(1)(A).

PROBLEM

2-10. Charles owns two parcels of land, the first with a $10,000 basis and $6,000 value and the second with a $3,000 basis and $4,000 value. Katie owns land with a $3,000 basis and $10,000 value. As part of a plan, Charles and Katie transfer their parcels of land to *X* Corp. in exchange for all *X* stock, each receiving half of that stock.

a. What are the tax consequences of the exchange to Charles, Katie, and *X* Corp.?
b. How do those consequences change if Charles' basis in the first parcel is $7,000, rather than $10,000, he receives $5,000 and one-third of the *X* stock, and Katie receives two-thirds of that stock?

5. *Securities*

Suppose *T* transfers property to *X* Corp. in exchange for an *X* Corp. debt instrument as part of a transaction that otherwise qualifies under §351. Certainly the debt instrument provides *T* with more continuity with the property transferred than an outright sale of the property for cash. If the transferee corporation is productive, *T* is more likely to be paid. Indeed, in some circumstances, a debt instrument may provide more continuity than stock. For financially disabled corporations, for example, debt ownership may provide greater ownership rights than stock ownership.

Until 1990, §351 granted nonrecognition upon the receipt of stock or securities (generally long-term debt instruments). The distinction between securities (i.e., qualifying property) and short-term debt (i.e., nonqualifying property) proved troublesome. Section 351 now draws a sharper line, providing that only the receipt of stock may qualify a transferor for nonrecognition treatment. Even so, it may not always be easy to determine whether a financial instrument constitutes stock or debt. See Bradshaw v. United States, page 61 infra.

Although §351 does not provide nonrecognition to a transferor who receives a debt instrument in exchange for appreciated property, it does not follow that the transferor is immediately taxable on the fair market value of the debt instrument received. See the discussion of installment reporting below.

Note that the distinction between short-term debt and debt securities is still important in the reorganization area. See page 399 infra.

6. *Boot and the Installment Method*

In a §351 transaction, if a transferor exchanges appreciated property for a combination of debt and stock, the debt constitutes boot. If, however, the transferor simply sells the property in exchange for the buyer's debt instrument, gain from the sale might be recognized under the installment method of §453 as the debt is paid off, not when the sale takes place. Because §351 may also require the transferor to recognize gain on the receipt of boot, the transferor may also use the installment method, when appropriate, to report gain in a §351 transaction. See Prop. Treas. Regs. §1.453-1(f)(3)(ii).

For example, suppose that *T* transfers land with a $120 basis and a $200 fair market value to *X* Corp. in a transaction that qualifies under §351. In exchange, *T* receives $100 of *X* stock and $100 of *X* debt. Although the debt constitutes boot, the transferor typically recognizes $80 of gain under §351(b) as *X* Corp. pays off the debt, rather than when the debt instrument is received.

Assume that *T*'s $80 gain can be reported under the installment method as the debt is paid off. *T*'s $120 basis is allocated to any stock received up to its fair market value (here, $100). See Prop. Treas. Regs. §1.453-1(f)(3)(ii) (treating the gain as recognized solely for purposes of applying §358(a)(1)). Any remaining basis ($20) is allocated to the debt, paving the way for *T* to recognize $80 of gain as the $100 debt instrument is paid off. *Id.* (also providing that as the transferor recognizes gain under the installment method, the corporate transferee increases its basis in the transferred assets).

A transferor cannot always report gain under the installment method when property is exchanged for transferee debt in a transaction qualifying under §351. For example, §453(g) restricts use of the installment method if depreciable property is transferred to a corporation by a transferor owning more than 50 percent of the stock of the corporation. Also, §453 does not apply to transfers of inventory or property held for sale to customers or to publicly traded debt instruments received by the transferor. See §453(b) and (f)(4). Even if installment reporting is available, §453(i) requires immediate recognition of any gain subject to depreciation recapture under §1245 or §1250. Finally, a transferor may elect out of installment reporting (if, for example, the transferor has an expiring loss deduction that will offset the gain). See §453(d).

PROBLEM

2-11. *A*, *B*, *C*, and *D* organize *X* Corp. by transferring the following:

	Transfers to X		*Receives from X*	
	Basis	*FMV*	*Shares*	*Cash*
A—cash	—	$10,000	10,000	$ 0
B—land/building	$50,000	$80,000	80,000	$ 0
C—inventory	$ 1,000	$10,000	5,000	$5,000
D—machinery	$15,000	$10,000	5,000	$5,000

With regard to *A*, *B*, *C*, *D*, and *X*, determine (1) the amount of realized and recognized gain or loss and (2) the applicable basis and holding period. How does your answer change as a result of the following alternatives (each considered independently)?

a. Suppose that *B* receives 80,000 shares of preferred stock.
b. Suppose *B* transferred services worth $80,000.
c. Suppose *B* transferred services worth $60,000 and property with a basis of $12,000 and a fair market value of $20,000.

d. Suppose *B* received from *X* Corp. $40,000 of stock and a debt instrument in the amount of $40,000 bearing an appropriate interest rate.
e. Suppose *B*'s transfer took place a year after the transfers of *A*, *C*, and *D*.
f. Suppose *D*'s transfer took place a year after those of *A*, *B*, and *C*.
g. Suppose *C*'s transfer took place three years after those of *A*, *B*, and *D* and that *B* purchased an additional 2,000 shares for $2,000 at that time.

D. INTERACTION OF §351 WITH OTHER CODE SECTIONS AND LEGAL DOCTRINES

Section 351 does not operate in a vacuum. Other code provisions and legal doctrines may affect the application of the provision. Indeed, there are a variety of situations where a taxpayer envisions more favorable treatment by seeking to avoid §351. In the first two cases that follow, the taxpayers tried to avoid the nonrecognition of §351. Why? As you read, try to determine why one taxpayer was successful while the other was not.

The third case in this section, *Hempt Bros.*, focuses on the relationship of §351 to assignment of income principles.

Bradshaw v. United States*

683 F.2d 365 (Ct. Cl. 1982)

Opinion

Bennett, Judge.

Both parties agree that there are only two questions for decision. The first is whether the transfer of real property to Castlewood, a [wholly owned] corporation, in exchange for installment obligations was a sale of the property to that corporation or, instead, was either a transfer of property to a controlled corporation solely in exchange for stock . . . of that corporation within the meaning of section 351 or a capital contribution to that corporation. [Discussion of second question omitted].

We find that the transfer of real property to Castlewood in exchange for installment obligations was a sale rather than a transfer governed by section 351 or a capital contribution. . . . Accordingly, we hold for the plaintiffs and against the defendant for the reasons hereafter stated.

I

On January 6, 1961, Thomas E. Swift (Thomas) purchased a tract of land, consisting of approximately 200 acres, in Dalton, Whitfield County, Georgia, for $60,000. Two dispositions of property out of this 200 acres were made by Thomas in the summer of 1968. The consolidated cases herein concern one of these

*Bradshaw, a party to the consolidated action, is not affected by this part of the court's opinion. — Eds.

dispositions, the transfer of 40.427 acres, subsequently known as Castlewood Subdivision (the subdivision), to Castlewood [Inc.] on July 29, 1968. The conservative fair market value of the subdivision on the date of transfer was $250,000. Thomas' adjusted basis in this portion of the property was $8,538. In exchange for the transfer, Thomas received from Castlewood five promissory notes (the Castlewood notes), each in the principal amount of $50,000 and bearing interest at the rate of 4 percent per annum. The first note matured on January 29, 1971, with each successive note maturing at 1-year intervals. Thomas received no down payment for the transfer, and no security or other collateral was taken for the purchase price. He elected to report his gain from the transaction on the installment method pursuant to section 453(b).

At the time of transfer, various opportunities were available to Thomas to dispose of the subdivision, including sale to third parties. While he had not developed property himself, Thomas was highly expert in real estate matters in the Dalton area. Based upon this knowledge, including knowledge of sales of other real estate in the vicinity of the subdivision, Thomas evaluated the prospects for the development of the subdivision to be bright, whether such development was undertaken by himself, by a corporation that he might organize, or by a third party. He considered the alternative opportunities available to him to dispose of the property and decided to develop the property himself through a corporation rather than sell it to a third party.

Consequently, Castlewood was organized and incorporated on July 29, 1968, under the laws of the State of Georgia, to obtain, subdivide, develop and sell lots in the subdivision. On July 29, 1968, Castlewood issued its Certificate No. 1, representing 50 shares of common stock, to Thomas in exchange for the transfer to the corporation of an automobile valued at $4,500. At all times relevant herein, Thomas was the sole shareholder of Castlewood and was responsible for conducting its business affairs. His expertise was available to and utilized by the corporation in its development of the subdivision, enabling it to minimize development costs and thus increase profits. . . .

From August 1970 to April 1973, Castlewood sold [18 lots in the subdivision] for an aggregate sales price of $239,880. It did not advertise the sale of these lots, use realtors, or pay sales commissions. The property sold had an allocated land cost (of the $250,000 purchase price) and development cost of $159,378.39, yielding a net return to the corporation of $80,501.11. Castlewood reported sales of lots on its federal income tax returns for the fiscal years ended July 31, 1971, July 31, 1972, and July 31, 1973. . . .

By statutory notice of deficiency dated September 20, 1976, the Commissioner determined that additional income tax was due from Castlewood for its 1971 and 1972 tax years, for the reason that the transfer of the subdivision to that corporation by Thomas was not a sale, as treated by the corporation on its tax returns, but rather a transfer of property solely in exchange for stock . . . within the meaning of section 351. Thus, he concluded that, pursuant to section 362, Castlewood's predevelopment basis in the property was equal to that of the transferor immediately before the transfer, or $8,538. This, in turn, increased Castlewood's taxable income on sales of lots. Additionally, the Commissioner concluded that no debtor-creditor relationship was established between Castlewood and Thomas, thereby disallowing certain deductions of interest paid . . . on the notes taken for the purchase price of the property. . . .

II

The first question concerns the proper tax treatment of Thomas' transfer of the subdivision to Castlewood in exchange for the five $50,000 promissory notes. If the transfer is treated as a sale, as plaintiff contends, then Castlewood's adjusted basis for its sales of the lots from the subdivision property would include the $250,000 purchase price (a cost basis), it would be allowed deductions of the interest paid on the notes and its taxable income would be generally as shown on its returns for the years in issue. However, if, as defendant claims, the transfer was not a sale but was either a transfer under section 351 or a contribution to the corporation's capital, then Castlewood's adjusted basis in the lots sold would be reduced to Thomas' original basis (a carryover basis) pursuant to section 362, it would be denied deductions of the interest paid on the notes and its taxable income would be generally as shown on the notice of deficiency issued with respect to it. The sale versus capital contribution problem arises from a situation which often confronts taxpayers with holdings in undeveloped real estate. It is not uncommon for a landowner with a large tract of land suitable for development to want to freeze as capital gain the appreciation in the value of the property that has accrued during its ownership. While an outright sale of the property achieves this result, it also deprives the landowner of any participation in the profits to be reaped from its ultimate development. On the other hand, if the landowner develops and sells the property himself, he runs the risk of being treated as a dealer of the property and any gain generated through sales, including the gain associated with the land's appreciation in value while undeveloped, is taxable to him at ordinary income rates. See, e.g., . . . Suburban Realty Co. v. United States, 615 F.2d 171 (5th Cir.), cert. denied, 449 U.S. 920 (1980).

In the face of such a dilemma, taxpayers have devised an apparently viable solution. By selling the real property to a controlled corporation, they can realize their capital gain on the appreciation which has accrued during their ownership and, at the same time, preserve their opportunity to later participate in the developmental profits as shareholders of the development corporation. Moreover, the corporation obtains a cost basis in the real property, thereby reducing the amount of ordinary income to be received from subsequent sales.

Not unexpectedly, the Commissioner has repeatedly challenged the characterization of such a transaction as a sale, instead maintaining that the transfer is, in reality, a capital contribution and that the transferee corporation is only entitled to a carryover basis for the property. See, e.g., Burr Oaks Corp. v. Commissioner, 365 F.2d 24 (7th Cir. 1966), cert. denied, 385 U.S. 1007 (1967); Aqualane Shores, Inc. v. Commissioner, 269 F.2d 116 (5th Cir. 1959). The two principal reasons asserted for denying the desired tax treatment to the corporation have their origin in the dual subparts of section 362(a). While the main thesis is that section 351 governs such a transaction and that the corporation's basis for the property is to be determined pursuant to section 362(a)(1), it is also maintained that, regardless of the applicability of section 351, the transfer to the corporation is, in substance, a contribution to capital and that the adjusted basis for the property is to be determined under section 362(a)(2). . . .

The proper characterization of a transaction, as a "sale" or a "capital contribution," is a question of fact to be decided as of the time of the transfer on the basis of all of the objective evidence. Gooding Amusement Co. v. Commissioner,

236 F.2d 159, 165 (6th Cir. 1956), cert. denied, 352 U.S. 1031 (1957). While the form of the transaction is relevant, we are required to examine all of the pertinent factors in order to determine whether the substance of the transaction complies with its form. Gregory v. Helvering, 293 U.S. 465, 469-70 (1935). The essential nature of the transaction is to be determined from a consideration of all of the surrounding circumstances. Piedmont Corp. v. Commissioner, 388 F.2d 886, 889 (4th Cir. 1968).

In this case, the objective evidence points to a sale. First, and foremost, the price paid for the subdivision reflected its actual fair market value. Since it has been stipulated that the value of the subdivision was $250,000, the very amount for which it was sold to Castlewood, the transfer cannot be considered a "pretextuous device" to divert the earnings and profits of the corporation, otherwise taxable as ordinary income, into sales proceeds taxable as capital gain. Piedmont Corp. v. Commissioner, 388 F.2d 886, 889 (4th Cir. 1968). The sales price did not constitute an inflated value for the property, and, thus, did not represent an attempt to transfer to Thomas any subsequent capital increment in the value of the property, nor any of the gain from its development. In this respect, the transfer was clearly a sale.

Additionally, the various formalities of a sale were strictly observed. The five instruments involved constituted negotiable instruments in the form of "notes" under Georgia law . . . , contained an unqualified obligation to pay the principal amount, with fixed maturity dates ranging from two and one-half to six and one-half years after the date of sale and bore a reasonable rate of interest. The notes were not subordinated to general corporate creditors and contained a means for collection at maturity, which was never utilized as the principal and interest were always paid as due until the Commissioner challenged the tax treatment of those payments. On these bases, the notes contained all of the traditional elements of sales-generated debt.

Even so, defendant asks that upon consideration of the economic substance of the transfer, the transaction be recast as a capital contribution. This is so, we are told, because Congress has dictated that no tax consequences shall attach to a transaction where direct ownership of property is changed into indirect ownership through a proprietary interest in a corporation. Thus, where the circumstances of a purported sale demonstrate that the transferor, in fact, retained a continuing interest in the property transferred, the transaction is more appropriately characterized as a capital contribution.

Defendant calls our attention to an alleged factual pattern to be discerned in those instances where it has been determined that the economic substance of a purported sale was actually a contribution to capital. In such cases, it is claimed, a newly formed, inadequately capitalized corporation received assets which were essential to its purpose, and which required at the outset substantial improvements to convert them into income-producing property. Whereas, in those cases holding that the transaction resulted in a sale, the transfer involved proven, income-producing assets. Defendant submits that the distinction drawn in these cases turns on the nature and degree of risk inherent in the transfer of unproven assets and that in such instances, because of the high degree of risk, the transferor is likely to have retained a continuing interest in the property transferred.

In the present case, defendant maintains, unproven real property was transferred to an untried, undercapitalized business in return for notes, which were to be satisfied from the proceeds expected to be generated through the sale of lots. From this, defendant urges that we conclude that the notes represented a continuing interest in the corporate business, for repayment was totally dependent upon the success of the enterprise.

We cannot quarrel with the policies underlying section 351, nor with its intended scope. However, even accepting defendant's premise that the prior cases can be meaningfully differentiated along the lines suggested, we are unable to agree with the conclusion defendant draws in this case. Rephrasing defendant's position, we are asked to find that the degree of risk herein was of the type normally associated with a capital contribution. Thus stated, the salient inquiry is whether the notes occupied the position of equity, the assets and prospects of the business being unable to assure payment of the debt according to its terms.

Admittedly, the stipulated facts show Castlewood to have been a "thin" corporation. Its initial capitalization consisted entirely of an automobile valued at $4,500. The corporation then issued five notes, each in the face amount of $50,000, in consideration for the subdivision property. While an additional $3,200 was contributed to Castlewood 4 months later, in practical terms it had no funds of its own with which to conduct business. . . . It cannot be refuted that Castlewood had a very high ratio of debt to equity. But the mere fact that a corporation is or is not thinly capitalized does not, per se, control the character of the transaction. See Gyro Eng. Corp. v. United States, 417 F.2d 437, 439 (9th Cir. 1969). . . . As these cases demonstrate, if the corporation is adequately capitalized for its intended purpose, then we are not prevented from treating the notes as valid debt.

The facts reveal that in addition to its formal capitalization, Castlewood anticipated having access to, did have access to, and utilized funds in the form of loans from C&S, the partnership owned by Thomas and his family, which served as Thomas' personal bank account. Castlewood also had access to an important resource in the expertise Thomas brought to the business, which allowed the corporation to minimize its development expenses. See Murphy Logging Co. v. United States, 378 F.2d 222, 224 (9th Cir. 1967). Given these resources, which were certainly adequate to finance the level of development activities undertaken, and the absence of any need to employ advertising or to use realtors, there was little reason for the corporation to maintain a large surplus of liquid capital. Under the circumstances, we cannot say that undercapitalization is fatal to plaintiff's position.

Integrally related to this discussion, as defendant recognizes, is the nature or quality of the risk assumed by the transferor. However, unlike defendant, we do not find the fact that what was sold to Castlewood was unimproved real estate to be necessarily indicative of a high degree of risk. Concomitantly, nor do we view repayment of the Castlewood notes to have been dependent upon the success of the business. Under the stipulated facts of this case, at the time of transfer, because of the character and location of the subdivision, there was a reasonable anticipation that the development of the property would succeed and yield a profit. And, as planned, the subdivision was developed, a cash flow generated and the notes paid, with interest, as due. . . . Moreover, at all times the value of the property was increasing, irrespective of its development, and, if necessary, the corporation could have borrowed the money against the property to pay off the notes. Clearly, it was always within Castlewood's ability to make payment as required. To be sure, as with any new venture, there was some risk of loss; but the evidence manifests that such risk was significantly reduced in this case. From the beginning, there existed a reasonable assurance of repayment of the notes regardless of the success of the business. To us, this is further indicia that the notes were debt, not equity.

The facts just do not support the inference that, in holding the Castlewood notes, Thomas was assuming the risk of loss normally associated with equity participation.

We are referred by defendant to, among others, Burr Oaks Corp. v. Commissioner, 365 F.2d 24 (7th Cir. 1966), cert. denied, 385 U.S. 1007 (1967), and Aqualane Shores, Inc. v. Commissioner, 269 F.2d 116 (5th Cir. 1959), two of the leading decisions to hold a purported sale to be a contribution to capital. In *Burr Oaks*, undeveloped land, intended for subdivision, was transferred to a newly formed corporation for more than twice its fair market value. In exchange therefor, the transferors received back 2-year promissory notes. Development costs ran extremely high and sales of lots were, at best, slow. Consequently, the notes were only partially paid at maturity and new notes were given for the unpaid balance. Moreover, some of the property was eventually retransferred to the noteholders at little or no cost. On these facts, the Seventh Circuit had no difficulty affirming the decision of the Tax Court, finding a strong inference that the transfer was an equity contribution where "payment to the transferors [was] dependent on the success of an untried undercapitalized business with uncertain prospects." 365 F.2d at 27. In *Aqualane Shores*, the land transferred to the development corporation was mangrove swamp. Thus, vast improvements were essential to its successful development, which, even then, was highly speculative. With its only source of revenue being the sale of lots, the corporation was forced to borrow substantial amounts of money in order to put the land in marketable condition. No payments on the notes taken back for the land were made for 4 years after maturity. On this basis, payment of the obligations to the transferors was deemed to be dependent upon and at the risk of the success of the venture, and the transfer subject to . . . the predecessor to section 351. 269 F.2d at 119-20.

The evidentiary basis of the present case, as previously set forth, contrasts sharply with these decisions. Unlike either case, the prospects for financial success were bright, such success was realized, and the corporation was always able to meet its obligations as they matured. Moreover, the promise of repayment was never in jeopardy, for the properties' self-liquidating potential guaranteed that repayment of the notes would not be subject to the fortunes of the business. In all major respects, the present case is more analogous to Piedmont Corp. v. Commissioner, 388 F.2d 886 (4th Cir. 1968), than to either *Burr Oaks* or *Aqualane Shores. Piedmont* involved successive transfers of options to purchase real property to a controlled corporation in exchange for unsecured promissory notes. The Fourth Circuit considered *Burr Oaks* and *Aqualane Shores*, but found both to be distinguishable. In reversing the decision of the Tax Court that the transfers were in effect a contribution to capital, the following were held to be determinative: (1) the facts indicated "some degree of certainty to the financial success of the venture"; (2) "a fair purchase price was paid"; (3) the corporation "paid the interest and installments of principal when due, promptly and regularly"; and (4) the corporation "did not retransfer any portion of any option, or any land which it acquired by exercise of an option" to the noteholders. Thereupon, the court concluded that "an evidentiary basis to disregard the purported sales as bona fide sales [was] lacking." 388 F.2d at 890-91.

These same factors appear in this case and, accordingly, we choose to be guided in our deliberations by *Piedmont*, rather than by *Burr Oaks* or *Aqualane Shores*. As supported by the record and confirmed by *Piedmont*, the transfer was in substance, as well as in form, a sale and not a capital contribution.

Defendant's remaining contention is that, notwithstanding a determination that the Castlewood notes were valid debt, the subject transaction falls within the literal provisions of section 351. . . .

We have already given our reasons as to why the Castlewood notes did not constitute a continuing proprietary interest in Castlewood and we will not repeat them here.

[The court's discussion of other issues including whether the notes constituted "securities" under then existing law is omitted.]

C-lec Plastics v. Commissioner

76 T.C. 601 (1981)

DRENNEN, Judge. . . .

The only issue for our decision is, for purposes of section 165(a), . . . to determine petitioner's adjusted basis in certain plastic molds and rings which were destroyed by fire.

FINDINGS OF FACT . . .

Edward D. Walsh (hereinafter Walsh) was the president and sole shareholder of petitioner at all times relevant herein.

Prior to May 31, 1970, petitioner, through the individual efforts of Walsh, created certain property which was used or sold to perform a contract with Physics International. The property consisted of 1 pattern mold, 3 master molds, 50 molds, 48 lite rings, and 1 plastic ring. (Hereinafter, this property will be referred to collectively as the molds.) The cost involved in creating the molds was deducted on petitioner's income tax return for its taxable year ended May 31, 1970.

On or about February 29, 1972, petitioner terminated the lease of its business premises and abandoned the molds along with various other properties. On or about the same date, Walsh took possession and acquired ownership of the abandoned molds. Walsh's basis in the molds for Federal income tax purposes and for purposes of this proceeding was at all times zero.

As of May 31, 1973, petitioner's bank account was overdrawn and it was in a cash-poor financial position. As of that date, petitioner's books and records showed that it owed $53,785.16 to Walsh. . . .

In early 1973, events occurred which indicated that a new market could emerge for products made with the molds and, thus, it became advantageous for petitioner to reacquire the molds.

On June 1, 1973, a special meeting of petitioner's board of directors was held. The corporate minutes of that meeting provide in pertinent part: . . .

> The Corporation in exchange for the molds and rings would issue common stock at the rate of $80.00 per share. If this proposal is accepted, Edward Walsh will purchase additional common stock to round the issuance to 500 shares and permit the Corporation to reduce the officers' loan account liability by $2,982.23. . . .

On or about June 1, 1973, Walsh reconveyed possession and ownership of the molds. At the same time, petitioner issued an additional 500 shares of common stock to Walsh. Additionally, a net reduction of $2,982.23 was made in the loan account. Walsh did not receive any cash or monetary consideration, nor any note or evidence of indebtedness from petitioner at the time he reconveyed the molds to petitioner; nor did petitioner pay Walsh any interest.

By journal entry in petitioner's books dated December 31, 1973, petitioner's acquisition of the molds was recorded by: (1) A debit of $37,017.77 in the research and development account; (2) a debit of $2,982.23 in the loan account; and (3) a credit of $40,000 in the common stock issued account. . . .

The molds were destroyed by fire on December 1, 1973. . . .

In the statutory notice of deficiency, respondent determined that petitioner had an adjusted basis of zero in the molds and, thus, was not entitled to any casualty loss deduction for the molds.

Walsh did not report any income arising out of his reconveyance of the molds to petitioner on his individual income tax returns for 1973, or any subsequent year.

Opinion

Section 165(a) allows a deduction for any loss sustained during the taxable year which is not compensated for by insurance or otherwise. There is no dispute that the molds were destroyed by fire, that no compensation was received or receivable therefor, and that any loss thereon is properly deductible under section 165(a). The only issue to be decided is the amount of that loss. Section 165(b) provides that the amount of the deductible loss is measured by the taxpayer's adjusted basis in the property as provided for in section 1011. See also sec. 1.165-7(b), Income Tax Regs. Thus, a determination of petitioner's adjusted basis in the molds is required. . . .

Petitioner argues that the general rule of sections 1011 and 1012 applies, resulting in an adjusted basis of $37,017.77 in the molds, because petitioner did not exchange its common stock for the molds but rather purchased the molds in an arm's-length transaction.

Based on the testimony of its only witness, Robert E. Williams (hereinafter Williams), petitioner's accountant, petitioner contends that on or about June 1, 1973, there were two separate transactions which were entered into for separate and different reasons. One transaction involved petitioner's issuance of $40,000 in common stock to Walsh in consideration for a like-amount debit to the loan account. This was done, petitioner contends, to improve its capital structure and preclude any allegation that it was thinly capitalized.

The second transaction was the purchase of the molds for the cash equivalent of a $37,017.77 credit to the loan account, which amount was in fact paid to Walsh by the conclusion of petitioner's taxable year ended May 31, 1976, at which time the loan account was zero. This purchase, petitioner contends, brings into operation the general rule of sections 1011 and 1012.

Petitioner explains the seemingly inconsistent December 31, 1973, journal entry concerning the acquisition of the molds, as an example of the "common practice" in recordkeeping, whereby the two transactions were "compounded" in one book entry and only the "net effect" thereof was shown. Similarly, petitioner explains the seemingly inconsistent corporate minutes of the special board of directors' meeting as the work of an unsophisticated corporate secretary who also only recorded the "net effect" of the two transactions.

In opposition to petitioner's contentions, respondent argues that the corporate minutes and books and records indicate that the only transaction was an exchange of the common stock for the molds and an incidental amount of cash (in the form of a debit to the loan account) and that such a transaction falls within the purview of section 351. Accordingly, since Walsh recognized no gain on the transfer, petitioner took Walsh's zero basis in the molds pursuant to section 362(a).

It has long been a principle of Federal income tax law that a transaction's substance rather than its form controls. See, e.g., Commissioner v. Court Holding Co., 324 U.S. 331 (1945); Minnesota Tea Co. v. Helvering, 302 U.S. 609 (1938); Gregory v. Helvering, 293 U.S. 465 (1935). . . .

Williams testified that Walsh approached him seeking advice as to effecting petitioner's acquisition of the molds from Walsh. Petitioner's cash-poor financial position precluded an outright cash purchase. Given petitioner's then-existing debt to Walsh in the amount of $53,785.16, Williams also considered it inadvisable for petitioner to purchase the molds solely on credit by increasing the amount it owed to Walsh. Williams testified that he accordingly recommended that petitioner issue $40,000 of common stock to Walsh in exchange for a $40,000 reduction in the loan account and that the petitioner then "purchase" the molds for $37,017.77 by increasing the loan account in an equal amount.

The only possible conclusion that can be drawn from Williams' testimony is that the two transactions were not separable but were two steps of an integrated whole. The impetus for both transactions was the need for petitioner to acquire the molds and there is nothing to suggest that one transaction would have been effected without the other. In substance, petitioner acquired the molds, and reduced its loan account in the amount of $2,982.23, and Walsh received an additional $40,000 in common stock. Despite the accountant's explanation of his "compounded" book entries, the book entries reflect precisely the action taken by the board of directors as reflected in the minutes of their meeting on June 1, 1973. Under these circumstances, to view the acquisition of the molds as a purchase for cash would be to ignore the best evidence of what was actually intended and what took place. That the transaction was "arm's length" in the sense that $37,017.77 may have been a reasonable price for the molds does not alter the basic substance of the transaction as an exchange of common stock for the molds. Moreover, it is of no import that petitioner did not intend for the transaction to qualify under section 351; that provision applies regardless of petitioner's intent. . . .

In this case, the evidence shows that both the substance and the form of the transaction support our conclusion that the molds were exchanged solely for petitioner's common stock and that the transaction falls within the purview of section 351. Thus, section 362 would apply and petitioner's adjusted basis in the molds would be the same as Walsh's, increased by any gain recognized by Walsh.

Furthermore, we do not believe it is necessary in resolving the issue presented to determine whether there were two transactions or one. Even if there were two transactions, it is clear that they were integrated components of a single whole, the substance of which was that petitioner acquired the molds and Walsh only received common stock. . . .

In summary, the carryover basis provision of section 362 results in petitioner's having an adjusted basis of zero in the molds, thereby precluding any casualty loss deduction under section 165.

Decision will be entered for the respondent.

NOTES

1. *Section 351 versus sale.* Section 351 by its terms is not an elective provision. Taxpayers, however, sometimes deliberately fail to comply with the formalities of §351 when noncompliance is to their benefit. Notice in *Bradshaw* that the formation of the corporation and the purported sale took place on the same day. In *C-lec Plastics* the issuance of stock and the purported sale also took place on the same day. Why was one taxpayer successful and the other unsuccessful in the quest to avoid §351 and its carryover basis provisions? Are formalities important?

Could the taxpayer in *C-lec Plastics* have argued that the tangible property transferred (i.e., the molds) embodied the transferor's services and must be so treated for §351 purposes? See the discussion of *James* at pages 15-16 supra. If the molds were not considered property for §351 purposes, how would that determination have helped the taxpayer?

In Kolkey v. Commissioner, 27 T.C. 37 (1956), aff'd, 254 F.2d 51 (7th Cir. 1958), the Tax Court established criteria for making the sale/§351 distinction:

> Was the capital and credit structure of the new corporation realistic? What was the business purpose, if any, of organizing the new corporation? Were the noteholders the actual promoters and entrepreneurs of the new adventure? Did the noteholders bear the principal risks of loss attendant upon the adventure? Were payments of "principal and interest" on the notes subordinated to dividends and to the claims of creditors? Did the noteholders have substantial control over the business operations; and, if so, was such control reserved to them as an integral part of the plan under which the notes were issued? Was the "price" of the properties, for which the notes were issued disproportionate to the fair market value of such properties? Did the noteholders, when default of the notes occurred, attempt to enforce the obligations?

In the following cases the court ruled that an attempted sale was a §351 transfer, thereby denying a stepped-up basis to the transferee for the reasons indicated: Hayutin v. Commissioner, 508 F.2d 462 (10th Cir. 1974) (undercapitalization, subordinated debt, excessive purchase price); Burr Oaks Corp. v. Commissioner, 365 F.2d 24 (7th Cir. 1966) (undercapitalization, speculative repayment of purported indebtedness); Nye v. Commissioner, 50 T.C. 203 (1968) (no business reason for separating attempted sale from §351 transfer).

Sale characterization was respected in the following: Murphy Logging Co. v. United States, 378 F.2d 222 (9th Cir. 1967) (despite unfavorable capitalization and a tax avoidance purpose); Piedmont v. Commissioner, 388 F.2d 886 (4th Cir. 1968) (notes bore reasonable interest, were not subordinated, and were paid).

Under §1239, any gain recognized by a transferor on the sale or exchange of property between certain related persons constitutes ordinary income if such property is depreciable in the hands of the transferee. For purposes of §1239, a person is deemed related to a corporation if the person owns, directly or indirectly, 50 percent or more of the value of the corporation's outstanding stock. Why didn't §1239 foil the taxpayer's attempt in *Bradshaw* to lock in a capital gain on the transfer of the real property to the transferee corporation? Consider whether the property was depreciable in the hands of the transferee corporation. See §§1221(a)(1) and 167(a).

Receipt of a stepped-up basis by the transferee is only one reason to prefer a sale over a §351 transaction. A transferor of property with an unrealized loss may seek recognition unavailable through §351. Even if a sale transaction is respected, the transferor must navigate §267, which prevents a loss deduction on a sale by an individual to a corporation, where the transferor directly or indirectly owns more than 50 percent in value of the outstanding stock of the enterprise. See also Higgins v. Smith, 308 U.S. 473 (1940), which may support a judicial expansion of §267.

One reason for a transfer as in *Bradshaw* is that the tax rate at the corporate level may be less than the rate at the individual level. But even if the applicable corporate tax rate is higher than the tax rate that would apply to an individual, will we still observe transactions like that in *Bradshaw*? Tax rates are not the only consideration. The corporate form offers non-tax advantages such as limited liability and perhaps easier access to financial markets. The use of a subchapter S corporation might provide use of the corporate form with individual tax rates. See Chapter 16.

From a tax standpoint, when would a sale to a corporation be preferable to a §351 transaction? There are a host of reasons why a sale might be more advantageous, aside from a lower tax rate at the corporate level. First, if the taxpayer has capital losses, those losses can offset only up to $3,000 of ordinary income. §1211(a). By selling appreciated property to a corporation, a taxpayer can generate a capital gain that will be fully absorbed by the capital losses. Even if the capital gain is not fully offset with capital losses, an individual taxpayer may prefer the preferential capital gains tax rate to the higher ordinary income rates that would apply if the taxpayer developed and sold the property in parcels. See §1(a)-(d) and (h). Another reason for a *Bradshaw*-type transaction might be an expectation of increased ordinary income rates in the future. A taxpayer might want to lock in a capital gain now rather than risk a higher ordinary income tax at a later point. Or a taxpayer might be willing to recognize gain on a sale in order to provide the purchasing corporation with a stepped-up basis under §1012, particularly if the taxpayer can postpone recognition through installment reporting.

2. *Contributions to capital by shareholders.* In *Bradshaw* the Service argued that the attempted sale was a contribution to capital. Had the Service prevailed, what would the consequences have been? Section 118 shields a corporation from recognition of income for contributions to the corporation's capital. The corporation's basis for the new capital is generally determined under §362(a) for transfers by shareholders. As explained in the following note, §362(c) provides a special rule for contributions "not contributed by a shareholder as such."

The shareholder who contributes capital does not recognize gain or loss on the contribution and can increase stock basis by the property contributed. Treas. Regs. §1.118-1. Should the basis increase be measured by the basis or by the fair market value of the property contributed?

Notice what would happen in *Bradshaw* and similar cases if the notes received by the "seller" were ignored because they were too speculative. Payments of what would otherwise be interest would be reclassified as dividends. What difference would this make to the recipient? How about to the payor? What happens when the corporation "retires the debt"? Normally, the recipient would have no income or perhaps a capital gain. §1271(a). Now the recipient faces the possibility of dividend treatment without basis offset on a failed redemption. See §302(d), discussed at page 155 infra.

The same consequences may befall a transferor and transferee whenever debt is reclassified as stock. See discussion of the debt-equity issue at pages 89-104 infra.

3. *"Contributions" to the capital of a corporation by nonshareholders.* Over the years, there has been confusion over the treatment to be afforded contributions by governmental agencies, community groups, and private persons to a business to encourage or assist the business in providing or expanding a service. The cases involve two basic issues for the recipient: (1) Is the contribution income? (2) Does the use of the contribution give rise to any tax benefits, such as a deduction for current expenses or basis?

The payment also creates tax issues for the contributor. If the contributor is a business and it subsidizes a railroad to extend service to a new area, is the grant a current business deduction or a capital expenditure? If a capital expenditure, it would ordinarily be recovered through a series of deductions over time—that is, depreciation deductions—unless it would last indefinitely (for instance, land). In the latter event, there is no basis benefit until the recipient sells the relevant asset. If the grantor is a charity, grants to private businesses to accomplish the aims of the charity, such as the prevention of community deterioration or providing new employment opportunities, might endanger its exemption.

The exclusion from income of nonshareholder contributions to capital derives from Edwards v. Cuba Railroad Co., 268 U.S. 628 (1925), in which the Court held that government subsidies to a railroad to induce the construction of railroad facilities were not taxable income within the meaning of the sixteenth amendment.

Since 1954, the Code has provided in §118 that gross income does not include any "contribution to capital," thus implicitly recognizing that contributions to capital can be received from nonshareholders. The general rule of §362(a) is that the corporation takes a tax basis in the contributed property equal to the transferor's basis. Section 362(c), however, provides that contributions by nonshareholders take a zero basis.

Before the enactment of §362(c), it was possible under the 1939 Code for the recipient of funds from nonshareholders to receive a double tax benefit. First, the amounts received were not recognized as income; second, the taxpayer was allowed to claim depreciation deductions on the contributor's basis. See Detroit Edison Co. v. Commissioner, 318 U.S. 98 (1943), and United States v. Chicago, Burlington & Quincy Railroad, 339 U.S. 583 (1950), permitting the depreciation. Section 362(c) laid to rest the depreciation issue by requiring a zero basis for nonshareholder contributions to capital. Section 362(c) did not resolve, however, whether a transfer should be characterized as a nontaxable contribution to capital by a nonshareholder or a taxable payment for services.

Under §118(a), a contribution to the capital of a corporation is excluded from its gross income. Section 118, codified in 1954 and intended to incorporate existing decisional law, deals with those transfers to a corporation that fall between genuine gifts, on one hand, and payments clearly for direct future services, on the other hand. The legislative history speaks of contributions to capital, as in the case where "the contributor expects to derive indirect benefits, the contribution cannot be called a gift; yet the anticipated future benefits may also be so intangible as to not warrant treating the contributions as a payment for future services." S. Rep. No. 1622, to accompany H.R. 8300 (Pub. L. No. 591), 83d Cong., 2d Sess. 18-19 (1954). See also Treas. Regs. §1.118-1.

The nature of a transferor's anticipated benefits was examined in Federated Department Stores v. Commissioner, 51 T.C. 500 (1968), aff'd, 426 F.2d 417 (6th Cir. 1970). In that case, a developer contributed money and land to a department store to induce its move into a new shopping center. The court concluded that the contribution provided only indirect and intangible benefits to the developer and was, therefore, a tax-free contribution of capital. Accord, May Department Stores Co. v. Commissioner, 33 T.C.M. (CCH) 1128 (1974), aff'd per curiam, 519 F.2d 1154 (8th Cir. 1975). But when payments have a reasonable connection with services that the recipient corporation's business provides, amounts received are treated as taxable income. John B. White, Inc. v. Commissioner, 55 T.C. 729 (1971), aff'd per curiam, 458 F.2d 989 (3d Cir. 1972) (subsidies from Ford Motor Co. to Ford automobile dealer to induce dealer to move showroom to new location were taxable income). The cases are not easily reconcilable. See Teleservice of Wyoming Valley v. Commissioner, 27 T.C. 722 (1957), aff'd, 254 F.2d 105 (3d Cir. 1958) (payments from prospective customers to finance construction costs to corporation operating community television antenna system were taxable income).

Sometimes receipts can be eliminated from income under what has been known as the conduit theory. In Seven Up Co. v. Commissioner, 14 T.C. 965 (1950), a soft-drink manufacturer received funds from bottlers who voluntarily contributed to an advertising campaign. The manufacturer was held to be a mere conduit for the funds, holding them solely as a trustee and required to disburse them for a specific purpose to benefit the bottlers. Therefore, the funds were not income to the manufacturer under §61. Accord, Ford Dealers Advertising Fund v. Commissioner, 55 T.C. 761 (1971), aff'd per curiam, 456 F.2d 255 (5th Cir. 1972). If the history of these cases seems confusing, see the concluding sentence of Judge Tannenwald's opinion in State Farm Road Corp. v. Commissioner, 65 T.C. 217 (1975), that in this area "a page of logic is worth a volume of history," taking note of Justice Holmes's statement that normally "a page of history is worth a volume of logic," New York Trust Co. v. Eisner, 256 U.S. 345, 349 (1921).

Section 118(b) provides no exclusion for contributions "in aid of construction or any other contribution as a customer or potential customer." The new provision reverses some of the prior cases, including Edwards v. Cuba Railroad Co., supra, which gave birth to §118.

Hempt Bros., Inc. v. United States

490 F.2d 1172 (3d Cir. 1974)

ALDISERT, Circuit Judge.

[A cash basis partnership transferred its assets to a newly formed corporation in exchange for all the corporation's stock in a transaction qualifying under §351. Among the transferred assets were $662,820 in accounts receivable with a $0 basis. The Service argued that the corporation, whose basis was $0 under §362, should recognize gain when the receivables were paid off. The taxpayer argued that the transferor partnership should have been taxed, a result that was precluded by the applicable statute of limitations.]

I

Taxpayer argues here, as it did in the district court, that because the term "property" as used in Section 351 does not embrace accounts receivable, the Commissioner lacked statutory authority to apply principles associated with

Section 351. The district court properly rejected the legal interpretation urged by the taxpayer.

The definition of Section 351 "property" has been extensively treated by the Court of Claims in E. I. DuPont de Nemours and Co. v. United States, 471 F.2d 1211, 1218-19 (Ct. Cl. 1973), describing the transfer of a non-exclusive license to make, use and sell area herbicides under French patents:

> Unless there is some special reason intrinsic to [Section 351] the general word "property" has a broad reach in tax law. . . . For section 351, in particular, courts have advocated a generous definition of "property," . . . and it has been suggested in one capital gains case that nonexclusive licenses can be viewed as property though not as capital assets. . . .

We see no adequate reason for refusing to follow these leads.

We fail to perceive any special reason why a restrictive meaning should be applied to accounts receivable so as to exclude them from the general meaning of "property." Receivables possess the usual capabilities and attributes associated with jurisprudential concepts of property law. They may be identified, valued, and transferred. Moreover, their role in an ongoing business must be viewed in the context of Section 351 application. The presence of accounts receivable is a normal, rather than an exceptional accoutrement of the type of business included by Congress in the transfer to a corporate form. . . .

The taxpayer next makes a strenuous argument that "[the] government is seeking to tax the wrong person." It contends that the assignment of income doctrine as developed by the Supreme Court applies to a Section 351 transfer of accounts receivable so that the transferor, not the transferee-corporation, bears the corresponding tax liability. It argues that the assignment of income doctrine dictates that where the right to receive income is transferred to another person in a transaction not giving rise to tax at the time of transfer, the transferor is taxed on the income when it is collected by the transferee; that the only requirement for its application is a transfer of a right to receive ordinary income; and that since the transferred accounts receivable are a present right to future income, the sole requirement for the application of the doctrine is squarely met. In essence, this is a contention that the nonrecognition provision of Section 351 is in conflict with the assignment of income doctrine and that Section 351 should be subordinated thereto. Taxpayer relies on the seminal case of Lucas v. Earl, 281 U.S. 111 (1930), and its progeny for support of its proposition that the application of the doctrine is mandated whenever one transfers a right to receive ordinary income.

On its part, the government concedes that a taxpayer may sell for value a claim to income otherwise his own and he will be taxable upon the proceeds of the sale. Such was the case in Commissioner v. P. G. Lake, Inc., 356 U.S. 260 (1958), in which the taxpayer-corporation assigned its oil payment right to its president in consideration for his cancellation of a $600,000 loan. Viewing the oil payment right as a right to receive future income, the Court applied the reasoning of the assignment of income doctrine, normally applicable to a gratuitous assignment, and held that the consideration received by the taxpayer-corporation was taxable as ordinary income since it essentially was a substitute for that which would otherwise be received at a future time as ordinary income.

Turning to the facts of this case, we note that here there was the transfer of accounts receivable from the partnership to the corporation pursuant to Section 351. We view these accounts receivable as a present right to receive future income. In consideration of the transfer of this right, the members of the partnership received stock — a valid consideration. The consideration, therefore, was essentially a substitute for that which would otherwise be received at a future time as ordinary income to the cash basis partnership. Consequently, the holding in *Lake* would normally apply, and income would ordinarily be realized, and thereby taxable, by the cash basis partnership-transferor at the time of receipt of the stock.

But the terms and purpose of Section 351 have to be reckoned with. By its explicit terms Section 351 expresses the Congressional intent that transfers of property for stock or securities will not result in recognition. It therefore becomes apparent that this case vividly illustrates how Section 351 sometimes comes into conflict with another provision of the Internal Revenue Code or a judicial doctrine, and requires a determination of which of two conflicting doctrines will control. . . .

While we cannot fault the general principle "that income be taxed to him who earns it," to adopt taxpayer's argument would be to hamper the incorporation of ongoing businesses; additionally it would impose technical constructions which are economically and practically unsound. None of the cases cited by taxpayer, including *Lake* itself, persuades us otherwise. In *Lake* the Court was required to decide whether the proceeds from the assignment of the oil payment right were taxable as ordinary income or as long term capital gains. Observing that the provision for long term capital gains treatment "has always been narrowly construed so as to protect the revenue against artful devices," 356 U.S. at 265, the Court predicated its holding upon an emphatic distinction between a conversion of a capital investment — "income-producing property" — and an assignment of income per se. "The substance of what was assigned was the right to receive future income. The substance of what was received was the present value of income which the recipient would otherwise obtain in the future." Ibid., at 266. A Section 351 issue was not presented in *Lake*. Therefore the case does not control in weighing the conflict between the general rule of assignment of income and the Congressional purpose of nonrecognition upon the incorporation of an ongoing business.

We are persuaded that, on balance, the teachings of *Lake* must give way in this case to the broad Congressional interest in facilitating the incorporation of ongoing businesses. As desirable as it is to afford symmetry in revenue law, we do not intend to promulgate a hard and fast rule. We believe that the problems posed by the clash of conflicting internal revenue doctrines are more properly determined by the circumstances of each case. Here we are influenced by the fact that the subject of the assignment was accounts receivable for partnership's goods and services sold in the regular course of business, that the change of business form from partnership to corporation had a basic business purpose and was not designed for the purpose of deliberate tax avoidance, and by the conviction that the totality of circumstances here presented fit the mold of the Congressional intent to give nonrecognition to a transfer of a total business from a noncorporate to a corporate form.

But this too must be said. Even though Section 351(a) immunizes the transferor from immediate tax consequences, Section 358 retains for the transferors a potential income tax liability to be realized and recognized upon a subsequent sale or exchange of the stock certificates received. As to the transferee-corporation, the tax basis of the receivables will be governed by Section 362. . . .

NOTES

1. *Assignment of income.* Nonrecognition under §351 can clash with the well-entrenched assignment of income doctrine developed through a series of Supreme Court cases. See, e.g., Lucas v. Earl, 281 U.S. 111 (1930); Helvering v. Horst, 311 U.S. 112 (1940). We have already seen that the transfer by a cash basis transferor of accounts receivable to a corporation will not trigger recognition at the time of the exchange if the standards of §351 are met. See page 11 supra. A decision reached on this point does not necessarily foreclose the recognition of income by the transferor *when the transferee collects.* Nevertheless, in transactions in which the assets of a going business are incorporated, courts have generally declined to invoke the assignment of income doctrine on collection by the transferee.

In contrast to *Hempt Bros., Inc.*, consider Brown v. Commissioner, 115 F.2d 337 (2d Cir. 1940). There, an attorney brought a lawsuit to collect fees for services rendered. A few months before settling the suit, he transferred the claim to a wholly owned corporation whose only asset was the claim and whose only purpose was to facilitate collection. Under these circumstances the court ruled that the transferor was taxable on the collection of the claim by the transferee. See also Weinberg v. Commissioner, 44 T.C. 233 (1965), aff'd per curiam, 386 F.2d 836 (9th Cir. 1967), where the court treated a sale of growing crops by a newly formed corporation as a sale by the shareholder-transferors who had made the transfer shortly before harvest.

In Rev. Rul. 80-198, 1980-2 C.B. 113, the Service approved of the results in both *Hempt* and *Brown,* citing a business purpose for incorporation, or lack thereof, as determinative. Notice that in the usual assignment of income situation, a taxpayer who assigns away income from the performance of services avoids taxation of that income. However, when the transferors in *Hempt* transferred the receivables to the transferee corporation, the assignment was not complete. Not only was the transferee corporation taxable when the receivables were collected, but the transferors were also taxed when the transferee corporation distributed the proceeds (or when the transferors sold their stock, the basis of which reflects the $0 basis in a cash basis taxpayer's accounts receivable). Perhaps it is the corporate double tax that underlies the court's willingness to sidestep the application of Lucas v. Earl in a §351 transaction.

2. *Tax benefit rule.* In Nash v. United States, 398 U.S. 1 (1970), accrual basis transferors exchanged receivables for stock. The Supreme Court held that there had been no "recovery" of a previously deducted bad debt reserve sufficient to trigger recognition by the transferors. In *Nash* the value of the stock received equaled the value of the receivables minus the bad debt reserve. If the value of the stock received exceeds the value of the property exchanged, the *Nash* rationale may not save the transferor from recognition under the tax benefit doctrine. See United States v. Bliss Dairy, 460 U.S. 370 (1983).

3. *Business purpose.* This ubiquitous doctrine will sometimes be invoked to ignore a purported §351 transfer. For example, in Rev. Rul. 60-331, 1960-2 C.B. 189, the Service disregarded an attempted transfer of stock in one corporation on which a dividend was due to a second corporation to try to qualify for the dividends-received deduction of §243. See also West Coast Marketing Corp. v. Commissioner, 46 T.C. 32 (1966), in which the court disregarded the formation

of a corporation solely for the purpose of qualifying the subsequent exchange of stock for nonrecognition under the reorganization provisions when the direct exchange of property would have subjected the transferor to capital gains treatment.

4. *Clear reflection of income.* In addition to judicially created doctrines, the Service has several statutory weapons in its arsenal. In Palmer v. Commissioner, 267 F.2d 434 (9th Cir. 1959), an individual taxpayer in the construction business, who had been reporting income on the completed contract method, transferred the business to a corporation shortly after a large payment was due for work done prior to the transfer. The court upheld the Commissioner's adjustment under §446(b), putting the transferor on the percentage of completion method of accounting, thereby allocating a large part of the income back to the taxpayer. See also Shore v. Commissioner, 631 F.2d 624 (9th Cir. 1980) (incorporation triggered §481 recognition).

In Rooney v. United States, 305 F.2d 681 (9th Cir. 1962), a husband and wife's farming business was incorporated under §351 after the transferors had taken deductions pertaining to the crop transferred. Employing §482, the court held that the deductions for business expenses could be denied to the transferors and allocated to the corporation, to be matched with the subsequently realized income to which the expenses related. For further discussion of §482, see page 508 infra.

5. *Organizational expenses.* Besides issuing stock, a new corporation must contend with a host of expenditures incident to its formation, such as legal fees for drafting the charter, bylaws, and stock certificates; accounting fees; expenses for the organizational meeting of directors or stockholders; and fees paid to the state of incorporation. Broadly, §248 permits a corporation to elect to amortize such "organizational expenses" over a period of 180 months. For a definition of "organizational expenditures," see §248(b) and Treas. Regs. §1.248-1(b)(2). Expenditures incurred in the process of raising capital—such as commissions and printing costs—are excluded from the reach of §248. Why? If the corporation does not elect to amortize under §248, presumably organizational expenses can be deducted in the year the corporation dissolves. See Bryant Heater Co. v. Commissioner, 231 F.2d 938 (6th Cir. 1956).

6. *Section 351 and redemptions.* For the interplay among §§351, 302, and 304, see page 209 infra.

7. *Section 351 and reorganizations.* There is an overlap between §351 and the provisions governing reorganizations. For example, suppose *T* wants to transfer appreciated property to *X* Corp. without recognizing gain. *T* is not a shareholder of *X* Corp. A direct attempt at a §351 transfer would leave *T* short of the control requirement. Suppose, though, that *T* and *X* Corp. together form Sub Corp., with *T* contributing the appreciated property and *X* Corp. all of its assets. Together the transferors hold all Sub Corp. stock. The final step is that the *X* Corp. shareholders receive Sub Corp. stock in exchange for their *X* Corp. stock. Assume that the *X* Corp. stock has not appreciated so that no gain is recognized by the shareholders on the exchange. Has *T* made an end run around the control requirements of §351? See Rev. Rul. 68-349, 1968-2 C.B. 143 (§351 nonrecognition unavailable to *T*).

8. *Section 351 and passive activity losses.* Suppose *B*, a transferor in a §351 transaction, transfers rental real estate that has been subject to the passive loss limitations under §469. Does the §351 transfer trigger suspended passive losses, thereby allowing *B* to use those losses to offset nonpassive income (such as portfolio income or income from services)? A taxable disposition of a passive activity triggers the use of any suspended losses against any type of income. §469(g).

The Senate Finance Committee report accompanying the Tax Reform Act of 1986 makes clear that a §351 transfer does not trigger the suspended losses because *B* retains an interest in the property. To the extent that there is taxable boot in the §351 transaction, the suspended passive losses can be used to offset that income. The suspended losses will be fully deductible when *B* disposes of her entire interest in the corporation.

PROBLEMS

2-12. *T*, a cash basis taxpayer, transfers real property and Microsoft stock to *X* Corp. in exchange for *X* stock in a transaction that qualifies under §351. Discuss the tax consequences to *T* and *X* Corp. in the following.

a. The real property has a basis of $200,000 and a fair market value of $900,000. It is subject to a liability of $500,000, which *X* will assume. The Microsoft stock has a basis of $100,000 and a fair market value of $70,000.
b. Suppose in (a) that *X* takes the property subject to the liability so that *T* remains liable on the underlying note. Suppose instead that *T* guarantees *X*'s payment of the liability.
c. Suppose in (a) that *T* borrows $200,000 from a bank and contributes the cash as part of the §351 transaction.
d. Suppose in (c) that *T* had borrowed $200,000 from *X* in an unrelated transaction. The loan bears a market rate of interest and the loan is due in 10 years. *T* contributes the loan proceeds as part of the §351 transaction.
e. Suppose in (a) that *T* makes a promissory note to *X* in the amount of $200,000 bearing a market rate of interest and transfers the note as part of the §351 transaction. The note is due in 10 years.

2-13. *T*, a cash basis taxpayer who operates a sole proprietorship, transfers $1,000 in uncollected accounts receivable (with a basis of $0) to *X*, a wholly owned corporation. In exchange, *T* receives $700 of *X* stock and *X*'s assumption of $300 of *T*'s accounts payable.

a. What are the tax consequences to *T* and *X*?
b. Suppose *T* is an accrual basis taxpayer transferring property with a basis of $0 and a fair market value of $1,000 in exchange for $700 of *X* stock and *X*'s assumption of $300 of *T*'s account payables. What are the tax consequences?
c. In (a), what are the tax consequences when *X* collects on the accounts receivable and pays off the accounts payable?

2-14. *T* owns all the stock of *X* Corp. *T* transfers to *X* Corp. a parcel of real estate with a basis of $100,000 and a fair market value of $500,000. In exchange, *T* receives an interest-bearing debt instrument due in five years. Following the transfer, *X* Corp. developed the property into 10 single-family dwellings, each of which was sold for $100,000. Ignoring the development costs, discuss the tax consequences of these transactions to *T* and *X* Corp.

3

Corporate Operation

A. CORPORATE TAX RATES AND BASE

1. *Taxable Entity*

For a discussion of when a corporation is treated as a separate taxable entity, see Chapter 15.

2. *Tax Rate*

Section 11 imposes graduated tax rates ranging from 15 percent to 35 percent on corporate taxpayers. The graduation is steep: Corporations with taxable income of more than $75,000 find themselves in the 34-percent bracket. The 35-percent bracket applies to corporate taxable income over $10 million. The little graduation that exists is eliminated for corporations with taxable income greater than $18,333,333. Those corporations are taxed at a flat 35-percent rate because Congress wanted to restrict the benefits of the lower rates to smaller businesses.

Section 11 implements this congressional policy in a somewhat convoluted manner. First, an additional tax is imposed on taxable income in excess of $100,000. The additional tax is equal to 5 percent of a corporation's income in excess of $100,000 up to a maximum additional tax of $11,750, which occurs at $335,000 of taxable income. The $11,750 figure represents the difference between taxing the first $75,000 of taxable income at a flat 34 percent rate ($25,500) and taxing it at the graduated rates ($13,750). As a corporation's taxable income increases from $100,000 to $335,000, the benefits of the reduced tax rates on the first $75,000 vanish. Note also that for taxable income in the range of $100,000 to $335,000, the marginal tax rate on the next dollar earned is not 34 percent but equals 34 percent plus the 5 percent surtax, or 39 percent.

A second provision of the same type phases out the 34-percent bracket for corporate taxpayers with taxable income exceeding $15 million. These taxpayers must pay 3 percent of taxable income in excess of $15 million or $100,000, whichever is less. Accordingly for taxpayers with taxable income between

$15,000,000 and $18,333,333, a 38-percent rate applies. If a taxpayer has taxable income exceeding $18,333,333, it pays tax at a flat 35-percent rate.

All of the above result in marginal rates as follow:

Taxable Income	*Rate*
Up to $50,000	15%
Over $50,000 but not over $75,000	25
Over $75,000 but not over $100,000	34
Over $100,000 but not over $335,000	39
Over $335,000 but not over $10,000,000	34
Over $10,000,000 but not over $15,000,000	35
Over $15,000,000 but not over $18,333,333	38
Over $18,333,333	35

Although §11(a) contains only slightly graduated tax rates, even that slight graduation is denied to "qualified personal service corporations," which are taxed at a flat 35-percent rate. A corporation is a qualified personal service corporation if it meets a function test and an ownership test. See §448(d). Under the function test, substantially all of the activities of the corporation must involve the performance of services in the fields of health, law, engineering, architecture, accounting, actuarial science, performing arts, or consulting. Under the ownership test, substantially all of the stock (by value) of the corporation must be held directly or indirectly by employees performing those services, by retired employees who performed those services in the past, by their estates, or by persons who hold stock in the corporation by reason of the death of such an employee or retired employee within the past two years.

Notice that the denial of graduated rates applies only to "qualified" personal service corporations, which are "qualified" to be treated more harshly in this regard than other corporations. The definition of qualified personal service corporations used in §§11(b) and 448(d) is quite narrow. Indeed §448 prohibits the use of the cash method of accounting by corporations except for the narrow category of corporations including qualified personal service corporations. §448(b) (also excepting farming businesses and corporations with no more than $5,000,000 of average annual gross receipts over the preceding three taxable years). Why would Congress use this narrow category to impose higher tax rates? Notice how Congress both giveth and taketh away. Qualified personal service corporations can use the cash method of accounting but cannot have the advantages of graduated rates. Why are qualified personal service corporations subject to a higher rate schedule than manufacturing or sales corporations? What policy reason, if any, justifies this discrimination?

While it is easy to categorize some businesses as qualified personal service corporations, such as incorporated doctors, dentists, lawyers, and accountants, the treatment of other businesses is not so clear. Are incorporated health clubs, nutritionists, and weight control clinics considered in the health field? Treas. Regs. §1.448-1T provides that health services do not include services not directly related to a medical field even if the services purportedly relate to the health of the recipient. Health clubs and spas are specifically excluded from coverage. Similar questions arise with respect to the performing arts. Under the regulation, performing arts services do not include services of managers or promoters or the activities of broadcasters. Athletes are not considered performing artists.

Perhaps the most uncertain area is consulting. According to the regulations, consulting is the giving of advice and counsel; sales and brokerage activities are not consulting. If compensation is contingent on the consummation of a transaction, any services performed in the transaction are not consulting services. For example, financial planners who are paid on the basis of advice are engaged in consulting and may be subject to the flat 35-percent rate while financial planners who are paid on the basis of trade orders in securities or commodities are not consulting.

3. *Taxation of Capital Gains and Losses*

For noncorporate taxpayers, §1(h) currently provides a rate ceiling of 20 percent on most long-term capital gain. Section 1201 accomplishes a similar (but less rewarding) function for corporations by providing an alternative tax for corporations with net capital gains in lieu of the tax imposed by §11 if the §1201 tax is less. This tax is the sum of (1) the §11 tax on the corporation's taxable income minus the net capital gains and (2) 35 percent of the net capital gains. That is, the maximum tax on corporate net capital gains is 35 percent—the same maximum rate for ordinary income. However, if the tax rate for ordinary income goes up, capital gains may only be taxed at a 35-percent rate.

Section 1201 is triggered if the rate of tax under §11 exceeds 35 percent. Suppose a corporation with $15 million of ordinary income earns a $500,000 capital gain. Does §1201 provide a top rate on the capital gain of 35 percent because the effective rate under §11 is 35 percent plus the 3 percent additional tax on the $500,000 gain? See §1201(a) (stating that the 35 percent rate is determined without regard to the last two sentences of §11(b)(1), which provide for the 3-percent and 5-percent surtaxes).

There are also some differences in the treatment of capital losses for corporations vis-à-vis other taxpayers. A corporation can deduct capital losses only to the extent of capital gains. §1211(a). No ordinary income can be offset by capital losses. Cf. §1211(b) (individuals can offset up to $3,000 of ordinary income with capital losses). Although individuals can carry unused capital losses forward indefinitely, corporations are generally given a three-year carryback period and a five-year carryforward period. §1212(a). The unused loss is carried back to the earliest year and then carried forward chronologically until the balance is used up or the carryforward period expires.

4. *Corporate Tax Base*

The §11 tax (or the §1201 tax) is applied to "taxable income." Although in most respects a corporation's taxable income is determined in the same manner as an individual's, there are some differences aside from the capital loss carryover provision discussed above. For individual taxpayers, "adjusted gross income" serves as a way station in moving from the calculation of gross income to taxable income. An individual's charitable, medical, and casualty loss deductions are all based on adjusted gross income. A corporation does not have an adjusted gross income. Instead, all appropriate corporate deductions are subtracted directly from gross income in arriving at taxable income.

Some deductions that are treated differently by individual and corporate taxpayers include the following:

1. The standard deduction allowed under §63(c) for individuals is not available for corporations, which instead must separately account for their deductions;
2. The personal exemption deduction under §151 is not available for corporations;
3. Personal deductions authorized under §§211-220 (including items such as medical expenses and alimony) do not apply to corporations, although §162 permits a corporation to deduct expenses incurred for the production of income not in a trade or business, expenses that for individuals are deductible under §212;
4. Under §170(b)(2), charitable contribution deductions are allowed to corporations up to 10 percent of taxable income (computed without regard to charitable deductions and several other items).

A number of provisions were enacted specifically to apply to corporate taxpayers. For example, Congress has shown concern over corporations' making large compensation payments to corporate officers in the event of a corporate takeover. These "golden parachutes" appear to some as a raid on the corporate treasury by its officers. To others the payments ensure that the officers will do what is best for the corporation in the event of a takeover attempt without worrying about personal consequences (e.g., the loss of a well-paying job).

Through the use of the tax system, Congress has raised the cost of making golden parachute payments. Section 280G denies a deduction for payments of "excessive" compensation to corporate officers triggered by changes in corporate control. Excessive payments are determined by comparing the payments with a designated base period. In addition, §4999 imposes an excise tax on the recipient equal to 20 percent of the "excessive" compensation.

A publicly held corporation also cannot deduct compensation paid to a "covered employee" in excess of $1 million if the compensation is "applicable employee remuneration." §162(m). The term "covered employee" refers to any employee who (1) as of the close of the taxable year is the chief executive officer (CEO) of the corporation, or (2) is one of the corporation's four highest compensated officers (other than the CEO) for the tax year. The term "applicable employee remuneration" refers to a covered employee's aggregate remuneration for services performed. The term does not apply, however, to commission payments or other performance-based compensation if (1) the performance goals are established by a compensation committee of the board of directors that has two or more outside directors; (2) the material terms of the compensation are approved by a majority vote of the shareholders before compensation is paid; and (3) the compensation committee certifies that the performance goals were satisfied. For example, compensation based on increases in stock price, market share, or earnings per share are not counted in determining the $1 million limit if the specified procedural requirements are satisfied. Notice that the limited deduction imposed by §162(m) applies to publicly held corporations, where there is accountability to outside directors and to the shareholders, but does not apply to privately held corporations, where there is more room for manipulation.

In October of 2008, Congress modified §162(m) and §280G to limit deductions for a corporate (or noncorporate) employer that participated significantly in the $700 billion federal "bailout" of Wall Street. If §162(m) applies, the employer cannot deduct more than $500,000 of a covered executive's compensation for any year. §162(m)(5)(A). Further, §280G may now apply to a covered executive's severance payments, even though not triggered by the employer's change of control. §280g(e). In either case, a covered executive includes the employer's CEO, its chief financial officer (CFO), and its three highest compensated officers (other than the CEO and CFO). §162(m)(5)(D).

With the increase of corporate takeover activity in the 1980s and 1990s, members of Congress voiced concern that regulation was needed to stem the tide. Although many commentators argue that takeovers are one of the free market's means of disciplining inefficient management and deploying corporate assets in the most efficient manner, others decry the dislocations to workers and communities caused by some takeovers and lament the amount of debt (i.e., leverage) used in some acquisitions.

There is no dispute, however, that Congress has looked to the tax laws as a means of regulating the market for corporate control. Section 279, enacted in 1969, disallows a deduction for corporate interest in excess of $5 million per year on specified "corporate acquisition indebtedness," defined to include certain convertible, subordinated debt. The effect of this provision is to make debt-financed takeovers less attractive. See page 337 infra.

More recent provisions have focused on all aspects of corporate acquisitions. Section 162(k) denies a deduction for any amount paid or incurred by a corporation to redeem its own stock. This provision is aimed at "greenmail" payments made by a corporation to a potential corporate "raider" to repurchase the "raider's" stock. Furthermore, §5881 imposes an excise tax of 50 percent on any gain or other income realized by the greenmail recipient. "Greenmail" is defined in §5881 as consideration paid by a corporation in redemption of its stock held for less than two years if the holder threatened a public tender offer. It is not clear that greenmail payments are "bad," but it is clear that the Code discourages such payments. See Macey and McChesney, A Theoretical Analysis of Corporate Greenmail, 95 Yale L.J. 133 (1985).

Section 382, discussed in more detail in Chapter 13, does not attempt to increase the direct cost of corporate acquisitions. Instead, this section limits the ability of acquiring corporations to use net operating losses of the acquired corporation to offset future income, thereby decreasing the attraction of some corporate takeovers. Note, however, that a purpose of §382 is to make it more likely that the use of the acquired corporation's losses will be unaffected by the acquisition.

In addition to the deductions discussed above, a corporation is entitled to a variety of tax credits. Perhaps the most significant one is the foreign tax credit. §§27 and 901. A corporation can offset any applicable U.S. federal income tax on income from foreign sources with foreign income taxes paid on that income. Credits are also available for research (§41), targeted jobs expenditures (§51), and rehabilitation and energy expenditures (§§46-48).

The preceding discussion of the corporate tax rate and base is aimed at domestic corporations (corporations created or organized in the United States or under the law of the United States or any state). Foreign corporations (corporations incorporated abroad) are subject to U.S. taxation on income that is connected in designated ways to the United States. See generally §§881 and 882. For example, a foreign corporation engaged in a trade or business in the United States is taxed in the same manner as a U.S. corporation on income that is "effectively connected" with the conduct of that U.S. trade or business (i.e., trade or business income). §882. The rules governing tax rates and base apply to such business income. A foreign corporation that has investment income from interest, dividends, rents, royalties, and so on is generally taxed at a flat rate of 30 percent (or in some cases, a lower treaty rate) on the gross amount of the payments. §881. No deductions are permitted. A foreign corporation can elect, however, to have rental payments for the use of U.S. real property taxed as business income that can be offset by appropriate deductions rather than being taxed at the flat 30-percent rate (or lower treaty rate). §882(d).

5. *Passive Loss Limitations*

In an effort to curtail investment solely or primarily for the purpose of securing tax benefits, Congress enacted §469, a provision that limits the deduction of passive activity expenses against other income (i.e., active business income or portfolio income). Any losses suspended as a result of the limitation can be carried forward and treated as deductions in the following year or can be taken when the taxpayer disposes of the entire interest in the passive activity. §469(b) and (g). In general, an activity is passive if it involves the conduct of a trade or business and if the corporation does not "materially participate" in the activity. By definition, a rental activity (e.g., ownership of an apartment building) is considered a passive activity regardless of the level of activity. An important exception, discussed below, applies for taxpayers in the real estate business.

Although an exhaustive discussion of the passive loss provisions is beyond the scope of a corporate tax course, the provisions do apply to certain personal service corporations and closely held corporations. Accordingly, a personal service corporation that also rents real estate may not be able to offset any active income from the performance of services with deductions from the real estate rental activity. A personal service corporation is defined as a corporation whose principal activity is the performance of personal services when such services are performed by an employee who owns any stock of the corporation. See §§469(j)(2) and 269A(b)(2).

In the case of a closely held corporation (other than a personal service corporation), the passive loss rules apply in modified form. §469(e)(2). Passive losses may be used to offset active business income but not portfolio income (e.g., interest, dividends, and royalties). *Id.* Broadly speaking, a closely held corporation is a corporation that has more than 50 percent in value of its outstanding stock owned by not more than five individuals. §§469(j)(1), 465(a)(1)(B), 542(a)(2).

A corporation's business is not a passive activity if the corporation materially participates in an activity, which occurs if one or more shareholders owning in the aggregate more than 50 percent of the outstanding stock of the corporation each materially participate. §469(h)(4). A shareholder materially participates if she spends more than 500 hours annually on the activity or if she meets one of the other tests specified under the regulations. Treas. Regs. §§1.469-1T(g), -5T. In addition, a corporation other than a personal services corporation materially participates in its business for a taxable year if the following requirements are met:

1. During the entire year, the corporation has at least one full-time management employee in the business;

2. During the entire year, the corporation has at least three full-time employees in the business, none of whom own more than 5 percent of the corporation's stock; and
3. For the year, the corporation's deductions under §§162 and 404 related to the business exceed 15 percent of its gross income from the business.

§469(h)(4)(B); §465(c)(7)(C).

If more than 50 percent of a closely held corporation's gross receipts for the taxable year are derived from real property trades or businesses in which the corporation materially participates, the rental activities are not considered passive. Then, associated losses can be used to offset nonpassive income. §469(c)(7)(A) and (D). A real property trade or business is any real property development, redevelopment, construction, reconstruction, acquisition, conversion, rental, operation, management, leasing, or brokerage trade or business. §469(c)(7)(C).

If passive losses are suspended, those losses can be taken in full when the taxpayer disposes (in a taxable transaction) of the entire interest in the passive activity. §469(g)(1). The reason for the rule is that prior to the disposition, it may be difficult to determine whether there has actually been economic gain or loss with respect to the activity. For example, allowable deductions may or may not exceed unrealized appreciation. Once a taxable disposition occurs, a final accounting can be made for the activity, accurately measuring that gain or loss.

Suppose a personal services corporation is also engaged in a rental real estate activity and that the deductions for the rental activity exceed the passive income from that activity by $20,000. Those excess deductions would not be allowed under §469. If the corporation then disposes of the rental real estate in a taxable transaction that produces a $15,000 gain, the suspended losses first apply against that gain. The remaining $5,000 of suspended loss can then reduce any other passive income. Finally, any unused suspended losses then reduce any other income or gain. §469(g). Suspended passive losses are not triggered when the passive activity interest is transferred to a related party. §469(g)(1)(B). On an installment sale, suspended losses can be recognized in proportion to the ratio of recognized gain on the sale for the taxable year to the overall gain from the sale of the property. §469(g)(3).

In general, suspended losses are not triggered by a nontaxable transfer such as a like-kind exchange (except to the extent of any gain recognized on the transaction) but instead may be triggered on disposition of the property received in the exchange. If an activity ceases to be passive (for example, the corporation no longer rents the property but uses it as part of its active service trade or business), any suspended losses can offset (i) net income from the formerly passive but now nonpassive activity or (ii) income from other passive activities. §469(f).

6. *Taxable Year and Accounting Methods*

In general, a corporation can choose any taxable year. §441(b). This flexibility has been exploited by taxpayers seeking to defer recognition of income for tax purposes. For example, prior to the enactment of §441(i), a personal service corporation was free to adopt any taxable year on its federal income tax return that conformed with its annual accounting period. A popular strategy was to adopt a January 31 business year. A doctor earning $200,000 a year might take a $10,000 monthly salary from the personal service corporation and take the remaining $80,000 as a January bonus. As a calendar year taxpayer, the doctor could defer the taxes on the bonus to the following year.

Under §441(i) a personal service corporation must adopt a calendar year unless the taxpayer receives approval from the Treasury Secretary for use of a different taxable year. An exception allows the use of a fiscal year if the deferral period is not more than three months (i.e., fiscal years ending in September through November). §444. See also §280H requiring certain minimum distributions. For purposes of these provisions, a personal service corporation is a corporation whose principal activity is the performance of services if those services are substantially performed by owner-employees who together own more than 10 percent (by value) of the corporation's stock. §269A(b)(1) and (b)(2); §441(i)(2).

Most corporations are prohibited from using the cash method of accounting. §448. In general, the accrual method of reporting more accurately reflects the economic results of a taxpayer's trade or business over a taxable year. Congress has, however, excepted certain entities from the prohibition against using the cash basis method, including farming businesses, qualified personal service corporations, and entities with average annual gross receipts of $5 million or less for a three-year testing period. §448(b).

A qualified personal service corporation is one that meets a function test and an ownership test. The function test is met if substantially all of the activities of the corporation are the performance of services in the fields of health, law, engineering, architecture, accounting, actuarial science, performing arts, or consulting. §448(d)(2)(A). Can you think of any policy reason to limit the cash basis method to these enterprises? The ownership test is met if substantially all the value of the outstanding stock of the corporation is owned by employees (present or retired). §448(d)(2)(B).

In some situations a corporation's method of accounting is modified to conform with the accounting method of shareholders. For example, §267(a)(1) prevents the deduction of losses on the sale or exchange of property between a corporation and a shareholder owning 50 percent (or more) in value of the corporation's stock. Section 267(a)(2) requires an accrual basis corporation to deduct compensation, interest, or another deductible payment when it is made rather than when it accrues in the following two circumstances: (i) when the payment is made to a cash basis, 50-percent shareholder or (ii) when it is made by a personal service corporation to any cash basis employee-owner. The purpose of this provision is to prevent a mismatching of deduction and income when the liability for payment accrues in one year, but actual payment is deferred to a subsequent year.

7. *Corporate Alternative Minimum Tax*

As you have already discovered, the Code is littered with provisions that provide tax incentives to engage in or abstain from various activities. Although Congress intends these provisions as broad-based incentives, it also sometimes tries to prevent any taxpayer from benefiting too much from an induced tax incentive. If 10 taxpayers engage in a particular tax-favored activity, each may be able to take a deduction because the activity is one that Congress has purposefully encouraged, but if one taxpayer engages in the activity tenfold, there may be limitations on the deduction even though in the aggregate the level of activity may be precisely what Congress intended. Rather than limit the deduction directly, in general Congress has opted for a minimum tax mechanism.

The alternative minimum tax (AMT) under §55 operates mechanically as a tax added on to the regular tax under §11. Conceptually, it is more accurate to think of the AMT as a shadow tax so that a corporation pays whichever is greater, the regular tax or the AMT. As compared with the regular tax under §11, the AMT has a broader tax base and a lower tax rate. In general, the tax base is the corporation's regular taxable income increased by the taxpayer's tax preferences and by certain other adjustments. §55(b)(2). The resulting amount is "alternative minimum taxable income" (AMTI), a term that seeks to identify the corporation's economic income before it behaves in a tax-induced manner. The AMTI is then reduced by an exemption amount and is subject to a 20-percent tax. §55(b)(1)(A). The exemption amount for corporations is $40,000, reduced by 25 percent of the amount by which AMTI exceeds $150,000. §55(d). Therefore, for a corporation with AMTI of $310,000 or more, no exemption is available.

The alternative minimum tax does not apply to a corporation with average annual gross receipts of $5 million or less for a three-year period. §55(e)(1). A corporation that meets this test continues to be exempt from the AMT as long as its average annual gross receipts for the previous three-year period do not exceed $7.5 million. *Id.*

The adjustments that must be made to the taxpayer's taxable income to arrive at AMTI are set out in §§56-58. For example, a portion of corporation's depreciation deductions may be treated as a tax preference that must be added to taxable income. §56(a)(1). The reason for the adjustment is Congress's concern that depreciation permitted under §168 as an investment incentive exceeds actual economic depreciation.

A significant preference affecting corporations is the adjustment for "adjusted current earnings" (ACE). §56(g). Congress was concerned that corporations such as General Electric Co. and W.R. Grace that reported substantial earnings to their shareholders for financial purposes (either through public reporting requirements or through voluntary disclosure) were able to report little or no earnings for tax purposes because of available deductions or credits (e.g., the foreign tax credit). Presumably, Congress regarded this phenomenon as a threat to taxpayer morale because appearances suggested that profitable corporations were escaping appropriate taxation.

Although adding back specific preferences to taxable income in arriving at AMTI addresses the problem somewhat, Congress has backstopped the process by requiring a corporation to add to its AMTI an amount equal to 75 percent of the excess of the corporation's ACE over its AMTI (computed without this ACE adjustment). ACE is defined as AMTI with a variety of adjustments intended to reflect a corporation's economic income available for distribution. §56(g)(4). For example, tax-exempt interest that increases a corporation's wealth is not included in the AMTI calculation but is added back for purposes of calculating the ACE. For a better understanding of the ACE adjustments, see the discussion of earnings and profits at page 113 infra.

In determining AMTI, taxable income is also adjusted by using the percentage of completion method of accounting, rather than the completed contract method, and using ratable, not accelerated, depletion in connection with mineral exploration. §56(a).

In attempting to reconstruct an economic tax base for purposes of determining minimum tax liability, an adjustment must be made to net operating losses. §56(a)(4). For AMT purposes, net operating losses tend to be overstated because they may reflect the tax preferences that the AMT is trying to address. Consequently, the AMT net operating loss is determined by adding to taxable income any tax preferences or adjustments. For example, if in year 1 a taxpayer has $20,000 of income and $35,000 of deductions, of which $10,000 is a preference item (such as accelerated depreciation), the AMT net operating loss for the year will be $5,000. §56(d). Thus, in any subsequent (or prior) year to which the loss may be carried, a $5,000 net operating loss deduction is allowed to reduce income subject to the AMT. Assume that in year 2 the taxpayer has $20,000 of AMTI before accounting for the AMT net operating loss. The taxpayer reduces AMTI to $15,000 by the AMT net operating loss deduction. §56(a)(4). The net operating loss deduction for the regular tax is not affected by this computation (that is, the taxpayer has a $15,000 loss carryover from year 1 for use against the regular tax). Moreover, the alternative tax net operating loss deduction cannot exceed 90 percent of AMTI. §56(d)(1)(A). Suppose that for the year in question a taxpayer has $10 million of AMTI and an AMT net operating loss of $11 million. The net operating loss reduces AMTI to $1 million, giving rise to $200,000 of AMT liability. The taxpayer may then carry forward $2 million of AMT net operating loss.

Once AMTI is determined, the tentative minimum tax equals 20 percent of the excess of AMTI over the exemption. §55(b)(1)(A). A taxpayer can in some cases then offset the tax with a specially computed foreign tax credit. §55(b)(1)(B). The credit is recomputed to account for any preferences that decreased U.S. source income and thereby increased the foreign tax credit. §59(a). Although conceptually the AMT applies if it is higher than the regular tax, under §55(a) the excess of the alternative minimum tax over the regular tax under §11 is added to the regular tax to determine total tax liability.

Section 53 allows a credit for a prior year's AMT liability. The credit is applied against a taxpayer's regular tax, not the AMT. The credit reflects that some of the tax preferences added to taxable income in determining AMTI involve the deferral of income (such as accelerated depreciation) rather than a permanent avoidance (such as percentage depletion). For example, taxpayers paying the AMT as a result of taking accelerated depreciation deductions potentially face a double penalty. First, the AMT must be paid. Then in a later year, the taxpayer loses a part of the deduction that would have been available if no accelerated depreciation had been taken (instead, that part was taken in the earlier year, giving rise to the AMT liability). The result is a higher regular tax in the later year.

The AMT credit is intended to allow the taxpayer in the later year to offset the "excess" regular tax liability with a prior year's AMT liability. The AMT credit can be carried forward indefinitely. The credit is allowed only with respect to liability arising as a result of deferral preferences (that is, preferences other than those that result in permanent exclusion of certain income for regular tax purposes). Accordingly, the amount of the AMT liability that can be credited is reduced by the AMT liability that would have arisen if the only applicable preferences were exclusion preferences.

PROBLEMS

3-1. How might a profitable U.S. corporation pay no U.S. taxes?

3-2. Suppose *X* Corp., a construction company engaged in a major project, in year 1 has no regular tax liability under its regular completed contract method of accounting. It does have $100,000 of AMT liability, principally because of §56(a)(3), which mandates the use of percentage of completion method of accounting for AMT purposes. In year 2, when the project is completed, *X* Corp.'s regular tax liability is $400,000 (there is no AMT liability in year 2). Why might *X* Corp. complain about this result? Does the Code offer any relief?

B. CAPITAL STRUCTURE

A corporation can raise capital either by issuing stock (equity) or by issuing a debt instrument in exchange for cash or property. In either case, an investor holds a financial instrument with a claim on corporate assets. The nature of those claims can be very different. A prototypical debt instrument provides that the borrower (i.e., the corporation) will repay the debt after a fixed term. Moreover, while the loan is outstanding, the borrower promises to pay the investor a fixed rate of interest regardless of the corporation's performance. Whether the corporation performs well or poorly, the return to the lender is fixed and, in the prototypical case, subject to little risk.

In contrast, the prototypical common stock instrument is riskier because it offers the holder no guarantees. Unlike the prototypical loan, there is no fixed date of repayment. Although interest is paid with respect to a debt instrument, stock ownership does not guarantee the receipt of dividends. Under state corporate law, creditors must be paid before any dividend distributions are made to shareholders. In many cases, the payment of dividends depends on the corporation's performance. The value of an investor's stock also depends on the performance of the corporation. If the corporation does well and is expected to do well in the future, typically the fair market value of the outstanding common stock increases. Conversely, if the corporation does poorly, the fair market value of the stock usually declines. At the extremes, prototypical debt has little risk and a limited upside potential; stock has more risk and an unlimited upside potential. Between these extremes is a bewildering assortment of financial instruments bearing various risk levels and expected profit levels.

In deciding whether to issue debt or equity, a corporation must consider both non-tax and tax factors. Many financial theorists believe that, taxes aside, the value of a corporation is independent of financial structure. See Modigliani and Miller, The Cost of Capital, Corporation Finance, and the Theory of Investment, Am. Econ. Rev. 261-267 (June 1958). Nevertheless, a corporation with a high ratio of outstanding debt to equity may find it difficult to obtain additional bank financing and attract future investors. Conversely, a corporation with little or no debt may be viewed as underperforming and may be a takeover candidate.

The following excerpt considers the effect of federal taxes on a corporation's financial structure.

Joint Committee on Taxation, Federal Income Tax Aspects of Corporate Financial Structures*

101st Cong., 1st Sess. (Jan. 18, 1989)

IV. Policy Issues

A. Tax Advantage of Debt Versus Equity

The total effect of the tax system on the incentives for corporations to use debt or equity depends on the interaction between the tax treatment at the shareholder and corporate levels.

The case of no income taxes.—In a simple world without taxes or additional costs in times of financial distress, economic theory suggests that the value of a corporation, as measured by the total value of the outstanding debt and equity, would be unchanged by the degree of leverage of the firm. This conclusion explicitly recognizes that debt issued by the corporation represents an ownership right to future income of the corporation in a fashion similar to that of equity. In this simple world there would be no advantage to debt or to equity and the debt-equity ratio of the firm would not affect the cost of financing investment.

Effect of Corporate Income Tax

Tax Advantages

Taxes greatly complicate this analysis. Since the interest expense on debt is deductible for computing the corporate income tax while the return to equity is not, the tax at the corporate level provides a strong incentive for debt rather than equity finance.

The advantages of debt financing can be illustrated by comparing two corporations with $1,000 of assets that are identical except for financial structure: the first is entirely equity financed; while the second is 50-percent debt financed. Both corporations earn $150 of operating income. The all-equity corporation pays $51 in corporate tax and retains or distributes $99 of after-tax income ($150 less $51). Thus, as shown in Table IV-A, the return on equity is 9.9 percent ($99 divided by $1,000).

The leveraged corporation is financed by $500 of debt and $500 of stock. If the interest rate is 10 percent, then interest expense is $50 (10 percent times $500). Taxable income is $100 after deducting interest expense. The leveraged corporation is liable for $34 in corporate tax (34 percent times $100) and distributes or retains $66 of after-tax income ($100 less $34). Consequently, the return on equity is 13.2 percent ($66 divided by $500). Thus, as shown in Table IV-A, increasing the debt ratio from zero to 50 percent increases the rate of return on equity from 9.9 to 13.2 percent.

* Footnotes omitted—Eds.

This arithmetic demonstrates that a leveraged corporation can generate a higher return on equity (net of corporate income tax) than an unleveraged company or, equivalently, that an unleveraged company needs to earn a higher profit before corporate tax to provide investors the same return net of corporate tax as could be obtained with [a leveraged] company. More generally, the return on equity rises with increasing debt capitalization so long as the interest rate is less than the pretax rate of return on corporate assets. This suggests that the Code creates an incentive to raise the debt-equity ratio to the point where the corporate income tax (or outstanding equity) is eliminated.

Table IV-A
Effect of Debt Financing on Returns to Equity Investment

Item	*All-equity corporation*	*50-percent debt-financed corporation*
Beginning Balance Sheet:		
Total assets	$1,000	$1,000
Debt	0	500
Shareholders' equity	1,000	500
Income Statement:		
Operating income	150	150
Interest expense	0	50
Taxable income	150	100
Income tax	51	34
Income after corporate tax	99	66
Return on Equity[1] (percent)	9.9	13.2

1. Return on equity is computed as income after corporate tax divided by beginning shareholders' equity.

Costs of Financial Distress

With higher levels of debt the possibility of financial distress increases, as do expected costs to the firm which occur with such distress. These additional costs include such items as the increase in the costs of debt funds; constraints on credit; expenditure or operating decisions; and the direct costs of being in bankruptcy. These expected costs of financial distress may, at sufficiently high debt-equity ratios, offset the corporate tax advantage to additional debt finance.

Effect of Shareholder Income Tax

The above analysis focuses solely on the effect of interest deductibility at the corporate level. Shareholder-level income taxation may offset to some degree the corporate tax incentive for corporate debt relative to equity.

Shareholder Treatment of Debt and Equity

The conclusion that debt is tax favored relative to equity remains unchanged if interest on corporate debt and returns on equity are taxed at the same effective rate to investors. In this case, the returns to investors on both debt and equity are reduced proportionately by the income tax; the advantage to debt presented by corporate tax deductibility remains. One noteworthy exception exists if the marginal investments on both debt and equity are effectively tax-exempt. Given the previously documented importance of tax-exempt pension funds in the bond and equity markets, this case may be of some importance.

Shareholder-Level Tax Treatment of Equity

In general, returns to shareholders and debtholders are not taxed the same. Although dividends, like interest income, are taxed currently, equity income in other forms may reduce the effective investor-level tax on equity below that on debt. First, the firm may retain earnings and not pay dividends currently. In general, the accumulation of earnings by the firm will cause the value of the firm's shares to rise. Rather than being taxed currently on corporate earnings, a shareholder will be able to defer the taxation on the value of the retained earnings reflected in the price of the stock until the shareholder sells the stock. [A stock sale has the advantage of not only deferring tax but also minimizing gain through a basis offset—EDS.]

Other aspects of capital gain taxation serve to reduce further the individual income tax on equity. Since tax on capital gain is normally triggered after a voluntary recognition event (e.g., the sale of stock), the taxpayer can time the realization of capital gain income when the effective rate of tax is low. The rate of tax could be low if the taxpayer is in a low or zero tax bracket because other income is abnormally low, if other capital losses shelter the capital gain, or if changes in the tax law cause the statutory rate on capital gains to be low. Perhaps most important, the step up in the adjusted tax basis of the stock upon the death of the shareholder may permit the shareholder's heirs to avoid tax completely on capital gains. For all these reasons, the effective rate of tax on undistributed earnings may be already quite low.

Corporations can distribute their earnings to owners of equity in forms that generally result in less tax to shareholders than do dividend distributions. Share repurchases have become an important method of distributing corporate earnings to equity holders. When employed by large publicly traded firms, repurchases of the corporation's own shares permit the shareholders to treat the distribution as a sale of stock (i.e., to obtain capital gain treatment, and recover the basis in the stock without tax). The remaining shareholders may benefit because they have rights to a larger fraction of the firm and may see a corresponding increase in the value of their shares. Thus, less individual tax will generally be imposed on a $100 repurchase of stock than on $100 of dividends. [Note that an individual currently may be taxed at the same rate (20 percent) on long-term capital gain from a stock sale and qualified dividend income. At the time of this report, the rate on dividend income could substantially exceed the long-term capital gain rate—EDS.] In addition, share repurchases allow shareholders to choose whether to receive corporate distributions by choosing whether to sell or retain shares, so as to minimize tax liability.

Acquisitions of the stock of one corporation for cash or property of another corporation provides a similar method for distributing corporate earnings out of corporate solution with less shareholder tax than through a dividend. The target shareholders generally treat the acquisition as a sale and recover their basis free of tax. For purposes of analyzing the individual tax effect of corporate earnings disbursements, this transaction can be thought of as equivalent to a stock merger of the target with the acquiror followed by the repurchase of the target shareholders' shares by the resulting merged firm. The result is similar to the case of a share repurchase in that cash is distributed to shareholders with less than the full dividend tax, except that two firms are involved instead of one.

Since dividends typically are subject to more tax than other methods for providing returns to shareholders, the puzzle of why firms pay dividends remains. Because dividends are paid at the discretion of the firm, it appears that firms cause their shareholders to pay more tax on equity income than is strictly necessary. Until a better understanding of corporate distribution policy exists, the role of dividend taxation on equity financing decisions remain uncertain.

To summarize, although the current taxation of dividends to investors is clearly significant, there are numerous reasons why the overall individual tax on equity investments may be less than that on interest income from debt. Since the effective shareholder tax on returns from equity may be less than that on debt holdings, the shareholder tax may offset some or all of the advantage to debt at the corporate level. . . .

This excerpt points out that at the corporate level, the payment of interest generates a deduction while the payment of dividends does not. At the shareholder level, although both interest and dividends received are taxable to the recipients, today dividends may be taxed at more favorable rates. See §1(h)(11). Further, shareholders holding equity can lessen, or in some cases eliminate, shareholder-level tax. The mere appreciation of a shareholder's stock is not a taxable event. By allowing accumulation at the corporate level, shareholders can defer any shareholder-level taxation. When shareholders eventually sell or exchange their stock, any gain is taxed at a capital gains rate, entitled to any capital gains preference that might exist. Moreover, upon the death of a shareholder, any appreciated stock takes a fair market value basis, permitting disposition without any recognition of gain.

Notwithstanding the advantages of equity at the shareholder level, the deductibility of interest payments at the corporate level may create a corporate bias in favor of debt over equity. But whether a financial instrument is treated as debt or equity is an issue that haunts our federal income tax system. Much may ride on the distinction, and yet the distinction is often difficult to make. After all, debt and equity are each paper representations of an interest in corporate assets. Although a debt instrument signifies a contractual relationship for repayment while stock provides residual rights for shareholders once creditors have been paid, the price of each kind of instrument reflects the associated risks. Is there a justification for treating debt differently from equity for tax purposes?

Whatever the theoretical answer to the previous question, the practical answer is that the two types of financial instruments are treated very differently. The characterization often determines (1) the gain to a transferor and the basis to the corporate transferee during the formation of a corporation (see Bradshaw v. United States, page 61 supra); (2) the treatment of the borrower (or issuer) as periodic payments are made to the instrument holder; and (3) the treatment of the instrument holder on surrender of the obligation.

The most significant difference in the treatment of debt and equity involves the second category above. The return on borrowed money (debt) typically is deductible as interest. §163. The return on stock (equity) constitutes a nondeductible dividend payment. To an instrument holder, both interest and dividends are includible as ordinary income, although an individual may be taxed on dividend income at the same rate as long-term capital gain. See §1(h)(11). For corporate instrument holders, §243 provides a deduction to the recipient of from 70 to 100 percent, depending on the degree of ownership. See discussion at page 118 infra.

Because interest is deductible by the corporation while dividends are not, there is a tax incentive for a corporation to raise needed capital through the issuance of debt rather than stock. Moreover, certain personal tax advantages will accrue to the organizers or principal owners of the corporation if they become creditors as well as stockholders. If the corporation prospers, it may pay off its debt, and the creditor-stockholders will realize income only to the extent that the payment exceeds the adjusted basis of the debt instruments paid off. The income, if any, will be capital gain. See §1271; §1222. If the organizers hold only stock, however, amounts distributed to them by the corporation as shareholders (including amounts paid for a pro rata reacquisition of stock) may be taxed as dividends with no basis offset. See the discussion of §302 in Chapter 5. For the use of debt in connection with corporate acquisitions, see page 331 infra.

In light of the advantages that debt can offer to corporate issuers, not surprisingly taxpayers often like to label financial instruments as debt. Notwithstanding the label, the Service will attempt to recharacterize an instrument if it resembles equity more than debt. The following case illustrates a typical situation.

Bauer v. Commissioner

748 F.2d 1365 (9th Cir. 1984)

Before Chambers, Hug, and Boochever, Circuit Judges.

Hug, Circuit Judge.

This case concerns a determination of whether cash payments by two stockholders to their wholly-owned corporation were loans or contributions to capital. The Commissioner of Internal Revenue contended that the payments by the stockholders were contributions to capital and not loans, as the stockholders and the corporation maintained. The documentation between the parties and the books of the corporation reflected the cash payments as loans and the periodic payments by the corporation as principal and interest payments to the stockholders. The corporation deducted the interest payments and the stockholders declared the interest payments as income and treated the principal payments as a return of capital. The Commissioner contended that because the stockholders' cash advances to the corporation were contributions to capital and not loans, the corporation could not deduct the claimed interest and the stockholders were required to treat the payments made to them as taxable dividends. The Commissioner assessed deficiencies accordingly. The stockholders and the corporation contested the assessments in the Tax Court and the cases were consolidated for trial. The Tax Court held for the Commissioner in each instance. On appeal, the sole issue is whether the Tax Court was clearly erroneous in holding that the stockholders' cash advances to the corporation were capital contributions rather than loans. We reverse.

Facts

The parties entered into a stipulation of facts, which we summarize here.

Philip Bauer and his father-in-law, Phillip Himmelfarb, are officers and sole stockholders of the Federal Meat Company ("Federal"). They formed Federal in 1958 with paid-in capital of $20,000. The initial and only stock issuance was 2,000 shares, of which Bauer owns 25 percent and Himmelfarb 75 percent. Federal is a custom slaughterer in the business of selling dressed meat to chain store buyers, retailers, and wholesalers. It buys live animals and has them custom slaughtered for fixed fees. Federal does not own a packing house, and it leases its premises and delivery equipment.

Since Federal's incorporation, and continuing throughout the years at issue, Bauer and Himmelfarb advanced various amounts of money to Federal. By the end of the calendar year 1958, a total of $102,650 had been advanced by Bauer and Himmelfarb. Numerous advances and repayments then occurred so that as of December 31, 1972, the net balance advanced by Bauer and Himmelfarb totaled $810,068. . . .

The parties treated all of the transactions as loans and repayments. Each advance to Federal was evidenced by a negotiable promissory note that was unsecured and was payable on demand. The notes carried a seven percent interest rate during 1972-1974 and a ten percent interest rate in 1976. The notes were not convertible into stock, nor were they subordinated to any other obligation. For each advance made to Federal, an amount representing "accrued interest payable" was entered in the corporate ledger at the end of each month as an addition to liabilities in the form of "outstanding loans payable-officers." Each year's total of accrued interest was paid within two and one-half months of the close of Federal's fiscal year. On its financial statements, Federal included the outstanding balances as a current liability labeled "loan payable-officers."

On its corporate federal income tax returns for the years at issue, Federal claimed interest expense deductions in the amounts of $79,638, $103,506, and $103,007, for its fiscal years ending April 30 of 1974, 1975, and 1976, respectively, for the amounts paid as interest to Bauer and Himmelfarb. These amounts, in turn, were reported by Bauer and Himmelfarb as interest income in the calendar year in which they were received. The amounts received from Federal characterized as loan principal repayments were not reported as income. These amounts for Bauer were: $65,000 in 1973, $25,000 in 1974, and $35,000 in 1975; for Himmelfarb, the amount was $75,000 in 1975. Bauer and Himmelfarb each received a yearly salary of $70,000 or $80,000. Federal has never paid dividends; the earnings of the corporation from its inception in 1958 were retained and reinvested to meet the continued growth of the corporation. By the end of the fiscal years in issue, the retained earnings were: 1974, $634,107; 1975, $657,973; and 1976, $486,092. (In the 1976 fiscal year, Federal suffered a net loss.)

The Tax Court concluded that the advances by Bauer and Himmelfarb to Federal were capital contributions and disallowed the interest deductions claimed by Federal on the ground that no debtor-creditor relationship was established to support treatment of the payments as interest. In addition, the principal payments made by Federal to Bauer and Himmelfarb were held to be taxable dividends. . . .

Analysis

The determination of whether an advance is debt or equity depends on the distinction between a creditor who seeks a definite obligation that is payable in any event, and a shareholder who seeks to make an investment and to share in the profits and risks of loss in the venture. . . . The outward form of the transaction is not controlling; rather, characterization depends on the taxpayer's actual intent, as evidenced by the circumstances and conditions of the advance. . . .

In 1969, Congress authorized the Secretary of the Treasury to prescribe regulations setting forth the factors to be considered in determining whether an advance is debt or equity. 26 U.S.C. §385. The Secretary did not issue such regulations until 1982. . . .* Here we must still be guided by the case law and by the five factors that Congress suggested, as part of the 1969 statute, might be included in the regulations. This court has identified eleven factors:

> (1) the names given to the certificates evidencing the indebtedness; (2) the presence or absence of a maturity date; (3) the source of the payments; (4) the right to enforce the payment of principal and interest; (5) participation in management; (6) a status equal to or inferior to that of regular corporate creditors; (7) the intent of the parties; (8) "thin" or adequate capitalization; (9) identity of interest between creditor and stockholder; (10) payment of interest only out of "dividend" money; and (11) the ability of the corporation to obtain loans from outside lending institutions.

A. R. Lantz Co., 424 F.2d at 1333. No one factor is controlling or decisive, and the court must look to the particular circumstances of each case. *Id.* "The object of the inquiry is not to count factors, but to evaluate them." Tyler v. Tomlinson, 414 F.2d 844, 848 (5th Cir. 1969). The burden of establishing that the advances were loans rather than capital contributions rests with the taxpayer. O. H. Kruse Grain & Milling v. Commissioner, 279 F.2d 123, 125 (9th Cir. 1960).

A. Ratio of Debt to Equity

In the present case, the Tax Court gave great weight to the eighth factor: whether Federal was adequately capitalized. The court found that Federal's debt-to-equity ratio was as high as 92 to 1 during the years in question and that Federal was seriously undercapitalized. The Tax Court found this to be a strong indication that the advances were capital contributions rather than loans. The Tax Court apparently based its finding of a debt-to-equity ratio of 92 to 1 on a paragraph of the Stipulation of Facts signed by the parties. That paragraph states:

> The ratio of stockholder debt to corporate stock was approximately 92 to 1 for the fiscal year ending April 30, 1976.

This is accurate insofar as it compares the ending debt owed to the stockholders in 1976 of $1,850,067 to their initial stock purchase in 1958 of $20,000. This is not a true or meaningful debt-to-equity ratio. First, it completely ignores the earnings that had been retained in the corporation as it grew over the 18-year period. The

* The regulations under §385 were withdrawn in 1984. See page 99 infra. In addition, they were not applicable to the years in controversy. — Eds.

stockholders' equity in a corporation is composed not only of the paid-in-capital, but also of the profits that have been generated and retained in the corporation as "retained earnings." Thus, if the debt-to-equity ratio were considered to be a comparison of stockholder loans to the correct calculation of stockholder equity including retained earnings in the corporation, this "debt-to-equity" ratio would be only 1.5 to 1 in 1974-1975 and 3.6 to 1 in 1976, as hereinafter shown.

The more meaningful debt-to-equity ratio compares the total liabilities to the stockholders' equity. The stockholders' equity would include both the initial paid-in capital and the retained earnings. Basically, the stockholders' equity is the difference between the assets and liabilities of the corporation.

Congress recognized this as the appropriate method of calculating the debt-to-equity ratio in enacting section 385.

> The debt-equity ratio of the issuing corporation for purposes of this test generally is determined by comparing the corporation's total indebtedness with the excess of its money and other assets over that indebtedness.

S. Rep. No. 552, 91st Cong., 1st Sess., *reprinted in* 1969 U.S. Code Cong. & Ad. News 1645, 2027, 2172. The calculation of Federal's debt-to-equity ratio for the years in question would therefore be as follows. In our view, the total debt-to-equity ratio is the appropriate ratio to review in determining whether a corporation is too thinly capitalized; however, we also show the stockholder debt-to-equity ratio for illustrative purposes. . . .

Total Debt-to-Equity Ratio
1974: \$1,410,603 divided by \$654,107 = 2.15 to 1
1975: \$1,952,944 divided by \$677,973 = 2.88 to 1
1976: \$3,880,642 divided by \$506,092 = 7.66 to 1

Stockholder Debt-to-Equity Ratio
1974: \$1,025,067 divided by \$654,107 = 1.56 to 1
1975: \$1,030,067 divided by \$657,973 = 1.56 to 1
1976: \$1,850,067 divided by \$506,092 = 3.65 to 1

Thus, during the years in question, the total debt-to-equity ratio, as reflected on the books of the corporation, was not 92 to 1, but ranged from a little over 2 to 1 to less than 8 to 1. The stockholder debt-to-equity ratio during those years was a minimum of 1.5 to 1 and a maximum of 3.6 to 1.

The purpose of examining the debt-to-equity ratio in characterizing a stockholder advance is to determine whether a corporation is so thinly capitalized that a business loss would result in an inability to repay the advance; such an advance would be indicative of venture capital rather than a loan. Gilbert v. Commissioner, 248 F.2d 399, 407 (2d Cir. 1957). Essentially, we are concerned with the degree of risk the loan presents to the lender and whether an independent lender, such as a bank, would be willing to make the loan. In addition to the numerical debt-to-equity ratio, other factors in the financial picture would also be important to an independent lender in analyzing the risk. Federal's history was that of a successful company whose increasing cash needs arose from growth, not a lack of profits or business reverses. Federal had virtually no fixed assets; its plant and equipment were leased. The assets were principally current assets which could be quickly turned into cash. At all times during the years in question, Federal's current assets exceeded all liabilities by at least $300,000, which presents a strong financial picture.

Federal's financial structure and these other factors indicate that Federal could readily have obtained a loan from a bank or other financial institution for the purpose for which the stockholders' loans were made, which was to finance inventory and accounts receivable. There is specific evidence in this case that one bank would have been willing to make these loans. In a letter from a vice president of Bank of America that was attached to the Stipulated Facts, the officer noted that it had dealt with Federal and was familiar with Federal's financing during the years in question and the bank was "ready to make bank loans for those amounts of officers' loans and/or more if Federal Meat Co. desired to use bank financing." The bank officer also noted that "in the event Federal wanted to liquidate during this period, Federal would have paid off its creditors, the bank, the officers' loans from conversion of its meat inventory, and accounts receivable within a three to four week cycle most likely without any need of selling the small amount of fixed assets."

Neither the numerical debt-to-equity ratio nor other factors in the analysis of the corporation's financial structure justify a conclusion that the advances should be characterized as venture capital rather than loans.

B. PROPORTIONAL HOLDINGS OF DEBT AND EQUITY

The Tax Court also gave weight to the alleged fact that Bauer and Himmelfarb had loaned Federal amounts that were roughly proportional to their respective capital investments. The court found that during the years in question Himmelfarb had advanced a total of $970,000 to Federal while Bauer had advanced $270,000, a ratio of about 3 1/2 to 1 as compared to the 3 to 1 ratio of their stockholdings. We agree that where a stockholder owns "debt" in the same proportion to which he holds stock in a certain corporation, the characterization as "debt" may be suspect. See *Gilbert*, 248 F.2d at 407. However, the Tax Court clearly miscalculated the amounts of Bauer's and Himmelfarb's advances to Federal.

The Tax Court looked only at the gross amount of Bauer and Himmelfarb's advances during the years in question. It failed to consider either the amount of the loans outstanding at the beginning of the three-year period or the effect of the repayments that Federal made during this period. At the beginning of the three-year period, Federal already owed $805,068 to Himmelfarb, but only $5,000 to Bauer. At the end of the period, the figures had grown to $1,700,068 and $150,000, a ratio of about 11 to 1. Even if the three-year period is considered in isolation — an approach that makes little sense given that the stockholders had been making loans to Federal since 1958 — the net amounts advanced by Himmelfarb and Bauer during that period were $895,000 and $145,000, respectively, a ratio of about 6 to 1. These figures simply will not support a finding that Bauer and Himmelfarb made advances to Federal in proportion to their capital investments.

C. OTHER FACTORS

The Tax Court also found it significant that all of Federal's shareholder debt was evidenced by demand notes with no fixed date of maturity. Although some repayments were made during the years in question, repayments never kept up with advances. We agree that lack of a fixed date of maturity on the debt instruments, together with continual growth of the debt, may suggest that there is no intention to make full repayment. But that one factor is not enough to carry the entire weight of this case. Many other factors favor the petitioners, as the Tax Court conceded: the existence of notes; fixed and reasonable interest rates; actual timely payment of interest; corresponding treatment of the interest as income by Bauer and Himmelfarb; the cash-flow demands of the custom slaughter business; and the lack of subordination of shareholder debt to other corporate debt. Additionally, this court concludes that Federal's ratio of debt to equity was within reasonable bounds and that Bauer and Himmelfarb did not own debt in proportion to their stockholdings.

Conclusion

The Tax Court erred in the basis of its calculation of Federal's debt-to-equity ratio. In reviewing the actual debt-to-equity ratio and the current assets in relation to the liabilities, and considering the general strength of the corporate financial picture, there is no reason to justify a conclusion that the loans were in fact "venture capital." Also, the record does not support the Tax Court's finding that Bauer and Himmelfarb made advances to Federal in rough proportion to their stockholdings. The documentation and the accounting procedures followed support the taxpayers' contention that the advances were loans. For these reasons and the other reasons above specified, we hold that the Tax Court's recharacterization of Federal's debt as equity is clearly erroneous, and the decision of the Tax Court is therefore reversed.

NOTES

1. *Statutory and regulatory classification of "equity" and "debt."* The House version of the 1954 Code contained definitions designed to indicate precisely what instruments would qualify for the interest deduction and for other tax privileges. But the Senate dropped these definitions, stating "Your committee believes that any attempt to write into the statute precise definitions which will classify for tax purposes the many types of corporate stocks and securities will be frustrated by the numerous characteristics of an interchangeable nature which can be given to these instruments." S. Rep. No. 1622, 83d Cong., 2d Sess. 42 (1954).

Despite this pessimistic conclusion, the Tax Reform Act of 1969 added §385 to the Code authorizing the Treasury to issue regulations to determine whether an interest in a corporation is to be treated "for purposes of this title as stock or indebtedness." The Treasury may take into account, along with other factors, the existence of a written unconditional promise to pay a sum certain and a fixed rate of interest, the subordination or preference over any indebtedness, the debt-equity ratio, the convertibility into stock, and the relationship between holdings of stock and of the interest in question. The Treasury has made three attempts to promulgate suitable regulations. Each attempt has been heavily criticized and ultimately withdrawn.

In some cases, the Service has been "whipsawed" by inconsistent treatment of financial instruments by the issuer and the holders. For example, the issuer might prefer to treat a financial instrument as debt in order to deduct the interest. A corporate holder of the instrument, however, may prefer to treat periodic distributions as dividends because of the dividends-received deduction in §243. See page 118 infra. Further, an individual holder may prefer to treat periodic distributions as dividends if the distributions would be treated as qualified dividend income taxed at preferential rates under §1(h)(11). See page 118 infra. Under §385(c)(1), the characterization by the issuer of an instrument as debt or equity is binding on the holders of the instrument. Section 385(c)(2), however, does permit a holder of an instrument to adopt an inconsistent treatment so long as such treatment is disclosed on the holder's tax return.

For some general guidance on factors that may be used to distinguish debt from equity, see Notice 94-47, 1994-1 C.B. 357.

2. *Judicial classification of "equity" and "debt."* In *Bauer* the court was concerned with the ratio of debt to equity. For those corporations whose outstanding debt far exceeds equity, debtholders would likely regard themselves as stockholders or potential stockholders because of the risk associated with repayment. Their chances of repayment would rise and fall with the success or failure of the corporation. See, e.g., Dobkin v. Commissioner, 15 T.C. 31 (1950), aff'd per curiam, 192 F.2d 392 (2d Cir. 1951); Burr Oaks Corp. v. Commissioner, 365 F.2d 24 (7th Cir. 1966). For well-capitalized corporations, the risk of default on outstanding debt instruments is lower.

There is no mathematical threshold for determining permissible debt-equity ratios. In Briggs Co. v. Commissioner, 1946 T.C.M. ¶46,109, a ratio of 4-to-1 was found excessive in light of surrounding financial considerations, whereas in Baker Commodities v. Commissioner, 48 T.C. 374 (1967), a ratio of 700-to-1 was upheld as justified because cash flow and earning power were sufficient to support repayment. A ratio of inside debt to equity that does not exceed 3-to-1 is likely to withstand attack. See B. Bittker and J. Eustice, Federal Income Taxation of Corporations and Shareholders ¶4.04[3] (7th ed. 2007). The withdrawn §385 regulations did not consider debt to be excessive if the inside debt/equity ratio did not exceed 3-to-1, and the outside ratio (i.e., debt held by all creditors) did not exceed 10-to-1.

In *Bauer*, the outcome hinged on how to measure the value of stock for purposes of determining the debt-equity ratio. Who has the stronger point: the Ninth Circuit, which used the fair market value of the outstanding stock (actually book value plus retained earnings), or the Tax Court, which used just the book value of the stock?

Thin capitalization is only one sign pointing toward recharacterizing debt as equity. For closely held corporations, when debt is owned in the same proportions as equity, the courts tend to scrutinize the situation closely. In *Bauer*, the ratio of stock held by the two shareholders was 3-to-1, while the ratio of new loans to the corporation incurred by the shareholders during the years in question was 3½-to-1. Why did the Ninth Circuit find that the holdings were not roughly proportionate?

Under the withdrawn §385 regulations, proportionality was deemed a key factor. Straight debt with no equity features held disproportionately would be respected as debt; proportionately held debt would be subject to much stricter scrutiny. Disproportionality was helpful to the taxpayer in Green Bay Steel v. Commissioner, 53 T.C. 451 (1969). Proportionality alone would not necessarily cause recharacterization. See, e.g., Litton Business Systems v. Commissioner, 61 T.C. 367 (1973), in which a parent corporation's advances to subsidiaries were held valid debt despite an absence of formalities. Interest was charged, the parent expected repayment, outside funding was available, and the subsidiary was not thinly capitalized. Compare United States v. Uneco, Inc., 532 F.2d 1204 (8th Cir. 1976).

Other factors considered by some courts when characterizing financial instruments include whether repayment in fact took place, whether formalities were observed when the "loan" was made, and whether the proceeds were used for "essential" assets. See Laidlaw Transportation, Inc. v. Commissioner, 98 T.C.M. 232 (1998) (equity found where related creditor corporation did not intend to request repayment on maturity dates and continually postponed maturity dates, and the debtor corporation used the borrowed funds to purchase essential assets). In *Bauer*, the Tax Court found that the loans were made during the formative stages of the corporation for essential operating assets and were therefore equity contributions. Should the timing of the loans be a factor?

3. *Hybrid securities: bifurcation.* When a corporation is unable to issue ordinary evidences of indebtedness, usually because of a fear of damaging its credit position, there have been attempts to get the same tax effect by issuing "hybrid" securities. These instruments often look like preferred stock to creditors, but it is hoped that they will be treated as bonds, debentures, or notes by the Service. Among the characteristics of such "hybrid" securities are the following: (a) They are often held only by shareholders and in the same proportions as the stock; (b) they may be transferable only with stock; (c) they have long maturities or no maturity dates; (d) the "interest" is geared to corporate income or is discretionary with the directors; (e) payment of the "interest" or "principal" (or both) is subordinated to the claims of general creditors; and (f) they are sometimes issued only to present stockholders and not for new consideration. If too many of these features are found, the instruments will be treated as preferred stock rather than as evidences of indebtedness.

The leading case on the subject is John Kelley Co. v. Commissioner, 326 U.S. 521 (1946). In that case, the nominal debt instruments provided for 8-percent interest, which was noncumulative, and payment was contingent on sufficient corporate earnings. The instruments matured in 20 years and were subordinate to all creditors. In determining that the hybrid instruments constituted debt, the Supreme Court reasoned that the corporation had a lot of outstanding stock and was not thinly capitalized.

In Farley Realty Corp. v. Commissioner, 279 F.2d 701 (2d Cir. 1960), a nonshareholder lent money to a corporation for the acquisition of a building. The obligation provided for a fixed payment of interest and a fixed maturity date. Furthermore, the lender was entitled to 50 percent of any appreciation on the sale of the building even if the sale took place after the maturity date. The court permitted a deduction for the fixed interest but not for the lender's share of the realized appreciation. But see Rev. Rul. 83-51, 1983-1 C.B. 48 (allowing a deduction for shared appreciation paid by a borrower to a lender on a home residence loan [i.e., a noncommercial context] with payment due upon sale of the residence or at the end of the 10-year loan term).

In Helvering v. Richmond, F & P.R.R., 90 F.2d 971 (4th Cir. 1937), the court permitted an interest deduction for guaranteed 7-percent dividend payments on preferred stock when the guaranteed dividends were a first lien on corporate assets ahead of all creditors. Payments in excess of the guaranteed amount were treated as nondeductible dividends.

Notwithstanding these cases, in general courts have resisted bifurcation. See generally Hariton, Distinguishing Between Equity and Debt in the New Financial Environment, 49 Tax L. Rev. 499 (1994). Several Code provisions, however, permit or mandate bifurcation. Section 385(a) authorizes regulations permitting the bifurcation of a corporate obligation as part equity and part debt. The legislative history of this provision explains, "[S]uch treatment may be appropriate in circumstances where a debt instrument provides for payments that are dependent to a significant extent (whether in whole or in part) on corporate performance, whether through equity kickers, contingent interest, significant deferral of payment, subordination, or an interest rate sufficiently high to suggest a significant risk of default." H.R. Rep. No. 247, 101st Cong., 1st Sess. 1235-1236 (1989).

Congress has also clamped down on the availability of a corporate interest deduction in connection with certain corporate takeovers by bifurcating certain high-yield discount obligations. See page 336 infra.

Another form of bifurcation is found in §163(j), the "earnings stripping" provision. If an interest expense is deductible but the recipient is not taxable upon receipt, there is a loss to the U.S. tax system as a whole and an incentive to borrow from tax-exempt lenders such as related foreign corporations and certain U.S. pension funds. Congress has addressed the practice of stripping away earnings of a taxable U.S. corporation through an interest payment to a tax-exempt related party by denying an interest deduction under specified circumstances.

Section 163(j) essentially disallows an interest deduction on "excess interest expense" of a payor corporation with a ratio of debt to equity in excess of 1.5-to-1 at the end of the tax year. See also §163(j)(2)(C) (for this purpose taking asset bases, not values, into account). "Excess interest expense" is defined as the amount by which the corporation's net interest expense exceeds 50 percent of its adjusted taxable income. Any interest deduction disallowed under §163(j) may be carried over to a subsequent year, when it may be deductible to the extent that there is no excess interest expense.

Can a financial instrument ever be bifurcated over time? That is, can an instrument that is considered equity when it is issued (e.g., because a corporation is thinly capitalized) be considered a debt instrument at a later time (e.g., when the corporation's debt-equity ratio improves)? For the possibility that an instrument may be a chameleon, see Edwards v. Commissioner, 50 T.C. 220 (1968) (notes that constituted bona fide debt in hands of original owners must be treated as equity in hands of purchasers, who had simultaneously purchased the stock of the obligor corporation when it was in a deficit position), rev'd, 415 F.2d 578 (10th Cir. 1969) (purchasers "took the capital financial structure as they found it," including valid debt); Cuyuna Realty Co. v. United States, 382 F.2d 298 (Cl. Ct. 1967) (debtor-creditor relationship changed with passage of time to equity-investor relationship).

4. *Hybrid securities: convertibility.* A debt instrument that is convertible into corporate stock contains both debt and equity features. A holder of the instrument may enjoy a fixed rate of return with relatively little risk, but the holder also has the right to share in future corporate growth by exercising the conversion privilege. As a general rule, a conversion feature by itself does not automatically result in the treatment of a financial instrument as equity. In Rev. Rul. 85-119, 1985-2 C.B. 60, a publicly traded debt instrument contained a conversion feature that was mandated by banking regulations. At maturity, the note was convertible into stock of the issuing corporation equal to the face value of the note. A holder could also elect to receive cash instead of stock. In determining that the note was a debt instrument (and that interest payments were deductible), the ruling highlighted the following factors: The note was publicly traded and not held in proportion to stock ownership; the issuing corporation was not thinly capitalized; the instrument had a fixed

maturity date; interest payments were not contingent on earnings; and instrument holders did not participate in corporate governance. The convertibility feature was not controlling because the amount of stock to be received was equal to the face value of the note.

In contrast, Rev. Rul. 83-98, 1983-2 C.B. 40, ruled that a nominal debt instrument was really an equity instrument, in part because the instrument contained a conversion feature. Under the conversion feature, a holder could convert the note to 50 shares of the issuer's stock (worth $1,000 at the time the instrument was issued) or receive $600 when the instrument matured. The issuer also had the right to call the instrument for $600 at any time. These conversion characteristics made it highly likely that holders would convert to stock.

Finally, §163(*l*) disallows a deduction for interest on financial instruments popularly called "equity contract notes." More precisely, it disallows a deduction for interest on a disqualified debt instrument, which is a corporate debt instrument payable (i.e., a substantial amount of either interest or principal) in equity of the issuer or a related party.

5. *Preferred stock versus debt.* If common stock and straight debt are the endpoints on the debt-equity spectrum, preferred stock is right in the middle. Typically, preferred stockholders receive fixed payments (like debtholders) and do not share in the growth of the issuing corporations (like debtholders). But preferred shareholders do not receive dividends until creditors have been paid (like common shareholders) and stand in line behind creditors in the event of liquidation (like common shareholders).

In Rev. Rul. 90-27, 1990-1 C.B. 50, the issue was whether a financial instrument was preferred stock or really a debt instrument (although labeled preferred stock). Typically, an issuer wants the instrument to be characterized as debt because of the interest deduction. But in contrast to *Bauer*, here the taxpayer (i.e., the shareholder, Corporation *Y*) wanted the financial instrument to be treated as preferred stock and the distributions to be treated as dividends. A corporation that receives dividends must include them in income but then can deduct a percentage of the dividends received. See §243, discussed at page 118 infra. In contrast, interest received on debt instruments is fully includible.

The ruling pointed out that the financial instruments were very much like short-term debt to the holders. The principal amount of the obligation in question was always $100,000, and the rate of return was adjusted every 49 days in accordance with the market to keep the fair market value of the instrument at $100,000. Nevertheless, the ruling noted that the equity features of the instruments outweighed the debt features. The holders were not entitled to receive a sum certain either on demand or on a specified date, and distributions could be made only in accordance with state law dividend requirements. Thus, the ruling concluded that the financial instruments were properly treated as equity.

6. *Retirement, redemption, and worthlessness.* The decision to issue debt or equity affects not only the characterization of the payments made on the obligation — whether such payments constitute interest or dividends — but also the treatment of the obligation itself on retirement or redemption. Generally, any gain (or loss) on the retirement of a debt instrument because of post-purchase fluctuation in the market interest rate will produce capital gain or loss. See §1271, but see §1276, which treats gain from pre-purchase fluctuation in the market interest rate as ordinary income. Gain (or loss) on the redemption of stock by a corporation may result in

ordinary or capital gain (or loss), depending on the successful navigation of the safe harbors of §302, which offer exchange treatment. See Chapter 5.

If retirement or redemption is unavailable because a corporation fails, then worthless stock, bonds, and other evidence of debt that are "securities" under §165(g)(2) ordinarily give rise to long- or short-term capital loss under §165(g)(1). Debt instruments that are not "securities" under §165(g)(2) are non-business bad debts and produce short-term capital losses under §166(d). See, e.g., Litwin v. United States, 983 F.2d 997 (10th Cir. 1993) (bad debt deduction allowed for advances by taxpayer with respect to his closely held business when taxpayer convinced the court that the corporation was formed to allow him to earn a salary).

In light of the attendant restrictions on capital losses imposed by §§1211 and 1212, Congress enacted §1244 in 1958, under which an individual's loss on "§1244 stock" can be deducted from ordinary income with certain limitations. The principal features of §1244 include the following: (1) Section 1244 stock must be issued by a corporation whose capital does not exceed $1 million; (2) only common stock qualifies; (3) the corporation must have been active for a period of time prior to the stock's worthlessness; (4) the stock must be issued to an individual for money or other property; (5) the aggregate amount that can be treated as an ordinary loss for any taxable year may not exceed $50,000 (or $100,000 for a taxpayer filing a joint return). See also §165(g)(3), which affords corporations ordinary losses for worthless securities in certain subsidiaries but does not apply if the corporation sells the securities.

PROBLEMS

3-3. *X* Corp., with only one class of stock outstanding, issues adjustable rate convertible notes with the following characteristics. The instruments are offered in exchange for either $1,000 or 50 shares of *X* Corp. stock (trading at $20 per share). The investor will receive annual payments equal to the dividends payable on 50 shares of *X* Corp. stock plus 2 percent of the $1,000 issue price ($20). The annual payment is guaranteed to be at least $60 and no more than $175 in all years. Stated differently, the investor is guaranteed a return of between 6 percent and 17.5 percent of face value. The notes are convertible at any time by the investor into 50 shares of *X* Corp. stock. If the investor chooses not to convert, the instrument will be redeemed for $600 at the end of 20 years. *X* Corp. retains an option to call the note for $600 at any time more than two years after issuance, although the investor can elect to convert if *X* Corp. exercises its option. *X* Corp. consults you about the tax treatment of the annual payments made on the instruments. See Rev. Rul. 83-98, 1983-2 C.B. 40.

3-4. *X* Corp., a U.S. corporation, borrows $10 million from *Y* Corp., its Dutch parent. Pursuant to an income tax treaty between the Netherlands and the United States, *Y* Corp. is not subject to U.S. taxation on its interest income. The loan has a 10-year term and bears a 10-percent rate, the market rate when the loan was made. Discuss the tax treatment of the interest payments made from *X* Corp. to *Y* Corp.

4

Distributions of Cash and Property

In Chapter 2 we looked at the formation of a corporation. Once in existence, a corporation reports income and takes deductions in much the same way individuals do. See pages 81-84 supra. At some point, however, the shareholders may want the corporation to distribute some or all of its earnings or even part of their capital contributions.

Section 61(a)(7) includes "dividends" in a taxpayer's gross income. But what are dividends? Certainly not every distribution by a corporation is a taxable dividend. Suppose *T* forms *X* Corp. with $100. At the end of its first year, *X* Corp. has lost $10 and holds $90 in assets. *T*, in need of cash, causes *X* Corp. to distribute $20. Is the distribution a dividend, subjecting *T* to tax? If not, what is it?

The labyrinth of statutory provisions governing this subject begins with §301(a), referring to distributions of "property," as defined by §317(a). This provision defines property primary by negation, excluding the corporation's own stock and stock rights, although it specifies that property includes cash, securities, and (unhelpfully) other property. Cf. Rev. Rul. 90-11, 1990-1 C.B. 10 (concluding that a corporation's adoption of a "poison pill" was not a distribution of "property" where the poison pill provided for the issuance of a separately tradable and valuable right to purchase preferred stock for every share of common stock, but only in the event of a hostile takeover attempt). Distributions of a corporation's stock or stock rights are governed by §305, discussed in Chapter 6. Note that §317 does not define property for purposes of §351.

Returning to §301(a), note as well that there must be a distribution of property by a corporation to a shareholder *with respect to its stock* for §301 to apply. Transfers such as salaries or debt repayment, even if the recipient is a shareholder, are not covered by §301(a) because they are not made "with respect to [the paying corporation's] stock." The amount of a distribution made with respect to a shareholder's stock is computed under §301(b). While the amount of a cash distribution is self-evident, distributions of property pose some questions. Is the amount distributed equal to the fair market value of the property, its basis to the corporation, or some other measure? How do liabilities encumbering the property affect the amount distributed? These issues are addressed at page 122 infra.

Once the "amount" of a distribution is determined, its tax treatment is governed by §301(c), which consists of three tiers: §301(c)(1), (c)(2), and (c)(3). Section 301(c)(1) states that dividends are to be included in gross income, a rule already announced in §61(a)(7). For the definition of "dividend," §301(c)(1) refers us to §316. Section 316(a) informs us that distributions out of current or accumulated "earnings and profits" will be treated as dividends. See §316(a)(1) and (2). Note that neither §316 nor any other Code provision comprehensively defines earnings and profits. Section 312 instructs us to increase or decrease earnings and profits to take account of various transactions but fails to tell us just what we are adjusting. See discussion at page 113 infra.

Returning to §301(c), a distribution, to the extent not treated as a dividend, is applied to reduce the adjusted basis of the taxpayer's stock. §301(c)(2). If the stock basis is reduced to zero, any remaining portion of the distribution is given sale or exchange treatment, resulting in capital gains if the stock is a capital asset. §301(c)(3)(A).

Section 301 and the related sections summarized above govern the tax treatment of the distributee shareholder. Distributions may also cause tax consequences to the distributing corporation. Is the distributing corporation taxable on a distribution of cash? On a distribution of appreciated property? Can it deduct a loss if the distributed property is worth less than its basis? How does a corporation determine its earnings and profits? Section 311 describes at least some aspects of these tax consequences to the distributing corporation. Historically, a distributing corporation was generally not taxed on a distribution of appreciated property. §311(a). The Tax Reform Act of 1986, however, radically altered this rule by providing that a distributing corporation will recognize gain on the distribution of any appreciated property. Moreover, distributions require adjustments to the corporation's earnings and profits account that may affect the tax consequences to the shareholders of *current and future* distributions. §312.

This quick trip through the distributions maze becomes slightly more bewildering when one realizes that we have encountered only some types of distributions, albeit the ones that are most frequently encountered. See §301(f) (for a cross-reference to other types of distributions). Stock distributions are governed by §305. Distributions in redemption or partial liquidation are governed by §302. Liquidations are governed by §§331-337. Distributions in connection with reorganizations are discussed in §§354-368. In Chapter 2 we already considered distributions in connection with the formation of a corporation.

This chapter is divided into four parts, each focusing on a different type of distribution: (1) cash distributions; (2) property distributions other than cash; (3) disguised or constructive dividends; and (4) intercorporate dividends. All of these subjects require an understanding of the concept of "earnings and profits," which is examined at the outset, in the context of a cash distribution.

A. CASH DISTRIBUTIONS

The Revenue Ruling that follows illustrates how the earnings and profits, once calculated, determine the amount of a dividend. The *Divine* case shows the importance of, and the uncertainty involved in, the calculation of earnings and profits.

Rev. Rul. 74-164

1974-1 C.B. 74

Advice has been requested concerning the taxable status of corporate distributions under the circumstances described below.

X corporation and *Y* corporation each using the calendar year for Federal income tax purposes made distributions of $15,000 to their respective shareholders on July 1, 1971, and made no other distributions to their shareholders during the taxable year. The distributions were taxable as provided by section 301(c) of the Internal Revenue Code of 1954.

Situation 1

At the beginning of its taxable year 1971, *X* corporation had earnings and profits accumulated after February 28, 1913, of $40,000. It had an operating loss for the period January 1, 1971 through June 30, 1971, of $50,000 but had earnings and profits for the entire year 1971 of $5,000.

Situation 2

At the beginning of its taxable year 1971, *Y* corporation had a deficit in earnings and profits accumulated after February 28, 1913, of $60,000. Its net profits for the period January 1, 1971 through June 30, 1971, were $75,000 but its earnings and profits for the entire taxable year 1971 were only $5,000.

Situation 3

Assume the same facts as in Situation 1 except that *X* had a deficit in earnings and profits of $5,000 for the entire taxable year 1971.

Situation 4

Assume the same facts as in Situation 1 except that *X* had a deficit in earnings and profits of $55,000 for the entire taxable year 1971.

Sections 301(a) and 301(c) of the Code provide, in part, that: (1) the portion of a distribution of property made by a corporation to a shareholder with respect to its stock which is a dividend (as defined in section 316), shall be included in the shareholder's gross income; (2) the portion of the distribution which is not a dividend shall be applied against and reduce the adjusted basis of the stock; and (3) the portion which is not a dividend to the extent that it exceeds the adjusted basis of the stock and is not out of increase in value accrued before March 1, 1913, shall be treated as gain from the sale or exchange of property.

Section 316(a) of the Code provides that the term "dividend" means any distribution of property made by a corporation to its shareholders out of its earnings and profits accumulated after February 28, 1913, or out of its earnings and profits of the taxable year computed as of the close of the taxable year without diminution by reason of any distribution made during the year, and without regard to the amount of earnings and profits at the time the distribution was made.

Section 1.316-2(a) of the Income Tax Regulations provides, in part, that in determining the source of a distribution, consideration should be given first, to the earnings and profits of the taxable year; and second, to the earnings and profits accumulated since February 28, 1913, only in the case where, and to the extent that, the distributions made during the taxable year are not regarded as out of the earnings and profits of that year.

Applying the foregoing principles, in Situation 1, the earnings and profits of *X* corporation for the taxable year 1971 of $5,000 and the earnings and profits accumulated since February 28, 1913, and prior to the taxable year 1971, of $40,000 were applicable to the distribution paid by it on July 1, 1971. Thus, $5,000 of the distribution of $15,000 was paid from the earnings and profits of the taxable year 1971 and the balance of $10,000 was paid from the earnings and profits accumulated since February 28, 1913. Therefore, the entire distribution of $15,000 was a dividend within the meaning of section 316 of the Code.

In Situation 2 the earnings and profits of *Y* corporation for the taxable year 1971 of $5,000 were applicable to the distribution paid by *Y* corporation on July 1, 1971. *Y* corporation had no earnings and profits accumulated after February 28, 1913, available at the time of the distribution. Thus, only $5,000 of the distribution by *Y* corporation of $15,000 was a dividend within the meaning of section 316 of the Code. The balance of such distribution, $10,000 which was not a dividend, applied against and reduced the adjusted basis of the stock in the hands of the shareholders, and to the extent that it exceeded the adjusted basis of the stock was gain from the sale or exchange of property.

In the case of a deficit in earnings and profits for the taxable year in which distributions are made, the taxable status of distributions is dependent upon the amount of earnings and profits accumulated since February 28, 1913, and available at the dates of distribution. In determining the amount of such earnings and profits, section 1.316-2(b) of the regulations provides, in effect, that the deficit in earnings and profits of the taxable year will be prorated to the dates of distribution.

Applying the foregoing to Situations 3 and 4 the distribution paid by *X* corporation on July 1, 1971, in each situation was a dividend within the meaning of section 316 of the Code to the extent indicated as follows:

Situation #3

Accumulated Earnings and Profits (E&P) [Jan. 1]	$ 40,000	
E&P deficit for entire taxable year ($5,000) Prorate to date of distribution [July 1] (1/2 of $5,000)	(2,500)	
E&P available [July 1]	$ 37,500	
Distribution [July 1] ($15,000)	(15,000)	taxable as a dividend
E&P deficit from [July 1-Dec. 31]	(2,500)	
[Accumulated E&P at end of year]	$ 20,000	

Situation #4

Accumulated E&P [Jan. 1]	$ 40,000	
E&P deficit for entire taxable year ($55,000) Prorate to date of distribution [July 1] (1/2 of $55,000)	(27,500)	
E&P available [July 1]	$ 12,500	
Distribution [July 1] ($15,000)	(12,500)	taxable as a dividend
E&P deficit from [July 1-Dec. 31]	(27,500)	
Accumulated E&P balance [Dec. 31]	$(27,500)	

Divine v. Commissioner

500 F.2d 1041 (2d Cir. 1974)

WATERMAN, Circuit Judge.

I . . .

The outcome of this case depends on our resolution of two legal issues. [Discussion of the first issue, involving collateral estoppel, is omitted.] Second, when, pursuant to the terms of statutory restricted stock options granted by a corporation to its employees, those employees, in exercising the options, purchased the stock for less than the stock's fair market value, should the corporation's "earnings and profits" under 316 of the Internal Revenue Code ("IRC" or "Code") be reduced by the difference between the fair market value of the stock so purchased and the prices paid by the employees? . . .

Rapid American Corporation (hereinafter "Rapid" or the "Corporation") is a publicly owned corporation. Its common stock during the years 1961 and 1962 was listed on the American Stock Exchange. As of January 31, 1963, Rapid had over 2,000 shareholders who held in the aggregate more than 2,000,000 shares of Rapid's common stock. Appellant Divine was one of those shareholders; his approximate holdings amounted to 37,000 shares in 1961 and rose to 40,000 in 1962.

During the years 1961 and 1962, Rapid made certain cash distributions, totaling some $840,840.53 in 1961, and $1,024,836.93 in 1962, to its shareholders. Appellant's portions of these disbursements were $18,501.40 in 1961 and $20,572.04 in 1962. Rapid advised the shareholders that the distributions did not have to be included by them in their individual personal income tax returns. This advice was predicated on the belief that Rapid's "earnings and profits" were insufficient to render these distributions dividends taxable as ordinary income to the recipients, but, rather, the recipients should consider the payments to be returns of capital and hence non-taxable.

At issue in this case is the manner in which Rapid's "current earnings and profits" and "accumulated earnings and profits" for its taxable years 1961 and 1962 should be computed. Specifically at issue is the correctness of a reduction of earnings and profits to account for purported "compensation expenses" measured by the "loss" Rapid absorbed in making "bargain" sales of its common stock to certain of its employees who possessed restricted stock options to purchase the stock.* Pursuant to the terms of these restricted stock options, during the period from January 1, 1957 to January 31, 1962, Rapid sold 174,395 shares of its common stock to some of its employees. Although these shares had a fair market value of $5,307,206, the corporation received only $1,889,360 from the employees who exercised their options. Rapid thus received $3,417,846 less for its stock than it could have received if the shares had been sold on the open market. In the period from February 1, 1962 to January 31, 1963 corporation employees purchased an additional 12,163 shares pursuant to the terms of options they held. Again, the prices paid by the employees, $155,388 in the aggregate, were substantially below the fair market value of the shares of stock, $363,914. It is argued that these differences of $3,417,846 and $208,526 represent compensation expense which should reduce corporate earnings and profits. . . .

II

[The collateral estoppel issue is omitted.]

III . . .

In this case the Commissioner claims that the cash distributions made to appellant by Rapid constitute "dividend" income which under §61 (a) (7) of the IRC is taxable to appellant as ordinary income. The word "dividend" is a term of art, the definition of which is found in §316 [of the] IRC: A "dividend" is "any distribution of property made by a corporation to its shareholders — (1) out of its earnings and profits accumulated after February 28, 1913, or (2) out of its earnings and profits of the [current] taxable year." Much to our chagrin, and that of many of our judicial ancestors, however, the Internal Revenue Code does not define the operative phrase "earnings and profits" or describe the manner in which that elusive quantity should be calculated. Congress could, and certainly should, rectify this deficiency by promulgating guidelines to assist the courts which must control the evolution of the concept. Be that as it may, such legislative guidelines do not now exist, so we must treat the problem as adequately as we can with the resources at our disposal.

Most of the commentators have experienced no difficulty in explaining what "earnings and profits" are not. For example, the term is synonymous with neither "corporate surplus," nor with "taxable income." Notably less successful have been the copious attempts to establish a coherent and workable scheme for determining when particular corporate transactions should reduce or increase a corporation's "earnings and profits." One of the most traditional approaches explains:

> Earnings and profits, on the other hand, are not defined by act; but they have a settled and well defined meaning in accounting. Generally speaking, they are computed by deducting from gross receipts the expense of producing them. Thus, under the ordinary method of accounting, in computing earnings and profits there

* Pursuant to the restricted stock option at issue, the amount of the "spread" was neither includible in gross income by the employees nor deductible by the corporate employer. — Eds.

> will be deducted, not only the items shown above, but others which are not, under the statute, deductible in computing taxable net income. In this classification may be listed such items as extraordinary expenses, charitable contributions, taxes paid the Federal Government, and taxes assessed against local benefits tending to increase the value of the property. Again, many items, such as interest upon the obligations of a state or political subdivision, tax-free Federal securities, and dividends from other corporations, must necessarily be considered in computing earnings and profits, though forming no part of taxable net income.

R. M. Weyerhaeuser, 33 B.T.A. 594, 597 (1935). . . . We propose . . . to determine whether . . . the option spread "loss" suffered by a corporation upon an employee's exercise of a stock option is an "expense of producing gross receipts," resulting in a reduction of "earnings and profits." . . .

Compensation paid to and received by the employees of a business are, of course, business "expenses of producing gross receipts" and therefore reduce earnings and profits. We must therefore ascertain whether the "bargain spread" existing when an employee exercises a stock option is a "compensation expense." Compensation of employees for past, present and future services represents one of the most fundamental and necessary expenses of operating a business. Payment may be made in myriad modes; it need not always be by way of cash disbursement. For instance, an employee may be paid in stock. In lieu of such an immediate transfer of stock to an employee the employee may instead be granted an option to purchase the employer corporation's stock at a fixed price per share from the company at some future date. Employees find the stock option to be a particularly attractive compensation device; in a rising market it gives the employee the opportunity to make a "bargain purchase." The question of whether the "bargain or option spread" (i.e., the difference between the option price and the fair market value of the stock at the time of the exercise of the option) existing at the time the option is exercised is compensatory in nature has been well settled for nearly twenty years. In Commissioner of Internal Revenue v. LoBue, 351 U.S. 243 (1956), the Supreme Court, noting that "it seems impossible to say that (the bargain transfer) was not compensation," *id.* at 247, commented upon this point:

> When assets are transferred by an employer to an employee to secure better services they are plainly compensation. It makes no difference that the compensation is paid in stock rather than in money.

Id. at 246-247.

When compensation is paid in its conventional form, cash, the magnitude of the expense (and, consequently, the reduction in earnings and profits) is easily visualized because there is an actual outflow of liquid corporate assets. When a bargain sale of stock to employees is made, however, both the existence and the extent of the corporate efflux are not as readily discernible. The same conceptual problems are presented when a corporation incurs an economic detriment when compensating employees by making awards of bonus stock to employees for the receipt of which the employees pay nothing into the corporate treasury. Yet the Service has twice ruled that the transfer of an employer's corporate stock to an employee as compensation produces for the transferor corporation a business expense deduction measured by the fair market value of the transferred stock, irrespective of whether that value exceeds the corporation's cost basis, if any, in the stock. Inasmuch as this deduction is allowed under §162, . . . these rulings appear to recognize that grants of bonus stock are expenses and have caused or should be considered as causing actual depletion of the corporate assets. Furthermore, these rulings demonstrate that the Service itself chooses to regard the *fair market value*, and not the cost basis, as one of the indices to be used in gauging the extent of the corporate expense incurred in compensating an employee by means of a direct award of stock. But the economic impact upon the corporation of the transfer of stock to employees pursuant to the exercise of employee stock options is in all important respects indistinguishable from the transfer of bonus corporation stock to employees. The only distinguishing feature of the option arrangement is that the employee pays something rather than nothing, but, it remains that in both instances, "at the end of these transactions, [the corporate] employer [is] worth . . . less to its stockholders." Commissioner of Internal Revenue v. LoBue, supra at 245. Accordingly, we would expect that the "bargain spread" would be considered to constitute a cognizable expense which would necessarily reduce earnings and profits. . . .

As a concluding comment, we reiterate our belief that the holding which we reach today is one which comports with economic reality and with the mechanics of operating a business. As the Seventh Circuit noted in Luckman v. Commissioner, [418 F.2d 381 (7th Cir. 1969)], if, instead of stock options, the corporation's employees had received cash there obviously would have been a cognizable corporate "expense." These stock options so granted were presumably the product of careful and deliberate negotiations between the corporation and the employees involved, and were apparently considered by the employees to be an acceptable, indeed, probably a superior, alternative to cash. In turn, the corporation undoubtedly expected to profit, and probably did profit, in precisely the same way it would have profited if it had awarded cash to those key employees, for, of course, this supplemental compensation to employees would normally cause the recipients to produce increased earnings and profits for the corporation.

In approaching a proper resolution of the tax issue here it is inequitable and unreasonable not to weigh the tangible corporate detriment resulting from the corporation's lost opportunity to sell the optioned stock to the public at its Fair Market Value, a detriment incurred in the hope that the grant of the options would result in producing added revenues. Moreover, in measuring the extent of the compensation, and the corresponding expense, by the amount of the excess of the Fair Market Value over the option price, realistic account is taken of the relationship between the employer and the employee. A company's revenues and profitability have a strong influence on the value of its stock and thus on the potential compensation accruing to the employee by virtue of the spread existing when the option he holds is exercised. Yet, typically, the employees who hold options are capable of increasing corporate revenues through their intensified labor and, insofar as such employees can affect corporate profitability, these same employees can indirectly influence the magnitude of their own compensation. Thus, the "bargain spread" does, in the form of increased employee compensation to the employees holding options, accurately reflect the economic detriment which the corporation has incurred in order, hopefully, to produce more revenue just like any other "development expense."

FRIENDLY, Circuit Judge (concurring and dissenting).

[Concurrence on collateral estoppel issue is omitted.]

The question in this case reduces to whether the "opportunity cost" incurred by Rapid in issuing the stock to the employees at less than its current market value rather than selling it to others is cognizable for purposes of reducing earnings and profits. There can be no claim that Rapid incurred out-of-pocket costs such as to reduce the earnings and profits available for distribution to shareholders. . . .

With all deference, I think the question can only be answered in the negative. Apart from the absence of evidence that Rapid could have sold the optioned stock at the market prices on the respective days of issuance, or would have done so, precisely the same sort of "cost" is incurred on the exercise of a warrant at a price below current market value, where no one suggests that this spread can be deducted from earnings and profits. The fact that here the options were issued to provide "incentive" to employees is not sufficient to support a different result. Selling stock at less than current market value does not impair the corporation's ability to make distributions without invading capital or paid-in surplus, which is what "earnings and profits" are mainly about. The effect of the exercise of an option, whether issued to an employee or to an outsider, at a "bargain spread" is to decrease the market price and, in some but not all instances, the book value of the shares of other stockholders. It has no adverse effect on the corporate accounts.

The petitioner's principal reliance is on two revenue rulings that, despite the general provision of §1032(a) prohibiting recognition of gain or loss on a corporation's receipt of money or property in exchange for stock (including treasury stock), a corporation may deduct as a business expense under §162 the fair market value of stock issued as compensation, whether the stock be treasury or theretofore unissued stock, Rev. Rul. 62-217, 1962-2 Cum. Bull. 59; Rev. Rul. 69-75, 1969-1 Cum. Bull. 52, with the presumable consequence that the same amount may be deducted from earnings and profits. Not only were these payments clearly compensation and nothing more, but the rulings can be rationalized on the basis that since the employee was subject to tax on the fair market value of the stock issued, allowing the deduction to the corporation was necessary to avoid unfairness. . . . By contrast, in the case of restricted stock options such as that before us, the employee escapes regular income taxation both when the option is issued and when it is exercised. There is therefore no reason to disregard the general principle of allowing no deduction, either from income or from earnings and profits, for mere loss of "opportunity costs." In substance [the restricted stock option] represented a trade-off. In return for the eagerly sought privilege of tax-free receipt and exercise of stock options by executives, the corporation would forego any deduction under §162 for the excess of the market value of the stock, when issued, over the option price. . . . There can be no fair doubt that the Congress that expressly ruled out use of the "bargain spread" to employees as a deduction would also have forbidden its use to reduce earnings and profits if it had ever considered the problem whether the "bargain spread" should enable the corporation to make a later distribution to stockholders as out of capital rather than from earnings and profits in the unusual case where this possibility might exist. . . .

I would affirm the judgment of the Tax Court.

NOTES

1. *"Earnings and profits."* It is a curious fact that the Code, ordinarily so prodigal in its use of words, never systematically defines the term "earnings and

profits" even though it is not a term that has a clear independent meaning outside of the Code. The term is partly explained by Treas. Regs. §1.312-6, and the effect of a number of transactions on earnings and profits is prescribed by the Code. See §§312 and 381(c)(2). The concept of earnings and profits is not the same as earned surplus for state law or financial reporting purposes. For example, a nontaxable distribution of common stock by a corporation decreases earned surplus but has no effect on earnings and profits. Otherwise, nontaxable stock dividends under Eisner v. Macomber, 252 U.S. 189 (1920), would clear away the corporation's earnings and profits account, allowing it to make nontaxable subsequent distributions of cash and property.

Similarly, the term "dividend" as defined for income tax purposes by §316(a) may not correspond with the term "dividend" under state law, so that a distribution may be a dividend under §316(a) although it impairs capital under state law. Conversely, it is possible for a distribution to constitute a dividend under state law without qualifying as a dividend under §316(a). In the former instance, the dividend will ordinarily be taxable to the stockholder under the "claim-of-right" doctrine, notwithstanding a potential liability to creditors under state law. See United States v. Lesoine, 203 F.2d 123 (9th Cir. 1953), holding that the claim-of-right doctrine requires that dividends be taxed in year of receipt even if the distribution may have been illegal under state law.

The determination of the earnings and profits account is often no simple feat, especially when the account must be traced through a series of corporate reorganizations or similar transactions. It may be necessary to go back many years to decide how a transaction should have been taxed under a now-interred income tax provision because of its effect on earnings and profits. See, e.g., Union Pacific Railroad v. United States, 524 F.2d 1343 (Cl. Ct. 1975), claiming that an accounting error affected earnings and profits between 1900 and 1907.

If a corporation is initially organized for cash, the reason for gearing the taxability of its distributions to its record of earnings and profits is clear enough. Until the corporation has engaged in profitable operations, any distribution to its original stockholders is a return of their investment rather than income. Once the corporation has realized profits, its distributions may pro tanto be fairly regarded as income to the stockholders.

The equity and logic of §§316 and 301(c) may be less clear if we assume that after a period of corporate profits, the stock changes hands, and that before additional earnings arise (the next day, if you will), there is a distribution to the new stockholder. Should the distribution be treated as a return of capital? Sections 316 and 301(c) are unrelenting: To the extent of earnings and profits, the surprised shareholder has realized income. This "miracle of income without gain"—the phrase is from Powell, Income from Corporate Dividends, 35 Harv. L. Rev. 363 (1922)—long ago was attested and explained by the Supreme Court in United States v. Phellis, 257 U.S. 156, 171-172 (1921):

> Where, as in this case, the dividend constitutes a distribution of profits accumulated during an extended period and bears a large proportion to the par value of the stock, if an investor happened to buy stock shortly before the dividend, paying a price enhanced by an estimate of the capital plus the surplus of the company, and after distribution of the surplus, with corresponding reduction in the intrinsic and market value of the shares, he was called upon to pay a tax upon the dividend received, it might look in

> his case like a tax upon his capital. But it is only apparently so. In buying at a price that reflected the accumulated profits, he of course acquired as a part of the valuable rights purchased the prospect of a dividend from the accumulation — bought "dividend on," as the phrase goes — and necessarily took subject to the burden of the income tax proper to be assessed against him by reason of the dividend if and when made. He simply stepped into the shoes, in this as in other respects, of the stockholder whose shares he acquired, and presumably the prospect of a dividend influenced the price paid, and was discounted by the prospect of an income tax to be paid thereon.

Note, however, that even though a buyer may anticipate a dividend, her discount for the tax on that dividend may not accurately reflect the tax that would have been paid by the buyer, because when the sale occurs, it may be unclear when any dividend may be paid or what the amount of the dividend may be.

2. *Source of distributions.* If a corporation has earnings and profits in a taxable year, any distribution in that year subject to §301 will be taxable pro tanto even though the corporation has a deficit from prior years equal to or exceeding the current year's profits. §316(a)(2). See Situation 2 of Rev. Rul. 74-164 at page 107 supra. This provision has a curious ancestry. It was enacted in 1936 as a relief measure when the undistributed profits tax was in effect. That tax was imposed on the undistributed part of corporate income, computed by deducting "dividends" from total income. Unless a deficit corporation could treat distributions out of current earnings as "dividends" for this purpose, it would be unable to avoid the undistributed profits tax no matter how large its distributions to stockholders. To enable such corporations to obtain a credit for "dividends" paid out of current earnings, §316(a) was enacted. Apparently, no thought was given to the effect of the new subsection apart from the undistributed profits tax. Nor was §316(a)(2) repealed when the short-lived undistributed profits tax was repealed.

Treas. Regs. §1.316-2 sets forth hierarchical rules for classifying distributions. Distributions are first deemed to come out of the corporation's current earnings and profits account. If the account is exhausted, then accumulated earnings and profits are tapped. If there is a deficit in the current earnings and profits account, distributions are deemed to be out of accumulated earnings and profits decreased by the current deficit prorated to the date of distribution unless the actual current deficit as of the transaction date can be ascertained. Rev. Rul. 74-164, above, illustrates these source rules. Note, though, that in Situation 3 of the ruling, the current deficit in the earnings and profits account is prorated even though the actual current deficit as of July 1, the distribution date, is known. Doesn't this treatment in the ruling conflict with Treas. Regs. §1.316-2? See also Rev. Rul. 69-440, 1969-2 C.B. 46, discussing priorities among distributions.

If there is more than one distribution during a taxable year, the current earnings and profits are prorated among the distributions for purposes of determining whether a distribution is a dividend. Accumulated earnings and profits, however, are allocated to distributions chronologically on a first come, first served basis. Treas. Regs. §1.316-2(b), (c).

As earnings and profits are distributed, the corporation decreases its earnings and profits account in accordance with §312(a). Note that a corporation cannot create an earnings and profits deficit through distributions. See §312(a) and Estate of Uris v. Commissioner, 605 F.2d 1258 (2d Cir. 1979). How then can there be a deficit in the earnings and profits account?

3. *Relationship of earnings and profits to taxable income.* Earnings and profits are intended to distinguish a corporation's profits from its shareholders' investment in the corporation. Thus, if the corporation enjoys an accession to wealth, it should increase its earnings and profits, while if it suffers a reduction in its wealth, it should reduce its earnings and profits. As with determinations of income, those accessions and reductions are accounted for only when realized (i.e., the mere appreciation or decline in value of a corporation's assets does not affect its earnings and profits).

Many compute earnings and profits by starting with taxable income. To convert taxable income into earnings and profits, three types of adjustments are necessary. First, some items excludible from taxable income are included in earnings and profits. They are included because they represent an accretion to the corporation that can be distributed without impairing the corporation's original capital. The items include proceeds from life insurance contracts under §101(a), interest on certain government obligations under §103, and amounts received through accident or health insurance for personal injuries to or sickness of insured employees under §104(a). See Treas. Regs. §1.312-6(b).

Section 312(n) contains some upwards adjustments to earnings and profits to ensure that earnings and profits conform more closely to economic income. For example, if a corporation sells property at a gain on the installment method, the entire gain goes into earnings and profits immediately even though there is deferred recognition of some or all of the gain. Similarly, a corporation that reports income and expenses attributable to a long-term contract on the completed contract method must use the percentage-of-completion method for earnings and profits purposes. Corporations using "last in, first out" (LIFO) accounting for inventory must adjust earnings and profits by the LIFO recapture amount.

Second, some items that are deductible in computing taxable income may not be deducted in computing earnings and profits. Often, these are "artificial" deductions in that no cash outlay is required that would deplete the earnings available for distribution. These items include the dividends-received deduction under §243 (which allows qualifying corporations to deduct from 70 percent to 100 percent of the amount of intercorporate dividends received) and the excess of accelerated over straight-line depreciation using recovery periods specified in §312(k). In addition, net operating losses under §172 and capital loss carrybacks under §1212 do not reduce earnings and profits because they represent a carryback or carryover of losses that reduced earnings and profits in the year in which they occurred.

Several provisions require a slower rate of deduction for earnings and profits purposes than for the purpose of computing gain or loss. For example, intangible drilling costs and mineral and development costs, to the extent deductible, must be capitalized and ratably amortized over 60 months for earnings and profits purposes. §312(n)(2). Special rules also apply for expenses amortizable under §§173 and 248 (see §312(n)(3)) and for construction period carrying charges. §312(n)(1).

Third, some items that cannot be deducted in determining taxable income are deducted in computing earnings and profits, because they represent a real drain on earnings available for distribution to shareholders. Included in this category are dividend distributions in prior years (but see §312(a)); federal income taxes;[1]

1. Treas. Regs. §1.312-6(a) provides that the method of accounting used to compute earnings and profits should be the same as that used for determining taxable income. Accordingly, a cash basis taxpayer cannot accrue a tax liability; for a cash basis taxpayer, earnings and profits are reduced only when taxes are paid, Mazzocchi Bus Co., Inc. v. Commissioner, 14 F.2d 923 (3d Cir. 1994).

excess charitable contributions (not deductible because of the 10-percent limitation of §170(b)); nondeductible expenses under §265; unreasonable compensation; and deductions disallowed on public policy grounds under §162(c), (e), (f), or (g). See Rev. Rul. 77-442, 1977-2 C.B. 264.

In *Divine*, the court faced an issue involving the third category—whether an item not deductible in computing taxable income (the difference between the cost of the stock and the fair market value of the stock) is deductible in computing earnings and profits.[2] The Tax Court tried its view twice and was reversed both times—once by the Seventh Circuit in Luckman v. Commissioner, 418 F.2d 381 (7th Cir. 1969), and once by the Second Circuit in *Divine*, although the Tax Court did convince Judge Friendly. Who is right, the majority or Judge Friendly? It is true that the purchase of stock by Divine did not deplete the cash or other property available for distribution to shareholders. If earnings and profits are intended to describe the corporation's ability to pay dividends, did the transaction in *Divine* impede the corporation's ability to pay dividends to all shareholders? If Divine had been paid compensation in cash and then used that cash, plus some other cash, to buy the corporation's stock, would there be doubts about the transaction's effect on earnings and profits? Is the cash distribution and purchase in economic substance different from the facts in *Divine*?

While *Divine* involves the effect on earnings and profits of a nondeductible item, in Bangor & Aroostook Railroad v. Commissioner, 193 F.2d 827 (1st Cir. 1951), the court confronted a discharge of indebtedness that went unrecognized—and hence was excluded from gross income—because of the taxpayer's election under the predecessors of §§108 and 1017. Since a reduction in basis accompanied the nonrecognition, the court ruled that there should be no increase in earnings and profits until the assets with the reduced basis were sold. See §312(f), relied on by the court, and §312(l)(1), which codified this result.

4. *The future of earnings and profits.* You may not need much convincing at this point that the concept of earnings and profits adds complexity to the Code. Moreover, if the purpose of the concept is to ensure that shareholders will not be taxed on the return of their capital, curious results abound for a stock purchaser receiving a distribution shortly after purchase and before the accumulation of any additional earnings. See page 115 supra. If there are accumulated earnings and profits, the distribution will be a dividend even though there have been no subsequent earnings following purchase. Finally, there is room for manipulation. For example, the impact of current earnings and profits where the corporation has an accumulated earnings and profits deficit sometimes can be avoided by postponing the distribution until the following year. If the corporation has no earnings in that year and still has an accumulated earnings and profits deficit, the distribution will be received tax free because it will fall under neither §316(a)(1) nor §316(a)(2). If a corporation can deplete its earnings and profits account, it may be able to borrow against appreciated property to make tax-free distributions to shareholders and then use the property's earnings to repay the loan.

2. *Divine* serves as a nice reminder of the *Golsen* rule—that the Tax Court by its own rules is not bound to follow a court of appeals decision unless appellate jurisdiction is in that circuit. See Golsen v. Commissioner, 54 T.C. 742, 757 (1970), aff'd without discussion of this issue, 445 F.2d 985 (10th Cir. 1971).

This combination of complexity, failure of purpose, and potential abuse has led some commentators, as well as some members of Congress from time to time, to consider a repeal of the earnings and profits concept, with relief for obvious distributions of capital. See Blum, The Earnings and Profits Limitation on Dividend Income: A Reappraisal, 53 Taxes 68 (1975); Colby, Blackburn, and Trier, Elimination of "Earnings and Profits" from the Internal Revenue Code, 39 Tax Law. 285 (1986). See also Staff of Senate Comm. on Finance, 99th Cong., 1st Sess., The Reform and Simplification of the Income Taxation of Corporations (1985). No change in this regard appears imminent, however.

5. *Relief from taxation of dividends.* Earnings and profits serve as the benchmark for measuring dividend income, thereby producing the "double tax"—taxation to the corporation earning income and taxation to shareholders on dividend distributions. See discussion of the double tax in Chapter 8.

There is a special allowance for dividends received by corporate shareholders to mitigate the multiple taxation of corporate earnings. This relief provision can be illustrated by considering the tax results that would prevail in its absence. If, for example, individual *A* owns all the stock in *P* Corp., which owns all the stock in *Q* Corp., earnings of *Q* Corp. might be subject to a triple tax by the time the earnings reach *A*. *Q* Corp. would be taxed when it earns income; *P* Corp. and then *A* would face taxation on the dividend. Since 1935, however, §243 (or a predecessor) has provided for a deduction by a corporation that is a shareholder of another corporation. Although §243 is a "deduction" provision, it provides, in effect, an exclusion for the shareholder-corporation (i.e., the corporation can deduct some portion of the dividend that has been received).

Currently, §243 permits a shareholder-corporation to deduct at least 70 percent of the dividend received from a domestic corporation. §243(a)(1). This provision at current rates makes the effective maximum tax rate on dividends received by a corporation 10.5 percent—that is, the highest corporate rate of 35 percent imposed on 30 percent of dividends received. If the recipient corporation owns 20 percent or more (by vote and value) of the stock of the distributing corporation, the deduction is increased to 80 percent. §243(a)(1) and (c). Notice that dividends paid on "portfolio stock" (i.e., when the receiving corporation owns less than 20 percent) are subject to a higher rate of tax on dividends.

The lowest rate on intercorporate dividends is available on distributions between affiliated corporations. An affiliated group of corporations can eliminate intragroup dividends from gross income entirely by electing to file consolidated returns under the relevant Code provisions. §§1501 et seq. Moreover, §243(a)(3) permits a 100-percent deduction for certain dividends for electing members of an affiliated group, as defined in §1504(a), who are willing to abide by certain restrictions. See §243(b)(3) (also requiring that the distribution be from earnings and profits for a year on each day of which the distributing and shareholder corporations were affiliated).

For a discussion of problems raised by the dividends-received deduction, see pages 145-153 infra.

6. *Qualified dividend income.* In addition, if an individual receives "qualified dividend income," she is taxed at a rate no greater than 20 percent on that income, the same rate as for long-term capital gain. §1(h)(11). However, qualified dividend income is still ordinary income, not long-term capital gain, and therefore it generally cannot be offset by capital loss. But see §1211(b) (allowing

a noncorporate taxpayer to offset up to $3,000 of ordinary income with net capital loss).

Qualified dividend income is a dividend paid on stock of a domestic corporation, or stock of certain foreign corporations, that meets the following added requirement: The shareholder must hold the stock for at least 61 days during the 121-day period that begins 60 days before the ex-dividend date (for common stock) or for at least 91 days during the 181-day period that begins 90 days before the ex-dividend date (for preferred stock). §1(h)(11)(iii) and §246(c). The ex-dividend date is the first date that the stock trades without the dividend.

PROBLEMS

4-1. Determine the tax consequences in the following situations:

a. On July 1 of year 2, *X* Corp., a calendar year taxpayer, made distributions of $20,000 to *A*, its sole shareholder, whose stock had a $5,000 basis. No other distributions were made in year 2. As of December 31 of year 1, *X* Corp. had no earnings and profits. In year 2, *X* Corp. had earnings and profits of $15,000 as of July 1, but only $5,000 for the entire year.
b. Suppose in (a) that *X* Corp. had an accumulated earnings and profits deficit of $15,000 as of December 31 of year 1.
c. Suppose in (a) that *X* Corp. had accumulated earnings and profits of $15,000 as of December 31 of year 1, and that in year 2, *X* Corp. had a $15,000 earnings and profits deficit on July 1, but a $5,000 earnings and profits account for the entire year.
d. Suppose in (c) that *X* Corp. had $15,000 of current earnings and profits as of July 1 of year 2, but a deficit of $20,000 for the entire year.

4-2. *X* Corp. is an accrual basis taxpayer. Compute its current earnings and profits from the following information. Assume that *X* Corp. is taxed at a flat 30-percent rate.

Gross income from business	$27,000
Dividend income	20,000
Interest on municipal bonds	9,000
Long-term capital gain	5,000
Contribution to capital	2,000
	$63,000
Wages, rent, office supplies	$15,000
Fines and kickbacks	7,000
Depreciation (excess over §168(g)(2) amount = $4,000)	6,000
Interest incurred to purchase municipal bonds	2,000
Dividends-received deduction	14,000
Capital losses	6,000
	$50,000
"Net"	$13,000

B. PROPERTY DISTRIBUTIONS

1. *The Effect of a Distribution of Property on the Distributing Corporation's Income*

Overview. Corporate income is subject to two levels of tax, as the United States employs a classic double tax system. When a corporation earns income, there is a corporate-level tax. When those earnings are distributed to the shareholders as dividends, there is a shareholder-level tax under §301. Similarly, if the corporation sells appreciated property and distributes the sales proceeds, there will typically be a corporate-level tax on the sale and shareholder-level tax on any dividend on the distribution of the sales proceeds. Note that the gain recognized by the corporation on the sale increases the corporation's earnings and profits, making it more likely that the distribution will be taxed as a dividend.

Suppose instead that the corporation distributes the appreciated property to its shareholders, who then sell the property. We know that the shareholders will have dividends equal to the fair market value of the property distributed if the corporation has sufficient earnings and profits. §301(b). If there are insufficient earnings and profits, the shareholders may escape dividend treatment, instead reducing their bases in the distributing corporation's stock. §301(c)(2). In any case, the distributed property will have a basis in the hands of the shareholders equal to its fair market value. §301(d). If the property is then sold, the shareholders will recognize no additional gain. To summarize, the shareholders will recognize, at most, one level of taxation (dividend treatment), and if there are insufficient earnings and profits, the shareholders may have no income as a result of the distribution and sale.

How will the corporation be treated on its distribution of appreciated property? To prevent the form of the transaction from dictating the tax consequences, there must be a corporate-level tax if the appreciated property is distributed and then sold, just as there is if the property is sold and the proceeds distributed. This conclusion promotes consistency in the double tax system. It is not, however, an endorsement of that system, the merits of which are explored in Chapter 8.

General Utilities ***doctrine.*** Note that a corporation has not always recognized gain on its distribution of appreciated property. In fact, nonrecognition was the rule for many years, a rule established in the seminal case, General Utilities & Operating Co. v. Helvering, 296 U.S. 200 (1935). In that case, General Utilities, a corporation, was poised to sell an appreciated asset. Realizing that its sale and its planned distribution of the sales proceeds would result in corporate-level and shareholder-level taxes, the corporation instead distributed the appreciated asset to its shareholders, who reported a shareholder-level dividend. Under the predecessor of §301(d), the shareholders took a fair market value basis in the distributed asset and reported no further gain when they sold the asset four days later to the purchaser at fair market value.

Before the Board of Tax Appeals (the predecessor to the Tax Court), the Commissioner asserted that the corporation should be taxed on the distribution, arguing that it had declared a dividend of $1 million and satisfied that obligation through a distribution of appreciated property. The trial court rejected that argument because in fact the corporation declared a dividend of the asset and not a dividend of cash. On appeal, the Commissioner added a second argument — that a sale of the property occurring immediately after the distribution should be attributed to the corporation, although made in form by the shareholders. (This rationale, commonly known as the *Court Holding Co.* doctrine, has been accepted where the corporation has negotiated the sale and then made a last-minute effort to avoid recognizing gain by distributing the property to its shareholders before the sale. See page 268 infra.) On this point, the court of appeals agreed with the Commissioner. In its Supreme Court brief, the Commissioner added a third argument — that a corporation must recognize taxable income on a distribution of appreciated property to its stockholders since the transfer was a "sale or other disposition" under what is now §1001.

The Supreme Court agreed with the Board of Tax Appeals that the distributed assets were not used to discharge a corporate debt. As to the second point, the Court held that it should have been raised at the trial court level and could not be belatedly argued before the appellate court. The government's third argument (i.e., the theory of realization-by-distribution) was not mentioned, and commentators disagreed about whether the third argument was rejected on the merits or passed over because it was advanced too late in the proceeding. Nevertheless, the former explanation of its fate became popular with the courts, and the *General Utilities* doctrine was born.

In 1954, Congress codified that doctrine in §311(a), which provides that no gain or loss is recognized to a corporation on a distribution of property with respect to its stock. In recommending the enactment of §311, the Senate Finance Committee Report noted that it intended to preserve exceptions to the doctrine exemplified by Commissioner v. First State Bank of Stratford, 168 F.2d 1004 (5th Cir. 1948).

In that case, a corporation was taxed under the assignment of income doctrine on income collected on debt instruments (not its own) distributed to its shareholders. The distributing corporation had taken bad debt deductions on the notes, but it distributed them to its shareholders when it appeared some amount would be collected. Although the shareholders actually collected the proceeds, the court taxed the distributing corporation on the collection, using assignment of income principles.

Following the enactment of §311(a), courts continued to chip away at the *General Utilities* doctrine. See, e.g., First Wisconsin Bankshares Corp. v. United States, 369 F. Supp. 1034 (E.D. Wis. 1973) (attributing income to a corporation following its contribution to charity of notes previously charged off as worthless using the tax benefit rule and the anticipatory assignment of income doctrine). See also Bush Brothers & Co. v. Commissioner, 668 F.2d 252 (6th Cir. 1982) (also applying the anticipatory assignment of income doctrine to attribute a shareholders' sale of distributed property to a corporation; note that the Tax Court reached the same result, reasoning that the corporation had an improper tax avoidance motive).

Gain recognized. Beginning in 1969, Congress began eroding the doctrine, adding exceptions to the nonrecognition rule of §311(a). By 1984, the exceptions to §311(a) all but swallowed the rule, and in 1986, Congress overturned most remaining vestiges of the *General Utilities* doctrine. Section 311(b) now provides that if a corporation distributes appreciated property (other than the distributing corporation's own obligation), it recognizes gain as if it had sold the property to the shareholder at fair market value.

Note that the gain recognized by the distributing corporation is not limited to post-incorporation appreciation. For example, suppose *B* forms *X* Corp. in a §351 transaction by exchanging property including one item with a basis of $100 and a fair market value of $500 for all the *X* Corp. stock. Before *X* Corp. earns any income, it distributes that item to *B*. Under §311(b), *X* Corp. must recognize the $400 of appreciation (the excess of $500, the property's value, over $100, its basis). The gain will be ordinary or capital, depending on the nature of the asset. Moreover, *X* Corp.'s earnings and profits account will increase from $0 to $400 (minus taxes paid by *X* Corp.) because *X* Corp.'s taxable income reflects the §311(b) gain. §312(b)(1). The increase in earnings and profits will cause *B* to recognize a dividend of about $400 under §301(c)(1). This phenomenon will doubtless precipitate some careful planning as indicated below.

If a corporation distributes property subject to a liability, the fair market value of the property distributed for purposes of §311(b)(1)(B) is not less than the amount of the liability. See §311(b)(2). See also §336(b) (for a comparable rule for liquidating distributions). For example, suppose *X* Corp. distributes property with a basis of $700 and a fair market value of $400 to *B*, a shareholder. The property is subject to a liability of $900. Under §311(b), *X* Corp. must recognize a $200 gain. Note that if there had been a sale, *X* Corp. would have recognized a $200 gain under Tufts v. Commissioner, 461 U.S. 300 (1983).

No loss recognized. A true repeal of the *General Utilities* doctrine would allow a distributing corporation to deduct a loss on the distribution of property with an adjusted basis that exceeds its fair market value. Suppose *X* Corp. held property with a basis of $700 and a fair market value of $200. If *X* Corp. sells the property, it will recognize a $500 loss. The distribution of the proceeds to the shareholders will be taxable to the shareholders under §301(c)(1) if there are sufficient earnings and profits after reducing taxable income by the amount of the loss. If, however, *X* Corp. distributes the property to its shareholders, §311(a) and (b) provide no loss deduction. Moreover, *X* Corp. does not decrease its earnings and profits by the built-in loss in the loss property before the shareholders compute their dividends under §301(c)(1). The shareholders will have a $200 dividend if there are sufficient earnings and profits. Finally, the shareholders will take the property with a basis of $200, its fair market value under §301(d). Notice that by mandating a fair market value basis, the Code forever eliminates the loss deduction.

Why do §311(a) and (b) disallow recognition of losses to the distributing corporation? Perhaps Congress was concerned that shareholders could cause their corporations to distribute "loss property" but retain "gain property." In this way corporations could exploit the realization doctrine by recognizing losses but deferring gains. If this was the concern, there are several responses. A corporation always has the power to exploit the realization doctrine by selling loss rather than gain property. Indeed, the limitation on capital loss deductions in §§1211 and 1212 is a response to that problem.

But it could be argued that the capital gains limitation is not sufficient when the loss property is transferred to a related party. Congress has addressed that problem as well by enacting §267, which prohibits the deduction of losses for exchanges between related parties. A corporation is considered related to any shareholder who owns, directly or indirectly, more than 50 percent in value of the corporation's stock. For a discussion of the attribution rules, see §267(b)(2), (c), and (f). A sale of loss property to a 25-percent shareholder, for example, will produce a deductible loss. Why didn't Congress treat all nonliquidating distributions as if the corporation had sold the property to the shareholders and allow §267 to determine the deductibility of losses? Could

Congress have worried that loss recognition would tempt the distributing corporation and shareholders to undervalue distributed property, producing phantom losses at the corporate level and understating dividend income at the shareholder level?

A side effect of not using §267 in connection with distributions of loss property is the basis consequence to the shareholders. Under §267, a purchaser takes a basis equal to cost—generally fair market value. But if the purchaser later sells the property at a gain, the loss that went unrecognized to the seller will be available to the purchaser to offset the gain. §267(d). There is no equivalent provision in §311.

Suppose *X* Corp. distributes two pieces of property to *B*, its shareholder. One has a basis of $200 and a fair market value of $900; the other has a basis of $900 and a fair market value of $200. Has *X* Corp. made a distribution of appreciated property? The answer is yes. Section 311 applies separately to each asset distributed. Thus, *X* Corp. recognizes a $700 gain but no loss.

Suppose *X* Corp., a partner in the *XY* partnership, wants to distribute a partnership interest to its shareholders and the interest has a value exceeding its basis. To decrease the amount of gain *X* must recognize under §311(b), *X* transfers loss property to the partnership. The effect of the transfer is to increase the corporation's basis in the partnership interest by the basis of the contributed property under §722 in a manner comparable to §358 in a §351 transaction, while the fair market value of the partnership interest increases by only the fair market value of the contributed property. The overall effect, if successful, would be to use the loss property to shield gain that would otherwise be recognized on the distribution. Section 311(b)(3) allows the Service to promulgate regulations that disregard the contribution of the loss property in determining the basis and fair market value of the distributed partnership interest.

Given the treatment to a distributing corporation of both gain and loss property, what strategies would you expect taxpayers to pursue? Suppose *X* Corp., with sufficient earnings and profits, wants to get a piece of property with a basis of $200 and a fair market value of $900 into the hands of *B*, its shareholder. A distribution will trigger gain at both the corporate and shareholder level. Suppose instead that *X* Corp. sells the property to *B*, who pays with a note bearing appropriate interest and payable in 10 years. If the transaction is respected, *X* Corp. will recognize no immediate gain on the sale because of installment reporting. §453. But consider the application of both §§267 and 1239. *B*, the purchaser, will have no gain on the acquisition of the property and will take a cost basis under §1012 of $900.

Later, if the shareholder defaults on the note, presumably the shareholder will recognize $900 of income as a discharge of indebtedness. §61(a)(12). The distributing corporation should be allowed to take a bad debt deduction under §166 for the $200 basis of the note. Consider first that this treatment is less onerous in absolute income terms than is dividend characterization in the year of the property's distribution because there is no corporate-level income (indeed there is a corporate-level loss) in the year of default. Moreover, *B* has had the benefit of deferral on the $900 of income that would be recognized at the shareholder level, although the deferred income may be taxed at a higher rate. Cf. §1(h)(11) (for preferential rates on dividends). Undoubtedly the Service may try to recharacterize the transaction as a distribution of the appreciated property followed years later by *B*'s contribution to capital when the note is paid.

If *X* Corp. wants to distribute property to *B* with a basis of $900 and a fair market value of $200, a similar strategy may be employed. *X* Corp. could declare a cash dividend and then satisfy the dividend with a distribution of the loss property.

See, e.g., Kenan v. Commissioner, 114 F.2d 217 (2d Cir. 1940) (satisfaction of a cash legacy with appreciated stock treated as a sale or disposition). Indeed, this technique is precisely what the Service accused the taxpayer of doing at the trial court in *General Utilities*. The Service presumably would argue that there never was an intention to pay a cash dividend and that the distribution of property cannot generate a loss under §311(b). Again consider the application of §267.

Suppose *X* Corp. had decided to distribute property with a basis of $900 and fair market value of $200 to shareholder *B*, who would then sell it to *P*. Immediately prior to the transaction, *X* Corp. decides to make the sale itself to *P* and to distribute the proceeds to *B*. This fact pattern is the converse of that presented in *General Utilities*. There, the distributing corporations made distributions before the sale took place. Here, the corporation sold the property and distributed the proceeds. One can expect that in appropriate circumstances the Service will reverse the argument that it relied on in these cases, claiming that actually the corporation distributed the property before the sale transpired. Such a recharacterization would deny the loss deduction to the distributing corporation. §311(b).

Taxpayers and their advisors have developed all manner of intricate ways of trying to avoid the repeal of *General Utilities*. See, e.g., Notice 2001-45, 2001-2 C.B. 129; Notice 94-93, 1994-2 C.B. 563; and Land, Strange Loops and Tangled Hierarchies, 49 Tax L. Rev. 53 (1993).

2. *The Effect of a Distribution of Property on the Distributing Corporation's Earnings and Profits*

Although we have looked at what goes into earnings and profits in general, we need to consider the effect of a distribution on the earnings and profits account. Until the repeal of the *General Utilities* doctrine, distributing corporations did not typically recognize gain on the distribution of appreciated property. Consequently, §312(a)(3) required earnings and profits to be decreased only by the adjusted basis of any property distributed because the appreciation never was taken into income by the corporation. With the repeal of the *General Utilities* doctrine, a corporation that distributes appreciated property must recognize the appreciation as income. The increase in taxable income results in an increase in earnings and profits. Therefore, it is appropriate to decrease the earnings and profits account after the distribution by the fair market value of the property distributed. Section 312(b)(2) accomplishes this result by substituting fair market value for adjusted basis in §312(a)(3) when appreciated property is distributed.

You may ask why Congress did not simply amend §312(a)(3) to read "fair market value" instead of "adjusted basis." The answer lies in the treatment of loss property. Because a distributing corporation does not take a loss into account for tax purposes when distributing property with a basis that exceeds its fair market value, it would be inappropriate to decrease earnings and profits only by the fair market value of the property distributed. Accordingly, §312(a)(3) allows the distributing corporation to decrease earnings and profits by the higher adjusted basis.

Section 312(b)(1) requires a corporation to increase its earnings and profits by any gain it recognizes under §311(b) on a distribution of appreciated property. Note that §312(b)(1) appears unnecessary, because a corporation would have been required to increase its earnings and profits for that gain without §312(b)(1).

To illustrate the workings of §312(b), suppose *X* Corp., with no earnings and profits, distributes property with a basis of $0 and a fair market value of $400 to its shareholders. *X* Corp. will have $400 of taxable income on the distribution under §311(b). For purposes of evaluating the tax consequences to the shareholders, *X* Corp.'s earnings and profits will increase by the $400 gain recognized (disregarding any tax on that gain). Therefore, the shareholders will have $400 of dividends under §301(c)(1). Following the distribution, *X* Corp.'s earnings and profits will be reduced from $400 to $0 under §312(b)(2) and (a)(3) because *X* Corp.'s earnings were fully distributed. Notice the sequence of the relevant tax events: Section 312(b)(1) increases earnings and profits, then the tax consequences to the shareholders are evaluated, and finally the earnings and profits account is decreased by the fair market value of the property distributed.

Finally, consider the effect of §312(a) on distributions of a specific type of property—a corporation's own note. For example, suppose *X* Corp., with $100,000 of accumulated earnings and profits, distributes its own notes with a $100,000 principal amount maturing in 10 years and bearing no interest. Assume further that the notes have an aggregate issue price of $20,000. *X* is not permitted to reduce its earnings and profits by the $100,000 principal amount in order to pave the way for future, potentially nontaxable cash distributions. Instead, §312(a)(2) now mandates a reduction by the $20,000 issue price. Each year, the corporation can reduce its taxable income and its earnings and profits by a portion of the original issue discount (i.e., accrued interest) on the notes. §163(e) (providing a deduction for original issue discount accrued during the year).

3. *The Effect of a Distribution of Property on Shareholders*

For both corporate and noncorporate distributees, §301(b)(1) specifies that the fair market value of property is the amount distributed for purposes of determining what constitutes a dividend under §§301(c) and 316. However, if the shareholder assumes a liability or takes property subject to a liability, the amount distributed is reduced (but not below zero) by the liability assumed (or taken subject to). §301(b)(2). The basis of property received by the distributee is its fair market value. §301(d).

If a corporation distributes an asset to *T* with a basis of $40 and a fair market value of $100, subject to a $70 mortgage, what is the amount distributed? See §301(b)(2). The basis of property received by distributees is its fair market value. §301(d). What is *T*'s basis in the asset received? Why isn't the basis reduced by the mortgage?

PROBLEMS

4-3. Discuss the tax consequences in the following, ignoring the quantitative effect of any corporate-level taxes on earnings and profits:

a. *X* Corp., a cash basis taxpayer with no earnings and profits, makes a distribution of property that has a basis of $3,000 and that *X* Corp. values at $3,000. The recipient is *B*, a shareholder whose basis in the *X* Corp. stock is $5,000. If the Service determines that the property has a value of $7,000, what are the tax consequences?
b. Suppose in (a) that the property has a fair market value of $7,000 but is subject to a mortgage of $8,000.
c. Suppose in (a) that *X* Corp. transfers the property to *B* in exchange for *B*'s $7,000 note.
d. Suppose in (a) that *X* Corp. has earnings and profits of $4,000 and that the property distributed by *X* Corp. has a basis of $7,000 and a fair market value of $3,000. What happens if the property increases in value after the distribution and then *B* sells the property for $7,000?
e. Suppose in (d) that *X* Corp. distributes the loss property and another piece of property with a basis of $3,000 and a fair market value of $7,000.
f. Suppose in (d) that *X* Corp. declares a $3,000 cash dividend and then distributes the loss property in satisfaction of the dividend.
g. Suppose in (d) that *P*, an unrelated purchaser, wants to buy the property. *X* Corp. negotiates the sale with *P*, sells the property for $3,000, and distributes the sales proceeds to *B*.
h. Suppose in (g) that *B* had negotiated the sale, *X* Corp. had planned to declare a dividend of the loss property so that *B* could execute the sale, but at the last moment, *X* Corp. decides to sell the property directly to *P* and to distribute the sales proceeds.

C. DISGUISED OR CONSTRUCTIVE DIVIDENDS

Dividend treatment is often an unattractive tax outcome for individual shareholders and their controlled corporations. Not only is the dividend taxable to the recipient as ordinary income (although often now at a preferential rate), but the distributing corporation does not get a deduction. Moreover, high-bracket shareholders who wish to transfer corporate funds to low-bracket relatives pay the income tax on the dividend and perhaps a gift tax on the transfer to the relative.

To avoid such unpleasantries, taxpayers often try to avoid dividend treatment while still pulling money out of corporate solution. Such attempts by taxpayers generally fall into two categories: (1) a distribution disguised as a deductible item to the distributing corporation even though it is taxable to the recipient, and (2) a distribution disguised as a nontaxable receipt for the recipient even though the corporation gets no deduction. Either category may be preferable to dividend characterization, which offers no deduction to the corporation and requires inclusion by the recipient. In a third category, which combines the first two, the corporation tries to deduct an expenditure while the shareholder excludes it.

The most common illustration of the first category is when a corporation pays excessive compensation to a shareholder-employee. If the corporation's characterization of the payment as compensation is successful, the payment generates a corporate deduction, even if it happens to be made to shareholders, because it is not a distribution "with respect to [the corporation's] stock" within the meaning of

§301(a). (The same is true for "excessive" interest and rental payments.) The stakes are nicely illustrated by the following passage from Mulcahy, Pauritsch, Salvador & Co., Ltd. v. Commissioner, 680 F.3d 867 (7th Cir. 2012):

> Corporate revenue paid as salary is deductible from corporate income and so is taxed only once, as income to the recipient, while revenue paid as a dividend is taxed at both the corporate and the personal level. Assume that corporate income is taxed at 34 percent, dividends at 15 percent, and personal income at 35 percent. If paid as a dividend, $100 of corporate income becomes $56.10 in the owner-employee's hands because the corporation pays a 34 percent tax on its income and then the owner-employee pays 15 percent on the $66 dividend, and $100 × .66 × .85 = $56.10. But if recharacterized as salary, the $100 in corporate income becomes $65.00 in the owner-employee's hands. The corporation would deduct the salary expense from its income, thus paying no tax on it; the owner-employee would pay a 35 percent tax; and $100 – (.35 × $100) is $65, which beats $56.10.

Section 162(a)(1) limits the compensation deduction to a "reasonable" allowance. In determining what is reasonable, courts generally have looked at a variety of factors, including the role of the recipient in the company, the comparative compensation of similarly situated employees of other companies, the character and condition of the company, the power of the recipient to control compensation levels, and internal consistency by the company (e.g., bonuses that are not part of a consistent program or that track the percentage of stock ownership may be suspect). For a discussion of these and other factors, see Elliots, Inc. v. Commissioner, 716 F.2d 1241 (9th Cir. 1983) (mere absence of dividend payments not conclusive as to whether compensation was "reasonable").

Corporate loans offer a common version of the second category. Loans produce no corporate deduction, but there is no shareholder inclusion. Predictably, the use of these and other techniques is limited only by the bounds of a taxpayer's imagination. Predictably, too, the Service will scrutinize transactions between shareholders and their closely held corporations to determine if the payment constitutes a "disguised" or "constructive" dividend.

The third category is illustrated by a corporation's payment of a shareholder's legal expenses in contesting a divorce that also threatened control of the business. See Dolese v. United States, 605 F.2d 1146 (10th Cir. 1979).

The cases and notes that follow offer a sampling of the litigation in the area of disguised or constructive dividends.[3] The recharacterization of a payment as a disguised dividend is by its nature a finding of fact, and examples abound in a wide variety of transactions. The following case — involving a bargain purchase — finds a constructive dividend, while the succeeding case — involving a service provided at cost — does not.

3. The term "constructive" dividend is a misnomer, since the shareholder receives an economic benefit from the corporation, even if the corporation makes a payment to another person.

Baumer v. United States

580 F.2d 863 (5th Cir. 1978)

Before Wisdom, Goldberg, and Rubin, Circuit Judges.

GOLDBERG, Circuit Judge.

This appeal presents a novel variation of the recurrent problem of determining the tax consequences of transactions between closely held corporations and their shareholders. Here a corporation granted an option to purchase a one-half interest in a parcel of real estate to the son of the corporation's sole shareholder for nominal consideration. In the proceedings below, the district court held that the grant of this option resulted in a constructive dividend from the corporation to the father, measured by the ascertainable value of the option. . . .

I. THE TRANSACTION

[The following fact statement appears in a later disposition of *Baumer* at 685 F.2d 1319-1320:

> On January 30, 1966, the Seven Eighty-Eight Greenwood Avenue Corporation (Corporation) contracted to purchase a parcel of residential property for $175,000. Erwin G. Baumer (Father) was the sole shareholder of Corporation. When Erwin H. Baumer (Son) learned of this transaction, he asked for an interest in the property and, in May, 1966, was given an option to purchase a one-half interest in the property. The term during which the option was exercisable was one year from its effective date and the exercise price was $88,000 plus five and one-half percent interest calculated from the effective date. In August, 1966, Corporation entered into a contract for the purchase of an adjacent piece of property for $25,000. Son was granted an amended option in January, 1967, which encompassed both properties. The exercise price for the new option was $100,000. The stated consideration for both options was $10, which Son did not recall having paid. Also in January, 1967, Corporation granted Pope & Carter Company, Inc. an option to purchase the properties for $500,000. In early December, 1968, Son exercised his option, giving a note to Corporation for $114,501.23, the entire option price [plus interest]. On December 27, 1968, Pope & Carter exercised its option. The sale by Son and Corporation to an assignee of Pope & Carter was closed on July 1, 1969. Son received $252,700 for his one-half interest in the properties.

The Commissioner determined that upon Son's exercise of his option in 1968, Father received a constructive dividend taxable to Father based on the difference between the exercise price of the option and the fair market value of the property. The Commissioner also determined that Son's gain on the sale of his one-half interest should be imputed to Corporation. The District Court ruled that imputation was not warranted.

The District Court determined that the option and its amendment were distributions of corporate property resulting in a constructive dividend to Father. The court assumed, without deciding, that the constructive dividend occurred when Son was granted the option in 1966 and at the time of its amendment in 1967, years not in issue in the proceedings. The District Court, however, found that the option had no ascertainable value at the time of its grant or its amendment. Therefore, under the open transaction doctrine of Burnet v. Logan 283 U.S. 404 (1931), the District

Court ruled that tax liability attached at the time the option was exercised in 1968. The court's valuation of the option was based on the consideration paid by Pope & Carter for [exercising] its option.]

II. Imputing Son's Income to Corporation

We first examine the government's contention that the sale by Corporation to Son of a one-half interest in the property immediately prior to the exercise of the Pope & Carter option was a sham transaction designed to shift half of Corporation's gain on that impending sale to Son. The government maintains that under the doctrine of Commissioner v. Court Holding Co., 324 U.S. 331 (1945), the district court should have taxed the Corporation on the entire gain from the sale to Pope & Carter. . . .

In the instant case, the district court concluded that the government's *Court Holding* theory was "inapplicable to the factual situation presented in this case," finding that the distribution of the option to Son occurred before a sale of the property was even contemplated, that Son was personally involved to a substantial extent in the development activity which led to the increased value of the Piedmont-Old Ivy properties, and that Son negotiated with Pope & Carter in his own behalf with respect to his interest in the properties. . . . Our review of the record convinces us that there is ample evidence to support the court's factual determinations. We therefore affirm the court's judgment that this transaction was not stricken by *Court Holding*'s selling virus.

In so holding we are not unaware of certain doubts raised by the government concerning the economic reality of the transactions between Corporation and Son. The government correctly notes that the corporation bore all the risks with respect to the zoning action, which was necessary to make the purchase a profitable venture. Son did not actually exercise his option and acquire title to the property until favorable zoning was obtained and the sale to Pope & Carter became a virtual certainty. Furthermore, Corporation actively participated in the negotiations with Pope & Carter which led to the sale of the Piedmont-Old Ivy properties. Son never expended a single cent on the transaction, either in acquiring the option or in exercising it. Indeed, the note Son gave Corporation as payment for the properties was modified shortly after its execution to allow a pass through to Corporation of Pope & Carter's payments to Son. The government further argues that, as a matter of law, the options granted by Corporation to Son were merely continuing offers to sell which did not transfer a present property interest to Son. Were this the case, no property interest would have been transferred from Corporation to Son until after the agreement with Pope & Carter was negotiated and virtually consummated by Corporation. To the extent Son participated in the negotiations before the sale from Father to Son, his activities would have been on behalf of Corporation since Son would have had no interest of his own. In such circumstances, a finding that the sale of Son's interest to Pope & Carter's assignee was made by Son, rather than by Corporation, would be difficult, if not impossible, to support. . . .

Nonetheless, there is other evidence in the record which supports the district court's findings and conclusions. . . . It is absurd to suggest that income may be imputed to the Corporation simply because it negotiated with third parties concerning this disposition *of its own interest* in the property. Instead, the crucial question becomes whether the Corporation "actively participated" in the sale of Son's share of the property. . . .

The court found that at the time the option was granted, Father and Son intended to use the property themselves "for a motel." This finding, supported by evidence in the record, indicates that no sale of the property was contemplated when Son received the property interest reflected by the option. This, in turn, supports the conclusion that the option was not merely a subterfuge designed to conceal Corporation's subsequent sale of the entire property, but instead was intended to pass an interest to Son which Son, and not Corporation, later disposed of in the sale to Pope & Carter.

The court's determination that Son, rather than Corporation, negotiated with respect to Son's interest in the property is further supported by evidence that Son was personally involved to a substantial extent in the development activity which led to the increased value of the properties. The district court found that these efforts were attributable to Son's belief that he had an interest in the property. The fact that Son had previously treated the option as constituting a personal property interest and had relied on this personal interest in developing the Piedmont-Old Ivy tracts strongly suggests that when Son later participated in the negotiations with Pope & Carter, he also did so in his own behalf. The prior treatment of a transaction by the parties is a relevant consideration, which in this case, supports the finding that Son, and not Corporation, negotiated with Pope & Carter with respect to Son's interest in the property.

In sum, we are not persuaded that the transactions at issue must necessarily be characterized as a sham, as less than bona fide, or as, "in substance," a sale by Corporation. . . . Accordingly, we affirm the court's decision not to impute income from that sale to Corporation under the *Court Holding* rationale.

III. The Option: Arm's-Length Transaction or Constructive Dividend?

Our conclusion that income from the sale of Son's interest in the Piedmont-Old Ivy property is not imputable to Corporation under *Court Holding* requires us to examine the government's alternative theory that the ascertainable value of property conferred by Corporation on Son without adequate consideration is taxable to Father as a constructive dividend. The district court substantially agreed with this theory and held that Father received a constructive dividend when Corporation granted the option to Son in 1966 and amended it in 1967. However, finding that the value of the option was not ascertainable in 1966 or 1967, the court deferred recognition of the dividend and liability for the tax until Son exercised his option in 1968. The court then valued the option with reference to the consideration paid by Pope & Carter for monthly extensions of its option.

Our review of the court's holding involves several distinct inquiries. In subsection III(A) we discuss why, as a general matter, the district court was correct in refusing to assume at once that a transaction between a corporation and the sole shareholder's son was an arm's-length transaction. We then consider in subsection III(B) whether constructive dividend treatment was warranted in this case. Finally, in subsection III(C) we examine the district court's valuation of the constructive dividend. . . .

A. JUDICIAL SCRUTINY OF TRANSACTIONS BETWEEN CLOSELY HELD CORPORATIONS AND THEIR SHAREHOLDERS: A GENERAL DISCUSSION

We begin by considering taxpayers' contention that the option to Son was granted by Corporation at a fair price in an arm's-length transaction. According to taxpayers, no tax consequences should attach either to the grant or to the exercise of the option. In taxpayers' view, Son's option should be treated no differently than the option granted to Pope & Carter. We conclude that this argument is untenable. In order to elucidate our views on the oft-perplexing problem of the conferral of benefits on a controlling shareholder by a closely held corporation, we begin with first principles.

Distributions of "property" made by a corporation to a shareholder with respect to its stock are dividends to the extent of the corporation's current and accumulated earnings and profits, . . . and must be included by the shareholder in gross income. [§§301(a), 301(c)(1), and 316].

In accordance with [the] broad definition of property, dividends may be "in cash or in kind, and may also result when the corporation makes a 'bargain sale' of its property to the shareholder at less than fair market value. When there is a 'bargain sale,' the shareholder receives a dividend in the amount of the difference between the fair market value and the price paid for the corporate property. . . ." Green v. United States, 460 F.2d 412, 419 (5th Cir. 1972). As the Supreme Court has recognized, "a sale, if for substantially less than the value of the property sold, may be as effective a means of distributing profits among stockholders as the formal declaration of a dividend." Palmer v. Commissioner, 302 U.S. 63 (1937). No such formal declaration is required for a shareholder to be charged with a constructive dividend. Crosby v. United States, 496 F.2d 1384 (5th Cir. 1974).

Two other guiding principles require mention at this stage. It is clear that the intent of the parties does not govern the characterization of a distribution. Instead, courts have looked to the economic *effect* of the transaction at issue in determining the existence of a dividend. It is also well settled that a dividend does not escape taxation "simply because it fails to pass through the hands of the particular taxpayer when . . . the dividend is diverted at the behest of the shareholder into the hands of others." Green v. United States, supra, 460 F.2d at 419, quoting Sammons v. United States, 433 F.2d 728, 730 (5th Cir. 1970), cert. denied, 402 U.S. 945 (1971). . . .

These expansive principles governing the treatment of constructive dividends reflect an awareness by Congress and the courts of the ingenious methods which have been devised by owners of closely held corporations trying to escape taxes at the corporate or shareholder level. . . . As a consequence, courts have generally examined dealings between a closely held corporation and its shareholders or relatives of shareholders with a jaundiced eye and microscopic vision. Such transactions are simply not entitled to the presumption that they are conducted at arm's length. Indeed, they call for special scrutiny. We suggest that the metaphor of a corporation and its sole shareholder walking arm-in-arm is more descriptive of reality than the vision of the corporation and shareholder holding each other apart at arm's length. . . .

B. THE GRANT OF THE OPTION AS A CONSTRUCTIVE DIVIDEND

Our inquiry is in two parts. First, we must focus on whether, in fact, the grant of the option conferred a benefit on Son by distributing valuable rights without consideration. If we determine that the option conferred such a benefit, we must then examine whether the resulting corporate distribution constituted a constructive dividend to Father. . . .

1. The Option: Valuable Rights or Fair Bargain?

Our initial task of valuing the option to determine whether the corporation distributed valuable rights to Son is greatly complicated by the unsettled state of the law in this area. Neither the Code nor the applicable case law provides clear guidance. Taxpayers maintain that under the Supreme Court's decision in Palmer v. Commissioner, 302 U.S. 63 (1937), there is no dividend if the exercise price of the option represents the fair market value of the underlying property at the time the option is issued, even if the value of the underlying property has appreciated greatly by the time the option is exercised. Taxpayers argue that the $100,000 exercise price of the option on the combined properties was a reasonable valuation of the fair market value of those properties at the time the option was granted to Son. Thus, according to taxpayers, no valuable rights constituting a dividend were distributed by Corporation.

The government responds first that taxpayer's argument rests on an erroneous reading of *Palmer*, and, second, that the 1954 Code has modified this aspect of the *Palmer* decision in any event. We agree with the government that the position contended for by taxpayers is justified neither by good sense nor by the applicable case law.

The Supreme Court's decision in *Palmer* has been a controversial one. In that case, a corporation distributed options, exercisable for 15 days, to its shareholders, entitling those shareholders to purchase from the corporation portfolio shares in a second corporation. On the date distribution of the option was authorized, the exercise price of the options equaled the market value of the portfolio shares. By the time the options were issued, eight days later, the market value of the portfolio shares had increased considerably.

The Court held first that under the Revenue Act of 1928, a shareholder who is granted an option to purchase portfolio shares is not subject to income tax on the receipt of the option, even though the option itself is valuable. "The mere issue of rights to subscribe and their receipt by stockholders, is not a dividend. No distribution of corporate assets or diminution of the net worth of the corporation results in any practical sense." 58 S. Ct. at 70. The Court then considered whether the shareholders would be taxable upon exercise of their option rights when a spread developed between the option price and the market value of the shares. The Court held that the exercise of these rights does not result in a dividend if the circumstances demonstrate "that distribution of corporate assets, effected by the sale, was not intended to be a means of distributing earnings, and that the price when fixed represented the fair market value of the property to be distributed." *Id.* at 71. Such a distribution "is not converted into a dividend by the mere circumstance that later, at the time of their delivery to the stockholders, [the assets] have a higher value." *Id.*

We recognize that this language appears to support taxpayers' contention that because the exercise price of Son's option equaled the fair market value of the property when the option was granted . . . , no dividend should result from either the grant or exercise of the option. The continuing vitality of this aspect of the *Palmer* decision under the 1954 Code, however, is far from self-evident. . . .

The 1954 Code . . . specifies the method for determining the value of a distribution. Under section 301(b)(1)(A), the amount of the distribution is measured by the *fair market value* of the property received. Thus, in the case at bar the amount of the distribution should be measured by the *fair market value* of the option, rather than by the spread between the exercise price and the value of the underlying property at the time of grant. . . . While that spread in some cases may approximate the fair market value of the option, here the duration of the option period and the likelihood of obtaining favorable rezoning must also be considered in determining the option's fair market value. . . . Thus the determination of whether the grant of the option conferred a benefit on Son is governed by the value of the option, rather than by the spread between the exercise price and the value of the underlying property.

Applying this standard, we are in complete agreement with the district court's finding that the rights granted under the option were of great value to Son. The option entitled Son to reap the benefits of the contemplated rezoning without incurring any of the risks associated with the real estate venture. He paid no consideration for his rights. If, during the two and one half year option period the properties appreciated in value, Son would realize a gain. If the value of the property decreased or remained the same, Son would be no worse off. Son was truly in a "heads I win, tails I don't lose" position. This "option privilege" represented valuable property to Son. . . .

Any doubts that Corporation distributed valuable rights to Son when it granted the option are dispelled by comparing Son's option with that received by Pope & Carter. Pope & Carter agreed to pay substantial amounts to keep its option open and, in addition, obligated itself to devote reasonable time and effort to obtaining favorable rezoning. In return it received the right to acquire the property for $500,000, a price far in excess of the fair market value of the property at the time the option was granted. Son's option, on the other hand, remained in effect for a longer period, imposed no obligations on Son, and allowed him to purchase a one-half interest in the property for only $100,000 plus 5 1/2 percent interest. Even if we ignore the fact that the amendment to Son's option, which extended the exercise period for an additional two years without increasing the exercise price, was granted a mere thirteen days before the grant of the Pope & Carter option . . . , it is apparent that in granting the option, Corporation conferred a benefit on Son by distributing valuable rights.

2. The Corporate Distribution: A Constructive Dividend?

Having concluded that Corporation distributed valuable rights to Son, we can easily dispose of taxpayers' contention that the grant of the option should not result in a constructive dividend to Father. . . .

Taxpayers maintain that the option was granted because of Corporation's interest in obtaining the benefit of Son's services. The evidence, however, more than adequately supports the conclusion that the grant of the option primarily served the personal interests of Father in his shareholder capacity. Indeed, taxpayers admit that the option was granted to satisfy the moral obligation of Father to compensate Son for taking advantage of a business opportunity Father had personally discouraged Son from pursuing. . . .

Since we hold that there is no clear error in the findings of the district court, we affirm the district court's conclusion that Father received a constructive dividend from the grant by Corporation to Son of the option on the Piedmont-Old Ivy property.

C. VALUING THE DIVIDEND

The final issue presented by this appeal is whether the district court properly valued Father's constructive dividend. In particular, questions have been raised concerning the district court's use of the consideration paid by Pope & Carter in valuing Son's option. To resolve this issue, we must first examine whether the dividend occurred upon the grant of the option or upon its exercise by Son. If we determine that *grant* of the option constituted a dividend, we must then consider both the district court's finding that the option had no ascertainable value at the time of grant and the Court's subsequent valuation of the option at the time of exercise in 1968. If, on the other hand, the dividend arose only upon Son's *exercise* of the option, we need only consider the proper valuation of the option at that time.

[The court ruled that the taxable event was the grant of the option but that since valuation was impossible at that time, the "open transaction" doctrine was appropriate. See Burnet v. Logan, 283 U.S. 404 (1931). However, the court rejected the district court's reliance on the value of the Pope & Carter option as evidence of the value of Son's option, because the options were different in duration, price, and required activity by the optionee.]

Thus in the instant case the option should be valued by subtracting the exercise price of approximately $100,000 from the fair market value of the underlying property when the option was exercised on December 6, 1968. . . . We therefore remand the case to the district court for a redetermination of the value of the constructive dividend taxable to Father.

IV. CONCLUSION

The concepts of imputed income and constructive dividend have been developed to prevent taxpayers from clothing their activities in tax-repellant garb. Both doctrines require courts to look behind the superficial or formal nature of a transaction. Application of these concepts in complicated tax cases involves the difficult task of characterizing elusive transactions. . . .

Here the district court found that Son, rather than Corporation, negotiated and consummated the sale of Son's interest in the Piedmont-Old Ivy property to Pope & Carter and therefore concluded that income from this sale should not be imputed to Corporation. The court also found that valuable rights were distributed by Corporation to Son without business purposes because of Father's position as the controlling shareholder of Corporation and therefore concluded that Father received a constructive dividend from Corporation. These factual determinations are supported by the record, and the court's ultimate conclusions rest on a correct application of the controlling law. These determinations are therefore affirmed. The court, however, failed to apply the proper standard for determining the value of Son's option at the time of exercise and therefore improperly computed the amount of Father's constructive dividend. Accordingly, this portion of the case must be remanded for further proceedings consistent with this opinion. The judgment of the district court is affirmed in part, reversed in part, and remanded in part.

Welle v. Commissioner

140 T.C. No. 19 (2013)

Marvel, Judge.

Respondent determined a deficiency of $10,620 in petitioners' Federal income tax and an accuracy-related penalty under section 6662(a) of $2,124 for 2006. The issues for decision are: (1) whether petitioner Terry J. Welle received a constructive dividend of $48,275 from his wholly owned subchapter C corporation, Terry Welle Construction, Inc. (TWC), in 2006; and (2) whether petitioners are liable for the accuracy-related penalty under section 6662(a).

Findings of Fact

. . . TWC is a construction company specializing in multifamily housing projects. For most jobs that closed during 2006 TWC had profit margins of 6% to 7%. Mr. Welle is the president and sole shareholder of TWC.

Petitioners owned lakefront property in Detroit Lakes, Minnesota, on which they planned to build a second home (lakefront home). In 2004 petitioners began construction of the lakefront home. To keep track of material and other construction costs, Mr. Welle caused TWC to open a "cost plus" job account on its books. Petitioners, however, personally contacted all of the subcontractors and building supply vendors that built or supplied materials for the lakefront home and acted as their own general contractors during its construction.

During the construction TWC paid the subcontractors and vendors directly, and its framing crew framed the lakefront home. Petitioners repaid TWC for all amounts paid to the subcontractors and also reimbursed TWC for its labor and overhead costs. TWC, however, did not charge petitioners, and petitioners did not pay to TWC, an amount equal to the customary profit margin that TWC used to calculate the contract price that it charged its unrelated clients (forgone profit).

Respondent determined that Mr. Welle received a qualified dividend of $48,275 from TWC in 2006, equal to the forgone profit.

Opinion

Respondent contends that Mr. Welle received a constructive dividend from TWC when TWC built petitioners' lakefront home without charging them an amount equal to its customary profit margin of 6% to 7%.

Petitioners contend that (1) Mr. Welle did not receive a constructive dividend because a shareholder does not receive a constructive dividend when a corporation provides services to the shareholder at cost; and (2) respondent's determination of the measure of any constructive dividend that Mr. Welle may have received was erroneous because the services that TWC provided to Mr. Welle were not comparable to the services that it provided to its unrelated clients. Because we decide on this record that Mr. Welle did not receive a constructive dividend, we need not address petitioners' second contention.

I. CONSTRUCTIVE DIVIDENDS GENERALLY

Section 61(a)(7) includes dividends in a taxpayer's gross income. Section 316(a) defines a dividend as any distribution of property that a corporation makes to its shareholders out of its earnings and profits accumulated after February 28, 1913, or out of its earnings and profits for the taxable year. Section 317(a) defines property as money, securities, and any other property except stock in the distributing corporation. We have held that, under some circumstances, the provision of services by a corporation to its shareholders constitutes "property" within the meaning of section 317(a). See Magnon v. Commissioner, 73 T.C. 980, 993 (1980) (citing Loftin & Woodard, Inc. v. United States, 577 F.2d 1206, 1214 (5th Cir. 1978), and Benes v. Commissioner, 42 T.C. 358, 379 (1964), aff'd, 355 F.2d 929 (6th Cir. 1966)).

"A constructive dividend arises '[w]here a corporation confers an economic benefit on a shareholder without the expectation of repayment, * * * even though neither the corporation nor the shareholder intended a dividend.' [citation omitted] The crucial concept in a finding that there is a constructive dividend is that the corporation has conferred a benefit on the shareholder in order to distribute available earnings and profits without expectation of repayment." Truesdell v. Commissioner, 89 T.C. 1280, 1295 (1987) (quoting Noble v. Commissioner, 368 F.2d 439, 443 (9th Cir. 1966), *aff'g* T.C. Memo. 1965-84. . . .

Where a corporation constructively distributes property to a shareholder, the constructive dividend received by the shareholder is ordinarily measured by the fair market value of the benefit conferred. . . . However, where fair market value cannot be reliably ascertained or there is evidence that fair market value is an inappropriate mode of measurement, the constructive dividend can be measured by the cost to the corporation of the benefit conferred. . . .

The Code does not define the term "earnings and profits." See sec. 316(a). . . . As we have previously observed, the calculation of earnings and profits is not easy or obvious. . . . For example, although section 1.312-6, Income Tax Regs., provides that a corporation must compute earnings and profits using the same method of accounting employed in computing taxable income, earnings and profits are not equivalent to taxable income. . . . The reason for this distinction is that earnings and profits is a broad concept "which the tax law has utilized 'to approximate a corporation's power to make distributions which are more than just a return of investment." Henry C. Beck Co. v. Commissioner, 52 T.C. at 6 (quoting Arthur R. Albrecht, *Dividends' and 'Earnings or Profits,* 7 Tax L. Rev. 157, 183 (1952)).

II. SERVICES PROVIDED BY A CORPORATION TO A SHAREHOLDER AT COST

Respondent contends that Magnon v. Commissioner, 73 T.C. 980, stands for the proposition that a shareholder receives a constructive dividend equal to the cost of the services provided to the shareholder by a corporation plus the corporation's customary profit margin. In Magnon v. Commissioner, 73 T.C. at 994-996, we held that the amount of the costs and overhead for electrical services provided by a corporation to a shareholder without expectation of repayment was a constructive dividend. But we did not hold, and the Commissioner did not assert, that the constructive dividend the shareholder received included an amount corresponding to the corporation's forgone profit.

Similarly, in [other] cases . . . , we held that amounts expended by the respective corporations in constructing homes for their shareholders constituted constructive dividends. But we did not hold, and the Commissioner did not assert, that the constructive dividends in those cases each included an amount corresponding to the respective corporations' forgone profit.

Respondent does not explain how a corporation's decision not to make a profit on services provided to a shareholder who fully reimburses the corporation for the cost of the services (including overhead) constitutes a distribution of property that reduces the corporation's earnings and profits under section 316(a), nor does respondent cite any cases supporting such a position. Respondent argues that his position follows from the general rule that constructive dividends are ordinarily measured by the fair market value of the benefit conferred. See *Ireland,* 621 F.2d at 737; Melvin v. Commissioner, 88 T.C. at 80-81. It appears to us, however, that respondent's argument skips an important analytical step required by section 316(a)—we must first find that there has been a distribution of property to the shareholder that reduces the corporation's current or accumulated earnings and profits. A finding that a shareholder received a constructive dividend from a corporation is only appropriate where "corporate assets are diverted to or for the benefit of a shareholder [citation omitted] in order to distribute available earnings and profits without expectation of repayment[.]" Truesdell v. Commissioner, 89 T.C. at 1295. . . .

We cannot see how TWC's provision of services to Mr. Welle at cost resulted in the diversion of corporate assets or the distribution of its earnings and profits. Moreover, we do not think that TWC's provision of services to Mr. Welle at cost was "in purpose or effect * * * an implement for the distribution of corporate earnings" and profits. See Palmer v. Commissioner, 302 U.S. at 70.

By contrast, in cases involving the bargain sale of property to a shareholder, we have held that the shareholder receives a constructive dividend equal to the excess of the fair market value over the sale price, . . . because the property being sold is an asset of the corporation and its sale for less than fair market value diverts actual value otherwise available to the corporation to or for the benefit of a shareholder. . . . Similarly, we have held that, where a corporation provides a shareholder with the use of corporate property and the shareholder does not fully and reasonably reimburse the corporation for its use, the shareholder has received a constructive dividend equal to the fair market value of the use of the property. See Melvin v. Commissioner, 88 T.C. at 80-81. In *Melvin,* however, we observed that incidental or insignificant use of corporate property may not justify a finding of a constructive dividend . . . and we specifically found that the taxpayer's personal use of the property was not incidental to the taxpayer's business use of the property[.] Melvin v. Commissioner, 88 T.C. at 82-83.

TWC maintained its corporate infrastucture and workforce for business purposes. Mr. Welle's use of TWC during the construction of petitioners' lakefront home was at most incidental to those purposes. The most that can be said about Mr. Welle's use of TWC is that he used the corporation as a conduit in paying subcontractors and vendors and that he obtained some limited services from corporate employees. Mr. Welle fully reimbursed the corporation for all costs, including overhead, associated with those services, and TWC did not divert actual value otherwise available to it by failing to apply its customary profit margin in determining the amount Mr. Welle had to reimburse the corporation.

We therefore conclude that this arrangement did not operate as a vehicle for the distribution of TWC's current or accumulated earnings and profits within the meaning of section 316(a).

III. CONCLUSION

We hold that Mr. Welle did not receive constructive dividend income when TWC provided services to him at cost and for which he timely paid. Accordingly, we do not sustain respondent's deficiency determination, and we thus need not decide whether an accuracy-related penalty under section 6662(a) would be appropriate. . . .

Decision will be entered for petitioners.

NOTES

1. *Shareholders' loans that may not be bona fide.* In Jaques v. Commissioner, 935 F.2d 104 (6th Cir. 1991), the taxpayer claimed that the proceeds received from the corporation were a loan that he intended to repay. The Tax Court found a dividend for federal tax purposes even though under state law no dividend distribution was permitted. Conversely, in Rev. Rul. 90-11, 1990-1 C.B. 10, the Service ruled that the adoption of a "poison pill" plan did not constitute a dividend for federal tax purposes even though the adoption of a plan was a dividend under state law.

In *Jaques*, the taxpayer did not repay the purported loans. Would repayment be conclusive proof that a loan was made? See Crowley v. Commissioner, 962 F.2d 1077 (1st Cir. 1992) (withdrawals by a minority shareholder treated as constructive dividend rather than a loan because of unrestricted withdrawal privilege, even though some repayments were made).

In Alterman Foods v. United States, 611 F.2d 866 (Cl. Ct. 1979), a corporate parent was saddled with dividend treatment on "advances" from its subsidiaries. Under the then applicable version of §243, the taxpayer was taxable on 15 percent of the constructive dividends. Among the factors relied on by the court were the paucity of historical dividends despite strong earnings and profits; the lack of a specified interest rate, promissory note, limit on the advances, or collateral; and a pattern of "advances" with no repayment from 57 subsidiaries. Compare Tollefsen v. Commissioner, 431 F.2d 511 (2d Cir. 1970), in which advances by a subsidiary to the controlling shareholder of the parent were treated as a dividend by the parent to the shareholder and not as a bona fide loan, with Gilbert v. Commissioner, 552 F.2d 478 (2d Cir. 1977), in which a bona fide loan from the corporation to shareholder was found because the shareholder had a clear intent to repay and promptly assigned assets sufficient to secure the amounts owed.

2. *Shareholders' loans with below-market interest rates.* Even bona fide loans to shareholders may result in disguised dividends if the loans bear no or inadequate interest. Suppose a corporation makes a bona fide loan to its shareholder but charges no interest.[4] In Dean v. Commissioner, 35 T.C. 1083 (1961), the court found no income to the borrower because any imputed income would be offset

4. The fact that there is no interest may count against "loan" characterization, but it is not conclusive. Thus, a "no-interest loan" is not a self-contradictory phenomenon.

with an interest deduction, but §7872 substantially alters the *Dean* rule. When the loan is a demand loan, the shareholder-borrower is deemed to have received a dividend of imputed interest, which in turn is repaid to the corporation-lender. For the borrower, there may be a wash if the interest is deductible. But see §265. Also consider §163(h), which denies a deduction in many instances for interest incurred for personal rather than business or investment purposes. For the lender, the dividend is not deductible, but the deemed interest received must be included in income each year the loan is outstanding.

If the loan is a term loan, the shareholder-borrower will be deemed to have received the difference between the loan principal and the present value of the payments due under the loan as a dividend. In accordance with the original issue discount rules of §§1271-1273, the borrower may be entitled to deduct the imputed interest over the term of the loan. The mirror image governs the corporation-lender. It is deemed to have made a dividend payment in the first year and to receive taxable interest payments over the life of the loan.

3. *Provision of services at cost. Welle* concluded that the sole shareholder (Welle) of a corporation (TWC) did not receive a constructive distribution when TWC provided Welle with services and Welle paid TWC's out-of-pocket costs, because TWC diverted no assets in providing the services.[5] That conclusion is inconsistent with §7872. As described in the previous note, under §7872, a corporation is treated as making a distribution to a shareholder when it makes an interest-free loan to the shareholder, even though the loan diverts no corporate assets. The lender does, however, relinquish any right to interest income (i.e., profit on the loan), just as a corporation, in providing services at cost, relinquishes any right to profits on those services. To be consistent with §7872, should Welle have been treated as receiving a constructive distribution (and TWC have been treated as receiving a payment equal to the distribution)?

The Tax Court in *Welle* was unable to find a "distribution" to the taxpayer when the corporation performed services for its shareholder and charged less than the fair market value of the services provided. This should remind you of the dissent of Judge Friendly in *Divine.* In that case, compensation was paid in the form of restricted stock, and the issue was what effect such a distribution should have on the corporation's earnings and profits. Judge Friendly in *Divine,* like Judge Marvel in *Welle,* could not find any reduction in the corporation's assets. Were you persuaded by this argument in *Divine*? Are you persuaded in *Welle*? If the shareholder in Welle had paid nothing for the corporation's services, the amount of the constructive dividend would have been the fair market value of the services provided by the corporation. If the shareholder pays less than fair market value for those services, how can there not be a constructive dividend equal to the excess of the fair market value of the services over the amount paid?

Assume that Welle is correct. By paying for just the cost of the services, Welle may have received an economic benefit (i.e., the excess of the value of those services over their cost). Cf. §132(a)(2) (providing for an exclusion of a qualified employee discount from gross income, implying that the discount may provide an economic benefit). If he did, should he have gross income equal to the value of that benefit?

5. In a similar vein, courts have been reluctant to assign income from a corporation to a shareholder who works for the corporation, arguably allowing a shareholder to shift income to the corporation. See page 516 infra.

See Commissioner v. Glenshaw Glass Co., 348 U.S. 426 (1955). Is there any provision in the Code that would exclude the value of that benefit from gross income? What would the character of any income be?

Finally, how confident are you that the payment made by Welle fully accounted for the cost of the services? For example, did it account for the benefit of TWC's workforce-in-place? Did it account for the decline in value of TWC's assets used to construct the lakefront property? On the other hand, could the Commissioner's litigating position have been correct when the Welles, in their personal capacities, appeared to act as general contractor for the construction?

4. *Bargain sale or purchase between corporation and shareholder.* A shareholder may also receive a disguised dividend if the shareholder makes a bargain purchase from the corporation (as *Baumer* illustrates) or makes an inflated sale to the corporation. The shareholder's dividend amount should equal the difference between the values of the property received and transferred, and the same rule should apply to corporate and noncorporate shareholders, despite outdated regulatory language that could be read to the contrary. See Treas. Regs. §1.301-1(j). The bargain purchase in *Baumer* was the purchase for $10 (which may never have been paid) of an option worth more than $10. How much more?

Suppose someone offers to sell you an option to buy property that has a fair market value of $100. The option has an exercise price of $70 and has a duration of five minutes. Chances are you will pay up to $30 for the option. Suppose, instead, that the exercise price is $100. You would probably pay nothing for this option, because it would cost you $100 if you chose to exercise it. In Palmer v. Commissioner, 302 U.S. 63, 71 (1937), the Supreme Court broadly stated, "The mere issue of rights to subscribe and their receipt by stockholders, is not a dividend." The court also ruled that the later exercise of the option when the property had appreciated in value was not a dividend. In *Palmer*, there was no spread between exercise price and fair market value of the property at the time the option was issued. Moreover, the option period was only 15 days. *Palmer* was limited to its facts by Commissioner v. Gordon, 391 U.S. 83, 90 n.4 (1968), in which the Court stated, "It has not . . . been authoritatively settled whether an issue of rights to purchase at less than fair market value itself constitutes a dividend, or the dividend occurs on the actual purchase." In Redding v. Commissioner, 630 F.2d 1169, 1182 (7th Cir. 1980), the court ruled that *Palmer* had been overruled by the enactment in 1954 of the "corporate distribution provisions as a whole" in circumstances in which there was a spread when the option was granted.

Suppose instead that there is no spread between the exercise price and the fair market value of the property, but the duration of the option is more than two years — the *Baumer* situation. Now is the option worth something? Suppose you pay $20 for the option. If the property decreases in value, you will not exercise the option and will not recoup your $20. If the property increases in value — say, to $200 — you will pay the $100 exercise price, ending up with an $80 profit. The longer the option period, the more valuable the option is, because of the increased likelihood that the optioned property will increase in value over that period. Is anything left of *Palmer* after *Redding* and *Baumer*?

In *Baumer*, why wasn't the option taxable to the shareholder when issued rather than when exercised? On remand the district court concluded that the option should be taxed in the year of receipt. This conclusion meant victory for the taxpayer because that year was not before the court. 518 F. Supp. 813 (N.D. Ga. 1981).

The taxpayer's celebration was short-lived as the court of appeals again reversed, holding that the law of the case dictated the use of the open transaction method. The district court was directed to find a dividend in the amount by which the fair market value at the time of exercise exceeded the exercise price. 685 F.2d 1318 (11th Cir. 1982). This reversal by the Eleventh Circuit is limited to the law of the case and does not suggest that in future cases the dividend consequences won't be determined in the year in which the option is granted if valuation is possible. See generally Jassy, Dividend Treatment of Distributions of Options to Acquire Assets of the Distributing Corporation, 34 Tax L. Rev. 607 (1979).

If *Baumer* had been decided under current law, would the distributing corporation have been taxed on the distribution of the option? See §311(b). If the distributing corporation should be taxed, when should it be taxed? How and when should the earnings and profits account be adjusted? In light of §311(b), would the Service need to rely on the *Court Holding Co.* doctrine? In Martin Ice Cream Co. v. Commissioner, 110 T.C. 189 (1998), the court refused to attribute a shareholder sale to the corporation under the *Court Holding Co.* doctrine, but found the corporation taxable under §311(b) on the distribution of the appreciated property to the shareholder.

Note that in *Baumer* the father was taxed even though the option was granted to the son. In Green v. United States, 460 F.2d 412 (5th Cir. 1972), a bargain element in a sale to the children of a shareholder-officer was held taxable to him even though he was a minority shareholder because he exerted substantial influence over the transaction.

Honigman v. Commissioner, 466 F.2d 69 (5th Cir. 1972), serves as a reminder that shareholders dealing with closely held corporations tread on dangerous ground. There, a shareholder was taxed on the difference between the actual purchase price and the court-determined fair market value on the corporation's purported sale of a deteriorating hotel to the shareholder. At trial, evidence was introduced that there was no other buyer, the purchasing shareholder was not in control of the corporation, and there was a valid business reason for the sale. The shareholder nevertheless was treated as receiving a disguised dividend because of the bargain purchase.

The flipside of the bargain purchase is the inflated sale to a controlled corporation. For example, if a sole shareholder of a corporation sells property worth $20,000 to the corporation for $70,000, the corporation may be deemed to make a $50,000 distribution to the shareholder.

5. *Transfers between commonly controlled corporations.* How should transfers for less than full consideration between commonly controlled corporations be treated? Suppose *A* owns all the stock of *X* Corp. and *Y* Corp. If *X* Corp. makes a purported loan to *Y* Corp. in circumstances suggesting that the funds are not to be repaid, how should the transaction be treated? Because *Y* Corp. owns no stock of *X* Corp., the transfer does not seem to be a distribution by *X* Corp. "with respect to its stock" to *Y* Corp. Instead, when transfers between commonly controlled corporations are recharacterized, there is a deemed distribution to the shareholder from one corporation followed by a deemed contribution of the property or cash by the shareholder to the other corporation. See Rev. Rul. 78-83, 1978-1 C.B. 79 (applying this characterization where a domestic corporation owned all stock of two foreign subsidiaries and one subsidiary transferred money to the other subsidiary). The analysis in *Gilbert* is typical of these cases. Often the court will first determine

whether there was a bona fide intercorporate loan. If not, the court will ask the extent to which the intercorporate contribution to capital had a business purpose or promoted the taxpayer's personal goals.

Compare Sammons v. Commissioner, 472 F.2d 449 (5th Cir. 1972) (concluding that a transfer by a parent corporation of funds to its nearly insolvent subsidiary so that the subsidiary could pay off the debt owed to the parent's controlling shareholder was a dividend to the shareholder because the purpose was to benefit the shareholder rather than the transferor) with Rapid Electric Co. v. Commissioner, 61 T.C. 232 (1974) (concluding that the extension of credit between two commonly owned corporations was held not a dividend to the sole shareholder because the transfer benefited the transferor corporation).

In Stinnett's Pontiac Service v. Commissioner, 730 F.2d 634 (11th Cir. 1984), the court found that a purported intercorporate loan from an automobile dealership to a Bahamian corporation constituted a constructive dividend to the common shareholder. The loan was unsecured and subordinated and had no terms of repayment. Furthermore, the court could discern no corporate purpose behind the loan. See also Sparks Nugget, Inc. v. Commissioner, 458 F.2d 631 (9th Cir. 1972) (excessive rent paid between commonly controlled corporations taxable to controlling shareholder).

6. *Unreasonable salaries or fees.* The allowance for a reasonable salary deduction under §162 has been interpreted by the Service and the courts to disallow, by inference, a deduction for any portion of salaries deemed excessive. Such excessive salaries may be reclassified as dividends if, as is often the case, the employee is also a shareholder and there are sufficient earnings and profits. See Mulcahy, Pauritsch, Salvador & Co., Ltd. v. Commissioner, 680 F.3d 867 (7th Cir. 2012) (in an entertaining case, concluding that "consulting fees" paid to owners of an accounting firm were disguised dividends).

What happens if there are insufficient earnings and profits? See Note 9 infra. In Charles McCandless Tile Service v. United States, 422 F.2d 1336 (Cl. Ct. 1970), the Court of Claims found that even reasonable salaries could be reclassified as dividends if the distributing corporation was profitable and had not made dividend distributions. In Laure v. Commissioner, 70 T.C. 1087 (1978), the Tax Court rejected the *McCandless* reasoning and upheld a large salary deduction even in the absence of dividends for an 18-year period. See also Rev. Rul. 79-8, 1979-1 C.B. 92 (insubstantial dividends alone do not cause denial of §162 deduction); Elliots, Inc. v. Commissioner, 716 F.2d 1241 (9th Cir. 1983) (*McCandless* rejected).

Shareholders sometimes contractually commit themselves to repay amounts deemed excessive by the Service. Their hope is that if the salary is held to be a dividend, the repayment of such amounts to the corporation will be a business expense deduction covered by §162. In Oswald v. Commissioner, 49 T.C. 645 (1976), under a corporate bylaw, a shareholder-officer was so obligated and was permitted a deduction. But in Pahl v. Commissioner, 67 T.C. 286 (1976), there was no *Oswald* contract provision requiring repayment; the excess salary was deemed a disguised dividend, and the repayment was labeled a capital contribution increasing basis.

Sometimes corporations try to use fee payments, rather than salaries, in lieu of dividends to distribute earnings in a manner that provides a §162 deduction. In Tulia Feedlot v. United States, 513 F.2d 800 (5th Cir. 1975), a corporation paid its directors a fee for guaranteeing a corporate loan; the guarantees were made by the director-shareholders in proportion to their stock ownership. The Court held this to be a constructive dividend, nondeductible by the corporation because no evidence was presented to show guarantors' fees were customary in the trade or that the fees were reasonable in amount. See also Olton Feed Yard v. United States, 592 F.2d 272 (5th Cir. 1979) (same result). In a later year and in a different jurisdiction, however, the same company prevailed when the fees were shown to be customary and were paid in proportion to the guarantees rather than the amount of stock owned. Tulia Feedlot v. United States, 52 A.F.T.R.2d 5702 (Cl. Ct. 1983).

7. *Corporate payment of expenses incurred to benefit the stockholder rather than the corporation.* Sometimes a controlling shareholder will cause a corporation to pay his personal expenses in the hope that the corporation can deduct what the shareholder cannot. In these situations, the courts look to see if the payment benefits "primarily" the corporation or the taxpayer. If the payment primarily benefits the shareholder, it may be treated as a nondeductible disguised dividend. For example, in American Properties v. Commissioner, 262 F.2d 150 (9th Cir. 1958), the court held that the expenses of designing, constructing, and racing speed boats, paid by a corporation with one shareholder, were not deductible under §162(a) by the corporation and constituted disguised dividends to the sole shareholder, who "had an insatiable desire for speed." In Magnon v. Commissioner, 73 T.C. 980 (1980), the sole shareholder received a constructive dividend when the corporation performed electrical contracting services on the shareholder's personal property.

In Dolese v. United States, 605 F.2d 1146 (10th Cir. 1979), payments by a corporation for legal fees and expenses in connection with a divorce of its sole shareholder were deemed constructive dividends. Those payments incurred to fight divorce proceedings that interrupted corporate business were, however, treated as a deductible expense by the corporation with no dividend treatment to the shareholder. But see Jack's Maintenance Contractors v. Commissioner, 703 F.2d 154 (5th Cir. 1983) (dividend to shareholder where corporation incurred legal expenses in defending shareholder against criminal tax evasion charges; benefit to shareholder far outweighed benefit to corporation).

When a court finds a constructive dividend, what is the measure of inclusion? See Ireland v. United States, 621 F.2d 731 (5th Cir. 1980) (amount of dividend from personal use of company plane based on private charter fare, not cost of operation). Cf. Treas. Regs. §1.61-21(b)(6) and (7) (providing that the value to an employee of an employer-provided noncommercial flight is based on arm's-length price unless the special valuation rule is used); *id.* at (g) (for the special valuation rule).

8. *Excessive compensation paid to the relatives of shareholders.* Section 162(a)(2) allows a corporation to deduct "a reasonable allowance for salaries or other compensation for personal services actually rendered." Suppose *X* Corp. is a family-owned corporation whose shareholders are Mom and Pop and *X* Corp. compensates Son and Daughter as though they were full-time employees when in fact they perform only minor services for the corporation during vacations. Why might the family choose to disperse corporate earnings in this fashion? How should the payments be treated? In this and similar cases, the transaction will be recharacterized as a dividend payment to Mom or Pop or both, followed by a gift from the shareholder(s) to Son and Daughter. See, e.g., Duffey v. Lethert, 316 F.2d 473 (D. Minn. 1963) (corporate "compensation" to sister of shareholder treated as dividend to shareholder when sister performed only occasional services). Note that in addition to possible dividend treatment, shareholders may have to file a gift tax return and pay a gift tax on the deemed gift.

Should the corporation or shareholders that participate in the diversion of corporate assets to nonworking employees be subject to civil or criminal fraud penalties? Does it matter if the corporation is wholly owned by the shareholders causing the diversion or whether there are outside shareholders?

9. *Constructive dividends and earnings and profits.* Suppose a taxpayer diverts corporate funds for personal use. Normally, there would be dividend consequences to the shareholder. But what is the result if the corporation has no current or accumulated earnings and profits? In Truesdell v. Commissioner, 89 T.C. 1280 (1987), the taxpayer's withdrawals from the corporation were treated by the Tax Court as constructive distributions. But in the absence of earnings and profits, the distributions were not taxable to the taxpayer. The court in *Truesdell* distinguished a nontaxable diversion from an *unlawful* diversion that is taxable regardless of the earnings and profits account. See, e.g., Leaf v. Commissioner, 33 T.C. 1093 (1960), aff'd per curiam, 295 F.2d 503 (6th Cir. 1961).

In Di Zenzo v. Commissioner, 348 F.2d 122 (2d Cir. 1965), the court ruled that the taxpayer (the sole shareholder) had no dividend and no §61 income in the absence of earnings and profits. See also Simon v. Commissioner, 248 F.2d 869 (8th Cir. 1957). For a holding to the contrary, see United States v. Miller, 545 F.2d 1204 (9th Cir 1976), in which the existence of earnings and profits was held not necessary in criminal fraud proceedings against taxpayer (not the sole shareholder) diverting corporate monies to himself. Can the cases be distinguished on the basis of whether funds were unlawfully diverted from another person, either another shareholder or a creditor? When a sole shareholder diverts funds from a corporation with no earnings and profits, who is the victim so long as no obligation to a creditor is breached? How is the shareholder enriched?

In Hagaman v. Commissioner, 958 F.2d 684 (6th Cir. 1992), the court affirmed the Tax Court's determination that a corporation should reduce its accumulated earnings and profits by the amount of constructive dividends deemed paid to the shareholders. The constructive dividends consisted of the fraudulent diversion of vending machine receipts and rental payments.

PROBLEMS

4-4. *T* is a shareholder of *X* Corp., a "start up" company producing computer software. In its early years, *X* Corp. experienced large research and development expenses. *X* Corp. makes an interest-free loan of $100,000 to *T*, its sole shareholder, payable on demand by *X* Corp. Discuss the tax consequences to both *X* Corp. and *T*.

4-5. *X* Corp., with a $5,000 earnings and profits deficit in year 1, issues to *B*, a shareholder, an option to buy a parcel of real estate at a price of $1,000, the property's fair market value and basis. The option has a three-year duration. In year 3, *B* exercises the option. At the time of exercise, the real estate had a fair market value of $3,000. Without accounting for *B*'s option exercise, *X* Corp. has no accumulated earnings and profits at the end of year 2 and no current earnings and profits in year 3. Discuss the tax consequences.

4-6. *A* owns all the stock in *X* Corp. and *Y* Corp. Each corporation runs a restaurant. *X* Corp. makes a $100,000 loan to *Y* Corp. Discuss the tax consequences.

4-7. *X* Corp. rents land from *A*, its sole shareholder, at an annual rental of $2,400, the fair rental value. The lease has a 10-year duration, and there are no renewal options. In year 5, *X* Corp. constructs a building on the property at a cost to *X* Corp. of $50,000. The building has a 20-year useful life, and the lease provides that all improvements made by the lessee revert to the lessor at the termination of the lease. At the end of the lease term, *A* enters into another lease with *X* Corp. at an annual rental of $3,600, the fair rental value for land and building. Is there a constructive dividend? When? Consider the applicability of §§109 and 1019. See Safeway Steel Scaffolds Co. v. United States, 590 F.2d 1360 (5th Cir. 1979).

D. INTERCORPORATE DIVIDENDS

If a corporate shareholder receives a dividend from a domestic corporation, it is entitled to a deduction of 70, 80, or 100 percent of the dividend received. See page 118 supra. But if the corporation simply sells the stock of that corporation at a gain, it includes the full amount of that gain in gross income and thus may be fully taxed on that gain. To minimize that tax, could the seller have the corporation distribute a dividend as a prelude to the sale?

Litton Industries, Inc. v. Commissioner

89 T.C. 1086 (1987)

Clapp, Judge.

Respondent determined a deficiency in petitioner's Federal corporate income tax for the year ended July 29, 1973 in the amount of $11,583,054. After concessions, the issue for decision is whether Litton Industries received a $30,000,000 dividend from Stouffer Corporation, its wholly owned subsidiary, or whether that sum represented proceeds from the sale of Stouffer stock to Nestle Corporation.

Findings of Fact

. . . On October 4, 1967, petitioner acquired all the outstanding stock of Stouffer Corporation (Stouffer), a corporation whose common stock was listed and traded on the New York stock exchange. Stouffer manufactured and sold frozen prepared food and operated hotels and food management services and restaurants. . . .

In early 1972, Charles B. Thornton (Thornton), the chairman of Litton's board of directors, Joseph Imirie, president of Stouffer, and James Biggar, an executive of Stouffer, discussed project "T.I.B.," i.e., the sale of Stouffer. In July 1972, Litton's board of directors discussed the mechanics and problems of selling Stouffer. As of August 1, 1972 Stouffer's accumulated earnings and profits exceeded $30,000,000. On August 23, 1972, Stouffer declared a $30,000,000 dividend which it paid to Litton in the form of a $30,000,000 negotiable promissory note, and at that time, Thornton believed that Litton would have no difficulty in receiving an adequate offer for Stouffer. Two weeks later, on September 7, 1972, petitioner announced publicly its interest in disposing of Stouffer. Subsequent to said announcement, Litton received inquiries from a number of interested sources, including TWA, Green Giant, investment banking houses, and business brokers about the possible purchase of all or part of the Stouffer business.

Beginning in mid-September 1972, Litton and several underwriters discussed the feasibility of a public offering of Stouffer Stock. In early September 1972, Litton negotiated with Lehman Brothers for a public offering of Stouffer stock, but Lehman Brothers decided not to participate in the offering. During October 1972, Litton, Stouffer and Merrill Lynch, a brokerage firm that thought Stouffer had an excellent outlook, prepared a public offering of Stouffer stock. During November 1972, petitioner, Stouffer, and Hornblower and Weeks prepared a partial public offering of Stouffer stock. Merrill Lynch had a policy of not effecting partial distributions of corporate subsidiaries and thus did not participate in the negotiations with Hornblower and Weeks. In mid-December 1972, Litton decided that a complete public offering was preferable and abandoned the idea of a partial public offering. The S-1 Registration Statement, which Stouffer filed with the Securities and Exchange Commission, stated that $30,000,000 of the proceeds would be used to pay the promissory note which Litton received as a dividend.

On March 1, 1973, Nestle Alimentana S.A. Corporation (Nestle), a Swiss corporation, offered to buy all of Stouffer's stock for $105,000,000. On March 5, 1973, Nestle paid Litton $74,962,518 in cash for all the outstanding stock of Stouffer and $30,000,000 in cash for the promissory note. Because Litton sold Stouffer to Nestle, the underwriters stopped work on the scheduled public offering.

Opinion

The issue for decision is whether the $30,000,000 dividend declared by Stouffer on August 23, 1972, and paid to its parent, Litton, by means of a negotiable promissory note was truly a dividend for tax purposes or whether it should be considered part of the proceeds received by Litton from the sale of all of Stouffer's stock on March 1, 1973. If, as petitioner contends, the $30,000,000 constitutes a dividend, petitioner may deduct 85 percent of that amount as a dividend received [deduction] pursuant to section 243(a), as that section read during the year at issue. However, if the $30,000,000 represents part of the selling price of the Stouffer stock, as contended by respondent, the entire amount will be added to the proceeds of the sale and taxed to Litton as additional capital gain. Respondent's approach, of course produces the larger amount of tax dollars.

The instant case is substantially governed by Waterman Steamship Corp. v. Commissioner, 50 T.C. 650 (1968), rev'd 430 F.2d 1185 (5th Cir. 1970), cert. denied 401 U.S. 939 (1971). Respondent urges us to follow the opinion of the Fifth Circuit, which in substance adopted the position of Judge Tannenwald's dissent (concurred in by three other judges) from our Court-reviewed opinion. If we hold for respondent, we must overrule our majority opinion in *Waterman Steamship*. Petitioner contends that the reasoning of the Fifth Circuit in *Waterman Steamship* should not apply since the facts here are more favorable to petitioner. Additionally, petitioner points out that several business purposes were served by the distribution here which provide additional support for recognition of the distribution as a dividend. For the reasons set forth below, we conclude that the $30,000,000 distribution constituted a dividend which should be recognized as such for tax purposes. We believe that the facts in the instant case lead even more strongly than did the facts in *Waterman Steamship* to the conclusion that the $30,000,000 was a dividend.

Accordingly, we hold that the Stouffer distribution to Litton was a dividend within the meaning of section 243(a).

In many respects, the facts of this case and those of *Waterman Steamship* are parallel. The principal difference, and the one which we find to be most significant, is the timing of the dividend action. In *Waterman Steamship*, the taxpayer corporation received an offer to purchase the stock of two of its wholly-owned subsidiary corporations, Pan-Atlantic and Gulf Florida, for $3,500,000 cash. The board of directors of Waterman Steamship rejected that offer but countered with an offer to sell the two subsidiaries for $700,000 after the subsidiaries declared and arranged for payments of dividends to Waterman Steamship amounting in the aggregate to $2,800,000. Negotiations between the parties ensued, and the agreements which resulted therefrom included, in specific detail, provisions for the declaration of a dividend by Pan-Atlantic to Waterman Steamship prior to the signing of the sales agreement and the closing of that transaction. Furthermore, the agreements called for the purchaser to loan or otherwise advance funds to Pan-Atlantic promptly in order to pay off the promissory note by which the dividend had been paid. Once the agreement was reached, the entire transaction was carried out by a series of meetings commencing at 12 noon on January 21, 1955, and ending at 1:30 P.M. the same day. At the first meeting the board of directors of Pan-Atlantic met and declared a dividend in the form of a promissory note in the amount of $2,799,820. The dividend was paid by execution and delivery of the promissory note. At 12:30 P.M., the board of directors of the purchaser's nominee corporation ("Securities") met and authorized the purchase and financing of Pan-Atlantic and Gulf Florida. At 1 P.M., the directors of Waterman authorized the sale of all outstanding stock of Pan-Atlantic and Gulf Florida to Securities. Immediately following that meeting, the sales agreement was executed by the parties. The agreement provided that the purchaser guaranteed prompt payment of the liabilities of Pan-Atlantic and Gulf Florida including payment of any notes given by either corporation as a dividend.

Finally at 1:30 P.M., the new board of directors of Pan-Atlantic authorized the borrowing of sufficient funds from the purchaser personally and from his nominee corporation to pay off the promissory note to Waterman Steamship, which was done forthwith. As the Fifth Circuit pointed out, "By the end of the day and within a ninety minute period, the financial cycle had been completed. Waterman had $3,500,000, hopefully tax-free, all of which came from Securities and McLean, the buyers of the stock." 430 F.2d at 1190. This Court concluded that the distribution from Pan-Atlantic to Waterman was a dividend. The Fifth Circuit reversed, concluding that the dividend and sale were one transaction. 430 F.2d at 1192.

The timing in the instant case was markedly different. The dividend was declared by Stouffer on August 23, 1972, at which time the promissory note in payment of the dividend was issued to Litton. There had been some general preliminary discussions about the sale of Stouffer, and it was expected that Stouffer would be a very marketable company which would sell quickly. However, at the time the dividend was declared, no formal action had been taken to initiate the sale of Stouffer. It was not until 2 weeks later that Litton publicly announced that Stouffer was for sale. There ensued over the next 6 months many discussions with various corporations, investment banking houses, business brokers, and underwriters regarding Litton's disposition of Stouffer through sale of all or part of the business to a particular buyer, or through full or partial public offerings of the Stouffer stock. All of this culminated on March 1, 1973, over 6 months after the dividend was declared, with the purchase by Nestle of all of Stouffer's stock. Nestle also purchased the outstanding promissory note for $30,000,000 in cash.

In the instant case, the declaration of the dividend and the sale of the stock were substantially separated in time in contrast to *Waterman Steamship* where the different transactions occurred essentially simultaneously. In *Waterman Steamship*, it seems quite clear that no dividend would have been declared if all of the remaining steps in the transaction had not been lined up in order on the closing table and did not in fact take place. Here, however, Stouffer declared the dividend, issued the promissory note and definitely committed itself to the dividend before even making a public announcement that Stouffer was for sale. Respondent argues that the only way petitioner could ever receive the dividend was by raising revenue through a sale of Stouffer. Therefore, respondent asserts the two events (the declaration of the dividend and then the sale of the company) were inextricably tied together and should be treated as one transaction for tax purposes. In our view, respondent ignores the fact that Stouffer could have raised sufficient revenue for the dividend from other avenues, such as a partial public offering or borrowing. Admittedly, there had been discussions at Litton about the sale of Stouffer which was considered to be a very saleable company. However, there are many slips between the cup and the lip, and it does not take much of a stretch of the imagination to picture a variety of circumstances under which Stouffer might have been taken off the market and no sale consummated. Under these circumstances it is unlikely that respondent would have considered the dividend to be a nullity. On the contrary, it would seem quite clear that petitioner would be charged with a dividend on which it would have to pay a substantial tax. Petitioner committed itself to the dividend and, thereby, accepted the consequences regardless of the outcome of the proposed sale of Stouffer stock. See Crellin v. Commissioner, 17 T.C. 781, 785 (1951), aff'd 203 F.2d 812 (9th Cir. 1953), cert. denied 346 U.S. 873 (1953).

Since the facts here are distinguishable in important respects and are so much stronger in petitioner's favor, we do not consider it necessary to consider further the opinion of the Fifth Circuit in *Waterman Steamship*.

The term "dividend" is defined in section 316(a) as a distribution by a corporation to its shareholders out of earnings and profits. The parties have stipulated that Stouffer had earnings and profits exceeding $30,000,000 at the time the dividend was declared. This Court has recognized that a dividend may be paid by a note. T. R. Miller Mill Co. v. Commissioner, 37 B.T.A. 43, 49 (1938), aff'd 102 F.2d 599 (5th Cir. 1939). Based on these criteria, the $30,000,000 distribution by Stouffer would clearly constitute a dividend if the sale of Stouffer had not occurred. We are not persuaded that the subsequent sale of Stouffer to Nestle changes that result merely because it was more advantageous to Litton from a tax perspective.

It is well established that a taxpayer is entitled to structure his affairs and transactions in order to minimize his taxes. This proposition does not give a taxpayer carte blanche to set up a transaction in any form which will avoid tax consequences regardless of whether the transaction has substance. Gregory v. Helvering, 293 U.S. 465 (1935). A variety of factors present here preclude a finding of sham or subterfuge. Although the record in this case clearly shows that Litton intended at the time the dividend was declared to sell Stouffer, no formal action had been taken and no announcement had been made. There was no definite purchaser waiting in the wings with the terms and conditions of sale already agreed upon. At that time, Litton had not even decided upon the form of sale of Stouffer. Nothing in the record here suggests that there was any prearranged sale agreement, formal or informal, at the time the dividend was declared.

Petitioner further supports its argument that the transaction was not a sham by pointing out Litton's legitimate business purposes in declaring the dividend. Although the code and case law do not require a dividend to have a business purpose, it is a factor to be considered in determining whether the overall transaction was a sham. TSN Liquidating Corp. v. United States, 624 F.2d 1328 (5th Cir. 1980). Petitioner argues that the distribution allowed Litton to maximize the gross after-tax amount it could receive from its investment in Stouffer. From the viewpoint of a private purchaser of Stouffer, it is difficult to see how the declaration of a dividend would improve the value of the stock since creating a liability in the form of a promissory note for $30,000,000 would reduce the value of Stouffer by approximately that amount. However, since Litton was considering disposing of all or part of Stouffer through a public or private offering, the payment of a dividend by a promissory note prior to any sale had two advantages. First, Litton hoped to avoid materially diminishing the market value of the Stouffer stock. At that time, one of the factors considered in valuing a stock, and in determining the market value of a stock was the "multiple of earnings" criterion. Payment of the dividend by issuance of a promissory note would not substantially alter Stouffer's earnings. Since many investors were relatively unsophisticated, Litton may have been quite right that it could increase its investment in Stouffer by at least some portion of the $30,000,000 dividend. Second, by declaring a dividend and paying it by a promissory note prior to an anticipated public offering, Litton could avoid sharing the earnings with future additional shareholders while not diminishing to the full extent of the pro rata dividend, the amount received for the stock. Whether Litton could have come out ahead after Stouffer paid the promissory note is at this point merely speculation about a public offering which never occurred. The point, however, is that Litton hoped to achieve some business purpose and not just tax benefits in structuring the transaction as it did.

Under these facts, where the dividend was declared 6 months prior to the sale of Stouffer, where the sale was not prearranged, and since Stouffer had earnings and profits exceeding $30,000,000 at the time the dividend was declared, we cannot conclude that the distribution was merely a device designed to give the appearance of a dividend to a part of the sales proceeds. In this case the form and substance of the transaction coincide; it was not a transaction entered into solely for tax reasons, and it should be recognized as structured by petitioner.

On this record, we hold that for Federal tax purposes Stouffer declared a dividend to petitioner on August 23, 1972, and, subsequently, petitioner sold all of its stock in Stouffer to Nestle for $75,000,000.

Decision will be entered under Rule 155.

NOTES

1. *Impact of dividends-received deduction on corporate shareholders.* In the discussion of disguised dividends at page 126 supra, the taxpayer was trying to disguise a dividend as some other type of transaction. Sometimes the tables are turned, and the taxpayer tries to hide some other transaction as a dividend. In Waterman Steamship Corp. v. Commissioner, 430 F.2d 1185 (5th Cir. 1970), the taxpayer found a

purchaser willing to pay $3.5 million for the stock of its subsidiary. The taxpayer, with a basis of $700,000 in the subsidiary's stock, was not thrilled with the prospect of a $2.8 million capital gain. Consequently, it restructured the transaction to have the subsidiary distribute a $2.8 million note as a dividend to taxpayer, followed by a sale of the subsidiary's stock to the purchaser for $700,000. The purchaser was to provide funds to the subsidiary to discharge the note (and it was not clear that the subsidiary had the means to otherwise satisfy the note). Because of the consolidated return provisions, the dividend, if respected, would have been tax free. See page 474 infra for a discussion of consolidated return provisions.

What were the anticipated tax consequences on the sale and later payment on the note? The Service argued successfully that the purported dividend should be ignored and that the purchaser should be deemed to have paid the full $3.5 million purchase price. Accord, Basic, Inc. v. United States, 549 F.2d 740 (Cl. Ct. 1977). But see TSN Liquidating Co. v. United States, 624 F.2d 1328 (5th Cir. 1980), in which the court refused to recharacterize a dividend of unwanted assets by a subsidiary to its parent even though the purchaser of the subsidiary's stock reinfused the subsidiary with cash following the purchase. Accord, Dynamics Corp. of America v. United States, 449 F.2d 402 (Cl. Ct. 1971) (distribution and sale were unconnected events).

In *Litton Industries*, how did the court distinguish *Waterman Steamship*? Is the distinction convincing if the reason Litton declared the dividend was to decrease its tax liability on its intended sale of stock? What were the so-called business reasons that justified dividend treatment in the court's view?

How would the result in *Litton Industries* have changed if the court had concluded that the note issued to Litton was properly treated as equity for tax purposes?

2. *Debt-financed portfolio stock.* The availability of the dividends-received deduction under §243 presents some tax arbitrage possibilities. For example, a shareholder-corporation could finance an investment in stock with borrowed funds, thereby enabling it to receive tax-favored dividend income while deducting the interest on the indebtedness. Suppose that stock of Blue Chip Corp. regularly pays dividends of $8 per year on its common stock selling for $100 per share, an 8-percent return. If Investment Corp. can borrow funds at 10-percent interest, should it borrow money to purchase stock of Blue Chip? Suppose Investment Corp. is in the 35-percent bracket and borrows $100 to buy one share of Blue Chip stock. The after-tax cost of borrowing $100 at 10 percent is $6.50 because of the interest deduction. The after-tax return on the $8 dividend is $7.16, assuming a 70-percent dividends-received deduction and therefore an $0.84 tax on the $2.40 that enters taxable income. The pretax losing proposition becomes a $0.66 posttax winner (i.e., $7.16 minus $6.50). Do we want a tax system that encourages purchases that would not be made in the absence of taxes?

In principle, Congress's response to the problem resembles §265, which prohibits an interest deduction for debt incurred to purchase tax-exempt securities. The primary mechanism employed by §246A (primary rather than exclusive because of the Treasury's power under §246A(f)), however, does not limit the interest deduction. Instead, the provision reduces the dividends-received deduction otherwise available under §§243-246 by a percentage related to the amount of debt used to purchase the stock. Thus, if a taxpayer purchases stock with some cash and some debt such that the "average indebtedness percentage" is 50 percent, the §243 deduction in the example above will be 35 percent rather than 70 percent. See §246A(a) and (d). Section 246A applies to "portfolio stock" only. Stock will not be considered portfolio stock if the corporate shareholder owns a sufficient interest in the subsidiary (e.g., at least 50 percent of its voting power and value). §246A(c)(2). Presumably, a substantial ownership interest in the subsidiary suggests that the parent is interested in more than the subsidiary's dividends: The corporations are likely to be part of a multicorporate structure. The enforcement difficulties that plague §265 are likely to dog §246A. In particular, it will be very difficult to ascertain "portfolio indebtedness," indebtedness directly attributable to investment in portfolio stock. §246A(d)(3). In general, portfolio indebtedness refers to debt incurred to finance the stock purchase or to debt incurred after the stock purchase if secured by the stock.

3. *Dividend-related losses.* Even if the purchase of stock is not financed with debt, tax arbitrage opportunities may still be present. For example, suppose *X* Corp., taxed at a 35-percent rate, purchases 100 shares of *Y* Corp. stock for $10,000 immediately before the dividend "record date." *Y* distributes a $1,000 dividend, which, after a 70-percent dividends-received deduction, results in $300 of taxable income to *X* and after-tax income of $895 (i.e., $1,000 minus $105 tax liability). *X* then sells the stock for $9,000 (i.e., the value of the stock reflects the dividend paid), recognizing a $1,000 capital loss, which offsets $1,000 of capital gain. In sum, *X*, which started with $10,000, ends up with $10,245 (i.e., $895 from the dividend, $9,000 from the stock sale, and $350 in taxes saved as a result of the $1,000 capital loss deduction). Two provisions impede this type of tax arbitrage.

Under §246(c), no dividends-received deduction is available unless the stock is held for more than 45 days (90 days for certain preferred stock). This holding period is tolled if the shareholder-corporation diminishes its risk of loss in specified ways. §246(c)(4). See Rev. Rul. 90-27, described at page 103 supra, and Progressive Corp. v. United States, 970 F.2d 188 (6th Cir. 1992) (purchase of stock and sale of a call option tolled the holding period). If the dividend to be received is extraordinarily large relative to the price of the stock, a shareholder-corporation may be able to satisfy the holding period of §246(c) with a minimal risk of loss. Accordingly, Congress enacted §1059, mandating a basis reduction for corporate shareholders in their stock on the receipt of "extraordinary dividends," as defined in §1059(c), if the stock on which the dividends are paid is sold before it has been held for two years.

For example, suppose *X* Corp. purchases common stock of *Y* Corp. for $10,000 on January 1, receives an "extraordinary dividend" of $2,000 on February 1, and sells the stock on March 1 for $8,000 (the January 1 value reduced by the amount of the dividend). *X* Corp. includes only $600 of the dividend in taxable income (70 percent of the dividend, or $1,400, is deducted under §243), and in the absence of §1059 would claim a $2,000 loss on the sale of the stock. See, e.g., Silco, Inc. v. United States, 779 F.2d 282 (5th Cir. 1986). Under §1059, *X* Corp. must reduce its stock basis by the $1,400 deducted under §243. On the sale, *X* Corp. will recognize a loss of $600 ($8,000 realized less basis of $8,600). This matches the gain reported on the dividend, an appropriate result because *X* Corp. ends up with $10,000, the amount with which it started.

"Extraordinary dividends" include dividends received by a taxpayer having ex-dividend dates within a 365-day period if in the aggregate they exceed 20 percent of the taxpayer's adjusted basis in the underlying stock. §1059(c)(3)(B). For this purpose, a taxpayer can use the fair market value of the stock on the day before the ex-dividend day, rather than adjusted basis, if the value can be established to the satisfaction of the Secretary. §1059(c)(4). For example, if a taxpayer has a stock basis of $100 and the fair market value of the stock is $900, a $40 dividend exceeds 20 percent of the adjusted basis but is less than 5 percent of fair market value. Thus, the alternative fair market value test could save the taxpayer from any basis reduction under §1059.

Further, for distributions on common stock, extraordinary dividends include dividends received by a taxpayer that have ex-dividend dates within an 85-day period and that exceed 10 percent of the taxpayer's adjusted basis in (or the value of) the underlying stock. §1059(c)(2) and (3). A comparable rule applies for dividends on preferred stock, except that the dividends received must exceed a 5 percent, rather than 10 percent, threshold. *Id.* But see §1059(e)(3) (limiting the basis reduction under §1059(a) for dividends on certain preferred stock for which the dividends are fixed and do not exceed 15 percent of the lesser of adjusted basis or liquidation preference).

Section 1059 can apply to any transaction taxed as a dividend including distributions in redemption of stock (see §302(d)), as well as redemptions through related corporations (see §304(a)). If a sale of stock in one corporation (called the issuing corporation) to another corporation (called the acquiring corporation) is taxed as a §301 distribution under §304(a)(1), the sale is recast as (1) a transfer of the stock sold for stock of the acquiring corporation, (2) which is then redeemed by the acquiring corporation in a transaction described in §302(d). If the shareholder engaging in this §304 transaction is itself a corporation (call it the "selling" corporation), the effect of this hypothetical stock acquisition and redemption is to ensure that if the selling corporation excludes more than its basis in the shares sold by reason of the §243 dividends received deduction, that excess will be taxable immediately as gain under §1059(a)(2).

For example, assume Parent Corp. owns all the outstanding stock of Brother Corp. with an adjusted basis of $5,000, as well as all the outstanding stock of Sister Corp. with an adjusted basis of $50,000, and assume that the fair market value of each subsidiary corporation equals $50,000. If Parent Corp. sells the stock of Brother Corp. to Sister Corp. for cash of $50,000, this transaction is a redemption by related corporations as described in §304(a)(1), and because Parent Corp. retains complete control of Brother Corp. after the transaction, it is taxable as a distribution under §304(a)(1) and §301.

Suppose that the combined earnings and profits of Brother and Sister exceed $50,000, so that the entire distribution is taxed as a dividend. See §§304(b)(2), 301(c)(1). Because the sale is treated as a distribution to which §301 applies, Parent Corp. is deemed to contribute its Brother Corp. stock to Sister Corp. for Sister Corp. stock, which is then redeemed in a redemption taxed as a dividend. See §304(a)(1). The Sister Corp. stock hypothetically received by Parent has a substituted basis of only $5,000 under §358(a)(1), so that the subsequent hypothetical $50,000 redemption produces not only a $50,000 dividend and a $50,000 dividends-received deduction but also a taxable gain of $45,000 under §1059(a)(2). Note in particular that it appears that Parent Corp. was unable to offset that gain with its preexisting basis in the stock of Sister Corp. that it actually owns.

4. *Dividends-received deduction and earnings and profits.* Cases such as *Litton Industries* and *Waterman Steamship* illustrate that shareholders that are corporations may prefer dividend treatment for distributions while individual shareholders may

try to avoid dividend treatment (because of no basis offset despite any favorable tax treatment under §1(h)(11)). As part of this tax schizophrenia, the earnings and profits concept has been broadened so that distributions to individual shareholders are more likely to be treated as dividends. For example, §312(n), discussed on page 116 supra, requires that certain items that are deferred for purposes of computing taxable income (e.g., installment sale gains) be taken into account for purposes of computing earnings and profits.

In contrast, any increase in earnings and profits from such an adjustment may be welcome by a corporate shareholder, raising a perceived concern. To illustrate the concern, suppose that in *Litton Industries*, Stouffer had no earnings and profits. If Stouffer had sold an asset on the installment method, thereby deferring any gain, the immediate increase in earnings and profits would permit the distribution of a dividend to Litton, thereby decreasing the capital gain that Litton would have to recognize on the sale of the Stouffer stock to Nestle.

Section 301(e) prevents this result, providing that adjustments to earnings and profits under §312(k) and (n) (other than (n)(7)) are not made for purposes of determining the taxable income (and adjusted basis) of any "20 percent corporate shareholder." This term refers to any corporation, entitled to a dividends-received deduction with respect to a distribution, that owns, directly or indirectly, stock possessing at least 20 percent of the total combined voting power or value (excluding nonvoting, nonconvertible preferred stock) of the distributing corporation. The effect of §301(e) is that a distribution that might have been a dividend generating a dividends-received deduction now will reduce the shareholder's basis in the distributing corporation's stock. In the example above, if the distribution to Litton was not a dividend but was treated as a return of basis under §301(c)(2), Litton would recognize the same gain on a sale to Nestle that it would have recognized had the distribution not taken place. That is, Nestle would pay less because of the distribution, but Litton's basis would be decreased by precisely the amount of the distribution.

PROBLEMS

4-8. *X* Corp. has owned all the stock of *Y* Corp. since its formation. The stock has a basis of $2 million and a fair market value of $5 million. *P* Corp. wants to purchase the stock of *Y* Corp. for $5 million. Before the sale, *Y* Corp. distributes a note to *X* Corp. in the amount of $3 million payable in one year. The note bears a market rate of interest. In light of *Y* Corp.'s debt obligation, *P* Corp. pays $2 million to *X* Corp. for the *Y* Corp. stock. Within a year of *P* Corp.'s purchase, *Y* Corp. pays *X* Corp. $3 million on the note. Discuss the tax consequences.

4-9. How would your analysis to the preceding question change if *Y* Corp. borrowed $3 million from an unrelated third party and distributed the loan proceeds, rather than distributing a $3 million note? Would your analysis be affected if the debt was guaranteed by *X* Corp. before the sale and *P* Corp. after the sale?

5

Redemptions and Partial Liquidations

A. TREATMENT OF SHAREHOLDERS

Corporate profit can become shareholder cash in a variety of ways. One possibility is for the corporation to distribute some of its profits to its shareholders as a dividend. Assuming the corporation has adequate earnings and profits, the shareholders must include the full amount of the distribution in gross income, §301, albeit for individuals at no more than a 20-percent tax rate.

Alternatively, a shareholder can sell some or all of her shares without waiting for a distribution. Here, too, the shareholder will turn some of her corporate investment into cash. Historically, the tax consequences of a dividend distribution — no recovery of basis and ordinary income rather than capital gain — were the opposite of the tax consequences of a sale of stock — tax-free recovery of basis followed by capital gain. Even now that most dividend distributions are taxed to individuals at the same rate as long-term capital gain, the sale of stock still offers an opportunity to recover basis as well as the possibility for recognition of loss.

How should a shareholder be taxed if she sells some or all of her shares *to the corporation*? On one hand, funds will come out of corporate solution just as if there had been a dividend declaration; in this respect, a sale of stock to the issuing corporation (a "redemption") differs from a sale of the stock to a third party. On the other hand, the shareholder's percentage ownership of the corporation may decrease as a result of the transaction; if so, the transaction can be likened to a sale of stock to a third party. Note, though, that if stock is redeemed pro rata from all the shareholders, their proportionate interests in the corporation remain unchanged — as is the case when ordinary dividends are paid. Thus, some redemptions resemble sales, while others resemble ordinary dividend distributions, and in §302, Congress attempts to distinguish redemptions resembling sales from those resembling dividends.

Before turning to §302, note the definition of a "redemption" in §317(b). A redemption in this context is the distribution of property by a corporation *in exchange for* its own stock. Certain redemptions are taxed to the selling shareholder under §302(a) as sales of stock, allowing the shareholder to be taxed under §§1001 et seq. Other redemptions are taxed to the selling shareholder under §302(d) as distributions subject to the rules of §301, yielding dividend income if the corporation has sufficient earnings and profits. In either event, the corporation is treated as making a distribution. Thus, if the property distributed to the selling shareholder includes non-cash property, then the corporation may recognize taxable gain (but not loss) as on any other nonliquidating distribution. See §311(a) and (b).

Consider the case of *X* Corp., having 10,000 shares of common stock outstanding, owned half by *P* and half by *Q*, who is unrelated to *P*. Suppose *X* Corp. has a fair market value of $100,000, and that *P*'s 5,000 shares are redeemed for $50,000 in cash. Assuming that *X* Corp. has at least $50,000 of accumulated earnings and profits, how should *P* be taxed? Because *P* no longer has any interest in the corporation, the effect of the redemption on *P* is the same as if he had sold his stock to *Q*. A redemption resulting in a complete termination of the shareholder's interest in the corporation is a compelling case for sale or exchange treatment, and Congress has recognized this in §302(b)(3). Note, though, that *Q* becomes the sole shareholder of the corporation without having paid out any additional personal funds; in effect, the corporation's payment to *P* has transformed *Q* from a 50-percent to a 100-percent owner (albeit in a company only half its former size). We will return (at pages 188-197, 231-232 infra) to the possible tax consequences to *Q* of this change in status.

At the opposite end of the spectrum is a redemption of part of the stock of a sole shareholder. Suppose *Q*, after the redemption of *P*'s stock, has *X* Corp. redeem half of his stock for $25,000. Has *Q*'s interest in *X* Corp. been changed? Although the number of shares that *Q* owns decreases from 5,000 to 2,500, his percentage ownership remains at 100. Under state law, the fact that *Q* surrendered half of his shares would cause some of the distribution to be charged to the corporation's capital or paid-in surplus account—if no shares had been surrendered, presumably the charge would be only to the corporation's earned surplus account. Should *Q*'s taxation turn on this distinction? In §302(b) (excluding the partial liquidation provision of §302(b)(4), discussed at pages 182-186 infra), Congress has elected to focus on the effect of a redemption on the recipient shareholder's relative ownership of the distributing corporation. Accordingly, the redemption of *Q*'s stock will be taxed as a distribution subject to the rules of §301, and, if *X* Corp. has at least $25,000 in earnings and profits, *Q* will treat the distribution entirely as a dividend.

Between these two extremes lies a morass; the courts have struggled with an endless variety of fact patterns, in each case attempting to distinguish redemptions taxable as exchanges from redemptions taxable as distributions. Particularly troublesome have been cases in which the shareholder whose stock is redeemed is related to the remaining shareholders. For example, what are the consequences if *P* and *Q* in the example above are husband and wife, mother and daughter, or brother and sister? As you read the following cases, keep in mind this distinction (between redemptions more closely resembling the sale of stock to a third party from those resembling receipt of a nonliquidating distribution from the corporation) that §302 and the courts are trying to draw. If you come away with the sense that no line can be found, reconsider whether nonliquidating corporate distributions should be taxed so differently from sales of corporate shares.

As you study §302, keep in mind that even without regard to the applicable tax rate, exchange treatment under §302(a) is in one critical respect more favorable than distribution treatment under §301. Exchange treatment allows the shareholders to offset the amount of the distribution by the basis of the stock surrendered, while (generally) no such offset is permitted against distributions taxable under §301.

1. *Complete Terminations under §302(b)(3)*

Seda v. Commissioner

82 T.C. 484 (1984)

Opinion

Fay, Judge. . . .

On October 15, 1957, petitioners [Mr. and Mrs. Seda] organized B & B Supply Company (herein the company), and, within two years after incorporation, they had acquired all of the company's stock. Mr. Seda was the company's president and chairman of the board and owned 22,910 shares of the company's stock. Mrs. Seda was a director, vice-president, and secretary and owned 1,010 shares of the company's stock.

The company was engaged in the business of selling garage doors as a wholesaler in Colorado and Wyoming. It purchased most of the garage doors from Frantz Manufacturing Co. (herein Frantz Co.). In addition to working for the company from approximately 1952 until April 1981, Mr. Seda also worked as a manufacturer's representative for Frantz Co., earning a three percent commission on all garage door sales he made to the company on behalf of Frantz Co.

Because of their declining health, in 1979 petitioners decided to terminate their ownership of the company. Their son James L. Seda (James) had worked for the company since 1973 and was ready to assume ownership and control of the company. On June 30, 1979, petitioners entered into a redemption agreement wherein the company redeemed all of petitioners' stock for $299,000 ($12.50 per share). Pursuant to the redemption agreement, the company also issued 1,000 shares of stock to James for $1,000. Thus, James was the sole shareholder of the company after the redemption. Petitioners resigned from their positions as officers and directors of the company on June 30, 1979.

Prior to signing the redemption agreement, petitioners hired an accountant to advise them with respect to the tax consequences of the redemption. The accountant advised them that in order to achieve long-term capital gain treatment they would have to terminate their relationship with the company completely. Because of James' insistence, however, Mr. Seda continued to work for the company after the redemption, and he continued to receive a salary of $1,000 per month. Neither petitioners nor James believed such employment would prevent petitioners from achieving long-term capital gain treatment in connection with the redemption of their stock. In June 1981, immediately after learning that his employment relationship could result in the gain from the redemption of his stock being taxed as ordinary income, Mr. Seda terminated his employment relationship with the company. Mrs. Seda never served as an employee, officer, or director of the company after the redemption.

The company has never paid a dividend, and its retained earnings as of June 30, 1978 were $202,455. . . .

The first issue is whether the redemption of all petitioners' stock in the company is taxable as a dividend distribution under section 301 or as long-term capital gain under section 302(a). Section 302(a) provides that a distribution of property to a shareholder by a corporation in redemption of stock will be treated as a sale or exchange of such stock if the redemption falls within one of four categories enumerated in section 302(b). If the redemption fails to so qualify, it is treated as a dividend distribution to the extent of the corporation's earnings and profits. See secs. 301 and 302(a).

Section 302(b)(3) provides that a shareholder is entitled to sale or exchange treatment if all his stock in the corporation is redeemed. For purposes of determining whether there has been a complete termination within the meaning of section 302(b)(3), the constructive stock ownership rules of section 318(a) will apply unless the requirements set out in section 302(c)(2)(A) are satisfied. Sec. 302(c)(1). Respondent contends that petitioners failed to effect a complete termination within the meaning of section 302(b)(3) because James' interest in the company after the redemption is attributable to petitioners pursuant to section 318(a)(1). Petitioners counter that James' interest is not attributable to them because they satisfied the requirements of section 302(c)(2)(A).

Section 302(c)(2)(A) provides in relevant part as follows:

> (A) In the case of a distribution described in subsection (b)(3), section 318(a)(1) shall not apply if—
>
> (i) immediately after the distribution the distributee has no interest in the corporation (*including an interest as officer, director, or employee*), other than an interest as a creditor,
> (ii) the distributee does not acquire any such interest (other than stock acquired by bequest or inheritance) within 10 years from the date of such distribution, and
> (iii) the distributee, at such time and in such manner as the Secretary by regulations prescribes, files an agreement to notify the Secretary of any acquisition described in clause (ii) and to retain such records as may be necessary for the application of this paragraph.

(Emphasis added.)

Focusing on the parenthetical language in section 302(c)(2)(A)(i), respondent's first argument is that petitioners are not entitled to the relief provided by section 302(c)(2)(A) because Mr. Seda remained an employee of the company after the redemption. Petitioners argue, however, that section 302(c)(2)(A)(i) does not prohibit all employment relationships. Thus, they contend that Mr. Seda's employment after the redemption was not the retention of a prohibited interest in the company. For the following reasons, we agree with respondent.

Congress' purpose in enacting section 302(c)(2) was to ensure that the family attribution rules would not prevent a bona fide severance of a shareholder's interest in a corporation from resulting in capital gains treatment. H. Rept. No. 1337, 83d Cong. 2d Sess., p. 36 (1954); S. Rept. No. 1622, 83d Cong., 2d Sess., p. 45 (1954). This Court has previously stated that it is reasonable to infer from the legislative history that in enacting section 302(c)(2)(A) Congress was primarily concerned with a situation where a redeeming shareholder retained a financial stake in the corporation or continued to control the corporation and benefit by its operations after making only a nominal transfer of his stock. Estate of Lennard v. Commissioner, 61 T.C. 554, 561 (1974).

Although section 302(c)(2)(A)(i) may not prohibit the retention of all employment relationships, it is clear that the level of employment engaged in by Mr. Seda herein is prohibited. After the redemption, Mr. Seda continued to work for the company for almost two years and received a salary of $1,000 per month. By receiving that salary Mr. Seda did retain a financial stake in the company. Moreover, petitioners have failed to show that Mr. Seda ceased to be involved in the management of the company after the redemption. The fact that petitioners did not know that Mr. Seda's continued employment would prevent them from achieving long-term capital gain treatment is unfortunate, but not controlling. Thus, we find that petitioners failed to satisfy section 302(c)(2)(A)(i).

Accordingly, James' interest in the company is attributable to petitioners and, therefore, petitioners failed to effect a complete redemption of all of their stock within the meaning of section 302(b)(3). Thus, the proceeds from the redemption are taxable under section 302(d) as a dividend distribution to the extent of the company's earnings and profits. . . .

Reviewed by the Court.

Simpson, Wiles, Wilbur, Chabot, Korner, Shields, Cohen and Swift, JJ., agree with the majority opinion.

WHITAKER, J., concurring.

While I concur in the result reached, the majority fails to apply the per se rule which, in my opinion, is mandated by the statute. Section 302(c)(1) and (2)(A)(i) prescribes that the family attribution rules may not be waived if after a redemption the former shareholder performs any services for, or receives any remuneration from, the redeeming corporation as an officer, director or employee. The parenthetical language of section 302(c)(2)(A)(i) — "(including an interest as officer, director, or employee)" — is neither ambiguous nor equivocal; it contains no qualification such as that suggested by the majority. Nothing in the statutory language or legislative history suggests that an "interest as officer, director, or employee" must be substantial to be prohibited. Rather, it contains a flat rule.

While Congress did not address directly the issue of whether a per se rule was to be applied in interpreting the parenthetical language of section 302(c)(2)(A)(i), it is clear that section 302(c) was intended to bring an element of certainty to an area that had become a confusing morass under prior law. Congress recognized that it was necessary to replace the difficult detailed factual inquiries that had become commonplace. With regard to corporate redemptions, the House Report states:

> . . . Redemptions of stock. — Under present law it is not clear when a stock redemption results in capital gain or ordinary income. . . .
>
> Your committee's bill sets forth definite conditions under which stock may be redeemed at capital-gain rates. . . .
>
> . . . At the present time a possible opportunity for tax avoidance results where redemptions are effected in the case of family-owned corporations. To prevent tax avoidance, but at the same time to provide definitive rules for the guidance of taxpayers, your committee has provided precise standards whereby under specific circumstances, a shareholder may be considered as owning stock held by members of his immediate family (or by partnerships, corporations, or trusts which he controls).

[H. Rept. 1337, 83d Cong., 2d Sess. 35-36 (1954).]

Section 302(c) thus was enacted as something of a "safe haven." Facts and circumstances must be considered in the application of some of the section 302(b) and (c) rules, such as the determination under section 302(b)(1) as to dividend equivalency, but we should not judicially modify the mechanical rules where they can be applied mechanically. Contrary to the majority's view, Congress did intend to "prohibit the retention of all employment relationships." In the context of Lewis v. Commissioner, 47 T.C. 129 (1966), I do agree with Judge Simpson that "Congress did not intend us to hold that an officer or director who performs no duties, receives no compensation, and exercises no influence has retained an interest in the corporation." 47 T.C. at 137 (Simpson, J., concurring). The principle of substance over form prevents us from applying the per se rule where no duties are performed and no compensation received by reason of status as an officer, director or employee. But where, as here, the facts are otherwise, the congressional attempt to achieve certainty should be allowed to operate. . . .

Dawson, Sterrett, Goffe, Nims, Parker, Hamblen, and Clapp, JJ., agree with this concurring opinion.

NOTES

1. *Constructive ownership of stock under §302(b)(3).* Although all the stock owned by Mr. Seda was redeemed, he failed to qualify under §302(b)(3) for exchange treatment on the redemption.[1] The complete termination provision of §302(b)(3) was inapplicable in this case solely because Mr. Seda's son owned stock in the corporation after the redemption, and this stock was attributed to Mr. Seda under §302(c)(1). Because of §302(c)(1), the constructive ownership rules of §318 generally apply to determinations of stock ownership under §302. The constructive ownership rules of §318 are discussed further at pages 165-166 infra.

One distinctive feature of the complete termination of interest provision in §302(b)(3) is the ability of the redeemed shareholder to waive application of the family attribution rules of §318(a)(1). See §302(c)(2). For such a waiver to be effective, however, the taxpayer must not retain, and must agree not to acquire for 10 years (other than by bequest or inheritance), any interest in the corporation other than as a creditor. If a taxpayer whose stock is redeemed fails to make the election provided by §302(c)(2), then the attribution rules will apply in full in determining whether the redemption qualifies under §302(b)(3). In *Seda,* the taxpayers filed a §302(c) election, but the retention of an interest in the corporation by Mr. Seda eviscerated the election's effect.

As part of electing out of the family attribution rules, a taxpayer must file an agreement under §302(c)(2)(A)(iii) that extends the statute of limitations with respect to his redemption. This agreement allows the Commissioner to reopen the redemption year and collect a deficiency if the taxpayer acquires a tainted interest in the corporation within 10 years.

Under §302(c)(2)(B), a taxpayer may not waive the family attribution rules if any of the redeemed stock was acquired within 10 years from a related person, "related" being defined by reference to §318(a). In addition, a taxpayer may not waive the family attribution rules if he transferred any stock within 10 years to such a related person. These two limitations do not apply, however, if the transfer of stock "did not have as one of its principal purposes the avoidance of federal income tax."

1. The opinion does not consider why Mrs. Seda failed to qualify under §302(b)(3). Is Mr. Seda's employment imputed to his wife?

Suppose *X* Corp. has 100 shares outstanding, all of which are owned by *H*. If *H* gives 10 shares to *W*, his wife, and then *W*'s 10 shares are immediately redeemed, §302(c)(2)(B)(i) operates to prevent *W* from avoiding application of the family attribution rules. Thus, *W* will be deemed to own 100 percent of *X* Corp.'s shares both before and after the redemption, and the redemption will be subject to the distribution rules of §301.

Suppose instead that *H* gives *W* all but 10 shares and then has his stock completely redeemed. Now *H* will seek to waive application of the family attribution rules, but §302(c)(2)(B)(ii) prevents him from doing so. *H* will thus be deemed to own 100 percent of the *X* Corp. stock both before and after the redemption and so will be taxed under the distribution rules of §301. Note, however, that §302(c)(2)(B) applies only to transfers that have "the avoidance of federal income tax" as one of their principal purposes. In Rev. Rul. 77-293, 1977-2 C.B. 91, the Service ruled that a transfer of appreciated stock to the taxpayer's son was not subject to §302(c)(2)(B) when made "solely for the purpose of enabling [the taxpayer] to retire while leaving the business to [his son]." See also Rev. Rul. 85-19, 1985-1 C.B. 94, in which the father gifted stock to his son and subsequently reacquired some of the gifted stock by purchase. The son's remaining stock was redeemed by the corporation, and he filed an election under §302(c)(2)(A)(iii) to waive the family attribution rules. The Service ruled that the waiver was valid because the resale of stock by the son to his father merely returned the stock to its original owner and was not undertaken to avoid tax.

2. *Retention or reacquisition of a tainted interest.* As *Seda* illustrates, a taxpayer desiring to waive the family attribution rules pursuant to §302(c)(2) must not retain (or acquire within 10 years) an interest in the corporation "other than an interest as a creditor." The concurring opinion of Judge Whitaker emphasizes that Congress seemingly drew a bright line in §302(c)(2)(A)(i) by specifically providing that an interest as an "officer, director, or employee" is proscribed. The majority opinion does not specifically embrace that reading of the statute. Judge Whitaker agrees that a nominal directorship entailing no duties and without compensation, the situation litigated in *Lewis,* is not a prohibited interest under §302(c)(2)(A)(i), and the majority in *Seda* condemn the minimal activity engaged in by the taxpayer in that case. What fact pattern might fall between *Lewis* and *Seda* to justify Judge Whitaker's concerns?

In Lynch v. Commissioner, 83 T.C. 597 (1984), the father was the sole shareholder of *X* Corp. He transferred some of the stock to his son, and thereafter *X* Corp. redeemed all the father's remaining stock. The father continued, as an independent contractor, to provide services to *X* Corp. under a consulting agreement. The father sought capital gain treatment on the redemption via §302(b)(3) and a waiver of the family attribution rules. Held, exchange treatment allowed because (1) an independent contractor is not an "employee" within the meaning of §302(c)(2)(A)(i), and (2) the father's transfer to his son did not have as one of its principal purposes the avoidance of federal income tax. What would the Tax Court's opinion in *Lynch* leave of *Seda* (other than a trap for the ill advised)? The court of appeals reversed the Tax Court in *Lynch,* saying that Congress sought certainty in this area of the law by enacting §302(c)(2)(A). 801 F.2d 1176 (9th Cir. 1986). Compare Cerone v. Commissioner, 87 T.C. 1 (1986), in which the Tax Court rejected a bright-line reading of §302(c)(2)(A), saying instead that a taxpayer who continues to perform services for his corporation after a redemption will fail §302(c)(2)(A) only if the taxpayer has a significant financial stake in, or continues to control, the corporation.

How should "creditor" status be defined in the context of §302(c)(2)(A)(i)? Under Treas. Regs. §1.302-4(d), a permissible creditor must have rights neither broader in scope than is necessary for the enforcement of her claim nor subordinate to the claims of general creditors. See Dunn v. Commissioner, 615 F.2d 578 (2d Cir. 1980). See also Lynch v. Commissioner, supra, in which a note was held not to run afoul of Treas. Regs. §1.302-4(d) even though the noteholder agreed, subsequent to the redemption, to subordinate his note to a new debt acquired by the corporation. Would a retiring shareholder be beyond the bounds of §302(c)(2)(A)(i) if he received a note of the corporation secured by corporate stock? What if the retiring shareholder could vote the stock upon default of the note?

In Rev. Rul. 77-467, 1977-2 C.B. 92, the Service ruled that a taxpayer could waive the family attribution rules under §302(c)(2) despite retaining his interest as lessor of the corporation's office building pursuant to a 10-year lease entered into five years before the taxpayer's redemption. The taxpayer's status was not a prohibited interest within the meaning of §302(c)(2)(A)(i) because "[t]he payments under the lease will not be dependent on [the corporation's] future earnings and will not be subordinate to the claims of [the corporation's] general creditors." Was Mr. Seda's salary as an employee any more dependent on future corporate earnings than the lease payments in Rev. Rul. 77-467? Remaining an employee of the corporation after the redemption plainly fails the congressionally delineated test of §302(c)(2)(A)(i). Does this suggest that the reasoning in Rev. Rul. 77-467 is flawed?

Can the family attribution rules be waived if the exiting shareholder retains the right to a lifetime pension from the corporation? If the pension is unfunded, the payments are unrelated to the corporation's future earnings, and the rights of the exiting shareholder are unsubordinated to the claims of general creditors of the corporation, then the answer is yes. Rev. Rul. 84-135, 1984-2 C.B. 80.

In a series of rulings, the Service has held that retention of the legal right to vote shares violates a §302(c)(2)(A) waiver even if the taxpayer has no equitable interest in the stock. See Rev. Rul. 81-233, 1981-2 C.B. 83 (custodian of stock under Uniform Gift to Minors Act); Rev. Rul. 71-426, 1971-2 C.B. 173 (retention of interest as trustee of voting trust). But see Rev. Rul. 79-334, 1979-2 C.B. 127 (appointment by will as trustee of trust holding stock not a forbidden "interest"); Rev. Rul. 72-380, 1972-2 C.B. 201 (executor of estate holding stock not a forbidden "interest").

3. *Corporate shareholders and §302.* When a corporate shareholder's stock is redeemed, the taxpayer and the Service often switch sides; the corporation usually prefers dividend treatment because of the generous dividends-received deduction pursuant to §243, and the Service prefers capital gains treatment. To avoid §302(b)(3), a corporate shareholder might arrange to have its stock redeemed in a series of redemptions, arguing that only the final redemption in the series should be taxable as a complete termination. In Bleily & Collishaw v. Commissioner, 72 T.C. 751 (1979), however, the Commissioner successfully argued that a series of redemptions should be combined and taxed as a single, complete termination of the corporate shareholder's interest. See also Rev. Rul. 77-226, 1977-2 C.B. 90, in which the Service found that a corporate shareholder had transacted a §302(b)(3) redemption by combining various steps in a complicated transaction. Can a noncorporate taxpayer "step" a series of redemptions together to qualify for exchange treatment under §302(b)(3)? See Benjamin v. Commissioner, 592 F.2d 1259 (5th Cir. 1979), in which the court refused to treat a partial redemption as part of a complete redemption because (1) there was no timeframe in which the "plan for total redemption"

was to be completed, and (2) the shareholder had wide discretion as to when the redemption would be completed. Cf. §302(b)(2)(D) (combining a series of redemptions in applying §302(b)(2) in certain cases).

PROBLEMS

5-1. *X* Corp. has a net value of $1 million and earnings and profits of $800,000. Of the 1,000 outstanding *X* shares, 500 are owned by Father with a basis of $600 per share, and 500 are owned by Son with a basis of $700 per share. Father would like to transfer the value of his interest to Son, and he contemplates the following four transactions: (a) Have the corporation redeem Father's stock and then give the proceeds to Son; (b) have the corporation redeem the stock from Father's estate after Father's death and devise the proceeds to Son; (c) give Father's stock to Son and then cause the corporation to redeem the stock gifted to Son; (d) devise the stock to Son and have the corporation redeem it after Father's death.

What are the tax consequences to Father and Son of each of these transactions?

5-2. In problem 5-1, suppose Father wants to pass the value of his stock on to Mother, his wife. Reconsider the tax consequences of each of the four transactions, assuming that Mother, rather than Son, will receive the value of Father's stock and that Mother, rather than Son, is a beneficiary of the estate.

2. *Substantially Disproportionate Redemptions under §302(b)(2)*

A less compelling case for exchange treatment than a complete redemption is a disproportionate redemption in which a shareholder's relative equity interest in the corporation is reduced significantly, though not to zero. Under §302(b)(2), a disproportionate redemption will qualify for exchange treatment under §302(a) if it satisfies the following three-part test: (1) The redeemed shareholder must own less than 50 percent of the total combined voting power of the corporation immediately after the redemption; (2) the shareholder's voting power after the redemption must be less than 80 percent of his former voting power; and (3) the shareholder's percentage ownership, by value, of all common stock (nonvoting as well as voting) must also be less than 80 percent of his former percentage ownership.

Consider the following example. Assume *E* Corp. has 300 shares of a single class of common stock outstanding, owned 70 percent (210 shares) by *P* and 30 percent (90 shares) by *Q*. If *P* and *Q* are unrelated and *E* Corp. redeems 20 shares of *Q*'s stock, will the redemption qualify under §302(b)(2)? The following table sets forth the relevant data.

	Total Shares Outstanding	*Q's Shares*	*Q's Percentage*
Pre-redemption	300	90	30
Post-redemption	280	70	25

Here, more than 20 percent of *Q*'s stock has been redeemed (20 of 90 shares), and *Q*'s percentage of ownership drops from 30 to 25. To qualify for sale or exchange treatment under §302(b)(2), *Q*'s ownership would have had to fall below 24 percent (because 80 percent of her prior 30 percent is 24 percent). Accordingly, *Q* does not meet the safe harbor test of §302(b)(2). This example displays the often overlooked fact that a redemption will not qualify under §302(b)(2) if only 20 percent of a shareholder's stock is redeemed: Because a redemption reduces the total number of shares outstanding as well as the number of shares held by the redeemed shareholder, the percentage of a taxpayer's shares that must be redeemed to qualify under §302(b)(2) always exceeds 20 percent and turns on the redeemed shareholder's pre-redemption percentage ownership of the corporation.

Now consider a more abstract example. *X* Corp. has 200 shares of voting stock outstanding, owned half by *K* and half by *L*. Assume that *K* and *L* are unrelated. What is the least number of shares that *K* must have redeemed if he is to qualify under §302(b)(2)? Before the redemption, *K* owns 100 of the 200 shares outstanding, or 50 percent. After the redemption, *K* must own less than 0.80 times 50 percent, or less than 40 percent. If *K* has *x* shares redeemed, then his post-redemption percentage of ownership will be $(100 - x)/(200 - x) \times 100$ percent.[2] To satisfy §302(b)(2), then, *K* must choose an *x* such that $(100 - x)/(200 - x) < 0.4$, and the smallest *x* satisfying this condition is 33.34. Accordingly, *K* must have at least 33.34 of his shares redeemed (and not merely a fraction more than 20 shares!) to qualify under §302(b)(3).[3]

Note the requirement imposed by the concluding paragraph of §302(b)(2)(C): Not only must the 80-percent test be satisfied as to all voting stock, but it also must be satisfied with respect to the shareholder's common stock taken alone. The Service has ruled that this "common stock" test is disregarded if a corporation redeems voting preferred stock of a shareholder who owns (actually and constructively) no common stock before the redemption. Rev. Rul. 81-41, 1981-1 C.B. 121. In addition, the Service has ruled that if multiple classes of common stock are outstanding, then the test of §302(b)(2)(C) will be applied to a shareholder's aggregate ownership of common stock rather than on a class-by-class basis. Rev. Rul. 87-88, 1987-2 C.B. 81. If the test were applied class by class, no redemption could qualify as substantially disproportionate unless shares of each class of stock were redeemed.

Suppose a corporation is equally owned by two shareholders. Although a pro rata redemption of the two shareholders' stock will fail to qualify for exchange treatment under §302(a), can they obtain such treatment if the corporation redeems a substantial portion of one shareholder's stock in one redemption and then redeems an equal portion of the other shareholder's stock in a second transaction? Under §302(b)(2)(D), a redemption that is part of a series of redemptions will not qualify under §302(b)(2) unless the series in total is "substantially disproportionate." See also Treas. Regs. §1.302-1(a)(3).

Suppose individual *A*, the controlling shareholder of *X* Corp., knows that *X* Corp. will in one month repurchase all the shares of individual *B*, a minority shareholder. How should *A* be taxed on a redemption that, viewed in isolation, satisfies the tests of §302(b)(2) but that would have failed those tests had the distribution to *A* come after the complete termination of *B*? For the Service's position that the distributions to *A* and to *B* must be treated as part of a single transaction, see Rev. Rul. 85-14, 1985-4 C.B. 92.

2. As this formula illustrates, in computing a shareholder's percentage of stock outstanding after the redemption, both the numerator and denominator must be reduced by the number of shares redeemed.

3. If T is the total number of shares outstanding just prior to the redemption and if N is the number of those shares held by the shareholder, then the number of shares needed to be redeemed to meet the 80-percent test under §302(b)(2) is any amount above NT/(5T–4N).

NOTES

1. *Constructive ownership of stock under §302.* By virtue of §302(c)(1), the constructive attribution rules of §318(a) apply to determinations under §302. The explicit reference in §302(c)(1) to §318(a) is important, for §318 does not apply except when "expressly made applicable." §318(a).

The constructive ownership rules of §318 consist of three main parts: attribution between family members, §318(a)(1); attribution *from* entities to their beneficial owners, §318(a)(2); and attribution *to* entities from their beneficial owners, §318(a)(3). In addition, holders of stock options are treated as owners of the optioned stock even though they have not yet exercised (and may never exercise) the option. §318(a)(4). Finally, §318(a)(5)(A) permits two or more attribution rules of §318 to be applied in sequence, resulting in a chain of attributed ownership.

The mechanics of §318 can best be gleaned from a number of examples. Assume *X* Corp. has 100 shares of common stock outstanding, owned 25 by *E*, 25 by *F*, 25 by the *T* trust, and 25 by the *P* partnership. While *E*, *F*, *T*, and *P* each actually own 25 percent of *X* Corp., their constructive (or deemed) ownership will depend on the relationships among them. For example, suppose *E* is a 60-percent partner in the *P* partnership. Now, *E* will have a total constructive ownership of 40 shares, 25 actually owned and 60 percent of the 25 shares owned by *P*. §318(a)(2)(A). *P*, however, will be deemed to own 50 shares, for all of *E*'s shares will be imputed to *P* under §318(a)(3)(A).

If *E* is also a beneficiary of the *T* trust, the matter becomes more complicated. Suppose *E*'s actuarially determined interest in the *T* trust is 80 percent of the trust's value. Then *E*'s total constructive ownership jumps by 20 shares to 60, for he must add 80 percent of the trust's holdings to his own under §318(a)(2)(B)(i). Furthermore, *P*'s constructive ownership also increases by 20 shares, for under §318(a)(5)(A), *E*'s constructive ownership can be imputed to a related party such as *P*, as is actual ownership.

Now assume *F* has the other 40-percent interest in the *P* partnership. *P*'s total constructive ownership will increase by 25 shares under §318(a)(3)(A). *F*'s total constructive ownership will increase to 35 shares, 25 actually owned and 10 constructively owned through attribution of 40 percent of *P*'s *actual* ownership. Why is *F* not deemed to own 40 percent of *P*'s *constructively* owned shares? Under §318(a)(5)(C), stock attributed *into* an entity under §318(a)(3) cannot then be reattributed *out of* the entity under §318(a)(2). A similar rule limits attribution under the family attribution rules more than once, so that, for example, there is no attribution between siblings via the chain: child 1 to parent to child 2. See §318(a)(5)(B). Note also that attribution to and from corporations is limited to its 50-percent shareholders. §318(a)(2)(C), (a)(3)(C).

Recall §302(c)(2), which allows a taxpayer to waive application of the family attribution rules to qualify under the complete termination safe harbor of §302(b)(3). Note that this waiver applies only to the attribution rules in §318(a)(1) — the *family* attribution rules — and that it applies only to determinations under §302(b)(3). In Rickey v. United States, 592 F.2d 1251 (5th Cir. 1979), it was held that an estate could waive the entity attribution rules of §318(a)(3) for purposes of §302(b)(3). In the legislative reports discussing §228 of the Tax Equity and Fiscal Responsibility Act of 1982, Congress indicated that the holding of *Rickey* was specifically disapproved.

Entities as well as individuals can waive the family attribution rules to qualify under §302(b)(3). See §302(c)(2)(C). Such a waiver might be appropriate when a trust completely terminates its interest in a corporation but the parent of a trust beneficiary continues to be a shareholder of the corporation. Note that the restrictions of §302(c)(2)(A)—a 10-year prohibition from acquiring a tainted interest in the corporation and the filing of an extension of the statute of limitations—are imposed on the entity and on all "related persons." See §302(c)(2)(C). A "related person" is any person to whom stock of the corporation is attributed under the family attribution rules of §318(a)(1) if that stock is further attributed to the entity under §318(a)(3). §318(c)(2)(C)(ii)(II).

2. *The case of the disappearing basis.* When a taxpayer receives an ordinary dividend, the basis of her shares is unaffected by the receipt, and gain or loss on a subsequent disposition of the shares, computed under §1001(a), will be the difference between the amount realized and the basis of the shares. A redemption of some or all of the taxpayer's shares that fails to qualify for exchange treatment under §302(a) similarly leaves the taxpayer's stock basis unaffected, but the taxpayer no longer has the redeemed shares for a later sale or other disposition. What happens to her basis in the redeemed shares? If it is lost, a §302(d) distribution is not the equivalent of an ordinary dividend; it is worse than one. See Treas. Regs. §1.302-2(c), stating that when a redemption of stock is treated as dividend, "proper adjustment of the basis *of the remaining stock* will be made with respect to the stock redeemed" (emphasis added), and note examples 1 to 3. But note that the shareholder may not own any shares after the redemption, as was true in *Seda.* What is the "proper adjustment" in a case such as *Seda*? See Levin v. Commissioner, 385 F.2d 521 (2d Cir. 1967) (transfer of basis to related shareholder).

This rule, that basis will be transferred to a related taxpayer when the shareholder whose stock is redeemed owns no stock after the transaction, can be exploited to produce some extreme results. Consider the case of related taxpayers *P* and *Q*, with each owning half of the stock of *X* Corp. Assume that *P* is a tax-indifferent party; that is, (1) *P* pays no tax because *P* is exempt under some applicable provision of the Internal Revenue Code, (2) *P* has sufficient current or carryover losses that current income is meaningless, or (3) *P* is not a citizen or resident of the United States and is not subject to U.S. taxation because of a specific statutory or treaty provision. Further, assume *Q is* subject to U.S. income taxation.

If *P*'s stock is completely redeemed by *X* Corp., the transaction may be treated as a distribution because *Q*, related to *P*, owns 100 percent of the corporation immediately after the transaction, and that ownership will be imputed to *P* under the attribution rules of §318. If *P*'s stock basis is treated as shifted to *Q*, then on a subsequent sale by *Q* of the *X* Corp. stock, *Q* will recognize less gain (or even a loss!) even though the dividend income to *P* yielded no revenue to the Treasury. Is there a fair solution to this problem? One possibility (suggested by the Treasury but ultimately withdrawn) is to give a capital loss to *P* when *Q* sells her shares rather than shift *P*'s basis.[4]

4. Proposed regulations offer a more nuanced approach. Instead of shifting the unused basis, the redeemed shareholder has a deferred loss equal to that basis amount, a loss that she would take into account on the first day that she would qualify under §302(b)(1), (2), or (3) if the stock ownership at the end of that day had been in place immediately after the redemption. See Prop. Treas. Regs. §1.302-5(a)(3) and (b)(4)(i); cf. *id.* at (b)(4)(ii) (for special rules for corporate shareholders).

PROBLEMS

5-3. *X* Corp. has one class of stock outstanding, stock owned by two unrelated individuals, *P* and *Q*. *P* owns 60 shares with a basis of $60 per share, and *Q* owns 40 shares with a basis of $70 per share. *X* has earnings and profits of $2,000, and the fair market value of each share is $100. What tax consequences does each of the following transactions have for *P*, *Q*, and *X* Corp.?

a. *P* sells 10 shares to *Q* for $1,000.
b. *P* sells 10 shares to *X* Corp. for $1,000.
c. *P* sells 21 shares to *X* Corp. for $2,100.
d. *P* sells 50 shares to *X* Corp. for $5,000.
e. Suppose in (d) that—
   i. *P* is *Q*'s sister.
   ii. *P* is *Q*'s mother.
   iii. *P* and *Q* are each 50-percent partners in the *PQ* Partnership.
   iv. *Q* is a corporation, and *P* owns 50 percent of the stock of *Q*. Unrelated shareholders own the other 50 percent.
   v. *Q* is a corporation, and *P*'s father owns 50 percent of the stock of *Q*. Unrelated shareholders own the other 50 percent.

5-4. *X* Corp. and *Y* Corp. each own 50 percent of the outstanding stock of *Z* Corp. Assume that *X* and *Y* are both wholly owned by individual *O*. *X* has an adjusted basis of $10,000 in its stock of *Z*, and *Y* has an adjusted basis of $15,000 in its stock of *Z*. *Z*'s assets consist of cash in the amount of $50,000 as well as business assets worth $50,000, and *Z* has earnings and profits of $90,000. What are the tax consequences to *X* and to *Y* if *Z* redeems the shares of *X* for $50,000 and then *Y* sells its *Z* shares to an unrelated third party for $50,000? How does this compare with a sale by *X* and *Y* of their *Z* shares to an unrelated third party?

5-5. *X* Corp. has one class of stock outstanding. *P* owns 60 *X* shares and *Q*, unrelated to *P*, owns the remaining 40 *X* shares. *X* Corp. redeems 45 of *P*'s shares and 35 of *Q*'s shares. Is either redemption described in §302(b)(2)? How would your analysis change if *Q*'s *X* stock was instead voting preferred stock and each share of *X* stock had one vote per share?

3. Redemptions Not Essentially Equivalent to a Dividend

A redemption that is neither a complete termination under §302(b)(3) nor substantially disproportionate under §302(b)(2) still can be taxed as an exchange at the shareholder level if, considering all the facts and circumstances, the redemption "is not essentially equivalent to a dividend." §302(b)(1). Until enactment of the 1954 Code, only this ambiguous language distinguished qualifying from nonqualifying redemptions, language interpreted in the following case.

United States v. Davis

397 U.S. 301 (1970)

Justice MARSHALL delivered the opinion of the Court.

In 1945, taxpayer and E. B. Bradley organized a corporation. In exchange for property transferred to the new company, Bradley received 500 shares of common stock, and taxpayer and his wife similarly each received 250 such shares. Shortly thereafter, taxpayer made an additional contribution to the corporation, purchasing 1,000 shares of preferred stock at a par value of $25 per share.

The purpose of this latter transaction was to increase the company's working capital and thereby to qualify for a loan previously negotiated through the Reconstruction Finance Corporation. It was understood that the corporation would redeem the preferred stock when the RFC loan had been repaid. Although in the interim taxpayer bought Bradley's 500 shares and divided them between his son and daughter, the total capitalization of the company remained the same until 1963. That year, after the loan was fully repaid and in accordance with the original understanding, the company redeemed taxpayer's preferred stock. . . .

[T]axpayer considered the redemption as a sale of his preferred stock to the company — a capital gains transaction under §302 of the Internal Revenue Code of 1954 resulting in no tax since taxpayer's basis in the stock equaled the amount he received for it. . . . According to the Commissioner, the redemption of taxpayer's stock was essentially equivalent to a dividend and was thus taxable as ordinary income under §§301 and 316 of the Code. Taxpayer paid the resulting deficiency and brought this suit for a refund. The District Court ruled in his favor. . . .

The Court of Appeals held that the $25,000 received by taxpayer was "not essentially equivalent to a dividend" within the meaning of that phrase in §302(b)(1) of the Code because the redemption was the final step in a course of action that had a legitimate business (as opposed to a tax avoidance) purpose. . . . We reverse.

The Internal Revenue Code of 1954 provides generally in §§301 and 316 for the tax treatment of distributions by a corporation to its shareholders; under those provisions, a distribution is includible in a taxpayer's gross income as a dividend out of earnings and profits to the extent such earnings exist. There are exceptions to the application of these general provisions, however, and among them are those found in §302 involving certain distributions for redeemed stock. . . .

Under subsection (a) of §302, a distribution is treated as "payment in exchange for the stock," thus qualifying for capital gains rather than ordinary income treatment, if the conditions contained in any one of the four paragraphs of subsection (b) are met. In addition to paragraph (1)'s "not essentially equivalent to a dividend" test, capital gains treatment is available where (2) the taxpayer's voting strength is substantially diminished, (3) his interest in the company is completely terminated. . . . Paragraph (4) is not involved here, and taxpayer admits that paragraphs (2) and (3) do not apply. Moreover, taxpayer agrees that for the purposes of §§302(b)(2) and (3) the attribution rules of §318(a) apply and he is considered to own the 750 outstanding shares of common stock held by his wife and children in addition to the 250 shares in his own name.

Taxpayer, however, argues that the attribution rules do not apply in considering whether a distribution is essentially equivalent to a dividend under §302(b)(1). According to taxpayer, he should thus be considered to own only

25 percent of the corporation's common stock, and the distribution would then qualify under §302(b)(1) since it was not pro rata or proportionate to his stock interest, the fundamental test of dividend equivalency. See Treas. [Regs.] §1.302-2(b). However, the plain language of the statute compels rejection of the argument. In subsection (c) of §302, the attribution rules are made specifically applicable "in determining the ownership of stock for purposes of this section." Applying this language, both courts below held that §318(a) applies to all of §302, including §302(b)(1) — a view in accord with the decisions of the other courts of appeals, a long-standing treasury regulation, and the opinion of the leading commentators.

Against this weight of authority, taxpayer argues that the result under paragraph (1) should be different because there is no explicit reference to stock ownership as there is in paragraphs (2) and (3). Neither that fact, however, nor the purpose and history of §302(b)(1) support taxpayer's argument. . . .

Indeed, it was necessary that the attribution rules apply to §302(b)(1) unless they were to be effectively eliminated from consideration with regard to §§302(b)(2) and (3) also. For if a transaction failed to qualify under one of those sections solely because of the attribution rules, it would according to taxpayer's argument nonetheless qualify under §302(b)(1). We cannot agree that Congress intended so to nullify its explicit directive. We conclude, therefore, that the attribution rules of §318(a) do apply; and, for the purposes of deciding whether a distribution is "not essentially equivalent to a dividend" under §302(b)(1), taxpayer must be deemed the owner of all 1,000 shares of the company's common stock.

II

After application of the stock ownership attribution rules, this case viewed most simply involves a sole stockholder who causes part of his shares to be redeemed by the corporation. We conclude that such a redemption is always "essentially equivalent to a dividend" within the meaning of that phrase in §302(b)(1) and therefore do not reach the Government's alternative argument that in any event the distribution should not on the facts of this case qualify for capital gains treatment.[8]

The predecessor of §302(b)(1) came into the tax law as §201(d) of the Revenue Act of 1921. . . . Enacted in response to this Court's decision that pro rata stock dividends do not constitute taxable income, Eisner v. Macomber, 252 U.S. 189 (1920), the provision had the obvious purpose of preventing a corporation from avoiding dividend tax treatment by distributing earnings to its shareholders in two transactions — a pro rata stock dividend followed by a pro rata redemption — that would have the same economic consequences as a simple dividend. Congress, however, soon recognized that even without a prior stock dividend essentially the same result could be effected whereby any corporation, "especially one which has only a few stockholders, might be able to make a distribution to its stockholders which would have the same effect as a taxable dividend." H.R. Rep. No. 1, 69th Cong., 1st Sess., 5. In order to cover this situation, the law was amended to apply

8. Of course, this just means that a distribution in redemption to a sole shareholder will be treated under the general provisions of §301, and it will only be taxed as a dividend under §316 to the extent that there are earnings and profits.

"(whether or not such stock was issued as a stock dividend)" whenever a distribution in redemption of stock was made "at such time and in such manner" that it was essentially equivalent to a taxable dividend. Revenue Act of 1926, §201(g), 44 Stat. 11. . . .

Unfortunately, however, the policies encompassed within the general language of §115(g)(1) and its predecessors were not clear, and there resulted much confusion in the tax law. . . .

By the time of the general revision resulting in the Internal Revenue Code of 1954, the draftsmen were faced with what has aptly been described as "the morass created by the decisions." Balenger v. United States, 301 F.2d 192, 196 (C.A.4 1962). In an effort to eliminate "the considerable confusion which exists in this area" and thereby to facilitate tax planning, H.R. Rep. No. 1337, 83d Cong., 2d Sess., 35, the authors of the new Code sought to provide objective tests to govern the tax consequences of stock redemptions. Thus, the tax bill passed by the House of Representatives contained no "essentially equivalent" language. Rather, it provided for "safe harbors" where capital gains treatment would be accorded to corporate redemptions that met the conditions now found in §§302(b)(2) and (3) of the Code.

It was in the Senate Finance Committee's consideration of the tax bill that §302(b)(1) was added, and Congress thereby provided that capital gains treatment should be available "if the redemption is not essentially equivalent to a dividend." . . . However . . . we find from the history of the 1954 revisions and the purpose of §302(b)(1) that Congress intended more than merely to re-enact the prior law.

In explaining the reason for adding the "essentially equivalent" test, the Senate Committee stated that the House provisions "appeared unnecessarily restrictive, particularly, in the case of redemptions of preferred stock which might be called by the corporation without the shareholder having any control over when the redemption may take place." S. Rep. No. 1622, 83d Cong., 2d Sess., 44. This explanation gives no indication that the purpose behind the redemption should affect the result. . . .

The intended scope of §302(b)(1) as revealed by this legislative history is certainly not free from doubt. However, we agree with the Government that by making the sole inquiry relevant for the future the narrow one whether the redemption could be characterized as a sale, Congress was apparently rejecting past court decisions that had also considered factors indicating the presence or absence of a tax-avoidance motive.[11] At least that is the implication of the example given. Congress clearly mandated that pro rata distributions be treated under the general rules laid down in §§301 and 316 rather than under §302 and nothing suggests that there

11. This rejection is confirmed by the Committee's acceptance of the House treatment of distributions involving corporate contractions—a factor present in many of the earlier "business purpose" redemptions. In describing its action, the Committee stated as follows:

> Your committee, as did the House bill, separates into their significant elements the kind of transactions now incoherently aggregated in the definition of a partial liquidation. Those distributions which may have capital-gain characteristics *because they are not made pro rata* among the various shareholders would be subjected, at the shareholder level, to the separate tests described in [§§301 to 318]. On the other hand, those distributions characterized by what happens solely at the corporate level by reason of the assets distributed would be included as within the concept of a partial liquidation. S. Rep. No. 1622, supra, at 49.

(Emphasis added.)

should be a different result if there were a "business purpose" for the redemption. . . .

Taxpayer strongly argues that to treat the redemption involved here as essentially equivalent to a dividend is to elevate form over substance. Thus, taxpayer argues, had he not bought Bradley's shares or had he made a subordinated loan to the company instead of buying preferred stock, he could have gotten back his $25,000 with favorable tax treatment. However, the difference between form and substance in the tax law is largely problematical, and taxpayer's complaints have little to do with whether a business purpose is relevant under §302(b)(1). It was clearly proper for Congress to treat distributions generally as taxable dividends when made out of earnings and profits and then to prevent avoidance of that result without regard to motivation where the distribution is in exchange for redeemed stock.

We conclude that that is what Congress did when enacting §302(b)(1). If a corporation distributes property as a simple dividend, the effect is to transfer the property from the company to its shareholders without a change in the relative economic interests or rights of the stockholders. Where a redemption has that same effect, it cannot be said to have satisfied the "not essentially equivalent to a dividend" requirement of §302(b)(1). Rather, to qualify for preferred treatment under that section, a redemption must result in a meaningful reduction of the shareholder's proportionate interest in the corporation. Clearly, taxpayer here, who (after application of the attribution rules) was the sole shareholder of the corporation both before and after the redemption, did not qualify under this test. The decision of the Court of Appeals must therefore be reversed and the case remanded to the District Court for dismissal of the complaint.

It is so ordered.

Reversed and remanded.

Mr. Justice Douglas, with whom Mr. Justice Brennan concurs, dissenting. . . .

[R]espondent's contribution of working capital in the amount of $25,000 in exchange for 1,000 shares of preferred stock with a par value of $25 was made in order for the corporation to obtain a loan from the RFC and that the preferred stock was to be redeemed when the loan was repaid. For the reasons stated by the two lower courts, this redemption was not "essentially equivalent to a dividend," for the bona fide business purpose of the redemption belies the payment of a dividend. . . .

When the Court holds it was a dividend, it effectively cancels §302(b)(1) from the Code. This result is not a matter of conjecture, for the Court says that in the case of closely held or one-man corporations a redemption of stock is "always" equivalent to a dividend. I would leave such revision to the Congress.

Henry T. Patterson Trust v. United States

729 F.2d 1089 (6th Cir. 1984)

Before Edwards and Krupansky, Circuit Judges, and Peck, Senior Circuit Judge.

Krupansky, Circuit Judge. . . .

Prior to 1969, Henry Patterson, Sr. was the sole shareholder and chief executive officer of Puritan [Laundry and Dry Cleaning Company]. In 1969, he gave forty shares of Puritan stock to each of his children—John, Hank and Ellen. At the time,

Ellen was married to Bill Hicks (Hicks), who, along with Hank, was employed by Puritan. Henry Patterson retained 200 shares of Puritan stock.

Bill Hicks was apparently a skilled business manager, while Hank Patterson (Hank) lacked effectiveness. Through the years, a bitter tension between Hicks and Hank developed, resulting in numerous altercations, one of which ended with Hank's hospitalization. At one point, John Patterson (John) participated in the management of the business but, because of the Hank-Hicks rivalry, John resigned and pursued a teaching career.

At trial, there was testimony that Henry Patterson desired that Hicks operate the company after Patterson's retirement. In early 1970, Patterson suffered a broken hip which forced him to remain away from the company. He designated Hicks to act as Puritan's president and general manager in his absence. Patterson's health continued to deteriorate and he died in November 1971.

In June 1971, Hicks presented the Puritan directors with a demand for an increase in salary and a proposal that they place all of the Puritan shares in a voting trust which Hicks would then control. The directors demurred and Hicks resigned. He immediately staged a slowdown of Puritan employees and persuaded the company's most substantial commercial accounts to demand that Puritan rehire him. Within ten days of Hicks' resignation, Puritan was on the verge of collapse. John, who had since returned to the business, contacted Hicks and negotiated a five-year employment contract with him.

Hicks' contract provided an increased salary, a profit sharing arrangement, and a five-year option to acquire eighty shares of Puritan stock. Hicks acquired five of those shares and his option on the remaining seventy-five shares remained open. At the same time, Hank also received a five-year contract.

During the ensuing five years, Puritan performed well but problems between Hank and Hicks became increasingly aggravated; Hank, John, and Ella Patterson, their mother, often were at odds with Hicks and his wife, Ellen. In the spring of 1976, the Patterson estate was closed. Henry Patterson had placed his 200 shares of Puritan stock in the Henry T. Patterson Trust (Trust) with his widow, Ella, as the beneficiary with the power to appoint the corpus at her death. Following the closing of the estate, the Puritan stock was thus distributed:

Henry T. Patterson Trust	200 Shares
Ella Patterson	25 Shares
Hank Patterson	40 Shares
John Patterson	40 Shares
Ellen (Patterson) Hicks	40 Shares
Bill Hicks	5 Shares
Lester Winkler	6 Shares

Hicks devised a two-step plan whereby he and his wife could obtain control of Puritan. First, Puritan would redeem the Trust shares and, following the redemption, Hicks would exercise his option and acquire an additional seventy-five shares. As a result, Hicks and his spouse would own 120 shares and the remaining shareholders would control only 111 shares, thus Hicks would acquire a controlling interest in Puritan.

The Reeves Bank, as Trustee, determined that if it refused to redeem the shares, Hicks would leave the company and eventually the Trust corpus would be worthless.

Thus, acting in what it perceived as the best interests of the Trust and the beneficiary, the Reeves Bank determined to accept the proposed redemption.

On April 2, 1976, the directors were presented with the proposal. The Trustee reported that it would be in Ella's best interest to redeem the shares and invest the proceeds. . . .

The Trust reported the transaction as a capital gains sale. Upon review, the Commissioner determined that the amount received by the Trust in the redemption, $190,000.00, was a dividend taxable as ordinary income under §301 of the Internal Revenue Code of 1954. . . .

[A]t issue here is the propriety, as a matter of law, of the district court's determination that the Trust's redemption was not essentially a dividend, as defined by §302(b)(1).

In United States v. Davis, 397 U.S. 301 (1970), the Supreme Court evaluated the intended scope of §302(b)(1). In that case, a sole shareholder caused part of his shares to be redeemed by the corporation; the Court concluded that such a redemption is always equivalent to a dividend and thus subject to ordinary income tax. However, the Court's examination of §302(b)(1)'s history is germane to the analysis of this appeal:

> It was clearly proper for Congress to treat distributions generally as taxable dividends when made out of earnings and profits and then to prevent avoidance of that result without regard to motivation where the distribution is in exchange for redeemed stock.
>
> We conclude that that is what Congress did when enacting §302(b)(1). If a corporation distributes property as a simple dividend, the effect is to transfer the property from the company to its shareholders without a change in the relative economic interests or rights of the stockholders. Where a redemption has that same effect, it cannot be said to have satisfied the "not essentially equivalent to a dividend" requirement of §302(b)(1). Rather, to qualify for preferred treatment under that section, a redemption must result in a meaningful reduction of the shareholder's proportionate interest in the corporation. Clearly, taxpayer here, who (after application of the attribution rules) was the sole shareholder both before and after the redemption, did not qualify under this test.

397 U.S. at 313.

As explicated by the Supreme Court, §302(b)(1) provides that corporate distributions which do not alter the shareholder's "relative economic interests or rights" will be taxed as a dividend, regardless of the form or nomenclature given the transactions. The test is to examine the change in the taxpayer's relationship to the corporation; §302(b)(1) is satisfied, under this test, if the examination establishes a "meaningful reduction" of the taxpayer's relative interests or rights in the company.

Whether a distribution by redemption of stock was "essentially equivalent to a dividend" for the purposes of the 1954 Code is a question of fact. The district court's factual determinations must be upheld on appeal if they are supported by substantial evidence within the record considered as a whole. . . .

To determine if the district court properly discerned a meaningful reduction in the Trust's interest and rights in Puritan, the starting point must be a comparison of the Trust's relative holdings prior to and after the redemption. As in United States v. Davis, supra, this comparison requires application of the attribution statutes.

Briefly stated, the 1954 Code provided that a trust constructively owned its shares plus the shares held by the beneficiary, including those shares which §318 attributed to the beneficiary. §§302(c), 318.

Applying this statute, it is readily apparent that prior to the redemption, the Trust constructively owned 345 shares of the Puritan company, computed from its own shares (200), Ella's holdings (25), and the shares owned by Ella's children (John — 40, Hank — 40, Ellen Hicks — 40). Following the redemption, the Trust's constructive holdings were reduced to 145 shares (25 owned by Ella, 120 held by her children). Only 11 other shares remained actually outstanding (Hicks — 5, Winkler — 6); therefore, the Trust held 345/356 shares, or 97%, before and 145/156 shares, or 93%, immediately after the redemption.

When the district court made this comparison it included the seventy-five option shares held by Hicks. Accordingly, the district court determined that the Trust held 80% of the company before redemption (345/431), and 62.8% after redemption (145/231). Because the Trust no longer controlled the company after the redemption (holding less than two-thirds of the stock), the district court concluded that the "meaningful reduction" test had been satisfied. The district court included the Hicks option in its calculations pursuant to the plain language of the attribution statute, §318(a)(4), which stated (emphasis added): "If *any* person has an option to acquire stock, such stock shall be considered as owned by such person."

On appeal, the Government urges that §318(a)(4) actually applies only to the taxpayer or to individuals whose shares are otherwise attributable to the taxpayer. The Government would therefore greatly narrow the scope of §318(a)(4). Under the Government's view of the statute, the Trust's ownership interest in Puritan was reduced only 4% as a result of the redemption, from 97 to 93%, which, it contends, was not meaningful as a matter of law.

"[I]n determining the scope of a statute, one is to look first at its language." Dickerson v. New Banner Institute, Inc., [460 U.S. 103, 100] (1983). . . ." Absent a clearly expressed legislative intention to the contrary, that language must ordinarily be regarded as conclusive." Consumer Product Safety Comm'n v. GTE Sylvania, Inc., 447 U.S. 102, 108 (1980). Further, "[i]t is axiomatic that where a statute is clear and unambiguous on its face, a court will not look to legislative history to alter the application of the statute except in rare and exceptional circumstances." Pope v. Rollins Protective Services Co., 703 F.2d 197, 206 (5th Cir. 1983). . . . Finally, "Congress is presumed to use words in their ordinary sense unless it expressly indicates the contrary." Davis Bros., Inc. v. Donovan, 700 F.2d 1368, 1370 (11th Cir. 1983). . . .

Nevertheless, the Government invites this court to examine the legislative history of §318(a)(4) and conclude that "any person" actually means only those "parties in the line of attribution." . . . The Government relies on the commentary in the "Detailed Discussion of Bill" portion of the Senate Report relative to §318(a)(3) (currently effective as §318(a)(4)). The commentary describes the operation of the relevant portions of the attributive statute in the following manner:

§318. Constructive Ownership of Stock

This section describes the area in which although in fact transactions related to stock ownership are in connection with a specific individual, ownership of stock is deemed to

> be in the hands of persons other than the person directly involved. Thus, for the purpose of determining whether a redemption of stock qualifies as a disproportionate redemption . . . consideration is given not only to the stock held by such person but also to stock owned by members of his family. . . .
>
> The area of constructive ownership includes members of the family, persons having interests in . . . trusts, . . . such . . . trusts, . . . and stock held under an option.
>
> In the family area (sec. 318(a)(1)) an individual is deemed to own stock owned by his parents, his children, and his grandchildren. . . . In the case of trusts, . . . the beneficiary or grantor is deemed to own his proportionate interest in the stock owned by the trust or estate and the trust or estate is deemed to own all of the stock owned by its beneficiaries or grantors. In any of the cases *above described* where stock, though not owned, is subject to an option, the holder of such option is deemed to own such stock (sec. 318(a)(3)).

S. Rep. No. 1622, 83d Cong., 2d Sess. 45 (emphasis added).

The Government urges that as a result of the commentary's apparent limitation of the option attribution rule to "the cases above described," "the Senate indicated its intent that §318(a)(3) (now §318(a)(4)) should be limited to parties in the line of attribution." The Internal Revenue Service has consistently followed the reasoning herein argued by the Government, see, e.g., Rev. Rul. 68-601, and the tax court has adopted the Service's view as well. However, only two appeals courts have addressed the issue and they, without analysis, adopted diverse positions.

In Friend v. United States, 345 F.2d 761 (1st Cir. 1965), the First Circuit's dictum indicated that that court believed that "Congress intended that section to apply only where options are held by the person whose shares are being redeemed." 345 F.2d at 764. In Sorem v. C.I.R., 334 F.2d 275, 280 (10th Cir. 1964), the court, again without analysis, applied the plain language of the options attribution provision of §318(a), and rejected the Government's view.

The Government argues that this court should defer to the Service's consistently-applied interpretation of the Code. However, while it is axiomatic that where statutory language remains vague even when illuminated by the legislative history, the construction offered by the agency charged with the enforcement of the statute will often be accorded dispositive weight, it is an equal principle that the agency may not so interpret the statute as to controvert its plain and unambiguous language. Except in "rare and exceptional circumstances," Rubin v. United States, supra, such as where Congress "expressly indicates" its intent that the plain meaning of the statutory language be avoided, Davis Bros., Inc. v. Donovan, supra, unambiguous statutory language "is to be regarded as conclusive." Dickerson v. New Banner Institute, supra.

Instantly, the Government asserts only the commentary of the Senate Report, reprinted above, as support for its construction of "any person" in §318(a)(4). The commentary falls short of a clear indication by Congress that the natural impact of the statutory language under review should be restrained. Accordingly, the district court appropriately included the option shares held by Hicks in determining the Trust's relative holdings prior to and following redemption.

It should be noted that, even if the Hicks shares were excluded, on the instant record the district court would have been entitled to enter the factual finding that the transaction under review was not essentially equivalent to a dividend and was therefore properly claimed as a capital gain. "The question whether a distribution in redemption of stock . . . is not essentially equivalent to a dividend . . . depends upon the facts and circumstances of each case." 26 C.F.R. §1.302-3(b) (1983 Treasury Regulations); United States v. Davis, supra. Obviously, one of the pertinent facts would be the relative holdings of the taxpayer as computed under §318's constructive stock ownership provisions, 26 C.F.R. §1.302(b). United States v. Davis. However, neither statutory enactment nor judicial construction would support the proposition that the resulting comparative calculation would become the exclusive and dispositive fact. In this case, the redemption effected "a change in the relative economic interests or rights" of all the stockholders of the Puritan company. Therefore, despite the fact that—excluding operation of §318(a)(4)—the Trust's relative holdings fell only 4% after redemption, under the unique facts and circumstances of this case, such was a "meaningful reduction" and the distribution was therefore not a dividend.

Accordingly, because substantial evidence supports the district court's factual determination that the transaction was not essentially equivalent to a dividend, the judgment below is affirmed.

NOTES

1. *The chain of attribution in* Patterson Trust. At issue in *Patterson Trust* was the taxation of the distribution in redemption of all of the shares owned by the trust. The trust could not qualify for exchange treatment under the complete termination safe harbor of §302(b)(3) because it constructively owned shares in the corporation after the redemption. Which shares did it constructively own?

Because Ella was a beneficiary of the trust, all her shares were attributed to the trust under §318(a)(3)(B)(i). Note that there is complete attribution from Ella to the trust regardless of her actuarial interest in the trust corpus. If, however, Ella had had only a remote contingent interest in the trust corpus, then there would have been *no* attribution under §318(a)(3)(B)(i).

Could the trust have filed an election under §302(c)(2)(C) and thereby have avoided all attribution from Ella? Recall that the §302(c)(2) waiver applies only to the *family* attribution rules of §318(a)(1). Because attribution from Ella to the trust arose under §318(a)(3), a §302(c) waiver would have had no effect on the attribution to the trust of the shares actually owned by Ella.

Not only are the shares actually owned by Ella attributed to the trust, but shares constructively owned by Ella may also be attributed to the trust under §318(a)(5)(A). Thus, the shares actually owned by Ella's children—Hank, John, and Ellen—are attributed to Ella and then to the trust under §318(a)(1)(A)(ii), (a)(3)(B)(ii), and (a)(5)(A). Although a §302(c)(2) waiver would avoid the attribution from Hank, John, and Ellen to Ella, that waiver applies only to determinations under §302(b)(3).

Are the shares actually owned by Hicks attributed to the trust? No. Although there can be attribution from Hicks to his wife, Ellen, see §318(a)(1)(A)(i), those shares cannot be further attributed from Ellen to her mother because of the anti-sidewise attribution limitation in §318(a)(5)(B) (prohibiting multiple application of the family attribution rules in one chain of ownership). Similarly, in computing Hicks's constructive ownership, there will be attribution of those shares actually owned by Ellen, see §318(a)(1)(A)(i), but he will not be attributed any shares

Ellen constructively owns only because of the family attribution rules. See §318(a)(5)(B).

The number of shares owned by Hicks was relevant in *Patterson Trust* because, for making determinations under §302(b)(2), a shareholder's percentage ownership is a function of the number of shares owned (actually and constructively) by the shareholder relative to the total number of shares outstanding. For computing the total number of shares outstanding, should shares attributed from one shareholder to another be counted twice? Did the court in *Patterson Trust* count any shares twice?

Under §318(a)(4), shares subject to an option are treated as owned by the person having the option. The Service argued in *Patterson Trust* that this provision was intended to ensure that a taxpayer could not qualify for exchange treatment on a redemption while possessing the ability to reacquire a substantial interest in the corporation by exercise of an option. Thus, according to the Service, §318(a)(4) is applicable only in determining the constructive ownership of the taxpayer receiving a distribution in redemption of some of his shares.

The court, however, refused to read §318(a)(4) as limited in this way. Accordingly, the court treated the option given to Hicks as shares constructively owned by him, thereby increasing the total number of shares outstanding. The effect of the court's interpretation of §318(a)(4) was to reduce the trust's pre- and post-redemption percentage of ownership of the corporation. Can the test of §302(b)(2) be manipulated through the strategic use of options as part of redemption transactions? See Bloom and Willens, How to Treat Option Shares Held by Third Parties in Planning for a Redemption, 62 J. Taxn. 80 (1985).

Suppose the option in *Patterson Trust* had been exercisable only after a specified period of time. Would §318(a)(4) still apply to the option? In Rev. Rul. 89-64, 1989-1 C.B. 91, the Service ruled that §318(a)(4) continues to apply. This ruling does not address the length of the specified period. If an option were exercisable only after 50 years, should the option fall under §318(a)(4)?

2. *The limited role of §302(b)(1).* As *Davis* indicates, the courts have given §302(b)(1) a narrow scope. In Levin v. Commissioner, 385 F.2d 521 (2d Cir. 1967), the court reviewed the legislative history of §302(b)(1) before concluding that "it was intended to play a modest role in the statutory scheme." The court agreed with the observation that the "major function" of §302(b)(1) was to immunize redemptions of minority holdings of (nonvoting) preferred stock, citing B. Bittker and J. Eustice, Federal Income Taxation of Corporations and Shareholders 291 (2d ed. 1966). But see Rev. Rul. 85-106, 1985-2 C.B. 116, in which the Service ruled that §302(b)(1) is inapplicable to the redemption of six of nine shares of preferred stock held by a trust when the trust owns, with attribution, 18 percent of the corporation's voting common stock both before and after the redemption.

What role should §302(b)(1) play? In Wright v. United States, 482 F.2d 600 (8th Cir. 1973), the court held that a redemption reducing a shareholder's ownership from 85 percent to 61.7 percent was not essentially equivalent to a dividend when state law imposed a two-thirds voting requirement on certain corporate actions. Cf. Rev. Rul. 78-401, 1978-2 C.B. 127, in which the Service ruled that a reduction in ownership from 90 percent to 60 percent was essentially equivalent to a dividend when no action requiring a supermajority was contemplated.

The Supreme Court wrote in *Davis* that "to qualify for preferred treatment under [§302(b)(1)], a redemption must result in a meaningful reduction of the shareholder's proportionate interest in the corporation." How great must a reduction be to be "meaningful"? The Service has ruled that a reduction in interest from 100 percent to 81 percent is not "meaningful." Rev. Rul. 73-2, 1973-1 C.B. 171. Was the court right in *Patterson Trust* when it said that a reduction of the trust's interest from 97 percent to 93 percent could be "meaningful"? Did the court confuse "meaningful" with "any"? Indeed, the court in *Patterson Trust* simply assumed that a reduction from 80 percent to 60 percent was "meaningful." Is this assumption subject to challenge?

In a pre-*Davis* case, the Second Circuit looked to the effect of a redemption on three aspects of stock ownership: (1) the right to vote, (2) the right to participate in nonliquidating distributions, and (3) the right to share in net assets on liquidation. Himmel v. Commissioner, 338 F.2d 815 (2d Cir. 1964). The Service has ruled that a redemption resulting in a reduction of these rights may satisfy the *Davis* "meaningful reduction" standard. Rev. Rul. 75-502, 1975-2 C.B. 111. A redemption of nonvoting preferred stock might reduce rights (2) and (3) but not (1), while a redemption of common stock with preferred stock outstanding might reduce (1) yet have little effect on (2) and (3). How should these different aspects of stock ownership be combined? Would it be appropriate to look to the relative change in fair market value of the redeemed shareholder's stock?

At best, the scope of §302(b)(1) is not altogether clear. At a minimum, it requires that the redeemed shareholder reduce her relative economic interest in the corporation. Beyond that requirement, the Service has focused on the redeemed shareholder's voting control (or lack of control) in implementing §302(b)(1). For example, the Service has ruled that a redemption qualified under §302(b)(1) when the redeemed shareholder exercised control over the corporation before the redemption but significantly reduced that control because of the redemption.[5] Further, the Service has concluded that a redemption qualified under §302(b)(1) in several cases when the redeemed shareholder reduced her relative economic interest *and* exercised no real control over the corporation both before and after the redemption.[6]

3. *Constructive ownership after* Davis. While the narrow issue before the Supreme Court in *Davis* was whether the attribution rules apply to determinations under §302(b)(1), language in the Court's opinion seems to speak to how those attribution rules should be applied to the whole of §302(b). Would it be proper, after *Davis,* to take into account evidence of a shareholder's estrangement from, or independence of, the persons whose shares would be imputed to him under §302(c)(1)? Compare David Metzger Trust v. Commissioner, 693 F.2d 459 (5th Cir. 1982) (family hostility cannot override attribution rules), aff'g 76 T.C. 42

5. See Rev. Rul. 75-502, 1975-2 C.B. 111 (concluding that a reduction from 57% to 50% was meaningful when a single, unrelated individual owned the remaining stock after the redemption); Rev. Rul. 76-364, 1976-2 C.B. 91 (finding a reduction meaningful when the redeemed shareholder lost the ability to join with any one of three other shareholders to control the corporation). Cf. Rev. Rul. 85-106, 1985-2 C.B. 116 (concluding that a redemption of nonvoting preferred did not qualify under §302(b)(1), because the shareholder could control the corporation both before and after the redemption by joining with two other shareholders); Rev. Rul. 77-81, 1977-1 C.B. 218 (concluding that a reduction in interest from 60% to 55% was not meaningful).

6. Rev. Rul. 76-385, 1976-2 C.B. 92 (shareholder's percentage interest in a large publicly traded corporation reduced from 0.0001118% to 0.0001018%); Rev. Rul. 75-512, 1975-2 C.B. 112 (minority shareholder exercised no control over the corporation); Rev. Rul. 56-183, 1956-1 C.B. 161 (shareholder's interest reduced from 11% to 9% and remaining stock owned by unrelated shareholders).

(1981) (court reviewed), with Haft v. Commissioner, 510 F.2d 43 (1st Cir. 1975) (remand to consider whether family hostility might mitigate attribution rules), and David Metzger Trust v. Commissioner, 76 T.C. 42, 80-84 (1981) (Tannenwald, J., concurring); see also Cerone v. Commissioner, 87 T.C. 1 (1986). If you conclude that "family hostility" should be taken into account to measure control, should control also be measured by considering stock owned by unrelated close friends (or a paramour)?

4. *Redemptions by publicly held corporations.* The development of both the statutory and judicial law of redemptions has focused on closely held corporations, which traditionally were the only corporations that customarily redeemed their shares. With increasing frequency, however, some publicly held corporations have embarked on large-scale programs of repurchasing their own shares. This practice and its tax implications have been described as follows:

> Thus, suppose that *X* Corporation, with one million shares of common stock outstanding, is a stable, non-growth company which annually generates $1 million of earnings after tax, or $1 per share. Unable to reinvest its earnings at a profitable rate of return, *X* decides to distribute the $1 million to its shareholders. The stock of *X*, which normally sells at 10 times earnings, is currently quoted at $11, i.e., normal value of $10 plus $1 per share available for distribution.
>
> If *X* distributes the $1 million as a dividend, and if the shareholders of *X* pay tax at an average rate of 30 percent, then the net wealth per share of an average shareholder following the distribution will be $10.70, i.e., normal value of *X* stock ($10) plus the after-tax value of the dividend ($0.70). In the alternative, if *X* uses the $1 million to repurchase its own shares at $11 per share, it will be able to retire approximately 90,909 shares at that price. Earnings per share will then rise to about $1.10 on the 909,991 shares that remain outstanding, and, with no change in the multiplier of 10, the value of the stock held by non-selling shareholders will be $11, as compared with an average net wealth per share of $10.70 if a dividend is paid. Shareholders who have chosen to resell their stock will hold $11 in cash for each share sold less any capital gain tax resulting from the sale, with the net proceeds varying from individual to individual depending on original cost.
>
> Without detriment to those who prefer to sell, but provided always that the only tax imposed is a capital gain tax on sellers disposing of appreciated shares, *X* Corporation can benefit non-selling shareholders by applying its "unwanted" cash assets to the retirement of outstanding stock instead of paying dividends. Aside from tax effects, though possibly bearing some relation thereto, share repurchase has the further advantage of providing an option to shareholders, since those who desire current income can obtain it by selling a portion of their shares, while those who do not can avoid it by retaining all of theirs.
>
> The critical assumptions that underlie the tax results just described are, first, that repurchase produces capital gain (or loss) for shareholders who choose to surrender their shares to the company, and second, that repurchase has no present tax consequences (other than the postponement of gain or loss) for those who do not. The Internal Revenue Service has thus far raised no question about the legitimacy of these results as a matter of law. They are also either ignored or taken for granted by the tax bar, presumably for the reason, mentioned above, that dividend equivalency problems are rarely associated with publicly held corporations.

Chirelstein, Optional Redemptions and Optional Dividends: Taxing the Repurchase of Common Shares, 78 Yale L.J. 739 (1969).

What is the statutory foundation for the first "critical assumption" (that capital gain treatment will be available to the tendering shareholder) identified by

Professor Chirelstein in the final paragraph of the extract? Is it necessarily the case that any redemption by a publicly held corporation is "substantially disproportionate" (or at least not essentially equivalent to a dividend)? Aren't the attribution rules equally applicable to the redemption of publicly held stock? See Bacon, Share Redemptions by Publicly Held Companies: A New Look at Dividend Equivalency, 26 Tax L. Rev. 283 (1971). As to the second "critical assumption" (that nontendering shareholders are unaffected by the redemption) identified by Professor Chirelstein, you should suspend your judgment until §305 is examined. In general, though, little attention has been focused on the tax consequences of a redemption to a nontendering shareholder. What alternatives are there? See Doernberg, The Taxation of Reinvested Corporate Earnings, 24 Wm. & Mary L. Rev. 1 (1982).

5. *Redemption of stock versus retirement of bonds.* Section 302 speaks of a redemption of "stock." On the repayment of corporate debt, the creditor has no gain or loss unless she receives more than her basis for the debt instrument. Even if there is a gain, the retirement of corporate bonds and other evidences of indebtedness is ordinarily a capital gain or loss transaction by virtue of §1271(a)(1), and there is no counterpart of §302 in the Code to treat the retirement of such creditor instruments as a distribution of earnings and profits. Once more (recall the discussion of equity and debt in Chapter 3), we find the Code smiling on the issuance of debt instruments instead of stock by the newly organized corporation and the ongoing, closely held corporation. Note the radically different treatment Davis would have received had the monies advanced for the preferred stock instead been contributed for bonds. See the penultimate paragraph in the *Davis* opinion. But the same criteria that turn ostensible bonds or debentures into stock so as to deny an interest deduction may also require the bonds to be treated as stock under §302.

6. *Redemption of §306 stock.* A possible end-run around §§302 and 301 takes the form of a sale of a shareholder's stock to an unrelated third party from whom the stock is later redeemed by the corporation. For example, how should a shareholder be taxed if he sells some of his shares in a closely held corporation to a third party subject to the understanding that the shares will be redeemed immediately? How definite must such an "understanding" be for the Commissioner to attribute the redemption to the selling shareholder? In any event, is the Commissioner likely to be able to discern the presence of a prearranged plan of redemption from the facts disclosed on the parties' tax returns? How should that difficulty be taken into account by an ethical tax planner?

A shareholder who tries this route to avoid §§302 and 301 may well find himself out of the frying pan and into the fire if he uses common stock as the bailout mechanism. What happens if, for example, the third party refuses to accede to the redemption? The tax-avoiding shareholder might end up with a stranger owning (and voting) a significant portion of the stock of his corporation. For this reason, sales of stock subject to prearranged redemptions will most often involve nonvoting preferred stock.

Section 306, dealing with the redemption or sale of certain classes of stock (primarily preferred stock issued as a stock dividend), is examined at page 233 infra. Consider also in this context the tax advantages of the gift of stock to a charitable organization in anticipation of redemption.

7. *Redemptions to pay death taxes.* Section 303, relating to distributions in redemption of stock to pay death taxes as well as funeral and administration expenses, first entered the Code in 1950. The general purpose of §303 is to protect

against forced sales of family businesses. Consider, for example, the case of a taxpayer who at death leaves a substantial estate composed predominantly of the stock of a closely held corporation. The decedent's executor will need cash for the payment of administrative expenses, funeral costs, the federal estate tax, and possibly a state inheritance tax. With such an illiquid estate, the executor may have no choice but to cause the corporation to redeem some of the estate's stock to raise the needed funds. Although the estate will have a fair market value adjusted basis in the stock pursuant to §1014, in the absence of §303 the estate might incur a tax liability on the redemption pursuant to §§301 and 302. Application of §303, though, will give exchange treatment to the estate on the redemption, thereby eliminating all tax liability by virtue of the basis step-up at death under §1014.

Although the simple example above describes the situation to which §303 was intended to speak, the benefits of §303 are available without any showing that the estate lacks sufficient liquid assets to cover its expenses. The benefit of §303, however, is available only to an estate in which stock of the redeeming corporation constitutes more than 35 percent of its gross value less the deduction provided by §§2053 and 2054 for taxes, expenses, debts, and losses, although the stock of two or more corporations can qualify under certain circumstances. §303(b)(2)(B). Section 303 can apply to taxpayers other than an estate, although it can only apply to owners of stock actually chargeable for debts, expenses, or taxes of the estate and only to the extent thereof.

In Rev. Rul. 87-132, 1987-2 C.B. 82, the Service adopted an expansive interpretation of the transactions covered by §303. An estate and an unrelated individual each owned 50 percent of the outstanding stock of a corporation. The estate wanted the benefits of §303 without diminishing its voting control over the corporation. Accordingly, the corporation declared a stock dividend of new nonvoting stock and then promptly redeemed two-thirds of the nonvoting stock issued to the estate. The Service ruled that this redemption was protected by §303, emphasizing that "the basis of the stock redeemed [was] determined by reference to the basis of the 'old stock' included in the estate."

Because the benefits of §303 are available only to substantial owners of a corporation, shareholders will sometimes seek to inflate their stock ownership beyond their actual holdings. For example, the taxpayer in Estate of Byrd v. Commissioner, 388 F.2d 223 (5th Cir. 1967), argued that the attribution rules of §318 could be applied to determinations under §303. Because §303 does not explicitly reference §318, however, the court held that application of the attribution rules to §303 determinations would be improper, relying on the first clause of §318(a).

How does §303 apply if stock is included in an estate because of §2035? In Rev. Rul. 84-76, 1984-1 C.B. 91, the Service ruled that §303 does not apply to redemptions of stock not actually owned by the decedent but includible in his gross estate under §2035(a) (transfers made within three years of death). The Service did rule, however, that such stock can be used to satisfy the 35-percent test of §303(b)(2)(A), thereby allowing stock actually owned by the decedent to qualify for §303 treatment.

Section 303 historically has played a minor role in the drama of subchapter C. Nonetheless, exchange treatment is important not only because of a preferential rate of tax but also because of the recovery of basis obtained prior to the recognition of any gain, however taxed. Because of the fair market value basis rule of §1014, applicable to property passing through the estate of a decedent, exchange treatment of postdeath redemptions often will avoid recognition of income altogether.

8. *Constructive redemptions.* Suppose a controlling shareholder sells stock at a gain to employees pursuant to a corporate stock bonus plan. Because the corporation had an obligation to sell stock to the employees under the stock bonus plan, the transaction presumably should be recharacterized as a transfer from the controlling shareholder to the corporation and then from the corporation to the employees. In fact, the Seventh Circuit adopted this approach, recharacterizing the transaction as if the corporation had redeemed the controlling shareholder's shares (producing ordinary income under §§302(d) and 301) followed by an issuance of stock by the corporation to the employees. Schneider v. Commissioner, 855 F.2d 435 (7th Cir. 1988).

PROBLEMS

5-6. *X* Corp. has one class of stock outstanding and earnings and profits exceeding $25,000. It redeems some of *B*'s *X* stock with a basis of $10,000 and value of $25,000. What are the tax consequences to *B* if—

a. *B* owns 54 percent of the *X* stock before the redemption and 50 percent after the redemption and—
   i. One other unrelated shareholder owns the remaining *X* stock; or
   ii. 50 other unrelated shareholders each own 1 percent of the *X* stock.
b. *B* owns 12 percent of the *X* stock before the redemption and 10 percent after the redemption and—
   i. One unrelated shareholder owns more than 50 percent of the *X* stock; or
   ii. *X* is a large publicly traded corporation and no other shareholder owns more than 0.05 percent of the *X* stock.

5-7. Reconsider problem 5-2(b) on page 163, but assume that Father's estate consists of the *X* Corp. stock as well as cash of $800,000 and that the federal estate tax imposed on Father's estate is $400,000. What are the tax consequences? Does your answer change if Father's estate consisted of only the *X* Corp. stock and $2 million of stock in a variety of other corporations? Assume Father's estate incurs no expenses described in §2053 or §2054.

4. *Partial Liquidations under §302(b)(4)*

If a redemption is a "partial liquidation" within the meaning of §302(b)(4), it is taxed to any noncorporate distributes as an exchange under §302(a). Partial liquidations are defined in §302(e), which makes clear (see §302(e)(1)(A)), unlike under §302(b)(1)-(3), that the redemption's *corporate-level* effects determine whether it is a partial liquidation.

Until 1982, the definition of a "partial liquidation" was found in §346. The Tax Equity and Fiscal Responsibility Act of 1982 repealed that section and moved the definition to §302(e). Although the language of §302(e) varies slightly from old §346, the variation is not substantive. Accordingly, the case law that developed under old §346 as well as the Treasury regulations promulgated under that section should be considered fully applicable to §302(b)(4).

The definition of a partial liquidation is found in §302(e)(1). While the language of subsection (e)(1)(A) mirrors the "not essentially equivalent to a dividend" language of §302(b)(1), the thrust of §302(e)(1)(A) differs substantially from that of §302(b)(1). Determinations under §302(b)(1) are made by looking to the effect of the redemption on the tendering shareholder and her interest in the redeeming corporation, and as the Supreme Court in *Davis* noted, any corporate purpose is irrelevant. In contrast, determinations under §302(e)(1)(A) are made solely by reference to the effect of (and reasons for) the redemption at the corporate level. Further, unlike §302(b)(1), §302(e) offers a more objective two-part test found in §302(e)(2) (and discussed below) that, if met, satisfies the "not essentially equivalent to a dividend" standard. (That standard is unlikely to have much impact because of the objective two-part test.)

Subsection (e)(1)(B) adds the dual requirement that a partial liquidation must be made "pursuant to a plan" and occur "within the taxable year in which the plan is adopted or within the next succeeding taxable year." Note that §302(e)(4) allows a partial liquidation to qualify for exchange treatment under §302(a) even if made pro rata to the distributing corporation's shareholders.

Rev. Rul. 60-322

1960-2 C.B. 118

Advice has been requested relative to the tax consequences of a proposed distribution by a corporation of cash, realized from the sale of United States Government bonds and excess inventories, to its stockholders under the circumstances described below.

M corporation has 3,800 shares of common stock, par value of 10*x* dollars per share, of which 200 shares are held in the treasury. The balance sheet indicates accumulated earnings of 1,500*x* dollars.

The corporation was engaged in the business of buying raw skins and tanning and selling the leather to a certain segment of the leather trade. It showed consistent profits until two years ago when the demand therefor suffered a serious, if not a permanent, decline. In an effort to revitalize the business, the corporation changed over to buying raw skins of another kind and tanning and selling the leather to another segment of the leather trade. However, the situation did not improve with the result that continuing losses were incurred and a large inventory of 5,000*x* dollars was accumulated.

Early in the year under consideration, *M* corporation determined that further purchases should be curtailed and inventories liquidated. Pursuant to this policy, the inventory was reduced to 3,000*x* dollars. In doing so, the corporation had sustained substantial operating losses. However, in view of the depressed state of the market and the grim future prospects, the process of liquidating its inventory is expected to be continued and the operations will be carried on at a modified basis with purchases kept at a minimum. In this manner, it is felt that the operating losses can be minimized and if the business decline continues, then a complete liquidation will eventually be voted by the stockholders. Accordingly, the *M* corporation proposes to redeem a portion of its stock with cash from the sale of United States Series

G bonds and from the proceeds of the inventories being liquidated in the ordinary course of business. . . .

Where a corporation has earnings available, in order for the distribution of assets by it to its shareholders to be treated as a partial liquidation, the distribution must result from a genuine contraction of the business of the corporation. See Joseph W. Imler v. Commissioner, 11 T.C. 836. . . . In the instant case, the earnings and profits of prior years were retained in the corporation and resulted in building up a large inventory and investment of funds in Government bonds.

Under the foregoing set of facts, it is held that neither the sale of investments nor the sale of a large part of the inventory in the ordinary course of business constitutes a genuine contraction of the business of the corporation. Accordingly, the proposed distribution of cash for the portion of the stock of *M* corporation to be redeemed will not constitute a distribution in partial liquidation within the purview of section [302(b)(4)] of the code. The provisions of section 301 will apply to this distribution and, accordingly, the distribution will be taxed as a dividend to the extent provided in section 316.

NOTES

1. *Corporate contractions.* Although §302(e) does not explicitly use the term "corporate contraction," that phrase has been the touchstone of a "partial liquidation" since before the first statutory treatment of partial liquidations. *Imler*, cited in Rev. Rul. 60-322, is the classic example of a contraction of a business.

> The principal building owned by the company had been damaged by fire in 1941. When the company undertook to repair the building it was found that, because of war conditions, the shortage of building materials, and high costs, it was advisable to abandon 2 damaged floors and reduce the 7-story building to one of 5 stories. The consequence was that the company found its facilities inadequate to carry on the retinning and soldering operations formerly engaged in. Moreover, these operations had proved unprofitable in recent experience because of the war conditions and shortage of necessary materials. For these reasons the company discontinued the retinning and soldering operations. This reduction in operations likewise reduced the amount of capital necessary for carrying on the business activities of the company. This was a bona fide contraction of the business operations and consequent reduction in capital used. The company thus had a real and legitimate purpose for reducing its outstanding capital stock.
>
> The motives of the corporation were all related to the above business purpose and were, therefore, legitimate and properly conceived. If the excess of insurance proceeds be set to one side, the surplus of the company had remained almost constant for 10 years. The company had followed a conservative dividend policy throughout its history and had not paid a dividend since 1934. The original issuance of the stock had occurred many years before and there was no connection between the issuance and the redemption of the same. There was no special circumstance or condition relating to the distribution excepting the fact that the company had in its hands the excess insurance proceeds, which formed the basis of the distribution. We are convinced that, except for the fire and excess insurance proceeds, there would have been no distribution.

11 T.C. 836, 840-841.

See Rev. Rul. 74-296, 1974-1 C.B. 80, distinguishing Rev. Rul. 60-322 and finding a genuine contraction in a change of business from a department store to a discount store. Here the taxpayer discontinued most of its operations and then changed the remaining business. Compare Estate of Chandler v. Commissioner, 22 T.C. 1158 (1954), aff'd, 228 F.2d 909 (6th Cir. 1955), in which a corporation distributed substantial cash in a pro rata partial redemption of its shares shortly after selling its general department store and opening a ladies' ready-to-wear store. Held, no valid partial liquidation because the distributed cash came from surplus rather than a reduction in working capital; the new store required as much working capital as did the prior department store.

In an effort to lend a degree of certainty to the concept of "corporate contraction," Congress as part of the 1954 Code enacted the predecessor of §302(e)(2) and (3). Unlike the "not essentially equivalent to a dividend" test of §302(b)(1) and §302(e)(1)(A), the "termination of a business" test in §302(e)(2) is intended to be objectively determinable. To meet the "termination" requirement, the corporation must distribute the assets, *or the proceeds*, of a business that was actively conducted for the five-year period immediately preceding the distribution, and immediately after the distribution it must continue to be engaged in a second trade or business with a similar five-year history. The concepts used by §302(e), and some of its problems, overlap with those of §355. Section 355 relates to so-called divisive reorganizations in which a corporation distributes to its shareholders the stock of a subsidiary corporation operating a going business while the parent corporation continues to operate another trade or business. See Chapter 11 infra.

Regulations under old §346 specify that an "active trade or business" be defined by reference to §355 and Treas. Regs. §1.355-1. New regulations have been promulgated under §355 defining an active trade or business since §346 was repealed, see Treas. Regs. §1.355-3. The examples in Treas. Regs. §1.355-3(c) are especially helpful in determining what activities rise to the level of an active trade or business.

Note that a qualified trade or business must have been conducted for at least five years prior to the partial liquidation. §302(e)(3)(A). If the distributing corporation did not conduct it for that entire period, some other taxpayer must have done so *and* the distributing corporation must have acquired the business in a tax-free transaction. See §302(e)(3)(B). Suppose *X* Corp. acquires all the stock of *Y* Corp. in a taxable purchase and then liquidates *Y* Corp. in a tax-free §332 liquidation. Has *X* acquired the business formerly conducted by *Y* in a transaction qualifying as tax free under §302(e)(3)(B)? See Treas. Regs. §1.355-3(b)(4)(i).

2. *Distributions of working capital.* The Service has ruled that in a genuine corporate contraction, a distribution in partial liquidation may include not only the net proceeds from a sale of the operating assets but also an amount of capital equal to the working capital attributable to the terminated business activity. Rev. Rul. 60-232, 1960-2 C.B. 115. At the same time, if a corporation reinvests the working capital of a ceased business in its other business, a subsequent distribution of cash will not be related back to the business cessation. Rev. Rul. 67-299, 1967-2 C.B. 138. See also Gordon v. Commissioner, 424 F.2d 378 (2d Cir. 1970), holding that a distribution of less than the entire proceeds received from the sale of an active trade or business cannot qualify as a partial liquidation.

3. *Surrender of shares.* Even if no shares are surrendered, as is true in an informal pro rata partial liquidation of a closely held corporation, the transaction may

nevertheless qualify as a redemption. See Fowler Hosiery v. Commissioner, 301 F.2d 394 (7th Cir. 1962). See also Joint Comm. on Taxn., General Explanation of the Tax Equity and Fiscal Responsibility Act of 1982, at 126 (1982). What portion of the shareholders' basis will be applied against the amount realized? See Rev. Rul. 57-334, 1957-2 C.B. 240. Is a distribution likely to qualify as a redemption described in §302(b)(1)-(3) if no shares are surrendered?

The discontinuance of a subsidiary's business and distribution of its assets (or the proceeds) to the shareholders of its parent may work a partial liquidation of the *parent* corporation. See Rev. Rul. 75-223, 1975-1 C.B. 109, clarified, Rev. Rul. 77-376, 1977-2 C.B. 107. But see Rev. Rul. 79-184, 1979-1 C.B. 143.

Consider, for example, the case of *ABC*, Inc., which operates a business and also owns all the stock of *XYZ*, Inc., which operates a second business. Suppose *XYZ* sells its business and distributes the proceeds to *ABC* in a liquidating distribution, which then distributes those proceeds to its own shareholders, all of whom are individuals. How will the distribution to *ABC* be taxed? How should the distribution to the shareholders of *ABC* be taxed?

4. *Corporate distributees.* Until 1982, exchange treatment for partial liquidations was available to corporate and noncorporate shareholders alike. Currently, corporate shareholders cannot qualify for sale or exchange treatment under the partial liquidation provision of §302(b)(4). See §302(b)(4)(A). For the most part, this limitation works in favor of corporate shareholders because of the dividends-received deduction provided by §243. Under §1059(e)(1)(A), however, a corporate shareholder receiving a distribution in redemption of stock that would qualify as a partial liquidation to a noncorporate shareholder must treat the distribution as an extraordinary dividend. Recall that, under §1059(a), a corporation must reduce its basis in stock held for less than two years by any extraordinary dividends received with respect to such stock. Thus, if §1059 applies, a partial liquidation to a corporate distributee eventually will produce the equivalent of sale or exchange treatment once the corporate distributee sells or exchanges its remaining stock. See the discussion of §1059 at pages 151-152 supra.

PROBLEM

5-8. Consider whether *T* qualifies for exchange treatment under §302(b)(4) on each of the following distributions.

a. *X* Corp. has operated a steel mill for many years. Because business has declined, *X* Corp. shuts down one of its furnaces, lays off 25 percent of its employees, and reduces production to 60 percent of its former capacity. *X* sells approximately 40 percent of its inventory as well as small machinery used with the closed furnace. The sale proceeds, as well as approximately 40 percent of *X*'s working capital, are distributed to *T* and to the other *X* shareholders pro rata. Is it relevant whether *T* is an individual or a corporation? Must the shareholders turn in a portion of their shares?
b. *Y* Corp. has operated a log mill and a lumber yard for 10 years. The fair market value of the log mill is $250,000. The entire output of the log mill is sent to the lumber yard, although that output accounts for only 25 percent of the lumber yard's inventory. *Y* sells the log mill and distributes the

proceeds to *T*, its 60-percent shareholder, in redemption of stock worth $200,000. Would it make a difference if *Y* had operated the lumber yard for only four years? If it had acquired the lumber yard four years ago?

c. *Z* Corp. has operated an ice cream parlor for 15 years. Seven years ago, a small food menu was added, and the seating capacity was expanded. The food operation now accounts for more than half of *Z*'s gross receipts and profits. *Z* Corp. distributes the ice cream equipment, ice cream trademark, and associated goodwill to *T*, its major shareholder in complete redemption of all of *T*'s stock. *T* will continue to run the ice cream business at a new location.

B. TREATMENT OF THE CORPORATION

As discussed at pages 120-124 supra, a corporation, as a general rule, recognizes gain but not loss on a nonliquidating distribution of property. §311(a) and (b). See Martin Ice Cream Co. v. Commissioner, 110 T.C. 189 (1998), where the Tax Court found a corporation taxable under §311(b) on the distribution of appreciated property to the shareholder in a redemption. Because redemptions under §302 are a subclass of the more general term "distributions," the redemption of stock with appreciated property ordinarily will result in recognition of gain to the distributing corporation.

If a corporation redeems some of its shares, the redemption may affect its earnings and profits in two ways. First, to the extent that gain is recognized by the redeeming corporation (because appreciated property is distributed), it will increase its earnings and profits pursuant to §312(b). Second, because the transaction involves a distribution of corporate assets, it must also reduce its earnings and profits, but the amount of the reduction will depend on how the redemption is taxed. If it is taxed under §301, the usual rule of §312(a) applies (i.e., earnings and profits are reduced (but not below zero) by the greater of the basis or value of each distributed asset). But what if the redemption is taxed to the shareholder as an exchange pursuant to §302(a)?

If a redemption is taxed to the distributee as an exchange, some part of the amount distributed might be treated as a distribution of the corporation's paid-in capital and not reduce earnings and profits. In fact, §312(n)(7) expressly limits the reduction of earnings and profits in just this way. Under §312(n)(7), if a redemption is taxed as an exchange, the distributing corporation limits its reduction in its earnings and profits to "an amount which is not in excess of the ratable share of the earnings and profits of [the] corporation . . . attributable to the stock so redeemed."

A conceptual difficulty arises, however, when the corporation has appreciated assets, for in such cases the amount distributed in redemption may exceed each redeemed share's allocable proportion of capital plus retained earnings, the excess being an allocable proportion of unrealized appreciation not yet reflected in the corporation's books or its earnings and profits account. Should this excess be charged, in whole or in part, to the corporation's earnings and profits account? See §312(n)(7). To understand the workings of that section, consider the following example taken from the conference report accompanying the 1984 Deficit Reduction Act.

X Corp. has outstanding 1,000 shares of class A common stock and 1,000 shares of class B common stock. Both classes are $10 par stock, and both were issued for $20 per share (for a total of $40,000). The class A stock has a preference as to dividends and on liquidation in a ratio of 2-to-1 over the class B stock, whereas only the class B stock votes. If *X* Corp. distributes $140,000 in cash in redemption of all the class A stock at a time when it has $120,000 in current and accumulated earnings and profits and assets with net value of $210,000 (i.e., with $50,000 of unrealized appreciation), then how much of the distribution should be charged to *X* Corp.'s earnings and profits?

The committee report specifically states that $80,000 should be charged to the corporation's earnings and profits, leaving only $60,000 to be applied against the corporation's capital account. The amount reducing the earnings and profits account is two-thirds of the corporation's total earnings and profits, a fraction determined by reference to the redeemed stock's preferential claim on the corporation's assets. The effect of §312(n)(7) is to allocate part of the corporation's earnings and profits account to each outstanding share, taking into account not only the total number of shares outstanding but also the legal priorities of each class of stock.

How should a corporation's earnings and profits be allocated between common stock and stock that is preferred and limited as to dividends and on liquidation (i.e., preferred stock)? According to the conference report,

> [N]o earnings and profits generally should be allocable to preferred stock which is not convertible [into common stock] or participating to any significant extent in corporate growth. Therefore, a redemption of such preferred stock should result in a reduction of the capital account only, unless the distribution includes dividend arrearages, which will reduce earnings and profits.

H.R. Rep. No. 861, 98th Cong., 2d Sess. 840, 1984-3 C.B. (vol. 2) 94.

What are the tax consequences if a corporation redeems a share of stock for less than the share's allocable portion of earnings and profits? For example, suppose a corporation has 100 shares of common stock outstanding and earnings and profits of $1,000. How should the redemption of one share for $7 affect the corporation's earnings and profits? Note the "not in excess of" language in §312(n)(7). According to the Senate Report accompanying the Deficit Reduction Act of 1984, "the committee does not intend that earnings and profits be reduced by more than the amount of a redemption." S. Rep. No. 169, 98th Cong., 2d Sess. 202 (1984).

C. REDEMPTIONS RELATED TO OTHER TRANSACTIONS

1. *Redemptions in Lieu of Buy-Sell Agreements*

In *Old Colony Trust Co. v. Commissioner*, 279 U.S. 716 (1929), the Supreme Court ruled that an employee had income when his employer paid the employee's federal income tax obligation pursuant to the employment contract. In another context, suppose that *A* and *B*, both shareholders of *X* Corp., agree that upon the death of either shareholder, the survivor agrees to purchase the shares from the estate of the deceased. But what happens if *B* dies and instead of *A* purchasing the shares, *X* Corp.

redeems the shares from *B*'s estate? Do *Old Colony* principles result in a deemed payment and taxation to *A* when *X* Corp. fulfills *A*'s obligation? Consider the following two cases.

Holsey v. Commissioner

258 F.2d 865 (3d Cir. 1958)

Before Maris, Goodrich and McLaughlin, Circuit Judges.

MARIS, Circuit Judge. . . .

J.R. Holsey Sales Company, a New Jersey corporation, was organized on April 28, 1936, as an Oldsmobile dealership. Taxpayer has been president and a director of the company since its organization. Only 20 shares were issued out of the 2,500 shares of no par value stock authorized; these 20 shares were issued to Greenville Auto Sales Company, a Chevrolet dealership, in exchange for all of the latter's right, title, and interest to the Oldsmobile franchise and other assets with respect to the franchise which had been owned and operated by the Greenville Company. The 20 shares issued were assigned a value of $11,000. Taxpayer's father, Charles V. Holsey, in 1936, owned more than two-thirds of the outstanding stock of the Greenville Company, and taxpayer was vice-president and a director of that corporation.

On April 30, 1936, taxpayer acquired from the Greenville Company an option to purchase 50% of the outstanding shares of the Holsey Company for $11,000, and a further option to purchase, within ten years after the exercise of the first option, all the remaining shares for a sum to be agreed upon. The Greenville Company owned all of the outstanding stock of the Holsey Company from its organization in 1936 until November, 1939, when taxpayer exercised his first option and purchased 50% of the outstanding stock of the Holsey Company for $11,000.

On June 28, 1946, the further option in favor of taxpayer was revised. Under the terms of the revised option, taxpayer was granted the right to purchase the remaining outstanding shares of the Holsey Company at any time up to and including June 28, 1951, for $80,000. The revised option was in favor of taxpayer individually and was not assignable by him to anyone other than a corporation in which he owned not less than 50% of the voting stock. On the date of the revision of this option, taxpayer's father owned 76% of the stock of the Greenville Company and taxpayer was a vice-president and director of that corporation. . . .

On January 19, 1951, taxpayer assigned his revised option to the Holsey Company; on the same date the Holsey Company exercised the option and paid the Greenville Company $80,000 for the stock held by it. This transaction resulted in taxpayer becoming the owner of 100% of the outstanding stock of the Holsey Company. In his income tax return for the year 1951, taxpayer gave no effect to this transaction.

The principal officers and only directors of the Holsey Company from April 28, 1936, to December 31, 1951, were taxpayer, his brother, Charles D. Holsey, and their father, Charles V. Holsey. On January 19, 1951, when the revised option was exercised, the earned surplus of the Holsey Company was in excess of $300,000.

The Oldsmobile franchise, under which the Holsey Company operated, was a yearly contract entered into by the Corporation and the manufacturer in reliance upon the personal qualifications and representations of taxpayer as an individual. It was the manufacturer's policy to have its dealers own all of the stock in dealership organizations.

The Commissioner determined that the effect of the transaction of January 19, 1951, wherein the Holsey Company paid $80,000 to the Greenville Company for 50% of the outstanding stock of the Holsey Company, constituted a dividend to taxpayer, the remaining stockholder. The Commissioner therefore asserted a deficiency against taxpayer in the sum of $41,385.34. The Tax Court sustained the Commissioner. 28 T.C. 962.

The question presented for decision in this case is whether the Tax Court erred in holding that the payment by the Holsey Company of $80,000 to the Greenville Company for the purchase from that company of its stock in the Holsey Company was essentially equivalent to the distribution of a taxable dividend to the taxpayer, the remaining stockholder of the Holsey Company. . . .

It will be observed that section [316(a)] defines a dividend as a distribution made by a corporation "to its shareholders." Accordingly unless a distribution which is sought to be taxed to a stockholder as a dividend is made to him or for his benefit it may not be regarded as either a dividend or the legal equivalent of a dividend. Here the distribution was made to the Greenville Company, not to the taxpayer. This the Government, of course, concedes but urges that it was made for the benefit of the taxpayer. It is true that it has been held that a distribution by a corporation in redemption of stock which the taxpayer stockholder has a contractual obligation to purchase is essentially the equivalent of a dividend to him since it operates to discharge his obligation. But where, as here, the taxpayer was never under any legal obligation to purchase the stock held by the other stockholder, the Greenville Company, having merely an option to purchase which he did not exercise but instead assigned to the Holsey Company, the distribution did not discharge any obligation of his and did not benefit him in any direct sense.

It is, of course, true that the taxpayer was benefited indirectly by the distribution. The value of his own stock was increased, since the redemption was for less than book value, and he became sole stockholder. But these benefits operated only to increase the value of the taxpayer's stock holdings; they could not give rise to taxable income within the meaning of the Sixteenth Amendment until the corporation makes a distribution to the taxpayer or his stock is sold. Eisner v. Macomber, 1920, 252 U.S. 189; Schmitt v. Commissioner of Internal Revenue, 3 Cir., 1954, 208 F.2d 819. In the latter case in a somewhat similar connection this court said (at page 821):

> During these years when Wolverine was buying its own shares it, of course, was subject to income tax as a corporation. Mrs. Green was subject to tax on whatever profit she made by the sale of these shares to the corporation. But what happened to warrant imposing a tax upon Schmitt and Lehren? If one owns a piece of real estate and, because of its favorable location in a city, the land becomes increasingly valuable over a period of years, the owner is not subject to income taxation upon the annual increase in value. In the same way, if a man owns shares in a corporation which gradually become more valuable through the years he is not taxed because of the increase in value even though he is richer at the end of each year than he was at the end of the year before. If he disposes of that which has increased, of course he must pay tax upon his profit. All of this is hornbook law of taxation; nobody denies it.

We think that the principle thus stated is equally applicable here. Indeed the Tax Court itself has so held in essentially similar cases.

The question whether payments made by a corporation in the acquisition and redemption of its stock are essentially equivalent to the distribution of a taxable dividend has been often before the courts and certain criteria have been enunciated. The most significant of these is said to be whether the distribution leaves the proportionate interests of the stockholders unchanged as occurs when a true dividend is paid. Ferro v. Commissioner of Internal Revenue, 3 Cir., 1957, 242 F.2d 838, 841. The application of that criterion to the facts of this case compels the conclusion that in the absence of a direct pecuniary benefit to the taxpayer the Tax Court erred in holding the distribution in question taxable to him. For in his case prior to the distribution the taxpayer and the Greenville Company each had a 50% interest in the Holsey Company whereas after it was over the taxpayer had 100% of the outstanding stock and the Greenville Company none.

The Government urges the lack of a corporate purpose for the distribution and the taxpayer seeks to establish one. But we do not consider this point for, as we have recently held, "It is the effect of the redemption, rather than the purpose which actuated it, which controls the determination of dividend equivalence." Kessner v. Commissioner of Internal Revenue, 3 Cir., 1957, 248 F.2d 943, 944. Nor need we discuss the present position of the Government that the transaction must be treated as a sham and the purchase of the stock as having been made by the taxpayer through his alter ego, the Holsey Company. For the Tax Court made no such finding, doubtless in view of the fact that at the time the taxpayer owned only 50% of the stock and was in a minority on the board of directors. On the contrary that court based its decision on the benefit which the distribution by the corporation to the Greenville Company conferred upon the taxpayer, which it thought gave rise to taxable income in his hands.

For the reasons stated we think that the Tax Court erred in its decision. The decision will accordingly be reversed and the cause remanded for further proceedings not inconsistent with this opinion.

McLaughlin, Circuit Judge (dissenting).

I think that the net effect of the facile operation disclosed in this case amounts to the distribution of a taxable dividend to the taxpayer. I do not think that the *Schmitt* decision controls here. Quite the contrary to the *Schmitt* facts, this taxpayer himself acquired a valuable option to buy the shares and solely on the theory of a gift of the option rights would make the corporation the true purchaser. I agree with the Tax Court that "The assignment of the option contract to J.R. Holsey Sales Co. was clearly for the purpose of having that company pay the $80,000 in exercise of the option that was executed for petitioner's personal benefit. The payment was intended to secure and did secure for petitioner exactly what it was always intended he should get if he made the payment personally, namely, all of the stock in J.R. Holsey Sales Co."

I would affirm the Tax Court decision.

Sullivan v. United States

363 F.2d 724 (8th Cir. 1966)

Before Vogel, Chief Judge, Blackmun, Circuit Judge, and Stephenson, District Judge.

Stephenson, District Judge.

[T]he taxpayer Sullivan purchased the assets of an automobile dealership in Blytheville, Arkansas in 1941. He then formed a corporation to operate the dealership. The individual who became resident manager of the dealership, Loy Eich, eventually acquired 120 shares of the 300 shares of stock outstanding — the rest being owned by taxpayer Sullivan. When Eich terminated his management of the dealership in February 1948, Sullivan purchased his 120 shares of stock. Thereafter, in September, 1948, Frank Nelson became the resident manager of the dealership under an arrangement which included an agreement permitting Nelson to acquire up to forty (40) per cent of the stock and further providing for taxpayer's repurchase of said stock upon Nelson's termination of his employment. After acquiring approximately 38% of the corporation's outstanding stock, Nelson announced his intention to depart from his position in 1956 and offered to sell his stock to taxpayer Sullivan. The corporation's Board of Directors then authorized the redemption of Nelson's stock by the corporation.

The ultimate question before the District Court involved a determination of whether the payment by the corporation in redemption of Nelson's stock constituted a taxable distribution to taxpayer Sullivan, the sole remaining stockholder of the corporation. The District Court found that taxpayer Sullivan was unconditionally and primarily obligated to purchase Nelson's stock in 1956 and that said stock was purchased by the Corporation out of profits distributable as a dividend and therefore held that the taxpayer constructively received income equivalent to a dividend in the amount paid by the Corporation for said stock, ($198,334.58). Initially, an interpretation of the memorandum agreement entered into by Sullivan and Nelson at the time the latter assumed his managerial functions is necessary. The agreement contained the following provisions:

> 6. TRANSFER OF SHARES OF STOCK. It is understood and agreed that Sullivan is permitting Nelson to buy stock in said corporation for the purpose of giving him a working interest only, and said Nelson agrees that said shares of stock cannot and will not be mortgaged, hypothecated or transferred by him, his heirs, executor, administrator or trustee to any person other than William J. Sullivan or such person as said Sullivan directs in writing. Any such sale, delivery or transfer to any other person, firm or corporation shall be null and void. Said Sullivan agrees that he will, within thirty (30) days after such shares have been offered for sale to him, accept the offer to sell, provided always that such shares shall be offered for sale at a price to be determined according to this contract.
>
> 7. TERMINATION OF CONTRACT. Said Nelson agrees that if he should terminate his employment or relationship with William J. Sullivan or employment by the said corporation, and if his connection and association with the corporation should cease or be terminated by Sullivan or the majority owners of the stock of the corporation, then said Nelson agrees to sell and transfer and deliver to Sullivan at the then book value all shares of stock owned by him in the Sullivan-Nelson Chevrolet Co. . . . If said contract is terminated by Nelson or Sullivan as herein provided or by the death of Nelson, the value of the stock owned by Nelson shall be fixed and determined as set up in paragraphs four and five of this agreement. If said Nelson should die or become so disabled by injury or sickness as to become incapable of managing and operating the business, then said Sullivan shall have the immediate and exclusive rights to purchase the stock owned by Nelson or by his heirs, administrators or executors in accordance with the

> terms of this contract. Title so (sic) said shares of stock shall automatically rest in Sullivan upon Nelson's death and said Sullivan shall be obligated to Nelson's personal representative or representatives for the value thereof as fixed by this agreement.

On the face of the agreement it would appear that Sullivan obligated himself to purchase Nelson's stock when it was offered to him for sale. The petitioner contends, however, that such an interpretation is contrary to the intention of the parties to the agreement and is not in conformity with the circumstances existing at the time the parties entered into the agreement. . . .[5]

At this juncture, the payment by the corporation to Nelson presents two basic questions: (1) Was that payment in actuality a dividend and therefore includable in Sullivan's gross income under §§61(a)(7), 316(a) and 301(c)(1) of the Internal Revenue Code? (2) If the payment is considered as a corporate redemption of stock, was the payment includable in Sullivan's gross income as being essentially equivalent to a dividend within the meaning of §302(b)(1)? This court has recognized that both questions are to be resolved as fact issues. Idol v. Commissioner of Internal Revenue, 319 F.2d 647 (8th Cir. 1963). If a finding is supported by substantial evidence on the record as a whole and is not against or induced by an erroneous view of the law, it will not be disturbed on appeal.

When an individual shareholder receives an economic benefit through a diversion of corporate earnings and profits, such a receipt may be taxed as a constructive dividend. This court set forth a criteria for determining whether a payment constitutes a constructive dividend in Sachs v. Commissioner of Internal Revenue, 277 F.2d 879, 882-883 (8th Cir. 1960):

> The motive, or expressed intent of the corporation is not determinative, and constructive dividends have been found contrary to the expressed intent of the corporation. The courts, as arbiters of the true nature of corporate payments, have consistently used as a standard the measure of receipt of economic benefit as the proper occasion for taxation. (footnote omitted)

This court has also adopted criteria for determining whether a redemption of stock is essentially equivalent to a dividend. See Heman v. Commissioner of Internal Revenue, 283 F.2d 227, 230-231 (8th Cir. 1960); United States v. Carey, 289 F.2d 531, 537 (8th Cir. 1961). While there is no sole decisive test in this connection, the several guidelines for the determination include "whether there is a bona fide corporate business purpose, whether the action was initiated by the corporation or by the shareholders, whether there was a contraction of the business, and whether there was a substantial change in proportionate stock ownership." Idol v. Commissioner of Internal Revenue, 319 F.2d 647, 651 (8th Cir. 1963). In addition, the Court has observed that the "net effect of the transaction is at least an important consideration in determining dividend equivalency." . . .

5. The taxpayer makes an alternative argument to the effect that, even if he was unconditionally obligated to purchase Sullivan's stock, subsequent events constituted a modification or novation of that agreement. Even if this contention is accepted, the court is at a loss as to how the taxpayer is aided. The novation or modification itself would be considered as resulting in an economic benefit and possible constructive dividend taxable against Sullivan. The taxpayer would be left in essentially the same position with respect to his possible tax liability.

The general net effect and the purpose of and circumstances surrounding the transaction involved herein must be carefully scrutinized to ascertain whether Sullivan received a taxable dividend. Prior to the transaction, Sullivan held approximately 62% of the shares outstanding while Nelson owned the remaining shares. As previously discussed, Sullivan was unconditionally obligated to purchase Nelson's stock if it was offered to him for sale. After the transaction was completed, the relevant facts were essentially as follows: (1) Sullivan's personal obligation had been discharged (2) Sullivan owned all of the outstanding shares of stock of the corporation (3) the corporation's assets were decreased by the amount paid to Nelson for his stock (4) Nelson's stock was held by the corporation as treasury stock. It is true that in terms of the financial worth of Sullivan's interest in the corporation, it was the same after the transaction as it was before.[7] The transaction still resulted in an economic benefit to Sullivan, however, because he was relieved of his personal obligation to purchase Nelson's stock. After careful consideration this court concludes that there was no corporate business purpose or other factor which justifies the taxpayer's position that as to him the payment must be considered a stock redemption and not the equivalent of a dividend.[8] On the facts of this case, Sullivan received a taxable dividend as the result of the corporation's purchase of Nelson's stock.

This court is aware that it is often difficult to distinguish true substance from mere form. Tax law places some weight and significance on form and the choice of one alternative rather than another for achieving a desired end is often critical and may be determinative of the tax effect of a transaction. Judge Becker's opinion comprehensively deals with the evidence and the applicable law of this case. The taxpayer has failed to establish grounds for reversal. The judgment of the District Court is affirmed.

NOTES

1. *Form and substance.* Are the facts of *Sullivan* so different from *Holsey* as to justify such diametric tax results? In each case, shares that the taxpayer might have purchased were in fact bought by the corporation. In *Sullivan*, the taxpayer had an obligation to purchase the shares, while in *Holsey* the taxpayer had only an option. These two cases should make clear that buy-sell agreements ought never require one shareholder to purchase the shares of another but instead should only require one shareholder *or the corporation* to purchase the shares. Since the pitfall of *Sullivan* can be avoided so easily, should the courts allow it to exist at all? One experienced jurist remarked in this context that he would "leave for another day [the possibility of creating] an exception to the now concretized standard of form over

7. Prior to the transfer of Nelson's stock Sullivan owned 186 shares of the 300 shares outstanding. His stock at this time was worth approximately $323,597.00. After the transfer, his 186 shares were the only outstanding stock of the corporation. Due to the corporate purchase of Nelson's stock, however, the value of the taxpayer's shares remained at approximately $323,597.00.

8. The taxpayer has strongly urged that there was a corporate business purpose motivating the purchase of Nelson's stock because of the valuable services received from him as resident manager of the corporation. The services had already been performed, however, when the stock was purchased. Moreover, it was Sullivan, not the corporation, who was obligated to purchase the stock. Under these circumstances, the District Court properly found that the purchase was not induced by a business purpose. The net effect of the transaction further indicates that a dividend was received by the taxpayer.

substance in [this area]." Jacobs v. Commissioner, 41 T.C.M. (CCH) 951 (1981) (Tannenwald, J.).

Suppose the shareholders of *X* Corp. agree that upon the death of any one shareholder, the remaining shareholders will purchase the decedent's stock from her estate. If the shareholders cancel this agreement and replace it with a provision that the corporation will purchase the shares of any deceased shareholder, will they have successfully overcome the *Sullivan* trap? Apparently so, at least if the novation occurs prior to the death of all shareholders. See Rev. Rul. 69-608, 1969-2 C.B. 42 (concluding that one shareholder received a constructive distribution when a corporation redeemed a second shareholder's stock if the first shareholder had a primary and unconditional obligation to purchase the redeemed stock when the redemption occurred). Thus, the *Sullivan-Holsey* distinction remains good law.

The same issue can arise in the context of divorce. For example, two divorcing spouses may own all stock of a corporation and under the divorce decree one spouse may be obligated to purchase the stock of the other. If, instead, the corporation purchases the stock, which spouse should be taxed on the redemption? Courts have applied differing standards in this context, with the result that in one case the redemption was not taxed to *either* spouse. Arnes v. United States, 981 F.2d 456 (9th Cir. 1992) (transferor spouse); Arnes v. Commissioner, 102 T.C. 522 (1994) (transferee spouse). To prevent future whipsaws, the regulations now generally provide that the same analysis applicable outside of the divorce context applies within it. Treas. Regs. §1.1041-2. Thus, the spouse with the unconditional obligation to purchase the shares generally should be taxed on the redemption. However, the regulations also provide that such an unconditional obligation will be ignored if so provided in a divorce decree, separation instrument, or written agreement between the spouses (or ex-spouses). In that case, the redemption's consequences would follow its form. Thus, the parties largely can control whether the form of the transaction will be respected or ignored, but in all events the parties must treat the transaction consistently.

PROBLEM

5-9. *X* Corp. has 120 shares of stock outstanding, 40 owned by *B*, 40 by *C*, and 40 by *D*, with each shareholder having an adjusted basis of $40 per share. *B* and *C* have agreed that if *C* predeceases *B*, upon *C*'s death, *B* will purchase *C*'s shares for their then-current fair market value. Subsequent to the signing of this agreement but prior to *C*'s death, *C* purchases the 40 shares owned by *D* for $100 per share. Upon *C*'s death, *C*'s estate tenders all 80 shares to *B* for their current value of $125 per share. *B* desires to purchase only 40 of those shares, although the estate argues that the agreement between *B* and *C* should be understood to require a purchase of all the shares *C* owned at death. To settle their differences, *B* agrees to purchase 40 of the 80 shares owned by *C*'s estate, and *X* Corp. agrees to redeem the other 40 shares. What are the tax consequences of these transactions to *B*, *C*, and *X* Corp., assuming *B* is an individual? How does the analysis change if *B* is a corporation? What steps could *B* take to increase the likelihood that a court would uphold a form of the transaction advantageous to *B*?

2. *Redemptions as Part of Bootstrap Acquisitions*

Redemptions are sometimes utilized to effect "shoestring" or "bootstrap" purchases of closely held corporations. For example, suppose *A*, who owns all the stock of a corporation, wishes to sell out to *B*, but *B* cannot finance the entire purchase. The corporation's assets include a substantial amount of cash and marketable securities. *A* sells part of his stock to *B*, and the corporation redeems the rest of *A*'s stock, using its cash and securities to make payment. Note that if part of *A*'s stock had been redeemed while *A* was the sole shareholder, then the redemption would have been essentially equivalent to a dividend. Despite this fact, it was held under the 1939 Code's predecessor to §302(b)(1) that a redemption following a sale, as described above, is a sale by *A* of his stock, not a dividend. Zenz v. Quinlivan, 213 F.2d 914 (6th Cir. 1954); Edenfield v. Commissioner, 19 T.C. 13 (1952). That result now seems assured under §302(b)(3).

The IRS acquiesced in these cases, although it announced that such transactions "will be closely scrutinized to determine whether the selling stockholder 'ceases to be interested in the affairs of the corporation' immediately after redemption." Rev. Rul. 54-458, 1954-2 C.B. 167.

A sale and redemption may be linked under what is now called the "*Zenz* doctrine." In Rev. Rul. 75-447, 1975-2 C.B. 113, the Service concluded that this doctrine also should apply under §302(b)(2), the "substantially disproportionate" rule. In the same revenue ruling, the Service concluded that the doctrine applies when the redemption precedes the sale as long as two events are "clearly part of an overall plan." See also Priv. Ltr. Rul. 2009-12-006 (Mar. 20, 2009) (concluding that the *Zenz* doctrine applies under §302(b)(1)). Note that if the redemption precedes the sale but the two events are linked, §302(b) is applied by taking into account stock ownership before the redemption and after the sale. Note as well that if a corporation redeems stock as part of a bootstrap acquisition using appreciated property, the corporation recognizes gain under §311(b).

What is the result if seller *A* does not wholly sever his relationship with the corporation? For example, he might continue to perform services under a profit-sharing agreement, or he might receive a percentage of the future profits as partial payment for his shares. Would the shareholder in either case have retained a forbidden "interest" in the corporation? Recall Seda v. Commissioner and the notes thereafter at pages 157-163 supra. And what about *B*? When the Service announced in Rev. Rul. 54-458, supra, that it would follow the *Zenz* case as to the seller, it went on to say that such redemptions "will . . . be examined to determine whether any payment by the corporation for stock has the effect of a dividend to the stockholders who remain interested in the corporation." Recall the *Holsey* and *Sullivan* cases, above.

When a redemption of stock owned by a corporation is taxed as a dividend, the 70 percent to 100 percent dividends-received deduction of §243 applies. See page 118 supra. But see Waterman Steamship Corp. v. Commissioner, 430 F.2d 1185 (5th Cir. 1970), discussed at page 149 supra, where an ostensible dividend paid by a subsidiary to its parent, coupled with a sale by the parent of its stock in the subsidiary to a third party, was viewed as an integrated transaction so that the "dividend" was recharacterized as part of the purchase price and not a dividend. As a result of the recharacterization, the parent had additional capital gain (or less capital loss) on the sale of the subsidiary stock.

PROBLEMS

5-10. *A* owns all the outstanding *X* Corp. stock — 100 shares with an aggregate basis of $40,000. The stock has a $100,000 fair market value. *P* wants to purchase *A*'s stock but has only $50,000. Assuming ample earnings and profits for *X* Corp., describe the tax consequences of each of the following situations:

a. *X* Corp. distributes $50,000 to *A*, who then sells her stock to *P* for $50,000.
b. *A* sells her stock to *P* for $100,000 (payable half in cash, half with a note). *P* then causes *X* Corp. to distribute $50,000 to her, using the cash to pay off the note. Would it matter if *X* Corp. redeemed some of *P*'s stock?
c. *A* sells 50 shares to *P* for $50,000, and then *X* Corp. redeems *A*'s remaining 50 shares for $50,000. What happens if the redemption precedes the sale?
d. If *A* were a corporation, how would *A* Corp. want to structure this transaction?

5-11. *B* owns 10 of the 100 outstanding shares of *X* Corp. with an adjusted basis of $50 per share and fair market value of $550 per share. While attending the *X* Corp.'s annual meeting, *B* slips and falls. *B* agrees not to sue *X* Corp. in exchange for a payment of $15,000. As part of that agreement, *B* agrees to sell all his stock back to *X* Corp. for $50 per share. What are the tax consequences of these transactions to *B* and to *X* Corp.? What is the result if *B* agreed to sell his shares not to *X* Corp. but to individual *C*, an individual owning 45 of the outstanding shares of *X* Corp.?

3. *Redemptions for More or Less than Stock Value*

Under some circumstances a corporation may repurchase its shares for more than those shares are worth. If the excess reflects a difference of opinion over valuation or a simple misjudgment, the entire amount paid should be treated as the cost of the shares and neither deducted nor capitalized. But what happens if the excess is paid because the corporation receives something from the tendering shareholder in addition to the shares? For example, the shareholder might agree not to purchase additional stock in the future (called a "standstill" agreement), or the shareholder, especially if she is an employee as well as a shareholder, might provide a covenant not to compete with the business of the company.

Under §162(k),[7] a corporation may not deduct any amount paid or incurred in connection with the redemption of its stock except for those items specified in §162(k)(2). See Fort Howard Corp. v. Commissioner, 103 T.C. 345 (1994). This provision was enacted in response to Five Star Manufacturing Co. v. Commissioner, 355 F.2d 224 (5th Cir. 1966), in which the corporation was permitted to deduct the full amount distributed in redemption of 50 percent of its outstanding stock on the theory that elimination of the shareholder-director whose stock was redeemed was essential for the corporation's survival. The decision in *Five Star Manufacturing* certainly seems wrong — in measuring a corporation's profit or loss, amounts paid in

7. This provision was originally enacted by the Tax Reform Act of 1986 as §162(*l*).

redemption of stock should be irrelevant—but the legislative response may be overbroad.

The legislative history of §162(k) provides that the phrase "in connection with" should be construed broadly to include legal, accounting, brokerage, transfer agent, appraisal, and similar fees incurred in connection with the redemption. After INDOPCO, Inc. v. Commissioner, 503 U.S. 79 (1992), might some part of the president's or comptroller's salary fall within the ambit of §162(k)?

The legislative history of §162(k) further provides that §162(k) should apply to amounts paid by the corporation for standstill agreements, whether lasting for a specified or indefinite time. Such amounts, often called "greenmail," might increase the value of the corporation's outstanding stock. If so, should the corporation be entitled to capitalize the greenmail, recovering it when the company is sold or liquidated? Although §162(k) does not speak to this issue, courts are unlikely to allow recovery of redemption premiums falling within §162(k) at *any* time. For an intriguing analysis of greenmail, see Macey and McChesney, A Theoretical Analysis of Greenmail, 95 Yale L.J. 13 (1985).

How should a redemption premium be treated under §162(k) if the corporation receives not only shares but also a noncompetition agreement from the tendering shareholder? In the absence of §162(k), an amount paid for a noncompetition agreement is amortized over 15 years, see §197, unless the covenant is not related to the acquisition of a business, see §197(d)(1)(E). If, however, the redemption and noncompetition agreements are parts of a single effort to eliminate an unhappy or uncooperative shareholder-employee, might not a court hold that the entire payment received by the departing shareholder-employee was made "in connection with" the redemption? In other contexts, courts have been willing to interpret the phrase "in connection with" surprisingly broadly. See Alves v. Commissioner, 79 T.C. 864 (1982), aff'd, 734 F.2d 478 (9th Cir. 1984). Note that §162(k) cannot apply if there is no redemption, so the tax treatment of payments for standstill agreements and similar arrangements not connected to a redemption is left open by §162(k).

A corporation might also pay less than full value for redeemed stock. Why might a tendering shareholder accept less than fair market value? The effect of receiving less than full value for redeemed shares is an increase in value of all post-redemption outstanding shares, so a shareholder who accepts less than full value for redeemed shares transfers some of her stock value to the other shareholders. To determine how such a transfer should be taxed, we must understand why such a transfer might be made. The following case concerns the most extreme situation, namely, a contribution of stock to the corporation by one shareholder without any return distribution.

Commissioner v. Fink

483 U.S. 89 (1987)

Justice Powell delivered the opinion of the Court.

The question in this case is whether a dominant shareholder who voluntarily surrenders a portion of his shares to the corporation, but retains control, may immediately deduct from taxable income his basis in the surrendered shares.

Respondents Peter and Karla Fink were the principal shareholders of Travco Corporation, a Michigan manufacturer of motor homes. Travco had one class of common stock outstanding and no preferred stock. Mr. Fink owned 52.2 percent, and Mrs. Fink 20.3 percent, of the outstanding shares. Travco urgently needed new capital as a result of financial difficulties it encountered in the mid-1970s. The Finks voluntarily surrendered some of their shares to Travco in an effort to "increase the attractiveness of the corporation to outside investors." Mr. Fink surrendered 116,146 shares in December 1976; Mrs. Fink surrendered 80,000 shares in January 1977. As a result, the Finks' combined percentage ownership of Travco was reduced from 72.5 percent to 68.5 percent. The Finks received no consideration for the surrendered shares, and no other shareholder surrendered any stock. The effort to attract new investors was unsuccessful, and the corporation eventually was liquidated.

On their 1976 and 1977 joint federal income tax returns, the Finks claimed ordinary loss deductions totaling $389,040, the full amount of their adjusted basis in the surrendered shares. The Commissioner of Internal Revenue disallowed the deductions. He concluded that the stock surrendered was a contribution to the corporation's capital. Accordingly, the Commissioner determined that the surrender resulted in no immediate tax consequences,* and that the Finks' basis in the surrendered shares should be added to the basis of their remaining shares of Travco stock. . . .

It is settled that a shareholder's voluntary contribution to the capital of the corporation has no immediate tax consequences. §263; [Treas. Regs.] §1.263(a)-2(f) (1986). Instead, the shareholder is entitled to increase the basis of his shares by the amount of his basis in the property transferred to the corporation. See §1016(a)(1). When the shareholder later disposes of his shares, his contribution is reflected as a smaller taxable gain or a larger deductible loss. This rule applies not only to transfers of cash or tangible property, but also to a shareholder's forgiveness of a debt owed to him by the corporation. [Treas. Regs.] §1.61-12(a) (1986). Such transfers are treated as contributions to capital even if the other shareholders make proportionately smaller contributions, or no contribution at all. See, e.g., Sackstein v. Commissioner, 14 T.C. 566, 569 (1950). The rules governing contributions to capital reflect the general principle that a shareholder may not claim an immediate loss for outlays made to benefit the corporation. Deputy v. du Pont, 308 U.S. 488 (1940); Eskimo Pie Corp. v. Commissioner, 4 T.C. 669, 676 (1945), aff'd, 153 F.2d 301 (C.A.3 1946). We must decide whether this principle also applies to a controlling shareholder's non pro rata surrender of portion of his shares. The Finks concede that a pro rata stock surrender, that by definition does not change the percentage ownership of any shareholder, is not a taxable event. Cf. Eisner v. Macomber, 252 U.S. 189 (1920) (pro rata stock dividend does not produce taxable income).

The Finks contend that they sustained an immediate loss upon surrendering some of their shares to the corporation. By parting with the shares, they gave up an ownership interest entitling them to future dividends, future capital appreciation, assets in the event of liquidation, and voting rights.[7] Therefore, the Finks contend, they are entitled to an immediate deduction. See §§165(a) and (c)(2). In addition, the Finks argue that any non pro rata stock transaction "give[s] rise to immediate

*More precisely, the surrender resulted in the recognition of no gain or loss. The surrender did have tax consequences — the basis of the surrendered shares was added to Fink's remaining shares and the corporation took a basis in the shares equal to Fink's basis. — Eds.

7. As a practical matter, however, the Finks did not give up a great deal. Their percentage interest in the corporation declined by only four percent. Because the Finks retained a majority interest, this reduction in their voting power was inconsequential. Moreover, Travco, like many corporations in financial difficulties, was not paying dividends.

tax results." For example, a non pro rata stock dividend produces income because it increases the recipient's proportionate ownership of the corporation. Koshland v. Helvering, 298 U.S. 441, 445 (1936). By analogy, the Finks argue that a non pro rata surrender of shares should be recognized as an immediate loss because it reduces the surrendering shareholder's proportionate ownership.

Finally, the Finks contend that their stock surrenders were not contributions to the corporation's capital. They note that a typical contribution to capital, unlike a non pro rata stock surrender, has no effect on the contributing shareholder's proportionate interest in the corporation. Moreover, the Finks argue, a contribution of cash or other property increases the net worth of the corporation. For example, a shareholder's forgiveness of a debt owed to him by the corporation decreases the corporation's liabilities. In contrast, when a shareholder surrenders shares of the corporation's own stock, the corporation's net worth is unchanged. This is because the corporation cannot itself exercise the right to vote, receive dividends, or receive a share of assets in the event of liquidation. . . .

A shareholder who surrenders a portion of his shares to the corporation has parted with an asset, but that alone does not entitle him to an immediate deduction. Indeed, if the shareholder owns less than 100 percent of the corporation's shares, any non pro rata contribution to the corporation's capital will reduce the net worth of the contributing shareholder.[10] A shareholder who surrenders stock thus is similar to one who forgives or surrenders a debt owed to him by the corporation; the latter gives up interest, principal, and also potential voting power in the event of insolvency or bankruptcy. But, as stated above, such forgiveness of corporate debt is treated as a contribution to capital rather than a current deduction. . . . The Finks' voluntary surrender of shares, like a shareholder's voluntary forgiveness of debt owed by the corporation, closely resembles an investment or contribution to capital. See B. Bittker & J. Eustice, Federal Income Taxation of Corporations and Shareholders §3.14, p. 3-59 (4th ed. 1979) ("If the contribution is voluntary, it does not produce gain or loss to the shareholder"). We find the similarity convincing in this case.

The fact that a stock surrender is not recorded as a contribution to capital on the corporation's balance sheet does not compel a different result. Shareholders who forgive a debt owed by the corporation or pay a corporate expense also are denied an immediate deduction, even though neither of these transactions is a contribution to capital in the accounting sense.[11] Nor are we persuaded by the fact that a stock surrender, unlike a typical contribution to capital, reduces the shareholder's proportionate interest in the corporation. This Court has never held that every change in a shareholder's percentage ownership has immediate tax consequences. Of course, a shareholder's receipt of property from the

10. For example, assume that a shareholder holding an 80 percent interest in a corporation with a total liquidation value of $100,000 makes a non pro rata contribution to the corporation's capital of $20,000 in cash. Assume further that the shareholder has no other assets. Prior to the contribution, the shareholder's net worth was $100,000 ($20,000 plus 80 percent of $100,000). If the corporation were immediately liquidated following the contribution, the shareholder would receive only $96,000 (80 percent of $120,000). Of course such a non pro rata contribution is rare in practice. Typically a shareholder will simply purchase additional shares.

11. It is true that a corporation's stock is not considered an asset of the corporation. A corporation's own shares nevertheless may be as valuable to the corporation as other property contributed by shareholders, as treasury shares may be resold. This is evidenced by the fact that corporations often purchase their own shares on the open market.

corporation generally is a taxable event. See §§301, 316. In contrast, a shareholder's transfer of property to the corporation usually has no immediate tax consequences.

The Finks concede that the purpose of their stock surrender was to protect or increase the value of their investment in the corporation. . . . They hoped to encourage new investors to provide needed capital and in the long run recover the value of the surrendered shares through increased dividends or appreciation in the value of their remaining shares. If the surrender had achieved its purpose, the Finks would not have suffered an economic loss. . . . In this case, as in many cases involving closely-held corporations whose shares are not traded on an open market, there is no reliable method of determining whether the surrender will result in a loss until the shareholder disposes of his remaining shares. Thus, the Finks' stock surrender does not meet the requirement that an immediately deductible loss must be "actually sustained during the taxable year." [Treas. Regs.]§1.165-1(b) (1986).

Finally, treating stock surrenders as ordinary losses might encourage shareholders in failing corporations to convert potential capital losses to ordinary losses by voluntarily surrendering their shares before the corporation fails. In this way shareholders might avoid the consequences of §165(g)(1), that provides for capital loss treatment of stock that becomes worthless. Similarly, shareholders may be encouraged to transfer corporate stock rather than other property to the corporation in order to realize a current loss. . . .[14]

We therefore hold that a dominant shareholder who voluntarily surrenders a portion of his shares to the corporation, but retains control, does not sustain an immediate loss deductible from taxable income. Rather, the surrendering shareholder must reallocate his basis in the surrendered shares to the shares he retains.[15] The shareholder's loss, if any, will be recognized when he disposes of his remaining shares. . . . We conclude only that a controlling shareholder's voluntary surrender of shares, like contributions of other forms of property to the corporation, is not an appropriate occasion for the recognition of gain or loss.

In this case we use the term "control" to mean ownership of more than half of a corporation's voting shares. We recognize, of course, that in larger corporations — especially those whose shares are listed on a national exchange — a person or entity may exercise control in fact while owning less than a majority of the voting shares. See Securities Exchange Act of 1934, §13(d), 48 Stat. 894, 15 U.S.C. §78m(d) (requiring persons to report acquisition of more than 5 percent of a registered equity security).

14. Our holding today also draws support from two other sections of the Code. First, §83 provides that, if a shareholder makes a "bargain sale" of stock to a corporate officer or employee as compensation, the "bargain" element of the sale must be treated as a contribution to the corporation's capital. . . . Second, if a shareholder's stock is redeemed — that is, surrendered to the corporation in return for cash or other property — the shareholder is not entitled to an immediate deduction unless the redemption results in a substantial reduction in the shareholder's ownership percentage. §§302(a), (b), (d); [Treas. Regs.] §1.302-2(c) (1986). Because the Finks' surrenders resulted in only a slight reduction in their ownership percentage, they would not have been entitled to an immediate loss if they had received consideration for the surrendered shares. §302(b). Although the Finks did not receive a direct payment of cash or other property, they hoped to be compensated by an increase in the value of their remaining shares.

15. The Finks remained the controlling shareholders after their surrender. We therefore have no occasion to decide in this case whether a surrender that causes the shareholder to lose control of the corporation is immediately deductible. In related contexts, the Code distinguishes between minimal reductions in a shareholder's ownership percentage and loss of corporate control. See §302(b)(2) (providing "exchange" rather than dividend treatment for a "substantially disproportionate redemption of stock" that brings the shareholder's ownership percentage below 50 percent); §302(b)(3) (providing similar treatment when the redemption terminates the shareholder's interest in the corporation).

For the reasons we have stated, the judgment of the Court of Appeals for the Sixth Circuit is reversed.

It is so ordered.

Justice BLACKMUN concurs in the result.

Justice WHITE, concurring.

Although I join the Court's opinion, I suggest that there is little substance in the reservation in footnote 15 of the question whether a surrender of stock that causes the stockholder to lose control of the corporation is immediately deductible as an ordinary loss. Of course, this case does not involve a loss of control; but as I understand the rationale of the Court's opinion, it would also apply to a surrender that results in loss of control. At least I do not find in the opinion any principled ground for distinguishing a loss-of-control case from this one.

Justice SCALIA, concurring in the judgment.

I do not believe that the Finks' surrender of their shares was, or even closely resembles, a shareholder contribution to corporate capital. Since, however, its purpose was to make the corporation a more valuable investment by giving it a more attractive capital structure, I think that it was, no less than a contribution to capital, an "amount paid out . . . for . . . betterments made to increase the value of . . . property," §263(a)(1), and thus not entitled to treatment as a current deduction.

[Dissenting opinion of Justice Stevens omitted.]

NOTES

1. *Stock surrenders and capital contributions.* The taxpayers in *Fink* argued that their non–pro rata stock surrenders were not capital contributions because nothing of value was added to the corporation's capital. Despite the remarks in footnote 11, surely it is the case that a corporation does not increase its wealth by the reacquisition of some of its shares. Were it otherwise, corporations could increase their wealth at will by coordinating pro rata stock surrenders. Moreover, because there is no significant difference between treasury stock and authorized but unissued stock — both can be sold to outside investors — the Court's comments in footnote 11 suggest authorizing additional stock as a fast way to corporate success. The Court's statement that reacquisition of corporate shares must increase corporate wealth or else corporations would not buy their own shares on the open market is a non-sequitur: Many transactions between corporations and their shareholders do not increase corporate capital (e.g., the declaration of dividends) but nevertheless are done for sound business reasons. If a corporation believes its shares are undervalued on the open market, it may purchase (redeem) some of its outstanding stock. This purchase shifts wealth from the selling shareholders to those who continue to hold stock of the corporation. Of course, no wealth — to the corporation or anyone else — is created by this activity.

2. *Stock surrenders and deductible losses.* Although it is true that the corporation gains nothing by reason of a stock surrender, it is equally true that the surrendering shareholder loses something. In *Fink,* the surrender of 80,000 shares resulted in the diminution of the Finks' ownership from 72.5 percent to 68.5 percent. If the corporation were worth $1 million, that would be a dollar loss of $40,000.

If the Finks lost value and the corporation did not gain it, then where did it go? To the other shareholders, of course. A non–pro rata stock surrender simultaneously reduces the percentage ownership of the surrendering shareholder and increases the value of all outstanding shares. If the surrendering shareholder continues to hold stock in the corporation, some of the value of the surrendered shares will reappear in the form of an increase in value of the remaining shares held by the surrendering shareholder.

Consider the case of a corporation, *X* Corp., with two shareholders, *A* and *B*. *A* owns 75 shares of *X* with an adjusted basis and fair market value of $100 per share, while *B* owns the remaining 25 shares of *X* with the same adjusted basis and fair market value. If *A* surrenders 50 of her shares, and still assuming that some loss deduction is appropriate, should *A* be entitled to a loss of $5,000? Note that the stock surrender reduced *A*'s ownership of a corporation worth $10,000 from 75 percent to 50 percent, for an economic loss of $2,500. That value is thus transferred to *B*, while the remaining value of the surrendered shares (also $2,500) remains with *A* in the form of an increase in value of her remaining shares.

Should §302 apply in *Fink*? A stock surrender is just a redemption for $0; if §302 applies to the transaction, then a loss will be allowed only if the shareholder qualifies under §302(a) via §302(b). Does this approach adequately respond to the Supreme Court's concerns articulated in *Fink*? Does it permit too great a loss deduction in some cases? Do you think §302 was intended to apply to stock surrenders?

Suppose a corporation redeems 10 shares for $80 when each share is worth $10. Should this be treated as a redemption of eight shares for full value and a surrender of two shares for no consideration? If so, then the redemption portion of the transaction would be tested under §302(b), while the basis of the two surrendered shares would be capitalized under *Fink*.

In Reynolds Metal Co. v. Commissioner, 105 T.C. 304 (1995), a parent corporation was denied a current capital loss deduction, and treated instead as making a capital contribution to its subsidiary, upon surrendering shares of stock in that subsidiary to creditors of the subsidiary.

PROBLEM

5-12. Individual *T* owns all 10 outstanding shares of *X* Corp. with an adjusted basis of $100 per share and fair market value of $75 per share. Unrelated individual *U* agrees to perform some accounting work for *X* Corp. in exchange for two shares of *X* Corp. from *T*. Assume the accounting work is worth $150. What are the tax consequences to *X* Corp., *T*, and *U* of the transfer of stock from *T* to *U*? Is it relevant whether *X* Corp. is authorized to issue more than 10 shares? How would your answers change if the transfer of stock from *T* to *U* were not for accounting services but instead for a covenant from *U* not to compete with *X* Corp. for a period of three years?

D. REDEMPTIONS BY RELATED CORPORATIONS — §304

A "redemption" under §317(b) is the sale of corporate stock back to the issuing corporation. A similar transaction, though not falling within the definition of §317(b), is the sale of stock to a corporation *related* to the issuing corporation.

For example, suppose individual *I* owns all the stock of *P* Corp., which in turn owns all the stock of *S* Corp. If *I* causes *P* to repurchase any of its stock, the transaction will be a "redemption" under §317(b), and, unless §302(b)(4) applies, the entire amount distributed will be taxed under the distribution rules of §301. If *I* instead sells some of his *P* stock to *S*, the transaction will not fall within the definition of a "redemption" even though the effect of the transaction is little different than a redemption of the stock by *P*.

In Rodman Wanamaker Trust v. Commissioner, 11 T.C. 365 (1948), aff'd, 178 F.2d 10 (3d Cir. 1949), the Tax Court held that such a sale of *P* stock to *S* does indeed qualify for exchange treatment because the redemption rules (now incorporated in §302) do not apply. In response, Congress added §115(g)(2) to the 1939 Code in order to close the loophole opened by *Rodman Wanamaker Trust*, and the substance of §115(g)(2) became the basis for current §304.

Section 304 addresses two related situations: (1) a taxpayer's sale of stock of one corporation to another corporation controlled by the taxpayer (i.e., the use of a brother-sister corporate pair), see §304(a)(1), and (2) the sale of parent stock to a subsidiary corporation as present in *Rodman Wanamaker Trust*, see §304(a)(2). In each case, §304(a) provides that the sale is subject to the redemption rules of §302 and, if the taxpayer fails to qualify for exchange treatment under §302(b), that the nominal sale will be recharacterized as a distribution subject to the rules of §301.

The following revenue ruling illustrates the basic operation of §304, focusing on what happens to the basis of stock surrendered by a shareholder in a §304 transaction that is treated as a distribution under §301.

Rev. Rul. 71-563

1971-2 C.B. 175

Advice has been requested regarding the federal income tax treatment of the transaction described below.

A, an individual, owns 100 shares of corporation *X* which is all the outstanding stock of *X*. *B*, the son of *A*, owns all the outstanding stock of Corporation *Y*. *A* sold 25 shares of stock of *X* to *Y* for cash. The purchase price of the *X* stock was its fair market value. The earnings and profits of *Y* exceeded the amount of cash paid by *Y* to *A* for the *X* stock.

Section 304(a)(1) of the Internal Revenue Code of 1954 provides that for purposes of section 302 and section 303 of the Code, if one or more persons are in control of each of two corporations and in return for property, one of the corporations acquires stock in the other corporation from the person so in control, then such property shall be treated as a distribution in redemption of the stock of the corporation acquiring such stock. . . .

Section 304(c)(1) of the Code provides that for purposes of section 304 of the Code control means the ownership of stock possessing at least 50 percent of the total combined voting power of all classes of stock entitled to vote, or at least 50 percent of the total value of shares of all classes of stock.

Section 304(c)(3) of the Code makes section 318(a) of the Code (relating to the constructive ownership of stock) applicable to section 304 of the Code, with certain modifications not here relevant, for the purposes of determining control under section 304(c)(1) of the Code. Section 318(a)(1)(A) of the Code provides, in pertinent part, that an individual is considered as owning the stock owned, directly or indirectly, by his children.

Section 318(a)(2)(C) of the Code provides, in pertinent part, that if 50 percent or more in value of the stock in a corporation is owned, directly or indirectly, by any person, such person is considered as owning the stock owned, directly or indirectly, by such corporation, in that proportion which the value of the stock which such person so owns bears to the value of all the stock in such corporation.

A actually owned 100 percent of the stock of *X* before the transaction and by the application of section 318(a)(1)(A) of the Code *A* is considered to have owned all of the stock of *Y* before the transaction. Accordingly, since *Y* acquired the stock of *X* for cash from a person (*A*) in control of both the issuing corporation (*X*) and the acquiring corporation (*Y*), the transaction is considered to be an acquisition of stock by a related corporation within the meaning of section 304(a)(1) of the Code and thus a redemption of the stock of *Y*, the acquiring corporation. See, in this connection, Coyle v. United States, 415 F.2d 488 (4th Cir. 1968).

Under section 1.304-2(a) of the Income Tax Regulations, the amount received by *A* is treated as a distribution of property under section 302(d) of the Code unless the distribution is to be treated as received in exchange for stock pursuant to section 302(a) or section 303 of the Code. Section 303 of the Code (relating to distributions in redemption of stock to pay death taxes) is not applicable in the instant case. Section 302(a) of the Code is applicable if the requirements of section 302(b) of the Code are satisfied.

Section 304(b)(1) of the Code provides that the applicability of section 302(b) of the Code is determined by reference to the stock of the issuing corporation, *X*. Through the application of section 318(a)(2)(C) of the Code, *B* owns the 25 shares of the stock of *X* held by *Y*. The ownership by *B* of the 25 shares of the stock of *X* is attributed to *A* by reason of application of section 318(a)(1)(A) of the Code. Therefore, after the transaction *A* still owns 100 percent of *X* and there is no complete termination of *A*'s interest in the stock of *X* within the meaning of section 302(b)(3) of the Code nor is there a substantially disproportionate redemption within the meaning of section 302(b)(2) of the Code.

The "not essentially equivalent to a dividend" test of section 302(b)(1) of the Code cannot be met since there has been no meaningful reduction in *A*'s proportionate interest in the stock of *X* as a result of the transaction. In determining the existence of a meaningful reduction, the constructive ownership rules of section 318 of the Code are applied (see United States v. Davis, 397 U.S. 301 (1970)).

The inapplicability of section 303 and section 302(a) of the Code results in the amount received by *A* being treated, pursuant to section 302(d) of the Code, as a distribution to which section 301 of the Code applies. Accordingly, the distribution is treated as a dividend to *A* from *Y* under section 301(c)(1) and section 316 of the Code. . . .

NOTES

1. *Overview.* Section 304 applies to the sale of the stock of a brother corporation to a sister corporation if one or more persons control each corporation and the sister corporation acquires brother stock for property from one or more of the controlling persons. §304(a)(1). If §304(a)(1) applies, such a person is treated as receiving the property in redemption of the acquiring corporation's stock. *Id.*

Section 304 also applies if a subsidiary acquires stock of the parent for property and the parent controls the subsidiary. §304(a)(2). The transferring shareholder is treated as receiving the property in redemption of the parent's stock. *Id.*

2. *"Control" under §304(c).* For purposes of §304, a person or persons "control" a corporation if they own at least 50 percent of the total voting power in the corporation *or* at least 50 percent of the total value of all shares of all classes of stock. §304(c)(1). In determining control, the attribution rules of §318 apply. See §304(c)(3). Note that, by virtue of §304(c)(3)(B), the reach of the attribution rules is broadened in the context of §304.

Suppose *X* Corp. has two classes of stock outstanding. Individual *T* owns all the shares of one class and none of the shares of the other class. The *X* Corp. stock owned by *T* gives *T* 40 percent of the vote but 60 percent of the fair market value of *X* Corp. If *T* sells some of the *X* stock to a corporation *T* controls, can §304 apply to the sale?

Section 304 will apply only if *T* controls both corporations, and control for purposes of §304(a) is defined in §304(c) to require "at least 50 percent of the total combined voting power of all classes of stock entitled to vote, or at least 50 percent of the total value of all classes of shares." *T* quite plainly fails the 50-percent-vote test, but does *T* satisfy the 50-percent-value test? If this test is applied separately to each class of stock, then *T* fails the test because *T* owns none of one of the two classes; if the value test is applied to the aggregate of all outstanding classes, then *T* satisfies it. Note that although Congress specified that all classes of stock are "combined" for determining the vote test, no similar specification appears in the value test. Nevertheless, in Rev. Rul. 89-57, 1989-1 C.B. 90, the Service held that the §304(c)(1) value test is applied to the aggregate value of stock held. Accordingly, *T* is deemed to control *X* Corp.

If a taxpayer sells stock of one corporation to a second corporation for stock of the second plus other property, it may be that the taxpayer did not control the purchasing corporation before the transaction but does control it afterward. Does §304 apply to such a transaction? Yes, under §304(c)(2), the stock received is taken into account in measuring control. Note, though, that §304 applies only to the "other property" received by the taxpayer, not to the stock of the purchasing corporation she receives. Why? Because §304(a) applies only to the exchange of stock for "property," and "property" does not include stock of the distributing (i.e., acquiring) corporation. §317(a).

Aficionados of the §318 attribution rules will observe that application of §318 to §304 is troublesome. Consider a taxpayer who owns 100 percent of the outstanding stock of two corporations, Brother and Sister. If this taxpayer sells some Brother stock to Sister, then it is clear that §304 will apply. But is §304(a)(1) or (a)(2) applicable? Although §304(a)(1) seems the obvious candidate, application of §318 causes the taxpayer's stock in Sister to be attributed to Brother (and vice versa), thereby making Brother and Sister into a parent-subsidiary pair (with either [or both?] as the parent [or subsidiary]). By its terms, §304(a)(1) defers to §304(a)(2). Thus, this sale of Brother stock to Sister seems to be taxed under §304(a)(2). Does it matter whether §304(a)(1) or (a)(2) applies? See Notes 2 and 4 infra.

Neither the courts nor the Service have been inclined to rearrange a brother-sister §304 transaction when the taxpayer's actual stock ownership placed him within the confines of §304(a)(1). See, e.g., Coyle v. United States, 415 F.2d 488 (4th Cir. 1968); Rev. Rul. 71-563 above. It appears safe to assume that the attribution rules of §318(a) will not be applied to remove a transaction from §304(a)(1) and place it into §304(a)(2). See also Broadview Lumber v. United States, 561 F.2d 698 (7th Cir. 1977).

3. *Application of §302(b) to a §304 transaction.* Sales of stock described in §304(a) are subject to the redemption rules of §§302 and 303. Assuming the inapplicability of §303 (discussed at pages 180-182 supra), the sale will qualify for exchange treatment under §1001 only if one of the tests in §302(b) is met. Otherwise, the proceeds received by the selling shareholder will be taxed according to the distribution rules of §301.

Pursuant to §304(b)(1), the tests of §302(b) are applied to the change (if any) in the shareholder's interest in the "issuing corporation" (i.e., the corporation whose shares are nominally being sold). Do not forget that the attribution rules of §318(a) are applicable to determinations under §302, even those triggered by §304. See Treas. Regs. §1.304-2(a).

Consider a taxpayer, *T*, who owns 60 of the 100 outstanding shares of Brother Corp. and 60 of the 100 outstanding shares of Sister Corp. How will *T* be taxed if she sells 20 shares of Brother stock (with a basis of $10 per share) to Sister for $15 per share?

T actually owned 60 percent of the outstanding stock of Brother prior to the sale. After the sale, *T* actually owned 40 shares and constructively owned 12 more through her ownership of Sister (60 percent of 20). See §318(a)(2)(C). Thus, *T*'s ownership of Brother dropped from 60 percent to 52 percent, so *T* cannot qualify under §302(b)(2) or (3) (*T* neither has gone below 80 percent of her former percentage ownership of Brother nor owns less than 50 percent of Brother after the redemption, thereby failing to qualify under §302(b)(2) on two grounds). Assuming, arguendo, the inapplicability of §302(b)(1) and (4), *T* will have received a distribution in the amount of $300 taxable under §301.

If *T* had sold 40 shares instead of 20, she would have qualified for exchange treatment under §302(a). A sale of 40 shares would bring *T*'s post-sale actual and constructive ownership down to 44 percent (20 percent actual ownership plus 60 percent of 40 percent, or 24 percent, constructive ownership), thereby qualifying her under §302(b)(2). As a consequence, *T* would have taxable gain of $200, that being the difference between her amount realized ($600) and her basis in the shares sold ($400).

The application of §304 to a sale of parent stock to its subsidiary corporation is similar, although the application of §318's attribution rules to the transaction is problematic. Consider the case of taxpayer *T* owning 60 of the 100 outstanding shares of Parent Corp., which in turn owns 100 percent of the stock of Sub Corp. How will *T* be taxed if he sells 30 shares of Parent to Sub?

Section 304(b)(1) requires that the tests of §302(b) be applied to *T*'s interest in Parent. His pre-sale ownership of Parent was 60 percent. His post-sale *actual* ownership was 30 shares. Can the shares sold to Sub be imputed back to *T*? The Service might seek to form a chain of attribution from Sub to Parent to *T*, but that would require attributing stock of Parent to itself. Treas. Regs. §1.318-1(b)(1) provides that "[a] corporation shall not be considered to own its own stock by reason of section 318(a)(3)(C) [attribution to corporations]." See D. Kahn, Basic Corporate Taxation §2.26(b) (3d ed. 1981).

Assuming that the Parent stock owned by Sub cannot be attributed to *T* through Parent, does that make *T*'s post-sale ownership of Parent only 30 percent? Under Treas. Regs. §1.304-3(a), the transaction is treated "as though the parent corporation had redeemed its own stock." Might not the Service argue that *T* should be treated as owning 30 of the 70 outstanding shares of Parent? Even in this case, however, *T* would still qualify for exchange treatment under §302(b)(2).

How should §302(b)(4) (applicable to redemptions in partial liquidation) be applied in the context of §304? Although §302(b)(4) surely applies to determinations under §§302 and 304, neither section specifies which corporation (the issuing corporation or the acquiring corporation) must engage in a partial liquidation. One court has held that the *acquiring* corporation must pass the test of §302(b)(4) if the shareholder is to obtain exchange treatment. See Blaschka v. United States, 393 F.2d 983 (Cl. Ct. 1968).

Suppose *F* and *F*'s son, *S*, own all the stock of *X* Corp. and *Y* Corp. *X* Corp. redeems all of *F*'s stock, and *F* waives the family attribution rules under §302(c)(2) in reporting the transaction as an exchange under §302(b)(3). Two years later, *F* sells his *Y* Corp. stock to *X* Corp. in a transaction governed by §304. Under §304(a)(1), *X* Corp. is treated as redeeming *F*'s *X* Corp. stock. Does this constructive redemption mean that *F* will be deemed to have acquired *X* Corp. stock in violation of §302(c)(2)(A)(iii)? The Service has ruled that the application of §304 does not cause *F* to run afoul of §302(c)(2)(A)(iii). Rev. Rul. 88-55, 1988-2 C.B. 45.

4. *Dividend income in a §304 transaction.* If a transaction described in §304(a)(1) (i.e., the brother-sister context) is taxed as a §301 distribution, the transferor and acquiring corporation are treated as follows: First, they are treated as if the transferor transferred the stock of the issuing (or target) corporation to the acquiror in a §351(a) transfer in exchange for acquiror stock. In a separate step, the acquiror is treated as redeeming that newly issued stock. This peculiar hypothetical redemption (which only arises if the transaction has *already* been determined to be taxable as a distribution so that the redemption rules of §302(b) are not implicated) is important if the transferor is itself a corporation; in such circumstances, this hypothetical redemption affects the transferor's tax treatment because the transaction may be taxed as an extraordinary dividend under §1059. See §1059(e)(1)(A) and pages 151-152 supra.

If a taxpayer subject to the rules of §304 has a sale recharacterized as a distribution pursuant to §302(d), then the amount of that distribution constituting a dividend will be determined by reference to the earnings and profits of both the issuing and the acquiring corporations. §304(b)(2). What is the function of the parenthetical in §304(b)(2)? Recall §312.

5. *Basis consequences of a §304 transaction.* If a taxpayer qualifies for exchange treatment in a §304 transaction, then her basis in the redeemed shares will be used to offset the sale proceeds. Furthermore, the acquiring corporation presumably will take a cost basis in those shares. But what happens if the taxpayer fails to qualify for exchange treatment and instead is subject to the distribution rules of §301?

In the case of a brother-sister §304 transaction, the transferor generally increases her basis in acquiror stock by her basis in the transferred target stock. That increase occurs in two steps. First, the transferor generally takes that basis in the hypothetical share deemed received in the deemed §351(a) transfer. §358(a). Cf. §362(e)(2)(C). On the deemed redemption, that basis then shifts to her acquiror stock. Treas. Regs. §1.302-2(c) (example 1). What happens if the taxpayer actually owns no stock of the acquiring corporation? One possibility would be to transfer the basis to the person whose stock was attributed to the taxpayer under §318. An alternate possibility is to increase the taxpayer's basis in any remaining shares of the issuing corporation. Which do you prefer? See Coyle v. United States, 415 F.2d 488 (4th Cir. 1968).

And what of the acquiring corporation? Because it is treated as receiving the stock of the issuing corporation in a §351(a) transfer, its basis in that stock generally equals the transferor's basis in the stock immediately before the transfer. §362(a). But see §362(e)(2) (providing that when property transferred by a transferor in a §351 exchange has a net built-in loss, that loss is eliminated either at the corporate level or, by election, at the shareholder level).

Once again, the basis consequences attending a parent-subsidiary §304 transaction are more complex than the brother-sister situation. Of course, if the shareholder qualifies for exchange treatment under §302(a), then the shareholder recovers his basis as an offset against the amount realized, and the acquiring corporation takes a cost basis. But if the transaction is subject to the distribution rules of §301, then what happens to the shareholder's basis in the stock transferred?

In Broadview Lumber Co. v. United States, 561 F.2d 698 (7th Cir. 1977), the Service argued that the transaction should be treated as a contribution to the capital of the subsidiary (acquiring) corporation by the taxpayer. The court observed, however, that Congress specifically limited such treatment to brother-sister transactions. The court then held that the subsidiary corporation takes the stock with a cost basis. What does this imply as to the shareholder's basis consequences? Cf. Rev. Rul. 70-496, 1970-2 C.B. 74, in which the Service ruled that a corporate taxpayer having no actual ownership of the acquiring corporation after a §304(a)(1) transaction simply loses its basis in the transferred shares.

6. *The relationship between §304 and §351.* If a taxpayer transfers stock of one corporation to a second corporation in exchange for stock of the acquiring corporation plus boot, it may be that both §351 and §304 apply to the transaction. These sections, however, have differing boot rules. Under §351, boot qualifies for exchange treatment and is taxable, if at all, only to the extent of gain on the transaction. Boot in a §304 exchange may be taxed as a dividend regardless of the amount of gain, if any, on the exchange. Because of the more favorable taxation of boot under §351, taxpayers have argued that §351 should override §304 when both are applicable. See, e.g., Haserot v. Commissioner, 46 T.C. 864 (1966), aff'd sub nom. Commissioner v. Stickney, 399 F.2d 828 (6th Cir. 1968).

Congress responded to this situation by providing that §304 overrides §351 (except with respect to certain acquisition indebtedness). See §304(b)(3). Once again, if the taxpayer receives only stock of the acquiring corporation without any boot, then §351 will be the exclusive taxing provision because stock of the acquiring corporation is not "property" for purposes of §304. See §317(a). Cf. Rev. Rul. 78-422, 1978-2 C.B. 129, in which an individual transferred encumbered stock of one controlled corporation to another controlled corporation in exchange for stock of the acquiring corporation. Held, receipt of stock in the acquiring corporation is a §351 transaction, but assumption by the acquiring corporation of the transferor's debt is like cash and therefore taxable under §304.

While §351 is supposed to defer to §304 by reason of §304(b)(3), Congress may have accidentally reversed that rule when it enacted the special rules for nonqualified preferred stock in §351(g). For purposes of §351(a) (providing for nonrecognition of gain or loss on the contribution of property to a controlled corporation in exchange for stock), receipt of nonqualified preferred stock is treated as boot rather than as stock. §351(g)(1)(A). However, for all other purposes, such nonqualified stock retains its character as stock. In particular, receipt of nonqualified preferred stock in a redemption by a related corporation is not taxable under §304 because for that provision *all* stock is excluded (§317(a)), even nonqualified preferred stock. Thus, a taxpayer can transfer stock of Brother Corp. to Sister Corp. for, say, common and nonqualified preferred stock of Sister, and any gain will be taxable as capital gain to the extent of the value of the nonqualified preferred stock received. The nonqualified preferred stock can then be sold to a third party (at no additional tax cost), and the taxpayer has avoided application of §304. This conclusion assumes, though, that the nonqualified preferred stock will not be tainted under §306 as well as taxed under §351(b) upon receipt, a result that is not at all clear from the statute. See §306(c)(3). How would the various statutory provisions apply if the taxpayer received *only* nonqualified preferred stock of Sister in exchange for the Brother stock?

PROBLEM

5-13. *F* sells 70 shares of *X* Corp. stock to *Y* Corp. for $100 per share. Prior to the sale, *F* owned all 100 outstanding shares of *X* Corp., with a basis of $25 per share. *X* Corp. and *Y* Corp. each have current and accumulated earnings and profits of $5,000. What are the tax consequences of the sale assuming the following situations?

a. *F* is the sole shareholder of *Y* Corp. Suppose instead of *F*, *P* Corp. is the sole shareholder of both *X* and *Y* Corp.
b. *F* owns 50 percent of the stock of *Y* Corp.
c. *F* owns no stock of *Y* Corp., but his son is the sole shareholder of *Y* Corp.
d. *F* is the sole shareholder of *Y* Corp.; *Y* Corp. has no current earnings and profits and has a $10,000 deficit accumulated earnings and profits account.
e. Reconsider your answers to (a) and (b) by assuming that *F* receives only $5,000 in cash and $5,000 in the form of *Y* Corp. stock.

In the following case, the relationship between the *Sullivan-Holsey* doctrine, supra page 188, and §304 is explored.

Citizens Bank & Trust Co. v. Commissioner

580 F.2d 442 (Cl. Ct. 1978)

Before Davis, Kunzig, and Bennett, Judges.

Opinion

Per Curiam. [T]he court agrees with the trial judge's recommended decision. . . .

Opinion of Trial Judge

Miller, Trial Judge. . . .

Plaintiff, John D. MacArthur (John), has at all pertinent times been the sole shareholder, chairman of the board of directors and chief executive officer of Bankers Life and Casualty Company (Bankers), an insurance company. Telfer MacArthur

(Telfer), plaintiff's brother, was experienced in the printing and publishing business and was president of Pioneer Publishing Company (Pioneer).

In its operations Bankers required a considerable amount of printed materials, such as applications, medical forms, advertising circulars, and policies. Up to 1950 it printed some of such materials itself, in the basement of its home office, and purchased others from various printing companies, including companies owned and operated by Telfer. During 1950, Telfer and plaintiff agreed to form a corporation, Brookshore Company, which they would jointly own and which would supply Bankers' printing needs at standard going rates. Telfer agreed to manage, staff and supervise Brookshore, and John agreed to furnish most of its capital and to have Bankers purchase its printing needs from it. Each was entitled to one-half of the outstanding stock. This agreement was effectuated in 1951.

In 1957, after Telfer had suffered a heart attack, he proposed to John that they enter into a mutual buy-out agreement. This agreement, executed June 29, 1957, acknowledged that they equally owned 2,235 of the outstanding 2,455 shares of Brookshore, and also all of the shares of Mackley Realty Company (Mackley), which they contributed to Brookshore. They agreed that upon the death of either, his estate was to sell his interest in Brookshore to the survivor and the survivor agreed to purchase such interest from the estate, at a stated price which increases with the passage of time prior to the date of death, with a maximum of $200,000 in the event death occurred after January 10, 1960.

Telfer died January 29, 1960. On February 10, 1960, John wrote to Telfer's widow, Elizabeth —

> As you undoubtedly know, Telfer insisted that I buy his half of Brookshore in the event of his death. I have every intention of keeping faith with him. When you make your final selection of a lawyer and qualify as executrix, let somebody in my office know and I will arrange to make the payment.

Thereafter, in February and March 1960, John requested Wayne R. Cook, an attorney employed by Bankers, to negotiate with Elizabeth and her attorneys in connection with fulfilling the terms and conditions of the 1957 agreement.

While never expressly repudiating its rights and obligations under the 1957 agreement, the representatives of the estate were not receptive to the $200,000 offer. Their reasons included the following:

(a) They believed that one-half of Brookshore, including its subsidiary, Mackley, was worth a great deal more than $200,000.

(b) They wanted additional indemnity agreements from John against various liabilities which the estate might incur, and they did not want to deal with Bankers because of the belief that an insurance company could not properly enter into an indemnity agreement, and

(c) They also wanted John to purchase from the estate for additional consideration Telfer's stock interest in Pioneer.

On March 24, 1960, an agreement was entered into between Elizabeth, individually and as executrix under Telfer's will, and John. Elizabeth was to deliver all of the shares of Brookshore to John or upon his written direction. In return, John was to pay concurrently to Elizabeth $200,000 and to release, indemnify and hold harmless Elizabeth and Telfer's estate against any loss arising out of any claims by himself, by the various corporations, and by Telfer's former wife. In addition, Elizabeth agreed forthwith to deliver to John or upon his written direction the remaining shares of Pioneer, which the estate owned, in exchange for an additional $175,000. The agreement was also approved by representatives of Bankers, Brookshore and Mackley to indicate their approval of the releases.

On the same day, pursuant to the agreement, Bankers issued a check in the sum of $375,000 to a bank and the latter in turn issued a cashier's check in the same amount payable to the estate of Telfer. Wayne Cook, on behalf of Bankers, delivered the check to Elizabeth's attorneys, and she deposited it in the estate's account. In return, Elizabeth's attorneys delivered the Brookshore, Mackley and Pioneer shares to Bankers.

It is stipulated that $200,000 of the $375,000 was for the Brookshore and Mackley shares and that the fair-market-value of such shares was at least $244,000.

The Commissioner of Internal Revenue determined that because the $200,000 payment satisfied John's obligation in the same amount and because Bankers had earnings and profits in excess of $200,000, Bankers' payment in that amount constituted a dividend to John. This is also defendant's primary position in this case.

In support of its position defendant relies on two cases, Sullivan v. United States, 363 F.2d 724 (8th Cir. 1966), cert. denied, 387 U.S. 905 (1967) and Wall v. United States, 164 F.2d 462 (4th Cir. 1947).

In *Sullivan* the taxpayer was the majority stockholder in a corporation in which there was only one other stockholder, Nelson. Sullivan had unconditionally agreed that upon Nelson's termination of his employment he would repurchase the stock from Nelson at book value. When Nelson did leave, instead of repurchasing the stock himself, Sullivan caused the corporation to do so. In agreeing with the Government that Sullivan had received a dividend in the amount of the corporation's payment to Nelson, the court concisely stated its rationale (363 F.2d at 729):

> After the transaction was completed, the relevant facts were essentially as follows: (1) Sullivan's personal obligation had been discharged (2) Sullivan owned all of the outstanding shares of stock of the corporation (3) the corporation's assets were decreased by the amount paid to Nelson for his stock (4) Nelson's stock was held by the corporation as treasury stock. It is true that in terms of the financial worth of Sullivan's interest in the corporation, it was the same after the transaction as it was before. The transaction still resulted in an economic benefit to Sullivan, however, because he was relieved of his personal obligation to purchase Nelson's stock.

(Footnotes omitted.)

In *Wall*, plaintiff was one of two equal shareholders. Plaintiff purchased the shares of the other shareholder for a cash down payment plus promissory notes payable in 10 successive years, with the stock to be held by trustees as security for the notes but otherwise for the benefit of plaintiff. After only a single year, the corporation assumed payment of the annual liability on the notes. Plaintiff transferred to the corporation his equity in the stock held by the trustees and the corporation entered such stock on its books as treasury stock. The court upheld the Government's position that the annual payments represented dividend income to plaintiff because (at 464) —

> [t]he transaction is regarded as the same as if the money had been paid to the taxpayer and transmitted by him to the creditor; and so if a corporation, instead of

> paying a dividend to a stockholder, pays a debt for him out of its surplus, it is the same for tax purposes as if the corporation pays a dividend to a stockholder, and the stockholder then utilizes it to pay his debt.

Neither of these decisions is authority for the defendant's position herein. They do support the idea that a corporation's satisfaction of its stockholder's debt gives him an economic benefit; but defendant ignores the fact that a payment to or for the benefit of a stockholder is not the only element of dividend. A dividend also necessitates a distribution of corporate earnings and profits. I.R.C. §316. Therefore, an exchange of assets of equal value which does not reduce corporate net worth cannot be a distribution of earnings and profits and hence is not a dividend.

This was made clear in Palmer v. Commissioner of Internal Revenue, 302 U.S. 63, 69-70 (1937), wherein the Court stated:

> While a sale of corporate assets to stockholders is, in a literal sense, a distribution of its property, such a transaction does not necessarily fall within the statutory definition of a dividend. For a sale to stockholders may not result in any diminution of its net worth and in that case cannot result in any distribution of its profits.
>
> [T]he bare fact that a transaction, on its face a sale, has resulted in a distribution of some of the corporate assets to stockholders, gives rise to no inference that the distribution is a dividend within the meaning of §[316]. To transfer it from one category to the other, it is at least necessary to make some showing that the transaction is in purpose or effect used as an implement for the distribution of corporate earnings to stockholders.

While the issue in *Palmer* was whether or not a sale of corporate property to stockholders resulted in a dividend to them, the principles underlying the decision are equally applicable to an exchange of property arising out of a purchase by a corporation. Both the courts and the Commissioner of Internal Revenue have ruled that a corporate payment of money or property to a stockholder to acquire corporate assets at a fair price does not reduce earnings and profits and is not a dividend.

For the same reasons, a corporation's assumption and payment of its stockholder's obligation to purchase from a third person an asset of equal or greater value cannot be deemed a dividend to the stockholder if the corporation acquires the asset. Just such a case was presented in Easson v. Commissioner of Internal Revenue, 294 F.2d 653 (9th Cir. 1961). There the taxpayer owned real property which was encumbered by a mortgage with respect to which the taxpayer was personally liable on the underlying notes. He transferred the property subject to the mortgage to a corporation in exchange for all its stock, but remained personally liable on the notes. The Commissioner contended that when the corporation made payments on the mortgage notes the taxpayer in effect received dividend income because such payments discharged taxpayer's legal obligation. The court rejected that contention with the following explanation (at 661):

> While the corporation may incidentally have benefited taxpayer by reducing the mortgage, it is clear that the corporation did not thereby distribute any assets. The corporation owned the apartment subject to the mortgage and as the mortgage decreased its equity in the apartment house increased. Thus when it took money out of cash and applied that amount to the mortgage, its net worth remained constant. Its total assets were unchanged because the credit to the cash account was offset by a corresponding debit to the fixed assets account.

And see also Stout v. Commissioner of Internal Revenue, 273 F.2d 345 (4th Cir. 1959).

Sullivan and *Wall* are distinguishable from the other cases discussed by the fact that the corporations there received no property in exchange for paying their stockholders' obligations. Because they received only their own stock, their net worth was reduced and they had to deplete their earnings and profits to make the payments. In substance, the transactions were stock redemptions in favor of the plaintiffs which were essentially equivalent to dividends and hence taxable as such. (See I.R.C. §302(b).) In *Sullivan*, as the extract from the opinion previously quoted shows, the court stated that it was a relevant fact that corporation's assets were decreased by its payment. In *Wall*, the taxpayer argued that because the shares acquired by virtue of the payments were kept in the corporate treasury they remained assets, but the court responded that irrespective of whether or not they were kept in the treasury (164 F.2d at 465), "As a practical matter, such shares are redeemed in the sense that they no longer constitute any liability of the corporation but represent nothing more than an opportunity to acquire new assets by a reissuance."

Since in return for the $200,000 payment to Telfer's estate Bankers received shares of Brookshore which had an agreed fair-market-value of at least $244,000, it is concluded that Bankers did not distribute any of its earnings and profits by virtue of having satisfied plaintiff's obligation to make such a purchase. Furthermore, the very fact that the purchase was such a bargain makes it difficult to understand how Bankers benefited plaintiff at all by taking over his opportunity to make the purchase. Indeed, the undisputed testimony was that Telfer's estate, the sellers, maintained in the negotiations that the $200,000 plaintiff offered was less than the fair value of their Brookshore shares and sought to avoid their agreement to sell them to plaintiff at such price. Thus it can hardly be said that plaintiff was benefited by being relieved of an "obligation," "liability" or "debt" in the onerous sense which those terms ordinarily connote.

Defendant argues alternatively that the $200,000 payment to Telfer's estate was a dividend pursuant to I.R.C. §304. . . .

Plaintiff and defendant agree that subsection 304(a)(1) is designed to prevent a stockholder who controls two corporations from drawing off accumulated corporate earnings through the device of selling part of his stock in one corporation to the other. Plaintiff had controlling interests in both corporations. Defendant contends that the 1960 transaction was the constructive equivalent of plaintiff obtaining the remaining 50 percent of Brookshore shares from Telfer's estate and then selling them to Bankers in return for Bankers assuming and paying plaintiff's obligation for the purchase price.

To apply section 304 in this manner would be to distort rather than to further the statutory purpose. The entire focus of the section is on closing a loophole. Sales proceeds received by a stockholder from a controlled corporation should be treated as dividend income rather than return of capital or capital gain if what the corporation acquires is nothing more than the stock of another corporation the same stockholder controls; for, under such circumstances, the sale is only a transfer from one pocket to another.

An obvious prerequisite for invoking subsection 304(a)(1) is that the stockholder must have received the sales proceeds. Here, however, when the transaction was completed the $200,000 sales proceeds were received by a third person, Telfer's estate, and not by plaintiff. The superseding of plaintiff's obligation to buy the stock at less than fair market value was not an assumption of a liability nor a benefit to plaintiff. It was a mere incident to Banker's payment and the estate's receipt of the purchase price.

Another prerequisite for application of the statute is that the stockholder must have owned the stock before the transfer; or else the corporation cannot have acquired it from him, but must have acquired it from a third person. Here, however, plaintiff did not own the additional 50 percent stock interest in Brookshore which was the subject of the acquisition by Bankers. Telfer's estate owned the shares and would not convey them to anyone until it received at least $200,000 in cash for them. Since it was Bankers and not plaintiff which paid the $200,000, there is no basis for imputing to plaintiff acquisition of the shares for himself or ownership at any time. Thus, Bankers necessarily acquired them from a third person and not from plaintiff.

It is concluded, therefore, that plaintiff is entitled to judgment. . . .

NOTES

1. *The constructive dividend under §301.* The court was correct, was it not, when it distinguished *Sullivan* by noting that the corporation did not redeem its own shares but rather purchased the shares of another corporation? A corporation's satisfaction of its shareholder's liability should not be a dividend (more accurately, a distribution subject to the rules of §301) if the shareholder transfers valuable property to the corporation in exchange, except to the extent that the shareholder's liability exceeds the fair market value of the transferred property. Because Bankers received for its $200,000 payment stock of Brookshore worth at least $244,000, there should be no constructive dividend under §301. Focusing on the language of §301, was the distribution in *Citizens Bank* made with respect to the taxpayer's stock or made in exchange for the Banker's stock that the corporation acquired?

2. *The dividend under §304.* Was the court correct when it wrote that "[a]n obvious prerequisite for invoking subsection 304(a)(1) is that the stockholder must have received the sales proceeds"? The effect of Bankers's $200,000 payment was to relieve the taxpayer from an obligation of the same amount; satisfaction of a taxpayer's liability has long been recognized as constructive receipt. Old Colony Trust Co. v. Commissioner, 279 U.S. 716 (1929). While it is true that the corporation received fair value for its payment, that value was in the form of stock of a corporation controlled by the taxpayer. Is not the exchange of stock of a controlled corporation for money or property, *or for the payment of an obligation,* precisely the situation addressed by §304?

6

Distributions of Stock

A. DISTRIBUTIONS OF STOCK AND STOCK RIGHTS UNDER §305

1. *The General Rule of Nontaxability under §305(a)*

In Eisner v. Macomber, 252 U.S. 189 (1920), the Supreme Court concluded that a provision treating a stock dividend as taxable to a shareholder was unconstitutional when the stock dividend was pro rata and the corporation had only one class of stock outstanding. Subject to the exceptions contained in §305(b), §305(a) continues the *Macomber* rule that stock dividends are nontaxable on receipt, and Congress has extended this rule to include the distribution of stock rights. §305(d)(1). Note, though, that the nonrecognition rule of §305(a) applies only to the distribution of a corporation's own stock (or rights to its stock) *made with respect to a shareholder's stock.* Distributions of stock as compensation to an employee or to pay off a debt of the corporation, for example, are not covered by §305, nor are distributions of stock by one corporation of stock in a second corporation. Such distributions, whether of stock or otherwise, will be taxed to the recipients under other provisions of the Code, usually §61. Cf. §83.

Although stock dividends may be received tax free under §305(a), that stock may be subject to substantial tax disabilities on disposition. Dividend stock (other than common stock received with respect to common stock) will be subject to the rules of §306 if it is received tax free under §305(a). See §306(c)(1)(A). These rules, discussed at pages 233-251 infra, may treat as ordinary income the entire amount realized for the stock on disposition. In some cases, in fact, §306 may produce harsher results than would have occurred if the stock dividend had simply been taxed on receipt under §305(b).

If a shareholder receives stock tax free under §305(a), then the basis in that stock is determined under §307(a). Section 307(a) requires an allocation of the old stock basis between the old and new shares. This allocation is made in proportion to the relative fair market values of each share. Treas. Regs. §1.307-1(a). Thus, if the underlying rationale for tax-free receipt of dividend stock is that the taxpayer's interest has undergone a change in form but not in substance, see the discussion of *Macomber* above, then the rule of §307(a) simply continues the identification of the old and new shares: The shareholder's old basis is allocated (without increase or decrease) among all shares constituting the new form of the old holding. How should the shareholder determine the holding period of the dividend stock? See §1223(5) (providing for tacking).

What effect should a distribution by a corporation of its own stock have on the corporation's earnings and profits if the distributed stock is received tax free by the shareholders under §305(a)? See §312(d)(1)(B).

2. *Exceptions to the General Rule: §305(b) and (c)*

a. Actual Distributions

Although §305(a) provides as a general rule that a shareholder excludes a stock dividend from gross income, the exceptions found in §305(b) almost swallow that nonrecognition rule. Section 305(b)(1) continues the pre-1969 rule that a distribution payable, at the election of any shareholder, in stock or property will be taxable regardless of the shareholder's choice. If she elects to receive property, then the distribution rules of §301 will apply directly. If she elects to receive stock, then the same distribution rules will apply by virtue of §305(b)(1). In these circumstances, Congress has taken the view that the shareholders electing to receive stock should be taxed as if they received cash that was then recontributed to the corporation in exchange for additional stock.

Section 305(b)(2) taxes the receipt of dividend stock if the effect of the stock dividend is to increase the proportionate corporate interests of some shareholders while giving other shareholders cash or other property. If a shareholder's right to future dividends is increased, then he has an increase in the earnings and profits of the corporation within the meaning of §305(b)(2)(B). Similarly, if a shareholder's right to participate in the corporation's eventual liquidating distribution is increased, then he has had an increase in his share of corporate assets. Because most preferred stock has a preference as to dividends and a limitation on liquidation, distributions *of* or *on* preferred stock often will cause a change in relative shareholder interests in the earnings and profits as well as in the assets of the corporation. The examples in Treas. Regs. §1.305-3(e) help clarify the potential scope of §305(b)(2). In particular, be certain that you understand why the distribution described in example 1 is subject to §305(b)(2) while the distribution described in example 2 is not.

A stock dividend cannot be taxable under §305(b)(2) unless shareholders not receiving the stock dividend receive cash or other property as part of the same transaction. This "companion distribution" requirement is easily satisfied because, under Treas. Regs. §1.305-3(b)(3), "there is no requirement that the shareholders receiving cash or property acquire the cash or property by way of a [formal] corporate distribution with respect to their shares, so long as they receive such cash or property in their capacity as shareholders." Distributions of stock and cash or property separated by more than three years, however, will be presumed to be unrelated for determinations under §305(b)(2). Treas. Regs. §1.305-3(b)(4). Why might Congress have limited taxation under §305(b)(2) to those disproportionate stock dividends having companion distributions? In what way are such stock dividends similar to those taxable under §305(b)(1)?

Section 305(b)(3) taxes stock dividends when some shareholders of common stock receive common stock while others receive preferred stock. Such distributions often will have the disproportionate effect described in §305(b)(2). Why will they not fall within that subsection? Recall the definition of "property" in §317(a), applicable to §§301-318.

Section 305(b)(4) applies to distributions of stock or stock rights made with respect to preferred stock (in common parlance, stock dividends "on" preferred stock). What is the reason for taxing such dividends? Should preferred on preferred stock dividends be tax free under the reasoning of *Macomber*?

The second clause in §305(b)(4) excludes from the rule of §305(b)(4) certain changes to the conversion ratio of preferred stock. The conversion ratio of convertible preferred stock is most often changed when a stock dividend is declared by the corporation on its common stock because, if the conversion ratio is not adjusted, the holders of the convertible preferred stock will have had their conversion rights diluted. Since a change in conversion ratio involves no actual distribution of stock or of stock rights, this final clause is misplaced. To be sure, changes in the conversion ratio of preferred stock can have the effect of a stock dividend, so such changes should, in appropriate circumstances, be treated as the equivalent of actual stock dividends. The taxation of constructive stock dividends, however, is addressed generally in §305(c), and the second clause in §305(b)(4) more appropriately belongs in that subsection. Section 305(c) is discussed at pages 227-233 infra.

Section 305(b)(5) taxes the distribution of convertible preferred stock. Suppose a corporation distributes preferred stock that is convertible into common stock. If some (but not all) of this stock is converted, then the effect of the distribution is a disproportionate distribution of common and preferred stock. Because disproportionate distributions of common and preferred stock are taxable under §305(b)(3), distributions of convertible preferred stock must also be taxable unless it is shown that the distribution will not have the effect described in §305(b)(2). Why does §305(b)(5) reference §305(b)(2) rather than §305(b)(3)?

The *Frontier Savings Association* case that follows explores the reach of §305(b)(1). Under what circumstances will a shareholder who has received a common stock dividend be taxable under §§305(b) and 301 because the shareholder is deemed to have elected to receive the stock rather than cash? While *Frontier Savings Association* focuses on §305(b)(1), Revenue Ruling 78-375, which follows *Frontier*, considers the impact of a dividend reinvestment plan (i.e., a DRIP) under both §305(b)(1) and (b)(2).

Frontier Savings Association v. Commissioner

87 T.C. 665 (1986), aff'd sub nom. Colonial Sav. Assn. v. Commissioner, 854 F.2d 1001 (7th Cir. 1988), acq., 1990-1 C.B. 1

SWIFT, Judge. . . .

Frontier Savings has been a member and stockholder of the Federal Home Loan Bank of Chicago (the "Chicago Bank") at all times since the organization of the Chicago Bank. . . .

The Federal Home Loan Bank system was designed primarily as a reserve credit facility for savings and loan associations and other home mortgage credit institutions. Savings and loan associations (such as Frontier Savings) and mutual savings banks that are members or stockholders in the district banks (hereinafter referred to as "members" or "member banks") are required by Federal law to maintain a certain capital stock ownership in the respective district banks of which they are members. The stock ownership requirements are determined at the end of each calendar year and are calculated with reference to each member bank's net home mortgage loans outstanding and total borrowings of each member from the district bank.

Each member bank generally must maintain a capital stock ownership interest in the district bank in an amount equal to at least one percent of the total outstanding balance of its home mortgage loans and at least equal to one-twelfth of total outstanding borrowings of the member bank from the district bank, as of December 31 of each year. Each share of stock in the district banks is valued by statute at its $100 par value. See 12 U.S.C. sec. 1426(b) and (c) (1978).

Based upon the above year-end calculations, member banks that are required to purchase additional stock of district banks must do so by January 31 of the following year at the par value of $100 per share. Member banks that own stock in district banks in excess of the required number of shares ("excess shares") may request that excess shares be redeemed by the district banks. . . .

At a meeting held on November 20, 1978, the board of directors of the Chicago Bank adopted a resolution to pay a 6.58-percent dividend to its stockholders of record as of December 31, 1978. Subject to the approval of the Federal Home Loan Bank Board, the resolution stated that the dividend would be paid in the form of shares of stock in the Chicago Bank. On December 22, 1978, the Director of the Office of District Banks, Federal Home Loan Bank Board, wrote a letter to the President of the Chicago Bank approving the stock dividend.

On December 22, 1978, the Chicago Bank mailed a bulletin to its member banks, informing them that a 6.58-percent stock dividend would be paid, with fractional shares to be paid in cash. The explanation made in the bulletin for paying a stock dividend, rather than a cash dividend, was as follows:

> (1) Providing a stock rather than a cash dividend may enable your association to defer the payment of income taxes on the value of the stock dividend. You may wish to consult your tax adviser for the proper handling of a stock dividend.
>
> (2) A stock dividend can be applied toward satisfying the stock investment requirement for members that experienced a growth in assets during 1978 or that will be required to purchase additional stock due to increased borrowings from the Bank.

The bulletin also explained that most member banks would be required to increase their stock holdings in the Chicago Bank due to that year's general increase in outstanding home mortgage loans. . . .

Enclosed with the December 22, 1978, bulletin mailed by the Chicago Bank to its member banks describing the 1978 stock dividend was a form entitled "Calculation of Bank Stock Requirement as of December 31, 1978." Using that form, each member bank could calculate the number of shares of stock it was required, under 12 U.S.C. sec. 1426(c) (1978), to own in the Chicago Bank as of December 31, 1978. If a member bank was required to purchase additional shares of stock, it could submit the form (reflecting the number of shares to be purchased) along with a check in payment therefor to the Chicago Bank. If the member bank held more shares than it legally was required to own, it could use the form to request the redemption of any excess shares. Although the Chicago Bank had no legal obligation to redeem excess shares, in prior years it routinely had done so.

On January 16, 1979, Frontier Savings completed the form calculating the number of shares of common stock in the Chicago Bank it was required to own based on its December 31, 1978, outstanding balance for home mortgage loans. That calculation indicated that Frontier Savings was required to purchase 678 additional shares of common stock in the Chicago Bank (after taking into account the shares received as part of the common stock dividend on December 29, 1978). Frontier Savings, therefore, sent a check in the amount of $67,800 to the Chicago Bank and 678 shares were credited to its stock account at the Chicago Bank. A new stock certificate was issued reflecting the ownership by Frontier Savings of a total of 10,332 shares of common stock in the Chicago Bank. During 1979, none of the shares of common stock in the Chicago Bank owned by Frontier Savings were redeemed or otherwise transferred.

Exclusive of the December 29, 1978, stock dividend received, on December 31, 1978, 195 of the 497 member banks owned sufficient shares of common stock in the Chicago Bank to meet their stock ownership requirements, and 302 member banks did not own sufficient shares to meet their stock ownership requirements. After receipt of the 1978 stock dividend, 69 member banks requested that the Chicago Bank redeem all or some of their excess shares. All such redemption requests were agreed to by the Chicago Bank and the following number of shares of common stock were redeemed by the Chicago Bank from its member banks in the months indicated:

Time Period	*Shares Redeemed*
December 1978	1,240
January 1979	62,575
February 1979	8,249
Remainder of 1979	22,256

During December of 1978 and 1979, 45 member banks redeemed a number of shares of stock in the Chicago Bank that was equal to or that exceeded the number of shares they received as their portion of the 1978 stock dividend. [A similar stock dividend and redemption occurred in late 1979 and early 1980.]

None of the shares of stock in the Chicago Bank received by Frontier Savings with respect to the 1978 and 1979 stock dividends were redeemed by the Chicago Bank or otherwise disposed of by Frontier Savings prior to 1982. In January of 1982, the Chicago Bank, at the request of Frontier Savings, redeemed 3,584 shares of its stock owned by Frontier Savings.

Opinion

The receipt of common stock dividends generally is not taxable to stockholders. Sec. 305(a). Where, however, dividends from a corporation are payable, at the election of the stockholders, in stock or property (such as cash), the receipt of dividends will be taxable to the stockholders under the provisions of section 301. Sec. 305(b)(1). In that circumstance the receipt of stock dividends will be taxable under sections 305(b)(1) and 301 regardless of whether the stockholders exercise their election to receive the dividends in cash or other property. Sec. 1.305-2(a), Income Tax Regs.

Respondent argues that by redeeming all of the common stock it was requested to redeem from its member banks in 1979 and 1980 (and apparently doing so in years before 1979), the Chicago Bank established such a policy and practice of redeeming excess stock upon request of the member banks that the member banks should be regarded as having had an "election" to receive the 1978 and 1979 stock dividends in cash. Respondent therefore argues that the stock dividends in question do not qualify for exemption from taxability under section 305(a) and should be taxable to the member banks under sections 305(b)(1) and 301. For the reasons explained below, we disagree. . . .

Congress vested in the district banks and in the Federal Home Loan Bank Board discretionary authority to redeem excess shares of common stock held by member banks. Our careful examination of the record herein satisfies us that the manner in which stock dividends were paid and redeemed in 1978 and 1979 by the Chicago Bank was consistent with that grant of discretionary authority and did not vest in the member banks the unilateral right to elect or to require the Chicago Bank to redeem excess shares upon request.

Respondent concedes that the Chicago Bank did not completely abdicate its discretionary authority to redeem its stock but respondent argues that authority was exercised so consistently in favor of redemption that member banks, as a practical matter, had the option or election to have excess shares redeemed at any time. Respondent contends that the option arose "from the circumstances of the distribution" citing section 1.305-2(a)(4), Income Tax Regs. As indicated, we have carefully examined the circumstances of the stock dividends in question and conclude that the member banks, including Frontier Savings, did not have the option or election to have the Chicago Bank redeem excess shares of common stock in the Chicago Bank.

In addition to the factors explained above, we think it significant that the stock dividends of the Chicago Bank were declared and distributed in late December of 1978 and 1979. Member banks, however, normally would not be able to determine until early in the following year (after actual distribution of the stock dividends) whether they would be able even to request a redemption of some of their common stock in the Chicago Bank. In other words, on the day of distribution of the stock dividends, member banks could not know (other than through estimates and projections) whether they would be required to retain the stock dividends they received as part of their required investments in the district bank or whether the stock dividends would qualify as excess shares, in which case redemption thereof, if requested, might occur depending on the decision of the Chicago Bank. . . .

We recognize that the issuance by the Chicago Bank in 1978 and 1979 of stock dividends instead of or in addition to cash dividends was motivated in part by tax considerations. We cannot conclude, however, on the facts before us that the stock dividends were a mere subterfuge for cash distributions or that the Chicago Bank had relinquished its discretionary authority to decline to grant stock redemption requests.

Respondent refers to Rev. Rul. 76-258, 1976-2 C.B. 95. Revenue Rulings are, of course, not binding on this Court. Estate of Lang v. Commissioner, 64 T.C. 404, 406-407 (1975), affd. 613 F.2d 770 (9th Cir. 1980). Respondent's litigating position herein is reflected in Rev. Rul. 83-68, 1983-1 C.B. 75. For the reasons explained above and under the facts of this case, we reject the conclusion reached therein that a history or practice of redemptions by the Chicago Bank makes the stock dividends received by petitioner herein taxable under sections 305(b)(1) and 301. . . .

Decisions will be entered under Rule 155.

Reviewed by the Court.

Sterrett, Goffe, Chabot, Nims, Parker, Whitaker, Korner, Shields, Hamblen, Cohen, Clapp, Jacobs, and Parr, JJ., agree with the majority opinion.

Simpson, J., dissents.

Gerber, Wright, and Williams, JJ., did not participate in the consideration of this case.

HAMBLEN, J., concurring.

I concur in the conclusion of the majority based upon the limited factual circumstances involved. If a discretionary act of the Board of Directors of a shareholder corporation to redeem stock dividends becomes a routine matter, it might, in my opinion, develop into an "option" that arises after the distribution or a distribution pursuant to a "plan." See secs. 1.305-2(a) and 1.305-3(b), Income Tax Regs. In such a situation, it seems the redemptions might be periodic rather than isolated. The broad rules of section 305 could invoke different considerations under other circumstances.

Sterrett, Cohen, and Jacobs, JJ., agree with this concurring opinion.

Rev. Rul. 78-375

1978-2 C.B. 130

Advice has been requested as to the treatment for federal income tax purposes of a "dividend reinvestment plan" where the shareholder may not only elect to receive stock of greater fair market value than the cash dividend such shareholder might have received instead, but also the shareholder may, through the plan, purchase additional stock from the corporation at a discount price which is less than the fair market value of the stock.

X is a corporation engaged in commercial banking whose shares of common stock are widely held and are regularly traded in the over-the-counter market. In order to raise additional equity capital for corporate expansion and to provide holders of *X*'s common stock with a simple and convenient way of investing their cash dividends and optional payments in additional shares of *X* common stock without payment of any brokerage commission, *X* established an automatic dividend reinvestment plan. An independent agent will administer the plan and will receive the stock from *X* in the manner described below on behalf of a participating shareholder.

The plan provides the following:

(1) Shareholders can elect to have all their cash dividends (less a quarterly service charge of $3x$ dollars that is paid to an independent agent of the shareholder) otherwise payable on common stock registered in the name of the shareholder automatically reinvested in shares of *X* common stock. The service charge is paid to the agent for administering the plan and maintaining the stock certificates for the shareholders. The shareholders who elect to participate in the plan acquire *X* stock at a price equal to 95 percent of the fair market value of such stock on the dividend payment date. The shareholder's option to receive a dividend in additional

common stock in lieu of a cash dividend is not transferable apart from a transfer of the common shares themselves.

(2) A shareholder who participates in the dividend reinvestment aspect of the plan as described in paragraph (1) above, in addition, has the option to invest additional amounts to purchase shares of *X* common stock at a price equal to 95 percent of the fair market value of such stock on the dividend payment date. Optional investments by a shareholder in any quarterly dividend period must be at least 4*x* dollars and cannot exceed 100*x* dollars. The shareholder's right to invest additional amounts under the plan is not transferable apart from a transfer of the common shares themselves.

There is no requirement to participate in the plan and shareholders who do not participate receive their cash dividend payments in full. Certain shareholders have chosen not to participate; therefore, they receive their regular quarterly cash dividend. While the plan continues in effect, a participant's dividends will continue to be invested without further notice to *X*.

Prior to the dividend payment date no cash dividend is available to either *X*'s participating or nonparticipating shareholders. On the dividend payment date the participant receives written notification that *X* is acting to effectuate the participant's option to receive stock on that date. The crediting on the plan account and notification to the participant of the exact number of shares acquired (including fractional shares) takes place shortly after the dividend payment date.

A participant may withdraw from the plan at any time, upon written request. Upon withdrawal, certificates for whole shares credited to the participant's account under the plan will be issued and a cash payment based upon the market value of the participant's fractional share interest will be paid by *X*, through the participant's agent, to the participant. As an alternative, the shareholder may request that all or part of the whole shares credited to its account in the plan be sold for the shareholder's account. The sale will be made by an independent agent acting on behalf of such participant and the proceeds of the sale (less any brokerage commission and transfer tax) will be forwarded to the participant. With regard to the whole shares, *X* will neither purchase any shares of a participant nor pay any expense attributable to the sale of such stock. Upon a request for sale of a participant's shares, a cash payment equal to the market value of the participant's fractional share interest will be paid by *X*, through the participant's agent, to the participant. The purpose of the payment of cash is to save *X* the trouble, expense, and inconvenience of issuing and transferring fractional shares and is not designed to give any particular group of shareholders an increased interest in the assets or earnings and profits of *X*. . . .

In the present case, the distributions made by *X* while the plan is in effect are properly treated as payable either in *X*'s stock or in cash at the election of *X*'s common shareholders within the meaning of section 305(b)(1) of the Code. . . .

The optional investment aspect of the present case results in an increase in the proportionate interests of the shareholders making the purchase at a 5 percent discount, and this event increases their proportionate interests in the assets or earnings and profits of *X* within the meaning of section 305(b)(2)(B) of the Code. Furthermore, the fact that *X* shareholders who do not participate in the plan receive cash dividends constitutes a receipt of property by those shareholders within the meaning of section 305(b)(2)(A).

Accordingly, under the circumstances described above, it is held as follows:

(a) A shareholder of *X* who participates in the dividend reinvestment aspect of the plan will be treated as having received a distribution to which section 301 of the Code applies by reason of the application of section 305(b)(1). Pursuant to section 1.305-1(b) of the regulations, the amount of the distribution to a participating shareholder (including participating corporate shareholders) will be the fair market value of the *X* stock received on the date of the distribution (sections 1.301-1(b) and (d)), plus, pursuant to section 301, 3*x* dollars, the service charge subtracted from the amount of the shareholder's distribution.

(b) The basis of the shares credited to the account of a participating shareholder pursuant to the dividend reinvestment aspect of the plan will equal the amount of the dividend distribution, as provided in section 301(c) of the Code, measured by the fair market value of the *X* common stock as of the date of the distribution both as to noncorporate and corporate shareholders, pursuant to section 301(d). Section 1.301-1(h)(1) and (2)(i) of the regulations. The quarterly service charge paid by a participant who is an individual for the production of income or for the management, conservation, or maintenance of property held for the production of income, is deductible in the year paid by such participant under section 212, provided the individual itemizes deductions. . . . The quarterly service charge, which is paid in carrying on a trade or business by a participant who is an individual, is deductible in the year paid by such participant under section 162. A participant who is a corporation may deduct the service charge under section 162.

(c) A shareholder of *X* who participates in the optional payment aspect of the plan will be treated as having received a distribution to which section 301 of the Code applies by reason of the application of section 305(b)(2). Pursuant to section 1.305-3(a) of the regulations, the amount of the distribution to a participating shareholder will be the difference between the fair market value on the dividend payment date of the shares purchased with the optional payment and the amount of the optional payment. Section 1.305-3(b)(2).

(d) The basis to the shareholder who participates in the optional payment aspect of the plan is the excess of fair market value of the shares purchased with the optional payment over the optional payment (provided that this deemed distribution is taxable as a dividend under section 301(c)(1) of the Code) . . . plus the amount of the optional payment, pursuant to section 1012.

(e) A participant in the plan will not realize any taxable income upon receipt of certificates for whole shares that were credited to the participant's account pursuant to the plan. . . . Any cash received by an *X* shareholder in lieu of a fractional share interest will be treated as a redemption of that fractional share interest, subject to the provisions and limitations of section 302 of the Code. . . .

(f) A participant will recognize gain or loss pursuant to section 1001 of the Code when shares are sold or exchanged on behalf of the participant upon the participant's withdrawal from the plan, or when the participant sells the shares after its withdrawal from the plan. In accordance with section 1001, the amount of such gain or loss will be the difference between the amount that the participant receives for the whole shares and the participant's tax basis. Any cash received by the participants, who withdraw from the plan, in lieu of their fractional share interests will be treated as a redemption of that fractional share interest, subject to the provisions and limitations of section 302. . . .

NOTES

1. *The shareholder's election under §305(b)(1).* What is the effect of the parenthetical expression in §305(b)(1)? See Treas. Regs. §1.305-2(a). Suppose a corporation issues two classes of common stock, class A and class B. The corporation's charter provides that dividends cannot be declared on one class without an equal dividend declaration on the other. Dividends on the class A stock will always be paid in cash, while dividends on the class B stock will always be paid in additional shares of class B. Has a shareholder, by choosing to purchase shares of class B rather than class A, "elected" to receive stock dividends in lieu of property so that §305(b)(1) will apply to all stock dividends he will receive? See Treas. Regs. §1.305-2(a)(4).

In *Frontier Savings Association*, the corporation annually declared a stock dividend and then habitually agreed to redeem shares as requested by its stockholders. The Tax Court did not find the requisite shareholder election in such circumstances, although Judge Hamblen added in the concurring opinion that such a routine could run afoul of §305 if the redemptions were "periodic rather than isolated." Yet §305(b)(1) nowhere limits its application to periodic stock dividends. Judge Hamblen apparently was focusing on the taxation of certain redemptions as constructive stock dividends pursuant to §305(c). See discussion of §305(c) at pages 231-233 infra. Even in the absence of a provision such as §305(c), might not a corporation's habitual practice of declaring a stock dividend, if always followed by an optional redemption, fall within the ambit of §305(b)(1)? Was the transaction in *Frontier* more legitimate because of the statutory obligation of the corporation's shareholders to purchase additional stock as their assets and outstanding loans increased? Is it relevant, under §305(b)(1), whether the corporation and shareholders had no tax avoidance motives for the transaction giving rise to an effective election by the shareholders to receive stock or property?

2. *Amount constituting dividend.* Distributions of stock falling within §305(b) will be subject to the property distribution rules of §301. To noncorporate and corporate shareholders alike, the "amount" of the distribution under §301(b) is the fair market value of the dividend stock. See Treas. Regs. §1.305-2(b) (example 2). Of that amount, the recipient shareholder will have a dividend to the extent of her pro rata share of the distributing corporation's earnings and profits. §§301(c)(1), 316(a). The excess amount of the distribution, if any, will be applied against the shareholder's old stock basis to the extent thereof, §301(c)(2), with any amount in excess of basis treated as though received "in exchange" for the old stock, §301(c)(3). See page 106 supra.

The rules of §305 generally apply to distributions by a corporation of its stock rights with respect to its stock. See §305(d)(1). As indicated by Rev. Rul. 78-375 above, the fair market value of an immediately exercisable right to buy stock equals the difference between the current fair market value of the corporation's stock and the amount the holder of the right must pay to acquire the stock. If a stock right cannot be exercised for a specified time, e.g., three or five years, then how should the right be valued? Cf. §83. If stock rights are received tax free under §305(a), then the shareholder must allocate a basis to them under §307. Note the special rule for stock rights received tax free that are worth less than 15 percent of the shareholder's old stock: Such rights have a zero basis unless the shareholder elects to allocate some of her old stock basis to them. §307(b). To prevent manipulation, if basis is allocated to distributed stock rights but those rights lapse, no loss to the shareholder is allowed. Rather, the basis of the lapsed rights flows back to the shareholder's stock. Treas. Regs. §1.307-1(a).

3. *The companion distribution requirement of §305(b)(2)(A).* A stock dividend increasing the proportionate share of the recipient shareholder's interest in the assets or earnings and profits of the corporation will not fall within §305(b)(2) unless some other shareholder receives a distribution of property. §305(b)(2)(A). Why should taxation of the dividend stock to the recipient shareholder turn on the existence of a companion distribution of property to another shareholder?

Is it likely that a stock dividend will be made to one shareholder (or to one group of shareholders) while the remaining shareholders receive nothing of value? Might a shareholder agree to a non–pro rata stock dividend to others if he will receive, as part of the deal, an increase in his salary as a corporate employee? See Treas. Regs. §1.305-3(b)(3) (companion distribution must be to a shareholder "in his capacity as a shareholder"). Would such a salary increase meet the companion distribution requirement of §305(b)(2)(A)? What is the risk that the Service will argue that the purported salary is properly characterized as a distribution on stock? Recall that in Treas. Regs. §1.305-3(b)(4) stock and property distributions separated by more than 36 months are presumed to be unrelated.

4. *The definition of preferred stock.* Subsections (3), (4), and (5) of §305(b) refer to "preferred" stock. The Code does not define "preferred stock," although Treas. Regs. §1.305-5(a) provides, in the context of §305(b)(4), that—

> [t]he term "preferred stock" generally refers to stock which, in relation to other classes of stock outstanding enjoys certain limited rights and privileges (generally associated with specified dividend and liquidation priorities) but does not participate in corporate growth to any significant extent. The distinguishing feature of "preferred stock" for the purposes of section 305(b)(4) is not its privileged position as such, but that such privileged position is limited and that such stock does not participate in corporate growth to any significant extent.

Does this definition of "preferred stock" comport with the underlying rationale of §305? Note in particular that nonvoting stock need not be "preferred" stock under this definition.

b. Constructive Distributions

Section 305(c) authorizes regulations that subject certain transactions that have the effect of a stock dividend to the rules of §305(b). The Treasury Department responded in 1973 with Treas. Regs. §1.305-7. Under that regulation, the following may be treated as a constructive distribution of stock taxable under §305: "a change in conversion ratio, a change in redemption price, a difference between redemption price and issue price, a redemption which is treated as a distribution to which §301 applies, or any transaction (including a recapitalization) having a similar effect on the interest of any shareholder."

Suppose a corporation has two classes of stock outstanding, common and convertible preferred. If a common stock dividend is declared on the common stock, then the value of the convertibility feature of the preferred will be reduced unless some provision is made to increase its conversion ratio. For example, if each share of the preferred is convertible into one share of common, and if a one-for-one common stock dividend is declared on the common, then the conversion ratio of the preferred stock must be adjusted so that each share of preferred stock can be converted into two shares of common stock. Such a change in conversion ratio to account for stock dividends is called an "antidilution" provision. Treas. Regs. §1.305-7 has special rules for antidilution provisions. Because of the wording of §305(b)(4), some of the antidilution rules also appear in Treas. Regs. §1.305-3(d). (Recapitalizations are also addressed in Treas. Regs. §1.305-3, but consideration of recapitalizations is deferred until pages 445-451 infra.)

The following revenue rulings illustrate the reach of §305(c). Revenue Ruling 78-60 concludes that dividend treatment under §§305(b) and 301 can apply to a shareholder who receives no actual distribution of stock. Section 305(c) lists a change in conversion ratio as an event that might constitute a constructive distribution, but §305(b)(4) contains an exception. Revenue Ruling 83-42 considers just how far that exception extends.

Rev. Rul. 78-60

1978-1 C.B. 81

Advice has been requested whether under section 302(a) of the Internal Revenue Code of 1954 the stock redemptions described below qualified for exchange treatment, and whether under section 305(b)(2) and (c) the shareholders who experienced increases in their proportionate interests in the redeeming corporation as a result of the stock redemptions will be treated as having received distributions of property to which section 301 applies.

Corporation *Z* has only one class of stock outstanding. The *Z* common stock is held by 24 shareholders, all of whom are descendants, or spouses of descendants, of the founder of *Z*.

In 1975, when *Z* had 6,000 shares of common stock outstanding, the board of directors of *Z* adopted a plan of annual redemption to provide a means for its shareholders to sell their stock. The plan provides that *Z* will annually redeem up to 40 shares of its outstanding stock at a price established annually by the *Z* board of directors. Each shareholder of *Z* is entitled to cause *Z* to redeem two-thirds of one percent of the shareholder's stock each year. If some shareholders choose not to participate fully in the plan during any year, the other shareholders can cause *Z* to redeem more than two-thirds of one percent of their stock, up to the maximum of 40 shares.

Pursuant to the plan of annual redemption, *Z* redeemed 40 shares of its stock in 1976. Eight shareholders participated in the redemptions. [No shareholder owned as much as 13 percent of the corporation's stock before or after the redemption. After the redemption, each shareholder actually and constructively owned at least 97 percent of his pre-redemption holding.]

Issue 1 . . .

None of the redemptions here qualified under section 302(b)(3) of the Code because all of the shareholders who participated in the redemptions continue to own stock of *Z*. Moreover, none of the redemptions qualified under section 302(b)(2) because none of the shareholders who participated in the redemptions experienced a reduction in interest of more than 20 percent, as section 302(b)(2)(C) requires. Therefore, the first question is whether the redemptions were "not essentially equivalent to a dividend" within the meaning of section 302(b)(1). . . .

In United States v. Davis, 397 U.S. 301 (1970), the Supreme Court of the United States said that for a redemption to qualify as not essentially equivalent to a dividend under section 302(b)(1) of the Code, the redemption must result in a meaningful reduction of the shareholder's proportionate interest in the corporation. The Court held that the business purpose of the redemption is irrelevant to this determination and that the ownership attribution rules of section 318(a) apply. Several of the shareholders of *Z* experienced reductions in their proportionate interests in *Z* (taking into account constructive stock ownership under section 318 of the Code) as a result of the 1976 redemptions. If their reductions were "meaningful," they are entitled to exchange treatment for their redemptions under section 302(a). Whether the reductions in proportionate interests were "meaningful" depends on the facts and circumstances.

In this case, an important fact is that the 1976 redemptions were not isolated occurrences but were undertaken pursuant to an ongoing plan for *Z* to redeem 40 shares of its stock each year. None of the reductions in proportionate interest experienced by *Z* shareholders as a result of the 1976 redemptions was "meaningful" because the reductions were small and each shareholder has the power to recover the lost interest by electing not to participate in the redemption plan in later years.

Accordingly, none of the 1976 redemptions qualified for exchange treatment under section 302(a) of the Code. All of the redemptions are to be treated as distributions of property to which section 301 applies.

Issue 2

Section 305(b)(2) of the Code provides that section 301 will apply to a distribution by a corporation of its stock if the distribution, or a series of distributions that includes the distribution, has the result of the receipt of property by some shareholders, and increases in the proportionate interests of other shareholders in the assets or earnings and profits of the corporation. . . .

Section 1.305-7(a) of the Income Tax Regulations provides that a redemption treated as a section 301 distribution will generally be treated as a distribution to which sections 305(b)(2) and 301 of the Code apply if the proportionate interest of any shareholder in the earnings and profits or assets of the corporation deemed to have made the stock distribution is increased by the redemption, and the distribution has the result described in section 305(b)(2). The distribution is to be deemed made to any shareholder whose interest in the earnings and profits or assets of the distributing corporation is increased by the redemption.

Section 1.305-3(b)(3) of the regulations provides that [a] distribution of property incident to an isolated redemption will not cause section 305(b)(2) to apply even though the redemption distribution is treated as a section 301 distribution.

Section 305 of the Code does not make the constructive stock ownership rules of section 318(a) applicable to its provisions.

The 16 shareholders of *Z* who did not tender any stock for redemption in 1976 experienced increases in their proportionate interests of the earnings and profits and assets of *Z* (without taking into account constructive stock ownership under section 318 of the Code) as a result of the redemptions. Shareholders *B* and *X*, who surrendered small amounts of their stock for redemption in 1976, also experienced increases in their proportionate interests. The 1976 redemptions were not isolated but were undertaken pursuant to an ongoing plan of annual stock redemptions. Finally, the 1976 redemptions are to be treated as distributions of property to which section 301 of the Code applies.

Accordingly, *B*, *X* and the 16 shareholders of *Z* who did not participate in the 1976 redemptions are deemed to have received stock distributions to which sections 305(b)(2) and 301 of the Code apply. See examples (8) and (9) of section 1.305-3(e) of the regulations for a method of computing the amounts of the deemed distributions.

Rev. Rul. 83-42

1983-1 C.B. 76

Issue

Is the distribution of common stock on convertible preferred stock, as described below, treated as the distribution of property to which section 301 of the Internal Revenue Code applies by reason of section 305(b)(4)?

Facts

X is a corporation that has both common and convertible preferred stock outstanding. The convertible preferred stock had been issued earlier in connection with the acquisition of an unrelated corporation. The convertible preferred stock is convertible into common stock according to a certain conversion ratio. The terms of the convertible preferred stock do not provide for anti-dilution protection by means of an increase in the conversion ratio made solely to take account of a stock dividend or stock split with respect to the stock into which such convertible stock is convertible.

On June 1, 1981, *X* distributed a 10 percent common stock dividend to the holders of its common stock. In addition, *X* distributed shares of its common stock to holders of its convertible preferred stock in order to offset the dilution of the holder's conversion rights. Dilution of the conversion rights of the holders of convertible preferred would have occurred but for the distribution of common stock to them because of the lack of a full adjustment in the conversion ratio of the preferred stock to reflect the stock dividend on the common stock.

Law and Analysis

Section 305(a) of the Code provides generally that gross income does not include the amount of any distribution of the stock of a corporation made by such corporation to its shareholders with respect to its stock, except as otherwise provided in section 305(b) or (c).

Section 305(b)(4) of the Code provides that section 305(a) will not apply to a distribution by a corporation of its stock, and the distribution will be treated as a distribution of property to which section 301 applies, if the distribution is with respect to preferred stock, other than an increase in the conversion ratio of convertible preferred stock made solely to take account of a stock dividend or stock split with respect to the stock into which such convertible stock is convertible.

Section 1.305-5(a) of the regulations states, in part, that under section 305(b)(4), a distribution by a corporation of its stock made with respect to its preferred stock is treated as a distribution of property to which section 301 applies unless the distribution is made with respect to convertible preferred stock to take into account a stock dividend, stock split, or any similar event which would otherwise result in the dilution of the conversion right.

The exception contained in section 305(b)(4) of the Code would permit *X* to adjust the conversion ratio of its preferred stock to eliminate the dilution which resulted from the 10 percent common stock dividend on June 1, but it will not permit an actual distribution of stock to the holders of preferred stock, even if undertaken for the same anti-dilution purposes. The "distribution" referred to in section 1.305-5(a) of the regulations is only the deemed distribution which is considered to result when the conversion ratio is adjusted for the purpose described in section 305(b)(4). All other distributions on preferred stock are taxable, as expressly provided by section 305(b)(4).

Holding

The distribution of *X* common stock to holders of its convertible preferred stock is a distribution to which section 301 of the Code applies by reason of section 305(b)(4).

NOTES

1. *Redemptions treated as stock dividends to non-redeemed shareholders.* The effect of any non–pro rata redemption of common stock is to increase the proportionate interests of the non-redeemed shareholders while giving the redeemed shareholders cash or other property. This effect, described in §305(b)(2), causes redemptions to be ideal candidates for constructive stock dividend treatment under §305(c). Two substantial limitations, however, are imposed on the Commissioner's ability to treat a redemption to one shareholder as a stock dividend to others.

First, Congress in §305(c) granted authority to tax redemptions as constructive stock dividends only when the redemptions are taxed to the redeemed shareholder under §301 (e.g., when the redemption fails to qualify for exchange treatment under §302(a) for want of qualification under §302(b)(1)-(4)). Even though redemptions taxed as exchanges may have the effect of increasing the non-redeemed shareholders' corporate interests, such redemptions are not described in §305(c). Indeed, under §302(b)(1)-(3), only those redemptions causing the most significant change in the proportionate interests of the shareholders can qualify for exchange treatment. Yet §305(c) cannot apply to such redemptions.

Second, even redemptions taxed as distributions under §301 will not cause the non-redeemed shareholders difficulty under §305(c) so long as the redemption is "an isolated redemption and is not a part of a periodic redemption plan." Treas. Regs. §1.305-3(e) (example 10). The statute makes no special distinction for "isolated" redemptions. Why has the Treasury Department so limited application of §305(c)? If a corporation distributes cash to shareholder *A* and stock to shareholder *B*, then shareholder *B* will be taxed pursuant to §305(b)(2). If the same result is accomplished by redeeming a part of the stock of shareholder *A*, then why should the taxation be different if the transaction is "isolated"?

In Rev. Rul. 77-19, 1977-1 C.B. 83, a corporation redeemed shares from deceased or retiring shareholders in 20 isolated transactions during the three prior years. It also redeemed the interests of minority shareholders. The Service ruled that the corporation was not engaged in a periodic redemption plan under §305(c) so as to trigger taxable constructive dividends to the continuing shareholders. Cf. Rev. Rul. 78-60, page 228 supra, in which the Service ruled that periodic small redemptions of stock pursuant to an ongoing plan of annual redemptions were taxable as dividends to the redeeming shareholders and as taxable distributions under §305(b)(2) and (c) to the continuing shareholders whose proportionate interests were increased thereby. See Dietzsch v. United States, 498 F.2d 1344 (Cl. Ct. 1974), in which an auto dealer, contractually obligated to use cash distributions from his corporation to purchase the stock of a co-shareholder in a program leading to eventual acquisition by the dealer of the entire ownership of the corporation, was held taxable on the distributions as a dividend. The court refused to view the various steps as an integrated transaction constituting a complete redemption of the co-shareholder and culminating in a tax-free stock dividend.

Some redemptions will not be subject to §305(c) because they are part of a transaction akin to a security arrangement. For example, in Rev. Rul. 78-115, 1978-1 C.B. 85, a corporation engaged in mandatory, periodic redemptions of nonparticipating, nonvoting stock that had been issued as partial consideration for a prior stock acquisition by the corporation. The Service ruled that such redemptions would not give rise to income to the non-redeemed shareholders under §305(c) because the redeemed stock was created solely to facilitate the prior acquisition when other forms of financing were unavailable. See also Treas. Regs. §1.305-3(e) (example 14).

Note that when §305(c) applies to a redemption, it does not automatically trigger the recognition of income to any shareholder: Transactions described in §305(c) are recharacterized by that section as distributions increasing the proportionate interests of one or more shareholders in their corporation. The tax consequences of such a deemed distribution must be determined under §305(a) and (b)(2).

2. *Adjustment in conversion ratio.* As made clear in Rev. Rul. 83-42, above, the only antidilution provision excluded from taxation under §305(b)(4) and (c) is an increase or decrease in the conversion ratio of convertible preferred stock to account for stock distributions on, or stock splits of, the stock into which the preferred may be converted. What are the consequences if the conversion ratio of convertible preferred stock is adjusted to account for cash dividends paid on the common or on the preferred stock? See Treas. Regs. §1.305-3(e) (example 7). To what possible abuse does this example speak? What is the result if the preferred shareholders exercise their conversion rights shortly after a cash dividend paid on the common? Cf. §305(b)(2).

Rev. Rul. 84-141, 1984-2 C.B. 80, discusses the consequences of a right given to holders of cumulative preferred stock to have dividend arrearages paid in common stock if cash dividends are unpaid for two consecutive quarters. The Service ruled that the holders of such cumulative preferred stock are subject to taxation under §305(c) and (b)(2) on the passage of two quarters in which the corporation fails to pay cash dividends. Because the holders of the preferred stock have an unqualified right to receive common stock in lieu of accrued dividends at that time, the Service ruled that they are taxable on the fair market value of the common stock they can elect to receive regardless of whether they elect to accept it.

PROBLEM

6-1. In the following, assume *X* Corp. has ample earnings and profits. Determine the tax consequences to *M* and *N* in the following situations:

a. *X* Corp. has two classes of stock outstanding. *M* holds 100 shares of common stock, and *N* holds 100 shares of nonconvertible preferred stock. *X* distributes:
   i. Common on common, but common shareholders can elect to receive cash instead of stock. Does it matter if all shareholders elect to receive stock?
   ii. Preferred on common and cash on preferred. Does it matter if the cash is distributed 18 months before or after the stock dividend?
   iii. Common on preferred and preferred on common.

b. *X* Corp. has two classes of stock outstanding. *M* owns 100 shares of class A common, and *N* owns 100 shares of class B common. The class A and B shares participate ratably in both current and liquidating distributions. *X* distributes:
   i. Cash on the class A common and class B common on the class B common. How would your answer change if each class of stock were entitled to 50 percent of current and liquidating distributions?
   ii. Cash in redemption of one-quarter (25 shares) of the class B common.
   iii. Class A common on the class A common and preferred stock on the class B common.

c. *X* Corp. has two classes of stock outstanding. *M* owns 100 shares of common, and *N* owns 100 shares of nonconvertible preferred. *X* distributes cash on the preferred and common on common. Would your answer change if the preferred stock were convertible into common stock?

B. TAINTING OF STOCK UNDER §306

Although the taxation rules of §305(b) and (c) may seem all-inclusive, they are not: Many stock dividends will be tax free under the general rule of §305(a). In particular, a pro rata distribution of nonconvertible preferred stock to all holders of common stock is tax free. To reinforce your comprehension of the last section, see if you can parse through the Code to arrive at this result.

How should the sale or redemption of shares received tax free as a stock dividend be taxed? Suppose a corporation has substantial earnings and profits that its sole shareholder would like to remove from corporate solution in the form of cash. A cash dividend could be declared, but that would produce ordinary income to the shareholder without any recovery of basis. In the absence of a partial liquidation, capital gain treatment on a redemption will be unavailable under §302(b)(1) under *Davis*, because the shareholder will continue to own all stock after the redemption. But suppose the shareholder follows a three-step plan: (1) declare a stock dividend of nonvoting preferred stock on her common shares, at the issue price at some point in the future; (2) sell this newly created preferred stock to an outside, unrelated purchaser for the issue price; and (3) cause the corporation to redeem this preferred stock shortly after the sale. If the preferred stock pays a sufficiently high (and guaranteed) dividend rate until redemption, the shareholder may have little difficulty in selling it. On that sale, the shareholder will claim basis recovery and capital gain, possibly taxed at preferential rates. The purchaser will claim exchange treatment on the redemption pursuant to the complete termination safe harbor of §302(b)(3), and, because the purchaser will have a basis in the preferred stock equal to the issue price, there will be no taxable gain on the redemption under §302(a).

If dividends are taxed at the same rate as long-term capital gain, then the tax benefit of such an end-run around §§301 and 302 is only the ability to offset some or all of the cash with the taxpayer's stock basis. Is that enough of a tax benefit to justify a statutory anti-abuse rule? Section 306, discussed below, was enacted when dividends were taxed much more harshly than net capital gain, and so the tax advantage from such a "preferred stock bailout" was dramatically greater. The *Chamberlain* case immediately following is typical of the analysis applied to such preferred stock bailouts when the stakes were high but Congress *had not yet enacted its statutory response in §306*. The *Fireoved* case, then, demonstrates how the analysis changes with the application of §306.

Chamberlin v. Commissioner

207 F.2d 462 (6th Cir. 1953)

Before Simons, Chief Judge, and McAllister and Miller, Circuit Judges.

MILLER, Circuit Judge.

Petitioner C. P. Chamberlin seeks a review of an income tax deficiency determined by the Respondent for the calendar year 1946, and sustained by the Tax Court. . . .

The Metal Moulding Corporation, hereinafter referred to as the Corporation, is a Michigan corporation engaged in the business of manufacturing metal mouldings and bright work trim used in the manufacture of automobiles. . . . From 1940 until December 20, 1946, the issued and outstanding common stock totaled 1,002 1/2 shares, of which Chamberlin and his wife together owned 83.8%. . . .

The business of the Corporation prospered, and after paying substantial cash dividends over a period of years, its balance sheet at the end of the first six months in 1946 reflected total assets of $2,488,836.53 and included in current assets $722,404.56 cash and $549,950 United States Government Bonds and notes.

On December 16, 1946, the Corporation's authorized capital stock was increased from $150,000 to $650,000, represented by 6,500 shares of $100 par value common stock. On December 20, 1946, a stock dividend was declared and distributed of five shares of common for each share of common outstanding, and the Corporation's accounts were adjusted by transferring $501,250 from earned surplus to capital account.

On December 26, 1946, the articles of incorporation were amended so as to authorize, in addition to the 6,500 shares of common stock, 8,020 shares of 4 1/2% cumulative $100 par value preferred stock. On December 28, 1946, a stock dividend was declared of 1 1/3 shares of the newly authorized preferred stock for each share of common stock outstanding, to be issued pro rata to the holders of common stock as of December 27, 1946, and the Company's accounts were adjusted by transferring $802,000 from earned surplus to capital account. The preferred stock was issued to the stockholders on the same day. Prior to the declaration of the preferred stock dividend, the Corporation at all times had only one class of stock outstanding.

On December 30, 1946, as the result of prior negotiations . . . all of the holders of the preferred stock, except the estate of Edward W. Smith, deceased, which owned 20 shares, signed a "Purchase Agreement," with The Northwestern Mutual Life Insurance Company and The Lincoln National Life Insurance Company, which instrument was also endorsed by the Corporation for the purpose of making certain representations, warranties and agreements. Under the "Purchase Agreement" 4,000 shares of the preferred stock was sold to each of the two insurance companies at a cash price of $100 per share plus accrued dividends from November 1st, 1946 to date of delivery. . . .

In the latter part of 1945, the Corporation's attorney and Chamberlin discussed with an investment firm in Chicago the possibility of selling an issue of preferred stock similar to the stock subsequently issued. The Corporation had such a large accumulated earned surplus it was fearful of being subjected to the surtax provided for by [§531], but at the same time Chamberlin, the majority stockholder, was not willing to have the Corporation distribute any substantial portion of its earned surplus as ordinary dividends because his individual income was taxable at high surtax rates. It was proposed that the issuance of a stock dividend to the stockholders and the sale of it by the stockholders would enable the stockholders to obtain accumulated earnings of the Corporation in the form of capital gains rather than as taxable dividends. . . .

The preferred stock contained the following provisions among others: The holders were entitled to cumulative cash dividends at the rate of $4.50 per annum payable quarterly beginning November 1, 1946; the stock was subject to redemption on any quarterly dividend date in whole or in part at par plus specified premiums and accrued dividends; it was subject to mandatory retirement in amounts not exceeding 2,000 shares on May 1, 1948 and 1,000 on May 1st on each succeeding year, depending upon the Corporation's net earnings for the preceding year, until fully retired on May 1, 1954. . . .

The Tax Court held that the issue of whether the stock dividend constituted income to the stockholders should be determined from a consideration of all the facts and circumstances surrounding the issuance of the dividend and not by a consideration limited to the characteristics of the stock declared as a dividend; that each case involving a stock dividend must be decided upon its own facts and circumstances as establishing whether the receipt of a particular kind of stock dividend was in fact taxable; that such a decision did not rest upon matters of form or nomenclature attending a stock dividend distribution but rather upon the real substance of the transaction involved; . . . but that considering the real substance of the transaction it was of the opinion that the stock dividend was not in good faith for any bona fide corporate business purpose, and that the attending circumstances and conditions under which it was issued made it the equivalent of a cash dividend distribution out of available earnings, thus constituting ordinary taxable income in the amount of the value of the preferred shares received. The Court also said that the real purpose of the issuance of the preferred shares was concurrently to place them in the hands of others not then stockholders of the Corporation, thereby substantially altering the common stockholders' pre-existing proportionate interests in the Corporation's net assets and thereby creating an entirely new relationship amongst all the stockholders and the Corporation. . . .

In our opinion, the declaration and distribution of the preferred stock dividend, considered by itself, falls clearly within the principles established in Towne v. Eisner, [245 U.S. 418 (1918)], and Eisner v. Macomber, [252 U.S. 189 (1920)], and is controlled by the ruling in the *Strassburger* case. Accordingly, as a preliminary matter, we do not agree with the Tax Court's statement that the stock dividend is taxable because as a result of the dividend and immediate sale thereafter it substantially altered the common stockholders' pre-existing proportional interests in the Corporation's net assets. The sale to the insurance companies of course resulted in such a change, but the legal effect of the dividend with respect to rights in the corporate assets is determined at the time of its distribution, not by what the stockholders do with it after its receipt. . . .

But respondent contends that the sale of the stock following immediately upon its receipt resulted in the stockholder acquiring cash instead of stock, thus making it a taxable dividend under Secs. 22(a) and 115(a), [1939] Internal Revenue Code. There are two answers to this contention.

A non-taxable stock dividend does not become a taxable cash dividend upon its sale by the recipient. . . . In none of the Supreme Court cases referred to above, dealing with the taxability of stock dividends, was the length of the holding period considered as a factor. Obviously, if the non-taxability of a stock dividend rests solely upon the principle that it does not alter the pre-existing proportionate interest of any stockholder or increase the intrinsic value of his holdings, the disposition of the stock dividend by the stockholder thereafter is not a factor in the determination.

The foregoing conclusion is supported by [§1223(5)], which provides that for the purpose of determining whether a non-taxable stock dividend which has been sold is a long-term capital gain there shall be included in the holding period the period for which the taxpayer held the stock in the distributing corporation prior to the receipt of the stock dividend. This necessarily recognizes that a stock dividend will often be sold before the expiration of six months after its receipt, and makes no distinction between a stock dividend held one day or for any other period less than six months. . . .

The other answer to the contention is that although the stockholder *acquired* money in the final analysis, he did not *receive* either money or property *from* the corporation. . . . The money he received was received from the insurance companies. It was not a "distribution" by the corporation declaring the dividend, as required by [§115(a), 1939 Code and §316(a), 1954 Code].

We come then to what in our opinion is the dominant and decisive issue in the case, namely, whether the stock dividend, which, by reason of its redemption feature, enabled the Corporation to ultimately distribute its earnings to its stockholders on a taxable basis materially lower than would have been the case by declaring and paying the usual cash dividend, was a bona fide one, one in substance as well as in form. . . .

It seems clear that it was an issue of stock in substance as well as in form. According to its terms, and in the absence of a finding that it was immediately or shortly thereafter redeemed at a premium, we assume that a large portion of it has remained outstanding over a period of years with some of it still unredeemed after nearly seven years. It has been in the hands of the investing public, free of any control by the corporation over its owners, whose enforceable rights with respect to operations of the corporation would not be waived or neglected. Substantial sums have been paid in dividends. The insurance companies bought it in the regular course of their business and have held it as approved investments. For the Court to now tell them that they have been holding a sham issue of stock would be most startling and disturbing news. . . .

If the transaction lacks the good faith necessary to avoid the assessment it must be because of the redemption feature of the stock, which, in the final analysis, is what ultimately permitted the distribution of the corporate earnings and is the key factor in the overall transaction. Redemption features are well known and often used in corporate financing. If the one in question was a reasonable one, not violative of the general principles of bona fide corporate financing, and acceptable to experienced bona fide investors familiar with investment fundamentals and the opportunities afforded by the investment market we fail to see how a court can properly classify the issue, by reason of the redemption feature, as lacking in good faith or as not being what it purports to be. . . .

Each case necessarily depends upon its own facts. The facts in this case show tax avoidance, and it is so conceded by petitioner. But they also show a series of legal transactions, no one of which is fictitious or so lacking in substance as to be anything different from what it purports to be. Unless we are to adopt the broad policy of holding taxable any series of transactions, the purpose and result of which is the avoidance of taxes which would otherwise accrue if handled in a different way, regardless of the legality and realities of the component parts, the tax assessed by the Commissioner was successfully avoided in the present case. We do not construe the controlling decisions as having adopted that view. . . .

Fireoved v. United States

462 F.2d 1281 (3d Cir. 1972)

Before Adams, Rosen, and Hunter, Circuit Judges.

Adams, Circuit Judge.

This appeal calls into question the application of section 306 . . . and the "first in-first out rule" to a redemption of preferred stock in a corporation by plaintiff, one of its principal shareholders. In particular we are asked to decide whether the transaction here had "as one of its principal purposes the avoidance of federal income tax," whether a prior sale of a portion of the underlying common stock immunized a like proportion of the section 306 stock from treatment as a noncapital asset and whether another block of the redeemed stock should be considered to represent stock not subject to section 306.

I. Factual Background

On November 24, 1948, Fireoved and Company, Inc. was incorporated for the purpose of printing and selling business forms. At their first meeting, the incorporators elected Eugene Fireoved, his wife, Marie, the plaintiffs, and a nephew, Robert L. Fireoved, as directors of the corporation. Subsequently, the directors elected Eugene Fireoved as president and treasurer and Marie Fireoved as secretary. . . . On December 31, 1948, in consideration for $100 cash, the corporation issued Eugene Fireoved 100 shares of common stock; for $500 cash, it issued him five shares of preferred stock; and in payment for automotive equipment and furniture and fixtures, valued at $6,000, it issued him an additional 60 shares of preferred stock.

In 1954, when Mr. Fireoved learned that his nephew, Robert, was planning to leave the business, he began discussions with Karl Edelmayer and Kenneth Craver concerning the possibility of combining his business with their partnership, Girard Business Forms, that had been printing and selling business forms for some time prior to 1954. Messrs. Fireoved, Edelmayer and Craver agreed that voting control of the new enterprise should be divided equally among the three of them. Because Mr. Fireoved's contribution to capital would be approximately $60,000 whereas the partnership could contribute only $30,000, it was decided that preferred stock should be issued to Mr. Fireoved to compensate for the disparity. In furtherance of this plan . . . the following corporate changes were accomplished: the name of the company was changed to Girard Business Forms; the authorized common stock was increased from 100 to 300 shares and the authorized preferred stock was increased to 1000 shares; Mr. Fireoved exchanged his 100 shares of common and 65 shares of preferred stock for equal amounts of the new stock; an agreement of purchase was authorized by which the company would buy all the assets of the Edelmayer-Craver partnership in return for 200 shares of common and 298 shares of preferred stock; and Mr. Fireoved was issued 535 shares of the new preferred stock as a dividend[6] on his 100 shares of common stock, thereby bringing his total holding of preferred stock to 600 shares to indicate his $60,000 capital contribution compared to the $29,800 contributed by the former partnership.

As the business progressed, Mr. Edelmayer demanded more control of the company. In response, Mr. Fireoved and Mr. Craver each sold 24 shares of common stock in the corporation to him on February 28, 1958.

On April 30, 1959, the company redeemed 451 of Mr. Fireoved's 600 shares of preferred stock at $105 per share, resulting in net proceeds to him of $47,355.[7] The gain from this transaction was reported by Mr. and Mrs. Fireoved . . . as a long term capital gain. Subsequently, the Commissioner . . . assessed a deficiency against the Fireoveds of $15,337.13 based on the Commissioner's view that the proceeds from the redemption of the 451 shares of preferred stock should have been reported as ordinary income and the tax paid at that rate based on section 306. . . .

6. At the time Mr. Fireoved received his stock dividend, the company had accumulated earnings and profits of $52,993.06

7. In 1959, the company had accumulated earnings and profits of $48,235.

II. Background of Section 306

Because we are the first court of appeals asked to decide questions of law pursuant to section 306, it is appropriate that we first examine the circumstances that led to the inclusion in 1954 of this section in the code. Generally, a taxpayer will benefit monetarily if he is able to report income as a long term capital gain rather than as ordinary income. Under normal circumstances a cash dividend from a corporation constitutes ordinary income to the shareholder receiving such money. Therefore, it would be to the advantage of a shareholder if a method could be devised by which the money could be distributed to him, that would otherwise be paid out as cash dividends, in a form that would permit the shareholder to report such income as a long term capital gain.

A temporarily successful plan for converting ordinary income to long term capital gain is described by the facts of Chamberlin v. C.I.R., 207 F.2d 462 (6th Cir. 1953). There a close corporation had assets of $2.5 million, approximately half of which were in the form of cash and government securities. To have distributed the cash not required in the operation of the business to the shareholders as a dividend would have subjected them to taxation at ordinary income rates. The corporation therefore amended its charter to authorize 8,020 shares of preferred stock to be issued to the shareholders as a dividend on their common stock. The accounts of the corporation were adjusted by transferring $802,000 from earned surplus to the capital account. While these corporate changes were taking place, negotiations occurred between the shareholders and two insurance companies for the purchase of the newly issued preferred stock. In addition, the corporation constructed a timetable for retirement of the preferred stock, which proved satisfactory to the purchasing companies. When the transaction was completed, the selling shareholders reported the gain they realized from the sale of the preferred stock to the insurance companies as a long term gain from the disposition of a capital asset. The Commissioner contended that the gain should have been reported as ordinary income and accordingly assessed a deficiency against the selling shareholders. The tax court agreed with the Commissioner. On review, the Sixth Circuit reversed, holding for the taxpayer thus giving the approval of a federal court to what has been termed "a preferred stock bail-out."

The legislative reaction to the *Chamberlin* decision was almost immediate, resulting in the addition of section 306 to the 1954 code, in order to prevent shareholders from obtaining the tax advantage of such bail-outs when such shareholders retain their ownership interests in the company. . . .

For tax purposes, Congress created a new type of stock known as section 306 stock. When a corporation having accumulated or retained earnings and profits issues a stock dividend which is not otherwise subject to taxation at the time of issuance (other than common on common), the stock received is section 306 stock. The effect of owning such stock is that on its redemption, if the corporation has sufficient retained earnings at that time, the gain* is taxed at ordinary income rates while any loss resulting may not be recognized for federal tax purposes. Section 306(b) sets forth several exceptions to the general rule which serve to remove the section 306 taint from stock disposed of under those circumstances.

*Gain or "amount realized"? — Eds.

Based on the history of section 306 and its plain meaning evidenced by the provisions, it is not disputed that the 535 shares of preferred stock issued to Mr. Fireoved as a stock dividend in 1954 were section 306 stock. Additionally, it is clear that in 1959, when the company redeemed 451 shares of Mr. Fireoved's preferred stock, the general provisions of section 306—aside from the exceptions—would require that any amount realized by Mr. Fireoved be taxed at ordinary income rates rather than long term capital gain rates, because the company had earnings at that time of $48,235—more than the $47,355 required to redeem the stock at $105 per share.

Thus, the questions to be decided on this appeal are (1) whether certain of the exceptions to section 306 apply to permit the Fireoveds' reporting their gain as a long term capital gain, and (2) whether 65 of the 451 shares redeemed are not section 306 stock because of the first in-first out rule of Treasury Regulation §1.1012-1(c).

III. Was the Distribution of the Stock Dividend "in Pursuance of a Plan Having as One of Its Principal Purposes Avoidance of Federal Income Tax"?

Mr. Fireoved asserts that the entire transaction should fall within the exception established by section 306(b)(4)(A). . . .

As a threshold point on this issue, the government maintains that because Mr. Fireoved never attempted to obtain a ruling from the "Secretary or his delegate" the redemption should be covered by section 306(a), and the district court should not have reached the question whether the exception applied to Mr. Fireoved. Mr. Fireoved urges that the district court had the power to consider the matter de novo, even without a request by the taxpayer to the secretary or his delegate. Because the ultimate result we reach would not be altered by whichever of these two courses we choose, we do not resolve this potentially complex procedural problem.

The district court, based on the assumption that it had the power to decide the question, found that although one of the purposes involved in the issuance of the preferred stock dividend may have been business related, another principal purpose was the avoidance of Federal income tax.

Mr. Fireoved's analysis of the facts presented in the stipulations would reach the conclusion that the *sole* purpose of the stock dividend was business related. He relies heavily on that portion of the stipulation which describes why the decision was made to combine his business with the Edelmayer-Craver partnership: "the partnership could provide the additional manpower which the expected departure of Robert L. Fireoved from the corporation would require. Additionally, the partnership needed additional working capital which the corporation had and could provide." Based primarily on the latter sentence, Mr. Fireoved asserts that the district court had no choice but to find that the transaction was business related and that it therefore had no avoidance incentive.

In making this argument, however, Mr. Fireoved overlooks the plain import of the language of section 306(b)(4). Whether the section requires the decision to be made by the secretary or the district court, it is clear that "one of [the] principal purposes" of the stock dividend was for "the avoidance of Federal income tax." The stipulation demonstrates no more than that the reorganized company required more capital than could be supplied by the partnership alone. The stipulation is completely in harmony with the following fact situation: after the partnership was combined with the corporation, the business required the $30,000 contributed by the partnership and all of the $60,000 Mr. Fireoved had in the corporation. Mr. Fireoved decided to take the stock dividend rather than to distribute the cash to himself as a dividend, and then to make a loan to the corporation of the necessary money because if he took the cash, he would subject himself to taxation at ordinary income rates. Therefore "one of the principal purposes" of the stock dividend would be for "the avoidance of federal income tax."

In a situation such as the one presented in this case, where the facts necessary to determine the motives for the issuance of a stock dividend are peculiarly within the control of the taxpayer, it is reasonable to require the taxpayer to come forward with the facts that would relieve him of his liability. Here the stipulation was equivocal in determining the purpose of the dividend and is quite compatible with the thought that "one of the principal purposes" was motivated by "tax avoidance." We hold then that the district court did not err in refusing to apply the exception created by section 306(b)(4)(A).[11]

IV. Did the Prior Sale by Mr. Fireoved of 24% of His Underlying Common Stock Immunize Such Portion of the Section 306 Stock He Redeemed in 1959?

The district court construed section 306(b)(4)(B) to mean that any time a taxpayer in Mr. Fireoved's position sells any portion of his underlying common stock and later sells or redeems his section 306 stock, an equivalent proportion of the section 306 stock redeemed will not be subject to the provisions of section 306(a). The government has appealed from this portion of the district court's order and urges that we reverse it, based on the history and purpose of section 306 and the particular facts here.

The stipulations indicate that, "on February 28, 1958, Fireoved and Craver each sold 24 shares of common stock in the corporation to Edelmayer," and that appropriate stock certificates were issued. From this fact, Mr. Fireoved reasons that his sale of 24 of his 100 shares of common stock was undertaken solely for the business purpose of satisfying Mr. Edelmayer's desire for more control of the corporation, and therefore he should be given the benefit of section 306(b)(4)(B). In addition, Mr. Fireoved contends that the disposition of his section 306 stock was related to a business purpose because he used part of the proceeds to pay off a $20,000 loan that the company had made to him.

Mr. Fireoved has the same burden here of showing a lack of a tax avoidance purpose that he had in section III supra. It is clear from the limited facts set forth in the stipulations that he has not established that the disposition of 24% of the 535 shares of the section 306 preferred stock he owned "was not in pursuance of a plan having as one of its principal purposes the avoidance of federal income

11. It is important to note that apparently both Mr. Fireoved, in prosecuting this action for a refund, and the government, in its defense, assumed that if the distribution and redemption of the preferred stock were not controlled by §306(a), the gain would be subject to taxation as a long term capital gain. This is not necessarily the case at all. Whether or not §306 governs the transaction, it nonetheless involves a redemption of stock by a corporation to which §302 could apply. Under the tests set out in §302(b)—the relevant one of which appears to be §302(b)(1)—Mr. Fireoved, who had the burden of proof, may well have been unable to show that the redemption was not "essentially equivalent to a dividend." . . . We hold, however, that it is now too late for the government to raise this issue.

tax."[12] More important, however, is that an examination of the relevant legislative history indicates that Congress did not intend to give capital gains treatment to a portion of the preferred stock redeemed on the facts presented here.

It is apparent from the reaction evinced by Congress to the *Chamberlin* case, supra, that by enacting section 306 Congress was particularly concerned with the tax advantages available to persons who controlled corporations and who could, without sacrificing their control, convert ordinary income to long term capital gains by the device of the preferred stock bail-out. The illustration given in the Senate Report which accompanied section 306(b)(4)(B) is helpful in determining the sort of transactions meant to be exempted by section 306(a):

> Thus if a shareholder received a distribution of 100 shares of section 306 stock on his holdings of 100 shares of voting common stock in a corporation and sells his voting common stock before he disposes of his section 306 stock, the subsequent disposition of his section 306 stock would not ordinarily be considered a tax avoidance disposition *since he has previously parted with the stock which allows him to participate in the ownership of the business.* However, variations of the above example may give rise to tax avoidance possibilities which are not within the exception of subparagraph (b). Thus if a corporation has only one class of common stock outstanding and it issues stock under circumstances that characterize it as section 306 stock, a subsequent issue of a different class of common having greater voting rights than the original common will not permit a simultaneous disposition of the section 306 stock together with the original common to escape the rules of subsection (a) of section 306.

S. Rep. No. 1622, 83d Cong., 2d Sess., 1954 U.S.C.C.A. News, pp. 4621, 4881 (emphasis added).

Thus, it is reasonable to assume that Congress realized the general lack of a tax avoidance purpose when a person sells *all* of his control in a corporation and then either simultaneously or subsequently disposes of his section 306 stock. However, when only a portion of the underlying common stock is sold, and the taxpayer retains essentially all the control he had previously, it would be unrealistic to conclude that Congress meant to give that taxpayer the advantage of section 306(b)(4)(B) when he ultimately sells his section 306 stock. *Cf.* United States v. Davis, 397 U.S. 301 (1970).

Shortly after Mr. Fireoved's corporation had been combined with the Edelmayer-Craver partnership, significant changes to the by-laws were made. The by-laws provided that corporate action could be taken only with the unanimous consent of all the directors. In addition, the by-laws provided that they could be amended either by a vote of 76% of the outstanding common shares or a unanimous vote of the directors. When the businesses were combined in late 1954, each of the directors held 1/3 of the voting stock, thereby necessitating a unanimous vote for

12. Consistent with Mr. Fireoved's sale of 24 shares of common stock in 1958 could have been his knowledge that one year later he would be selling his section 306 stock and a desire on his part to avoid taxation at ordinary income rates. As noted later in the opinion, the sale of just 24 shares was enough so that he retained effective control—in the form of veto power—over the corporation. Moreover, the fact that Mr. Fireoved needed $20,000 of the proceeds to pay off a loan to the corporation would not meet his burden. The proceeds of the redemption totaled $47,355. Thus, although $20,000 of the redemption may not have been to avoid taxes, we can ascribe no purpose other than tax avoidance to the receipt of the additional $27,355. Therefore, since one of the principal purposes of the redemption of 451 shares of preferred stock was "the avoidance of Federal income tax," Mr. Fireoved may not take advantage of §306(b)(4)(B) for any part of the redemption.

amendment to the by-laws. After Messrs. Fireoved and Craver each sold 24 shares of common stock to Mr. Edelmayer, Mr. Fireoved held 25 1/3% of the common (voting) stock, Mr. Craver 25 1/3% and Mr. Edelmayer 49 1/3%. It is crucial to note that the by-laws provided for a unanimous vote for corporate action, and after the common stock transfer, the by-laws were capable of amendment only by a unanimous vote because no two shareholders could vote more than 74 2/3% of the common stock and 76% of the common stock was necessary for amendment. Thus, although Mr. Fireoved did sell a portion of his voting stock prior to his disposition of the section 306 stock, he retained as much control in the corporation following the sale of his common stock as he had prior to the sale. Under these circumstances it is not consonant with the history of the legislation to conclude that Congress intended such a sale of underlying common stock to exempt the proceeds of the disposition of section 306 stock from treatment as ordinary income. Accordingly, the district court erred when it held that any of the preferred shares Mr. Fireoved redeemed were not subject to section 306(a) by virtue of section 306(b)(4)(B).

V. Does the Rule of First in–First out Mean That 65 of the 451 Redeemed Shares Were Those Which Mr. Fireoved Acquired When He Incorporated His Business in 1948 and Thus Should Not Be Treated as Section 306 Stock?

The district court held that 65 of 451 shares of preferred stock that Mr. Fireoved redeemed in 1959 represented the original shares issued to him in 1948 and were not, therefore, section 306 stock, and that the proceeds from their sales should be treated as a long term capital gain. The court reached this conclusion by applying Treas. Reg. §1.1012-1(c). This regulation provides that when an individual acquires shares of the same class of stock in the same corporation on different dates and for different prices, sells a portion of those shares, and cannot adequately identify which lots were sold, for the purpose of determining the basis and the holding period, the first shares acquired are deemed to be the first shares sold.

Both the district court and Mr. Fireoved reason that the 65 preferred shares he received in 1948 were the first such shares owned by him. In 1954, when the corporation was recapitalized, Mr. Fireoved surrendered his certificate for 65 shares, received a 535 share stock dividend and was issued a certificate representing 600 shares of preferred stock. When he disposed of 451 shares in 1959, it was impossible to identify which shares of the 600 share certificate were being sold. By applying the convenient tool of section 1.1012-1(c), one might conclude that the 65 original shares were sold first because they were received first.

Superficially, this analysis appears to be correct. However, it overlooks the existence of section 1223(5) of the code and the regulations issued pursuant thereto. This section governs the transaction in question because section 307 required Mr. Fireoved to allocate his investment in the underlying common stock between the stock and the preferred stock issued as a dividend. Section 1223(5) is then clear in that it will apply to all situations in which an allocation of basis has occurred pursuant to section 307. These provisions broadly state that the holding period for stock received as a stock dividend is equal to the period for which the underlying stock was held. Applying this test we discover that the preferred stock dividend of 535 shares was issued with respect to the original 100 shares of common received by Mr. Fireoved. Therefore, the holding period for the 535 shares dividend relates back to the date on which the underlying common was issued. Coincidentally, the original 65 shares of preferred stock were issued on the same date as the common. Because the constructive date of issuance for all of the 600 shares of preferred stock owned by Mr. Fireoved is identical, neither the 65 shares nor the 535 shares are first in, but rather are in at the same time.

Since it is impossible adequately to identify which shares were sold when Mr. Fireoved redeemed 451 shares of preferred stock, we hold that a pro rata portion of the 65 shares were redeemed in 1959. In other words, the percentage of the 600 shares of preferred which were not section 306 stock may be represented by the fraction 65/600. That percentage of the 451 shares redeemed in 1959, therefore, would not be section 306 stock. . . .

The revenue rulings that follow consider what constitutes preferred stock for purposes of §306. Stock labeled common stock might be treated for federal income tax purposes as preferred stock, and vice versa.

Rev. Rul. 81-91

1981-1 C.B. 123

Issue

Is the class B stock described below "section 306 stock" within the meaning of section 306(c) of the Internal Revenue Code?

Facts

A corporation has outstanding a single class of common stock held by 10 individuals, each of whom owned 20 shares. For valid business reasons the corporation entered into a plan of recapitalization under which each outstanding share of common stock was surrendered to the corporation in exchange for one share of new class A stock plus one share of new class B stock of the corporation.

The recapitalization was a reorganization defined in section 368(a)(1)(E) of the Code and the exchanges were nontaxable under section 354(a)(1).

Each share of the class A and class B stock had a par value of 10*x* dollars. The class B shares were entitled to an annual cumulative dividend of 6 percent of par value payable before any dividend was payable on the class A shares, and a prior right to repayment up to par value in the event of liquidation. After the satisfaction of the class B stock's preferences, each share of class A and class B stock shared equally as to dividends and on liquidation. Each class of shares carried equal voting rights and neither class was by its terms redeemable.

Law and Analysis

Section 306(c)(1)(B) of the Code provides, in part and in effect, that "section 306 stock" is any stock, except common stock, that is received by a shareholder pursuant to a plan of reorganization under section 368 with respect to the receipt of which gain or loss to the shareholder was to any extent not recognized by reason of section 354, but only to the extent that the effect of the transaction is substantially the same as the receipt of a stock dividend.

The term "common stock" as used in section 306 of the Code is not defined in that section or the related regulations. In determining whether newly issued stock is "common stock" for purposes of section 306, the "preferred stock bailout" abuse Congress sought to prevent by enactment of that section provides guidance. . . . A bailout occurs if shareholders, through section 306 stock or some other device, withdraw a corporation's earnings and profits at the more favorable tax rates for capital gains. The potential for a preferred stock bailout exists if the shareholders receive a pro rata distribution of two classes of stock in a recapitalization when the corporation has earnings and profits, and the stock of one class, because of its terms, can be disposed of without a surrender by the shareholders of significant interests in corporate growth. Thus, stock is other than "common stock" for purposes of section 306 not because of its preferred position as such, but because the preferred position is limited and the stock does not participate in corporate growth to any significant extent.

The class B stock enjoys voting rights on an equal basis with the class A stock, the only other class of stock outstanding. After satisfaction of its preference to dividends and as to assets in the event of liquidation, the class B stock shares equally with the class A stock. These rights in the class B stock to participate in corporate growth are significant. Thus, a sale of the class B stock cannot occur without a loss of voting control and interest in the unrestricted growth of the corporation. Therefore, the bailout abuse that Congress sought to prevent by the enactment of section 306 cannot be effected through a sale of the class B stock.

Holding

The class B stock is "common stock" and is, therefore, excepted from the definition of section 306 stock under section 306(c)(1)(B) of the Code. . . .

Rev. Rul. 76-387

1976-2 C.B. 96

Advice has been requested whether, under the circumstances set forth below, the class A nonvoting common stock is "common stock" for purposes of section 306(c)(1)(B) of the Internal Revenue Code of 1954.

Corporation *X* had outstanding class A nonvoting common stock, class B voting common stock, and nonvoting preferred stock. The preferred stock was limited and preferred as to dividends, had no dividends in arrears, had a fixed liquidation preference, and was "section 306 stock" within the meaning of section 306(c) of the Code. Neither the class A nor the class B stock was limited or preferred with respect to dividends or distributions in liquidation and neither had a preference over the other in any respect. The only difference between the two classes of common stock was that the class B stock had voting rights while the class A stock did not. Neither the class A stock nor the class B stock was by its terms redeemable.

X desired to simplify its corporate structure by eliminating the preferred stock. Pursuant to a plan of recapitalization, the holders of the preferred stock exchanged such stock solely for shares of class A stock of equal value. The transaction qualified as a reorganization (recapitalization) under section 368(a)(1)(E) of the Code and no gain or loss was recognized to the exchanging shareholders pursuant to section 354. There was no intent to redeem the class A stock when the exchange was made.

Section 306(c)(1)(B) of the Code provides, in part, that "section 306 stock" is any stock, except common stock, that is received by a shareholder in exchange for other "section 306 stock" in pursuance of a plan of reorganization under section 368 with respect to the receipt of which gain or loss to the shareholder was to any extent not recognized. Therefore, if the class A stock in the instant case is "common stock," it is not "section 306 stock" within the meaning of section 306(c)(1)(B). Neither the Code nor the Income Tax Regulations define "common stock" for purposes of section 306.

In determining whether newly issued stock is "common stock" for purposes of section 306 of the Code, the bailout abuse Congress sought to preclude by enactment of that section provides guidance. . . . A bailout occurs if the stockholders can dispose of their stock in question without a loss of voting control and interest in the unrestricted equitable growth of the corporation.

While the class A nonvoting common stock in the instant case can be disposed of without a loss of voting control in *X*, it cannot be disposed of without the shareholder parting irretrievably with an interest in the unrestricted equitable growth of *X* represented by such stock.

Accordingly, the class A nonvoting common stock in the instant case is "common stock" for purposes of section 306(c)(1)(B) of the Code. . . .

NOTES

1. *The legislative response to the "preferred stock" bailout.* Section 306 is aimed squarely at the *Chamberlin* type of preferred stock "bailout" — that is, the conversion of potential dividend income into capital gain without diluting the shareholder's equity or control (other than by the restrictions imposed on the shareholder by the holders of the preferred shares). Note that §306 stock includes more than just preferred stock received tax free as a stock dividend. It includes, for example, preferred stock that is received tax free in a reorganization if the receipt of such stock "was substantially the same as the receipt of a stock dividend." §306(c)(1)(B)(ii). The §306 taint does not, however, attach to stock received in a taxable distribution. §301(c)(1)(A).

Under §306, the price of tax-free receipt of stock is, in general, ordinary income on disposition. In *Chamberlin,* the preferred stock was worth $100 per share when issued, and the amount of the distribution was fully covered by earnings and profits. Had §306 been applicable to the sale of that stock, the first $100 per share received by the taxpayers for the preferred stock would have been fully includible in their gross incomes. Only the excess, if any, could qualify for sale or exchange treatment. See §306(a)(1)(B). Note, however, that no loss can be recognized. §306(a)(1)(C).

Query whether §306 would have been necessary had the reasoning of the Tax Court in *Chamberlin* been followed and the various steps viewed as an integrated transaction. Note also that the Tax Reform Act of 1969 substantially reduced the scope of §306 by enlarging the class of stock dividends subject to taxation at the time of distribution under §305. The pro rata distribution of nonconvertible preferred stock to the common shareholders, however, remains tax free, and such stock dividends generally give rise to §306 stock. See Rev. Proc. 77-37, 1977-2 C.B. 568, on the requirements for issuing ruling letters concerning whether convertible preferred stock is §306 stock.

2. *Definition of "§306 stock."* The definition of "§306 stock" is found in §306(c). Section 306(c)(1)(A) is the anti-*Chamberlin* rule, for it imposes a §306 taint on preferred stock received tax free under §305(a).

Preferred stock received tax free in a reorganization (or in a §355 divisive distribution) will also be §306 stock if it is received tax free and if the transaction substantially has the effect of a stock dividend. §306(c)(1)(B). Thus, the §306 net extends to certain reorganizations. (Discussion of reorganizations is deferred until page 339.) When preferred stock of an acquired corporation that is not "§306 stock" is exchanged for preferred stock of the acquiring corporation of equal value and with substantially similar terms, the preferred stock of the acquiring corporation is not "§306 stock" within the meaning of §306(c)(1)(B). Rev. Rul. 88-100, 1988-2 C.B. 46.

Under §306(c)(1)(C), a §306 taint is not removed by transferring §306 stock in a carryover basis transaction. For example, §306 stock received as a gift or in a §351 transaction is §306 stock. Stock received from a decedent, however, will not be §306 stock because of the fair market value basis rule of §1014. What is the effect of giving §306 stock to a tax-exempt charity? See Rev. Rul. 76-396, 1976-2 C.B. 55 (concluding that §170(e) limits the deduction to the fair market value of the stock less the ordinary income component).

Section 306(c)(2) provides a long-standing rule that no §306 taint will attach to stock received in a distribution in which, had money been distributed instead of stock, no portion of the distribution would have been a dividend. Thus, tax-free stock dividends cannot produce §306 stock if the corporation had no accumulated earnings and profits at the time of the distribution and no current earnings and profits for the year of the distribution. This rule recognizes that it is the preferred stock bailout to which §306 speaks: If cash could have been "bailed out" without dividend treatment, then stock distributed in lieu of cash will work no end-run around the §301 distribution rules.

Section 306(c)(3) coordinates §304 and §306, preventing an abuse of the §306(c)(2) rule. Suppose a taxpayer transfers stock of one controlled corporation (*X* Corp.) to a second controlled corporation (*Y* Corp.) in exchange for preferred stock of *Y* in a transaction qualifying under §351. Because *Y* stock is not "property" for purposes of §304 (see §317(a)), this transaction is excluded from the definition of §304. If the stock so received is subsequently sold or redeemed, then the effect of the acquisition and disposition could be to bail out earnings and profits of the corporations.

Such stock-for-stock exchanges are addressed by §306(c)(3). Stock (other than common stock) received in such an exchange will be §306 stock if, had cash been distributed in lieu of the stock, the shareholder would have received dividend treatment under §304. Thus, positive earnings and profits of either controlled corporation will cause noncommon stock received in such an exchange to be characterized as §306 stock.

If a taxpayer receives both nonqualified preferred stock and other stock (i.e., either common or "qualified" preferred stock), then the transaction may fall within

§351(b) with the nonqualified preferred stock as boot. §351(g)(1)(B). Can such nonqualified preferred stock that is taxable upon receipt also be tainted under §306(c)(3)? Treasury has in the past been willing to limit application of §306(c) when to do otherwise would be inconsistent with the statutory scheme. See Treas. Reg. §1.306-3(f). Might this be another appropriate occasion in which to limit the reach of §306(c)? And if a taxpayer received *only* nonqualified preferred stock, would the §306(c) taint apply?

Note that common stock distributed on common stock is not §306 stock. §306(c)(1)(A). Why not? What is common stock? According to Rev. Rul. 81-91, page 244 supra, and Rev. Rul. 76-387, page 245 supra, common stock for purposes of §306 is any stock that participates without substantial restrictions in the future growth of the corporation. Does this definition of "common" stock adequately respond to the preferred stock bailout abuse? Is it consistent with the statutory language employed by Congress? Should it be consistent with the definition of "common" stock for purposes of §305? See Treas. Regs. §1.305-5(a), discussed in Note 4, page 227 supra.

Will a bailout using common stock necessarily succeed? The Commissioner will, in such circumstances, be forced to relitigate *Chamberlin.* See Rosenberg v. Commissioner, 36 T.C. 716 (1961) (recharacterizing sale of stock by shareholders as sale of stock by corporation followed by distribution of proceeds to old shareholders). The taxpayer will, however, have a new argument: By enacting the detailed rules of §306, Congress may have preempted the field. Should such a legislative preemption argument be accepted in this context?

3. *Disposition of §306 stock.* Section 306(a) provides one rule for disposition of §306 stock by redemption and another rule for all other dispositions (such as sales and exchanges). The redemption rule is simple: If a corporation redeems a shareholder's §306 stock, then the shareholder is subject to the distribution rules of §301 with respect to the amount realized (not gain) on the redemption. §306(a)(2). Thus, if the corporation has sufficient earnings and profits at the time of the redemption, then the entire amount received by the shareholder can be fully includible at ordinary rates as a dividend.

If §306 stock is disposed of in a transaction other than a redemption, the rule is more complex. Under §306(a)(1), the amount realized in exchange for the §306 stock is treated as ordinary income, but only to the extent of the stock's ratable share of the corporation's earnings and profits as of the time of the distribution of the §306 stock.

For example, suppose *X* Corp. has 100 shares of common stock outstanding, equally divided between *A* and *B.* Assume that these shares are worth $40 per share, that *A*'s basis in each share is $20, and that *X* Corp. has earnings and profits of $1,500. What are the tax consequences to *A* if *X* Corp. declares a stock dividend payable as one share of $100 nonconvertible preferred stock for each five shares of common stock outstanding?

No gain is recognized on the stock dividend by virtue of §305(a). Under §307(a), *A* must allocate some of his basis in the common stock to the newly received preferred stock. That allocation is made in proportion to the relative fair market values of the common and preferred stock. Treas. Regs. §1.307-1(a).

Before the stock dividend, *X* Corp. had 100 shares of common stock outstanding with aggregate fair market value of $4,000. After the distribution, an additional 20 shares of $100 par value preferred stock also are outstanding. Assuming that the preferred stock is worth par, then the aggregate value of the outstanding preferred is $2,000, which leaves only $2,000 in value for the common. Accordingly, one consequence of the stock dividend is to reduce the value of *X* Corp.'s common stock from $40 to $20 per share.

A now has $1,000 in common stock (50 shares at $20 per share) and $1,000 in value in preferred stock (10 shares at $100 per share), so he must allocate basis equally between the common and preferred stock. Because the total to be allocated is $1,000, *A* takes a basis of $10 per share in the common stock and $50 per share in the preferred stock. Is the preferred stock tainted under §306? Yes. See §306(c)(1)(A).

Suppose *A* sells his 10 shares of preferred stock for $105 per share. How will he be taxed? Absent §306, *A* would have a capital gain on each share of $105 minus $50, or $55. Under §306(a)(1), we must compute the difference between (1) *A*'s amount realized on the sale and (2) the amount that would have been a dividend had cash been distributed in lieu of the preferred stock.

The fair market value of the preferred stock was $2,000. If cash of $2,000 had been distributed in lieu of the preferred stock, there would have been a dividend to *A* and *B* of $1,500, the amount of *X* Corp.'s earnings and profits. Because 20 shares of preferred stock were distributed, each share's "ratable share" (see §306(a)(1)(A)(ii)) of the dividend would have been $75.

Under §306(a)(1)(A), *A* will recognize $75 of the $105 amount realized per share as ordinary income. No further gain is recognized by *A* because the remaining $30 per share of amount realized is less than his basis in the stock (which is $50 per share). See §306(a)(1)(B). No loss can be recognized, §306(a)(1)(C), so *A* may add the unrecovered basis in the preferred stock (viz., $20 per share) to his basis in the common stock. See Treas. Regs. §1.306-1(b)(2) (example 2).

The rules for the redemption of §306 stock differ from those applicable to dispositions of §306 other than in redemption. When §306 stock is redeemed, the earnings and profits of the corporation at the time of redemption are relevant. See §§306(a)(2), 301(c)(1). For other types of dispositions, earnings and profits of the corporation at the time of the issuance of the §306 stock are important. See §306(a)(1)(A)(ii). The corporation's earnings and profits at time of issuance can be important even if the §306 stock is redeemed, for the absence of such earnings and profits can remove the stock from §306 ab initio. See §306(c)(2).

4. *Exceptions to the §306 rules.* The draconian rules just described are modified by the exceptions of §306(b). If the shareholder disposes of her entire stock interest (determined by applying the constructive ownership rules of §318) under circumstances set out in §306(b)(1), she can avoid the automatic ordinary income treatment. A redemption of §306 stock in partial or complete liquidation will also relieve the shareholder of §306 disabilities. §306(b)(2)(B).

An exchange of §306 stock in a nontaxable transaction (such as a tax-free reorganization or a §1036 exchange) is not a taxable disposition subject to the rules in §306(a). See §306(b)(3). The stock received on the exchange ordinarily will be §306 stock unless it is common stock issued in a reorganization. See §306(c)(1)(B) and (C). A conversion of §306 stock into common stock will eliminate the §306 taint if the detailed rules of §306(e) are met. Those rules generally remove the taint from §306 stock if it is converted into common stock not further convertible into other stock or property.

Section 306(b)(4) describes two circumstances in which the disposition of §306 stock will not be subject to the rules of §306(a). Section 306(b)(4)(A) absolves a shareholder who establishes to the satisfaction of the Secretary of the Treasury (or the Secretary's delegate) that the distribution as well as the redemption or other disposition did not have, as one of its principal purposes, the avoidance of federal income taxes. If the taxpayer sells (or otherwise disposes of) the non-§306 stock at the same time as, or prior to, disposing of the §306 stock, then the taxpayer need convince the Secretary of the Treasury only that the disposition of the §306 stock did not have tax avoidance as one of its principal purposes. §306(b)(4)(B).

In a series of prior revenue rulings, the Service had ruled that §306 stock is not disposed of in pursuance of a tax avoidance plan whenever the stock is widely held. In Rev. Rul. 89-63, 1989-1 C.B. 90, the Service ruled that a shareholder may encounter liability under §306(a) upon disposition of stock of even a widely held corporation unless the shareholder can establish the absence of a tax avoidance motive.

The court in *Fireoved* was able to avoid a difficult procedural question raised by §306(b)(4): May a taxpayer litigate his qualification for §306(b)(4) characterization, or is an appeal to the Secretary of the Treasury his only avenue of relief under that section? The language of §306(b)(4) supports the latter reading, although the courts traditionally have sought to impose *some* judicial review on every exercise of administrative discretion. See, e.g., Crowell v. Benson, 285 U.S. 22 (1932); Johnson v. Robinson, 415 U.S. 361 (1974). When Congress has deliberately granted broad discretion to an administrative agent, the scope of judicial review is appropriately narrow. Surely a taxpayer would have the right to challenge an adverse administrative determination under §306(b)(4) as arbitrary, capricious, or the result of bias or prejudice. But the taxpayer in *Fireoved* sought a favorable judicial determination under §306(b)(4) despite having failed to seek an administrative ruling under that section. Given the clear statement of administrative discretion in §306(b)(4), should not such a failure on the part of the taxpayer have foreclosed judicial review of the issue?

If a taxpayer disposes of §306 stock in a transaction that qualifies as a complete termination of interest under §306(b)(1), then he automatically avoids the harsh rules of §306(a). To so qualify, though, the taxpayer must terminate his interest in the corporation actually and constructively. See §306(b)(1)(A)(iii) and §§306(b)(1)(B), 302(c)(1). If a taxpayer reduces to zero his actual interest in the corporation but continues to have a constructive interest in the corporation, then he may seek an administrative ruling under §306(b)(4)(B). See Rev. Rul. 77-455, 1977-2 C.B. 93, in which a father owned a majority of the corporation's common stock and all the corporation's preferred stock subject to a §306 taint. The father sold some of his common and preferred stock to his son, who already held part of the common, and some to an unrelated party. The balance of the father's stock was redeemed by the corporation. The Service ruled that §306(b)(1) did not apply (because of the rules of constructive ownership) but that §306(b)(4) did apply because the father had terminated his actual interest in the corporation.

In Pescosolido v. Commissioner, 91 T.C. 52 (1988), a graduate of Deerfield Academy and Harvard College gave 1,500 shares of appreciated §306 stock to the two institutions and deducted the fair market value of the stock. The IRS, pursuant to §170(e)(1)(A), limited the deduction to the taxpayer's basis in the stock because the stock would not have produced long-term capital gain if sold. Relying on §306(b)(4), the taxpayer argued that the stock would not have produced "tainted" ordinary income if sold because there was no tax avoidance on the distribution or disposition. The Tax Court ruled for the IRS, concluding that the taxpayer was aware that the consequences of the charitable contribution deduction would be the avoidance of ordinary income on the bailout of corporate earnings.

In *Fireoved*, the taxpayer sold a part of his non-§306 stock prior to the disposition of his §306 stock. His prior sale of common stock did not, however, reduce his voting interest in the corporation below that amount necessary to give him a veto over corporate decisions. The court held that under these circumstances the disposition of some of the voting common did not remove the §306 taint from even a proportionate share of the §306 stock. See Rev. Rul. 75-247, 1975-1 C.B. 104, following *Fireoved* in interpreting §306(b)(4)(B).

5. *A comparison of §305 and §306.* The success of the preferred stock bailout in *Chamberlin* turned on two key facts: (1) that the distribution of the preferred stock dividend was tax free on receipt and (2) that the sale of the dividend stock produced capital gain. This abuse could have been prevented either by taxing the stock dividend or by tainting the dividend stock. Which method should Congress have adopted? Do you agree with the congressional decision to employ both methods, sometimes taxing the stock dividend under §305(b) and other times tainting the dividend stock under §306? If, as a general rule, a tax liability should be imposed only when funds are available to pay the tax, is taxation of stock dividends ever appropriate?

PROBLEMS

6-2. *X* Corp. has 100 shares of stock outstanding, 80 owned by *B* and 20 by *C*. *B* and *D*, an unrelated party, form *Y* Corp., with *B* contributing his *X* stock to *Y* in exchange for 80 shares of *Y* common and 800 shares of *Y* $10 par-value nonconvertible preferred. *D* contributes $2,000 in cash for 20 shares of *Y* common and 200 shares of *Y* $10 par-value nonconvertible preferred. If the fair market value of the *X* stock is $100 per share and *X* has earnings and profits of $5,000, how much of the *Y* common and preferred stock is §306 stock in the hands of *B* and *D*? How does your answer change if *B* receives only 50 percent of the stock of *Y* Corp.?

6-3. *A* and *B* organize *X* Corp. in 1995, each contributing $10,000 in cash in return for 100 shares of common stock. In July 2010, *X* declared a dividend payable in nonconvertible preferred stock: one share of the preferred stock for each share of common stock. At the date of distribution, the preferred stock had a fair market value of $200 per share. Immediately prior to the distribution, the common stock was worth $500 per share. On January 1, 2010, *X* had accumulated earnings and profits of $15,000, and *X* had $5,000 in current earnings and profits for 2010. On January 1, 2014, *X* had accumulated earnings and profits of $45,000, and *X* had $5,000 current earnings and profits for 2014. Determine the tax consequences of each of the following situations:

a. In February 2014, *A* sold all her preferred stock to *P* for $11,000, and in January 2015 she sold her common stock to *Q* for $40,000.
b. In February 2014, *X* redeemed all of *A*'s preferred stock for $11,000.
c. In (b) above, *X* also redeemed 50 shares of *A*'s common stock for $20,000.
d. In (c) above, assume there was neither accumulated nor current earnings and profits for 2010. How would your answer change if there had been $1 of current earnings and profits?

7

Liquidations

When a shareholder transfers property to a corporation in a §351 exchange solely for stock, she recognizes no gain or loss. §351(a). The price of this nonrecognition is the preservation of the shareholder's net unrecognized built-in gain in the bases in the assets transferred to the corporation. §362(a). Cf. §362(e)(2) (eliminating net built-in loss at either the corporate or shareholder level). One might expect a similar statutory structure governing liquidations — that when the corporation is liquidated, no gain or loss would be recognized, but the shareholders would succeed to the corporation's basis in the assets distributed.

Alas, life is not so simple. A complete liquidation is ordinarily a recognition event for both the distributing corporation and the shareholders. The distributing corporation generally recognizes gain or loss on the distribution of its assets as if those assets were sold to the shareholders at their fair market values, and each shareholder generally recognizes gain or loss on the difference between the fair market value of the property received on the distribution and the shareholder's stock basis.

One reason for the nonrecognition pattern on incorporation and the recognition pattern on liquidation may be that there is a continuity of investment in moving a business from unincorporated to incorporated solution, but the same continuity of investment is ordinarily absent when the taxpayer liquidates the business. Often, the business has come to a halt, and the liquidated assets will either be sold for use in another business or used for personal purposes. A liquidation also represents the last opportunity to tax the shareholders on any earnings and profits accumulated by the corporation. Consequently, since 1924 Congress has provided that most often a liquidation will be a taxable event to shareholders. In many but not all respects a liquidation will be treated as if the shareholders sold the corporation's stock back to the corporation and the corporation sold the assets distributed to the shareholders. Note that the liquidation rules apply even if the shareholders continue the corporation's business after liquidation.

This chapter focuses on two common liquidation patterns. The first pattern, governed primarily by §§331 and 336, is embodied in the general rule summarized above (and discussed further at Section A infra). For example, suppose *X* Corp. has assets with an aggregate basis of $100 and a fair market value of $500. The sole shareholder, *A*, has a basis in the stock of $200. On liquidation *X* Corp. recognizes gain of $400 under §336. Disregarding any tax on *X* Corp.'s gain, the gain recognized by *A* equals the difference between the fair market value of the property received and the basis of the surrendered stock, or in this example $300. *A*'s basis in each asset received is its fair market value. §334(a). Note now (although it is discussed in more detail below) that historically a liquidating corporation recognized no gain or loss on a liquidation. The Tax Reform Act of 1986 repealed this application of the *General Utilities* doctrine in the liquidation context.

The second pattern involves the liquidation of a subsidiary by a parent corporation (see Section B infra). The subsidiary's assets remain in corporate solution, but the corporate structure has been simplified. Recognizing this continuity, Congress requires that neither the distributing corporation nor parent corporation recognize gain or loss. To illustrate, assume that *A* in the example above is a corporation rather than an individual. On the liquidation, *X* Corp., the liquidating corporation, recognizes no gain under §337(a), and *A* Corp., the parent corporation, recognizes no gain under §332(a). As the price for (or benefit of) nonrecognition, *A* Corp. takes transferred bases in *X* Corp.'s assets under §334(b) (here, an aggregate $100 basis). Furthermore, *A* Corp. will succeed to certain significant tax attributes of *X* Corp. See §381. Note that this pattern of taxation is available only if, among other things, the parent corporation controls the subsidiary within the meaning of §332(b).

The two liquidation patterns outlined above do not operate in a vacuum. Events before, during, and after a liquidation must be considered in evaluating the tax consequences of the liquidation itself. Historically, statutory responses to events preceding or following a liquidation were found in former §337 and §338. Former §337 addressed the liquidating corporation's sale of assets before a liquidation (see page 268 infra). Be sure not to confuse former §337 with current §337. As explained below, the two provisions are unrelated. Section 338, in part, deals with the purchase of stock by a corporate shareholder, in some cases, before liquidation (see page 307 infra).

The liquidation rules apply to distributions in "complete liquidation" of a corporation. Such a distribution "is one of a series of distributions in redemption of all stock of the corporation pursuant to a plan." §346(a).

That definition, however, does not pinpoint when a liquidation begins, although the regulations offer some guidance. See Treas. Regs. §1.332-2(c) (providing that the status of liquidation exists when the corporation has adopted a plan of liquidation and ceased to be a going concern, and its remaining activities are merely for the purpose of winding up its affairs). A liquidation can occur without a corporation's selling all of its assets, and a distribution in kind may be a liquidating distribution. See Rev. Rul. 63-107, 1963-1 C.B. 71. Further, it is not necessary that a liquidating corporation dissolve under state law. Moreover, a formal plan of liquidation need not be adopted. See, e.g., Kennemer v. Commissioner, 96 F.2d 177 (5th Cir. 1938). Nevertheless, failure to formally adopt a plan of liquidation may tempt the Service: The early distributions may be treated as dividends rather than as liquidating distributions. See, e.g., Estate of Maguire v. Commissioner, 50 T.C. 130 (1968).

Within what timeframe must a liquidating distribution be effected to constitute a "complete liquidation"? What corporate activities will be inconsistent with a state of liquidation? Although there is no formal requirement, the longer the process and the more active the liquidating corporation, the more likely the Service will treat the distributions as dividends to the extent of earnings and profits. See Cleveland v. Commissioner, 335 F.2d 473 (3d Cir. 1964) (conduct of business by corporation after distributions rendered them dividends). But see Estate of Fearon v. Commissioner, 16 T.C. 385 (1951) (liquidating distribution more than 23 years after plan adopted respected; court found corporation had tried to dispose of assets). Regardless of the liquidation pattern, tax lawyers often use the three-year period set forth in §332 as a guide for the liquidation timeframe.

Consider the following case, which provides an overview of what constitutes a liquidation and how gain or loss is determined.

Rendina v. Commissioner

United States Tax Court, T.C. Memo 1996-392

Memorandum Findings of Fact and Opinion

Beghe, Judge:

Findings of Fact

. . . In 1986, petitioner and Thomas J. Ackerman (Ackerman), a construction contractor, formed WSAI as a general business corporation under Ohio law, for the purposes of constructing and selling 18 condominium units in Willoughby, Ohio. WSAI was operated as a C corporation. Petitioner and Ackerman each paid WSAI approximately $250 for an equal number of common shares of WSAI.

In 1987 and 1988, WSAI constructed the 18 condominium units, known as "South Wood Condominiums" (South Wood). South Wood consists of two-story townhouses, built in clusters of six units in each of three buildings.

WSAI financed the construction of South Wood primarily with borrowed funds. The funds used by WSAI consisted of a loan from Security Federal Savings and Loan of approximately $740,000, petitioner's deposits in WSAI's checking account of approximately $41,200, and approximately $68,000 in loans from three of petitioner's accounting clients: William and Mary Foss (the Fosses), Vito and Adella Navar (the Navars), and Frank and Benette Posa (the Posas). The principal amounts of the loans from the Fosses, Navars, and Posas were $53,000, $10,000, and $5,000, respectively. The loan checks were made to WSAI, and deposited in WSAI's checking account at National City Bank. WSAI issued promissory notes to the lenders, providing that interest would be paid at a rate of 12 percent per year. . . .

Toward the end of 1988, two of the 18 units remained unsold. Petitioner and Ackerman orally agreed that WSAI would transfer title to the two remaining condominium units to petitioner in consideration of petitioner's assumption of the Foss, Navar, and Posa notes, and petitioner's discharge of WSAI's "debt" owed to him.

In December 1988, WSAI transferred South Wood's two remaining condominium units to petitioner. Petitioner did not report any income or gain from the receipt of the two condominium units on his 1988 Federal income tax return, but did report a taxable dividend from WSAI in the amount of $90. . . .

With the transfer of the last two condominium units to petitioner in 1988, WSAI no longer held business assets, and ceased to be a going concern. Upon transfer of all 18 condominium units in 1988, WSAI ceased doing business, but did not formally dissolve. Its charter was revoked in 1990 for nonpayment and nonfiling of Ohio franchise tax returns.

In April 1989, petitioner sold one of the units for $67,900.

Following his receipt of the last two South Wood condominium units, petitioner gave the Fosses, Navars, and Posas the option of either having their loans repaid, or of having the loan obligations taken over by Canterbury Construction Co. (Canterbury), an S corporation wholly owned by petitioner that is in the business of real estate construction and development. The note holders chose to have Canterbury take over the loan obligations and to continue receiving interest payments. While petitioner did not, in his individual capacity, issue promissory notes to any of the note holders, Canterbury issued new notes to the Fosses, Navars, and Posas sometime after April 1989, and began making interest payments on the notes.

The loans to the Posas and Navars, in the principal amounts of $15,000 and $10,000, respectively, have been paid. As of the date of filing of the petition, the Fosses still held a note issued by Canterbury on which they were receiving interest payments. . . .

OPINION

The substantive tax question before us is whether petitioner's receipt of two condominium units, during the taxable year 1988, was a taxable distribution from WSAI. Respondent determined that petitioner's receipt of the last two units was a dividend in the amount of $135,800 during the taxable year 1988. Petitioner contended that his receipt of the units was not taxable to him because it was offset by discharge of WSAI's debt to him, and his assumption of the Foss, Navar, and Posa notes. Petitioner also maintained that his receipt of the two units could not be a dividend because WSAI had no earnings and profits.

Petitioner, in his reply brief, raised the alternative argument that he received the condominium units in de facto liquidation of WSAI, which would entitle him to use the basis of his WSAI stock to compute his gain on the distribution, if we should determine that his payments into WSAI represented equity rather than debt. Because it appeared to us that this position might have greater merit than the primary position of either of the parties, we had them address this newly raised issue in supplemental briefs.

I. Lack of Prejudice to Respondent in Addressing Liquidation

[discussion omitted]

II. De Facto Liquidation

Applying the three-pronged test of Estate of Maguire v. Commissioner, 50 T.C. 130, 140 (1968): (1) Whether there is a manifest intention to liquidate; (2) whether there is a continuing purpose to terminate corporate affairs; and (3) whether the activities of the corporation and its shareholders are directed toward that objective, we are convinced that WSAI and its shareholders displayed a manifest intention to liquidate and continuing purpose to terminate corporate affairs, and that the activities of WSAI and its shareholders were directed to that end. See Olmsted v. Commissioner, T.C. Memo. 1984-381.

Neither the Code nor the regulations to section 331 define the term "complete liquidation." However, as we noted in Olmsted v. Commissioner, T.C. Memo. 1984-381, the regulations under section 332 (governing subsidiary liquidations) contain a definition of "complete liquidation" under section 332 that applies equally to section 331:

> A status of liquidation exists when the corporation ceases to be a going concern and its activities are merely for the purpose of winding up its affairs, paying its debts and distributing any remaining balance to its shareholders. A liquidation may be completed prior to the actual dissolution of the liquidating corporation. However, legal dissolution of the corporation is not required. Nor will the mere retention of a nominal amount of assets for the sole purpose of preserving the corporation's legal existence disqualify the transaction.

[Sec. 1.332-2(c), Income Tax Regs.]

Respondent maintains that petitioner never liquidated WSAI. In support of her position, respondent relies on Haley Bros. Constr. Corp. v. Commissioner, 87 T.C. 498, 515-516 (1986). In *Haley Bros. Construction Corp.*, the corporation at issue, Marywood Corp., was not dissolved formally in accordance with State law, and continued to maintain a checking account. We held that there was no liquidation because there was a business purpose for the continued existence of Marywood, which continued to be operated in accordance with that business purpose, holding and selling real property, maintaining a checking account, paying expenses, and filing tax returns. Moreover, the continued corporate existence of Marywood served the purpose of insulating its parent corporation from liabilities on a mortgage and in pending litigation.

In the case at hand, there was no business purpose for WSAI to continue operating. WSAI did not file a corporate tax return for 1988, and, with the sale or distribution of all of the condominium units, WSAI had no further assets of any consequence.

We are unpersuaded by respondent's assertion that, because WSAI continued some activities through the beginning of 1989, it did not liquidate. Complete liquidation can occur despite an extended liquidation process, and several earlier opinions of this court have upheld liquidations despite protracted time frames. See, e.g., Estate of Maguire v. Commissioner, supra; T. T. Word Supply Co. v. Commissioner, 41 B.T.A. 965 (1940); Olmsted v. Commissioner, supra. In order for complete liquidation treatment to apply, it is not essential that a formal plan of liquidation be adopted or that the corporation dissolve, as long as there is a manifest intention to liquidate that is carried out. Genecov v. United States, 412 F.2d 556 (5th Cir. 1969); Stamler v. Commissioner, 145 F.2d 37 (3d Cir. 1944), affg. 45 B.T.A. 37 (1941); Kennemer v. Commissioner, 96 F.2d 177, 178 (5th Cir. 1938), affg. 35 B.T.A. 415 (1937); Olmsted v. Commissioner, supra; Silverman v. Commissioner, T.C. Memo. 1971-143; see Bittker & Eustice, Federal Income Taxation of Corporations & Shareholders, par. 10.02, at 10-9 (6th ed. 1994); 11 Mertens, Law of Federal Income Taxation, sec. 42.06, at 53 (1992 rev.).

Respondent maintains that petitioner has failed to provide the necessary books and records to support his position regarding the liquidation of WSAI. Although we agree with respondent that there are gaps in the record, we believe that it contains sufficient evidence to sustain our conclusion that WSAI was liquidated in 1988. The intentions of petitioner and Ackerman to liquidate WSAI at the end of 1988 were apparent from the sales of WSAI's assets, its cessation of business, and the agreement of petitioner and Ackerman that WSAI would distribute the last two condominium units to petitioner, in consideration of petitioner's assumption of the corporation's liabilities to its lenders and his recovery of his investment out of the balance. With that final distribution, WSAI held title to no further assets of any substantial consequence. With the exception of interest payments made through the beginning of 1989 WSAI engaged in no further activities.

Finally, respondent argues that petitioners made no disclosure of any kind on their 1988 individual income tax return regarding the receipt of the two condominium units as a liquidating distribution, as required by section 1.331-1(d), Income Tax Regs., which states,

> In every case in which a shareholder transfers stock in exchange for property to the corporation which issued such stock, the facts and circumstances shall be reported on his return unless the property is part of a distribution made pursuant to a corporate resolution reciting that the distribution is made in liquidation of the corporation and the corporation is completely liquidated and dissolved within one year after the distribution. See section 6043 for requirements relating to returns by corporations.

Section 1.331-1(d), Income Tax Regs., does not impair our ultimate conclusion that a de facto liquidation did occur during the taxable year 1988 in the case at hand. Although section 1.331-1(d), Income Tax Regs., appears to complement section 6043 and section 1.6043-1, Income Tax Regs., thereunder, providing for the filing of Form 966 (Corporate Dissolution or Liquidation) by a corporation that adopts any resolution or plan of liquidation, the filing of Form 966 is not a condition of liquidation treatment under any provision of the Internal Revenue Code. Maguire v. Commissioner, 222 F.2d 472, 478 (7th Cir. 1955), revg. 21 T.C. 853 (1954); Murphy v. Commissioner, T.C. Memo. 1996-59; see also Fowler Hosiery Co. v. Commissioner, 36 T.C. 201 (1961), affd. 301 F.2d 394 (7th Cir. 1962). We are satisfied that section 1.331-1(d), Income Tax Regs., like the regulation under section 6043, is directory only. While compliance with these regulations serves the evidentiary function of supporting the conclusion that a distribution was received in a corporate liquidation, and helps to avoid controversies of the sort we now deal with, we regard them as playing only a facilitating role. Petitioner's compliance with section 1.331-1(d), Income Tax Regs., is not a condition precedent to our treating the distribution of the condominium units to petitioner as a liquidating distribution.

We are convinced that the agreement of the WSAI shareholders, petitioner and Ackerman, for the distribution of the last two condominium units to petitioner, in consideration of his taking care of the corporate liabilities and recovering his own investment, manifested WSAI's intention to liquidate, and that that intention was carried out in the informal winding-up of WSAI's affairs that followed.

III. Computation of Gain

Having found that WSAI was liquidated in 1988, we turn to the tax treatment of petitioner's receipt of the condominium units. Section 331(a) provides that amounts received by a shareholder in complete liquidation of a corporation shall be treated as "full payment in exchange for the stock," considering a liquidating distribution, in effect, as a sale by the shareholder of his stock to the corporation.

Bittker & Eustice, Federal Income Taxation of Corporations & Shareholders, at 10-4, 10-5 (6th ed. 1994); S. Rept. 398, 68th Cong., 1st Sess. 11 (1924), 1939-1 C.B. (pt. 2) 266, 274. As a result, the shareholder computes gain or loss under section 1001(a) by subtracting the adjusted basis of his stock from the amount realized (the fair market value of the distribution), and reports the difference as capital gain or loss if the stock is a capital asset in his hands.

To compute petitioner's gain, we first look at the value of the condominium units distributed to determine the amount realized. We then look at whether petitioner's deposits into the WSAI checking account were loans or equity investments; concluding that they are equity rather than debt, we add them to petitioner's basis in his WSAI stock, rather than treating them as liability offsets to the amount realized. We also look at whether petitioner assumed, or took subject to, WSAI liabilities, because the amount realized under section 1001 on the liquidation exchange is the net value of the distribution, and that amount must be reduced by the amount of liabilities assumed or taken subject to. See Ford v. United States, 160 Ct. Cl. 417, 311 F.2d 951 (1963). We then subtract the basis of petitioner's shares from the amount realized on the distribution to compute his gain.

A. Value of Condominium Units Distributed

Respondent maintains that petitioner received a taxable distribution of $135,800, or the value of the two condominium units received. Petitioner maintains that he gave value equivalent to that of the condominium units. Petitioner's position throughout this proceeding has been that the value of the condominium units was no more than $109,200 — the sum of what he argues were the amount of the WSAI liabilities that he assumed and his deposits into the WSAI account.

We disagree with petitioner's estimate of the value of the condominium units received. The average selling price of the other 14 condominium units was $66,915. Four months after the distribution, petitioner sold one of his condominium units for $67,900.

Petitioner has not convinced us that the fair market value of his condominium units should be less than the average selling price of the other units sold, or $66,915. Thus, we find the fair market value of the condominiums transferred to petitioner to be $133,830.

B. Basis of WSAI Shares: Debt v. Equity

Respondent maintains that no loan or other value was given by petitioner to WSAI. However, the deposit records of National City Bank, where WSAI maintained a checking account, indicate that petitioner deposited $41,200 into WSAI's account. Because the books and records of WSAI were not made available, we must look to such documentary evidence as bank statements, as well as the testimony of witnesses, in considering whether petitioner gave value to WSAI. Hagaman v. Commissioner, T.C. Memo. 1987-549. We are satisfied that petitioner's deposits into the WSAI account constitute value that resulted in cost to be taken into account in determining petitioner's gain on the receipt of the condominium units.

While the analysis would vary, depending on whether the investment in the corporation were debt or equity, the net tax effect to petitioner would be the same. If petitioner's investment in the corporation were a loan, WSAI's transfer of property to petitioner in satisfaction of the loan would not be governed by section 331 to that extent. This is because the transfer would not be "in payment for" petitioner's stock.

In such a case, the corporation merely would be repaying the loan, receiving equal value in exchange for the transfer, resulting in no taxable event for the transferee. See Citizens Bank & Trust Co. v. United States, 217 Ct. Cl. 606, 580 F.2d 442 (1978); J. Hofert Co. v. United States, 23 AFTR 2d 69-845, 69-1 USTC par. 9220 (C.D. Cal. 1969).

If petitioner's investment were equity, petitioner would be entitled to increase his basis in his WSAI shares by the amount of the investment. Under this scenario, petitioner would subtract his basis from the amount of the distribution; if the distribution should exceed petitioner's basis, the excess would be treated as capital gain from sale of the stock.

In Donisi v. Commissioner, 405 F.2d 481, 483 (6th Cir. 1968), affg. T.C. Memo. 1967-62, the court noted that, although the intention of the parties weighs heavily in determining whether advances are loans, proof of such intent is to be found in "the arrangements concerning the normal security, interest and repayment or efforts to secure the same." In Austin Village, Inc. v. United States, 432 F.2d 741, 745 (6th Cir. 1970), the court relied on the fact that there was no unconditional promise to repay the loans, no fixed schedule of payments, and no security given for issuance of the loans.

In the case at hand, none of the factors are present that would tend to show that petitioner reasonably expected WSAI to repay the "loan" in accordance with terms in line with those generally prevailing in the business community. See Nassau Lens Co. v. Commissioner, 308 F.2d 39 (2d Cir. 1962), remanding 35 T.C. 268 (1960). Moreover, no interest payments to petitioner were made or provided for. See Texas Farm Bureau v. United States, 725 F.2d 307, 313-314 (5th Cir. 1984). If petitioner had been a true lender, he would have provided for interest payments. Curry v. United States, 396 F.2d 630, 634 (5th Cir. 1968).

We find that petitioner's $41,200 of deposits into the WSAI checking account was a contribution to the capital of WSAI. Because petitioner was a shareholder of WSAI, his $41,200 of contributions to capital is reflected in an increased basis for his WSAI stock. Sec. 1.118-1, Income Tax Regs. Thus, petitioner's basis in his WSAI stock was $41,450.

Petitioner's amount realized from the distribution of the condominium units should be reduced by the amount of the corporation's liabilities to the Posas, Fosses, and Navars that petitioner agreed to assume, and for whose discharge he made the necessary arrangements. Thus, after subtracting the assumed liabilities of $68,000 from the $92,380 gain ($133,830 amount realized minus $41,450 adjusted basis), petitioner's realized capital gain is $24,380.

Decision will be entered under Rule 155.

NOTES

The taxpayer's successful litigating position was almost an afterthought. The Service had claimed that the distribution of the two condominium units was a dividend, which at the time would have been taxable at ordinary income rates. Cf. §1(h)(11) (now providing that an individual's qualified dividend income is taxed at the same rate as long-term capital gain). The taxpayer initially replied that the amount distributed should be reduced by corporate liabilities that were assumed and a corporate debt owed to the taxpayer. Alternatively the taxpayer argued that there were no earnings and profits. The court never got to these issues, ruling instead that even in the absence of a declared intention to liquidate, the distribution was a liquidating distribution.

In computing the shareholder's gain on the liquidation, why did the court state that from a tax perspective it did not matter whether the funds advanced by the shareholder to the corporation constituted debt or equity? What steps could the taxpayers in *Rendina* have taken to easily avoid litigation?

As you read the material that follows, consider whether the liquidating corporation in *Rendina* should have reported gain or loss on the distribution. Then again, the corporation apparently never filed a return for the year in question and never reported the gain on the sale of the other 16 units. The Service apparently was seeking more than $100,000 in unpaid taxes and penalties. So the taxpayer in this case as a transferee faces bigger problems that were not resolved in this litigation.

A. SECTION 331 LIQUIDATIONS

1. *Treatment of Shareholders*

a. Exchange Treatment under §331

Section 331(a)(1) provides that on a complete liquidation of a corporation, a shareholder is treated as receiving any liquidating distributions in exchange for the shareholder's stock. The shareholder realizes and recognizes gain or loss on the difference between the adjusted basis of the stock surrendered and the value of what is received. See §1001. That gain or loss is capital gain or loss if the stock is a capital asset in the shareholder's hands. See §1222. Thus, the earnings and profits account, so critical to the tax status of the distributions of a going concern, becomes irrelevant when the distribution is in complete liquidation. The analogy for §331(a)(1) is a sale by the stockholder of the shares to a third party. Is this analogy valid? Consistent with the recognition of gain or loss, §334(a) provides that the basis of property received in complete liquidation is its fair market value at the time of the distribution.

b. Treatment of Liabilities

If a shareholder assumes a corporate liability or takes property subject to a liability as part of a liquidating distribution, the shareholder's amount realized is reduced by the amount of those liabilities. Cf. §301(b)(2) (distribution reduced by liability assumed by the shareholder). See Rev. Rul. 59-228, 1959-2 C.B. 59. For example, suppose *X* Corp. holds two assets: depreciable real property with a basis of $4,000 and a fair market value of $11,000, and inventory with a basis of $2,000 and a fair market value of $5,000. The real property is subject to a $7,000 mortgage. *T*, the sole shareholder, has a basis in her *X* Corp. stock of $3,000. If *X* Corp. liquidates, *T* would recognize a $6,000 gain ($9,000 amount realized [or $16,000 aggregate value of distributed property minus $7,000 liabilities assumed] less $3,000 basis), and her basis in the land and inventory would be $11,000 and $5,000, respectively. §334(a). What would be *T*'s gain or loss on a sale of these assets at fair market value? Does *T*'s taxable gain or loss on the *X* stock and distributed assets correspond to her economic gain?

Suppose a liquidating corporation distributes assets with a fair market value of $10,000 subject to a disputed liability for patent infringement. What is the amount distributed? If the liability cannot be valued, it will not be taken into account in valuing the distributed assets. Suppose two years later the shareholder pays the liability, which turns out to be $3,000. What is the nature of the deduction? See Arrowsmith v. Commissioner, 344 U.S. 6 (1952).

c. Contingent Assets

In some cases, the assets distributed may themselves be difficult to value even though there are no disputed liabilities. For example, if *X* Corp.'s only asset is a contingent contract right that is not valued on liquidation, the gain to the shareholders will remain "open" on the authority of Burnet v. Logan, 283 U.S. 404 (1931), until the contracts can be valued. In Rev. Rul. 58-402, 1958-2 C.B. 15, the Service announced that it "will continue to require valuation of contracts and claims to receive indefinite amounts of income, such as those acquired with respect to stock in liquidation of a corporation, except in rare and extraordinary cases." See also Treas. Regs. §1.1001-1(a). In Commissioner v. Carter, 170 F.2d 911 (2d Cir. 1948), a shareholder on liquidation received oil brokerage contracts that the parties stipulated had no ascertainable fair market value. Later, the shareholder collected commissions of $35,000 under the contracts. Is the gain ordinary or capital? The Second Circuit permitted the taxpayer capital gains treatment. Compare Waring v. Commissioner, 412 F.2d 800 (3d Cir. 1969), in which a patent royalty contract was valued on liquidation. Consequently, future payments to shareholder in excess of the §334(a) basis were treated as ordinary income in the absence of a sale or exchange. See also Likins-Foster Honolulu Corp. v. Commissioner, 840 F.2d 642 (9th Cir. 1988) (Commissioner applied the open transaction doctrine to the liquidating corporation's claim for condemnation proceeds).

Section 453(j)(2) and Treas. Regs. §15A.453-1(d)(2)(iii) now attempt to curtail sharply the use of the open transaction doctrine. Can a taxpayer elect out of §453 and the above regulation? See §453(d).

d. Installment Notes

If a liquidating corporation distributes installment notes in a §331 liquidation, the liquidating corporation must recognize the difference between the adjusted basis and the fair market value of the notes. §453B. Under some circumstances, the shareholders do not have to immediately take gain into account related to the distributed notes. §453(h). Instead, the former shareholders can treat payments on the notes as installment payments for the stock, thereby deferring the gain. This treatment for shareholders applies only if the sale or exchange that resulted in the installment obligation occurred during a 12-month period beginning on the date a plan of liquidating was adopted. Further, the liquidation must take place within the same period. Installment obligations for the sale of inventory are accorded this treatment only if there is a bulk sale to one purchaser in one transaction. Installment sale reporting is not available if the stock of the liquidating corporation is publicly traded. §453(k)(2).

If §453(h) does not apply, a shareholder of a liquidating corporation must treat the fair market value of any installment note distributed as an amount realized on the exchange of stock in the liquidating corporation.

e. Allocation of Stock Basis to Liquidating Distributions

If a shareholder acquires stock on different dates or at different prices, gain or loss is determined separately for each block. Treas. Regs. §1.331-1(e).

Further, if a shareholder receives a series of liquidating distributions, the shareholder recovers basis before recognizing gain. Rev. Rul. 68-348, 1968-2 C.B. 141. See also Rev. Rul. 85-48, 1985-1 C.B. 126. Cf. §301(c)(2) and (3). Thus, the shareholder recognizes gain only as the aggregate distributions allocable to a share exceed the share's basis. Under the same principle, the shareholder recognizes no loss until the final liquidating distribution. For example, if *A* holds stock with a $5,000 basis and receives liquidating distributions of $4,000 in year 1 and $4,000 in year 2, *A* recognizes no gain in year 1, recovering $4,000 of his $5,000 stock basis, and recognizes a $3,000 gain in year 2. If, instead, *A*'s basis is $10,000 and the year 2 distribution is the final one, then *A* recovers $4,000 of his $10,000 stock basis in year 1 and recognizes a $2,000 loss in year 2. Note that although §267(a)(1) generally disallows loss deductions on the sale or exchange of property between a shareholder and a corporation in which the shareholder owns directly or indirectly more than 50 percent of the stock, shareholder losses incurred on the complete liquidation of a corporation are exempted.

2. *Treatment of Liquidating Corporation*

a. Recognition of Gain or Loss at the Corporate Level

In a nonliquidating distribution, when a corporation distributes property with a value exceeding adjusted basis, it recognizes gain equal to that excess. §311(b)(1). It does not recognize loss, however, when it distributes loss property. §311(a). Generally, however, when a corporation makes a liquidating distribution, it recognizes gain or loss.

Under §336(a), a liquidating corporation recognizes gain or loss as if the property distributed is sold to the distributee at fair market value. The effect of §336(a) is to ensure a corporate-level tax even on pre-incorporation appreciation. Suppose *B* forms *X* Corp. by contributing property with a $1,000 basis and $9,000 fair market value in exchange for all the *X* Corp. stock in a transaction that qualifies under §351. On the exchange, *X* Corp. takes a $1,000 basis in the property under §362(a), and *B* takes a $1,000 basis in the stock under §358. If *X* Corp. liquidates, the distributing corporation will recognize an $8,000 gain under §336(a), and *B* will recognize an $8,000 gain under §§331 and 1001. *B* will take a $9,000 basis in the property distributed under §334(a).

Why should §336 require a corporate-level tax on this pre-incorporation appreciation? Could Congress have written §336(a) in a manner that would exclude pre-incorporation appreciation? Congress did so in the case of pre-incorporation losses, as is discussed below.

If the property had a $1,000 fair market value when *B* formed *X* Corp. and then increased in value to $9,000 prior to the liquidation, there is a stronger argument for a double tax on the liquidation—stronger in the sense that to the extent our corporate taxation system is a double tax system, it is not unreasonable to treat a corporation's built-in gains (and losses) in the same manner as recognized gains (or losses), if those built-in gains (or losses) arose during the corporation's existence.

When §336(a) treats the property as if it were sold to the shareholders, are the provisions generally associated with a sale invoked as well? For example, §1239 provides that in the case of a sale between certain related parties, any gain recognized shall be treated as ordinary if the property would be depreciable in the hands of the transferee. Section 1239(b) and (c)(1)(A) treat a corporation and a 50-percent (by value) shareholder as related. Suppose, for example, that *X* Corp. makes a liquidating distribution of an apartment building to *B*, its sole shareholder. The building has a $100,000 basis and a $500,000 fair market value and is not subject to depreciation recapture because *X* Corp. used the straight-line method for depreciation. Assume the building is a capital asset in *X* Corp.'s hands. When *X* Corp. distributes the property, is the $400,000 gain that *X* Corp. must recognize a capital gain or ordinary income? It appears that §1239 applies and that *X* Corp. has ordinary income.

Section 336 does not apply to all liquidating distributions, including a liquidation that is part of a reorganization. §336(c). Suppose *X* Corp. transfers all its assets to *Y* Corp. in exchange for *Y* stock and then liquidates in a transaction described in §368(a). If *X* Corp. distributes the appreciated *Y* Corp. stock to its shareholders, it recognizes no gain or loss on the distribution. §361(c)(1).

b. Treatment of Liabilities

In general, if a corporation distributes property in complete liquidation, it is treated as selling the distributed property for its fair market value, a rule generally unaffected by whether the distributed property is encumbered by a liability. §336(a). For example, assume that *X* Corp. makes a liquidating distribution of an asset with a $50,000 basis and $90,000 fair market value to an individual shareholder, and the shareholder assumes a $30,000 liability as part of the liquidation. Under §336(a), *X* Corp. recognizes a $40,000 gain (the excess of the asset's value over its basis). The result to *X* Corp. is the same if the assumed liability is $65,000, rather than $30,000.[1] Note that *X* Corp. does not have any cancellation of indebtedness income. Why not?

1. The consequences to the shareholder differ, however. When the shareholder assumes a $30,000 liability, the shareholder's amount realized on the *X* stock is $60,000 ($90,000 value of property received minus $30,000 liability assumed). In contrast, when the shareholder assumes a $65,000 liability, the shareholder's amount realized on the *X* stock is only $25,000 ($90,000 value of property received minus $65,000 liability assumed).

What happens if the property distributed in complete liquidation is encumbered by a liability in excess of its fair market value? Under §336(b), the liquidating corporation's amount realized for the distributed property is not less than the amount of the liability. In effect, §336(b) codifies the result in Tufts v. Commissioner, 461 U.S. 300 (1983). Suppose that *X* Corp. owns property with a $100,000 basis and a $400,000 fair market value that is subject to a $600,000 liability. A distribution of that property will trigger a $500,000 corporate-level gain, which will be capital or ordinary depending on the nature of the property distributed. What will the amount realized be for purposes of evaluating the tax consequences to the shareholders?

c. Treatment of Corporate-Level Losses

A distributing corporation generally recognizes gain and loss on a liquidating distribution, while it recognizes gain but not loss on a nonliquidating distribution. Compare §336(a) with §311(a) and (b). The dissimilar treatment may be justified because of the following difference between the two types of distributions. In a nonliquidating distribution, the distributing corporation may "cherry pick" the assets to be distributed. Thus, it may choose to distribute "loss" property to recognize loss, while retaining "gain" property and deferring gain. In contrast, in a liquidating distribution, the distributing corporation distributes all of its property—any "gain" property as well as any "loss" property.

Even for a liquidating distribution, Congress has been concerned that taxpayers would exploit the loss allowance by artificially creating corporate-level losses. Congress addressed that concern in §336(d)(1) and (2), a response that seems too broad, however, following the enactment of §362(e)(2). Despite that enactment, §336(d)(1) and (2) remain in the Code.

Consider the following example to illustrate why Congress may have enacted §336(d)(1) and (2) and why §362(e)(2) makes those sections sometimes unnecessary.

Suppose *B* owns all the stock of *X* Corp., and *X*'s assets have a $70,000 basis and $100,000 fair market value. Assume *B*'s *X* stock basis is also $70,000. *B* holds a piece of property with a $130,000 basis and $50,000 fair market value. If *X* Corp. liquidated, it would recognize a $30,000 gain under §336(a), and *B* would recognize a $30,000 gain under §331.

Suppose instead that *B* exchanges the loss property for additional *X* Corp. stock in a transaction that qualifies under §351. (A contribution to capital will achieve the same results.) If §362(e)(2) does not apply to that transaction, *B*'s $80,000 built-in loss in the transferred asset will be duplicated in *B*'s basis in the *X* Corp. stock and in *X* Corp.'s basis in the asset: Under §358, *B*'s basis in the *X* stock increases to $200,000, and under §362, *X* Corp.'s total basis in the assets increases to $200,000. Now when *X* Corp. liquidates, it is treated as if it sold the property to its shareholder in the aggregate for $150,000, its fair market value. Assuming that §336(d)(1) and (2) do not apply, *X* Corp. recognizes an overall $50,000 loss under §336. Further, *B* recognizes a $50,000 loss under §331. Those losses allow both *X* Corp. and *B* to offset other taxable income. Note that *B*'s basis in the loss property after the liquidation is $50,000, its fair market value under §334(a). But *B* will gladly surrender a higher basis in exchange for a double loss deduction—once by *X* Corp. and once by *B*.

Section 336(d)(1) and (2) target that double loss deduction, but so does §362(e)(2). If §362(e)(2) applies to the §351 transaction in the example above, under the general rule of §362(e)(2)(A), *X* Corp. takes a $50,000 basis in the transferred asset, and *B* takes a $200,000 basis in the *X* stock. Then, on the liquidation, *X* recognizes an overall $30,000 gain, while *B* recognizes a $50,000 loss. If *X* Corp. and *B* instead make the election provided in §362(e)(2)(C), *X* Corp. takes a $130,000 basis in the transferred asset, and *B* takes a $120,000 basis in the *X* stock. Then, on the liquidation (assuming that §336(d)(1) and (2) do not apply), *X* Corp. recognizes an overall $50,000 loss, while *B* recognizes a $30,000 gain. Thus, in either case, §362(e)(2) eliminates the double loss. See page 58 supra for a discussion of §362(e)(2).

Like §362(e)(2), §336(d)(1) and (2) address duplicate loss. Under §336(d)(1), the liquidating corporation cannot recognize a loss on a distribution to a "related person" if the distribution is not pro rata or if the property distributed is "disqualified property." A "related person" is defined by reference to §267. Under §336(d)(1)(B), "disqualified property" is property acquired by the liquidating corporation in a transaction to which §351 applied (or as a capital contribution) within five years of the distribution date.

Thus, if the distributee is a related person, a liquidating corporation cannot recognize a loss unless it distributes the loss property pro rata among its shareholders.[2] Even if there is a pro rata distribution, the liquidating corporation cannot recognize a loss on a distribution of "disqualified property" to a related person.

The "disqualified property" rule, like §362(e)(2), is an "anti-stuffing" provision that targets the creation of duplicate loss at the shareholder and corporate levels. However, the two rules may operate in concert to reach an untoward (and likely unintended) result. Consider the example above. Assume that *B* and *X* Corp. make the §362(e)(2)(C) election but that *B* is a related person and the contributed loss asset is disqualified property. Then, §336(d)(1) literally applies to *X* Corp. when it distributes the loss asset in liquidation. If it applies, *X* Corp. does not recognize its $80,000 loss on the asset, and both *B* and *X* Corp. recognize an overall $30,000 gain on the liquidation. Thus, §336(d)(1) and §362(e)(2) operate together to eliminate not only the duplicate loss but any loss associated with the loss asset.

Notice as well that even if the property declines in value while held by the liquidating corporation, no loss is permitted. Suppose *B* owns all the stock of *X* Corp. In year 4, *B* contributes to *X* Corp. additional property with a $30,000 basis and a $50,000 fair market value. In year 7, *B* decides to liquidate *X* Corp. At the time of the liquidating distribution, the property still has a $30,000 basis, but it has declined in value to $10,000. Section 336(d)(1)(B) appears to preclude *X* Corp. from recognizing a loss under §336(a). Perhaps future regulations will soften the provisions in obvious nonabuse cases and will better coordinate §362(e)(2) and §336(d).

As a final note, §336(d)(1)(B) also applies if the basis of property is determined by reference to the basis of property acquired in the described transaction. Thus, if a liquidating corporation acquires property in a §351 transaction three years prior to a liquidation, it cannot avoid the impact of §336(d)(1)(B) by exchanging the acquired property for like-kind property under §1031 prior to liquidation, because the basis of property acquired in a §1031 transaction is determined by looking to the basis of the property exchanged. §1031(d).

2. Instead of this related party rule, could Congress simply have provided that a liquidating corporation was treated as if it sold the property to its shareholders at fair market value and §267 was amended to apply to that deemed sale?

Section 336(d)(2) restricts a liquidating corporation's loss and is also an "anti-stuffing" rule aimed at preventing double deductions. The rule is triggered by a distribution, *sale, or exchange* of property acquired in a §351 transaction (or as a contribution to capital) if the following additional condition is met: The property's acquisition was "part of a plan a principal purpose of which was to recognize loss by the liquidating corporation with respect to such property in connection with the liquidation." §336(d)(2)(B)(i). Property acquired by the liquidating corporation "after the date two years before the date a corporation adopts a plan of liquidation" is presumed to have been acquired with that principal purpose. §336(d)(2)(B)(ii).[3]

Although no regulations have been published to date, the legislative history suggests that regulations should exempt nonabusive transfers occurring within the two-year period. It gives as examples of nonabusive transfers contributions of property to be used in the corporation's trade or business or contributions of property during the first two years of a corporation's existence. Suppose, however, that the §351 exchange occurs more than two years before a plan of liquidation is adopted but it has a loss recognition motive. The conference report states that "[the provision disallowing a loss] will apply only in the most rare and unusual cases under such circumstances." H.R. Rep. No. 841, 99th Cong., 2d Sess. (1986).

If §336(d)(2) applies, the liquidating corporation is not automatically denied the entire loss deduction relating to offending property. Instead, for purposes of determining loss, the basis of the property is decreased by the excess of the basis of the asset on the date of contribution over its fair market value at that time. §336(d)(2)(A). Suppose that one year before the adoption of a plan of liquidation, *X* Corp. acquires, in a §351 transaction, property that has a $50,000 basis and $30,000 fair market value. The property continues to decline in value, and on the date of the liquidating distribution, it has a fair market value of $18,000. Assuming that *X* Corp. takes a $50,000 basis in the property, and §336(d)(2) (but not §336(d)(1)) applies, *X* Corp. will be able to recognize a loss of $12,000 — the decline that occurred while it held the property.[4]

Suppose *X* Corp. acquires loss property in a §351 transaction. Within two years of the acquisition, *X* Corp. sells the property at a loss. Three years after the acquisition, *X* Corp. adopts a plan of liquidation and liquidates. Can *X* Corp. recognize the loss on the sale of the property?

d. Costs of a Liquidation

Thus far we have focused on the liquidating corporation's gain or loss resulting from the property distributed. How does the liquidating corporation treat the costs of liquidation? The costs associated with preparing and carrying out a plan of liquidation are deductible by the corporation as ordinary and necessary business expenses. See Connery v. United States, 460 F.2d 1130 (3d Cir. 1972); for the treatment of similar expenses in a reorganization context, see page 395 infra.

3. Note that the two-year rule of §336(d)(2)(B) looks to the date of adoption of a plan of liquidation, while the five-year rule of §336(d)(1)(B) looks to the date of distribution.

4. Why doesn't §336 or §311 adopt a similar rule for pre-incorporation gain property, thereby limiting recognition to gain that occurred while the property was held by the corporation?

3. *The* Court Holding Co. *Doctrine and Former §337*

Commissioner v. Court Holding Co.

324 U.S. 331 (1945)

Mr. Justice Black delivered the opinion of the Court.

An apartment house, which was the sole asset of the respondent corporation, was transferred in the form of a liquidating dividend to the corporation's two shareholders. They in turn formally conveyed it to a purchaser who had originally negotiated for the purchase from the corporation. The question is whether the Circuit Court of Appeals properly reversed the Tax Court's conclusion that the corporation was taxable under [§61] for the gain which accrued from the sale. . . .

The respondent corporation was organized in 1934 solely to buy and hold the apartment building which was the only property ever owned by it. All of its outstanding stock was owned by Minnie Miller and her husband. Between October 1, 1939 and February, 1940, while the corporation still had legal title to the property, negotiations for its sale took place. These negotiations were between the corporation and the lessees of the property, together with a sister and brother-in-law. An oral agreement was reached as to the terms and conditions of sale, and on February 22, 1940, the parties met to reduce the agreement to writing. The purchaser was then advised by the corporation's attorney that the sale could not be consummated because it would result in the imposition of a large income tax on the corporation. The next day, the corporation declared a "liquidating dividend," which involved complete liquidation of its assets, and surrender of all outstanding stock. Mrs. Miller and her husband surrendered their stock, and the building was deeded to them. A sale contract was then drawn, naming the Millers individually as vendors, and the lessees' sister as vendee, which embodied substantially the same terms and conditions previously agreed upon. One thousand dollars, which a month and a half earlier had been paid to the corporation by the lessees, was applied in part payment of the purchase price. Three days later, the property was conveyed to the lessees' sister.

The Tax Court concluded from these facts that, despite the declaration of a "liquidating dividend" followed by the transfers of legal title, the corporation had not abandoned the sales negotiations; that these were mere formalities designed "to make the transaction appear to be other than what it was," in order to avoid tax liability. The Circuit Court of Appeals drawing different inferences from the record, held that the corporation had "called off the sale, and treated the stockholders" sale as unrelated to the prior negotiations.

There was evidence to support the findings of the Tax Court, and its findings must therefore be accepted by the courts. Dobson v. Commr., 320 U.S. 489. . . . On the basis of these findings, the Tax Court was justified in attributing the gain from the sale to respondent corporation. The incidence of taxation depends upon the substance of a transaction. The tax consequences which arise from gains from a sale of property are not finally to be determined solely by the means employed to transfer legal title. Rather, the transaction must be viewed as a whole, and each step, from the commencement of negotiations to the consummation of the sale, is relevant. A sale by one person cannot be transformed for tax purposes into a sale by another by using the latter as a conduit through which to pass title. To permit the true nature of a transaction to be disguised by mere formalisms, which exist solely to alter tax liabilities, would seriously impair the effective administration of the tax policies of Congress. . . .

The decision of the Circuit Court of Appeals is reversed, and that of the Tax Court affirmed.

It is so ordered.

Reversed.

NOTES

1. Court Holding Co. When *Court Holding Co.* was decided, former §336 provided that a corporation recognized no gain or loss on a liquidating distribution, a rule that embodied the *General Utilities* doctrine. However, if the corporation sold an asset, it recognized gain or loss. Suppose that *X* Corp. owns a piece of undeveloped land with a $60 basis and $100 fair market value. The sole shareholder, *A*, owns stock with a $30 basis and $100 fair market value. If *X* Corp. liquidated, it recognized no gain under former §336, but *A* recognized a $70 gain under §§61, 1001, and 331. Further, *A* took a $100 basis in the property pursuant to §334(a). If *A* then sold the property for $100, no further gain was recognized. What happened if the sale was attributed to the corporation as was the case in *Court Holding Co.*?

Court Holding Co. was limited by United States v. Cumberland Public Service Co., 338 U.S. 451 (1950), in which the shareholders first attempted to sell the stock of their corporation. The buyer refused to buy the stock, perhaps because the buyer did not want to assume any undisclosed liabilities to which the corporation was subject. The shareholders then offered to and did sell the assets that they acquired by liquidating the corporation. The Court of Claims held that the sale was made by the shareholders rather than the corporation. The Supreme Court affirmed, stating that, as in *Court Holding Co.*, it relied on the factual finding made by the lower court. The distinction was a delicate one: In *Court Holding Co.* the decision to liquidate seemed to come at the last moment solely for tax avoidance purposes, while in *Cumberland* the plan for a liquidation came early enough for the lower court to find that a genuine liquidation had in fact taken place.

In 1954, in response to the confusion created by *General Utilities, Court Holding Co.*, and *Cumberland,* former §337 was enacted to eliminate the corporate-level tax, a tax eliminated whether the sale of assets was made by the corporation before the liquidation or by the shareholders after the liquidation.

2. *Purpose of former §337.* Under former §337 (omitting some technical detail), if a liquidating corporation sold an asset in connection with the liquidation, it generally recognized no gain or loss. (Note that current §337 has nothing to do with former §337.) Former §337 therefore made the order of the asset sale and liquidation more neutral, eliminating the concern raised by *Court Holding Co.* Whether the corporation sold the asset and distributed the sales proceeds or the corporation distributed the asset and the shareholders sold it, under former §337, the corporation recognized no gain or loss. In either case, however, the shareholders recognized gain or loss on the liquidation. See §331.

Former §337 also mitigated a concern with loss selectivity. Before it was enacted, a well-advised corporation would sell loss assets, recognizing loss, but distribute gain assets in liquidation, eliminating gain. Former §337 prevented the corporation from recognizing loss on its sale of a loss asset in connection with the liquidation.

3. *Repeal of the* General Utilities *doctrine and former §337.* When Congress repealed the *General Utilities* doctrine, the need for the anti-*Court Holding Co.* provision of former §337 disappeared. Suppose *X* Corp. holds assets with a basis of $40,000 and a fair market value of $90,000. If purchaser *P* wants to buy the assets, the tax consequences to *X* Corp. and its shareholders on a liquidation followed by a sale are a tax at the corporate level under §336 and a tax on the shareholder level. Section 331. If *X* Corp. were to sell the assets and distribute the proceeds, logically there also should be a corporate-level and shareholder-level tax. The need for former §337 protection arose only because former §336 gave the liquidating corporation nonrecognition.

Whether both a corporate- and shareholder-level tax on liquidation is appropriate or not, certainly one of the benefits of the repeal of former §337 is the elimination of some of the contentious areas outlined in the previous Note. No longer does a specially drafted nonrecognition provision apply to a sale in connection with a liquidation. Such a sale will be governed by §1001, producing a gain or loss that will be recognized under §1001(c).

4. Court Holding Co. *after the repeal of* General Utilities. With the repeal of the *General Utilities* doctrine under the Tax Reform Act of 1986, you might wonder what, if anything, is left of the *Court Holding Co.* doctrine. Now that a corporation is taxed whether it sells or distributes property, is there a need to recharacterize a purported distribution followed by a sale as a sale followed by a distribution, or vice versa?

First, the *Court Holding Co.* rule — that steps in an integrated transaction are stepped together — applies in a variety of tax-motivated transactions. For example, a *Court Holding Co.* analysis may be helpful in determining whether the control requirement is satisfied in §351 transactions in which a shareholder sells the stock received immediately after the transfer of receipt of the stock. See page 31 supra.

Second, even in the liquidation context, the *Court Holding Co.* doctrine endures. Suppose *B* owns all the *X* Corp. stock with a basis of $2,000 and a fair market value of $5,000. Among its assets, *X* Corp. owns and has owned for several years an asset with a basis of $5,000 and a fair market value of $1,000. *P*, an unrelated purchaser, wants to buy the asset and starts to negotiate with *B* for the sale. The original negotiations contemplate the liquidation of *X* Corp. followed by a sale of the asset by *B*. Before the liquidation, *X* Corp. sells the asset to *P* and then distributes the proceeds.

If the transaction is respected, *X* Corp. will recognize a $4,000 loss on the sale under §1001 because it is unlikely that §336(d)(2) will apply to property acquired by the liquidating corporation more than two years before the adoption of the plan of liquidation. *B* will recognize a $3,000 gain on the liquidation under §§331 and 1001. If the transaction is not respected, the Service might recharacterize the transaction as a liquidation followed by a sale. In that event, *X* Corp. would recognize no loss on the liquidating distribution if the property were acquired by *X* Corp. within the five-year period ending on the date of the distribution. Section 336(d)(1). *B* would still recognize a $3,000 gain under §§331 and 1001. *B* would take a $1,000 basis in the asset under §334(a) and would recognize no gain or loss on the sale to *P*.

Characterizing the steps as a liquidation followed by a sale deprives *B* (and *B*'s wholly owned corporation) of a loss deduction. The *Court Holding Co.* doctrine will continue to function in this and other situations in which differing tax consequences hinge on which taxpayer sold assets.

5. *A corporate triple tax?* The U.S. corporate tax system seeks to tax corporate earnings twice — once when earned by the corporation and once when distributed

to individual shareholders. To reinforce this double taxation paradigm, Congress has enacted §243 to provide a dividends-received deduction for dividends received by a shareholder-corporation. See page 118 supra.

The repeal of the *General Utilities* doctrine creates the potential for a triple tax in a liquidation context, however. Suppose *B* owns all the stock of *X* Corp., a holding company, and *X*'s sole asset is all the stock of *Y* Corp. *P*, an unrelated purchaser, seeks to acquire all of *Y* Corp.'s assets (all of which are appreciated). Suppose *P* buys the *Y* Corp. stock from *X* Corp., and then *B* and *P* liquidate their corporations. *X* Corp. has already recognized gain on the sale of the *Y* Corp. stock (single tax), and *B* will recognize gain on the liquidation under §§331 and 1001 (double tax). *P* will recognize no gain on the liquidation of *Y* Corp. because *P* took a cost basis in the *Y* Corp. stock purchased from *X* Corp. When *P* liquidates *Y* Corp., the liquidating corporation will recognize gain (triple tax).

The triple tax could have been avoided if *Y* Corp. had sold its assets directly to *P*, followed by a liquidation of *Y* Corp. and then *X* Corp. On the sale, *Y* Corp. would recognize gain (single tax). When *Y* Corp. liquidates into its parent *X* Corp., no gain is recognized. See the discussion of §§337 and 332 at page 272 infra. *B* recognizes gain on the liquidation of *X* Corp. (double tax).

In both examples above, *P* ends up with the assets having a fair market value basis, and *B* ends up with cash. The triple tax possibility puts a premium on form and would undoubtedly precipitate *Court Holding Co.* arguments about who sold what. In §336(e), Congress has authorized the Treasury to promulgate regulations that will treat the sale of *Y* Corp. stock by *X* Corp. as if the *Y* Corp. assets were sold instead. Treasury has recently finalized those regulations. If *X* Corp. and *Y* Corp. joined in making a §336(e) election in the example above, *Y* Corp. would be deemed to sell its assets, and *X* Corp. would recognize no gain or loss on its sale of *Y* stock (single tax). The *Y* Corp. assets would then take a fair market value basis whether or not *P* liquidated *Y* Corp. Although *X* Corp. would recognize no gain or loss on its sale of the *Y* Corp. stock itself, *B* would recognize gain on the liquidation of *X* Corp. (double tax). This treatment, which would reduce the triple tax to a double tax, could only be available if the target corporation (i.e., *Y* Corp.) met the substantial ownership tests under §1504(a)(2) (80 percent voting control and 80 percent of total value of outstanding stock). See page 474 infra for a more detailed discussion of the §336(e) regulations.

6. *Growth of S corporations and other transparent entities.* The repeal of the *General Utilities* doctrine has upped the ante for operating in corporate form—at least in corporate form under subchapter C. Taxpayers now have several choices in addition to operating through a C corporation. For example, a taxpayer can operate through a partnership that is transparent (i.e., not a taxpaying entity for tax purposes). Alternatively, a taxpayer can operate through a limited liability company or other entity where the taxpayer has "checked the box" to have the entity taxed as a transparent entity. See the discussion of the "check-the-box" regulations at pages 499-501. Also, subchapter S, discussed in Chapters 16-18, offers qualifying taxpayers the advantages of corporate form with only a single shareholder level of taxation. Generally, there is no corporate-level taxation for an S corporation. This difference in treatment, combined with the repeal of the *General Utilities* rule, heightens the attraction of subchapter S status for a corporation contemplating a liquidation.

Suppose *X* Corp. with appreciated assets is planning to sell its assets and then liquidate. The sale will result in a corporate-level gain, and, assuming the *X* Corp. stock is appreciated, the liquidation will produce a shareholder-level gain under

§§331 and 1001. Suppose instead that immediately prior to the sale and liquidation, *X* Corp. elects to be taxed under subchapter S. In the absence of a remedial provision, *X* Corp. would not be taxed on the gain and instead would allocate that gain among its shareholders who would report and pay tax on the gain. However, the shareholders would also increase their stock bases by the allocated gain and would therefore recognize correspondingly less gain on the liquidation. The effect of the S election would be avoidance of a corporate-level tax.

Section 1374, discussed further in Chapter 18, now imposes a corporate-level tax equal to the highest rate under §11 (or §1201 if applicable) on any net gain (built-in gain) arising prior to the conversion from a C corporation to an S corporation that is recognized by the corporation through sale or distribution, currently within five years after the date on which the S election took place. Any gain will be presumed to be a built-in gain unless the taxpayer can establish that the appreciation accrued after the conversion.

PROBLEM

7-1. Determine the tax consequences in the following situations.

a. *X* Corp. is owned by unrelated individuals, *A* and *B*, who hold 80 percent and 20 percent, respectively, of the outstanding *X* Corp. stock. *A*'s stock has a $300,000 basis and an $800,000 fair market value. *B*'s stock has a $600,000 basis and a $200,000 fair market value. *X* Corp. holds two assets. Asset 1 has a $200,000 basis and a $500,000 fair market value. Asset 2 has an $800,000 basis and a $500,000 fair market value. Both assets were transferred to *X* Corp. in a §351 transaction two years ago. At that time, asset 2 had a basis of $800,000 and a fair market value of $900,000. *X* Corp. has accumulated earnings and profits of $100,000, but no current earnings and profits. What are the tax consequences if *X* Corp. liquidates, distributing the assets pro rata (i.e., *A* gets 80 percent of asset 1 and 80 percent of asset 2)?
b. In (a), suppose asset 2 had an $800,000 basis and a $700,000 fair market value at the time of the §351 transfer.
c. In (b), suppose the §351 transfer took place six years before the liquidation.
d. In (c), suppose *X* Corp. distributes all of asset 2 and a $300,000 interest in asset 1 to *A* and the remaining $200,000 interest in asset 1 to *B*.
e. In (a), suppose *A* and *B* are planning to sell the assets after liquidation. Does it matter whether *X* Corp. makes the sale and then distributes $1 million in cash or *A* and *B* make the sale following liquidation? In (b), would it matter?
f. If *A* is a corporation, how does your answer to (a) change?

B. SUBSIDIARY LIQUIDATIONS AND RELATED PROVISIONS

1. *Section 332 Liquidations*

Sections 332 and 337 provide in substance that a parent and subsidiary corporation recognize no gain or loss on the subsidiary's liquidation. These provisions, enacted in an earlier form in 1936, were proposed by the Treasury as a measure to encourage the simplification of elaborate corporate structures. In the absence of such a nonrecognition provision, a parent corporation could eliminate subsidiary corporations only by paying a tax under §331, assuming appreciation in the value of the subsidiary's stock. Further, if a subsidiary distributed appreciated assets in the liquidation, it would have to recognize any gain (and pay tax) as well. §336.

Note that §332 by its terms is not optional; moreover, it provides for the nonrecognition of both gain and loss. Although the technical requirements of §332 allow taxpayers often to avoid its nonelective nature when they so desire, the *Associated Wholesale Grocers* case that follows shows that the ability to manipulate §332 is not unrestrained.

Section 332's basis provision, §334(b), does not follow the usual practice of giving the property received on a tax-free exchange the same basis as the property given up—here, the stock of the subsidiary. For an example of the general rule, see §358, which applies to an exchanging shareholder in a §351 transaction. Instead, §334(b) ordinarily requires the transferee (the parent corporation) to take over the basis of the transferor—its subsidiary—in the distributed assets. Does this unusual principle seek to treat the parent as though it had operated the business, ab initio, without the intervening subsidiary's corporate veil? Note that the basis rule of §334 is consistent with the carryover basis rule applied to transferees in §351 transactions and in certain mergers, in which the transferee is considered the successor to the transferor.

Taken together, the nonrecognition principle of §332 and the carryover basis rule of §334(b) in effect remove from tax consideration any gain or loss unrecognized by the parent. Consider the following two situations:

	A	*B*
Parent's stock basis	$10,000	$10,000
Subsidiary's asset basis	3,000	17,000
Fair market value of subsidiary's assets	8,000	13,000

In situation *A* the parent has an unrecognized $2,000 loss in the stock of its subsidiary; if the subsidiary liquidates and §332 applies, the parent will recognize no loss on the liquidation and will hold the subsidiary's assets with a basis of $3,000, thereby producing a gain if the parent should then sell the assets. Conversely, in situation *B* the parent has a potential $3,000 gain in the subsidiary's stock. If the subsidiary liquidates and §332 applies, the parent will recognize no gain and the parent will take a $17,000 basis in the subsidiary's assets, which will produce a $4,000 loss if the parent then sells the assets.

Associated Wholesale Grocers, Inc. v. United States

927 F.2d 1517 (10th Cir. 1991)

BRORBY, Circuit Judge. . . .

The material facts are not in dispute. In 1976, Super Market Developers, Inc. ("Super Market Developers") made a tender offer for all of the outstanding stock of Weston Investment Co. ("Weston"), a publicly traded holding company which owned a number of corporate supermarkets. Super Market Developers acquired approximately 99.97 percent of the total outstanding shares of Weston by 1980. The management of Super Market Developer's parent corporation, Associated Wholesale Grocers, Inc. ("Associated Grocers"), subsequently decided it was not in their best interests to own and operate grocery stores through subsidiary corporations. . . .

One of Weston's subsidiaries was Weston Market, Inc. ("Weston Market"), a grocery managed by Thomas Elder. In 1980, Mr. Elder expressed to taxpayer his interest in buying Weston Market. Taxpayer advised Mr. Elder that it was not interested in a transaction solely involving the stock or operating assets of Weston Market, but that it would be willing to continue discussions.

The parties eventually structured a disposition of Weston's stock which, taxpayer hoped, would enable it both to cash out Weston's minority shareholders without paying a premium and to recognize a substantial loss in the value of Weston's assets[1] when it sold Weston Market. The transaction took the form of two agreements between Super Market Developers and Elder Food Mart, Inc. ("Elder, Inc."), a corporation organized by Mr. Elder to facilitate the purchase of Weston Market. Both agreements were signed on December 11, 1980, and consummated on December 23, 1980.

Under the "Agreement and Plan of Merger," Weston was merged into Elder, Inc., with Elder, Inc. as the surviving corporation. Elder, Inc. exchanged $300,000 in cash and a non-interest bearing demand promissory note, with a face value of $9,049,703, for the Weston stock. The minority shareholders were entitled to receive $28.50 per share, or more, depending on their pro rata share of the cash and note exchanged for Weston stock.

Under the "Agreement and Plan of Reorganization," which took effect "immediately following the time of effectiveness of the merger," Super Market Developers bought back all the assets acquired by Elder, Inc. under the merger agreement except for the stock of Weston Market. In exchange for those assets, Super Market Developers paid "an amount equal to the principal amount of the promissory note . . . plus an amount equal to the cash received by the [minority] shareholders."

Taxpayer treated the transaction as a taxable sale of Weston's assets and declared a tax loss under I.R.C. §1001(a). Because the transaction brought Super Market Developers $2,353,258 less than its cost basis in the stock of Weston, the taxpayer reported that amount as a long-term capital loss in its 1980 consolidated federal income tax return and sought to carry back portions of the loss to each of the three prior years. The IRS denied the loss, concluding the transaction was not a sale but rather a complete liquidation of taxpayer's subsidiary, Weston. As such, the IRS concluded, recognition of the loss was barred by I.R.C. §332. The IRS assessed a deficiency which the taxpayer paid.

Upon the IRS's denial of taxpayer's claim for refund, taxpayer filed suit in the United States District Court for the District of Kansas. The district court applied the step transaction doctrine in holding that §332 bars the recognition of taxpayer's

1. Taxpayer was concerned by the difference between Super Market Developer's cost basis in the Weston stock — the amount it had paid for the stock, $11,727,716 — and the carryover basis representing the market value of Weston's assets, $9,374,458. Under I.R.C. §334, taxpayer would get the carryover basis for Weston's assets upon a complete liquidation of Weston.

loss. *Grocers,* 720 F. Supp. at 890. The court granted summary judgment in favor of the government. *Id.* This appeal followed. . . .

Arguments on Appeal

The issue presented is whether, as a matter of law, the transaction of December 23, 1980 constitutes a taxable sale or other disposition of Weston's assets under I.R.C. §1001(a) or a non-taxable complete liquidation of Weston under I.R.C. §332.

Taxpayer argues the district court erred in accepting the government's characterization of the transaction as a non-taxable liquidation under §332, and in applying the step transaction doctrine to reach that conclusion. Taxpayer advances five reasons in support of its argument: (1) the transaction does not meet the enumerated requirements of §332; (2) case law rejects application of the step transaction doctrine in the §332 context; (3) this transaction was supported by business purposes which bar application of the step transaction doctrine; (4) even if it is applicable, the step transaction doctrine was improperly applied by the district court; and (5) application of the step transaction doctrine in this case will produce the harsh result of forever depriving taxpayer of the recognition of its tax loss. We now address those contentions.

I. Internal Revenue Code §332

. . . The nonrecognition exception of §332 applies or, in other words, a distribution is considered to be in complete liquidation of a subsidiary, only if:

(1) the asset-receiving or "parent" corporation owns, on the date of the adoption of the plan of liquidation and continuously until the receipt of the assets upon liquidation, at least 80 percent of the total voting power and value of the subsidiary (§332(b)(1)); and
(2) the subsidiary distributes its property in complete cancellation or redemption of its stock (§332(b)(2), (3)); and
(3) the subsidiary transfers all of its property to the parent either:
    (a) within the taxable year (in which case the shareholders' adoption of the resolution authorizing the distribution of assets in complete cancellation or redemption of stock is considered an adoption of a plan of liquidation) (§332(b)(2)), or
    (b) in a series of distributions in accordance with a plan of liquidation under which all property is distributed within three years from the close of the year in which the first distribution is made. (§332(b)(3).)

See I.R.C. §332(b)(1)-(b)(3); 11 J. Mertens, The Law of Federal Income Taxation, §42.42 at 113-14 (1990); *cf.* Matter of Chrome Plate, Inc., 614 F.2d 990, 994 (5th Cir. 1980).

The significance of the statute in this dispute is apparent: if §332 applies, taxpayer cannot recognize its loss. If §332 is inapplicable, however, taxpayer is entitled to a substantial tax refund.

Taxpayer argues §332 is inapplicable for three reasons: the 80 percent ownership requirement was not continuously met; all of the assets of the subsidiary were not transferred to the parent; and taxpayer did not adopt a plan of liquidation. We will consider these arguments in turn.

II. 80% STOCK OWNERSHIP REQUIREMENT

The stock ownership requirement is found in §332(b)(1), which specifies an 80 percent voting and value requirement. That requirement is not specifically at issue here, as parties agree that taxpayer owned 99.97 percent of Weston's stock until the transactions occurred on December 23, 1980.

At issue is the continuity requirement of §332(b)(1)—whether taxpayer "has continued to be at all times until the receipt of the property" qualified under the 80 percent voting and value test. As explained by Treasury Regulation:

> The recipient corporation must have been the owner of the specified amount of such stock on the date of the adoption of the plan of liquidation and have continued so to be at all times until the receipt of the property. If the recipient corporation does not continue qualified with respect to the ownership of stock of the liquidating corporation and if the failure to continue qualified occurs at any time prior to the completion of the transfer of all the property, the provisions for the nonrecognition of gain or loss do not apply to any distribution received under the plan.

Treas. Reg. §1.332-2(a). The question, then, is whether taxpayer continued qualified with respect to the ownership of Weston stock until taxpayer received Weston's assets.

Section 332(b)(1) and Treas. Reg. §1.332-2(a) each direct our inquiry to two time periods: "the date of the adoption of the plan of liquidation" and "all times until the receipt of the property." We assume for the purposes of the first inquiry that the adoption of the "Agreement and Plan of Merger" by Weston shareholders on December 20, 1980 was an adoption of a plan of liquidation. Taxpayer undisputedly owned 99.97 percent of Weston's stock at that time.

The key dispute concerns the effect of the merger and reorganization transactions on December 23, 1980—the date on which taxpayer received the property of its subsidiary. Taxpayer argues that because all of Weston's assets were transferred to Elder, Inc. and all of Weston's stock was cancelled under the merger, taxpayer's ownership of Weston stock was cut off before it received Weston's property. Therefore, taxpayer argues, because taxpayer owned no Weston stock when it subsequently received the property of its subsidiary under the reorganization, it did not continue qualified with respect to stock ownership under §332(b)(1).

The government urges this court to disregard Elder, Inc.'s transitory ownership of Weston by applying the step transaction doctrine in holding that the merger and reorganization "should be collapsed and viewed as a single transaction for tax purposes." The district court agreed and "view(ed) the execution of the two integrated agreements as one transaction which did not effect a bonafide sale of stock and conclude(d), as a matter of law, that Super Market Developers, at all relevant times, owned more than 80 percent of the outstanding shares of Weston. . . ." 720 F. Supp. at 890.

A. The Step Transaction Doctrine

"The step-transaction doctrine developed as part of the broader tax concept that substance should prevail over form." American Potash & Chem. Corp. v. United

States, 399 F.2d 194, 207, 185 Ct. Cl. 161; see also Security Indus. Ins. Co. v. United States, 702 F.2d 1234, 1244 (5th Cir. 1983); Rosenberg, Tax Avoidance and Income Measurement, 87 Mich. L. Rev. 365, 400 (1988) [hereinafter Rosenberg]. Under the step transaction doctrine:

> interrelated yet formally distinct steps in an integrated transaction may not be considered independently of the overall transaction. By thus "linking together all interdependent steps with legal or business significance, rather than taking them in isolation," federal tax liability may be based "on a realistic view of the entire transaction."

Commissioner v. Clark, 489 U.S. 726, 738 (1989) (quoting 1 B. Bittker, Federal Taxation of Income, Estates and Gifts & 4.3.5, p. 4-52 (1981)). . . .

Courts and commentators have identified several tests which are used with varying frequency in determining whether to apply the step transaction doctrine. Most sources identify three tests: see, e.g., *Security Indus.*, 702 F.2d at 1244-45 (identifying the "end result," "interdependence," and "binding commitment" tests); McDonald's Restaurants of Illinois, Inc. v. Commissioner, 688 F.2d 520, 524-25 (7th Cir. 1982) (same); 11 J. Mertens, The Law of Federal Income Taxation, §§43.254-43.256 (1990) (same); Comments, Step Transactions, 24 U. Miami L. Rev. 60, 62-66 (1969) (identifying the "time," "intention," and "interdependency" tests). Others differ: see, e.g., King Enters., Inc. v. United States, 418 F.2d 511, 516 (Ct. Cl. 1969) (identifying "end result" and "interdependence" as the "two basic tests"); Schwartz, Liquidation-Reincorporation: A Sensible Approach Consistent with Congressional Policy, 38 U. Miami L. Rev. 231, 240 n.33 (1984) (same). The "end result" and "interdependence" tests are the most frequently applied. See *Security Indus.*, 702 F.2d at 1244, and Rosenberg, at 409, respectively.

Under the "end result" test, "purportedly separate transactions will be amalgamated into a single transaction when it appears that they were really component parts of a single transaction intended from the outset to be taken for the purpose of reaching the ultimate result." *King Enters.*, 418 F.2d at 516 (quoting Herwitz, Business Planning, 804 (1966)). The "end result" test, like the substance over form principle, is particularly pertinent to cases involving a series of transactions designed and executed as parts of a unitary plan to achieve an intended result. Such plans will be viewed as a whole regardless of whether the effect of so doing is imposition of or relief from taxation. The series of closely related steps in such a plan are merely the means by which to carry out the plan and will not be separated. . . .

The "interdependence test" requires an inquiry as to "whether on a reasonable interpretation of objective facts the steps were so interdependent that the legal relations created by one transaction would have been fruitless without a completion of the series." Paul & Zimet, "Step Transactions," Selected Studies in Federal Taxation 200, 254 (2d Series 1938), quoted in *King Enters.*, 418 F.2d at 516, and *Security Indus.*, 702 F.2d at 1244. The "interdependence test" focuses on the relationship between the steps, rather than on the "end result." *McDonald's Restaurants*, 688 F.2d at 524. Disregarding the tax effects of individual steps under this test is, therefore, "especially proper where . . . it is unlikely that any one step would have been undertaken except in contemplation of the other integrating acts. . . ." Kuper v. Commissioner, 533 F.2d 152, 156 (5th Cir. 1976).

We now consider taxpayer's claim that relevant case law bars the use of step transaction analysis in the context of §332. Taxpayer most heavily relies on Granite Trust Co. v. United States, 238 F.2d 670 (1st Cir. 1956), a taxpayer refund suit involving the liquidation of a corporate subsidiary. In *Granite Trust,* the First Circuit considered whether to allow the taxpayer to avoid the nonrecognition provisions of I.R.C. §112(b)(6) (1939), the predecessor to modern code section 332.

Taxpayer Granite Trust Company (Granite) expected to realize losses upon the liquidation of its wholly owned subsidiary, Building Corp. Granite therefore took two steps to avoid the nonrecognition provisions of §112(b)(6). First, Granite sold 20.5 percent of Building Corp.'s stock in order to circumvent the 80 percent ownership requirement of §112(b)(6). *Id.* at 672. Second, after adopting a liquidation plan, Granite sold twenty shares of stock and donated two shares to charity. *Id.* at 673. The dispositions were intended to circumvent the "second condition" of §112(b)(6), one which was not included in modern code section 332. See *id.* at 672 n.1, 675. That condition allowed recognition of gains or losses where the parent corporation, within a specified time period, disposed of stock in the subsidiary without making countervailing acquisitions. *Id.* at 675. The *Granite Trust* court ruled on the merits only as to the second step, and allowed taxpayer to recognize its loss. See *id.* at 675.

Because *Granite Trust*'s decision in favor of the taxpayer hinged on a provision which is no longer present in the Code, *Granite Trust* is not dispositive in this case. However, to the extent the *Granite Trust* court discussed provisions of §112(b)(6) which are still contained in modern §332, some of its reasoning is persuasive.

Granite prevailed over the government's arguments against its recognition of losses. First, the government advanced the "end-result" test in urging the court to ignore the intermediate steps in Granite Trust's liquidation of Building Corp. *Id.* at 674. The court rejected that argument, stating "the very terms of §112(b)(6) make it evident that it is not an 'end-result' provision, but rather one which prescribes specific conditions for the nonrecognition of realized gains or losses, conditions which, if not strictly met, make the section inapplicable." *Id.* at 675. The court found support in the legislative history of both §112(b)(6) (1939) and §332 (1954), and concluded "that taxpayers can, by taking appropriate steps, render the subsection applicable or inapplicable as they choose, rather than be at the mercy of the Commissioner on an 'end-result' theory." *Id.* at 676. The "interdependence test" was neither argued nor discussed.

Second, the government argued that there were in fact no valid sales made by the taxpayer, "that the sales of stock by [Granite Trust] should be ignored on the ground that they were not bona fide, and that the taxpayer therefore retained 'beneficial ownership.'" *Id.* at 677. . . .

The court ultimately concluded that because the facts "showed legal transactions not fictitious or so lacking in substance as to be anything different from what they purported to be," the sales must be given effect in the administration of §112(b)(6). *Id.* at 678. Therefore, the taxpayer was able to recognize the loss and claim a substantial tax refund.

In the present case, taxpayer asserts that *Granite Trust* and the legislative history discussed therein stand as a complete bar to any application of step transaction analysis in the context of §332. We disagree. As an initial matter, the First Circuit considered only the "end result" formulation of the step transaction doctrine. 238 F.2d at 675. As noted, the "interdependence test" was neither argued nor considered in *Granite Trust.*[7] The legislative history discussed in *Granite Trust* is equally silent as to the "interdependence test." *Id.* at 675-77. Taxpayer fails to appreciate the differences between, and the different functions performed by, the "interdependence" and "end result" tests. As the "interdependence" test addresses the relationship between, and therefore the integrity of, intermediate steps in a complex transaction, its application is not precluded by *Granite Trust*'s conclusion that a narrow focus on a transaction's "end result" is inappropriate in the context of §112(b)(6).

Furthermore, although the First Circuit concluded from the legislative history that "taxpayers can, by taking appropriate steps, render the subsection applicable or inapplicable as they choose," *id.* at 676, we think taxpayer misinterprets that conclusion. The nonrecognition mandated by §332 is not optional at the election of taxpayers within the reach of that section. . . . Steps taken by the taxpayer . . . are not immunized from "the question . . . whether the transaction under scrutiny is in fact what it appears to be in form." Chisholm v. Commissioner, 79 F.2d 14, 15 (2d Cir. 1935). . . .

Appellant also relies on Commissioner v. Day & Zimmermann, Inc., 151 F.2d 517 (3rd Cir. 1945), another case where a taxpayer was able to recognize a loss despite §112(b)(6). Yet the Third Circuit did not address the step transaction doctrine in *Day & Zimmerman.* The court took pains to verify the bona fides of the questioned transaction, and emphasized "there was no understanding of any kind between [the stock purchaser] and Day & Zimmerman by which the latter retained any sort of interest in the securities or proceeds therefrom. . . ." 151 F.2d at 519. After a detailed analysis of the motivations of the actors, the court concluded, "the facts before us so manifestly point to the legitimacy of the . . . purchase of stock that they offer no alternative but to accept that view of the transaction." *Id.*

Granite Trust discussed the significance of *Day & Zimmermann* in terms which indicate the preferred mode of analysis:

> The significant thing in the case is its ultimate rationale that the purported sales of stock to the treasurer were in fact sales, notwithstanding the tax motive which prompted the corporation to enter into the transaction; from which it would seem to be irrelevant how the transfer was arranged, or whether or not it occurred at a public auction or exchange, so long as the beneficial as well as legal title was intended to pass and did pass.

238 F.2d at 676 (emphasis added). Thus *Day & Zimmermann* reaffirms the necessity of determining whether the substance of a transaction matches its form. . . .

B. Business Purpose

. . . The law is unclear as to the relationship between the step transaction doctrine and the business purpose requirement. Our survey of the relevant cases suggests that no firm line delineates the boundary between the two. Most cases applying

7. Taxpayer argues that because the *Granite Trust* transactions "clearly" would have met the interdependence test had it been applied, the court's failure to use that test constitutes proof that it believed all forms of the step transaction doctrine to be inapplicable to §112(b)(6). We decline to indulge in such speculative reasoning.

the step transaction doctrine, far from identifying business purpose as an element whose absence is prerequisite to that application, do not even include discussion of business purpose as a related issue. In some cases, the existence of a business purpose is considered one factor in determining whether form and substance coincide. In others, the lack of business purpose is accepted as reason to apply the step transaction doctrine. We have found no case holding that the existence of a business purpose precludes the application of the step transaction doctrine.

We therefore reject the contention that a valid business purpose bars application of step transaction analysis in this context. "A legitimate business goal does not grant [a] taxpayer carte blanche to subvert Congressionally mandated tax patterns." *Kuper*, 533 F.2d at 158. Moreover, we share the government's skepticism as to the alleged significance of taxpayer's claimed business purpose — that of cashing-out certain minority shareholders who collectively owned no more than 0.03 percent of Super Market Developer's stock. Having thus rejected taxpayer's arguments against the applicability of step transaction analysis, we now apply it to the disputed transaction.

C. Step Transaction Analysis Applied

. . . We are mindful of "the central purpose of the step transaction doctrine: ensuring that the tax consequences of a particular transaction turn on substance rather than form." *Security Indus.*, 702 F.2d at 1245. Under the "interdependence test" we focus primarily on the relationship between the steps, *McDonald's Restaurants*, 688 F.2d at 524, and in so doing inquire whether "'the steps were so interdependent that the legal relations created by one transaction would have been fruitless without a completion of the series.'" *Security Indus.*, 702 F.2d at 1244 (quoting Paul & Zimet, "Step Transactions," in Selected Studies in Federal Taxation 200, 254 (2d Cir. 1938)). We find sufficient evidence of interdependence in the merger and reorganization agreements to answer that question conclusively.

The "Termination" clause included in the merger agreement is itself a strong indication of interdependence. That clause states:

> *Termination.* If the Agreement and Plan of Reorganization dated as of December 11, 1980, which has been entered into between the Surviving Corporation [Elder Food Mart, Inc.] and Weston Investments, Inc., . . . a Missouri corporation, is terminated prior to the Merger Date, then this Agreement of Merger shall simultaneously terminate without further action by the parties hereto.

Under the express terms of the merger agreement, the legal relations it created were entirely contingent on the continuing force of the reorganization agreement. Thus, the merger agreement would bear no fruit unless the two-step series could be completed.

The "Purchase and Sale" clause contained in the plan of reorganization is another manifestation of the relationship between the two steps. It provides:

> The Buyer [Super Market Developers] agrees to purchase from the Seller [Elder, Inc.] and the Seller agrees to sell to the Buyer all of the assets of every kind and description acquired by the Seller pursuant to the Agreement of Merger, except for the shares of common stock of Weston. As part of the consideration to the Seller for the purchase described in this paragraph, the Buyer agrees to assume and discharge all of the

> obligations and liabilities of the Seller which were formerly the obligations and liabilities of the Merging Corporation [Weston] and which became the obligations and liabilities of the Seller pursuant to the Agreement of Merger.

So interdependent were the two steps that the parties who drafted the agreement setting forth the second step did not think it necessary to separately list the assets (valued at over nine million dollars) which were bought and sold, or the obligations and liabilities which were assumed and discharged therein — they simply referenced the first agreement "attached hereto."

We also consider the timing of the steps in assessing their interdependence. Again, that matter was squarely addressed by the parties to the transactions. Under the terms of the reorganization agreement:

> The merger shall become effective at, and the Merger Date shall mean, *for the purpose of this Agreement and the Agreement of Merger,* the close of business on the date when the Agreement of Merger is filed with the Secretary of State of the State of Missouri in accordance with Missouri law. The closing of the transactions provided for herein shall take place on the date (the "Closing Date") which is the same day as the Merger Date *immediately following* the time of effectiveness of the merger.

(Emphasis supplied.) This provision is remarkable for at least two reasons. First, it allows virtually no time to pass between the effectiveness of the two steps which taxpayer vociferously argues are separate transactions. Second, the plan of reorganization actually sets forth the time at which the merger (supposedly a separate transaction controlled by a second agreement) will become effective. . . .

D. Substance Over Form

In giving effect to the substance of the overall transaction, we ignore acts taken in intermediate steps which the taxpayer has itself undone with subsequent steps. We also treat as significant the existence of an understanding between the parties that an interest in the assets transferred would be retained by the taxpayer. See *Granite Trust,* 238 F.2d at 677; *Day,* 151 F.2d at 519. The transaction of December 23, 1980 involved two steps — the "merger" of Weston into Elder, Inc. and the "reorganization" of Super Market Developers and Elder, Inc. Under the first step, Elder, Inc. paid taxpayer $300,000 cash and a promissory note for all of Weston's assets. The shares of minority shareholders were also converted to cash. Under the second step, taxpayer "immediately" bought back the same assets except for Weston Market, paying "an amount equal to the principal amount of the promissory note . . . plus an amount equal to the cash received by the [minority] shareholders." Excepting the exchange of Weston Market for $300,000, all acts were undone: taxpayer got back the other assets; Elder, Inc. got the value of the note back; and taxpayer fully reimbursed Elder, Inc. for cashing out the minority shareholders.

The transparent form of the transaction fails to obscure its obvious substance: Elder, Inc. bought Weston Market for $300,000 cash, and Weston was liquidated. In light of this transactional substance, we reject taxpayer's claim to have disposed of Weston's stock before Weston's assets were distributed. Accordingly, taxpayer did continue qualified with respect to Weston stock ownership in the meaning of §332.

III. Asset Distribution and Liquidation Plan

Taxpayer also argues the requirements of §332 were not met because all of Weston's assets were not transferred to Super Market Developers, and because the shareholders of Weston adopted a plan of merger, rather than a plan of liquidation. This argument is, of course, premised on the transactional form which we have rejected in favor of substance. . . .

Taxpayer argues, however, that because some but not all of Weston's assets were distributed to Super Market Developers, there was no transfer of all the property under the statute. Taxpayer further argues "Elder, Inc. kept the Weston Market subsidiary stock and, unlike a liquidation of Weston, [Super Market Developers] and the other individual shareholders of Weston did not receive stock of all of the subsidiaries owned by Weston." Taxpayer cites no authority in support of its argument.

Given our holding that the step whereby Weston stock was briefly transferred to Elder, Inc. must be disregarded, this argument is rejected. First, there was a resolution authorizing the distribution of Weston's assets in complete cancellation or redemption of all its stock — the shareholders of Weston approved the Plan of Merger by majority vote on December 20, 1980. Under the transactions of December 23, 1980, Weston stock was cancelled or redeemed and its shareholders — both Super Market Developers and the minority shareholders — received payment in distribution of Weston's assets. Second, Elder, Inc. did not "keep" the stock of Weston Market, as taxpayer suggests, because when the form of the transaction is ignored, the substance of the transaction is that Elder, Inc. did not buy Weston stock — it bought Weston Market. . . .

Finally, taxpayer's objection to the alleged "harshness" of the nonrecognition of its tax loss is insufficient to sustain its claim. We must apply the tax effects of the tax code to transactional substance, not form.

Conclusion

As the substance of the disputed transaction met the requirements of I.R.C. §332, no gain or loss shall be recognized. The district court's Order of September 19, 1989 granting summary judgment in favor of the government and denying taxpayer's motion for summary judgment is hereby affirmed.

NOTES

1. *80-percent stock ownership.* Section 332(b)(1) requires (through §1504(a)(2)) that the parent own stock (a) that possesses at least 80 percent of the total voting power of the stock of the subsidiary and (b) that has a value equal to at least 80 percent of the total value of the stock of the subsidiary. See §1504(a)(4) (not counting for purposes of §1504(a)(2) stock that is nonvoting, nonconvertible, and limited and preferred as to dividends). The stock must be held continuously from the date of adoption of a plan of liquidation until the receipt of the property.

If a parent lacks the necessary 80-percent control, can it come within the ambit of §332 by acquiring stock immediately before the liquidation? Compare Rev. Rul.

75-521, 1975-2 C.B. 120 (purchase from other individual shareholders just prior to plan of liquidation upheld), with Rev. Rul. 70-106, 1970-1 C.B. 70 (redemption of minority shareholder in order to boost parent over 80-percent mark failed where redemption was part of the liquidation plan). See also George L. Riggs, Inc. v. Commissioner, 64 T.C. 474 (1975) (redemption of stock to qualify under §332 permitted). Suppose *S*, an individual, owns all the stock of *X* Corp. and *Y* Corp., each of which in turn owns 50 percent of *Z* Corp. If *Z* Corp. is liquidated, can *X* and *Y* rely on §332? Consider the applicability of §318.

If a parent can acquire stock to avail itself of §332, can it dispose of stock to avoid §332? Suppose a parent corporation has a basis of $10,000 in the stock of its wholly owned subsidiary, which owns a single asset with a basis of $12,000 and a fair market value of $8,000. Can the parent sell 21 percent of the subsidiary's stock to an unrelated purchaser in order to recognize the loss on the subsequent liquidation? In Commissioner v. Day & Zimmermann, Inc., 151 F.2d 517 (3d Cir. 1945), a parent sold enough stock in its subsidiary to reduce its ownership below the 80-percent standard. The shares were sold at a public auction to the parent's treasurer, who paid a fair market value price with his own funds. Even though the parent's sole purpose was to avoid §332, the court upheld the transaction. See also Granite Trust Co. v. United States, 238 F.2d 670 (1st Cir. 1956) (contribution of two shares worth $130 to charity allowed parent successfully to avoid §332 even though charity surrendered the shares in liquidation four days after receipt); Priv. Ltr. Rul. 201014002 (Apr. 9, 2010) (applying the principles of *Granite Trust* to find a §331 liquidation).

The freedom to structure a liquidation under either §331 or §332 also gains support from §338. Under that section, if an 80-percent domestic corporate shareholder sells target stock and a §338 election is made for the sale, the shareholder may elect to either recognize or avoid gain or loss on its stock sale. Compare §338(g) with §338(h)(10). The election essentially offers the shareholder the choice between §331 and §332 treatment. See pages 307-313 infra for a further discussion of §338.

Nevertheless, *Associated Wholesale Grocers* sharply reminds taxpayers that the ability to manipulate §332 is not without limitation. Did the court convince you that the earlier decisions in *Granite Trust* and *Day & Zimmermann* were distinguishable, or should the court simply have refused to follow those decisions? Is it significant that in those earlier cases there really was a disposition by the taxpayer, while in *Associated Wholesale Grocers* there was only a transitory disposition followed by an immediate repurchase?

Could the taxpayer have structured the transaction differently to achieve its desired result? Why didn't Super Market Developers first buy out the minority shareholders in Weston and then sell enough stock in Weston to Elder, Inc., to allow Elder, Inc., to receive the Weston Market stock on a liquidation of Weston while all the other assets were distributed to Super Market Developers? Would the sale of Weston stock to Elder, Inc., have been enough to bring Super Market Developers below the 80-percent ownership threshold for purposes of §332? The court determined that the Weston Market stock had a value of $300,000 and that Super Market Developers sold the Weston assets for $9,349,703 and purchased back all the assets of Weston (except Weston Market) for $9,049,703.

For a checklist of information to be submitted to the Service in connection with a request for a ruling on the liquidation of a controlled subsidiary, see Rev. Proc. 90-52, 1990-2 C.B. 626.

2. *Timing of distribution.* For §332 to apply, the liquidation must take place within one of two prescribed time periods. The liquidation must occur either within one taxable year (§332(b)(2)) or within three years after the close of the year during which the first distribution is made (§332(b)(3)). Could the taxpayer in *Associated Wholesale Grocers* have avoided the application of §332 by spreading out the liquidating distributions?

In Cherry-Burrell Corp. v. United States, 367 F.2d 669 (8th Cir. 1966), the court liberally permitted the liquidation to qualify under §332, even though the liquidation was not completed within the requisite time period, because the delay was involuntary. What is the effect of a taxpayer's deliberate effort to avoid the timing requirements? In Service Co. v. Commissioner, 165 F.2d 75 (8th Cir. 1948), the court held that a parent could not intentionally avoid §332 through noncompliance with the recordkeeping requirements of Treas. Regs. §1.332-6. But suppose the parent spreads the subsidiary's distributions out over more than four years. Might the Service try to argue that there was constructive receipt by the parent?

3. *Basis, holding period, and carryovers.* As noted above, the parent's basis in the assets received on liquidation is the subsidiary's basis. §334(b). If a distributing subsidiary recognizes gain on a distribution to a parent corporation in a §332 liquidation (e.g., a distribution to a foreign parent corporation, see §367(e)(2)), a corresponding increase in the distributee's basis occurs under §334(b).

Because a parent corporation determines its basis in a subsidiary asset by taking into account the subsidiary's basis, the parent inherits the subsidiary's holding period for the asset. See §1223(2). In addition, the parent typically inherits the subsidiary's tax attributes under §381(a), including loss carryovers and the earnings and profits account. But see §269(b), discussed at page 468 infra, which can deny the parent a loss carryover under some tax avoidance circumstances.

4. *Minority shareholders.* Because §332 applies only to parent corporations, minority shareholders must look to other provisions — typically, §§331(a) and 1001 — to determine their gain or loss on liquidation.

5. *Treatment of liquidating subsidiary.* Section 332(a) provides tax consequences only to the shareholder-parent on liquidation of a subsidiary. What are the tax consequences to the liquidating subsidiary? Current §337 (not to be confused with former §337) provides that the liquidating corporation recognizes no gain or loss on the distribution to an 80-percent distributee in a §332 liquidation.

If the parent corporation is not taxable on its income, the nonrecognition rule will not apply. In this situation, it makes sense for the subsidiary to recognize gain or loss, because nonrecognition would be tantamount to permanent exclusion. For example, if the parent corporation is fully tax exempt, the liquidating subsidiary must recognize gain or loss in accordance with §336. Section 337(b)(2)(A).

This recognition exception does not apply (so the liquidating subsidiary does not recognize gain or loss) when the property distributed will be used in an unrelated trade or business of the tax-exempt organization. §337(b)(2)(B). Nonrecognition makes sense because the parent would be taxed on gains in connection with such unrelated activities. §§511 and 512. If the property ceases to be used in an unrelated trade or business, the tax-exempt organization will be taxed at that time on the lesser of the built-in gain at the time of liquidation or the difference between fair market value and adjusted basis at the time of cessation. Similarly, if the parent-corporation is a foreign corporation beyond the reach of U.S. federal taxation, a liquidating corporation may be taxed in accordance with §336. §367(e)(2).

Suppose *Y* Corp. has only one class of stock outstanding, of which 80 percent is owned by *X* Corp. and 20 percent by *B*, an individual. If *Y* Corp. liquidates, it recognizes no gain or loss on the property distributed to *X* Corp. But §337 does not apply to a liquidating distribution made to shareholders other than the 80-percent distributee. Under §336(a) and (d)(3), the liquidating corporation recognizes gain but not loss on the distribution of any asset to a minority shareholder. In providing the loss rule in §336(d)(3), Congress presumably intended to prevent a liquidating corporation from selectively recognizing loss and deferring gain by distributing gain property to the corporate parent but loss property to a minority shareholder. Thus, Congress treated a liquidating distribution to minority shareholders like a nonliquidating distribution under §311. This position seems reasonable, because a §332 nontaxable liquidation treats the subsidiary and parent like one corporation in which the minority shareholders, in effect, have their stock redeemed.

Section 337(b) contains another provision affecting the treatment of the liquidating subsidiary. Ordinarily, if a taxpayer transfers appreciated property in satisfaction of a debt, gain must be recognized. See, e.g., United States v. Davis, 370 U.S. 65 (1962). But if the transfer occurs in the context of a §332 liquidation, it might be very difficult to distinguish a taxable transfer from a subsidiary to a parent-creditor to satisfy the outstanding indebtedness from a nontaxable transfer in exchange for stock. Accordingly, §337(b) provides for nonrecognition of gain or loss on a distribution of property to a parent-creditor to satisfy an indebtedness. Section 334(b)(2) provides that the parent takes the subsidiary's basis in that property. But see §1.332-7 (providing that the parent recognizes gain or loss on the debt satisfaction). Cf. §1041 in an unrelated context involving transfers between spouses.

6. *Overlap with reorganization provisions.* For a discussion of the relationship of subsidiary liquidations to reorganizations, see page 394 infra.

PROBLEM

7-2. Individuals *A* and *B* own all the stock of *X* Corp., which runs a factory that produces thermostatic devices. *X* Corp. also owns all the stock of *Y* Corp., which runs two businesses as separate unincorporated divisions. Division 1 produces and sells electricity from solar panels; division 2 produces air conditioners. The primary asset of division 1 is undeveloped land on which the solar panels are situated. The primary asset of division 2 is a factory that produces air conditioners. *P* Corp., owned by individuals *C* and *D*, wants to acquire the assets of division 2. *A* and *B* would like to liquidate *Y* Corp. and operate both the thermostatic device business and solar panel business as unincorporated divisions of *X* Corp.

X Corp.'s basis in the *Y* Corp. stock is $650,000. The division 1 assets of *Y* Corp. have a combined basis of $700,000 and a fair market value of $400,000. The assets of division 2 have a combined basis of $60,000 and a fair market value of approximately $100,000. Consider the tax consequences of the following alternative methods of satisfying the goals of the parties.

a. *X* Corp. liquidates *Y* Corp. and then sells the division 2 assets to *P* Corp.
b. *Y* Corp. distributes the division 1 assets to *X* Corp. and sells the division 2 assets to *P* Corp. *Y* Corp. then liquidates.

c. *Y* Corp. sells all its assets to *P* Corp. for approximately $500,000. *P* Corp. pays cash for the division 2 assets and issues a note for $400,000 for the division 1 assets. The note bears interest at the market rate and is due in 10 years. *X* Corp. then liquidates *Y* Corp. Sometime after *P* Corp.'s acquisition and the liquidation, *X* Corp. purchases the division 1 assets from *P* Corp. for $400,000, payable by a note.
d. *Y* Corp. sells the division 1 assets to *X* Corp. for $400,000 and sells the division 2 assets to *P* Corp. *Y* Corp. then liquidates.
e. *X* Corp. sells to *P* Corp. stock in *Y* Corp. equal to the fair market value of the division 2 assets held by *Y* Corp. *X* Corp. and *P* Corp. then liquidate *Y* Corp., with the division 1 assets distributed to *X* Corp. and the division 2 assets distributed to *P* Corp.
f. *Y* Corp. adopts a plan of liquidation, sells the division 2 assets to *P* Corp. for cash, and then distributes the division 1 assets and the cash, completing the liquidation in 18 months.

8

Integration of the Corporate and Individual Income Taxes

A. THE INCIDENCE AND EFFECTS OF THE CORPORATE TAX

Although corporations are the nominal payors of the corporate income tax, in substance that tax is paid directly or indirectly by individuals. We know this must be true because corporations are fictional entities, and when we speak of a "corporation" we really are using that term as a convenient shorthand for a collection of contracts and legal relationships among shareholders, debt holders, employees, suppliers, and customers. Accordingly, when a tax is levied on a corporation, the burden of that levy is shared by these groups of individuals, with some bearing a greater and others a lesser share of that burden.

No theory tells us precisely how the corporate tax is shared among the various possible groups of individuals. On one hand, it might be the case that the wages paid to employees and the costs paid to suppliers would be the same even if there were no corporate tax. If so, then the corporate tax is borne only by the stockholders and bondholders as well as by the corporation's consumers. On the other hand, the incidence of the corporate tax might lie on the employees alone or, possibly, on the shareholders and customers. Ultimately, this is an empirical question but unfortunately a very complex one. Accordingly, economists can estimate the incidence of the corporate tax only if they make significantly simplifying assumptions.[1] The true incidence of the corporate tax remains to this day a mystery.

If we do not know who bears the burden of the corporate tax, why do we have one? After all, the revenue collected by the corporate tax could be replaced with some alternate levy such as an increased estate and gift tax or individual income tax, the incidence of which may be easier to determine. Presumably the burden of taxation in this country should be fair, and while different people may have different notions of fairness in this context, so long as we do not know who bears the corporate tax, we cannot with confidence assert that its burden is imposed in accordance with *anyone's* concept of fairness.

1 See, e.g., Klein, The Incidence of the Corporation Income Tax: A Lawyer's View of a Problem in Economics, 1965 Wis. L. Rev. 576.

A cynic might suggest that we have a corporate tax precisely because its incidence is unknown. Raising taxes is difficult for politicians: Although most of us may not mind taxes imposed on other people, few of us willingly accept higher taxes imposed on ourselves. Indeed, because most tax increases are imposed on a well-defined group of individuals while the benefits of those tax revenues are spread among the entire electorate, it is easier for opponents of a tax to band together and lobby against an increase than it is for proponents to lobby in favor.

The incidence of the corporate tax is uncertain, so the possible return to voters who choose to fight it may be slight. Accordingly, the financial incentive to lobby against the corporate tax is diminished. Indeed, so long as voters perceive the corporate tax as imposed only on people other than themselves, it offers politicians the opportunity to raise funds seemingly without taking those funds from anyone.

Even without knowing the precise incidence of the corporate tax, we can make some observations. So long as the corporate tax is paid, it is borne by someone; so long as it is borne by someone, the tax system discourages investment in the corporate form. In addition, because of the way in which the corporate tax is implemented, it may encourage some forms of corporate behavior over others. The following excerpts from two Treasury Department reports identify possible distortions in economic behavior caused by imposition of the corporate tax. Latent within the first discussion is the assumption that the corporate tax is borne exclusively by corporate shareholders. This assumption undoubtedly is false to some extent, but it also is likely true to a great extent. As you read the excerpts, you might seek to identify the extent to which their conclusions depend on knowledge of the incidence of the corporate tax.

Integration of the Individual and Corporate Tax Systems: Taxing Business Income Once 3-11

Treasury Department Report 1992

The classical corporate income tax system distorts three economic and financial decisions: (1) whether to invest in noncorporate rather than corporate form, (2) whether to finance investments with debt rather than equity, and (3) whether to retain rather than distribute earnings. Apart from corporate and investor level tax considerations, nontax benefits and costs also influence those decisions. To the extent that the classical tax system distorts the choice of organizational form, financial structure, and dividend policy, economic resources can be misallocated.

. . . In deciding whether to undertake an investment, firms require that the investment provide a sufficient after-tax return to compensate investors. The cost of capital is the pre-tax rate of return that is sufficient to cover operating expenses, taxes, economic depreciation, and the investor's required after-tax rate of return. Thus, the cost of capital depends in part on the return firms must pay to suppliers of debt or equity capital to attract funds. The cost of capital also depends in part on such factors as tax rates, the investment's economic depreciation rate, the capital cost recovery deductions allowed on the investment, the inflation rate, and the source of financing for the investment. Because a higher cost of capital makes certain investments unprofitable, corporate and individual income taxes reduce investment incentives by raising the cost of capital. . . .

Organizational Form

A simple example illustrates the effect of the current corporate tax system on investment decisions. Suppose that an investor requires an after-tax rate of return of 8 percent and the investor's effective tax rate is 20 percent. An equity investment in a noncorporate enterprise must earn a return high enough to pay tax at the investor's rate (20 percent) and still yield the required 8 percent after-tax return.[11] The noncorporate investment must therefore earn a 10 percent pre-tax rate of return (net of depreciation) in order to cover the investor's income taxes and meet the required return ($0.10 \times (1 - 0.20) = 0.08$). However, if the corporate tax rate is 34 percent and the corporation distributes all of its income, the cost of capital of an equity financed investment in the corporate sector in the above example is 15.2 percent. This 15.2 percent pre-tax return yields an 8 percent return after paying both the corporate tax and the investor level tax on dividends ($0.152 \times (1 - 0.34) \times (1 - 0.20) = 0.08$). Since fewer investments can earn the higher required return (15.2 percent as opposed to 10 percent), the corporate tax discourages investment in the corporate sector by raising the cost of capital.

More complex calculations support this result. For example, a Congressional Research Service report estimates, under realistic assumptions, the total effective Federal income tax rate on corporate equity (taking into account both corporate level and shareholder level taxes) to be 48 percent, compared to 28 percent for noncorporate equity. Therefore, some corporations fail to undertake investments that would be profitable if the tax burden on corporate and noncorporate investments were the same. . . .

International comparisons add perspective on the effect of the corporate tax on the U.S. corporate sector. One measure is the ratio of corporate investment to investment in housing, which provides a comparison of resource allocation in different economies. . . . Throughout the period [1976-1989], the United States has had a lower ratio [of corporate gross fixed investment relative to private residential housing investment] than the United Kingdom. Although the U.S. ratio exceeded that for Japan and Australia until the early 1980s, corporate investment relative to housing has tended upwards over the whole period for Japan and Australia while the ratio for the United States has remained fairly stable, except for the 2 years following the Economic Recovery Tax Act of 1981 [when the ratio dropped significantly]. Indeed, for the last 4 years for which data are available, the United States has had essentially the lowest corporate investment per dollar of housing investment of any of the four nations. . . .

Another useful international comparison is the spread between the pre-tax return on corporate investment and the cost of funds in the United States and other countries. This spread, or corporate "tax wedge," generally depends upon the type of asset acquired, the corporate tax rate, the capital recovery allowances, the rate of inflation, and various other country specific factors. Table 1.1 [which is omitted] presents a listing of preliminary [Organisation for Economic Co-operation and Development] calculations of the 1991 corporate tax wedge based on a standard mix of assets and sources of funding for a manufacturer located in several

11. This simple example abstracts from other factors affecting the cost of capital, including: (i) differences between tax and economic depreciation; (ii) differences in tax rates among investors; and (iii) inflation.

OECD member countries. According to these data, the corporate tax wedge in the United States is higher than in France or Germany, is approximately the same as in the U.K., and is lower than in Canada and Japan.

Corporate Capital Structure

Corporations have three alternatives for financing new investments: (1) issuing new equity, (2) using retained earnings, or (3) issuing debt. There can be important nontax benefits and costs of alternative corporate financing arrangements, and the tax system should avoid prejudicing financial decisions.

The current classical corporate tax system discriminates against equity financing of new corporate investment. . . . Because of the two levels of taxation of corporate profits, the cost of equity capital generally exceeds the cost of debt capital. The Congressional Research Service estimates, under realistic assumptions, the total effective Federal income tax rate on corporate debt to be 20 percent, compared with 48 percent for corporate equity. Moreover, the total effective tax rate for debt financed corporate rather than for equity financed corporate investment encourages the use of debt by corporations, assuming nontax factors that affect financing decisions do not change.

If a corporation borrows from an individual to finance an investment, the corporation deducts the interest payments from its taxable income and is therefore not taxed on the investment's pre-tax return to the extent of the interest payments, although the lender is taxable on the interest at the individual tax rate. Consequently, to the extent that corporations finance investment with debt, current law does not distort the choice between investment in the corporate and noncorporate sectors. Using the assumptions in the numerical example set forth under "Organizational Form," above, for a 100 percent debt financed corporate investment, the cost of capital is 10 percent ($0.10 \times (1 - 0.2) = 0.08$, the required rate of return). This cost is well below the 15.2 percent cost of capital for equity financed investments for corporations that distribute income as dividends, and is the same as the cost of capital for a noncorporate investment.

Historical data show U.S. corporate debt to be at relatively high levels by post-war standards, with some, but not all, measures growing at an unusually rapid pace in the 1980s. Because there is no single, universally agreed-upon measure of debt, the discussion below considers trends based on alternative measures.

One group of debt measures focuses on corporate balance sheets: the ratio of debt to total assets. The debt to asset ratio can be computed using either book value (the par value of debt and the historical cost of assets as reported for financial accounting purposes) or market value. . . . This ratio grew from 43 percent in 1948 to 61 percent in 1989. Although the ratio generally increased over the postwar period, it declined sharply beginning in 1975 and continued through the mid 1980s. Following that decrease, the ratio began to rise again and by 1989 had reached a post-war high of 61 percent. In 1989, this book-value debt to asset ratio was more than 17 percentage points higher than in 1980, but only 10 percentage points higher than the pre-1980s peak of 51 percent reached in 1973.

. . . Like the book-value measure, the market-value ratio indicates that corporate debt has generally increased since 1961. . . .

A second measure of leverage focuses on the importance of debt in corporations' sources of additional funds rather than corporations' total outstanding debt. . . . Over the entire postwar period, equity finance was dominant. For nonfinancial corporations, retained earnings and new equity issues accounted for roughly 78 percent of funds raised. Debt provided the balance, divided about equally between private issues (bank loans and private placements) and public issues (bonds). Relative financing patterns changed during the 1980s. While corporations continue to rely heavily on retained earnings, they have sharply adjusted the composition of external finance. Most notably, corporations have undertaken substantial repurchases of equity, financed mainly with debt. . . . The increase in nonfinancial corporate debt during the 1980s was largely matched by a reduction in outstanding equity. [N]onfinancial corporations relied significantly more on internal funds (retained earnings) during the 1980s than was the case for the postwar period as a whole.

Recent evidence suggests that share repurchases have contributed to the increase in corporate debt. Rather than simply replacing dividends, repurchases have been financed primarily by debt, which results in higher interests costs. Increased share repurchases, therefore, account for part of the recent increases in net interest payments, and may be viewed as one method that firms have used to reduce their corporate tax liabilities. [B]y 1990, over one quarter of the interest payments of nonfinancial corporations was attributable to increased share repurchases. . . .

Debt finance may have nontax benefits. Analysts most sanguine about high levels of corporate debt and debt-service burdens typically maintain that the discipline of debt is desirable because it gives lenders indirect means to monitor the activities of managers. This need for supervision owes to the separation between ownership and management that is characteristic of the traditional corporate structure.

A disadvantage of higher debt levels is that they can increase nontax costs of debt, including costs associated with financial distress. Even when corporations avoid formal bankruptcy proceedings, they incur costs when they cannot meet their interest obligations or when debt covenants restrict operating flexibility. The costs include extra demands on executives' time, supply disruptions, declines in customers' confidence, and, frequently, significant legal fees. Corporations therefore must evaluate the tax and nontax benefits of additional debt relative to these costs. Tax-induced distortions in capital structure can entail significant efficiency costs.

Corporate Dividend Distributions

The current system of corporate taxation also may distort a corporation's choice between distributing or retaining earnings and, if amounts are distributed, whether they are paid in the form of a nondividend distribution, such as a share repurchase. Differences in effective tax rates on dividends and retained earnings are significant.

Assessing the efficiency costs of such tax differentials requires an analysis of motives for corporate dividend distributions in the presence of relatively high taxes on such dividends compared to capital gains. This Report assumes that corporate dividends offer special nontax benefits to shareholders that offset their tax disadvantage,[26] and, accordingly, that corporations set dividend payments so that the incremental nontax benefit of dividends paid equals their incremental tax cost. Under this assumption, the amount of dividends paid out is expected to decrease as the tax burden on dividends relative to capital gains increases; empirical studies are consistent with this prediction. Investor level taxes on dividends also raise the cost of capital (and thereby reduce investment) to the extent that corporations pay out earnings as dividends. Thus, under the assumption used in this Report, dividend taxes reduce the payout ratio and real investment incentives.

The growth in share repurchases in the last decade supports this view of the linkage between the corporate tax and corporate dividends. Share repurchases provide a means of distributing corporate earnings with, in many cases, more favorable shareholder level tax treatment than dividend distributions. While a shareholder pays tax on the full amount of a dividend at ordinary income rates, the shareholder generally pays tax on the proceeds of a share repurchase only to the extent they exceed share basis and, in some cases, at a preferential capital gains rate. Share repurchases increased substantially from 1970 to 1990, growing from 1.2 billion (or 5.4 percent of dividends) to 47.9 billion (or 34 percent of dividends), and peaking in 1989 at 65.8 billion (or 47 percent of dividends).

Investing in America's Future: Report of the Department of Treasury on the Economic Effects of Cutting Dividend and Capital Gains Taxes in 2003 (March 14, 2006)

Double Taxation of Corporate Income

The tax system imposes a heavy tax burden on equity-financed corporate investment through the double tax on corporate income. Corporate income from a newly equity-financed project is subject to two layers of tax. First, the corporate tax is paid on earnings at the firm level at a maximum rate of 35 percent. For income distributed as a dividend, the second layer of tax is paid by individual shareholders at a maximum rate of 15 percent. Alternatively, shareholders pay tax at a maximum statutory rate of 15 percent on the appreciation in stock value that arises from corporate earnings that are retained and reinvested in the firm.* The total tax on corporate income is calculated by combining these two layers of tax. For corporate income distributed to shareholders as dividends, the combined tax can be nearly

26. This assumption is controversial, since not all economic models of the effects of taxation on dividend payments maintain that nontax benefits are associated with dividend payments. There are two leading explanations why corporations continue to pay dividends in spite of the greater investor level tax burden on dividends than on capital gains attributable to retained earnings or share repurchases: the "traditional view" and the "new view." The "traditional view" asserts that dividends offer nontax benefits to shareholders that offset their tax [dis]advantage. Accordingly, dividend taxes distort payout decisions and raise the cost of capital. The "new view" assumes that dividend payments offer no nontax advantages to shareholders and that corporations have no alternative to dividends for distributing funds to shareholders. Under this assumption, dividend taxes reduce the value of the firm, but do not affect firms' dividend or investment decisions. This Report adopts the framework suggested by the "traditional view." . . .

* Currently, the maximum individual rate for qualified dividend income and long-term capital gain on stock is 20 percent. — Eds.

45 percent (not counting state and local taxes).[2] For corporate income that is retained by the firm and realized by a shareholder as a capital gain, the combined tax rate can be nearly 40 percent, after accounting for deferral.[3] The double tax on corporate profits affects economic decisions in a number of important ways that may reduce corporate investment, encourage debt finance over equity finance, discourage the payment of dividends, and discourage investment generally.

Economists often use marginal effective tax rates to measure the impact of taxes on investment decisions. Marginal effective tax rates summarize how various provisions in the tax code, including the statutory tax rate, depreciation deductions, interest deductions, deferral of tax liability, and both the individual and corporate levels of tax, affect the after-tax rate of return to a new investment. In other words, marginal effective tax rates estimate the extra share of an investment's economic income needed to cover taxes over its lifetime. In addition to the double taxation of equity-financed corporate investment, many types of investment face uneven tax treatment because of the various ways tax rates, depreciation deductions, deferral of tax, and inflation, interact and lead to different effective tax rates on different types of investment.

Table 1 shows the marginal effective tax rates on different types of investment by type of financing and economic sector for both current law and for the case with increased dividend and capital gains tax rates that would occur if the shareholder tax cuts enacted as part of the 2003 Jobs and Growth Act were allowed to expire.[4] Currently, the overall effective tax rate on an investment is 17.3 percent economy-wide, and 25.5 percent for investment within the business sector. The effective tax rate in the corporate sector is 29.4 percent, nearly 50 percent higher than the effective tax rate for the non-corporate sector because of the double tax on corporate profits. Equity-financed investment in the corporate sector faces an effective tax rate of 39.7 percent, while a debt-financed investment is effectively subsidized at a rate of 2.2 percent.

Table 1. Marginal Effective Tax Rates for Different Types of Investment

Effective Tax Rates (percent)	*Current Law**	*Without Lower Dividends and Capital Gains Tax Rates**
Economy wide	17.3	19.1
Business Sector	25.5	28.1
Corporate	29.4	33.5
Debt financed	(2.2)	(2.2)
Equity financed	39.7	44.2
Non-corporate	20.0	20.0
Owner-occupied housing	3.5	3.5

Source: Department of the Treasury, Office of Tax Analysis.

*The estimates of the effective marginal tax rates under current law and with the expiration of the lower tax rates on dividends and capital gains do not incorporate the deduction for certain production activities enacted as part of the American Jobs Creation Act of 2004.

2. The formula for computing the total tax equals $t_c + (1 - t_c) * t_d$, where t_c is the corporate rate (35 percent) and t_d is the dividend tax rate (15 percent). Without the dividend tax cut, the total rate could be as high as $0.35 + (1 - 0.35) * 0.35 = 58$ percent.

3. The effective tax rate on capital gains is lower than the effective rate on dividends because of the ability to defer the tax on capital gains until realized.

4. In other words, the comparison is between current law marginal effective tax rates assuming that dividend and capital gains cuts are permanent, and the marginal effective tax rates that occur under current law if the dividend and capital gains rates were not in place.

Without the reduction in the double tax on corporate profits enacted as part of the 2003 Jobs and Growth Act, the overall effective marginal tax rate on investment economy wide would be 10 percent higher (i.e., 19.1 percent) than under current law. The effective marginal tax rate for investment in the business sector would also be about 10 percent higher (i.e., increasing to 28.1 percent) than under current law. . . .

Economic Effects of the Dividend Tax Cuts

Effect on Dividend Payouts

The economics literature suggests dividend payments are sensitive to the difference between the effective tax rates on dividends and capital gains. By reducing the distortion in the treatment of dividends and capital gains, the 2003 Jobs and Growth Act should increase dividend payments. One study estimates that dividends will eventually increase by approximately 30 percent.[8] The empirical evidence on actual dividend payments has found that dividend payments have increased significantly as a result of the tax cut.

Several studies indicate that prior to the recent dividend tax cuts, corporations were steadily reducing dividend payments over the past two decades. One study documented that the portion of firms paying cash dividends in their sample fell from 66.5 percent in 1978 to 20.8 percent in 1999.[9] Other studies have found that aggregate payout ratios have been more stable, as the remaining dividend paying firms are large and profitable, but these ratios also declined in the decade preceding the 2003 tax cut.[10] These trends of declining dividends reversed beginning in 2003 at the time the dividend tax cuts were enacted. One study found that the dividend tax cut increased regular dividend payments by publicly traded corporations by approximately 20 percent by the end of the second quarter in 2004.[11] The same study found that the portion of firms paying dividends increased from under 20 percent in 2002 to almost 25 percent by the middle of 2004. Similarly, . . . the percent of firms in the S&P 500 paying dividends declined from 94 percent in 1980 to 70 percent in 2002, but has since increased to 77 percent.

Recent data from Standard and Poor's (S&P) indicate that these dividend increases have continued through 2004 and 2005. Among the approximately 7,000 publicly owned companies that report dividends to S&P, 1,745 reported an increase in dividends in 2004, a 7.2 percent increase over 2003. For the first 9 months of 2005, 1,446 firms reported dividend increases, a 12.4 percent increase from the same period in 2004. In 2004, dividends paid by S&P 500 companies

8. Poterba, James. 2004. "Taxation and Corporate Payout Policy," *American Economic Review* Vol. 94, No. 2, pp. 171-175.

9. Fama, Eugene F., and Kenneth R. French. 2001. "Disappearing Dividends: Changing Firm Characteristics or Lower Propensity to Pay," *Journal of Financial Economics*, 60:3-43.

10. For example, see Gustavo Grullon and Roni Michealy. 2002. "Dividends, Share Repurchases, and the Substitution Hypothesis," *The Journal of Finance*, Vol. LVII, No. 4, pp. 1649-1684.

11. Chetty, Raj, and Emmanuel Saez. 2005. "Dividend Taxes and Corporate Behavior: Evidence from the 2003 Dividend Tax Cut," *Quarterly Journal of Economics*, Vol. CXX, No. 3, pp. 791-833. As with the previous two studies, financial and utility companies are excluded from the sample. The 20 percent figure is likely to increase over time and suggests a faster adjustment than previously estimated by Poterba (2004).

reached a record level of $181 billion (not counting Microsoft's special one-time payout of $32.6 billion), an increase of 13 percent over 2003. In 2005, dividend payments set another record of $203 billion, an increase of 12.4 percent over 2004. Dividend payments by S&P 500 companies were up 36.5 percent in 2005 as compared to 2002.

It is too early to know whether these dividend increases represent a long-term change in corporate payout policies. An important factor is whether firm managers and shareholders believe that the lower tax rate on dividends will remain in place in the future. . . .

NOTES

1. *Market response to the corporate tax.* One might expect that the imposition of a corporate tax would drive the corporate form out of existence. That is, because the corporate tax can be avoided by operating a business in noncorporate form, all businesses would avoid the corporate tax by a simple change in organization. We see, though, that the corporation thrives. How can this be so?

Even though use of the corporate form increases the income taxes levied on a business enterprise, the corporate form may nonetheless be the most efficient choice. First, it is a *familiar* form of organization, and familiarity in this context may allow the organization to raise capital more cheaply than otherwise. For example, one alternative to the corporation is a Massachusetts Business Trust. Because this form of business organization is uncommon outside of the northeastern United States, such a trust may need to educate potential investors before they will be willing to provide funds to the enterprise. This education (in the form of advertising, additional solicitation materials, or whatever) represents an additional cost of capital, a cost of capital that use of the more familiar corporate form would have avoided.

Use of the corporate form can offer other benefits. Many state laws offer benefits to corporations that are unavailable to other business organizations. See, e.g., Commissioner v. Bollinger, page 502 infra, in which state law provides corporations more complete access to capital markets than it does to other potential borrowers. Perhaps most important, corporations offer limited liability for their investors, centralized management, continuity of life for the enterprise without regard to the circumstances (such as death or bankruptcy) of investors, and easy transferability of investment interests (i.e., shares).

In the early 1980s, several large corporations raised the possibility of liquidating and then reforming in partnership form to avoid the imposition of future corporate taxes. In response, Congress enacted §7704 providing that most publicly traded partnerships will be taxed as corporations. As a result, entities that want access to the public capital market cannot avoid taxation as a corporation by changing their form of organization.

2. *Relief from the corporate tax.* Not all corporations are subject to the corporate tax. Certain corporations, called "S corporations," generally pay no tax but instead pass their items of income and deduction through to their shareholders for inclusion on the shareholders' individual returns. For these corporations there is no corporate tax (except to the extent they have income attributable to a prior taxable year when they were not S corporations, see §§1374-1375). Not all corporations are

eligible for S status. S corporations may not have more than 100 shareholders nor may they have a corporate shareholder or a foreign shareholder. §1361(b)(1). In addition, S corporations may not have more than one class of stock outstanding. §1361(b)(1)(D). These and other restrictions limit the feasibility of S corporations in many circumstances. S corporations are discussed further beginning in Chapter 16.

Another form of business organization is the limited liability company. Limited liability companies are much like corporations in that they offer limited liability to their owners just as corporations offer limited liability to their shareholders. In addition, limited liability companies can have centralized management, as do corporations. In essence, a limited liability company is a corporation chartered under a state law that dispenses with the purely formal step of "incorporation." Thus, the state act authorizing the existence of a limited liability company avoids the terms "incorporation," using instead something like "organization" or "formation." Although a limited liability company must file papers equivalent to articles of incorporation, because they are called "articles of organization" or something similar, the company is not in a technical sense a corporation. See page 501 infra.

Under current law, an unincorporated entity with more than one owner can choose to be taxed as either a corporation or a pass-through entity. See Treas. Regs. §301.7701-3(a). If a limited liability company does not choose to be taxed as a corporation (i.e., as a nontransparent entity subject to an entity-level tax) and it has more than one owner, then it will be taxed as a partnership (i.e., treated as a transparent entity). A partnership is not subject to tax at the entity level but instead passes its items of income and deduction through to its owners for inclusion on their individual returns. See Chapter 19 infra. The ability of taxpayers to form limited liability companies under state law, which are transparent for federal income tax purposes, is a self-help method of integration. As described above, though, if interests in such an entity are publicly traded, §7704 provides (with limited exceptions) that the entity will be taxed as a corporation regardless of its characterization under state law.

There are additional self-help methods for taxpayers that are operating in corporate form. Even in the absence of formal relief from the corporate tax, the burden of the tax is lessened to the extent that a corporation can make deductible interest payments.

B. METHODS OF INTEGRATION

Is there a simple way to eliminate the double tax burden imposed on profits earned in corporate form? One might think that simple elimination of the corporate tax would be the ideal solution, but in fact the problem is considerably more difficult. Indeed, if the corporate tax were repealed, then corporate investments would offer a significant tax advantage over noncorporate investments.

In general, the exchange of one investment for another is a taxable transaction. To be sure, exceptions are made for certain like-kind property, see §1031, and for involuntary conversions, see §1033, but for the most part, a taxpayer cannot roll one investment into another without the recognition of gain or loss. If, however, the corporate tax were repealed, then investments made through corporations could be exchanged for other investments without the imposition of tax so long as the rollover was done by the corporation and not by the shareholder.

For example, suppose individual *B* creates *X* Corp. by contributing $10,000. *X* Corp. then purchases rental property, and assuming the corporate tax has been repealed, that rental income goes untaxed until distributed by *X* Corp. Thus, *X* Corp. might invest its rents in some new investment (say, a bond fund), and no tax will yet be due. Had *B* purchased the real estate directly, the rents would have been taxable upon receipt as would the bond interest.

To continue this example, *X* Corp. might eventually sell its rental property at a gain, and if the corporate tax were repealed, then no tax on that gain would be due. *X* Corp. could, for example, take the sale proceeds and invest in some unrelated enterprise, all without the imposition of any tax. Of course, taxes will be imposed on *B* when *X* Corp. eventually makes distributions, but until that time, *B* enjoys a deferral opportunity as compared with noncorporate investments. Of course, if *B* should die while holding the *X* Corp. stock, the liquidation of *X* Corp. into *B*'s estate may escape taxation. See §§1014, 336, and 331.

If we are to make the income tax neutral with respect to the form that an investment takes, simply repealing the corporate income tax will not work. Instead, we need to find some way to integrate the corporate and individual income taxes so that income is taxed once, and only once, and at the proper time, whether earned within or without the corporate structure.

Complete integration of the individual and corporate income taxes is achieved when the taxable events of the corporation are reported directly by the corporation's shareholders as they arise. Taxation of S corporations, discussed more completely beginning in Chapter 16, as well as of partnerships, governed by subchapter K, is an example of such direct reporting. Implementing a system of complete integration, however, is administratively difficult if the number of investors is large and their relationship to the investment complex, as is the case when a corporation has multiple classes of stock outstanding.[2] Two leading scholars have described the debate concerning integration of the corporate and individual income taxes as a clash between idealists and pragmatists.[3]

In considering ways in which the corporate and individual income taxes can be integrated, it is important to keep in mind that appreciation in corporate assets can be realized either by a corporate sale of the assets or by a shareholder sale of stock. To ensure that corporate investments do not offer deferral opportunities, presumably we should tax such appreciation at the earlier of its realization at the corporate and shareholder levels. To avoid the imposition of a corporate double tax, however, we must not tax that realization a second time when recognized at the other level. In the partnership context, these two concerns are addressed by the optional basis adjustment in §743(b). In any proposal to fully integrate the corporate and individual income taxes, some similar mechanism must be included.

The following excerpt offers two possible means of partial integration, that is, of integrating the corporate and individual income taxes with respect to distributed funds only. Under both proposals, undistributed corporate earnings would be subject to a corporate-level tax much as they are today. For a discussion of the

2. See, e.g., Sunley, Corporate Integration: An Economic Perspective, 47 Tax L. Rev. 621, 625 (1992).

3. Break and Pechman, Relationship Between the Corporation and Individual Income Taxes, 28 Natl. Tax J. 341, 341 (1975); see also Yin, Corporate Tax Integration and the Search for the Pragmatic Ideal, 47 Tax L. Rev. 431 (1992).

relative merits of full versus partial integration, see C. McLure, Must Corporate Income Be Taxed Twice 2-12 (1979).

Reporter's Study of Corporate Tax Integration 50-57

American Law Institute (Federal Income Tax Project 1993)

There are three basic methods of accomplishing the results of integration with respect to distributed corporate earnings: shareholder credit, dividend deduction, and split rates.

A. Shareholder Credit Integration

Under the most common form of integration abroad, shareholders would treat dividend payments just as wage earners now treat wage payments subject to withholding. Cash dividends received would be increased (or "grossed up") by the amount of federal income tax paid by the corporations on the earnings distributed as dividends, just as cash wages are increased by amounts withheld. An eligible shareholder would compute the tax at his regular rate on the gross dividend, and a tax credit would be available for the amount of the gross-up, just as a credit is now available for withholding on wages. Complete implementation of this system would result in the corporate tax becoming simply a withholding tax on individual income earned through corporate entities.

Consider a corporation that receives $100 in taxable income and pays $30 in corporate taxes (assuming a 30 percent corporate tax rate). [Consider] how distributions of $70 and $20 of after-tax corporate income would be treated by shareholders whose tax rates were 20 percent or 40 percent. The grossed-up dividend is equal to the cash dividend (i.e., the dividend net of corporate taxes) divided by $1 - c$, where c equals the corporate tax rate. Equivalently, the gross dividend equals the net dividend multiplied by $1/(1 - c)$, which equals 1.429 when the corporate tax rate is 30 percent. If all corporations were taxed at the same rate, a single gross-up rate could be used by all shareholders for all dividends for all corporations. Having included the gross dividend in income, the shareholder applies his personal tax rate (p) and reduces the resulting tax by the shareholder credit attributable to corporate tax payments. The credit is always the cash dividend times $c/1 - c$, which would be .429 if c were 30 percent. Once again, if all corporations paid tax at the same rate, shareholder credits on all dividends could be determined by applying the same rate. As a result of the gross-up and credit, distributed after-tax corporate earnings are taxed to shareholders at a rate of $(p - c)/(1 - c)$, eliminating the separate burden of the corporate tax . . . .

. . . With a $70 distribution after corporate taxes, each shareholder is in the position he would be in if he had earned $100 on individual account [and received a $30 tax credit]; with a $20 cash distribution each shareholder is treated as though $29 of income had been earned on individual account [and a $9 tax credit had been received]. Achieving those results for the 20 percent taxpayer in our example would require that the credit could be used against taxes generated by other income or, if there were no other such taxes, that the credit be refundable. "Shareholder credit integration" along these lines is often referred to abroad as "imputation" because the corporate tax rate is imputed to the shareholder through the gross-up and credit. . . .

As these examples indicate, the shareholder credit leaves the additional cash flow from integration in the hands of shareholders if the corporation does not adjust its dividend payments in response to the shareholder credit. The credit mechanism is therefore sometimes said to be a superior form of integration because the benefits of integration can be denied foreign and tax-exempt shareholders by making the credit nonrefundable to such shareholders.

B. Dividend Deduction

Integration could also be accomplished by permitting a corporate deduction for amounts paid as dividends, just as a deduction is now permitted for amounts paid as interest. The immediate effect of the deduction would be to increase the corporation's cash flow, although some of that benefit might be passed on to its shareholders in the form of increased dividends. In the example illustrated in Table 4, equivalent results would be achieved under a dividend deduction if the cash distribution were increased by 42.0 percent, from \$70 to \$100 and from \$20 to \$29.

As the dividend deduction method initially results in more cash at the corporate level, it is sometimes advocated as a superior form of integration on the ground that one of the purposes of integration is to provide additional incentives for corporate capital formation. On the other hand, one of the method's defects is sometimes said to be its automatic extension of the benefits of integration to tax-exempt and foreign shareholders, as compared with the possibility of denying imputation credits to such investors under shareholder credit integration. Finally, a dividend deduction would be simpler from the perspective of shareholders, because dividends would not be subject to a withholding mechanism, as they would be under imputation.

C. Split Rates

An alternative method of integration is to levy a corporate tax on distributed earnings at a rate below that applied to retained earnings. Complete integration with respect to distributed corporate earnings would require a tax rate of zero on distributions and would be indistinguishable from a full dividend deduction. Less-than-complete integration would involve a tax rate on distributed earnings greater than zero but lower than the rate for retained earnings, making it indistinguishable from a partial deduction for dividends. . . .

D. Equivalence of Integration Methods

The differences in cash flow under the shareholder credit and dividend deduction methods depend on the assumption that there will be no change in the amount of cash dividends paid by corporations in response to integration. To the extent cash dividends were reduced under the shareholder credit or increased under the dividend deduction, precisely the same results could obtain under either alternative. A choice between the two methods thus depends, in part, on the effect of imperfections in the capital markets and on whether those imperfections suggest that it would be better to have the initial increase in cash flow at the shareholder or the corporate level.

If, for enforcement purposes, a withholding tax on dividends was desirable under the dividend deduction method, that withholding tax would serve the same function as an equivalent rate corporate tax under the shareholder credit. The two integration methods would then be equivalent not only in their ultimate effect assuming perfect capital markets, but also in their immediate result. Under the dividend deduction the shareholder would include in income not only the cash dividends received, but also the withholding tax collected by the corporation, which is precisely the same process as that involved in grossing up the dividend under the shareholder credit. Likewise, the corporate tax on distributed earnings plus the withholding tax on distributed earnings under the dividend deduction would equal the corporate tax due under the shareholder credit. . . .

Although the substantive results are the same under the two methods, the difference in labels might cause different legal, regulatory, or accounting consequences. For instance, the amount of the "dividend" paid for various purposes might differ. . . . Because part of the tax is characterized as "withholding" under the dividend deduction, the dividend appears to be the gross amount before withholding; under the shareholder credit, the dividend appears to be the cash distribution, net of corporate taxes. [Any] portion of the tax paid by the corporation might therefore be subject to different treatment by regulatory authorities or under tax treaties because it could be characterized as withholding (and therefore paid on behalf of shareholders) under the dividend deduction, but as a corporate tax under the shareholder credit mechanism.

There may also be differences in public perceptions regarding the two methods of distribution-related integration. One possibility is illustrated by the case of Jacques Chaban-Delmas, who as Prime Minister of France was attacked in the press for paying no personal income taxes for several years in the late 1960s, when no net taxes were due because of offsetting imputation credits. The possibility that high income individuals might appear not to be paying taxes would be less likely under a dividend deduction system, but it would be easier to argue that a corporation paid no or little taxes due to the deduction. . . .

NOTES

1. *The Treasury's proposal.* As the Reporter's study indicates, the shareholder credit method and the dividend deduction method of partially integrating the corporate and individual income taxes are functionally equivalent. And as that study also points out, most of the world currently employs the shareholder credit method of integration. It therefore came as a surprise to many when the Treasury recommended (in a portion of the report not excerpted above) that the United States adopt the dividend deduction method of integration. The reason underlying this recommendation was the Treasury's belief that the shareholder credit method is significantly more complex to implement than the dividend deduction method. This belief seems unusually parochial in light of the substantial international experience to the contrary. Furthermore, adopting a method of integration at odds with what most of the world does presents additional difficulties when a corporation earns profits in one country and then distributes those profits to a shareholder residing in a different country. See generally van Raad, Approaches to Internationally Integrated Taxation of Distributed Corporate Income, 47 Tax L. Rev. 613 (1992).

2. *The role of subchapter S in an integrated tax world.* Professor Martin Ginsburg has suggested that the provisions for S corporations should continue even if Congress adopts a shareholder credit or dividend deduction method of partial integration. Ginsburg, Maintaining Subchapter S in an Integrated Tax World, 47 Tax L. Rev. 665 (1992). Professor Ginsburg justified this proposal in his inimitable fashion as follows:

> Someone once suggested that the one thing that makes subchapter S look really good is subchapter K, the awesomely complex partnership tax provisions. The notion, to which I am much persuaded, is that subchapter S — setting aside the foolish complexity attracted when the S corporation has a subchapter C history — reflects a sensible and successful balance under which the investor surrenders flexibility, precision, and any claim for deduction in excess of her investment, and in exchange is absolved from ever having to master or to be mastered by anything like the partnership provisions' miserable contributed property rules or, worse, the "hot asset" distribution rules.
>
> I suggest that if subchapter K qualifies as an historic justification for subchapter S, general integration under any Treasury or ALI [American Law Institute] prototype will qualify as a modern, new justification for subchapter S. The familiar K-S trade off, flexibility and precision for simplicity, and more particularly the way the Code expresses that tradeoff, appears exceedingly attractive when integration is center stage.

47 Tax L. Rev. at 670.

For a contrasting reply to Professor Ginsberg, see Schenk, Complete Integration in a Partial Integration World, 47 Tax L. Rev. 697 (1992).

3. *Corporate tax integration proposals.* Corporate tax integration proposals continue to make their appearance in tax policy and legislative debates. As noted above, many smaller businesses can help themselves to corporate tax integration by operating as limited liability companies or subchapter S corporations. Some of the "flat tax" reform proposals introduced in Congress in recent years contain integration proposals. For example, Senator Spector introduced the Flat Tax Act of 1999 in the Senate, and Representative Armey introduced similar legislation in the House. Both bills would achieve integration through a flat rate combined with shareholders excluding dividends from their tax base. See also GAO, Report on Impact of Alternative Tax Systems (January 14, 1998); Polito, Dual-Approach Tax Integration: Issues for Discussion, 73 Tax Notes 1213 (1996); Dodge, A Combined Mark-to-Market and Pass-through Corporate-Shareholder Integration Proposal, 50 Tax L. Rev. 265 (1995).

PROBLEMS

8-1. *X* Corp. intends to make a $100,000 investment in a new enterprise. *X* Corp. can raise the funds for this investment by issuing preferred stock or bonds. Assume the investment will yield 12 percent annually for five years and then will be returned to *X* Corp. Assuming the preferred stock can be sold if it offers a 10 percent annual return, while bonds must pay 11 percent annual interest to be marketable, which should *X* Corp. issue? Assume *X* Corp. is in the 33.3- percent tax bracket.

8-2. What effect on interest rates would you expect to see if the individual and corporate taxes were completely integrated? Partially integrated?

9

Taxable Acquisitions

Suppose *X* Corp. holds non-cash assets with a $300,000 basis and a $900,000 fair market value as well as $210,000 in cash. *B*, an individual, owns all the *X* Corp. stock with a $400,000 basis. *P*, an unrelated purchaser, wants to acquire *X* Corp. stock or assets in a fair market value purchase. Among the acquisition choices available are the following:

1. An asset purchase in which either
   a. *X* Corp. sells its assets to *P*, remains in existence, and reinvests the net sales proceeds;
   b. *X* Corp. sells its assets to *P* and then liquidates; or
   c. *X* Corp. liquidates, and *B* sells the former *X* Corp. assets to *P*.
2. A stock purchase in which *P* buys the stock of *X* Corp. from *B* and either
   a. liquidates *X* Corp.; or
   b. continues to hold *X* Corp. as a subsidiary.

These options are not the only ones for *P* and *B*. Under the nontaxable reorganization provisions discussed in Chapter 10, *B* may exchange the *X* Corp. stock for *P* stock, if *P* is a corporation, or for stock in a corporation set up by *P* to consummate the acquisition. Alternatively, *X* may be able to merge into *P* or a subsidiary of *P* in a nontaxable reorganization. The advantage of a nontaxable reorganization is, not surprisingly, that it is nontaxable. If a reorganization can be nontaxable, why would taxpayers ever structure a taxable acquisition? The answer lies in the stringent requirements, imposed by the Code, that a transaction must meet to qualify as a nontaxable reorganization. Often taxpayers cannot meet, or choose not to meet, the requirements. For example, if *B* insists on receiving cash, rather than stock of *P* or of a corporation set up by *P*, the transaction will be treated as a taxable acquisition.

A. ASSET PURCHASE

1. *Overall Tax Treatment*

In the example above, if *P* acquires the non-cash assets from *X* Corp. for $900,000, *X* Corp. must recognize a $600,000 overall gain on the sale ($900,000 amount realized for the non-cash assets less $300,000 basis). If *X* Corp. is taxable at a 35-percent rate, the tax is $210,000, which *X* Corp. may pay with its cash. If *X* Corp. then liquidates, *B* recognizes a $500,000 gain under §§331 and 1001 ($900,000 amount realized less $400,000 basis). If *B* is taxable on the gain at a 20-percent rate (i.e., the maximum rate on long-term capital gain generated by a stock sale), *B* pays tax of $100,000 and ends up with $800,000. *P*'s aggregate basis in the assets purchased is $900,000. §1012. If *P* is a corporation, and *X* merges into *P* in accordance with the state merger laws in a transaction in which *B* receives cash, then the transaction is treated for tax purposes as a sale of the *X* assets followed by a liquidation of *X*. See West Shore Fuel, Inc. v. United States, 598 F.2d 1236 (2d Cir. 1979). See also Rev. Rul. 69-6, 1969-1 C.B. 104 (reaching the same conclusion). Again, *X* Corp. recognizes gain on the sale of its assets, and *B* recognizes gain on *X*'s liquidation.

Suppose *X* Corp. sells the assets to *P* using the installment method of reporting. §453. Generally, when a corporation makes a liquidating distribution of an installment note, the corporation must include any remaining deferred gain in income. §453B. The shareholders generally must treat the fair market value of the note as an amount realized with respect to the stock. The shareholders take a basis in the notes equal to their fair market value. Rev. Rul. 66-280, 1966-2 C.B. 304.

Under an important exception, the shareholders may account for the notes under the installment method. This exception applies when shareholders receive installment obligations arising from a sale or exchange of corporate assets after the adoption of a plan of liquidation if the liquidation is completed within 12 months of the adoption. §453(h). In this circumstance, shareholders recognize gain on the installment notes as they are paid. If the installment obligation arises from the sale of inventory, however, installment reporting is available to shareholders only if substantially all the inventory is sold in bulk to a single purchaser. Also, if depreciable property is sold to a party related to a shareholder (e.g., a relative or a corporation more than 50 percent owned by the shareholder), installment reporting is not available. §453(g).

If, instead of selling its assets to *P* or merging into *P*, *X* Corp. first liquidates, and then *B* sells the former *X* Corp. assets to *P*, the tax consequences are comparable to the asset sale or merger. On the liquidation, *X* Corp. recognizes a gain of $600,000 under §336, incurring a $210,000 tax, which it pays with the available cash.[1] *B* is taxed on the difference between the $900,000 fair market value of the *X* Corp. assets, and *B*'s $400,000 stock basis. After paying taxes of $100,000, which *B* has in a bank account, *B* ends up with the former *X* Corp. assets with a fair market value and basis of $900,000. §301(d). When *B* sells those assets to *P*, *B* recognizes no further gain, and *P* takes an aggregate cost basis of $900,000 in the assets. §1012.

Notice that in both taxable acquisition patterns there are two levels of taxation—corporate-level taxation of *X* Corp. and shareholder-level taxation of *B*. In exchange for these two levels of taxation, *P* acquires the *X* Corp. assets with a stepped-up cost basis. As explained in Section B, it is possible for *P* to acquire *X* Corp. through a stock purchase with only a shareholder-level tax, but if there is no corporate-level tax, *P* does not take a stepped-up basis in the corporate assets.

1. Alternatively, *X* Corp. could liquidate, distributing its assets (including cash) subject to the corporate tax liability.

2. *Allocation of Purchase Price*

Both the seller and the buyer may have an interest in the allocation of the purchase price to the various assets sold. For the seller (whether it is *X* Corp. or *B*), gain or loss and the character of that gain or loss (i.e., capital or ordinary) is determined asset by asset. For the buyer, *P*, the allocation of the $900,000 purchase price determines how much basis is allocated to depreciable assets, inventory, and other nondepreciable assets.

Historically, the parties to a sale often had adverse interests in allocating the purchase price among assets. Sellers wanted to allocate as much of the purchase price as possible to assets yielding tax-favored capital gain, such as land and goodwill. In contrast, buyers benefited from allocating as much as possible to inventory, depreciable property (e.g., buildings, equipment), and amortizable intangibles (e.g., covenants not to compete) to decrease the amount of ordinary income that the buyer would have to recognize in the future. Because of these adverse interests, the Service typically respected negotiated purchase agreements that specifically allocated the purchase price to each asset sold. A buyer and seller were bound by the agreement unless mistake, undue influence, fraud, or distress were shown. See, e.g., Commissioner v. Danielson, 378 F.2d 771 (3d Cir. 1967).

Agreements often contain no specific allocation of purchase price. In these situations the seller and buyer historically have taken inconsistent positions, whipsawing the government. For example, a buyer often allocated a portion of the purchase price to a covenant not to compete, which was amortizable over the life of the covenant (but produced ordinary income to the seller), while the seller wanted to allocate a portion of the purchase price to goodwill, which resulted in capital gain to the seller (but was not amortizable by the buyer). Also, if little or no differential existed between the rate of tax on capital gain and ordinary income, a seller often did not care about the allocation of purchase price and, along with the buyer, "ganged up" on the Service.

Code §1060 now requires a specific method of allocation that must be followed by both seller and buyer in the case of "any applicable asset acquisition." An "applicable asset acquisition" is any transfer (direct or indirect) of assets that constitute a trade or business and with respect to which the transferee's basis in the purchased assets is determined wholly by reference to the consideration paid for the assets (i.e., cost basis). §1060(c). Assets constitute a trade or business if, among other things, goodwill or going concern value could attach to the assets under any circumstances. Treas. Regs. §1.1060-1(b)(2)(i)(B).

Under the regulations, the consideration is allocated among the assets using a residual, seven-tier allocation method described in Treas. Regs §1.338-6(b). (See Treas. Regs. §1.1060-1, which cross-references Treas. Regs. §1.338-6.) The consideration is first reduced by the amount of Class I assets. The remainder is then allocated, in order, among Class II assets, then Class III assets, then Class IV assets, then Class V assets, and then Class VI assets, to the extent of, and in proportion to, the fair market value of the assets in each class. Any residual is allocated to Class VII assets.[2]

2. Thus, if the consideration to be allocated exceeds the aggregate value of all assets other than Class VII assets, each asset other than a Class VII asset is allocated an amount equal to its fair market value. Anything left over (i.e., the residual) is allocated to Class VII assets.

The seven classes of assets are as follows: Class I comprises cash, bank deposits, and similar assets. Class II covers certificates of deposits, U.S. government securities, and readily marketable stock or securities. Class III includes accounts receivable, mortgages, and credit card receivables that arise in the ordinary course of business. Class IV applies to stock in trade or inventory of a taxpayer, Class VI assets include all §197 intangibles except goodwill and going concern value, which make up Class VII. Class V is reserved for all other assets (i.e., assets not in Classes I-IV or Classes VI-VII).

Some allocation disputes under §1060 may be lessened by the enactment of §197, which generally requires 15-year straight-line amortization for all purchased intangibles. This provision is more favorable than prior law with respect to previously unamortizable intangibles such as goodwill. It is less favorable, however, for intangibles that were previously amortizable over shorter periods of time, such as covenants not to compete. The assets covered by §197 include the following: goodwill and going concern value; workforce in place; customer lists and other customer-based intangibles; favorable contracts with suppliers and other supplier-based intangibles; business books and records and any other information base; patents, copyrights, formulas, processes, know-how, designs, and similar items; computer software; franchises, trademarks, and trade names; licenses, permits, and other governmental rights; and covenants not to compete.

Some assets are specifically excluded from §197. These include the following: off-the-shelf intangibles (e.g., computer software sold in stores); interests in tangible property leases (e.g., a lease premium); interests in debt obligations; certain intangibles requiring contingent payments (e.g., payments for a franchise based on productivity); financial interests; interests in land; and fees for professional services (e.g., *INDOPCO*-type expenses). Some intangibles, like patents, copyrights, and covenants not to compete, are covered by §197 only when there is a related acquisition of the assets or, in some cases, the stock of an incorporated business.

Even though both goodwill and a covenant not to compete are amortizable over 15 years under §197, there may be incentives for buyers and sellers of assets to allocate purchase price to goodwill rather than a covenant not to compete. First, the sale of goodwill produces capital gain that may be taxed to an individual at a maximum 20-percent rate; payments for a covenant not to compete may be taxed to an individual at a maximum 39.6-percent rate if the seller is in the highest tax bracket. Second, for financial reporting purposes, goodwill may be amortizable over 40 years, while a covenant not to compete is amortizable over the life of the agreement. Consequently, allocation to goodwill produces higher earnings for financial reporting purposes.

B. STOCK PURCHASE

1. *Individual Purchaser*

Suppose that, instead of purchasing the assets of *X* Corp. either from *X* Corp. or from *B* after *X* Corp. liquidates, *P* purchases the *X* Corp. stock from *B* for $900,000.[3]

3. Although *X* Corp. has assets worth $1,110,000, if *P* anticipates that *X* Corp. will soon either sell its assets or liquidate (thereby recognizing a gain), *P* would not pay more for the *X* Corp. stock than for the purchase of the assets directly. If *P* does not anticipate either the asset sale by, or liquidation of, *X* Corp., *P*

On the sale, *B* recognizes a gain of $500,000, pays tax of $100,000, and ends up with $800,000 of cash. Notice that *P* has acquired *X* Corp. stock, and, compared with the asset purchases described above, there has been only a shareholder-level tax rather than both a shareholder-level and corporate-level tax. But also notice that *P* has acquired (indirectly through *X* Corp.) assets (other than the cash) that still have an aggregate $300,000 basis. In an asset purchase, *P* acquires the *X* Corp. assets with an aggregate basis of $900,000.

If *P*, an individual, wants to step up the basis of the *X* Corp. assets to $900,000, *P* can do so, but only if a corporate-level tax is paid. If, after buying *B*'s *X* Corp. stock, *P* liquidates *X* Corp., under §336 *X* Corp. recognizes a $600,000 gain on the liquidation and incurs a tax liability of $210,000, which is paid with *X* Corp.'s cash. *P* has no gain on the liquidation under §§331 and 1001 because *P*'s basis in the *X* Corp. stock is $900,000, which is equal to the fair market value of the distributed assets. *P*'s aggregate basis in those assets is $900,000. §334(a).

Obtaining a higher basis in *X* Corp.'s assets may benefit *P*. If the assets are depreciable, the depreciation deductions in the aggregate will be larger (although the recovery periods may be longer). Even if the assets are not depreciable, *P* will have less gain or a larger loss deduction if the assets are sold. But *P* can acquire a stepped-up basis in the *X* Corp. assets only if *X* Corp. recognizes a corporate-level gain on the liquidation. Typically, a taxpayer will not trade immediate income recognition for future tax benefits (e.g., larger depreciation deductions), unless those future benefits have a present value exceeding the immediate tax cost of recognition. That equation may favor *P*, however, if *X* Corp. has a net operating loss carryover. Then, a liquidation might provide a higher asset basis at no (or a reduced) immediate tax cost. Also, if *X* Corp.'s assets have bases that exceed fair market value, its liquidation may allow *X* Corp. an immediate loss (and tax benefit) that *P* may gladly trade for a lower fair market value basis in the assets received in the liquidation.

2. *Corporate Purchaser: §338*

If *P*, a corporation (*P* Corp.), merely purchases the *X* Corp. stock from *B* and retains that stock, the tax consequences will be the same as if *P* were an individual. In either case, *X* Corp. recognizes no gain and retains its $300,000 aggregate asset basis, and the purchaser takes a cost basis in the *X* stock. If *P* is an individual and chooses to liquidate *X* Corp., *X* Corp. recognizes gain, and *P* takes stepped-up bases in the *X* assets. §§331, 334(a), 336. In contrast, if *P* is a corporation and liquidates *X* Corp., *X* Corp. recognizes no gain, and *P* Corp. inherits *X* Corp.'s historic asset bases, rather than taking stepped-up bases in the assets. §§332, 334(b), 337. See page 272 supra. *P* Corp. can obtain stepped-up bases in the *X* Corp. assets by purchasing them directly, but can *P* Corp. somehow obtain stepped-up bases if it purchases *B*'s *X* Corp. stock?

Because of §338, it can. Under that section, *P* Corp. may make an election that allows *X* Corp. to take stepped-up bases in its assets, but at the cost of *X* Corp.'s recognizing the gain inherent in its assets. Thus, from a tax standpoint (but not

---

may be willing to pay up to $1,110,000 for *X* Corp. The actual purchase price is a function of the demand for the *X* stock.

necessarily a non-tax business standpoint), *P* Corp. treats its stock purchase in significant ways like an asset purchase.

A corporation may make a §338 election for its acquisition of target corporation stock if, within a 12-month period, it purchases an affiliated interest in target stock. An affiliated interest in target stock is at least 80 percent of the voting power and at least 80 percent (by value) of all target stock (disregarding nonvoting, nonconvertible, preferred stock, limited as to dividends). See §1504(a)(2).

A §338 election affects the target and, depending on its form, the target shareholders. A "regular" §338 election does *not* affect the target shareholders; they recognize gain or loss on the sale under §1001, just as if no election had been made. Their consequences may be affected, however, if a special election is made under §338(h)(10), an election available only in limited circumstances. With the §338(h)(10) election, the selling target shareholders generally are treated as receiving their consideration in liquidation of the target.[4] Thus, if the purchasing corporation acquires the target stock from one corporate shareholder, with a §338(h)(10) election, the shareholder recognizes no gain or loss on its receipt of the sales proceeds. See §332.

With either the regular §338 or §338(h)(10) election, the target corporation is deemed to do the following for federal income tax purposes: First, it is deemed to make a taxable sale of its assets. Next, the target, treated as a newly formed subsidiary of the purchasing corporation, is deemed to purchase those assets. Note, however, that for non-tax purposes, the purchaser simply acquires target stock, and the target does not sell or purchase its assets.

In the example above, if *P* Corp. purchases all *X* Corp. stock and makes a §338 election, *X* Corp. is first deemed to sell all of its assets. Next, *X* Corp. is treated as a newly formed subsidiary of *P* Corp. for federal income tax purposes and is deemed to purchase those assets. In other words, *X* Corp. sells the assets to itself. As a result of this circular fiction, *X* Corp. recognizes a $600,000 gain and takes a $900,000 basis in its non-cash assets.

As the example illustrates, under §338, a purchasing corporation secures a cost basis in the target corporation's assets without liquidating the target. If the purchaser then liquidates the target, §§332, 334, and 337 apply to the liquidation, and the purchaser inherits the target corporation's asset bases, bases that were stepped up because of the deemed asset sale. Thus, §338 makes the form of an acquisition (stock or asset purchase) more tax neutral to the purchasing corporation.

The regular §338 election had more importance before the repeal of the *General Utilities* doctrine. Before the repeal, it was possible under §338 to obtain a fair market value basis with limited corporate-level gain recognition. Since the repeal, corporate-level gain is fully recognized on the deemed sale, and the §338(h)(10) election has assumed the greater prominence.

It often makes sense to make a §338(h)(10) election (if it is available). Suppose, in the example above, that *S* Corp. owns all *X* Corp. stock with a $300,000 basis. If *P* Corp. buys the *X* Corp. stock for $900,000, and no §338 election is made for the

4. That special rule does not apply to "minority" shareholders. For this purpose, minority shareholders are target shareholders other than members of the selling consolidated group, the selling affiliate, or S corporation shareholders. Treas. Regs. §1.338(h)(10)-1(d)(6)(i). Just as with a regular §338 election, a minority shareholder recognizes gain or loss on her sale or exchange of target stock included in the qualified stock purchase. *Id.* at (d)(6)(ii). Further, to the extent a minority shareholder retains target stock, nothing happens. *Id.* at (d)(6)(iii).

purchase, *S* Corp. recognizes a $600,000 gain, but *X* Corp. has no gain and retains its $300,000 aggregate asset basis. If, however, a §338(h)(10) election is made, *S* Corp. recognizes none of its realized gain on the *X* stock sale, while *X* Corp. recognizes a $600,000 gain and takes a $900,000 aggregate asset basis. Thus, in this example, a §338(h)(10) election produces the same corporate-level gain as without a §338 election, but with the added benefit of a $600,000 step up in *X* Corp.'s aggregate asset basis.

If a §338(h)(10) election cannot be made, typically no §338 election is better than a regular §338 election. Under current law, if the regular election is made, *X* Corp. gets a stepped-up basis in its assets only if it recognizes its $600,000 gain, and the *X* shareholders recognize gain or loss on their sales of *X* stock. Generally, *P* Corp. will not make a §338 election to have *X* Corp. recognize gain now in order to obtain a stepped-up basis that may increase tax benefits in the future.

In some situations, though, a regular §338 election may still make sense. Suppose that *X* Corp. has a $300,000 basis in its assets worth $900,000 but also has a net operating loss (NOL) carryforward of $600,000. If *P* Corp. makes a regular §338 election, *X* Corp.'s $600,000 gain will be offset by the NOL, *X* Corp. will incur no tax on the deemed sale, and *X* Corp. will take a $900,000 aggregate basis in its assets on its deemed purchase. The $900,000 basis, rather than a $300,000 basis, may allow larger depreciation deductions, thereby decreasing *X* Corp.'s taxable income (or it may decrease gain or increase deductible loss on a sale of the assets). But even if *X* Corp. has such an NOL, a §338 election may not be advisable: Often *P* Corp. may be able to use *X* Corp.'s NOL after *P* Corp. liquidates *X* Corp., or perhaps *X* Corp. can use its own NOL against future earnings. See §§381 and 382 at page 456 infra. If *X* Corp.'s NOL is about to expire, however, a §338 election may provide a net present-value tax benefit.

A regular §338 election may also be advantageous if *X* Corp. has an aggregate built-in loss in its assets. Then, the deemed sale produces a loss that can be carried back and produce an immediate tax refund.

Finally, a regular §338 election may be useful when *P* Corp. purchases a foreign target corporation with appreciated assets. The gain on the deemed §338 sale is not usually taxable in the United States (or abroad), and the stepped-up basis on the deemed purchase may result in lower U.S. taxation on any eventual distribution from the target to *P* Corp. The higher asset basis may, in turn, result in greater depreciation deductions, lower earnings and profits, and therefore a smaller dividend upon eventual distribution.

NOTES

1. *Qualified stock purchases.* To make a §338 election, the purchasing corporation must acquire an affiliated interest in the target corporation by "purchase." §338(d)(3). "Purchase," as defined in §338(h)(3), generally includes all acquisitions other than "transferred" or "exchanged" basis transactions. For example, acquisitions by gift or in a §351 transaction do not qualify. In addition, a "purchase" does not include an acquisition from a related party. §338(h)(3)(A)(iii).

The affiliated target stock interest must be acquired by purchase within a 12-month acquisition period that begins with the date of the first acquisition by purchase. See §338(h)(1). That purchase of stock is a "qualified stock purchase," and the date on which the affiliated interest is first acquired is the "acquisition date." §338(d)(3) and (h)(1).

2. *Election.* Either the regular §338 or §338(h)(10) election may be made any time on or before the 15th day of the ninth month following the month that includes the acquisition date. The election is irrevocable. See §338(g)(3). The regular election is made exclusively by the purchasing corporation. See generally Treas. Regs. §1.338-3 for the §338 election requirements.

A §338(h)(10) election, however, must be made jointly by the purchasing corporation and target shareholders. Treas. Regs. §1.338(h)(10)-1(c)(3). Note that a §338(h)(10) election can be made only if the purchasing corporation acquires target stock from—

1. A consolidated group that includes the target corporation as a subsidiary on the acquisition date;
2. A domestic corporation that owns an affiliated interest in the target corporation on the acquisition date; or
3. S corporation shareholders, but the target corporation must have been an S corporation immediately before the acquisition date.

See Treas. Regs. §1.338(h)(10)-1(b) and (c)(1).

3. *Target gain or loss on deemed sale.* With a regular §338 election, any gain (or loss) recognized by the target corporation on its deemed asset sale cannot be offset by losses (or gains) of affiliates in either the selling or purchasing groups. §338(h)(9). But see Treas. Regs. §1.338-10(a)(1) and (4) (providing that a deemed sale return may combine all "deemed sale" gains and losses of targets that belonged to the same consolidated group and were acquired by the purchasing corporation on the same acquisition date). However, if a §338(h)(10) election is made for a target that was a subsidiary of a selling consolidated group, the target's gain (or loss) from the deemed sale can be offset by (or offset) other group members' losses (or gains). Treas. Regs. §1.338(h)(10)-1(d)(7).

4. *Operation of §338.* The deemed sale by the target corporation, set forth in §338(a)(1), will trigger gain or loss recognition. In the aggregate, the target assets are deemed sold for the "aggregate deemed sales price" (ADSP). Treas. Regs. §1.338-4. A major component of ADSP is the amount paid by the purchasing corporation for the target stock in the qualified stock purchase. If the purchasing corporation purchases less than all target stock (but still the requisite affiliated interest), the amount paid is proportionately increased to reflect what the payment would have been if all target stock had been purchased. See Treas. Regs. §1.338-4(c)(1).

Return to our example, in which *X* Corp. holds assets with a $300,000 basis and $900,000 fair market value. If *P* Corp. acquires all stock of *X* Corp. for $900,000 and makes the election, a $600,000 gain will be recognized, and *X* Corp.'s basis in its non-cash assets will become $900,000. Suppose *P* Corp. purchases 80 percent of the *X* Corp. stock for $720,000. If the election is made, *X* Corp. will still be deemed to receive $900,000 in the deemed asset sale ($720,000/.8) and thus will still recognize a $600,000 gain.

Turning from the deemed sale to the deemed purchase, we find even more complexity. The rules contained in §338(a)(2) and (b) determine the basis that the target takes in its assets following the deemed purchase. The rules specially deal with two phenomena: First, a purchasing corporation may not purchase all target stock, but the target will still be deemed to sell and purchase all of its assets; second, the purchasing corporation may hold "nonrecently purchased stock." That stock is all target stock held by the purchasing corporation on the acquisition date but not acquired in the qualified stock purchase. §336(b)(6)(B). All other target stock then held by the purchasing corporation is "recently purchased stock." §338(b)(6)(A).

Section 338(b) accounts for those two different types of target stock in computing "adjusted grossed-up basis" (AGUB), which becomes the aggregate basis of the target's assets following the deemed purchase. Treas. Regs. §1.338(b)-5. A major component of AGUB is the sum of the purchasing corporation's basis in recently purchased stock and its basis in nonrecently purchased target stock. If the purchasing corporation holds less than all target stock on the acquisition date, its basis in its recently purchased stock is proportionately increased ("grossed up") for the AGUB computation to reflect what the basis would have been if all remaining target stock not held by the purchaser had been purchased. §338(b)(4).

In our example, there is no nonrecently purchased stock, because all *X* stock held by *P* Corp. was acquired by purchase within the 12-month acquisition period. Section 338(b)(1)(A) and (b)(4) provide that if *P* Corp. pays $900,000 for that stock, *X* Corp.'s aggregate basis in its assets following the deemed purchase will be $900,000, or (*P* Corp.'s basis in the *X* Corp. stock) × 100 percent/100 percent, the same basis as if *P* Corp. had purchased the assets directly. If *P* Corp. acquires 80 percent of the *X* Corp. stock for $720,000, the new basis of the *X* Corp. assets will still be $900,000, or $720,000 (*P* Corp.'s basis in the *X* Corp. stock) × 100 percent/80 percent. Note that the new basis of the *X* Corp. assets is the same regardless of whether *P* Corp. purchases 80 or 100 percent because in either case *X* Corp. will recognize a $600,000 gain.

The complexity increases when nonrecently purchased stock is introduced, because it must be excluded from the gross-up calculation. Suppose in our example that *P* Corp. acquires 80 percent of *X* Corp. stock for $720,000 during the acquisition period and that *P* Corp. holds an additional 8 percent of the *X* Corp. stock (acquired before the acquisition date) with a basis of $20,000 and a fair market value of $72,000 on the acquisition date. The remaining 12 percent of the stock continues to be held by *B*. If *P* Corp. makes a regular §338 election after purchasing 80 percent of the *X* Corp. stock, *X* Corp.'s basis in its assets will equal $848,000, or the grossed-up basis for the recently purchased stock ($828,000 or $720,000 [purchase price of the stock] × 92 percent/80 percent[5]) plus its $20,000 basis in the nonrecently purchased stock. Notice that the basis in the target's assets reflects that $52,000 of appreciation has not been recognized on *P*'s nonrecently purchased *X* Corp. stock.

In the previous example, however, *P* Corp. can elect to fully step up the basis of the target's assets to $900,000 by recognizing gain on the nonrecently purchased stock (i.e., the 8-percent holding). In the example, if *P* Corp. made the gain recognition election, gain would be the difference between the $20,000 basis

5. The numerator in the fraction (92%) equals the percentage of *X* stock by value that is not nonrecently purchased stock and the denominator (80%) equals the percentage of *X* stock by value that is recently purchased stock.

and the $72,000 deemed sales price under §338(b)(3) ($828,000 × 8 percent/92 percent). The effect of this election is to increase the basis for the nonrecently purchased stock to $72,000, which, when added to the $828,000 grossed-up basis, provides a full $900,000 basis. The cost of this additional corporate-level step-up in asset basis is recognition of what otherwise could eventually be shareholder-level gain.

Note that losses are not recognized if a gain recognition election is made for nonrecently purchased stock. Treas. Regs. §1.338-5(d)(3)(iii). Note, as well, that if a §338(h)(10) election is made, a gain recognition election is deemed to have been made for any nonrecently purchased stock. Treas. Regs. §1.338(h)(10)-1(d)(1).

5. *Adjustments for liabilities.* Both the ADSP and the AGUB for the target are increased by the target's liabilities at the beginning of the day after the acquisition date, including any tax liability from the deemed sale. Treas. Regs. §1.338-4(b)(1)(ii); *id.* at (d)(1); Treas. Regs. §1.338-5(b)(1)(iii); *id.* at (e)(1). Suppose in our example that *X* Corp.'s assets have a fair market value of $900,000 but are subject to a liability of $200,000. Further, assume that *P* Corp. purchases all the *X* Corp. stock for $700,000 (i.e., the net value of *X* Corp.). Thus, if *P* Corp. makes a §338 election, *X* Corp. still recognizes a gain of $600,000 and then takes a $900,000 basis in the assets it is deemed to sell to itself. Treas. Regs. §1.338-4(d).

Note that any tax liability resulting from the deemed sale by *X* Corp., if not assumed by the sellers, will be treated as a liability that increases *X* Corp.'s amount realized on the deemed sale (i.e., the aggregate deemed sales price or the ADSP) and its asset basis on its deemed purchase (i.e., the adjusted grossed-up basis or the AGUB). In effect, the tax liability inherent in *X* Corp.'s appreciated assets probably reduced the cash *P* Corp. was willing to pay for the *X* Corp. stock in the same manner as would a mortgage on its assets.

6. *Contingent liabilities.* The ADSP on the target's sale to itself may not initially equal the AGUB on the deemed purchase. For example, there may be some contingent liabilities that are taken into account in determining gain but cannot be immediately reflected in the purchaser's basis. General tax principles determine when liabilities are taken into account to determine a target's gain and its subsequent basis on the deemed sale. Treas. Regs. §1.338-5. Some contingent liabilities that may not initially be reflected in the AGUB may later be reflected when an adjustment is appropriate under general tax principles. Treas. Regs. §1.338-5(b)(2)(ii).

7. *Allocation of the ADSP and AGUB.* In the example above, if *X* Corp. holds only one asset, the allocation of the amount realized and basis (i.e., the ADSP and AGUB) on a deemed §338 sale by *X* Corp. to itself is straightforward. If *X* Corp. holds more than one asset (including intangible assets such as goodwill), those amounts must be allocated among the assets. In general, the regulations require that the seven-tier residual method be used. Treas. Regs. §1.338-6(b). This is the same method of allocation mandated by §1060 on asset sales. See page 305 supra.

Note that there are special rules to allocate the AGUB if the purchasing corporation holds appreciated nonrecently purchased target stock but does not make a gain recognition election. Treas. Regs. §1.338-6(c)(3).

Suppose *P* Corp. purchases the stock of *X* Corp. from *X*'s shareholder, *B*. The stock has a basis of $300,000 and a fair market value of $700,000. *P* Corp. pays $1 million in exchange for the stock and *B*'s covenant not to compete for five years. Under §197, *P* Corp. must amortize the amount paid for the covenant not to compete over the statutory 15-year period rather than the five-year period of the covenant itself. Note that because the *X* Corp. assets carry over their bases when *P* Corp. purchases the *X* Corp. stock from *B*, §197 does not permit *X* Corp. to amortize any amount allocated to goodwill even though *X* Corp.'s assets may be stepped up for accounting purposes. If *P* Corp. makes a §338 election, §197 will apply to *X* Corp.'s deemed sale to itself. Any amount of the purchase price allocated to goodwill or other intangibles will be amortizable over a 15-year period.

8. *Consistency requirements and deemed elections.* Section 338(e) and (f) present purchasing corporations with an all-or-nothing choice regarding §338. If a §338 election is made, it applies not only to the target corporation but also to any "target affiliates" (§338(g)(6)) whose stock is purchased during the "consistency" period. §338(f). The consistency period is the period that spans one year before the acquisition period, the 12-month acquisition period (up to the acquisition date), and one year following the acquisition date. §338(h)(4).

If a purchasing corporation makes a §338 election with respect to a qualified stock purchase of a target corporation, §338(f) deems a §338 election to be made for any qualified stock purchase of a target affiliate within the consistency period. However, the regulations "interpreting" this rule all but eliminate this deemed election. Treas. Regs. §1.338-8(a)(6).

The statute also literally provides that if a purchasing corporation does not make a §338 election, it will be deemed to have made an election if, during the consistency period, it acquires any asset of the target or a target affiliate. §338(e). This deemed election prevents a purchasing corporation from stepping up the basis of desired assets by purchasing them directly while preserving the basis of other assets (and perhaps avoiding gain) by not electing §338. The regulations, however, take a completely different approach.

Instead of deeming a §338 election, the regulations sometimes require the purchasing corporation (or an affiliate) to take a carryover basis in assets acquired from the target (or a lower-tier affiliate). For example, suppose *T* Corp. holds two assets: undeveloped land with a $100,000 basis and a $600,000 fair market value, and a building with a $300,000 basis and a $700,000 fair market value. *T* Corp. is owned by *S* Corp., which has a $200,000 basis in the *T* Corp. stock. *P* Corp. wants to acquire *T* Corp. and to step up the basis of the building (to increase the depreciation deductions) but not that of the undeveloped land. Suppose *P* Corp. buys the building for $700,000 directly from *T* Corp.; six months later, after the $700,000 has been distributed to *T* Corp.'s shareholders or paid as compensation to *T* Corp.'s employees, *P* Corp. buys the *T* Corp. stock from *S* Corp. for $600,000. Under Treas. Regs. §1.338-8(d), if *S* Corp. and *T* Corp. filed consolidated returns, *P* Corp. will take a $300,000 carryover basis in the building.

Despite the literal language of §338(e), the regulations no longer permit the Service to impose a deemed §338 election. Moreover, §338(e) generally only applies when the target is a subsidiary in a consolidated group. Treas. Regs. §1.338-8(a).

PROBLEMS

T Corp., a profitable corporation, has the following assets and liabilities:

Assets	*Basis*	*FMV*
Portfolio of marketable securities	$ 20,000	$ 50,000
Inventory	30,000	200,000
Equipment ($50,000 §1245 recapture)	100,000	150,000
Land	150,000	300,000
Building (no recapture)	175,000	340,000
Patent	25,000	60,000
	$500,000	$1,100,000
Liabilities		
Bank loan		$ 200,000

A owns 50 shares of *T* Corp. stock with a basis of $300,000; *B* owns 40 shares of *T* Corp. stock with a basis of $200,000; *C* owns 10 shares of *T* Corp. stock with a basis of $50,000.

The shareholders of *T* Corp. have decided to sell the business to *P*. Ignoring the quantitative effects of the tax consequences, outline the tax considerations in the following alternatives:

9-1. *P*, an individual, pays $1.2 million to *T* Corp. for all its assets and assumes *T* Corp.'s bank loan. *T* Corp. then liquidates.

9-2. In 9-1, suppose *P* issues a $1.2 million note (bearing appropriate interest).

9-3. In 9-1, suppose *P* pays $1.2 million to the shareholders to purchase their stock in *T* Corp., and *T* Corp. does not liquidate.

9-4. In 9-3, suppose *P* decides to liquidate *T* Corp.

9-5. In 9-3, suppose *P* is a corporation (*P* Corp.). Suppose further that *P* Corp. borrowed the funds used to purchase the stock, thereby generating interest deductions in excess of the income of *P* Corp. and *T* Corp. combined.

9-6. In 9-5, suppose *T* Corp. has a $700,000 NOL that is about to expire.

9-7. In 9-5, suppose that *P* Corp. decides to liquidate *T* Corp.

9-8. Suppose *P* Corp. purchases the land and building from *T* Corp. for $700,000. Eleven months later, *P* Corp. purchases the stock of *T* Corp. for $1 million.

9-9. Suppose *A*, *B*, and *C* own the stock of *H* Corp., the only asset of which is the *T* Corp. stock. *H* Corp. and *T* Corp. file a consolidated return. *H* Corp.'s basis in the *T* Corp. stock is $200,000. *T* Corp. sells its assets to *P* Corp. (which assumes *T* Corp.'s liability) for $1 million and then liquidates. *H* Corp. then liquidates.

9-10. In 9-9, suppose that prior to any asset sale, *T* Corp. liquidates, and then *H* Corp. liquidates. *A*, *B*, and *C* then sell the former *T* Corp. assets to *P* Corp. for $1 million.

9-11. In 9-10, suppose that rather than an asset sale, *P* Corp. purchases the stock of *T* Corp. from *H* Corp. for $1 million.

3. *Section 336(e)*

Section 338 cannot apply if an individual purchases target stock, a result that is more likely an oversight than a deliberate policy choice. However, under recently published regulations, the seller (or sellers) of target stock may be able to make an election under §336(e) to produce results for the target like under §338. If a §336(e) election is made for a target, the target is deemed to sell its assets and typically deemed to purchase its assets as a new corporation, just like under §338.

In fact, the §336(e) regulations employ a structure and principles like those under the §338(h)(10) regulations, using those regulations as a template. Despite many similarities, the two regulatory regimes differ in several ways, however, including the following: First, §338(h)(10) looks to the purchase of a target stock interest, while §336(e) focuses on its disposition. Second, for §338(h)(10) to apply to a non-S corporation target, the target must be a member of the consolidated group or affiliated with a selling domestic corporation on the acquisition date. See Treas. Regs. §1.338(h)(10)-1(b)(2)-(3); *id.* at (c)(1). In contrast, under the §336(e) regulations, a §336(e) election may be made for the target even if it is not affiliated with the selling corporation or a member of the selling consolidated group on the corresponding date. See Treas. Regs. §1.336-2(a); *id.* at (b)(1)(iii)(A); *id.* at (k), example 6.

A §336(e) election can be made only for a qualified stock disposition, which occurs when a domestic corporation or S corporation shareholders dispose of an affiliated interest in a domestic corporation over a 12-month period. Treas. Regs. §1.336-1(b)(6)(i). An affiliated interest in target stock is at least 80 percent of the voting power and at least 80 percent (by value) of all target stock (disregarding nonvoting, nonconvertible, preferred stock, limited as to dividends). See §1504(a)(2).

A §336(e) election affects the target and often affects the target shareholders. The selling target shareholders generally are treated as receiving their consideration in liquidation of the target.[6] As with a §338(h)(10) election, if the purchasers acquire the target stock from one corporate shareholder, the shareholder typically recognizes no gain or loss on the receipt of the sales proceeds. See §332.

If a §336(e) election is made, the target is deemed to do the following for federal income tax purposes. First, it is deemed to make a taxable sale of its assets. Second, it is deemed to purchase those assets, generally as a newly created corporation.[7] As with a §338 election, for non-tax purposes, the purchasers simply acquire target stock and the target does not sell or purchase its assets.

For example, suppose that *P* Corp. owns all *X* stock with a $300,000 basis and $900,000 value and *X* Corp. owns assets with a $300,000 basis and $900,000 value and also has $210,000 in cash. If *P* Corp. sold all of its *X* stock to Fred for $900,000 and made a §336(e) election for the sale, *X* Corp. would be deemed to sell its non-cash assets for $900,000, recognizing a $600,000 gain and then deemed to purchase those assets as a new corporation for $900,000, taking an aggregate $900,000 basis in those assets. Finally, the "old" *X* Corp. is deemed to liquidate into *P* Corp. and typically §332 applies to that deemed liquidation and *P* Corp. succeeds to historic tax attributes of *X* Corp. See §381.

6. If a §336(e) election is made for a transaction to which §355(d)(2) or (e)(2) applies in whole or in part, the target is not deemed to liquidate. Treas. Regs. §1.336-2(b)(2)(i)(*1*).

In addition, note that "minority" shareholders are not deemed to receive a liquidating distribution. For this purpose, minority shareholders are target shareholders other than members of the selling consolidated group, the selling affiliate, or S corporation shareholders. Treas. Regs. §1.336-2(d)(1). A minority shareholder recognizes gain or loss on her sale or exchange of target stock. *Id.* at (d)(2). To the extent a minority shareholder retains target stock, nothing happens. *Id.* at (d)(3).

7. If a §336(e) election is made for a transaction to which §355(d)(2) or (e)(2) applies in whole or in part, the target is not treated as a new corporation in acquiring its assets. Treas. Regs. §1.336-2(g)(1).

Note that if Alice owned all *X* stock and sold that stock to Fred, a §336(e) election could not be made for the sale, unless *X* Corp. was an S corporation. If no §336(e) election were made, Fred could achieve a stepped-up basis in the *X* assets only by liquidating *X* Corp. See §334(a).

NOTES

1. *Qualified stock disposition.* To make a §336(e) election, the seller or sellers must transfer an affiliated interest in the target corporation by disposition. Treas. Regs. §1.336-1(d)(6)(i). Generally, all transferred target stock is transferred by disposition, except for stock transferred in transferred or exchanged basis transactions or to a related party.[8]

The affiliated interest must be sold by disposition within a 12-month disposition period that begins with the first sale, exchange, or distribution included in the qualified stock disposition. See *id.* at (b)(7). That affiliated transfer is a "qualified stock disposition" and the date on which the affiliated interest is first transferred is called the "disposition date." *Id.* at (b)(6)(i) and (8).

If a qualified stock disposition of a target is also a qualified stock purchase for which a §338 election may be made, a §336(e) election generally cannot be made for the disposition. Treas. Regs. §1.336-1(b)(6)(ii)(A).

2. *Election.* Once made, a §336(e) election is irrevocable. Treas. Regs. §1.336-2(a). In certain cases, however, it may be unclear whether a transaction is a qualified stock disposition. In those cases, the appropriate persons may make a "protective" §336(e) election in connection with the transaction. The protective election will be binding if the transaction turns out to be a qualified stock disposition; otherwise, it will have no effect. *Id.* at (j).

Who makes the election depends on whether the seller (or sellers) and target are members of the same consolidated group, the target is an S corporation, or the target is neither an S corporation nor a subsidiary in a consolidated group. If the seller or sellers and target are members of a consolidated group, the sellers and target must enter into a written, binding agreement to make a §336(e) election. *Id.* at (h)(1). The group's common parent must then attach the §336(e) election statement to its timely filed return for the taxable year that includes the disposition date. *Id.*

If the target is neither a member of a consolidated group nor an S corporation, the §336(e) election is made as follows: The seller and target must enter into a written, binding agreement to make a §336(e) election, and the seller and target each must then attach the §336(e) election statement to its timely filed return for the taxable year that includes the disposition date. *Id.* at (h)(2).

Finally, if the target is an S corporation, the election is made as follows: The target and all S corporation shareholders, whether or not they dispose of stock in the qualified stock purchase, must enter into a written, binding agreement to make a §336(e) election. *Id.* at (h)(3). The target must then attach the §336(e) election statement to its timely filed federal income tax return (including extensions) for the taxable year that includes the disposition date. *Id.*

8. *Id.* at (b)(5)(i). Note, however, that if stock is distributed in a §355 transaction in which the full amount of stock gain is recognized under §355(d)(2) or (e)(2), the stock is transferred in a disposition as long as it is transferred to a person who is not a related person. *Id.* at (b)(5)(ii).

3. *Target gain or loss on deemed sale.* If a §336(e) election is made for a target that was a subsidiary of a selling consolidated group, the target's gain (or loss) from the deemed sale can be offset by (or offset) other group members' loss (or gain). See *id.* at (k), example 6.

4. *Operation of §336(e).* If a §336(e) election is made for a qualified stock disposition of the target, the target is deemed to sell its assets, recognizing gain or loss. Generally, the target recognizes its gain or loss on the deemed sale, unless its stock has been distributed by the seller during the 12-month disposition period. In that exceptional case, a fraction of the target's net loss is disallowed, a fraction that broadly reflects the percentage (by value) of the distributed target stock. *Id.* at (b)(1)(i)(B)(*2*)(*i*).

In the aggregate, the target assets are deemed sold for the aggregate deemed asset disposition price (ADADP). *Id.* at (b)(1)(i)(A). A major component of the ADADP is the grossed-up basis of recently disposed target stock, which is the following sum: (i) the amount realized on the sale or exchange of recently disposed target stock plus (ii) the fair market value of recently disposed target stock distributed in the qualified stock disposition.[9] If less than all target stock is recently disposed stock, this component is proportionately increased, dividing the sum in the previous sentence by the percentage of target stock that is recently disposed. *Id.* at (c)(1)(ii).

Return to our example, in which *X* Corp. holds assets with a $300,000 basis and $900,000 value. If Fred purchases all of the *X* Corp. stock from *P* Corp. for $900,000 and *P* Corp. makes a §336(e) election for the disposition, *X* Corp. is deemed to sell its assets for $900,000, recognizing a $600,000 gain. If, instead, Fred purchases only 80 percent of the *X* stock for $720,000, *X* Corp. will still be deemed to sell its assets for $900,000 ($720,000/.8) and thus will still recognize a $600,000 gain.

Turning from the deemed sale to the deemed purchase, the target is deemed to purchase its assets for the adjusted grossed-up basis (AGUB). In computing the AGUB, it is necessary to account for two phenomena: First, the purchasers may not acquire all target stock, but the target will still be deemed to sell and purchase all of its assets; second, a purchaser may hold "nonrecently disposed stock."[10]

The AGUB includes as a major component the sum of the purchasers' aggregate basis in recently disposed and nonrecently disposed target stock. If less than all target stock is held by the purchasers, the basis in recently disposed target stock is increased (grossed-up) as follows: That basis is multiplied by a fraction, the numerator of which equals the percentage (by value) of target stock that is *not* the purchasers' nonrecently disposed target stock and the denominator of which equals the percentage (by value) of target stock that is recently disposed target stock. Treas. Regs. §1.338-5(c).

In our example, there is no nonrecently disposed stock, because *P* Corp. disposes of all *X* stock to Fred in the qualified stock disposition. If Fred pays $900,000 for all *X*

9. Treas. Regs. §1.336-3(b)(1)(i); *id.* at (c)(i). Recently disposed target stock is target stock (i) that is not held by the seller, a member of the seller's consolidated group, or an S corporation shareholder immediately after the disposition date and (ii) that was disposed of by the seller, a member of the seller's consolidated group, or an S corporation shareholder during the 12-month disposition period. Treas. Regs. §1.336-1(b)(17).

10. Treas. Regs. §1.336-4(b); §1.338-5(b)(1). Nonrecently disposed target stock is target stock (i) that is not recently disposed target stock and (ii) that is held on the disposition date by a purchaser or person related to the purchaser who on that date actually and constructively owns at least 10 percent of total voting power or value of target stock. Treas. Regs. §1.336-1(b)(18) (noting that ownership is determined by applying §318(a) (other than §318(a)(4)).

stock, the AGUB and therefore *X* Corp.'s aggregate basis in its assets equals $900,000. If *P* Corp. sells only 80 percent of the *X* stock to Fred for $720,000, retaining a 20-percent block, *X* Corp.'s assets will still have an aggregate $900,000 basis or $720,000 (Fred's basis in his purchased *X* stock) divided by 80 percent.

The result changes when nonrecently disposed target stock is introduced, because it must be excluded from the gross-up calculation. Suppose in our example that during the 12-month disposition period, Mary and Fred, who are unrelated, each acquire 40 percent of *X* Corp. stock for $360,000 and that Fred holds an additional 8 percent of the *X* Corp. stock (acquired before the start of the 12-month disposition period) with a basis of $20,000 and a fair market value of $72,000 on the disposition date. The remaining 12 percent of the stock continues to be held by *P* Corp. If *P* Corp. makes a §336(e) election for the disposition, *X* Corp.'s basis in its assets will equal $848,000, or the grossed-up basis for the recently disposed stock ($828,000 or $720,000 [purchase price of the stock] × 92 percent/80 percent) plus Fred's $20,000 basis in the nonrecently disposed stock. Treas. Regs. §1.336-4(c)(1); Treas. Regs. §1.338-5(c)(1). Note that the basis in the target's assets reflects that $52,000 of appreciation has not been recognized on Fred's nonrecently disposed *X* Corp. stock. Note as well that on the deemed asset sale, *X* Corp. will still recognize a $600,000 gain.

In the previous example, however, Fred may elect to fully step up the basis of the target's assets to $900,000 by recognizing gain on his nonrecently disposed stock (i.e., the 8-percent holding). In the example, if Fred makes the gain recognition election, the gain would be the difference between the $20,000 basis and the $72,000 deemed sales price under §338(b)(3) ($828,000 × 8 percent/92 percent). The effect of this election is to increase the basis for the nonrecently disposed stock to $72,000, which, when added to the $828,000 grossed-up basis, provides a full $900,000 basis. The cost of this additional corporate-level step-up in asset basis is recognition of what otherwise could eventually be shareholder-level gain.

Note that losses are not recognized if a gain recognition election is made for nonrecently disposed stock. Treas. Regs. §1.338-5(d)(3)(iii). Note, as well, that this election is deemed made by any 80-percent purchaser or any person related to the 80-percent purchaser. Treas. Regs. §1.336-4(c)(2). A gain recognition election must actually be made by any other purchaser. *Id.* at (c)(3).

5. *Adjustments for liabilities.* Both the ADADP and the AGUB for the target are increased by the target's liabilities at the beginning of the day after the acquisition date, including any tax liability from the deemed sale. Treas. Regs. §1.336-3(b)(1); §1.336-4(b); §1.338-5(b)(1)(iii); *id.* at (e)(1). Suppose in our example that *X* Corp.'s assets have a fair market value of $900,000 but are subject to a liability of $200,000. Further, assume that Fred purchases all the *X* Corp. stock for $700,000 (i.e., the net value of *X* Corp.). Thus, if *P* Corp. makes a §336(e) election, *X* Corp. still recognizes a gain of $600,000 and then takes a $900,000 basis in the assets it is deemed to sell to itself.

Note that any tax liability resulting from the deemed sale by *X* Corp., if not assumed by the sellers, will be treated as a liability that increases *X* Corp.'s amount realized on the deemed sale (i.e., the ADADP) and its asset basis on its deemed purchase (i.e., the AGUB). In effect, the tax liability inherent in *X* Corp.'s appreciated assets probably reduced the cash Fred was willing to pay for the *X* Corp. stock in the same manner as would a mortgage on its assets.

6. *Contingent liabilities.* The ADADP on the target's sale to itself may not initially equal the AGUB on the deemed purchase. For example, there may be some contingent liabilities that are taken into account in determining gain but cannot be immediately reflected in the purchaser's basis. General tax principles determine when liabilities are taken into account to determine a target's gain and its subsequent basis on the deemed sale. Treas. Regs. §1.336-3(a); Treas. Regs. §1.336-4(a). Some contingent liabilities that may not initially be reflected in the AGUB may later be reflected when an adjustment is appropriate under general tax principles. Treas. Regs. §1.338-5(b)(2)(ii).

7. *Allocation of the ADADP and AGUB.* In the example above, if *X* Corp. holds only one asset, the allocation of the amount realized and basis (i.e., the ADADP and AGUB) on a deemed §336(e) sale by *X* Corp. to itself is straightforward. If *X* Corp. holds more than one asset (including intangible assets such as goodwill), those amounts must be allocated among the assets. In general, the regulations require that the seven-tier residual method be used. Treas. Regs. §1.336-3(a); Treas. Regs. §1.336-4(a); Treas. Regs. §1.338-6(b). This is the same method of allocation mandated by §1060 on asset sales. See page 305 supra.

8. *Consistency rule.* In general, the principles of consistency rules under §338 apply for a qualified stock disposition for which no §336(e) election is made. Treas. Regs. §1.336-1(a)(2). Those principles are modified in one important respect: The asset consistency rules may apply to an asset that is owned immediately after the acquisition and on the disposition date by a person that acquires at least 5 percent of the target stock in the qualified stock disposition or by a person related to such a purchaser, even if that person is not a corporation. *Id.* Thus, the consistency rules for a qualified stock disposition are broader than for a qualified stock purchase.

For example, if *P* Corp. makes a qualified stock disposition of its *X* stock, selling all of that stock to Fred, no §336(e) election is made for the disposition, and Fred also purchases an asset from *X* Corp. before the disposition, Fred may be required to take a carryover basis in that asset under the §336(e) consistency rules. In contrast, if *Y* Corp., Fred's wholly owned corporation, acquired the *X* stock from *P* Corp. in a qualified stock purchase and Fred purchased an asset from *X* Corp. before the acquisition, the §338 consistency rules would *not* apply. It is not clear why the consistency rules under §336(e) are broader than those under §338.

C. BOOTSTRAP ACQUISITIONS

For a discussion of the tax consequences of bootstrap acquisitions in connection with a sale of a business, see page 328 infra.

D. EXPENSES IN CONNECTION WITH AN ACQUISITION

INDOPCO, Inc. v. Commissioner

503 U.S. 79 (1992)

Justice Blackmun delivered the opinion of the court.

In this case we must decide whether certain professional expenses incurred by a target corporation in the course of a friendly takeover are deductible by that corporation as "ordinary and necessary" business expenses under section 162(a) of the federal Internal Revenue Code.

I

. . . Petitioner INDOPCO, Inc., formerly named National Starch and Chemical Corporation and hereinafter referred to as National Starch, is a Delaware corporation that manufactures and sells adhesives, starches, and specialty chemical products. In October 1977, representatives of Unilever United States, Inc., also a Delaware corporation (Unilever), expressed interest in acquiring National Starch, which was one of its suppliers, through a friendly transaction. National Starch at the time had outstanding over 6,563,000 common shares held by approximately 3700 shareholders. The stock was listed on the New York Stock Exchange. Frank and Anna Greenwall were the corporation's largest shareholders and owned approximately 14.5% of the common. The Greenwalls, getting along in years and concerned about their estate plans, indicated that they would transfer their shares to Unilever only if a transaction tax-free for them could be arranged.

Lawyers representing both sides devised a "reverse subsidiary cash merger" that they felt would satisfy the Greenwalls' concerns. Two new entities would be created—National Starch and Chemical Holding Corp. (Holding), a subsidiary of Unilever, and NSC Merger, Inc., a subsidiary of Holding that would have only a transitory existence. In an exchange specifically designed to be tax-free under section 351, Holding would exchange one share of its nonvoting preferred stock for each share of National Starch common that it received from National Starch shareholders. Any National Starch common that was not so exchanged would be converted into cash in a merger of NSC Merger, Inc., into National Starch.

In November 1977, National Starch's directors were formally advised of Unilever's interest and the proposed transaction. At that time, Debevoise, Plimpton, Lyons & Gates, National Starch's counsel, told the directors that under Delaware law they had a fiduciary duty to ensure that the proposed transaction would be fair to the shareholders. National Starch thereupon engaged the investment banking firm of Morgan Stanley & Co., Inc., to evaluate its shares, to render a fairness opinion, and generally to assist in the event of the emergence of a hostile tender offer.

Although Unilever originally had suggested a price between $65 and $70 per share, negotiations resulted in a final offer of $73.50 per share, a figure Morgan Stanley found to be fair. Following approval by National Starch's board and the issuance of a favorable private ruling from the Internal Revenue Service that the transaction would be tax-free under section 351 for those National Starch shareholders who exchanged their stock for Holding preferred, the transaction was consummated in August 1978.[2]

Morgan Stanley charged National Starch a fee of $2,200,000, along with $7,586 for out-of-pocket expenses and $18,000 for legal fees. The Debevoise firm charged

2. Approximately 21% of National Starch common was exchanged for Holding preferred. The remaining 79% was exchanged for cash.

National Starch $490,000, along with $15,069 for out-of-pocket expenses. National Starch also incurred expenses aggregating $150,962 for miscellaneous items — such as accounting, printing, proxy solicitation, and Securities and Exchange Commission fees — in connection with the transaction. No issue is raised as to the propriety or reasonableness of these charges.

On its federal income tax return for its short taxable year ended August 15, 1978, National Starch claimed a deduction for the $2,225,586 paid to Morgan Stanley, but did not deduct the $505,069 paid to Debevoise or the other expenses. Upon audit, the Commissioner of Internal Revenue disallowed the claimed deduction and issued a notice of deficiency. Petitioner sought redetermination in the United States Tax Court, asserting, however, not only the right to deduct the investment banking fees and expenses but, as well, the legal and miscellaneous expenses incurred.

The Tax Court, in an unreviewed decision, ruled that the expenditures were capital in nature and therefore not deductible under section 162(a) in the 1978 return as "ordinary and necessary expenses." National Starch and Chemical Corp. v. Commissioner, 93 T.C. 67 (1989). The court based its holding primarily on the long-term benefits that accrued to National Starch from the Unilever acquisition. *Id.*, at 75. The United States Court of Appeals for the Third Circuit affirmed, upholding the Tax Court's findings that "both Unilever's enormous resources and the possibility of synergy arising from the transaction served the long-term betterment of National Starch." National Starch and Chemical Corp. v. Commissioner, 918 F.2d 426, 432-433 (1990). In so doing, the Court of Appeals rejected National Starch's contention that, because the disputed expenses did not "create or enhance . . . a separate and distinct additional asset," see Commissioner v. Lincoln Savings & Loan Assn., 403 U.S. 345, 354 (1971), they could not be capitalized and therefore were deductible under section 162(a). 918 F.2d, at 428-431. We granted certiorari to resolve a perceived conflict on the issue among the Courts of Appeals.[3]

II

Section 162(a) of the Internal Revenue Code allows the deduction of "all the ordinary and necessary expenses paid or incurred during the taxable year in carrying on any trade or business." In contrast, section 263 of the Code allows no deduction for a capital expenditure — an "amount paid out for new buildings or for permanent improvements or betterments made to increase the value of any property or estate." The primary effect of characterizing a payment as either a business expense or a capital expenditure concerns the timing of the taxpayer's cost recovery: While business expenses are currently deductible, a capital expenditure usually is amortized and depreciated over the life of the relevant asset, or, where no specific

3. Compare the Third Circuit's opinion, 918 F.2d, at 430, with NCNB Corp. v. United States, 684 F.2d 285, 293-294 (C.A.4 1982) (bank expenditures for expansion-related planning reports, feasibility studies, and regulatory applications did not "create or enhance separate and identifiable assets," and therefore were ordinary and necessary expenses under section 162(a)), and Briarcliff Candy Corp. v. Commissioner, 475 F.2d 775, 782 (C.A.2 1973) (suggesting that *Lincoln Savings* "brought about a radical shift in emphasis," making capitalization dependent on whether the expenditure creates or enhances a separate and distinct additional asset). See also Central Texas Savings & Loan Assn. v. United States, 731 F.2d 1181, 1184 (C.A.5 1984) (inquiring whether establishment of new branches "creates a separate and distinct additional asset" so that capitalization is the proper tax treatment).

asset or useful life can be ascertained, is deducted upon dissolution of the enterprise. Through provisions such as these, the Code endeavors to match expenses with the revenues of the taxable period to which they are properly attributable, thereby resulting in a more accurate calculation of net income for tax purposes. See, e.g., Commissioner v. Idaho Power Co., 418 U.S. 1, 16 (1974).

In exploring the relationship between deductions and capital expenditures, this Court has noted the "familiar rule" that "an income tax deduction is a matter of legislative grace and that the burden of clearly showing the right to the claimed deduction is on the taxpayer." Interstate Transit Lines v. Commissioner, 319 U.S. 590, 593 (1943); Deputy v. Du Pont, 308 U.S. 488, 493 (1940); New Colonial Ice Co. v. Helvering, 292 U.S. 435, 440 (1934). The notion that deductions are exceptions to the norm of capitalization finds support in various aspects of the Code. Deductions are specifically enumerated and thus are subject to disallowance in favor of capitalization. See sections 161 and 261. Nondeductible capital expenditures, by contrast, are not exhaustively enumerated in the Code; rather than providing a "complete list of nondeductible expenditures," *Lincoln Savings*, 403 U.S., at 358, section 263 serves as a general means of distinguishing capital expenditures from current expenses. See Commissioner v. Idaho Power Co., 418 U.S., at 16. For these reasons, deductions are strictly construed and allowed only "as there is a clear provision therefor." New Colonial Ice Co. v. Helvering, 292 U.S., at 440; Deputy v. Du Pont, 308 U.S., at 493.

The Court also has examined the interrelationship between the Code's business expense and capital expenditure provisions. In so doing, it has had occasion to parse section 162(a) and explore certain of its requirements. For example, in *Lincoln Savings*, we determined that, to qualify for deduction under section 162(a), "an item must (1) be 'paid or incurred during the taxable year,' (2) be for 'carrying on any trade or business,' (3) be an 'expense,' (4) be a 'necessary' expense, and (5) be an 'ordinary' expense." 403 U.S., at 352. See also Commissioner v. Tellier, 383 U.S. 687, 689 (1966) (the term "necessary" imposes "only the minimal requirement that the expense be 'appropriate and helpful' for 'the development of the taxpayer's business,'" quoting Welch v. Helvering, 290 U.S. 111, 113 (1933)); Deputy v. Du Pont, 308 U.S. 488, 495 (1940) (to qualify as "ordinary," the expense must relate to a transaction "of common or frequent occurrence in the type of business involved"). The Court has recognized, however, that the "decisive distinctions" between current expenses and capital expenditures "are those of degree and not of kind," Welch v. Helvering, 290 U.S., at 114, and that because each case "turns on its special facts," Deputy v. Du Pont, 308 U.S., at 496, the cases sometimes appear difficult to harmonize. See Welch v. Helvering, 290 U.S., at 116.

National Starch contends that the decision in *Lincoln Savings* changed these familiar backdrops and announced an exclusive test for identifying capital expenditures, a test in which "creation or enhancement of an asset" is a prerequisite to capitalization, and deductibility under section 162(a) is the rule rather than the exception. We do not agree, for we conclude that National Starch has overread *Lincoln Savings*.

In *Lincoln Savings*, we were asked to decide whether certain premiums, required by federal statute to be paid by a savings and loan association to the Federal Savings and Loan Insurance Corporation (FSLIC), were ordinary and necessary expenses under section 162(a), as Lincoln Savings argued and the Court of Appeals had held, or capital expenditures under section 263, as the Commissioner contended. We found that the "additional" premiums, the purpose of which was to provide FSLIC with a secondary reserve fund in which each insured institution retained a pro rata interest recoverable in certain situations, "serve to create or enhance for Lincoln what is essentially a separate and distinct additional asset." 403 U.S., at 354. "As an inevitable consequence," we concluded, "the payment is capital in nature and not an expense, let alone an ordinary expense, deductible under section 162(a)." Ibid.

Lincoln Savings stands for the simple proposition that a taxpayer's expenditure that "serves to create or enhance . . . a separate and distinct" asset should be capitalized under section 263. It by no means follows, however, that *only* expenditures that create or enhance separate and distinct assets are to be capitalized under section 263. We had no occasion in *Lincoln Savings* to consider the tax treatment of expenditures that, unlike the additional premiums at issue there, did not create or enhance a specific asset, and thus the case cannot be read to preclude capitalization in other circumstances. In short, *Lincoln Savings* holds that the creation of a separate and distinct asset well may be a sufficient but not a necessary condition to classification as a capital expenditure. See General Bancshares Corp. v. Commissioner, 326 F.2d 712, 716 (C.A.8) (although expenditures may not "result in the acquisition or increase of a corporate asset, . . . these expenditures are not, because of that fact, deductible as ordinary and necessary business expenses"), cert. denied, 379 U.S. 832 (1964).

Nor does our statement in *Lincoln Savings*, 405 U.S., at 354, that "the presence of an ensuing benefit that may have some future aspect is not controlling" prohibit reliance on future benefit as a means of distinguishing an ordinary business expense from a capital expenditure. Although the mere presence of an incidental future benefit — "*some* future aspect" — may not warrant capitalization, a taxpayer's realization of benefits beyond the year in which the expenditure is incurred is undeniably important in determining whether the appropriate tax treatment is immediate deduction or capitalization. See United States v. Mississippi Chemical Corp., 405 U.S. 298, 310 (1972) (expense that "is of value in more than one taxable year" is a nondeductible capital expenditure); Central Texas Savings & Loan Assn. v. United States, 731 F.2d 1181, 1183 (C.A.5 1984) ("While the period of the benefits may not be controlling in all cases, it nonetheless remains a prominent, if not predominant, characteristic of a capital item."). Indeed, the text of the Code's capitalization provision, section 263(a)(1), which refers to "permanent improvements or betterments," itself envisions an inquiry into the duration and extent of the benefits realized by the taxpayer.

III

In applying the foregoing principles to the specific expenditures at issue in this case, we conclude that National Starch has not demonstrated that the investment banking, legal, and other costs it incurred in connection with Unilever's acquisition of its shares are deductible as ordinary and necessary business expenses under section 162(a).

Although petitioner attempts to dismiss the benefits that accrued to National Starch from the Unilever acquisition as "entirely speculative" or "merely incidental," the Tax Court's and the Court of Appeals' findings that the transaction produced significant benefits to National Starch that extended beyond the tax year in question are amply supported by the record. For example, in commenting on the merger with Unilever, National Starch's 1978 "Progress Report" observed that the company would "benefit greatly from the availability of Unilever's enormous resources, especially in the area of basic technology." App. 43. See also *id.*, at 46 (Unilever "provides new opportunities and resources"). Morgan Stanley's report to the National Starch board concerning the fairness to shareholders of a possible business combination with Unilever noted that National Starch management "feels that some synergy may exist with the Unilever organization given a) the nature of the Unilever chemical, paper, plastics and packaging operations . . . and b) the strong consumer products orientation of Unilever United States, Inc." *Id.*, at 77-78.

In addition to these anticipated resource-related benefits, National Starch obtained benefits through its transformation from a publicly held, freestanding corporation into a wholly owned subsidiary of Unilever. The Court of Appeals noted that National Starch management viewed the transaction as "swapping approximately 3500 shareholders for one." 918 F.2d, at 427; see also App. 223. Following Unilever's acquisition of National Starch's outstanding shares, National Starch was no longer subject to what even it terms the "substantial" shareholder-relations expenses a publicly traded corporation incurs, including reporting and disclosure obligations, proxy battles, and derivative suits. The acquisition also allowed National Starch, in the interests of administrative convenience and simplicity, to eliminate previously authorized but unissued shares of preferred and to reduce the total number of authorized shares of common from 8,000,000 to 1,000. See 93 T.C., at 74.

Courts long have recognized that expenses such as these, "'incurred for the purpose of changing the corporate structure for the benefit of future operations are not ordinary and necessary business expenses.'" General Bancshares Corp. v. Commissioner, 326 F.2d, at 715 (quoting Farmers Union Corp. v. Commissioner, 300 F.2d 197, 200 (C.A.9), cert. denied, 371 U.S. 861 (1962)). See also B. Bittker & J. Eustice, Federal Income Taxation of Corporations and Shareholders, pp. 5-33 to 5-36 (5th ed. 1987) (describing "well-established rule" that expenses incurred in reorganizing or restructuring corporate entity are not deductible under section 162(a)). Deductions for professional expenses thus have been disallowed in a wide variety of cases concerning changes in corporate structure.[7] Although support for these decisions can be found in the specific terms of section 162(a), which require that deductible expenses be "ordinary and necessary" and incurred "in carrying on any trade or business," courts more frequently have characterized an expenditure as capital in nature because "the purpose for which the expenditure is made has to do with the corporation's operations and betterment, sometimes with a continuing capital asset, for the duration of its existence or for the indefinite future or for a time somewhat longer than the current taxable year." General Bancshares

7. See, e.g., McCrory Corp. v. United States, 651 F.2d 828 (C.A.2 1981) (statutory merger under 26 U.S.C. section 368(a)(1)(A)); Bilar Tool & Die Corp. v. Commissioner, 530 F.2d 708 (C.A.6 1976) (division of corporation into two parts); E.I. du Pont de Nemours & Co. v. United States, 432 F.2d 1052 (C.A.3 1970) (creation of new subsidiary to hold assets of prior joint venture); General Bancshares Corp. v. Commissioner, 326 F.2d 712, 715 (C.A.8) (stock dividends), cert. denied, 379 U.S. 832 (1964); Mills Estate, Inc. v. Commissioner, 206 F.2d 244 (C.A.2 1953) (recapitalization).

Corp. v. Commissioner, 326 F.2d, at 715. The rationale behind these decisions applies equally to the professional charges at issue in this case.

IV

The expenses that National Starch incurred in Unilever's friendly takeover do not qualify for deduction as "ordinary and necessary" business expenses under section 162(a). The fact that the expenditures do not create or enhance a separate and distinct additional asset is not controlling; the acquisition-related expenses bear the indicia of capital expenditures and are to be treated as such.

The judgment of the Court of Appeals is affirmed.

It is so ordered.

NOTES

1. *Form of the transaction.* This transaction was structured as a taxable reverse subsidiary (or triangular) merger. In some cases, a reverse subsidiary merger can be tax free to the participants. See page 385 infra. If this had been a tax-free reverse subsidiary merger, the shareholders of National Starch would have exchanged their stock for stock in Holding when NSC Merger merged into National Starch. Then, former National Starch shareholders, along with Unilever, would have owned stock of Holding, which in turn would have owned National Starch. Shareholders owning 79 percent of the National Starch stock, however, apparently wanted cash rather than Holding stock. If the parties attempted a tax-free reverse subsidiary merger in which shareholders of 79 percent of the National Starch stock received cash, all the shareholders would have been taxable, including those that exchanged 21 percent of the National Starch stock for Holding Stock.

To secure tax-free treatment for the 21 percent exchanging stock for stock, the parties agreed to a two-step transaction. First, Unilever and those National Starch shareholders desiring a stock-for-stock exchange formed Holding, with Unilever receiving voting common stock in exchange for the cash it transferred, and National Starch shareholders receiving nonvoting preferred stock in exchange for their National Starch stock. This transaction qualified under §351, providing nonrecognition for those National Starch shareholders making the exchange. See Rev. Rul. 84-71, 1984-1 C.B. 106 (confirming that result). Then, the remaining National Starch shareholders received cash for their stock when NSC Merger, Inc. merged into National Stock. This part of the transaction was treated as a redemption of the shareholders of National Starch. Rev. Rul. 78-250, 1978-1 C.B. 83. Each of these shareholders likely was taxable on the difference between her adjusted basis in the National Starch stock and the cash received. Before undertaking this two-step transaction, the parties requested and received a private letter ruling from the Service. See Priv. Ltr. Rul. 7839060 (June 28, 1978).

2. *Regulatory response to INDOPCO.* Concerned that *INDOPCO* created more uncertainty than it resolved, Treasury issued regulations to deal with amounts paid to facilitate a capital restructuring or acquisition of a trade or business. See Treas. Regs. §1.263-5. Among other things, the regulations may apply to costs

related to friendly takeovers, hostile takeovers, and defenses to hostile takeovers (e.g., seeking a white knight).

The regulations require a taxpayer to capitalize an amount paid to "facilitate" 10 types of transactions, including the following:

(i) An acquisition of a trade or business (whether the taxpayer is the acquirer or target);
(ii) An acquisition of an ownership interest in the taxpayer by someone other than the taxpayer;
(iii) An acquisition by the taxpayer of an ownership interest in a business entity if the taxpayer and business entity are related immediately after the acquisition;
(iv) A stock issuance; or
(v) A borrowing.

Treas. Regs. §1.263(a)-5(a). See also Treas. Regs. §1.263(a)-4(c) (for rules relating to the capitalization of costs related to the taxpayer's acquisition of an ownership interest in a business entity generally); *id.* at (e) (for rules relating to the capitalization of transaction costs). A cost "facilitates" a transaction "if it is paid in the process of investigating or otherwise pursuing the transaction." Treas. Regs. §1.263(a)-5(b)(1). But see *id.* at (d)(1) (providing as a simplifying convention that a taxpayer is not required to capitalize employee compensation, overhead, and certain de minimis costs). See also *id.* at (c)(6) (providing that an amount paid to integrate the business operations of a target with the acquirer does not facilitate a transaction).

Note that the taxpayer is generally not required to capitalize costs incurred at a preliminary stage of a covered transaction. Those costs must relate to activities performed before the earlier of the date that—

(i) Representatives of the acquirer and target execute a letter of intent, exclusivity agreement, or similar written document; or
(ii) The taxpayer's board of directors approve the material terms of the transaction, as tentatively agreed to by representatives of the acquirer and target.

Id. at (e)(1) (providing additional rules for noncorporate taxpayers). But see *id.* at (e)(2) (for certain "preliminary" costs that must be capitalized, including the amount paid (i) to secure an appraisal or fairness opinion, (ii) to structure the transaction, and (iii) to prepare and review documents to effectuate the transaction). A covered transaction includes the taxable acquisition of the assets of a trade or business or of an ownership interest in a business entity. *Id.* at (e)(3).

3. *Friendly takeovers.* If stock or assets of a target corporation are acquired in a friendly takeover, the target must capitalize any amount paid to facilitate the transaction. *Id.* at (l) (example 9) (for the target). The regulations require capitalization even if the transaction provides no discernible long-term benefits to the target.

Note that if a takeover results in the target's capitalization of expenses and the acquirer purchases target stock, a §338 election may eliminate the impact of capitalization. See page 307 supra. Under the election, the capitalized expenditures should either be added to the basis of the assets deemed sold or reduce the deemed sales price.

4. *Hostile takeovers.* Some, but not all, of a target corporation's costs to defend against a hostile takeover may be capitalized. For example, the following target costs must be capitalized: amounts paid to investigate and complete a "defensive" recapitalization, any amount paid for a fairness opinion on the prospective hostile takeover, and any amount paid to conduct due diligence following the preliminary stage of any proposed acquisition by a white knight. *Id.* (example 11(iv) and (v) and example 12(ii)). In contrast, the following target costs are not capitalized: legal fees paid to seek an injunction against a prospective hostile takeover, investment banking fees paid to search for a white knight, and any amount paid to conduct due diligence during the preliminary stage of any proposed acquisition by a white knight. Treas. Regs. §1.263(a)-5(l) (example 11(ii) and (iii) and example 12(ii)).

If the target corporation is not required to capitalize its costs to defend against a hostile takeover, those costs may be deductible. By analogy, for example, expenses incurred by a corporation to defend itself in a proxy contest are deductible. See, e.g., Rev. Rul. 67-1, 1967-1 C.B. 28. But see Treas. Regs. §1.212-1(k) (expenses to defend title to property must be capitalized). In other cases, corporate expenditures to defend the corporation are deductible. See, e.g., Dolese v. United States, 605 F.2d 1146 (10th Cir. 1979) (corporate expenses incurred in a divorce proceeding).

Note that a target may pursue several defensive strategies before consummating one strategy and abandoning the rest. If an abandoned strategy and the consummated strategy are not mutually exclusive,[11] the target may deduct the capitalized costs of the abandoned strategy under §165(a). *Id.* at (c)(8); *id.* at (l) (example 3(iii)). See A.E. Staley Manufacturing Co. v. Commissioner, 119 F.3d 482 (7th Cir. 1997) (fees paid in an unsuccessful effort to defeat a hostile tender offer deductible as an abandonment loss). See also Rev. Rul. 73-580, 1973-2 C.B. 86.

If, however, those strategies are mutually exclusive, the cost of the abandoned strategy is deemed to facilitate the consummated strategy. Treas. Regs. §1.263(a)-5(c)(8). In that case, that cost is added to the capitalized cost of the consummated strategy. By way of illustration, assume that *T* Corp. initially resists a takeover attempt by *H* Corp. *T* Corp. pursues a white knight, *W* Corp., and the two corporations execute a letter of intent. Later, *H* Corp. sweetens its offer to *T* Corp. convincing *T* Corp. to terminate the *W* Corp. deal. To do so, however, *T* Corp. must pay *W* Corp. a $10 million fee. Because *T* Corp. could not be acquired by both *H* Corp. and *W* Corp., the two acquisitions are mutually exclusive, and *T* Corp. must capitalize its $10 million termination payment as a cost to facilitate its acquisition by *H* Corp. See *id.* at (l) (example 13) (illustrating that case).

5. *Loan fees.* Most acquisitions are financed with debt. For the purchaser, the cost of obtaining debt financing (such as fees for negotiating the loan and drafting loan documents and commitment fees) must be capitalized. *Id.* at (a)(9). Because that cost facilitates the borrowing but not the acquisition, the cost is amortized over the term of the loan. Rev. Rul. 70-359, 1970-2 C.B. 103; Rev. Rul. 70-360, 1970-2 C.B. 103. See also §1.263(a)-5(c)(1) (providing that a cost to facilitate a borrowing does not facilitate another transaction); *id.* at (l) (example 2) (illustrating that rule).

11. Abandoned and consummated strategies are not mutually exclusive if both strategies could have been completed at the same time. See *id.* at (l) (example 14).

6. *Organizational expenses.* A new corporation can deduct up to $5,000 of its organizational expenses when it begins business and can amortize any remaining organizational expenses over the subsequent 180 months. §248.

E. CORPORATE ACQUISITIONS AND THE USE OF DEBT

Joint Committee on Taxation, Federal Income Tax Aspects of Corporate Financial Structures

101st Cong., 1st Sess. (Jan. 18, 1989)

III. Examples of Transactions That Increase Debt or Reduce Equity, and Tax Consequences

There are various transactions which can increase the debt of a corporation or reduce its equity. The discussion below describes broad categories of these transactions and uses examples to illustrate their tax consequences. The examples assume that no restrictions on interest deductions or other tax benefits stemming from interest expenses apply. In many cases, however, such limitations are applicable. . . .

Although there are significant tax reasons which may lead a corporation to engage in these transactions, such transactions may also be motivated by reasons apart from Federal income tax considerations. For example, such transactions may be undertaken to increase the value of a corporation's stock, to enhance earnings per share calculations, to concentrate common stock holdings, to create treasury stock, as a defensive maneuver to ward off a takeover, or for other reasons. . . .

C. Acquisitions including leveraged buyouts

The acquisition of one corporation by another corporation may be structured in many different ways. An acquiring corporation may acquire control of the "target" corporation or it may acquire a small interest in the stock of another corporation as an investment. The acquiring corporation may finance the acquisition with debt (either by a new borrowing of the necessary funds or by keeping an old borrowing outstanding), or with its own retained earnings, or with funds contributed as new equity capital by investors.

An acquisition of the control of a target company may be a hostile or friendly transaction. It may be structured as an acquisition of the stock of the target company or an acquisition of the assets of the target company. The target company may continue to operate as an independent company in the same manner as before it was acquired, or it may be absorbed into the acquiring company or other companies owned by the acquiring company, or it may cease operations entirely and its assets be divided and sold.

1. Stock Acquisitions out of Retained Earnings

A corporation may finance the acquisition of the stock of another corporation with internally generated funds (i.e., its retained earnings). The purchase of the stock has no tax consequences to the shareholders of the purchasing corporation. Likewise, there are no tax consequences to the acquired corporation as a result of the acquisition. [But cf. §§382-384.] The taxable shareholders of the acquired corporation recognize any gain or loss on the sale of their shares.

There are generally no immediate tax consequences to the purchasing corporation as a result of the transaction. However, the total amount of funds in corporate solution, the earnings of which are subject to a corporate-level tax, may be reduced by the amount spent for the acquisition to the extent that shares are acquired by the acquiring corporation from noncorporate shareholders. Moreover, no compensating additional corporate tax may arise when earnings of the acquired corporation are distributed to the acquiring corporation. This is because earnings of the target company which are distributed to the acquiring corporation as dividends will either be nontaxable under the consolidated return rules, or, if the corporations do not file a consolidated return, will be eligible for the dividends received deduction.

2. Debt-Financed Stock Acquisitions Including Leveraged Buyouts

A corporation may finance the acquisition of another corporation's stock by borrowing. The acquiring corporation may borrow using its own assets as security for the loan or it may borrow using the assets of the target company as security for the loan. In either case, debt has been substituted for equity at the corporate level. When the debt is secured by the acquired corporation's assets, the transaction is more likely to be called a "leveraged buyout."

Description

A leveraged buyout refers to a particular type of debt-financed acquisition of a "target" corporation. The purchasers borrow most of the purchase price of the target company, using the assets of the target company as security for the loan. After the acquisition, the target corporation may be able to service the debt obligation out of its cash flow from operations or the purchaser may sell the assets of the target company and use the proceeds to retire the debt.

A leveraged buyout may occur in many different contexts and may be used by many different types of purchasers. The leveraged buyout, also sometimes called a bootstrap acquisition, has long been used to acquire private (i.e., closely held) corporations. More recently, leveraged buyouts have been used to acquire large public companies. A public company may be "taken private" through a leveraged buyout if the purchasers of the target public corporation are a relatively small group of investors. If the purchasers of the target corporation in a leveraged buyout include the current management of the target company, the transaction is sometimes called a "management buyout." A division or a subsidiary of a company also may be purchased through a leveraged buyout.

A leveraged buyout of a target company is usually accomplished by a debt-financed tender offer by the existing corporation for its outstanding publicly held stock, or, alternatively, by a tender offer for the target corporation's stock by a largely debt-financed shell corporation established for this purpose. The target corporation will repurchase its stock from its shareholders or the shell corporation will buy all the stock of the target corporation.[76] If a shell corporation is used, the target corporation and the shell corporation will typically merge immediately after the acquisition.

As mentioned above, most of the funds for a leveraged buyout transaction are borrowed, with the purchasers contributing only a small amount of their own funds as equity. Lenders for these transactions have been banks, investment banks, insurance companies, pension funds, and pools of investors. Debt terms reflect the degree of leverage and the loan security involved. Some of the debt incurred frequently is below investment grade, i.e., so-called "junk" bonds.

Tax Consequences

A leveraged buyout is generally a taxable transaction with respect to the shareholders of the target corporation.[77] Taxable shareholders selling their stock recognize gain or loss on the sale of their shares.[78] There are no immediate tax consequences of a leveraged buyout at the corporate level since generally neither the repurchase by the target corporation of its own shares nor the purchase of the target corporation's shares by a shell corporation followed by the merger of the target and shell corporation is a taxable transaction. [But cf. §312(n)(7).]

The primary tax consequences of a leveraged buyout to the target corporation arise from the fact that the equity of the corporation has been replaced by debt. Income of the target corporation once paid to investors as nondeductible dividends on stock is instead paid to creditors as tax-deductible interest on debt. As a result of the interest deductions generated by the borrowing in a leveraged buyout, the target corporation may have little, if any, taxable income in the years following a leveraged buyout and may claim loss carrybacks producing a refund of taxes paid prior to the acquisition. Because the target corporation pays little, if any, of its operating income as Federal income taxes, the portion of the target corporation's income that was once being paid to the Federal government as Federal income taxes may instead be redirected to increase investor returns. However, to the extent increased investor returns are paid to taxable shareholders or holders of debt, there may be an increase in investor-level Federal income taxes paid.

Example III-C

[Company *M*, with 99,000 shares of stock outstanding and no debt, has $1.5 million annual income. *M*'s federal income tax is $510,000 ($1.5 million × .34), leaving $990,000 of after-tax income, or earnings of $10 per share. *M*'s stock trades at

76. Shareholders of the target company typically receive a premium for their stock above the price at which the stock has been trading on the market.

77. Of course, there will be no tax imposed on those shareholders that are not subject to U.S. income tax on their income, i.e., certain foreign investors and tax-exempt investors such as pension funds.

78. Taxable shareholders will generally recognize gain (i.e., the excess of the amount received over their basis in the stock) because acquirors typically pay a substantial premium for stock in a leveraged buyout transaction.

$80 per share (or 8 times earnings per share).] Company *M* is acquired in a leveraged buyout. The acquirors pay $120 per share of stock, or 50 percent more than the price at which the stock has been trading on the market, for a total price of $11.88 million. Taxable selling shareholders recognize gain or loss on the sale of their shares.

The acquirors put up $880,000 of their own funds and raise the remaining $11 million of the purchase price by issuing notes paying 12 percent interest to be secured by the assets of Company *M*. The annual income of Company *M* after the leveraged buyout is unchanged.

The distribution of the operating income of Company *M* before and after the leveraged buyout is as follows:

	Before	*After*
Company *M* shareholders	$ 990,000	$ 0
Bondholders	0	1,320,000
Acquirors	0	118,800
Corporate income taxes	510,000	61,200
Total operating income	$1,500,000	$1,500,000

The leveraged buyout has redistributed the income stream of Company *M*. [T]he acquirors of Company *M*, rather than all the shareholders (in the case of a distribution with respect to stock) or the continuing shareholders of Company *M* (in the case of a stock redemption) receive the profit of $118,800. Company *M* shareholders who before the transaction received $990,000 a year in dividends now receive no distributions. New bondholders receive interest of 12 percent on $11 million, or $1.32 million. This is one third more than the entire amount of Company *M*'s after-tax income before the leveraged buyout, even though the operating income of Company *M* is the same before and after the leveraged buyout.

The taxable income of Company *M* has, however, been reduced from $1.5 million to $180,000 ($1.5 million minus $1.32 million) because most of the income of the company is paid out to investors as interest rather than dividends. Federal income taxes are thereby reduced from $510,000 to $61,200. Acquirors make an after-tax profit of $118,800 (pre-tax profit of $180,000 reduced by Federal income tax of $61,200), a 13.4 percent return on their $880,000 equity investment. The income tax reduction of $448,800 exactly pays for the increased returns to investors (bondholders and the acquirors) as a result of the leveraged buyout. Depending on whether the increased investor returns are paid to taxable shareholders or holders of debt, there may be an increase in investor-level Federal income taxes paid.*

* The engine that drives this example is the assumption that the Company *M* stock initially sells for $80 per share and can be redeemed for $120 per share. Is this a realistic assumption? The example assumes that *M*'s pretax borrowing cost is 12 percent; presumably its rate of return on investment would be higher than 12 percent. Even assuming that the rate of return on investment is 12 percent, *M*'s assets should be worth $12,500,000 ($1,500,000/0.12) to produce the assumed annual pretax profit of $1,500,000. Yet the market seems to value the corporation at only $7,920,000 (99,000 shares × $80 per share).

Why might the market value of *M* be so much below its asset value? There may be a host of reasons. Perhaps the expected cost of a corporate-level tax is one reason. Also, stock may be undervalued because of information failure in the marketplace, or perhaps the assets are not efficiently deployed, and transactions costs prevent a more efficient deployment. In any case, the example not surprisingly shows that if you can borrow at 12 percent to purchase an investment (i.e., *M* stock) that provides a return of almost 19 percent ($1,500,000 income/(99,000 shares × $80 per share)), it's a good deal.

Actual Transactions

Leveraged buyouts of public companies have greatly increased in recent years, and the amounts involved in such transactions have risen dramatically. The largest leveraged buyout transaction to date is the proposed acquisition of RJR Nabisco by the investment firm of Kohlberg Kravis Roberts & Co. ("KKR") for nearly $25 billion. It is expected that this acquisition will be completed by February 1989. Other large leveraged buyout transactions include the acquisition of Beatrice Companies by KKR for $6.25 billion in April 1986, and the management buyout of R.H. Macy & Co., Inc. for $3.5 billion in July 1986.

Newspaper reports indicate that out of the approximately $25 billion needed for the RJR Nabisco acquisition, more than $22.5 billion will be borrowed. Secured bank debt will account for approximately $17.5 billion of the borrowing, with most of the remainder being provided by investment banking firms. A pool of investors organized by KKR will put up $1.5 billion as an equity investment. It has been reported that KKR will contribute approximately $15 million of its own funds as equity. RJR Nabisco shareholders will be paid $109 for each share of common stock. This is almost twice the price at which the stock was trading immediately prior to the announcement of the possible sale of the company. It has been reported that due to increased interest deductions, RJR Nabisco could save up to $682 million annually in Federal and state income taxes and be able to seek the refund of additional amounts of taxes paid in prior years due to the carryback of net operating losses. Other reports have projected the annual savings at $370 million.

In the Beatrice transaction, each common shareholder received $50 per share ($40 in cash). This price of $50 per share was 45 percent higher than the market value of the stock one month prior to the announcement date of the first offer. Financing for the Beatrice leveraged buyout included $6.5 billion in debt and $1.35 billion in equity capital. Four billion dollars of the debt was lent by banks and $2.5 billion came from a new issue of high yield bonds. The equity came from two sources. Six hundred million came from a buyout fund organized by KKR and subscribed to by institutional investors and $750 million came from converting existing common stock to a new issue of preferred stock.

In the Macy transaction, each common share of stock outstanding received $68 in cash. This price of $68 per share was 55 percent higher than the market value of the stock one month prior to the announcement date of the first offer. On completion of the Macy leveraged buyout, the management group held 20 percent of the new company stock and an additional 20 percent was held by General Electric Co.'s credit union. Financing for the Macy leveraged buyout totaled approximately $3.7 billion. Out of this amount, almost $3.2 billion was debt: $770 million was lent from banks, $1.625 billion came from new issues of high yield bonds, and $800 million came from notes secured by mortgages. The remaining $500 million of the financing consisted of $200 million of excess cash of Macy's and $300 million was equity capital contributed by the acquirors.

Notice that in this example the government receives less in corporate taxes when debt is used. The example assumes that the benefits of this tax reduction are shared by the shareholders and the debt holders. As noted at page 287 supra, however, the reduction in taxes might also inure to employees, suppliers, customers, etc. Regardless of who benefits from the tax reduction, tax liability is lowered through the use of debt. — Eds.

D. ROLE OF OVERFUNDED PENSION PLANS AND ESOPS IN LEVERAGED BUYOUTS

1. Overfunded Pension Plans

In the case of a leveraged buyout, the assets in the overfunded pension plan of the target company may represent a source of capital to help finance the acquisition. An overfunded pension plan represents a pool of assets that may make a company a target for a takeover. Conversely, this pool of assets may be used by the company to ward off a hostile takeover. In recent years, some companies with significantly overfunded pension plans have been acquired by other companies. After the acquisition, the acquiring company terminated the overfunded pension plan and used the excess assets partially to finance the takeover. An overfunded plan represents an attractive source of cash even if the value of the assets are included in the purchase price.

Another possibility is that a company will itself terminate an overfunded pension plan to assist its efforts to thwart a hostile takeover attempt.

Consider the following example:

Example III-D

Corporation *K* is a widely held public corporation. *K* maintains a qualified defined benefit pension plan for the exclusive benefit of its employees. The trust is currently overfunded by approximately $100 million on a termination basis. That is, if the trust is terminated, its assets would exceed the present value of the benefits accrued under the plan by *K* employees up to the date of plan termination. LBO Fund (*L*) wants to acquire *K*.

Under almost any form of acquisition, *L*, subject to some limitations, could cause *K* to terminate its pension plan. The termination would enable *L*, directly or indirectly, to obtain the $100 million. It could be used to assist *L* in paying for the acquisition, for general corporate purposes, or for any other purpose. While the $100 million would be included in the gross income of *K* upon termination of the plan, any net operating losses and loss carryovers of *K* could be used to offset that income. A nondeductible 15 percent excise tax would also apply to the reversion.*

If *K*'s current management wanted to prevent an acquisition, it might terminate the plan itself and make use of the proceeds. *K* might be a less attractive takeover candidate in that event, for it would not have $100 million in readily available cash as an inducement to a potential acquiror.

This utilization of excess pension assets is not peculiar to a leveraged buyout, but is potentially available in any takeover or merger transaction. In addition, any pool of liquid assets, not just excess pension assets, would be attractive to potential acquirors.

2. Employee Stock Ownership Plans (ESOPs)

A leveraged ESOP can be used by an employer as a technique of finance to obtain funds for working capital or plant expansion, or as a means of financing a

* Congress has increased the excise tax rate to at least 20%. §4980(a). The rate increases to 50%, unless the employer provides adequate plan benefits to employees. §4980(d). — Eds.

leveraged buyout. Use of this financing technique can result in a lower cost of borrowing than would be available if conventional debt or equity financing were used. In a typical transaction, the employer enters into a contract with the ESOP to sell the ESOP a specified number of shares of its stock. The ESOP borrows the funds needed to purchase the shares from a bank or other lender and pays them to the employer in exchange for the stock. In subsequent years, the employer makes tax-deductible cash contributions to the ESOP in the amount necessary to amortize the loan principal and interest payments thereon.

A leveraged ESOP may be used not only to provide the company with working capital but also to finance an acquisition of the stock or assets of another corporation. In a typical case, a leveraged ESOP maintained by the acquiring corporation or its subsidiary borrows funds in an amount equal to the amount needed to acquire the target corporation. The proceeds of the loan are used to purchase employer securities from the employer. The employer (or the subsidiary) then uses the proceeds of the sale to purchase the stock or assets of the target company.

One variation of this leveraged-ESOP financing technique is for the employer to purchase target stock, either directly or through a subsidiary, using funds borrowed from a financial institution or other lender. Once the acquisition has been completed, the newly acquired subsidiary establishes a leveraged ESOP. The ESOP borrows money and purchases stock in the subsidiary from the subsidiary (or from the acquiring corporation). The acquiring corporation then uses the proceeds of this sale to pay off the original acquisition loan. The subsidiary makes annual, deductible contributions sufficient to amortize the ESOP loan and pay interest.

Recently, leveraged ESOPs have been used in some situations to thwart hostile corporate takeover attempts. Leveraged ESOPs have also been used to accomplish leveraged buyouts by persons desiring to take the company private.

The establishment of an employee stock ownership plan (ESOP) may reduce the costs of financing a leveraged buyout, as evidenced by the following example.

Example III-E

Partnership *R* purchases Target Company *X* for $3.0 billion, financed by $2.4 billion of debt and $600 million of equity capital. As part of the buyout agreement, *X* establishes an ESOP for its employees. *X* borrows $250 million from a commercial lender and secures the loan by mortgages and asset pledges. *X* then lends $250 million to the ESOP on substantially the same terms as the terms of *X*'s loan from the commercial lender. The ESOP uses the loan proceeds to purchase $250 million of *X*'s stock.

The ESOP pays off the loan with contributions made by *X* in subsequent years. Such contributions will equal the annual principal and interest payments required by the ESOP on the loan from *X*. As the ESOP makes such loan payments, *X* uses the payments to satisfy its repayment requirements to the commercial lender.

Under present law, the contributions of *X* to the ESOP, which equal the principal and interest payments on *X*'s loan to the ESOP, generally are deductible under the rules governing deductions for contributions to qualified pension plans. Consequently, if an ESOP is established by *X*, *X* may deduct both the principal and interest payments on its loan. This result can be illustrated by comparing the following 2 cases:

Case 1.—*X* borrows $250 million from lender *A*. Only the interest on *X*'s payments to *A* are deductible.

Case 2.—*X* establishes an ESOP, which borrows $250 million from lender *A* and uses the proceeds to purchase capital stock from *X*. *X*'s payments to the ESOP equal the principal and interest payments on the ESOP's loan from *A*. *X*'s payments are fully deductible.

In case 2, *X* has, in effect, borrowed $250 million from a lender and gets the benefit of a full deduction for its loan repayments. A further advantage of the use of an ESOP in the buyout of *X* is the special interest exclusion allowed under present law (sec. 133). [(Note that §133 has been repealed.—Eds.)] The commercial lender who loans $250 million to *X* is entitled to exclude from gross income 50 percent of the interest it receives on the loan. Typically, this tax benefit is passed on partially to the borrower in the form of a reduced cost of borrowing (i.e., rest rate on the loan).

A potential disadvantage of the use of an ESOP in this case is that the employees of *X* will receive an equity interest in *X*. As the ESOP loan is repaid, the stock of *X* purchased by the ESOP will be allocated to the accounts of the ESOP participants. Thus, the ownership of the shares acquired through the ESOP ultimately will be transferred to the ESOP participants. The advantages of using the ESOP to finance a leveraged buyout or other transaction may not outweigh the disadvantage of transferring equity interests to employees.

Actual Transactions

Leveraged ESOPs have been used in a variety of corporate financing transactions. For example, the Procter and Gamble Company plans to add $1 billion (financed by debt) to its existing ESOP (thereby giving the ESOP a 20-percent interest in the company's common stock) in a transaction designed to provide substantial tax benefits and to offer a shield against a threat of hostile takeover. Similarly, the recent establishment of the J. C. Penney Company ESOP is widely viewed as an effort to deter a hostile takeover.

Leveraged ESOPs have also been used to accomplish leveraged buyouts by persons desiring to take a company private. The leveraged ESOP of Parsons Corporation accomplished such a result.

IV. Policy Issues . . .

C. Risks of Excessive Corporate Debt

1. Implication of Excessive Debt for Financial Stability and Economic Growth

Overview

Increased corporate indebtedness potentially has significant implications for the financial health of investors and issuers of the debt as well as for the economy as a whole. Corporate issuers with increased indebtedness must devote larger proportions of earnings and cash flow to interest payments. If leverage ratios are high, and if sales decline or expenses increase, firms may be forced to sell assets, reduce wage costs, or reduce capital and research expenditures. If such actions are insufficient to restore liquidity, debt restructuring or bankruptcy can result. Furthermore, losses incurred by investors holding the corporate debt of troubled firms could adversely affect their own balance sheets. If bankruptcies and debt restructurings are greater than expected, the negative effects could extend beyond distressed lenders and borrowers and reduce employment, income and growth in the economy as a whole. However, increased corporate indebtedness and even increased risk are not necessarily adverse developments, and there is by no means consensus among experts about the significance of increased debt. Some consider it an impending crisis; others consider it to be just one more aspect of financial innovation; yet others consider it as ultimately improving economic efficiency.

NOTES

1. *Acquisition indebtedness.* In the late 1960s, Congress expressed concern over acquisition activity that involved the use of various types of debt instruments, often convertible into common stock of the acquiring corporation. To discourage the use of debt in such acquisitions, Congress enacted §279, which disallows an interest deduction to an acquiring corporation on specified "corporate acquisition indebtedness." Essentially, "corporate acquisition indebtedness" is a debt obligation issued by an acquiring corporation to acquire a specified amount of stock or assets (i.e., two-thirds of the value of the trade or business assets) of another corporation if the following conditions are met:

1. The obligation is subordinated to trade creditors or unsecured creditors;
2. The obligation is convertible into stock of the acquiring corporation (or is part of an investment unit that includes an option to acquire stock of the acquiring corporation); and
3. The ratio of debt to equity exceeds 2:1 or the projected earnings of the acquiring corporation (or in some cases the combined corporations) do not exceed three times the interest paid or incurred with respect to the obligation.

If an acquiring corporation can avoid any one of these requirements, then §279 does not apply. For example, if the debt is not subordinated to trade creditors, §279 does not apply. If all three requirements are satisfied, §279 denies an interest deduction in excess of $5 million paid on such corporate acquisition indebtedness. Accordingly, at a 7-percent interest rate, a corporation could have more than $70 million of debt outstanding without triggering §279.

2. *High-yield discount obligations.* In the aftermath of the stock market plunge of 1987, Congress acted again to curb the perceived misuse of corporate debt to fund major acquisitions, although its actions have a narrow scope. An interest deduction may be denied to issuers of any "applicable high-yield discount obligation." This type of obligation typically has an issue price that is significantly lower than the redemption price. The spread between the issue price and the redemption price is original issue discount (OID). Normally, an issuer of an OID bond accrues and deducts (and the lender includes) the spread over the life of the bond even though payment is not made until maturity. §§1272-1273. A related instrument is the

"payment in kind" (PIK) bond, an instrument for which payments are in the form of other debt or stock of the issuer, rather than cash. Both the high-yield and PIK bonds are attractive to issuers, because they promise deductions before any cash outlay is required.

Section 163(e)(5) divides the OID amount on these bonds between an interest portion that is deductible only when paid and a disqualified portion for which no deduction is allowed but that may qualify for a dividends received deduction for a corporate lender. This approach is a compromise between treating the instrument as equity (i.e., periodic payments would not be deductible) and treating it as debt. An "applicable high-yield discount obligation" is defined as an instrument with: (a) a maturity date of more than five years, (b) a yield to maturity that is at least 5 percentage points more than a designated federal rate, and (c) "significant original issue discount." §163(i).

3. *Debt-financed net operating losses.* At the same time Congress enacted §163(e)(5), it added a provision targeting the use of tax refunds to finance leveraged buyouts. These tax refunds were generated by the acquiring corporation's carryback of net operating losses (NOLs) generated after the acquisition. §172. In debt-financed acquisitions, interest deductions often generated the NOL and resulted in a tax refund. Broadly speaking, Congress limited the carryback of interest expense incurred because of a takeover.

Section 172(h) limits the carryback of NOLs if the losses are created (or increased) by interest deductions attributable to a "corporate equity reduction transaction" (CERT). A CERT is either a "major stock acquisition" or an "excess distribution." In general, a "major stock acquisition" is a planned acquisition by a corporation of 50 percent or more of the voting power or value of stock in another corporation. §172(h)(3)(B). An "excess distribution" is an unusually large distribution relative to the distributing corporation's distribution history or net worth. §172(h)(3)(C).

If the CERT limitation applies, (and the limitation may apply as much as two years after the year in which the CERT occurs) interest attributable to the CERT cannot be carried back to a year before the CERT. See §172(b)(1)(E)(ii). A de minimis rule provides that the limitation applies only if the interest expense in question equals or exceeds $1 million. §172(h)(2)(D).

4. *Integration.* The limited statutory provisions discussed above may have the effect of limiting the use of debt in acquisition activity in some specific cases, but even taken together the attempts are uneven and certainly are complicated. A more general and principled approach to the debt-equity problem may be the integration of corporate and individual income taxes. Under some integration proposals, the tax differences between debt and equity would be either eliminated or lessened, thereby substantially removing tax incentives for debt-financed acquisitions.

For a discussion of integration, see Chapter 8.

10

Acquisitive Reorganizations

A. INTRODUCTION

In a broad sense, a corporate reorganization can mean any rearrangement of corporate activity, including the division of a single corporation into two or more entities, the combination of two or more corporations into a single entity, and the continuation of a corporation's business by new shareholders. Sales of corporate shares and sales of corporate assets are thus "reorganizations" in this broad sense.

Consider the following example of an acquisitive corporate reorganization. Acquiring Corp. seeks to obtain the business assets of Target Corp. To this end, Acquiring purchases the productive assets of Target, paying with cash, stock and securities of Acquiring, or some combination. Target then distributes the consideration received from Acquiring, along with its remaining assets, if any, to its shareholders in exchange for their Target stock.

In the absence of any special provisions, this transaction will be taxable at both the corporate and shareholder levels. First, Target Corp. will recognize gain or loss on the assets it sells to Acquiring Corp. as well as on the assets it does not sell but instead distributes as part of its liquidating distribution. See §§1001, 336. Second, the Target shareholders will recognize gain or loss on the exchange of their shares for the distributed assets to the extent that the adjusted basis in their shares differs from the fair market value of the assets they receive. §331.

One might question whether one or both levels of taxation is appropriate. For example, suppose the consideration used by Acquiring Corp. consisted exclusively of its own common stock so that, in the liquidating distribution of Target Corp., the Target shareholders exchanged their Target shares for Acquiring shares. Although this exchange works a change in the form of the shareholders' investment, it may have little real impact on the substance of their investment: They continue to own stock of a corporation conducting the business formerly conducted by Target.

In §368(a), Congress has defined types of reorganizations for which taxation at one or both levels is avoided. Note that in other sections Congress has allowed businesses to undergo a change in form without imposing tax. Section 351, for example, permits the tax-free incorporation of assets, and §721 performs a similar role in partnership formations. The reorganization provisions reflect a similar congressional attitude for corporate combinations and divisions. In this chapter we will look at the provisions associated with combining two or more corporations — that is, we will examine the acquisitive reorganization provisions.

As you will soon discover, these reorganization provisions are exceedingly complex. Much of this complexity results from the conflicting congressional desires to (1) permit a mere change in the form of a corporate enterprise to be effected without immediate taxation while (2) not allowing the sale of a business to escape taxation simply because the business is incorporated. Although Congress and the courts have sought to develop reasonable ways to distinguish nontaxable corporate reorganizations from taxable sales of corporate enterprises, the current statutory and judicial framework often seems to exalt form (and early tax advice) over substance.

Section 368(a) merely defines what constitutes a reorganization; the tax consequences for acquisitive reorganizations that flow from these definitions are found elsewhere. For shareholders, the cornerstone of reorganization taxation is §354(a)(1). To obtain nonrecognition under §354(a)(1), a shareholder must exchange "stock or securities" solely for "stock or securities," the exchange must be "in pursuance of a plan of reorganization," and both the stock or securities surrendered and received must be "in a corporation a party to a reorganization." See also §356 (allowing a shareholder to receive other property (i.e., boot) but at the cost of recognizing realized gain up to the boot's value).

For these purposes, stock represents an equity interest in a corporation, and a security is a debt interest or stock right. Note that not all corporate debt interests qualify as "securities" under §354(a)(1), and Congress has failed to define this important term. Transactions that constitute "reorganizations" are defined with specificity in §368(a), and a "party" to a reorganization is defined in §368(b). These crucial definitions have been litigated extensively, particularly early in their development, and the resulting judicial gloss on the statutory provisions has proved substantial.

Before turning to the judicial gloss (now expanded through substantial regulations), we will map the statutory terrain. The principal definition of a "reorganization" is in §368(a)(1), and the various different forms of reorganizations described in that subsection are usually referred to without the preface "§368(a)(1)." Thus, we have A through G reorganizations (described in §368(a)(1)(A)-(G)), and the acquisitive reorganizations include the types A through D, which are discussed in this section. Note that some D reorganizations are divisive transactions (where one corporation is split into two) and those transactions are discussed in the next chapter.

An A reorganization is a "statutory merger or consolidation." In a merger, one corporation (usually called the "acquiring" or "surviving" corporation) acquires the assets of another corporation (usually called the "target" corporation), and all outstanding target shares are canceled, with the former target shareholders receiving some form of consideration usually including some combination of cash, stock, and debt of the acquiring corporation, or stock and debt of a corporation controlling the acquiring corporation. Thus, if Target Corp. merges into Acquiring Corp., Target will disappear, and Acquiring will end up with the Target assets.

In a consolidation, two corporations join together to form a new, third corporation. Thus, *X* Corp. and *Y* Corp. might consolidate into *Z* Corp., with *Z* owning the combined assets of *X* and *Y*. All stock of *X* and *Y* will be canceled, and the former *X* and *Y* shareholders will receive consideration usually including some combination of cash, stock, and debt of *Z*.

An A reorganization must occur by operation of state, federal, or foreign law. The operative statute requires consent by the target shareholders and sometimes by the acquiror shareholders as well. The statute also often imposes various procedural requirements to ensure that all affected parties (often including workers) are adequately apprised of the event. The non-tax aspects of these federal merger statutes are irrelevant to the tax consequences of the transaction, except that the parties must comply with relevant non-tax law to fall within the ambit of §368(a)(1)(A). Note that not all statutory mergers and consolidations qualify as A reorganizations: Courts have added additional requirements beyond the (minimal) requirements imposed by the language of §368(a)(1)(A).

A C reorganization is sometimes called the "de facto merger provision" because a C reorganization has a similar effect as an A reorganization without necessarily being a merger. In a C reorganization, the acquiring corporation must acquire "substantially all" of the target assets and then the target corporation generally must liquidate, distributing any of its assets not transferred to the acquiring corporation as well as whatever consideration was paid by the acquiring corporation for the target's assets. If the acquiring corporation uses its own stock as payment, the former target shareholders will become shareholders of the acquiring corporation.

A B reorganization differs from A and C reorganizations, because it is an acquisition of stock, not assets. In a B reorganization, after the stock exchange, the acquiring corporation must control the target corporation, so that the target becomes a subsidiary of the acquiring corporation. Because the B reorganization is a stock acquisition, it involves no corporate-level tax for the target, even in the absence of special taxing provisions, since the target assets do not change hands. Further, the former target shareholders generally avoid recognition of gain (and of loss, although that is typically no advantage) on the exchange of their shares with the acquiring corporation.

Section 368(a)(2) has several provisions expanding the basic reorganization definitions to allow the use of parent stock in an A reorganization even though the parent's controlled subsidiary combines with the target. In addition, and for reasons understood only by looking to the history of the reorganization provisions, part of the definition of a C reorganization is found in §368(a)(2). Section 368(b) defines the term "party to a reorganization," and as provisions have been added to §368(a)(2) that expand the use of parent-subsidiary pairs, so too have §368(b) and associated regulations been amended to expand the concept of a party to the reorganization. Section 368(c) defines control, a definition that we first encountered in studying §351.

Section 368 is nothing more than a *definitional* section: It contains no provision specifying the taxation of the various parties. In Chapter 2 you were briefly introduced to §354, the basic shareholder-level taxing provision. Section 356 addresses the shareholder taxation of boot, while §361 plays both roles at the corporate level (and §357 specifies circumstances in which the assumption of a liability is treated as nonqualifying property). The associated basis rules are in §358 (for shareholders) and §§358 and 362 (for the corporate parties to the reorganization). As with most nonrecognition provisions in the Code, the reorganizations defer, rather than eliminate, realized but not recognized gain or loss.

B. JUDICIAL REQUIREMENTS

For a transaction to be treated as an acquisitive reorganization, it must meet not only the statutory definition of a reorganization under §368(a) but generally also certain judicial requirements: An acquisitive reorganization must have a continuity of interest, continuity of business enterprise, and a valid business purpose. We next consider those judicial requirements.

1. Continuity of Interest

A merger or other corporate combination qualifies as a §368(a) reorganization only if it has continuity of interest. This standard is met if "a substantial part of the value of the proprietary interest in the target corporation [is] preserved in the reorganization." Treas. Regs. §1.368-1(e)(1). Thus, the target shareholders must have a continuing, entrepreneurial interest in the combined venture.[1]

This standard raises two questions:

1. What type of consideration preserves the target shareholder's proprietary interest?
2. How much qualifying consideration is needed for a transaction to be a reorganization?

The first question was answered in a series of Supreme Court cases in the 1930s and 1940s, as the Court developed the "continuity of interest" doctrine.

a. Continuity-Preserving Consideration

Despite any explicit statutory requirement, the Supreme Court concluded that a merger could not be an A reorganization if it lacked continuity of interest. In Pinellas Ice & Cold Storage Co. v. Commissioner, 287 U.S. 462 (1933), the seller corporations, in exchange for their assets, received cash plus well-secured promissory notes of the purchasing corporation payable in less than four months. The Supreme Court concluded that the transaction constituted a taxable sale rather than a tax-free reorganization, stating, "Certainly, we think that to be within the [definition of a reorganization] the seller must acquire an interest in the affairs of the purchasing company more definite than that incident to ownership of its short-term purchase-money notes." 287 U.S. at 470.

Two years later, in Helvering v. Minnesota Tea Co., 296 U.S. 378 (1935), the Court upheld the tax-free status of a transfer by a corporation of substantially all of its assets for voting trust certificates (worth about $540,000) representing 18,000 shares of common stock of another corporation as well as about $425,000 in cash.

1. For continuity of interest to be met, a substantial proprietary interest in the target corporation must be preserved in the reorganization. Because other types of target interests could also be preserved (e.g., debt interests), it may be more precise to label this requirement "continuity of proprietary interest." However, because the regulations name the requirement "continuity of interest," we do as well. Do not forget, however, that the requirement focuses on the preservation of proprietary interests.

The 18,000 shares represented about 7 1/2 percent of the outstanding stock of the transferee, a publicly held corporation. Because of this substantial reduction in the transferor's control over the transferred assets, the Board of Tax Appeals had denied reorganization treatment to the transaction. In coming to the opposite conclusion, the Supreme Court restated the rule of *Pinellas* and then wrote,

> True it is that the relationship of the taxpayer to the assets conveyed was substantially changed, but this is not inhibited by the statute. Also, a large part of the consideration was cash. This, we think, is permissible so long as the taxpayer received an interest in the affairs of the transferee which represented a material part of the value of the transferred assets.

296 U.S. at 386. Thus, the Court measured continuity by looking to the percentage of consideration received in the exchange that was acquiror stock, not the percentage of acquiror stock held after the exchange.

Minnesota Tea left open the questions (1) what constitutes an "interest in the affairs of the transferee" and (2) how much of such an interest is a "material part" of the value transferred. The first of these two questions was answered in large part by John A. Nelson & Co. v. Helvering, 296 U.S. 374 (1935), and LeTulle v. Scofield, 308 U.S. 415 (1940).

In *LeTulle*, all the assets of a corporation were conveyed for $50,000 in cash plus $750,000 in bonds of the transferee payable serially over 11 years. The Supreme Court characterized the transaction as a sale, holding that "[w]here the consideration is wholly in the transferee's bonds, or part cash and part such bonds, we think it cannot be said that the transferor retains any proprietary interest in the enterprise." 308 U.S. at 420-421. In *John A. Nelson & Co.*, however, the Court upheld the reorganization treatment of a transfer by a corporation of substantially all of its assets for $2 million cash plus nonvoting preferred stock of the transferee worth about $1.25 million. The preferred stock was redeemable as well as nonvoting, but the Court held that the statute had no requirement of participation by the transferor in the transferee's management.

The line of cases from *Pinellas* through *LeTulle* stands for the proposition that for a transaction to qualify as a "reorganization," the target shareholders must receive some stock (a "material part") of the acquiror in the exchange. Thus, the continuity of interest requirement may be met if the target shareholders exchange target voting common stock for acquiror nonvoting, preferred stock. The requirement cannot be met, however, if the target shareholders receive no stock, even if they receive a long-term debt interest.

NOTES

1. *Bright-line rule.* Does this rule make sense? Is the distinction between nonvoting preferred stock and subordinated debt sufficiently important to warrant so great an emphasis? Consider Roebling v. Commissioner, 143 F.2d 810 (3d Cir. 1944), involving a corporation whose assets had been leased to a second corporation on a 900-year lease calling for annual rent of $480,000. The lessor corporation was merged into the lessee, and the shareholders of the lessor exchanged their stock for 100-year bonds of the lessee paying in aggregate $480,000 per year of interest. The

exchanging shareholders argued that their relationship to the underlying assets was no more distant under the 100-year bonds than it had been under the 900-year lease, but the court, relying on *LeTulle* and related cases, held that no reorganization occurred.

2. *Qualifying stock.* Which corporation's stock preserves continuity in an acquisitive reorganization? Generally, the stock that preserves continuity is issued by the corporation that acquires the target stock or assets. See Treas. Regs. §1.368-1(b). In certain situations, however, the Code allows stock of a corporation that controls the acquiring corporation to preserve continuity. See §368(a)(1)(B) (parenthetical language); §368(a)(1)(C) (parenthetical language); §368(a)(2)(D) and (E). For convenience in the discussion below and depending on the context, stock that preserves continuity is called "qualified stock," and the corporation that issues that stock is called the "issuing corporation."

3. *Mergers of mutual banks.* In Paulsen v. Commissioner, 469 U.S. 131 (1985), a state-chartered savings and loan association merged into a federally-chartered savings and loan. Before the merger, the state-chartered entity had "guaranty stock" outstanding that gave its owners all rights to the association's assets upon liquidation but no practical rights to dividends. The federally-chartered entity had no capital stock outstanding but instead was owned by its depositors and borrowers. Pursuant to the merger, the guaranty stock of the state-chartered entity was exchanged for passbook interests in the continuing enterprise at a rate of one $12 passbook for every share of guaranty stock owned.

The Supreme Court held that the transaction was not an "A" reorganization because the former guaranty share owners received no proprietary interest in the acquiring entity: Although the passbook interests had some equity aspects, the debt aspects predominated. The taxpayer had relied on Revenue Ruling 69-3, 1969-1 C.B. 103, which held that a merger of one federally-chartered mutual savings and loan association into another qualified as an "A" reorganization when the target shareholders exchanged passbook accounts of the target entity for equal-value passbook accounts of the acquiring entity. The Supreme Court distinguished this ruling as follows:

> When two [federally-chartered] associations merge, the shares [that is, the passbooks] received are essentially identical to the shares given up. As long as the cash value of the shares on each side of the exchange is the same, the equity interest by the shares received—though small—is equivalent to the equity interest represented by the shares given up.

Is the Supreme Court's opinion in *Paulsen* consistent with *Roebling*? If the continuity of interest doctrine speaks only to the form of consideration *received* in the exchange, then how can it be that the Supreme Court is willing to sanction the tax-free merger of a mutual savings and loan into a mutual savings and loan while refusing the same tax treatment to a stock savings and loan merging into a mutual savings and loan? For a thoughtful criticism of the continuity of interest doctrine, ending with the suggestion that the doctrine be eliminated, see Wolfman, "Continuity of Interest" and the American Law Institute Study, 57 Taxes 840 (1979).

In *Paulsen*, the issue before the court was whether a transaction meeting all the statutory requirements of a "reorganization" should nevertheless be taxed as a sale. Given the precision of the definitions in §368, should the courts ask for more? When these cases were decided, the only relevant guidance was Treas. Regs. §1.368-1(b), which then stated,

> In order to exclude transactions not intended to be included, the specifications of the reorganization provisions of the law are precise. Both the terms of the specifications and their underlying assumptions and purposes must be satisfied in order to entitle the taxpayer to the benefit of the exception from the general rule.

Try to identify these "underlying assumptions and purposes." Can they be articulated with sufficient clarity to guide a court through the maze of §368?

b. Quantity of Continuity-Preserving Consideration

The cases discussed above did not answer how much qualifying consideration is needed for a transaction to be a reorganization, an issue considered in the following case:

Kass v. Commissioner

60 T.C. 218 (1973), aff'd without opinion, 491 F.2d 749 (3d Cir. 1974)

DAWSON, Judge. . . .

The only issue for decision is whether petitioner, a minority shareholder of an 84-percent-owned subsidiary, must recognize gain upon the receipt of the parent's stock pursuant to a statutory merger of the subsidiary into the parent. . . .

For a period greater than 6 months prior to 1965, petitioner had owned 2,000 shares of common stock of Atlantic City Racing Association (herein called ACRA). . . .

ACRA was a New Jersey corporation which was formed in 1943 and which was engaged in the business of operating a racetrack. Its total authorized and outstanding stock consisted of 506,000 shares of common stock. It has approximately 500 stockholders. Track Associates, Inc. (herein called TRACK), is a New Jersey corporation which was formed on November 19, 1965. The total authorized capital stock of TRACK consisted of 500,000 shares of common stock. Its original capitalization consisted of 202,577 shares. Over 50 percent of the original issue was acquired by the Levy family and 8 percent was acquired by the Casey family. The remaining stock went to 18 other individuals. The Levys and the Caseys were also minority shareholders (whether computed separately or as a group) in ACRA. Their purpose in forming TRACK was to gain control over ACRA's racetrack business. They wanted to do away with ACRA's cumbersome capital structure and institute a new corporate policy with regard to capital improvements and higher purses for the races. Control was to be gained by establishing TRACK and then by (1) having TRACK purchase at least 80 percent of the stock of ACRA and (2) subsequently merging ACRA into TRACK.

The Levys acquired 48,300 shares of TRACK stock (out of the total original capitalization of 202,577 shares) in exchange for stock of ACRA. The Caseys acquired 3,450 shares in exchange for their ACRA stock. Together the Levys and Caseys purchased an additional 70,823 shares of TRACK stock as part of the original capitalization.

On December 1, 1965, TRACK offered to purchase the stock of ACRA at $22 per share, subject to the condition that at least 405,000 shares (slightly more than 80 percent of ACRA's outstanding shares) be tendered. As a result of this tender offer, which terminated on February 11, 1966, 424,764 shares of ACRA stock were received and paid for by TRACK. A total of 29,486 shares of ACRA stock were not tendered.

The board of directors of TRACK approved a plan of liquidation providing for the liquidation of ACRA by way of merger into TRACK. . . . At a special meeting of the shareholders of ACRA held on March 8, 1966, the aforementioned plan of liquidation and joint agreement were adopted. A copy of the notice of the meeting was sent to the petitioner, and it notified petitioner of the rights of a dissenting stockholder under New Jersey corporate law.

The merger having taken place, the remaining shares of ACRA that were not sold pursuant to the tender offer or the dissenting shareholder provisions were exchanged for TRACK stock, 1 for 1. The petitioner exchanged 2,000 shares of ACRA stock, with a fair market value at the time of $22 per share, for 2,000 shares of TRACK stock. She did not report any capital gain in connection with this transaction.

Petitioner contends that the merger of ACRA into TRACK, although treated at least in part as a liquidation at the corporate level, is at her level, the shareholder level, (1) a true statutory merger and (2) a section 368(a)(1)(A) reorganization, occasioning no recognition of gain on the ensuing exchange. . . . Respondent, on the other hand, argues that the purchase of stock by TRACK and the liquidation of ACRA into TRACK, which took the form of a merger, must be viewed at all levels as an integrated transaction; that the statutory merger does not qualify as a reorganization because it fails the continuity-of-interest test; and that, as a consequence, petitioner falls outside of section 354(a)(1) and must recognize gain pursuant to section [1001]. . . .

Respondent does not take the position that a statutory merger, such as the one we have here, can never qualify for reorganization-nonrecognition status. . . . Rather, his position is simply that the merger in question fails to meet the time-honored continuity-of-interest test. We agree with this and so hold. . . .

Reorganization treatment is appropriate when the parent's stock ownership in the subsidiary was not acquired as a step in a plan to acquire assets of the subsidiary: the parent's stockholding can be counted as contributing to continuity-of-interest, so that since such holding represented more than 80 percent of the stock of the subsidiary, the continuity-of-interest test would be met. Reorganization treatment is inappropriate when the parent's stock ownership in the subsidiary was purchased as the first step in a plan to acquire the subsidiary's assets in conformance with the provisions of section 334(b)(2).* The parent's stockholding could not be counted towards continuity-of-interest, so . . . there would be a continuity-of-interest of less than 20 percent. (Less than 20-percent continuity would be significantly less continuity-of-interest than that allowed in John A. Nelson Co. v. Helvering, 296 U.S. 374 (1935).) In short, where the parent's stock interest is "old and cold," it

* Under old §334(b)(2), a corporation could purchase 80 percent or more of the stock of a target corporation and then liquidate the target and obtain a stepped-up basis in the former target assets without the imposition of a corporate-level tax. That provision has been repealed, and §338 was enacted in its place. One central feature of the former §334(b)(2) was that the step-up in basis could be obtained only by liquidating the target. — EDS.

may contribute to continuity-of-interest. Where the parent's interest is not "old and cold," the sale of shares by the majority of shareholders actually detracts from continuity-of-interest.

In petitioner's case, TRACK's stock in ACRA was acquired as part of an integrated plan to obtain control over ACRA's business. The plan called for, first, the purchase of stock and, second, the subsidiary-into-parent merger. Accordingly, continuity-of-interest must be measured by looking to all the pre-tender offer stockholders rather than to the parent (TRACK) and the nontendering stockholders only; and by that measure the merger fails and petitioner must recognize her gain. . . .

Faced with the general rule as to the applicability of the continuity-of-interest test, petitioner makes the following arguments, which we will deal with separately.

One, the continuity-of-interest doctrine should not be applied because TRACK was formed by a few stockholders in ACRA in order to purchase the business and, in the process, to acquire a stepped-up basis for as many of the assets as possible via section 334(b)(2). "In effect, the situation was the same as the sale of stock by some shareholders to other shareholders." The petitioner meets herself coming, so to speak, when making this argument. Confronted with the problem of how to characterize the second event in the present two-event transaction, she contends that the transaction was a true statutory merger in both form and substance, at least insofar as she, a minority shareholder, was concerned. Now, confronted with the continuity-of-interest problem, she would have us treat the transaction in a manner inconsistent with the characterization previously given to the transaction, that of a merger. Further, the parties to these events (the selling shareholders of ACRA, the organizers of TRACK, and the nontendering, nondissenting shareholders such as the petitioner) chose the steps that were followed. To allow one of them in a separate proceeding to characterize the facts as being in substance something else would lay the groundwork for an enormous amount of "whipsawing" by and against both taxpayers and the Government.

Two, in applying the continuity-of-interest test, if it is applied, the purchase of stock by TRACK and the subsequent merger should not be viewed as steps in an integrated transaction because the choice of merger over liquidation as a second step had independent significance to the minority shareholders and either choice would have suited TRACK. By so arguing, the petitioner attempts in effect to avoid the step-transaction doctrine and thus to limit the application of the continuity-of-interest test. If the merger can be separated from the stock purchase, the continuity-of-interest test might be applicable only with regard to ACRA's shareholders at the time of the statutory merger, namely, the parent corporation, TRACK, and the minority shareholders, including petitioner. We note at least one flaw: The choice — liquidation or merger — did make a difference to TRACK. If it had liquidated ACRA, TRACK would not have received all of ACRA's assets. Some of the assets would have gone to the minority shareholders, and it would have had to have purchased them from these shareholders at an additional price. By choosing to merge ACRA into itself, it was able to avoid this and other problems.

Three, if the purchase and merger are to be viewed as parts of a single transaction for continuity and reorganization purposes, then the incorporation of TRACK should also be integrated into the transaction for section 351 purposes; thus the petitioner should be viewed as having participated in a tax-free section 351 transaction along with the Levys and Caseys. Briefly, the answer to this argument is that while the purchase and the merger were interdependent events, petitioner's exchange of ACRA stock for TRACK stock was not "mutually interdependent" with the incorporation transfers made by the Levys, Caseys, and 18 other individuals. American Bantam Car Co., 11 T.C. 397, 405-407 (1948), affirmed per curiam 117 F.2d 513 (C.A.3, 1949). . . .

Four, assuming that the continuity-of-interest test is applied, it is met where all 16 percent of the stockholders of ACRA exchanged their stock for a total of 35 percent of the stock of TRACK. The 16-percent figure (really 16.04 percent) is the sum of the percentage of ACRA stock transferred to TRACK at the time of TRACK's formation (10.22 percent) plus the percentage of ACRA stock exchanged for TRACK stock following the statutory merger (5.82 percent). Fortunately, we need not engage in a game of percentages since the continuity figure argued for by petitioner, 16 percent, is not "tantalizingly" high. . . .

Finally, we emphasize that the petitioner is not any worse off than her fellow shareholders who sold their stock. She could have also received money instead of stock had she chosen to sell or to dissent from the merger. The nonrecognition of a realized gain is always an important matter. We hold that petitioner is not entitled to such favorable treatment in this case.

Reviewed by the Court. . . .

NOTES

1. *Aggregate test. Kass* illustrates that the continuity of interest test looks to the consideration received by target shareholders in the aggregate, not on a shareholder-by-shareholder basis. See Rev. Proc. 77-37 (§3.02), 1977-2 C.B. 568 (setting out an aggregate test); Rev. Rul. 66-224, 1966-2 C.B. 114 (continuity requirement met where two 25-percent shareholders were cashed out, while the other two 25-percent shareholders received stock of the acquiring corporation). See also Reilly Oil Co. v. Commissioner, 189 F.2d 382 (5th Cir. 1951) (31 percent of transferor's shareholders elected to receive cash). Thus, Kass recognized her realized gain, even though she received solely acquiror stock in the exchange.

2. *Fairness.* If a shareholder receives solely cash in an exchange, the shareholder recognizes gain or loss, even if the reorganization as a whole meets the continuity of interest test. If the transaction fails that test, all shareholders (including those receiving only stock) lose the benefit of tax-free treatment. Is this distinction fair? The court in *Kass* ended its opinion with the observation that Kass was "not any worse off than her fellow shareholders who sold their stock." Although that observation is true, it fails to recognize the injustice that has been worked on Kass: The other shareholders were appropriately taxed to the extent that they cashed out, but Kass did nothing but continue her corporate investment in equity form and so arguably should be entitled to nonrecognition on the exchange.

3. *Amount of qualifying consideration.* Judicial and administrative guidance provides no bright-line standard for the minimum *quantity* of qualified stock target shareholders must receive in the transaction. Historically, the Service ruled that a prospective corporate combination met the continuity requirement only if the taxpayer represented the following: The former target shareholders would receive qualified stock "equal in value, *as of the effective date of the reorganization,* to at least *50 percent* of the value of all of the formerly outstanding [target] stock . . . as of the

same date." Rev. Proc. 77-37 (§3.02), 1977-2 C.B. 568 (emphasis added). Practitioners argued that the 50-percent threshold should be lowered to reflect current business practice. They also argued that qualified stock should be valued when the acquisition agreement became binding, at least if the target shareholders' rights in the qualified stock became fixed on that date.

Treas. Regs. §1.368-1(e)(2) addresses both concerns. The regulation clarified that the continuity of interest requirement could be met if the target shareholders received qualified stock that in the aggregate comprised *40 percent* of the total consideration. See Treas. Regs. §1.368-1(e)(2)(v) (example 1) (concluding that 40 percent continuity is sufficient). Cf. *id.* (example 11) (concluding that 28.57 percent continuity is not sufficient).

Further, the regulation provides that if the contract to effect the potential reorganization has fixed consideration, continuity is measured on the last business day before the date the contract becomes binding. *Id.* at (e)(2)(i). A contract has fixed consideration if it provides the number of shares of each class of qualified stock and any other property (identified by value or specific description) to be exchanged for *all* target stock or for *each share of* target stock. *Id.* at (e)(2)(iii)(A). There are special rules to deal with modifications of the contract and contingent consideration. Note that if the agreement does not provide for fixed consideration, continuity is measured as of the acquisition's effective date.

4. *Pre- and post-reorganization continuity.* The cases discussed above did not address the impact of pre-reorganization sales of target stock or post-reorganization sales of qualified stock, two issues that confused the courts for many years. The confusion was caused by a misplaced focus on the *consideration received by the target shareholders.* With that focus, continuity of interest could be threatened when historic target shareholders sold their target stock before, or their qualified stock after, the potential reorganization. See McDonald's v. Commissioner, 688 F.2d 520 (7th Cir. 1982), rev'g 76 T.C. 972 (1981).

Treas. Regs. §1.368-1(e)(1) now shifts the focus to the *consideration furnished by the acquiring corporation.* Under the regulation's general rule, pre- or post-reorganization sales of stock for disqualified consideration are disregarded in measuring continuity of interest.

This general rule has two exceptions. First, sales of target or qualified stock in connection with the potential reorganization are taken into account if made directly or indirectly to the issuing corporation or a related corporation. Treas. Regs. §1.368-1(e)(1)(i) and (e)(3). Broadly speaking, a corporation is related to the issuing corporation if, immediately before or after the relevant stock acquisition, it is (1) a direct or indirect 50-percent subsidiary of the issuing corporation or (2) a member of the same affiliated group. Treas. Regs. §1.368-1(e)(4) (determining affiliation without regard to §1504(b)).

Second, if a target shareholder receives a distribution (including a redemption distribution) before the reorganization, the distribution is disregarded unless §356 applies to the distribution (or would if the shareholder had received qualified stock in the reorganization). Treas. Regs. §1.368-1(e)(1)(ii). An example suggests that §356 does not apply to such a distribution unless it is funded by the issuing corporation. Treas. Regs. §1.368-1(e)(7) (example 9).

For example, consider the merger of a target into an acquiring corporation in which the target shareholders receive exclusively acquiror stock, but, as part of the same plan, the acquiring corporation redeems most or all of that stock for cash. In substance, the acquiror has paid mostly cash in the merger, and the regulations properly adopt that view. Treas. Regs. §1.368-1(e)(7) (example 4(i)). The result is the same if the acquiror acquires the target stock for cash immediately before the merger. Treas. Regs. §1.368-1(e)(7) (example 4(ii)).

Nor can an acquiror avoid that result by having a related corporation make the stock purchase. Suppose that *T* Corp. merges into *A* Corp., and the *T* Corp. shareholders receive solely *A* stock in the merger, but, as part of the same plan, *B* Corp. purchases that *A* stock for cash. If *A* and *B* have a common parent, *P* Corp. (so that they are members of an affiliated group), the *T* shareholders will be deemed to receive solely cash in the merger, and the merger will lack continuity of interest. See Treas. Regs. §1.368-1(e)(7) (example 4(iii)).

5. Continuity of interest and §338. In *Kass*, TRACK purchased a controlling interest in ACRA stock and then liquidated ACRA by merger, acquiring a stepped-up basis in the ACRA assets under §334(b)(2). Essentially, the ACRA stock purchase and merger were integrated and treated as a taxable asset purchase, a characterization consistent with treating Kass as making a taxable transfer of her stock.

In 1982, Congress replaced §334(b)(2) with §338 (a section considered in more detail in Chapter 9). Through §338, a purchasing corporation can elect to treat a qualified stock purchase of target stock like either a stock or asset purchase, whether or not it liquidated the target. To preserve that election, Congress recognized that the stock purchase and any subsequent liquidation had to be treated as independent steps for federal income tax purposes. See H.R. Conf. Rep. No. 760, 97th Cong., 2d Sess. 536 (1982). See also Rev. Rul. 90-95, 1990-2 C.B. 67. Stated differently, the policy of §338 requires that if a purchasing corporation acquires a target in a qualified stock purchase and as part of the same plan liquidates the target, the target recognizes gain or loss and its assets take a cost basis only if a §338 election is made.

However, if the stock purchase and liquidation were treated consistently as independent steps, it would allow an end-run around the continuity of interest requirement. To illustrate why, consider the following example: *P* Corp. acquires 80 percent of the only class of *T* Corp. stock for cash. As part of the same plan, *T* Corp. merges into *P* Corp., and the remaining historic *T* shareholders receive *P* stock.

If the stock purchase and merger were treated as fully independent steps for tax purposes, the first step would be a taxable sale, and the *T* shareholders selling their *T* stock for cash would recognize gain or loss. But the second step, the merger, could qualify as a tax-free reorganization, because *P* Corp. would be treated as an historic *T* shareholder for continuity of interest purposes. At the corporate level, *T* Corp. would recognize neither gain nor loss and *P* Corp. would acquire *T*'s assets at their historic asset bases, results consistent with the policy underlying §338. However, at the shareholder level, the remaining *T* shareholders (i.e., the shareholders in Kass's position) would enjoy nonrecognition on their exchange of *T* stock for *P* stock, a result inconsistent with the continuity of interest requirement. Overall, only 20 percent of the original *T* shareholders would receive qualifying stock, certainly too low a percentage to meet that continuity requirement.

Why not treat the stock purchase and merger as steps in an integrated transaction? Then, because only 20 percent of the *T* stock would be exchanged for *P* stock, the continuity requirement could not be met and the transaction could not qualify as a tax-free reorganization. At the shareholder level, recognition would be the order of the day for all *T* shareholders (including those in Kass's position). At the corporate level, however, *T* Corp. would be treated as making a taxable sale of its assets and *P* Corp. would take a cost basis in those assets. However, because the stock purchase would be a qualified stock purchase but no §338 election would be made, that integrated treatment would contravene the policy of §338.

Thus, the transaction presents a conundrum: If its steps are fully integrated, it may act as an end-run around §338, while if its steps are treated as fully independent, the transaction may circumvent the continuity of interest requirement. The regulations resolve the dilemma by splitting the baby. The two steps are integrated to determine the consequences of the potential reorganization to the target corporation, the corporation acquiring the target assets, and the purchasing corporation (i.e., the corporation purchasing the target stock). Because the purchasing corporation is treated as an historic target shareholder, the transaction is treated as a tax-free reorganization by those corporations.[2] However, to determine the consequences to the original target shareholders, the stock purchase and merger may be treated as part of one transaction (i.e., integrated) and be taxable. See Treas. Regs. §1.338-3(d)(1); *id.* at (d)(5), example (v). Thus, in our example, *T* Corp. enjoys nonrecognition, *P* Corp. takes a transferred basis in the *T* assets, but all original *T* shareholders, including those receiving *P* stock, recognize gain or loss.

c. Continuity of Business Enterprise

Because the rationale for tax-free treatment of a reorganization is that the transaction is best viewed as a mere change in form of the business enterprise, can a corporate acquisition be tax free if the issuing corporation does not continue the historic business of the acquired corporation? At one time, the Service argued against tax-free treatment in such circumstances, although the courts regularly rejected the Service's position. See, e.g., Bentsen v. Phinney, 199 F. Supp. 363 (S.D. Tex. 1961) (concluding that the doctrine of business continuity requires only that the assets of the acquired corporation be used in *some* business after the transaction). In Rev. Rul. 63-29, 1963-1 C.B. 77, the Service acquiesced in the reasoning of cases like *Bentsen*, holding that the amalgamation of a toy company and a steel company into a single corporation could qualify as a reorganization.

The regulations now formally require that an acquisitive reorganization satisfy a continuity of business enterprise requirement. That requirement is satisfied if the issuing corporation either continues a significant historic business of the target *or* uses a significant portion of the target's historic assets in a business. Treas. Regs. §1.368-1(d)(1). See also *id.* at (d)(3)(iii) (providing that significance is based on the facts and circumstances). See also *id.* at (d)(5) (examples 1 and 10-12) (apparently concluding that if the issuing corporation owns at least one-third of the historic target assets, it will be treated as owning a "significant" portion of those assets).

For this purpose, an issuing corporation is treated as owning the assets of, and conducting the businesses of, each member of its qualified group. *Id.* at (d)(4)(i). Its qualified group includes (i) the issuing corporation, (ii) any corporation in which the issuing corporation directly owns stock meeting the requirements of

2. See Treas. Regs. §1.338-3(d)(2); *id.* at (d)(5), example (i)-(iv). Note that in our example, *P* Corp. is both the corporation acquiring the *T* assets and the corporation purchasing the *T* stock. This regulatory regime would also apply if *T* Corp. merged into *S* Corp., a controlled *P* subsidiary. Then, *S* Corp. would be the corporation acquiring the *T* assets while *P* Corp. would be the corporation purchasing the *T* stock.

§368(c),[3] and (iii) any other corporation in which qualified group members together own that amount of the corporation's stock. Treas. Regs. §1.368-1(d)(4)(ii). Additional rules attribute partnership assets or businesses in certain cases to the issuing corporation. See *id.* at (d)(4)(iii)(B) and (D).

As an example, this continuity requirement is met if target has three business of equal value, sells two of them, and then merges into an acquiring corporation. *Id.* at (d)(5) (example 1) (continuity met when the acquiror continues one of three significant lines of business). However, the requirement is not met when all target assets are sold in connection with the purported reorganization, and the historic target business is discontinued. See *id.* at (d)(5) (example 4 and 5). See also *id.* at (d)(2)(iii) (providing that a target's historic business is not one that it enters into as part of the plan of reorganization).

Note that nothing in the regulations requires that the acquiring corporation continue its own historic business or use its own historic assets in any capacity. Rev. Rul. 81-25, 1981 C.B. 65. In considering the continuity of business enterprise requirement, you should recognize that labeling one corporation as the "acquiring" corporation and another as the "acquired" corporation may be a matter of indifference. For example, if *A* Corp. and *B* Corp. merge, the decision to make *A* Corp. or *B* Corp. the survivor often will turn on such factors as which corporation has more goodwill associated with its name or whether either corporation owns an asset (such as a favorable long-term lease) that is difficult to transfer. Should the continuity of business enterprise requirement focus only on the continued use of the *acquired corporation's* assets when the reorganization involves a minnow swallowing a whale?

d. Business Purpose

The doctrines of continuity of interest and continuity of business enterprise were developed by the courts to deny tax-free reorganization status to transactions that closely resembled sales. Similarly, the business purpose doctrine was developed early on to deny tax-free status to transactions that meet all the formal requirements of a "reorganization" but lack a valid non-tax business purpose. The business purpose requirement is often traced to Gregory v. Helvering, 293 U.S. 465 (1935), one of the most famous opinions in the tax law.

In 1928, Gregory owned all the outstanding shares of the United Mortgage Corporation (UMC Corp.), which in turn owned 1,000 appreciated shares of the Monitor Securities Corporation. Gregory sought to effect a sale of the Monitor shares at a tax cost of only a capital gain tax at the shareholder level.

Had UMC Corp. distributed the Monitor shares to Gregory as a simple dividend, she would have recognized dividend income on the distribution because UMC Corp. had adequate earnings and profits, dividend income that was then taxed at ordinary rates. (UMC Corp. would have recognized no gain on the distribution because in 1928 the Code contained no provision similar to §311(b).) To avoid this ordinary income, taxed at regular rates, Gregory adopted the following strategy:

3. An issuing corporation would meet that requirement if it owned stock possessing at least 80 percent of the voting power of the other corporation and also owned at least 80 percent of each class of the other corporation's nonvoting stock. §368(c) and Rev. Rul. 59-259, 1959-1 C.B. 115.

First, Gregory had UMC Corp. form a new corporation, Averill Corp., by transferring the Monitor shares to Averill in exchange for all the Averill stock. The Averill stock was immediately distributed to Gregory from UMC Corp. Finally, within one week, the newly formed Averill Corp. was liquidated and the Monitor shares were distributed to Gregory in complete liquidation of Averill.

If form were followed and the statute applied literally, Gregory would have achieved her intended result. The reorganization statute at the time provided that a "reorganization" included "a transfer by a corporation of all or a part of its assets to another corporation if immediately after the transferor or its stockholders or both are in control of the corporation to which the assets are transferred." Accordingly, the formation of Averill Corp. met the formal requirements of a "reorganization." In addition, the statute provided that a distribution "in pursuance of a plan of reorganization, to a shareholder in a corporation a party to a reorganization, [of] stock or securities in such corporation or in another corporation a party to the reorganization, without the surrender by such shareholder of stock or securities in such corporation, [results in] no gain to the distributee from the receipt of such stock or securities." Thus, if the statute were followed literally, Gregory received the stock of Averill without tax. The final step in the plan, the complete liquidation of Averill, was taxable to Gregory, but because she was taxed at capital gain rates on the property distributed in complete liquidation, she had obtained her goal of stepping up the basis in the Monitor shares to fair market value at the cost of a single, capital gain tax. Gregory was able to sell the Monitor shares to a third party without realizing or recognizing further gain.

The Supreme Court, however, denied reorganization status to the transaction:

> [T]he facts speak for themselves and are susceptible of but one interpretation. The whole undertaking, though conducted according to the terms of the [statute], was in fact an elaborate and devious form of conveyance masquerading as a corporate reorganization, and nothing else. The rule which excludes from consideration the motive of tax avoidance is not pertinent to the situation, because the transaction upon its face lies outside the plain intent of the statute. To hold otherwise would be to exalt artifice above reality and to deprive the statutory provision in question of all serious purpose.

Judge Learned Hand, author of the circuit court opinion in the *Gregory* case also denying reorganization status to the transaction, shortly thereafter wrote of the case:

> In Gregory v. Helvering . . . , the incorporators adopted the usual form of creating corporations; but their intent, or purpose, was merely to draught the papers, in fact not to create corporations as the court understood that word. That was the purpose which defeated their exemption, not the accompanying purpose to escape taxation; that purpose was legally neutral. Had they really meant to conduct a business by means of the two reorganized companies, they would have escaped whatever other aim they may have had, whether to avoid taxes, or to regenerate the world.

Chisholm v. Commissioner, 79 F.2d 14, 15 (2d Cir. 1935).

Line drawing and analysis in this area are difficult. Compare Judge Hand's later comments:

> The doctrine of Gregory v. Helvering . . . means that in construing words of a tax statute which describes commercial or industrial transactions we are to understand

> them to refer to transactions entered upon for commercial or industrial purposes and not to include transactions entered upon for no other motive but to escape taxation.

Commissioner v. Transport Trading & Terminal Corp., 176 F.2d 570, 572 (2d Cir. 1949).[4]

Although *Gregory* involved a divisive corporate reorganization, the business purpose doctrine can play an important role in acquisitive reorganizations as well. For an example of the interplay among the business purpose doctrine, the divisive reorganization provisions, and the acquisitive reorganization provisions, see Helvering v. Elkhorn Coal Co., 95 F.2d 732 (4th Cir. 1937). In *Elkhorn*, the taxpayer transferred some of its assets to a newly formed subsidiary, and the subsidiary's stock was then distributed to the taxpayer's shareholders, much as in *Gregory*. By itself, such a transaction qualified as a tax-free divisive D reorganization. Then, however, the taxpayer transferred its remaining assets to an unrelated corporation in exchange for voting stock of this company, a transaction that, standing on its own, would constitute an acquisitive C reorganization. Finally, the taxpayer completely liquidated, distributing the stock of the acquiring corporation. (At the time, the subsequent liquidation was not required as part of the C reorganization. Under current §368(a)(2)(G), the liquidation of the transferor corporation is mandatory.)

The statute then provided, as it does now, that a corporation must transfer "substantially all" of its properties to qualify as a C reorganization. By spinning off part of its assets to a newly formed corporation immediately before the nominal C reorganization, the taxpayer effectively circumvented the "substantially all" requirement. Because the creation of the subsidiary had no purpose other than to qualify the transaction as a tax-free reorganization, the transaction as a whole lacked the proper "spirit." Accordingly, the taxpayer's transfer of its assets to the acquiring corporation in exchange for voting stock of the acquiror, as well as the subsequent complete liquidation, was held to be a taxable event.

Although a transaction is unlikely be challenged under the business purpose doctrine if it has a substantial non-tax business purpose, the doctrine has gained new prominence because of the statutory enactment of the economic substance doctrine. Under §7701(o), for any transaction where the economic substance doctrine is relevant, the transaction is treated as having economic substance only if—

> (i) It changes in a meaningful way (apart from Federal income tax effects) the taxpayer's economic position; and
> (ii) The taxpayer has a substantial non-Federal income tax purpose for entering the transaction.

§7701(o)(5)(A). In other words, if a transaction where economic substance is relevant lacks a meaningful profit motive or a substantial non-tax business purpose, its tax benefits are not allowable. Section 7701(o) resolves a dispute that raged in the courts about whether economic substance required both a profit motive and non-tax business purpose, adopting the government's view that both are required.

4. See also Marvin A. Chirelstein, Learned Hand's Contribution to the Law of Tax Avoidance, 77 Yale L.J. 440 (1968) (discussing *Gregory*'s scope). What was most suspect about the *Gregory* transaction was the creation and immediate destruction of the Averill Corp. Under the step-transaction doctrine, United Mortgage Corp. could have been treated as simply distributing the Monitor Securities stock.

In addition, as an adjunct to §7701(o), Congress added substantial penalties for a transaction that lacks economic substance. It is then subject to a tax penalty of 20 or 40 percent on the portion of the underpayment of tax attributable to that failure. §6662(a) (providing for the 20-percent penalty); *id.* at (i) (increasing the penalty to 40 percent for any non-disclosed economic substance transaction). Most concerning for many, these are strict liability penalties; there is no reasonable cause exception.

Despite the enactment of §7701(o), there remain many unanswered questions about the economic substance doctrine. Those questions include when the doctrine is "relevant" to a transaction; when a transaction promises a "meaningful" change in a taxpayer's economic position; over what period of time that change should be measured; when a non-tax purpose is substantial; and so on. The government has announced that it will not address these or similar questions through regulations nor will it publish a list of transactions (sometimes called an "angels" list) that, it believes, will typically satisfy the doctrine. Thus, it appears that these questions will be answered over time by the courts on a case-by-case basis.

However, transactions that met the economic substance doctrine before the enactment of §7701(o) should continue to do so after its enactment. §7701(o)(5)(C) (providing that the determination of whether the economic substance doctrine is relevant to a transaction is made as if §7701(o) had never been enacted). Thus, even though a reorganization may provide tax benefits to its participants, those benefits are ones intended by the Code, and a reorganization typically should not be subject to challenge under the doctrine merely because of those benefits.

PROBLEMS

10-1. Would the transaction described in *Kass* now qualify as a reorganization under Treas. Regs. §1.368-1(e)? Would there by a better way to structure the transaction so as to ensure tax-free treatment to Mrs. Kass?

10-2. Determine whether the following transactions satisfy the continuity of interest requirement (in (a) and (b)) or continuity of business enterprise requirement (in (c)).

a. *X* Corp. has 100 shares outstanding, 40 owned by *A*, 40 by *B*, and 20 by *C*. The fair market value of *X* Corp. stock is $100 per share. *Y* Corp. is owned by 10 individuals. For every dollar of stock held by the *Y* shareholders, they each hold four dollars in 20-year notes of *Y*. *X* Corp. merges into *Y* Corp., with *A*, *B*, and *C* receiving two shares of *Y* stock (worth $100 per share) and an $800 20-year note of *Y* for every 10 shares of *X* stock tendered. What is the result if *A* and *B* receive only notes, and *C* receives only stock? Could there be a "reorganization" as to *C* alone?

b. *F* owns all the stock of *M* Corp., and *G* owns all the stock of *N* Corp. *M* Corp. is worth $1 million, and *N* Corp. is worth $100,000. *M* and *N* consolidate into newly formed *O* Corp., with *F* receiving 100 shares of class A common and *G* receiving 10 shares of class B common. Both classes have equal rights to dividends and on liquidation and both vote. The corporation, however, can redeem the class B shares at any time. What is the result if the class A shares can be redeemed at any time? If the class B shares can be redeemed for 80 percent of their fair market value?

c. *L* Corp. has lost money in the computer business for several years, and *P* Corp. is a profitable publisher of children's books. What are the consequences if *L* merges into *P*, with the *L* shareholders receiving stock of *P*, assuming that most of the *L* assets will be sold, and *P* Corp. will not enter the computer business? If the merger is structured such that *P* merges into *L*, once again assuming that the *L* assets will be sold, and only publishing will continue? If *L* and *P* formally consolidate into new corporation *LP*?

10-3. *T* Corp. merges into *A* Corp., with the *T* shareholders receiving solely *A* stock. Shortly thereafter, *X* purchases all of the *A* stock received by the former *T* shareholders. *X* has at all times owned all *A* stock (except for the *A* stock received by former *T* shareholders in the merger).

a. Does this transaction meet the continuity of interest requirement? Does it matter whether *X* is a corporation or an individual?
b. Does the transaction meet the continuity of business enterprise requirement if, as part of the same plan, *A* Corp. transfers the *T* assets to *S* Corp., its wholly owned subsidiary? How about if *A* Corp. owns all *S* voting common stock (worth $1 billion) but none of its nonvoting preferred stock (worth $100,000)?

C. DEFINITIONAL ISSUES

In analyzing whether a transaction is a reorganization, you first look to the transaction as a whole, asking whether it fits within one of the specific reorganization definitions and also meets the judicial requirements. If you conclude that a reorganization has occurred, you determine the parties' tax consequences by looking to §354, §356, §357, §358, §361, and §362, among other sections. If you conclude that a transaction is not a reorganization, do not assume that it is fully taxable. For example, a failed reorganization may be a nontaxable liquidation under §332 or described in §351. As a last warning, be sure to consider *all* the reorganization provisions before labeling a transaction as failing to qualify for reorganization treatment, for failure to qualify under one provision does not preclude qualification under other provisions. See page 373 infra.

Section 368(a) provides the definitions for the seven types of tax-free reorganizations, and §368(a)(1)(A)-(D) defines acquisitive reorganizations, the combination of two or more corporations. Each type of reorganization has somewhat different qualifications, and there is some overlap among the various types. Aside from §368(a)(2)(A) (providing that a reorganization qualifying as both a C and a D be treated as a D) and §368(a)(3)(C) (providing that a reorganization qualifying as a G must be treated as a G), the Code does not determine which type takes priority. No rule of priority is needed, though, because the applicable taxing provisions generally do not distinguish among the various types of reorganizations.

The choice of the proper type of reorganization is often governed by important non-tax factors. For example, because of contingent liabilities of the transferor corporation, the acquiring corporation may prefer a C to an A or B; preservation of certain rights or licenses of the acquired corporation may require using a B; state and federal securities law requirements may vary depending on the form chosen; shareholder approval of both the transferor and the acquiring corporation are usually required in an A—expensive and time-consuming procedures in the case of publicly held corporations—whereas only approval by shareholders of the transferor may be required in a B or C; appraisal rights for dissenters are more easily awarded in a B than in an A or C. As the various criteria for the different types of reorganizations are examined, keep in mind that the underlying purpose of the criteria in any reorganization should be to separate a nonrecognition change in form from a taxable sale or exchange.

1. *The A Reorganization: Statutory Mergers and Consolidations*

A transfer of assets by one corporation to another corporation meets the statutory requirements of §368(a)(1)(A) if the transfer is effected under a statute or statutes necessary to effect a merger or consolidation and the following two events occur simultaneously:

1. All target assets (other than those distributed in the transaction) and all target liabilities (other than those satisfied or discharged in the transaction) become assets and liabilities of a corporation; and
2. The target ceases its separate legal existence.

Treas. Regs. §1.368-2(b)(1)(ii). For this purpose, if a target merges into a disregarded entity, it is treated as merging into any corporation deemed to own the disregarded entity's assets immediately after the transaction. Treas Regs. §1.368-2(b)(1)(i)(C) and (ii)(A); *id.* at (b)(1)(iii) (example 2). Note that an A reorganization may involve domestic corporations, foreign corporations, or a mix of domestic and foreign corporations.

PROBLEMS

10-4. Which of the following transactions meet the statutory definition of an A reorganization? In each case, under applicable law, all *T* assets and all *T* liabilities become assets and liabilities of *X* and simultaneously *T* ceases to exist.

a. *T* is a corporation and *X* is a corporation;
b. *T* is a corporation and *X* is a disregarded entity wholly owned by *Y*, a corporation;
c. *T* is a corporation and *X* is a disregarded entity wholly owned by *Y*, a partnership;
d. *T* is a disregarded entity wholly owned by *Z*, a corporation, and *X* is a corporation.

10-5. *X* Corp. acquires all *T* stock and as of the effective time of the acquisition elects to treat *T* as a disregarded entity. Does the transaction meet the statutory definition of an A reorganization? See Treas. Regs. §1.368-2(b)(1)(iii) (example 9).

2. *The B Reorganization: Stock for Stock*

In a B reorganization, the acquiring corporation acquires stock of the target corporation and must control the target (but not necessarily wholly own it) immediately after the acquisition. The sole consideration that can be used by the acquiring corporation is its voting stock (or the voting stock of its parent). The voting stock may be common, preferred, or a combination of the two, but voting stock of both the acquiring corporation and its parent cannot be used. See Treas. Regs. §1.368-2(c). Unless there are prohibited pre- or post-reorganization stock sales, the continuity of interest doctrine will be satisfied in a B reorganization, because solely stock is used.

The acquiring corporation must control the target corporation immediately after the acquisition. That is, the acquiror must own at least 80 percent of the total combined voting power of target stock plus at least 80 percent of the total number of shares of each other class of target stock. §368(c); Rev. Rul. 59-259, 1959-1 C.B. 115.

In a B reorganization, the acquiror need not acquire a block of target stock in the acquisition that constitutes control. For example, assume that *A* Corp. historically has owned 30 percent of the only class of *T* Corp.'s stock. If *A* Corp. acquires an additional 51-percent block of *T* stock solely for its voting stock, the acquisition may be a B reorganization. Note, however, that the earlier acquisition of the 30-percent block, if independent of the later acquisition, would not be a B reorganization. See Treas. Regs. §1.368-2(c). This example illustrates that a "creeping acquisition" of control can qualify as a B reorganization (sometimes called a "creeping" B reorganization). In addition, an increase in ownership by a corporation that already has actual 80-percent control can also qualify as a B reorganization.

The main obstacle to a B reorganization is that the acquiring corporation cannot acquire any target stock for boot. See, however, Rev. Rul. 77-271, 1977-2 C.B. 116, in which a taxpayer exchanged stock of the target company for voting stock of equal market value of the acquiring company and, as part of the agreement, entered into an employment contract in exchange for additional shares of the acquiring corporation. The transaction was treated as a valid stock-for-stock exchange qualifying as a valid B and a separate employment arrangement in which the stock received was taxed as compensation income. A contract for fair cash salary for services to be rendered also is not treated as boot.

Although the acquiring corporation in a B reorganization must use only voting stock as consideration for the stock of the target corporation, no similar limitation is placed on the acquiring corporation's ability to acquire non-stock interests in the target corporation (such as debt instruments and stock options). See Rev. Rul. 70-269, 1970-1 C.B. 82 (stock options); Rev. Rul. 70-41, 1970-1 C.B. 77 (debt securities); Rev. Rul. 69-91, 1969-1 C.B. 106 (convertible debentures). Further, an exchange of securities for securities can be tax free under §354 as part of the reorganization even though the exchange of securities is ignored for determining whether the transaction qualifies as a "B" reorganization as a stock-for-stock exchange. Rev. Rul. 98-10, 1998-1 C.B. 643.

Payment by the acquiring corporation of the target corporation's share of reorganization expenses (such as legal, accounting, appraisal, printing, and registration fees) is also not treated as boot in a B reorganization. At the same time, similar expenses of the target shareholders may not be paid by the acquiring corporation without disqualifying the transaction as a B. Rev. Rul. 73-54, 1973-1 C.B. 187.

Chapman v. Commissioner

618 F.2d 856 (1st Cir. 1980)

Before Coffin, Chief Judge, Campbell and Bownes, Circuit Judges.

Levin H. CAMPBELL, Circuit Judge. . . .

We must decide whether the requirement of Section 368(a)(1)(B) that the acquisition of stock in one corporation by another be solely in exchange for voting stock of the acquiring corporation is met where, in related transactions, the acquiring corporation first acquires 8 percent of the acquiree's stock for cash and then acquires more than 80 percent of the acquiree in an exchange of stock for voting stock. The Tax Court agreed with the taxpayers that the latter exchange constituted a valid tax-free reorganization. Reeves v. Commissioner, 71 T.C. 727 (1979). . . .

The events giving rise to this dispute began in 1968, when the management of ITT, a large multinational corporation, became interested in acquiring Hartford [Fire Insurance Company] as part of a program of diversification. In October 1968, ITT executives approached Hartford about the possibility of merging the two corporations. This proposal was spurned by Hartford, which at the time was considering acquisitions of its own. In November 1968, ITT learned that approximately 1.3 million shares of Hartford, representing some 6 percent of Hartford's voting stock, were available for purchase from a mutual fund. After assuring Hartford's directors that ITT would not attempt to acquire Hartford against its will, ITT consummated the $63.7 million purchase from the mutual fund with Hartford's blessing. From November 13, 1968 to January 10, 1969, ITT also made a series of purchases on the open market totalling 458,000 shares which it acquired for approximately $24.4 million. A further purchase of 400 shares from an ITT subsidiary in March 1969 brought ITT's holdings to about 8 percent of Hartford's outstanding stock, all of which had been bought for cash.

In the midst of this flurry of stock-buying, ITT submitted a written proposal to the Hartford Board of Directors for the merger of Hartford into an ITT subsidiary. . . . Received by Hartford in December of 1968, the proposal was rejected in February of 1969. A counterproposal by Hartford's directors led to further negotiations, and on April 9, 1969 a provisional plan and agreement of merger was executed by the two corporations. . . .

[The merger plan, however, was not approved by the Connecticut Insurance Commissioner, and ITT instead executed a stock-for-stock exchange. In that exchange, Hartford shareholders transferred a controlling interest in Hartford stock solely for ITT voting preferred stock.]

Concluding that the entire transaction [did not constitute] a nontaxable reorganization, the Service assessed tax deficiencies against a number of former Hartford shareholders who had accepted the exchange offer. Appellees, along with other taxpayers, contested this action in the Tax Court, where the case was decided on appellees' motion for summary judgment. For purposes of this motion, the taxpayers conceded . . . that the initial cash purchases of Hartford stock had been made for the purpose of furthering ITT's efforts to acquire Hartford. . . .

I

The single issue raised on this appeal is whether "the acquisition" in this case complied with the requirement [of a B reorganization] that it be "solely for . . . voting stock." It is well settled that the "solely" requirement is mandatory; if any part of "the acquisition" includes a form of consideration other than voting stock, the transaction will not qualify as a (B) reorganization. See Helvering v. Southwest Consolidated Corp., 315 U.S. 194, 198 (1942) ("'Solely' leaves no leeway. Voting stock plus some other consideration does not meet the statutory requirement."). The precise issue before us is thus how broadly to read the term "acquisition." The Internal Revenue Service argues that "the acquisition . . . of stock of another corporation" must be understood to encompass the 1968-69 cash purchases as well as the 1970 exchange offer. If the IRS is correct, "the acquisition" here fails as a (B) reorganization. The taxpayers, on the other hand, would limit "the acquisition" to the part of a sequential transaction of this nature which meets the requirements of subsection (B). They argue that the 1970 exchange of stock for stock was itself an "acquisition" by ITT of stock in Hartford solely in exchange for ITT's voting stock, such that after the exchange took place ITT controlled Hartford. Taxpayers contend that the earlier cash purchases of 8 percent, even if conceded to be part of the same acquisitive plan, are essentially irrelevant to the tax-free reorganization otherwise effected.

The Tax Court accepted the taxpayers' reading of the statute, effectively overruling its own prior decision in Howard v. Commissioner, 24 T.C. 792 (1955), rev'd on other grounds, 238 F.2d 943 (7th Cir. 1956). The plurality opinion stated its "narrow" holding as follows:

> We hold that where, as is the case herein, 80 percent or more of the stock of a corporation is acquired in one transaction, in exchange for which only voting stock is furnished as consideration, the "solely for voting stock" requirement of section 368(a)(1)(B) is satisfied.

. . . The plurality treated as "irrelevant" the 8 percent of Hartford's stock purchased for cash, although the opinion left somewhat ambiguous the question whether the 8 percent was irrelevant because of the 14-month time interval separating the transactions or because the statute was not concerned with transactions over and above those mathematically necessary to the acquiring corporation's attainment of control.

II

For reasons set forth extensively in section III of this opinion, we do not accept the position adopted by the Tax Court. . . . As explained below, we find a strong implication in the language of the statute, in the legislative history, in the regulations, and in the decisions of other courts that cash purchases which are concededly "parts of" a stock-for-stock exchange must be considered constituent elements of the "acquisition" for purposes of applying the "solely for . . . voting stock" requirement of Section 368(a)(1)(B). We believe the presence of nonstock consideration in such an acquisition, regardless of whether such consideration is necessary to the gaining of control, is inconsistent with treatment of the acquisition as a nontaxable reorganization. . . .

III

A . . .

We begin with the words of the statute itself. The reorganization definitions contained in Section 368(a)(1) are precise, technical, and comprehensive. They were intended to define the exclusive means by which nontaxable corporate reorganizations could be effected. See Treas. Reg. §1.368-1 (1960); 3 J. Mertens, The Law of Federal Income Taxation §20.86 at 364 (1972). In examining the language of the (B) provision, we discern two possible meanings. On the one hand, the statute could be read to say that a successful reorganization occurs whenever Corporation *X* exchanges its own voting stock for stock in Corporation *Y*, and, immediately after the transaction, Corporation *X* controls more than 80 percent of *Y*'s stock. On this reading, purchases of shares for which any part of the consideration takes the form of "boot" should be ignored, since the definition is only concerned with transactions which meet the statutory requirements as to consideration and control. To take an example, if Corporation *X* bought 50 percent of the shares of *Y*, and then almost immediately exchanged part of its voting stock for the remaining 50 percent of *Y*'s stock, the question would arise whether the second transaction was a (B) reorganization. Arguably, the statute can be read to support such a finding. In the second transaction, *X* exchanged only stock for stock (meeting the "solely" requirement), and after the transaction was completed *X* owned *Y* (meeting the "control" requirement).

The alternative reading of the statute — the one which we are persuaded to adopt — treats the (B) definition as prescriptive, rather than merely descriptive. We read the statute to mean that the entire transaction which constitutes "the acquisition" must not contain any nonstock consideration if the transaction is to qualify as a (B) reorganization. In the example given above, where *X* acquired 100 percent of *Y*'s stock, half for cash and half for voting stock, we would interpret "the acquisition" as referring to the entire transaction, so that the "solely for . . . voting stock" requirement would not be met. We believe if Congress had intended the statute to be read as merely descriptive, this intent would have been more clearly spelled out in the statutory language.

We recognize that the Tax Court adopted neither of these two readings. For reasons to be discussed in connection with the legislative history which follows, the Tax Court purported to limit its holding to cases, such as this one, where more than 80 percent of the stock of Corporation *Y* passes to Corporation *X* in exchange solely for voting stock. The Tax Court presumably would assert that the 50/50 hypothetical posited above can be distinguished from this case, and that its holding implies no view as to the hypothetical. . . . In order to distinguish the 80 percent case from the 50 percent case, it is necessary to read "the acquisition" as referring to at least the amount of stock constituting "control" (80 percent) where related cash purchases are present. Yet the Tax Court recognized that "the acquisition" cannot always refer to the conveyance of an 80 percent bloc of stock in one transaction, since to do so would frustrate the intent of the 1954 amendments to permit so-called "creeping acquisitions."

The Tax Court's interpretation of the statute suffers from a more fundamental defect, as well. In order to justify the limitation of its holding to transactions involving 80 percent or more of the acquiree's stock, the Tax Court focused on the *passage* of control as the primary requirement of the (B) provision. This focus is misplaced. Under the present version of the statute, the *passage* of control is entirely irrelevant; the only material requirement is that the acquiring corporation have control immediately after the acquisition. As the statute explicitly states, it does not matter if the acquiring corporation already has control before the transaction begins, so long as such control exists at the completion of the reorganization. Whatever talismanic quality may have attached to the acquisition of control under previous versions of the Code, see Part III B infra, is altogether absent from the version we must apply to this case. In our view, the statute should be read to mean that the related transactions that constitute "the acquisition," whatever percentage of stock they may represent, must meet both the "solely for voting stock" and the "control immediately after" requirements of Section 368(a)(1)(B). Neither the reading given the statute by the Tax Court, nor that proposed as the first alternative above, adequately corresponds to the careful language Congress employed in this section of the Code.

B

The 1924 Code defined reorganization, in part, as "a merger or consolidation (including the acquisition by one corporation of at least a majority of the voting stock and at least a majority of the total number of shares of all other classes of stock of another corporation, or substantially all of the properties of another corporation)." Pub. L. No. 68-176, c. 234, §203(h)(1), 43 Stat. 257. Although the statute did not specifically limit the consideration that could be given in exchange for stock or assets, courts eventually developed the so-called "continuity of interest" doctrine, which held that exchanges that did not include some quantum of stock as consideration were ineligible for reorganization treatment for lack of a continuing property interest on the part of the acquiree's shareholders. See, e.g., Cortland Specialty Co. v. Commissioner, 60 F.2d 937, 939-40 (2d Cir. 1932), cert. denied, 288 U.S. 599 (1933); Pinellas Ice Co. v. Commissioner, 287 U.S. 462, 470 (1933).

Despite this judicial development, sentiment was widespread in Congress that the reorganization provisions lent themselves to abuse, particularly in the form of so-called "disguised sales." . . . The Senate Finance Committee . . . propos[ed] to retain these provisions, but with "restrictions designed to prevent tax avoidance." S. Rep. No. 558, 73d Cong., 2d Sess. 15. . . . One of these restrictions was the requirement that the acquiring corporation obtain at least 80 percent, rather than a bare majority, of the stock of the acquiree. The second requirement was stated in the Senate Report as follows: "the acquisition, whether of stock or of substantially all the properties, must be in exchange solely for the voting stock of the acquiring corporation." *Id.* at 17. The Senate amendments were enacted as Section 112(g)(1) of the Revenue Act of 1934. . . .

Congress revised this definition in 1939 in response to the Supreme Court's decision in United States v. Hendler, 303 U.S. 564 (1938), which held that an acquiring corporation's assumption of the acquiree's liabilities in an asset-acquisition was equivalent to the receipt of "boot" by the acquiree. Since virtually all asset-acquisition reorganizations necessarily involve the assumption of the acquiree's liabilities, a literal application of the "solely for . . . voting stock" requirement would have effectively abolished this form of tax-free reorganization. In the Revenue Act of 1939, Congress separated the stock-acquisition and asset-acquisition provisions in order to exempt the assumption of liabilities in the latter category of cases from the "solely for . . . voting stock" requirement. . . .

The next major change in this provision occurred in 1954. In that year, the House Bill, H.R. 8300, would have drastically altered the corporate reorganization sections of the Tax Code, permitting, for example, both stock and "boot" as consideration in a corporate acquisition, with gain recognized only to the extent of the "boot." . . . The Senate Finance Committee, in order to preserve the familiar terminology and structure of the 1939 Code, proposed a new version of Section 112(g)(1), which would retain the "solely for . . . voting stock" requirement, but alter the existing control requirement to permit so-called "creeping acquisitions." Under the Senate Bill, it would no longer be necessary for the acquiring corporation to obtain 80 percent or more of the acquiree's stock in one "reorganization." The Senate's proposal permitted an acquisition to occur in stages; a bloc of shares representing less than 80 percent could be added to earlier acquisitions, regardless of the consideration given earlier, to meet the control requirement. The Report of the Senate Finance Committee gave this example of the operation of the creeping acquisition amendment:

> [C]orporation *A* purchased 30 percent of the common stock of corporation *W* (the only class of stock outstanding) for cash in 1939. On March 1, 1955, corporation *A* offers to exchange its own voting stock, for all the stock of corporation *W* tendered within 6 months from the date of the offer. Within the 6 months period corporation *A* acquires an additional 60 percent of the stock of *W* for its own voting stock. As a result of the 1955 transactions, corporation *A* will own 90 percent of all of corporation *W*'s stock, No gain or loss is recognized with respect to the exchanges of the *A* stock for the *W* stock.
>
> 1954 Senate Report, supra, at 273. . . . See also Treas. Reg. §1.368-2(c) (1960).

At the same time the Senate was revising the (B) provision (while leaving intact the "solely for . . . voting stock" requirement), it was also rewriting the (C) provision to explicitly permit up to 20 percent of the consideration in an asset acquisition to take the form of money or other nonstock property. See . . . §368(a)(2)(B). The Senate revisions of subsections (B) and (C) were ultimately passed, and have remained largely unchanged since 1954. . . . Proposals for altering the (B) provision to allow "boot" as consideration have been made, but none has been enacted.

As this history shows, Congress has had conflicting aims in this complex and difficult area. On the one hand, the 1934 Act evidences a strong intention to limit the reorganization provisions to prevent forms of tax avoidance that had proliferated under the earlier revenue acts. This intention arguably has been carried forward in the current versions through retention of the "solely for . . . voting stock" requirement in (B), even while the (C) provision was being loosened. On the other hand, both the 1939 and 1954 revisions represented attempts to make the reorganization procedures more accessible and practical in both the (B) and (C) areas. In light of the conflicting purposes, we can discern no clear Congressional mandate in the present structure of the (B) provision, either in terms of the abuses sought to be remedied or the beneficial transactions sought to be facilitated. At best, we think Congress has drawn somewhat arbitrary lines separating those transactions that resemble mere changes in form of ownership and those that contain elements of a sale or purchase arrangement. In such circumstances we believe it is more appropriate to examine the specific rules and requirements Congress enacted, rather than some questionably delineated "purpose" or "policy," to determine whether a particular transaction qualifies for favorable tax treatment. . . .

C

Besides finding support for the IRS position both in the design of the statute and in the legislative history, we find support in the regulations adopted by the Treasury Department construing these statutory provisions. We of course give weight to the statutory construction contemporaneously developed by the agency entrusted by Congress with the task of applying these laws. The views of the Treasury on tax matters, while by no means definitive, undoubtedly reflect a familiarity with the intricacies of the tax code that surpasses our own. . . .

D

Finally, we turn to the body of case law that has developed concerning (B) reorganizations to determine how previous courts have dealt with this question. Of the seven prior cases in this area, all to a greater or lesser degree support the result we have reached, and none supports the result reached by the Tax Court. [A]fter carefully reviewing the precedents, we are satisfied that the decision of the Tax Court represents a sharp break with the previous judicial constructions of this statute, and a departure from the usual rule of stare decisis, which applies with special force in the tax field where uncertainty and variety are ordinarily to be avoided.

Of the seven precedents, the most significant would seem to be Howard v. Commissioner, 238 F.2d 943 (7th Cir. 1956), rev'g, 24 T.C. 792 (1955), which stands out as the one case before *Reeves* that specifically addressed the issue raised herein. In *Howard*, the Truax-Traer Coal Company acquired 80.19 percent of the outstanding stock of Binkley Coal Company solely in exchange for Truax-Traer voting stock. At the same time and as part of the same plan of acquisition, Truax-Traer purchased the other 19.81 percent of Binkley's stock for cash. The taxpayers, former shareholders of Binkley who had exchanged their shares solely for voting stock, sold some of the Truax-Traer stock they had received in August 1950, the same year as the exchange. The Commissioner, treating the exchange as a taxable event and not a reorganization, employed a new holding period, beginning with the effective date of the exchange, and treated the taxpayers' gain on their sale of the Truax-Traer stock as a short-term capital gain. The Tax Court sustained the Commissioner, concluding the exchange had not been made "solely for . . . voting stock," as required by the 1939 Act, even though the cash purchases were not essential to Truax-Traer's acquisition of control. 24 T.C. at 804.

The Seventh Circuit, after reviewing the legislative history of Section 112(g)(1)(B) of the 1939 Code, agreed with the Tax Court's conclusion that the presence of cash purchases prevented the transaction from meeting the "solely" requirement of the statute. . . . The principal linchpin of the Seventh Circuit's decision was Helvering v. Southwest Consolidated Corp., 315 U.S. 194 (1942), in which the Supreme Court denied tax-free treatment to an asset acquisition under the 1934 Act because a substantial amount of the consideration was given in the form of stock warrants and cash. The Court first noted that under the law existing before 1934, this transaction would have been a perfectly valid tax-free reorganization. The revised statute, . . . had made the continuity of interest test much stricter, however:

> Congress has provided that the assets of the transferor corporation must be acquired in exchange "solely" for "voting stock" of the transferee. "Solely" leaves no leeway. Voting stock plus some other consideration does not meet the statutory requirement.

315 U.S. at 198. The Seventh Circuit noted that in the 1934 Act the asset and stock acquisition reorganizations were dealt with in the same clause both in the statutory language and in the legislative history. It therefore seemed reasonable to the Seventh Circuit to conclude that the Supreme Court's "no leeway" rule for asset acquisitions applied with equal force to stock acquisitions.

Appellees argue that *Southwest Consolidated* is distinguishable from the present facts, and, implicitly, that it should not have been relied on by the *Howard* court. This argument rests, in our view, on a strained reading of *Southwest Consolidated.* The taxpayers point out that the nonstock consideration in that case amounted to 37 percent of the total consideration, by the Tax Court's reckoning. Further, they say that the stock and nonstock consideration could not be separated where one bundle of assets was exchanged for one bundle of consideration, so that *Southwest Consolidated* was essentially a mixed consideration case. We disagree. Had the Supreme Court chosen to decide the issue of whether "substantially all" the assets of one corporation were obtained solely for voting stock, it could have allocated the consideration on a proportional basis, much as the Tax Court did in making its calculations. The Supreme Court did not consider, however, whether the voting stock consideration was sufficient to cover "substantially all" the assets, so that Section 112(g)(1)(B) would be satisfied. The Court determined rather that the presence of *any* nonstock consideration in the acquisition negated the possibility of a valid tax-free reorganization. While the facts were such that the Court could have reached the same result on another rationale, this does not detract from the weight of its words. The Seventh Circuit was, in our opinion, justified in resting its holding by analogy on the decision in *Southwest Consolidated.* . . .

Besides questioning its lineage, the Tax Court plurality made three attempts to distinguish the *Howard* case or undercut its holding. First, the Tax Court argued that *Howard* was a case in which "some stockholders involved in the one exchange transaction . . . received cash." 71 T.C. at 737. The impact of this distinction is less than clear. There was no finding in *Howard* that any stockholder received both cash and stock for the same shares. In both *Howard* and this case, more than 80 percent of the shares were exchanged for stock only, and additional shares were purchased for cash. The only possible meaning of the Tax Court's statement is that it did not consider the 1968-69 cash purchases and the 1970 exchange offer part of "one exchange transaction." Yet the taxpayers' specific concession on motion for summary judgment was that the two events should be assumed to constitute "parts of the 1970 exchange offer reorganization." We do not see how *Howard* can be distinguished from the present case other than on a finding that the cash and stock transactions here were unrelated as a matter of law, a finding the Tax Court specifically declined to make. (As we are remanding this latter issue to the Tax Court, we take no position on it now.)

The Tax Court's second attack on *Howard* . . . is equally unpersuasive. The fact that one shareholder of Binkley (the acquiree) received voting stock for some of its shares and cash for other shares, so that the 80 percent necessary for control was not acquired from shareholders receiving only stock, was not relied on by the Seventh Circuit. Furthermore, the focus of the statute is on the consideration furnished in the exchange, not on the consideration received by a particular shareholder. . . . Indeed, in this case there is no proof that some of ITT's earlier market purchases were not made from shareholders of Hartford who later exchanged other shares for ITT's voting stock. . . .

Even were we doubtful as to the correctness of the result reached in *Howard* (and we are not), we would nonetheless be reluctant to see a rule of tax law which has stood virtually unchallenged by courts for 25 years discarded so unceremoniously. As the dissenting judges of the Tax Court noted, much tax planning must proceed on the basis of settled rules. Avoidance of risk and uncertainty are often the keys to a successful transaction. Transactions may have been structured on the basis of *Howard,* with cash intentionally introduced to prevent reorganization treatment. Where a long standing tax rule of this sort is not clearly contrary to Congressional intent or markedly inconsistent with some generally accepted understanding of correct doctrine, we think the proper body to make changes aimed at improving the law is Congress, and not the courts. The complex and delicate judgments as to proper tax policy, and the balancing of interests between corporations, their shareholders, and the public, required to formulate appropriate rules in this area are not the proper province of courts. . . .

Our reading of the statute is reinforced by another more recent circuit decision as well. In Mills v. Commissioner, 331 F.2d 321 (5th Cir. 1964), rev'g, 39 T.C. 393 (1962), the issue was whether cash payments for fractional shares in an exchange prevented a nontaxable reorganization. General Gas Corporation, the acquiror, offered the three taxpayers, sole stockholders in three small gas corporations, shares of General common stock in exchange for all of their stock. The number of General shares to be exchanged at a value of $14 per share was to be determined by measuring the net book value of the three small corporations. In the event the purchase price was not evenly divisible by 14, cash was to be paid in lieu of fractional shares. As a result, each taxpayer received 1,595 shares of General stock and $27.36 in cash. The Tax Court held this transaction invalid as a tax-free reorganization, declining to adopt a de minimis rule. 39 T.C. at 400. The Fifth Circuit agreed that cash could not form any part of the consideration in a (B) reorganization, but concluded in reversing the Tax Court that the fractional-share arrangement was merely a bookkeeping convenience and not an independent part of the consideration. 331 F.2d at 324-25.

Taxpayers, and the Tax Court, argued that *Mills* was distinguishable, despite its sweeping language, because each shareholder of the acquired corporations received both stock and cash in the exchange. We have discussed earlier our reasons for rejecting any rule premised on the consideration received by the acquiree's shareholders. If *Mills* were distinguishable at all, it would be only because the consideration for some of the shares in *Mills* consisted of both stock and cash. But even this distinction evaporates when one notes that the one share in each exchange for which a fractional share would have been necessary never constituted more than 20 percent of the stock of any one of the acquiree corporations (since each shareholder held at least six shares in each corporation). In every exchange it was theoretically possible to identify a bloc of more than 80 percent of the stock of the acquiree which was exchanged solely for the voting stock of the acquiring corporation. Thus, in the only case raising the issue now before us under the 1954 Code, the Tax Court accepted as a premise that no cash was permissible as consideration in a (B) reorganization, even where the facts showed that control had passed solely for voting stock.

IV

We have stated our ruling, and the reasons that support it. In conclusion, we would like to respond briefly to the arguments raised by the Tax Court, the District Court of Delaware, and the taxpayers in this case against the rule we have reaffirmed today. The principal argument, repeated again and again, concerns the supposed lack of policy behind the rule forbidding cash in a (B) reorganization where the control requirement is met solely for voting stock. It is true that the Service has not pointed to tax loopholes that would be opened were the rule to be relaxed as appellees request. We also recognize, as the Tax Court and others have highlighted, that the rule may produce results which some would view as anomalous. For example, if Corporation *X* acquires 80 percent of Corporation *Y*'s stock solely for voting stock, and is content to leave the remaining 20 percent outstanding, no one would question that a valid (B) reorganization has taken place. If Corporation *X* then decides to purchase stock from the remaining shareholders, the *Howard* rule might result in loss of nontaxable treatment for the stock acquisition if the two transactions were found to be related. See 71 T.C. at 740-41. The Tax Court asserted that there is no conceivable Congressional policy that would justify such a result. Further, it argued, Congress could not have felt that prior cash purchases would forever ban a later successful (B) reorganization since the 1954 amendments, as the legislative history makes clear, specifically provided that prior cash purchases would not prevent a creeping acquisition.

While not without force, this line of argument does not in the end persuade us. First of all, as already discussed, the language of the statute, and the longstanding interpretation given it by the courts, are persuasive reasons for our holding even in the absence of any clear policy behind Congress' expression of its will. Furthermore, we perceive statutory anomalies of another sort which the Tax Court's rule would only magnify. It is clear from the regulations, for example, that a corporation which already owned as much as 80 percent of another's stock, acquired solely for cash, could in some circumstances acquire all or a part of the remainder solely for voting stock as a valid (B) reorganization. Why, then, could not as little as 10 percent of an acquisition constitute a (B) reorganization, if made solely for voting stock, even though the remaining transactions totaling more than 80 percent were made for nonstock consideration? If it is true that Congress did not view related cash transactions as tainting a stock-acquisition reorganization, why would it enact a "solely for . . . voting stock" requirement at all, except to the extent necessary to prevent mixed consideration of the sort employed in the "disguised sales" of the twenties?

Possibly, Congress' insertion of the "solely for . . . voting stock" requirement into the 1934 Act was, as one commentator has suggested, an overreaction to a problem which could have been dealt with through more precise and discriminating measures. But we do not think it appropriate for a court to tell Congress how to do its job in an area such as this. If a more refined statutory scheme would be appropriate, such changes should be sought from the body empowered to make them. While we adhere to the general practice of construing statutes so as to further their demonstrated policies, we have no license to rework whole statutory schemes in pursuit of policy goals which Congress has nowhere articulated. Appellees have not shown us any reason to believe that reaffirmation of the settled rule in this area will frustrate the Congressional purpose of making the (B) reorganization provision generally available to those who comply with the statutory requirements.

A second major argument, advanced primarily by the district court in Pierson [v. United States, 472 F. Supp. 957 (D. Del. 1979), rev'd sub nom. Heverly v. Commissioner, 621 F.2d 1227 (3d Cir. 1980)], is that the previous cases construing this statute are suspect because they did not give proper weight to the changes wrought by the 1954 amendments. In particular, the court argued the liberalization of the "boot" allowance in (C) reorganizations and the allowance of creeping (B) acquisitions showed that Congress had no intent or desire to forbid "boot" of up to 20 percent in a (B) reorganization. As we have discussed earlier, we draw the opposite conclusion from the legislative history. Liberalization of the (C) provision shows only that Congress, when it wished to do so, could grant explicit leeway in the reorganization rules. . . .

A third argument asserts that reliance on the literal language of the 1954 Code, and in particular a focus on the interpretation of "acquisition," is unjustified because the 1954 Code was not intended to alter the status of (B) reorganizations under the 1934 and 1939 Codes. According to this argument, the acquisition of at least 80 percent of the acquiree's stock solely for voting stock was allowed under the pre-1954 version, and must still be allowed even though the present statute refers only to "the acquisition . . . of stock" with no percentage specified. This argument assumes the answer to the question that is asked. As *Howard* and *Southwest Consolidated* illustrate, it has been the undeviating understanding of courts, until now, that the pre-1954 statutes did not allow cash or other "boot" in a (B) reorganization. It cannot be inferred that Congress left intact a rule which never existed by enacting language inconsistent with such a rule.

Finally, we see no merit at all in the suggestion that we should permit "boot" in a (B) reorganization simply because "boot" is permitted in some instances in (A) and (C) reorganizations. Congress has never indicated that these three distinct categories of transactions are to be interpreted in pari materia. In fact, striking differences in the treatment of the three subsections have been evident in the history of the reorganization statutes. We see no reason to believe a difference in the treatment of "boot" in these transactions is impermissible or irrational. . . .

The case will be remanded to the Tax Court for further proceedings consistent with this opinion. . . .

NOTES

1. *The* Chapman *decision.* Notice how the taxpayer in *Chapman* waged a double-barreled attack against the *Howard* adverse precedent. Not only did the taxpayer seek to distinguish *Howard,* but the case cited for support by the *Howard* court (Helvering v. Southwest Consolidated Corp.) also was distinguished. By this technique, the taxpayer offered the court the opportunity to overrule or distinguish the adverse precedent of *Howard.*

The court stated that it could discern no clear policy argument supporting one side's interpretation over the other. In that light, was the court's decision to adopt a narrow construction of the statute a good one, particularly when a "corporate reorganization" (in the colloquial sense) was effected? The Tax Court seemingly has accepted the *Chapman* construction of §368(a)(1)(B). Clark v. Commissioner, 86 T.C. 138, 142 n.5 (1986).

In fact, the Service argued that there was a good policy reason for rejecting the taxpayer's argument in this case. A voting block of 10 percent to 15 percent of a publicly held corporation often produces effective control. By purchasing about 8 percent of Hartford's stock, ITT was able to force on the Hartford board of directors a merger that it had already rejected on almost the same terms. Counsel for the government argued on appeal that a proper interpretation of the statute should not permit such "gunboat diplomacy." Would such a policy argument have been a proper basis for the court's holding?

The effect of the circuit court's decision in *Chapman* was to remand the case to the Tax Court for trial on the merits. While petitions for certiorari in *Chapman* and a related case were pending, however, the case was settled with ITT's agreement to make a one-time payment of $18.5 million to the U.S. Treasury. Why would ITT, which was not a party to the action, agree to pay the settlement? What should the tax consequences of this settlement have been to the former Hartford shareholders? In fact, the settlement included the provisions that ITT would not deduct the settlement payment and that no tax deficiencies would be asserted against the former Hartford shareholders. These shareholders, though, were bound to carry over their Hartford stock basis into their ITT stock.

In Rev. Rul. 85-139, 1985-2 C.B. 123, the Service ruled that the solely-for-voting-stock requirement of a B reorganization is not met when the acquiring corporation exchanges its voting stock for 90 percent of the target corporation's stock and a wholly owned subsidiary of the acquiring corporation acquires 10 percent of the target's stock for cash. Is the emphasis placed by *Chapman* and Rev. Rul. 85-139 on the "transaction" justified? To what extent should motives matter?

In Rev. Rul. 69-294, 1969-1 C.B. 110, *X* Corp. owned all the outstanding stock of *Y* Corp. *Y* Corp., in turn, owned more than 80 percent of the outstanding stock of *Z* Corp. To obtain direct ownership of 100 percent of *Z*, *X* caused *Y* to liquidate, and *X* immediately thereafter acquired the minority stock in *Z* for its own voting stock. The Service ruled that the latter exchange was taxable and did not qualify as a B reorganization because *X*, as part of a single unified transaction, had acquired all the stock of *Z* but not "solely for" *X* voting stock. The reasoning was that more than 80 percent of the *Z* stock was received in exchange for its *Y* stock. Cf. Treas. Regs. §1.368-2(d)(4)(i) (for an arguably contrary rule for C reorganizations).

Suppose a corporation adopts a "poison pill," an anti-takeover provision giving shareholders the right to purchase at a bargain price additional shares of the company (or of any acquiring company) if there is a hostile takeover. Can the corporation now participate as the acquiring corporation in a B reorganization, or will the poison pill attached to its stock constitute impermissible non-stock consideration? The Service has consistently ruled that the poison pill rights do not constitute non-stock consideration. See Priv. Ltr. Rul. 9125013; Priv. Ltr. Rul. 8925087; Priv. Ltr. Rul. 8808081.

2. *Contingent stock.* An acquiring corporation in a merger may, in addition to issuing shares of stock outright to the shareholders of the target company, promise to pay additional shares on the occurrence of certain contingencies. The type of contingencies may be, for example, the earnings performance of the target

company over some specified future period or the trading value of its stock. The use of contingent stock allows the parties to exploit differing expectations of the future to strike a deal that otherwise would be unobtainable. See H. Raiffa, The Art and Science of Negotiation 91-107 (1982).

Contingent rights to acquire stock that are issued in connection with a reorganization have been treated as stock rather than boot. See Carlberg v. United States, 281 F.2d 507 (8th Cir. 1960); Hamrick v. Commissioner, 43 T.C. 21 (1964). Rev. Proc. 77-37, 1977-2 C.B. 568, provides guidelines for advanced rulings when contingent or escrowed stock is involved. The most important of these relates to the maximum number of shares whose receipt can be made contingent (50 percent of the total that can be issued) and the time during which the contingencies must be resolved (five years). See also Rev. Proc. 84-42, 1984-1 C.B. 521 (amplifying Rev. Proc. 77-37).

Section 483 creates interest income in the case of contingent stock deferred for more than one year after the exchange unless interest is provided for in the form of additional shares. Solomon v. Commissioner, 570 F.2d 28 (2d Cir. 1977); accord, Jeffers v. United States, 556 F.2d 986 (Cl. Ct. 1977); Catterall v. Commissioner, 68 T.C. 413 (1977), aff'd sub nom. Vorbleski v. Commissioner, 589 F.2d 123 (3d Cir. 1978). But in Rev. Rul. 70-120, 1970-1 C.B. 124, the Service ruled that deferred payments do not exist in a reorganization in which bonus stock is issued in each shareholder's name and then is placed in escrow if the shareholders can vote the shares and receive dividends even though they may later be divested of the bonus shares. The result is that interest income under §483 can be avoided if all the stock is issued initially even though some is in effect made contingent by being placed in an escrow. Why? Note that under the regulations, the interest portion imputed on contingent stock is not treated as boot and will not destroy the tax-free status of the reorganization. Treas. Regs. §§1.483-2(a)(2), 1.483-2(b)(3)(i), and 1.483-1(b)(6) (examples 7 and 8).

3. *Dissenters.* In Rev. Rul. 68-285, 1968-1 C.B. 147, the Service concluded that a transaction qualified as a B reorganization even though one-quarter of the target shareholders dissented. The dissenters received cash from an escrow account established by the target. Nondissenting shareholders received solely acquiror voting stock in exchange for their target stock. Because the acquiror did not pay the dissenters or reimburse the target, directly or indirectly, for the escrow payments, it was treated as acquiring the target stock solely for its voting stock.

4. *Cash in lieu of fractional shares.* In Rev. Rul. 66-365, 1966-2 C.B. 116, the Service ruled that cash paid in lieu of issuing fractional shares will not be regarded as boot consideration in an acquisitive reorganization. This favorable ruling is limited, however, to those cases in which the cash is not a separately bargained-for consideration. In what circumstances might cash in lieu of fractional shares be separately bargained for? See also Rev. Rul. 69-34, 1969-1 C.B. 105, and Rev. Rul. 74-36, 1974-1 C.B. 85, extending this rule to E and F reorganizations.

PROBLEM

10-6. Determine whether the following transactions are "reorganizations" within the meaning of §368(a)(1)(B).

a. To ensure a ready source of newsprint, News Corp. purchases 85 percent of the stock of Paper Co. for cash. One year later, News Corp. acquires the remaining stock of Paper Co. in exchange for its own voting preferred stock. What is the result if News Corp. used voting stock of its parent corporation? Of its wholly owned subsidiary? Could News Corp. use its own nonvoting common stock? Can News Corp. pay the cost of registering the stock received by the shareholders of Paper Co.?

b. *T* owns all 100 outstanding shares of *Z* Corp. The shares have an aggregate value of $100,000 and are subject to a mortgage of $15,000 incurred by *T* to remodel her home. Big Corp. acquires all the stock of *Z* by exchanging 85 shares of its $1,000 par value voting preferred for the *Z* shares and assuming the outstanding debt. What is the result if it took the shares subject to the debt, but *T* remained personally liable on it?

3. *The C Reorganization: Stock for Assets*

An acquisition of target assets may qualify as a C reorganization if it meets the following statutory requirements:

1. The acquiror must acquire "substantially all" of the properties of the target corporation.
2. The acquiror must acquire the target assets using solely its voting stock or solely the voting stock of a corporation that controls the acquiror. Stock of both corporations cannot be used. For this purpose, target liabilities are disregarded.
3. The target must distribute all of its properties in liquidation, unless the government waives the distribution requirement.

§368(a)(1)(C) and (a)(2)(G). See Rev. Proc. 89-50, 1989-2 C.B. 631 (for circumstances under which the Service may waive the distribution requirement).

Accordingly, the C reorganization, like a statutory merger, is an asset acquisition. As in a B reorganization (and unlike a statutory merger), however, Congress has limited the allowable consideration in a C reorganization to voting stock of the acquiring corporation or its parent. §368(a)(1)(C) (parenthetical language).

In United States v. Hendler, 303 U.S. 564 (1938), the Supreme Court held that the assumption by the acquiring corporation of a target liability constituted boot. Because most businesses encumber their assets, the practical effect of the *Hendler* decision was to eliminate the C reorganization as a viable possibility. Congress responded by adding to the definition of a C reorganization that the acquiring corporation's assumption of a liability (or taking property subject to a liability) will not cause the transaction to lose its reorganization status. See §368(a)(1)(C). A further anti-*Hendler* rule was enacted in §357, discussed at pages 39-41 supra in the context of §351 incorporations and at page 403 infra in the context of reorganizations.

The technical traps of the reorganization provisions are vividly illustrated by some problems that have arisen under §368(a)(1)(C)'s requirement that the acquiring corporation acquire "substantially all of the properties" of another corporation.

In Bausch & Lomb Optical Co. v. Commissioner, 267 F.2d 75 (2d Cir. 1959), the acquiring corporation owned 79 percent of the transferor corporation. The parent issued its stock for all the assets of the subsidiary, and the subsidiary then liquidated. The parent received back 79 percent of the newly issued stock, and the minority shareholders of the subsidiary became shareholders of the parent. Should the acquisition have been taxed as a C reorganization?

The court held that the transaction did not qualify as a C reorganization, because the parent acquired 79 percent of the subsidiary's assets in exchange for stock of the subsidiary as part of the liquidation. Only the remaining 21 percent was acquired for voting stock of the parent. Therefore, the parent received less than "substantially all" of the subsidiary's properties in exchange for its own stock, and it did not acquire the subsidiary's properties solely for its voting stock.

Regulations have overturned *Bausch & Lomb Optical.* Treas. Regs. §1.368-2(d)(4). See also Treas. Regs. §1.368-1(e)(1) and (7) (example 7) (illustrating that the continuity of interest requirement is satisfied to the extent the acquiror exchanges target stock for a direct interest in target assets). Note that if the acquisition in *Bausch & Lomb Optical* had been effected by merger, it could have qualified as an A reorganization.

NOTES

1. *"Substantially all" of the properties.* Under Rev. Proc. 77-37 (§3.01), 1977-2 C.B. 568, for advance ruling purposes, the Service will consider the "substantially all" requirement to be met by the transfer of at least 70 percent of the target's gross assets and 90 percent of its net assets. The 70-percent test is met if assets with a value equal to 70 percent of all target assets are transferred, while the 90-percent test is met if net assets with a value equal to 90 percent of all net assets are transferred. Net assets are gross assets less liabilities. For example, if *X* Corp. owns assets with aggregate fair market value of $1 million subject to liabilities of $200,000, it has $1 million of gross assets and $800,000 of net assets. Thus, if *X* transfers $720,000 or more in value of its assets to the acquiring corporation and the acquiring corporation assumes no *X* liabilities, the transfer will satisfy both the gross and net asset tests.

The judicial interpretation of the "substantially all" requirement may be more relaxed than the Service's ruling guidelines. The transferor corporation in an acquisitive D reorganization, discussed infra, must also transfer substantially all of its assets in the reorganization. See §354(b)(1)(A). In that context, a transfer of all the operating assets of the transferor has been held to satisfy the substantially all test even when the value of those assets, as a percentage of the net worth of the corporation, has been low. See Smothers v. United States, page 375 infra (15 percent); Armour, Inc. v. Commissioner, 43 T.C. 295 (1961) (51 percent).

2. *The boot relaxation rule of §368(a)(2)(B).* While the "solely for voting stock" requirement is absolute for a B reorganization, Congress has provided for a C reorganization that property other than stock may be used as consideration if at least 80 percent of the fair market value of the acquired corporation's assets is acquired for voting stock. §368(a)(2)(B). In determining whether 80 percent of all property is acquired for voting stock, any liabilities assumed by the acquiring corporation are treated as money or other property. Thus, if the value of the transferor's properties is $100,000 subject to liabilities of $15,000, the acquiring

corporation would be limited to paying $5,000 in money or other property in addition to assuming the liabilities. If the liabilities were $21,000, the only consideration allowed in a C reorganization would be voting stock. Because most businesses have substantial liabilities, the boot possibilities for C reorganizations are practically nonexistent.

Can a failed B reorganization be converted into a successful C reorganization by prompt liquidation of the acquired subsidiary? For example, suppose *A* Corp. acquires all the stock of *T* Corp. in exchange for its voting stock worth $1 million plus cash of $100,000. Because of the cash, the acquisition is not a B reorganization. But suppose *A* promptly liquidates *T* Corp. Can the transaction be viewed as an indirect asset acquisition qualifying as a C reorganization? See American Potash & Chemical Corp. v. United States, 399 F.2d 194 (Cl. Ct.), aff'd, 402 F.2d 1000 (Cl. Ct. 1968) (failed B reorganization followed by liquidation of subsidiary cannot qualify as a C reorganization); Rev. Rul. 67-274, 1967-2 C.B. 141 (B reorganization followed by liquidation of acquired corporation taxed as a C reorganization). Should ITT have attempted to convert its Hartford acquisition into a C reorganization? Might Hartford's liabilities have prevented that characterization?

3. *Contingent stock.* In Rev. Rul. 78-376, 1978-2 C.B. 149, *X* Corp. acquired substantially all of the assets of *Y* Corp. in a C reorganization. *A*, the sole shareholder of *Y*, received shares of *X*, a portion of which were placed in escrow as security pending the resolution of a contingent liability of *Y*. When the amount of the liability was determined, the escrowed shares had doubled in value. The agreement provided that the number of shares to be returned to *X* would be based on the amount of the liability and the value of the escrowed stock on the date of return. The Service ruled that *A* recognized gain on return of the shares equal to the excess of the fair market value of the shares not returned (which was equal to the liability) over their adjusted basis. *A*'s basis in the remaining shares was increased by the amount of the claim satisfied. Cf. Rev. Rul. 76-42, 1976-1 C.B. 102, in which no gain was recognized on the return of escrowed shares because the number of shares returned was based on their initial negotiated value, and, therefore, the shareholder could receive no benefit or detriment from any changes in the fair market value of the escrowed stock returned. Are these two rulings consistent even assuming the validity of the rationale of the latter?

Although escrowed stock is not treated as boot, stock rights, options, and warrants are not considered to be stock but "equity" securities. See Treas. Regs. §1.354-1(e); Helvering v. Southwest Consolidated Corp., 315 U.S. 194 (1942) (warrants). Why should the use of escrowed stock be permissible in B and C reorganizations while stock rights, options, and warrants are not?

PROBLEM

10-7. Determine whether the following transactions meet the statutory requirements of a C reorganization.

a. Target Corp. owns assets with a fair market value of $200,000 subject to debts of $50,000. Acquiring Corp. exchanges its voting stock worth $150,000 for the Target assets subject to the debt, and Target promptly liquidates. What are the consequences if Acquiring Corp. paid Target

Corp. $50,000 to discharge the debts as part of the acquisition? If Acquiring Corp. uses cash of $25,000 and takes the assets subject to $25,000 of debt? How do your answers change if the debt was only $30,000?

b. Suppose in (a) that Acquiring Corp. exchanges voting stock of its Parent Corp. (rather than its own voting stock) for the Target Corp. assets and that after the exchange Acquiring Corp. transfers the assets acquired from Target Corp. to Holding Corp., a wholly owned subsidiary of Acquiring Corp. Assume Acquiring Corp. is a wholly owned subsidiary of Parent Corp.

c. Suppose in (b) that the Target assets are transferred directly by Target Corp. to Holding Corp., instead of being first transferred to Acquiring Corp. and then dropped by Acquiring Corp. down to Holding Corp.

4. *The Nondivisive D Reorganization*

The D reorganization at first blush seems peculiar in that it contemplates a *transfer* of assets from one corporation to another rather than an *exchange* of assets for stock or some other valuable consideration. Note, though, that such a transfer will not qualify as a D reorganization unless the transferor corporation (or its shareholders) controls the transferee corporation. By virtue of §368(a)(2)(H), "control" for a D reorganization is defined in §304(c)—a 50-percent-vote or value test—rather than the 80-percent tests in §368(c) applicable to the other types of reorganization. Were there no more to it than this, a nondivisive D reorganization would be a transfer of assets between a (broadly defined) brother-sister or parent-subsidiary pair.

But there is more. A transfer of assets to a corporation controlled by the transferor (or its shareholders) will not qualify as a D reorganization unless the asset transfer is accompanied by a distribution of stock or securities described in §354, §355, or §356. The two basic forms of D reorganizations are (1) those qualifying by virtue of a §354 distribution and (2) those qualifying by virtue of a §355 distribution. (D reorganizations qualifying under §356 are simply one of the two basic forms in which the distribution includes some boot as well as stock and securities.) We will consider only the first form of the D reorganization here; the second form—a D reorganization qualifying under §355—effects a divisive reorganization and is discussed in the next chapter.

A D reorganization qualifying with a §354 distribution must satisfy the requirements of §354(b)(1). That section requires that the transferor corporation must transfer substantially all of its assets and then liquidate. The transferor may, but need not, receive stock, securities, or other property in exchange for its assets; whatever it receives, plus all assets not transferred, must be distributed in a complete liquidation.

The D reorganization qualifying with a §354 distribution is often called an "acquisitive" D reorganization because the transferee corporation is controlled by the same shareholders who controlled the transferor, §368(a)(1)(D), and it ends up with at least substantially all of the transferor's assets, §354(b)(1). The substantially all requirement of the acquisitive D, as well as the forced liquidation of the transferor corporation, should remind you of the C reorganization. Both C and D reorganizations include the following features: (1) an exchange of substantially all of the assets of one corporation for stock of another corporation and (2) the immediate liquidation of the transferor corporation. The difference between the two is that continuity of interest is generally ensured in a C reorganization by requiring that 80 percent of the stock received by the transferor corporation be voting stock in the acquiring corporation (or in its parent), while continuity in a D reorganization is ensured by requiring that the shareholders of the transferor corporation control the acquiring corporation immediately after the transaction. Note that some overlap between C and D reorganizations is contemplated, and when such overlap occurs, the transaction is treated as a D reorganization. §368(a)(2)(A).

Although reorganization treatment often favors taxpayers, historically it has often been the Commissioner who argues in favor of the acquisitive D, and the taxpayer who argues for taxable liquidation treatment. See *Smothers*, below. A taxable liquidation could result in capital gain, taxed at preferential rates for individuals, while the acquisitive D could result in dividend income. Because qualified dividend income is now taxed under §1(h)(11) at preferential long-term capital gains rates, the Commissioner may less frequently press that argument.

However, the acquisitive D reorganization is also used by the Commissioner to attack liquidation-reincorporations. For example, were *T* to liquidate *X* Corp. and then reincorporate the operating assets, the Commissioner would argue that the effect of the liquidation-reincorporation was an acquisitive D reorganization in which the liquid assets were distributed as boot. In such a case, however, the Commissioner faces the preliminary difficulty of identifying the distribution of stock or securities by the transferor required by §354(b)(1)(B). What argument would you advise the Commissioner to make?

Smothers v. United States

642 F.2d 894 (5th Cir. 1981)

Before Wisdom, Garza and Reavley, Circuit Judges.

Wisdom, Circuit Judge. . . .

This dispute arises from the dissolution of one of [the Smothers'] wholly-owned business corporations. The taxpayers contend that the assets distributed to them by that corporation should be taxed at the capital gain rate applicable to liquidating distributions. The Internal Revenue Service (IRS) counters by characterizing the dissolution as part of a reorganization, thereby rendering the taxpayers' receipt of the distributed assets taxable at ordinary income rates. The district court viewed the transaction as a reorganization and ruled for the IRS. We affirm.

I

In 1956, [the Smothers] and an unrelated third party organized Texas Industrial Laundries of San Antonio, Inc. (TIL). The Smothers owned all of its outstanding stock from 1956 through the tax year in issue, 1969. TIL engaged in the business of renting industrial uniforms and other industrial cleaning equipment, such as wiping cloths, dust control devices, and continuous toweling. It owned its own laundry equipment as well.

Shortly after the incorporation of TIL, the taxpayers organized another corporation, Industrial Uniform Services, Inc. (IUS), specifically to oppose a particular competitor in the San Antonio industrial laundry market. The taxpayers owned all of the stock of IUS from the time of its organization until its dissolution. Unlike TIL, IUS did not own laundry equipment; it had to contract with an unrelated company to launder the uniforms it rented to customers. J. E. Smothers personally managed IUS, as well as TIL, but chose not to pay himself a salary from IUS in any of the years of its existence.

IUS evidently succeeded in drawing business away from competing firms, for TIL purchased its main competitor in 1965. IUS continued in business, however, until 1969. On the advice of their accountant, the taxpayers then decided to dissolve IUS and sell all of its non-liquid assets to TIL. On November 1, 1969, IUS adopted a plan of liquidation in compliance with I.R.C. §337, and on November 30, it sold the following assets to TIL for cash at their fair market value (stipulated to be the same as their book value):

Assets	*Amount*
Noncompetitive covenant	$ 3,894.60
Fixed assets	491.25
Rental property	18,000.00
Prepaid insurance	240.21
Water deposit	7.50
Total	$22,637.56[3]

The noncompetitive covenant constituted part of the consideration received by IUS from its purchase of a small competitor. The fixed assets consisted of incidental equipment (baskets, shelves, and a sewing machine), two depreciated delivery vehicles, and IUS's part interest in an airplane. The rental property was an old apartment building in Corpus Christi on land with business potential. These assets collectively represented about 15% of IUS's net value. The parties stipulated that none of these assets were necessary to carry out IUS's business.

After this sale, IUS promptly distributed its remaining assets to its shareholders, the taxpayers, and then dissolved under Texas law:

Assets	*Amount*
Cash (received from TIL)	$ 22,637.56
Cash (of IUS)	2,003.05
Notes receivable	138,000.00
Accrued interest receivable	35.42
Claim against the State of Texas	889.67
Liabilities assumed	(14,403.35)
Total	$149,162.35

TIL hired all three of IUS's employees immediately after the dissolution, and TIL continued to serve most of IUS's customers.

In computing their federal income tax liability for 1969, the taxpayers treated this distribution by IUS as a distribution in complete liquidation within §331(a)(1). Accordingly, they reported the difference between the value of the assets they

3. The parties stipulated that the purchase price was $22,637.56, and the district court found that as a fact. The items listed add to $22,633.56, however. We ignore the discrepancy and accept the stipulation.

received in that distribution, $149,162.35, and the basis of their IUS stock, $1,000, as long-term capital gain. Upon audit, the IRS recharacterized the transaction between TIL and IUS as a reorganization within §368(a)(1)(D), and therefore treated the distribution to the taxpayers as equivalent to a dividend under §356(a)(2). Because IUS had sufficient earnings and profits to cover that distribution, the entire distribution was therefore taxable to the Smothers at ordinary income rates. The IRS timely assessed a $71,840.84 deficiency against the Smothers. They paid that amount and filed this suit for a refund.

The district court held that the transaction constituted a reorganization and rendered judgment for the IRS. . . .

II

Subchapter C of the Internal Revenue Code broadly contemplates that the retained earnings of a continuing business carried on in corporate form can be placed in the hands of its shareholders only after they pay a tax on those earnings at ordinary income rates. That general rule is, of course, primarily a consequence of §301, which taxes dividend distributions as ordinary income. The Code provides for capital gain treatment of corporate distributions in a few limited circumstances, but only when there is either a significant change in relative ownership of the corporation, as in certain redemption transactions, or when the shareholders no longer conduct the business themselves in corporate form, as in true liquidation transactions. The history of Subchapter C in large part has been the story of how Congress, the courts, and the IRS have been called upon to foil attempts by taxpayers to abuse these exceptional provisions. Ingenious taxpayers have repeatedly devised transactions which formally come within these provisions, yet which have the effect of permitting shareholders to withdraw profits at capital gain rates while carrying on a continuing business enterprise in corporate form without substantial change in ownership. This is just such a case.

The transaction in issue here is of the genus known as liquidation-reincorporation, or reincorporation. The common denominator of such transactions is their use of the liquidation provisions of the Code, which permit liquidating distributions to be received at capital gain rates, as a device through which the dividend provisions may be circumvented. Reincorporations come in two basic patterns. In one, the corporation is dissolved and its assets are distributed to its shareholders in liquidation. The shareholders then promptly reincorporate all the assets necessary to the operation of the business, while retaining accumulated cash or other surplus assets. The transaction in this case is of the alternate form. In it, the corporation transfers the assets necessary to its business to another corporation owned by the same shareholders in exchange for securities or, as here, for cash, and then liquidates. . . . If formal compliance with the liquidation provisions were the only necessity, both patterns would enable shareholders to withdraw profits from a continuing corporate business enterprise at capital gain rates by paper-shuffling. Unchecked, these reincorporation techniques would eviscerate the dividend provisions of the Code.

That result can be avoided by recharacterizing such transactions, in accordance with their true nature, as reorganizations. A reorganization is, in essence, a transaction between corporations that results merely in "a continuance of the proprietary interests in the continuing enterprise under modified corporate form"—a phrase that precisely describes the effect of a reincorporation. Lewis v. Commissioner, 1 Cir. 1949, 176 F.2d 646, 648. Congress specifically recognized that the throw-off of surplus assets to shareholders in the course of a reorganization can be equivalent to a dividend, and if so, should be taxed as such. §§356(a)(1)-(2). The reincorporation transactions described above result in a dividend payment to the shareholders in every meaningful financial sense. The assets retained by the shareholders therefore should be taxed as dividends as long as the transaction can be fitted within the technical requirements of one of the six classes of reorganizations recognized by §368(a)(1).

In general, reincorporation transactions are most easily assimilated into §368(a)(1)(D) ("D reorganization"), as the IRS attempted to do in this case. A transaction qualifies as a D reorganization only if it meets six statutory requirements:

(1) There must be a transfer by a corporation (§368(a)(1)(D));
(2) of substantially all of its assets (§354(b)(1)(A));
(3) to a corporation controlled by the shareholders of the transferor corporation, or by the transferor corporation itself (§368(a)(1)(D));
(4) in exchange for stock or securities of the transferee corporation (§354(a)(1));
(5) followed by a distribution of the stock or securities of the transferee corporation to the transferor's shareholders (§354(b)(1)(B));
(6) pursuant to a plan of reorganization (§368(a)(1)(D)).

On this appeal, the taxpayers concede that the transaction in issue meets every technical prerequisite for characterization as a D reorganization, except for one. They argue that since the assets sold by IUS to TIL amounted to only 15% of IUS's net worth, TIL did not acquire "substantially all of the assets" of IUS within the meaning of §354(b)(1)(A).

We hold to the contrary. The words "substantially all assets" are not self-defining. What proportion of a corporation's assets is "substantially all" in this context, and less obviously, what "assets" are to be counted in making this determination, cannot be answered without reference to the structure of Subchapter C. To maintain the integrity of the dividend provisions of the Code, "substantially all assets" in this context must be interpreted as an inartistic way of expressing the concept of "transfer of a continuing business."[I]t is in a sense simply a limited codification of the general nonstatutory "continuity of business enterprise" requirement applicable to all reorganizations.

This interpretation finds support in the history of §368(a)(1)(D) and §354(b)(1)(A). The Internal Revenue Code of 1939 had no provision equivalent to the "substantially all assets" requirement, and courts almost uniformly approved attempts by the IRS to treat reincorporation transactions as reorganizations within the predecessor of §368(a)(1)(D) in the 1939 Code. The "substantially all assets" requirement of §354(b)(1)(A) and the amendment of §368(a)(1)(D) incorporating that requirement were added during the 1954 recodification as part of a package of amendments aimed at plugging a different loophole—the bail-out of corporate earnings and profits at capital gains rates through divisive reorganizations. There is no indication that Congress wished to relax the application of the reorganization provisions to reincorporation transactions. Indeed, the committee reports indicate the contrary. The Senate report accompanying the bill that contained the "substantially all assets" requirement of §354(b)(1)(A) and the parallel amendment to §368(a)(1)(D) stated that the purpose of those changes was only "to insure that the tax consequences of the distribution of stocks or securities to shareholders or security holders in connection with divisive reorganizations will be governed by the requirements of section 355." The report expressly noted that except with respect to divisive reorganizations, the reorganization provisions "are the same as under existing law and are stated in substantially the same form." Even more significantly, the original House version of the 1954 Code contained a provision specifically dealing with reincorporation transactions. That provision was dropped in conference because the conferees felt that such transactions "can appropriately be disposed of by judicial decision or by regulation within the framework of the other provisions of the bill." As the court said in Pridemark, Inc. v. Commissioner, 4 Cir. 1965, 345 F.2d 35, 40, this response shows that "the committee was aware of the problem and thought the present statutory scheme adequate to deal with it." By implication, this passage approved the IRS's use of the predecessor of §368(a)(1)(D) to meet the problem, and shows that the "substantially all assets" amendment was not thought to restrict its use.

Courts have almost unanimously so interpreted the "substantially all assets" language. Moreover, they have also interpreted the other technical conditions for a D reorganization in ways that accomplish the congressional intent to reach reincorporation transactions. For example, the literal language of §368(a)(1)(D) and §§354(a), 354(b)(1)(B) requires that the transferee corporation "exchange" some of its "stock or securities" for the assets of the transferor, and that those items be "distributed" to the shareholders of the transferor, before a D reorganization can be found. Yet both of those requirements have uniformly been ignored as "meaningless gestures" in the reincorporation context, in which the same shareholders own all the stock of both corporations. Smothers does not even challenge the applicability of that principle here.

Properly interpreted, therefore, the assets looked to when making the "substantially all assets" determination should be all the assets, and only the assets, necessary to operate the corporate business — whether or not those assets would appear on a corporate balance sheet constructed according to generally accepted accounting principles. Two errors in particular should be avoided. Inclusion of assets unnecessary to the operation of the business in the "substantially all assets" assessment would open the way for the shareholders of any enterprise to turn dividends into capital gain at will. For example, if we assume that "substantially all" means greater than 90%, a corporation need only cease declaring dividends and accumulate surplus liquid assets until their value exceeds 10% of the total value of all corporate assets. The shareholders could then transfer the assets actively used in the business to a second corporation owned by them and liquidate the old corporation. Such a liquidating distribution would be a dividend in any meaningful sense, but an interpretation of "substantially all assets" that took surplus assets into account would permit the shareholders to treat it as capital gain. Indeed, such an interpretation would perversely treat a merely nominal distribution of retained earnings as a dividend, but would permit substantial distributions to be made at capital gain rates. Courts therefore have invariably ignored all surplus assets and have focused on the operating assets of the business — the tangible assets actively used in the business — when making the "substantially all assets" assessment.

Second, exclusion of assets not shown on a balance sheet constructed according to generally accepted accounting principles from the "substantially all assets" assessment would offer an unjustified windfall to the owners of service businesses conducted in corporate form. The most important assets of such a business may be its reputation and the availability of skilled management and trained employees, none of which show up on a standard balance sheet. Other courts have correctly recognized that in appropriate cases those intangible assets alone may constitute substantially all of the corporate assets. Otherwise, for example, a sole legal practitioner who owns nothing but a desk and chair could incorporate himself, accumulate earnings, and then set up a new corporation and liquidate the old at capital gain rates — as long as he is careful to buy a new desk and chair for the new corporation, rather than transferring the old.

When these principles are applied to this case, it is plain that "substantially all of the assets" of IUS were transferred to TIL, and that the transaction as a whole constituted a reorganization. TIL and IUS were both managed and wholly owned by Smothers. By the nature of its business, IUS was wholly a service enterprise; indeed, the parties stipulated that none of the tangible assets of IUS were necessary to the operation of its business. The extent to which those tangible assets were transferred to TIL is therefore entirely irrelevant. IUS's most important assets — its reputation, sales staff, and the managerial services of Smothers — were all transferred to TIL. TIL rehired all three of IUS's employees immediately after IUS's liquidation, and continued to serve IUS's old customers. The same business enterprise was conducted by the same people under the same ownership, and the only assets removed from corporate solution were accumulated liquid assets unnecessary to the operation of the business. To treat this transaction as other than a reorganization would deny economic reality; to permit Smothers to extract the retained earnings of IUS at capital gain rates would make a mockery of the dividend provisions of the Internal Revenue Code.

We do not perceive ordinary income treatment here to be particularly harsh, or a "tax trap for the unwary." It places the Smothers only in the position they would have been in if they had extracted the retained earnings of IUS as the Code contemplates they should have by periodically declaring dividends.

Affirmed.

Garza, Circuit Judge, dissenting.

After carefully reading the majority's opinion, I find that I must respectfully dissent. Unlike my Brothers, who apparently feel that it is their duty to "plug loopholes," I would remain content in applying the tax law as it reads leaving the United States Congress to deal with the consequences of the tax law as it has been drafted. The only issue before this Court on appeal is whether or not IUS transferred "substantially all of its assets" to TIL. Instead of dealing with this straightforward question, the majority has made a case of evil against liquidation-reincorporation abuses and, in an attempt to remedy every such perceived abuse, they have relieved the Congress of its burden to change the law heretofore requiring that "substantially all" of a corporation's assets be transferred to now read that "only those assets necessary to operate the corporate business" be transferred in order to meet the "D reorganization" requirements. Essentially, the majority has changed the definition of "substantially all assets" to mean only "necessary operating assets." I believe if Congress had meant "necessary operating assets" it would have said so instead of specifically requiring that "substantially all" of the assets be transferred. In my mind "substantially all" plainly means *all* of the assets except for an *insubstantial* amount. Under such a definition, the sale of 15% of IUS's assets to TIL could hardly be defined as "substantially all" of IUS's assets.

However, even after having redefined "substantially all" to mean "necessary operating assets," the IUS liquidation still falls short of the "D reorganization" requirements because the stipulated facts are that absolutely none of the assets sold from IUS to TIL were necessary operating assets for either corporation. Faced with an absence of a proper factual setting, the majority goes on to define necessary operating assets as including a corporation's intangible assets. Now while a sale of intangible assets might be an appropriate consideration in determining whether or not "substantially all" assets of a corporation have been transferred, such a consideration simply has no bearing in this case. All of the assets transferred to TIL were depreciated tangible objects sold at book value after which IUS completely ceased all business operations. There simply was no other transfer of IUS's intangible assets as a continuing business.

The majority has placed great emphasis on the fact that three of IUS's route salesmen were subsequently employed by TIL and that Mr. Smothers' managerial services were available to TIL. Regardless of whether or not these facts enhanced TIL's business, the fact remains that neither the route salesmen or Mr. Smothers' services were *transferred* as assets from one corporation to another. After IUS ceased business its route salesmen were free to seek any employment they desired. Likewise, Mr. Smothers was never obligated to perform services for TIL. From these facts I cannot agree that there was a transfer of a continuing business. The majority imputes adverse tax consequences to IUS's stockholders simply because TIL offered new employment to the route salesmen who were unemployed upon cessation of IUS's business operations. [The majority forces future stockholders, in the Smothers' position, to choose between unfavorable tax consequences and helping secure future employment for loyal and deserving employees.]

Although the Internal Revenue Service has never questioned the bona fides of IUS's liquidation, the majority has gone beyond the stipulated facts by characterizing the liquidation as a tax avoidance scam. I simply cannot agree. After starting from scratch, Mr. Smothers worked for over a dozen years refraining from drawing salary in order that IUS could pay its taxes, employees and other operating expenses and in order for IUS to become a successful self-sustaining business enterprise. Mr. Smothers was successful but, now that he no longer could devote his service to IUS, his years of labor are now labeled by the majority as a mere "paper shuffle." I do not share the majority's attitude.

The reasons for my position can be more easily understood by a simple review of the bottom-line facts. After IUS began showing a profit and started accumulating a cash surplus, instead of immediately investing in a building or in other equipment for its operations, it continued its operations as before. Now, if IUS had purchased real property or depreciable personal property for its operations (instead of leasing as it had been) and had sold these properties pursuant to its plan of liquidation, certainly no argument would be made that the money initially invested in those properties should have been declared by IUS as dividends. However, instead of investing its accumulations, IUS simply put them in its bank account as the tax laws allow and presumably faced any tax consequences posed by such an accumulation.

After IUS ceased operations, was liquidated, and its assets distributed to its stockholders in exchange for their stock, the I.R.S. issued a deficiency, not because IUS was reorganized within the meaning of . . . §368(a)(1)(D), but rather because the I.R.S. felt the accumulated earnings of IUS coupled with long-term capital gains rates applicable to the stock exchange provided an undesirable windfall to IUS's stockholders. In essence, the I.R.S. sought to expand the "D reorganization" provisions, lessen the availability of long-term capital gains treatment to . . . stockholders, and totally ignore the purpose of the tax upon improperly accumulated surplus as provided in . . . §531. The majority seeks to do equity for the I.R.S. position by "treating" the IUS liquidation as a "D reorganization." I do not believe the taxpayers or the tax laws are served by upholding an I.R.S. deficiency for the sole purpose of "plugging loopholes." The lesson to be learned from the majority's opinion is clear—future corporations faced with similar circumstances need only invest their otherwise accumulated surplus in some method other than savings. In the process of liquidation they need sell whatever assets exist to third parties unrelated to their stockholders and their stockholders should make no effort to find future employment for the corporation's employees.

It seems to me that in its attempt to "plug" a perceived "loophole," the majority is giving this Court's imprimatur to a variation of the same so-called "mockery" of the tax laws sought to be prevented by its opinion.

For these reasons, I respectfully dissent.

NOTES

1. *The control requirement.* For a transaction to be an acquisitive D reorganization, shareholders of the target corporation must control the acquiring corporation within the meaning of §304(c). §368(a)(2)(H). Persons control a corporation within the meaning of §304(c) if they own at least 50 percent of the total voting power or value of the corporation's stock. §304(c)(1). See also §304(c)(3) (determining stock ownership for this purpose by applying the constructive ownership rules of §318 with some modifications).

2. *Continuity of interest and distribution requirement.* Can there be an "all-cash" acquisitive D reorganization? Consider the following transaction: *B* owns all stock of *X* Corp. and *Y* Corp., *X* Corp. sells all of its assets to *Y* Corp. for cash, and *X* Corp. liquidates, distributing the cash to *B*. Even though *B* receives no stock in the transaction, the transaction is a D reorganization. See Treas. Regs. §1.368-2(l)(3) (example 1).

Does the result in the preceding example mean that the continuity of interest requirement for acquisitive D reorganizations may be relaxed? The answer is yes if all of the target and acquiror stock is owned by the same shareholders in identical proportions, because the issuance of stock in that situation would be a meaningless gesture.

Note that no stock or securities are distributed to *B* in the example above, contrary to a possible reading of §354(b)(1)(B). However, Treas. Regs. §1.368-2(l)(2)(i) deems the acquiror to issue a nominal share to the target that is distributed to the target shareholders, meeting the distribution requirement. A nominal share is deemed issued if, subject to a de minimis exception, the same person or persons own all of the target stock and acquiror stock in identical proportions.

Treas. Regs. §1.368-2(l)(2) (also applying §318 attribution rules to determine ownership and disregarding ownership of §1504(a)(4) stock). See also *id.* at (l)(3) (example 2) (treating a mother and son as one individual for this purpose). Could the deemed distribution of a nominal share result in gain? Cf. §311(b).

3. *Substantially all of the assets.* The court in *Smothers* was willing to treat 15 percent of the transferor corporation's assets as "substantially all" because the 15 percent at issue included all the corporation's operating assets. To the same effect, see Moffatt v. Commissioner, 363 F.2d 262 (9th Cir. 1966) (64.52 percent); Armour, Inc. v. Commissioner, 43 T.C. 295 (1964) (51 percent). Are these courts, as Judge Garza argued in dissent in *Smothers*, giving insufficient deference to the words used by Congress in §354(b)(1)?

Liquidation of the transferor corporation was not required as part of a C reorganization until 1984. Until then, the C reorganization did not so closely resemble the nondivisive D reorganization. Given the current similarity of the C and nondivisive or acquisitive D reorganizations, should the interpretation of "substantially all" in §368(a)(1)(C) be informed by these judicial decisions explicating the terms of an acquisitive D reorganization? If some but not all of the assets of *T* Corp. are transferred to *A* Corp. in exchange for voting stock of *A*, and *T* then liquidates, is the transaction more like a sale than a continuation of *T*'s business? If the shareholders of *T* lack control of *A* (so that the transaction is not an acquisitive D), is the transfer of all the operating assets of *T* more like a sale than a reorganization? Recall Rev. Proc. 77-37, discussed at page 372 supra, in which for advance ruling purposes "substantially all" means 70 percent of a corporation's gross assets and 90 percent of its net assets.

4. *The transfer requirement.* A service-intensive business may have few or no operating assets. Suppose such a business operating in corporate form is completely liquidated, followed by the formation of a corporation engaged in a similar business employing the same workers and servicing the same clients or customers. Can the Commissioner attack such an arrangement as an acquisitive D reorganization? Under the definition of a D reorganization in §368(a)(1)(D), the transferor corporation must "transfer" substantially all of its assets to the acquiring corporation. In the example posed above, have the employees or customers been "transferred" within the meaning of §368(a)(1)(D)?

It has been suggested that employees cannot be "transferred" in this sense. Warsaw Photographic Associates, Inc. v. Commissioner, 84 T.C. 21 (1985). But in Moffatt v. Commissioner, 363 F.2d 262 (9th Cir. 1966), it was held employees could be so "transferred." See also Simon v. Commissioner, 644 F.2d 339 (5th Cir. 1981), in which a nonassignable franchise right was "transferred" within the meaning of §368(a)(1)(D) when the franchise liquidated and the franchise reissued to a corporation controlled by shareholders of the liquidated corporation. Cf. §197(d)(1)(C)(i) (providing that workforce in place is a §197 intangible; because §197 deals with asset acquisitions, the section presumes that workforce in place may be transferred).

PROBLEM

10-8. *P* Corp. owns operating assets worth $300,000 as well as investment real estate worth $700,000. *F* owns all the stock of *P* Corp. *P* transfers all its assets to

Q Corp. in exchange for common stock of *Q* worth $800,000 and cash of $200,000. *P* then liquidates, distributing the *Q* stock and cash to *F*. Before the transaction, *Q* was wholly owned by individual *S*. After the transaction, *F* owns 40 percent of *Q*, and *S* owns 60 percent. Is this transaction a "reorganization" within the meaning of §368? What would the result be if *P* did not transfer the real estate, receiving in exchange for the operating assets stock of *Q* worth $300,000 and representing a 20-percent interest? Is it relevant whether *F* and *S* are father and son?

5. *Remote Continuity*

Historically, a merger (or other transaction) was disqualified as a §368 reorganization if the acquired assets were transferred by the acquiring corporation to a controlled subsidiary. See Groman v. Commissioner, 302 U.S. 82 (1937); Helvering v. Bashford, 302 U.S. 454 (1938). This "remote" continuity problem has been addressed in several ways in the Code and regulations.

Section 368(a)(2)(C) states that an A, B, C, or G reorganization is not disqualified merely because the assets or stock acquired in a transaction are "dropped down" to a subsidiary controlled by the acquiring corporation. See also §368(c) (defining control). For example, suppose that *X* Corp. merges into *Y* Corp., and *Y* Corp. transfers the *X* Corp. assets to *S1*, *Y* Corp.'s controlled subsidiary. If the merger otherwise qualifies as an A reorganization, it will not be disqualified by that asset drop-down.

Treas. Regs. §1.368-2(k) interprets §368(a)(2)(C) to illustrate, rather than limit, permissible drop-downs and other transfers of target assets or stock in a §368(a) reorganization. For instance, in the example above, the *X-Y* merger could still be an A reorganization if *S1* also dropped the *X* assets to *S2*, its controlled subsidiary, *S2* then dropped those assets to *S3*, its controlled subsidiary, and so on.

This liberal interpretation of §368(a)(2)(C) is hard to square with the words of the statute. Under §368(a)(2)(C), authority to drop down assets is confined to the A, B, C, and G reorganizations, a list that notably excludes D reorganizations. Nonetheless, the Service ruled that the benefit of §368(a)(2)(C) extends to D reorganizations on the theory that "§368(a)(2)(C) is permissive and not exclusive or restrictive." Rev. Rul. 2002-85, 2002-2 C.B. 986. To be sure, it is hard to see a principled reason why a post-reorganization transfer of assets to a controlled subsidiary ought to disqualify an otherwise valid D reorganization. But that appears to be exactly what Congress intended by excluding the D reorganization in §368(a)(2)(C). Indeed, in the parenthetical language in §368(a)(2)(A), Congress expressly provided that a transaction qualifying as both a C and a D reorganization could get the benefit of §368(a)(2)(C), language that would be unnecessary if D reorganizations already qualified for that benefit.

Nevertheless, for *any* §368 reorganization, the regulation provides that drop-downs of assets or stock of the target or acquiring corporation do not disqualify the transaction as a reorganization (or cause it to be recharacterized) if the following requirements are met:

1. The continuity of business enterprise requirement of §1.368-1(d) continues to be satisfied after the drop-downs;

2. If stock of the target or acquiring corporation is dropped down, the corporation remains a member of the issuing corporation's qualified group; and
3. The target or acquiring corporation does not cease to exist in connection with the drop-downs.

Treas. Regs. §1.368-2(k)(1)(ii). (For a discussion of the continuity of business enterprise requirement and qualified groups, see pages 351-352 supra.)

A companion rule under Treas. Regs. §1.368-2(k)(1)(i) applies to direct or indirect distributions (i.e., push-ups) of target assets or stock. Under that rule, for any §368 reorganization, a push-up of stock or assets does not disqualify a transaction as a reorganization (or cause it to be recharacterized) if the following requirements are met: First, the continuity of business enterprise requirement must continue to be met. Second, if target stock is distributed, the distribution must be of less than all target stock acquired in the transaction and the target must remain a member of the issuing corporation's qualified group. If, instead, assets are distributed (or deemed distributed), the distribution cannot be deemed a liquidation, a determination made by disregarding all non-target assets of the distributing corporation. If assets are both dropped down and pushed up, those transfers are tested under the push-up rule. *Id.* at (k)(1)(ii)(A).

6. *Triangular Reorganizations*

Because of the "drop-down" rule, a parent may acquire target stock or assets in a §368 reorganization and drop the stock or assets to a controlled subsidiary without jeopardizing reorganization treatment. Could the parent group save costs and minimize the group's exposure to target liabilities by having the subsidiary acquire the target stock or assets directly but still have the target shareholders receive parent stock in a tax-free reorganization?

Before 1954, such a direct subsidiary acquisition did not qualify as a tax-free reorganization. In 1954, Congress begin making piecemeal amendments to the Code to permit these "triangular" reorganizations. It first amended the definition of a C reorganization—adding the parenthetical phrase of §368(a)(1)(C)—to permit use of parent stock. Later, it made a similar statutory change to permit the use of parent stock in a B reorganization. These B or C reorganizations are called "parenthetical" or "triangular" B or C reorganizations.

One reason for the widespread use of subsidiaries in the reorganization context is that state law may require the shareholders of the acquiring corporation as well as the shareholders of the target corporation to vote their approval of the reorganization, a requirement especially likely in the case of an A reorganization. If the acquiring corporation is publicly held, however, the cost of obtaining shareholder consent may be prohibitive. By using a subsidiary as the nominal acquiring corporation, only the vote of the subsidiary's shareholders—usually the board of directors of the parent company—is needed.

Although there is no parenthetical A reorganization, §368(a)(2)(D) plays that role. Under this provision, a transaction may qualify as an A reorganization if the target merges into a subsidiary but the target shareholders receive stock of the parent, a corporation that controls the subsidiary. §368(a)(1)(A) and (a)(2)(D).

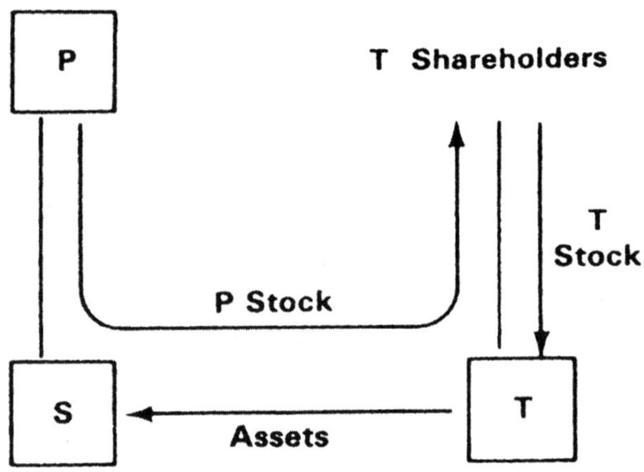

Figure 10-1

In the merger, no subsidiary stock may be used and the subsidiary must acquire substantially all of the target assets. §368(a)(2)(D)(i) and (ii). See Figure 10-1.

It may make sense, instead, to merge the subsidiary into the target corporation. For example, the target might be the lessee on a favorable long-term lease that terminates unless the target survives any merger. Can the merger of the subsidiary into the target qualify as an A reorganization if the target shareholders exchange their stock for stock of the parent, a corporation that controls the subsidiary?

Section 368(a)(2)(E) allows use of parent stock in such a merger. It requires the following:

1. In the transaction, former shareholders of the target (which survives the merger) must exchange, for parent voting stock, a controlling interest in the target stock.
2. After the transaction, the target must hold substantially all of its assets and substantially all of the merged subsidiary's assets.

See Treas. Regs. §1.368-2(j). See Figure 10-2.

Reorganizations described in §368(a)(2)(D) are called "forward triangular (or subsidiary) mergers," while reorganizations described in §368(a)(2)(E) are called "reverse triangular (or subsidiary) mergers." Both subsidiary mergers must qualify as mergers under §368(a)(1)(A). See Treas. Regs. §1.368-2(b)(1)(ii) (for the merger definition). Further, as with all acquisitive reorganizations, both forms of triangular mergers must satisfy the judicial requirements, including continuity of interest.

PROBLEM

10-9. Determine whether the following transactions are "reorganizations" within the meaning of §368:

a. Corner Grocery Corp. is acquired by the *BQ* National Chain in the following steps. *BQ* forms a wholly owned subsidiary Sub Corp., and Corner Grocery

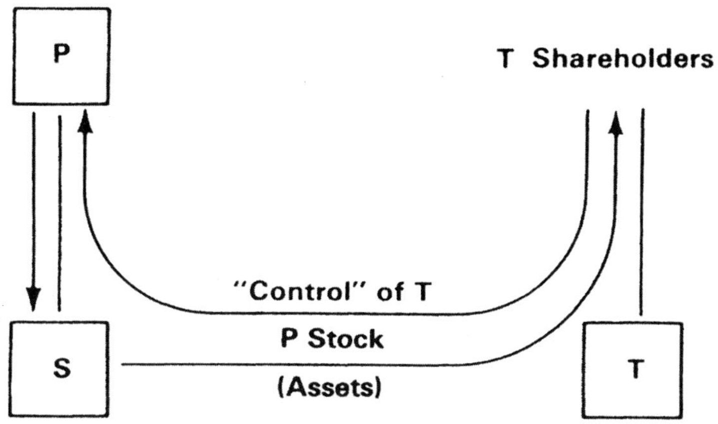

Figure 10-2

then merges into Sub Corp., with the shareholders of Corner Grocery receiving their consideration half in the form of *BQ* voting preferred stock and half in debentures of *BQ*. What are the consequences if the debentures were debt of the subsidiary? If the stock had been nonvoting?

b. Suppose in (a) that Corner Grocery owns a favorable lease that cannot be transferred. Accordingly, the transaction is structured as follows. *BQ* forms Sub Corp. by contributing *BQ* preferred stock. Sub Corp. is then merged into Corner Grocery, with *BQ* receiving 1,000 shares of Corner Grocery voting stock in exchange for its shares of Sub Corp. At the same time, the former shareholders of Corner Grocery exchange all their common stock of Corner Grocery for the *BQ* preferred owned by Sub Corp. How does your answer change if the former owners of Corner Grocery also owned nonvoting preferred stock in Corner Grocery and those preferred shares remain outstanding after the merger?

7. *Multi-Step Mergers*

Sometimes, a merger is accomplished in two steps. In the first step, the acquiring corporation acquires all or part of the target corporation's stock, and in the second, the target merges into the acquiring corporation. If properly structured, the two-step merger has the following advantage: After the first step, the acquiror, by voting its target shares in favor of the merger, is practically assured that the merger will gain shareholder approval. If the two steps are part of an overall plan and the judicial requirements for a reorganization are met, the Service generally treats the two steps, in substance, as an A reorganization. See Rev. Rul. 2001-46, 2001-2 C.B. 321 (citing King Enterprises, Inc. v. United States, 418 F.2d 511 (Ct. Cl. 1969), and J.E. Seagram Corp. v. Commissioner, 104 T.C. 75 (1995)). See also Rev. Rul. 2001-26, 2001-1 C.B. 1297.

Recall, however, that if the first step (i.e., the stock acquisition) is a qualified stock purchase, the stock acquisition and subsequent liquidation by merger may be treated, at least in part, as separate steps for tax purposes. See page 350 supra. How should we determine whether the stock acquisition is a qualified stock purchase?

Should we consider the stock acquisition by itself or look to the transaction as a whole? The Service makes this determination by looking to the transaction as a whole.

For example, suppose that *T* Corp. has one class of stock outstanding and that *P* Corp. acquires the *T* stock by merging its newly formed, wholly owned subsidiary, *N* Corp., into *T* Corp. The *T* shareholders receive 70 percent *P* voting stock and 30 percent cash in exchange for their *T* stock. As part of the same plan, *T* Corp. then merges into *P* Corp. Standing alone, the *N-T* merger would be treated as a stock acquisition and would be a qualified stock purchase. If, however, the step transaction doctrine applied, the *T* stock acquisition and *T-P* merger would qualify as a multi-step A reorganization, and the stock acquisition would not be a qualified stock purchase. See §338(h)(3)(A)(ii) (providing that stock acquired in a §354 or §356 exchange is not acquired by purchase).

The Service concluded in a similar case that the step transaction doctrine applied, because its application did not violate the policy behind §338. Rev. Rul. 2001-46, 2001-2 C.B. 321. It reasoned that §338 was intended to be the sole method to treat a stock purchase like a taxable asset purchase, quoting legislative history to that effect. Because the transaction, as stepped together, was treated as a §368 reorganization, the target (*T* Corp. in our example) did not recognize gain or loss nor were its asset bases stepped up. See §361(b); §362(b). In other words, the transaction was not treated like a taxable asset acquisition, and applying the step transaction doctrine did not circumvent the policy behind §338. Thus, the Service concluded, the step transaction doctrine should apply in that case to determine whether the stock acquisition was a qualified stock purchase.[5]

How does the step transaction doctrine apply in the converse case when the stock acquisition, standing alone, would not be a qualified stock purchase but, if the step transaction doctrine applied, it would be? Consider the following revenue ruling:

Rev. Rul. 2008-25

2008-1 C.B. 986

This ruling discusses an integrated transaction where stock of a target corporation is acquired in a taxable reverse subsidiary merger, followed by liquidation of target. The ruling addresses the proper treatment and application of the step transaction doctrine in light of the policies behind section 338 of the Code.

Issue

What is the proper Federal income tax treatment of the transaction described below?

5. By regulation, however, the step transaction doctrine does not apply to a stock acquisition and planned liquidation if (i) the stock acquisition would be a qualified stock purchase if it were treated as a separate step and (ii) a §338(h)(10) election is made. Treas. Regs. §1.338(h)(10)-1(c)(2).

Facts

T is a corporation all of the stock of which is owned by individual *A*. *T* has 150*x* dollars worth of assets and 50*x* dollars of liabilities. *P* is a corporation that is unrelated to *A* and *T*. The value of *P*'s assets, net of liabilities, is 410*x* dollars. *P* forms corporation *X*, a wholly owned subsidiary, for the sole purpose of acquiring all of the stock of *T* by causing *X* to merge into *T* in a statutory merger (the "Acquisition Merger"). In the Acquisition Merger, *P* acquires all of the stock of *T*, and *A* exchanges the *T* stock for 10*x* dollars in cash and *P* voting stock worth 90*x* dollars. Following the Acquisition Merger and as part of an integrated plan that included the Acquisition Merger, *T* completely liquidates into *P* (the "Liquidation"). In the Liquidation, *T* transfers all of its assets to *P* and *P* assumes all of *T*'s liabilities. The Liquidation is not accomplished through a statutory merger. After the Liquidation, *P* continues to conduct the business previously conducted by *T*.

Law . . .

Section 1.368-1(a) generally provides that in determining whether a transaction qualifies as a reorganization under §368(a), the transaction must be evaluated under relevant provisions of law, including the step transaction doctrine.

Section 1.368-2(k) provides, in part, that a transaction otherwise qualifying as a reorganization under §368(a) shall not be disqualified or recharacterized as a result of one or more distributions to shareholders (including distribution(s) that involve the assumption of liabilities) if the requirements of §1.368-1(d) are satisfied, the property distributed consists of assets of the surviving corporation, and the aggregate of such distributions does not consist of an amount of assets of the surviving corporation (disregarding assets of the merged corporation) that would result in a liquidation of such corporation for Federal income tax purposes.

Rev. Rul. 67-274, 1967-2 C.B. 141, holds that an acquiring corporation's acquisition of all of the stock of a target corporation solely in exchange for voting stock of the acquiring corporation, followed by the liquidation of the target corporation as part of the same plan, will be treated as an acquisition by the acquiring corporation of substantially all of the target corporation's assets in a reorganization described in §368(a)(1)(C). The ruling explains that, under these circumstances, the stock acquisition and the liquidation are part of the overall plan of reorganization and the two steps may not be considered independently of each other for Federal income tax purposes. See also, Rev. Rul. 72-405, 1972-2 C.B. 217.

Rev. Rul. 2001-46, 2001-2 C.B. 321, holds that, where a newly formed wholly owned subsidiary of an acquiring corporation merged into a target corporation, followed by the merger of the target corporation into the acquiring corporation, the step transaction doctrine is applied to integrate the steps and treat the transaction as a single statutory merger of the target corporation into the acquiring corporation. Noting that the rejection of step integration in Rev. Rul. 90-95, 1990-2 C.B. 67, and §1.338-3(d) is based on Congressional intent that §338 replace any nonstatutory treatment of a stock purchase as an asset purchase under the Kimbell-Diamond doctrine, the Service found that the policy underlying §338 is not violated by treating the steps as a single statutory merger of the target into the acquiring corporation because such treatment results in a transaction that qualifies as a reorganization in which the acquiring corporation acquires the assets of the target corporation with a carryover basis under §362, rather than receiving a cost basis in those assets under §1012. (In Kimbell-Diamond Milling Co. v. Commissioner, 14 T.C. 74, aff'd per curiam, 187 F.2d 718 (1951), cert. denied, 342 U.S. 827, 72 S. Ct. 50, 96 L. Ed. 626 (1951), the court held that the purchase of the stock of a target corporation for the purpose of obtaining its assets through a prompt liquidation should be treated by the purchaser as a purchase of the target corporation's assets with the purchaser receiving a cost basis in the assets.) . . .

Section 338 was enacted in 1982 and was "intended to replace any nonstatutory treatment of a stock purchase as an asset purchase under the Kimbell-Diamond doctrine." H.R. Conf. Rep. No. 760, 97th Cong, 2d Sess. 536 (1982), 1982-2 C.B. 600, 632. Stock purchase or asset purchase treatment generally turns on whether the purchasing corporation makes or is deemed to make a §338 election. If the election is made or deemed made, asset purchase treatment results and the basis of the target assets is adjusted to reflect the stock purchase price and other relevant items. If an election is not made or deemed made, the stock purchase treatment generally results. In such a case, the basis of the target assets is not adjusted to reflect the stock purchase price and other relevant items.

Rev. Rul. 90-95 (Situation 2), holds that the merger of a newly formed wholly owned domestic subsidiary into a target corporation with the target corporation shareholders receiving solely cash in exchange for their stock, immediately followed by the merger of the target corporation into the domestic parent of the merged subsidiary, will be treated as a qualified stock purchase of the target corporation followed by a §332 liquidation of the target corporation. As a result, the parent's basis in the target corporation's assets will be the same as the basis of the assets in the target corporation's hands. The ruling explains that even though "the step-transaction doctrine is properly applied to disregard the existence of the [merged subsidiary]," so that the first step is treated as a stock purchase, the acquisition of the target corporation's stock is accorded independent significance from the subsequent liquidation of the target corporation and, therefore, is treated as a qualified stock purchase regardless of whether a §338 election is made. Thus, in that case, the step transaction doctrine was not applied to treat the transaction as a direct acquisition by the domestic parent of the assets of the target corporation because such an application would have resulted in treating a stock purchase as an asset purchase, which would be inconsistent with the repeal of the Kimbell-Diamond doctrine and §338.

Section 1.338-3(d) incorporates the approach of Rev. Rul. 90-95 into the regulations by requiring the purchasing corporation (or a member of its affiliated group) to treat certain asset transfers following a qualified stock purchase (where no §338 election is made) independently of the qualified stock purchase. In the example in §1.338-3(d)(5), the purchase for cash of 85 percent of the stock of a target corporation, followed by the merger of the target corporation into a wholly owned subsidiary of the purchasing corporation, is treated (other than by certain minority shareholders) as a qualified stock purchase of the stock of the target corporation followed by a §368 reorganization of the target corporation into the subsidiary. As a result, the subsidiary's basis in the target corporation's assets is the same as the basis of the assets in the target corporation's hands.

Analysis

If the Acquisition Merger and the Liquidation were treated as separate from each other, the Acquisition Merger would be treated as a stock acquisition that qualifies as a reorganization under §368(a)(1)(A) by reason of §368(a)(2)(E), and the Liquidation would qualify under §332. However, as provided in §1.368-1(a), in determining whether a transaction qualifies as a reorganization under §368(a), the transaction must be evaluated under relevant provisions of law, including the step transaction doctrine. In this case, because *T* was completely liquidated, the §1.368-2(k) safe harbor exception from the application of the step transaction doctrine does not apply. Accordingly, the Acquisition Merger and the Liquidation may not be considered independently of each other for purposes of determining whether the transaction satisfies the statutory requirements of a reorganization described in §368(a)(1)(A) by reason of §368(a)(2)(E). As such, this transaction does not qualify as a reorganization described in §368(a)(1)(A) by reason of §368(a)(2)(E) because, after the transaction, *T* does not hold substantially all of its properties and the properties of the merged corporation.

In determining whether the transaction is a reorganization, the approach reflected in Rev. Rul. 67-274 and Rev. Rul. 2001-46 is applied to ignore *P*'s acquisition of the *T* stock in the Acquisition Merger and to treat the transaction as a direct acquisition by *P* of *T*'s assets in exchange for 10*x* dollars in cash, 90*x* dollars worth of *P* voting stock, and the assumption of *T*'s liabilities.

However, unlike the transactions considered in Rev. Rul. 67-274, 72-405 and 2001-46, a direct acquisition by *P* of *T*'s assets in this case does not qualify as a reorganization under §368(a). *P*'s acquisition of *T*'s assets is not a reorganization described in §368(a)(1)(C) because the consideration exchanged is not solely *P* voting stock and the requirements of §368(a)(2)(B) are not satisfied. Section 368(a)(2)(B) would treat *P* as acquiring 40 percent of *T*'s assets for consideration other than *P* voting stock (liabilities assumed of 50*x* dollars, plus 10*x* dollars cash). See Rev. Rul. 73-102, 1973-1 C.B. 186 (analyzing the application of §368(a)(2)(B)). *P*'s acquisition of *T*'s assets is not a reorganization described in §368(a)(1)(D) because neither *T* nor *A* (nor a combination thereof) was in control of *P* (within the meaning of §368(a)(2)(H)(i)) immediately after the transfer. Additionally, the transaction is not a reorganization under §368(a)(1)(A) because *T* did not merge into *P*. Accordingly, the overall transaction is not a reorganization under §368(a) . . . .

In this case, further application of the approach reflected in Rev. Rul. 67-274, integrating the acquisition of *T* stock with the liquidation of *T*, would result in treating the acquisition of *T* stock as a taxable purchase of *T*'s assets. Such treatment would violate the policy underlying §338 that a cost basis in acquired assets should not be obtained through the purchase of stock where no §338 election is made. Accordingly, consistent with the analysis set forth in Rev. Rul. 90-95, the acquisition of the stock of *T* is treated as a qualified stock purchase by *P* followed by the liquidation of *T* into *P* under §332.

Holding

The transaction is not a reorganization under §368(a). The Acquisition Merger is a qualified stock purchase by *P* of the stock of *T* under §338(d)(3). The Liquidation is a complete liquidation of a controlled subsidiary under §332 . . . .

NOTES

1. *Partial application of the step transaction doctrine.* In Rev. Rul. 2008-25, the Service concluded that the step transaction doctrine applied only to characterize the stock acquisition as a qualified stock purchase, not to characterize the transaction as a whole. The broader application of the doctrine would have been inconsistent with the policy behind §338, allowing a transaction that included a qualified stock purchase to be treated like a taxable asset purchase without a §338 election. Thus, under the step transaction doctrine, the stock acquisition was treated as a qualified stock purchase, but that doctrine did not more broadly apply to treat the stock acquisition and liquidation together like an asset purchase. Instead, the stock acquisition and liquidation were treated as separate steps, with the stock acquisition being taxable and the liquidation tax free under §332 and §337.

2. *Impact of Rev. Rul. 2008-25.* Standing alone, the merger of *X* into *P* qualified as a §368(a)(2)(E) reorganization. Then, if the requirements of Treas. Regs. §1.368-2(k)(1)(i) were met, that merger and the subsequent liquidation could be treated as separate steps for tax purposes. Why did the Service conclude that Treas. Regs. §1.368-2(k)(1)(i) did not apply? Whose tax consequences were affected by that conclusion?

D. TAXATION

1. *Overview*

If a reorganization has occurred, the tax consequences for the reorganizing corporations are described in §§357, 358, 361, 362, 1032, and 1223(2), while the consequences for target shareholders are described in §§354, 356, 358, and 1223(1). Other sections implicated by a tax-free reorganization include §§269, 381, and 382, sections discussed in Chapter 13.

In general, these rules provide that gain or loss is not recognized and that basis is continued unchanged. The acquiring corporation takes the acquired assets with a transferred basis, and neither the target nor acquiring corporation generally recognizes gain or loss. If a target shareholder exchanges target stock solely for qualified stock, the shareholder recognizes no gain or loss and takes the same basis in the stock received as the stock surrendered in the exchange. If the shareholder receives other property in addition to qualified stock (i.e., she receives boot), the shareholder may recognize gain, but not loss.

These rules all refer to "parties" to a reorganization, defined in §368(b). At the corporate level, the reorganization provisions apply only to corporations that are parties to the reorganization. See §361. At the shareholder level, nonrecognition will apply only to exchanges of stock and securities of corporations that are, once again, parties to the reorganization.

The corporate parties to a reorganization are specified in §368(b). When the 1954 Code was enacted, §368(b) contained only the first sentence of the current provision. As Congress expanded the definition of a reorganization, it also expanded the definition of parties to a reorganization in §368(b).

Parties to a reorganization include—

1. Both corporations if one corporation acquires the stock or assets of a second corporation (as in an A merger or in a B or C reorganization);
2. Any consolidated corporations and the resulting corporation in an A consolidation;
3. The parent of the acquiring corporation in a triangular B, triangular C, or §368(a)(2)(D) reorganization;
4. The parent of the merged corporation in an §368(a)(2)(E) reorganization; and
5. The controlled subsidiary to which assets or stock are dropped pursuant to §368(a)(2)(C).

§368(b).

2. *Corporate-Level Taxation*

Issues that arise in the corporate-level taxation of reorganizations include (a) recognition of gain or loss by the transferor corporation; (b) recognition of gain or loss by the acquiring corporation; (c) the bases and holding periods of the assets acquired by the acquiring corporation; (d) for triangular reorganizations, the parent's basis in subsidiary stock; and (e) the tax treatment of expenses incurred by the corporate parties incident to the reorganization. These issues are discussed below. Chapter 13 discusses the impact of the reorganization on net operating losses, earnings and profits accounts, and other tax attributes of corporations.

a. The Transferor Corporation's Gain or Loss

Section 361 governs the recognition of gain and loss by the transferor corporation.[6] Section 361(a) and (b) deal with the transferor corporation's exchange of its assets with the acquiring corporation. Section 361(c) deals with the transferor corporation's distribution of property to its shareholders or creditors.

Under §361(a), the transferor corporation recognizes no gain or loss on its exchange of property solely for the stock and securities of another corporate party to the reorganization. For this purpose, if the acquiring corporation assumes the transferor's liabilities, that assumption is generally disregarded. §357(a). But see §357(b) (providing that the assumption is treated as the payment of boot if a liability is assumed for a tax avoidance purpose).

If the transferor corporation receives other property (boot) in addition to qualifying stock and securities, the transferor recognizes no gain or loss if the boot is distributed as part of the reorganization. §361(b)(1)(A). Note that a distribution to a creditor *satisfies* this requirement. §361(b)(3). Because the transferor corporation almost always liquidates as part of the reorganization (see

6. In every acquisitive asset reorganization other than a §368(a)(2)(E) reorganization, the transferor corporation is the "target." In a §368(a)(2)(E) reorganization, the corporation that survives the merger is the "target."

§368(a)(2)(G)(ii) for the possible exception), gain recognition by the transferor corporation is unlikely. But see §357(b) (treating a liability assumed as boot; no distribution of this boot is possible). Note that the transferor corporation never recognizes loss on the exchange. §361(b)(2).

A transferor corporation may recognize gain but not loss on its distribution of property as part of the reorganization. §361(c). The distribution might include three classes of property: (1) stock, stock rights, or debt obligations of a party to the reorganization received in the reorganization, (2) other property (i.e., boot) acquired from the acquiring corporation, and (3) property held by the transferor corporation and not transferred to the acquiring corporation as part of the reorganization.

The interests described in class (1) are "qualified property" under §361(c)(2)(B), and the transferor corporation recognizes no gain on their distribution. §361(c)(1). See also *id.* at (c)(3) (treating a transfer of qualified property to a creditor in connection with a reorganization as a distribution). The transferor corporation also recognizes no gain on its distribution of the boot described in class (2), because the boot's basis equals its fair market value (assuming that the distribution occurs just following the boot's receipt). §358(a)(2) and (f). However, the transferor corporation recognizes gain on its distribution of any asset described in class (3), to the extent the asset has a fair market value in excess of its adjusted basis. §361(c)(2)(A). Note that the usual rules applicable to complete liquidations do not apply in this context. §361(c)(4).

Could a transferor corporation deduct any amount transferred to a shareholder in connection with the reorganization? Compare I.R.S. A.O.D, (Aug. 5, 2013), 2013 TNT 140-17 (concluding that payments to preferred shareholders to forego their redemption rights were nondeductible under §162(k) and also under §361(c) if the payments were made pursuant to a plan of reorganization) with Rev. Rul. 62-217, 1962-2 C.B. 59 (concluding that a corporation was entitled to a deduction for compensation that it paid using its stock despite §1032(a)).

b. The Acquiring Corporation's Gain or Loss

Under §1032, a corporation recognizes no gain or loss on its acquisition of property for its stock or stock rights (whether or not in connection with a reorganization). Under general principles, it recognizes no gain or loss when it acquires assets for cash, its newly issued debt or securities, or the assumption of liabilities. Thus, the acquiring corporation recognizes no gain or loss to the extent it acquires assets in the reorganization in exchange for its stock, stock rights, securities, or debt or for cash or the assumption of liabilities.

If, however, the acquiring corporation uses non-cash boot to acquire assets in the reorganization, it generally recognizes gain or loss on that exchange. See §1001. But that gain or loss is not recognized to the extent another nonrecognition section applies to the exchange. See, e.g., §1031.

In a triangular reorganization, there is generally no Code section that prevents the acquiring subsidiary from recognizing gain on its use of parent stock. Treas. Regs. §1.1032-2(c) provides, however, that the subsidiary recognizes no gain or loss on its use of stock acquired from the parent as part of the plan of reorganization. See also Rev. Rul. 57-278, 1957-1 C.B. 124 (reaching the same conclusion).

c. The Acquiring Corporation's Bases and Holding Periods in Acquired Assets

In A, C, and acquisitive D reorganizations, the acquiring corporation takes a basis in transferor assets acquired equal to the transferor's basis plus any gain recognized by the transferor on the exchange. §362(b). In a B or triangular B reorganization, the acquiring corporation succeeds to the shareholders' bases in the target stock. §362(b). See also §358(e). In either case, because the acquiring corporation determines its basis in the transferred property by looking to the transferor's basis, it tacks the transferor's holding period. §1223(2).

d. The Parent's Basis in Subsidiary Stock Following a Triangular Reorganization

In a triangular reorganization, the target shareholders receive parent stock even though the target stock or assets are acquired by the parent's subsidiary or, in a reverse subsidiary merger, the subsidiary merges into the target. Treas. Regs. §1.358-6 describes the basis consequences of triangular reorganizations to the parent, which generally are as follows:

In a triangular B reorganization, the parent's basis in its subsidiary stock is increased by the target shareholders' aggregate adjusted basis in the acquired target stock. See Treas. Regs. §1.358-6(c)(3). In a triangular C reorganization and a forward triangular merger, the parent increases its basis in the subsidiary stock by the net basis of the target assets. That net basis equals the excess, if any, of (i) the aggregate basis of the acquired target assets over (ii) the amount of target liabilities assumed in the transaction (or to which acquired target assets were subject). *Id.* at (c)(1).

In a reverse subsidiary merger, the parent determines its basis in the target stock under one of two methods. Under the method that generally applies, its basis in the target stock equals (i) its basis in the subsidiary stock immediately before the transaction plus (ii) the net basis of the target assets. *Id.* at (c)(2)(i)(A). But see *id.* at (c)(2)(B) and (C) (for adjustments if less than all target stock is acquired or if the parent owned target stock before the transaction). If the transaction also qualifies as a §351 transfer or a B reorganization, the parent can choose alternatively to determine its basis in the acquired target stock as if it acquired that stock in a B reorganization. Treas. Regs. §1.358-6(c)(2)(ii).

If the parent supplies less than all consideration in the reorganization, the adjustments described above are reduced (but not below zero) by the fair market value of the other consideration exchanged in the reorganization but not provided by the parent. *Id.* at (d) (disregarding assumed liabilities for this purpose).

e. Corporate Expenses

Lastly, consider the tax treatment of any expenses incurred by the corporate parties to a reorganization. Those expenses might include attorney and accountant fees as well as printing costs of a prospectus and related documents. Similar expenses often are incurred in connection with an initial incorporation, and under §248, up to $5,000 of these expenses can be immediately deducted and the remainder can be amortized over a period of 180 months. No similar provision, however, authorizes the amortization of reorganization expenses. See the discussion of *INDOPCO* at page 319 supra.

f. Examples

These reorganization provisions are difficult, not only because they are technically complex but also because they are spread among many tax sections. You must refer back and forth among the various sections to determine the consequences of a reorganization to all the corporate parties, a skill that is mastered only through practice. An example of the technique used to analyze the corporate-level tax effects of a reorganization follows. Remember that a similar exercise should be performed to determine the shareholder-level tax effects.

X Corp. and *T* Corp. execute the following transaction: *T* transfers most of its assets, worth $98,000, to *X* in exchange for (1) *X* voting stock worth $80,000, (2) *X* securities worth $8,000, (3) real estate worth $5,000, and (4) the assumption by *X* of a $5,000 *T* liability. *X*'s adjusted basis in the real estate is $3,500. Immediately after the exchange, *T* distributes the *X* stock and securities, the real estate, and its remaining asset, an investment asset with a $1,200 adjusted basis and $2,000 fair market value, to its shareholders in complete liquidation. Assume that *T*'s basis in the transferred assets totals $60,000, that *T*'s shareholders do not own a significant amount of *X* stock before or after the transaction, that none of the assets *T* transfers to *X* are real estate, and that *X* has no plan to sell or dispose of the former *T* assets.

Is this transaction a reorganization? For a transaction to be an acquisitive reorganization, it must meet the three judicial requirements. The transaction meets the continuity of interest requirement, because 80 percent of the consideration is *X* stock. It also meets the continuity of business enterprise requirement, because *X* acquires (and plans to retain) all of *T*'s historic business assets. Assume that the business purpose requirement is met.

The transaction also meets the statutory requirements of a C reorganization. *X* acquires substantially all of *T*'s assets (98% of the net and gross value of those assets) and, except for the boot paid, uses solely its voting stock. Further, *T* liquidates as part of the transaction. Even though the *T* shareholders receive boot, the boot relaxation rule applies because *X* acquires at least 80 percent of the *T* assets for its voting stock (in fact acquiring exactly 80%). Thus, the transaction meets the statutory and judicial requirements for a C reorganization. Note that one additional dollar of boot in lieu of stock would have disqualified the transaction as a C reorganization.

How is *T* taxed? *T* computes its realized gain or loss on each asset transferred to *X* under §1001, but none of its realized gain or loss is recognized. §361(b). On its distribution of the assets received from *X*, *T* recognizes no gain or loss, either because the distributed assets are qualified property (the *X* stock and securities) or because they have a fair market value basis (the real estate). §361(c)(1) and (2). On its distribution of its retained asset, however, *T* recognizes an $800 gain, the excess of the asset's $2,000 value over its $1,200 basis. §361(c)(2).

How is *X* taxed? Under §1032 and general principles, *X* recognizes no gain or loss on its acquisition of *T* assets acquired for its stock, securities, and the assumption of *T*'s liability. However, *X* recognizes its realized $1,500 gain ($5,000 amount realized less $3,500 basis) on its exchange of its real estate for *T* assets.

What is *X*'s basis in the assets acquired from *T*? Under §362(b), *X* takes *T*'s basis in each transferred asset plus any gain recognized by *T* on its transfer of assets to *A*. Because *T* recognized no gain on that transfer, *X*'s basis in each *T* asset equals *T*'s basis in the asset.

PROBLEM

10-10. *T* Corp. has 1,000 shares of common stock outstanding, owned 60 percent by *A* and 40 percent by *B*. *A* and *B* each have a basis of $100 per share in their *T* stock. *T* owns a factory with a $300,000 adjusted basis and $800,000 fair market value, subject to a $500,000 mortgage. *T* also owns inventory with a $100,000 adjusted basis and $200,000 fair market value. *P* Corp., a widely held, publicly traded corporation, wishes to acquire all the *T* assets in a tax-free reorganization. Discuss the tax consequences to *P* and to *T* of each of the following:

a. *P* transfers $500,000 of its voting preferred stock to *T* in exchange for all the assets subject to the mortgage, followed by the complete liquidation of *T*.
b. *P* transfers $400,000 of its voting common stock to *T* Corp. in exchange for half the inventory and the factory subject to the mortgage. *T* then completely liquidates, distributing both the *P* stock and the remaining inventory to its shareholders pro rata.
c. *P* transfers $400,000 of its voting common stock and $100,000 of its long-term bonds to *T* in exchange for all its assets subject to the mortgage, followed by a complete liquidation of *T*.
d. How would your answers to (c) change if there had been no mortgage on the factory, and *P* had transferred $900,000 of its voting stock as well as $100,000 of securities? If *P* had transferred voting stock worth $900,000 plus Microsoft stock with a $50,000 adjusted basis and $100,000 fair market value?

3. *Shareholder-Level Taxation*

In a reorganization, the taxation of the target shareholders is governed by §§354, 356, 358, 1001(a), and 1223(1). Because the acquiring corporation shareholders make no exchange, they recognize no gain or loss as a consequence of the reorganization (unless §305(c) applies).

If, as part of a plan of reorganization, a target shareholder exchanges stock of the target, which is a party to the reorganization, solely for stock of another party to the reorganization (i.e., qualified stock), the shareholder recognizes no gain or loss. §354(a)(1). If the shareholder receives property in addition to qualified stock (i.e. boot), however, the shareholder recognizes no realized loss and recognizes gain equal to the smaller of (i) the value of the boot received and (ii) the realized gain. §356(a)(1). Note that if a target shareholder receives solely boot in exchange for target stock, the shareholder typically recognizes gain or loss under §1001.[7]

The shareholder's basis in the qualified stock received equals (1) the shareholder's basis in the target stock surrendered in the exchange, plus (2) any gain recognized on the exchange (including as a dividend), minus (3) the value of any boot received. §358(a)(1). The shareholder takes a fair market value basis in any boot received. §358(a)(2). Finally, the shareholder's holding period for the qualified stock received in the exchange includes her holding period for the target stock surrendered in the exchange if (as is likely) that target stock was a capital asset. §1223(1).

Suppose, for example, that *N* Corp. merges into *O* Corp. in a statutory merger qualifying as an A reorganization. The terms of the merger provide that each *N* shareholder will receive one share of *O* common stock, one share of *O* preferred stock, and $5 in cash for each *N* share surrendered.

If *T* owns one share of *N* stock before the merger, how will *T* be taxed on the exchange? To compute *T*'s realized gain or loss, we must know *T*'s adjusted basis in the *N* share and the fair market value of the *O* shares. Assume that *T*'s basis in the *N* share is $20, that the *O* common is worth $40, and that the *O* preferred is worth $10. Thus, *T* has realized a $35 gain on the exchange ($55 amount realized minus $20 basis).

Although *T*'s exchange is not described in §354(a) because *T* receives cash, it is described in §356(a). Under §356(a)(1), *T* recognizes $5 of the $35 realized gain (the smaller of the boot's value and the realized gain).

T's basis in the *O* common and preferred stock is determined under §358. Under §358(a), *T*'s combined basis in the two shares equals $20 (the *N* stock basis) − $5 (boot) + $5 (dividend or gain), or $20. That amount is allocated between the *O* shares in proportion to their fair market values, so that 40/50ths (80%, or $16) is allocated to the *O* common, and 10/50ths (20%, or $4) is allocated to the *O* preferred. See §358(b)(1); Treas. Regs. §1.358-1, -2. Note that if *T* had received non-cash boot, its basis would equal its fair market value. §358(a)(2).

If *T* held the *N* stock exchanged as a capital asset, *T*'s holding period for the *O* stock received would include *T*'s holding period for the *N* stock exchanged. §1223(1).

NOTES

1. *Receipt of nonqualified preferred stock.* "Nonqualified preferred stock" is defined in §351(g)(2) as preferred stock that does not participate in the growth of the corporation to any significant extent. Further, to be "nonqualified" such preferred stock must include a redemption feature making it only a short-term interest in the corporate enterprise or must have a dividend rate tied to interest rates or some equivalent index, thereby making the stock much like debt.

7. Rev. Rul. 74-515, 1974-2 C.B. 118, concludes that §302 applies to a target shareholder receiving solely boot in an acquisitive asset reorganization. Thus, that target shareholder is deemed to receive the boot in redemption of her target stock, and typically the redemption should be described in §302(b). Then, the shareholder would be deemed to sell or exchange her target stock, recognizing gain or loss under §1001. See §302(a).

Nonqualified preferred stock received as part of an acquisitive reorganization will be tax free to the extent that it is received in exchange for other nonqualified preferred stock or for securities. However, to the extent that nonqualified stock is received in exchange for stock other than nonqualified preferred stock (which includes all common stock and much preferred stock), it is taxed as boot under §354(a)(2)(C). Note, though, that if stock is treated as "nonqualified preferred stock," that treatment is relevant only to shareholder-level taxation; at the corporate level, no distinction is drawn between nonqualified preferred stock and other forms of equity. Thus, an acquiring corporation could use exclusively voting nonqualified preferred stock in a B or C reorganization with the result that the acquisition would be fully tax free at the corporate level despite being fully taxable at the shareholder level.

Suppose that in a B reorganization, *X* Corp. acquired all of the shares of *T* Corp. in exchange for its voting stock. In the exchange, *A* transferred one share of *T* stock with an $11,000 basis and a $1,000 fair market value solely for one share of *X* stock. Assume that the *X* stock, but not the *T* stock, is nonqualified preferred stock. What are the tax consequences of *A*'s exchange to *A* and *X* Corp.?

2. *Securities as qualifying property.* Section 354 provides for the tax-free receipt of stock *or securities* by a shareholder in connection with a reorganization. A debt security is a debt instrument, but not all debt instruments are "securities" for this purpose. If nonrecognition is granted on the theory that the taxpayer has changed an investment in form only, why shouldn't all debt be treated as boot? The answer seems to be that some corporate debt gives the holder as much or more of an interest in the future performance of the assets transferred as a stock interest. Debt obligations that qualify for nonrecognition treatment are referred to as "securities." The leading case on the definition of a security is Camp Wolters Enterprises v. Commissioner, 22 T.C. 737, 751 (1954), aff'd, 230 F.2d 555 (5th Cir. 1956), in which the Tax Court stated,

> The test as to whether notes are [debt] securities is not a mechanical determination of the time period of the note. Though time is an important factor, the controlling consideration is an overall evaluation of the nature of the debt, degree of participation and continuing interest compared with similarity of the note to a cash payment.

Prior to the Installment Sales Revision Act of 1980, the distinction between a debt security and a note could be very significant. The receipt of a note was immediately taxable to the transferor whereas the receipt of a debt security was not. As indicated at page 59 supra, this distinction in tax treatment has been removed, although other differences in tax treatment remain.

The most important factor separating debt securities from nonqualifying debt is the length of maturity of the obligation. Notes with a five-year term or less rarely will qualify as debt securities, while obligations with a term of 10 years or more seem likely to qualify. Cf. Rev. Rul. 2004-78, 2004-2 C.B. 108 (concluding that acquiror debt with a two-year term was a debt security when it was exchanged for a target debt security with two years remaining on its original 15-year term). In the following cases, obligations were classified as debt securities: Parkland Place Co. v. United States, 354 F.2d 916 (5th Cir. 1966) (10-year 6-percent interest-bearing note where no interest paid); Nye v. Commissioner, 50 T.C. 203 (1968) (10-year note); Camp Wolters Enterprises v. Commissioner, supra (five- and nine-year subordinated notes). Notes were not treated as debt securities in the following cases:

Bradshaw v. United States, 683 F.2d 365 (5th Cir. 1982) (notes maturing annually for five years); Adams v. Commissioner, 58 T.C. 41 (1972) (2 1/4-year note); Raich v. Commissioner, 46 T.C. 604 (1966) (demand note retired within four years).

As the court in *Camp Wolters* points out, the maturity date is not the only consideration. Consider D'Angelo Associates v. Commissioner, 70 T.C. 121 (1978), in which a demand note was held a debt security. No interest and only half of the principal of the note had been paid after 16 years. In addition, the corporation did not have sufficient liquid assets to retire the debt. Rental income was to provide funds for repayment. Finally, the note was subordinated to another liability encumbering the transferred assets. The open-ended maturity date of the note in combination with the other features gave the transferor "a continuing participation in the affairs of the debtor corporation." See also United States v. Mills, 399 F.2d 944 (5th Cir. 1968) (one-year unsecured notes where renewal expected; jury decision).

3. *Debt securities as boot.* Although §354(a)(1) classifies the exchange of stock and securities solely for stock and securities as a nonrecognition event, the receipt of acquiror debt securities is sometimes, but not always, tax free. The exchange is tax free if a target security holder exchanges a target debt security solely for qualified stock or solely for a qualified debt security of the same (or smaller) principal amount. §354(a) and (b)(1)(A). However, if the debt security holder receives more debt principal than she transfers in the reorganization, the value of that excess is treated as boot under §356. §354(a)(2)(A)(i). Further, if a target shareholder transfers target stock and receives qualified stock and a qualified debt security in exchange, the entire amount of the security received is treated as boot. §354(a)(2)(A)(ii) and §356(d)(2)(B).

Consider example 4 of Treas. Regs. §1.356-3(b). Under a plan of reorganization, *D* exchanges a debt security with principal amount of $1,000 for 100 shares of stock plus a debt security with principal amount of $1,200 and a fair market value of $1,100. The excess principal amount of the debt security received is $200, and the fair market value of that amount is $1,100 × (200/1,200), or $183.33. Accordingly, *D* can recognize gain of up to $183.33 on the exchange.

4. *Equity securities.* Securities also include rights issued by a party to the reorganization to acquire its stock, and in applying §§354 and 356(d)(2)(B), such an "equity" security is treated as having "no principal amount." Treas. Regs. §1.354-1(e). Thus, in an acquisitive reorganization, if a person exchanges target stock for qualified stock and stock rights, the person recognizes no gain or loss. The result is the same if a person exchanges target stock rights solely for qualified stock rights or for a combination of qualified stock and stock rights. However, if a person exchanges target stock solely for qualified stock rights, the exchange is not described in §354 or §356, but it may be one to which §302 applies. See Rev. Rul. 74-515, 1974-2 C.B. 118.

5. *Allocation of boot.* Under §356, a target shareholder recognizes realized gain in an acquisitive reorganization to the extent of boot received but recognizes no realized loss. Because the target shareholder computes her recognized gain share-by-share, she must allocate any boot received among the target shares surrendered. That allocation follows the terms of the exchange, if those terms are *economically reasonable.* Treas. Regs. §1.356-1(b). See also *id.* at (d) (example 4). In the absence of such terms, the boot is allocated pro rata among the surrendered shares of target stock (i.e., in proportion to the shares' fair market values). *Id.* at (b). See also *id.* at (d) (example 3). Consistent rules apply to determine the shareholder's basis in the qualified stock received in the exchange. See Treas. Regs. §1.358-2.

As the following example illustrates, this regime affords target shareholders considerable latitude to recognize gain. Suppose that *A* owns two shares of *T* stock. Share 1 has a $10 basis, and Share 2 has a $40 basis. In an acquisitive reorganization, *A* exchanges those shares for one share of *X* stock worth $50 and $50 cash. If the terms of the exchange do not provide for an allocation of the boot, the boot is allocated equally to each share. *A* recognizes an overall $35 gain, a $25 gain on Share 1 (the smaller of *A*'s $40 realized gain and the $25 cash received) and a $10 gain on Share 2 (the smaller of *A*'s $10 realized gain and the $25 cash received). If, under the terms of the exchange, the boot is allocated entirely to Share 1, *A* recognizes a $40 gain (the smaller of *A*'s $40 realized gain and the $50 cash received). If, instead, the boot is allocated entirely to Share 2, *A* recognizes a $10 gain (the smaller of *A*'s $10 realized gain and the $50 cash received).

Note that if Share 2 had a $60, rather than a $40, basis, and the entire $50 boot was allocated to Share 2, *A* would recognize no loss. §356. More troubling, *A*'s excess basis disappears, at least under the current position of the Service.

6. *Characterization of gain.* Does a shareholder who receives boot as part of a reorganization recognize capital gain or ordinary income? Usually, the character of gain recognized on an exchange described by §356(a)(1) is determined by reference to the property given up. For example, if the stock and securities surrendered were all capital assets held longer than one year, any gain recognized would be long-term capital gain. This general rule, however, is limited by §356(a)(2).

Under §356(a)(2), if some gain must be recognized and the exchange has the effect of a distribution of a dividend, the taxpayer must treat any gain recognized as dividend income, up to the taxpayer's ratable share of the earnings and profits of the corporation. This section poses two difficult questions: When does an exchange have the effect of a "distribution of a dividend"? In computing the earnings and profits limitation, which corporation's earnings and profits should be used?

In Clark v. Commissioner, 489 U.S. 726 (1985), the Supreme Court held that when a shareholder of the target corporation in an acquisitive reorganization receives boot in addition to qualifying property, the shareholder should be taxed as if she received additional stock in place of the boot and then had this additional stock redeemed with the boot actually received by the shareholder. The character of the shareholder's gain is then determined by reference to the redemption rules of §302 as applied to this hypothetical redemption.

Suppose that *T* Corp. merges into *A* Corp. when each share of *T* Corp. stock and *A* Corp. stock is worth $50. Assume that, before the merger, individuals *P*, *Q*, and *R* own stock in *T* Corp. and *A* Corp. as follows:

	Number of Shares	
	T Corp.	*A Corp.*
P	60	0
Q	60	90
R	0	30
	120	120

In the merger, *P* receives $1,500 in cash and 30 shares of *A* Corp. stock, while *Q* receives $2,500 in cash and 10 shares of *A* Corp. stock. Accordingly, after the merger,

A Corp. has 160 shares of stock outstanding, of which *P* owns 30, *Q* owns 100, and *R* owns 30.

Following the approach adopted by the Supreme Court in *Clark*, we treat the transaction as if *P* and *Q* received only stock in the reorganization and then some of that stock was redeemed. Because each share of *A* Corp. is worth $50, the $1,500 boot received by *P* corresponds to 30 shares of *A* Corp., and the $2,500 boot received by *Q* corresponds to 50 shares of *A* Corp. Accordingly, we treat the transaction as if *P* and *Q* each received 60 shares of *A* Corp. stock in the reorganization and then 30 of *P*'s shares and 50 of *Q*'s shares were redeemed.

Thus, before the deemed redemption, *A* Corp. is treated as having 240 shares outstanding, 60 owned by *P*, 150 owned by *Q*, and 30 owned by *R*. The effect of the hypothetical redemption is to reduce *P*'s ownership of *A* Corp. from 25 percent (60 of 240 shares) to 18.75 percent (30 of 160 shares) and to leave *Q*'s ownership of *A* Corp. at 62.5 percent (from 150 of 240 shares to 100 of 160 shares). On this redemption, *P* will qualify for exchange treatment under §§302(b)(2) and 302(a) but *Q* will receive dividend income (assuming adequate earnings and profits) under §§302(d) and 301.

7. *Measuring earnings and profits.* If a taxpayer is considered to receive boot that has the effect of a distribution of a dividend, should the amount of the dividend be determined by reference to the earnings and profits of the target corporation, the acquiring corporation, or both? In Wright v. United States, 483 F.2d 600 (8th Cir. 1973), the court held that only the earnings and profits of the target could be used, a view that the Service has rejected. Rev. Rul. 75-83, 1975-1 C.B. 112. The Supreme Court in *Clark* did not determine the proper measure of earnings and profits because in that case the distribution of boot did not have the effect of a dividend, but the Tax Court had the following to say on this issue: "There is no reason why the redemption cannot be considered as having been made by one corporation with the consequences to be measured by the earnings and profits of another corporation." Clark v. Commissioner, 86 T.C. 138 (1986), aff'd, 828 F.2d 221 (4th Cir. 1987), aff'd, 489 U.S. 726 (1989); see also American Manufacturing Co. v. Commissioner, 55 T.C. 204 (1970) (no combination allowed); Atlas Tool Co. v. Commissioner, 614 F.2d 860 (3d Cir. 1980) (same); Davant v. Commissioner, 366 F.2d 874 (5th Cir. 1966) (combination allowed); Rev. Rul. 70-274, 1970-1 C.B. 81 (same). Indeed, because the approach adopted by the Supreme Court in *Clark* treats the redemption as part of the full reorganization, it would seem appropriate to make the earnings and profits of *both* corporations available for dividend income. Compare the earnings and profits computation in §304(b)(2).

8. *Dividend income versus dividend gain.* Section 356(a)(2) has one structural aspect that is difficult to justify. If the receipt of boot is a dividend equivalent, it is still the *gain*, rather than the amount of the boot, that is taxable as ordinary income under §356(a)(2). If the effect of the boot is the receipt of a dividend, why is the taxpayer allowed basis recovery before recognizing income? Indeed, if there is no gain on the exchange, the taxpayer will not recognize any income under §356(a)(2) regardless of the amount of the boot or dividend equivalency.

PROBLEMS

10-11. Discuss the shareholder-level tax consequences of the transactions described in problem 10-10.

10-12. *X* Corp. has 100 shares outstanding, 50 owned by individual *A* and 50 by individual *B*. *Y* Corp. also has 100 shares outstanding, 80 owned by *B* and 20 by individual *C*. *X* Corp. has earnings and profits of $1,000, and *Y* Corp. has earnings and profits of $1,500. *A*'s basis in the *X* Corp. stock is $20 per share; *B*'s basis in the *X* Corp. stock is $10 per share; *B*'s basis in the *Y* Corp. stock is $10 per share; *C*'s basis in the *Y* Corp. stock is $30 per share. The shares of *X* and *Y* are worth $50 per share.

X Corp. merges into *Y* Corp. under applicable state law. As part of the merger, *A* receives $1,000 in cash and 30 shares of *Y*. *B* receives $1,500 in cash and 20 shares of *Y*. Accordingly, the ownership of *Y* Corp. after the merger is as follows: *A* owns 30 shares, *B* owns 100 shares, and *C* owns 20 shares.

What are the tax consequences to *A* and *B* of this merger? Assume that *A*, *B*, and *C* are unrelated to one another.

E. THE STATUS OF CREDITORS IN CORPORATE REORGANIZATIONS

The materials in this chapter focus primarily on the consequences of a corporate reorganization to the combining corporations and the shareholders of the target corporation (i.e., the corporation whose stock or assets is transferred). Almost always, however, the target corporation will have creditors. How are those creditors affected by the reorganization? Do they recognize gain or loss if they surrender their claims and in exchange receive stock or securities of the acquiring corporation or other claims against it?

At the outset it should be noted that the creditors will not necessarily participate in the reorganization exchange. For example, in a B reorganization, the creditors of the target corporation may simply ride through the reorganization, preserving intact their claims against their respective debtors.

Alternatively, the acquiring corporation may assume the target corporation's liabilities or take the properties subject to those liabilities, still without any formal exchange by the creditors. Ordinarily, this will not constitute boot to the transferee. §357. Nor will creditors recognize gain or loss because their claims have not been paid, retired, or exchanged. Treas. Regs. §1.1001-3(e)(4)(i)(B). Moreover, §368(a)(1)(C) states explicitly that the requirement that the acquisition be solely for the acquiring corporation's voting stock in a C reorganization is not breached by the corporation's assuming liabilities or taking property subject to liabilities.

Frequently, however, there will be a formal exchange. The creditors may surrender bonds, debentures, or notes of one corporation and receive stock or securities of another corporation. In general, the exchange will qualify under §354. One difficulty that may arise is that short-term notes (whether given up or received) may not qualify as "securities." See pages 399-400 supra. But see Treas. Regs. §1.1001-3(e)(4)(i)(B) (providing that a target creditor recognizes no gain or loss if the acquiror is merely substituted as the debtor as part of an acquisitive asset reorganization).

There may be other problems as well. If in conjunction with a B reorganization (stock for stock) the acquiring corporation issues bonds in exchange for bonds of the target corporation, will the transaction fall outside of §368(a)(1)(B) on the grounds that it is not "solely" for voting stock? If the stock-for-stock exchange qualifies, will the bondholders' exchange be "in pursuance of a plan of reorganization" under §354(a)(1)? See Rev. Rul. 70-41, 1970-1 C.B. 77 (exchange of debt of the acquired corporation for stock of the acquiring corporation incident to B reorganization is taxable). Similarly, in a C reorganization, if the acquiring corporation issues its own evidences of indebtedness to creditors of the target corporation instead of merely assuming the liabilities, should the transaction lose its status as a reorganization?

F. REORGANIZATIONS OF INSOLVENT OR FINANCIALLY DISTRESSED CORPORATIONS

Under prior law, a transfer of all or part of a corporation's assets to another corporation pursuant to a court-approved plan under the Bankruptcy Act could qualify for tax-free treatment under separate rules applicable to "insolvency reorganizations." In the Bankruptcy Tax Act of 1980, Congress ended the separate regime for debtor corporations in a title 11 (bankruptcy) case, adding a new category of tax-free corporate reorganization under §368(a)(1)(G): the G reorganization. Congress made this change to encourage and facilitate the rehabilitation of bankrupt debtor corporations. As a consequence, many prior law requirements for tax-free treatment were removed, parties were given additional flexibility in structuring the acquisition, and, most importantly, the acquiring corporation was permitted to succeed to the tax attributes of the acquired corporation (such as its net operating loss carryovers). S. Rep. No. 1035, 96th Cong., 2d Sess. 34-25 (1980).

As is often the case, change is not without its problems. Although there are benefits to the G reorganization, qualifying transactions must also conform to certain statutory and judicial requirements imposed on all tax-free reorganizations. It is apparent that many of these regular tax reorganization requirements cannot be easily adapted and applied to the unique circumstances faced by a bankrupt corporation.

Difficulties aside, the G reorganization is the most flexible of the acquisitive tax-free reorganization provisions. It is a hybrid provision that borrows most of its characteristics from the other acquisitive reorganization provisions. It is similar to an A reorganization (a state law merger) in that it requires two corporations, and the only limit on the nature of consideration used by the acquiring corporation is the judicial continuity of interest doctrine discussed at the beginning of this chapter. State law merger requirements, however, need not be met. It is similar to a C reorganization in that it contemplates an acquisition of assets of one corporation by another corporation, but it does not require an exchange of assets solely (as relaxed by statute) for voting stock of the acquiring corporation. It is most like an acquisitive D reorganization, except that it does not require that the shareholders of the acquired corporation also "control" the acquiring corporation.

A G reorganization is defined as (1) a transfer of assets (2) by one corporation to another corporation in a title 11 (bankruptcy) or similar case (3) followed by a distribution as described in §354, §355, or §356 of the consideration received in the transaction. Each of these three requirements is discussed below.

A G reorganization requires that a corporation transfer all or a part of its assets to another corporation, provided one of the corporations is in a bankruptcy (or similar) case and provided the transfer occurs pursuant to a plan of reorganization approved by the bankruptcy court. §368(a)(3)(B). Thus, the transfer of stock of the debtor corporation to its creditors in satisfaction of their claims will not qualify as a G reorganization (although such a transaction may have no adverse tax consequences). Similarly, out-of-court transactions, chapter 7 liquidating cases, and foreign reorganizations are ineligible.

For example, suppose Loss Corp. is hopelessly insolvent. Immediately before filing a bankruptcy petition, Loss Corp. agrees to transfer all its assets to Public Corp. in exchange for Public Corp. common stock; Loss Corp. will then distribute the stock received to its creditors in satisfaction of their claims. This acquisition will not qualify as a G reorganization because it did not occur within a title 11 or similar case. Accordingly, the transaction will be tax free only if it meets the standards of one of the other acquisitive reorganization provisions such as the A, C, or D.

As a second example, suppose Loss Corp. is in a chapter 11 bankruptcy case. Loss Corp.'s plan of reorganization provides for a transfer of cash and certain nonoperating assets to secured creditors and of all newly authorized common stock to its unsecured creditors. All previously authorized outstanding common stock is canceled. Loss Corp.'s plan will not qualify as a G reorganization because Loss Corp. has not transferred its assets to another corporation. Although not qualifying as a G reorganization, this transaction likely qualifies for tax-free treatment as an E recapitalization, a form of tax-free reorganization discussed in Chapter 12. See S. Rep. No. 1035, 96th Cong., 2d Sess. 36 (1980).

Section 354(b) also requires that substantially all of the assets of the acquired corporation be transferred to the acquiring corporation. In the context of the C reorganization, the Service requires (for advanced rulings) that at least 90 percent of the net assets and 70 percent of the gross assets be transferred in the reorganization. Rev. Proc. 77-37 (§3.01), 1977-2 C.B. 568. Congress has indicated that the substantially all requirement should be interpreted liberally in the context of the G reorganization in view of the underlying purpose of the provision to facilitate the rehabilitation of financially troubled corporations. Accordingly, substantially all of the assets of the debtor corporation may be acquired even if the debtor sells assets to pay creditors or to rearrange its business affairs so as to obtain creditor approval of its plan of reorganization. S. Rep. No. 1035, 96th Cong., 2d Sess. 36-36 (1980). In private rulings, the Service has relaxed its definition of "substantially all" in the context of a G reorganization. See Priv. Ltr. Rul. 9313020 (Apr. 2, 1993); Priv. Ltr. Rul. 8726055 (Mar. 31, 1987).

In addition to the substantially all requirement, §354(a) requires that stock or securities of the acquiring corporation be distributed to a holder of stock or securities of the acquired corporation. If holders of securities in the acquired corporation actually receive stock or securities (or if shareholders in the acquired corporation actually receive stock) in the acquiring corporation pursuant to the plan of reorganization, the transaction should qualify as a G reorganization even if the value of the stock or securities received represents a small percentage of the value of the total equity consideration given in the transaction. Thus, the threshold exchange requirement of §354(a) should be satisfied if one security holder receives stock or securities (or if one shareholder receives stock) pursuant to the plan of reorganization. The threshold exchange requirement of §354(a) will not be satisfied, however, if (as is often true in the typical corporate bankruptcy) all the old stock of the debtor corporation is canceled (because there is no equity left), and the acquiring corporation's stock is distributed to short-term creditors whose debt instruments are not debt securities. But cf. Treas. Regs. §1.368-1(e)(6) (treating unsecured creditors of financially troubled corporations as equity holders in certain cases).

For example, suppose Loss Corp. is in a chapter 11 bankruptcy case. Loss Corp.'s plan of reorganization provides for the transfer of substantially all of its assets to Public Corp. in exchange for Public Corp. common stock with fair market value of $450 and cash of $550. The plan calls for the transfer of cash and certain nonoperating assets to secured creditors and for the distribution of all the Public Corp. common stock to Loss Corp.'s unsecured creditors. One unsecured creditor holds a 10-year bond with a locomotive printed on the face of the certificate. Assume that a locomotive is clear evidence that the bond is a "security" for tax purposes. The old Loss Corp. common stock is canceled, and the shareholders receive nothing under the plan. Because substantially all of the assets were acquired by Public Corp. in exchange for an amount of common stock that should satisfy the continuity of interest doctrine, and because at least one Loss Corp. security holder received stock pursuant to the plan, the transaction should qualify as a tax-free G reorganization.

The transaction in this example would not qualify as a G reorganization if all of Loss Corp.'s unsecured creditors held only short-term debt. One possible way to avoid this technical trap in the statute is to convert the claims of the creditors into stock of the acquired debtor corporation before the G reorganization is consummated, relying on Helvering v. Alabama Asphaltic Limestone Co., 315 U.S. 179 (1942). In that case, the Supreme Court held that creditors of an insolvent corporation who received stock of a reorganized corporation had a "continuing interest" because, under the full priority rule of bankruptcy proceedings, they had "effective command over the disposition of the properties" of the old corporation.

In Neville Coke & Chemical Co. v. Commissioner, 148 F.2d 599 (3d Cir. 1945), however, the court held that noteholders of a reorganized corporation who exchanged their notes for debentures and common stock could not claim nonrecognition of their gain under what is now §354. The court relied on *Pinellas* and *LeTulle* as establishing that notes received on an exchange do not evidence a continuing interest in the enterprise and are not "securities." It then held that the notes are equally deficient if given up in the exchange. The debtor was in financial difficulties at the time of the exchange, but the court was unwilling to find that the creditors already owned the entire equity, and in fact the old stockholders did participate in the exchange. If, however, the creditors of a distressed corporation in reorganization received stock or securities evidencing a proprietary interest in the enterprise, is it not probable that the claims they gave up, whatever their form, already represented in economic reality a proprietary interest in the assets? For a forceful statement of this view, see Griswold, "Securities" and "Continuity of Interest," 58 Harv. L. Rev. 705 (1945).

Regulations now adopt that view, and in applying the continuity of interest requirement for a G reorganization (and for certain transactions involving an insolvent target), a creditor's interest may be treated as a proprietary interest. Recall that to satisfy this continuity requirement, holders of the target's proprietary interests must receive qualified stock as a significant part of their consideration in the transaction. This requirement should be met if those holders receive qualified stock that in the aggregate comprises 40 percent of their total consideration. See Treas. Regs. §1.368-1(e)(2)(v), example 1 (concluding that 40-percent continuity is sufficient).

A creditor's claim against the target may be treated as a proprietary interest if the target is under the jurisdiction of the court in a title 11 or similar case. Treas. Regs. §1.368-1(e)(6)(i) (also providing for that treatment if the target is insolvent (i.e., its liabilities exceed the value of its assets immediately before the potential reorganization)). In that case, the target's proprietary interest holders are divided into two groups: (i) the most senior class of target creditors that receives qualified stock in the transaction (the "senior creditors") and (ii) more junior target creditors and target shareholders. See *id.* at (e)(6)(ii). Each claim of a junior creditor or target shareholder is treated in whole as a proprietary interest. *Id.* at (e)(6)(i).

The treatment of a senior creditor's claim depends on the consideration received by senior creditors as a group. If those creditors receive solely qualified stock in the transaction, each senior creditor's claim is treated in whole as a proprietary interest. *Id.* If, however, the senior creditors receive consideration in addition to qualified stock, a senior creditor's interest is bifurcated, treated in part as debt and in part as a proprietary interest. The part treated as a proprietary interest equals the percentage (by value) of the total consideration received by senior creditors that is qualified stock.[8]

For example, suppose that *P* Corp. acquires all assets of *L* Corp. in a transaction that qualifies as a G reorganization as long as the continuity of interest requirement is met. Before the acquisition, *L* Corp. has $10 million of long-term debt and $20 million of trade debt, and the trade debt is junior to the long-term debt. As part of the bankruptcy plan, the long-term creditors receive $5 million in cash and $5 million worth of *P* stock, while the trade creditors receive $5 million in cash. In measuring continuity, *one-half* of each long-term creditor's interest and *all* of each trade creditor's interest are treated as proprietary interests. Thus, the total amount received for the *L* Corp. proprietary interests equals $10 million ($5 million for the long-term creditors' interests plus $5 million for the trade creditors' interests).

Suppose first that each long-term creditor receives (by value) one-half cash and one-half *P* stock. In total, therefore, each long-term creditor is deemed to receive solely *P* Corp. stock for its proprietary interest in *L* Corp. (i.e., $5 million of *P* stock in total). Thus, $5 million out of $10 million (or half) of the total consideration received for the *L* Corp. proprietary interests in *L* Corp. is *P* stock, and the transaction meets the continuity of interest requirement.

Suppose, instead, that half of the long-term creditors receive solely cash for their interests while the other half receive solely *P* stock. In total, therefore, half of the long-term creditors are deemed to receive cash for their *L* Corp. proprietary interests (worth $2.5 million), while half receive solely *P* stock (also worth $2.5 million). Thus, only $2.5 million out of $10 million (or 25 percent) of total consideration received for the *L* Corp. proprietary interests is *P* stock, too little to satisfy the continuity of interest requirement. Treas. Regs. §1.368-1(e)(2)(v) (examples 2(ii) and 4) (concluding that 25% continuity is not sufficient).

In addition to the continuity of interest requirement, a G reorganization must meet other judicial requirements imposed on all tax-free corporate reorganizations,

8. *Id.* at (e)(6)(ii)(A) (also adding, however, that if there is only one class of creditors, the amount of stock received by that class cannot be de minimis when compared to the total consideration received in the transaction by the target, its shareholders, and its creditors). Thus, a G reorganization will have 100-percent continuity of interest if (i) each senior creditor receives solely stock (or the same ratio of stock to non-stock consideration) for its claim and (ii) no junior claim receives non-stock consideration.

including continuity of business enterprise and business purpose. These are discussed at pages 342-356 supra. Finally, if a transaction qualifies as both a G reorganization and a different reorganization under another provision (or under §332 or §351), the transaction is treated as qualifying only as a G reorganization. §368(a)(3)(C).

PROBLEM

10-13. *L* Corp. is involved in a bankruptcy proceeding. As part of the court-supervised plan of reorganization, Big Corp. transfers its preferred stock worth $50,000 to *L* Corp. in exchange for *L*'s fully depreciated operating assets. *L* Corp. then liquidates, distributing the Big Corp. preferred stock and its nonoperating assets (short-term certificates of deposit with adjusted basis of $22,000 and fair market value of $25,000) to its sole debtholder, *H*, in complete satisfaction of *L*'s $100,000 debt to *H*. The shareholders of *L* Corp. receive nothing, and their stock in *L* Corp. is canceled. What are the tax consequences of this transaction to Big Corp., to *H*, to *L*, and to the former shareholders of *L*?

G. POLICY

Recall that the initial justification for the reorganization provisions was that a corporate rearrangement should be taxable if it resembles a sale but should be tax free if it more closely appears to be a mere change in form of the business enterprise. From that relatively simple notion has grown the complexity you have just discovered.

The simple fact is that most corporate acquisitions can be structured either as reorganizations or as taxable transactions. Although not formally elective, reorganization status is practically a matter of choice. The detailed rules of the Code seeking to distinguish tax-free reorganizations from taxable sales have little effect beyond increasing the transaction and uncertainty costs to taxpayers contemplating acquisitive transactions.

Those corporate rearrangements qualifying as reorganizations under §368 are, in general, tax free at both the corporate and shareholder level. Nonqualifying transactions will be taxable at one or both levels, depending on the form selected by the parties. On one hand, a corporate acquisition structured as the sale of shares by the acquired corporation's shareholders will be taxed at the shareholder level only (unless a §338 election is made): Because the corporate assets are not formally transferred, no corporate-level tax is imposed. On the other hand, sale by the target of its assets will produce a corporate-level tax, but the shareholders of the target corporation will be safe from taxation until the sale proceeds are distributed.

At the corporate level, this distinction makes little sense. Any bulk transfer of corporate assets is a rearrangement of the business enterprise. Tax-free treatment of any such transaction, *however effected*, arguably is an appropriate incident to the change in form of a business. So long as asset basis is preserved, no corporate-level tax is avoided (unless corporate-level gain can be indefinitely postponed). If the corporate parties desire a step-up in basis and are willing to be taxed on the transaction as the price for that step-up, that result should also be acceptable to the Treasury. Section 338 has adopted this elective approach to rearrangements of corporate control effected by sale of the target corporation's stock. If Congress permitted the bulk sale of corporate assets to go untaxed with an accompanying carryover basis rule, the tax treatment of corporate reorganizations would become fully elective.

At the shareholder level, the appropriate taxation seems to turn on what each shareholder receives in the reorganization. That is, the exchange of stock and securities for stock and securities incident to a corporate acquisition ought to be tax free regardless of what other shareholders receive. Kass, for example, should have been entitled to nonrecognition even though most of her co-shareholders properly were taxed.

Accordingly, shareholder-level taxation should be independent of corporate-level taxation: Whether the corporate parties elect nonrecognition or taxable exchange is a matter of indifference to the shareholders. Further, the taxation of each shareholder should be independent of the taxation of all other shareholders: In particular, the continuity of interest should be abolished. These basic reforms, along with several others, have been proposed by the American Law Institute. See ALI, Federal Income Tax Project: Subchapter C — Proposals on Corporate Acquisitions and Dispositions (1982). In turn, the ALI reforms largely were embraced by the Senate Finance Committee. See Staff of the Senate Finance Committee, The Subchapter C Revision Act of 1985, 99th Cong., 1st Sess. (Comm. Print 1985). Alas, these reforms have not been adopted nor are they likely to be adopted in the near future.

11

Divisive Reorganizations

A. TAXATION UNDER §355

1. *Overview*

In a divisive reorganization, one corporation distributes the stock of a second corporation that it controls immediately before the distribution. §355(a)(1)(A). See also §368(c) (defining control). The controlled corporation may be an existing corporation or it may be newly formed with assets contributed by the distributing corporation as part of the transaction.[1] Whether a divisive reorganization involves an existing or newly formed controlled corporation, §355 defines its principal characteristics.

For §355 to apply to a distribution, not only must the distributing corporation control the distributed corporation immediately before the distribution, three additional statutory hurdles must be navigated: the "device" restriction of §355(a)(1)(B), the "active business" limitation of §355(a)(1)(C), and the "distribution" requirement of §355(a)(1)(D). In addition, the regulations impose a "business purpose" requirement, sometimes the most troublesome hurdle of all. These requirements all reflect that a divisive reorganization, if unchecked, has the potential for tax abuse — the bailout of earnings and profits at preferential rates and with basis recovery.

If the statutory and regulatory requirements for a divisive reorganization are met, the distribution of stock of the controlled corporation will be tax free to both the shareholders and to the distributing corporation. See §355(c)(1) and §361(c)(1) (for the distributing corporation); §355(a) (for the shareholder). If the distributing corporation also distributes boot, both the corporation and shareholder may recognize gain (or, for the shareholder, have dividend income). §355(c)(2) and §361(c)(2) (for the distributing corporation); §356(a) and (b) (for the shareholder).

1. The asset contribution may be described in §368(a)(1)(D). Then, the asset contribution and stock distribution are sometimes referred to as a "divisive D" or "D/355" reorganization. Note that when the text refers to "divisive reorganization," that reference includes all transactions described in §355, whether or not also described in §368(a)(1)(D).

2. *Potential Abuse*

To understand §355, you need to understand the abuse it is intended to forestall. Suppose *X* Corp. has been successful for many years, so that it has substantial earnings and profits as well as substantial cash and liquid assets. The shareholders of *X* Corp. would like to get some of its profits into their hands without recognizing dividend income. Of course, a shareholder could sell stock at capital gain rates, or redemptions could be structured to obtain the same effect, but in either case the favorable capital gain treatment is obtained only at the cost of giving up some control of the corporation and its future profit-making capability.

Consider the following plan: *X* Corp. creates new Sub Co. in a §351 transaction, transferring its cash and liquid investments to Sub Co. in exchange for all of Sub Co.'s stock. The Sub Co. stock is then distributed by *X* Corp. to its shareholders, and, if that distribution were tax free to *X* Corp. and to its shareholders, Sub Co. could then liquidate; by this mechanism the cash and liquid assets of *X* Corp. would be removed from corporate solution at capital gain rates and with recognition of income only after recovery by the shareholders of their basis in the Sub Co stock. Or, instead of liquidating Sub Co., the shareholders could sell their stock in Sub Co. to obtain capital gains, and the purchasers would have a cost basis in the Sub Co. stock so that its assets could be bailed out in the future without difficulty.

Note that the effect of placing the *X* Corp. assets in a separate corporation (Sub Co.) allows the *X* Corp. shareholders to part with their Sub Co. stock without relinquishing any control over the operating assets of *X* Corp. As we saw when we looked at redemptions,[2] and again at stock dividends,[3] a shareholder should be able to avoid dividend treatment only by reducing ownership of the ongoing profit-making ability of the corporation. If divisive reorganizations permitted the tax-free separation of operating assets from investment assets, earnings and profits could be bailed out with abandon.

To ensure that corporate divisions do not become bailouts, §355 imposes three distinct hurdles. First, the active trade or business requirement of §355(a)(1)(C) mandates that each of the corporations after the division be engaged in a longstanding active trade or business. Thus, the transaction cannot simply separate operating assets from investment assets. Second, the device limitation of §355(a)(1)(B) provides that the transaction cannot be used "principally as a device for the distribution of earnings and profits." This broadly worded provision allows the courts to police divisive transactions with an eye toward the underlying policy of §355; in addition, it has allowed Treasury to promulgate a business purpose test in the regulations. Third, the distribution requirement of §355(a)(1)(D) limits tax-free treatment to divisive transactions in which the corporations separate completely: With limited exceptions, the distributing corporation cannot retain any ownership of the corporation whose stock it is distributing. Without this requirement, the distributing shareholders might be able to sell an indirect interest in the controlled corporation, by selling distributing corporation stock, and enjoy capital gain (or loss). These three requirements are discussed below.

2. See Chapter 5.
3. See Chapter 6.

In all §355 transactions, one corporation distributes stock and securities of one or more other corporations, thereby converting a parent-subsidiary structure into a brother-sister structure. In the language of §355, the corporation distributing the stock and securities is called the "distributing" corporation, and the corporations whose stock and securities are distributed are called the "controlled" corporations. In a §355 transaction, there is only one distributing corporation, but there can be one or more controlled corporations.

3. *The Active Trade or Business Requirement*

Section 355(a)(1)(C), by incorporating §355(b), requires that both the distributing corporation and the controlled corporations be engaged immediately after the transaction in the active conduct of trades or businesses that have been conducted for at least five years.[4] The purpose of this five-year requirement is—

> to prevent the corporate earnings of one business from being drawn off . . . and put into a new business and thereby, through the creation of a marketable enterprise, convert what would normally have been dividends into [a nontaxable distribution of stock that is] readily saleable by the shareholders.

Rev. Rul. 59-400, 1959-2 C.B. 114 (obsoleted by Rev. Rul. 2003-99, 2003-2 C.B. 388).

Should the active trade or business requirement be met when one business is split between two corporations? How about if profits are used to "expand" a business? Consider the following case and revenue ruling:

Coady v. Commissioner

33 T.C. 771 (1960), aff'd per curiam, 289 F.2d 490 (6th Cir. 1961)

TIETJENS, Judge: . . .

The issue for decision is whether the transfer by the Christopher Construction Company of a portion of its assets to E. P. Coady and Co. in exchange for all of the Coady Company's stock, and the subsequent distribution by the Christopher Company of such Coady stock to petitioner in exchange for his Christopher stock, constituted a distribution of stock qualifying for tax-free treatment on the shareholder level under the provisions of section 355 of the 1954 Internal Revenue Code.

All of the facts were stipulated, are so found, and are incorporated herein by this reference. . . .

Christopher Construction Co., an Ohio corporation, is now engaged, and for more than 5 years prior to November 15, 1954, was engaged, in the active conduct of a construction business primarily in and around Columbus, Ohio. In an average year the Christopher Company undertook approximately 6 construction contracts, no

4. In a split-up, the distributing corporation does not survive, and the active trade or business requirement is met if (i) immediately before the distribution, the distributing corporation has no assets other than stock or securities in the controlled corporations and (ii) immediately after the distribution, each controlled corporation is engaged in the active conduct of a trade or business. §355(b)(1)(B).

one of which lasted for more than 2 years. Its gross receipts varied between $1,500,000 and $2,000,000 per year.

At its central office, located at 16 East Broad Street in Columbus, the Christopher Company kept its books of account, paid its employees, prepared bids for its jobs, and, excepting minor amounts of tools and supplies, made its purchases. In addition, it maintained temporary field offices at each jobsite. It also maintained a central repair and storage depot for its equipment. Equipment in use on particular jobs was kept at the jobsite until work was terminated. Then, it would either be returned to the central depot or moved to another jobsite.

At all times material hereto, the stock of the Christopher Company was owned by M. Christopher and the petitioner. For a number of years, petitioner owned 35 per cent of that stock and Christopher owned 65 per cent. However, on April 19, 1954, petitioner purchased 15 per cent of the total stock from Christopher. From that date until November 15, 1954, each owned 50 per cent of the company's stock.

Sometime prior to November 15, 1954, differences arose between the petitioner and Christopher. As a result, they entered into an agreement for the division of the Christopher Company into two separate enterprises. Pursuant to that agreement, the Christopher Company, on November 15, 1954, organized E. P. Coady and Co., to which it transferred the following assets, approximating one-half the Christopher Company's total assets:

A contract for the construction of a sewage disposal plant at Columbus, Ohio, dated June 1, 1954.
A part of its equipment.
A part of its cash, and certain other items.

In consideration for the receipt of these assets, E. P. Coady and Co. transferred all of its stock to the Christopher Company. The Christopher Company retained the following assets, which were of the same type as those transferred to E. P. Coady and Co.:

A contract for a sewage treatment plant in Charleston, West Virginia.
A part of its equipment.
A part of its cash.

Immediately thereafter, the Christopher Company distributed to the petitioner all of the stock of E. P. Coady and Co. held by it in exchange for all of the stock of the Christopher Company held by petitioner. The fair market value of the stock of E. P. Coady and Co. received by petitioner was $140,000. His basis in the Christopher Company stock surrendered was $72,500.

Since the distribution, both E. P. Coady and Co. and the Christopher Company have been actively engaged in the construction business.

On their 1954 Federal income tax return, petitioner and his wife reported no gain or loss on the exchange of the Christopher Company stock for the stock of E. P. Coady and Co.

Respondent determined that petitioner realized a capital gain on that exchange in the amount of $67,500, 50 per cent of which was taxable in 1954.

Petitioner contends that the distribution to him of the E. P. Coady and Co. stock qualified for tax-free treatment under the provisions of section 355 of the 1954

Code, arguing that it was received pursuant to a distribution of a controlled corporation's stock within the meaning of that section.

Respondent on the other hand maintains petitioner's receipt of the Coady stock did not fall within those distributions favored by section 355, inasmuch as the 5-year active business requirements of 355(b) were not met. More particularly he argues that section 355 does not apply to the separation of a "single business"; and, inasmuch as the Christopher Company was engaged in only one trade or business (construction contracting), the gain realized by petitioner upon receipt of the Coady stock was taxable. As authority for his position respondent points to that portion of his regulations which expressly provides that section 355 does not apply to the division of a single business.*

Thus, the issue is narrowed to the question of whether the challenged portion of the regulations constitutes a valid construction of the statute, or whether it is unreasonable and plainly inconsistent therewith. Though this appears to be a case of first impression, the question has not gone without comment. . . .

Section 355 of the 1954 Code represents the latest of a series of legislative enactments designed to deal with the tax effect upon shareholders of various corporate separations. Where the 1939 Code contained three sections, 112(b)(3), 112(b)(11), and 112(g)(1)(D), which controlled the tax impact of these exchanges, present law groups the statutory requirements into two sections, 355 and 368(c). A careful reading of section 355, as well as the Finance Committee report which accompanied its enactment, reveals no language, express or implied, denying tax-free treatment at the shareholder level to a transaction, otherwise qualifying under section 355, on the grounds that it represents the division or separation of a "single" trade or business. . . .

The active business requirements of 355(b)(1) prohibit the tax-free separation of a corporation into active and inactive entities. Section 355(b)(1)(A) extends the provisions of §355(a) only to those divisive distributions where the distributing corporation and the controlled corporation are engaged immediately after the distribution in the active conduct of a trade or business. In the case of those distributions which involve liquidation of the transferor, 355(b)(1)(B) requires that immediately before the distribution the transferor have no assets other than stock or securities in the controlled corporations, and that immediately thereafter each of the controlled corporations is engaged in the active conduct of a trade or business. Neither 355(b)(1)(A) nor (B) concerns itself with the existence of a plurality of businesses per se; rather both speak in terms of a plurality of corporate entities engaged in the active conduct of a trade or business, a distinction we believe to be vital in light of provisions of 355(b)(2). . . .

Respondent maintains that a reading of 355(b)(2)(B) in conjunction with the requirement of 355(b)(1) that both "the distributing corporation, *and* the controlled corporation . . . , [be] engaged immediately after the distribution in the active conduct of a trade or business" (emphasis supplied) indicates Congress intended the provisions of the statute to apply only where, immediately after the distribution, there exist two separate and distinct businesses, one operated by the distributing corporation and one operated by the controlled corporation, both of

* This regulation has been repealed. — Eds.

which were actively conducted for the 5-year period immediately preceding the distribution. In our judgment the statute does not support this construction.

[T]he only reference to plurality appears in section 355(b)(1), and deals with corporate entities, not businesses. Recognizing the divisive nature of the transaction, subsection (b)(1) contemplates that where there was only one corporate entity prior to the various transfers, immediately subsequent thereto, there will be two or more *corporations.* In order to insure that a tax-free separation will involve the separation only of those assets attributable to the carrying on of an active trade or business, and further to prevent the tax-free division of an active corporation into active and inactive entities, subsection (b)(1) further provides that each of the surviving corporations must be engaged in the active conduct of a trade or business.

A careful reading of the definition of the active conduct of a trade or business contained in subsection (b)(2) indicates that its function is also to prevent the tax-free separation of *active* and *inactive* assets into *active* and *inactive* corporate entities. This is apparent from the use of the adjective "such," meaning beforementioned, to modify "trade or business" in subsection (b)(2)(B), thus providing that the trade or business, required by (b)(2)(B) to have had a 5-year active history prior to the distribution, is the same trade or business which (b)(2)(A) requires to be actively conducted immediately after the distribution. Nowhere in (b)(2) do we find, as respondent suggests we should, language denying the benefits of section 355 to the division of a single trade or business.

Nor can respondent derive support for his position by reading subsections (b)(1) and (b)(2) together, inasmuch as the plurality resulting therefrom is occasioned, not by any requirement that there be a multiplicity of businesses, but rather by the divisive nature of the transaction itself: i.e., one corporation becoming two or more corporations. Moreover, from the fact that the statute requires, immediately after the distribution, that the surviving corporations each be engaged in the conduct of a trade or business with an active 5-year history, we do not think it inevitably follows that each such trade or business necessarily must have been conducted on an individual basis throughout that 5-year period. As long as the trade or business which has been divided has been actively conducted for 5 years preceding the distribution, and the resulting businesses (each of which in this case, happens to be half of the original whole) are actively conducted after the division, we are of the opinion that the active business requirements of the statute have been complied with.

Respondent argues his construction of section 355 is confirmed by the report of the Senate Committee on Finance which accompanied the 1954 Internal Revenue Code. He refers us to that portion of the report which provides:

> Present law contemplates that a tax-free separation shall involve only the separation of assets attributable to the carrying on of an active business. Under the House bill, it is immaterial whether the assets are those used in an active business but if investment assets, for example, are separated into a new corporation, any amount received in respect of such an inactive corporation, whether by a distribution from it or by a sale of its stock, would be treated as ordinary income for a period of 10 years from the date of its creation. Your committee returns to existing law in not permitting the tax free separation of an existing corporation into active and inactive entities. It is not believed that the business need for this kind of transaction is sufficiently great to permit a person in a position to afford a 10-year delay in receiving income to do so at capital

> gain rather than dividend rates. Your committee requires that *both* the business retained by the distributing company and the business of the corporation the stock of which is distributed must have been actively conducted for the 5 years preceding the distribution, a safeguard against avoidance not contained in existing law. [Emphasis supplied.]

He argues that use of the term "both," with reference to the business retained by the distributing corporation and that operated by the controlled corporation, indicates that Congress intended there be in operation and existence during the 5 years preceding the distribution two or more separate and distinct businesses. We do not agree.

A reading of the quoted section of the report in its entirety reveals that the committee was addressing itself to the nature and the use of the particular assets which were transferred (active v. inactive), rather than to any distinction between one or more businesses. This is obvious when the entire paragraph is considered in the light of its topic sentence. The committee notes that under present law only assets attributable to the carrying on of an active trade or business may be separated tax free. After acknowledging a departure from this requirement in the House bill, the committee disapproves of the position taken by the House, and indicates it is returning to existing law by not permitting the tax-free separation of a corporation into active and inactive entities, and strengthens this provision by requiring that both the business retained by the distributing corporation and that of the controlled corporation must have been actively conducted for 5 years preceding the distribution. The excerpt makes no mention of trades or businesses per se.

Respondent next argues the regulations upon which he relies are entitled to additional stature due to the fact that the Technical Amendments Act of 1958 (72 Stat. 160), which was intended to eliminate unintended benefits and hardships contained in the 1954 Code, was enacted subsequent to their promulgation, and, while making extensive changes in many sections of the statute, made no change in section 355. He relies upon the rule which attributes congressional approval to long-standing regulations under a section of the Internal Revenue Code where the section has been often amended without a revision of its administrative interpretation. See Lykes v. United States, 343 U.S. 118 (1952), rehearing denied 343 U.S. 937 (1952).

We note that the final regulations under subchapter C of the 1954 Code became effective on December 2, 1955, and that the Technical Amendments Act of 1958 was enacted on September 2, 1958. Further we note that section 355 has not been amended since its enactment in August of 1954. Thus, it is apparent that the challenged regulations have neither the longevity nor the congressional approval alluded to in Lykes v. United States, supra.

There being no language, either in the statute or committee report, which denies tax-free treatment under section 355 to a transaction solely on the grounds that it represents an attempt to divide a single trade or business, the Commissioner's regulations which impose such a restriction are invalid, and cannot be sustained. Commissioner v. Acker, 361 U.S. 87 (1959).

Finally, respondent argues that there is presently pending in Congress legislation (H.R. 4459) which would revise section 355(a)(1)(B) so as to permit a nontaxable distribution if either: (1) The active business requirements of 355(b) are met; or (2) it is established to the satisfaction of the Secretary or his delegate that the distribution is not made for the purpose of avoiding tax. As interpretative of this pending legislation, respondent directs our attention to a report dated December 11, 1958, of The Advisory Group on Subchapter C of the Internal Revenue Code of 1954, appointed by the House Subcommittee on Internal Revenue Taxation, wherein it is stated at page 65:

> It is further provided in section 355(a)(1)(B)(ii) of the proposed revision that even though the transaction does not otherwise qualify under section 355 because of failure to satisfy the active business requirements or the 20 percent distribution requirement, it will nevertheless qualify under section 355 if it is established to the satisfaction of the Secretary or his delegate that the distribution is not in pursuance of a plan having as one of its principal purposes the avoidance of Federal income tax. *For example, even if the controlled corporation and the distributing corporation are not engaged in separate businesses, the Secretary or his delegate might find that a division of a single business qualifies under section 355, particularly where after the division certain stockholders will own stock in only one of the corporations and the remaining stockholders will own only stock in the other corporation.* Permitting some latitude in administration of the section should serve to prevent a rigid interpretation of the requirements of clause (i). [Emphasis supplied.]

Relying on the italicized language, respondent argues that under the law as presently written, the division of a single trade or business does not qualify for tax-free treatment under section 355.

The short answer to this argument is that *pending* legislation in no way is binding on this Court. Until enacted, H.R. 4459 represents a course of action Congress may or may not take. Moreover, the cited report was not prepared by any congressional committee, but rather by an advisory group appointed to assist in a study of subchapter C of the 1954 Code. Quite possibly, the proposed revision of section 355 was occasioned by the restrictive nature of the Commissioner's regulations, rather than by any interpretation of the nature of existing law. In any event, respondent's reliance upon either the bill or the report as indicative of existing law is misplaced.

Inasmuch as the parties treat the distribution as otherwise qualifying under section 355 for tax-free treatment, and inasmuch as we have found that portion of the regulations denying application of section 355 to the division of a single business to be invalid, we conclude that petitioner properly treated the distribution to him of the stock of E. P. Coady and Co. as a nontaxable transaction.

No evidence having been introduced with respect to the addition to tax under section 294(d)(2) of the 1939 Code, it is sustained subject to our holding on the above issue.

Reviewed by the Court.

Decision will be entered under Rule 50.

Pierce, J., dissents.

[Dissents by Judges Harron and Atkins omitted.]

Rev. Rul. 2003-38

2003-1 C.B. 811

Corporation *D* has operated a retail shoe store business, under the name "D," since Year 1 in a manner that meets the requirements of §355(b) of the Internal Revenue Code. *D*'s sales are made exclusively to customers who frequent its retail stores in shopping malls and other locations. *D*'s business enjoys favorable name recognition, customer loyalty, and other elements of goodwill in the retail shoe market. In Year 8, *D* creates an Internet web site and begins selling shoes at retail on the web site. To a significant extent, the operation of the web site draws upon *D*'s experience and know-how. The web site is named "D.com" to take advantage of the name recognition, customer loyalty, and other elements of goodwill associated with *D* and the *D* name and to enhance the web site's chances for success in its initial stages. In Year 10, *D* transfers all of the web site's assets and liabilities to corporation *C*, a newly formed, wholly owned subsidiary of *D*, and distributes the stock of *C pro rata* to *D*'s shareholders. Apart from the issue of whether the web site is considered an expansion of *D*'s business and therefore entitled to share the business's five-year history at the time of the distribution in Year 10, the distribution meets all the requirements of §355 . . . .

In determining whether an active trade or business has been conducted by a corporation throughout the five-year period preceding the distribution, the fact that a trade or business underwent change during the five-year period (for example, by the addition of new or the dropping of old products, changes in production capacity, and the like) shall be disregarded, provided that the changes are not of such a character as to constitute the acquisition of a new or different business. Section 1.355-3(b)(3)(ii). In particular, if a corporation engaged in the active conduct of one trade or business during that five-year period purchased, created, or otherwise acquired another trade or business in the same line of business, then the acquisition of that other business is ordinarily treated as an expansion of the original business, all of which is treated as having been actively conducted during that five-year period, unless that purchase, creation, or other acquisition effects a change of such character as to constitute the acquisition of a new or different business. *Id.* . . .

Rev. Rul. 2003-18, 2003-7 I.R.B. 467, concludes that the acquisition by a dealer engaged in the sale and service of brand *X* automobiles of a franchise (and the assets needed) to sell and service brand *Y* automobiles is an expansion of the brand *X* business and does not constitute the acquisition of a new or different business under §1.355-3(b)(3)(ii) because (i) the product of the brand *X* automobile dealership is similar to the product of the brand *Y* automobile dealership, (ii) the business activities associated with the operation of the brand *X* automobile dealership (*i.e.*, sales and service) are the same as the business activities associated with the operation of the brand *Y* automobile dealership, and (iii) the operation of the brand *Y* automobile dealership involves the use of the experience and know-how that the dealer developed in the operation of the brand *X* automobile dealership . . . .

The product of the retail shoe store business and the product of the web site are the same (shoes), and the principal business activities of the retail shoe store business are the same as those of the web site (purchasing shoes at wholesale and reselling them at retail). Selling shoes on a web site requires some know-how not associated with operating a retail store, such as familiarity with different marketing approaches, distribution chains, and technical operations issues. Nevertheless, the web site's operation does draw to a significant extent on *D*'s existing experience and know-how, and the web site's success will depend in large measure on the goodwill associated with *D* and the *D* name. Accordingly, the creation by *D* of the Internet web site does not constitute the acquisition of a new or different business under §1.355-3(b)(3)(ii). Instead, it is an expansion of *D*'s retail shoe store business. Therefore, each of *D* and *C* is engaged in the active conduct of a five-year active trade or business immediately after the distribution. See Rev. Rul. 2003-18 and §1.355-3(c), Examples (7) and (8). . . .

The creation by a corporation engaged in the retail shoe store business of an Internet web site that sells shoes at retail constitutes an expansion of the retail shoe store business rather than the acquisition of a new or different business under §1.355-3(b)(3)(ii). . . .

NOTES

1. *Vertical divisions.* As *Coady* illustrates, the active trade or business requirement can be met by dividing one active trade or business into two, sometimes called a vertical division. See also Treas. Regs. §1.355-3(c) (example 4), expressly allowing a vertical division.

2. *Satisfying the five-year requirement.* Although the businesses must have been conducted for five years prior to the transaction, they need not have been conducted by the distributing corporation or by the controlled corporation during that entire period. That is, the requirement can be met if one or both of the businesses were acquired during the five-year period. Both businesses must, however, have been actively conducted by *someone* during the preceding five years, and acquisition of the businesses by the distributing corporation or by the controlled corporation must not have occurred within the five-year period unless the acquisition was tax free. See §355(b)(2)(C). Further, control of the controlled corporation must not have been acquired within that five-year period, unless the acquisition was tax free. §355(b)(2)(D).

For example, suppose *X* Corp. has actively engaged in the toy manufacturing business for more than five years. Three years ago it acquired a software distributing company, Sub Co., in a tax-free B reorganization; Sub Co. had been actively conducting the software distributing business for more than two years before the reorganization. The distribution by *X* Corp. of the Sub Co. stock will satisfy the active trade or business requirement of §§355(a)(1)(C) and 355(b). Note, however, that if *X* Corp. had purchased the Sub Co. stock in a taxable transaction, the requirement of §355(b)(2)(D) would not be met.

Consider the following variation on this example. Once again, suppose *X* Corp. acquired the Sub Co. stock in a tax-free B reorganization, but now assume Sub Co. acquired the software distributing business one year before in a taxable transaction and has no other business. Now, the distribution of Sub Co. stock by *X* Corp. will fail the active trade or business test by reason of §355(b)(2)(C). See also the example in Treas. Regs. §1.355-3(b)(4)(ii). The effect of §355(b)(2)(C) is to require that all transfers of the trades or businesses used by the taxpayer to satisfy the requirements of §355(a)(1)(C) occurring during the five-year testing period be by way of tax-free transactions, including §351 formations and §368(a)(1) reorganizations.

3. *Business expansions.* Note that the limitation of §355(b) applies to the acquisition of a *business,* not to the acquisition of particular *assets.* As Rev. Rul. 2003-38 illustrates, the active trade or business requirement may be met even if a business is expanded through taxable asset purchases during the five-year period preceding a vertical division of the expanded business.

For example, suppose again that *X* Corp. has actively engaged in the business of manufacturing toys for more than five years. Suppose further that one year ago *X*

Corp. purchased for cash in a fully taxable transaction all the assets of one of its competitors in the toy manufacturing business and that these assets were then used to form a wholly owned subsidiary, Sub Co., in a §351 transaction. *X* Corp. can distribute the stock of Sub Co. without violating the active trade or business requirement because both the distributing corporation (*X* Corp.) and the controlled corporation (Sub Co.) are actively conducting the toy manufacturing business immediately after the transaction, and *X* Corp. had been actively conducting this business for more than five years. That is, §355(b) does not prohibit the distribution of a part of a business representing a recent expansion, even if the expansion was by purchase, so long as the expansion continues the historic business of the distributing company. See Treas. Regs. §1.355-3(c) (examples 7 and 8).

Consider again Rev. Rul. 2003-38. Was the Service too quick to conclude that the internet operation was a business expansion of the bricks-and-mortar operation? Does the ease with which the two operations apparently were separated give you any concern? Would you be more concerned if Corporation *D* had purchased an existing internet business, instead of creating the internet operation from scratch?

4. *Separate affiliated groups.* Let us consider one more variation on this theme. Suppose *X* Corp. does not acquire the assets of one of its competitors but instead acquires the stock of one of its competitors (Sub Co.). Historically, the distribution of the Sub Co. stock did not satisfy §355(b) because of the language in §355(b)(2)(D). See also Nelson v. Commissioner, 61 T.C. 311 (1973); Boettger v. Commissioner, 51 T.C. 324 (1968). Currently, however, that stock acquisition should be treated as a purchase of assets and a business expansion under the "separate affiliated group" rule of §355(b)(3). See Prop. Treas. Regs. §1.355-3(b)(3)(ii); *id.* at (b)(4); *id.* at (d)(2) (example 20). Under that rule, in determining whether a corporation engages in the active conduct of a trade or business, the corporation essentially is treated as conducting any business conducted within its separate affiliated group. §355(b)(3)(A) (more precisely, treating the separate affiliated group as one corporation). A corporation's separate affiliated group is the affiliated group that would be determined under §1504(a) (without regard to §1504(b)) if the corporation were the group's common parent. §355(b)(3)(B).

5. *Comparing partial liquidations and divisive reorganizations.* If the distributing corporation or the controlled corporation is liquidated, the effect of the §355 distribution and subsequent liquidation is the same as a partial liquidation. It should come as no surprise, then, that both divisive distributions and partial liquidations include an active trade or business requirement. Cf. §355(b) with §302(e)(2). Unfortunately, the terms of these two provisions are not precisely the same — there is nothing like §355(b)(2)(D) in §302(e).

6. *Functional divisions and divisions of integrated businesses.* In a functional division, two different facets of one business are separated into two corporations. A valid functional division satisfies the technical tests of §355, provided that after the division both companies remain operating entities engaged in the active conduct of a business. If the division creates a passive corporation, the active business requirement is not met, and the division will not be tax free under §355. In Rafferty v. Commissioner, 452 F.2d 767 (1st Cir. 1971), no active business was found when the spun-off corporation's activity after the division involved leasing back real estate to its parent. The court found the economic activities were an investment rather than an active trade or business. But compare King v. Commissioner, 458 F.2d 245 (6th Cir. 1972), finding an active business when the corporation's only source of income

was a long-term net lease of realty to the parent; there the real property was fit for only a single use, was needed in the business, and, therefore, was not suitable for a bailout.

Treas. Regs. §1.355-3(b)(2)(iii) states that whether a trade or business is actively conducted is a question of fact but that generally the corporation must perform active and substantial management and operational functions. See also Rev. Rul. 86-125, 1986-2 C.B. 57, in which the Service ruled that the rental of an office building does not constitute an active trade or business when the property is managed by an independent contractor rather than by employees of the corporation. Cf. Rev. Rul. 2007-42, 2007-28 I.R.B. 44 (attributing the business of a partnership to a passive partner when the partner held a significant interest in the partnership).

Suppose a coal mine sells coal only to its owner, a steel mill, which in turn sells steel only to its owner, a manufacturer of automobiles. May the coal mine be spun off to the shareholders of the automobile manufacturer? May the steel mill be spun off? While there was doubt under the old regulations, the current regulations contain examples of such horizontal divisions of an integrated business that meet the active conduct test. See examples 10-12 of Treas. Regs. §1.355-3(c). In the vertical division, there was the question as to whether the statute permitted a division of a single business into two businesses, which has been answered affirmatively by *Coady.* In a functional division (e.g., the company sells machinery and its subsidiary services such machinery), there is first the question as to whether after the division both entities are engaged in an active trade or business, as in *Rafferty* and *King.* Even if the answer is affirmative, the second question is whether each business is properly "aged." In *Burke* and *Lockwood* the spun-off business could tack on the parent's history to meet the aging requirement while in *Boettger* it could not. The integrated business division asks whether there can be an active conduct of a trade or business if there are no outside customers. Compare Groetzinger v. Commissioner, 480 U.S. 23 (1987) (full-time gambler betting on his own account was engaged in a trader business for purposes of §§62(1) and 162).

Note that under Treas. Regs. §1.355-2(d)(2)(iv)(C), the division of an integrated business may be considered a "device" for the distribution of earnings and profits if one of the post-separation corporations engages in a business that has as its principal function the service of the other post-separation corporation, if this captive business can be sold without adversely affecting the primary business. What is the rationale behind this limitation?

7. *Cash-rich split-off.* Finally, can §355 apply to a so-called "cash-rich" split-off? Is there a requirement that a specific percentage of the assets of the distributing or controlled corporation be active business assets? Generally, neither the case law, Code, regulations, nor administrative guidance, imposes any specific percentage requirement for active business assets. However, under §355(g), a special rule applies if either the distributing or controlled corporation is a "disqualified investment corporation" and after the purported §355 transaction a person owns at least a 50-percent interest in the corporation. §355(g) (also applying the §318 attribution rules to determine stock ownership). Then, neither §355 nor §356 applies to the distribution of controlled corporation stock. *Id.* (Instead, §311 would apply to the distributing corporation and §301 or §302, as appropriate, to its shareholders.) For this purpose, a corporation is a disqualified investment corporation if at least two-thirds of its assets are specified investment assets. See §355(g)(2).

4. *The Device Limitation*

The "device" language of §355(a)(1)(B) stems from congressional recognition that the existence of the active conduct of a trade or business is not sufficient assurance that the division of an existing corporation will not be used as a bailout. Even the most active trade or business can be sold. In addition to objective tests, Congress included the catchall subjective "device" test as another weapon against a division serving as a vehicle for a bailout.

The regulations under §355 list three factors that offer evidence of a "device." Treas. Regs. §1.355-2(d)(2). First, the regulations state that a distribution that is pro rata or substantially pro rata bears close resemblance to a dividend and therefore presents the greatest opportunity for abuse. But cf. §355(a)(2)(A) (providing that §355(a) should be applied "without regard to . . . whether or not the distribution is pro rata").

The second "device" factor is a post-distribution sale or exchange. §355(a)(1)(B) and Treas. Regs. §1.355-2(d)(2)(iii). The regulations provide that if such a sale or exchange is negotiated or agreed on before the distribution, the sale or exchange is substantial evidence of a "device." Given the second parenthetical in §355(a)(1)(B), should a pre-arranged sale or exchange be treated as conclusive evidence of a "device"? In answering this question, note that the regulations also ordinarily treat a sale discussed by the parties and reasonably anticipated by them as a sale agreed on before the distribution, regardless of whether a sale was negotiated before the distribution. Treas. Regs. §1.355-2(d)(2)(iii)(B)-(D).

The third factor under the regulations indicating that the distribution is a device for the distribution of earnings and profits is the "nature, kind, amount and use" of the assets of the distributing and controlled corporations. The regulations recognize that spinning off liquid assets or other assets not used in the distribution corporation's trade or business should not qualify for tax-free treatment. This aspect of the "device" limitation overlaps the active trade or business requirement, discussed below

The regulations also list factors that show or help show that a distribution is not a device for the distribution of earnings and profits. Treas. Regs. §1.355-2(d)(3) and (5). For example, if neither the distributing corporation nor the controlled corporation has earnings and profits, the distribution will not be treated as a "device." This regulatory concession certainly seems justified: No corporate distribution can bail out earnings and profits if there are no earnings and profits to begin with. More generally, a distribution will not be considered a "device" if, in the absence of §355, the distribution would not be taxable as a dividend to the distributees because it would qualify as an exchange under §302(a) or §303. Do not forget, however, that avoiding the "device" restriction of §355(a)(1)(B) does not guarantee qualification under §355: the transaction must still meet the other requirements of §355.

Note that individuals are now taxed at long-term capital gains rates on many dividend distributions. See §1(h)(11). Does that preferential tax on dividends suggest that "device" should no longer be a concern under §355? Was Congress concerned with the amount of any income, as well as its character?

5. *Business Purpose*

A sufficient business purpose for a distribution offers evidence that the distribution is not a device. Treas. Regs. §1.355-2(d)(3)(ii). How may the absence of a business or non-business motive for the distribution be taken into account? In Commissioner v. Wilson, 353 F.2d 184 (9th Cir. 1965), the court discerned neither a business nor non-business motive for the division and refused to upset the Commissioner's determination that the corporate division was a "device" because of the absence of a discernible motive for the transaction. Had there been a finding of a tax avoidance motive, of course, the taxpayer would have been no better off. But what would be the outcome if the trial court had found that the motive behind the division was wholly non-tax related? In Rafferty v. Commissioner, 452 F.2d 767 (1st Cir. 1971), a closely held corporation was divided to facilitate non-tax estate planning. The court upheld the Commissioner's characterization of the transaction as a device on the theory that non-tax personal motives of a taxpayer cannot protect a transaction that has a considerable potential for bailing out earnings and profits at capital gain rates.

Note that in *Wilson* the Court required a business purpose notwithstanding the arguably more specific device language of §355. Is the requirement of a business purpose redundant? Not if the device language is limited to facts that constitute evidence of a bailout, e.g., a prearranged sale. The business purpose requirement can preclude from §355 those divisions that have a potential bailout in the future and that are not explained by non-tax reasons. The ambiguity of such divisions is resolved in the regulations by assuming that their underlying purpose is a bailout. Is *Wilson* clear support for such an across-the-board approach? One might raise the question why putting oneself in the position for a future bailout should be allowed even with a valid purpose. But note that the business activities separated in *Wilson* could originally have been put into two corporations separately owned by the shareholders; these problems would never have arisen in such an arrangement. This is the perplexing question in the corporate division area mentioned at the outset. Regulations have explicitly incorporated the *Wilson* rule that the absence of a business purpose, even if there is no tax avoidance purpose, will be fatal to the reorganization. See Treas. Regs. §1.355-2(b)(1).

By regulation, therefore, a valid business purpose, called a "corporate" business purpose, is a separate requirement for §355 transactions: The transaction must be motivated by some non-federal income tax business purpose of the corporate enterprise. Treas. Regs. §1.355-2(b)(2).

Examples of corporate business purposes are found in Treas. Regs. §1.355-2(b)(5) (examples 1, 2, 5, and 8). Those purposes include compliance with an antitrust order, resolution of a shareholder stalemate, and facilitation of a public offering. See generally Treas. Regs. §1.355-2(b)(5) (examples 1 and 2); Rev. Rul. 85-122, 1985-2 C.B. 118. See also Rev. Proc. 96-30, 1996-1 C.B. 696 (suggesting other valid business purposes, including distributions to (i) provide an equity interest to a key employee, (ii) facilitate borrowing, (iii) achieve significant cost savings, (iv) resolve management, systemic, or other problems caused by operating different businesses in one corporation or group (the "fit and focus" rationale), (v) facilitate an acquisition, and (vi) reduce risk).

The relationship between a corporate business purpose and a "device" is found in Treas. Regs. §1.355-2(d)(3)(ii). The regulations now impose a best-fit requirement: The transaction will fail §355 if the business purpose could be accomplished in a tax-free manner without involving the distribution of stock, unless each alternative transaction is impractical or unduly expensive. Treas. Regs. §1.355-2(b)(3).

The regulations also provide that a corporate business purpose does not include the reduction of federal taxes even if that reduction would come about other than from a bailout or similar transaction to which §355 speaks. Treas. Regs. §1.355-2(b)(2). In particular, the regulations provide that a distribution made to facilitate an election under subchapter S is not protected by §355 for want of a valid business purpose. Treas. Regs. §1.355-2(b)(5) (example 6).

This aspect of the regulations should be subject to challenge. Note that the statute fails to include an explicit "business purpose" requirement. Accordingly, such a requirement can be defended only as an attempt to further the purpose of §355. Is there any suggestion that §355 was intended to limit the number of subchapter S elections? Surely the ghost of Gregory v. Helvering has reappeared once too often if the Treasury feels secure in promulgating regulations exorcising all divisive transactions motivated by any attempt to minimize federal taxes even without the dangers to which §355 speaks.

In Rev. Rul. 85-122, 1985-2 C.B. 118, the Service ruled that the business purpose requirement of §355 is met if an unprofitable ski resort is separated from a profitable golf and tennis resort to meet the recommendation of the securities underwriter advising the corporation on marketing of debentures of the golf and tennis resort. And in Rev. Rul. 85-127, 1985-2 C.B. 119, the Service ruled that the business purpose requirement is met when two active businesses are split apart to retain the services of a key employee of one of the two businesses.

Note that the Service no longer issues advance rulings on business purpose. Rev. Proc. 2003-48 (§4.01), 2003-2 C.B. 86. It is possible that the Service's failure to issue advance rulings on business purpose will lead to a gradual erosion of the business purpose requirement.

6. *Shareholder Versus Corporate Business Purpose*

The regulations state that a transaction does not qualify under §355 if carried out for purposes not germane to the business of the corporations. Treas. Regs. §1.355-2(b)(2) states that when the business purpose serves the shareholder as well as the corporation, there may be no problem, but if the transaction is undertaken solely for the personal reasons of the shareholder, the distribution will not qualify under §355. Note Parshelsky's Estate v. Commissioner, 303 F.2d 14 (2d Cir. 1962), suggesting the business purpose could be a shareholder purpose rather than a corporate business purpose, but the Court in *Rafferty*, Note 6 in the active trade or business discussion supra, rejected the suggestion that a shareholder investment purpose was sufficient. This issue pervades the entire reorganization area.

In Rev. Rul. 88-34, 1988-1 C.B. 115, *X* Corp. owned all the stock of *Y* Corp. The president of *Y* Corp. had recently retired, and individual *A* was identified as a prospective new president. *A* insisted that he receive an equity interest in *Y* Corp. as part of his compensation without acquiring any interest in *X* Corp. To facilitate the transfer of *Y* stock to *A*, *X* Corp. spun off *Y* Corp. by distributing the *Y* stock pro rata to the *X* shareholders. The Service ruled that the spin-off of *Y* Corp. satisfied the business purpose test of former Treas. Regs. §1.355-2(c) because "the distribution enables the subsidiary corporation [*Y* Corp.] to hire the key employee it believes is necessary to the continued success of the business." Without knowing more about *A*'s reasons for insisting on acquiring an interest in *Y* but not in *X*, has a shareholder purpose been transmuted into a corporate purpose? The current regulations take a somewhat more skeptical view of these transactions. See Treas. Regs. §1.355-2(b)(5) (example 8).

7. *The Distribution Requirement*

By virtue of §355(a)(1)(D), the distributing corporation must either distribute all the stock and securities that it holds in the controlled corporation or distribute an amount of stock constituting "control" (as defined by §368 (c)) *and* must satisfy the Treasury that the retention of stock in the controlled corporation was not part of a tax avoidance plan. Why this emphasis on a complete, or nearly complete, separation of the two corporations?

Consider individual *T*, who owns all the outstanding stock of *X* Corp. *X* has actively conducted two distinct businesses for more than five years. *X* transfers one of its two businesses to newly formed *Y* Corp. in exchange for common and callable preferred stock of *Y*, and the *Y* common stock is then distributed to *T*. If this transaction qualified as a tax-free divisive D reorganization, *T* would be in a position to bail out earnings and profits of *Y* Corp. by selling the stock of *X*. To see why, observe that *X* Corp.'s assets include preferred stock of *Y* Corp., so a sale of *X* would include a sale of the *Y* preferred. A purchaser of *X* would pay *T* not only for the value of the *X* operating assets but also for the value of the *Y* preferred stock, and *T* would have only a capital gain on this sale. When the *Y* preferred stock is then redeemed, the bailout is complete. To avoid this type of transaction, Congress placed the "control" requirement in §355(a)(1)(D). Why doesn't §306 handle this abuse?

In Commissioner v. Gordon, 391 U.S. 83 (1968), the distribution of the requisite 80-percent control of the distributed corporation took place in two steps (occurring in 1961 and 1963), and the court held that §355 was not satisfied; the first distribution (of less than 80 percent) was independent in the sense that a further distribution, though contemplated, was not promised or required by the plan. Another issue in the case—whether a distribution of stock pursuant to the exercise of stock rights qualifies under §355—was left unanswered by the court. On remand it was held that the stock rights did not constitute stock within §354(a), 424 F.2d 378 (2d Cir. 1970). Note that the regulations now provide that stock rights are generally treated as securities for purposes of §355. Treas. Regs. §1.355-1(c).

8. *Forms of Divisive Transactions*

Corporate divisions have generated a lexicon of colorful labels, namely, the "spin-off," the "split-off," and the "split-up." A *spin-off* is a distribution by a parent corporation of the stock of a controlled subsidiary, where parent shareholders end up owning a brother/sister pair. A *split-off* occurs when the parent distributes the stock of its controlled subsidiary in redemption of some of the parent stock (even if the redemption is pro rata). Finally, a *split-up* occurs where the parent liquidates and its sole assets immediately before the liquidation were the stock of controlled subsidiaries. The economic consequences to *X*'s stockholders of all three methods are practically identical.

Both the split-off and the split-up can be useful when feuding shareholders seek to go their separate ways. For example, suppose *X* Corp. is owned equally by individuals *A* and *B*. If *A* and *B* often disagree on important corporate questions, they may decide to sever their business relationship by dividing their business between two companies. On one hand, if *X* Corp. transfers half of its assets to newly formed *Y* Corp., whose stock is distributed to *B* in exchange for his stock in *X*, then a split-off has been used to divide *X*. On the other hand, if *X* Corp. transfers half of its assets to *Y* Corp. and half to *Z* Corp. and then distributes the *Y* stock to *A* and the *Z* stock to *B* in complete liquidation, a split-up has been used to accomplish the same end.

With one exception, §355 treats all divisive reorganizations the same way. It is applicable both to distributions (spin-offs) and to exchanges (split-ups and split-offs). Moreover, the old corporation can distribute (a term that is defined to include exchanges) the stock and securities of a controlled corporation that it already owns or one created expressly to effect the corporate division. The requirements of §355 that are of particular interest are those in §355(a)(1)(B) and §355(b). Note that §354(b) prevents divisive reorganizations from avoiding the more restrictive provisions of §355 by qualifying under §354.

Not all corporate divisions will be "reorganizations" within the meaning of §368(a)(1). If the division is effected by transferring assets to a newly created subsidiary and then distributing the subsidiary's stock, the transaction is a D reorganization qualifying by virtue of a distribution described in §355. If the division is effected by distributing stock of an existing subsidiary without transferring assets as part of the plan, §355 will be applicable to the distribution of the subsidiary's stock without application of §368(a)(1)(D). Although all forms of divisive rearrangements are referred to as "divisive reorganizations," the touchstone of such a transaction is not qualification under §368(a)(1)(D) but application of §355. The tax treatment of a §355 distribution, however, can turn on whether the transaction is a "reorganization" under §368(a)(1)(D).

9. *Taxation of Divisive Transactions*

Section 355(a)(1) permits a shareholder exchanging stock or securities for stock or securities in a divisive transaction to defer recognition of gain (and loss) realized on the exchange. It plays the same role for divisive transactions that §354(a)(1) plays for acquisitive reorganizations. And like §354, gain (but not loss) will be recognized by a shareholder receiving boot or excess securities. See §§356(a), 356(b), 355(a)(3).

Under some circumstances, boot in a divisive transaction will be taxed under the same rule governing boot in an acquisitive reorganization. In particular, dividend income is limited to the amount of gain realized on the transaction. See §356(a)(2). If the divisive transaction is structured as a *distribution* rather than as an *exchange*, however, the rule of §356(b) applies, subjecting not the gain but the value of the boot received to taxation as a dividend. See also Treas. Regs.

§1.356-2(a). In light of §355(a)(2) permitting pro rata exchanges in a divisive transaction, an astute taxpayer should always be able to avoid the harsh rule of §356(b).

How is the corporation taxed in a §355 transaction? One would expect that the distribution of stock and securities would be tax free and that gain (but not loss) would be recognized on the distribution of other property ("boot"). If the divisive transaction happens to be a D reorganization (that is, if a newly formed subsidiary was created and spun off), current law produces these results under §361(c)(1) (nonrecognition on distribution of stock or securities) and §361(c)(2) (recognition of gain but not loss on distribution of other property). If the transaction is not a "reorganization" because the controlled corporation is preexisting, the same taxation will result under §355(c).

As a general rule, however, boot includes stock of the controlled corporation acquired in a taxable transaction within five years of the distribution. §355(b)(3)(B) (sometimes called the "hot" stock rule). This general rule does not apply if (i) the controlled corporation is an affiliated subsidiary of the distributing corporation after the acquisition (but before the distribution) or (ii) the distributing corporation acquires the controlled stock from another member of an affiliated group that includes the distributing corporation. Treas. Regs. §1.355-2(g). Note that the exception practically swallows the general rule. The general rule applies in the relatively rare case where the distributing corporation acquires stock of the controlled corporation but the two corporations are not affiliated at any time after the acquisition and before the distribution. Compare §368(c) (control definition) with §1504(a)(2) (affiliation definition).

Suppose *X* Corp. has for many years owned 90 percent of the only class of stock of *Y* Corp., which engages in an active trade or business. The remaining 10 percent of the *Y* Corp. stock was acquired by *X* one year ago in a taxable transaction. If *X* distributes all the *Y* stock to its shareholders, will the distribution be tax free under §355? Because *X* and *Y* were affiliated after *X* acquired the 10-percent interest in *Y* stock but before the distribution, the exception to the general rule applies, and none of the distributed stock is treated as boot. See Treas. Regs. §1.355-2(g)(5) (example 2).

Section 355 imposes no restriction on the type of stock or securities that can be distributed in a divisive reorganization. If debt securities are distributed, however, they will constitute boot under §356(d) to the extent their principal amount exceeds the principal amount of any securities that are surrendered; if preferred stock is distributed, it may be tainted by §306(c)(1)(B). See §356(e). See, e.g., Rev. Rul. 77-335, 1977-2 C.B. 95, where in a §355 spin-off by a parent of the subsidiary's common and preferred stock, the preferred was §306 stock. The ruling stated that §306 status is determined by reference to the earnings and profits of the distributing corporation—i.e., the parent. Section 355(a)(4) refers to §356 for the treatment of boot; §356(a) determines the amount of gain to be recognized and how it is to be taxed; §356(c) prohibits recognition of loss. See Rev. Rul. 74-516, 1974-2 C.B. 121, abandoning the automatic dividend rule in reorganization boot distributions and adopting instead a dividend equivalence test under the principles of §302(b)(1).

How should earnings and profits be allocated between the distributing and the controlled corporations? See §312(h). When the controlled corporation is newly formed, Treas. Regs. §1.312-10 provides that the earnings and profits "generally" should be made in proportion to the fair market value of the business or businesses retained by the distributing corporation as compared with the value of the business or businesses transferred to the controlled corporation.

10. Predistribution Purchases

Suppose *P* Corp. owns 100 percent of the outstanding stock of Sub Corp., and assume the Sub Corp. stock constitutes 25 percent of the value of *P* Corp. Further, assume the Sub Corp. stock is worth $250,000, and *P* Corp.'s adjusted basis in the Sub Corp. stock equals $100,000. *T* Corp. would like to acquire Sub Corp. without the imposition of a corporate-level tax.

If a distribution by *P* Corp. of the Sub Corp. stock will qualify under §355, *P* and *T* can adopt the following plan: First, *T* Corp. will purchase 25 percent of the outstanding shares of *P* Corp. Second, after waiting a sufficient time to satisfy the continuity of interest requirement of Treas. Regs. §1.355-2(c), *P* Corp. will distribute its Sub Corp. stock to *T* in redemption of *T*'s stock of *P*. If §355 applied without limitation, *T* would acquire Sub Corp. from *P* without the imposition of a corporate-level tax; yet *T*'s basis in the Sub Corp. stock would equal its fair market value of $250,000 (because that is what *T* Corp. paid for the *P* Corp. stock it purchased, which was then redeemed). Before the transaction, the Sub Corp. stock had a basis of only $100,000 in the hands of *P* Corp. Thus, *T* Corp. has effectively purchased a corporate asset (the Sub Corp. stock) without the selling corporation (*P* Corp.) recognizing any gain. Cf. Treas. Regs. §1.355-2(c)(1) (as an independent requirement, providing that shareholders of the distributing corporation must own stock establishing continuity of interest in each of the distributing and controlled corporations after the separation).

Section 355(d) responds to this type of transaction not by disqualifying the transaction under §355 but instead by forcing the distributing corporation (here, *P* Corp.) to recognize gain on the distribution of the stock of the controlled corporation (here, Sub Corp.). Note that §355(d) will apply if, immediately after the transaction, a shareholder holds 50 percent or more of the distributing corporation *or* of the controlled corporation if that interest was acquired within five years and was acquired by "purchase," which is defined quite broadly in §355(d)(5).

What is the abuse to which §355(d) speaks? In general, one corporation cannot transfer an appreciated asset to another person without the imposition of a corporate-level tax. To be sure, there are exceptions to this rule for tax-free reorganizations, as discussed in Chapter 10. Aside from these exceptional cases, the transfer of an asset from one corporation to another person is a recognition event for the transferor corporation.

In the example above, the Sub Corp. stock initially held by *P* Corp. ended up in the hands of *T* Corp. Yet, were §355 to apply to the transaction, there would be no taxation to *P* Corp. The legislative history of §355(d) indicates that this type of transaction is inconsistent with the repeal of the *General Utilities* doctrine, discussed at page 120 supra.

The broad reach of §355(d) has been cut back substantially by regulations. Under Treas. Regs. §1.355-6(b)(3)(i), a transaction described in §355(d)(2) will not be subject to §355(d)(1) if the effect of the transaction is not to "increase direct or indirect ownership in the distributing corporation or any controlled corporation by a disqualified person" nor to "provide a disqualified person with a purchased basis in the stock of any controlled corporation." In this context a "disqualified person" is anyone who holds, directly or indirectly, disqualified stock constituting a 50-percent or greater interest in the corporation. Treas. Regs. §1.355-6(b)(3)(ii) (providing that disqualified stock is stock purchased [or attributable to stock purchased] within the five-year period preceding the distribution). For a thorough discussion of this complex regulation, see Cummings, Section 355(d) Proposed Regulations Provide Meaningful Safe Harbors, 91 J. Taxation 5 (1999).

11. Nonqualifying Transactions

If a spin-off does not qualify under §355, and if the fair market value of the distributed stock exceeds its adjusted basis, gain will be recognized by the distributing corporation. §311(b). In addition, the distribution falls under §301 and will be taxed as a dividend to the extent of the distributing corporation's earnings and profits. But suppose the nonqualifying distribution takes the form of a split-up. Such a transaction amounts to a complete liquidation of the distributing corporation and presumably will be taxed as any other corporate liquidation. Can a taxpayer argue that a *successful* split-up should be taxed as a complete liquidation rather than as a §355 division, particularly if the distribution includes boot? See Telephone Answering Service Co. v. Commissioner, 63 T.C. 423 (1974), aff'd, 546 F.2d 423 (4th Cir. 1976), especially footnote 14. See also Rev. Rul. 84-71, 1984-1 C.B. 106, in which the Service ruled that §351 could apply to a transfer that was part of a larger acquisitive transaction failing to qualify for reorganization treatment.

12. Criss-Cross Transactions

If *A* owns 50 percent of the stock of *X* Corp. and of *Y* Corp., and *B* owns the other 50 percent of *X* and *Y*, can they employ §355 to effect a rearrangement of their investments so that *A* will become the sole owner of *X* and *B* the sole owner of *Y*? What might be the mechanics of such a division? Treas. Regs. §1.355-4 holds such a transaction taxable, and the cases have generally integrated the various steps and found such a transaction taxable. See Portland Manufacturing Co. v. Commissioner, 56 T.C. 58 (1971), aff'd, 75-1 U.S.T.C. (CCH) ¶ 9449; Kuper v. Commissioner, 61 T.C. 624 (1974), aff'd, 533 F.2d 152 (5th Cir. 1976); Atlee v. Commissioner, 67 T.C. 395 (1976), following *Portland.* Contra, Badanes v. Commissioner, 39 T.C. 410 (1962), allowing such a division. Can §355 be used to accomplish an exchange under which *A*, owning all the stock of *X* Corp., and *B*, owning all the stock of *Y* Corp., each succeed in becoming the sole owner of the other's corporation? Rev. Rul. 71-336, 1971-2 C.B. 299, prohibits a somewhat similar plan. But see Rev. Rul. 77-11, 1977-1 C.B. 93, for a successful way of dividing two 50-percent-owned brother-sister corporations of differing size, *X* and *Y*, owned equally by *A* and *B*, by a non–pro rata split-off. *X* Corp. transferred 1,850*x* dollars in assets representing half of its net worth to *Z*, a newly formed corporation, for 1,850 shares of *Z*'s voting common stock. *Y* Corp. transferred 350*x* dollars in assets representing half of its net worth to *Z* for 350 shares of *Z*'s voting common stock. Section 351 covered these exchanges. *X* then distributed all the *Z* stock to *B* in exchange for all of *B*'s stock in *X*. Because *X* distributed a controlling interest in the *Z* stock and because the other requirements of §355 were met, this exchange was tax free. *Y* then distributed all of its *Z* stock to *B* in exchange for all of *B*'s stock in *Y*. A capital gains tax on *B*'s gain was payable on this exchange because *Y* could not distribute a controlling interest in *Z*. (Note that today *Y* would also be taxed under §311(b).) As a result, *A* owned all the stock of *X* and *Y* without tax, and *B* owned all the stock of *Z* at the cost of the tax incurred on the exchange with *Y* Corp.

PROBLEMS

11-1. For the past 15 years, *X* Corp. has engaged in the business of heavy construction. *X* Corp. transfers half of the company's heavy machinery and other operating assets along with one long-term contract to newly formed *Y* Corp. in exchange for all of *Y* Corp.'s stock, and this stock is promptly distributed pro rata to the shareholders of *X* Corp. Immediately after the transaction, both corporations actively conduct the business formerly conducted by *X* Corp. It is anticipated that *Y* Corp. will be liquidated within the taxable year.

a. Does the distribution of *Y* Corp. stock qualify as a tax-free divisive reorganization under §368(a)(1)(D) and §355?
b. Does the analysis change if it is *X* Corp. that will be liquidated and its assets distributed in the near future?

11-2. *A* and *B* each own 50 percent of the stock of *X* Corp. *A*'s basis in the *X* stock is $600, and *B*'s stock basis is $1,400. *X* Corp. carries on (and has carried on for more than five years) two lines of business: (a) the manufacture and sale of computer games (Gameco division) and (b) the manufacture and sale of denim sleepwear (Denco division). The assets of each division have a value of $2,000 and adjusted basis of $800. No liabilities exist, and there are joint earnings and profits of $1,000.

a. On January 1, 1988, *X* transfers all the Gameco assets to newly formed *Y* Corp. in exchange for all of *Y*'s stock. *X* also transfers all its Denco assets to newly formed *Z* Corp. in exchange for all of *Z*'s stock. *X* then liquidates and distributes the *Y* and *Z* stock ratably to *A* and *B*. What are the tax consequences to *A* and *B*?
b. Suppose instead that *X* transferred the Gameco assets to *Y* Corp. and retained the Denco assets. Immediately thereafter, *X* distributes the *Y* stock to *A* in exchange for all of *A*'s stock in *X*.
c. What are the results if *X* transfers the Gameco assets to *Y* and then distributes the *Y* stock equally to *A* and *B*?
d. How do your answers to (b) change if most of the assets of Gameco consist of appreciated securities traded on the New York stock exchange?
e. How do your answers to (b) change if Denco was purchased three years before with profits from Gameco? If *X* had purchased the stock of Holding Corp. three years before with profits from Gameco, with Holding Corp.'s only asset then being stock of Denco, and, shortly after *X*'s acquisition of the Holding Corp. stock, Holding Corp. liquidated under §332 so that *X* acquired the stock of Denco under §332?

11-3. Parent Corp. owns as its sole assets the entire outstanding stock of Sub-1 Corp., Sub-2 Corp., and Sub-3 Corp. *X*, *Y*, and *Z* each purchase one-third of the outstanding shares of Parent Corp. and Parent Corp. subsequently distributes the stock of Sub-1 to *X*, the stock of Sub-2 to *Y*, and the stock of Sub-3 to *Z*. What are the tax consequences of the distributions to Parent Corp., *X*, *Y*, and *Z*? How would your answers change if the distributions had been pro rata so that *X*, *Y*, and *Z* each ended up with a one-third interest in Sub-1, Sub-2, and Sub-3? Assume each corporation has actively conducted a trade or business for more than five years.

11-4. *X* Corp. purchases all the outstanding stock of *Y* Corp. for $200,000. *Y* Corp.'s assets include all the outstanding stock of *Z* Corp. with an adjusted basis of $60,000 and fair market value of $100,000. Three years later, *P* Corp. acquires all the outstanding stock of *Y* Corp. from *X* Corp. in exchange for its own voting preferred stock in a transaction described in §368(a)(1)(B). How are *P* Corp. and *Y* Corp. taxed if *Y* Corp. distributes all its stock in *Z* Corp. one year after the *P*-*X* B reorganization, assuming the active business requirement of §355(a)(1)(C) is met?

B. VARIATIONS

Although Congress intended §355 to be the exclusive vehicle granting tax-preferred treatment to divisive transactions, taxpayers wishing to avoid the strict limitations of §355 have sought to fit their corporate divisions within the umbrella of less restrictive provisions. Consider the transaction in Bhada v. Commissioner, 89 T.C. 959, 976 (1987), aff'd, 892 F.2d 39 (6th Cir. 1989):

> *P* Corp. owns all the stock of . . . *S* Corp. . . . The value of *P* is ten times greater than the value of *S*. The *P* shareholders desire to cash in on the stock of *S* at capital gains rates. To this end, *S* Corp. offers to exchange newly created shares of itself (the same class of stock) . . . to *P*'s shareholders for shares of *P* on a value-for-value basis.

Formally, the transaction looks like an exchange at the shareholder level, taxable under §1001. To *S* Corp., on the other hand, it is simply a distribution of its own stock for property, a tax-free event under §1032(a). If the transaction is taxable to the shareholders and §304(a)(2) does not apply, the shareholders will recognize capital gain (or loss) on their exchange.[5]

Section 304(a)(2) does not apply to the distribution, because that provision applies only to the distribution of "property," and "property" for purposes of §304 does not include stock of the distributing corporation. §317(a). Although the Service has argued that *P* Corp. should be treated as the distributing corporation in the transaction, the courts have refused to read §304(a)(2) that way. See, e.g., Bhada v. Commissioner, 89 T.C. 959, 976 (1987), aff'd, 892 F.2d 39 (6th Cir. 1989).

In *Bhada*, a stock-for-stock exchange turned the parent-subsidiary pair into a brother-sister pair (albeit with cross-ownership between the brother and sister) and so had the effect of a divisive reorganization. Had the Tax Court held that stock of the distributing corporation (i.e., the subsidiary) constituted "property" for the application of §304(a), the transaction might have been taxed as a distribution, just as a failed §355 transaction is taxed. Unfortunately, the court ruled that §304(a) did not cover the stock of the distributing corporation because of §317(a). Thus, the transaction effected a tax-free divisive reorganization without

5. Note that because *S* Corp. distributes its own stock, the transaction does not fall under §355 even though the transaction does have a divisive impact.

having to satisfy the hurdles imposed by §355. Although the Tax Court acknowledged that its holding might create an end-run around §355, it wrote, "[W]e decline to adopt an interpretation of section 304 in contravention of the language of the statute and its legislative history." 89 T.C. at 977.

Thus, the transaction described above may allow the *P* Corp. shareholders to avoid the restrictions of §355, including the device and active trade or business requirements. By selling the *S* Corp. stock after the transaction, the shareholders will end up with cash, but at a tax cost of only capital gain.

PROBLEM

11-5. *X* Corp., a successful corporation with substantial earnings and profits, has 100 shares of stock outstanding, wholly owned by individual *B*. *B* owns 50 of these shares with an adjusted basis of $10 per share and the other 50 shares with an adjusted basis of $1,000 per share. Assume each share of *X* Corp. is worth $1,000. *X* Corp. transfers cash of $50,000 to newly formed *Y* Corp. in exchange for 100 shares of *Y* Corp. stock. One year later, *B* transfers the 50 shares of *X* Corp. stock having an adjusted basis of $1,000 per share to *Y* Corp. in exchange for 100 shares of *Y* Corp. common stock. What are the tax consequences of this exchange to individual *B*? How will *B* be taxed if her stock of *Y* Corp. is subsequently redeemed?

Commissioner v. Morris Trust

367 F.2d 794 (4th Cir. 1966)

Before Haynsworth, Chief Judge, J. Spencer Bell, Circuit Judge, and Stanley, District Judge.

HAYNSWORTH, Chief Judge.

Its nubility impaired by the existence of an insurance department it had operated for many years, a state bank divested itself of that business before merging with a national bank. The divestiture was in the form of a traditional "spin-off," but, because it was a preliminary step to the merger of the banks, the Commissioner treated their receipt of stock of the insurance company as ordinary income to the stockholders of the state bank. We agree with the Tax Court, that gain to the stockholders of the state bank was not recognizable under §355 of the 1954 Code.

In 1960, a merger agreement was negotiated by the directors of American Commercial Bank, a North Carolina corporation with its principal office in Charlotte, and Security National Bank of Greensboro, a national bank. [T]hough American was slightly larger than Security, it was found desirable to operate the merged institutions under Security's national charter, after changing the name to North Carolina National Bank. . . .

For many years, American had operated an insurance department. This was a substantial impediment to the accomplishment of the merger, for a national bank is prohibited from operating an insurance department except in towns having a population of not more than 5000 inhabitants. To avoid a violation of the national banking laws, therefore, and to accomplish the merger under Security's national charter, it was prerequisite that American rid itself of its insurance business.

The required step to make it nubile was accomplished by American's organization of a new corporation, American Commercial Agency, Inc., to which American transferred its insurance business assets in exchange for Agency's stock which was immediately distributed to American's stockholders. At the same time, American paid a cash dividend fully taxable to its stockholders. The merger of the two banks was then accomplished.

Though American's spin-off of its insurance business was a "D" reorganization, as defined in §368(a)(1), provided the distribution of Agency's stock qualified for nonrecognition of gain under §355, the Commissioner contends that the active business requirements of §355(b)(1)(A) were not met, since American's banking business was not continued in unaltered corporate form. He also finds an inherent incompatibility in substantially simultaneous divisive and amalgamating reorganizations.

Section 355(b)(1)(A) requires that both the distributing corporation and the controlled corporation be "engaged immediately after the distribution in the active conduct of a trade or business." There was literal compliance with that requirement, for the spin-off, including the distribution of Agency's stock to American's stockholders, preceded the merger. The Commissioner asks that we look at both steps together, contending that North Carolina National Bank was not the distributing corporation and that its subsequent conduct of American's banking business does not satisfy the requirement.

A brief look at an earlier history may clarify the problem. . . .

Nonrecognition of gain in "spin-offs" was introduced by the Revenue Act of 1924. Its §203(b)(3), as earlier Revenue Acts, provided for nonrecognition of gain at the corporate level when one corporate party to a reorganization exchanged property solely for stock or securities of another, but it added a provision in subsection (c) extending the nonrecognition of gain to a stockholder of a corporate party to a reorganization who received stock of another party without surrendering any of his old stock. Thus, with respect to the nonrecognition of gain, treatment previously extended to "split-offs" was extended to the economically indistinguishable "spin-off."

The only limitation upon those provisions extending nonrecognition to spin-offs was contained in §203(h) and (i) defining reorganizations. The definition required that immediately after the transfer, the transferor or its stockholders or both be in control of the corporation to which the assets had been transferred, and "control" was defined as being the ownership of not less than eighty percent of the voting stock and eighty percent of the total number of shares of all other classes of stock.

With no restriction other than the requirement of control of the transferee, these provisions were a fertile source of tax avoidance schemes. By spinning-off liquid assets or all productive assets, they provided the means by which ordinary distributions of earnings could be cast in the form of a reorganization within their literal language.

The renowned case of Gregory v. Helvering, 293 U.S. 465, brought the problem to the Supreme Court. The taxpayer there owned all of the stock of United Mortgage Corporation which, in turn, owned 1000 shares of Monitor Securities Corporation. She wished to sell the Monitor stock and possess herself of the proceeds. If the sale were effected by United Mortgage, gain would be recognized to it, and its subsequent distribution of the net proceeds of the sale would have been a dividend to the taxpayer, taxable as ordinary income. If the Monitor stock were distributed to the taxpayer before sale, its full value would have been taxable to her as ordinary income. In order materially to reduce that tax cost, United Mortgage [transferred] the Monitor stock to a new corporation, Averill, the stock of which was distributed to the taxpayer. Averill was then liquidated, and the taxpayer sold the Monitor stock. She contended that she was taxable only on the proceeds of the sale, reduced by an allocated part of her cost basis of United Mortgage, and at capital gain rates.

The Supreme Court found the transaction quite foreign to the congressional purpose. It limited the statute's definition of a reorganization to a reorganization of a corporate business or businesses motivated by a business purpose. It was never intended that Averill engage in any business, and it had not. Its creation, the distribution of its stock and its liquidation, the court concluded, was only a masquerade for the distribution of an ordinary dividend, as, of course, it was. . . .

Underlying such judicially developed rules limiting the scope of the nonrecognition provisions of the Code, was an acceptance of a general congressional purpose to facilitate the reorganization of businesses, not to exalt economically meaningless formalisms and diversions through corporate structures hastily created and as hastily demolished. Continuation of a business in altered corporate form was to be encouraged, but immunization of taxable transactions through the interposition of shortlived, empty, corporate entities was never intended and ought not to be allowed.

While these judicial principles were evolving and before the Supreme Court declared itself in Gregory v. Helvering, an alarmed Congress withdrew nonrecognition of gain to a stockholder receiving securities in a spin-off. It did so by omitting from the Revenue Act of 1934, a provision comparable to §203(c) of the Revenue Act of 1924.

Nonrecognition of gain to the stockholder in spin-off situations, however, was again extended by §317(a) of the Revenue Act of 1951, amending the 1939 Code by adding §112(b)(11). This time, the judicially developed restrictions upon the application of the earlier statutes were partially codified. Nonrecognition of gain was extended "unless it appears that (A) any corporation which is a party to such reorganization was not intended to continue the active conduct of a trade or business after such reorganization, or (B) the corporation whose stock is distributed was used principally as a device for the distribution of earnings and profits to the shareholders of any corporation a party to the reorganization."

If this transaction were governed by the 1939 Code, as amended in 1951, the Commissioner would have had the support of a literal reading of the A limitation, for it was not intended that American, in its then corporate form, should continue the active conduct of the banking business. From the prior history, however, it would appear that the intention of the A limitation was to withhold the statute's benefits from schemes of the Gregory v. Helvering type. It effectively reached those situations in which one of the parties to the reorganization was left only with liquid assets not intended for use in the acquisition of an active business or in which the early demise of one of the parties was contemplated, particularly, if its only office was a conduit for the transmission of title. The B limitation was an additional precaution intended to encompass any other possible use of the device for the masquerading of a dividend distribution.

The 1954 Code was the product of a careful attempt to codify the judicial limiting principles in a more particularized form. The congressional particularization extended the principles in some areas, as in the requirement that a business, to be considered an active one, must have been conducted for a period of at least five years ending on the distribution date and must not have been acquired in a taxable transaction during the five-year period. In other areas, it relaxed and ameliorated them, as in its express sanction of non-pro rata distributions. While there are such particularized variations, the 1954 Code is a legislative reexpression of generally established principles developed in response to definite classes of abuses which had manifested themselves many years earlier. The perversions of the general congressional purpose and the principles the courts had developed to thwart them, as revealed in the earlier cases, are still an enlightening history with which an interpretation of the reorganization sections of the 1954 Code should be approached.

Section 355(b) requires that the distributing corporation be engaged in the active conduct of a trade or business "immediately after the distribution." This is in contrast to the provisions of the 1951 Act, which, as we have noted, required an intention that the parent, as well as the other corporate parties to the reorganization, continue the conduct of an active business. It is in marked contrast to §355(b)'s highly particularized requirements respecting the duration of the active business prior to the reorganization and the methods by which it was acquired. These contrasts suggest a literal reading of the post-reorganization requirement and a holding that the Congress intended to restrict it to the situation existing "immediately after the distribution."

Such a reading is quite consistent with the prior history. It quite adequately meets the problem posed by the Gregory v. Helvering situation in which, immediately after the distribution, one of the corporations held only liquid or investment assets. It sufficiently serves the requirements of permanence and of continuity, for as long as an active business is being conducted immediately after the distribution, there is no substantial opportunity for the stockholders to sever their interest in the business except through a separable, taxable transaction. If the corporation proceeds to withdraw assets from the conduct of the active business and to abandon it, the Commissioner has recourse to the back-up provisions of §355(a)(1)(B) and to the limitations of the underlying principles. At the same time, the limitation, so construed, will not inhibit continued stockholder conduct of the active business through altered corporate form and with further changes in corporate structure, the very thing the reorganization sections were intended to facilitate.

Applied, to this case, there is no violation of any of the underlying limiting principles. There was no empty formalism, no utilization of empty corporate structures, no attempt to recast a taxable transaction in nontaxable form and no withdrawal of liquid assets. There is no question but that American's insurance and banking businesses met all of the active business requirements of §355(b)(2). It was intended that both businesses be continued indefinitely, and each has been. American's merger with Security, in no sense, was a discontinuance of American's banking business, which opened the day after the merger with the same employees, the same depositors and customers. . . . There was a strong business purpose for both the spin-off and the merger, and tax avoidance by American's stockholders was neither a predominant nor a subordinate purpose. In short, though both of the transactions be viewed together, there were none of the evils or misuses which the limiting principles and the statutory limitations were designed to exclude.

We are thus led to the conclusion that this carefully drawn statute should not be read more broadly than it was written to deny nonrecognition of gain to reorganizations of real businesses of the type which Congress clearly intended to facilitate by according to them nonrecognition of present gain.

The Commissioner, indeed, concedes that American's stockholders would have realized no gain had American not been merged into Security after, but substantially contemporaneously with, Agency's spin-off. Insofar as it is contended that §355(b)(1)(A) requires the distributing corporation to continue the conduct of an active business, recognition of gain to American's stockholders on their receipt of Agency's stock would depend upon the economically irrelevant technicality of the identity of the surviving corporation in the merger. Had American been the survivor, it would in every literal and substantive sense have continued the conduct of its banking business.

Surely, the Congress which drafted these comprehensive provisions did not intend the incidence of taxation to turn upon so insubstantial a technicality. Its differentiation on the basis of the economic substance of transactions is too evident to permit such a conclusion.

This, too, the Commissioner seems to recognize, at least conditionally, for he says that gain to the stockholders would have been recognized even if American had been the surviving corporation. This would necessitate our reading into §355(b)(1)(A) an implicit requirement that the distributing corporation, without undergoing any reorganization whatever, whether or not it resulted in a change in its corporate identity, continue the conduct of its active business.

We cannot read this broader limitation into the statute for the same reasons we cannot read into it the narrower one of maintenance of the same corporation identity. The congressional limitation of the post-distribution active business requirement to the situation existing "immediately after the distribution" was deliberate. Consistent with the general statutory scheme, it is quite inconsistent with the Commissioner's contention.

The requirement of §368(a)(1)(D) that the transferor or its stockholders be in control of the spun-off corporation immediately after the transfer is of no assistance to the Commissioner. It is directed solely to control of the transferee, and was fully met here. It contains no requirement of continuing control of the transferor. Though a subsequent sale of the transferor's stock, under some circumstances, might form the basis of a contention that the transaction was the equivalent of a dividend within the meaning of §355(a)(1)(B) and the underlying principles, the control requirements imply no limitation upon subsequent reorganizations of the transferor.

There is no distinction in the statute between subsequent amalgamating reorganizations in which the stockholders of the spin-off transferor would own 80% or more of the relevant classes of stock of the reorganized transferor, and those in which they would not. The statute draws no line between major and minor amalgamations in prospect at the time of the spin-off. Nothing of the sort is suggested by the detailed control-active business requirements in the five-year predistribution period, for there the distinction is between taxable and non-taxable acquisitions, and a tax free exchange within the five-year period does not violate the active business-control requirement whether it was a major or a minor acquisition. Reorganizations in which no gain or loss is recognized, sanctioned by the statute's control provision when occurring in the five years preceding the spin-off, are not prohibited in the postdistribution period. . . .

Nor can we find elsewhere in the Code any support for the Commissioner's suggestion of incompatibility between substantially contemporaneous divisive and amalgamating reorganizations. The 1954 Code contains no inkling of it; nor does its immediate legislative history. The difficulties encountered under the 1924 Code and its successors, in dealing with formalistic distortions of taxable transactions into the spin-off shape, contain no implication of any such incompatibility. Section 317 of the Revenue Act of 1951 . . . did require an intention that the distributing corporation continue the conduct of its active business, but that transitory requirement is of slight relevance to an interpretation of the very different provisions of the 1954 Code and is devoid of any implication of incompatibility. If that provision, during the years it was in effect, would have resulted in recognition of gain in a spin-off if the distributing corporation later, but substantially simultaneously, was a party to a merger in which it lost its identity, a question we do not decide, it would not inhibit successive reorganizations if the merger preceded the spin-off.

The Congress intended to encourage six types of reorganizations. They are defined in [section] 368 and designated by the letters "A" through "F." The "A" merger, the "B" exchange of stock for stock and the "C" exchange of stock for substantially all of the properties of another are all amalgamating reorganizations. The "D" reorganization is the divisive spin-off, while the "E" and "F" reorganizations, recapitalizations and reincorporations, are neither amalgamating nor divisive. All are sanctioned equally, however. Recognition of gain is withheld from each and successively so. Merger may follow merger, and an "A" reorganization by which *Y* is merged into *X* corporation may proceed substantially simultaneously with a "C" reorganization by which *X* acquires substantially all of the properties of *Z* and with an "F" reorganization by which *X* is reincorporated in another state. The "D" reorganization has no lesser standing. It is on the same plane as the others and, provided all of the "D" requirements are met, is as available as the others in successive reorganizations. . . .

A decision of the Sixth Circuit appears to be at odds with our conclusion. In *Curtis* [v. United States, 336 F.2d 714 (6th Cir. 1964)], it appears that one corporation was merged into another after spinning-off a warehouse building which was an unwanted asset because the negotiators could not agree upon its value. The Court of Appeals for the Sixth Circuit affirmed a District Court judgment holding that the value of the warehouse company shares was taxable as ordinary income to the stockholders of the first corporation.

A possible distinction may lie between the spin-off of an asset unwanted by the acquiring corporation in an "A" reorganization solely because of disagreement as to its value and the preliminary spin-off of an active business which the acquiring corporation is prohibited by law from operating. We cannot stand upon so nebulous a distinction, however. We simply take a different view. The reliance in *Curtis* upon the Report of the Senate Committee explaining §317 of the Revenue Act of 1951, quite dissimilar to the 1954 Code, reinforces our appraisal of the relevant materials.

To the extent that our own decision in [Helvering v. Elkhorn Coal Co., 95 F.2d 732 (4th Cir. 1937)] is relevant, it tends to support our conclusion, not to militate against it.

Elkhorn was one of the interesting cases which contributed to the development of the judicial principles which served, as best they could, to confine pretensive arrangements in the early days long before adopting of the 1954 Code. Mill Creek Coal Company wanted to acquire for Mill Creek stock one of the mining properties of Elkhorn. Had the bargain been effectuated, directly, it would have been clearly a taxable transaction, for Elkhorn had other mining properties. In an attempt to avoid the tax, Elkhorn's other properties were spun-off to a new Elkhorn; old Elkhorn conveyed its remaining properties to Mill Creek for stock and by successive transactions, Elkhorn stockholders wound up owning stock in new Elkhorn which owned all of old Elkhorn's mining properties, except the ones transferred to Mill Creek, and the Mill Creek stock received by old Elkhorn. They were in precisely the same position as they would have been in if old Elkhorn had transferred the Mill Creek properties to Mill Creek for stock. It was an obviously transparent attempt to circumvent the requirement that substantially all of the properties must be transferred to qualify for nonrecognition in what would now be classified as a "C" reorganization.

The contention in *Elkhorn* was not that its stockholders realized gain on the spin-off. The opinion denying a rehearing, particularly, suggests the absence of recognizable gain as a result of the spin-off. It approved the recognition of gain as a result of the subsequent "C" reorganization.

It is difficult now to envision any other result in *Elkhorn,* since the stockholders' purpose of formalistic transformation of a clearly taxable transaction into the form of a series of untaxable transactions was so blatant. Nothing of the sort is represented here. Interestingly, however, *Elkhorn* would question the recognition of gain in the merger exchange here, as to which the Commissioner wisely makes no contention under the 1954 Code, not recognition of gain at the earlier spin-off step. As to the first step, the *Elkhorn* opinion appears to oppose the Commissioner's present position.

For the reasons which we have canvassed, we think the Tax Court . . . correctly decided that American's stockholders realized no recognizable taxable gain upon their receipt in the "D" reorganization of the stock of Agency.

Affirmed.

NOTES

1. Morris Trust *and* Elkhorn Coal. The court in *Morris Trust* argued that its decision was supported by its prior opinion in *Elkhorn Coal,* in which a divisive reorganization followed by a C reorganization was held taxable. In *Morris Trust,* a divisive reorganization followed by an A reorganization was held tax free. Given that a C reorganization is nothing but a de facto merger (that is, a de facto A reorganization), can these two decisions be squared?

In *Elkhorn Coal* the Commissioner sought to tax the shareholders on the transfer made pursuant to the nominal C reorganization. In *Morris Trust,* however, he sought to recharacterize the initial divisive reorganization as a taxable transaction. Was that the Commissioner's fatal error in *Morris Trust*? Would the court in *Morris Trust* have sustained a challenge to the tax-free status of the merger of American into Security?

Congress has limited the C reorganization to acquisitions of "substantially all" the transferor corporation's assets. If a C reorganization could be preceded by a tax-free divisive D reorganization, the transferor could spin off any unwanted assets before transferring its remaining assets to the acquiring corporation, thereby circumventing the C reorganization's "substantially all" requirement. *Elkhorn Coal* refused to permit the "substantially all" limitation to be emasculated in this way. Would a contrary decision have been so bad? What abuse might the Commissioner fear?

2. *The statutory symmetries of §355.* The court in *Morris Trust* recognized that if the spin-off had been followed by a merger of the insurance company rather than of the bank, the spin-off would have failed to satisfy the requirement in §368(a)(1)(D) that the shareholders be in control of the spun-off company immediately after the transaction. The court said, however, that there is no similar requirement that the shareholders control the distributing corporation immediately after the transaction. Because a divisive D reorganization involves splitting one corporation into two, it would be peculiar for a control requirement to be imposed on the shareholders with respect to only one of the resulting corporations.

Section 368(a)(1)(D) requires that the shareholders control the spun-off corporation immediately after the transaction. There is no explicit requirement that they also control the distributing corporation for the simple reason that the shareholders *by definition* already control it—they are, after all, its shareholders. Simply put, a divisive reorganization contemplates that the shareholders of the spin-off corporation be former (and perhaps current) shareholders of the distributing corporation.

To be sure, the shareholders might sell or exchange their stock in the distributing corporation immediately after the transaction, but if they do so, the tax-free status of the transaction will be in jeopardy under the "device" language of §355(a)(1)(B). See also Treas. Regs. §1.355-2(c) (the continuity of interest requirement). Indeed, the same statutory provision forbids the planned sale or exchange of the stock of either the distributing corporation or of the spun-off corporation. Thus, to meet the express requirement of a divisive D reorganization, former shareholders of the distributing corporation must control both corporations after the transaction.

The effect of following a divisive reorganization with an acquisitive reorganization is to introduce new shareholders into the transaction. If these new shareholders acquire a sufficient interest in one of the corporations so as to cause the former shareholders to lose "control," the transaction will fail to meet the condition imposed on divisive reorganizations under §355(a)(1)(B). Yet the Treasury has promulgated a regulation under §355 stating that a planned exchange will not run afoul of the "device" language in §355(a)(1)(B) if the exchange is tax free under the reorganization provisions. Treas. Regs. §1.355-2(d)(2)(iii)(E). What weight does this regulation give to the inner parenthetical in §355(a)(1)(B)? Where does this regulation leave *Elkhorn Coal*? Does a tax-free exchange after a divisive reorganization present an opportunity for abuse?

3. *The statutory response to* Morris Trust. Section 355(e) was enacted in 1997 for two principal reasons: First, Congress believed "[i]n cases in which it is intended that new shareholders will acquire ownership of a business in connection with a spin off, the transaction more closely resembles a corporate level disposition of the portion of the business that is acquired." Second, rejecting the asymmetries in *Morris Trust,* Congress "believe[d] that the differences in treatment of certain transactions following a spin-off, depending upon whether the distributing or controlled corporation engages in the transaction, should be minimized.

Consider the following: *B* Corp., a state-chartered bank, has owned for many years all the stock of *I* Corp., an insurance company. The stock of *I* Corp. is distributed to the shareholders of *B* Corp., and then *B* converts to a national bank. Some time after the conversion, Acq. Corp. acquires all *B* Corp. stock in a B reorganization. Assume that the spin-off of *I* Corp. was a necessary prelude to the Acq. Corp.'s acquisition.

Assuming the active trade or business requirement of §355(a)(1)(C) is met, the distribution by *B* Corp. of the *I* Corp. stock should satisfy all the requirements of §355(a)(1). Indeed, the device language of §355(a)(1)(B) should not be implicated because no stock of the distributing corporation (i.e., *B*) and no stock of the controlled corporation (i.e., *I*) is sold as part of the transaction. However, if the former *B* Corp. shareholders own too little Acq. Corp. stock after the stock acquisition, the distribution by *B* Corp. of the *I* Corp. stock could be taxable at the corporate level (although it will remain tax free at the shareholder level) under §355(e).

If §335(e) applies to a distribution, the distributing corporation will recognize any gain on its distribution of appreciated, controlled stock. Section 355(e) is triggered if an otherwise tax-free distribution under §355 is part of a plan for one or more persons to acquire 50-percent or more control (by vote or value) of the distributing corporation or of the controlled corporation. See also §355(e)(4)(C)(ii) (for this purpose, applying §318(a)(2)(C) to attribute stock to any shareholder, not just a 50-percent or greater shareholder). Although §355(e)(2)(B) presumes that any transfer of control occurring less than two years before or after the spin-off is part of such a plan, the regulations are more forgiving. They contain nine safe harbors under which a distribution and acquisition do not trigger §355(e). See Treas. Regs. §1.355-7(d). For example, a distribution and later acquisition will not be considered part of a plan if—

1. The distribution is motivated in whole or substantial part by a business purpose other than the acquisition of the acquired corporation; and
2. The acquisition occurs more than six months after the distribution and there is no prohibited activity during the period that begins one year before, and ends six months after, the distribution.

Id. at (d)(1) (Safe Harbor I). Further, a distribution and later acquisition will not be considered part of a plan if there is no prohibited activity at the time of, and within one year after, the distribution. *Id.* at (d)(3) (Safe Harbor III). For these purposes, prohibited activities include an agreement, understanding, arrangement, or substantial negotiations concerning the acquisition or a similar acquisition.

In the example above, if following Acq. Corp.'s acquisition of the *B* Corp. stock, the former *B* Corp. shareholders own 50 percent or less of the vote or value of Acq. Corp. (see §355(e)(4)(A) incorporating §355(d)(4)) and none of the safe harbors apply, gain (but not loss) will be recognized to *B* on the spin-off as if *B* had sold the *I* Corp. stock for its fair market value. And note that the same taxation would result if new shareholders acquired 50-percent or more control of *I* Corp. rather than of *B* Corp.

The legislative history of §355(e) makes clear that no adjustment should be made to the basis of any corporate assets as a result of this taxation. This makes little sense and has the result of imposing a triple tax on corporate earnings: once under §355(e) on the distribution by the distributing corporation of the stock of the controlled corporation, a second time at the corporate level when the controlled corporation sells the appreciated assets or otherwise earns income from them, and a third time when the shareholders sell or exchange the distributed stock of the controlled corporation. One would expect that the controlled corporation would get a step-up in the basis of its assets if the distributing corporation is taxed under §355(e), just as would occur if the assets had simply been sold in a taxable transaction. Nonetheless, the effect of §355(e) apparently is to demand an eventual extra corporate-level tax as the price for obtaining shareholder level deferral (under §355(a)) on the transaction, unless the distributing corporation is eligible for and makes a §336(e) election. The election would avoid a triple tax, eliminating the distributing corporation's gain on controlled corporation stock but requiring the controlled corporation to recognize gain or loss on its assets at the time of the distribution. See §1.336-2(b)(2)(i); *id.* at (b)(2)(iii)(A). But see *id.* at (b)(2)(ii) (for a limitation on loss recognition). Section 336(e) elections are described beginning at page 314 supra.

Not all transfers of control will trigger taxation under §355(e). If the new shareholders acquiring control of the distributing or of the controlled corporation already had control of the other corporation, taxation under §355(e) will be avoided. See §355(e)(3)(A)(iv). And, of course, the actual distribution under §355(a) works a transfer of control (from the distributing corporation to its shareholders), but that inevitable transfer of control is irrelevant under §355(e)(3)(A)(ii).

Although §355(e) is triggered by the transfer of corporate control, certain asset acquisitions are treated as control transfers. Under §355(e)(3)(B), tax-free asset acquisitions (such as a tax-free merger or C reorganization) are equated to stock transfers for purposes of §355(e). Note that both taxable and tax-free stock transfers can trigger §355(e), but only tax-free asset transfers can have that effect. This rule makes sense because §355(e) imposes a corporate-level tax on the transaction, and if the assets were transferred in a taxable transaction, the corporate-level tax would have already been incurred.

This example should make clear that §355(e) is both more and less than a congressional rejection of the *Morris Trust* case. *Morris Trust* held that a tax-free transfer of control in the distributing corporation is not a "device" within the meaning of §355(a)(1)(B) and that holding remains good law. On the other hand, taxation at the corporate level under §355(e) is triggered if post-distribution control of the distributing corporation or of the controlled corporation is transferred in any manner. Thus, this rule applies to tax-free acquisitions (including tax-free asset transfers as occurred in *Morris Trust*) and to taxable transactions. Note, though, that nothing in §355(e) limits the device language in §355(a)(1)(B) so that a prearranged taxable transfer of control might invalidate the entire transaction under §355(a)(1)(B), thereby subjecting the transaction to taxation at both the corporate and individual levels.

Because §355(e) subjects the distributing corporation to taxation on any appreciation in the stock of the controlled corporation, at least one asymmetry remains. Suppose *P* Corp. owns two businesses, a toy business with assets having an adjusted basis of $500,000 and a fair market value of $900,000 and a software business with assets having an adjusted basis and a fair market value of $300,000. If *P* Corp. wishes to divide these two business under §355 and then transfer control of one of the two to new investors, it can do so without paying any toll under §355(e) by transferring the assets of the software business to a newly formed corporation and then distributing the stock of the newly formed corporation to its shareholders under §355.

To be sure, when control of either business is relinquished, §355(e) will be implicated, but because the software assets were unappreciated, no taxation results. Had *P* Corp. instead spun off the assets of the toy business, §355(e) would have forced *P* to recognize a gain on the spin-off of $400,000.

4. *Some concluding thoughts on §355.* The corporate division problem is another example of some of the internal conflicts or strains of the present system of taxing corporations and their shareholders. If *A* forms two separate corporations and lets them grow independently, *A* is free to deal separately with them. But if *B* starts the same business activities in a single corporation, it will be difficult for *B* to separate them later without adverse tax consequences: A distribution from *B*'s corporation of one of its businesses, even in corporate form, resembles a dividend. *B* will argue that she should be allowed to achieve the same results as *A* so long as she keeps the business activities in "corporate solution," but unless the distribution passes the complicated tests of §355, it will not be tax free.

Confusion stems from the corporate system's allowing the retention of earnings without a direct tax on shareholders. If stock is sold, earnings to the extent reflected in the sale price are usually taxed at the shareholder level as capital gains. But if the earnings are distributed to the shareholder by an ongoing corporation, they are taxed as dividends. A tax-free division of a single corporation with retained earnings into two separate corporations gives the shareholder the potential to sell one at capital gains rates, the economic equivalent of a dividend distribution from the original corporation. Recall §302(b)(4) and the circumstances under which part of a business enterprise may be distributed at capital gains rates as a partial liquidation.

PROBLEM

11-6. *X* Corp. has actively conducted two businesses for more than five years. Business 1 is worth $500,000 and *X*'s adjusted basis in the assets of business 1 is $400,000. Business 2 is also worth $500,000, and *X*'s adjusted basis in the assets of business 2 is $250,000. All of *X*'s outstanding stock is owned by *Y* with an adjusted basis of $600,000.

a. Assume that *Y* purchased half of the shares of *X* Corp. three years ago for $450,000. *X* intends to create a new subsidiary, *S*, and then transfer one of the two businesses to *S*. As part of that transaction, *X* will then distribute all of the shares of *S* to *Y*. What are the tax consequences of this transaction to *X*, *Y*, and *S*, assuming that the assets of business 1 are transferred to *S*? How does your answer change if it is the assets of business 2 rather than of business 1 that are transferred to *S*?
b. Assume that *Y* has owned all of the *X* Corp. stock for more than five years. *X* will spin off one of the businesses as described in part (a) above and then merge the corporation owning business 1 (*X* or *S*) into a publicly traded corporation in an "A" reorganization. Does it matter which business is transferred to *S*? Why?

12

One-Party Reorganizations

A. RECAPITALIZATIONS

A recapitalization, in general, refers to a readjustment of the capital structure of a single, existing corporation. Because the term "recapitalization" is not defined in the Code, at the margins, its scope may be uncertain. Many types of conversions have been swept into its meaning by cases and rulings. As with other tax-free reorganizations, discussed in Chapters 10 and 11, the assumptions underlying nonrecognition are that the stock received in a recapitalization is a continuation of the old investment with a mere change in form and that gain or loss consequently should not be recognized, except as to boot received in the exchange.

The classic recapitalization occurs when a closely held family corporation has older owners close to retirement age who wish to transfer the opportunity for growth to younger managers, often their children. Typically, the recapitalization in that case will involve an exchange of the older owners' common stock for preferred. This exchange, sometimes called an "estate freeze," suits the estate planning needs of the retiring owners by keeping future equity appreciation out of their estates while retaining for them, in more secure form, their capital in the corporation. In addition, dividends on the preferred stock may provide the older owners with a stable retirement income. The recapitalization also suits the younger managers, who are eager to be rewarded for their efforts with the equity growth of the corporation but are unable to buy significant amounts of the old common stock. Risk of future loss also will be transferred to the new equityholders because the preferred stock has a preferred position over the common.

Another common type of recapitalization, filling a much different need and with a host of problems beyond the scope of this discussion, occurs with a financially distressed corporation. In such a case, the debtors and shareholders may together recapitalize the company's debt and equity structure, or they may contribute their debt and equity interests to a new corporation. See pages 404-408 infra.

If an exchange of stock for stock is treated as a tax-free recapitalization, the substitute basis rules of §358 apply so that the basis of the stock received remains the same as the stock surrendered. In a recapitalization, the corporation usually retains all of its tax attributes — e.g., no change in the basis of its assets, no effect on its earnings and profits. The corporation's tax existence, in other words, continues without interruption. Thus, there is no special provision for the carryover of tax attributes (such as a net operating loss), and the rules of §381 applicable to most reorganizations generally do not apply to recapitalizations.

Section 305(b) and (c) can make taxable certain disproportionate recapitalization exchanges when the effect of the transaction is a non–pro rata stock dividend. The Service does not, however, usually raise the §305(b) and (c) problems in the isolated recapitalization of a closely held corporation. See Rev. Rul. 75-93, 1975-1 C.B. 101, in which a disproportionate recapitalization exchange did not trigger §305(c) because it was not part of a plan to periodically increase equity interests. To the same effect, see Gen. Couns. Mem. 39088 (Dec. 7, 1983). See also Treas. Regs. §1.305-3(e) (examples 10, 11, and 12).

Recapitalizations can cover a variety of stock exchanges. For examples, see Treas. Regs. §1.368-2(e) as well as the following: common stock for preferred stock, Rev. Rul. 74-269, 1974-1 C.B. 87, and preferred stock for common stock, Rev. Rul. 77-238, 1977-2 C.B. 115. Recall from page 246 supra that an exchange of common stock for preferred stock may cause the preferred to be §306 stock under §306(c)(1)(B).

Recapitalizations also can include exchanges of bonds as well as of stock. The Service has ruled that convertible bonds may be exchanged for stock of the same corporation without recognition. See Rev. Rul. 72-265, 1972-1 C.B. 122. Bonds may be exchanged for bonds, and there is no original issue discount (see §1273) on a bond-for-bond and bond-for-stock recapitalization. See Rev. Rul. 77-415, 1977-2 C.B. 311. In Rev. Rul. 77-437, 1977-2 C.B. 28, the Service ruled that a debtor corporation recognized income from the cancellation of indebtedness on a bond exchange to the extent that the face value of the old bonds exceeded the face value of the new bonds.

A controversial problem in the recapitalization area has been how to treat the exchange of stock for bonds, as illustrated in *Bazley* below. It always has been clear that if a corporation simply distributes its own debt securities on its stock and has adequate earnings and profits, the distribution is a taxable dividend. See page 120 supra. But the status of debt securities issued by a corporation in the course of a corporate recapitalization has been less clear. The 1939 Code provided (as does the "general rule" laid down in §354(a)(1) of the 1954 Code) that no gain or loss was recognized if stock or securities of a corporation that was a party to a "reorganization" were exchanged for stock and securities of the same corporation; the 1939 Code, like §368(a)(1)(E) of the current Code, defined a "reorganization" to include a recapitalization. Suppose, then, that a corporation "recapitalized" by calling in its outstanding common stock and issuing in exchange other common stock (with a different par value or some other alteration of rights) plus bonds, debentures, or notes. Should the transaction be a tax-free exchange of the old stock for the new stock and bonds or other debt instruments? Should it be treated as a taxable sale or exchange? As a dividend of the debt instruments? *Bazley* considers this problem. For the effect of §354(a)(2) enacted in 1954, see the Note following *Bazley*.

Bazley v. Commissioner

331 U.S. 737 (1947)

Mr. Justice FRANKFURTER delivered the opinion of the Court. . . .

[T]he Commissioner of Internal Revenue assessed an income tax deficiency against the taxpayer for the year 1939. Its validity depends on the legal significance of the recapitalization in that year of a family corporation in which the taxpayer and his wife owned all but one of the Company's one thousand shares. These had a par value of $100. Under the plan of reorganization the taxpayer, his wife, and the holder of the additional share were to turn in their old shares and receive in exchange for each old share five new shares of no par value, but of a stated value of $60, and new debenture bonds, having a total face value of $400,000, payable in ten years but callable at any time. Accordingly, the taxpayer received 3,990 shares of the new stock for the 798 shares of his old holding and debentures in the amount of $319,200. At the time of these transactions the earned surplus of the corporation was $855,783.82.

The Commissioner charged to the taxpayer as income the full value of the debentures. The Tax Court affirmed the Commissioner's determination, against the taxpayer's contention that as a "recapitalization" the transaction was a tax-free "reorganization" and that the debentures were "securities in a corporation a party to a reorganization," "exchanged solely for stock or securities in such corporation" "in pursuance of a plan of reorganization," and as such no gain is recognized for income tax purposes. [§§368(a)(1)(E) and 354(a)(1).*] The Tax Court found that the recapitalization had "no legitimate corporate business purpose" and was therefore not a "reorganization" within the statute. The distribution of debentures, it concluded, was a disguised dividend, taxable as earned income under [§§61(a) and 301]. 4 T.C. 897]. The Circuit Court of Appeals for the Third Circuit, sitting en banc, affirmed, two judges dissenting. 155 F.2d 237.

Unless a transaction is a reorganization contemplated by [§368(a)], any exchange of "stock or securities" in connection with such transaction, cannot be "in pursuance of the plan of reorganization" under [§354]. While [§368(a)] informs us that "reorganization" means, among other things, "a recapitalization," it does not inform us what "recapitalization" means. "Recapitalization" in connection with the income tax has been part of the revenue laws since 1921. . . . Congress has never defined it and the Treasury Regulations shed only limited light. Treas. Regs. [§1.368-2(e)(1)-(4)]. One thing is certain. Congress did not incorporate some technical concept, whether that of accountants or of other specialists, into [§368(a)], assuming that there is agreement among specialists as to the meaning of recapitalization. And so, recapitalization as used in [§368(a)] must draw its meaning from its function in that section. It is one of the forms of reorganization which obtains the privileges afforded by [§368(a)]. Therefore, "recapitalization" must be construed with reference to the presuppositions and purpose of [§368(a)]. It was not the purpose of the reorganization provision to exempt from payment of a tax what as a practical matter is realized gain. Normally, a distribution by a corporation,

*Section 354(a)(2), which greatly limits the general rule of §354(a)(1), was not enacted until 1954.—EDS.

whatever form it takes, is a definite and rather unambiguous event. It furnishes the proper occasion for the determination and taxation of gain. But there are circumstances where a formal distribution, directly or through exchange of securities, represents merely a new form of the previous participation in an enterprise, involving no change of substance in the rights and relations of the interested parties one to another or to the corporate assets. As to these, Congress has said that they are not to be deemed significant occasions for determining taxable gain. . . .

In a series of cases this Court has withheld the benefits of the reorganization provision in situations which might have satisfied provisions of the section treated as inert language, because they were not reorganizations of the kind with which [§354], in its purpose and particulars, concerns itself. See Pinellas Ice & Cold Storage Co. v. Commissioner, 287 U.S. 462; Gregory v. Helvering, 293 U.S. 465; LeTulle v. Scofield, 308 U.S. 415. . . .

Since a recapitalization within the scope of [§368] is an aspect of reorganization, nothing can be a recapitalization for this purpose unless it partakes of those characteristics of a reorganization which underlie the purpose of Congress in postponing the tax liability.

No doubt there was a recapitalization of the Bazley corporation in the sense that the symbols that represented its capital were changed, so that the fiscal basis of its operations would appear very differently on its books. . . . What is controlling is that a new arrangement intrinsically partake of the elements of reorganization which underlie the Congressional exemption and not merely give the appearance of it to accomplish a distribution of earnings. . . .

What have we here? No doubt, if the Bazley corporation had issued the debentures to Bazley and his wife without any recapitalization, it would have made a taxable distribution. Instead, these debentures were issued as part of a family arrangement, the only additional ingredient being an unrelated modification of the capital account. The debentures were found to be worth at least their principal amount, and they were virtually cash because they were callable at the will of the corporation which in this case was the will of the taxpayer. One does not have to pursue the motives behind actions, even in the more ascertainable forms of purpose, to find, as did the Tax Court, that the whole arrangement took this form instead of an outright distribution of cash or debentures, because the latter would undoubtedly have been taxable income whereas what was done could, with a show of reason, claim the shelter of the immunity of a recapitalization-reorganization. . . .

A "reorganization" which is merely a vehicle, however elaborate or elegant, for conveying earnings from accumulations to the stockholders is not a reorganization under [§368]. This disposes of the case as a matter of law, since the facts as found by the Tax Court bring them within it. And even if this transaction were deemed a reorganization, the facts would equally sustain the imposition of the tax on the debentures under [§356(a)(1) and (2)]. Commissioner v. Estate of Bedford, 325 U.S. 283. . . .

Other claims raised have been considered but their rejection does not call for discussion.

Judgments affirmed.

Mr. Justice Douglas and Mr. Justice Burton dissent in both cases for the reasons stated in the joint dissent of Judges Maris and Goodrich in the court below. Bazley v. Commissioner, 3 Cir., 155 F.2d 237, 244.

NOTES

1. *The 1954 changes in §354.* Although the 1954 Code continued the general nonrecognition rule for shareholder exchanges incident to reorganizations, it added §354(a)(2) limiting nonrecognition to cases in which the principal amount of securities (debt instruments) received does not exceed the principal amount of debt instruments surrendered. By virtue of §354(a)(2), in conjunction with §356(a) and (d), the debentures in *Bazley* would have been taxed as boot even if the transaction had been treated as a reorganization, because no debt instruments were surrendered.

Does §354(a)(2) render *Bazley* obsolete? Securities constituting boot received in a reorganization may be taxed under the installment sale provisions. See §453(f)(6) (last sentence). If such taxation is available, gain will be deferred until payment on the securities is received. See §453(c). But if under *Bazley* an exchange is held to be a distribution taxable under §301 rather than a recapitalization, installment sale treatment is unavailable and the securities will be taxable on receipt. Accordingly, *Bazley* is still important for its gloss on the definition of a "recapitalization." Note that installment sale treatment is not available for securities that are "readily tradable." §453(f)(4)-(5).

Securities received as boot in a reorganization will not qualify for installment sale treatment under §453(f)(6) if receipt of the securities has the effect of a dividend. See §356(a)(2). Recall *Clark*, page 401 supra, defining dividend equivalency. For a discussion of the relationship between the reorganizations provisions and the installment sale provisions, see Siegel, Installment Sales — Relationship to Section 385 Regulations, Section 337 Sales, and Other Concepts, 40 N.Y.U. Inst. Fed. Tax. ch. 46, at §46.06 (1982). See also Prop. Regs. §1.453-1(f)(2).

2. *The effect of* Bedford. *Bedford*, cited by the Supreme Court in *Bazley*, involved these facts: Under a recapitalization plan, a shareholder exchanged 3,000 shares of cumulative preferred stock (par value $100) for 3,500 shares of cumulative preferred stock (par value $75), 1,500 shares of common stock (par value $1), and $45,240 of cash. The shareholder's gain (the difference between the adjusted basis of the shares given up and the value of the stock plus cash received) was $139,740. The corporation's earnings and profits were sufficient to cover the entire cash distribution. The government admitted that the transaction was a reorganization exchange, and the taxpayer admitted that the cash was property not permitted to be received tax free — i.e., boot. The only issue was whether under what is now §356(a)(1) and (2) the boot should be taxed as capital gain — like a sale of stock for cash — or as a dividend. The Court, conceding that the matter was not "wholly free from doubt," concluded that because the corporation had earnings and profits, the distribution of cash had "the effect of the distribution of a taxable dividend." The result of *Bedford* became generally known as the automatic dividend rule. That rule has now become discredited. See pages 401-402 supra.

3. *The "dividend limited to gain" rule of §356.* In citing §356 and *Bedford* as an alternative route to the same result reached by the "no reorganization" route, the Court in *Bazley* may have overlooked the fact that §356(a) requires boot to be treated as a dividend only if, and to the extent that, the taxpayer realizes a gain on the exchange itself. For example, suppose individual *A* owns the 100 outstanding shares of *X* Corp. with an adjusted basis and fair market value of $100 per share. What are the tax consequences under §§354 and 356 if *A* exchanges all the stock for 50 shares

of newly issued common stock worth $40 per share plus securities with a fair market value of $8,000, assuming that the exchange constitutes a "recapitalization" within the meaning of §368(a)(1)(E)? Because there is no gain (within the meaning of §1001(a)) on the exchange, *A* recognizes no income under §356 despite the presence of boot.

Turning to *Bazley*, the value of the stock and securities received may well have exceeded the taxpayer's basis for the stock surrendered, but the Tax Court made no finding to this effect. Even if there had been such a finding, the amount of the taxpayer's gain might have been less than the value of the distributed securities. Under the Supreme Court's holding in *Bazley*, the taxpayer recognized the full value of the securities received as income without any offset for his basis in the stock turned in. Accordingly, even a taxpayer captured by the excess securities rule of §354(a)(2) may profit by arguing in favor of reorganization treatment for the exchange.

4. *Use of debt in a corporation's capital structure.* On incorporation, corporations often issue bonds or debentures to the incorporators, in addition to stock, so that the corporation can lay a foundation for the deduction of interest under §163. See pages 89-104 supra. Moreover, the bonds can be retired at the capital gain rate under §1271, while the redemption of stock would be open to the Pandora's box of §302. See pages 155-187 supra. In addition, an accumulation of surplus by the corporation to pay off the indebtedness, unlike an accumulation for the purpose of redeeming stock, may be permissible under §531, see pages 489-490 infra. *Bazley* and §354(a)(2) mean that a corporation that does not issue debt securities for these purposes to its shareholders at the time of incorporation will not find it easy to rectify its error in a tax-free manner later.

5. *Bankruptcy workouts and other debt restructurings.* When a corporation's financial health becomes impaired, the rights of creditors often are increased. For example, the failure of a corporation to make interest payments when due may entitle bondholders to take control of the company's board of directors. If the corporation's fortunes do not improve, the creditors may seek to restructure their interests in the enterprise; in the extreme case, the creditors may seek to oust the shareholders entirely.

Consider the situation in which a corporation replaces its outstanding debt with new debt having different terms. For example, short-term, low-interest notes might be replaced with long-term, higher-interest bonds. What are the tax consequences of such a debt swap?

Under Treas. Regs. §1.1001-3, "a significant modification of a debt instrument . . . is deemed to result in an exchange of the original instrument." Accordingly, gain or loss can be recognized by the debtholder. If, for example, the value of the debt received exceeds the holder's adjusted basis in the debt surrendered, gain will be recognized on the exchange. This might be the case when the corporation's distress has been reflected in the market price of its notes so that current holders of those notes may have paid significantly less than face value. The definition of a "significant modification" is contained in Treas. Regs. §1.1001-3(e).

The transaction will also be taxable to the debtor corporation, which raises the possibility of cancellation of indebtedness income to the corporation if it substitutes current low value debt for outstanding obligations initially issued for face value. Thus, if a corporation exchanges bonds with an $800 issue price for each $1,000 short-term note outstanding, the corporation will recognize $200 of cancellation of indebtedness income on each exchange. See §108(e)(10)(A). Generally, unless the exchange occurs while the corporation is insolvent or in a bankruptcy proceeding, the cancellation of indebtedness income will be included in gross income immediately. See §§61(a)(12), 108(a). If the insolvency exception applies, the amount included in gross income will be limited to the extent of the debtor corporation's insolvency. Section §108(a)(3).

A corporation might also swap stock for debt. To the extent that the value of such stock is less than the adjusted issue price of the surrendered debt, once again the corporation will recognize cancellation of indebtedness income, except to the extent that §108 applies. See §108(e)(8). Further, if application of §108 to an insolvent or bankrupt corporation permits the corporation to exclude some or all of its cancellation of indebtedness income, the corporation will be forced to reduce its tax attributes (including its tax credits, NOL carryovers, and adjusted basis) as the tax "payment" for the exclusion. See §108(b).

B. REINCORPORATIONS

Suppose a corporation changes the state of its incorporation. Formally, the shareholders must relinquish their old shares in exchange for new ones. Should such an exchange be a taxable event? In a case that antedated special statutory treatment for corporate reorganizations, the Supreme Court held that the reincorporation of General Motors Corporation from New Jersey to Delaware (coupled with a transfer of $5 million from the corporation's earned surplus account to its capital account and minor changes in the terms of the corporation's preferred stock) was a taxable event to shareholders exchanging General Motors (New Jersey) common stock for General Motors (Delaware) common stock. Marr v. United States, 268 U.S. 536 (1925).

The definition of a "reorganization" now includes such reincorporations and other changes in the identity or form of one corporation. See §368(a)(1)(F). The taxable year of any corporation reincorporated under §368(a)(1)(F) does not end, and as with recapitalizations, the limitations applicable to the carryover of tax attributes in a reorganization are generally not applicable to such reincorporations. See, e.g., §381(b) and pages 456-457 infra. Until the Tax Equity and Fiscal Responsibility Act of 1982, F reorganizations were not expressly limited to mere changes in the form, identity, or place of incorporation of a *single* corporation, and case law had treated the amalgamation of multiple corporations as an F reorganization so long as there was a sufficiently high percentage of common ownership. See, e.g., Davant v. Commissioner, 366 F.2d 874 (5th Cir. 1966); Reef Corp. v. Commissioner, 368 F.2d 125 (5th Cir. 1966). The Conference Report accompanying TEFRA of 1982 included the following:

> This limitation [added to §368(a)(1)(F)] does not preclude the use of more than one entity to consummate the transaction provided only one operating company is involved. The reincorporation of an operating company in a different State, for example, is an F reorganization that requires that more than one corporation be involved.

H.R. Conf. Rep. No. 760, 97th Cong., 2d Sess. 541 (1982). *Cf.* 1996 WL 33320990 (IRS FSA) (Mar. 4, 1996) (suggesting that an F reorganization can involve two corporations if one of the corporations has no "tax history"). Accordingly, regardless of the extent of common ownership or control, the amalgamation of two or more operating corporations cannot be an F reorganization. See pages 374-383 supra for application of the D reorganization in such circumstances.

Finally, a corporation does not engage in an F reorganization if its existing shareholders or assets change. How is a purported F reorganization treated if it is part of a larger transaction in which those changes occur? Consider the following revenue ruling:

Rev. Rul. 96-29

1996-1 C.B. 50

Do the transactions described below qualify as reorganizations under §368(a)(1)(F) of the Internal Revenue Code?

Facts

Situation 1. *Q* is a manufacturing corporation all of the common stock of which is owned by twelve individuals. One class of nonvoting preferred stock, representing 40 percent of the aggregate value of *Q*, is held by a variety of corporate and noncorporate shareholders. *Q* is incorporated in state *M*. Pursuant to a plan to raise immediate additional capital and to enhance its ability to raise capital in the future by issuing additional stock, *Q* proposes to make a public offering of newly issued stock and to cause its stock to become publicly traded. *Q* entered into an underwriting agreement providing for the public offering and a change in its state of incorporation. The change in the state of incorporation was undertaken, in part, to enable the corporation to avail itself of the advantages that the corporate laws of state *N* afford to public companies and their officers and directors. In the absence of the public offering, *Q* would not have changed its state of incorporation. Pursuant to the underwriting agreement, *Q* changed its place of incorporation by merging with and into *R*, a newly organized corporation incorporated in state *N*. The shares of *Q* stock were converted into the right to receive an identical number of shares of *R* stock. Immediately thereafter, *R* sold additional shares of its stock to the public and redeemed all of the outstanding shares of nonvoting preferred stock. The number of new shares sold was equal to 60 percent of all the outstanding *R* stock following the sale and redemption.

Situation 2. *W*, a state *M* corporation, is a manufacturing corporation all of the stock of which is owned by two individuals. *W* conducted its business through several wholly owned subsidiaries. The management of *W* determined that it would be in the best interest of *W* to acquire the business of *Z*, an unrelated corporation, and combine it with the business of *Y*, one of its subsidiaries, and to change the state of incorporation of *W*. In order to accomplish these objectives, and pursuant to an overall plan, *W* entered into a plan and agreement of merger with *Y* and *Z*. In accordance with the agreement, *Z* merged with and into *Y* pursuant to the law of state *M*, with the former *Z* shareholders receiving shares of newly issued *W* preferred stock in exchange for their shares of *Z* stock. Immediately following the acquisition of *Z*, *W* changed its place of organization by merging with and into *N*, a newly organized corporation incorporated in state *R*. Upon *W*'s change of place of organization, the holders of *W* common and preferred stock surrendered their *W* stock in exchange for identical *N* common and preferred stock, respectively.

Law and Analysis

Section 368(a)(1)(F) provides that a reorganization includes a mere change in identity, form, or place of organization of one corporation, however effected. This provision was amended by the Tax Equity and Fiscal Responsibility Act of 1982, Pub. L. No. 97-248, in order to limit its application to one corporation. Certain limitations contained in §381(b), including those precluding the corporation acquiring property in a reorganization from carrying back a net operating loss or a net capital loss for a taxable year ending after the date of transfer to a taxable year of the transferor, do not apply to reorganizations described in §368(a)(1)(F) "in recognition of the intended scope of such reorganizations as embracing only formal changes in a single operating corporation." H.R. Rep. No. 760, 97th Cong., 2d Sess. 540, 541 (1982). Although a change in the place of organization usually must be effected through the merger of one corporation into another, such a transaction qualifies as a reorganization under §368(a)(1)(F) because it involves only one operating corporation. The 1982 amendment of §368(a)(1)(F) thus overruled several cases in which a merger of two or more operating corporations could be treated as a reorganization under §368(a)(1)(F). . . .

A transaction does not qualify as a reorganization under §368(a)(1)(F) unless there is no change in existing shareholders or in the assets of the corporation. However, a transaction will not fail to qualify as a reorganization under §368(a)(1)(F) if dissenters owning fewer than 1 percent of the outstanding shares of the corporation fail to participate in the transaction. Rev. Rul. 66-284, 1966-2 C.B. 115.

The rules applicable to corporate reorganizations as well as other provisions recognize the unique characteristics of reorganizations qualifying under §368(a)(1)(F). In contrast to other types of reorganizations, which can involve two or more operating corporations, a reorganization of a corporation under §368(a)(1)(F) is treated for most purposes of the Code as if there had been no change in the corporation and, thus, as if the reorganized corporation is the same entity as the corporation that was in existence prior to the reorganization. . . .

In Rev. Rul. 69-516, 1969-2 C.B. 56, the Internal Revenue Service treated as two separate transactions a reorganization under §368(a)(1)(F) and a reorganization under §368(a)(1)(C) undertaken as part of the same plan. Specifically, a corporation changed its place of organization by merging into a corporation formed under the laws of another state and, immediately thereafter, it transferred substantially all of its assets in exchange for stock of an unrelated corporation. The ruling holds that the change in place of organization qualified as a reorganization under §368(a)(1)(F).

Accordingly, in *Situation 1*, the reincorporation by *Q* in state *N* qualifies as a reorganization under §368(a)(1)(F) even though it was a step in the transaction in which *Q* was issuing common stock in a public offering and redeeming stock having a value of 40 percent of the aggregate value of its outstanding stock prior to the offering.

In *Situation 2*, the reincorporation by *W* in state *N* qualifies as a reorganization under §368(a)(1)(F) even though it was a step in the transaction in which *W* acquired the business of *Z*. . . .

PROBLEMS

12-1. *X* Corp. has 100 shares of common stock outstanding, 80 owned by *A* and 20 by *B*. The fair market value of the *X* Corp. stock is $100 per share, and *X* Corp. has substantial earnings and profits. *A*'s basis in the *X* Corp. stock is $20 per share, while *B*'s basis in the *X* Corp. stock is $40 per share. What are the tax consequences to *A*, *B*, and *X* Corp. of the following alternative transactions?

a. As part of a single transaction, *A* exchanges all her *X* Corp. stock for 800 shares of newly issued, nonvoting preferred stock (worth $10 per share), and *B* exchanges all his *X* Corp. stock for 100 shares of newly issued common stock.
b. As part of a single transaction, *A* exchanges her *X* Corp. stock for 20 shares of a new class of common stock and long-term bonds with face amount and fair market value of $6,000. *B* exchanges his *X* Corp. stock for 20 shares of the newly issued common stock. How would your answer change if *A*'s basis in the *X* Corp. stock were $100 per share?
c. How would your answers to (b) change if *B* were *A*'s son?

12-2. *Y* Corp., doing poorly but not yet insolvent, acquires its outstanding, long-term bonds having an issue price of $1 million in exchange for 800 shares of newly issued preferred stock with par value and fair market value of $1,000 per share. What are the tax consequences of the exchange to *Y* Corp.? How would your answer change if the exchange were made pursuant to a conversion privilege in the cancelled bonds?

12-3. *Z* Corp. has outstanding 20-year unsecured bonds with a face value of $100,000 and fair market value of $70,000. What are the tax consequences to *Z* Corp. and to its bondholders if it exchanges these instruments for secured bonds having the same face value and bearing the same interest rate and maturity? What is the result if the new secured bonds have a face value and fair market value of $70,000?

13

Combining Tax Attributes: Net Operating Losses and Affiliated Corporations

A. CARRYOVER OF TAX ATTRIBUTES

In transactions covered by §§351, 355, and 368, the Code has specific provisions relating to the carryover of basis for property transferred or stock exchanged. Thus, §358 provides, generally speaking, for a transfer of the adjusted basis of exchanging shareholders to the new stock or securities acquired by them. Similarly, §362 provides, generally speaking, that property acquired by a corporation in connection with a §351 transaction or in connection with a reorganization has the same basis as the property had in the hands of the transferor. See also §1223 relating to the holding period of property received in connection with such transactions.

Corporations have a great many more tax attributes than basis and holding periods of assets. Different corporations will employ different accounting methods, will have elected certain methods of depreciation with respect to property, will have positive or negative earnings and profits accounts, may or may not have foreign tax credits, and may or may not have unused investment tax credit carryovers or net operating loss carryovers. Consistent with the philosophy of the nonrecognition provisions such as §§351, 355, and the transactions to which §368 applies, these tax attributes should remain undisturbed after such transactions. One would also expect similar rules to apply in the case of those special combinations consisting of liquidations of controlled subsidiaries into their parents to which §§332, 337, and 334(b) apply.

Thus, if a subsidiary liquidates into its parent in a liquidation described in §332, one would expect that after the liquidation, in calculating whether distributions were made out of earnings and profits, one would look to the combined earnings and profits of the two corporations. Section 381 (providing for carryover of tax attributes in certain tax-free exchanges) and other provisions of the Code generally carry out such expected results.

It should be noted, however, that when a corporation sells its assets in a taxable sale and liquidates but the liquidation is not described in §332, the attributes of the former corporation are obliterated by the transaction. Similarly, when a corporation makes an election under §338 (but not §338(h)(10)) to be treated as if it sold its assets to itself, the former corporation's attributes are obliterated. See pages 307-313 supra for a discussion of §338. Thus, in certain cases a §338 election will involve a trade-off between a step-up in basis and the loss of certain tax attributes. For example, if a corporation purchases stock of a subsidiary with appreciated assets and a large net operating loss, a §338 election may be inadvisable in some cases but not in others. By not making the election the purchaser would not be able to step up the bases of the subsidiary's assets, but the net operating loss (NOL) would be preserved (but its use may be indirectly restricted). On the other hand, if a §338 election were made, the gain recognized on the deemed sale can be offset by an NOL, thereby providing a step-up in basis at no tax cost.

The foregoing simplified discussion has ignored the problems created over many decades by what some call the "traffic" in corporations having substantial net operating losses and corporations having other desirable tax attributes (for example, high-basis, low-value assets). Individuals having business deductions in excess of income can carry those losses back or forward as prescribed by §172 but cannot readily sell these tax benefits to others. When such net operating loss carryovers are lodged in a corporate entity, however, sale of the loss is no more difficult than the sale of the stock of the corporation—provided that the tax attributes are not reduced or restricted by the transfer of the stock.

This "trafficking" in loss corporations has been resisted by the Treasury and the Congress for a number of decades, as described below.

1. *Section 381*

Section 381 provides for the carryover of tax attributes from a transferor corporation to an acquiring corporation in certain transactions. The transactions covered are (1) a liquidation of a controlled subsidiary described in §332 and (2) A, C, or F tax-free reorganizations as well as nondivisive D and G reorganizations. Note that in a §368(a)(1)(B) stock-for-stock reorganization, there is no need for the rules of §381, because the corporate existence of the acquired company continues even though an exchange occurs at the shareholder level. The same holds true for §368(a)(1)(E) recapitalizations. In other words, §381 deals, as its opening sentence states, with "the acquisition of assets of a corporation by another corporation." See Baicker v. Commissioner, 93 T.C. 316 (1989) (no carryovers in a divisive reorganization; not a §381 transaction).

The attributes inherited in a qualified transaction are subject to the operating rules of §381(b). Section 381(b) provides that the taxable year of the transferor closes on the date of distribution or transfer, defined as the date when the distribution or transfer is completed or when substantially all the property has been transferred and the transferor ceases all activities other than liquidating activities. Treas. Regs. §1.381(b)-(1)(b). Section 381(b)(3) provides that the acquiring corporation may not carry back a post-acquisition net operating loss or net capital loss to a pre-acquisition year of the transferor. Here the rules do not impinge on the carryover of the transferor's attributes to the transferee but instead block the transferee's use of its own losses—e.g., against income of a transferor corporation for a year before the merger. See also the discussion of CERTS at page 337 supra. Note that the rules of §381(b) do not apply to an F reorganization. See page 451 supra. Why is there no need to close the taxable year of the transferor or to limit the carryback of post-acquisition losses in an F reorganization?

Suppose that in a forward triangular merger, *X* Corp. merges into Sub. Corp, a wholly owned subsidiary of *Y* Corp., and the former *X* Corp. shareholders receive *Y* Corp. stock. See page 385 supra. If Sub Corp. incurs an NOL after the acquisition, can that NOL be carried back, or does §381(b)(3) prevent the carryback? In Bercy Industries, Inc. v. Commissioner, 640 F.2d 1058 (9th Cir. 1981), the court permitted the carryback even though the reorganization was not a B, E, or F reorganization. See §381(b) and Treas. Regs. §1.381(a)-1(b)(3)(i). Notwithstanding what seems to be clear legislative language, the court had little difficulty reaching this result when Sub Corp. was merely a shell. Should a court reach the same result in a triangular merger if Sub Corp. is not a shell?

Section 381(c) lists numerous tax attributes of the transferor that carry over to the transferee. Of these, the most prominent one that will be discussed in greatest detail is the net operating loss carryover of §381(c)(1). Note that although loss carryovers are transferred to the transferee, they can be used only against the transferee's future income. Other important inherited attributes include the transferor's earnings and profits. §381(c)(2). Under §381(c)(2)(A), the earnings and profits or deficit in earnings and profits of the transferor carry over to the transferee, but under §381(c)(2)(B), an inherited deficit in earnings and profits may be applied only against the transferee's post-transfer earnings and profits and not against the transferee's accumulated earnings and profits.

Under §381(c)(4) the acquiring corporation must continue to use the transferor's accounting method if both corporations have been using the same method. When the acquiring and transferor corporations use different methods, the regulations specify the appropriate method to be used. See Treas. Regs. §1.381(c)(4)-(1)(c) and (d). Specific accounting provisions are provided under §381(c)(5) for inventories, under §381(c)(6) for depreciation allowance computation, under §381(c)(8) for installment obligations, and under §381(c)(16) for assumed expense liabilities.

2. *Section 382*

Suppose in year 1, the first year of its existence, *X* Corp. operates at a $100 loss (i.e., deductions exceed income by $100). In year 2, *X* Corp. produces $100 of income. Overall, *X* Corp. has $0 of income, and its tax consequences should reflect that, but strict adherence to the annual accounting concept would prevent *X* Corp. from offsetting income in year 2 with the loss from year 1. Nevertheless, the Code permits *X* Corp. to carry forward its year 1 loss to offset its year 2 income. §172. Similarly, if *X* Corp. had earned $100 of income in year 1 and had suffered a $100 loss in year 2, the year 2 loss could be carried back to offset the year 1 income (i.e., *X* Corp. would file an amended return for year 1). Under §172(b), a corporation can generally carry a loss back two years and forward 20 years if necessary, using up the loss in the earliest years in which income is sufficient to absorb the loss.

Now suppose *X* Corp. has a $100 loss in year 1, and *Y* Corp. has $100 of income in year 1. If *X* Corp. merges into *Y* Corp., and the *X* Corp. shareholders receive *Y* Corp. stock, should *Y* Corp. be able to use the $100 loss to offset the $100 of income? After all, if *X* Corp. could carry its losses back and forward, why should it not be permitted to carry its losses sideways to offset *Y* Corp.'s income? This situation gives rise to the concern that the merger of *X* into *Y* Corp. may be motivated significantly by the presence of the NOLs. For example, suppose *X* Corp.'s assets at the time of the merger are worth $0. Even so, if *Y* Corp., pays taxes at a 35-percent rate, it may be willing to exchange up to $35 of *Y* Corp. stock for the *X* Corp. stock in the merger if it can use the *X* Corp. NOL and save $35 in taxes.

Although it is by no means clear that such a tax-motivated purchase is economically inefficient, Congress has since 1954 wrestled with the perceived problem of "trafficking" in NOLs. On one hand, the carryover provisions perform an averaging function that allows corporations to overcome the limits of our annual accounting system. On the other hand, when NOLs are used to offset totally unrelated income (such as the acquisition of a corporation solely to obtain its NOLs), perhaps no legitimate averaging function is performed.

To address these concerns, §382 adopts the following approach: After a substantial ownership change, the amount of the NOL of the loss corporation that can be used is not directly limited. Instead, the earnings that can be offset by an NOL are limited annually to a percentage of the loss corporation's value, determined immediately before the ownership change. This limitation-on-earnings approach is intended to approximate the results that would occur if a loss corporation's assets were combined with those of a profitable corporation in a partnership having the following attributes: Only the loss corporation's share of the partnership's income could be offset by the corporation's NOL carryforward. See §704(c). Further, the loss corporation's share of the partnership's income would be limited to earnings generated by the assets contributed by the loss corporation. To achieve a similar result, §382(f) prescribes an objective rate of return (the federal long-term tax-exempt rate) on the value of the corporation's net equity. The annual limitation, then, equals that prescribed rate multiplied by the value of the loss corporation's equity immediately before the ownership change. §382(b).

For example, suppose *X* Corp., a calendar year taxpayer, has a $1 million NOL carryforward. On January 1 of year 1, all the stock of *X* Corp. is sold in a transaction that triggers §382. On that date, the value of *X* Corp.'s stock was $500,000, and the applicable rate of return was 10 percent. In year 1 (and for each year thereafter), *X* Corp. could offset $50,000 (10 percent × $500,000) of income with the NOL carryforward. The same limitation would apply if *X* Corp. were merged into another corporation so long as an ownership change occurred as defined in §382(g). To the extent that *X* Corp. does not earn enough in year 1 (or a subsequent year) to absorb the $50,000 amount, the excess loss is carried forward to the succeeding year and is added to the $50,000 NOL limitation allowed in that year. §382(b)(2). The Notes that follow consider the details of §382.

The §382 limitation, although somewhat artificially determined, applies regardless of the actual performance of a loss company. For example, suppose all the stock of *L* Corp., a loss corporation, is sold by *B* to *P* in a transaction that triggers §382. After the acquisition, the amount of income that can be offset by the pre-acquisition NOLs is determined under §382 (i.e., the value of *L* Corp. multiplied by the federal long-term tax-exempt rate). This limitation applies even if *L* Corp. after the acquisition produces more income than the §382 limitation deems produced. Conversely, if *L* Corp. is merged into *P* Corp. in a transaction that triggers §382, *P* Corp. can offset income as determined under §382 even though the assets of the former *L* Corp. do not in fact produce that amount of income. Thus, the federal long-term tax-exempt rate is an imperfect proxy for the actual return on the assets; it may produce too large or too small a deduction. Once the §382 limitation is determined, however, it is used every year until the pre-change NOLs are used up or the 20-year carryforward limitation of §172 is reached.

For a thorough analysis of §382 and its legislative history, see Berry Petroleum Co. v. Commissioner, 104 T.C. 584 (1995).

NOTES

1. *Ownership changes.* Section 382 applies if an "ownership change" occurs. §382(a), (j), (k)(3). An ownership change arises if the percentage of stock of a loss corporation owned by one or more 5 percent shareholders has increased by more than 50 percentage points over the testing period. §382(g). Note that a series of unrelated transactions may be aggregated to constitute an "ownership change" but that all such transactions must have occurred during the testing period, which is generally three years. §382(i).

An ownership change occurs when there is more than a 50-percentage point change, not more than a 50-percent change. To illustrate, suppose *A* owns 20 percent of *L* Corp. If *A* acquires additional stock bringing *A*'s ownership to 31 percent, no ownership change has occurred even though *A* has increased his ownership of *L* Corp. by more than 50 percent. For an ownership change to occur, *A* would have to increase ownership in *L* Corp. to more than 70 percent.

An ownership change may result from an "owner shift" or an "equity structure shift." §382(g). There are no substantive differences between an owner shift and an equity structure shift and no observable reason for the distinction. Treas. Regs. §1.382-2T(e)(2)(iii).

An owner shift includes any change in stock ownership by "5 percent shareholders" (those holding 5 percent or more in value of corporate stock before or after the change). For purposes of the 5-percent rule, all non–5 percent shareholders are aggregated as a single 5 percent shareholder. §382(g)(4)(A). Owner shifts may occur in the following transactions: a purchase of stock from existing shareholders or the corporation; a §351 exchange; a redemption; an exercise of stock conversion rights; or a combination of the foregoing.

For example, assume that the stock of *L* Corp. is publicly traded and that no shareholder owns 5 percent or more of its stock. No owner shift will occur so long as no person becomes a 5 percent shareholder. That is, random trading does not bring about an owner shift because *L*'s one 5 percent shareholder (i.e., the group of all of the *L* shareholders, who are treated as one shareholder because they are all non–5 percent shareholders) owns 100 percent before and after each trade. If, however, all the stock of widely held *L* Corp. is purchased by *A*, *B*, and *C*, none of whom were previous shareholders and each of whom acquires a one-third stock interest, a more than 50 percent owner shift occurs because their ownership has gone from 0 percent to 100 percent.

Similarly, if *L* Corp. — closely held by *A*, *B*, and *C*, each of whom is a one-third shareholder — makes a public offering so that 51 percent of the stock will be held by non–5 percent shareholders, a more than 50 percent owner shift will occur because all the stock owned by non–5 percent shareholders is treated as being owned by one 5 percent shareholder, and that interest increases from 0 percent to 51 percent.

An "equity structure shift" includes any tax-free reorganization (other than a divisive D, an F, or a divisive G reorganization). §382(g)(3). A more than 50 percent equity shift occurs if after the shift, the percentage of stock held by one or more of the new loss corporation's 5 percent shareholders is at least 50 percentage points more than the percentage of the old loss corporation's stock held by them during the testing period. The old loss corporation is the corporation with NOLs before the reorganization; the new loss corporation is the corporation entitled to use the NOLs after the reorganization. §382(k)(2) and (3).

To illustrate an equity structure shift, suppose *L* Corp., a loss corporation, is merged into *P* Corp. in a tax-free transaction with *P* Corp. surviving. No shareholder of either corporation is a 5 percent shareholder. In the merger, the former *L* shareholders receive 49 percent of the stock of *P*, and the remaining stock of *P* is owned by *P* shareholders unrelated to the *L* shareholders. There has been a more than 50 percent equity structure change of *L* because the *P* shareholders (all of whom are non–5 percent shareholders and are therefore lumped together as a single 5 percent shareholder) have gone from 0 percent owners of *L* to 51 percent shareholders of the new loss corporation. Had the former *L* shareholders received at least 50 percent of the *P* stock, the merger of *L* into *P* would not, by itself, have triggered an ownership change.

You may recall that in the context of an owner shift, all less than 5 percent shareholders are aggregated and treated as a single 5 percent shareholder so that the constant buying and selling of a publicly traded corporation's stock does not cause problems under §382. In a reorganization (i.e., an equity structure shift), however, there may be two groups of less than 5 percent shareholders that are separately aggregated — the shareholders of the acquired and acquiring corporations. Each of these groups is treated separately for purposes of testing an ownership change. §382(g)(4)(B). Otherwise all reorganizations involving publicly held corporations would escape §382. Accordingly in the previous example, an ownership change occurs when the less than 5 percent shareholders of the acquiring corporation, as a group, become greater than 50-percent owners of the new loss corporation.

The relevant testing period used for determining whether an ownership change has occurred generally spans the three years preceding any owner shift or equity structure shift. §382(i)(1).[1] Therefore, a series of unrelated transactions occurring during the testing period together may constitute an ownership change. In measuring whether an ownership change has occurred during the testing period, it is necessary to measure the difference between each 5 percent shareholder's percentage ownership immediately after the close of the testing date and her lowest percentage ownership during the testing period. Treas. Regs. §1.382-2T(c)(1). For example, suppose *X* Corp. has 200 shares of common stock owned by *A* (100 shares), *B* (50 shares), and *C* (50 shares). On January 2 of year 1, *A* sells 60 shares to *B*. On January 1 of year 3, *A* purchases *C*'s entire interest in *X* Corp. Overall, *B*, a 5 percent shareholder, has increased his interest by 30 percentage points (from 25 percent ownership to 55 percent ownership). *A* has decreased her ownership percentage from 50 percent to 45 percent; *C* has decreased his ownership from 25 percent to 0 percent. At first glance, it appears that the 5 percent shareholders together have

1. If an ownership change has occurred earlier, the testing period for determining whether a second ownership change has occurred begins the day after the first change has occurred. §382(i)(2).

increased their ownership by only 30 percentage points, not the more than 50 percentage points necessary to trigger §382. *A*'s percentage ownership from his lowest ownership during the testing period, however, has increased from 20 percent after the sale to *B* to 45 percent after the purchase from *C*. This increase of 25 percentage points when added to the 30 percentage point increase for *B* now triggers the restrictions under §382. See Treas. Regs. §1.382-2T(c)(4).

For both owner shifts and equity structure changes, a series of transactions during the testing period may trigger the operation of §382. For example, suppose the following events occur in year 1: *B*, an individual, purchases 40 percent of the stock of *L*. *L* then is merged into *P*—which is wholly owned by *B*—in a tax-free transaction. In exchange for their stock in *L*, the *L* shareholders (none of whom except *B* was a 5 percent shareholder) receive stock with a value representing 60 percent of the *P* stock (*B* receives 24 percent, the other shareholders 36 percent). The merger triggers an ownership change, because immediately after the merger, *B* owned 64 percent of the combined entity (40 percent by virtue of *B*'s ownership of P before the merger plus 24 percent received in the merger), which is more than 50 percentage points over 0 percent, the lowest percentage in *L* owned by *B* during the testing period.

2. *Constructive ownership.* As case #1, suppose that *B* owns all the stock of *L* Corp., a corporation with NOLs, and all the stock of *P* Corp. If *P* Corp. acquires all the *L* Corp. stock in a B reorganization, *P* Corp. has gone from a 0 percent shareholder in *L* Corp. to a 100 percent owner. Section 382 should not apply here, however, because there really has not been a change in ownership (i.e., *B* continues to own both corporations). Conversely, as case #2, suppose that *B* owns all the stock of *H* Corp., which in turn owns all the stock of *L* Corp. *P* Corp. is wholly owned by *C*, an individual who is unrelated to *B*. *B* sells the stock of *H* Corp. to *P*. Here, §382 should apply because of a change in ultimate ownership from *B* to *C* even though *H* Corp.'s direct ownership of *L* Corp. has remained at 100 percent.

Generally, changes in percentage ownership are determined by looking to the individuals who constructively own stock of the loss corporation. Under §382(l)(3), the constructive ownership rules of §318 apply with modification in determining owner shifts and equity structure changes. Stock owned by entities (e.g., corporations, partnerships, trusts) is deemed owned by their shareholders or beneficiaries in proportion to their interests in the entity. In case #1 above, because *B*, the ultimate beneficiary of *L* Corp.'s NOLs, remained a 100 percent shareholder of *L* Corp., §382 does not limit the carryover of *L* Corp.'s NOLs. Similarly, suppose the stock of *X* Corp., a publicly traded corporation, is not owned by any 5 percent shareholders. If *X* Corp. distributes to its shareholders pro rata all the stock of its wholly owned subsidiary, *Y* Corp., no ownership change occurs. Through the attribution rules, the shareholders of *X* Corp. owned 100 percent of *Y* Corp. before the transaction and 100 percent after. In case #2, when *P* purchases the stock of *H* Corp., which owns *L* Corp., even though *H* Corp.'s direct ownership of *L* Corp. has not changed, the ultimate beneficiary of *L* Corp.'s NOLs has changed. *C* has gone from being a 0 percent owner of *L* Corp. to being a 100 percent owner because *C* is deemed to own the *L* Corp. stock that *H* Corp. owns (i.e., *C* owns *P* Corp., which owns *H* Corp., which owns *L* Corp.).

For an illustration of the constructive ownership rules, see Treas. Regs. §1.382-2T(g)(4), (example 1).

3. *Definition of stock.* Generally, in measuring whether an ownership change has occurred, all stock except certain preferred stock is taken into account. §382(k)(6). The excluded stock is stock described in §1504(a)(4), that is stock that is not entitled to vote, is limited and preferred as to dividends, does not participate in corporate growth to any significant extent, has redemption and liquidation rights that do not exceed the issue price (except for a reasonable redemption premium), and is not convertible. Note that stock labeled "common" stock may be treated as "preferred" stock, and stock labeled "preferred" stock may be treated as "common" stock for purposes of this rule. The Secretary has broad discretion in deciding what stock is counted in determining whether an ownership change has occurred. §382(k)(6). See Treas. Regs. §1.382-2T(f)(18)(ii), which contains a test for identifying when stock is not counted for purposes of §382. See also Treas. Regs. §1.382-2T(f)(18)(iii), which treats certain "debt" instruments as equity.

The preferred stock provision is intended legislatively to reverse the result in Maxwell Hardware Co. v. Commissioner, 343 F.2d 713 (9th Cir. 1965). In that case, a loss corporation's old shareholders retained common stock representing more than 50 percent of the corporation's value, thereby avoiding the application of former §382. New shareholders, however, received special preferred stock that carried with it 90 percent participation in earnings attributable to newly contributed property. As currently constructed, §382 would apply in *Maxwell Hardware* because the new shareholders went from 0 percent to 100 percent participating stock ownership even though the stock they received was called preferred stock.

4. *Options.* Generally, in determining whether an ownership change has occurred, a stock option is deemed exercised only if it was issued or transferred for an "abusive" principal purpose. See generally Treas. Regs. §1.382-4(d)(1) and (2). An option may be deemed exercised if it has that abusive purpose and satisfies an ownership, control, or income test. Treas. Regs. §1.382-4(d)(2)(i). However, those tests generally do not apply to many commercially reasonable stock purchase agreements, security arrangements in typical lending transactions, typical compensatory stock options, and options exercisable only upon a shareholder's death, disability, or retirement. *Id.* at (d)(7)(i)-(v).

5. *Continuity of business.* Following an ownership change, a loss corporation's NOL carryforwards (including applicable built-in losses) are disallowed unless during the two-year period following the ownership change the new loss corporation either (1) continues the old loss corporation's historic business or (2) uses a significant portion of the old loss corporation's assets in a business. §382(c). (This continuity requirement is similar to the requirement that must be satisfied to qualify as a tax-free reorganization under §368. Treas. Regs. §1.368-1(d). See page 342 supra.) The purpose of this continuity requirement is to try to distinguish acquisitions motivated by loss trafficking from those motivated by acceptable business purposes. An extreme example of tax-motivated behavior is the subject of Alprosa Watch Corp. v. Commissioner, 11 T.C. 240 (1948). In that case, a shareholder purchased the stock of a loss corporation, sold the assets back to the original shareholders, and infused the corporation with a new business. The court, prior to any version of §382, allowed the use of NOLs to offset post-acquisition income. How would this situation be treated under §382?

6. *Section 382 limitation.* For any taxable year after the change date (that is, the date of a triggering ownership change), the amount of a loss corporation's taxable income for any year that can be offset by a pre-change loss cannot exceed the §382

limitation. §382(a). The §382 limitation is an amount equal to the value of the loss corporation before the exchange multiplied by the federal long-term tax-exempt rate in effect on the change date. §382(b), (f). Once the §382 limitation is computed, it stays in effect regardless of fluctuations in the federal long-term tax-exempt rate.

If the §382 limitation amount exceeds taxable income, the excess carries over. §382(b)(2). For example, suppose the §382 limitation amount for *L* Corp. with $1 million in NOLs is $100,000 per year. In the first year after an ownership change, the new loss corporation produces $70,000 of income, all of which is offset by the NOL carryover. In the second year, the new loss corporation can use $130,000 of the NOLs to offset income produced. In some situations, even though §382 does not directly result in the permanent loss of NOLs, the §382 limitation, combined with the 20-year carryforward limitation in §172, does result in a loss of NOLs. In the example above, if *L* Corp. had $3 million of NOLs, and the §382 limitation is $100,000 per year, the new loss corporation will be unable to use at least $1 million of the NOLs to offset post-ownership change income.

a. *The federal long-term tax-exempt rate.* Under §382, the federal long-term tax-exempt rate must be multiplied by the value of the loss corporation to determine whether NOLs are limited. By specifying use of the long-term rate for federal obligations, Congress intended to provide a reasonable risk-free rate of return that a loss corporation could obtain in the absence of a change of ownership. Congress discounted the long-term *taxable* rate on federal obligations, however, by requiring the use of the long-term *tax-exempt* rate on federal obligations. This requirement was intended to take into account the fact that the purchase price of the loss corporation's stock reflects not only asset value but also the value of the NOLs themselves. Accordingly, Congress attempted to balance overvaluation of the worth of the loss corporation with undervaluation of the rate of return on the loss corporation's assets.

b. *The value of the loss corporation.* Generally, in computing the §382 limitation, the value of the corporation is the value of its stock (including any preferred stock) immediately before the ownership change. §382(e)(1). This value may be reduced, however, if the loss corporation (i) has substantial nonbusiness assets, (ii) redeems its stock in connection with the ownership change, or (iii) receives a capital contribution in contemplation of the ownership change.

An "anti-stuffing" rule under §312(l)(1) addresses the last point. Because a loss corporation's ability to use its NOLs increases as its value increases, the shareholders of a loss corporation may have an incentive to make capital contributions to the loss corporation to increase its value immediately before an ownership change. Congress has discouraged this technique through §312(l)(1), under which the loss corporation's value is reduced by any capital contribution made "as part of a plan, a principal purpose of which is to avoid or increase" the §382 limitation. Although a finding of principal purpose is based on the facts and circumstances, this anti-stuffing rule does not apply to contributions made (i) on formation of the corporation (if the incorporated assets did not have a net unrealized built-in loss), (ii) before its first loss year, or (iii) in exchange for stock issued for services. See H.R. Rep. No. 841, at Sess. II-189; Notice 2008-78, 2008-41 I.R.B. 851 (also describing some safe harbors and announcing that future regulations will contain those rules).

Congress was also concerned that the value of a loss corporation might be inflated because of investment assets held by the loss corporation to generate income to be offset by the corporation's business NOLs. See Berry Petroleum Co. v. Commissioner, 104 T.C. 584 (1995) (exploring what constitutes nonbusiness assets). The general aim of §382 is to limit the use of acquired NOLs to offset a hypothetical level of income generated by the loss corporation's business assets. To the extent that a loss corporation's investment assets inflate the use of the NOLs, §382's purpose is circumvented. Section 382(l)(4) provides that if at least one-third of a loss corporation's assets consist of nonbusiness assets, the value of the corporation for purposes of the §382 limitation does not include the net value of the nonbusiness assets (i.e., their gross value reduced by any attributable indebtedness). In applying this one-third test, stock of a 50 percent or more owned subsidiary is not considered a nonbusiness asset. Instead, §382(l)(4)(E) adopts a "look-through" rule that deems the appropriate percentage of the subsidiary's assets to be owned by the parent.

The anti-stuffing and nonbusiness asset rules both attack steps taken to inflate the value of a loss corporation *before* an ownership change. In contrast, the redemption rule considers *post-change* redemptions of a loss corporation's stock that diminish its value. Under the redemption rule, the value of the loss corporation is reduced to account for any redemption or other corporate contraction that occurs "in connection with" an ownership change. §382(e)(2). The effect of the redemption rule is to discourage (or at least not encourage) "bootstrap" acquisitions in which the purchasers finance the acquisition of a loss corporation with the corporation's own assets. See Berry Petroleum Co. v. Commissioner, 104 T.C. 584 (1995) (exploring the definition of what constitutes a "corporate contraction").

7. *Special rules for insolvent or bankrupt corporations.* If a corporation is insolvent, its value may be $0, effectively eliminating all NOLs after an ownership change under the general rule of §382(a). Section 382(l)(5) provides a decidedly more favorable rule for corporations involved in bankruptcy or similar proceedings if at least 50 percent of the loss corporation's stock immediately after the ownership change is owned by former shareholders and certain historic long-term creditors. Under §382(l)(5), the ownership change does not limit use of the bankrupt corporation's pre-change losses, subject to two caveats. First, §382(l)(5) may require a significant reduction in the pre-change losses and excess credits that can be carried forward to post-change years. §382(l)(5)(B). In addition, if a second ownership change occurs within two years after the initial change, the §382 limitation is reduced to zero. Because of those caveats, a loss corporation may elect not to have §382(l)(5) apply. §382(l)(5)(H) (for the election).

If §382(l)(5) does not apply (by election or otherwise), §382(l)(6) applies to the ownership change of a bankrupt corporation. If §382(l)(6) applies, the bankrupt corporation's pre-change loss is subject to a §382 limitation, but in computing that limitation, the corporation's value is specially determined. That value equals the smaller of (i) the value of the corporation's stock immediately *after* the ownership change, or (ii) the gross value of its pre-change assets immediately *before* the ownership change. Treas. Regs. §1.382-9(j). See also *id.* at (k) and (l) (describing how the special valuation rules considered in Note 6(b) apply to a §382(l)(6) transaction).

8. *Built-in gains.* The purpose of §382 is to limit the use of a loss corporation's NOLs to the income deemed to be produced by the loss corporation. The income that can be offset by the NOLs is not only the expected future income from operations but also any inherent gain in a loss corporation's appreciated assets. Section

382(h)(1)(A) allows a loss corporation with a "net unrealized built-in gain" to increase its §382 limitation by a "recognized built-in gain" for any taxable year within the five-year period beginning on the change date (the recognition period). See Notice 90-27, 1990-1 C.B. 336 (recognition period extended for an installment sale). "Net unrealized built-in gain" is defined as the amount by which the value of a corporation's assets exceeds their aggregate basis immediately before the ownership change. A "recognized built-in gain" is defined as any gain recognized on the disposition of an asset during the recognition period if the taxpayer establishes that the asset was held by the loss corporation before the change date and that the gain accrued before the change date. See Notice 2003-65, 2003-40 I.R.B. 747 (providing two safe harbors to quantify recognized built-in gains, a §338 approach and a §1374 approach). The recognized built-in gain for any year cannot exceed the net unrealized built-in gain reduced by the recognized built-in gains for prior years in the recognition period.

9. *Built-in losses.* The term "prechange loss" to which §382(a) applies includes NOL carryforwards arising before the change year, the allocable portion of a corporation's NOLs for the year in which the change occurs, and certain recognized built-in losses and deductions. §382(d), (h)(1)(B). Built-in losses and deductions are limited, because, like NOLs, they may provide an incentive for a purchaser to acquire a loss corporation. For example, a corporation interested in purchasing a loss corporation with $1 million of NOLs might also be interested in purchasing a corporation with no NOLs but having assets with an aggregate basis of $1.1 million and fair market value of $100,000. The purpose of the restrictions on built-in losses is to curtail trafficking in a corporation with built-in loss assets that can be sold to offset the acquiring corporation's income from other sources. Under §382(h)(1)(B), if a loss corporation has a net unrealized built-in loss, recognized built-in losses during the five-year recognition period (in total up to the net unrealized built-in loss) are treated as pre-change losses and are therefore subject to the §382 limitation. For instance, suppose that an ownership change occurs in year 1, there is a net unrealized built-in loss attributable to a loss asset, and that asset is sold and the loss recognized in year 2. The loss will be subject to the §382 limitation along with pre-change NOLs. A de minimis rule ignores a corporation's net unrealized built-in loss (or gain) if it does not exceed the lesser of (a) 15 percent of the fair market value of the assets of the corporation or (b) $10 million. §382(h)(3)(B).

"Net unrealized built-in loss" is defined as the amount by which the aggregate adjusted bases of a corporation's assets exceeds the fair market value of the assets immediately before the ownership change. A "recognized built-in loss" is any loss recognized on the disposition of an asset during the five-year recognition period except to the extent the taxpayer can prove either that the asset was not held by the loss corporation immediately before the change date or that the loss exceeds the built-in loss in the asset on the change date. §382(h)(2)(B).

Depreciation or amortization deductions during the five-year recognition period are treated as recognized built-in losses to the extent attributable to the excess of adjusted basis over fair market value. §382(h)(2)(B). Also, amounts that accrue before the change date but are allowable as deductions after such date (such as deductions deferred under §267, §465, or §469) are treated as built-in losses. §382(h)(6).

10. *Anti-abuse rules.* Section 382 does not alter the continuing application of §269 (see pages 468-470 infra). Moreover, §382(m) authorizes the Secretary to

prescribe regulations to prevent avoidance of §382 through the use of related persons, pass-through entities, or other intermediaries. See, e.g., Treas. Regs. §1.382-2T(k)(4).

3. *Section 383*

Section 383(a) authorizes the Secretary to promulgate regulations that will limit capital loss carryforwards under §1212 to the taxable income of the loss corporation not exceeding the §382 limitation. Any capital loss carryforward used in a post-change year will reduce the §382 limitation that is applied to pre-change losses. Similar rules are adopted for excess credits (e.g., the alternative minimum tax credit under §53 or the foreign tax credit under §901) and passive activity losses.

4. *Section 384*

Section 382 does not inhibit a loss corporation from acquiring a profitable corporation if the acquisition does not cause an ownership change for the loss corporation. That acquisition does not involve a direct trafficking in losses. For example, suppose that *L* Corp., a loss corporation owned by *B*, acquires the stock of *P* Corp., a profitable corporation owned by *C*, for cash, and assume that *L* Corp. and *P* Corp. are both members of the same consolidated group and combine their income and loss on a consolidated return. The ability of *L* Corp. to use its pre-acquisition NOLs to offset *P* Corp.'s post-acquisition income, including gain recognized on any built-in gain assets, is not inhibited by §382. The same is true if *P* Corp. were merged into *L* Corp. so long as no ownership change in *L* Corp. takes place.

But suppose that *P* Corp. is a "burnt-out" tax shelter—an entity that has produced depreciation deductions and that now has a large built-in gain because the bases of its assets have been adjusted downward under §1016 while the property's fair market value has not decreased correspondingly. For example, assume that after generating depreciation deductions, *P* Corp. has depreciable assets with an aggregate basis of $50,000 and a fair market value of $300,000, subject to a $250,000 mortgage liability. If *P* Corp. sells the assets, the taxes on the $250,000 gain will exceed the $50,000 of cash that *P* Corp. can expect to receive on an arm's-length sale.

Suppose, instead, that *L* Corp. acquires the *P* Corp. stock, and either the corporations file a consolidated return or *P* Corp. merges into *L* Corp. In the absence of a remedial provision, *L* Corp.'s preexisting NOLs can be used to offset gain generated by the post-acquisition sale of the *P* Corp. assets. *L* Corp. may be happy to pay up to $50,000 in cash to make the acquisition, while *C*, the *P* Corp. shareholder, may be happy to receive any cash for his stock. To the extent *L* Corp. has paid more for the *P* Corp. stock because of its NOLs, *L* Corp. has shared the tax benefit of its NOLs with *C*.

Congress, unhappy with this technique of "laundering" the built-in gain from the sale of assets with pre-existing NOLs, enacted §384. That section originated as an effort to deny the use of any pre-acquisition NOLs by a loss corporation to offset any built-in gains of an acquired corporation recognized during a five-year recognition period following an acquisition. But the provision was broadly drafted so that it also applies to a corporation with built-in gains that acquires a corporation with pre-acquisition NOLs. Even though §382 might permit the use of some NOLs by the acquiring corporation in this situation, §384 may apply to deny their use against recognized built-in gains of the acquiring corporation.

Section 384 applies if one corporation acquires control of another corporation and either corporation is a gain corporation (i.e., a corporation with net unrealized built-in gain at the time of acquisition). Control is defined, broadly speaking, as stock representing at least 80 percent of vote and value of the acquired corporation. §384(c)(5). Section 384 also applies to an asset acquisition if the acquisition qualifies as a tax-free A, C, or acquisitive D reorganization. If both the acquiring and the acquired corporations were part of the same control group under §1563 (using a 50-percent-ownership test) at all times during the previous five-year period (or the term of a corporation's existence, if shorter), §384 will not apply.

If §384 is applicable, the provision denies the use of any "preacquisition loss" of a loss corporation (but not of the gain corporation) to offset any "recognized built-in gain" of the gain corporation during the five-year recognition period. §384(a). In the examples above, *L* Corp.'s NOLs cannot be used to offset gain recognized on the sale of *P* Corp.'s appreciated assets. The term "preacquisition loss" includes NOLs and net unrealized built-in losses that are recognized during a five-year recognition period. §384(c)(3)(A). The term "recognized built-in gain" refers to any gain on the disposition of an asset during a five-year recognition period except to the extent that it can be established that the asset was not held by the gain corporation on the acquisition date or that the gain was attributable to post-acquisition appreciation. §384(c)(1)(A).

In some cases, §§382 and 384 overlap; in others, one or neither of the provisions applies. Suppose *B* owns all the stock of *L* Corp., a company with NOLs, and *C*, unrelated to *B*, owns all the stock of *P* Corp., a company with built-in gains. If *L* Corp. purchases all the stock of *P* Corp. and together they file a consolidated return, §382 will not prevent the use of *L* Corp.'s losses against *P* Corp.'s future income because there is no ownership change for *L* Corp. Section 384, however, will prevent the use of the NOLs to offset any built-in gains recognized by *P* Corp. during the five-year recognition period.

If, instead, *L* Corp. merges into *P* Corp., and *C* ends up with more than 50 percent of the surviving corporation, §382 will limit the use of *L* Corp.'s NOLs, and §384 will also apply to limit any NOLs allowable under §382 that would otherwise be used to offset any of *P* Corp.'s recognized built-in gains. If *P* Corp. had no built-in gains before the merger, only §382 would apply to limit the use of the NOLs. If, in the preceding example, *L* Corp. and *P* Corp. were both long-standing subsidiaries of *H* Corp., neither §382 nor §384 would apply to limit the use of the NOLs.

Suppose *L* Corp. and *P* Corp., which are unrelated, form a joint venture partnership, *LP*, which attempts to allocate income under the partnership agreement disproportionately to *L* Corp. As a technical matter, there has been no triggering event for purposes of §382 or §384. Nevertheless, Congress has given the Service authority to apply these loss limitation principles in abuse situations. §§382(m)(3), 384(f)(1).

5. *Section 269*

Enacted in 1943, §269 provides for the disallowance of tax benefits when tax avoidance is the principal purpose for—

1. A person or persons acquiring control of a corporation; or
2. A corporation acquiring property of another corporation, not controlled by the acquiror or its shareholders, in a carryover-basis acquisition.

Section 269, which can apply to either an asset acquisition or a stock acquisition, provides the Service with a potentially powerful weapon because it applies subjectively: The provision can apply when the acquirer (or persons controlling the acquirer) possesses a "bad" state of mind. Under §269(a), for example, the Service can disallow the deduction of an NOL carryover if the control of a corporation or corporate assets was acquired for the principal purpose of avoiding or evading federal income tax by securing a deduction. To invoke §269, there are two requirements: (1) an acquisition and (2) a motive (i.e., tax avoidance as "the" principal purpose). The presence of §§382-384 does not limit the application of §269. Treas. Regs. §1.269-7. Therefore, it is possible that NOLs otherwise allowed under §382 may nevertheless be disallowed under §269.

On its face, §269 seems to cover the acquisition by a profitable business of a loss corporation with an NOL carryover. But does the provision apply to an acquisition of a profitable business by a loss corporation?

Commissioner v. British Motor Car Distributors

278 F.2d 392 (9th Cir. 1960)

Before Pope, Hamlin and Merrill, Circuit Judges.

MERRILL, Circuit Judge.

The taxpayer corporation incurred losses while engaged in the business of selling home appliances. It disposed of all its assets and the corporate shares were then sold to new owners, who used the corporation to operate a previously going automobile business. The question here presented is whether the taxpayer is entitled to carry over the losses incurred in the old business, where it is clear that the principal purpose of the acquisition of the taxpayer by the new owners was to avoid taxes.* The Tax Court, five judges dissenting, ruled in the affirmative. . . .

British Motor Car Company was a partnership consisting of Kjell H. Qvale, who had an 85 per cent interest, and his wife, who had a 15 per cent interest. The partnership had existed from about May 1, 1948, and engaged, in San Francisco, in the business of importing, distributing and selling foreign automobiles and parts. On September 11, 1951, the partnership submitted an offer to counsel for the Empire Home Equipment Company, in which the former offered to buy the outstanding stock of the corporation from its then owners for $21,250.00, upon the

* The tax years in question predate the enactment of §382.—EDS.

conditions, inter alia, that the corporation would increase its authorized capital and change its name. The offer was accepted. On November 2, 1951, Empire changed its name to British Motor Car Distributors, Ltd. On November 30, 1951, the partnership acquired all the outstanding shares of stock and immediately thereafter transferred its net assets (exclusive of the acquired shares) to the corporation in exchange for an additional 15,923 shares of stock. It is not claimed that there was any business purpose in the acquisition.

In the tax years ending October 31, 1952, and October 31, 1953, the corporation operated profitably in the automobile business. In its income and excess profits tax returns for those years, it carried forward the net operating losses that it had sustained in the appliance business in its fiscal years ending in 1949, 1950 and 1951. . . .

The Tax Court, in its construction of [§269(a)], adhered to its view as expressed in T.V.D. Company, 27 T.C. 879, 886, following the dictum in Alprosa Watch Company, 11 T.C. 240, to the effect that "it is manifest from the unambiguous terms of [§269] that it applies only to an acquiring corporation." The court points out that here the corporation is seeking to make use of its own previous loss; that it is the corporation, and not its new stockholders, which is securing the benefit of the deduction. *Alprosa Watch* is quoted to the effect that [§269(a)] "would seem to prohibit the use of a deduction, credit or allowance only by the acquiring person or corporation and not their use by the corporation whose control was acquired."

We do not read the language of the section, "securing the benefit of a deduction," as applying only to the actual taking of such deduction by the taxpayer. We should be closing our eyes to the realities of the situation were we to refuse to recognize that the persons who have acquired the corporation did so to secure *for themselves* a very real tax benefit to be realized by them *through* the acquired corporation and which they could not otherwise have realized.

This is not, as the corporation protests, a disregard of its corporate entity. Since [§269(a)] is expressly concerned with the persons acquiring control of a corporation, we must recognize such persons as, themselves, having a significant existence or entity apart from the corporation they have acquired. To ignore such independent entity simply because such persons are also the stockholders of their acquisition is to ignore the clear demands of [§269(a)]. It is not the fact that they are stockholders which subjects them to scrutiny. Rather, it is the fact that they are the persons specified by the section: those who have acquired control of the corporation. They may not escape the scrutiny which the section demands by attempting to merge their identity with that of their acquisition.

Section [§269(a)] contemplates that it shall not be limited to corporate acquirers. While Clause (2) is specifically limited to corporate acquirers, Clause (1) deals with "persons" as acquirers. That Clause (1) is to include noncorporate acquirers could not be more clearly implied. Nor do we find any sound reason, if this device for tax avoidance is to be struck down, for doing the job only when the tax avoider is a corporation. Legislative history indicates that a much broader construction was intended.[3]

3. H.R. No. 871, 78th Congress, First Session (1944 Cum. Bull. 901, 938):

> This section is designed to put an end promptly to any market for, or dealings in, interests in corporations or property which have as their objective the reduction through artifice of the income or excess profits tax liability.

To limit the effect of [§269(a)] to cases in which the taxpayer is seeking to deduct as its own a loss incurred by another would seem to limit Clause (1) to corporate acquirers. Who but a corporation could claim as its own a loss which had been incurred by an acquired corporation? Certainly an individual could not do so. The construction here contended for by the taxpayer corporation would then clearly frustrate legislative purpose. . . .

The corporation contends, as stated by the Tax Court, that the benefit to the stockholders (as distinguished from that to the corporate taxpayer) is too tenuous to bring the section into play. Tenuous or not, it is the benefit which actuated these persons in acquiring this corporation and is thus the very benefit with which this section is concerned. It is not for the courts to judge whether the benefit to the acquiring persons is sufficiently direct or substantial to be worth acquiring. That judgment was made by the acquirers. The judicial problem is whether the securing of the benefit was the principal purpose of the acquisition. If it was, the allowance of the deduction is forbidden.

Judgment reversed. The deductions claimed by the taxpayer are disallowed and judgment is entered for the Commissioner.

NOTES

1. *Acquisition requirement.* In *British Motor Car,* the stock of a floundering, inefficient corporation was sold, and the new owners changed the operation of the business to make it more efficient. Under these circumstances, should §269 come into play? Does the tax system create a disincentive for an inefficient business to become efficient, or does it simply remove tax benefits from consideration in a business decision, forcing the decision to rise or fall on its own merits?

It is now clear that §269 applies not only when NOL carryovers are acquired by a profitable business but also when the *benefits* of an NOL carryover are exploited by a loss corporation acquiring a profitable business. See also Vulcan Materials Co. v. United States, 446 F.2d 690, 698 (5th Cir. 1971). How would *British Motor Car* be decided under §382? Notice that the partnership that owned 0 percent of British Motor Car Distributors before the transaction in question owns 100 percent afterwards. Note that even if §382 would apply to this situation today, §269 might also apply to deny the use of the NOLs permitted by §382. Treas. Regs. §1.269-7.

The crux of the devices which have come to the attention of your committee has been some form of acquisition on or after the effective date of the Second Revenue Act of 1940, but the devices take many forms. Thus, the acquisition may be an acquisition of the shares of a corporation, or it may be an acquisition which follows by operation of law in the case of a corporation resulting from a statutory merger or consolidation. The person, or persons, making the acquisition likewise vary, as do the forms or methods of utilization under which tax avoidance is sought. Likewise, the tax benefits sought may be one or more of several deductions or credits, including the utilization of excess profits credits, carry-overs and carry-backs of losses or unused excess profits credits, and anticipated expense of other deductions. In the light of these considerations, the section has not confined itself to a description of any particular methods for carrying out such tax avoidance schemes but has included within its scope these devices in whatever form they may appear. For similar reasons, the scope of the terms used in the section is to be found in the objective of the section, namely, to prevent the tax liability from being reduced through the distortion or perversion effected through tax avoidance devices. . . .

If you conclude that both §§382 and 269 would apply in *British Motor Car* because of the ownership change, can §269 ever apply in a situation where §382 does not? Suppose *L* Corp., a loss corporation, acquires *P* Corp., a profitable corporation. If *L* Corp. and *P* Corp. file a consolidated return, the Service may in some circumstances argue that §269 prevents the use of *L* Corp.'s NOLs to offset *P* Corp.'s post-acquisition income. For example, if the former shareholders of *P* Corp. continue to exercise real control over *P* Corp.'s governance even though *L* Corp. has acquired enough control to permit consolidated reporting, §269 may apply. See, e.g., Briarcliff Candy Corp. v. Commissioner, 54 T.C.M. 667 (1987).

The acquisition test under §269 is triggered by either of the following: (1) Any person or persons acquire sufficient stock to hold at least 50 percent of either the total combined voting power or total value of all shares (§269(a)(1)) or (2) a corporation acquires property of another corporation with a carryover basis (§269(a)(2)). Section 269(a)(2) is used primarily to disallow NOL carryovers resulting from a corporate reorganization with an improper purpose involving unrelated corporations. Generally, an acquisitive reorganization would activate the carryover basis rule of §362 and would, in the absence of §269, enable the acquiring corporation to carry over the acquired corporation's tax attributes under §381. If the transferor is controlled directly or indirectly by the acquirer or its shareholders immediately before the acquisition, §269 does not apply. §269(a)(2). Accordingly, a merger between commonly controlled corporations will not result in the loss of any NOL carryovers. See Rev. Rul. 66-214, 1966-2 C.B. 98.

For a discussion of the acquisition requirement, see Hermes Consolidated, Inc. v. United States, 14 Cl. Ct. 398 (1988) (acquisition structured to avoid the 50-percent threshold was successful).

2. *Tax avoidance motive.* The term "evasion or avoidance of tax," though not defined, is not restricted to behavior that would precipitate criminal or civil fraud penalties. Treas. Regs. §1.269-1(b). Acquiring an NOL carryover that the acquiror would not otherwise enjoy will result in the avoidance of tax that would otherwise be paid on the profits of the acquiror. Note, however, that tax avoidance must be "the principal purpose" — the purpose that exceeds any other purpose in importance — often a difficult standard for the Service to meet. See Treas. Regs. §1.269-3(a). Determining the principal purpose is a question of fact. The regulations describe certain transactions that will ordinarily indicate the proscribed purpose. See, e.g., Treas. Regs. §1.269-3(b)(1), setting forth an example quite similar to the facts in *British Motor Car.*

Because tax reduction is often a motive behind an acquisition of a business with favorable tax attributes, what business purpose will suffice as a principal purpose of the acquisition? One typical business purpose for the acquisition of corporate control is the seller's insistence that the acquirer purchase stock rather than assets. See Glen Raven Mills v. Commissioner, 59 T.C. 1 (1972), a court-reviewed opinion in which the seller's insistence on a package deal in conjunction with some other factors was sufficient to constitute the principal purpose of the acquisition. What is the result if the *purchaser* insists on acquiring stock? For other business purposes, see American M.A.R.C., Inc. v. United States, 19 A.F.T.R.2d 929 (C.D. Cal. 1967) (a genuine belief that the acquired business could be turned around); Fairfield Communities Land Co. v. Commissioner, 47 T.C.M. (CCH) 1194 (1984) (acquisition of loss corporation to obtain cash and broaden the shareholder base); Clarksdale Rubber Co. v. Commissioner, 45 T.C. 234 (1965) (expansion of acquiror's business); Naeter Brothers Publishing Co. v. Commissioner, 42 T.C. 1 (1964) (combined operation favored by lenders).

Suppose an acquisition is 40 percent motivated by tax avoidance, 30 percent motivated by a desire for expansion, and 30 percent motivated by a desire to "go public" (which the acquisition would allow). Is tax avoidance the primary motive, or in making that determination, can a corporation combine all non-tax motives? In U.S. Shelter Corp. v. United States, 13 Cl. Ct. 606 (1987), the court allowed the corporation to combine the non-tax motives, concluding that §269 did not apply.

Authority is split with respect to whether §269 applies to losses incurred after an acquisition. Compare Borge v. Commissioner, 405 F.2d 673 (2d Cir. 1968) (§269 can apply to post-acquisition losses), with Herculite Protective Fabrics Corp. v. Commissioner, 387 F.2d 475 (3d Cir. 1968) (post-acquisition losses were true economic loss to acquirer and not subject to §269).

3. *Section 269(b).* Recall that pursuant to §§332 and 334(b), a parent liquidating a subsidiary generally recognizes no gain or loss but inherits the subsidiary's basis in its assets. See pages 272-285 supra. Under §381(a)(1), a parent can succeed to the tax attributes of its liquidated subsidiary as well. If the parent has purchased the stock of a subsidiary, the parent can make an election under §338 to step up (or step down) the basis of the subsidiary's assets. See discussion at pages 310-313 supra. If the election is made, the subsidiary loses its tax attributes, including any NOL carryovers (although the NOLs can offset any gain on the deemed §338 sale). If no election is made and the subsidiary is liquidated, the parent might succeed to the subsidiary's tax attributes, including its NOL carryovers. See §381.

Under §269(b)(1), the Service can disallow any deduction or other tax attribute that otherwise would be acquired if (1) there is a qualified stock purchase, (2) a §338 election is not made, (3) the acquired corporation is liquidated pursuant to a plan adopted within two years of acquisition, and (4) the principal purpose of the liquidation is tax avoidance. The liquidation of a newly purchased subsidiary ordinarily indicates that the principal purpose of the liquidation is tax avoidance, in the absence of evidence to the contrary. H.R. Rep. No. 432 (pt. II), 98th Cong., 2d Sess. 1623 (1984).

4. *Relationship between §§269 and 382.* Section 382 is triggered by objective criteria, §269 by a subjective tax avoidance purpose. Because of its breadth, §269 can apply to disallow an NOL carryover that would not be disallowed under §382. Treas. Regs. §1.269-7. Indeed, deliberate avoidance of §382(a) may indicate that use of the NOL carryovers was the principal purpose for the acquisition. Luke v. Commissioner, 351 F.2d 568 (7th Cir. 1965). Conversely, the application of §382 may suggest the absence of a tax avoidance purpose.

PROBLEMS

13-1. *B* owns all the stock of *L* Corp., which has $2 million of NOL carryovers. *P* Corp. is a profitable business that earns approximately $300,000 a year. What effect does each of the following transactions have on the NOL carryovers?

a. *B* contributes sufficient cash to *L* Corp. to enable *L* Corp. to purchase the assets of *P* Corp.

b. *L* Corp. sells all its assets and uses the proceeds to purchase the assets of *P* Corp.
c. *L* Corp. acquires the stock of *P* Corp. for cash, *P* Corp. liquidates, and *L* Corp. continues to operate *P* Corp.'s profitable business.

13-2. Discuss the application of §382 in the following situations:

a. *L* Corp., a corporation with NOL carryforwards, is closely held by four unrelated individuals, *A*, *B*, *C*, and *D*, each of whom owns 25 percent of the *L* Corp. stock. There is a public offering of *L* Corp.'s stock. No person who purchases stock in the offering acquires 5 percent or more, and none of *A*, *B*, *C*, or *D* acquires any additional stock. As a result of the offering, the new shareholders own stock representing 60 percent of the outstanding *L* Corp. stock. Consider the restrictions, if any, on *L* Corp.'s use of the NOL carryforwards.
b. Suppose in (a) that *L* Corp. is publicly held, with no shareholder owning more than 2 percent of the outstanding stock.
c. Suppose *L* Corp. is wholly owned by *B*. *L* Corp. merges into *P* Corp., a publicly held corporation in which no shareholder owns more than a 2-percent interest. After the merger, *B* owns 60 percent of *P* Corp. Two years later, *P* Corp. sells additional stock to *C* equal to 50 percent of the stock value.

13-3. Determine the tax consequences in the following situations:

a. *X* Corp. is wholly owned by individual *A*, and its stock has a value of $3,000; *X* Corp. has NOL carryforwards of $10,000. *Y* Corp. is wholly owned by individual *B*, and its stock has a value of $9,000; *Y* Corp. has NOL carryforwards of $100. *Z* Corp. is owned by individual *C*, and its stock has a value of $18,000; *Z* Corp. has no NOL carryforwards. *X* Corp., *Y* Corp., and *Z* Corp. consolidate into *W* Corp. in a transaction that qualifies under §368(a)(1)(A). The applicable long-term tax-exempt rate on such date is 10 percent. As a result of the consolidation, *A* receives 10 percent of *W* stock, *B* receives 30 percent, and *C* receives 60 percent. *W*'s taxable income before any reduction for its NOLs is $1,400. Consider whether the NOLs can be used to offset *W*'s income.
b. Suppose in (a) that *X* Corp. holds an asset with a basis of $1,000 and a fair market value of $1,600 at the time of the consolidation. The asset is sold by *W* in year 1, thereby producing $600 of *W*'s $1,400 of taxable income.
c. Suppose in (a) that *X* Corp. holds an asset with a basis of $1,600 and a fair market value of $1,000 at the time of the consolidation. The asset is sold by *W*. Excluding this transaction and the use of any NOLs, *W* Corp. has taxable income of $2,000.

13-4. *L* Corp., a loss company with pre-acquisition losses, is wholly owned by *B*. *P* Corp., a profitable corporation with built-in gains, is wholly owned by *C*. Consider whether §382 or §384 or both apply in the subparts below and what tax consequences follow.

a. *L* Corp. purchases all the *P* Corp. stock for cash and does not elect §338.
b. Suppose in (a) that *L* Corp. makes a §338 election for the *P* stock purchase.
c. *P* Corp. purchases all the *L* Corp. stock for cash and does not elect §338.
d. *L* Corp. merges into *P* Corp., and *B* ends up with 60 percent of the *P* Corp. stock.
e. Suppose in (d) that *B* ends up with 40 percent of the *P* Corp. stock.
f. Suppose *L* Corp. and *P* Corp. form *L-P*, a joint venture partnership. Under the *L-P* partnership agreement, much of the *L-P* income is allocated to *L* Corp.

B. AFFILIATED CORPORATIONS

In principle, every corporation reports its income and deductions separately from other corporations. But see §482 (authorizing the Service to allocate tax items among related taxpayers to prevent tax evasion or clearly reflect income). For a discussion of §482, see pages 508-516 infra. The consolidated return provisions offer an exception to this principle, allowing several corporations to combine their income and loss.

Why would individuals choose to operate a business or businesses through multiple corporations rather than through a single corporation? There may be a host of reasons—both non-tax and tax motivated. Some of the non-tax reasons for maintaining, acquiring, or forming multiple corporations include (1) minimizing potential tort liability (see Walkovszky v. Carlton, 18 N.Y.2d 414 (1966) [ownership of taxi fleet in many corporations, each owning only one or two cabs]); (2) avoiding regulatory restraints on combining businesses within a single corporation; (3) avoiding state law complications; (4) securing more favorable contractual arrangements; (5) seeking to alleviate labor problems; and (6) maintaining the existence of corporate goodwill.

Using multiple corporations may also offer tax advantages, including (1) the ability to use different taxable years or make different tax elections; (2) the reallocation of income to avoid progressive tax rates; (3) the availability of multiple tax benefits, such as the accumulated earnings tax credit; (4) more favorable disposition of unwanted assets, e.g., through a tax-free spin-off (see Chapter 11 supra); and (5) greater flexibility with regard to earnings and profits and shareholder distributions. Many of these tax advantages have been limited for related corporations, however. See Chapter 15.

Despite these possible tax advantages, an affiliated group of corporations often elects to file a single return that combines the income, deductions, gain, and loss of its members. See §§1501-1504. A group that makes this election is called a consolidated group. Note that only corporations controlled by a common parent corporation may make the election. Thus, if *B*, an individual, owns the stock of *X* Corp. and *Y* Corp., the two corporations may not elect to file a consolidated return. If *B* owns the stock of *H* Corp., *H* Corp. owns the stock of *X* Corp. and *Y* Corp., and the corporations are otherwise eligible to do so, they may elect to file a consolidated return.

Once the election is made for a taxable year, the consolidated group must continue to file on a consolidated basis unless the Commissioner consents to a discontinuance or the group terminates. Treas. Regs. §1.1502-75(a)(2) and (c). Under a broad statutory grant (§1502), the Treasury has promulgated detailed regulations that describe how a consolidated group applies the Code. As the Code has become more complex, so have the consolidated return regulations. These regulations constitute the "law" of consolidated returns, and by electing to file consolidated returns, a group consents to the regulations. See §1501.

NOTES

1. *Eligibility for filing.* A consolidated return may be filed by an "affiliated group" of corporations. Under §1504, that term means certain "includible" corporations linked through specified stock ownership requirements. Most corporations are includible, with certain exceptions such as tax-exempt corporations, certain life insurance companies, many foreign corporations, regulated investment companies, and S corporations. §1504(b) (defining includible corporations). But see United States Padding Corp. v. Commissioner, 865 F.2d 750 (6th Cir. 1989) (subsidiary formed to comply with foreign government practice and policy was an includible corporation). If a consolidated return election is made by an affiliated group, all group members must join in filing a consolidated return.

More specifically, an affiliated group includes its common parent and subsidiaries, and a subsidiary is (a) any corporation in which the common parent owns an affiliated interest, and (b) any other corporation in which other members collectively own an affiliated interest. §1504(a)(1). For this purpose, an affiliated interest in a corporation is at least 80 percent of the total voting power of its stock plus at least 80 percent of the total value of its stock. §1504(a)(2). See Alumax, Inc. v. Commissioner, 109 T.C. 133 (1997) (interpreting the 80-percent-voting-control requirement of §1502(a)). Note that the direct ownership requirement rules out corporations owned by an individual or group of individuals or by a nonincludible corporation.

Under the stock ownership rules of §1504(a), "stock" does not include nonvoting, nonconvertible, "pure vanilla" preferred stock described in §1504(a)(4). Subsidiaries often issue such stock to raise outside equity capital without jeopardizing their right to join in the group's consolidated return. Under §1504(a)(5), options are generally ignored in determining eligibility unless not treating the option as exercised would result in substantial federal tax savings and it is reasonably certain that the option will be exercised. Treas. Regs. §1.1504-4.

Even with a statutory definition of "affiliated group," some courts have denied the privilege of filing consolidated returns to a corporation that acquires another corporation solely to use its tax attributes on a consolidated return. For example, in Elko Realty Co. v. Commissioner, 29 T.C. 1012, aff'd per curiam, 260 F.2d 949 (3d Cir. 1958), a successful corporation acquired the stock of two other corporations that had been operating at a loss. Relying in part on the business purpose principle of Gregory v. Helvering, page 352 supra, the court denied the parent's right to file a consolidated return in the absence of a business purpose for the acquisition. See also R.P. Collins & Co. v. United States, 303 F.2d 142 (1st Cir. 1962) (§269 used to deny loss deductions on consolidated return). But see Zanesville Investment Co. v. Commissioner, 335 F.2d 507 (6th Cir. 1964) (consolidated returns permitted when post-affiliation losses of some members offset income from other members).

In light of the current regulations that restrict the use of pre-affiliation and some post-affiliation net operating losses regardless of acquisition purpose, is the approach of the court in *Elko Realty* still appropriate? See Treas. Regs. §§1.1502-15, 1.1502-21, 1.1502-22. Even when these restrictions apply, the regulations do not deny consolidated return treatment as did the court in *Elko Realty*.

2. *Election to file a consolidated return and other accounting considerations.* A consolidated return may be filed only if all affiliated corporations consent. §1501. Once an election is made, the affiliated group must continue to file on a consolidated basis unless the Commissioner grants permission to discontinue for "good cause," even if new members join the group. Treas. Regs. §1.1502-75(a)(2).

The taxable year for a consolidated group is based on the common parent's annual accounting period. In general, subsidiaries must adopt the parent's period. Treas. Regs. §1.1502-76(a)(1). But the subsidiaries are not required to adopt the accounting method of the common parent. Instead, each member of the group employs the method that it would use if it filed a separate return. Treas. Regs. §1.1502-17(a). But see *id.* at (c) (for an anti-avoidance rule).

If a corporation is a member of a consolidated group during any part of the group's year, the corporation is severally liable for the entire tax of the group for that year. Treas. Regs. §1.1502-6(a). But see *id.* at (b) (for a limited exception). This liability cannot be avoided or reduced by intercompany agreements, but such agreements will be effective as between the parties and are frequently used by consolidated group members. See Rev. Rul. 73-605, 1973-2 C.B. 109 and Treas. Regs. §1.1502-6(c).

3. *Computation of consolidated taxable income: in general.* A consolidated group combines the tax items of its members in computing its overall tax. Through this combination, a consolidated group may offset one member's loss against another member's income, the main benefit of filing consolidated returns. In this significant way, the group is treated like a single entity for federal income tax purposes.

A consolidated group's tax liability is based on its "consolidated taxable income" (CTI). Using CTI, the group computes its gross consolidated tax liability in accordance with §§11, 541, 531, 1201, and so on. Finally, it subtracts any available consolidated credits, including the investment credit or foreign tax credit. Treas. Regs. §1.1502-2.

A group's CTI for any taxable year includes the common parent's tax items for the whole year and each subsidiary's tax items for the portion of that year for which it was a member. Treas. Regs. §1.1502-76(b). Thus, if a subsidiary leaves or enters a consolidated group during the group's year, the subsidiary's items must be allocated between its separate and consolidated periods. *Id.*

A group's CTI is the sum of each member's separate taxable income (STI) plus a number of consolidated items. Treas. Regs. §1.1502-11(a). Broadly speaking, a member's STI includes all of its tax items except for those computed on a consolidated basis. Treas. Regs. §1.1502-12. Tax items computed on a consolidated basis (i.e., as if the group was a single corporation) include net operating loss, capital gain and loss, §1231 gain and loss, any charitable contribution deduction, and any dividends-received deduction. *Id.* For example, if a consolidated group has two members, *P* and *S*, and *S* has $100 of §1231 loss while *P* has $150 of §1231 gain, that gain and loss will be characterized as long-term capital gain and loss, because the group, as a whole, has a net §1231 gain. See Treas. Regs. §1.1502-23 (for the computation of the consolidated net §1231 gain or loss); §1231(a)(1).

A member computes its STI under the Code as a separate corporation but with several modifications. In addition to excluding any items computed on a consolidated basis, it takes into account other rules in the consolidated return regulations that affect income (and loss) computations. For example, STI is computed by considering rules relating to intercompany transactions, excess loss accounts, investment basis adjustments, earnings and profits, and various consolidated loss limitations. Treas. Reg. §1.1502-11.

4. *Intercompany transactions.* One of the most significant aspects of the consolidated return regulations is their treatment of transactions between members, called intercompany transactions. To the extent possible, the intercompany transaction rules treat members like divisions of a single corporation. Thus, an intercompany transaction is not intended to create, eliminate, defer, or accelerate the group's income as a whole. Treas. Regs. §1.1502-13(a)(1). Some highlights of these complicated rules are described below.

A consolidated group accounts for intercompany transactions using two main rules, the "matching" and "acceleration" rules. See Treas. Regs. §1.1502-13(c) and (d). Under the matching rule, the timing, holding period, and attributes of tax items related to an intercompany transaction are accounted for using a single-entity approach. However, the location and amount of those items are determined by treating the members as separate corporations. Treas. Regs. §1.1502-13(a)(2).

An intercompany transaction is a transaction between corporations that are members immediately after the transaction. *Id.* at (b)(1)(i). Note that Treas. Regs. §1.1502-13 refers to the member transferring property (e.g., by sale, lease, or loan) or providing services in an intercompany transaction as "S" and the member receiving the property or services as "B." See Treas. Regs. §1.1502-13(b)(1). For convenience, this description does as well.

Broadly stated, the matching rule is intended to assure that the overall income or loss of the group is unaffected by an intercompany transaction until S or B deals with an outsider. Under the matching rule, S takes its income, gain, or loss on the intercompany transaction into account as B takes its "corresponding" items into account under its separate accounting method. Treas. Regs. §1.1502-13(c)(2)(i). See also *id.* at (b)(3) (defining B's corresponding items as its income, gain, deduction, or loss from the intercompany transaction or from the property acquired in that transaction). The amount that S takes into account reflects the difference for the year between B's actual tax items and what those items would have been if S and B had been divisions of a single corporation and the intercompany transaction had occurred between those divisions. See Treas. Regs. §1.1502-13(b)(4).

For example, assume that S holds land with a $6,000 basis and $9,000 value and sells the land to B for $9,000. Under §1001(c), S recognizes a $3,000 gain, and under §1012, B takes a $9,000 basis in that land. Under the matching rule, however, S's $3,000 gain is deferred (i.e., not then reported on the group's consolidated return). If B sells the land to another member, S's gain continues to be deferred. Treas. Regs. §1.1502-13(j)(4). Suppose, however, that B sells the land to an unrelated nonmember, X, for $11,000. On the sale, B recognizes a $2,000 gain, S also takes its $3,000 gain into account, and both gains are reported on the group's return. S takes its $3,000 gain into account because it fully reflects the difference between B's actual gain ($2,000), and what B's gain would have been if S and B had been divisions of a single corporation ($5,000). If they had been divisions, B would have acquired the land with a $6,000 basis and therefore would have recognized a $5,000 gain on the sale.

Suppose that B had sold the land to X on the installment basis and could report its $2,000 gain using the installment method. See §453. The matching principle also requires that S takes its gain into account on the installment method as B reports its gain on the installment sale. Treas. Regs. §1502-13(c)(7)(ii) (example 5). For example, under the installment method, if B reports half of its gain in the year of the sale, S would take half of its gain into account that year as well.

Suppose that instead of S's selling land to B, S sold B a depreciable asset, still realizing a $3,000 gain. Assume that for the first year after the sale, B's actual depreciation deduction on the asset is $600, but if S and B had been divisions of a single corporation, its depreciation deduction would have been only $400. In that first year, S must take into account $200 of its $3,000 gain, reflecting the difference between B's actual depreciation deduction ($600) and what its deduction would have been if S and B had been divisions ($400). Treas. Regs. §1.1502-13(c)(7)(ii) (example 4). Further, because B's depreciation deductions can offset ordinary income, the matching principle requires that S's income must also be ordinary. See Treas. Regs. §1.1502-13(c)(4)(i).

Note that the matching rule does not always defer S's tax items. For example, assume that at the beginning of year 1, S loans B $100, with B obligated to pay S $5 interest at the end of each year for 10 years, when the principal amount of the loan must be repaid. Assume that each year, B deducts the $5 interest payment. S also takes $5 of interest income into account each year, reflecting the $5 difference between B's actual interest deduction ($5) and what its deduction would have been if S and B had been divisions of a single corporation ($0) (because there can be no loan between divisions for tax purposes). Thus, in this example, S and B account for the items on the loan under Treas. Regs. §1.1502-13 just as they would have if they were not members of the same consolidated group.

Consider again the example where S sells land with a $6,000 basis to B for $9,000, and S defers its $3,000 gain under the matching rule. Would S be able to continue deferring its gain if either S or B left the consolidated group but B retained the land? The answer is no, because of the acceleration rule, a kind of "last clear chance" rule. Under that rule, S must take its intercompany items into account immediately before it first becomes impossible to treat S and B as divisions of a single corporation. Treas. Regs. §1.1502-13(d)(1)(i)(A). Stated differently, S must take its intercompany items into account once the matching rule can no longer apply. Thus, if either S or B left the group, it would no longer be possible to treat S and B as divisions of a single corporation, and S's $3,000 deferred gain would be "triggered."

Because the consolidated return regulations provide their own recognition and nonrecognition rules for intercompany transactions, they also provide that many of the Code's more general provisions do not apply in the consolidated context. Thus, there are no §1031 exchanges between members of a consolidated group, Treas. Regs. §1.1502-80(f), and §304 does not apply to sales between consolidated corporations, Treas. Regs. §1.1502-80(b). On the other hand, many anti-abuse provisions continue to apply to intercompany transactions including §§269, 482, and 1091. Treas. Regs. §1.1502-13(a)(4).

5. *Intercompany distributions.* An intercompany distribution is an intercompany transaction to which §301 applies. Treas. Regs. §1.1502-13(f)(2)(i). Typically, the shareholder member excludes the entire intercompany distribution from gross income, no matter how the distribution is treated under §301(c). *Id.* at (f)(2)(ii) (excluding the distribution to the extent it results in a negative adjustment under

the investment adjustment rules, described below). The shareholder member also takes a basis in any distributed property equal to its fair market value. §301(d).

The distributing member recognizes any gain *or* loss on an intercompany distribution, because the regulations provide that the principles of §311(b) apply to loss as well as gain. Treas. Regs. §1.1502-13(f)(2)(iii). The member accounts for that recognized gain or loss under the matching and acceleration rules described in Note 4. Section 311(a) continues to apply to a member's §301 distribution to a *nonmember*, however, so that a distributing member does not recognize loss on that distribution.

Most intercompany liquidations of solvent subsidiaries are described in §332. Under that section, a shareholder member recognizes no gain or loss on its receipt of a liquidating distribution. Note that for §332 to apply to a shareholder, the shareholder must own an affiliated interest in the liquidating corporation, and for this purpose, a consolidated group member is deemed to own all stock owned by the group. Treas. Regs. §1.1502-34. Thus, §332 may apply to all distributions to shareholder members in an intercompany liquidation.

In a §332 liquidation, the liquidating corporation recognizes no gain or loss on any liquidating distributions to which §337 applies, and it recognizes gain and may recognize loss on its other liquidating distributions. §337(a); §336(a); but see §336(d)(1). Cf. §336(d)(3). For §337 to apply to an intercompany liquidating distribution, the shareholder member must *actually* own an affiliated interest in the liquidating subsidiary, since the special consolidated ownership rule discussed above does not apply. See §337(c) (second sentence). Thus, the liquidating subsidiary recognizes any gain and may recognize any loss on an intercompany distribution *other than* to an actual "80-percent" shareholder member. That recognized amount will be deferred and taken into account by the shareholder members under the matching rule. See Treas. Regs. §1.1502-13(j)(2) (describing successors). To the extent that the liquidating corporation does not recognize gain or loss on a §332 intercompany liquidating distribution of property, the distributee member takes a transferred basis in the property, preserving that gain or loss. §334(b)(1).

Note that if one member has sold subsidiary stock to another member at a gain, that gain is deferred under the matching rule. Treas. Regs. §1.1502-13(c). If the subsidiary then liquidates under §332, the selling member must take the deferred gain into account, even though the stock never left the group. Treas. Regs. §1.1502-13(f)(4). However, this harsh result may be mitigated under several regulatory elections. *Id.* at (f)(5); *id.* at (c)(6)(ii).

6. *Investment basis adjustments and excess loss accounts.* A consolidated group adjusts its basis in subsidiary stock to reflect the subsidiary's tax items. Cf. §705(a) (for similar adjustments to a partner's basis in a partnership interest). These basis or "investment" adjustments are intended to prevent the subsidiary's tax items from being taken into account a second time when the group sells its subsidiary stock. See Treas. Regs. §1.1502-32(a)(1).

Under the investment adjustment system, a shareholder member increases its basis in subsidiary stock for positive adjustments and decreases that basis for negative adjustments. *Id.* at (b)(2). The subsidiary's taxable and tax-exempt income results in positive adjustments and its absorbed losses, noncapital, nondeductible expenses, and distributions result in negative adjustments. See *id.* at (b)(3). For example, suppose that *P* and *S* are members of a consolidated group and *P* owns all *S* stock with a $200 basis. In a taxable year, *S* has $100 of taxable income and $50 of tax-exempt income and *S* makes a $60 distribution to *P*. *P*'s basis in its *S* stock will be increased by $90 to $290, reflecting the excess of the $150 of taxable and tax-exempt income (the positive adjustments) over the $60 distribution (the negative adjustment).

Each year, those adjustments are allocated among the subsidiary's shares, including shares owned by nonmembers. *Id.* at (c)(1). (An amount allocated to a share owned by a nonmember has no effect on that share's basis, however. *Id.*) Broadly speaking, the allocations are made among subsidiary shares in a manner intended to reflect changes in value of the shares. See generally *id.* at (c)(2) and (3).

To treat a consolidated group more like a single entity, the consolidated return regulations allow a member to have a *negative basis* in subsidiary stock, called an excess loss account or ELA. See generally Treas. Regs. §1.1502-19. Because of this mechanism, a group can take into account all of a subsidiary's losses in, and exclude all subsidiary distributions from, CTI, even if the losses and distributions exceed the group's positive basis in subsidiary stock. However, the group must include the ELA in income if, for example, it sells the subsidiary stock to a nonmember. Treas. Regs. §1.1502-19(b)(1)(i) and (c)(1).

For instance, assume that *P* has a $30 basis in the stock of *S*, its wholly owned subsidiary, and that *P* and *S* join in filing a consolidated return. If *S* suffers a $50 loss that the group absorbs, *P*'s *S* stock will have a $20 ELA ($30 starting basis minus $50 absorbed loss). If *P* later sells the *S* stock for $25, it will recognize a $45 gain—the $25 sales proceeds plus the $20 ELA. The group's overall $5 tax loss related to *S* ($50 of losses less $45 stock gain) matches *P*'s $5 economic loss on its *S* stock investment—$30 paid for the stock less $25 received on the sale.

7. *Subsidiary stock loss.* After the *General Utilities* doctrine was repealed, some consolidated groups used the investment adjustment rules to create noneconomic loss in subsidiary stock. They also structured transactions to enjoy a subsidiary stock loss and a duplicate subsidiary asset loss. Concerned with both noneconomic and duplicate losses, Treasury responded with the subsidiary loss disallowance rules.

Under Treas. Regs. §1.1502-20, first issued in 1990, a group's loss on subsidiary stock was generally disallowed to the extent it exceeded the sum of three factors. Treas. Regs. §1.1502-20(c) (2001) (laying out those factors). Although the three factors were intended to allow the group to recognize its economic loss when it sold the subsidiary stock, in practice, they proved less than perfect.

Treas. Regs. §1.1502-20 was invalidated, at least in part, by Rite Aid Corp. v. United States, 255 F.3d 1359 (Fed. Cir. 2001). Treasury quickly withdrew the regulation and, after several intervening steps, has replaced it with Treas. Regs. §1.1502-36.

Treas. Regs. §1.1502-36 addresses both noneconomic loss and loss duplication with three main rules that may apply on the group's transfer of subsidiary stock at a loss, rules that are technically masterful but extraordinarily complex. First, under Treas. Regs. §1.1502-36(b), the group may redetermine its basis in transferred and non-transferred subsidiary stock, a rule that complements the investment adjustment rules of Treas. Regs. §1.1502-32 and is an analog to §704(c). Second, the group's loss on subsidiary stock may be disallowed, in whole or in part, under a basis-reduction rule found in Treas. Regs. §1.1502-36(c). Technically, under that rule, the group reduces its basis of subsidiary stock, with the reduction intended to avoid noneconomic loss. Even with the basis-redetermination and basis-reduction rules, a group could dispose of subsidiary stock at a loss but the loss could be duplicated in subsidiary tax attributes (like basis). To the extent of that duplication, the attribute-reduction rule, found in Treas. Regs. §1.1502-36(d), requires the subsidiary (and perhaps lower-tier corporations) to reduce tax attributes, including NOL carryovers and basis.

8. *Limitations on consolidated reporting.* If a group acquires a new member with loss carryovers, the use of those carryovers may be restricted under §382 and the separate return limitation year or "SRLY" rules. Generally, a group's use of a member's pre-consolidation or SRLY loss carryovers is limited to the member's *cumulative* contribution to the group's CTI. Treas. Regs. §1.1502-21(c)(1)(i). See also Treas. Regs. §1.1502-15 (describing how the SRLY rules apply to a new member's built-in deductions). If the loss member is acquired as part of a subgroup, the SRLY limitation is applied by looking to the subgroup as a whole, not just the loss member. *Id.* at (c)(2). Similar rules exist for other tax attributes. See Treas. Regs. §1.1502-4(f) (foreign tax credit carryovers); Treas. Regs. §1.1502-22(c) (capital loss carryovers).

The reach of the SRLY rule is substantially limited by the overlap rule. See Treas. Regs. §1.1502-15(g); Treas. Regs. §1.1502-21(g). Under the overlap rule, the SRLY limitations generally do not apply if a member joins the group in a transaction that causes §382 to apply or within six months of such a transaction.

Section 382 may also apply to the group as a whole, and Treas. Regs. §§1.1502-90-1.1502-99 describe that application. If a loss consolidated group has an ownership change, it will generally apply §382 like a single corporation. Treas. Regs. §1.1502-91(a)(1). See pages 457-466 supra for a general discussion of §382. To compute its consolidated §382 limitation, the group determines its value as the aggregate value of each member's stock, other than stock owned directly or indirectly by any member. Treas. Regs. §1.1502-93(b)(1). Thus, the group's value includes the value of the stock held by nonmembers.

A group has an ownership change if its common parent has an ownership change, and as a general rule, this determination is made by considering only changes in the ownership of common parent stock. (This general rule is referred to as the "parent change" method.) Treas. Regs. §1.1502-92(b)(1). A loss group may also have an ownership change in rare cases under a supplemental method. See *id.* at (c) (for a description of the supplemental method).

9. *Advantages and disadvantages of consolidated reporting.* The notable advantage of an affiliated group's filing consolidated returns is that one member's loss may offset another member's income. Further, intercompany distributions are tax free to the distributee member, and the gain and loss recognized by the distributor member are deferred under the intercompany transaction rules.

The notable disadvantage is that the group must cope with the complex and lengthy consolidated return regulations. Further, once a group begins filing a consolidated return, it must continue filing those returns. In addition, members cannot adopt different taxable years or make inconsistent elections. Finally, a group's loss on its sale of subsidiary stock may be disallowed.

Thus, the consolidated return regulations offer consolidated groups a mixed blessing. Nevertheless, many affiliated groups will elect consolidated status so that one member's loss can offset another member's income, the often irresistible lure of consolidation.

PROBLEMS

13-5. Forco, a foreign corporation that cannot make use of U.S. tax benefits, is planning a new U.S. venture to be operated through *L* Corp. It is expected that *L* Corp. will generate tax losses in its first several years. To make use of the expected losses, Forco finds a U.S. partner, *P* Corp., a profitable U.S. corporation. Forco and *P* Corp. form *L* Corp., with Forco receiving preferred stock with a fair market value of $800,000 and *P* Corp. receiving common stock with a fair market value of $200,000. The preferred stock is preferred as to dividends and on liquidation, but it has an adjustable rate feature whereby the level of dividends is set by reference to certain yields of U.S. Treasury obligations. In addition, this preferred stock is convertible into another class of preferred stock, identical in all respects to the outstanding preferred except that the adjustable rate feature references different U.S. Treasury obligations. Can *L* Corp. and *P* Corp. file a consolidated return allowing *P* Corp. to offset its profits with *L* Corp.'s losses? Consider §1504(a).

13-6. *P* Corp. has three wholly owned subsidiaries having the following items of income and loss:

	X	*Y*	*Z*
Ordinary business income (loss)	$300	($80)	$ 40
§1231 gains (loss)	80	40	(40)
Capital gains (loss)	20	40	(100)
§170 contributions	60		

What is the group's consolidated taxable income?

13-7. In problem 13-6, what are the tax consequences of the following transactions?

a. *P* Corp. leases computer software from *X* Corp., paying an annual $300 royalty.
b. *P* Corp. pays interest of $60 to *Y* Corp. on an intercorporate loan.
c. *P* Corp. owns land with a $300 basis. In Year 1, it sells that land to *Z* Corp. for $400, the land's fair market value. *Z* Corp. resells the land in year 2 to an unrelated party for $650.
d. Suppose in (c) that *Z* Corp. sells the property on the installment method.
e. Suppose in (c) that the property sold to *Z* Corp. is depreciable property that *Z* Corp. uses in its trade or business. *Z* Corp. depreciates the property using a straight-line method over 10 years.

13-8. Discuss the tax consequences of the following situations:

a. *P* Corp. owns all the stock of *X* Corp., with which it files a consolidated return. *P* Corp.'s basis in the *X* Corp. stock is $100. In year 1, *X* Corp. earns $30 and makes no distribution. In year 2, *X* Corp. earns $20 and makes a $50 distribution to *P* Corp.
b. Suppose in (a) that in year 1, *P* Corp. earns $200 and *X* Corp. has a net operating loss of $160. In year 2, *P* Corp. earns $100, and *X* Corp. suffers a $140 loss. *P* Corp. sells its *X* Corp. stock in year 3 for $80.

14

Penalty Provisions

The heart and soul of subchapter C is that distributed corporate earnings from operations should be taxed twice — once when the corporation earns them and again when they are distributed. Historically, it was also Congress's intention that both taxes should be at ordinary income rates. The propriety or impropriety of these guiding principles has been explored in Chapter 8.

Of course, Congress did not intend that all corporate earnings be taxed twice. For example, *X* Corp. might earn $10,000, which is taxed as ordinary income at corporate rates. Rather than distributing the earnings in the form of a dividend, *X* Corp. might accumulate the earnings, thereby increasing the value of the outstanding stock. Further, so long as *X* Corp. made no distribution, the cash that otherwise would have been paid in taxes by a dividend-receiving shareholder can continue to earn income, thereby providing shareholders with the benefits of deferral. Moreover, if an *X* shareholder died, the shareholder's estate took a "stepped-up" basis in its *X* stock, and *X* often could redeem that stock without a shareholder-level tax. See §302(a); §303(a).

Aware that subchapter C contains the seeds of its own circumvention, Congress has enacted various penalty provisions to keep taxpayers on the straight and narrow. In this chapter we will consider two: the accumulated earnings tax (§§531-537) and the personal holding company tax (§§541-547). These taxes are levied on the corporation in addition to normal corporate taxes (e.g., §§11 and 55).

A. ACCUMULATED EARNINGS TAX

What tax pressures are there on corporations and their shareholders to accumulate income? Historically corporate tax rates have been lower than individual tax rates. Before 1982, the maximum rate for individuals was 70 percent, while corporations were taxed at a 46 percent maximum rate. This differential led some individuals to incorporate their businesses and to accumulate earnings at the corporate level for eventual distribution at a time when the individual was in a lower tax bracket. During the period of accumulation, the taxpayer might gain access to the earnings through loans.

Even with a 35-percent top rate for both individuals and corporations, accumulation can be an attractive strategy. Once a corporation has earned and paid tax on income, the choice to distribute or retain that income depends on several factors, including the rate at which the distribution would be taxed and any current or projected future differential between corporate and individual tax rates. Although distributions to individuals historically were taxed at ordinary income rates, they are often currently taxed at a preferential capital gains rate, possibly encouraging distributions. See §1(h)(11) (taxing qualified dividend income at no greater than a 20-percent rate). Still, because corporate tax rates are graduated, a corporation may pay taxes at a lower effective rate than an individual pays, an incentive to accumulate not distribute. Compare §1 with §11. Further, accumulation allows the corporation and shareholders to postpone tax on the distribution, enabling the corporation to invest the postponed tax. For example, suppose a corporation has $1,000 available for distribution. Suppose further that the corporation is taxed at a 35-percent rate while its shareholder is taxed at a 31-percent rate on ordinary income. Even though the individual is taxed at a lower rate than the corporation, the corporation should not necessarily distribute the $1,000. If there is a distribution, the $1,000 distribution is taxed to the shareholder (assume at a 20-percent rate), resulting in only $800 left to generate income. Note as well, that a corporation with an elderly, significant shareholder may also have an incentive to accumulate earnings. If the shareholder dies still owning the stock, the stock will take a "stepped-up" basis. §1014. The shareholder's estate (or heirs) can then sell the stock with little or no tax, despite any corporate accumulation.

The accumulated earnings tax is a penalty tax imposed by Congress to discourage individuals from using a corporation to accumulate earnings and avoid (or defer) dividends taxable at the shareholder level. The motive triggering the tax is the accumulation of earnings beyond the reasonable needs of the business—a question of fact turning on subjective intent. The base of the accumulated earnings tax in any taxable year is the corporation's "accumulated taxable income" for that year, a term that must be distinguished from "earnings and profits" either of the current year or accumulated from prior years. Section 535 defines "accumulated taxable income" as taxable income less (1) the dividends-paid deduction of §561 and (2) the unused portion, if any, of the one-time accumulated earnings credit ($250,000 for most corporations). §535(c). The credit generally allows accumulation of $250,000 with impunity. Certain adjustments are made to taxable income under §535(b) to account for the fact that taxable income does not necessarily reflect dividend-paying capacity. Accordingly, taxable income is reduced by income taxes paid. Taxable income also is reduced by nondeductible charitable contributions, capital losses, net capital gain, and the taxes attributable thereto. Ignored in the computation of accumulated taxable income are intercorporate dividends-received deductions, net operating loss deductions, partially tax-exempt interest, and capital loss carryovers because they merely affect the computation of tax liability but do not absorb cash available for dividends. Section 531 imposes a 20-percent tax on accumulated taxable income.

The accumulated earnings tax is essentially focused on cash available for distribution. Only cash that is not needed or used for the reasonable needs of the business is considered available for distribution. Further, if cash is unavailable for distribution to shareholders because it is invested in other assets not needed in the business, those unnecessary assets may be counted as unreasonably accumulated and available for distribution. Treas. Regs. §1.537-2. For example, the Service is likely to maintain that cash used to make loans to shareholders or their relatives or to purchase a portfolio of stocks or properties unrelated to the corporation's business is the equivalent of cash on hand that could have, and should have, been paid out to shareholders. But if a corporation's earnings are used to buy a new business, to expand the present business, to meet working capital needs, to retire stock of a minority shareholder, or to pay off business debt, the corporation may be able to avoid imposition of the accumulated earnings tax. A thinly capitalized business with debt borrowed from outside sources may not have difficulty with the §531 tax because the repayment of debt is a reasonable business need. It has also been held that the §531 penalty cannot be imposed on a corporation that could have easily borrowed funds but chose instead to forgo dividends and build up cash to meet its business needs. See, e.g., Myron's Enterprises v. United States, 548 F.2d 331, 335 n.6 (9th Cir. 1977).

NOTES

1. *Unreasonable accumulations.* Section 532(a) imposes the accumulated earnings tax on corporations that accumulate earnings to avoid taxes. Section 533 presumes that accumulation "beyond the reasonable needs of the business" reflects the improper tax avoidance motive. What constitutes the "reasonable needs of the business" is discussed in the Notes that follow. But even if we know the reasonable needs of the business, to determine whether an accumulation is improper we need to know more than the earnings and profits account. When a corporation accumulates income in a year under scrutiny, it is not enough to compare reasonable business needs with earnings and profits to determine whether current accumulation is appropriate. The earnings and profits account may be misleadingly large or small. See Technalysis Corp. v. Commissioner, 101 T.C. 397 (1993) (large accumulations evaluated in the context of a risky and highly competitive business).

In Ivan Allen Co. v. United States, 422 U.S. 617 (1975), the taxpayer, which engaged in the business of selling office furniture and supplies, was profitable during the years in question but paid dividends that were substantially less than taxable income. The parties agreed that taxpayer had reasonable business needs for operating capital. The parties further stipulated that if taxpayer's marketable securities were valued at cost, there was no unreasonable accumulation under §533(a). However, if the marketable securities were evaluated at fair market value, the taxpayer would be deemed to have accumulated earnings beyond reasonable business needs.

The Court ruled that the securities should be evaluated at fair market value, and concluded that the taxpayer was guilty of unreasonable accumulation. Although unrealized appreciation does not increase a corporation's accumulated taxable income under §§531 and 535 or its earnings and profits, the unrealized appreciation can serve as evidence that current accumulations of earnings and profits are unreasonable because the securities could be sold at fair market value to meet the needs of the business. The Court emphasizes the liquidity of the investment assets as the key factor. Should the result be different if the taxpayer had illiquid investment assets? Presumably, the valuation of the assets would reflect their illiquidity.

The Court rejected the taxpayer's argument that looking at fair market value in effect violates the realization doctrine by forcing the taxpayer to sell the stock to meet the conceded business needs. The realization doctrine does not stretch that far, however. The unrealized appreciation was used solely as a yardstick to determine if current accumulations were necessary. Moreover, the possibility of forced sale was too speculative because a taxpayer might not have to sell the property (e.g., the corporation might be able to borrow on the security of the property).

Finally, in dicta that is relevant in many areas of taxation, the Court was not bothered by the fact that its decision may conflict with standard accounting practice; it noted, "The Court has not hesitated to apply the congressional policy underlying a revenue statute even when it does conflict with an established accounting practice."

Contrast *Ivan Allen* with Electric Regulator Corp. v. Commissioner, 336 F.2d 339 (2d Cir. 1964), in which earnings and profits at first glance seemed more than ample to meet business needs, but closer analysis revealed that prior earnings and profits had been reinvested in the corporation and that current accumulations were necessary to meet business needs. Indeed, as the court in *Electric Regulator* pointed out, had the corporation made the dividend distributions that the Service required, corporate assets would have been insufficient to meet reasonable business needs. In addition to focusing on accumulation of earnings and profits, it is equally important to consider what assets are on hand to meet the reasonable business needs.

2. *Burden of proof: presumptions.* Under §532(a), a corporation is subject to the accumulated earnings tax if it is "formed or availed of for the purpose of avoiding the income tax with respect to its shareholders . . . by permitting earnings and profits to accumulate instead of being divided or distributed." What is the relationship between this provision and the statutory presumptions — if that is what they are — of §533(a) (unreasonable accumulation shall be "determinative of the purpose to avoid the income tax with respect to shareholders" unless the corporation proves to the contrary by a preponderance of evidence) and §533(b) (if corporation is a mere holding company or investment company, this fact shall be "prima facie evidence of the purpose to avoid the income tax")?

Section 534 allows the taxpayer to shift the burden of proof to the government in Tax Court proceedings. Before mailing a notice of deficiency, the government may send a notification informing the taxpayer that the proposed notice of deficiency includes an amount imposed under §531. See Myco Industries v. Commissioner, 98 T.C. 270 (1992) (Commissioner's notice was not adequate to shift burden of proof to taxpayer because the notice failed to state the years for which the tax was asserted). The taxpayer may then submit a statement setting forth the grounds on which it will rely to prove it has not been accumulating unreasonably. The Tax Court will ordinarily rule in advance on the sufficiency of the taxpayer's §534(c) statement (Rule 142(e) of Rules of Practice). If the statement is sufficient, or if the notification has not been sent by the government, the burden is on the Service. Why is this procedure limited to Tax Court proceedings? For a §534(c) statement held insufficient because of vagueness, see Rutter v. Commissioner, 81 T.C. 937 (1983).

The purpose behind the notification procedure of §534 presumably is to encourage administrative resolution of accumulated earnings tax issues. We know that the burden of proof will be on the Commissioner for failure to notify the taxpayer of an impending deficiency notice based on §531. Where should the burden be placed if the Commissioner sends notification but then asserts a deficiency before the taxpayer has replied to the notification? See Manson Western Corp. v. Commissioner, 76 T.C. 1161 (1981).

In United States v. Donruss Co., 393 U.S. 297 (1969), the government argued that to rebut the presumption of §533(a), the taxpayer must establish by a preponderance of the evidence that tax avoidance was not "one of the purposes" for accumulating earnings beyond the reasonable needs of the business. In contrast, the taxpayer argued that the presumption could be rebutted by showing that tax avoidance was not the "dominant, controlling, or impelling" reason for the accumulation. The Court accepted the government's interpretation, saying that the taxpayer's interpretation "would exacerbate the problems that Congress was trying to avoid" by the statutory emphasis on the reasonableness of the accumulation rather than on the "vagaries of corporate motive." The taxpayer's construction "would allow taxpayers to escape the tax when it is proved that at least one other motive was equal to tax avoidance. We doubt that such a determination can be made with any accuracy, and it is certainly one which will depend almost exclusively on the interested testimony of corporate management." 393 U.S. at 308. In Technalysis Corp. v. Commissioner, 101 T.C. 397 (1993), however, the taxpayer won in spite of the court's finding that accumulation exceeded reasonable business needs because the court found no tax avoidance purpose.

Will a finding of a shareholder deadlock be sufficient to rebut the §533 presumption of an improper purpose? In Atlantic Properties v. Commissioner, 519 F.2d 1233 (1st Cir. 1975), four of the five shareholders representing 75 percent of the vote wanted a dividend distribution, while one shareholder representing the other 25 percent wanted to accumulate. The corporate bylaws required an 80-percent vote for dividend distribution. The court found the corporation subject to the accumulated earnings tax. The same result was reached in Hedberg-Freidheim Contracting Co. v. Commissioner, 251 F.2d 839 (8th Cir. 1958), in which two shareholders were deadlocked. Compare Casey v. Commissioner, 267 F.2d 26 (2d Cir. 1959), in which two shareholders were deadlocked, but an unreasonable accumulation was not found.

3. *Reasonable needs of the business: anticipated needs.* Section 537(a)(1) provides that the term "reasonable needs of the business" includes the "reasonably anticipated needs of the business." It was enacted in 1954, and the Senate Report on the 1954 Code (page 318) says of §537,

> It is intended that this provision will make clear that there is no requirement that the accumulated earnings be invested immediately in the business so long as there is an indication that future needs of the business require such accumulation. In any case where there exists a definite plan for the investment of earnings and profits, such corporation need not necessarily consummate these plans in a relatively short period after the close of the taxable year. However, where the future needs of the business are uncertain or vague, or the plans for the future use of the accumulations are indefinite, the amendment does not prevent application of the accumulated earnings tax.

The Senate Report also states (pages 69-70),

> If the retention of earnings is justified as of the close of the taxable year, subsequent events should not be used for the purpose of showing that the retention was unreasonable in such year. However, subsequent events may be considered to determine whether the corporation actually intended to consummate the plans for which the earnings were accumulated.

For cases in which §537(a)(1) has been construed, see Motor Fuel Carriers v. United States, 559 F.2d 1348 (5th Cir. 1977) (reversing Tax Court finding that plans too indefinite though later consummated); Cheyenne Newspapers v. Commissioner, 494 F.2d 429 (10th Cir. 1974) (accumulations prohibited for contingencies that were unreasonable); Bahan Textile Machinery Co. v. United States, 453 F.2d 1100 (4th Cir. 1972) (plans too vague and loans to shareholder's relatives indicated prohibited purpose); Sterling Distributors v. United States, 313 F.2d 803 (5th Cir. 1963) (plans sufficiently definite even though later abandoned); Vulcan Steam Forging Co. v. Commissioner, 35 T.C.M. (CCH) 110 (1976) (possible relocation of business justified accumulations for three years, but not for fourth year when relocation plans were abandoned). See also Myron's Enterprises v. United States, 548 F.2d 331 (9th Cir. 1977), in which taxpayer-lessee had made offers for six years to purchase property from lessor and had, during the six years, accumulated funds for the purchase and remodeling. The court of appeals found the plans were sufficiently definite and reversed the district court, which had held that reasonable needs must be reduced by the amount the sole shareholder would have been willing to lend the corporation.

In this era of high damage awards, can a corporation claim that accumulation is necessary to protect against liability? Treas. Regs. §1.537-1(f) sets forth a list of factors for determining whether an accumulation for anticipated product liability losses is reasonable. Some of the factors include (1) previous product liability experience, (2) the extent of commercial product liability insurance, (3) the income tax consequences of the taxpayer's product liability losses, and (4) the taxpayer's future potential liability in light of reasonable expansion plans.

4. *Reasonable needs of the business: working capital needs.* The cases of Bardahl Manufacturing Corp. v. Commissioner, 24 T.C.M. (CCH) 1030 (1965), and Bardahl International Corp. v. Commissioner, 25 T.C.M. (CCH) 935 (1966), created a statistical formula for determining the reasonably anticipated working capital needs of a business for an operating cycle. The operating cycle is the period of time required to convert cash into inventory, inventory into accounts receivable, and accounts receivable into cash, and the length of the cycle depends on the type of business involved. For example, if three months elapse from the purchase of the inventory to the receipt of payment in cash for the goods manufactured and sold, then the working capital needs are 25 percent of total annual operating costs and costs of goods sold. In addition to the amount of working capital so determined, *Bardahl I* recognized the need for funds to pay for such items as the cost of plant expansion, the stockpiling of raw materials, and notes and other liabilities payable in one year (including accrued income taxes). The *Bardahl* formula is now relied on as a guide to determine permissible accumulations, but it is not always rigidly applied, Thompson Engineering Co. v. Commissioner, 80 T.C. 672 (1983) (*Bardahl* formula inappropriate to measure business needs of mechanical contractor without routine operating cycle), rev'd, 751 F.2d 191 (6th Cir. 1985) (Tax Court impermissibly substituted its judgment for that of taxpayer). In Delaware Trucking Co. v. Commissioner, 32 T.C.M. (CCH) 105 (1973), the court found as reasonable the working capital needs for one cycle plus an additional 75 percent of that amount for anticipated increased labor costs and other costs resulting from inflation. See also Hughes, Inc. v. Commissioner, 90 T.C. 1 (1988) (working capital less than business needs; no accumulated earnings tax liability).

5. *Reasonable business needs: diversification.* What is "the" business, as this term is used in §533(a)? The regulations state that a corporation's business "is not merely that which it has previously carried on but includes, in general, any line of business which it may undertake." Treas. Regs. §1.537-3(a). Does this mean that a small grocery store may aspire to become a department store or a nationwide chain of

stores—or to monopolize the manufacture and sale of widgets? The regulations under the 1939 Code, Treas. Regs. 118, §39.102-3(a), included the sentence just quoted but went on to warn that "a radical change of business when a considerable surplus has been accumulated may afford evidence of a purpose to avoid the surtax." This sentence was dropped in 1959. In defining "reasonable needs," the regulations speak favorably of an accumulation "to acquire a business enterprise through purchasing stock or assets" but disapprove of "investments in properties or securities which are unrelated to the activities of the business of the taxpayer corporation." Treas. Regs. §§1.537-2(b)(2), 1.537-2(c)(4).

If the business needs of another corporation can be taken into account, must the relationship between the corporations be that of parent-subsidiary, or will a brother-sister affiliation be sufficient? See Treas. Regs. §1.537-2(c)(3); Latchis Theaters v. Commissioner, 214 F.2d 834 (1st Cir. 1954) (accumulations to aid brother-sister corporation not sufficient reason). But compare Inland Terminals v. United States, 477 F.2d 836 (4th Cir. 1973), in which a subsidiary's accumulations to meet the business needs of its parent corporation were held to qualify as reasonable accumulations.

In Chaney & Hope, Inc. v. Commissioner, 80 T.C. 263 (1983), an individual, Mr. Hope, owned all the stock of brother-sister corporations. One corporation was engaged in the construction business; the other held large amounts of liquid assets. The brother-sister corporations were established for a variety of non-tax business reasons. Both corporations agreed to indemnify the Travelers Indemnity Co., the company furnishing the bonding required on construction projects. Travelers insisted that both corporations sign the indemnity agreement. The court determined that the accumulations by one corporation to help the other corporation were unreasonable.

In *Chaney & Hope*, the court conceded that the total amount accumulated by the brother-sister corporations was reasonable in light of the bonding requirements. Why then should the taxpayer lose merely because of the nature of the corporate structure when, if Mr. Hope had operated with one corporation, the accumulation would have been reasonable? Note also that if the corporations had been parent-subsidiary, the accumulation would have been reasonable. Treas. Regs. §1.537-3(b). Through the attribution rules, isn't every brother-sister relationship a parent-subsidiary relationship as well? See page 206 supra. Do the attribution rules apply to §531? In Hughes, Inc. v. Commissioner, 90 T.C. 1 (1988), the court held that a corporation is not liable for the accumulated earnings tax when earnings were accumulated to purchase the stock of an affiliated corporation, the taxpayer's primary customer, as part of a strategy to prevent a takeover of the purchased corporation.

6. *Reasonable business needs: payment of corporate debts.* In Helvering v. Chicago Stock Yards Co., 318 U.S. 693 (1943), involving a one-person corporation that was accumulating earnings for the purpose, among others, of paying off certain obligations of its subsidiaries, the Court suggested that the taxpayer's stockholder, if the taxpayer's surplus had been distributed to him, could equally well have paid off the obligations in question. Does this suggest that, despite a corporation's capital requirements, the §531 tax may be imposed if the earnings could have been distributed to the stockholders and reinvested by them in the corporation? What would this do to the reasonable business needs test in §535(c)? In Smoot Sand & Gravel Corp. v. Commissioner, 241 F.2d 197 (4th Cir. 1957), this suggestion was rejected on

a showing that a distribution would have been subject to a tax rate of 89 percent in the shareholder's hands.

If at the time of organization, the corporation issues both common stock and notes or bonds to its organizers, is accumulation for the retirement of the debt at or before maturity a reasonable need of the business? Note the reference in Treas. Regs. §1.537-2(b)(3) to a "sinking fund for the purpose of retiring bonds issued by the corporation." In *Chicago Stock Yards Co.*, there is a suggestion that the existence of long-term obligations might not be a satisfactory excuse for the accumulation of surplus if the obligations might be readily refinanced at the due date. Despite this suggestion, the payment of corporate debts is often regarded as a reasonable need of the business without regard to the possibility of refinancing the obligations. See, e.g., Gazette Telegraph Co. v. Commissioner, 19 T.C. 692 (1953), involving a corporation that on organization (a) issued common stock of a par value of $250,000 and 10-year promissory notes of a face amount of $250,000 to its organizers and (b) borrowed $400,000 from a bank, to acquire assets of a net value of about $900,000. Within about four years, both the notes and the bank loan were paid off. The court found that the notes were bona fide, that the capitalization was not too thin, and that the future intended repayment of the obligations was a reasonable need of the business that justified the accumulation of earnings.

7. *Reasonable needs of the business: redemptions.* In general, redemption of common or preferred stock will not be regarded as a proper reason for accumulating surplus. See Pelton Steel Casting Co. v. United States, 251 F.2d 278 (7th Cir. 1958) (accumulation to redeem majority interest shareholder not for reasonable needs of the business). Special circumstances, however, might justify an accumulation for the purpose of reducing shareholders' interests. See Technalysis Corp. v. Commissioner, 101 T.C. 397 (1993) (accumulation for purposes of funding stock buyback program to support market for taxpayer's stock was held reasonable business need); Gazette Publishing Co. v. Self, 103 F. Supp. 779 (E.D. Ark. 1952) (elimination of potentially disruptive minority stock interest); Mountain State Steel Foundries v. Commissioner, 284 F.2d 737 (4th Cir. 1960) (accumulation to redeem stock may be a reasonable business need). More recently, in Technalysis Corp. v. Commissioner, 101 T.C. 397 (1993), the court ruled that a corporation with accumulated earnings beyond its reasonable business needs was not subject to §531 when the accumulation was made to redeem shares at some future time in accordance with a general redemption plan. See §537(a)(2) and (3) and §537(b) permitting accumulations to redeem stock under §303 (redemption to pay death taxes, etc., discussed at page 180 supra) and under the "excess business holdings" provisions applicable to tax-exempt private foundations.

Suppose *X* Corp. with accumulated earnings and profits earns $500,000 in year 5. That year, *X* Corp. redeems all the stock of shareholder *A*. Assume the redemption reduces the current earnings and profits account to zero. See §312(n)(7). Prior to year 5, the accumulated earnings and profits were not deemed unreasonable. Can *X* Corp. face accumulated earnings tax liability for its year 5 activities if no earnings and profits accumulated in year 5? Recall that the base of the accumulated earnings tax is accumulated taxable income, §535, not earnings and profits for the year.

Even if the taxpayer manages to get rid of its earnings and profits for the year in question, apparently there may still be accumulated earnings tax liability. In GPD, Inc. v. Commissioner, 508 F.2d 1076 (6th Cir. 1974), the sole shareholder followed a pattern, over a period of years, of donating some of his shares of the corporation's stock to charity and later causing the corporation to redeem the stock from the charity. The redemptions in the tax year in question eliminated the corporation's current earnings and profits. The Tax Court held the accumulated earnings tax to be improper for the year. The circuit court reversed and assessed §531 liability. The court reasoned that normally, if there is no surplus cash on hand at the end of a year, there will be no accumulated earnings tax liability. Here, there was none, but there had been cash generated during that year that was found to be used for a nonbusiness purpose, i.e., the redemption of shares from the charity. Because there was accumulated taxable income for the year, the liability was imposed. A distribution of a dividend to shareholders reduces accumulated taxable income (and earnings and profits), §535(a), but a §302(a) redemption as in *GPD, Inc.* does not reduce accumulated taxable income. See §§535(a), 561, and 562. For a case following *GPD, Inc.*, see Lamark Shipping Agency, Inc. v. Commissioner, 81 T.C.M. (CCH) 284 (1981). Notwithstanding the circuit court's reasoning in *GPD, Inc.*, it does seem odd to proclaim liability for accumulating income when the corporation has not accumulated any income for the year in question. See Doernberg, The Accumulated Earnings Tax: The Relationship between Earnings and Profits and Accumulated Taxable Income in a Redemption Transaction, 34 Fla. L. Rev. 715 (1982). Also, should accumulation for charitable purposes be treated as an impermissible purpose under the statute?

8. *The minimum accumulated earnings credit.* By virtue of §535(c)(2)(A), a corporation may accumulate up to $250,000 of earnings and profits (overall, not annually) without being subject to the accumulated earnings tax. Of course, accumulation in excess of $250,000 is permitted if the taxpayer can show the accumulation is necessary to meet the reasonable needs of the business. Only the $250,000 minimum credit, however, is allowed to a corporation that is a "mere holding or investment company," §535(c)(3). Section 535(c)(1) does not allow these companies to accumulate based on the reasonable needs of the business. See Rev. Rul. 77-368, 1977-2 C.B. 201 (need for liquidity cannot be considered for investment or holding company).

When the Economic Recovery Tax Act of 1981 increased the minimum credit from $150,000 to $250,000, the $150,000 credit was retained for corporations whose "principal function . . . is the performance of services in the field of health, law, engineering, architecture, accounting, actuarial science, performing arts, or consulting." See §532(c)(2)(B). Why do these corporations receive a smaller credit than a mere investment corporation that has no business whatsoever?

To discourage the multiplication of corporate entities as a means of multiplying the allowable credit, §1551 was amended to apply to the accumulated earnings credit as well as to limit the use of the lower corporate rates. See also §243(b) (treating certain life insurance companies as component members [rather than excluded members] of a control group if an affiliated group makes an election under §243(b) to claim the 100-percent deduction for dividends from those companies).

9. *Publicly held corporations and the accumulated earnings tax.* How likely is it that §531 will be applied to a publicly held corporation? See Trico Products Corp. v. Commissioner, 137 F.2d 424 (2d Cir. 1943), and Trico Products Corp. v. McGowan, 169 F.2d 343 (2d Cir. 1948), in which, although there were more than 2,000 stockholders, six stockholders owned about two-thirds of the total shares. After the

taxpayer paid a total of about $3.2 million in §531 surtaxes and interest, a minority stockholder brought a stockholder's derivative action against the directors for subjecting the corporation to the §531 penalty. The action was settled by a payment of about $2.5 million by the defendants to the corporation. See Mahler v. Trico Products Corp., 296 N.Y. 902, 72 N.E. 622 (1947).

See Golconda Mining Corp. v. Commissioner, 507 F.2d 594 (9th Cir. 1974), in which it was held that the accumulated earnings tax could not be applied to a publicly held company unless a small group of shareholders controlled at least 50 percent of its stock. The position of the Service is that, in an appropriate case, there is no legal impediment to applying §531 to a publicly held corporation. See Rev. Rul. 75-305, 1975-2 C.B. 228. Apparently, Congress agreed with the Service. In 1984 Congress enacted §532(c), which states that the accumulated earnings tax may be imposed on a corporation without regard to the number of shareholders. The Conference Report indicates, however, that it may be difficult to establish the requisite tax avoidance motive in the case of a widely held operating company in which no individual or group has legal or effective control.

In Technalysis Corp. v. Commissioner, 101 T.C. 397 (1993), the court in dicta commented that widely held corporations can be subject to the accumulated earnings tax if the proscribed purposes exist. Technalysis itself had approximately 1,500 shareholders, but approximately 30 percent of the stock was held by the five members of the board of directors.

PROBLEM

14-1. Does an individual shareholder ever have an incentive to accumulate income in a corporation if the shareholder's marginal tax rate is lower than the corporate marginal tax rate?

B. PERSONAL HOLDING COMPANY TAX

The personal holding company tax is another weapon that the Commissioner has, along with the accumulated earnings tax, to curtail the practice of accumulating profits in a corporation to avoid individual tax rates. The tax was enacted in 1934 to reach passive investment income and personal services earnings that are allowed to accumulate in a corporation. The personal holding company tax is a mechanical one, and tax avoidance motives are irrelevant or statutorily presumed. It therefore is possible to stumble unwittingly into being a personal holding company.

Two tests are applied to determine if income is personal holding company income: the stock ownership test and the income test, both set out in §542(a). The tax generally applies to closely held corporations because, under the stock ownership test, more than 50 percent of the value of the stock must be owned directly or indirectly by five or fewer individuals. To make the ownership determination, the attribution rules of §544 apply. Under the income test, at least 60 percent of "adjusted ordinary gross income" must be personal holding company income under §543(a), a term discussed in the following Notes.

The rate of tax imposed on undistributed personal holding company income is 20 percent. §541. Because the purpose of the tax is not to raise revenue but to encourage dividend distributions from personal holding companies, relief is available under the dividends-paid deduction and the deficiency dividend provisions described in Note 4.

NOTES

1. *Sixty percent of adjusted ordinary gross income test.* Since 1964, the income test has required that at least 60 percent of the corporation's adjusted ordinary gross income for the taxable year be personal holding company income. §542(a)(1). Before 1964, the comparable requirement was 80 percent. To compute adjusted ordinary gross income, ordinary gross income is first defined by excluding from gross income the gains from the sale or other disposition of capital assets and §1231(b) assets. §543(b)(1). Then adjustments to ordinary gross income are made by subtracting allowable deductions for depreciation, taxes, interest, and rent from rental income and mineral royalties. §543(b)(2). These adjustments are intended to determine whether the rental activities substantially contribute to the corporation's net income or constitute high gross/low net income activities, engaged in to minimize the importance of the corporation's other personal holding company income. Under §543(b)(2)(C), interest on condemnation awards, judgments, and tax refunds and interest earned by certain dealers in U.S. securities is also excluded. The following items are included in adjusted ordinary gross income: dividends; interest; royalties including special rules for mineral, oil, and gas royalties and copyright royalties; produced film rents; rental payments from a 25-percent or more shareholder; personal service contract payments; and income from trusts and estates. §543(a).

2. *Personal holding company income.* Section 543(a) is the product of congressional efforts to distinguish the "tainted" personal holding company income from income that offers a "legitimate" reason to operate in corporate form.

In RAS of Sand River, Inc. v. Commissioner, 935 F.2d 270 (6th Cir. 1991), the taxpayer was wholly owned by a single individual. Although a written contract between the taxpayer and its customer for engineering services did not designate a particular person to perform the work or give the customer the right to designate who would perform the services, the court found that an oral agreement with the customer required the sole shareholder to perform the engineering services (and was a tainted personal service contract payment). The court was not influenced by the fact that the shareholder's services were not unique or irreplaceable.

Other categories of personal holding company income pose difficult interpretative problems as well. In Allied Industrial Cartage Co. v. Commissioner, 647 F.2d 713 (6th Cir. 1981), an individual owned all the stock in two corporations — one of which leased trucks and real estate to the other corporation. The Service argued that the rental income was personal holding company income under §543(a)(6). The court held that the use of the rental property could not be attributed to the individual because a business nexus existed for the corporate arrangement and no personal benefit accrued to the shareholder. See also Silverman & Sons Realty Trust v. Commissioner, 620 F.2d 314 (1st Cir. 1980).

In *Allied Industrial Cartage,* the contours of §543(a)(6) were at issue. That provision is aimed at rents paid by shareholders to a corporation for the use of an incorporated yacht, country home, or similar property. Can a shareholder avoid §543(a)(6) by arranging for a controlled corporation to rent the property? See the discussion of disguised dividends at page 126 supra.

Section 543(a)(2) treats certain other rental payments as personal holding company income. To distinguish receipts from an active rental business from passive rental receipts, the provision invokes a special formula. The adjusted income from rents is included as personal holding company income unless the rents amount to 50 percent or more of adjusted ordinary gross income (an "active" rental business), and the dividends paid at least equal the amount by which non-rent personal holding company income for the year exceeds 10 percent of its ordinary gross income. (Who dreams up these formulas?) If a taxpayer fails the numerical tests, can it still argue that the rental business is "active" by demonstrating a high level of services rendered in connection with the rental activities? See Eller v. Commissioner, 77 T.C. 934 (1981) (when the §543(a)(2) tests were not met, income from operation of commercial shopping center and mobile home park was personal holding company income despite level of services; exhaustive review of the area).

Copyright royalties are considered personal holding company income under §543(a)(4). See Irving Berlin Music Corp. v. United States, 487 F.2d 540 (Cl. Ct. 1973), in which licensing receipts were found to be royalties for use of copyright property, subject to tax as personal holding company income, and not compensation for services. Cf. Rev. Rul. 75-202, 1975-1 C.B. 170, in which a transfer of the exclusive right to a copyright, subject to a contingent reversion, was held a sale and therefore did not give rise to personal holding company income.

Other categories of personal holding company income include dividends, interest, royalties (other than royalties from minerals, oil, gas, or copyrights), and annuities (§543(a)(1)); mineral, oil, and gas royalties (§543(a)(3)); produced film rents (§543(a)(5)); and income from trusts and estates (§543(a)(8)).

It is not always easy to distinguish royalties from other payments. In Dothan Coca-Cola Bottling Co. v. United States, 745 F.2d 1400 (11th Cir. 1984), the court held that amounts paid to the taxpayer by subbottlers constituted rent for the use of tangible real and personal property rather than royalties for the use of the taxpayer's franchise. The payments were 20 cents per gallon of Coke syrup sold by the taxpayer to the subbottlers. Although adjusted income from rents can constitute personal holding company income, the Service conceded that the rents did not meet the personal holding company income requirements of §543(a)(2).

In this digital age, one important concern is whether income received by a computer software company from licensing arrangements is personal holding company income. Section 543(a)(1) excepts certain software royalties if the corporation receiving the royalties (1) is actively engaged in the business of developing computer software; (2) derives at least 50 percent of its gross income from such software; (3) incurs substantial trade or business expenses; and (4) distributes most of its passive income other than the royalties. See §543(a)(1) and (d).

3. *Stock ownership test.* Recall that in addition to the personal holding company income requirement, there is also a stock ownership requirement — that at any time during the last half of the taxable year, more than 50 percent in value of the corporation's outstanding stock is owned, directly or indirectly, by or for not more than five individuals. §542(a)(2). Some trusts and tax-exempt organizations are considered "individuals" under §542(a)(2), presumably because they are susceptible to

domination by the other shareholders. Note that if fewer than 10 individuals own all stock of a corporation, the stock ownership test is automatically satisfied.

In determining stock ownership, the constructive ownership rules of §544 apply, and those rules differ in some respects from §318. For example, there is attribution between siblings and no 50-percent threshold for attribution from corporations.

4. *Dividends-paid deduction; deficiency dividend procedure.* Under §545, the base for the tax is the corporation's taxable income with certain adjustments. The adjustments include decreasing taxable income by the amount of taxes paid, net capital gains reported, and the deduction described in §561. The §561 deduction equals the sum of (i) the dividends paid during the taxable year (and to a limited extent within two and one-half months of the last day of the taxable year), (ii) consent dividends determined under §565, and (iii) the dividend carryover of §564. Dividends paid in property will qualify for a reduction under Treas. Regs. §1.562-1(a) to the extent of the property's adjusted basis at the time of distribution. This regulation was upheld in Fulman v. United States, 434 U.S. 528 (1978). Are *Fulman* and the regulation still sound law in light of the changes in §311 repealing the *General Utilities* doctrine? If a corporation's taxable income is increased on the distribution of appreciated property, shouldn't the dividends-paid deduction be an amount equal to the adjusted basis plus any gain recognized to the corporation on the distribution? See §312(b). Otherwise the distribution of appreciated property may actually increase a corporation's personal holding company tax liability.

After the corporation's liability for personal holding company tax has been determined, the corporation may mitigate or eliminate that tax liability under the deficiency dividend procedure of §547, but the liability for interest and penalties is not eliminated by this procedure. Section 547 permits the corporation to make a dividend distribution to shareholders on which the shareholders are taxed currently, and the corporation may use this distribution to reduce its already determined past personal holding company liability. The deficiency dividend procedure can produce a dividend to a shareholder even on a liquidation. See §331(b) and §316(b)(2)(B).

5. *Consolidated groups.* With some exceptions, a consolidated group computes its personal holding company tax using "consolidated" adjusted ordinary gross income and "consolidated" personal holding company income. See §542(b); §1.542-4. However, neither the statute nor regulations describe these consolidated computations, leaving many questions unanswered.

6. *Regulated investment companies, mutual funds, and real estate investment trusts.* Certain regulated investment companies (including mutual funds) may elect under subchapter M (§§851-855) to be subject to corporate taxation on only their undistributed income. These corporations, which must distribute currently at least 90 percent of their income, are treated as conduits through which the income from investments passes to their stockholders, and their long-term capital gains retain that character on distribution to the stockholders.

Sections 856-858 provide that certain real estate investment trusts (REITs) that distribute a specified percentage of current income are treated as corporations, with the important exception that distributed income is taxed to the beneficiaries rather than to the trust. The conduit concept is patterned on the treatment of regulated investment companies. The rules relating to and the treatments of regulated investment companies and REITs differ in important ways from those corporations electing subchapter S, discussed in Chapter 16.

15

The Corporation as a Separate Taxable Entity

A. DEFINITION OF A CORPORATION

1. *Morrissey v. Commissioner*

Morrissey v. Commissioner, 296 U.S. 344 (1935), considered whether a trust should be treated as an association taxed as a corporation. The petitioners set up the trust to develop some tracts of land and to construct and operate a golf course. The trustees were authorized to buy, sell, lease, and operate the land owned by the trust; to construct and operate the golf course and club house; to make loans and investments; and to manage the property as if they were the owners. The trustees had no power to bind the beneficiaries. Beneficial interests in the trust were evidenced by transferable certificates. The trust was to continue for 25 years and was not terminated by the death of a trustee or beneficiary. During the years before the court, the trust developed the land, sold some of the lots, and constructed a golf course and club house, which were transferred to a corporation in exchange for its stock. The trustees leased and operated the golf facilities from the corporation for some time, but later their activities were confined to the collection of installments on the lots that were sold, the receipt of dividends from the incorporated golf facilities, and distributions to beneficiaries.

The Supreme Court held that the corporate income tax was properly imposed on the trust, which was deemed an "association" for tax purposes. See §7701(a)(3), which defines "corporation" to include "association." The characteristics necessary to tax a business enterprise as an association were set forth by the Court as follows: (a) associates, (b) an objective to carry on a trade or business, (c) continuity of life of the enterprise, (d) centralized management representing the owners, (e) limited liability for the owners, and (f) free transferability of ownership interests.

2. *Professional Corporations*

The Service was successful in arguing for association status in *Morrissey*. Subsequent to the *Morrissey* decision, however, certain taxpayers sought the sanctuary of association status for tax purposes even though that classification carried with it the possibility of a corporate-level tax. Doctors and other professionals practicing in unincorporated associations or partnerships wanted association status to take advantage of qualified pension and profit-sharing plans, then only available to corporate employees. Because most states prohibited the incorporation of professionals, many professionals formed associations adhering to the *Morrissey* characteristics. In this setting, the Service found itself arguing against association status. In Kintner v. United States, 216 F.2d 418 (9th Cir. 1954), the Ninth Circuit ruled that a professional medical service association was a corporation for federal tax purposes even though a state law prohibited the practice of medicine by corporations. For a good review of the history of professional corporations, see Richland Medical Association v. Commissioner, 953 F.2d 639 (4th Cir. 1992).

3. *The Association Regulations*

In 1960, the Service reacted to defeats in *Kintner* and other cases by enacting Treas. Regs. §301.7701-2, which codified the basic characteristics of an association described in *Morrissey*. These regulations set forth two prerequisites to association status: (1) an objective to carry on business for profit and (2) associates, although associates may be ignored in the one-person corporation or sole proprietorship situation. In lieu of an uncertain weighing of the various *Morrissey* factors, the regulations further provided a mechanical numbers test. An unincorporated organization would not be classified as an association unless the organization had three of four listed corporate characteristics: continuity of life, centralization of management, limited liability, and free transferability of ownership interests. These characteristics were defined in a manner stacked against corporate classification.

In light of the strict federal regulations, professionals lobbied state legislatures to enact professional corporation statutes permitting operation in corporate form. The Service's reaction to this turn of events was to issue specific regulations in 1965 intended to ignore the professional corporation statutes for federal tax purposes. The 1965 regulations were struck down as arbitrary, legislative in nature, and discriminatory by all courts that considered them. See, e.g., Kurzner v. United States, 413 F.2d 97 (5th Cir. 1969); O'Neill v. United States, 410 F.2d 888 (6th Cir. 1969); United States v. Empey, 406 F.2d 157 (10th Cir. 1969). When the solicitor general decided not to apply for certiorari in *Kurzner*, the Service announced that it would no longer contest this issue. See Rev. Rul. 70-101, 1970-1 C.B. 278, listing the state statutes that were recognized as conferring corporate status on professional service organizations. Subsequent rulings added state statutes as they were enacted to the list set out in Rev. Rul. 70-101. In 1977, the 1965 regulations were revoked.

Despite recognition as a corporation, the personal service corporation and its shareholder-employees may be subject to a reallocation of income under principles developed in cases such as Lucas v. Earl. See Sargent v. Commissioner, 93 T.C. 572 (1989). See also page 516 infra.

4. **Larson** *and Limited Partnerships*

While the Service was still waging war to make federal corporate status unavailable for professionals, it found itself fighting to impose corporate status on certain noncorporate enterprises — limited partnerships. Relying on the restrictive association regulations, limited partnerships could operate much like corporations but easily escape that classification. These limited partnerships were used to market "tax shelters" to individual investors who might not otherwise be able to make such investments on their own. The partnership form was ideal because it allowed limited partners to take their pro rata shares of partnership losses or credits, which could then be used to offset income from other sources and thereby shelter income. Often the losses in the early years of a partnership exceeded a partner's actual cash investment in the partnership.[1] Faced with these proliferating "tax shelter" cases, the Service argued that a limited partnership should be taxed as a corporation under some circumstances, in which case the entity's losses would not pass through to the partners but could be used only by the entity.

In the absence of congressional guidance, courts faced a difficult task in determining the tax treatment of limited partnerships. Compare Zuckman v. United States, 524 F.2d 729 (Cl. Ct. 1975) (holding a limited partnership not an association) with Larson v. Commissioner, 65 T.C. No. 10 (1975) (*Larson I*) (holding a fairly typical California limited partnership an association). Even though the *Larson I* opinion was withdrawn for reconsideration within a month after its issuance, it created a near panic among some real estate groups. *Larson II* (Larson v. Commissioner, 66 T.C. 159 (1976)), however, came as a relief to many taxpayers. In *Larson II,* the court applied the four-factor test of the regulations rigidly and without giving greater weight to any one factor over any other.

Larson II concluded that an entity was characterized as an association only if it had more corporate than noncorporate characteristics. In an apparent response to *Larson II,* the Treasury in 1977 proposed, and in the ensuing clamor immediately thereafter withdrew, new regulations that would have classified most limited partnerships as associations. Several days after withdrawal, then-Secretary William Simon announced that regulations would not be reproposed. In April 1979, the Treasury agreed to follow *Larson II.*

The *Zuckman* and *Larson II* opinions reflected that courts appeared unwilling to reclassify an entity when the taxpayers managed to satisfy the existing regulations on a technical or literal level. Such an approach was close to saying that "form is form," i.e., if a state adopted the UPA or the ULPA and the partnership agreement adhered to either act, the partnership form would be acknowledged for tax purposes. The result was that taxpayers and their counsel were usually able to arrange the transaction to get the desired results, i.e., association or partnership status.

5. *The "Check-the-Box" Regulations*

In 1996, the Service quit this classification battle by issuing new regulations that permit eligible business entities in many cases to elect the type of classification they desire. Treas. Regs. §301.7701-3(a). Under the regulations, an eligible business

1. The ability of a partner to take loss deductions stems in part from the *Crane* doctrine, which allows purchase indebtedness to be included in basis, thereby increasing depreciation deductions. See Crane v. Commissioner, 331 U.S. 1 (1949). While there may be a day of reckoning for the partner who receives large loss deductions in the early years, there has been no shortage of genius in finding ways to postpone or avoid that day or at least make it less painful by qualifying for capital gains treatment on any recapture. Note that the ability of partners to take loss deductions may now be restricted under the passive activity rules of §469.

entity is a business entity that is unincorporated and is not an association (i.e., an entity that previously elected to be taxed as a corporation under Treas. Regs. §301.7701-3), insurance company, bank, political/governmental entity, or entity otherwise subject to special treatment under the Code. Treas. Regs. §301.7701-2(b)(3)-(7).

A business entity other than an eligible business entity is treated as a corporation. Additionally, partnerships whose interests are publicly traded or for which there is a secondary market are generally treated as corporations, ineligible for the election. §7704. Further, the regulations provide a list of specific foreign entities that are deemed "per se" corporations and therefore precluded from electing out of corporate classification. See Treas. Regs. §301.7701-2(b)(8).

An eligible business entity, in contrast, is offered the classification election. It may elect to be treated as a corporation for federal tax purposes. See Treas. Regs. §301.7701-3(c). Absent that election, under a default rule, an eligible domestic entity with two or more members is treated as a partnership for federal tax purposes, and one with a single owner is treated as a disregarded entity (that is, treated as transparent like a sole proprietorship, branch, or division of the owner). Treas. Regs. §301.7701-3(b)(1). (Entities that are disregarded are sometimes referred to as "tax nothings.") The default rules for foreign eligible entities are more complicated as they are determined by the liability exposure of the organization's members. *Id.* at (b)(2).

Once a business entity has elected to change its classification, it generally cannot change its classification again during the following 60 months. This prohibition does not apply to the initial classification of a new entity because the initial classification is not a change. Treas. Regs. §301.7701-3(c)(1)(iv). Further, if new owners acquire more than 50 percent of the entity's interests during the 60-month period, the Service may allow a change in classification. *Id.*

Because a reclassification may involve a taxable conversion, the advantages of reclassification must be weighed against the potential tax costs. For example, if a partnership elects to be treated as a corporation for tax purposes, it is deemed to contribute all of its assets and liabilities to the corporation in exchange for the corporation's stock and then to distribute the stock to its partners in liquidation. Treas. Regs. §301.7701-3(g)(1)(i). A corporation that elects to be treated as a partnership is deemed to distribute all of its assets and liabilities to its shareholders in liquidation, and the shareholders are then deemed to contribute the assets and liabilities to a newly formed partnership. Treas. Regs. §301.7701-3(g)(1)(ii). If a corporation with a single owner elects to be disregarded, it is deemed to distribute all of its assets and liabilities in liquidation to its single owner. Treas. Regs. §301.7701-3(g)(1)(iii). Finally, if a disregarded entity elects to be treated as a corporation, its owner is deemed to contribute all of the entity's assets and liabilities to the corporation in exchange for the corporation's stock. Treas. Regs. §301.7701-3(g)(1)(iv).

The "check-the-box" regulations are relatively clear and concise by modern standards, simplifying the classification problem immensely. In the past, a knowledgeable financial planner could typically choose the desired business classification by jumping through the requisite hoops set by the old regulations, effectively making the choice elective. The new regulations have just made the election explicit, eliminating the prior formalities and their attendant costs.

However, the ease of choosing to operate as a transparent (e.g., partnership or disregarded entity) or nontransparent (e.g., corporation) entity from Treasury's point of view may offer too much freedom, particularly in the international context, where taxpayers may be able take tax advantage of entities classified one way for U.S. tax purposes and a different way for foreign tax purposes. An entity that is transparent for U.S. tax purposes and nontransparent for foreign tax purposes is sometimes referred to as a "hybrid entity." An entity that is nontransparent for U.S. tax purposes and transparent for foreign tax purposes is sometimes referred to as a "reverse hybrid."

6. *Limited Liability Companies*

A multiple-owner limited liability company (LLC) combines the corporate benefit of limited liability for its owners and, unless otherwise elected under the check-the-box regulations, the partnership's tax advantage of pass-through treatment for federal income tax purposes. To form an LLC, articles of organization (not incorporation) must be filed with the appropriate state authority. An LLC is owned by "members" rather than by shareholders or partners. In some cases, an LLC must have at least two members, but many states permit single-member LLCs. Corporations, partnerships, LLCs, trusts, estates, and other entities, as well as individuals, may be members. Contributions to an LLC in exchange for a membership interest may be made in the form of cash, property, the use of property, services, or any other valuable consideration. In some states, contributions may also be made in the form of a promissory note or other binding obligation.

An LLC may not be required to have an operating agreement. Some states, however, require the adoption of an operating agreement and specify certain mandatory provisions. In the absence of an operating agreement, an LLC is governed by its articles and state law. Provisions relating to an LLC's affairs generally may be included in an operating agreement to the extent that they are not inconsistent with state law or the LLC's articles. Typically, LLC statutes rely on "default rules," or statutory provisions that apply unless an LLC's articles or operating agreement specifies otherwise, specifications that may customize the LLC to suit the needs of its members.

Members of an LLC are usually permitted under state law to customize both distribution of cash and property and allocation of profits and losses to the members through the operating agreement or the articles. In the absence of any financial provisions in the operating agreement or in the articles, distributions are generally made, and profits and losses are allocated on a proportional basis in accordance with the members' respective contributions.

One of the major advantages of an LLC is that it provides limited liability to all its members and managers. The typical state act provides that an individual or entity does not have any personal obligation for the liabilities of an LLC solely by reason of being a member, manager, or other agent of the LLC. Some states permit a member to waive limited liability. The ability to insulate an LLC member from personal liability as a member, regardless of management activities, is one of the primary distinctions between an LLC and a limited partnership. For example, under the Revised Uniform Limited Partnership Act (RULPA), a limited partner who participates in the partnership's management can become personally liable for partnership obligations.

Unless an operating agreement or the articles provide to the contrary, a membership interest is assignable in whole or in part. The assignment of a membership interest enables the assignee only to receive, to the extent assigned, the distributions from the LLC to which the assignor would otherwise be entitled. For the assignee to participate in the management and affairs of the LLC and to exercise other membership rights, the remaining members may have to unanimously consent to the assignee's admission as a member.

B. DUMMY CORPORATIONS

The check-the-box regulations do not formally permit a corporation to choose to be taxed as a transparent entity. But can a taxpayer that has chosen to operate in corporate form under applicable state law nevertheless ignore that form for federal tax purposes?

Commissioner v. Bollinger

485 U.S. 340 (1988)

Justice SCALIA delivered the opinion of the Court.

Petitioner the Commissioner of Internal Revenue challenges a decision by the United States Court of Appeals for the Sixth Circuit holding that a corporation which held record title to real property as agent for the corporation's shareholders was not the owner of the property for purposes of federal income taxation. 807 F.2d 65 (1986). We granted certiorari . . . to resolve a conflict in the courts of appeals over the tax treatment of corporations purporting to be agents for their shareholders. . . .

I

Respondent Jesse C. Bollinger, Jr., developed, either individually or in partnership with some or all of the other respondents, eight apartment complexes in Lexington, Kentucky. (For convenience we will refer to all the ventures as "partnerships.") Bollinger initiated development of the first apartment complex, Creekside North Apartments, in 1968. The Massachusetts Mutual Life Insurance Company agreed to provide permanent financing by lending $1,075,000 to "the corporate nominee of Jesse C. Bollinger, Jr." at an annual interest rate of eight percent, secured by a mortgage on the property and a personal guaranty from Bollinger. The loan commitment was structured in this fashion because Kentucky's usury law at the time limited the annual interest rate for noncorporate borrowers to seven percent. Ky. Rev. Stat. §§360.010, 360.025 (1972). Lenders willing to provide money only at higher rates required the nominal debtor and record title holder of mortgaged property to be a corporate nominee of the true owner and borrower. On October 14, 1968, Bollinger incorporated Creekside, Inc., under the laws of Kentucky; he was the only stockholder. The next day, Bollinger and Creekside, Inc., entered into a written agreement which provided that the corporation would hold title to the apartment complex as Bollinger's agent for the sole purpose of securing financing, and would convey, assign, or encumber the property and disburse the proceeds thereof only as directed by Bollinger; that Creekside, Inc., had no obligation to maintain the property or assume any liability by reason of the execution of promissory notes or otherwise; and that Bollinger would indemnify and hold the corporation harmless from any liability it might sustain as his agent and nominee.

Having secured the commitment for permanent financing, Bollinger, acting through Creekside, Inc., borrowed the construction funds for the apartment complex from Citizens Fidelity Bank and Trust Company. Creekside, Inc., executed all necessary loan documents including the promissory note and mortgage, and transferred all loan proceeds to Bollinger's individual construction account. Bollinger acted as general contractor for the construction, hired the necessary employees, and paid the expenses out of the construction account. When construction was completed, Bollinger obtained, again through Creekside, Inc., permanent financing from Massachusetts Mutual Life in accordance with the earlier loan commitment. These loan proceeds were used to pay off the Citizens Fidelity construction loan. Bollinger hired a resident manager to rent the apartments, execute leases with tenants, collect and deposit the rents, and maintain operating records. The manager deposited all rental receipts into, and paid all operating expenses from, an operating account, which was first opened in the name of Creekside, Inc., but was later changed to "Creekside Apartments, a partnership." The operation of Creekside North Apartments generated losses for the taxable years 1969, 1971, 1972, 1973, and 1974, and ordinary income for the years 1970, 1975, 1976, and 1977. Throughout, the income and losses were reported by Bollinger on his individual income tax returns.

Following a substantially identical pattern, seven other apartment complexes were developed by respondents through seven separate partnerships. For each venture, a partnership executed a nominee agreement with Creekside, Inc., to obtain financing. (For one of the ventures, a different Kentucky corporation, Cloisters, Inc., in which Bollinger had a 50 percent interest, acted as the borrower and titleholder. For convenience, we will refer to both Creekside and Cloisters as "the corporation.") The corporation transferred the construction loan proceeds to the partnership's construction account, and the partnership hired a construction supervisor who oversaw construction. Upon completion of construction, each partnership actively managed its apartment complex, depositing all rental receipts into, and paying all expenses from, a separate partnership account for each apartment complex. The corporation had no assets, liabilities, employees, or bank accounts. In every case, the lenders regarded the partnership as the owner of the apartments and were aware that the corporation was acting as agent of the partnership in holding record title. The partnerships reported the income and losses generated by the apartment complexes on their partnership tax returns, and respondents reported their distributive share of the partnership income and losses on their individual tax returns.

The Commissioner of Internal Revenue disallowed the losses reported by respondents, on the ground that the standards set out in National Carbide Corp. v. Commissioner, 336 U.S. 422 (1949), were not met. The Commissioner contended that *National Carbide* required a corporation to have an arm's-length relationship with its shareholders before it could be recognized as their agent. Although not all respondents were shareholders of the corporation, the Commissioner took the position that the funds the partnerships disbursed to pay expenses should be deemed contributions to the corporation's capital, thereby making all respondents constructive stockholders. Since, in the Commissioner's view, the corporation rather than its shareholders owned the real estate, any losses sustained by the ventures were attributable to the corporation and not respondents. Respondents sought a redetermination in the United States Tax Court. The Tax Court held that the corporations were the agents of the partnerships and should be disregarded for tax purposes. Bollinger v. Commissioner, 48 T.C.M. 1443 (1984), ¶ 84,560 P-H Memo T.C. On appeal, the United States Court of Appeals for the Sixth Circuit affirmed. 807 F.2d 65 (1986). We granted the Commissioner's petition for certiorari.

II

For federal income tax purposes, gain or loss from the sale or use of property is attributable to the owner of the property. *See* Helvering v. Horst, 311 U.S. 112, 116-117 (1940); Blair v. Commissioner, 300 U.S. 5, 12 (1937); see also Commissioner v. Sunnen, 333 U.S. 591, 604 (1948). The problem we face here is that two different taxpayers can plausibly be regarded as the owner. Neither the Internal Revenue Code nor the regulations promulgated by the Secretary of the Treasury provide significant guidance as to which should be selected. It is common ground between the parties, however, that if a corporation holds title to property as agent for a partnership, then for tax purposes the partnership and not the corporation is the owner. Given agreement on that premise, one would suppose that there would be agreement upon the conclusion as well. For each of respondents' apartment complexes, an agency agreement expressly provided that the corporation would "hold such property as nominee and agent for" the partnership, App. to Pet. for Cert. 21a, n.4, and that the partnership would have sole control of and responsibility for the apartment complex. The partnership in each instance was identified as the principal and owner of the property during financing, construction, and operation. The lenders, contractors, managers, employees, and tenants — all who had contact with the development — knew that the corporation was merely the agent of the partnership, if they knew of the existence of the corporation at all. In each instance the relationship between the corporation and the partnership was, in both form and substance, an agency with the partnership as principal.

The Commissioner contends, however, that the normal indicia of agency cannot suffice for tax purposes when, as here, the alleged principals are the controlling shareholders of the alleged agent corporation. That, it asserts, would undermine the principle of Moline Properties v. Commissioner, 319 U.S. 436 (1943), which held that a corporation is a separate taxable entity even if it has only one shareholder who exercises total control over its affairs. Obviously, *Moline*'s separate-entity principle would be significantly compromised if shareholders of closely held corporations could, by clothing the corporation with some attributes of agency with respect to particular assets, leave themselves free at the end of the tax year to make a claim — perhaps even a good-faith claim — of either agent or owner status, depending upon which choice turns out to minimize their tax liability. The Commissioner does not have the resources to audit and litigate the many cases in which agency status could be thought debatable. Hence, the Commissioner argues, in this shareholder context he can reasonably demand that the taxpayer meet a prophylactically clear test of agency.

We agree with that principle, but the question remains whether the test the Commissioner proposes is appropriate. The parties have debated at length the significance of our opinion in National Carbide Corp. v. Commissioner, supra. In that case, three corporations that were wholly owned subsidiaries of another corporation agreed to operate their production plants as "agents" for the parent, transferring to it all profits except for a nominal sum. The subsidiaries reported as gross income only this sum, but the Commissioner concluded that they should be taxed on the entirety of the profits because they were not really agents. We agreed, reasoning first, that the mere fact of the parent's control over the subsidiaries did not establish the existence of an agency, since such control is typical of all shareholder-corporation relationships, *id.*, at 429-434; and second, that the agreements to pay the parent all profits above a nominal amount were not determinative since income must be taxed to those who actually earn it without regard to anticipatory assignment, *id.*, at 435-436. We acknowledged, however, that there was such a thing as "a true corporate agent . . . of an owner-principal," *id.*, at 437, and proceeded to set forth four indicia and two requirements of such status, the sum of which has become known in the lore of federal income tax law as the "six *National Carbide* factors":

> [1] Whether the corporation operates in the name and for the account of the principal, [2] binds the principal by its actions, [3] transmits money received to the principal, and [4] whether receipt of income is attributable to the services of employees of the principal and to assets belonging to the principal are some of the relevant considerations in determining whether a true agency exists. [5] If the corporation is a true agent, its relations with its principal must not be dependent upon the fact that it is owned by the principal, if such is the case. [6] Its business purpose must be the carrying on of the normal duties of an agent.

Id., at 47 (footnotes omitted).

We readily discerned that these factors led to a conclusion of nonagency in *National Carbide* itself. There each subsidiary had represented to its customers that it (not the parent) was the company manufacturing and selling its products; each had sought to shield the parent from service of legal process; and the operations had used thousands of the subsidiaries' employees and nearly $20 million worth of property and equipment listed as assets on the subsidiaries' books. *Id.*, at 425, 434, 438, and n.21.

The Commissioner contends that the last two *National Carbide* factors are not satisfied in the present case. To take the last first: The Commissioner argues that here the corporation's business purpose with respect to the property at issue was not "the carrying on of the normal duties of an agent," since it was acting not as the agent but rather as the owner of the property for purposes of Kentucky's usury laws. We do not agree. It assuredly was not acting as the owner in fact, since respondents represented themselves as the principals to all parties concerned with the loans. Indeed, it was the lenders themselves who required the use of a corporate nominee. Nor does it make any sense to adopt a contrary-to-fact legal presumption that the corporation was the principal, imposing a federal tax sanction for the apparent evasion of Kentucky's usury law. To begin with, the Commissioner has not established that these transactions were an evasion. Respondents assert without contradiction that use of agency arrangements in order to permit higher interest was common practice, and it is by no means clear that the practice violated the spirit of the Kentucky law, much less its letter. It might well be thought that the borrower does not generally require usury protection in a transaction sophisticated enough to employ a corporate agent — assuredly not the normal modus operandi of the loan shark. That the statute positively envisioned corporate nominees is suggested by a provision which forbids charging the higher corporate interest rates "to a corporation, the principal asset of which shall be the ownership of a one (1) or two (2) family dwelling," Ky. Rev. Stat. §360.025(2) (1987) — which would seem to prevent use of the nominee device for ordinary home-mortgage loans. In any event, even if the transaction did run afoul of the usury law, Kentucky, like most States, regards only the lender as the usurer, and the borrower as the victim. *See* Ky. Rev. Stat. §360.020 (1987) (lender liable to borrower for civil penalty), section 360.990 (lender guilty of misdemeanor). Since the Kentucky statute imposed no penalties upon the borrower for allowing himself to be victimized, nor treated him as in pari delictu, but to the contrary enabled him to pay back the principal without any interest, and to sue for double the amount of interest already paid (plus attorney's fees), see Ky. Rev. Stat. section 360.020 (1972), the United States would hardly be vindicating Kentucky law by depriving the usury victim of tax advantages he would otherwise enjoy. In sum, we see no basis in either fact or policy for holding that the corporation was the principal because of the nature of its participation in the loans.

Of more general importance is the Commissioner's contention that the arrangements here violate the fifth *National Carbide* factor — that the corporate agent's "relations with its principal must not be dependent upon the fact that it is owned by the principal." The Commissioner asserts that this cannot be satisfied unless the corporate agent and its shareholder principal have an "arm's-length relationship" that includes the payment of a fee for agency services. The meaning of *National Carbide*'s fifth factor is, at the risk of understatement, not entirely clear. Ultimately, the relations between a corporate agent and its owner-principal are always dependent upon the fact of ownership, in that the owner can cause the relations to be altered or terminated at any time. Plainly that is not what was meant, since on that interpretation all subsidiary-parent agencies would be invalid for tax purposes, a position which the *National Carbide* opinion specifically disavowed. We think the fifth *National Carbide* factor — so much more abstract than the others — was no more and no less than a generalized statement of the concern, expressed earlier in our own discussion, that the separate-entity doctrine of *Moline* not be subverted.

In any case, we decline to parse the text of *National Carbide* as though that were itself the governing statute. As noted earlier, it is uncontested that the law attributes tax consequences of property held by a genuine agent to the principal; and we agree that it is reasonable for the Commissioner to demand unequivocal evidence of genuineness in the corporation-shareholder context, in order to prevent evasion of *Moline*. We see no basis, however, for holding that unequivocal evidence can only consist of the rigid requirements (arm's-length dealing plus agency fee) that the Commissioner suggests. Neither of those is demanded by the law of agency, which permits agents to be unpaid family members, friends, or associates. *See* Restatement (Second) of Agency §§16, 21, 22 (1958). It seems to us that the genuineness of the agency relationship is adequately assured, and tax-avoiding manipulation adequately avoided, when the fact that the corporation is acting as agent for its shareholders with respect to a particular asset is set forth in a written agreement at the time the asset is acquired, the corporation functions as agent and not principal with respect to the asset for all purposes, and the corporation is held out as the agent and not principal in all dealings with third parties relating to the asset. Since these requirements were met here, the judgment of the Court of Appeals is affirmed.

Justice Kennedy took no part in the consideration or decision of this case.

NOTES

Justice Scalia's opinion is refreshing in its unwillingness to submerge the Court in an abstract test or a game of words involving the fifth *National Carbide* factor. Instead, the opinion finds a genuine principal-agent relationship in the existence of a written agreement when the property was acquired, in the fact that the corporation functioned as an agent for all purposes, and in the fact that the corporation held itself out as an agent in all third-party dealings.

Why wasn't the Court bothered by the argument that the decision was furthering evasion of state usury laws? Did Kentucky mean to prohibit the type of arrangements made by the taxpayers, or did the law have a more limited purpose?

Not all cases involving the agency issue concern corporations formed for the purpose of circumventing state usury limitations. See, e.g., Elot H. Raffety Farms v. United States, 511 F.2d 1234 (8th Cir. 1975) (the court of appeals recognized a corporation even though it was used only to avoid a foreign law requirement prohibiting conduct of a business by aliens). In Interstate Transit Lines v. Commissioner, 319 U.S. 590 (1943), a parent corporation was denied a deduction under §162(a) for a payment to its wholly owned subsidiary to defray the subsidiary's operating deficit for the taxable year, despite the fact that by contract it was entitled to the subsidiary's profits and was obliged to reimburse the subsidiary for its losses. The Court held that the subsidiary's operating deficit was not an expense of the parent's business. The case was complicated by the fact that the subsidiary was organized to engage in operations (intrastate transportation in California) that were forbidden to the parent because it was a foreign corporation. The Court was not called on to decide whether the parent's payments should be treated as an additional investment in the subsidiary.

PROBLEM

15-1. Management Corp. is in the business of managing real estate investments made by limited partnerships in which it serves as the general partner. The limited partnerships are organized by Management Corp., which is compensated for both its management and organizational services. For a variety of reasons, banks making mortgage loans to the partnerships generally prefer that title to the property be held by a corporation. Management Corp. performs that function for the partnerships, which in turn compensate the corporation for its role. When Management Corp. performs this function, it represents to everyone it deals with that it is serving as an agent for the partnership. What else do you need to know to determine whether the corporation or the partnership is entitled to any deductions arising from the real estate activities?

C. REALLOCATION OF INCOME AND RELATED ISSUES

When corporate tax rates are lower than the top individual tax rates, individuals have incentives to allocate income to corporations they control. Moreover, historically corporations have offered pension incentives to owner-employees not available to individual entrepreneurs. For example, prior to 1982, the pension opportunities available to employees of corporations far exceeded those available to the self-employed. In response to this disparity, professionals such as doctors and lawyers created wholly owned professional service corporations for which they would work. These corporations would be in the business of hiring out their sole employee (the doctor or lawyer) to his prior employer. The income that the corporation received was paid to its sole employee partly in cash and partly in the form of a lucrative pension plan. Thus, the professional service corporation often was used solely to obtain greater pension benefits.

Personal service corporations also offer income-splitting opportunities. For example, an architect might work exclusively for her professional service corporation for a salary far less than the fees received by the corporation for her services. Because the corporation will deduct the architect's salary under §162 as an ordinary and necessary business expense, the corporation's taxable income will be only that proportion of its receipts that it retains. The architect's taxable income, on the other hand, will equal her salary. By dividing receipts between herself and her corporation, no income goes untaxed, but the architect's compensation is taxed between two taxpayers, thereby taking advantage of two sets of progressive rates to reduce the total tax liability.

The allocation of income phenomenon is not restricted to shareholders trying to shift income to controlled corporations; it is a dominant issue for intercorporate allocations as well. In many cases, U.S. corporations subject to U.S. taxation have an incentive to shift income to a related foreign corporation that may not be subject to U.S. taxation and is often subject to little foreign taxation. For example, suppose a U.S. corporation with a foreign subsidiary in a low-tax jurisdiction manufactures thermostats at a cost of $100 that it sells to the subsidiary, which resells the thermostats to unrelated purchasers in the subsidiary's jurisdiction at a price of $500. If the U.S. parent charges the subsidiary $140 for the thermostats, it will have $40 subject to U.S. taxation. The $360 gain the subsidiary realizes on the resale is typically not subject to U.S. taxation. Often the Service in this type of situation will attempt to reallocate some of the subsidiary's income to the U.S. parent.

1. *Section 482 in General*

Section 482 authorizes the Service to allocate gross income, deductions, and credits among related taxpayers to the extent necessary to prevent evasion of taxes or to clearly reflect the income of related taxpayers. The regulations implementing §482 are based on the principle that transactions between related parties should be evaluated on an "arm's length" basis—that is, how unrelated parties would structure the transaction.

Section 482 can apply whenever two taxpayers are "owned or controlled directly or indirectly by the same interests." In determining control, the Service focuses on the realities of the situation rather than on whether there is formal legal control. Treas. Regs. §1.482-1(i)(4). Section 482 can apply to domestic and foreign corporations, but because of the steep graduation in §11, there is often little to be gained by allocating income between related U.S. corporations. In the international context, §482 is often applied to allocate income from a foreign subsidiary to a U.S. parent. The provision also applies, however, in the converse situation to allocate income from a foreign parent to a U.S. subsidiary or between commonly owned corporations, one foreign and one domestic.

The arm's-length character of a transaction between related parties (i.e., a controlled transaction) is best tested by comparing the results of the transaction in question with the results of unrelated taxpayers engaged in comparable transactions under comparable circumstances (i.e., uncontrolled transactions). The use of comparables is important in most of the arm's-length methods described below. For two transactions to be considered comparable, an uncontrolled transaction need not be identical. When necessary, a reasonable number of adjustments may be made to account for material differences between a controlled and an uncontrolled transaction.

Comparability of two transactions can be established by looking at the following factors: functions, risks, contractual terms, economic conditions, and property or services. Treas. Regs. §1.482-1(d)(1). Each of these factors is weighed to determine how compatible two transactions are and what appropriate adjustments may be necessary. See Treas. Regs. §1.482-1(d)(3).

The reallocation principles of §482 are best understood in the context of specific types of transactions. What follows is a summary of the principles that can apply to some of the more basic transactions addressed by the regulations. In any situation involving §482, the result is heavily dependent on the facts, but taxpayers receive little guidance from the decided cases. The regulations attempt to provide more certainty in reallocating income, but uncertainty still abounds. This uncertainty has made reallocation of income one of the most pervasive tax problems faced by multinational corporations.

a. Sales of Tangible Property

When Parentco, a U.S. corporation, sells goods to Subco, a foreign subsidiary, and Subco resells the goods to unrelated purchasers, the Parentco's gain on its sale to Subco for U.S. tax purposes is determined in accordance with the arm's-length price that an unrelated purchaser would have paid under the same circumstances. The same is true if Parentco is a foreign parent corporation that sells goods to Subco, its wholly owned U.S. subsidiary, which resells to unrelated purchasers in the United States, or if the foreign and U.S. corporations have a common parent corporation. The regulations detail the following pricing methods: the comparable uncontrolled price method, the resale price method, the cost plus method, and the comparable profits method. Treas. Regs. §1.482-3. Under some circumstances other methods are also permitted.

In a world with perfect information available at no cost, all methods would generate the identical allocation between the parent and subsidiary corporation. A comparable transaction involving unrelated parties transacting at an arm's-length price is the best method of allocation. If that information is not available, working backward from the ultimate price charged by Subco to an unrelated purchaser may produce an arm's-length price for the sale from Parentco to Subco (i.e., the resale price method). If that information is not available, perhaps an arm's-length price can be determined by working forward from the actual manufacturing cost incurred by Parentco (i.e., cost plus method).

Under the "best method rule" of the regulations, the arm's-length price for a particular transaction should be determined using the method that provides the most reliable measure of an arm's-length result—hardly a shocking rule. Treas. Regs. §1.482-1(c)(1). For example, use of the resale price method may be appropriate when a manufacturer sells products to a controlled distributor that, without further processing or the use of significant intangibles, resells the products in uncontrolled transactions. Use of the cost plus method may be appropriate when a manufacturer sells products to a controlled taxpayer that resells after further processing or the use of significant intangibles. In either case, however, the comparable uncontrolled price method, if data are available, may provide the most accurate measure of an arm's-length price.

Comparable uncontrolled price method. Under the comparable uncontrolled price method, the price for tax purposes deemed paid by Subco to Parentco is based on the price in "uncontrolled sales" made by Parentco to unrelated buyers. Treas. Regs. §1.482-3(b)(1). An uncontrolled sale might include a sale made by Parentco to an unrelated purchaser if, like Subco, the purchaser is not an end-user. Comparable sales of the same product between two unrelated parties may also provide relevant information. In determining comparability, differences in the product or the circumstances surrounding the sale (e.g., volume discounts, geographic market, whether the purchaser is a wholesaler or retail customer) are taken into account. For unique products or products in which the seller has a virtual monopoly, there may be no comparable uncontrolled prices.

Resale price method. The regulations also permit use of the resale price method, and it is ordinarily used when the related purchaser does not add significant value to the product (e.g., if the purchaser is merely a distributor). Treas. Regs. §1.482-3(c)(1). It is not ordinarily used, however, where the related purchaser uses intangible property to add substantial value to the goods sold. *Id.*

The resale price method is intended to measure the value of the distribution function performed by a related purchaser. Under this method, the deemed transfer price equals the applicable resale price charged to unrelated purchasers, minus an appropriate gross profit. Treas. Regs. §1.482-3(c)(2)(i) and (ii). The appropriate gross profit is determined by multiplying the applicable resale price by an appropriate gross profit margin, which is essentially profit as a percentage of gross sales in uncontrolled transactions. *Id.* at (c)(2)(iii).

Cost plus method. The cost plus method is ordinarily used in cases involving the manufacture, assembly, or other production of goods sold to a related purchaser, but where the related purchaser adds substantial value to the goods. See Treas. Regs. §1.482-3(d)(1). Under this method, the deemed transfer price equals the sum of the seller's costs plus an appropriate gross profit markup. *Id.* at (d)(2).

Comparable profits method. The comparable profits method is based on the principle that similarly situated taxpayers will tend to earn similar returns over a reasonable period of time. The comparable profits method determines arm's-length consideration for a controlled transfer of property based on objective measures of profitability (profit-level indicators) derived from uncontrolled taxpayers that engage in similar activities with other uncontrolled taxpayers. Treas. Regs. §1.482-5(a).

An arm's-length range of comparable operating profits is determined by applying the profit-level indicators to the tested party. A controlled transaction will be considered arm's length if the tested party's actual operating profits are within the arm's-length range of the comparable operating profits. See generally Treas. Regs. §1.482-5(b). See also Treas. Regs. §1.482-1(e)(2). The tested party can be either party to a controlled transaction — generally the one that provides the simplest, and therefore the most easily compared, operations. Treas. Regs. §1.482-5(b)(2)(i).

Profit-level indicators are financial ratios that measure the relationships among profits, costs incurred, and resources employed. *Id.* at (b)(4). For example, the rate of return on capital employed is the ratio of operating profit to operating assets. *Id.* at (b)(4)(i). This measure may provide an acceptable profit-level indicator if the tested party has substantial fixed assets or working capital. Other financial ratios that may serve as profit-level indicators include the ratio of operating profit to sales and the ratio of gross profit to operating expenses. *Id.* at (b)(4)(ii). For a comparable uncontrolled company that has gross profits of $140 and operating expenses of $100, for example, the ratio of gross profits to operating expenses is 1.4. If the tested party has operating expenses of $50, then one point in the arm's-length range of comparable operating profits is $70 (1.4 times $50).

In an example taken from the regulations, the comparable profit method is used to determine the transfer price for an intercompany sale of goods. Treas. Regs. §1.482-5(e) (example 1). Foreign Parent (FP) manufactures consumer products. A U.S. subsidiary (USSub) purchases these products for distribution in the United States. Similar products are produced by other companies but none of them is sold to uncontrolled taxpayers. Because no comparable uncontrolled transactions exist and because there is insufficient data for use of either the cost plus or resale price methods, the comparable profits method is used by the Service to verify the price paid by USSub to FP for the tangible property purchased in 1996.

USSub is selected as the tested party because its activities are less complex than FP's. USSub has the following financial profile:

	1994	*1995*	*1996*	*Average*
Sales	500,000	560,000	500,000	520,000
Cost of goods sold	393,000	412,400	400,000	401,800
Operating expenses	80,000	110,000	106,600	98,200
Operating profit	27,000	37,600	(4,600)	20,000

To test the transfer price paid by USSub to FP for the consumer products, the Service would identify comparable parties to USSub (i.e., wholesale distributors in the same industry segment that perform similar functions and assume similar risks). Because working capital plays a significant role in generating operating profit, the Service might choose the rate of return on capital as a profit-level indicator. Calculating the average ratio of operating profits (OP) to operating assets (OA) for each of the uncontrolled distributors and multiplying that ratio by the average operating assets of USSub for the three-year testing period leads to the following comparable operating profits (COP) for USSub:

Unrelated Distributor	*OP/OA*	*USSub COP*
A	1.7%	$ 8,840
B	3.1	16,120
C	3.8	19,760
D	4.5	23,400
E	4.7	24,440
F	4.8	24,960
G	4.9	25,480
H	6.7	34,840
I	9.9	51,480
J	10.5	54,600

If the Service determines that the products sold by the distributors are not similar enough to allow the use of all the comparable operating profits, top and bottom comparable operating profits will be lopped off, and the "interquartile" range (i.e., the 25th to the 75th percentile) of results will be used. In this example, the interquartile range is $19,760 to $34,840. Because USSub's reported average operating income of $20,000 falls within this range, the 1996 transfer pricing used by USSub is accepted by the Service even though there is an operating loss for 1996. If USSub's average operating income for the three-year period were $0, the Service would determine a transfer price that would increase USSub's operating profit to the median of the arm's-length range for 1996.

Other methods. All the methods just described and those described below relating to transactions other than sales depend in part on the availability of comparable transactions. Comparables are often difficult to locate, whether in the context of sales, services, or rentals of tangible property or licenses of intangible property. Moreover, product sales often are interrelated to the licensing of intangibles (e.g., manufacturing patents) used to produce the products. The difficulty in determining arm's-length prices for interrelated items has led to the development of alternative income allocation approaches used for determining the price of intercompany sales of inventory as well as royalty rates on intercompany licenses. Treas. Regs. §1.482-3(e). An appropriate method might include an allocation of overall profit based on an acceptable rate of return on invested capital or on a comparison of rates of return to operating costs.

b. Services

When one corporation performs services that result in a benefit to a related corporation, the arm's-length price for the services is determined under one of seven methods. See Treas. Regs. §1.482-9(l) (calling these services "controlled service transactions"). In applying these methods, the best method rule also applies.

Service cost method. This method applies to low-margin services, such as back-office operations. Under this method, the arm's-length price for these services is their cost with no markup. *Id.* at (b)(1). This method applies to services for which the median comparable markup on total service costs, as determined under the regulations, is not more than 7 percent. *Id.* at (b)(3)(ii).

Comparable uncontrolled services price (CUSP) method. This method compares the amounts charged for a controlled service and for comparable uncontrolled services.

Id. at (c)(1). This method should be the best method if "an uncontrolled transaction has no differences from the controlled transaction that would affect the price, or if there are only minor differences that have a definite and reasonably ascertainable effect on price and for which appropriate adjustments are made." *Id.* at (c)(2)(ii)(A). If "there are material differences for which reliable adjustments cannot be made," however, this method "ordinarily" is not the best method. *Id.*

Gross services margin method. The "gross services margin" method determines the arm's-length price of a controlled services transaction by looking to the gross profit margin realized in comparable uncontrolled transactions. *Id.* at (d)(1). This method may be used when a member of a controlled group acts as an agent for another member in connection with a transaction with an unrelated person. *Id.* It may also be used when one controlled group member acts as an intermediary, contracting to provide services to an unrelated person but using another member to actually perform some portion of those services. *Id.*

Cost of services plus method. Under this method, the arm's-length price is determined by comparing the gross profit markup in comparable controlled and uncontrolled transactions. *Id.* at (e)(1). This method is ordinarily used when the service provider provides the same or similar services to both controlled and uncontrolled parties. *Id.* (cautioning that this method "is ordinarily not used where the controlled services transaction involves a contingent-payment arrangement").

The comparable profit method. With some modifications, this method is the same as the one described above for sales. See Treas. Regs. §1.482-5; Treas. Regs. §1.482-9. See also *id.* at (f)(2)(ii) (adding that relevant profit indicators also include the ratio of operating profit to total service costs). This method may apply if the tested party is the one providing the services; however, it does not apply if that party is the one receiving the services. *Id.* at (f)(2)(i).

Under this method, no adjustment is made to the operating income of a taxpayer if the income falls within the arm's-length range of results, which is a range of operating incomes for similar taxpayers. If the operating income does not fall within the arm's-length range, adjustments may be made in a taxpayer's transfer price to place the taxpayer within the arm's-length range.

The profit split method. This method evaluates the allocation of the combined operating profit or loss attributable to one or more controlled transactions between controlled taxpayers. *Id.* at (g)(1). Whether that allocation is arm's length is based on the relative value of each controlled taxpayer's contribution to that combined operating profit or loss. *Id.*; Treas. Regs. §1.482-6(a). That relative value is determined in a manner that reflects the functions performed, risks assumed, and resources employed by each participant in the relevant business activity. Treas. Regs. §482-9(g)(1); Treas. Regs. §1.482-6(b).

Other methods. Another method, not specified above, may be used if "it provides the most reliable measure of an arm's length result under the principles of the best method rule." Treas. Regs. §1.482-9(h)(1). Among other things, the method should take into account economically similar transactions involving unrelated parties. *Id.*

c. Rentals of Tangible Property

When a taxpayer leases tangible property (e.g., machinery, equipment, real estate) to a related taxpayer but the lessee does not pay an arm's-length rental, appropriate allocations may be made to reflect an arm's-length rental. Treas. Regs. §1.482-2(c)(1). An arm's-length rental is the amount that would have been charged on a transaction between unrelated parties. *Id.* at (c)(2)(i). If the owner of a lease makes the property available to a related entity through a sublease, the arm's-length price generally is an amount equal to the owner's deductions (i.e., rent, maintenance, utilities, etc.). *Id.* at (c)(2)(iii)(A). See also *id.* at (c)(2)(iii)(B) (for some exceptions). There is no deemed profit in the sublease situation.

d. Licenses of Intangible Property

Payments to a related party for a license or transfer of an intangible may be reallocated by the Service if the payments are not deemed to be at arm's length. Intangible property for purposes of §482 includes any patent, invention, formula, process design, pattern, know-how, copyright, trademark, franchise, license, or contract. Treas. Regs. §1.482-4(b) (adding that the intangible must have substantial value independent of the services of any individual). Methods for determining an arm's-length price for the transfer of an intangible include the comparable uncontrolled transaction (CUT) method, the comparable profits method (CPM), the profit split method (PSM), and "unspecified" methods. Treas. Regs. §1.482-4(a). See also Treas. Regs. §1.482-7 (for methods of determining taxable income in connection with a cost sharing arrangement).

The comparable uncontrolled transaction method. Under the comparable uncontrolled transaction method, the arm's-length consideration for a controlled transfer of intangible property (i.e., transactions between related parties) is equal to the consideration charged in a comparable uncontrolled transaction (i.e., transactions between unrelated parties). Treas. Regs. §1.482-4(c). An uncontrolled transaction is considered comparable to a controlled transaction if the intangibles to be compared are used in the connection with similar products or processes in the same general market or industry and have similar profit potential. *Id.* at (c)(2)(iii)(B). In addition, comparability is also based on the economic terms under which the transactions take place. *Id.* These rules are intended to ensure that the circumstances surrounding the controlled and uncontrolled transactions are comparable.

The comparable profit method. This method was described above for sales. See Treas. Regs. §1.482-5. Under this method, no adjustment is made to the operating income of a taxpayer if the income falls within the arm's-length range of results, which is a range of operating incomes for similar taxpayers. If the operating income does not fall within the arm's-length range, adjustments may be made in a taxpayer's transfer price to place the taxpayer within the arm's-length range.

The profit split method. This method was described above for services. It evaluates the allocation of the combined operating profit or loss attributable to one or more controlled transactions between controlled taxpayers. Whether that allocation is arm's length is based on the relative value of each controlled taxpayer's contribution to that combined operating profit or loss. Treas. Regs. §1.482-6(a). That relative value is determined in a manner that reflects the functions performed, risks assumed, and resources employed by each participant in the relevant business activity. *Id.* at (b).

Periodic adjustments. Payments to a related party for a license or transfer of an intangible must be "commensurate with the income" attributable to the intangible.

§482 (second sentence). The practical effect of the "commensurate with" language is that royalty arrangements between related parties can be periodically adjusted by the Service to reflect changing market conditions. For example, royalty payments deemed received by a U.S. corporation from intangible property licensed to its foreign subsidiary might be adjusted periodically to reflect how the property actually performs in the hands of the licensee. If, five or ten years after the original license, the intangible becomes extremely valuable, that increase in value (i.e., increased sublicensing royalties or increased sales of property incorporating the intangible) may be taxable to the licensor even if the royalty rates at the time of the original license were reasonable under the facts known at that time. This provision represents an extraordinary view of what an arm's-length transaction is — substituting an ex post determination for an ex ante determination. The fact that a royalty agreement at the time it was concluded provided for arm's-length payments does not guarantee that an adjustment will not be made in a subsequent year. Treas. Regs. §1.482-4(f)(2).

e. Loans

Like other transactions between related parties, a loan from one corporation to a related corporation must be made at arm's length; otherwise, the Service may reallocate interest income between the parties. If U.S. Co. makes a loan to Subco, its foreign subsidiary, and charges inadequate interest, U.S. Co. has effectively transferred the earning of interest beyond U.S. tax jurisdiction. Conversely, if Subco lends money to U.S. Co. and charges an artificially high interest rate, the interest deduction otherwise available to U.S. Co. diverts income to Subco. To prevent this assignment of income, the Service generally imposes an arm's-length interest rate. Cf. §7872.

2. *The Interplay of §482 and Foreign Law*

The purpose of §482 is to force taxpayers for tax purposes to deal at arm's length with related parties. Suppose, however, that related parties are prohibited from setting an arm's-length price because of a foreign government law or regulation. For U.S. tax purposes, should §482 apply notwithstanding the impossibility of paying an arm's-length price?

In Procter & Gamble Co. v. Commissioner, 961 F.2d 1255 (6th Cir. 1992), Procter and Gamble (P&G) owned all the stock of Procter and Gamble A.G. (AG), a Swiss corporation engaged in marketing P&G's products in countries where P&G did not have a marketing subsidiary. AG licensed and paid royalties to P&G for the use of P&G's patents, trademarks, tradenames, knowledge, and assistance. AG, in turn, sublicensed the patents, etc., to its subsidiaries throughout Europe and the Middle East. The income earned by AG from its sublicensing activities was taxable directly to P&G under the controlled foreign corporation provisions (§§951-959). AG organized a Spanish subsidiary, Gamble Espana, S.A. (Espana) to manufacture and sell its consumer and industrial products in Spain. The Tax Court found that during the years in question, Spain prohibited the payment of royalties from Espana to AG.

Notwithstanding the Spanish prohibition against royalty payments to a parent corporation, the Service determined that a royalty equal to 2 percent of Espana's net sales should be allocated to AG (and therefore be taxable to P&G). The Service reasoned that no taxpayer would give away the right to use property in an arm's-length transaction. The only reason AG was willing to forgo a royalty payment from Espana was that, as a parent corporation, AG would reap the benefit of Espana's use of the royalty property in the form of increased stock value. A nonshareholder-licensor would not agree to license the use of its property unless it received royalty payments in exchange; otherwise, the income produced by the transferred property would inure to the benefit of the licensee's shareholders. Indeed, Spanish law recognized this fact by permitting the payment of royalties to unrelated licensors. Accordingly, there can be little doubt that it was the relationship of AG to Espana that gave rise to the uncompensated use of P&G's property.

Although the relationship of AG to Espana made the transaction possible, it was the existence of Spanish law that made the royalty payment impossible. Relying on the Supreme Court holding in Commissioner v. First Security Bank of Utah, 405 U.S. 394 (1972) (income shifted from a bank to a captive insurance company could not be allocated under §482 because receipt of insurance commissions by the bank would have violated U.S. banking laws), the Tax Court in *Procter & Gamble* concluded that the Service could not allocate income between related corporations when the purported misallocation was caused by foreign law. As a result of the Tax Court's decision, Procter & Gamble did not have to report royalty income deemed received by AG. See Texaco v. Commissioner, 98 F.3d 825 (5th Cir. 1996).

A danger arises in allowing foreign law to impede the application of §482. It is not difficult to imagine that some taxpayers may actually encourage (and be willing to pay for) foreign governments to prevent certain arm's-length payments between related taxpayers if the upshot is lower overall taxes. Should the United States allow foreign law to govern what is taxable in the United States when, under the arm's-length principle of §482, the United States considers income to be subject to U.S. taxation?

PROBLEM

15-2. USCO, a large U.S. oil company doing business in Saudi Arabia, is prohibited under Saudi law from selling any oil for more than $12 a barrel. The prohibition does not extend to resale by any purchaser from USCO. USCO's costs of exploration are $9 a barrel. USCO sells the oil at $12 a barrel to Subco, a wholly owned subsidiary located in Finland, a low-tax jurisdiction. Subco then resells the oil to independent purchasers at a price of $100 a barrel. Can the Service reallocate any of Subco's profits to USCO? Consider Commissioner v. First Security Bank of Utah, 405 U.S. 394 (1972), and Procter & Gamble Co. v. Commissioner, 961 F.2d 1255 (6th Cir. 1992). Should *First Security* apply in an international context?

3. *Income Shifting and the Assignment of Income Doctrine*

Historically, the use of personal service corporations, discussed at page 508 supra, was motivated in part by the opportunities to lower income by dividing profits between a corporation and owner-employees. In Rubin v. Commissioner, 429

F.2d 650 (2d Cir. 1970), the Tax Court's application of the assignment of income doctrine to a taxpayer and his personal service corporation was reversed. Despite this reversal, the Tax Court continued to sustain assignment of income challenges to personal service corporations. The Tax Court was reversed again in Foglesong v. Commissioner, 621 F.2d 865 (7th Cir. 1980) (*Foglesong I*) (a chemical engineer owned 98 percent of a personal services corporation), and it finally conceded in Keller v. Commissioner, 77 T.C. 1014 (1981), that the assignment of income doctrine cannot be used to reallocate income away from a corporation to its employee-shareholder so long as the corporation is a viable entity. In *Keller* and in *Foglesong I*, the Tax Court observed that because §482 could apply to a taxpayer who worked as an employee for his controlled corporation, application of the assignment of income doctrine would be redundant.

In *Foglesong I*, the circuit court gave the following explanation for why the assignment of income doctrine could not be used to reattribute income reported by Foglesong's corporation to Foglesong.

> Personal service corporation tax cases reveal a tension between "the principle of a graduated income tax . . . and the policy of recognizing the corporation as a taxable entity distinct from its shareholders in all but extreme cases." Rubin v. Commissioner, 429 F.2d 650, 652 (2d Cir. 1970). The impact of the graduated income tax is eroded when income is split artificially among several entities or over several tax years. The assignment of income doctrine under Section 61 (as formulated by Lucas v. Earl) seeks to recognize "economic reality" by cumulating income diffused among several recipients through "artificial" legal arrangements. The attribution of income to its "true earner" is simply a species of recognizing "substance" over "form."
>
> But, if the issue is one of attributing the income of a corporation to its sole stockholder-employee who "really" earned it, we encounter the important legal policy of the law favoring recognition of the corporation as a legal person and economic actor. . . .
>
> Under the circumstances of this case, we think it inappropriate to attempt to weigh "business purpose" against "tax avoidance motives" in a determination whether the assignment of income doctrine of Lucas v. Earl should apply, in effect, to substantially disregard the corporate form. [T]o apply Lucas v. Earl in this fashion under the circumstances present here is effectively (and more realistically) to nullify the determination that the Corporation is a viable, taxable entity and not a sham. . . .

Do you agree with the majority in *Foglesong I* that application of the assignment of income doctrine would have been tantamount to disregarding the corporate entity? Recall that Foglesong was not the sole shareholder of the corporation. If the corporation had been held a sham, would all the income have been includible by Foglesong? In his dissenting opinion in *Keller*, Judge Wilbur wrote, 77 T.C. at 1042: "Mere existence — either of Mrs. Earl or petitioner's corporation — does not carry automatic immunity from the assignment of income doctrine." If Foglesong had signed the same employment documents with his sister rather than with the corporation, could the assignment of income doctrine have been applied? Suppose his sister owned a large chemical engineering firm?

In Sargent v. Commissioner, 93 T.C. 572 (1989), the court ruled that hockey players were employees of their hockey teams notwithstanding that they had formed personal service corporations that contracted with the teams. *Keller* was distinguished on the ground that there was no issue as to who was the employer.

Foglesong I held out the promise that §482 could apply to allocate income between a personal services corporation and an employee-owner. But in

Foglesong v. Commissioner, 691 F.2d 848 (7th Cir. 1982) (*Foglesong II*), the court ruled that §482 did not apply where an owner-employee worked exclusively for the corporation because the owner-employee under these circumstances did not operate a separate trade or business to which income could be allocated under §482. But see Haag v. Commissioner, 855 F.2d 855 (8th Cir. 1988) (rejecting *Foglesong II* and allocating much of the income of a corporation performing medical services to the owner-employee doctor). See also Rev. Rul. 88-38, 1988-1 C.B. 246 (the Service will not follow *Foglesong* on the separate business issue).

PROBLEM

15-3. Rock Star earns between $500,000 and $1 million in royalties and salary under a contract with Recording Co. To defer recognition of most of this income until after Rock Star's greatness fades, Rock Star agrees to work exclusively for Deferral Corp., a wholly owned corporation of Rock Star's tax lawyer. Assume Deferral Corp. is located in the Cayman Islands, and its income is not subject to any U.S. or foreign income taxation. Deferral Corp. agrees to transfer to Rock Star each year a lifetime annuity that pays $75,000 per year and is worth $750,000. Thus, after one year, Rock Star will receive $75,000 for life, after two years, Rock Star will receive $150,000 for life, and so on. The contract between Rock Star and Deferral Corp. can be canceled at the beginning of each year by either party.

a. How should Rock Star and Deferral Corp. be taxed if Deferral Corp. enters into a new contract with Recording Co. after the old contract expires, obligating Rock Star to record and perform for Recording Co. on the same terms as before?
b. Suppose Recording Co. refuses to sign with anyone other than Rock Star. Rock Star accordingly signs with Recording Co. and then assigns all his rights and obligations under the Recording Co. contract to Deferral Corp. in exchange for the lifetime annuity. How should Rock Star and Deferral Corp. be taxed?

4. *Denial of Tax Benefits under §269A*

Although Congress in 1982 substantially equalized the pension benefits available to employees and the self-employed, thereby removing a major incentive to form a personal services corporation, it also enacted §269A. That section resembles §482 by providing for income and deduction reallocations rather than tax benefit denial. But it is triggered by forming or acquiring control of a corporation with a principal purpose of avoiding tax or obtaining benefits otherwise unobtainable. The Conference Committee wrote of §269A, "The conferees intend that the provisions [of §269A] overturn the results reached in cases like Keller v. Commissioner, 77 T.C. 1014 (1981), where the corporation served no meaningful purpose other than to secure tax benefits which would not otherwise be available." H.R. Rep. No. 760, 97th Cong., 2d Sess. (1986).

Suppose a husband, *H*, and wife, *W*, simultaneously graduate from law school. They form *WH* Corp., for which each works and in which each is a 50-percent shareholder. The corporation then hires out its two employees to two separate law firms for $50,000 per year. The corporation pays *H* and *W* only $35,000 each and retains (and pays taxes on) $30,000. Will this device reduce *H* and *W*'s overall tax liability? Can the Commissioner wage a successful challenge to the scheme under §269A?

5. The "Graduated Bracket Amount" and §1561(a)

For some corporations, the corporate income tax rates are progressive. See page 79 supra. Just as individual taxpayers might seek to assign income to family members in lower tax brackets, so too might affiliated corporations seek to divide profits among several related entities to take advantage of the graduated corporate rates available to low-profit corporations. In §1561(a), Congress has provided that the "component members" of a "control group" must share a single run through the corporate progressive rates. A "control group" consists of a parent and its controlled subsidiaries, §1563(a)(1); brother-sister corporations, §1563(a)(2); or three or more corporations, each of which is a member of a parent-subsidiary group or a brother-sister group and one of which is a common parent corporation, §1563(a)(3). The "component members" of controlled groups are defined in §1563(b). See §1561. Suppose *A* owns 40 percent, and *B* owns 60 percent of the stock of *X* Corp., and *A* owns all the stock of *Y* Corp. Are *X* Corp. and *Y* Corp. a brother-sister controlled group, or must there be a commonality of control? See §1563(a)(2); United States v. Vogel Fertilizer Co., 455 U.S. 16 (1982).

II

SUBCHAPTER S CORPORATIONS

16

S Corporations: Overview

A. INTRODUCTION

In this chapter we begin our study of S corporations. Most corporations, called C corporations (see §1361(a)(2)), are treated as taxpayers independent of their shareholders. Some corporations, called S corporations (see §1361(a)(1)), file an informational return but do not (with some exceptions) pay income taxes. Instead, an S corporation's items of income and deduction are passed through to its shareholders who generally report these items directly on their income tax returns.[1] This chapter and the two following it are concerned exclusively with the taxation of such S corporations.

Subchapter C of the Internal Revenue Code, §§301-385, provides most of the provisions governing the interaction between shareholders and their corporations, C corporations and S corporations alike. Subchapter S, §§1361-1378, adds those provisions specially applicable to S corporations. One important aspect of the taxation of S corporations is the coordination of the rules in these two subchapters. Indeed, §1371(a)(1) provides, "Except as otherwise provided in this title, and except to the extent inconsistent with this subchapter, subchapter C shall apply to an S corporation and its shareholders." Accordingly, we will examine sections in both subchapters C and S, but when examining a provision in subchapter C, our emphasis will be on its application to S corporations.

There are two basic models upon which pass-thru taxation can be designed: the entity model and the aggregate model. Under a pure entity model, the entity computes its taxable income without reference to any tax attributes of its beneficial owners. That is, the entity's basis in its assets is independent of any asset basis of its shareholders or partners, the entity has a taxable year and method of accounting independent of the taxable years and accounting methods of its owners, and so on. Once the entity's taxable income or loss is computed, it is passed through to its owners.

Under a pure aggregate model, the entity has no tax attributes of its own and does not compute a taxable income. Instead, the entity is treated as no more than an

1. The Code uses the term "pass-thru" to refer to the allocation of tax items from an S corporation (or partnership) to its owners.

aggregate of its owners, so that, for example, it has no independent basis in its assets but instead uses the aggregate of its owners' bases. Thus, a separate depreciation schedule must be maintained for each owner's interest in each entity asset, each owner may have a distinct holding period for each asset, and so on. Although a pure aggregate approach to pass-thru taxation is possible, in practice it would be cumbersome to implement.

Subchapter K constructs a modified entity model for the taxation of partnerships and their partners. Computationally, we treat a partnership as an entity separate from its partners having its own tax attributes including basis, taxable year, and accounting method. However, much of subchapter K is devoted to injecting some of the aggregate model into the mixture.

For example, §§722-723 ensure that initial aggregate inside basis equals initial aggregate outside basis. Further, the rules of §§705 and 752 struggle to preserve this equality. Indeed, the optional basis adjustments of §§734(b) and 743(b) can ensure that the equality between aggregate inside and aggregate outside bases is maintained despite excess distributions and dispositions of partnership interests. Equality of aggregate inside and outside bases minimizes the impact of the partnership on the taxation of its partners.[2]

Similarly, distributions from a partnership to a partner, as well as contributions from a partner to a partnership, usually are not taxable events. Thus, transfers of partnership property generally are taxable only when a nonpartner is involved. See §§721, 731; but see §§702(a)(2), 704(c)(1)(B), 737. Once again the rules of subchapter K seek to make a partnership transparent to taxation of its partners.

The taxation of S corporations is much closer to a pure entity model. Although aggregate inside basis may initially equal aggregate outside basis, that equality will be broken once the S corporation incurs debt. There is, in other words, no precise corporate analog to §752. But cf. §1366(d) (limiting the allocable loss that a shareholder can take into account to the shareholder's aggregate basis in S corporation stock *and* debt). Distributions of property from a corporation to a shareholder are generally taxable to the entity (and through it, to its shareholders), and contributions to a corporation can be taxable depending on the ownership interests of the contributing shareholders. There are no optional basis adjustments akin to §§734(b) and 743(b). In fact, even the assignment of income doctrine gives way to the relatively pure entity model of subchapter S in that pre-contribution unrealized gain and loss in contributed assets is shifted away from the contributing shareholder to the other shareholders: there is no provision equivalent to §704(c). Finally, the flexibility for which partnership taxation is most noted is absent from subchapter S because there are no special allocations of corporate-level income and deductions. Thus, subchapter S is very different from subchapter K.

But there are also similarities because each subchapter implements a form of pass-thru taxation. Pass-thru taxation requires that a distributive share of income (by whatever name) must increase outside basis, while a distributive share of loss must have the opposite effect. This is true in both subchapter K and subchapter S, and it *must* be true if entity-level income and loss are to be recognized once and only once. Thus, our inspection of subchapter S will reveal the corporate analogs of

2. See page 593 infra.

partnership outside basis, distributive shares, and outside basis adjustments. The remainder of this chapter presents an overview of the taxation of S corporations, emphasizing the similarities to and differences from the taxation of partnerships.

But before that overview begins, one more detail should be mentioned. A corporation can be a C corporation at some times and an S corporation at other times. To be sure, most corporations begin and end as one type or the other without any mid-life changes. But a C corporation is permitted to file an S corporation election, and an S corporation's election may terminate, and in either event transition issues arise. This chapter as well as the next considers only S corporations wholly lacking all C corporation history. In Chapter 18, we look at the problems faced by existing C corporations filing an S corporation election as well as the problems of S corporations whose elections terminate.

B. THE S CORPORATION ELECTION

Kean v. Commissioner

469 F.2d 1183 (9th Cir. 1972)

BYRNE, JR., District Judge:

Appellants, petitioners in the Tax Court, were shareholders in Ocean Shores Bowl, Inc., hereinafter referred to as Bowl, a Washington corporation. They appeal from a judgment of the Tax Court, 51 T.C. 337, invalidating Bowl's election under Subchapter S, . . . and disallowing petitioners' deductions on their personal tax returns of their pro rata shares of Bowl's 1962 and 1963 net operating losses.

Bowl was formed on March 20, 1962 and had only one class of stock issued and outstanding. On October 30, 1962 Bowl filed a timely election to be taxed as a small business corporation pursuant to [§1362]. Consents to such election were contemporaneously filed by all of the shareholders of record and their wives. As a result of the election, Bowl's net operating losses of $15,316 for the short taxable year 1962 and $56,638.28 for 1963 were deducted in pro rata shares by petitioners on their 1962 and 1963 personal income tax returns.

Some Bowl debentures and 125 shares of Bowl stock were held in the name of petitioner, William MacPherson. He and his brother, petitioner Murdock MacPherson, were engaged in the real estate business in a company called MacPhersons, Inc. Each brother owned 45% of the stock of MacPhersons, Inc. with the remaining 10% being held by their mother. William and Murdock MacPherson had many joint investments which were conducted without any written agreement. Whoever initiated the investment would normally be responsible for its management. Neither held a power of attorney for the other. The books and records of MacPhersons, Inc. were maintained by its employee, Donald Minkler.

On their 1962 joint income tax return William MacPherson and his wife deducted the net operating loss of Bowl accruing to the 125 shares in William's name. In 1963 William MacPherson and his wife deducted one half of the net operating loss for that year attributed to said shares while Murdock MacPherson and his wife deducted the other one half on their joint return. In 1964 the William MacPhersons and the Murdock MacPhersons each reported the sale of one half of the 125 shares of Bowl stock and one half of the Bowl debentures. All of these returns were prepared by Donald Minkler.

A 1965 Internal Revenue Service audit disclosed that the 125 shares of Bowl stock and Bowl debentures, issued to William MacPherson in 1962, were purchased with a MacPhersons, Inc. check. The cost of the purchase was charged on the books of MacPhersons, Inc. equally against the drawing accounts of William and Murdock. Murdock MacPherson has never been repaid by William MacPherson for the amounts taken out of his drawing account to pay for the stock and debentures.

Murdock MacPherson was not a shareholder of record of Bowl. Neither he nor his wife were mentioned in the Subchapter S election filed with the Internal Revenue Service in October, 1962; nor did they file a consent to the election. None of the other shareholders knew that Murdock MacPherson was involved in any way with Bowl until the 1965 audit.

The Tax Court held that Bowl's Subchapter S election was invalid because Murdock MacPherson, as a beneficial owner of Bowl stock, was a shareholder within the meaning of [§1362] and had not consented to the corporation's election. Based on this finding, the court disallowed petitioners' deduction of their pro rata shares of the corporation's net operating losses.

Subchapter S of the Internal Revenue Code of 1954 allows a small business corporation, as defined by [§1361], to elect to be exempt from corporate income taxes with the consequence that its shareholders are taxed directly on the corporation's earnings or may deduct the corporation's losses. Section [1362(a)(2)] provides that the corporation's election is "valid only if all persons who are shareholders . . . consent to such election."

Petitioners contend that since Murdock MacPherson was not a shareholder of record and was not able to exercise any rights as a shareholder under Washington law, he was not a "shareholder" under [§1362]. We disagree. The question of who is a shareholder as the term is used in Subchapter S must be determined by federal rather than state law. . . . Treasury Regulation §1.1371-1(d)(1), implementing Subchapter S, states that "Ordinarily, the persons who would have to include in gross income dividends distributed with respect to the stock of the corporation are considered to be shareholders of the corporation."*

Petitioners challenge the validity of this regulation on the ground that it has no statutory basis and is in conflict with the legislative history. They rely on a portion of the report of the Senate Finance Committee discussing Subchapter S which stated:

> An election may be made to supply the tax treatment provided by this new subchapter only if all of the shareholders consent to this election. For this purpose the shareholders are those of record as of the first day of the taxable year in question, or if the election is made after that time, shareholders of record when the election is made.

S. Rep. No. 1900, 85th Cong., 2nd Sess., p. 87.

* This regulation has been withdrawn and more specific guidance is now provided. See Treas. Regs. §1.1362-6(b). See also Treas. Regs. §1.1361-1(e)(1) (for language similar to the quoted language in the text). — Eds.

The Tax Court in Alfred N. Hoffman, 47 T.C. 218, 235 (1966), aff'd sub nom. Hoffman v. Commissioner of Internal Revenue, 391 F.2d 930 (5th Cir. 1968), in considering the contention that a shareholder of record rather than the beneficial owner of the stock must consent to the Subchapter S election, discussed the report of the Senate Finance Committee as follows:

> While this use of the words "of record" furnishes some support for petitioner's position, it is entirely inconsistent with the basic congressional purpose to tax the undistributed corporate income only to the persons who are accountable for dividends paid by the corporation, and those persons are the real owners of the stock whether or not they are the shareholders "of record." In the circumstances, we must rely upon the all pervasive legislative purpose and not upon the foregoing fragmentary phrase in the committee report.

Subchapter S allows shareholders of a small business corporation to elect alternative tax consequences resulting from stock ownership. Without a Subchapter S election the corporation is liable for corporate taxes, the shareholders cannot deduct corporate losses, and only distributed dividends are subject to the personal income tax. If the election is made, the corporation is exempt from corporate taxes and the shareholders may deduct corporate net operating losses but must pay personal income tax on all corporate income whether distributed or not. The desirability of a Subchapter S election depends upon the individual tax considerations of each shareholder. The final determination of whether there is to be an election should be made by those who would suffer the tax consequences of it. . . .

A treasury regulation which supplies the definition that Congress omitted must be sustained unless unreasonable and obviously inconsistent with the statute. Bingler v. Johnson, 394 U.S. 741, 89 S. Ct. 1439, 22 L. Ed. 2d 695 (1969); Commissioner of Internal Revenue v. South Texas Lumber Co., 333 U.S. 496. Treasury Regulation §1.1371-1(d)(1) is consistent with the basic purpose of Subchapter S and reasonably implements the legislative mandate.

We conclude, as did the Tax Court, that William and Murdock MacPherson jointly invested in the 125 shares of Bowl stock issued to William MacPherson. Murdock MacPherson was the beneficial owner of one half of that stock in William MacPherson's name and must be considered a "shareholder" for the purpose of [§1362]. Murdock MacPherson's failure to file a consent invalidates Bowl's Subchapter S election. Therefore, petitioners were not entitled to deduct their pro rata shares of Bowl's net operating loss for 1962 and 1963. . . .

Finally, petitioners contend that the District Director abused the discretion reposed in him by Treas. Reg. §1.1372-3(c)* and that the Tax Court erred in refusing to review the exercise of the District Director's discretion.

After the judgment of the Tax Court finding that Bowl's Subchapter S election was invalid due to Murdock MacPherson's failure to consent, petitioners requested of the District Director an extension of time, pursuant to Treas. Reg. §1.1372-3(c), in which to file consents. All the petitioners offered to file new consents for the years 1962 and 1963.

The District Director denied the request. Petitioners then filed a motion in the Tax Court for retrial, further trial or reconsideration, seeking a review of the discretion exercised by the District Director. The Tax Court denied the motion.

* Treas. Regs. §1.1372-3(c) has been reissued as Treas. Regs. §1.1362-6(b)(3)(iii). — Eds.

The District Director advised petitioners that he was rejecting the request for an extension because the Tax Court had "issued an opinion in these cases . . . and because we do not feel the circumstances of this matter meet the requirements of Regs. §1.1372-3(c)."

The fact that the Tax Court had issued an opinion invalidating Bowl's Subchapter S election was not a basis for refusing to allow petitioners an extension of time to file consents. At the time the opinion was filed, no request had been made to the District Director and nothing in the opinion precluded him from granting a subsequent request for extension.

Additionally, there is no valid basis for the District Director's determination that the requirements of Treas. Reg. §1.1372-3(c) had not been met. Under the regulation the failure to file a consent will not invalidate the Subchapter S election and an extension of time to file new consents should be granted if it is shown to the satisfaction of the District Director that: (1) there was reasonable cause for the failure to file such consent, and (2) the government interest will not be jeopardized by treating the Subchapter S election as valid. There was reasonable cause for Murdock MacPherson's failure to file a timely consent. Murdock MacPherson was not a shareholder of record. He believed that whatever ownership interest he had in the shares did not necessitate his consent to Bowl's election. When the Internal Revenue Service disagreed with this position, the petitioners sought a judicial determination. Until the Tax Court issued its opinion, Murdock MacPherson did not know that his consent was required to consummate Bowl's election under [§1362]. Furthermore, there is nothing to indicate that any government interest is jeopardized by now validating the Subchapter S election.

At the time of the Subchapter S election, petitioners, other than possibly the MacPhersons, did not know or have reason to suspect that Murdock MacPherson had any ownership interest in Bowl's stock. The District Director's failure to exercise his discretion so as to allow petitioners to file their consents deprives eight taxpayers of deductions taken in good faith ten years earlier and saddles each taxpayer with a substantial liability for back taxes. It is apparent that Treas. Reg. §1.1372-3(c) was promulgated to prevent the harsh result reached in cases of this kind.

The District Director abused his discretion by arbitrarily refusing to allow petitioners an extension of time in which to file their consent to Bowl's Subchapter S election. Mensik v. C.I.R., 328 F.2d 147 (7th Cir. 1964); Bookwalter v. Mayer, 345 F.2d 476 (8th Cir. 1965).

We affirm the opinion of the Tax Court, except with regard to its refusal to review the exercise of the District Director's discretion, and order the District Director to grant petitioners an extension of time to file the consents pursuant to Treas. Reg. §1.1372-3(c).

Rev. Rul. 86-110

1986-2 C.B. 150

Issue

If a corporation's election to be an S corporation is automatically terminated because the corporation inadvertently had one or more ineligible shareholders for a limited period of time before discovery and correction, is the corporation treated as continuing to be an S corporation under section 1362(f) of the Internal Revenue Code during the period when it had one or more ineligible shareholders?

Facts

X corporation is an electing small business corporation. *A*, the majority shareholder of *X*, on advice of counsel, transferred shares of *X* stock to two irrevocable trusts for the benefit of *A*'s minor children. Neither trust was an eligible shareholder under section 1361(c)(2) or section 1361(d)(3) of the Code because neither trust was treated by sections 671 through 679 as entirely owned by an individual that is a citizen or resident of the United States and because each trust had more than one income beneficiary. Thus, under section 1362(d)(2), the transfer of stock to the trusts resulted in an automatic termination of the S corporation election.

It was not *A*'s desire or expectation to terminate the election when the transfer of the stock was made to the trusts. *A* acted on the advice of counsel that such transfers would not jeopardize the Subchapter S election, and *A* would not have made the transfers but for this advice. *X* and its shareholders continued to file returns and report income in a manner consistent with their belief that the election was still in effect.

Within a reasonable period of time after discovery of the termination, *A* took steps to correct the problem so that *X* once more qualified as a small business corporation. In addition *X*, and each shareholder of *X*, agreed to make any adjustments required by the Service with respect to such period as the Service might specify.

Law and Analysis

Section 1361(a) of the Code provides that the term "S corporation" means, with respect to any tax year, a small business corporation for which an election under section 1362(a) is in effect.

Section 1361(b)(1) of the Code defines a "small business corporation" as a domestic corporation that is not an ineligible corporation and does not (A) have more than 35 shareholders, (B) have as a shareholder, a person (other than an estate and other than a trust described in section 1361(c)(2)) that is not an individual, (C) have a nonresident alien as a shareholder, and (D) have more than one class of stock.

Section 1361(c)(2) of the Code provides that four types of domestic trusts may be shareholders of an S corporation: a trust that is treated as owned by an individual who is a citizen or resident of the United States; a trust that was treated as owned by an individual who was a citizen or resident of the United States immediately before the death of the deemed owner and that continues in existence after such death, but only for the 60-day period (or 2-year period if the entire corpus of the trust is includible in the gross estate of the deemed owner) beginning on the day of the deemed owner's death; a trust with respect to stock transferred to it pursuant to the terms of a will, but only for the 60-day period beginning on the day on which such stock is transferred to it; and a trust created primarily to exercise the voting power of stock transferred to it.

Section 1361(d) of the Code provides that a qualified subchapter S trust can be treated as a trust described in section 1361(c)(2) if a beneficiary of the trust makes an election for such treatment. A qualified subchapter S trust is a trust the terms of which require that (i) during the life of the current income beneficiary, there shall be only one income beneficiary of the trust; (ii) any corpus distributed during the life of the current income beneficiary may be distributed only to such beneficiary; (iii) the income interest of the current income beneficiary in the trust shall terminate on the life of the current income beneficiary, the trust shall distribute all of its assets to such beneficiary. In addition, all the income of the trust must be distributed (or required to be distributed) currently to one individual who is a citizen or resident of the United States.

Section 1362(d)(2) of the Code provides that an election under section 1362(a) will be terminated whenever (at any time on or after the first day of the first taxable year for which the corporation is an S corporation) the corporation ceases to be a small business corporation.

Section 1362(f) of the Code provides that if (1) an election by any corporation is terminated under section 1362(d)(2) or (3) of the Code, (2) the Secretary determines that the termination was inadvertent, (3) no later than a reasonable period of time after discovery of the terminating event, steps are taken so that the corporation is once more a small business corporation, and (4) the corporation, and each person who was a shareholder during the period specified under section 1362(f), agree to make such adjustments (consistent with the treatment of the corporation as an S corporation) as may be required by the Secretary with respect to that period, then, notwithstanding the terminating event, such corporation will be treated as continuing to be an S corporation during the period specified by the Secretary.

S. Rep. No. 97-640, 97th Cong., 2d Sess. 12 (1982), 1982-2 C.B. 718, 723, discusses section 1362(f) of the Code. It states in part:

> If the Internal Revenue Service determines that a corporation's subchapter S election is inadvertently terminated, the Service can waive the effect of the terminating event for any period if the corporation timely corrects the event and if the corporation and the shareholders agree to be treated as if the election has been in effect for such period.

Under the facts presented, since *A* transferred stock to trusts that are ineligible shareholders under section 1361(b)(1) of the Code, *X* ceased to be a small business corporation, thereby terminating its S corporation election. However, the termination was inadvertent. *A* acted on advice of counsel and would not have made the transfers but for this advice. Further, *A* took the necessary steps to correct the problem within a reasonable time after discovery of the termination and *X* and its shareholders agreed to make such adjustments as may be required by the Secretary.

Holding

The S corporation is treated as continuing to be an S corporation under section 1362(f) of the Code for the period specified by the Service during which it had one or more ineligible shareholders.

NOTES

1. *Eligibility.* For a corporation to be taxed as an S corporation, it must be a "small business corporation" as defined in §1361(b) and it must file an election pursuant to §1362(a). Despite the name, the definition of a small business corporation is not based in any way on the size of the corporation's business. "Small" in this context refers to the number of shareholders. A "small business corporation" under §1361(b) cannot have more than 100 shareholders, and a husband and wife (and their estates) are treated as a single shareholder, as are all family members (and their estates). §1361(c)(1). Family members include any common ancestor, lineal descendants of that ancestor, and their spouses or former spouses. §1361(c)(1)(B)(i). See also *id.* at (c)(1)(C) (treating the following as children by blood: adopted children, certain individuals lawfully placed for adoption with an individual, and certain foster children). However, to be a common ancestor of a family, a person can be no more than *six* generations removed from the youngest generation of shareholders who would be included in the family. *Id.* at (c)(1)(B)(ii) and (iii). In other words, a family includes all persons who have a common ancestor (even if dead) in the preceding six generations. Treas. Regs. §1.1361-1(e)(3) (for the date when this "six-generation" test is applied). Note that although all members of a family are treated as one shareholder for purposes of the 100-shareholder limit, each member must still qualify as an S corporation shareholder.

Other requirements are (1) the corporation must be domestic; (2) all shareholders must be individuals, estates, certain qualifying trusts (see §1361(c)(2)); pension, profit-sharing, or stock bonus plans qualifying under §401; or charitable organizations (see §1361(c)(6)); (3) no nonresident alien may be a shareholder; and (4) the corporation may have only one class of stock outstanding. In addition, the corporation must not be an ineligible corporation (i.e., not an insurance company, a financial institution that uses the reserve method for accounting for bad debts, a §936 corporation, a DISC, or a former DISC). See §1361(b)(2).

2. *Election.* If a corporation satisfies these requirements, it may file an election to be taxed as an S corporation. Every shareholder must consent to this election, §1362(a)(2), although once made, the election need not be ratified by shareholders who acquire stock after the election is filed. Because the effect of an S corporation election is to pass-thru and tax shareholders on the corporation's income, requiring unanimous shareholder consent eliminates any possible argument that taxing a shareholder on the corporation's income violates the Constitution.

If an S corporation election is filed during the first 2½ months of the corporation's taxable year, the election can be effective for the current year or for the subsequent year, whichever the corporation prefers. But see §1362(b)(2) (for certain cases where the election cannot be effective for the current year). If the election is filed more than 2½ months into a taxable year, it automatically becomes effective for the subsequent year. §1362(b). Once filed, an election continues until it is revoked or the corporation ceases to be a "small business corporation." See §1362(c). And once an S corporation's subchapter S election terminates, the corporation is prohibited from filing a new election for five taxable years, unless the Service consents to the new election. §1362(g).

3. *Revocation and termination.* An S corporation may file a revocation of its election so long as shareholders holding more than one-half of its shares agree. §1362(d)(1). Note that this does *not* require consent by a majority of the shareholders:

if, for example, one shareholder owns 51 of the 100 outstanding shares of the corporation, that shareholder alone has the ability to terminate the S corporation election, and the remaining shareholders have no say in the matter. The revocation may specify a prospective date, although like the election itself, a revocation can be effective for the current taxable year if filed within the first 2½ months of the year.

Even if an eligible corporation makes a late election or makes no election at all for the current year, that corporation may nevertheless be treated as an S corporation if the Secretary of the Treasury determines that the failure to make a timely election was due to reasonable cause. §1362(b)(5). The Service has adopted a surprisingly generous interpretation of its authority under this provision. See Treas. Regs. §1.1362-4 (describing inadvertent terminations and inadvertent invalid elections). See also Rev. Proc. 2003-43, 2003-1 C.B. 998, supplemented by Rev. Proc. 2007-62 I.R.B. 786.

An S corporation election will be terminated without regard to its shareholders' desires if the corporation fails to satisfy the requirements of a small business corporation. For example, if one shareholder sells her shares to several others, the total number of shareholders may exceed 100, immediately terminating the S corporation election. Similarly, a shareholder could sell her stock to an impermissible trust, a nonresident alien, or a partnership, and again the S corporation election would be terminated.

It might be the case that the corporation accidentally terminates its S corporation election under §1362(d)(2). As Rev. Rel. 86-110 illustrates, if the corporation can convince the Internal Revenue Service that the termination was inadvertent, S corporation status can be restored without legal interruption. §1362(f). However, the Service may require of the corporation and of its shareholders any adjustments the Service deems appropriate.

Note that the provisions governing the S corporation election plainly contemplate that a corporation could spend part of its existence as a C corporation and part as an S corporation. In this and the next chapter, we will consider only those corporations electing to be taxed as S corporations throughout their existence; the taxation of an S corporation having a C corporation history is substantially more complex. For example, such S corporations can terminate their S corporation election by having too much passive income. §1362(d)(3).

PROBLEMS

16-1. *S* Corp. is an S corporation having 101 actual shareholders, including one married couple, *H* and *W*. *H* and *W* are about to become divorced from one another. Will their divorce have any impact on the other *S* Corp. shareholders?

C. FORMATION

Because no special rules govern the formation of an S corporation, the general rules of subchapter C apply. Under §351, a person may recognize no gain or loss on the transfer of property to a corporation solely in exchange for the corporation's stock. However, unlike partnerships in which a similar rule is unconditional, §351 imposes an additional requirement: for the transfer to be tax-free to the transferor, the transferor, together with any others who transfer property in the same exchange, must "control" the corporation immediately after the exchange. See §351(a). For this purpose, "control" means ownership of stock possessing at least 80 percent of the vote as well as ownership of at least 80 percent of the shares of each class of nonvoting stock. See §368(c); Rev. Rul. 59-259, 1959-2 C.B. 115.

Note that in determining control, all shares owned by the transferors immediately after the exchange are counted, including any shares owned before the exchange. For example, suppose *S* Corp. has 100 shares outstanding, all of a single class, 25 owned by individual *X* and 75 by individual *Y*. If *Y* and individual *Z* transfer property to the corporation in exchange for 25 shares apiece, the transaction falls under §351 because the transferor group (individuals *Y* and *Z*) owns 125 of the 150 outstanding shares (over 83%) immediately after the exchange.

When a person transfers property to a corporation solely for its stock, and §351 applies to the exchange, the transferor generally takes a basis in the stock received equal to the aggregate basis of the property transferred. §358(a). But see §362(e)(2)(C) (for an exception). This result should come as no surprise: because no realized gain or loss is recognized on the exchange, basis remains the same, a rule that corresponds to §722 in the partnership context. The shareholder's stock basis preserves her realized but unrecognized gain or loss on the exchange.

If §351 does not apply to a person's exchange of property for stock (e.g., because the transferor group lacks control), the person recognizes any realized gain or loss on the transfer. See §1001(c). Further, if a person provides services for stock, she has income equal to the stock's value. In either case, the shareholder takes a fair market value basis in the stock received. The effect of this rule is to increase the shareholder's net basis by the amount of income or gain (or reduce it by the amount of loss) recognized on the transaction.

A corporation does not recognize gain or loss on the exchange of its stock for property (or for services), whether or not the transaction falls within §351. See §1032. Given the double tax regime implemented by subchapter C, this rule makes sense: Because the corporation has not engaged in any productive activity simply by receiving property for its stock, it should not yet be taxed on any income. This rule also makes sense in the pass-thru context of subchapter S: there is no need to tax transactions between a pass-thru entity and its owners; taxation can (but need not) wait until a transaction occurs between the entity or its owners and a third party.[3]

Although the corporation's immediate tax consequences are independent of §351, the corporation's basis in the assets acquired from the shareholder is not. If §351 applies to a transferor-shareholder, the corporation generally takes a transferred or carryover basis in the transferred assets. §362(a). However, if the transaction falls outside of §351, the corporation takes a fair market value basis in those assets. Thus, immediately following incorporation, the shareholders' aggregate stock basis generally equals the corporation's aggregate net asset basis, whether or not §351 applies to the incorporation.

However, basis equivalence is not the standard for a §351 exchange where, under §362(a), the corporation would take an aggregate basis in a shareholder's

3. See page 588 infra.

property that exceeded its value. Then, as a general rule under §362(e)(2), that built-in loss is eliminated at the corporate level, but preserved at the shareholder level. The shareholder and corporation may elect, instead, to preserve the built-in loss at the corporate level but eliminate it at the shareholder level. §362(e)(2)(C). Although there are many twists and turns, that election may be unwise for an S corporation and its shareholders, because if the corporation recognized the built-in loss, its shareholders would reduce their stock bases by the same amount. See §1367(a)(2)(B). Their sale of that stock could then eliminate any overall benefit from the loss.

For purposes of §351, "property" does not include services. §351(d)(1). Some assets, notably patents, copyrights, and accounts receivable, may owe most of their value to personal effort. When such an asset is contributed to a corporation in exchange for stock, some may question whether "property" or "services" have been transferred to the corporation and thus whether §351 should apply to the transaction. For the most part, the courts have construed the term "property" broadly under §351. See, e.g., Hempt Brothers, Inc. v. United States, 490 F.2d 1172 (3d Cir. 1974) (accounts receivable constitute "property").

D. PASS-THRU OF CORPORATE INCOME AND DEDUCTION

An S corporation is generally not a taxpayer.[4] Like a partnership, an S corporation computes its income, loss, deductions, and other tax items and then passes those items through to its owners. See §1363(b) (providing that an S corporation generally determines its taxable income in the same manner as an individual). Its owners are its shareholders, and each shareholder reports a proportion of the corporation's income, loss, and deductions based on the shareholder's relative ownership of the corporation's outstanding shares. For example, if shareholder *X* owns 15 of the 100 outstanding shares of *S* Corp.'s outstanding stock, *X* reports 15 percent of *S* Corp.'s taxable income or loss. If a shareholder's percentage of stock ownership changes during the year, as a general rule, the corporation's income is allocated ratably to each day of the year and then passed through to each shareholder in proportion to the shareholder's ownership interest on each day. §1377(a)(1). Cf. §1377(a)(2); Treas. Regs. §1.1368-1(g) (for circumstances where income may be allocated under a closing of the books).

As in the partnership context, the character of items of income and deduction recognized by the corporation and passed through to its shareholders is preserved. For example, capital gain recognized by the corporation will be reported as capital gain by the shareholders, and charitable contributions made by the corporation will be treated as charitable deductions of the shareholders. §1366(a)-(b); cf. §702(a)-(b).

An S corporation must allocate its tax items among its shareholders in proportion to their stock ownership. §1366(a)(1). In contrast, a partnership has much more flexibility to allocate its tax items among its partners, limited only by the

4. An S corporation with a C corporation history may sometimes be a taxpayer, however. See pages 569-576 infra.

requirement that allocations have "substantial economic effect."[5] This flexibility is wholly missing under subchapter S. In fact, corporate income must be apportioned according to stock interests, even in the face of assignment of income concerns.

For example, suppose individuals *X* and *Y* form *S* Corp., with *X* contributing $10,000 cash and *Y* contributing inventory with a $6,000 adjusted basis and $10,000 fair market value. Each receives 50 shares of *S* Corp. stock, so that when the inventory is sold, each is allocated and reports half of the $4,000 gain realized on the sale. In the partnership arena and consonant with assignment of income concerns, pre-contribution appreciation in the contributed assets must be allocated all to the contributing partner under §704(c). Thus, if *X* and *Y* instead formed a partnership, *Y* would be allocated the entire $4,000 gain on the inventory. In subchapter S, however, the gain is allocated between *X* and *Y* in proportion to relative stock ownership.

A shareholder increases her stock basis for her allocable share of income and decreases her stock basis for her allocable share of losses and deductions. See §1367(a). These adjustments prevent a shareholder from taking her allocable share of S corporation income and loss into account again when she sells her stock.[6] The adjustments under §1367(a) parallel those under §705. Both provisions require a basis increase for taxable income and tax-exempt income and a basis decrease for losses, deductions, and nondeductible, noncapitalizable expenses like illegal bribes and kickbacks. §1367(a).

An S corporation's items of income and deduction are passed through to its shareholders on the last day of the corporation's taxable year. §1366(a)(1). Accordingly, shareholders whose taxable years do not coincide with that of the corporation will enjoy some deferral, with the greatest deferral enjoyed by those shareholders whose taxable years end just prior to the close of the corporation's taxable year.[7]

Under §1378, however, an S corporation is not free to choose its taxable year. Unless the S corporation can convince the Service that it has a sufficient business purpose to justify some other taxable year, an S corporation must use the calendar year as its taxable year. Although this rule eliminates deferral opportunities for calendar year taxpayers, it mandates deferral for fiscal year taxpayers beyond that enjoyed by most taxpayers. Of course, because most shareholders of S corporations must be individuals,[8] and individuals invariably are calendar year taxpayers, restricting S corporation's use of fiscal years should present little real opportunity for deferral.

Pass-thru of corporate loss is limited to a shareholder's outside basis. §1366(d). However, in this situation outside basis includes not only the shareholder's stock basis but also her basis in certain corporate debt. While the limitation of §1366(d) operates much like §704(d), limiting the pass-thru of partnership loss to the partner's outside basis, the §1366(d) concept of debt basis makes the S corporation limitation considerably more complex. This complexity is deferred until the next chapter.[9]

5. See page 598 infra.
6. See §705 for the comparable partnership rule.
7. See page 845 infra.
8. For some exceptions, see §1361(c)(2)-(3) and page 531 supra.
9. See page 553 infra.

PROBLEM

16-2. Individuals *X*, *Y*, and *Z* form *XYZ* Corp., an S corporation. *X* contributes Blackacre with a $600 adjusted basis and a $1,000 fair market value in exchange for 100 shares of *XYZ* Corp. *Y* contributes inventory with a $2,000 adjusted basis and $1,000 fair market value in exchange for 100 shares of *XYZ* Corp. *Z* contributes cash of $100 and services worth $900 in exchange for 100 shares of *XYZ* Corp.

a. How are *X*, *Y*, and *Z* taxed on their contributions?
b. What are the tax consequences to the corporation and to each shareholder if the corporation sells each of the contributed assets sometime during the corporation's first taxable year? Assume that the corporation has no income or loss other than from disposition of the contributed property. Also consider the impact of an election under §362(e)(2)(C).
c. What happens if each shareholder sells his or her *XYZ* stock for $1,000 at the end of the first taxable year?

E. NONLIQUIDATING DISTRIBUTIONS

The entity-level taxation of nonliquidating distributions made by S corporations to its shareholders could not be more different from the partnership scheme implemented by §§731-733. In general, if an S corporation distributes appreciated property, it recognizes gain as if it sold the property to the distributee for fair market value. That is, the corporation recognizes the appreciation in the property at the time of distribution. §311(a)-(b)(1). This corporate gain, like all corporate income, is then passed through to the corporation's shareholders at the close of the taxable year. Note, however, that an S corporation does not recognize loss on a nonliquidating distribution. §311(a). Because a shareholder takes a fair market value basis in any distributed property, §301(d), if an S corporation distributes loss property, the built-in loss disappears.

A shareholder recognizes gain on a distribution only if the value of the property distributed to the shareholder exceeds her stock basis. §1368(b). This result is the same for a C corporation shareholder who receives a distribution from a C corporation with no earnings and profits. See §301(c)(2) and (3). Cf. §731(a)(1) (requiring a partner to recognize gain on a distribution, but only to the extent that *cash* distributed (or deemed distributed) exceeds her outside basis). To account for the distribution, the distributee must reduce her stock basis (but not below zero) by the value of the property distributed. §1367(a)(2).[10]

When a corporation distributes appreciated property, it recognizes gain that is allocated among its shareholders, including the distributee. Can the distributee use the stock basis increase for that allocated gain to reduce any gain she otherwise would recognize on the distribution? For example, suppose individual *X* owns 50 percent of the outstanding stock of *S* Corp. with an adjusted basis of $10,000 in that

10. More precisely, the shareholder reduces her stock basis by the portion of the distribution not included in income. §1367(a)(2)(A).

stock. What are the tax consequences to *X* if *S* Corp. distributes Blackacre to *X* when Blackacre is worth $12,000 and has an adjusted basis to *S* Corp. of $8,000?

A possible (unpleasant) result might be that—

1. *X* recognizes a $2,000 gain on the distribution, because Blackacre's value ($12,000) exceeds *X*'s $10,000 stock basis by $2,000; and
2. *X* is also taxed on an additional $2,000 of corporate-level income, her 50-percent share of *S* Corp.'s $4,000 recognized gain on Blackacre.

Could *X*, instead, *first* adjust her *S* Corp. stock basis to account for her $2,000 allocable share of *S* Corp.'s gain on Blackacre, and *then* account for the distribution? With this ordering, *X*'s stock basis would increase by $2,000, from $10,000 to $12,000, and she would recognize no gain on the distribution of Blackacre, worth $12,000.

The more favorable ordering is supported by §1368(d)(1). It provides that "[i]n the case of any distribution made during the taxable year," the distributee-shareholder determines her stock basis "with regard to" any §1367(a)(1) adjustments for the taxable year. Under §1367(a)(1), a shareholder increases her stock basis for her allocable share of the S corporation's income for the taxable year, including for any gain recognized on a distribution. Because that income passes through to the shareholder on the last day of the corporation's taxable year (§1366(a)(1)), the shareholder also increases her stock basis on the last day of the year. Thus, §1368(d)(1) implies that a shareholder cannot determine the consequences of a distribution until the close of the corporation's taxable year and that the shareholder accounts for the distribution only after increasing her stock basis under §1367(a)(1).

Regulations make clear that the shareholder-level tax consequences of a distribution cannot be determined until the close of the corporation's tax year. As a consequence, later activities of the corporation can affect the shareholder's tax treatment of a mid-year distribution. Consider the following example taken from the Treas. Regs. §1.1368-3 (example 2):

> *A*, an individual, owns all 10 outstanding shares of *S* Corp. with adjusted basis of $1 per share. *S* Corp. is a calendar-year S corporation. On March 1, *S* makes a distribution of $38 in cash to *A*. For the entire year, *A*'s pro rata share of items described in §1367(a)(1) is $50, and *A* increases basis in each share of *S* stock by $5 ($50/10) to $6. Thus, *A* recognizes no gain on the distribution, because *A*'s basis in each share ($6) at the end of the year exceeds the distribution on that share ($3.80 or $38/10). *A* reduces each share's basis by $3.80, from $6 to $2.20.

The regulatory example goes on to illustrate that after *A* accounts for the distribution, she next accounts for any share of noncapitalizable, nondeductible expenses and finally accounts for any share of losses and deductions. Treas. Regs. §1.1368-3 (example 2).

This treatment is similar to how an advance is treated under subchapter K but different from how a "regular" distribution is treated. Under §731(a), a "regular" distribution of cash to a partner is taxable to the partner to the extent the amount of cash distributed exceeds the partner's *pre-distribution* outside basis. In subchapter S, we use the shareholder's *year-end* outside (i.e., stock) basis adjusted first for the shareholder's pass-thru items of income.

Reconsider the example above but assume that the distribution consists of property having an adjusted basis to the corporation of $10 and a fair market value of $38 and that *S* Corp.'s only income for the year results from the distribution. The distribution will not result in any recognition to *A*, because *A*'s year-end stock basis, after adjusting for pass-thru income, is $38,[11] and that amount is sufficient to absorb the entire $38 value of the distribution. *A*'s stock basis will end up at $0, reflecting an increase of $28 for pass-thru income and a decrease of $38 for the distribution. See §1367(a)(1)(A), (2)(A).

This treatment is also consistent with the final sentence of §1368(d), which makes clear that gain from the distribution in excess of stock basis is determined before adjusting stock basis downward for pass-thru of loss pursuant to §1367(a)(2). Thus, positive basis adjustments are made prior to computing the tax consequences of a distribution even though negative adjustments are made after the computation. This ordering rule minimizes the likelihood that a taxpayer will be forced to recognize gain on a distribution in a year in which the S corporation loses money.

For example, suppose individual *X* owns one share of stock in an S corporation with an adjusted basis of $10 as of the beginning of the year. If the corporation has no income or deductions for the year, a distribution of $10 or less to *X* will be tax free, §1368(b)(1), while a distribution in excess of that amount will produce income to *X* in the amount of the excess, §1368(b)(2).

But what if the corporation has net income or loss for the year? If the corporation distributes $12 to *X* during the year, and *X*'s share of the corporation's net income is $3 for the year, then *X* will recognize no gain on the distribution, because the §1367(a)(1) positive stock basis adjustment for *X*'s share of the earnings is made *prior to* determining the tax consequences to *X* of the distribution. §1368(d) (final sentence). On the other hand, if the corporation distributes only $9 to *X*, the corporation has a net loss for the year, and *X*'s share of that net loss for the year is $3, *X* still has no gain on the distribution because the §1367(a)(2) negative stock basis adjustment is made only after determining the tax consequences of the distribution. That is, the distribution reduces *X*'s stock basis to $1, so that *X* can report only $1 of her share of the corporation's loss, and the remaining $2 is deferred under §1366(d), subject to the debt rule of §1366(d)(1)(B). §§1366(d)(1), 1367(b)(2).

Note that if the shareholders' aggregate basis in their S corporation stock equals the S Corporation's net basis in its assets, that equality will be broken if the S corporation distributes property to a shareholder with a value exceeding the shareholder's stock basis. In subchapter K, this equality also can be broken by a distribution, though it will be reestablished if the partnership has a §754 election in effect.[12] Because S corporation distributions of property as well as of cash can break the equality, and because there is no subchapter S equivalent to §754, the inside/outside bases equality is more likely to disappear for S corporations than it is for partnerships.

PROBLEM

16-3. What are the tax consequences to the three shareholders and to the corporation if *XYZ* in problem 16-2(b) above distributes cash of $6 per share to each shareholder halfway into the corporation's first taxable year?

11. The amount equals the prior stock basis of $10 plus pass-thru income of $28 for a total of $38.
12. See page 807 infra.

F. DISPOSITIONS OF SHARES AND LIQUIDATING DISTRIBUTIONS

1. *Disposition of Stock Not in Redemption*

The disposition of stock in an S corporation is taxed just like the disposition of stock in a C corporation. That is, gain or loss is recognized on each share equal to the difference between the amount realized and the shareholder's adjusted basis in the share. See §1001. However, a disposition of stock in an S corporation is more complex because the disposition (1) affects the pass-thru of corporate-level tax items to the selling shareholder and (2) may affect how that shareholder treats distributions. Because distributions and pass-thrus of corporate-level tax items affect stock basis, a shareholder who sells stock of an S corporation cannot determine gain or loss on the sale until the close of the corporation's taxable year.

If a person disposes of shares in an S corporation, the disposition affects the allocation of the corporate-level items to the shareholder. Under §1377(a)(1), a corporate-level item for a year is apportioned equally to each day of the year and then allocated pro rata among the shares outstanding on that day. For example, suppose individual *A* owns 50 of the 100 outstanding shares of *S* Corp., an S corporation using the calendar year as its taxable year. On June 30, *A* sells 25 of those shares to individual *B*. If the corporation has net taxable income for the year of $2,000, *A* must report $750 on her individual return: $500 for six months ownership of 50 percent of *S* Corp. and $250 for six months ownership of 25 percent of *S* Corp.[13]

Suppose that *A* had sold all 50 of her shares in *S* Corp. on June 30. Now, *A* reports only $500 of *S* Corp.'s income, equal to half of the income for half the year. Note that it does not matter *when S* Corp. earned the income. Thus, *A* reports the same $500, whether *S* Corp. earned $1,000 in each half year or *S* Corp. lost $1,000 in the first six months and then earned $3,000 in the last six months. Because corporate tax items are ratably allocated to each day of the corporation's taxable year, it is irrelevant when during the year the corporation accrued or received any particular item.

A shareholder who sells her entire interest in an S corporation during the corporation's taxable year might prefer that her share of the corporation's tax items not be affected by post-sale corporate activities. If the corporation, the seller, and all buyers agree, they may elect to treat the corporation's taxable year as ending on the date of sale as to those shareholders, with a new taxable year beginning on the following day. §1377(a)(2). If such an election is filed, the outgoing shareholder will be taxable on her share of corporate activities occurring only on or before the day she terminates her interest in the S corporation. Similarly, the incoming shareholder will be taxable on her share of corporate activities occurring after the sale.[14]

A disposition of some or all of a shareholder's stock in an S corporation also affects the taxation of distributions made to the selling shareholder before the sale

13. For ease of computation, June 30 is treated as the midpoint of the year.

14. See also Treas. Regs. §1.1368-1(g) (providing that the corporation may elect to close its taxable year in the case of a qualifying disposition of its stock; this election affects all shareholders).

of the stock. Recall that distributions of cash or property are tax free to the distributee-shareholder to the extent that the amount of the distribution does not exceed the distributee-shareholder's stock basis. §1368(b)(1). Recall also that it is the shareholder's stock basis as of the close of the corporation's taxable year that is used in this comparison. The shareholder increases her stock basis for pass-thru items of income, accounts for the distribution, and then decreases her stock basis for pass-thru items of loss and deduction.

If a shareholder sells some or all of her shares during the taxable year, §1367(a) adjustments to the basis of the transferred shares for pass-thru items of income and deduction as well as the downward basis adjustments for all prior distributions are effective immediately prior to the stock transfer. Treas. Regs. §1.1367-1(d)(1). For example, assume that individual *A* owns 40 of the 100 outstanding shares of *S* Corp., an S corporation using the calendar year as its taxable year. As of January 1, *A* owns these 40 shares with an adjusted basis of $10 per share. On June 30, *A* sells 15 of her 40 shares to individual *C* for $15 per share. During the entire calendar year, *S* Corp. earns $200.

To compute *A*'s gain (or loss) on the sale of the 15 shares, we must know *A*'s adjusted basis in those shares. We begin with *A*'s adjusted basis of $10 per share as of the beginning of the calendar year. We then increase that adjusted basis for *A*'s share of the corporation's income. Treating June 30 as the midpoint of the year, $100 of the corporation's income is allocated to the period from January 1 through June 30, and the remaining $100 is allocated to July 1 through December 31. Accordingly, each of the 100 outstanding shares is allocated $1 for the first half of the year, so that *A*'s stock basis as of June 30 is increased to $11 per share. Thus, the sale of 15 shares for $15 per share yields a taxable gain of $4 per share, or $60 total gain. In addition, *A* must report $65 of pass-thru income for the year ($40 for the first half plus $25 for the second half).

Assume in addition that *A* received a distribution of $80 sometime during the first half of the year. Now, we must adjust the basis of the transferred shares not only for the pass-thru income allocable to the pre-transfer period but also for the distribution. The tax effect of the $80 distribution is to reduce *A*'s stock basis by $80 total, or $2 per share. Accordingly, *A*'s adjusted basis in the shares as of the date of sale is now $9,[15] producing a taxable gain of $6 per share or $90 total. Individual *A* still reports pass-thru income of $65 on her individual return.

To make this example even more complicated, assume that *A* uses a fiscal year ending August 31 as her taxable year. This wrinkle means that *A* must report her gain from the sale of the 15 shares in one taxable year and her share of the pass-thru income in the next taxable year. Further, *A* cannot compute her gain from the stock sale until the close of the corporation's taxable year (i.e., until sometime after December 31), which is after *A*'s individual tax return is due! *A* must estimate her stock gain and pay her taxes based on that estimate. If (as is likely) her estimate is not perfect, she must file an amended return showing additional income or seeking a refund.

15. This $9 per share adjusted basis is computed as follows: initial basis of $10 plus pass-thru income of $1 less distribution of $2 equals $9.

PROBLEMS

16-4. How does your answer to problem 16-3 above change if shareholder *X* sells 35 of her shares to shareholder *Y* and 35 of her shares to shareholder *Z* one-quarter of the way into the year? What if the sale takes place three-quarters of the way into the year? Assume in each case that the sale price is $12 per share.

16-5. *S* Corp. is an S corporation using the calendar year as its taxable year. As of January 1, individual *I* owns all 100 outstanding shares of *S* Corp. with an adjusted basis of $10 per share. On March 1 of the same year, *S* Corp. distributes Blackacre to *I*. At the time of the distribution, *S* Corp. has an adjusted basis in Blackacre of $5,000, and Blackacre is worth $17,000. What are the tax consequences of this distribution, assuming that in addition to the distribution: (a) *S* Corp. recognizes taxable income for the year of $3,000? (b) *S* Corp. recognizes a net loss for the year of $2,000? (c) *S* Corp. recognizes taxable income for the year of $3,000, and *S* Corp. redeems half of *I*'s shares for $15 per share on July 1?

16-6. How does your answer to problem 16-5(a) above change if the corporation's adjusted basis in Blackacre immediately prior to the distribution is $20,000, rather than $5,000?

2. *Redemptions of Stock*

A corporation redeems its stock when it buys the stock from a shareholder. §317(b). The redemption's effect on the shareholder depends on the shareholder's ownership interest in the corporation. At one extreme, consider the case of a shareholder holding all 100 outstanding shares of *X* Corp. If this shareholder sells, for example, 10 of the shares back to the corporation, the shareholder's relationship to the corporation is essentially unchanged: both before and after the transaction, the shareholder owns 100 percent of the corporation. Accordingly, one would expect this redemption to be taxed like a non-redemption (i.e., simple) distribution of property from the corporation to the shareholder (i.e., the stock transfer would be ignored), and that (usually) is the case.[16]

At the other extreme, consider the case of a shareholder selling every share she owns back to the corporation in exchange for cash. Once the redemption is complete, the shareholder has no further relationship with the corporation. From the shareholder's perspective, this transaction is identical to a sale of the shares to a third party, and the shareholder in this case usually is taxed as if the sale had been made to a third party.

As an intermediate case, consider a shareholder *D* owning 60 of 120 outstanding shares in *X* Corp. If *D* sells 30 shares back to the corporation (i.e., if the corporation redeems 30 shares), *D*'s interest in the corporation drops from one-half (60 of 120) to one-third (30 of 90). This redemption resembles both a distribution and a sale in some respects. Had the sale been to a third party, *D*'s interest would have dropped from one-half to one-fourth (30 of 120). Thus, the redemption reduced *D*'s

16. Under some circumstances, the shareholder's taxation of a redemption does not turn on the effect of the transaction on the shareholder's interest in the corporation. See §§302(b)(4) (partial liquidations), 303 (redemptions to pay death taxes). In those cases, even a sole shareholder can treat the redemption as an exchange.

proportionate share of corporate control *less than* an equivalent sale. However, a simple distribution with no tender of shares would have left *D*'s interest at one-half, so that this redemption had more effect on *D*'s ownership of the corporation than that of a simple distribution. In other words, when some but not all of the stock of a partial owner of a corporation is redeemed, the effect of the redemption on the shareholder's interest in the corporation is less than that of a sale but more than that of a simple distribution.

The taxation of redemptions is governed by §302.[17] If the redemption of a shareholder's stock is described in §302(b)(1)-(4), the shareholder is treated as selling the redeemed stock for the redemption proceeds. §302(a). Thus, the shareholder recognizes gain or loss equal to the difference between the amount realized and her adjusted basis in the redeemed shares. Note that the redemption may affect the taxation of any simple distributions to the shareholder and the shareholder's allocable portion of pass-thru income and loss.

If the transaction does *not* fall within §302(b) the shareholder is taxed as if the redemption proceeds had been received in a simple distribution. Thus, as long as the shareholder's stock basis (presumably all the stock, not just the redeemed shares) equals or exceeds the amount of the distribution, the shareholder recognizes no gain. However, if the amount of the distribution exceeds the shareholder's stock basis, the shareholder recognizes gain equal to that excess. The shareholder reduces her stock basis (but not below zero) by the amount of the distribution. See §1367(a)(2)(A). Note that any unused basis in the redeemed shares flows into the shareholder's remaining shares. Treas. Regs. §1.302-2(c).

Section 302(b) is a complicated provision more fully covered in Chapter 5. What follows is an overview of major aspects of §302(b). Recall that the constructive ownership rules generally apply to determine stock ownership under §302(b) and that if a redemption is described in §302(b), the shareholder is treated as selling or exchanging the redeemed shares. See §302(a) and (c)(1).

A redemption is described in §302(b)(3) if it terminates the shareholder's entire interest in the corporation. Usually, this means that the corporation redeems every share of stock held by the shareholder. However, if, as part of a clear plan, a corporation redeems some of the shareholder's shares, and the shareholder sells her remaining shares to an unrelated third party, the redemption is described in §302(b)(3).

A redemption is described in §302(b)(2) only if it meets the following three-part test:

1. Immediately after the redemption, the shareholder must own less than 50 percent of the corporation's voting stock;
2. The percentage of voting stock owned by the shareholder immediately after the redemption must be less than 80 percent of that percentage immediately before the redemption; and
3. The percentage of all stock owned by the shareholder immediately after the redemption must be less than 80 percent of that percentage immediately before the redemption.

17. Some distributions are taxed under §303. See pages 180-182 supra.

To see how these tests work, reconsider the case of shareholder *D* whose stock interest drops from 60 of 120 shares to 30 of 90 shares.[18] Assume that all of the corporation's stock is voting stock. Because *D* owns less than 50 percent of the corporation's stock after the redemption (i.e., less than 45 of the outstanding shares), *D* passes the first test of §302(b)(2). The second test requires that we compare *D*'s pre-redemption ownership percentage (60 of 120 shares, or 50%), with *D*'s post-redemption ownership percentage (30 of 90 shares, or 33.33%). Because 80 percent of *D*'s pre-redemption ownership percentage is 40 percent (i.e., 80% of 50% is 40%), *D* passes the second test of §302(b)(2) as well as the first test. Because the corporation has only one class of stock and it is all voting stock, the third test is the same as the second. Accordingly, the redemption is described in §302(b)(2), and *D* is treated as selling his stock under §302(a).

Reconsider the example but assume that the corporation redeems only 20 of *D*'s shares, so that *D*'s ownership interest drops from 50 percent (60 of 120) to only 40 percent (40 of 100). Once again, *D* passes the first test under §302(b)(2) (because *D* owns less than 50% of the voting shares after the redemption). However, *D* fails the second and third tests, because his ownership immediately after the redemption (40%) is not less than 80 percent of his ownership percentage before the redemption (80% of 50%). (In fact, the two amounts are exactly equal.) Accordingly, the redemption is not described in §302(b)(2). It may be described in §302(b)(1), however.

Note that the second and third tests of §302(b)(2) are *not* satisfied by a redemption of 20 percent of a shareholder's stock. In the example above, the redemption of 20 of *D*'s 60 shares is a redemption of 33.33 percent of *D*'s shares, yet *D* fails to qualify under §302(b)(2). Section 302(b)(2), instead, compares *D*'s ownership percentage in the corporation before the redemption with his ownership percentage in the corporation after the redemption.

Section 302(b)(1) plays a minor role in the taxation of redemptions, in large part because a Supreme Court case limits it to redemptions effecting a "meaningful reduction" in the shareholder's ownership of the corporation. United States v. Davis, 397 U.S. 301 (1970). As it now stands, §302(b)(1) has very little application outside of redemptions of preferred stock, transactions not arising in subchapter S by virtue of the one class of stock limitation. And §302(b)(4), applicable only to "partial liquidations," requires a corporate contraction under the narrow terms of §302(e). Of the four provisions in §302(b), only §302(b)(4) does *not* look to the redemption's effect on the shareholder's ownership interest in the corporation.

S corporation shareholders often have different stakes in a redemption than individual C corporation shareholders. An individual C corporation shareholder may prefer sale treatment, which allows basis recovery and capital gain, instead of nonsale treatment, where the entire distribution may be taxed as a dividend. Cf. §1(h)(11) (taxing qualified dividend income at the same rate as long-term capital gain). However, an S corporation shareholder may prefer nonsale treatment, because it may allow basis recovery but avoid gain.[19]

The effect of a redemption on the redeeming corporation does not turn on application of §302—that section governs only the shareholder's taxation. To the

18. See page 541 supra.

19. Because of the dividends-received deduction available to corporate shareholders (see §243), the stakes for a corporate shareholder of a C corporation in a redemption are in some ways like those of an S corporation shareholder.

corporation, a distribution in redemption of stock is simply a distribution, so that the corporation recognizes any gain (but not loss) in the distributed property. §311(a) and (b) (determining the gain or loss on an asset-by-asset basis). Of course, any gain so recognized is passed through to the shareholders.

3. Liquidating Distributions

When a corporation liquidates — that is, when it distributes all of its assets to its shareholders in exchange for all of its outstanding shares — the transaction technically is a distribution in redemption of stock. That technical description nicely indicates how the transaction is taxed: for the corporation it is taxed in some ways like a nonliquidating distribution, while for the shareholder it is taxed like a redemption that qualifies as a complete termination of interest.

Consider first the corporation. Recall that nonliquidating distributions of appreciated property produce recognition of income to the distributing corporation as if the property had been sold to a third party. This taxation continues for liquidating distributions, and it reflects an important difference between subchapter S and subchapter K. Under subchapter K, contributions and distributions generally are not taxable. Rather, taxation waits until property is transferred outside of the partnership family.

C corporations are taxpayers independent of their shareholders, and a transaction between a C corporation and one or more of its shareholders usually is a taxable event. Although S corporations generally avoid the double tax of C corporations, they retain the independent status upon which the corporate double tax is founded. Thus, for most purposes, an S corporation's shareholders are treated like unrelated parties, so that, for example, a distribution of property from the corporation to a shareholder is taxed like a sale of the property by the corporation to an unrelated individual. Recall that a nonliquidating distribution is not taxed precisely equivalent to a sale because the corporation cannot recognize loss on a nonliquidating distribution. A liquidating distribution is taxed more like a sale because the corporation often (but not always) can recognize a loss on the liquidating distribution of property having an adjusted basis in excess of fair market value. Of course, any corporate gain or loss recognized on the distribution will flow through to the shareholders, producing pass-thru income or loss as well as stock basis adjustments.

In general, an S corporation recognizes gain or loss on a liquidating distribution as if the property were sold for its fair market value. §336(a). However, loss will not be recognized if the distribution is made to a 50 percent or greater shareholder and either (1) is not pro rata or (2) consists of property acquired by the corporation in a §351 transfer (or as a contribution to capital) less than five years before the liquidating distribution. §336(d)(1). In addition, loss on property can disappear if the property was acquired by the S corporation in a §351 transfer (or as a contribution to capital) for the purpose of recognizing a corporate loss on the property. §336(d)(2).[20]

20. This last limitation applies only to the extent of the loss built into the property at the time of acquisition by the corporation. See §336(d)(2)(A).

To the shareholders, a liquidating distribution will be treated as a taxable exchange of their shares for assets distributed in the complete liquidation. Recall that §302(b)(3) provides exchange treatment (via §302(a)) for distributions resulting in a complete termination of a shareholder's interest in the corporation. Because a liquidating distribution results in a complete termination of every shareholder's interest within the meaning of §302(b)(3), exchange treatment should be available and the shareholders should take the distributed assets with fair market value bases. This is in fact the result. §331(a); §334(a). Note that under §1366, each shareholder is allocated her share of the S corporation's gain or loss on the liquidation. Under §1367, the shareholder adjusts her stock basis to account for that gain or loss (and any other tax items for the year of the liquidation). The shareholder uses that basis, as adjusted, to determine her gain or loss on the liquidation.

17

S Corporations: Selected Topics

A. ONE CLASS OF STOCK

Every system of pass-thru taxation needs a mechanism for allocating the entity's income and loss among its owners. For partnerships, that mechanism is §704. Most partnership income can be allocated among the partners as they see fit, subject only to the "substantial economic effect" test of §704(b). However, to address concerns with assignment of income, under §704(c), the partnership must specially allocate gain or loss on contributed property if the property, when contributed, had a basis-value disparity. Much of the flexibility and complexity of subchapter K can be traced to these two provisions.

Because an S corporation must have "one class of stock" (§1361(b)(1)(D)), its income and loss must be allocated in proportion to stock ownership. Thus, this "one class of stock" rule avoids the complexity of §704(b)-(c) but lacks its flexibility.

A corporation is treated as having one class of stock if "all outstanding shares of stock [of the corporation] confer identical rights to distribution and liquidation proceeds." Treas. Regs. §1.1361-1(*l*)(1). In particular, different shares may have different voting rights without violating the one class of stock requirement. §1361(c)(4).

NOTES

1. *Shareholder agreements.* Especially in closely held corporations, shareholders often sign agreements restricting their rights to transfer their stock. For example, an employee may be required to sell her stock to another shareholder or back to the corporation if she terminates her employment. Sale and redemption agreements triggered by death, bankruptcy, or divorce also are common. If a shareholder signs such an agreement, do the restrictions transform the shareholder's stock into a second, impermissible class of stock?

In general, the answer is no. Under the regulations, "[t]he determination of whether all outstanding shares of stock confer identical rights to distribution and liquidation proceeds is made based on the corporate charter, . . . applicable state law, and binding agreements relating to distribution and liquidation proceeds."

Treas. Regs. §1.1361-1(*l*)(2)(i). The regulations specify that these "governing instruments" do not include buy-sell agreements, agreements restricting the transferability of shares, and similar arrangements unless (1) a principal purpose of the agreement is to circumvent the one class of stock requirement and (2) the agreement establishes a purchase price that, at the time the agreement is entered into, is significantly in excess of or significantly below the fair market value of the stock. Treas. Regs. §1.1361-1(*l*)(2)(iii)(A).[1] Further, bona fide agreements to redeem or purchase shares at death, divorce, disability, or termination of employment are disregarded in determining whether a corporation's shares confer identical rights. Treas. Regs. §1.1361-1(*l*)(2)(iii)(B).

The regulations offer several examples applying these rules. For example, suppose an S corporation enters into an agreement providing that distributions to its shareholders will be made in such proportions as to ensure that each shareholder will receive the same amount after taking into account state tax burdens. Thus, shareholders residing in Texas (which imposes no state income tax) will receive $100 per share, while shareholders in Georgia (which imposes a state income tax of as much as 6%) receive $106.38 per share.[2]

In this example, the corporation will be treated as having *more than* one class of stock outstanding because a binding agreement relating to distribution proceeds is a "governing instrument," and this governing instrument alters distribution rights so that those rights are not identical among all outstanding shares. An opposite result would be reached if the corporation declared equal distributions but then withheld differing amounts in accordance with differing state withholding laws. In this latter circumstance, the amounts withheld would constitute constructive distributions so that the total actual and constructive distribution amount for each shareholder would be equal. Cf. examples (6) and (7) of Treas. Regs. §1.1361-1(*l*)(2)(v).

As a second example, suppose an S corporation distributes 50 percent of its taxable income within three months of the close of its taxable year, and suppose further that this distribution must be made in the same proportion as the corporation's taxable income is reported. If individual *A* owned all 100 outstanding shares of the corporation at the beginning of the corporation's taxable year and sold 50 of those shares halfway through the year to individual *B*, the distribution would be made 75 percent to *A* and 25 percent to *B*.

Does this arrangement create a second class of stock? Note that the corporate distribution is *not* made in proportion to stock ownership *as of the date of the distribution*. Although one might think that the outstanding shares do not have identical rights with respect to distributions and therefore constitute more than a single class of stock, the regulations specifically permit distributions to be made in proportion to varying stock ownership during the year. Treas. Regs. §1.1361-1(*l*)(2)(iv) (noting that if the distributions are not made "within a reasonable time after the close of the taxable year," the distributions may be recharacterized but will not create a second class of stock).

2. *Corporate debt as a second class of stock.* A shareholder investment in the form of debt often offers tax advantages over investment in the form of equity. For

1. These regulations also state that agreements that provide for the purchase or redemption of stock at book value or at a price between book value and fair market value will not be considered as establishing a price significantly in excess of or below the fair market value of the stock. *Id.*

2. A 6% tax imposed on $106.38 equals $6.38, so that the after-tax amount equals $100.00.

example, periodic returns on debt (i.e., interest) are deductible to the corporation while periodic returns on equity (i.e., dividends) are not. Similarly, payments in retirement of corporate debt qualify for exchange treatment (i.e., recovery of basis followed by capital gain) while payments in retirement of corporate equity must pass the hurdles of §302(b) to be assured exchange treatment.

Ever seeking to protect the federal fisc, the Commissioner often asserts that shareholder debt should be reclassified (and taxed) as equity. For an S corporation and its shareholders, the usual advantages of debt over equity disappear, because the corporation generally does not pay tax. Nonetheless, the Commissioner might seek to reclassify nominal debt as equity to challenge the very validity of the corporation's subchapter S election: If nominal debt is reclassified as equity, could it be treated as a second class of stock that then terminates the S corporation election?

One important aspect of the regulations is that if a corporate instrument is not nominally classified as equity (i.e., debt, call options, and other financial instruments), it will not violate the one class of stock requirement unless (1) the instrument is reclassified as equity under general principles of tax law, and (2) a principal purpose of issuing the instrument is to circumvent the rights to distribution or liquidation conferred on the corporation's outstanding shares by the governing instruments or to circumvent the limitation on eligible shareholders. Treas. Regs. §1.1361-1(*l*)(4)(ii)(A). Further, debt instruments owned only by the corporation's shareholders in proportion to their stock holdings (and for that reason more likely to be reclassified as equity) are not treated as a second class of stock under these regulations.[3] As a corollary, no debt held by the sole owner of an S corporation can violate the one class of stock rule. *Id.* at (*l*)(4)(ii)(B)(*2*). See also *id.* at (*l*)(4)(ii)(B)(*1*) (for a safe harbor for certain short-term unwritten advances).

Even corporate debt failing these standards can still avoid being classified as a second class of stock if it is a written, unconditional promise to pay a sum certain on demand or on a specific due date if (1) the interest due on the debt is not contingent on the corporation's profits, the payment of dividends, the borrower's discretion, or similar factors; (2) the debt is not convertible into corporate equity; and (3) the debt is held only by an individual (other than a nonresident alien) or a trust or estate allowed to be a shareholder of an S corporation under §1361(c)(2). §1361(c)(5); Treas. Regs. §1.1361-1(*l*)(5)(i). This safe harbor for "straight debt" is available even to debt subordinated to other debt of the corporation. Treas. Regs. §1.1361-1(*l*)(5)(ii). This safe harbor is also available to indebtedness held by "a person which is actively and regularly engaged in the business of lending money"; that is, "straight debt" can be held by financial institutions even though financial institutions are not eligible shareholders of an S corporation. See §1361(c)(5)(B)(iii).

PROBLEM

17-1. Does an S corporation have more than one class of stock (a) if all employee-shareholders are required to sell their stock back to the corporation at book value upon termination of employment; (b) if all married couples who

3. Note that in this case, a shareholder's allocable share of the S corporation's interest expense from the debt is matched by offsetting interest income on the debt.

purchase stock must provide upon purchase a buy-sell agreement (upon whatever terms they desire) automatically effective upon divorce and separation; (c) if, should the corporation miss two consecutive interest payments on its long-term debt, holders of that debt automatically receive voting, preferred stock (none of which is outstanding currently); (d) if highly compensated employees receive bonuses in the form of "phantom stock," that being the nontransferable right to receive additional salary as dividends are paid in proportion to those dividends and the right to receive, upon termination of employment, a lump sum equal to the increase (if any) in the value of the corporation's stock from the time the phantom stock was issued until termination of employment; or (e) if any employee-shareholder who is fired for cause must sell her stock to the corporation at cost?

B. QUALIFIED SUBCHAPTER S SUBSIDIARIES

A subsidiary of an S corporation can be treated for income tax purposes like a division of its S corporation parent if it meets the following four requirements:

1. It is a domestic corporation;
2. All of its stock is held by its S corporation parent;
3. It is not an ineligible corporation (i.e., not an insurance, a financial institution that uses the reserve method of accounting for bad debts, a §936 corporation, a DISC, or a former DISC); and
4. Its S corporation parent makes an appropriate election.

§1361(b)(3)(B). A subsidiary that meets these requirements is called a "qualified subchapter S subsidiary" or "QSub." Because a QSub is not treated as a corporation separate from its parent, its assets, liabilities, and tax items are treated as assets, liabilities, and tax items of its parent. §1361(b)(3)(A). See also Treas. Regs. §1.1361-4(a). QSubs offer a liability shield to S corporations and their shareholders without imposition of a second level of tax. For example, suppose that an S corporation has an active but risky business as well as substantial investment assets. If the business and investment assets are held by a single corporation, the investment assets are exposed to creditors of the risky business. If, instead, the risky business is placed in a QSub, the QSub may shield the investment assets from that liability exposure.[4] However, the S Corporation parent is treated as holding the assets of the risky business for federal income tax purposes. As this example demonstrates, the QSub's dual nature — transparent for income tax purposes but respected for state law purposes — provides a fertile field for planning.

NOTES

1. *Election.* The S corporation parent may make a QSub election for an eligible subsidiary at any time during the taxable year. Treas. Regs. §1.1361-3(a)(3). The

4. Note that placing the *investment assets* in the QSub would not eliminate that exposure, because the QSub stock, as an asset of the S corporation parent, could be used to satisfy creditors' claims arising out of the risky business.

election may be effective no more than 2½ months before, or 12 months after, the date of filing. *Id.* at (a)(4). If no effective date is specified on the election form, the election is effective on the date the form is filed. *Id.* Thus, an S corporation may acquire a C corporation in the middle of the year, and if the C corporation is otherwise eligible, elect to treat it as a QSub immediately. See *id.* at (a)(5) (example).

2. *Effect of the election.* If an S corporation makes a valid QSub election for a subsidiary, the subsidiary will be deemed to liquidate into the S corporation. Treas. Regs. §1.1361-4(a)(2)(i). However, "[t]he tax treatment of the liquidation or of a larger transaction that includes the liquidation will be determined under the Internal Revenue Code and general principles of tax law, including the step-transaction doctrine." *Id.* See also *id.* at (a)(2)(iii) (providing that the making of the QSub election may be deemed the adoption of a plan of liquidation); *id.* at (a)(2)(v) (in determining stock ownership, disregarding options, debt instruments, and other arrangements that are not considered stock for purposes of §1361). Cf. *id.* at (a)(5) (for some transitional relief).

For example, if an S corporation forms a subsidiary and makes a valid QSub election for the subsidiary effective on the date of formation, the transfer of assets to the subsidiary and its deemed liquidation will be disregarded. *Id.* at (a)(2)(i). Instead, the subsidiary will be deemed to be a QSub from its inception.

Suppose, instead, that an S corporation acquires all stock of a solvent C corporation in a qualified stock purchase and does not make a §338 election for the purchase, but elects to treat the target as a QSub as of the date of the purchase. The stock purchase and deemed liquidation are treated as separate steps for tax purposes. Rev. Rul. 90-95, 1990-2 C.B. 67. The target C corporation is treated as distributing all of its assets to its S corporation parent in a liquidating distribution to which §§332 and 337 should apply. *Id.* at (a)(2)(ii) (example 1).

Suppose, finally, that the target is a solvent S corporation, instead of a C corporation, the S corporation acquiror does not make a §338 election for the purchase, and, as of the date of the purchase, elects to treat the target as a QSub. The stock purchase and deemed liquidation still should be treated as separate steps for tax purposes, and the target corporation still should be treated as distributing all of its assets to its S corporation parent in a liquidating distribution to which §332 and §337 generally should apply. Importantly, however, because the target's liquidation is deemed to occur at the beginning of the acquisition date immediately following the termination of the target's S election, there is no time during which the target is deemed to be a C corporation. Cf. §1374.

Note that if QSub elections for tiered subsidiaries are effective on the same date, the S corporation may specify the order of their liquidations. Treas. Regs. §1.1361-4(b)(2). If no order is specified, the liquidations are deemed to occur from the bottom up. *Id.*

3. *Termination.* An S corporation parent may revoke a QSub election for its subsidiary at any time. Treas. Regs. §1.1361-3(b)(1). The revocation can be effective up to 2½ months before, or 12 months after, the revocation is filed. Treas. Regs. §1.1361-3(b)(2). A QSub election is also terminated if the corporation ceases to be an eligible entity, its parent ceases to own all of its stock, or its parent ceases to be an S corporation. §1361(b)(3)(C). Treas. Regs. §1.1361-5(a). Cf. §1362(d)(2) (for similar circumstances in which a corporation's S corporation status terminates).

Following the termination of a QSub election, by revocation or otherwise, a new QSub election cannot be made, broadly speaking, for five years, unless the Service waives this five-year requirement. §1361(b)(3)(D). See also Treas. Regs. §1.1361-3(b)(4) (not imposing this five-year requirement if a revocation is effective on the first day that the QSub election was to be effective).

When a QSub election terminates, the former QSub is treated as a new corporation that acquires its assets from the S corporation parent in exchange for its stock and the assumption of its liabilities. §1361(b)(3)(C). Treas. Regs. §1.1361-5(b)(1)(i). The tax treatment of this exchange (or any larger transaction that includes the exchange) is determined under the Code and general principles of tax law. *Id.* The following examples illustrate those points. In each example, assume that *X*, an S corporation, owns all stock of *Y*, a QSub, and that *Y* has only one class of stock outstanding.

First, assume that *Z*, unrelated to *X*, transfers property to *Y* in exchange for 21 percent of the *Y* stock. Because *Z* acquires *Y* stock, *Y* ceases to be a QSub. Consequently, *Y* is treated as a new corporation, acquiring its assets in exchange for its stock. Because *X* and *Z* are co-transferors, transfer property to *Y* in deemed or actual exchange for *Y* stock, and control *Y* immediately after the exchange, §351 applies to their exchanges. *Id.* at (b)(3) (example 3).

Changing the facts slightly, assume that *X* sells 21 percent of the *Y* stock to *Z*. Because of the sale, *Y* ceases to be a QSub and is treated as a new corporation, acquiring all of its assets in exchange for its stock. *X* is treated as selling an undivided 21-percent interest in each of the *Y* assets to *Z*, recognizing gain or loss. *X* and *Z* are then deemed to contribute the *Y* assets to a new corporation in a §351 exchange. §1361(b)(3)(C)(ii).

Suppose instead that *X* merges into *Y*. *Y*'s QSub election terminates, but the merger is treated as an F reorganization. Treas. Regs. §1.1361-5(b)(3) (example 8).

Finally, assume that *X* sells all of the *Y* stock to *Z*, a C corporation. *X* is treated as selling the *Y* assets to *Z*, and *Z* is treated as transferring those assets to *Y* in exchange for the *Y* stock. *Id.* at (b)(3) (example 9). Cf. Rev. Rul. 70-140, 1970-1 C.B. 73 (adopting a recharacterization of this sort for a similar transaction). The result would be the same if *Z* were an S corporation, unless *Z* elected to treat *Y* as a QSub immediately after the purchase. If *Z* made that election, the deemed formation and liquidation of *Y* would be disregarded and *Z* would be treated simply as acquiring the *Y* assets. See Treas. Regs. §1.1361-5(b)(3) (example 9); Rev. Rul. 2004-85, 2004-2 C.B. 189.

4. *Planning opportunities.* A QSub has many of the non-tax business advantages of other disregarded entities. For a discussion of those advantages, see pages 492-502, supra. A QSub, as a corporation, also offers some potential tax advantages. See Treas. Regs. §1.1361-5(b)(3) (example 4) (illustrating that a distribution of all QSub stock may be a nontaxable §355 distribution, rather than a taxable distribution of assets); *id.* at (d)(3) (example 8) (illustrating that the merger of the parent S corporation into its QSub may be treated as an F reorganization). Note that an S corporation parent may effectively "convert" a QSub into another type of disregarded entity by forming the entity and merging the QSub into it. *Id.* at (d)(3) (example 2) (illustrating that such a merger is disregarded for federal tax purposes).

The principal advantage of a QSub is that it offers liability protection at no potential additional tax cost. Suppose that Old Corp., an S Corporation, runs two businesses, a risky business and a secure business. The Old Corp. shareholders want to insulate the assets of the secure business from the liabilities of the risky business. However, because of loan restrictions, the assets of risky business cannot be transferred until the loans are fully repaid. How can the Old Corp. shareholders achieve their goal?

If Old Corp. simply transfers the assets of the secure business to a QSub, the transfer will not achieve the intended purpose, because the assets of the secure business will still be at risk (indirectly through the QSub stock). That purpose could be achieved if Old Corp. transferred the assets of the risky business to a QSub, but loan restrictions block that transfer. There is at least one viable alternative, however:

1. The shareholders of Old Corp. form a new S corporation (New Corp.) and transfer their Old Corp. stock to New Corp., so that Old Corp. becomes New Corp.'s wholly owned subsidiary;
2. New Corp. makes a QSub election for Old Corp. that is effective upon the transfer; and
3. Old Corp. distributes the assets of the secure business to New Corp. in a state-law dividend.

Both the stock transfer and asset distribution should avoid federal income tax. The stock transfer should be treated as a nontaxable F reorganization. See *id.* at (d)(3) (example 8). The asset distribution is a non-transaction for federal income tax purposes, because Old Corp.'s assets are treated as owned by New Corp. Overall, therefore, these steps help to protect the assets of the secure business from the risks associated with the risky business at little or no tax cost.

PROBLEM

17-2. *S* Corp., an electing S corporation, owns all the outstanding stock of two C corporations, Brother Corp. and Sister Corp. Brother and Sister each own half of the outstanding shares of Child Corp., also a C corporation. Can *S* Corp. file a QSub election for Brother, Sister, and Child?

C. STOCK AND DEBT BASIS

Suppose Debtor borrows $100 from Lender. To Lender, the loan is an asset, and Lender's basis in the loan is the amount of cash that Lender can receive for the loan without recognizing gain. See §1001(a). Here, Lender can receive the $100 principal amount back from Debtor without recognizing gain. Accordingly, Lender's basis in the loan must be $100. Indeed, if Lender receives less than $100 back from Debtor, Lender will be entitled to a bad debt deduction (see §166(a)(2)), a result fully consistent with ascribing a $100 basis to Lender's loan.

When Debtor uses the borrowed proceeds to purchase property, Debtor will take a cost basis in the property acquired. Thus, the effect of the loan is to give $100 of basis to both Lender and to Debtor; for Lender, basis is in the right to repayment; for Debtor, basis is in the borrowed proceeds or in property acquired with those proceeds. A borrowing transaction thus produces a doubling of total basis.[5]

Pass-thru of an S corporation loss is limited to a shareholder's outside basis, but for this purpose, the shareholder may use both her equity and debt basis to absorb such losses. §1366(d).[6]

Equity basis is just stock basis. Debt basis is shareholder's basis, if any, in loans she has made to the S corporation. That is, debt basis refers to basis enjoyed by the shareholder not in her capacity as shareholder but rather in her capacity as lender. Of course, if the shareholder has made no loans to the corporation, debt basis is zero.

Losses allocated to a shareholder first reduce equity basis before reducing debt basis. §1366(b)(2)(A). Because of the basis reduction for debt, an S corporation shareholder may recognize gain on the sale of that debt to a third party even if the third party pays less than face value. For example, if the lending shareholder has used a note's basis to absorb pass-thru loss, that basis is not available on the note's sale. There is, then, no doubling of basis but only a shifting of basis.

Note that debt basis is available *only* for absorbing pass-thru loss and not for absorbing distributions. An S corporation shareholder who receives a distribution of cash or property in excess of stock basis must report the excess as gain,[7] and in this context only true stock basis is counted. Debt basis is simply irrelevant in computing a shareholder's income from a distribution.

Income allocated to an S corporation shareholder increases the shareholder's outside basis. §1367(a)(1).[8] How is this income allocated if the shareholder has both debt and stock basis? Subchapter S provides a simple ordering rule: If pass-thru losses have reduced a shareholder's debt basis, subsequent pass-thru income will first increase debt basis to the extent of the reduction, and the balance, if any, will be allocated to stock basis. §1367(b)(2)(B).

For example, suppose individual *A* forms *S* Corp., an S corporation, by contributing $10,000 in exchange for 100 shares of *S* Corp. stock. In addition, *A* loans $40,000 to *S* Corp., and the loan is respected for tax purposes (i.e., the loan is not treated as equity). If the corporation distributes $15,000 to *A*, *A* must report $5,000 of income because the amount of the distribution exceeds *A*'s stock basis by that amount. §1368(b). A reduces her stock basis to zero. §1367(a)(2).

Suppose that the corporation invests its remaining cash of $35,000 in some activity, and suppose further that this activity produces a loss of $5,000 the following

5. More accurately, no doubling of basis occurs because Debtor has a negative basis in the debt itself. That is, Debtor will have to repay the principal amount of the debt without receiving a deduction for the payment or increasing the basis of any asset. Debtor sometimes is said to have a $100 "sisab" (backward basis) in the repayment obligation to make clear that Debtor's tax relationship to the loan transaction is the inverse of Lender's relationship. The remainder of this discussion ignores Debtor's backward basis (sisab) in the loan.

6. To the extent the losses exceed the aggregate debt and equity basis, they are suspended and treated as losses incurred by the corporation and allocated to the shareholder in the succeeding year. §1366(d)(2). Cf. §704(d). Generally, only the shareholder may use any suspended loss. But see §1366(d)(2)(B) (providing that a suspended loss may be shifted to a spouse or former spouse in a §1041 transfer); Treas. Regs. §1.1366-2(a)(5)(ii) (describing the shift).

7. See page 586 supra.

8. Outside basis adjustments for allocated income, loss and deduction are the linchpin of pass-thru taxation. See pages 588-590 supra.

year. Although *A*'s stock basis is zero, the $5,000 loss may pass through to *A* because it can be absorbed by *A*'s debt basis. That is, *A* reports the $5,000 loss on her individual return and reduces her debt basis by $5,000, from $40,000 to $35,000.

If the corporation recognizes $8,000 of income the following year, that income will pass through to *A* and will increase outside basis. Because debt basis is restored before equity basis, the first $5,000 of pass-thru income restores *A*'s debt basis to $40,000. §1367(b)(2)(B). The balance, or $3,000, increases *A*'s stock basis from zero to $3,000. Any future pass-thru of income will increase *A*'s stock basis *only* (unless *A*'s debt basis subsequently is reduced): Debt basis is not increased under §1367(b)(2)(B) above its original amount.

As this example makes clear, debt basis is important despite the absence of a provision like §752. Shareholders, then, will fight for recognition of debt basis even in circumstances when it is less than clear that the statute authorizes it. In particular, shareholders often seek debt basis when they are not lenders but only guarantors of third-party debt. Should such guarantors be treated as lenders for purposes of §1366(d)?

Estate of Leavitt v. Commissioner

875 F.2d 420 (4th Cir. 1989)

MURNAGHAN, Circuit Judge:

The appellants, Anthony D. and Marjorie F. Cuzzocrea and the Estate of Daniel Leavitt, Deceased, et al., appeal the Tax Court's decision holding them liable for tax deficiencies for the tax years 1979, 1980 and 1981. Finding the appellants' arguments unpersuasive, we affirm the Tax Court.

I

As shareholders of VAFLA Corporation, a subchapter S corporation during the years at issue, the appellants claimed deductions under [§1366] to reflect the corporation's operating losses during the three years in question. The Commissioner disallowed deductions above the $10,000 bases each appellant had from their original investments.

The appellants contend, however, that the adjusted bases in their stock should be increased to reflect a $300,000 loan which VAFLA obtained from the Bank of Virginia ("Bank") on September 12, 1979, after the appellants, along with five other shareholders ("Shareholders-Guarantors"), had signed guarantee agreements whereby each agreed to be jointly and severally liable for all indebtedness of the corporation to the Bank. At the time of the loan, VAFLA's liability exceeded its assets, it could not meet its cash flow requirements and it had virtually no assets to use as collateral. The appellants assert that the Bank would not have lent the $300,000 without their personal guarantees.

VAFLA's financial statements and tax returns indicated that the bank loan was a loan from the Shareholders-Guarantors. Despite the representation to that effect, VAFLA made all of the loan payments, principal and interest, to the Bank. The appellants made no such payments. In addition, neither VAFLA nor the

Shareholders-Guarantors treated the corporate payments on the loan as constructive income taxable to the Shareholders-Guarantors.

The appellants present the question whether the $300,000 bank loan is really, despite its form as a borrowing from the Bank, a capital contribution from the appellants to VAFLA. They contend that if the bank loan is characterized as equity, they are entitled to add a *pro rata* share of the $300,000 bank loan to their adjusted bases, thereby increasing the size of their operating loss deductions. Implicit in the appellants' characterization of the bank loan as equity in VAFLA is a determination that the Bank lent the $300,000 to the Shareholders-Guarantors who then contributed the funds to the corporation. The appellants' approach fails to realize that the $300,000 transaction, regardless of whether it is equity or debt, would permit them to adjust the bases in their stock if, indeed, the appellants, and not the Bank, had advanced VAFLA the money. The more precise question, which the appellants fail initially to ask, is whether the guaranteed loan from the Bank to VAFLA is an economic outlay of any kind by the Shareholders-Guarantors. To decide this question, we must determine whether the transaction involving the $300,000 was a loan from the Bank to VAFLA or was it instead a loan to the Shareholders-Guarantors who then gave it to VAFLA, as either a loan or a capital contribution.

Finding no economic outlay, we need not address the question, which is extensively addressed in the briefs, of whether the characterization of the $300,000 was debt or equity.

II

To increase the basis in the stock of a subchapter S corporation, there must be an economic outlay on the part of the shareholder. See Brown v. Commissioner, 706 F.2d 755, 756 (6th Cir. 1983), affg. T.C. Memo 1981-608 (1981) ("In similar cases, the courts have consistently required some economic outlay by the guarantor in order to convert a mere loan guarantee into an investment."); Blum v. Commissioner, 59 T.C. 436, 440 (1972) (bank expected repayment of its loan from the corporation and not the taxpayers, i.e., no economic outlay from taxpayers).[7]

A guarantee, in and of itself, cannot fulfill that requirement. The guarantee is merely a promise to pay in the future if certain unfortunate events should occur. At the present time, the appellants have experienced no such call as guarantors, have engaged in no economic outlay, and have suffered no cost.

The situation would be different if VAFLA had defaulted on the loan payments and the Shareholders-Guarantors had made actual disbursements on the corporate indebtedness. Those payments would represent corporate indebtedness to the shareholders which would increase their bases for the purpose of deducting net operating losses under [§1366(d)(1)]. *Brown*, 706 F.2d at 757. See also Raynor v. Commissioner, 50 T.C. 762, 770-71 (1968) ("No form of indirect borrowing, be it

7. Even the Eleventh Circuit case on which the appellants heavily rely applies this first step. See Selfe v. United States, 778 F.2d 769, 772 (11th Cir. 1985) ("We agree with *Brown* inasmuch as that court reaffirms that economic outlay is required before a stockholder in a Subchapter S corporation may increase her basis.").

guaranty, surety, accommodation, comaking or otherwise, gives rise to indebtedness from the corporation to the shareholders until and unless the shareholders pay part or all of the obligation.").

The appellants . . . argue that the "loan" is not really a loan, but is a capital contribution (equity). . . . However, the appellants once again fail to distinguish between the initial question of economic outlay and the secondary issue of debt or equity. Only if the first question had an affirmative answer, would the second arise.

The majority opinion of the Tax Court, focusing on the first issue of economic outlay, determined that a guarantee, in and of itself, is not an event for which basis can be adjusted. It distinguished the situation presented to it from one where the guarantee is triggered *and actual payments are made.* In the latter scenario, the first question of economic outlay is answered affirmatively (and the second issue is apparent on its face, *i.e.*, the payments represent indebtedness from the corporation to the shareholder as opposed to capital contribution from the shareholder to the corporation). To the contrary is the situation presented here. The Tax Court, far from confusing the issue by discussing irrelevant matters, was comprehensively explaining why the transaction before it could not represent any kind of economic outlay by the appellants.

The Tax Court correctly determined that the appellants' guarantees, unaccompanied by further acts, in and of themselves, have not constituted contributions of cash or other property which might increase the bases of the appellants' stock in the corporation.

The appellants, while they do not disagree with the Tax Court that the guarantees, standing alone, cannot adjust their bases in the stock, nevertheless argue that the "loan" to VAFLA was in its "true sense" a loan to the Shareholders-Guarantors who then theoretically advanced the $300,000 to the corporation as a capital contribution. The Tax Court declined the invitation to treat a loan and its uncalled-on security, the guarantee, as identical and to adopt the appellants' view of the "substance" of the transaction over the "form" of the transaction they took. The Tax Court did not err in doing so.

Generally, taxpayers are liable for the tax consequences of the transaction they actually execute and may not reap the benefit of recasting the transaction into another one substantially different in economic effect that they might have made. They are bound by the "form" of their transaction and may not argue that the "substance" of their transaction triggers different tax consequences. Don E. Williams Co. v. Commissioner, 429 U.S. 569, 579-80 (1977); Commissioner v. National Alfalfa Dehydrating & Milling Co., 417 U.S. 134, 149 (1974).[9] In the situation of guaranteed corporate debt, where the form of the transaction may not be so clear, courts have permitted the taxpayer to argue that the substance of the transaction was in actuality a loan to the shareholder. See *Blum*, 59 T.C. at 440.

9. On the other hand, the Commissioner is not so bound and may recharacterize the nature of the transaction according to its substance while overlooking the form selected by the taxpayer. Higgins v. Smith, 308 U.S. 473, 477 (1940). In doing so, the Commissioner usually applies debt-equity principles to determine the true *nature* of the transaction. As the *Selfe* court noted:

> This principle is particularly evident where characterization of capital as debt or equity will have different tax consequences. Thus in *Plantation Patterns* the court held that interest payments by a corporation on debentures were constructive stockholder dividends and could not be deducted by the corporation as interest payments. There, the former Fifth Circuit recharacterized debt as equity at the insistence of the Commissioner.

Selfe, 778 F.2d at 773.

However, the burden is on the taxpayer and it has been a difficult one to meet. That is especially so where, as here, the transaction is cast in sufficiently ambiguous terms to permit an argument either way depending on which is subsequently advantageous from a tax point of view.

It is important to note that those cases did not involve the question posed here of whether an economic outlay existed because it clearly did. Actual payments were made. The only question was what was the nature of the payments, debt or equity.

In the case before us, the Tax Court found that the "form" and "substance" of the transaction was a loan from the Bank to VAFLA and not to the appellants:

The Bank of Virginia loaned the money to the corporation and not to petitioners. The proceeds of the loan were to be used in the operation of the corporation's business. Petitioners submitted no evidence that they were free to dispose of the proceeds of the loan as they wished. Nor were the payments on the loan reported as constructive dividends on the corporation's Federal income tax returns or on the petitioners' Federal income tax returns during the years in issue. Accordingly, we find that the transaction was in fact a loan by the bank to the corporation guaranteed by the shareholders.

Whether the $300,000 was lent to the corporation or to the Shareholders/Guarantors is a factual issue which should not be disturbed unless clearly erroneous. Finding no error, we affirm.

It must be borne in mind that we do not merely encounter naive taxpayers caught in a complex trap for the unwary. They sought to claim deductions because the corporation lost money. If, however, VAFLA had been profitable, they would be arguing that the loan was in reality from the Bank to the corporation, and not to them, for that would then lessen their taxes. [Is this true?—EDS.] Under that description of the transaction, the loan repayments made by VAFLA would not be on the appellants' behalf, and, consequently, would not be taxed as constructive income to them. See Old Colony Trust Co. v. Commissioner, 279 U.S. 716 (1929) (payment by a corporation of a personal expense or debt of a shareholder is considered as the receipt of a taxable benefit). It came down in effect to an ambiguity as to which way the appellants would jump, an effort to play both ends against the middle, until it should be determined whether VAFLA was a profitable or money-losing proposition. At that point, the appellants attempted to treat the transaction as cloaked in the guise having the more beneficial tax consequences for them.

Finally, the appellants complain that the Tax Court erred by failing to apply debt-equity principles[11] to determine the "form" of the loan. We believe that the Tax Court correctly refused to apply debt-equity principles here, a methodology

11. . . . The appellants correctly state that the First, Fifth and Ninth Circuits have all applied traditional debt-equity principles in determining whether a shareholder's guarantee of a corporate debt was in substance a capital contribution. See Casco Bank & Trust Co. v. United States, 544 F.2d 528 (1st Cir. 1976), cert. denied, 430 U.S. 907 (1977); Plantation Patterns v. Commissioner, 462 F.2d 712 (5th Cir. 1971), cert. denied, 409 U.S. 1076 (1972); Murphy Logging Co. v. United States, 378 F.2d 222 (9th Cir. 1967). What the appellants fail to point out, however, is that those cases each involved activated guarantees, i.e., actual advances or payments on defaults. Therefore, the issue in those cases was not whether the taxpayer had made an "investment"—an economic outlay—in the corporation. The investment was admitted. The issue in those cases asked what was the nature of the investment—equity or debt. None of those cases involved the disallowance of deductions claimed by a shareholder pursuant to [§1366] for his or her share of an electing corporation's operating losses where there had simply been no economic outlay by the shareholder under the guarantee.

which is only relevant, if at all,[12] to resolution of the second inquiry—what is the nature of the economic outlay. Of course, the second inquiry cannot be reached unless the first question concerning whether an economic outlay exists is answered affirmatively. Here it is not.

The appellants, in effect, attempt to collapse a two-step analysis into a one-step inquiry which would eliminate the initial determination of economic outlay by first concluding that the proceeds were a capital contribution (equity). Obviously, a capital contribution is an economic outlay so the basis in the stock would be adjusted accordingly. But such an approach simply ignores the factual determination by the Tax Court that the Bank lent the $300,000 to the corporation and not to the Shareholders-Guarantors.

The appellants rely on Blum v. Commissioner, 59 T.C. 436 (1972), and Selfe v. United States, 778 F.2d 769 (11th Cir. 1985), to support their position. However, the appellants have misread those cases. In *Blum,* the Tax Court declined to apply debt-equity principles to determine whether the taxpayer's guarantee of a loan from a bank to a corporation was an indirect capital contribution. The Tax Court held that the taxpayer had failed to carry his burden of proving that the transaction was in "substance" a loan from the bank to the shareholder rather than a loan to the corporation. The *Blum* court found dispositive the fact that "the bank expected repayment of its loan from the corporation and not the petitioner." *Blum,* 59 T.C. at 440.

With regard to *Selfe,* the Tax Court stated:

> [T]he Eleventh Circuit applied a debt-equity analysis and held that a shareholder's guarantee of a loan made to a subchapter S corporation may be treated for tax purposes as an equity investment in the corporation where the lender looks to the shareholder as the primary obligor. We respectfully disagree with the Eleventh Circuit and hold that a shareholder's guarantee of a loan to a subchapter S corporation may not be treated as an equity investment in the corporation absent an economic outlay by the shareholder.

The Tax Court then distinguished *Plantation Patterns,* 462 F.2d 712 (5th Cir. 1972), relied on by *Selfe,* because that case involved a C corporation, reasoning that the application of debt-equity principles to subchapter S corporations would defeat Congress' intent to limit a shareholder's pass-through deduction to the amount he or she has actually invested in the corporation.

The Tax Court also distinguished *In re Lane,* 742 F.2d 1311 (11th Cir. 1984), relied on by the *Selfe* court, on the basis that the shareholder had actually paid the amounts he had guaranteed, i.e., there was an economic outlay. In *Lane,* which involved a subchapter S corporation, the issue was "whether advances made by a shareholder to a corporation constitute debt or equity. . . ." *Id.* at 1313. If the advances were debt, then Lane could deduct them as bad debts. On the other hand, if the advances were capital, no bad debt deduction would be permitted.

12. In a [§1366] subchapter S corporation case, the inquiry whether or not the economic outlay, assuming there is one, is debt or equity appears not to matter since the economic outlay, regardless of its characterization as debt or equity, will increase the adjusted basis. . . . There are no different tax consequences from the point of view of the taxpayer on the narrow issue of what amount of net operating losses may be deducted. Therefore, application of debt-equity principles in a case such as this one appears to be a red herring. However, we do not reach that issue because the Tax Court's factual finding that the appellants have shown no economic outlay on their part is not clearly erroneous.

Thus, the issue of adjusted basis for purposes of flow-through deductions from net operating losses of the corporation was not at issue. There was no question of whether there had been an economic outlay.

Although *Selfe* does refer to debt-equity principles, the specific issue before it was whether any material facts existed making summary judgment inappropriate. The Eleventh Circuit said:

> At issue here, however, is not whether the taxpayer's contribution was either a loan to or an equity investment in Jane Simon, Inc. The issue is whether the taxpayer's guarantee of the corporate loan was in itself a contribution to the corporation [as opposed to a loan from the bank] sufficient to increase the taxpayer's basis in the corporation.

The *Selfe* court found that there was evidence that the bank primarily looked to the taxpayer and not the corporation for repayment of the loan.[17] Therefore, it remanded for "a determination of whether or not the bank primarily looked to Jane Selfe [taxpayer] for repayment [the first inquiry] and for the court to apply the factors set out in *In re Lane* and section 385 to determine if the taxpayer's guarantee amounted to either an equity investment in or shareholder loan to Jane Simon, Inc. [the second inquiry]." *Id.* at 775. The implications are that there is still a two-step analysis and that the debt-equity principles apply only to the determination of the characterization of the economic outlay, once one is found.

This particular situation is not before us and we decline to address the question of whether a guarantee can be an economic outlay when accompanied by pledged collateral.

Granted, that conclusion is clouded by the next and final statement of the *Selfe* court: "In short, we remand for the district court to apply *Plantation Patterns* and determine if the bank loan to Jane Simon, Inc. was in reality a loan to the taxpayer." *Id.* To the degree that the *Selfe* court agreed with *Brown* that an economic outlay is required before a shareholder may increase her basis in a subchapter S corporation, *Selfe* does not contradict current law or our resolution of the case before us. Furthermore, to the extent that the *Selfe* court remanded because material facts existed by which the taxpayer could show that the bank actually lent the money to her rather than the corporation, we are still able to agree. It is because of the *Selfe* court's suggestion that debt-equity principles must be applied to resolve the question of whether the bank actually lent the money to the taxpayer/shareholder or the corporation, that we must part company with the Eleventh Circuit for the reasons stated above.

In conclusion, the Tax Court correctly focused on the initial inquiry of whether an economic outlay existed. Finding none, the issue of whether debt-equity

17. The loan officer so stated during deposition testimony. Furthermore, the bank originally extended a credit line to the taxpayer in consideration of her pledge of 4500 shares of stock in another corporation. When her business was later incorporated, the bank converted the loans made on the existing credit line to corporate loans, accompanied by taxpayer's agreement guaranteeing the corporation's indebtedness to the bank. The Eleventh Circuit noted that "a guarantor who has pledged stock to secure a loan has experienced an economic outlay to the extent that that pledged stock is not available as collateral for other investments." *Id.* at 772 n.7. Thus, upon remand, the district court could determine that there was an economic outlay on that basis alone, before deciding whether the form of the loan was to the taxpayer or to the corporation.

principles ought to apply to determine the nature of the economic outlay was not before the Tax Court. The Tax Court is

Affirmed.

NOTES

1. *The rights of guarantors and lenders.* The *Leavitt* court recognized that the issue before it was a difficult one. A guarantor of corporate debt is liable on the debt in the sense that the guarantor will be called upon to pay the debt if the corporation is unable to do so. Thus, if the corporation cannot repay the loan, the guarantor will be poorer by the amount of the debt. In this sense, the guarantor is in the same economic position as a shareholder who makes a loan to the same corporation: if the corporation is unable to pay the debt, the lending shareholder will suffer the loss of repayment without an ability to pass that loss on to anyone else. The statute explicitly gives debt basis to such a shareholder-lender, and because a shareholder-guarantor is in a virtually identical economic position, the shareholder's claim to debt basis for the guarantee is at least colorable.

However, there *are* differences between a guarantor and a lender that go unstated by the shareholder's argument. As we have discussed, a shareholder-lender has basis in the debt, basis that can be shifted by operation of §1366(d) into the shareholder's stock. A shareholder-guarantor, however, has no such basis. Accordingly, there is no basis to shift into equity basis for the guarantor. See also Prop. Treas. Regs. §1.1366-2(a)(2)(ii) (which would confirm that a guarantee does not create basis, including for purposes of §1366(d)) (REG-134042-07, 77 Fed. Reg. 34884 (June 12, 2012)).

2. *Implications of the taxpayer's argument.* Suppose a shareholder-guarantor were given debt basis for the guarantee, and suppose further that this debt basis were then used by the shareholder to absorb passed-thru corporate loss under §1366(d). If the corporation then repaid the debt (that is, made full payment to the lender, not to the shareholder-guarantor), it must be the case that the guarantor recognizes income. That is, we would be forced to treat extinguishment of the guarantee as income to the extent that the shareholder received and used debt basis under §1366(d). Although this certainly could be done, we usually do not think of debtor repayment as a taxable event to a guarantor.[9]

3. *Analysis of the government's argument.* There may be little economic difference between a shareholder-lender and a shareholder-guarantor. The court in *Leavitt* nonetheless held that a shareholder-guarantor is unable to exploit the debt basis advantage of §1366(d) explicitly made available to shareholder-lenders. The court distinguished lenders from guarantors by observing that lenders make an actual outlay corresponding to their economic risk of loss while guarantors, although bearing the same risk of loss, make no such outlay.

This distinction by the *Leavitt* court is *at best* thin. In many cases the shareholder-lender obtains the cash loaned to the corporation by borrowing from a third party.

9. Although if a guarantor is called upon to make good on her guarantee, and she then receives payment from the debtor, such payment will be taxable to the extent the guarantor deducted the initial payment. Use of the guarantee to absorb passed-thru corporate loss would thus play the same role as did the deduction arising from payments made by the guarantor.

Indeed, in those cases, the third-party lender often pays the loan proceeds directly to the corporation. In such circumstances the court's distinction between the nominal shareholder-lender and a shareholder-guarantor, based upon actual outlay, seems meaningless.

Indeed, tax law rarely turns on physical outlay although it often turns on economic reality. To be sure, for cash basis taxpayers actual cash flow is crucial in determining the timing of income and deduction. But cash basis accounting is an anomaly, a concession to simplify accounting for individuals and small businesses. Usually, tax consequences are independent of cash flow. For example, a taxpayer's basis in purchased property is "cost" under §1012, where cost includes not only actual outlays but also promises to make outlays in the future; that is, purchase money debt goes into basis. If tax consequences should follow economic reality unless Congress explicitly directs otherwise, how should *Leavitt* have come out?

Two arguments in favor of allowing a shareholder-guarantor to increase debt basis by reason of the guarantee often are advanced. The first is that a loan from a third party to an S corporation should be treated as made to a shareholder-guarantor *if* the third-party lender looks primarily to the shareholder-guarantor for repayment. Indeed, the *Selfe* court seemed to adopt this view.

On this theory, a court should seek to determine whether the loan, nominally made to the corporation, would not have been made but for the guarantee by one or more shareholders. Yet, what if the loan would have been made without the guarantee but not on the same terms? For example, what if the effect of a guarantee is to allow the corporation to borrow at a lower interest rate? So long as the corporation has any assets whatsoever, the lender can look to some extent to the corporation for repayment. Presumably, a lender who makes a loan to a corporation and then obtains a shareholder guarantee can and will look to both the corporation and the guarantor for repayment, and it is unrealistic to focus on one to the exclusion of the other.

4. *Partnership analogies.* The second argument advanced for allowing shareholder-guarantors to obtain debt basis for their guarantees is based on subchapter K's treatment of debt. Under §752, partnership debt increases outside basis of the partners as they share economic risk of loss. If this rule were to apply to S corporation debt guaranteed by a shareholder, such debt would be allocated to the guarantor-shareholder.[10]

Yet this analogy understates the dissimilarities between the treatment of entity debt in subchapters K and S. In subchapter K, §752 provides that *all* entity debt must increase outside basis. Given that mandate in §752, the regulations then provide that recourse partnership debt is allocated among the partners as they share economic risk of loss. Nonrecourse partnership debt is allocated differently, generally in accordance with partnership profits interests.[11] The structural aspect of §752 is not that partnership debt is allocated as the partners share risk — the sharing of

10. Because no shareholder is liable on corporate debt absent a guarantee, a shareholder guarantee of corporate debt is equivalent to a partner's guarantee of a nonrecourse debt. Under the rules of §752, partnership nonrecourse debt guaranteed by a partner is allocated to the guarantor-partner. See page 666 supra.

11. See page 666 supra.

nonrecourse debt proves that assertion false — but rather that *all* partnership debt, recourse and nonrecourse alike, increases outside basis.

This basic feature of §752 — not how partnership debt is allocated among the partners but rather that *all* debt must be allocated somehow — reinforces the transparency metaphor upon which subchapter K is based. As a general rule, partnership aggregate inside basis equals aggregate outside basis. To be sure, there can be exceptions to this rule, especially if a §754 election is not in place.[12] But for the most part this equality holds true, and it helps ensure that existence of the partnership will not affect the timing of income and deduction to the partners. For example, the equality of aggregate inside and outside basis means that sufficient outside basis will exist to absorb all pass-thru partnership-level deductions. Absent §752, partnership losses from leveraged property would be unavailable to the partners because of §704(d).

Subchapter S follows no transparency metaphor, and an S corporation's aggregate inside basis will not, as a rule, equal aggregate outside basis. Because there is no provision in subchapter S analogous to §752, it is a mistake to read into subchapter S any of the incidental allocation rules following from application of §752. That is, because there is no general rule in subchapter S providing that entity level borrowing increases outside basis, it is a mistake to read into subchapter S the partnership allocation rule that entity debt is allocated as partners share risk.

5. *A final note on* Leavitt. The analysis to this point still leaves us with no good answer to the question at issue in *Leavitt.* Internal Revenue Code §1366(d) allows a shareholder of an S corporation to deduct pass-thru losses to the extent of the shareholder's equity and debt basis. This provision makes no mention of shareholder guarantees, and because it functions wholly differently from §752, an analogy to subchapter K offers little support. But, as discussed above, a shareholder guarantee of corporate third-party debt is in many ways the equivalent of a direct loan from the shareholder-guarantor. So should the guarantee contribute to the shareholder's debt basis for purposes of §1366(d)?

The premise of §1366(d) seems to be that a shareholder of an S corporation should be permitted to deduct her share of pass-thru losses to the extent of the shareholder's investment in the corporation. By explicitly including both equity and debt investment in §1366(d), Congress has taken the welcome if unusual step of recognizing that equity and debt are but two bands in a single spectrum. That is, investing in corporate equity and investing in corporate debt both reflect a shareholder's decision to seek profit from the corporation's business activity, with the difference between equity and debt largely being a greater or lesser risk of nonpayment and a greater or lesser possible profit.

From this perspective, a shareholder guarantee of corporate debt is similar to both equity and debt investments in that the guarantee represents a shareholder decision to place capital at risk in the venture. However, the guarantee is unusual in that it offers no opportunity for profit: Unless the shareholder-guarantor is compensated for the guarantee, the best that the shareholder-guarantor can hope for is that the guarantee will prove unnecessary. Of course, such uncompensated guarantees usually are made not out of disinterested generosity but to improve the

12. See Chapter 27 infra.

prospects of the shareholder's equity (and debt, if any) investment in the corporation.

Economically, then, a shareholder guarantee of an S corporation's third-party debt is an additional investment of the shareholder in the corporate activity made to maintain or improve the shareholder's existing investment. Whether an investment is made with the shareholder's own funds, directly borrowed funds, or implicitly borrowed funds (i.e., by guaranteeing third-party debt) should be substantively irrelevant. By including both debt and equity investments within its embrace, §1366(d) represents a triumph of substance over form. The *Leavitt* court unfortunately emphasized just the reverse, and so the decision seems wrong. Note, however, that proposed regulations would follow *Leavitt.* Prop. Treas. Regs. §1.1366-2(a)(2)(ii) (REG-134042-07, 77 Fed. Reg. 34884 (June 12, 2012)).

A formalistic way around the *Leavitt* decision is for a shareholder to borrow funds from a third party (such as a bank) and then reloan the proceeds to the S corporation on identical terms. In this way, the S corporation will bear the economic cost of repayment, and the shareholder will suffer the burden of repayment only if the corporation is unable to make good on its obligation. This is in essence the relationship that arises when the corporation borrows from the third party directly with a shareholder guarantee. Courts have split on the efficacy of this back-to-back loan transaction. Compare Miller v. Commissioner, T.C. Memo 2006-125 (respecting a back-to-back loan transaction), with Oren v. Commissioner, 357 F.3d 854 (8th Cir. 2004) (rejecting a back-to-back loan transaction as not satisfying the "economic outlay" test). Proposed regulations have moved away from the "economic outlay" standard in the context of back-to-back loans in favor of asking whether the corporate loan is "bona fide." Prop. Treas. Regs. 1.1366-2(a)(2)(i) (adding that whether debt is bona fide is determined under general tax principles and depends on all facts and circumstances).

PROBLEM

17-3. Individual *X* forms *S* Corp., an S corporation, by contributing cash of $10,000 in exchange for 100 shares of *S* Corp. stock. In addition, *X* contributes $15,000 to the corporation in exchange for a bond. During its first year, *S* Corp. borrows $75,000 from Big Bank, and this debt is guaranteed by *X.* Also during that year, it distributes $20,000 to *X.* For the entire year, *S* Corp. recognizes a taxable loss of $12,000. What are the tax consequences to *X* of the distribution, and how much of the corporation's loss can *X* claim on her individual return? How might *X* have improved her tax position without significantly changing the transactions?

D. ASSIGNMENT OF INCOME CONCERNS

1. *Pre-Contribution Appreciation and Related Problems*

Although the one class of stock rule ensures that an S corporation's income and loss will be allocated among its shareholder's in proportion to ownership interests, it plays havoc with assignment of income concerns. For example, suppose individuals

X and *Y* form *XY* Corp., an S corporation, with *X* contributing cash of $10,000 and *Y* contributing Blackacre with a $6,000 adjusted basis and $10,000 fair market value. If each shareholder receives 10 shares of *XY* stock in exchange for the contribution, they will each report one-half of the corporation's earnings. Accordingly, if the corporation's only taxable activity is a sale of Blackacre for its current value of $10,000, each shareholder will report $2,000 of gain on her individual return and will increase outside basis by the same amount. By contributing Blackacre to the corporation in anticipation of sale, *Y* is able to shift half of the gain on Blackacre to *X*. In the partnership context, *Y* would be taxable on the full $4,000 of gain under §704(c).

Assume that the corporation invests its $20,000 in Whiteacre, and that when Whiteacre increases in value to $30,000, *Y* sells her shares of stock to *Z*. *Z* is acquiring one-half of a corporation now worth $30,000, and assume that *Z* will pay $15,000 for those shares.[13] If Whiteacre is subsequently sold for $30,000, half of the $10,000 gain will be allocated to, and reported by, *Z* even though no corporate asset has appreciated since *Z* bought in to the enterprise. The sale of shares from *Y* to *Z* did not so much work a shift of income as a doubling: *Y* was taxed implicitly on her share of the increase in value of Whiteacre when she sold her stock to *Z*, and *Z* is taxed again on that increase in value when Whiteacre is sold to a third party and the gain is passed through to the shareholders. Of course, this income will adjust *Z*'s stock basis upward from $15,000 to $20,000, so that *Z* will enjoy an offsetting loss should she sell her stock immediately thereafter. But because *Y*'s share of gain from Whiteacre is taxed to *Z* upon disposition of the property by the corporation, and the offsetting loss is deferred until *Z* sells her shares, *Z* may suffer a present-value cost: The tax on the gain precedes the tax benefit from the loss. In the partnership context, this timing problem could be avoided by the partnership filing an election under §754 so that *Z*'s purchase of *Y*'s interest in the venture would trigger an optional basis adjustment under §743(b).

2. *Family Ownership and §1366(e)*

Suppose Mother forms *S* Corp., an S corporation, by contributing cash of $10,000 in exchange for 100 shares. As the corporation begins to turn a profit, Mother gives some or all of the shares to her children. Because the corporation's income is taxed to its shareholders, the effect of the stock transfer is to shift some or all of the corporation's income from Mother to her children. Does this run afoul of the assignment of income doctrine?

In general, the answer is no. Recall that income from property can be shifted by a transfer of the income-producing property. See, e.g., Blair v. Commissioner, 300 U.S. 579 (1941). The corporation's profit is just one form of income from property, and transfer of the stock is the transfer of the income-producing property. Transfer of the corporation's stock is, in general, no more abusive than a transfer of the initial $10,000 cash.

13. *Z* may pay less because of Whiteacre's $10,000 built-in gain, half of which, when recognized, will be allocated to *Z* and reported on *Z*'s individual return. Among other things, the price reduction will depend on *Z*'s estimate of the present-value cost of the tax on that allocable gain.

But what if the corporation's profit is derived in part from Mother's labor. For example, suppose that *S* Corp. is in the business of accounting, and it provides accounting services to its customer by hiring Mother, a public accountant. If Mother is paid only a small salary for her efforts, much of the value of Mother's services will be reported as corporate profit and will be passed through and taxed to the children.

In those circumstances, the Commissioner may reallocate some of the corporation's income back to Mother to more accurately reflect her contribution to the enterprise. §1366(e). Indeed, if Mother has transferred all of her shares so that she is no longer a shareholder, the Commissioner may still allocate some of the corporation's profit directly to Mother to approximate a fair salary for her services. Section 1366(e) broadly authorizes the Commissioner to reallocate income if one member of a family is undercompensated for services or the use of capital by an S corporation owned in whole or in part by other family members. See also Treas. Regs. §1.1366-3(a) (defining the family of a shareholder to include the shareholder's spouse, ancestors, lineal descendants, and any trust for the primary benefit of any of those persons). This section is similar to, but far broader than, §704(e)(2), a section targeted at family partnerships.

PROBLEM

17-4. Individuals *A* and *B* form *Z* Corp., an S corporation, with *A* contributing a copyright with an adjusted basis of $0 (because *A* wrote the manuscript) and a fair market value of $5,000, and *B* contributing depreciable machinery with an adjusted basis of $3,000 and fair market value of $5,000. In return, each individual receives 50 shares of *Z* Corp. common stock. Assume the machinery is depreciable over five years on a straight-line basis.

a. If the corporation sells the machinery immediately for $5,000, how is the $2,000 gain allocated between *A* and *B*?
b. If *B* cleans and repairs the machinery so that its value increases to $6,000 and the corporation then sells it for that amount, how is the gain allocated between *A* and *B*?
c. If the corporation is entitled to a $600 depreciation deduction for its first taxable year, how is that deduction allocated between *A* and *B*?

E. SALES OF STOCK AND §336(e) AND §338(h)(10) ELECTIONS

If the shareholders of an S corporation sell an affiliated interest in their stock (i.e., stock possessing at least 80 percent of total vote and value), they may be able to elect to treat the stock sale for tax purposes in many ways as an asset sale by joining in an election under §338(h)(10) or §336(e). If either election is made, the S corporation and its shareholders are treated for tax purposes as if the S corporation sold its assets to a newly formed subsidiary of the buyer and then liquidated, distributing the sales proceeds to its shareholders.

With either election, the selling target shareholders may couple the non-tax advantages of a stock sale with the tax advantages of an asset sale. For example, for business purposes, it is often easier to transfer the target's stock rather than its assets, and a stock transfer is more likely to preserve the target's goodwill and other assets (such as licenses) but avoid real property transfer taxes. For tax purposes, because the target is deemed to sell and then buy back its assets, its assets take a cost basis, a result that eliminates a possible layer of tax. Because of that tax benefit, the selling target shareholders may be able to exact a greater sales price. Although the election may result in no additional tax to a target shareholder, that is not always true. For example, because of the election, a shareholder may substitute ordinary income for long-term capital gain.

A §338(h)(10) election may be made jointly by the S corporation shareholders and the buyer if the shareholders sell an affiliated interest in their stock on one day to a corporate buyer in a qualified stock purchase (as defined in §338(h)(3)).[14] A §336(e) election may be made jointly by the S corporation shareholders and the target if the shareholders sell an affiliated interest in their stock over a 12-month period to purchasers in a qualified stock disposition (as defined in Treas. Regs. §1.336-1(b)(6)(i)).[15] If the corporation qualifies as a small business corporation after the deemed purchase, it may be treated as an S corporation, but only if a new S election is made. Treas. Regs. §1.336-2(b)(1)(ii).

Whether a §336(e) or §338(h)(10) election is made, because the S corporation is deemed to sell its assets, all the rules applicable to assets sales are implicated. These rules include the tax on built-in gains under §1374 (discussed in the following chapter) and the depreciation recapture rules of §§1245 and 1250. Of course, if the S corporation owns some ordinary income assets, one disadvantageous effect of the §336(e) or §338(h)(10) election is that some of the sales gain will be includible as ordinary income.

A selling S corporation shareholder adjusts her stock basis to account for her allocable share of gain or loss on the deemed asset sale. §1367. See also Treas. Regs. §1.338(h)(10)-1(d)(3)(i); Treas. Regs. §1.336-2(b)(1)(iii)(A).[16] Then, on the deemed liquidation, the shareholder recognizes gain or loss, measured by the difference between the sales proceeds received and her adjusted basis in the S corporation stock. §331. See also Treas. Regs. §1.338(h)(10)-1(d)(4)(i) and (d)(5)(i); *id.* at (d)(5)(iii) (providing that the target shareholder does not recognize additional gain or loss on the sale of target stock in the qualified stock purchase); Treas. Regs.

14. Treas. Regs. §1.338(h)(10)-1(c). The buyer actually acquires the S corporation stock, so that the S corporation becomes the buyer's subsidiary. For federal income tax purposes, however, the S corporation is treated as a new corporation that buys its assets in the §338 deemed asset sale. For a fuller discussion of §338, see pages 307-313 supra.

15. If the sale constitutes both a qualified stock purchase and qualified stock disposition, it is treated as a qualified stock purchase, ineligible for a §336(e) election. Treas. Regs. §1.336-1(b)(6)(ii)(A). For example, if the S corporation shareholders sold an affiliated interest in the S corporation stock to unrelated individuals over a 12-month period, the sale would be a qualified stock disposition. If, instead, they sold that stock to a single corporation, it would be a qualified stock purchase. For a fuller discussion of §336(e), see pages 314-319 supra.

16. For a § 336(e) election to be made for an S corporation target, its shareholders must dispose of the target's stock over a 12-month period. See Treas. Regs. §1.336-1(b)(6)(ii). In contrast, a §338(h)(10) election may be made for an S corporation target only if the relevant purchases all occur on one day. See Treas. Regs. §1.338(h)(10)-1(b)(4). Perhaps because the §336(e) regulations are modeled on the §338(h)(10) regulations, they fail to answer a number of questions that may arise when the relevant dispositions occur over time, including the following: If S corporation shareholders sell their target stock in a series of steps to individuals and the target remains an S corporation, will a buyer or seller take the target's tax items into account that arise between a stock sale and the deemed asset sale? If the shareholders sell their stock in a series of steps to a corporation but a §336(e) election is made, will the target's S corporation status remain in effect through the deemed asset sale?

§1.336-2(b)(1)(i)(A) (providing a comparable result). If an S shareholder does not sell her target stock, she is still deemed to receive a liquidating distribution, recognizing gain or loss, and then deemed to buy back that stock on the day after the acquisition or disposition date for its fair market value. Treas. Regs. §1.338(h)(10)-1(d)(5)(i); *id.* at (d)(5)(ii) (providing that the price deemed paid is pegged to the price paid for the purchased stock); Treas. Regs. §1.336-1(b)(1)(v) (providing a comparable result).

The §336(e) or §338(h)(10) election can play an important role in the sale of an S corporation. What is surprising is that, under the explicit language of the statute, each election is available only if the target is a subsidiary in an affiliated group, a definition excluding S corporations. But see §338(i) (providing regulatory authority "as necessary or appropriate to carry out the purposes of" §338).

PROBLEMS

17-5. Individual *B* owns all the outstanding shares of *S* Corp., an S corporation. *B* agrees to sell the stock of *S* Corp. to Acquiring Corp. for $1,000,000, payable half down and half in the form of an interest-bearing installment obligation payable in two years. *B*'s adjusted basis in her *S* Corp. shares is $400,000, and that is *S* Corp.'s adjusted basis in its assets. If *B* files an election under §338(h)(10), how much gain does *B* report in the year of sale?

17-6. Individual *T* owns all of the outstanding shares of *X* Corp., an S corporation. *T*'s *X* stock has a $1,000,000 basis and *X*'s assets also have a $1,000,000 basis. *A* Corp. proposes to buy *T*'s *X* stock for $5,000,000. If the sale is consummated as proposed *T* will recognize a long-term capital gain of $4,000,000. Assume that *T* is taxed at a 20-percent rate on long-term capital gain and a 40-percent rate on ordinary income, while *X* Corp. is taxed at a 35-percent rate on its taxable income after *A* Corp. purchases the *X* stock.

a. Assuming all of the property owned by *X* Corp. is inventory, what is the least increase in purchase price that *T* should demand for agreeing to join in making an election under §338(h)(10)? What is the maximum increase in the purchase price that *A* Corp. should agree to if that election is made? If individual *A*, rather than *A* Corp., made the purchase, *A* was taxed at a 40-percent rate on ordinary income, and a §336(e) election were made, but *X* Corp. remained an S corporation, what is the maximum increase in price that *A* should agree to?
b. Assuming that the assets of *X* Corp. will be depreciable immediately following the sale on a straight-line basis over four years whether an election is made or not, what is the dollar benefit to *A* Corp. of an election under §338(h)(10) (ignoring the time value of money)?

18

Transition Issues

A. FROM C CORPORATION TO S CORPORATION

An existing C corporation can elect S corporation status so long as it satisfies the requirements set forth in §1361(b) relating to the maximum number of shareholders (100), maximum number of classes of shares outstanding (1), and so on. As discussed above,[1] an election under §1362 will be effective for the corporation's next taxable year unless the corporation wishes the election to be effective for its current taxable year and the election is filed within the first two and one-half months of the year. Once the election is effective, the corporation is subject to subchapter S and is taxed as described previously. However, because the corporation has a C corporation history, it is also subject to some special subchapter S rules to transition from C corporation to S corporation status.

1. Shareholder Taxation of Distributions

In general, profits earned by a C corporation are taxed twice, once when earned by the corporation and a second time when distributed to the corporation's shareholders. However, not all distributions from a C corporation to its shareholders are taxable dividends: distributions exceeding the corporation's earnings and profits are treated as a return of the shareholder's capital to the extent of the shareholder's stock basis, with any excess taxed as gain from the sale or exchange of shares of stock. §301(c). Every C corporation must maintain an "earnings and profits" account, and distributions will be taxed as dividends only to the extent of this account.

When an existing C corporation with a positive earnings and profits account elects S corporation status, distributions of post-election earnings should be passed through tax free to the shareholder-distributees. However, distributions out of the corporation's pre-election earnings and profits account should be treated as dividends under subchapter C's regime. Section 1368(c) adopts a pro-taxpayer rule: Distributions are, in general, assumed to be out of post-election earnings to the extent of such earnings; only after all post-election earnings have been exhausted

1. See page 531 supra.

are distributions treated as coming from pre-election earnings and profits. To keep track of the corporation's post-election earnings, the statute defines an "accumulated adjustments" account (often called the "AA" account, or simply the "AAA"), which must be maintained by each S corporation with accumulated earnings and profits (i.e., positive C corporation earnings and profits). See §1368(e)(1). This AA account reflects, with one modification, the corporation's post-election undistributed earnings.

Recall that distributions of S corporations having no C corporation history are taxed to the distributee-shareholders under §1368(b). Under this provision, the distribution is tax free to the extent of the shareholder's stock basis, with any excess treated as gain from the sale or exchange of shares. This same provision applies to S corporations having a C corporation history if the corporation has no accumulated earnings and profits.

If, however, the corporation has accumulated earnings and profits, distributions are taxed to its shareholder-distributees under §1368(c), and that section divides distributions into three tiers:

Tier 1. First, distributions are taxed under §1368(b) to the extent paid out of the corporation's accumulated adjustments account; that is, such distributions are taxed like all distributions made by S corporations without accumulated earnings and profits. §1368(c)(1).

Tier 2. Second, distributions in excess of a corporation's accumulated adjustments account are taxed as dividends to the extent of the corporation's accumulated earnings and profits account. §1368(c)(2).

Tier 3. Third, to the extent distributions exceed *both* the corporation's accumulated adjustments account *and* the corporation's earnings and profits account, distributions are taxed under §1368(b) (i.e., the same as tier 1 distributions). §1368(c)(3).

Consider the following example: *X* Corp. files an S corporation election effective January 1 of year 1. As of that date, *X* Corp. has accumulated earnings and profits of $10,000. All outstanding shares of *X* Corp. are owned by individual *J* with an aggregate stock basis of $12,000. During year 1, *X* Corp. recognizes $6,000 of taxable income and makes distributions totaling $30,000.

First, the $6,000 of post-election income pass through to shareholder *J* and increase her stock basis to $18,000. Second, of the $30,000 distributed to *J*, $6,000 is received tax free under §§1368(c)(1) and 1368(b) (i.e., under tier 1), reducing *J*'s stock basis back to $12,000. Of the remaining $24,000 distributed to *J*, $10,000 is taxed as a dividend under §1368(c)(2) (i.e., under tier 2), reducing *X* Corp.'s earnings and profits to $0 and leaving *J*'s stock basis at $12,000. The remaining $14,000 is taxed under §§1368(c)(3) and 1368(b) (i.e., under tier 3), so that $12,000 is received tax free, and $2,000 is taxed as gain from the sale or exchange of *J*'s shares, with *J*'s stock basis reduced to $0.

If *X* Corp. should recognize, say, $2,000 of income in year 2, it can then distribute up to that amount tax free under §1368(c)(1) because recognition of income increases the corporation's accumulated adjustments account. Indeed, if *X* Corp. earns $2,000 in year 2 and distributes less than $2,000 in that year, *X* Corp.'s accumulated adjustments account will remain positive and can absorb distributions in subsequent years.

An S corporation's accumulated adjustments account may be reduced below zero by corporate losses. For example, suppose *Y* Corp. has earnings and profits of $10,000 and an accumulated adjustments account of $7,000. If the corporation distributes $5,000, that amount is treated as a distribution of pass-thru income under §1368(c)(1) and reduces *Y* Corp.'s accumulated adjustments account down to $2,000. If the corporation recognizes a taxable loss of $5,000 in the next year, the accumulated adjustments account is reduced to negative $3,000, so that any distribution during this year will be taxed as a dividend to the extent of the corporation's $10,000 earnings and profits. Further, if the corporation earns only $1,000 in the following year, the accumulated adjustments account remains negative (i.e., negative $2,000), so again tier 1 is unavailable to shelter distributions. Thus, if the corporation distributes $1,000 during that year and has at least $1,000 of earnings and profits, the full $1,000 will be taxed as a dividend. Even though the corporation distributes no more than it earns during the year, the distribution will be taxable to its distributee-shareholders as a dividend.

Recall that tax-exempt income of an S corporation increases its shareholders' stock bases so that tax-exempt income will not be taxable when distributed or indirectly upon disposition of the shares. Nevertheless, tax-exempt income does *not* increase an S corporation's accumulated adjustments account. To understand the impact of this rule, consider the following example:

Z Corp. files an S corporation election effective January 1 of year 1. As of that date, *Z* Corp. has earnings and profits of $5,000. All of the outstanding shares of *Z* Corp. are owned by individual *M* with an aggregate adjusted basis of $12,000. During year 1, *Z* Corp. recognizes no taxable income or loss but receives tax-exempt income of $1,000. In addition, *Z* Corp. distributes $500 to *M*.

Under §1367(a)(1)(A), the tax-exempt income increases *M*'s stock basis by $1,000, from $12,000 to $13,000. However, the tax-exempt income does not increase *Z* Corp.'s accumulated adjustments account, so that account remains at $0. Thus, the entire distribution is taxed under §1368(c)(2) (i.e., under tier 2) as a dividend to *Z* and reduces the corporation's earnings and profits account to $4,500. *M*'s stock basis remains at $13,000.

Do not conclude from this example that the tax-exempt income received by the corporation will be taxed as a dividend when distributed to *M*. It will not be: All post-election income of the corporation will be received by *M* tax free under the pass-thru/basis adjustment mechanism of §§1367(a)(2)(A) and 1368(b)(1). When a corporation has both pre-election earnings and profits and post-election income, an ordering rule determines if distributions are deemed to come first out of the pre- or post-election accounts. Section 1368(c) provides that ordering rule.

Recall that the effect of the three tiers in §1368(c) is to provide that distributions are assumed to come first out of the accumulated adjustments account and, once that account is exhausted, out of pre-election earnings and profits. Because post-election tax-exempt income does not increase the corporation's accumulated adjustments account, distributions will be deemed to come out of pre-election earnings and profits before they are assumed to come out of post-election tax-exempt income. Distributions out of post-election tax-exempt income still come out tax free to the shareholders under tier 3. In contrast, a distribution of post-election taxable income comes out tax free but under tier 1. Thus, distributions out of post-election tax-exempt income get the same treatment to the shareholders as does post-election taxable income, but such distributions are deemed to be made *last*, after the accumulated adjustments account and the earnings and profits account are both depleted. Because post-election tax-exempt income does not increase the corporation's earnings and profits account, its distribution will not result in additional dividend income.

If the shareholders of an S corporation having accumulated earnings and profits so elect, the ordering rule of §1368(c)(1)-(2) can be reversed, so that distributions are assumed to come out of earnings and profits before the accumulated adjustments account. This election can be made on an annual basis and requires the consent of all shareholders receiving a distribution during the year. §1368(e)(3). Because the effect of such an election is to accelerate dividend income to the shareholders, it rarely is made. However, certain disabilities sometimes are imposed on an S corporation that has accumulated earnings and profits, and these disabilities may be avoided by depleting the corporation's earnings and profits. These disabilities are discussed below in Section A.3.

PROBLEM

18-1. *X* Corp., a C corporation using the calendar year as its taxable year, elects S corporation status effective January 1 of year 1. As of that day, the corporation has accumulated earnings and profits of $8,000. During year 1, the corporation recognizes net taxable income of $6,000 and net tax-exempt income of $4,000. Also during that year, the corporation distributes $20,000 to its shareholders at the rate of $5,000 per calendar quarter (distributed February 14, May 15, August 15, and November 15, $2,500 to each of its two shareholders). As of January 1 of year 1, shareholder *P* owns 50 shares with an adjusted basis of $20 per share, and shareholder *Q* owns 50 shares with an adjusted basis of $100 per share. What are the tax consequences of these distributions to each shareholder?

2. *Corporate-Level Tax on Built-In Gains*

Suppose a C corporation owns substantially appreciated property. If this corporation sells the property, it will recognize gain, and if it distributes the proceeds, the shareholders will have dividend income. Thus, two taxes may be owed: one on the corporate-level gain and a second on the shareholder-level dividend income. If the corporation sells the property and then files an S corporation election, both taxes still may be incurred: the first as a C corporation and the second upon eventual distribution because of §1368(c)(2). But suppose the corporation files an S corporation election before selling the property. So long as the election is effective *before* the sale of the property, the corporation's gain will not increase its accumulated earnings and profits account because the gain will be recognized *after* the corporation's earnings and profits account is closed by the election.

To inhibit corporations from electing S corporation status to avoid the double tax on appreciated property, Congress enacted §1374. This section, applicable during the corporation's "recognition period," imposes an annual tax equal to the corporation's "net recognized built-in gain" for the year times the highest corporate income tax rate (currently 35 percent). §1374(d)(7)(A) (providing, in general, that the corporation's recognition period is the first 10 years of its existence); *id.* at (d)(7)(B) (for special rules for taxable years beginning in 2009-2011); *id.* at (d)(7)(C) (providing for taxable years beginning in 2012-2013 that the recognition period is just five years). This tax can be understood only by working through the definitions in §1374(d).

Look first at §1374(d)(1). A corporation's "net unrealized built-in gain" equals the excess of the fair market value over the adjusted basis of all corporate assets owned by the corporation when its S corporation election becomes effective. See also §1374(d)(8) (for a special rule that applies if, for example, a C corporation merges into an S corporation in a §368 reorganization). "Net unrealized built-in gain" is thus fixed in amount once the election becomes effective and need not be recomputed each year.

As the corporation sells or exchanges the assets that it held when its S corporation election became effective, it realizes and recognizes its unrealized built-in gains and losses. During the corporation's recognition period, the corporation computes the excess, if any, of its recognized built-in gains for the year over its recognized built-in losses, and this excess is called its "net recognized built-in gain."[2] These amounts, adjusted for certain items of income and loss, are then netted to form the corporation's "net recognized built-in gain" for the year. As a limitation, however, net recognized built-in gain for a year cannot exceed the excess of the net *unrealized* built-in gain over the net recognized built-in gain taken into account in prior years. §1374(c)(2).

The §1374 tax is then imposed on the net recognized built-in gain or, if less, on the corporation's total taxable income for the year. §1374(d)(2)(A). The taxable income limitation should come into play only if the corporation recognizes a net loss for the year, excluding recognized built-in gains and losses. Note that if that limitation applies, any amount that escapes the §1374 tax because of the limitation is treated as recognized built-in gain the next year. See §1374(d)(2)(B). Thus, all of the corporation's net unrealized built-in gain should eventually be subjcct to the §1374 tax, unless the corporation holds property beyond the recognition period.

If an S corporation is subject to the §1374 tax on built-in gains, the amount of the tax so imposed is treated as a loss of the corporation for the year in which the tax is imposed. §1366(f)(2). As a result, the amount of the tax is passed through to the corporation's shareholders like any other corporate loss, with the character of the loss determined by reference to the built-in gains upon which the §1374 tax was imposed.

PROBLEM

18-2. *Y* Corp., a C corporation using the calendar year as its taxable year, owns four capital assets with adjusted bases and fair market values as follows:

Asset	*Adjusted Basis*	*Fair Market Value*
Asset 1	$5,000	$8,000
Asset 2	5,000	3,000
Asset 3	5,000	2,000
Asset 4	5,000	9,000

2. Post-election appreciation does not contribute to the computation of "recognized built-in gain," see §1374(d)(3), and post-election reduction in value does not add to "recognized built-in loss," see §1374(d)(4).

Y Corp. elects S corporation status effective January 1 of year 1. During year 1, *Y* Corp. sells assets 1 and 2 for $6,000 and $3,000. During year 2, *Y* Corp. sells asset 3 for $2,000. During year 3, *Y* Corp. sells asset 4 for $10,000. Compute the corporation's tax under §1374 for years 1-3.

3. *Disabilities Associated with Passive Investment Income*

Consider the case of a C corporation having substantial earnings and profits when its S corporation election becomes effective. Because of the ordering rule of §1368(c), the shareholder-level tax on those earnings will be deferred until all post-election taxable income has been distributed. Congress apparently feels that this deferral is inappropriate if the corporation amounts to no more than an incorporated pocketbook: If the corporation has too much passive investment income, it will be subject to a special corporate-level tax and can even lose its status as an S corporation. However, because these penalties apply only to S corporations having accumulated earnings and profits, they can be avoided by distributing out the earnings and profits before or after the election is effective. Of course, if an S corporation retains earnings and profits, the penalties may apply until those earnings and profits are fully distributed. To expedite distributions of its earnings and profits, an S corporation may elect under §1368(e)(3) to treat its distributions as coming first out of its earnings and profits, rather than its accumulated adjustments account.[3]

NOTES

1. *Corporate tax on excessive passive income.* Section 1375 imposes a tax on an S corporation having accumulated earnings and profits if its "passive investment income" exceeds 25 percent of its "gross receipts" for the year. (For convenience, that excess is referred to as "excess" passive investment income.) Generally, "passive investment income" includes rents, royalties, dividends, interest, and annuities. §1362(d)(3)(C)(i). But see §1362(d)(3)(C)(ii)-(v) (for some exceptions). Further, "gross receipts" generally include the total amount that the corporation receives or accrues under its method of accounting, unreduced by returns, costs of goods sold, and deductions. Treas. Regs. §1.1362-2(c)(4)(i). However, gross receipts include only capital gain net income from the disposition of capital assets (other than stocks and securities) and only gains (not losses) from sales or exchanges of stocks or securities. §1362(d)(3)(B).

When §1375 imposes a tax on an S corporation, the tax equals (a) the corporation's "excess net passive income" multiplied by (b) the highest corporate income tax rate (currently 35%). "Excess net passive income" equals the following amount:

$$\frac{\text{excess passive investment income} \times \text{net passive income}}{\text{passive investment income}}$$

3. See page 572 supra.

where "passive investment income" and "excess passive investment income" are defined above, and "net passive income" is passive investment income less deductions directly connected with the production of that income. §1375(b)(2) (defining net passive income).[4] Any §1375 tax reduces the amount of the corporation's passive investment income passed through to the corporation's shareholders. §1366(f)(3).

Consider the following example: *Z* Corp. is an S corporation with accumulated earnings and profits. During the current taxable year, the corporation has passive investment income of $50,000, deductions directly connected with the production of that income of $10,000, and total gross receipts of $100,000.[5]

Section 1375 imposes a tax on the S corporation, because its passive investment income ($50,000) exceeds 25 percent of its gross receipts ($25,000 or 25 percent of $100,000). The corporation's excess passive investment income equals that excess, or $25,000. Its net passive income equals $40,000, the excess of its passive investment income ($50,000) over the expenses directly connected with the production of that income ($10,000).

Thus, the corporation's excess net passive income equals

$$\frac{\$25{,}000 \times \$40{,}000}{\$50{,}000}$$

or $20,000.[6] The tax under §1375 is then imposed on this amount at the highest corporate income tax rate (currently 35 percent) for a total tax of $7,000.

Note that this tax is not imposed unless the corporation has accumulated earnings and profits. Suppose that an S corporation believes that it lacks accumulated earnings and profits and invests most or all of its funds in passive-income producing assets. Suppose, however, that the Service then audits the corporation for a C corporation year. If this audit yields even one dollar of accumulated earnings and profits, the corporation may now be subject to the §1375 tax. To be sure, had the corporation known of the additional accumulated earnings and profits, it would have distributed them, but without that knowledge, it now appears trapped.

Section 1375(d) offers a possible remedy. The Service may waive the §1375 tax if the following two conditions are met: First, the S corporation must have determined in good faith that it had no accumulated earnings and profits. Second, it must distribute the unanticipated accumulated earnings and profits within a "reasonable" time after they are discovered. §1375(d). Of course, if the corporation has a positive accumulated adjustments account, an election under §1368(e)(3) may be necessary.[7]

2. *Forced termination of S corporation status.* Although §1375 imposes a corporate-level tax on excessive passive investment income received by an S corporation with accumulated earnings and profits, the tax should encourage such a

4. Note, however, that the corporation's excess net passive income under §1375 cannot exceed the corporation's taxable income. §1375(b)(1)(B). For this purpose, the corporation's taxable income is computed without allowance for any net operating loss deduction under §172 and the deductions in §§241-249 (excluding the deduction in §248 for organizational expenditures). *Id.*

5. Assume that the corporation has no other deductions. Thus, its taxable income equals $90,000.

6. Because the corporation's taxable income for the year is $90,000, excess net passive investment income is not limited by §1375(b)(1)(B).

7. See page 572 supra.

corporation to distribute out its earnings and profits or reduce its passive investment income. However, any corporation willing to pay the §1375 tax faces possibly an even greater burden. Under §1362(d)(3), if an S corporation with accumulated earnings and profits has passive investment income exceeding 25 percent of its gross receipts for three consecutive taxable years, the corporation's election as an S corporation terminates. As with §1375, "passive investment income" is gross receipts from "royalties, rents, dividends, interest, and annuities," §1362(d)(3)(D)(i), with some exceptions (see §1362(d)(3)(D)(ii)-(v)).

Because the forced termination in §1362(d)(3) is so easy to avoid, it rarely applies. However, because its impact is so severe, one should be certain to avoid it. As with the corporate-level tax in §1375, the forced termination under §1362(d)(3) applies only to corporations with accumulated earnings and profits. Accordingly, S corporations without accumulated earnings and profits may simply ignore §1362(d)(3), and any other S corporation can make §1362(d)(3) less likely to apply by electing under §1368(e)(3) to treat its distributions as coming first out of its accumulated earnings and profits.

PROBLEM

18-3. *M* Corp. is an S corporation having $100 of accumulated earnings and profits. In year 1, *M* Corp. has gross receipts of $160,000, of which half are from active business operations and half are royalty income. *M* Corp. also has $60,000 of deductions, of which $40,000 are allocable to the business operations and $20,000 are allocable to the royalty income. Compute *M* Corp.'s tax liability under §1375 as well as its taxable income for the year.

4. *No Carryover from C Year to S Year*

If a C corporation incurs capital losses in excess of its capital gains, the excess may not be deducted but instead is carried back or forward to a taxable year or years in which excess capital gains are recognized. §§1211(a), 1212(a). Similarly, if a C corporation incurs operating deductions in excess of taxable income, the excess is carried backward or forward as a net operating loss deduction. See §172. However, in no event may an excess capital loss, a net operating loss, or any other carryover be carried from a year in which a corporation is a C corporation to a year in which the corporation is an S corporation to reduce income allocable to a shareholder. §1371(b)(1). But see §1374(b)(2) (allowing carryovers from C corporation years to offset net recognized built-in gain for purposes of §1374). Note that no carryover of any kind can originate in any year when the corporation is an S corporation. §1371(b)(2). As a result, there are no carryovers from S years to C years or from S years to other S years. However, losses allocated to a shareholder but limited by §1366(d) may be available for the shareholder's use for a short time after the corporation's subchapter S election terminates. See §1366(d)(3).[8]

8. See page 578 infra.

B. FROM S CORPORATION TO C CORPORATION

A corporation's status as an S corporation can terminate by revocation under §1362(d)(1), by the corporation failing to meet the standards of §1361(b) (see §1362(d)(2)), or by receipt of excessive passive investment income if the corporation has accumulated earnings and profits (see §1362(d)(3)). Regardless of the method of termination, the results are the same: If the termination is effective on a date other than the last day of the corporation's taxable year, the taxable year is divided into two short taxable years.[9] The first short taxable year ends on the day preceding the date of termination of the S corporation's election, §1362(e)(1)(A), and the second short taxable year begins on the following day, §1362(e)(1)(B). By this mechanism, there is no taxable year during which the corporation is sometimes an S corporation and sometimes a C corporation. The two short years together are sometimes referred to as the "S termination year." §1362(e)(4).

Recall that when a corporation with accumulated earnings and profits becomes an S corporation, distributions out of pre–S corporation earnings and profits are taxed as dividends, while distributions out of S corporation earnings are generally treated as a return of basis. See §1368(c). When an S election terminates, a similar issue arises because distribution of pre-termination earnings should be taxed as basis recovery, while post-termination distributions should be taxed as dividends. Unfortunately, the rule is not so simple.

Under §1371(e)(1), a post-termination distribution on a shareholder's stock may be tax free up to the smaller of the corporation's accumulated adjustments account and the shareholder's stock basis. However, to qualify for this treatment, the distribution must be paid in cash during the post-termination transition period.[10] §1371(e)(1). Further, the shareholder must reduce her stock basis by the amount of this tax-free distribution. *Id.* See also §1371(e)(2) (for an election to not apply §1371(e)(1)). All other distributions are taxed under §301, the section generally applicable to distributions from C corporations. Thus, distributions made after the close of the post-termination transition period are subject to §301 even if the corporation's accumulated adjustments account has not been fully depleted.

Note that post-termination gains and losses will not affect the corporation's accumulated adjustments account. In addition, post-termination distributions of property (i.e., of anything other than cash) are taxed under §301 even if the property was acquired or appreciated while the corporation was an S corporation. Accordingly, if a corporation is contemplating changing from an S corporation to a C corporation, it may make sense to distribute the property before the change if the property is likely to be sold in the near future.

Finally, recall that tax-exempt income of an S corporation does not add to its accumulated adjustments account. §1368(e)(1)(A). When a C corporation

9. A termination under §1362(d)(3) for excessive passive investment income necessarily is effective on the first day of the corporation's taxable year. §1362(d)(3)(A)(ii). Terminations under §1362(d)(1) by revocation and under §1362(d)(2) by ceasing to be a small business corporation need not be effective on the first day of the corporation's taxable year. See §§1362(d)(1)(C), 1362(d)(2)(B).

10. The "post-termination transition period" begins on the first day that the corporation is no longer an S corporation and ends at the later of (i) one year after that date or (ii) the due date for the federal income tax return (including extensions) for the corporation's final taxable year as an S corporation. §1377(b)(1). See also *id.* at (b)(1)(B) and (C) (for special rules relating to audits and the unintended termination of the S election).

transitions to an S corporation, this peculiarity affects the order in which corporate distributions are deemed to be paid out of accumulated earnings and profits or out of S corporation earnings.[11] When the transition is the other way, though, the exclusion of tax-exempt income from the corporation's accumulated adjustments account has a more dramatic impact: A post-termination distribution of the tax-exempt income will always be taxed under subchapter C's §301. This result occurs because the relief offered by §1371(e)(1) to post-termination distributions of S earnings extends only to the extent of the corporation's accumulated adjustments account. Because tax-exempt income does not enter the accumulated adjustments account, its distributions are unprotected by §1371(e)(1).

Although the transition from S to C status brings little tax relief, there is one positive aspect. If the corporation had a prior C history, and if there is a surviving net operating loss carryover from that earlier C period, it can be used by the corporation in its reincarnation as a C corporation. Although §1371(b)(1) prohibits carryovers from C years to S years, there is no prohibition on carryovers from C years to C years, even if several S years are sandwiched in between. However, those S years count to determine whether the carryover has expired. §1371(b)(3).

Although S corporation losses generally pass through to the shareholders, §1366(d)(1) limits the pass-thru to the extent of a shareholder's stock and debt basis. If a corporation's status as an S corporation terminates, any losses suspended by application of §1366(d)(1) can be claimed by the affected shareholders in the following year, subject to the limitation that such losses cannot exceed their stock basis at that time. §1366(d)(3). Of course, any losses so claimed must reduce stock basis, §1366(d)(3)(C), just as they would if subchapter S were applicable in full (see §1367(a)(2)(B)).

11. See page 571 supra.

III

SUBCHAPTER K PARTNERSHIPS

19

The Structure of Partnership Taxation

In this chapter we will look at the taxation of the four basic transactions in the life of a partnership: formation, daily business activity, nonliquidating distributions, and final disposition of the investment (liquidation of the partnership and sales of partnership interests). Those factual patterns that complicate understanding of the basic rules — encumbered property or the acquisition of partnership debt, for example — will be deferred. Having seen how the basic pieces fit together in simple circumstances, you will be better able to appreciate the nuances of subchapter K's treatment of the more complex transactions.

A. NOTE ON LIMITED LIABILITY COMPANIES

The rules of subchapter K apply to those entities falling within the definition of a "partnership" in §761(a). While a full examination of this definition is better postponed until later, it is worth noting at this point that a "partnership" for tax purposes can include many entities not classified as "partnerships" under relevant local law. And while incorporated entities are explicitly excluded from the §761(a) definition of a "partnership," there is no statutory requirement that a partnership include even a single member whose liability for debts of the entity is unlimited. That is, the statutory language of §761(a) includes the possibility of partnerships consisting exclusively of owners insulated from obligations of the entity.

Such organizations are called "limited liability companies," or LLCs for short. LLCs offer investors the non-tax advantage of limited liability equivalent to the better-known corporate veil. They also offer investors the tax advantages of pass-thru taxation available under subchapter K. While the precise requirements of an LLC vary state by state, most states permit the investors in an LLC (usually called "members" rather than shareholders or partners) substantial flexibility in structuring management of the organization. For example, one LLC might be run by majority vote of its members, much like a general partnership, while another LLC might be run by a manager or management company as is common for corporations and limited partnerships.

For a tax lawyer, the name given to an organization is relatively unimportant as compared with its tax status under federal law. That does not mean, though, that a tax lawyer can ignore the state law distinctions between general partnerships, limited partnerships, LLCs, and similar organizations even though all can be taxable as partnerships under subchapter K. For example, the partnership tax rules for allocating entity-level debt among partners is influenced by the extent of each partner's potential liability for repayment of such debts. Thus, for this purpose members of an LLC are treated like limited partners. Note that members of LLCs are treated like limited partners in this context not because they are (or are not) called "limited partners" but rather because they have the same substantive rights and obligations as limited partners with respect to entity-level debt.

There is at least one area of the Code in which the name given to a partner may determine the tax consequences of a transaction. Under §736(b)(3)(B), special rules generally favorable to the partnership apply to certain retirement payments made to a "general" partner. Because this provision of the Code has no particular relationship to entity debt, it is unclear if the specification of a "general" partner in §736(b)(3)(B) should be understood as requiring unlimited liability for entity-level obligations, participation in day-to-day management of the entity's activities, or some other characteristic usually part of a "general" partnership interest under state law. We will return to an examination of §736 later, but as you read various provisions of subchapter K and the regulations interpreting it, keep in mind that not all entities taxed as partnerships will have members who neatly fall under the traditional labels of general and limited partner.

B. THE PASS-THRU OF PARTNERSHIP INCOME

The most basic rule of subchapter K is in §701, which reads, "A partnership as such shall not be subject to the income tax imposed. . . . Persons carrying on business as partners shall be liable for income tax only in their separate or individual capacities." Despite this absolute rule of nontaxation, it does make sense to speak of a partnership's income. Consistent with the entity model of pass-thru taxation, under §703 a partnership computes its taxable income *as if* it were a taxable entity. For example, if a partnership owns rental real estate, it might include rents and deduct maintenance, interest, and depreciation.

Once the partnership's taxable income is computed, that income is allocated among the various partners for inclusion on their individual returns. A partner's share of partnership income is called her "distributive" share. See §702, §704. The term "distributive share" is one of the great misnomers in the Internal Revenue Code because a partner's distributive share is what is *included* on the partner's individual return and bears no necessary relation to any amount actually *distributed* to the partner.

For example, a partnership agreement might provide that no funds will be distributed to any partner during the first five years of the partnership. Thus, the first five years will see no partnership *distributions.* Nevertheless, there will be *distributive shares* each year because, as the partnership earns (or loses) income, the partners must include (or deduct) it on their individual returns. Do not confuse distributive shares with actual distributions or anything else of the sort. To be sure, it would have been easier if distributive shares had been called "allocative shares" or something similar. "Distributive share" is the statutory term, though, and so "distributive share" is the term we use.

Partnership taxation, then, is a two-step dance. In step 1, we compute the entity's taxable income. In step 2, we allocate that income among the partners. And nowhere is the independence of the two steps more clearly set out than in the Supreme Court's opinion in United States v. Basye.

United States v. Basye

410 U.S. 441 (1973)

Mr. Justice POWELL delivered the opinion of the Court.

I

Respondents, each of whom is a physician, are partners in a limited partnership known as Permanente Medical Group, which was organized in California in 1949. Associated with the partnership are over 200 partner physicians, as well as numerous nonpartner physicians and other employees. In 1959, Permanente entered into an agreement with Kaiser Foundation Health Plan, Inc., a nonprofit corporation providing prepaid medical care and hospital services to its dues-paying members.

Pursuant to the terms of the agreement, Permanente agreed to supply medical services for the 390,000 member-families, or about 900,000 individuals, in Kaiser's Northern California Region which covers primarily the San Francisco Bay area. In exchange for those services, Kaiser agreed to pay the partnership a "base compensation" composed of two elements. First, Kaiser undertook to pay directly to the partnership a sum each month computed on the basis of the total number of members enrolled in the health program. That number was multiplied by a stated fee, which originally was set at a little over $2.60. The second item of compensation — and the one that has occasioned the present dispute — called for the creation of a program, funded entirely by Kaiser, to pay retirement benefits to Permanente's partner and non-partner physicians.

The pertinent compensation provision of the agreement did not itself establish the details of the retirement program; it simply obligated Kaiser to make contributions to such a program in the event that the parties might thereafter agree to adopt one. As might be expected, a separate trust agreement establishing the contemplated plan soon was executed by Permanente, Kaiser, and the Bank of America Trust and Savings Association, acting as trustee. Under this agreement Kaiser agreed to make payments to the trust at a predetermined rate, initially pegged at 12 cents per health plan member per month. Additionally, Kaiser made a flat payment of $200,000 to start the fund and agreed that its pro rata payment obligation would be retroactive to the date of the signing of the medical service agreement.

The beneficiaries of the trust were all partner and nonpartner physicians who had completed at least two years of continuous service with the partnership and who elected to participate. The trust maintained a separate tentative account for each beneficiary. As periodic payments were received from Kaiser, the funds were allocated among these accounts pursuant to a complicated formula designed to take into consideration on a relative basis each participant's compensation level, length of service, and age. No physician was eligible to receive the amounts in his tentative account prior to retirement, and retirement established entitlement only if the participant had rendered at least 15 years of continuous service or 10 years of continuous service and had attained age 65. Prior to such time, however, the trust agreement explicitly provided that no interest in any tentative account was to be regarded as having vested in any particular beneficiary. The agreement also provided for the forfeiture of any physician's interest and its redistribution among the remaining participants if he were to terminate his relationship with Permanente prior to retirement. A similar forfeiture and redistribution also would occur if, after retirement, a physician were to render professional services for any hospital or health plan other than one operated by Kaiser. The trust agreement further stipulated that a retired physician's right to receive benefits would cease if he were to refuse any reasonable request to render consultative services to any Kaiser-operated health plan.

The agreement provided that the plan would continue irrespective either of changes in the partnership's personnel or of alterations in its organizational structure. The plan would survive any reorganization of the partnership so long as at least 50% of the plan's participants remained associated with the reorganized entity. In the event of dissolution or of a nonqualifying reorganization, all of the amounts in the trust were to be divided among the participants entitled thereto in amounts governed by each participant's tentative account. Under no circumstances, however, could payments from Kaiser to the trust be recouped by Kaiser: once compensation was paid into the trust it was thereafter committed exclusively to the benefit of Permanente's participating physicians. . . .

During the years from the plan's inception until its discontinuance in 1963, Kaiser paid a total of more than $2,000,000 into the trust. Permanente, however, did not report these payments as income in its partnership returns. Nor did the individual partners include these payments in the computations of their distributive shares of the partnership's taxable income. The Commissioner assessed deficiencies against each partner-respondent for his distributive share of the amount paid by Kaiser. . . .

The Commissioner premised his assessment on the conclusion that Kaiser's payments to the trust constituted a form of compensation to the partnership for the services it rendered and therefore was income to the partnership. And, notwithstanding the deflection of those payments to the retirement trust and their current unavailability to the partners, the partners were still taxable on their distributive shares of that compensation. Both the District Court and the Court of Appeals disagreed. They held that the payments to the fund were not income to the partnership because it did not receive them and never had a "right to receive" them. They reasoned that the partnership, as an entity, should be disregarded and that each partner should be treated simply as a potential beneficiary of his tentative share of the retirement fund. Viewed in this light, no presently taxable income could be attributed to these cash basis taxpayers because of the contingent and forfeitable nature of the fund allocations.

We hold that the courts below erred and that respondents were properly taxable on the partnership's retirement fund income. This conclusion rests on two familiar principles of income taxation, first, that income is taxed to the party who earns it and that liability may not be avoided through an anticipatory assignment of that income, and, second, that partners are taxable on their distributive or proportionate shares of current partnership income irrespective of whether that income is actually distributed to them. The ensuing discussion is simply an application of those principles to the facts of the present case.

II

Section 703 of the Internal Revenue Code of 1954, insofar as pertinent here, prescribes that "[t]he taxable income of a partnership shall be computed in the same manner as in the case of an individual." Thus, while the partnership itself pays no taxes, §701, it must report the income it generates and such income must be calculated in largely the same manner as an individual computes his personal income. For this purpose, then, the partnership is regarded as an independently recognizable entity apart from the aggregate of its partners. Once its income is ascertained and reported, its existence may be disregarded since each partner must pay tax on a portion of the total income as if the partnership were merely an agent or conduit through which the income passed.[8]

In determining any partner's income, it is first necessary to compute the gross income of the partnership. One of the major sources of gross income, as defined in §61(a)(1) of the Code, is "[c]ompensation for services, including fees, commissions, and similar items." There can be no question that Kaiser's payments to the retirement trust were compensation for services rendered by the partnership under the medical service agreement. These payments constituted an integral part of the employment arrangement. The agreement itself called for two forms of "base compensation" to be paid in exchange for services rendered — direct per-member, per-month payments to the partnership and other, similarly computed, payments to the trust. . . .

Yet the courts below, focusing on the fact that the retirement fund payments were never actually received by the partnership but were contributed directly to the trust, found that the payments were not includable as income in the partnership's returns. The view of tax accountability upon which this conclusion rests is incompatible with a foundational rule, which this Court has described as "the first principle of income taxation: that income must be taxed to him who earns it." Commissioner v. Culbertson, 337 U.S. 733, 739-740 (1949). The entity earning the income — whether a partnership or an individual taxpayer — cannot avoid taxation by entering into a contractual arrangement whereby that income is diverted to some other person or entity. . . .

Permanente's agreement with Kaiser, whereby a portion of the partnership compensation was deflected to the retirement fund, is certainly within the ambit of Lucas v. Earl. The partnership earned the income and, as a result of arms'-length

8. There has been a great deal of discussion in the briefs and in the lower court opinions with respect to whether a partnership is to be viewed as an "entity" or as a "conduit." We find ourselves in agreement with the Solicitor General's remark during oral argument when he suggested that "[i]t seems odd that we should still be discussing such things in 1972." The legislative history indicates, and the commentators agree, that partnerships are entities for purposes of calculating and filing informational returns but that they are conduits through which the taxpaying obligation passes to the individual partners in accord with their distributive shares. . . .

bargaining with Kaiser, was responsible for its diversion into the trust fund. The Court of Appeals found the *Lucas* principle inapplicable because Permanente "never had the right itself to receive the payments made into the trust as current income." 450 F.2d. at 114. In support of this assertion, the court relied on language in the agreed statement of facts stipulating that "[t]he payments . . . were paid solely to fund the retirement plan, and were not otherwise available to [Permanente]. . . ." Ibid. Emphasizing that the fund was created to serve Kaiser's interest in a stable source of qualified, experienced physicians, the court found that Permanente could not have received that income except in the form in which it was received.

The court's reasoning seems to be that, before the partnership could be found to have received income, there must be proof that "Permanente agreed to accept less direct compensation from Kaiser in exchange for the retirement plan payments." Apart from the inherent difficulty of adducing such evidence, we know of no authority imposing this burden upon the Government. . . .

III

Since the retirement fund payments should have been reported as income to the partnership, along with other income received from Kaiser, the individual partners should have included their shares of that income in their individual returns. §§61(a)(13), 702, 704. For it is axiomatic that each partner must pay taxes on his distributive share of the partnership's income without regard to whether that amount is actually distributed to him. . . .

The courts below reasoned to the contrary, holding that the partners here were not properly taxable on the amounts contributed to the retirement fund. This view, apparently, was based on the assumption that each partner's distributive share prior to retirement was too contingent and unascertainable to constitute presently recognizable income. It is true that no partner knew with certainty exactly how much he would ultimately receive or whether he would in fact be entitled to receive anything. But the existence of conditions upon the actual receipt by a partner of income fully earned by the partnership is irrelevant in determining the amount of tax due from him. The fact that the courts below placed such emphasis on this factor suggests the basic misapprehension under which they labored in this case. Rather than being viewed as responsible contributors to the partnership's total income, respondent-partners were seen only as contingent beneficiaries of the trust. In some measure, this misplaced focus on the considerations of uncertainty and forfeitability may be a consequence of the erroneous manner in which the Commissioner originally assessed the partners' deficiencies. The Commissioner divided Kaiser's trust fund payments into two categories: (1) payments earmarked for the tentative accounts of nonpartner physicians; and (2) those allotted to partner physicians. The payments to the trust for the former category of nonpartner physicians were correctly counted as income to the partners in accord with the distributive-share formula as established in the partnership agreement.[16] The latter payments to the tentative accounts of the individual partners, however, were improperly allocated to each partner

16. These amounts would be divided equally among the partners pursuant to the partnership agreement's stipulation that all income above each partner's drawing account "shall be distributed equally."

pursuant to the complex formula in the retirement plan itself, just as if that agreement operated as an amendment to the partnership agreement.

The Solicitor General, alluding to this miscomputation during oral argument, suggested that this error "may be what threw the court below off the track." It should be clear that the contingent and unascertainable nature of each partner's share under the retirement trust is irrelevant to the computation of his distributive share. The partnership had received as income a definite sum which was not subject to diminution or forfeiture. Only its ultimate disposition among the employees and partners remained uncertain. For purposes of income tax computation it made no difference that some partners might have elected not to participate in the retirement program or that, for any number of reasons, they might not ultimately receive any of the trust's benefits. Indeed, as the Government suggests, the result would be quite the same if the "potential beneficiaries included no partners at all, but were children, relatives, or other objects of the partnership's largesse." The sole operative consideration is that the income had been received by the partnership, not what disposition might have been effected once the funds were received.

IV

In summary, we find this case controlled by familiar and long-settled principles of income and partnership taxation. There being no doubt about the character of the payments as compensation, or about their actual receipt, the partnership was obligated to report them as income presently received. Likewise, each partner was responsible for his distributive share of that income. We, therefore, reverse the judgments and remand the case with directions that judgments be entered for the United States.

It is so ordered.

Mr. Justice Douglas dissents.

In theory, once a partnership's income is computed there are two ways in which it can be allocated among the partners. For example, if *X* is a one-third partner in the *XYZ* partnership, we could allocate to *X* one-third of each item of income, deduction, credit, and loss *or* we could allocate to *X* one-third of some net figure combining all of these items. It is easiest to think of the allocation item by item. Thus, *X* might be allocated $10,000 of the partnership's $30,000 of income, $5,000 of the partnership's $15,000 of interest expense, etc. In fact, though, the Code uses a slightly different method, passing some items through to the partners as individual items and others combined into one net figure.

In general, we net together all partnership level items whose tax status does not depend on non-partnership tax items appearing on a partner's individual return. For example, a partnership might make a "charitable contribution" within the meaning of §170(c) to a qualified educational institution. Such contributions generally are deductible up to 50 percent of a taxpayer's adjusted gross income. See §170(b)(1)(A), §170(b)(1)(F). Accordingly, we cannot know the extent to which the partnership's contribution is deductible without knowing each partner's adjusted gross income as well as all other charitable contributions made by (or allocable to) each partner. We do not net the charitable contribution against the partnership's taxable income but rather allocate it as a distinct item among the partners. In the language of §703(a)(1), charitable contributions are "separately stated" items.

As a second example, suppose a partnership has $20,000 of ordinary income, $6,000 of (ordinary) deduction, and $10,000 of long-term capital loss. If this partnership has two equal partners, individuals *A* and *B*, how should the partners account for the partnership's items of income and loss?

If the $10,000 of capital loss had been an ordinary deduction, we would simply net the partnership items together to produce $4,000 of partnership taxable income. Our co-partners would then report $2,000 apiece. However, because the loss is capital, we cannot simply net it against the partnership's ordinary income: With certain limitations, capital loss cannot offset ordinary income. See §§1211-1212. Accordingly, the tax effect of the partnership capital loss will depend on each partner's individual tax status. For example, if partner *A* has some additional capital gain to be reported on her individual return, *A*'s share of the partnership's capital loss can offset that gain. Capital gain and loss, therefore, are separately stated items (see §702(a)(1)-(2)), so that partners *A* and *B* will each report $7,000 of partnership income from the non–separately stated items and $5,000 of long-term capital loss.

PROBLEM

19-1. Individuals *X* and *Y* form the *XY* partnership to perform charitable work in local hospitals. A good-hearted citizen transfers a 30-year treasury bond to the partnership to help it pay for its activities. The terms of the transfer provide, however, that all of the bond interest must be used for charitable purposes or the bond automatically reverts to its prior owner. At the end of the year, *X* and *Y* report no income from *XY* on their individual returns even though the bond paid interest. *X* and *Y* attach a statement to their returns saying, "We have no bond income this year for two reasons. First, the partnership owns the bond, not us. We have never owned it and will never own it. Therefore, we have no income from it. Second, all the bond interest will go to charitable uses. Because none of it will be used personally, we should not have to report any income." What do you think of these arguments?

C. FORMATION AND OPERATION OF THE PARTNERSHIP

The rules governing partnership formation are in §721, §722, and §723. They provide that the contribution of property to a partnership in exchange for a partnership interest is not a taxable event to the partnership or to the contributing partner. Further, they provide for a double carry-over basis: the partnership carries over the contributing partner's basis in the asset, and the partner carries over the asset basis into her partnership interest. Be sure to note that these rules apply not only to contributions forming the partnership but also to subsequent contributions (so-called mid-stream contributions) made by new or continuing partners.

Consider the following example. *P*, *Q*, and *R* form the *PQR* partnership by making the following contributions:

	Property	*Adjusted basis*	*Fair market value*
P	Blackacre	$10,000	$10,000
Q	Whiteacre	$ 8,000	$10,000
R	Greenacre	$15,000	$10,000

In a financial sense, the partners have made equivalent contributions of property worth $10,000 apiece. In a tax sense, though, the contributions are quite distinct: *Q* has contributed appreciated property while *R* has contributed loss property. *P*'s basis in her partnership interest (her "outside" basis) will be $10,000, *Q*'s basis will be $8,000, and *R*'s will be $15,000. Of course, the partnership will take a carry-over basis in each contributed asset for a combined asset basis (the partnership's combined "inside" basis) of $33,000.

One effect of this double carry-over basis rule is that any appreciation or loss in contributed property existing at the time of contribution will be built into the contributing partner's outside basis. For example, if *Q* sells her partnership interest for $10,000 shortly after acquiring it, she will recognize a gain of $2,000. Recognition of that gain is appropriate because *Q* has, in effect, simply sold Whiteacre for $10,000, and had that sale been made directly, *Q* would have recognized a gain of $2,000.

While §722 gives us each partner's initial basis in her partnership interest, §705 informs us that these bases will change as the partnership makes or loses money. Suppose, for example, that Blackacre increases in value and is then sold by the partnership for $25,000. Assuming this is the only taxable event of the year, the partnership will have taxable income of $15,000 (amount realized of $25,000 less adjusted basis of $10,000) and each partner's distributive share will be $5,000. Accordingly, each partner will report $5,000 on her individual return and, pursuant to §705(a)(1)(A), each partner will increase her outside basis by the same amount. This basis adjustment is needed to ensure that partnership gains and losses are not recognized twice, once when recognized by the partnership and a second time upon disposition by the partner of her partnership interest.

For example, suppose partner *P* sells her interest in the year after Blackacre is sold but before any funds have been distributed. Because the fair market value of the partnership's assets now totals $45,000 ($25,000 in cash, $10,000 worth of Whiteacre, and $10,000 worth of Greenacre), *P*'s one-third interest should sell for $15,000. Should *P* recognize gain on the sale of her partnership interest for its fair market value of $15,000?

The answer is no, and the easiest way to see that is to look at *P*'s cash flow over the life of the partnership. *P* contributed property with an adjusted basis of $10,000. She received no distributions from the partnership and then received $15,000 upon disposition of her interest. Thus, her in-flow of receipts exceeded the adjusted basis of her contribution by $5,000, and so *P* should recognize $5,000 of income over the life of the partnership. Because she already has recognized that amount of income, there should be no further gain or loss when she sells her partnership interest.

This cash-flow analysis tells us that *P*'s outside basis must be $15,000 when she sells her partnership interest. How do we reach that result under the Code? Section

705(a)(1)(A) provides for a basis increase equal to the partner's distributive share of taxable income. For every dollar of partnership income the partner reports on her individual return, the partner's outside basis goes up by the same amount. This basis adjustment ensures that income taxed to the partner when earned by the partnership will not be taxed a second time upon disposition of the partnership interest.

Should there be an outside basis adjustment for a partner's distributive share of tax-exempt income? Suppose individuals *A* and *B* form the *AB* partnership by contributing $5,000 apiece. The partnership invests its $10,000 in a municipal, tax-exempt bond paying 10-percent interest per year. In the first year, the partnership receives interest of $1,000. What effect should this have on the partners' outside bases?

The partnership is now worth $11,000, so that each partner's half interest is worth $5,500. If *A* sells her partnership interest for that amount, she will recognize gain of $500 unless she is entitled to a basis increase for her share of the partnership's tax-exempt income. If we do not provide such a basis increase, the tax-exempt interest will in fact be taxable to *A*, albeit not when earned by the partnership but only when *A* sells her interest. To keep the interest entirely tax exempt, *A* is given an upward basis adjustment for her share of tax-exempt interest just as for taxable income. See §705(a)(1)(B). In the case of taxable income, this basis adjustment eliminates a second tax on the income; in the case of tax-exempt income, the basis adjustment eliminates a first tax on the income.

Just as outside basis is adjusted upward for distributive share of taxable income, so too outside basis is adjusted downward for distributive share of taxable losses (and all other deductions). §705(a)(2)(A). Similarly, the counterpart of tax-exempt income, nondeductible, noncapitalizable expenses (such as illegal bribes and kickbacks) also produces a downward basis adjustment. These downward basis adjustments can never produce a negative outside basis, see §705(a)(2) (parenthetical), because a partner's distributive share of losses cannot exceed his outside basis. §704(d).

PROBLEM

19-2. Return to the *XY* charitable partnership of problem 19-1 above. Assuming the transfer of the bond is properly treated as a gift under §102, what tax consequences, if any, should there be to *X*, *Y*, and *XY* as a result of this gift of the bond? What if the donor's adjusted basis in the bond had been $800, and the fair market value of the bond had been $1,000?

D. NONLIQUIDATING DISTRIBUTIONS

Nonliquidating distributions (also sometimes called current distributions) are, in general, nontaxable to the distributee partner. §731(a). Because the rules applicable to cash distributions and property distributions differ somewhat, we will consider first a nonliquidating distribution of (non-cash) property.

Suppose *X* is a member of the *XYZ* partnership with an outside basis of $10,000. Further, suppose that the partnership distributes Purpleacre to *X* when Purpleacre has a basis in the partnership's hands of $6,000 and a fair market value of $7,500.

Under §731(a)(1)-(2), *X* will not recognize gain or loss on the distribution. Indeed, loss can never be recognized on a nonliquidating distribution and gain can be recognized only if the distribution includes (or is deemed to include) cash. Because the distribution is not a taxable event to *X*, it cannot increase or decrease her basis. However, because *X* now owns two assets (Purpleacre and her partnership interest) when before she owned only one (the partnership interest), *X*'s pre-distribution outside basis of $10,000 is allocated between the two assets.

Under §732(a)(1), *X* carries over the partnership's $6,000 basis in Purpleacre. And under §733(2), *X* reduces her outside basis by that $6,000 down to $4,000. The effect of these rules is not to change *X*'s overall basis amount (it remains at $10,000) but simply to divide it between the partnership interest and the newly acquired Purpleacre.

What if Purpleacre had a basis to the partnership of $12,000? If we gave *X* a carry-over basis of $12,000 in Purpleacre, we would have to give *X* a negative $2,000 outside basis to preserve the $10,000 total. Outside basis can never go negative, so we adopt a different allocation scheme. *X* takes a basis in Purpleacre of only $10,000, see §732(a)(2), and reduces her outside basis to zero. Note that the transaction remains tax free; the only thing that changes is the allocation of *X*'s pre-distribution outside basis between the post-distribution partnership interest and the distributed asset (Purpleacre). You should also note that the fair market value of Purpleacre plays no role in the taxation of *X* (at least until *X* sells or exchanges it in a taxable transaction).

We can restate the rules of §§731-733 as they apply to nonliquidating distributions of property (not cash!) as follows: No gain or loss is recognized and the distributee partner allocates her pre-distribution outside basis to the asset up to the partnership's pre-distribution basis in the asset. Any outside basis left over remains as outside basis. The effect of these rules is to preserve any gain or loss inherent in the property despite the distribution. If we gave the distributee partner a basis higher than carryover, recognition of income could be deferred by distributing an appreciated asset in anticipation of sale. If the distributee partner is given a basis lower than carryover (as is done when the distributee partner's outside basis cannot absorb the full carryover), recognition of income may be accelerated.

The rules applicable to current distributions of cash work almost identically. Suppose *X* receives $6,000 of cash. Under §731(a), no gain or loss is recognized, and under §733(1), *X* reduces her outside basis by the $6,000 down to $4,000. Recognizing that cash implicitly always has a basis equal to face (or fair market) value, *X* is taxed just as if she received property with an adjusted basis to the partnership of $6,000.

But what if *X* receives cash of $12,000? Had the cash been other property, we would simply give it a lower than carry-over basis of $10,000 and reduce *X*'s outside basis to zero. But because cash cannot have a lower than face-value basis, this technique will not work when *X* receives the cash. We could give *X* a negative $2,000 outside basis, but the Code eschews negative basis. Accordingly, we force *X* to recognize $2,000 of income and reduce *X*'s outside basis only to zero. Recognition of income replaces the negative basis.

Thus, the difference between the rules governing nonliquidating distributions of property and those governing nonliquidating distributions of cash is that the distribution of property with a basis exceeding the distributee partner's outside basis results in a basis adjustment to the distributed property, see §732(a)(2). In the case of a distribution of cash in excess of the distributee partner's outside basis, recognition of income substitutes for the basis adjustment. See §731(a)(1).

The effect of these rules is to preserve, as much as possible, the equality of aggregate inside basis with that of aggregate outside basis. The equality begins with the double carry-over basis rule of §§722-723: Both outside basis and inside basis are initially set equal to the adjusted basis of contributed property. This equality continues with the basis adjustment rules of §705: Recognition of partnership income (taxable or tax exempt) occurs when inside basis goes up and causes, by reason of §705(a)(1)(A), outside basis to go up dollar for dollar. Similarly, recognition of partnership loss (taxable or tax exempt) occurs when inside basis goes down and causes, by reason of §705(a)(2)(A), outside basis to go down. Accordingly, the initial equality of aggregate inside and outside bases continues as the partnership engages in its day-to-day business activities.

For example, suppose *X* and *Y* form the *XY* general partnership by contributing $10,000 apiece. Aggregate inside basis begins at $20,000 (treating cash as having basis equal to face) as does aggregate outside basis ($10,000 per partner). If the partnership earns $1,000 during its first year, that amount will pass through to the partners presumably 50-50 (or $500 apiece) and will increase aggregate outside basis to $21,000. Inside basis is now $21,000 (the initial inside basis of $20,000 plus the $1,000 earned during the year), so aggregate inside and outside bases are equal.

The distribution rules of §§731-733 continue this equality, albeit with some exceptions. When property is distributed by the partnership to a partner, partnership inside basis decreases by the adjusted basis of the distributed property because the partnership no longer owns the property. And under the rule of §732(a)(1), that asset basis continues in the hands of the distributee partner, and, under §733(2), it also reduces outside basis by the same amount. Thus, the reduction to inside basis equals the §733(2) reduction in outside basis so equality is preserved. If cash is distributed, the same result is obtained under §733(1).

For example, suppose *XY* distributes $1,000 to *X*. No gain or loss is recognized by *X*, §731(a), and *X* reduces her outside basis from $10,500 to $9,500. Thus, aggregate outside basis totals $20,000 (*X*'s outside basis of $9,500 plus *Y*'s outside basis of $10,500). Inside basis also equals $20,000, since that was the initial value of the inside basis and all current earnings have been distributed.

However, the equality of aggregate inside and outside bases is not preserved if property is distributed having an adjusted basis in the hands of the partnership in excess of the distributee partner's pre-distribution outside basis. Recall that in such circumstances the distributee partner takes a basis in the property equal to her pre-distribution outside basis and outside basis is reduced to zero. §732(a)(2), §733(2). Thus, inside basis is reduced by the adjusted basis of the asset in the hands of the partnership (because the asset no longer is owned by the partnership), while aggregate outside basis is reduced only by the distributee partner's pre-distribution outside basis.

For example, suppose the *XY* partnership invests $15,000 of its remaining $20,000 (after the distribution to *X*) in bonds of company *C*. If those bonds are then distributed to partner *Y*, inside basis will decline from $20,000 to $5,000 (because the bonds are no longer owned by the partnership). Under §732(a)(2), *Y* will take a basis in the bonds of $10,500 and will reduce her basis to zero (see

§733(2)). Outside basis will then stand at $9,500 ($9,500 for *X* and $0 for *Y*), which is $4,500 higher than inside basis.

The same problem occurs if cash is distributed to a partner in an amount sufficient to trigger recognition of income under §731(a)(1). Recall that a distribution of cash will produce income to the distributee partner only if the partner receives cash in excess of her pre-distribution outside basis. In such circumstances, the distribution reduces aggregate inside basis by the amount of the cash distributed while outside basis is reduced only by the distributee partner's pre-distribution outside basis (because outside basis cannot be reduced below zero). In short, the only time a distribution will break the equality between aggregate inside and outside bases is when the distributee partner's outside basis is too small to absorb the partnership's basis in the distributed property.

Why is the equality between aggregate inside and outside bases important? If one or more individuals own some property, gain or loss on disposition of the property is determined by comparing the amount realized on the disposition with the owner's (or owners') adjusted basis in the property. If this same piece of property is contributed to a partnership, the double carry-over basis rule of §§722-723 ensures that disposition by the partnership will have the same tax consequences as would disposition of the property outside the partnership. The equality between aggregate inside and outside bases, in short, gives to the entity model of pass-thru taxation much of the feel of the aggregate model without losing the simplifying structure of the entity.

If the partnership were given a basis in the property lower than its former basis in the hands of the contributing partner, more gain would be recognized upon disposition by the partnership than would have been recognized directly by the contributing partner. Conversely, if the partnership were given a basis in the property higher than its former basis in the hands of the contributing partner, less gain would be realized by a partnership disposition than by disposition directly by the partner. In short, the double carry-over basis rule of §§722-723 ensures that contribution of property to a partnership is as transparent (to the tax system) as possible.

The double carry-over basis rule of §§722-723 further ensures that an individual does not profit (or lose) by contributing property to a partnership shortly before selling the partnership interest. Indeed, the amount of gain or loss realized by all partners if they sold all their partnership interests is precisely equal to the gain realized by the partnership if it sold all its assets, so long as aggregate inside and outside bases are equal. If we think of the partners as each having undivided interests in the mass of partnership assets, then each partner's individual outside basis is simply her share of the partnership's aggregate inside (asset) basis.

As we have seen, the equality between aggregate inside and aggregate outside bases occasionally can be broken. This should suggest that the equality is not an essential feature of pass-thru entity taxation. That is correct: Inside basis rules affect only the timing of recognition of income and loss and so can be varied without great penalty. For example, the relationship between aggregate inside basis and aggregate outside basis is much more attenuated under subchapter S than under subchapter K.

Recognition of income by a partnership has both good and bad tax effects for the partners. The bad effect is that the partners must report that income on their individual returns in proportion to their distributive shares. The good effect is that this recognition increases the partners' outside bases so that future recognition of income is reduced (or future recognition of loss is increased). Because partnership recognition of income and loss is determined by inside basis, any change to inside basis will have offsetting effects, one immediate and one deferred.

For example, suppose assets contributed to a partnership were given a basis equal to fair market value rather than carryover. For appreciated assets, this rule would produce less gain (or more depreciation) to the partnership and through it to the partners. Thus, the partners would report less income in the short run.

However, reporting less income now means reporting more income later because of the basis rules of §705. Recognition of pass-thru income results in an outside basis increase, so that a fair market value basis rule for contributed, appreciated assets would leave the partners with lower outside bases, lower outside bases that ultimately will produce additional gain. The gain that was not recognized by the partnership on disposition of the asset, in other words, will be recognized by the partners on disposition of their partnership interests. Thus, a disparity between aggregate inside and outside bases does not mean that income will be counted twice (or lost), but that income will be accelerated or deferred.

While the inside basis rules could be changed without affecting the total amount of income recognized by a partner over the life of the partnership, the same is not true of the outside basis rules. When property is contributed to a partnership, the contributing partner carries the asset basis into her partnership interest. This is an essential structural rule of taxation: Because the partner does not recognize gain or loss on the partnership formation, the partner's asset basis must be preserved in the interest acquired.

For example, recall the *PQR* partnership formed as follows:

	Property	*Adjusted basis*	*Fair market value*
P	Blackacre	$10,000	$10,000
Q	Whiteacre	$ 8,000	$10,000
R	Greenacre	$15,000	$10,000

As a result of the carry-over outside basis rule in §722, if *Q* sells her partnership interest for its fair market value of $10,000 shortly after formation of the partnership, she will recognize a gain of $2,000. Recognition of $2,000 of gain is appropriate because *Q* has, in effect, sold Whiteacre for $10,000.

Any rule other than carryover would result in too much or too little income to *Q*. For example, giving *Q* a fair market value basis in her partnership interest would permanently exclude all pre-contribution asset appreciation (and loss) from the tax base.

Consider the following example: *P* and *Q* co-own Blackacre with a combined adjusted basis of $10,000 and a fair market value of $14,000. They contribute Blackacre to the newly formed *PQ* partnership and become equal partners. *If P and Q are given initial outside bases equal to the fair market value of the property contributed* (i.e., of $7,000 each instead of $5,000 under §722), will the $4,000 pre-contribution asset appreciation permanently escape taxation?

Suppose the partnership sells Blackacre for its fair market value of $14,000. The partnership will recognize $4,000 of income (because its basis in the property was carryover, see §723), and that income will pass through to (i.e., be reported by) the partners. Accordingly, *P* and *Q* will each report $2,000 of income from the sale of Blackacre.

In addition, *P* and *Q* will each increase their outside bases by the gain recognized. §705(a)(1). Since we assumed (contrary to §722) that each partner began with an outside basis of $7,000, each partner's outside basis will equal $9,000 once Blackacre is sold. However, the partnership has but $14,000 in cash (that being the sale proceeds), so that each partnership interest is worth $7,000. In other words, each partner has a $9,000 adjusted basis in a partnership interest worth $7,000.

As a result, a sale by *P* or *Q* of her partnership interest will produce a taxable loss of $2,000. This loss just offsets the prior income recognized by each partner when Blackacre was sold by the partnership. The net effect, then, is a wash: for each partner, $2,000 of income is reported when Blackacre is sold by the partnership, and $2,000 of loss is reported when the partnership interest is sold by the partner. Thus, over the life of the partnership, the pre-contribution appreciation of $4,000 is exempted from tax.

PROBLEMS

19-3. Ten individuals form the *P* partnership as equals by contributing $10,000 apiece. *P* uses this $100,000 to purchase some commercial real estate. During the first year, *P* turns an operating profit of $30,000. Half of this is distributed pro rata to the partners, and the other half is retained as a reserve. If one of the partners then sells her 10-percent interest in *P* for $15,000, how much gain should she report on the sale?

19-4. Individual *C* is a one-quarter partner in the *CDEF* partnership. *C* receives a current distribution of property worth $20,000 and with an adjusted basis to the partnership of $14,000. What are the tax consequences to *C* of this distribution if *C*'s outside basis at the time of the distribution equals

a. $35,000?
b. $15,000?
c. $10,000?
d. How would your answers change if the distribution consisted of $20,000 in cash?

19-5. Individual *H* has a $10,000 outside basis in her interest in the *PQ* partnership. The partnership owns Blackacre with an adjusted basis of $12,000 and a fair market value of $18,000. The partnership will distribute Blackacre to *H* as well as cash of $6,000. How will *H* be taxed if

a. Blackacre and the cash are distributed as two separate distributions, with the cash first?
b. Blackacre and the cash are distributed in two separate distributions, with Blackacre first?
c. Blackacre and the cash are distributed as part of a single transaction?
d. From these problems, would you characterize the distribution rules as cash-first or cash-last? Which is most favorable to taxpayers?

E. DISPOSITIONS OF PARTNERSHIP INTERESTS

A partner can exit the venture in a variety of ways: The partner might sell her partnership interest to a third party, she might receive a liquidating distribution in cash or in property, or she might sell her interest to one or more existing partners (who may have received cash or property from the partnership that is then used to purchase the partnership interest). Few special provisions apply to the sale of a partnership interest: Gain or loss is computed by comparing the amount realized by the selling partner with her adjusted basis in her partnership interest, §741, the same computation generally applicable to taxable exchanges by reason of §1001. The character of that gain or loss as ordinary or capital will turn on the character of the assets held by the partnership. See §751(a). To properly tax the selling partner on her share of the partnership's unrealized cash basis items accruing prior to the sale, the selling partner's distributive share of those items is computed and includible by the selling partner. See §706(c)(2).

A liquidating distribution is conceptually a sale of the partnership interest back to the partnership (and through it to the other partners). Despite this, a liquidating distribution is taxed more like a current distribution than a sale. Thus, gain and loss generally are not recognized on a liquidating distribution even if the value of the property received by the terminating partner exceeds her outside basis. Rather, the exiting partner pushes her basis in the partnership interest into the distributed property, thereby ensuring that any gain or loss realized on the liquidating distribution is built into the basis of the property distributed. See §731(a), §732(b).

20

Determining Distributive Shares

A partnership is not a taxpayer, §701; rather, it computes its taxable income as if it were a taxpayer and then passes through its tax items to its partners. §702. The portion of the entity-level items that a partner includes on her individual tax return is called the partner's "distributive share." §702. "Distributive" share, then, is what each partner reports on her individual tax return, and it bears no necessary relationship to amounts actually distributed to the partner. "Distributive" share is thus an unfortunate choice of words: "allocable share" or something similar would have been far less confusing. But "distributive share" is what Congress used, and so we must use it as well.

Under §704(a), each partner's distributive share is determined by reference to the partnership agreement. Further, this section provides that a partner's distributive share may be specified item by item, so that partner *X* might have a 30-percent share of rents, a 25-percent share of royalties, and a 50-percent share of losses. Thus, §704(a) gives the partners great flexibility in allocating the partnership's tax items among themselves.

The term "partnership agreement" is defined in §761(c) to include all amendments made by the partners up to the time that the partnership tax return is due to be filed (not including extensions). As a result, it specifically allows the partners to allocate the partnership tax items with hindsight. Thus, distributive shares need not be defined until the partnership's income and loss is known and the nonpartnership tax status of the partners is determined. This definition in §761(c), when combined with the rule of §704(a), seemingly encourages the partners to allocate partnership tax items in ways guaranteed to minimize the partners' aggregate tax liability.

Section 704(a) is unusual in that it expressly allows the partners, through amendment of the partnership agreement, to manipulate tax items. Usually, taxpayers adjust non-tax items such as property rights, rental agreements, and sale terms, and then the tax consequences follow from these non-tax arrangements. Here, though, the partners are given the power to say which partner reports how much of each tax item in a way that seemingly has nothing to do with any economic reality.

As should be expected, there are limitations. The partners' distributive shares as reflected in the partnership agreement will not be given effect if they lack "substantial economic effect." §704(b). The "substantial economic effect" test has come to stand for the proposition that allocations must be consistent with the underlying economic arrangements of the partners (the economic effect requirement, see Treas. Regs. §1.704-1(b)(2)(ii)(a)) and must affect the dollar amounts to be received by the partners from the partnership independent of tax consequences (the substantiality requirement, see Treas. Regs. §1.704-1(b)(2)(iii)(a)).

The Treasury Department has promulgated a voluminous regulation (Treas. Regs. §1.704-1(b)) covering the substantial economic effect test. That regulation divides the test into two separate components: an economic effect test and a substantiality test. You may have heard that mastery of the substantial economic effect test is one of the most difficult parts of the tax law, and rightly so. Nevertheless, if looked at properly, drafting allocation provisions can become almost mechanical. In fact, drafting allocation provisions that pass tax muster is remarkably straightforward. What causes much of the difficulty is drafting provisions that reflect the economic arrangements desired by the partners.

The term "special allocation" (although not defined in the Code or regulations) commonly is used to describe any tax allocation other than one corresponding to the partner's general interest in the partnership. For example, if two partners agree to allocate all tax items equally between them except that depreciation deductions will be allocated exclusively to one partner, we say that the depreciation deductions have been specially allocated.

While the term "special allocation" is generally accepted, you should be careful when using it because it is premised on the naive notion that partners *have* a general interest in the partnership. If partner *X* is allocated 15 percent of the partnership's ordinary income, 20 percent of the partnership's capital gain, and 30 percent of the partnership's losses, then there is no way to describe *X*'s interest in the partnership by some general percentage. We will see that many provisions of subchapter K and the early regulations implicitly assume that each partner has some determinable general interest in the partnership. Yet there is nothing to prevent a partnership from allocating each item separately on a year-by-year basis.

A "bottom line" allocation is an allocation of the partnership's net income or loss. See Treas. Regs. §1.704-1(b)(1)(vii). Thus, rather than allocate the partnership's income and deductions item-by-item, bottom line allocations divide the net total. Such bottom line allocations are specifically authorized by §704(b). If a partnership agreement contains bottom-line allocations, the tax consequences to the individual partners of a particular event cannot be determined until the close of the partnership's taxable year.

A. BASIC MAINTENANCE OF CAPITAL ACCOUNTS

A "capital account"[1] must be maintained for each partner according to the rules set forth in Treas. Regs. §1.704-1(b)(2)(iv). The capital account maintenance rules

1. More accurately, a "§704(b) capital account." Partnerships may need to keep other capital accounts for non-tax reasons. For example, in addition to the §704(b) capital accounts, a partnership that disseminates audited financial statements likely will maintain an alternate set of capital accounts based on generally-accepted accounting principles (usually called "GAAP capital accounts").

help enforce the substantial economic effect limitation on partnership allocations. If these rules are not followed, tax allocations specified in the partnership agreement may be disregarded by the Service. Treas. Regs. §1.704-1(b)(2)(iv)(a). Note in particular that each partner has a single capital account even if the partner owns several interests in the partnership. Treas. Regs. §1.704-1(b)(2)(iv)(b).

Just like a partner's outside basis, a partner's capital account begins with the partner's contribution to the partnership and is adjusted for distributions and further contributions of property as well as for distributive share of income and loss. Treas. Regs. §1.704-1(b)(2)(iv)(b). However, while initial outside basis equals the adjusted basis of contributed property, initial capital accounts begin at the *fair market value* of contributed property. Treas. Regs. §1.704-1(b)(2)(iv)(d). Thus, the capital account balances measure the economic (rather than tax) relationship between the partners.

The partnership must also maintain a table of values for its assets, and these values (called the "book" value of the assets) correspond to the values used to construct the partners' capital accounts. As a result, the aggregate value of the partners' capital accounts should always equal the aggregate book value of the partnership's assets (less partnership liabilities). This common value represents the *net book value* of the partnership: The capital accounts divide that value among the owners' interests, whereas the book values of the assets divide it among the various partnership assets.

Booking in contributed property at fair market value ensures that the contributing partner gets full credit for the value of her contribution. For example, suppose *A* and *B* form the *AB* general partnership with *A* contributing cash of $10,000 and *B* contributing Blackacre with a fair market value of $10,000 but an adjusted basis of only $6,000. *B* surely expects to be an equal partner with *A* because they have each contributed $10,000 in value to the partnership. *B*'s capital account is credited with the full value of Blackacre, and so the two partners begin with equal capital accounts reflecting their equality.

Of course, if Blackacre increases in value, say to $12,000, neither *A*'s nor *B*'s capital account will reflect the true value of the partner's interest in the partnership. As with outside basis, capital accounts are not adjusted simply because property appreciates (or declines) in value. Accordingly, partnership capital accounts reflect the *book* value of partnership property and do not (in general) reflect any unrealized appreciation or loss accruing after the property was acquired by the partnership.

There are, however, occasions when the partners must take into account the current fair market value of some or all partnership assets, and when they do so, the assets will be booked up (or down) to current fair market value. For example, if the partnership distributes property to one of its partners, the distributee partner's capital account must be reduced by the full fair market value of the distributed property. Treas. Regs. §1.704-1(b)(2)(iv)(e)(1). Accordingly, the distributed property is booked to current value immediately prior to the distribution. *Id.*

There are additional rules governing capital account maintenance, see generally Treas. Regs. §1.704-1(b)(2)(iv), and there are other differences between capital accounts and outside bases, see Treas. Regs. §1.704-1(b)(2)(iv)(c) (treatment of liabilities), §1.704-1(b)(2)(iv)(f) (revaluations of property), §1.704-3 (contributed property). But to understand the basics of the substantial economic effect test, we have what we need. We will return to capital account maintenance throughout these materials as we cover specific transactions.

PROBLEM

20-1. *B* and *W* form the *BW* general partnership. *B* contributes Blackacre with an adjusted basis of $20,000 and a fair market value of $25,000. *W* contributes Whiteacre with an adjusted basis of $28,000 and a fair market value of $25,000. *B* and *W* agree to allocate all items of gain or loss equally. During the first year, *BW* earns $10,000 from renting Blackacre but loses $6,000 from the operation of Whiteacre. The partnership makes no distributions. What are the partners' capital accounts after the first year?

B. ECONOMIC EFFECT I: THE GENERAL TEST

The substantial economic effect test is divided under the regulations into two components: the economic effect test and the substantiality test. Treas. Regs. §1.704-1(b)(2)(i). We will postpone until later an examination of the second (substantiality) of these two tests (set forth in Treas. Regs. §1.704-1(b)(2)(iii)). Remember, though, that partnership allocations will not be valid unless they pass both tests.

Under the *general test for economic effect,* see Treas. Regs. §1.704-1(b)(2)(ii)(b), allocations have economic effect if three conditions are met. First, capital accounts must be properly maintained. Treas. Regs. §1.704-1(b)(2)(ii)(b)(1). Second, liquidation proceeds[2] must be distributed in accordance with final capital account balances. Treas. Regs. §1.704-1(b)(2)(ii)(b)(2). Third, any partner with a capital account deficit at the time of liquidation of her partnership interest must have an unqualified obligation to restore the amount of that deficit (within 90 days of liquidation of the interest) for distribution to creditors of the partnership or to other partners. Treas. Regs. §1.704-1(b)(2)(ii)(b)(3). This deficit restoration obligation may arise from the partnership agreement or otherwise. For example, state law may impose such an obligation on the partners.

Note that this regulation ties "distributive share" (i.e., partnership allocation of income and deductions) to liquidating distributions. Furthermore, because nonliquidating distributions affect capital account balances, Treas. Regs. §1.704-1(b)(2)(iv)(b), nonliquidating distributions influence partnership allocations as well. What underlies these rules is an attempt to relate partnership allocations to the economic arrangements among the partners.

In order for an allocation to have economic effect, it must be consistent with the underlying economic arrangement of the partners. That is, in the event there is an economic benefit or economic burden that corresponds to an allocation, the partner to whom the allocation is made must receive such economic benefit or bear such economic burden. Treas. Regs. §1.704-1(b)(2)(ii)(a).

What does this mean? Suppose that a partnership earns $100 of income, and suppose further that this item of income is allocated under the partnership agreement to partner *P.* If capital accounts are maintained properly, this allocation will

2. The "liquidation" of a partnership interest means a distribution or series of distributions that terminate the partner's interest in the venture. §761(d). The liquidation of a particular interest in a partnership does not imply that all interests are being liquidated as part of the same transaction.

result in a $100 increase in *P*'s capital account. And if liquidation proceeds will be distributed in accordance with final capital accounts, then *P* will receive $100 more at liquidation (if not before) by reason of the allocation. The upward capital account adjustment, in other words, ensures that the economic benefit (receipt of more dollars) follows the tax allocation (inclusion of more income).

Consider the following partnership agreement. *A* and *B* each contribute $100 to the *AB* partnership. The partnership purchases business equipment for $200, and assume that this equipment is depreciable at the rate of $40 per year for five years. *A* and *B* will share equally all income, but *B* will be allocated all of the depreciation deductions. If the partnership has rental income of $60 per year, what will the partnership books look like after five years?

At formation, the partnership capital accounts will equal $100 for each partner. The first year's activities produce taxable income of $60 and a depreciation deduction of $40. Allocating the income 50-50 between *A* and *B* and allocating the depreciation entirely to *B* produces capital accounts of $130 for *A* and $90 for *B*:

A	*B*	
$100	$100	Starting values
30	30	Distributive share of income
0	(40)	Distributive share of depreciation
$130	$90	Totals

Asset	Book value
Equipment	$160
Cash	60
Total	$220

After five years, the partnership capital accounts will be $250 for *A* and $50 for *B*:

A	*B*	
$130	$90	Carryover
120	120	Distributive share of income
0	(160)	Distributive share of depreciation
$250	$50	Totals

Asset	Book value
Equipment	$ 0
Cash	300
Total	$300

B was allocated all of the depreciation deductions. The economic burden associated with depreciation is risk of diminution in value of the depreciable property. Thus, economic effect requires that *B* bear that economic risk. Has this happened? Assume that the property has declined in value as it has been depreciated. That is, assume the equipment has declined to zero value. The partnership now holds cash of $300 ($60 per year received times five years) and nothing else of value. Liquidation proceeds thus can be distributed to the partners in accordance with final capital account balances: *A* will be entitled to $250, and *B* will be entitled to $50.

Have the tax consequences worked out? Each year of the five years, *A* included $30 of income. Over five years, *A* thus included $150 of income. Upon liquidation, *A* receives $250 in cash, and that is precisely $150 more than *A* invested. Thus, *A* can and does receive the liquidating distribution with no further tax consequences, ultimately receiving one dollar of cash for every dollar of partnership income allocated to her.

As for *B*, each year *B* included $30 of income and deducted $40 of depreciation. Thus, *B*'s net result was $10 of deduction per year. Over the five years, then, *B* deducted $50 more than *B* included, and that is the precise amount of money *B* lost in the venture ($100 invested less $50 received upon liquidation). Thus, *B*'s liquidating distribution properly has no tax consequences to *B*: The economic effect of the tax allocations ensured that the tax consequences were felt as the income was earned (and as the depreciation was claimed) over the five years.

Consider for a moment what would have happened if the partners had allocated all tax items the same way but had provided (in violation of the general test for economic effect) that liquidation proceeds were to be distributed equally to *A* and to *B* regardless of final capital account balances. In this case, each partner would receive $150 in cash upon liquidation. As for *A*, such a liquidation would produce a taxable loss of $100 because the amount of money distributed would be less than *A*'s pre-liquidation outside basis. The reverse would be true for *B*: The distribution would produce a taxable gain of $100 because the cash distributed would exceed *B*'s pre-liquidation outside basis.

Absence of economic effect means, in other words, that the distribution of liquidation proceeds will result in gain or loss to the partners. A partner recognizing income on a liquidating distribution would (like *B*) have been allocated too little income (or too much loss) during the life of the partnership. Note that the absence of economic effect does not result in phantom income or loss *over the life of the partnership*.[3] The outside basis rules in §705 ensure that whatever economic effect is lacking during the life of the partnership will be corrected upon liquidation. Economic effect is about the timing of partnership tax items. From another perspective, economic effect is about the amount each partner will receive upon liquidation: So long as capital accounts are properly maintained and liquidation proceeds are properly distributed, *any* set of partnership allocations will have economic effect under the general test.

Reconsider the last *AB* example but assume that the partnership recognizes no income in any year. Thus, the only tax item is a deduction of $40 per year for five years. At the end of that time, the partnership capital accounts will stand at $100 for *A* and negative $100 for *B*:

A	*B*	
$100	$100	Contributions
0	(200)	Distributive share of depreciation
$100	($100)	Totals

Asset	Book value
Equipment	$0
Cash	0
Total	$0

3. "Phantom income" means taxable income without receipt of an equivalent economic receipt (usually of cash).

Assuming once again that the equipment declines in value to zero, the partnership will have no assets. Liquidation proceeds must be distributed in accordance with final capital account balances, but where is the $100 due *A* to come from? From *B*, of course, because a capital account deficit must be restored at liquidation under the rules of the general test for economic effect. Note that *B* deducted $40 per year times five years, or $200 total. *B* lost her entire investment of $100 and, because of the capital account deficit restoration obligation, *B* will lose another $100 upon liquidation. *A*, on the other hand, will have lost nothing and will receive $100—precisely the amount initially invested—at liquidation.

You should now have a feel for what the regulations mean when they say that the partner given a tax allocation must also receive the associated economic benefit or burden. The benefit associated with an allocation of income is the right to receive more funds, while the burden associated with a deduction is risk of loss of funds. By reflecting tax allocations in properly maintained capital accounts, economic benefits and burdens follow tax allocations.

Although economic benefits and burdens must follow tax allocations, it sometimes happens that anticipated burdens do not materialize. In particular, the economic burden associated with depreciation deductions is the risk of diminution in value of the property. Often, depreciable property does not decline in value as quickly as its depreciation schedule suggests. In such cases, careful drafting of the partnership agreement can ensure that no partner bears an economic burden in excess of that actually incurred by the partnership.

For example, suppose that *A* and *B* form the *AB* partnership by contributing $5,000 each. The partnership will invest its $10,000 in depreciable property, and all depreciation deductions will be allocated to *A*. All other tax items will be allocated equally between *A* and *B*.

Assume that the partnership has no income or loss each year other than a $2,000 depreciation deduction. After two years, the capital accounts will be $1,000 for *A* and $5,000 for *B*:

A	*B*	
$5,000	$5,000	Cash contributions
(2,000)	0	Year 1 depreciation
(2,000)	0	Year 2 depreciation
$1,000	$5,000	Totals

Asset	Book value
Equipment	$6,000
Total	$6,000

Suppose the partnership now sells its property for $9,000 in anticipation of liquidation. As a result of the sale, the partnership recognizes a gain of $3,000, allocable under the partnership agreement equally between the partners. Accordingly, final capital accounts will be $2,500 for *A* and $6,500 for *B*:

A	*B*	
$1,000	$5,000	Carryover
1,500	1,500	Distributive share of gain
$2,500	$6,500	Totals

Asset	Book value
Cash	$9,000
Total	$9,000

A has reported $4,000 of deduction and $1,500 of income for a net loss of $2,500, and that is the correct measure of *A*'s economic loss. However, the partnership lost only $1,000 on the property; after all, it purchased the property for $10,000 and subsequently sold it for $9,000. Why is *A* losing $2,500 when the partnership lost only $1,000?

A's excess loss arises because the $3,000 dispositional gain was allocated 50-50 while the depreciation deductions were allocated entirely to *A*. Note that the taxable gain from disposition of the property is not the result of an increase in the value of the property. Rather, it represents a tax payback of the amount of depreciation claimed ($4,000) in excess of the true decline in value of the property ($1,000). To avoid this unfairness to *A*, the partnership agreement should allocate the entire gain back to *A*, resulting in final capital accounts of $4,000 for *A* and $5,000 for *B*:

A	*B*	
$1,000	$5,000	Carryover
3,000	0	Chargeback of gain
$4,000	$5,000	Totals

Asset	Book value
Cash	$9,000
Total	$9,000

This *gain chargeback* ensures that *A* suffers no loss beyond that suffered by the partnership. In this example, *A* suffers an economic loss of $1,000 over the life of the partnership. That loss is appropriate, however, because the partnership's property declined in value by that $1,000 and, because *A* was specially allocated all depreciation deductions, *A* must bear that loss.

Consider the following arrangement: *P* and *Q* form the *PQ* partnership with *P* contributing cash of $25,000 and *Q* contributing cash of $75,000. The partnership uses its cash of $100,000 to purchase depreciable business property. The partnership agreement provides (1) all cost recovery deductions (i.e., depreciation) will be allocated to *Q*; (2) all operating income and loss (excluding cost recovery deductions) will be allocated 25 percent to *P* and 75 percent to *Q*; and (3) all gain or loss from the eventual sale of the business property will be allocated 50 percent to *P* and 50 percent to *Q*. Assume that the cost of the business property is recovered at a rate of $10,000 per year for 10 years and that the partnership has income each year (excluding the cost recovery deduction) of $12,000.

At the start of the partnership, the capital accounts begin at $25,000 for *P* and $75,000 for *Q*. As a result of the activities in year 1, *P*'s distributive share will include $3,000 of income while *Q*'s distributive share will include $9,000 of income and $10,000 of deduction. Accordingly, the capital accounts will become $28,000 for *P* and $74,000 for *Q*:

P	*Q*	
$25,000	$75,000	Cash contributions
3,000	9,000	Distributive share of income
0	(10,000)	Distributive share of depreciation
$28,000	$74,000	Totals

Asset	Book value
Equipment	$ 90,000
Cash	12,000
Total	$102,000

The partnership now owns business property with book value of $90,000 as well as cash of $12,000. If the partners wish to distribute that cash in a nonliquidating distribution, how much must go to *P*? The answer, and this is important, is that the tax allocations do not specify or restrict how nonliquidating distributions are to be made. The partners could choose to distribute as much or as little of the $12,000 cash as they see fit, and if they choose to distribute any, they can do so to *P* and *Q* in any proportions. *Tax allocations ("distributive shares") do not determine current distributions.*

Assume the partners decide to distribute the entire $12,000 in the same proportion as that income was allocated. In that case, $3,000 will be distributed to *P*, and $9,000 will be distributed to *Q*. As a result of these distributions, the books will become $25,000 for *P* and $65,000 for *Q*:

P	*Q*	
$28,000	$74,000	Carryover
(3,000)	(9,000)	Distribution
$25,000	$65,000	Totals

Asset	Book value
Equipment	$90,000
Cash	0
Total	$90,000

Suppose the partnership sells its business property immediately at the beginning of year 2 for its initial cost of $100,000. As a result of that sale, the partnership will recognize a gain of $10,000, allocable under the partnership agreement $5,000 to *P* and $5,000 to *Q*. If the partnership now liquidates, the final (pre-liquidation) capital account balances will be $30,000 for *P* and $70,000 for *Q*:

P	*Q*	
$25,000	$65,000	Carryover
5,000	5,000	Distributive share of gain
$30,000	$70,000	Totals

Asset	Book value
Cash	$100,000
Total	$100,000

It should come as no surprise that final capital account balances precisely equal the cash available for distribution: If the partnership owns nothing but cash, the requirement that liquidating proceeds be distributed in accordance with final capital account balances is premised on this equality. But consider the following: Has *Q* been treated fairly?

From one perspective *Q* has been treated fairly: Over the life of the partnership, *Q* included (net) $4,000 of income and made an economic profit of the same amount. To see this, recall that *Q* reported $9,000 of income and $10,000 of deduction at the end of the first year and reports $5,000 at the end of the second year as a result of the pre-liquidation sale. The net effect of these transactions is income of $4,000.

As for *Q*'s economic profit, *Q* invested $75,000. *Q* received back $9,000 at the end of year one and $70,000 upon liquidation of the partnership, producing a net economic profit of $4,000. Thus, *Q* has been treated fairly in the sense that *Q*'s tax situation properly reflects his economic situation.

But ignore taxes for a moment and look at what happened to *Q*. The partnership agreement provides that *Q* will be allocated three-quarters of all operating profit. The partnership in fact made $12,000 of operating profit, yet *Q* comes away from the partnership with only $4,000. What went wrong?

By allocating all cost recovery deductions to *Q*, *Q* was forced to bear the risk that the business property would decline in value. The property did not decline in value, though, but instead produced a tax gain (but no economic gain) at disposition. By allocating *Q* all depreciation but only half of the resulting gain, *Q*'s capital account suffered a net decline of $5,000 (that is, $10,000 decrease from the cost recovery deduction less $5,000 from *Q*'s half of the dispositional gain).

By allocating all the depreciation deductions to *Q*, *Q* was forced to bear the economic risk of diminution in value of the business property: Had it gone down in value, the loss would have been borne by *Q*. That risk of loss was reflected in *Q*'s capital account by a downward adjustment of $10,000. When that loss did not mature, *Q* should have received an upward adjustment of the same amount. However, because the partnership agreement did not include the appropriate gain chargeback, *Q*'s capital account received only half of the upward adjustment. Had there been a gain chargeback provision in the agreement, *Q* would have paid for his excess depreciation deductions by including an offsetting amount of income. Without the gain chargeback, *Q* pays for the depreciation by actually losing money.

How should this partnership agreement have been written? The easy answer is: however the partners want it. Unfortunately, determining exactly what the partners have in mind often is difficult. For example, partners rarely will request a gain chargeback provision directly. However, the same partners when shown an example demonstrating the effect of a gain chargeback often will agree that such a provision is needed to effectuate their intentions. The most effective way to ascertain the partners' intentions is to present them with a series of hypotheticals (losses followed by gains, gains followed by losses, extreme losses, extreme gains, refinancing of the partnership property, etc.) and ask them to decide what non-tax results they desire. Once those desires are known, drafting the corresponding tax allocations should be relatively straightforward.

This brings up another important point in drafting the tax provisions of a partnership agreement. The tax allocations in a partnership agreement divide the partnership's profit and loss among the partners: what is allocated to one partner is unavailable to the others. Thus, the allocations form the rules of a zero-sum game, and like any such game, not all players can be winners at the same time. For example, if you suggest a gain chargeback provision to *P* and *Q* in the example above, then you are helping *Q* but hurting *P*. Which partner is your client? If the partner*ship* is your client, then why are you helping one partner over another?

There is nothing wrong with being the partnership's lawyer in its dealing with persons outside the partnership, but you cannot represent more than one partner in preparing a partnership agreement without a conflict of interest. At a minimum, you must thoroughly explain the conflict to each of the partners in writing and advise them to seek independent counsel. This is best done in the initial representation and fee agreement letter sent to and signed by all parties. Such advice, though, often will be taken as a lawyer's attempt to multiply fees needlessly. Whether you insist on independent representation (and thereby risk losing the transaction to some lawyer less concerned with ethical considerations) or agree to represent all partners as best you can (and thereby face the risk of future recriminations and lawsuits) is one of the great difficulties in the practice of partnership tax law. Even great lawyers have made mistakes in this area. Most clients, though, will appreciate your professionalism.

Let us recap the *general* test for economic effect. First, capital accounts must be properly maintained. See Treas. Regs. §1.704-1(b)(2)(ii)(b)(1), §1.704-1(b)(2)(iv). The easiest way to ensure that capital accounts are maintained properly in partnership agreements you write is *not* to provide detailed maintenance rules in the agreement. Rather, you should incorporate the regulations by reference, writing "Capital accounts will be maintained in accordance with the rules in Treasury Regulation section 1.704-1(b)" or something similar.

Second, upon liquidation of the partnership (or of any partner's interest in the partnership), proceeds must be distributed in accordance with final capital account balances. Treas. Regs. §1.704-1(b)(2)(ii)(b)(2). Once again, detailed rules are not needed in the partnership agreement itself. Rather, include a sentence such as "Upon liquidation of one or more interests in the partnership, liquidation proceeds will be distributed in proportion to final capital account balances as adjusted for the distribution." The "as adjusted" language refers to adjustments made to reflect any disparities between book value and tax basis. See Treas. Regs. §1.704-1(b)(2)(iv)(f)(5)(ii).

Third, each partner must have an unqualified obligation to restore a capital account deficit upon liquidation of her interest. Treas. Regs. §1.704-1(b)(2)(ii)(b)(3). Although this obligation need not arise directly from the partnership agreement (for example, state law may impose such an obligation on general partners), it is a good practice to explicitly declare the obligation in the partnership agreement. By making the deficit restoration obligation specific, there is less chance that incoming partners will be misled. In addition, you will avoid arguing the niceties of state law with an aggressive revenue agent auditing the partnership.

NOTES

1. *Exceptions to the liquidation requirement.* While the general test for economic effect requires that the amount of a liquidating distribution equal the exiting partner's capital account balance, there is an exception to that rule. Under the final

paragraph of Treas. Regs. §1.704-1(b)(2)(ii)(b), an exiting partner may sell her partnership interest to other partners or to the partnership "pursuant to an agreement negotiated at arm's length by person's who have materially adverse interests and if a principal purpose of such . . . sale is not to avoid the principles of [the requirement of economic effect]." For example, a partner owning only a small interest in the partnership may wish to leave, and a fair market appraisal of the partnership interest might include discounts for lack of control and marketability. So long as the valuation is bona fide, a liquidating distribution should not jeopardize the partnership's allocations under §704(b). Note that this regulation expressly provides that the exception does not apply to distributions made in liquidation of the partnership as a whole.

2. *Drafting suggestion: tax definitions.* One of the requirements of economic effect is that capital accounts be maintained properly. Many partnership agreements include detailed capital account maintenance rules in an attempt to comply with this requirement. A better way to draft a partnership agreement is to include a statement such as, "A capital account will be maintained for each partner in accordance with applicable Treasury Regulations" (where "Treasury Regulations" is suitably defined in the partnership agreement). This avoids the possibility that a typing error will cause the partnership agreement to be inconsistent with the capital account maintenance rules (now found in Treas. Regs. §1.704-1(b)(2)(iv)) and allows for the possibility that those rules might change during the life of the partnership.

3. *Drafting suggestion: allocation provisions or liquidating distributions.* The economic effect regulations tacitly assume that partnership agreements will include a set of "waterfall" allocation provisions. Such a set of provisions allocates gain or loss (or an item of gain or loss) in tiers. Such a provisions might read, "The partnership's Net Income is allocated, first, to *X*, in an amount equal to 10 percent of *X*'s average Capital Account balance for the year, and, second, any remaining Net Income 45 percent to *X* and 55 percent to *Y*." Consistent with the general test for economic effect, the partnership agreement also will include a statement that upon the liquidation of any interest in the partnership, the exiting partner will receive the positive amount of his capital account balance, if any, or must repay within 90 days the negative amount of his capital account balance, if any.

The problem with such waterfall allocation schemes is the consequence of error. Depending on the economic arrangements among the partners, waterfall allocations can become very complicated. If they are misdrafted, the ending capital account balances will differ from what the partners anticipated. Because liquidating distributions are controlled by final capital account balances, a mistake in the allocation provisions will affect not only the tax obligations of the partners but also the actual dollars they will receive.

To ensure that no drafting error mistranslates the partners' economic arrangements, some partnership agreements are drafted in a very different way. These agreements specify how all distributions (current and liquidating) must be made, and then the tax allocations are left unspecified. In addition, a provision is included saying that the allocations must have economic effect. Each year, the accountant for the partnership will then ask the following question: "If the partnership had liquidated at the end of this year, how much would each partner have received?" Once that is determined, the accountant must then figure out a set of allocations that brings each partner's capital account at year end to these hypothetical totals.

For complicated partnership, this can be an extremely complex (and expensive) annual task. Note, though, that if it is done incorrectly it will affect only the taxes that each partner pays rather than the value each partner will receive in liquidation. Such distribution-driven agreements are sometimes described as having "targeted," "forced," or "fill-up" allocations.

4. *Drafting suggestion: check the translation!* The most difficult part of drafting partnership tax allocation provisions is ensuring that the economic agreement of the partners has been translated properly into the partnership agreement's tax language. There is no foolproof way to ensure all errors have been avoided, but one important thing to do is to test the tax allocations against hypothetical fact patterns by using a spreadsheet. Construct a few possible futures (money is made every year, money is lost every year, money is made and then lost, etc.), and determine how the partnership's cash will be distributed under the agreement as drafted. Then have the partners agree that the examples you have constructed accurately reflect their understanding. *Have the partners sign the examples and keep a signed copy for your records.* You may wish to include the examples as an appendix to the partnership agreement as an aid in interpreting the agreement.

PROBLEMS

20-2. *P* and *Q* form the *PQ* partnership. They agree on a set of bottom-line allocations: (1) If there is a net loss for the year, it will be allocated 60 percent to *P* and 40 percent to *Q*, and (2) if there is net income for the year, it will be allocated 50 percent to *P* and 50 percent to *Q*. Are the partners' capital accounts *time dependent* in the sense that they turn on not only how much income and loss the partnership recognizes but also on the year in which items of income and loss are recognized?

20-3. *X* and *Y* form the *XY* Travel Agency, a general partnership, by contributing $10,000 each. They agree to split losses equally but, because *X* is a more experienced travel agent than *Y*, they agree to allocate 60 percent of the profits to *X* and 40 percent to *Y*. Assuming that these allocations should apply to economic gains and losses, write the tax allocation provisions for the *XY* partnership. (*Hint*: Make sure your provisions work properly if there is loss in year one and profit in year two, then consider what happens if there is profit in year one and loss in year two.)

C. ECONOMIC EFFECT II: THE ALTERNATE TEST

Although the general test for economic effect is satisfactory for many partnerships, its deficit restoration obligation will be unacceptable to some partners, especially to limited partners (and to members of limited liability companies) for whom liability is statutorily limited. A limited partner makes an initial contribution to the partnership and agrees to make further contributions up to a stated maximum. That maximum can be as little as zero or as much as the partners agree, but whatever the amount, the existence of any limitation on a partner's obligation to contribute additional funds to the partnership is inconsistent with the unlimited deficit restoration requirement of the general test for economic effect. Allocations to limited partners, then, can never satisfy the general test for economic effect.

The alternate test for economic effect dispenses with the requirement of an unlimited deficit restoration obligation. In its place, three new requirements are imposed: (1) An allocation may drive the partner's capital account negative only to the extent that the partner can be required to make further capital contributions;[4] (2) future events that would reduce a partner's capital account when they occur must be entered into the partner's capital account as soon as they reasonably can be anticipated (the look-ahead requirement); and (3) if the partner's capital account becomes negative in an amount beyond the maximum amount that the partner can be required to contribute to the partnership, partnership income must be allocated to the partner as quickly as possible to bring her capital account back up (the qualified income offset provision).

Rev. Rul. 97-38

1997-2 C.B. 69

Issue

If a partner is treated as having a limited deficit restoration obligation under §1.704-1(b)(2)(ii)(c) of the Income Tax Regulations by reason of the partner's liability to the partnership's creditors, how is the amount of that obligation calculated?

Facts

In year 1, *GP* and *LP*, general partner and limited partner, each contribute $100*x* to form limited partnership *LPRS*. In general, *GP* and *LP* share *LPRS*'s income and loss 50 percent each. However, *LPRS* allocates to *GP* all depreciation deductions and gain from the sale of depreciable assets up to the amount of those deductions. *LPRS* maintains capital accounts according to the rules set forth in §1.704-1(b)(2)(iv), and the partners agree to liquidate according to positive capital account balances under the rules of §1.704-1(b)(2)(ii)(b)(2).

Under applicable state law, *GP* is liable to creditors for all partnership recourse liabilities, but *LP* has no personal liability. *GP* and *LP* do not agree to unconditional deficit restoration obligations as described in §1.704-1(b)(2)(ii)(b)(3) (in general, a deficit restoration obligation requires a partner to restore any deficit capital account balance following the liquidation of the partner's interest in the partnership); *GP* is obligated to restore a deficit capital account only to the extent necessary to pay creditors. Thus, if *LPRS* were to liquidate after paying all creditors and *LP* had a positive capital account balance, *GP* would not be required to restore *GP*'s deficit capital account to permit a liquidating distribution to *LP*. In addition, *GP* and *LP* agree to a qualified income offset, thus satisfying the requirements of the alternate test for economic effect of §1.704-1(b)(2)(ii)(d). *GP* and *LP* also agree that no allocation will be made that causes or increases a deficit balance in any partner's capital account in excess of the partner's obligation to restore the deficit.

4. Plus, as we'll see, by the amount of the partner's share of the partnership's "minimum gain" and "partner minimum gain."

LPRS purchases depreciable property for $1,000*x* from an unrelated seller, paying $200*x* in cash and borrowing the $800*x* balance from an unrelated bank that is not the seller of the property. The note is recourse to *LPRS*. The principal of the loan is due in 6 years; interest is payable semi-annually at the applicable federal rate. *GP* bears the entire economic risk of loss for *LPRS*'s recourse liability, and *GP*'s basis in *LPRS* (outside basis) is increased by $800*x*. See §1.752-2.

In each of years 1 through 5, the property generates $200*x* of depreciation. All other partnership deductions and losses exactly equal income, so that in each of years 1 through 5 *LPRS* has a net loss of $200*x*.

Law and Analysis

... To come within the safe harbor for establishing economic effect in §1.704-1(b)(2)(ii), partners must agree to maintain capital accounts under the rules of §1.704-1(b)(2)(iv), liquidate according to positive capital account balances, and agree to an unconditional deficit restoration obligation for any partner with a deficit in that partner's capital account, as described in §1.704-1(b)(2)(ii)(b)(3). Alternatively, the partnership may satisfy the requirements of the alternate test for economic effect provided in §1.704-1(b)(2)(ii)(d). *LPRS*'s partnership agreement complies with the alternate test for economic effect.

The alternate test for economic effect requires the partners to agree to a qualified income offset in lieu of an unconditional deficit restoration obligation. If the partners so agree, allocations will have economic effect to the extent that they do not create a deficit capital account for any partner (in excess of any limited deficit restoration obligation of that partner) as of the end of the partnership taxable year to which the allocation relates. §1.704-1(b)(2)(ii)(d)(3) (flush language).

A partner is treated as having a limited deficit restoration obligation to the extent of: (1) the outstanding principal balance of any promissory note contributed to the partnership by the partner, and (2) the amount of any unconditional obligation of the partner (whether imposed by the partnership agreement or by state or local law) to make subsequent contributions to the partnership. §1.704-1(b)(2)(ii)(c).

LP has no obligation under the partnership agreement or state or local law to make additional contributions to the partnership and, therefore, has no deficit restoration obligation. Under applicable state law, *GP* may have to make additional contributions to the partnership to pay creditors. However, *GP*'s obligation only arises to the extent that the amount of *LPRS*'s liabilities exceeds the value of *LPRS*'s assets available to satisfy the liabilities. Thus, the amount of *GP*'s limited deficit restoration obligation each year is equal to the difference between the amount of the partnership's recourse liabilities at the end of the year and the value of the partnership's assets available to satisfy the liabilities at the end of the year.

To ensure consistency with the other requirements of the regulations under §704(b), where a partner's obligation to make additional contributions to the partnership is dependent on the value of the partnership's assets, the partner's deficit restoration obligation must be computed by reference to the rules for determining the value of partnership property contained in the regulations under section 704(b). Consequently, in computing *GP*'s limited deficit restoration obligation, the value of the partnership's assets is conclusively presumed to equal the book basis of those assets under the capital account maintenance rules of §1.704-1(b)(2)(iv). See §1.704-1(b)(2)(ii)(d) (value equals basis presumption applies for purposes of determining expected allocations and distributions under the alternate test for economic effect); §1.704-1(b)(2)(iii) (value equals basis presumption applies for purposes of the substantiality test); §1.704-1(b)(3)(iii) (value equals basis presumption applies for purposes of the partner's interest in the partnership test); §1.704-2(d) (value equals basis presumption applies in computing partnership minimum gain).

The *LPRS* agreement allocates all depreciation deductions and gain on the sale of depreciable property to the extent of those deductions to *GP*. Because *LPRS*'s partnership agreement satisfies the alternate test for economic effect, the allocations of depreciation deductions to *GP* will have economic effect to the extent that they do not create a deficit capital account for *GP* in excess of *GP*'s obligation to restore the deficit balance. At the end of year 1, the basis of the depreciable property has been reduced to \$800*x*. If *LPRS* liquidated at the beginning of year 2, selling its depreciable property for its basis of \$800*x*, the proceeds would be used to repay the \$800*x* principal on *LPRS*'s recourse liability. All of *LPRS*'s creditors would be satisfied and *GP* would have no obligation to contribute to pay them. Thus, at the end of year 1, *GP* has no obligation to restore a deficit in its capital account.

Because *GP* has no obligation to restore a deficit balance in its capital account at the end of year 1, an allocation that reduces *GP*'s capital account below \$0 is not permitted under the partnership agreement and would not satisfy the alternate test for economic effect. An allocation of \$200*x* of depreciation deductions to *GP* would reduce *GP*'s capital account to negative \$100*x*. Because the allocation would result in a deficit capital account balance in excess of *GP*'s obligation to restore, the allocation is not permitted under the partnership agreement, and would not satisfy the safe harbor under the alternate test for economic effect. Therefore, the deductions for year 1 must be allocated \$100*x* each to *GP* and *LP* (which is in accordance with their interests in the partnership).

The allocation of depreciation of \$200*x* to *GP* in year 2 has economic effect. Although the allocation reduces *GP*'s capital account to negative \$200*x*, while *LP*'s capital account remains \$0, the allocation to *GP* does not create a deficit capital account in excess of *GP*'s limited deficit restoration obligation. If *LPRS* liquidated at the beginning of year 3, selling the depreciable property for its basis of \$600*x*, the proceeds would be applied toward the \$800*x* *LPRS* liability. Because *GP* is obligated to restore a deficit capital account to the extent necessary to pay creditors, *GP* would be required to contribute \$200*x* to *LPRS* to satisfy the outstanding liability. Thus, at the end of year 2, *GP* has a deficit restoration obligation of \$200*x*, and the allocation of depreciation to *GP* does not reduce *GP*'s capital account below its obligation to restore a deficit capital account.

This analysis also applies to the allocation of \$200*x* of depreciation to *GP* in years 3 through 5. At the beginning of year 6, when the property is fully depreciated, the \$800*x* principal amount of the partnership liability is due. The partners' capital accounts at the beginning of year 6 will equal negative \$800*x* and \$0, respectively, for *GP* and *LP*. Because value is conclusively presumed to equal basis, the depreciable property would be worthless and could not be used to satisfy *LPRS*'s \$800*x* liability. As a result, *GP* is deemed to be required to contribute \$800*x* to *LPRS*. A contribution by *GP* to satisfy this limited deficit restoration obligation would increase *GP*'s capital account balance to \$0.

Holding

When a partner is treated as having a limited deficit restoration obligation by reason of the partner's liability to the partnership's creditors, the amount of that obligation is the amount of money that the partner would be required to contribute to the partnership to satisfy partnership liabilities if all partnership property were sold for the amount of the partnership's book basis in the property.

NOTES

1. *The alternate test and economic effect.* To understand the alternate test for economic effect, consider the following example. *G* and *L* form the *GL* limited partnership with *G* the general partner and *L* the limited partner who cannot be required to make further contributions to the partnership. The partners each contribute cash of $5,000, and the partnership agreement provides that losses will be allocated 70 percent to *L* and 30 percent to *G*. If the partnership incurs $8,000 of deductible expenses in its first year, how will the capital accounts stand?

Each partner's capital account will begin at $5,000. The first year's deduction of $8,000 is allocated $5,600 to *L* and $2,400 to *G* under the partnership agreement. Accordingly, *L*'s capital account will show a deficit of $600 while *G*'s capital account will stand at positive $2,600. Is there anything wrong?

If $8,000 is lost during the partnership's first year, then only $2,000 of value remains within the partnership. If the partnership were to liquidate immediately after the conclusion of its first year, there would be only $2,000 to distribute but *G*'s capital account balance would be $2,600. Assuming we distribute the entire $2,000 to *G*, *G* still ends up $600 short: Although *G* deducted only $2,400 during the life of the partnership, *G* will have suffered an economic loss of $3,000. This disparity between the *tax loss reported* by *G* and the *economic loss borne* by *G* is the touchstone of a lack of economic effect.[5]

We see the same lack of economic effect if we look at *L*. During the life of the partnership, *L* deducted $5,600. But *L*'s economic loss is only $5,000 because that was the amount of *L*'s initial investment and *L* cannot be required to contribute additional funds. The goal of the alternate test of economic effect is to ensure that *L* cannot deduct more than her maximum possible economic loss.

When one partner's capital account is negative while another's is positive, an immediate liquidation will force one partner to reimburse the other. If the partner with a negative capital account balance has no unconditional deficit restoration obligation, full reimbursement may be impossible. This is the situation that the alternate test for economic effect tries to avoid. Note that we cannot say with certainty that *G* will bear some of the loss allocated to *L*. If, for example, the partnership turns a profit in subsequent years, then *L*'s capital account may become positive, and so *G* would not bear any of the loss allocated to *L*.

5. If these allocations were upheld despite their lack of economic effect, we would force *L* to recognize a gain of $600 on liquidation of the partnership, and we would allow *G* to recognize a loss of the same amount. Once again, absence of economic effect means only that a liquidating distribution of cash will produce gain or loss to the partners. Economic effect is about the *timing* of income and deductions; it is not about the total amount of income and deductions recognized over the life of the partnership (including the tax consequences of the liquidation).

But we cannot know that *L*'s capital account will increase in the future, and without that knowledge, *G* might bear some of *L*'s loss. This possibility violates the regulation's standard of economic effect, see generally Treas. Regs. §1.704-1(b)(2)(ii), and so the tax allocations, as reflected in the partnership agreement, are not fully valid. To the extent that economic effect is lacking, the partners' distributive shares will be redetermined to correspond with the economics of the transaction.

This does not mean that the partnership agreement is wholly inoperative. As to the first $5,000 of loss allocated to *L*, economic effect is present. It is only as to the last $600 of loss—that is, as to the loss that makes *L*'s capital account negative despite her lack of any obligation to make further contributions to the partnership—that economic effect is lacking. Thus, only the last $600 of loss will be reallocated to *G*. As the regulations make clear, allocations that are in part valid and in part invalid will be set aside only as to the invalid component. See, e.g., Treas. Regs. §1.704-1(b)(5) (example 1(iv)).

2. *The look-ahead requirement.* To appreciate the significance of the look-ahead requirement of the alternate test, consider what happens if the partnership distributes half of its cash (i.e., $1,000) at the beginning of its second year. Assume that the first year's deduction of $8,000 has been allocated $5,000 to *L* and $3,000 to *G* to preserve economic effect. If the $1,000 is distributed, for example, 70 percent to *L* and 30 percent to *G*, the effect of the distribution will be to reduce *L*'s capital account to negative $700 and to reduce *G*'s capital account to positive $1,700.

Once again *L*'s capital account has become negative, and because *L* cannot be required to restore a capital account deficit, this means that something has gone wrong. *L*'s net contribution to the partnership has been $4,300 (initial contribution of $5,000 less cash distributed to *L* of $700), yet *L* has deducted $5,000 of partnership losses. *L*'s share of partnership deductions has thus exceeded the maximum economic loss *L* can be forced to bear.

Yet we made no allocations (to *L* or to *G*) in the second year: what caused the problem was the $700 reduction in *L*'s capital account resulting from the distribution, not from an allocation of loss. Does that mean that the Commissioner can challenge the cash distribution as lacking economic effect?

Certainly not! The substantial economic effect test of §704(b) applies only to distributive shares—that is, to tax allocations—and not to anything else. The Commissioner has no authority to challenge a partnership's distributions or any other non-tax aspect of its business. Accordingly, the Commissioner is helpless in year 2 and must hope that *L*'s capital account deficit is eliminated prior to actual liquidation of *L*'s interest in the partnership.

The look-ahead provision of the alternate test, see Treas. Regs. §1.704-1(b)(2)(ii)(d)(4), seeks to avoid this situation where a partner lacking an unlimited capital account deficit restoration obligation suffers a capital account reduction from a non-tax item (such as from a cash distribution). The look-ahead provision requires that *L*'s capital account be adjusted downward immediately once it is known with reasonable certainty that an event in the future will cause a capital account reduction. Thus, if we knew upon formation of the partnership that $700 would be distributed to *L* in year 2, we would start *L*'s capital account at *L*'s contribution of $5,000 less the future $700 reduction, or at $4,300. The effect of this reduction is to limit *L*'s maximum share of the deduction in year 1 to $4,300. That is, by looking ahead to future events, we limit *L*'s share of tax losses so that her capital account will be sufficient to absorb those future events when they occur.

What events must be anticipated in this way? Although you might think that all future distributions would be subject to the look-ahead provision, in fact that is not the case. Most partnerships only distribute cash as it is earned, and in such cases the capital account reduction from the distribution is precisely offset by the capital account increase from the distributive share of earnings. Only distributions in excess of distributive share of income—such as a distribution from a refinancing of partnership property—will cause a net reduction in capital accounts. Accordingly, only distributions in excess of distributive shares must be anticipated under the look-ahead provision, and a failure to anticipate such a distribution will violate the alternate test for economic effect if the distribution was reasonably expected to be made. There are other non-tax activities of the partnership that can cause a net reduction in a partner's capital account, see generally Treas. Regs. §1.704-1(b)(2)(iv)(f), but they are too unusual or complex to be considered here.

By limiting tax allocations of losses and requiring immediate downward adjustments for future events that will decrease capital accounts, the alternate test for economic effect avoids, as much as possible, the situation in which a partner's capital account deficit exceeds her obligation to make future contributions to the partnership. Nevertheless, such a situation might occur. For example, an *unanticipated* distribution of cash in excess of distributive share of income might occur. In such circumstances, the regulations require that the limited partner be allocated income as soon as possible to bring her capital account back up. The provision in the partnership agreement providing for such an allocation of income is called a "qualified income offset" provision, a mandatory aspect of any partnership agreement if one or more partners lacks an unqualified obligation to restore a capital account deficit upon liquidation.

3. *Conditional deficit restoration obligations and cancellation of indebtedness income.* In Rev. Rul. 97-38 above, the general partner's capital account deficit restoration obligation was limited to repaying amounts owed to nonpartner creditors. As a result, the general partner's conditional restoration obligation was treated as limited to the excess, if any, of the outstanding debt over the book value of the partnership's property. Note that if the debt is repaid or forgiven, the partner's deficit restoration obligation drops to zero. Note further that if the book value of the property changes, the amount of the partner's limited deficit restoration obligation changes as well. This is important to remember in the context of reverse allocations, discussed later.

If the debt is forgiven, the partnership will recognize income from the discharge of indebtedness under §61(a)(12). This income must be allocated in accordance with economic effect, and because neither partner will have a deficit restoration obligation at that time, the income will be subject to allocation under the partnership's qualified income offset provision, at least to the extent of the limited partner's negative capital account balance immediately before the debt discharge. See Rev. Rul. 92-97, 1992 C.B. 124. Note: The partnership cannot exclude any of the income under §108(a) because that section is applied at the partner level. §108(d)(6).

PROBLEMS

20-4. *M* and *N* form the *MN* limited liability company by contributing cash of $10,000 each. *MN* purchases Purpleacre for $100,000, using its cash of $20,000 and signing a fully recourse note for $80,000. Neither partner is obligated to contribute additional funds to the venture except as specifically agreed to by the partners. Each partner agrees to restore any deficit in her capital account upon liquidation of her interest in the partnership only to the extent necessary to repay third-party creditors. Assume the partnership has no income or deductions other than depreciation from Purpleacre.

a. How may the partnership allocate the first $10,000 of depreciation?
b. How may the partnership allocate the second $10,000 of depreciation?
c. How may the partnership allocate the third $10,000 of depreciation?

20-5. *G* and *L* form the *GL* limited partnership with *G* as the general partner and *L* as the limited partner. *G* contributes cash of $60,000, and *L* contributes cash of $60,000. The partnership uses its initial cash of $120,000 to open an art gallery. The partnership agreement provides that *L* cannot be required to contribute additional funds to the partnership for three years. After then, *L*'s maximum contribution is $10,000. The partnership allocates income and losses 20 percent to *G* and 80 percent to L. If the partnership loses $30,000 per year for each of its first four years, how much of each year's loss is properly allocated to *G*? What are the capital account balances after four years?

20-6. *X* and *Y* form the *XY* general partnership, with *X* contributing cash of $100 and *Y* contributing cash of $900. Each partner is obligated to restore a capital account deficit only in favor of third-party creditors. The partnership borrows $9,000 and uses its cash of $10,000 to purchase depreciable property; each year for five years, the property generates $2,000 of depreciation. The partners agree to allocate all items of loss and deduction 10 percent to *X* and 90 percent to *Y* and all items of income 50 percent to *X* and 50 percent to *Y*. The partners also agree to a qualified income offset provision. After four years, the partnership's property is transferred to the lender and the remainder of debt is discharged. How should the $7,000 income from the cancellation of indebtedness be allocated between *X* and *Y*?

D. ALLOCATIONS WITH RESPECT TO CONTRIBUTED PROPERTY

1. *Allocations to the Contributing Partner under §704(c)(1)(A)*

For clarity of presentation, all the examples in this section involve the contribution of appreciated or loss property as part of the formation of a partnership. The rules of §704(c)(1)(A) apply, however, whenever appreciated or loss property is contributed under §721.[6]

Suppose *P* and *Q* form the *PQ* general partnership. *P* contributes cash of $10,000, and *Q* contributes property with fair market value of $10,000 but

6. See generally Howard E. Abrams, Adding a New Cash Partner to an Operating Partnership (pt. 2), Business Entities 38 (Mar.-Apr. 2002); Howard E. Abrams, Adding a New Cash Partner to an Operating Partnership (pt. 1), Business Entities 28 (Jan.-Feb. 2002).

adjusted basis of only $6,000. As you already know, the opening books of the partnership read:

P		*Q*		
CA	OB	CA	OB	
$10,000	$10,000	$10,000	$6,000	Contribution

Under the rule of §704(c)(1)(A), the built-in gain of $4,000 must be allocated to *Q*. For example, if the property is subsequently sold for $12,000, the first $4,000 of gain must be allocated to *Q* (under §704(c)(1)(A)), and the remaining $2,000 of gain may be allocated however the partners agree (under §704(b)). Assume that the partners agree to split equally all gain and loss (including any gain resulting from post-contribution appreciation of the property), except as required otherwise by §704(c)(1)(A). How will the partnership books read after sale of the property for $12,000?

There is a tax gain of $6,000, of which the first $4,000 is allocated entirely to *Q*, and the remaining $2,000 of gain is allocated $1,000 to *P* and $1,000 to *Q*. In total, then, $1,000 is allocated to *P*, and $5,000 is allocated to *Q*. Under §705, these allocations of gain affect the partners' outside bases, bringing each partner's outside basis to $11,000. However, there is book gain of only $2,000 (remember that the property was booked in at its fair market value at time of contribution), allocable $1,000 to *P* and $1,000 to *Q*. When book gain or loss differs from tax gain or loss, capital accounts are adjusted by the amount of *book gain*. See Treas. Regs. §1.704-3(b). Accordingly, each partner's capital account is increased by $1,000 to $11,000. (If we had increased *Q*'s capital account by her share of the tax gain, she would have received capital account credit for the pre-contribution appreciation twice, once when the property was contributed and a second time on sale.)

A similar analysis would be followed if the property had had a built-in loss when it was contributed to the partnership. For example, suppose the property contributed by *Q* had a fair market value of $10,000 but an adjusted basis of $14,000. The opening books of the partnership would read:

P		*Q*		
CA	OB	CA	OB	
$10,000	$10,000	$10,000	$14,000	Contribution

If the property is immediately sold by the partnership for its fair market value of $10,000, there will be a tax loss of $4,000, allocable entirely to *Q* under §704(c). However, there will be no book gain or loss, so neither partner's capital account will be adjusted by reason of the sale. Thus, following the sale, the partnership will have $20,000 in cash, and each partner's outside basis and capital account will equal $10,000.

If the §704(c)(1)(A) property is depreciable, an additional level of complexity is introduced. Assume once again that *P* contributes cash of $10,000, and that *Q* contributes property with a fair market value of $10,000 but an adjusted basis of only $6,000. Assume in addition that the property is depreciable using the straight-line method over five years, so that the partnership is entitled to a depreciation deduction of $1,200 per year for five years.

To determine the proper allocation of this $1,200 per year, we first must determine the proper allocation of the partnership's "book depreciation." Treas. Regs. §1.704-1(b)(2)(iv)(g)(3) provides that "book depreciation . . . with respect to an item of partnership property is the amount that bears the same relationship to the book value of such property as the depreciation . . . computed for tax purposes . . . bears to the adjusted tax basis of such property." Therefore, because tax depreciation is one-fifth of the partnership's adjusted basis in the property each year, book depreciation is one-fifth of the property's book value (or $2,000) per year. That is, had the property's adjusted basis been equal to its fair market value at time of contribution, the partnership would be entitled to a tax depreciation deduction of $2,000 per year.

We allocate this book depreciation to the partners under the terms of the partnership agreement subject to the rules of §704(b); thus, in this case we allocate it 50-50, or $1,000 to each partner. Next, we allocate to the *noncontributing* partner as much tax depreciation as equals her share of the book depreciation. This allocation of $1,000 to *P* is reasonable: After all, it is not *P*'s fault that the tax basis is below its book value. Lastly, we allocate the remaining tax depreciation—in this case, $200 per year—to *Q*, the contributing partner. See Treas. Regs. §1.704-1(c)(2)(i) (example 1).

Look at what happens to the partnership's books. At formation, the books stand as follows:

P		*Q*		
CA	OB	CA	OB	
$10,000	$10,000	$10,000	$6,000	Contribution

After one year (assuming there is no partnership income or loss other than the depreciation deduction), the books read:

P		*Q*		
CA	OB	CA	OB	
$10,000	$10,000	$10,000	$6,000	Contribution
(1,000)	(1,000)	(1,000)	(200)	Depreciation
$ 9,000	$ 9,000	$ 9,000	$5,800	Totals

After the second year (again assuming that there is no partnership income or loss other than the depreciation deduction), the books read:

P		*Q*		
CA	OB	CA	OB	
$9,000	$9,000	$9,000	$5,800	Carryover
(1,000)	(1,000)	(1,000)	(200)	Depreciation
$8,000	$8,000	$8,000	$5,600	Totals

Note that *Q*'s book/tax disparity began at $4,000 and is reduced by $800 per year. Accordingly, after five years the property will be fully depreciated and the book/tax disparity will be eliminated. At that time, the books will read:

P		Q		
CA	OB	CA	OB	
$8,000	$8,000	$8,000	$5,600	Contribution
(3,000)	(3,000)	(3,000)	(600)	Depreciation
$5,000	$5,000	$5,000	$5,000	Totals

Despite the complexity of these rules, the basic scheme should be apparent. The noncontributing partner is (or partners are) allocated as much tax depreciation as she would receive had there been no §704(c)(1)(A) problem at contribution. Whatever depreciation is left over then is allocated to the contributing partner.

To make sure you understand how this rule works, consider the following variation. Once again *P* contributes cash of $10,000, and *Q* contributes property worth $10,000. However, this time the property has an adjusted basis of $20,000 thus representing a built-in loss. Assuming that the property is depreciable over five years using the straight-line method, how should the depreciation be allocated?

There is book depreciation of $2,000 per year, allocated under the partnership agreement (and subject to the rules of §704(b)) equally between the partners; that is, $1,000 to each. The noncontributing partner (namely *P*) is allocated tax depreciation equal to her share of book depreciation, and the remaining $3,000 of tax depreciation is allocated to the contributing partner, *Q*.

The opening books of the partnership will read:

P		Q		
CA	OB	CA	OB	
$10,000	$10,000	$10,000	$20,000	Contribution

After one year, the books will read:

P		Q		
CA	OB	CA	OB	
$10,000	$10,000	$10,000	$20,000	Contribution
(1,000)	(1,000)	(1,000)	(3,000)	Depreciation
$ 9,000	$ 9,000	$ 9,000	$17,000	Totals

After five years, the books will read:

P		Q		
CA	OB	CA	OB	
$ 9,000	$9,000	$9,000	$17,000	Carryover
(4,000)	(4,000)	(4,000)	(12,000)	Depreciation
$ 5,000	$5,000	$5,000	$ 5,000	Totals

Once again, we eliminate the book/tax disparity by treating the noncontributing partner as if there were no §704(c)(1)(A) problem and by allocating whatever is left over to the contributing partner.

PROBLEM

20-7. What would be the tax consequences to the *PQ* partnership if property, contributed with a fair market value of $10,000 and an adjusted basis of $6,000 and depreciable using the straight-line method over five years, were sold for $8,000 after it had been depreciated by the partnership for two years?

Let us return to nondepreciable §704(c) property, and consider what happens if the property turns around in value. For example, suppose that *P* contributes cash of $10,000 to the *PQ* partnership, and *Q* contributes property with a fair market value of $10,000 and an adjusted basis of $6,000. What are the tax consequences to *P* and *Q* if the property is subsequently sold by the partnership for $7,000?

Q's capital account begins at $10,000 to reflect not only *Q*'s after-tax investment in the property ($6,000) but also the pre-contribution appreciation ($4,000). The property then declines in value post-contribution, and the partners have agreed to share partnership losses equally. The partnership agreement requires that each partner be allocated one-half of the book loss, reducing each capital account to $8,500. But how do we allocate the tax gain of $1,000. Even if we allocate all of the tax gain to *Q*, there will be a book/tax disparity for both partners, because the final books will be:

P		*Q*		
CA	OB	CA	OB	
$10,000	$10,000	$10,000	$6,000	Contribution
(1,500)	0	(1,500)	0	Book loss
0	0	0	1,000	Tax gain
$ 8,500	$10,000	$ 8,500	$7,000	Totals

With $17,000 of cash now in the partnership, these books show that *P* and *Q* are equal partners (each will receive $8,500 on liquidation) and that each suffered an economic loss of $1,500. However, because outside bases do not equal capital accounts, tax aspects of the partnership have not followed economic aspects. What caused the book/tax disparities was the sale that produced a *book loss* but a *tax gain*. Without any tax loss to match the book loss, tax allocations in the year of sale could not correspond to the book allocations. The only way to eliminate the book/tax disparity is to make up equal and offsetting tax allocations for *P* and *Q*: If we gave *P* a tax allocation of $1,500 of loss and *Q* an additional $1,500 of gain, the books would be in balance.

Historically, the regulations have imposed a "ceiling" limitation on allocations under §704(c)(1)(A) such that the partners cannot be allocated more tax income or loss than is recognized by the partnership. See generally Treas. Regs. §1.704-3(b). In the example above, when the property is sold for $7,000, the tax gain recognized by the partnership equals $1,000. Accordingly, application of the ceiling limitation means that the partnership must allocate only that amount of tax gain and no more between the partners. In particular, they cannot allocate an extra $1,500 of gain to contributing partner *Q*. Furthermore, because no tax loss is recognized by the partnership, no tax loss can be allocated to any partner.

a. The Traditional Method

Regulations promulgated under §704(c) provide three alternatives that can be used to respond to the problems caused by the ceiling limitation: (1) the *traditional method,* Treas. Regs. §1.704-3(b); (2) the *traditional method with curative allocations,* Treas. Regs. §1.704-3(c); and (3) *the remedial allocation method,* Treas. Regs. §1.704-3(d). The traditional method is the simplest: When the ceiling limitation is encountered, do nothing. Thus, in the example immediately above in which property is contributed to the partnership with a fair market value of $10,000 and then is sold for $7,000, under the traditional method the book/tax disparities for *P* and *Q* will remain until the partnership is liquidated.

b. The Traditional Method with Curative Allocations

The traditional method with curative allocations uses other partnership taxable income or deductions of consistent character to eliminate any book/tax disparity caused by the ceiling limitation. For example, suppose in the *PQ* example above that the partnership recognizes additional income of $3,000 in the year it disposes of the property contributed by *Q*. Consistent with the partnership agreement, allocation of this additional income should be $1,500 to *P* and $1,500 to *Q*, both for book purposes and for tax purposes. However, if we allocate this income equally for book purposes but entirely to *Q* for tax purposes, this disparate book/tax allocation will just offset the book/tax disparity caused by the ceiling limitation; thus, it cures the book/tax disparity caused by the ceiling limitation. Putting this curative allocation into the partnership's books produces:

P		*Q*		
CA	OB	CA	OB	
$10,000	$10,000	$10,000	$ 6,000	Contribution
(1,500)	0	(1,500)	1,000	Sale
1,500	0	1,500	3,000	Cure
$10,000	$10,000	$10,000	$10,000	Totals

Just as we used unrelated partnership income to form the curative allocation, we can use unrelated partnership loss to the same effect. For example, suppose the partnership had an unrelated loss of $3,000 in the year that the partnership sold the property contributed by *Q*. We could allocate this loss equally between the partners for book purposes but entirely to *P* for tax purposes and thereby eliminate the book/tax disparities. Such a curative allocation of loss would leave the partnership books at:

P		*Q*		
CA	OB	CA	OB	
$10,000	$10,000	$10,000	$6,000	Contribution
(1,500)	0	(1,500)	1,000	Sale
(1,500)	(3,000)	(1,500)	0	Cure
$ 7,000	$ 7,000	$ 7,000	$7,000	Totals

Indeed, any combination of unrelated income and loss totaling $3,000 can cure the book/tax disparity caused by application of the ceiling limitation, and the regulations do not express a preference for income over loss or vice versa. Of course the regulations do not authorize curative allocations in any amount greater than that needed to eliminate the book/tax disparities. Treas. Regs. §1.704-3(c)(3)(i); see also Treas. Regs. §1.704-3(c)(4) (example 1(iii)). In particular, even if there is insufficient income and loss to cure a book/tax disparity caused by the ceiling limitation in one year, a curative allocation may not be made in a subsequent year. Treas. Regs. §1.704-3(c)(3)(i). Note also that "[a] partnership may limit its curative allocations to allocations of one or more particular tax items (e.g., only depreciation from a specific property or properties) even if the allocation of those available items does not offset fully the effect of the ceiling rule." Treas. Regs. §1.704-3(c)(1).

The ceiling limitation can arise in surprising circumstances. Suppose that the adjusted basis of *Q*'s contributed property is only $4,000, and once again assume that this property is depreciable over five years using the straight-line method. The partnership is entitled to an annual depreciation deduction of $800 per year although book depreciation equals $2,000 per year.

Because the partnership agreement makes *P* and *Q* equal partners, for book purposes each partner must be allocated one-half of the book depreciation each year. That is, each partner's capital account must be reduced by $1,000 annually. For tax purposes, §704(c)(1)(A) requires that we allocate depreciation so as to take account of the variance between the property's value and adjusted basis at time of contribution. As we have seen, that means we should allocate tax depreciation to the noncontributing partner in an amount equal to her share of the book depreciation. Any tax depreciation remaining should then be allocated to the contributing partner. Because the noncontributing partner is *P*, this means that we should allocate tax depreciation to *P* of $1,000. However, the partnership's total depreciation for the year is only $800, and application of the ceiling limitation means that we cannot allocate more depreciation to *P* than the partnership recognizes. Accordingly, after one year the partnership's books will read:

P		*Q*		
CA	OB	CA	OB	
$10,000	$10,000	$10,000	$4,000	Contribution
(1,000)	(800)	(1,000)	0	Depreciation
$ 9,000	$ 9,200	$ 9,000	$4,000	Totals

The effect of the ceiling limitation in year 1 is to create a permanent book/tax disparity of $200 for each partner. If this continues for the remaining four years of the property's depreciable life, then the partnership's books will be:

P		*Q*		
CA	OB	CA	OB	
$9,000	$9,200	$9,000	$4,000	Carryover
(4,000)	(3,200)	(4,000)	0	Depreciation
$5,000	$6,000	$5,000	$4,000	Totals

Once again, the regulations permit this to happen, so that the partners can have permanent book/tax disparities that will trigger recognition of income (to *Q*) and loss (to *P*) upon disposition of their partnership interests. Partner *P*, though, presumably would prefer that the book/tax disparity be eliminated by means of annual curative allocations, and the regulations allow that choice as well. That is, if the partnership has unrelated income of $400 each year of the appropriate character, the partners may agree to allocate that income entirely to *Q* for tax purposes even though it is allocated equally between the partners for book purposes. Treas. Regs. §1.704-3(c)(3)(iii). Similarly, the partners should be permitted to make annual curative allocations of loss, allocating $400 of loss each year to *P* for tax purposes but allocating it equally between *P* and *Q* for book purposes. Note, though, that the partners must be consistent year to year, Treas. Regs. §1.704-3(c)(2), so that if curative allocations are eschewed in the first year they cannot be made in subsequent years.

c. The Remedial Allocation Method

In addition to the traditional method and the traditional method with curative allocations, the regulations offer a third alternative for handling book/tax disparities under §704(c)(1)(A): the remedial allocation method. Under this method, depreciable appreciated property contributed to a partnership in exchange for a partnership interest is divided into two components, one unappreciated and one with zero basis. For example, if depreciable property is contributed with an adjusted basis of $4,000 and fair market value of $10,000, the remedial allocation method acts as if two properties had been contributed, one with an adjusted basis and fair market value of $4,000 and a second with an adjusted basis of $0 and fair market value of $6,000. Further, this second, zero-basis property is treated as if newly purchased by the partnership, so that its depreciation schedule does not carry over from the contributing partner but instead starts fresh. See Treas. Regs. §1.704-3(d)(2).

In any year in which the ceiling limitation causes a book/tax disparity, the partners cure the disparity by manufacturing tax allocations to cure. Treas. Regs. §1.704-3(d)(1). These tax allocations will net to zero among all the partners, because the ceiling limitation always causes offsetting book/tax disparities. For example, assume *P* and *Q* form the *PQ* general partnership as equal partners, with *P* contributing cash of $10,000 and *Q* contributing depreciable property with an adjusted basis of $4,000 and fair market value of $10,000. *P* and *Q* have agreed to use the remedial allocation method to eliminate any book/tax disparities caused by the ceiling limitation. Assume the depreciable property has a remaining useful life of five years, and assume also that the partners have agreed to recover the excess book depreciation (i.e., the $6,000 excess of fair market value over adjusted basis) using the straight-line method. Finally, assume that the property has a statutory recovery period of 10 years if newly placed in service

In the first year, there is $800 of tax depreciation. The book depreciation, though, equals $1,400: The partnership recovers $4,000 of book value over the five years remaining on the contributing partner's depreciation schedule, and it recovers $6,000 of the book value over a fresh, 10-year statutory recovery period using (by assumption in this example) the straight-line method. Thus, book depreciation in the first year equals $800 plus $600, or $1,400, allocated $700 per partner according to the partnership agreement. Accordingly, tax depreciation must be allocated $700 to *P* and $100 to *Q*, and there is no ceiling limitation problem caused in year 1.

The analysis in years 2 through 5 is the same as in year 1. Thus, after five years the partnership books stand as follows:

P		*Q*		
CA	OB	CA	OB	
$10,000	$10,000	$10,000	$4,000	Carryover
(700)	(700)	(700)	(100)	First year
(2,800)	(2,800)	(2,800)	(400)	Years 2-5
$ 6,500	$ 6,500	$ 6,500	$3,500	Totals

In years 6-10, there is no tax depreciation, but there is book depreciation of $600 per year. This book depreciation is allocated equally between *P* and *Q* according to the partnership agreement, and thus it creates a $300 per year book/tax disparity for each partner. Under the remedial allocation method, each partner reports an offsetting remedial tax allocation that cures the book/tax disparity without regard to other partnership income. Thus, assuming the partnership has no taxable activity in years 6 through 10, *P* includes a remedial allocation of $300 per year of deduction, and *Q* reports $300 of ordinary income. This continues for each of the years 7-10, fully eliminating the book/tax disparity.

P		*Q*		
CA	OB	CA	OB	
$6,500	$6,500	$6,500	$3,500	Start
(300)	0	(300)	0	Year 6
0	(300)	0	300	Remedy
(1,200)	(1,200)	(1,200)	1,200	Years 7-10
$5,000	$5,000	$5,000	$5,000	Totals

A partnership can elect to use the remedial allocation method with respect to *any* contributed property even if there otherwise would be no ceiling limitation issue. For example, reconsider the *PQ* example in which *Q* contributes property with a fair market value of $10,000 and an adjusted basis of $6,000 amortizable over five years. If the partners agree to allocate the depreciation equally, then *P*'s annual tax depreciation will be $1,000 while *Q*'s annual tax depreciation will be $200, and the ceiling limitation will never be encountered. Nonetheless, the partnership can elect to use the remedial allocation method for this property. Thus, although the remedial allocation method is one of the three §704(c) recovery methods, it also is an alternate method of computing book and tax depreciation from contributed property.

Because the remedial allocation method violates the ceiling limitation, it arguably is inconsistent with §704(c)(1)(A). Perhaps in recognition of this, the regulations provide that the Commissioner cannot require any partnership to use the remedial allocation method even if the method adopted by the partnership is unreasonable within the meaning of the anti-abuse rule in Treas. Regs. §1.704-3(a)(10). See Treas. Regs. §1.704-3(d)(5)(ii).

NOTES

1. *Transfer of a built-in loss.* In §704(c)(1)(C), Congress has provided that any built-in loss in contributed property can be taken into account only by the contributing partner and that all other partners must be treated as if the contributed property had basis equal to value at the time of contribution. This provision plainly ensures that a partnership cannot be used to shift a built-in loss from one partner to another, but how does it differ from the more general rule of §704(c)(1)(A)? While the legislative history of §704(c)(1)(C) is none too clear, this section should be understood as speaking to the transferee of a partnership interest who receives the partnership interest from a partner who previously contributed loss property.

For example, suppose *X* contributes loss property to the *P* partnership and then sells her interest in the partnership to *Y*. Under the general rule of Treas. Regs. §1.704-1(b)(2)(iv)(*l*), *Y* assumes the capital account of *X*. Section 704(c)(1)(C), however, denies the built-in tax loss to *Y*. The same loss denial would occur if *X* gifted the partnership interest to *Y* or contributed the partnership interest to *Y* Corp. in a transaction described in §351. And while it is true that the same loss denial might be triggered by the application of §743(d), this latter provision can on occasion be avoided. Section 743 is discussed in more detail in Chapter 27. Note that §704(c)(1)(C) has overruled the loss portion of Treas. Regs. §1.704-3(a)(7).

2. *Contribution of nonamortizable intangibles.* Many types of intangible assets are nonamortizable if acquired other than in connection with the acquisition of a trade or business. Such assets include self-created goodwill, going concern value, business books and records, patents, and copyrights. See §197(c)(2). If such nonamortizable §197 intangibles are contributed to a partnership, then they remain nonamortizable in the hands of the partnership. However, if the partnership elects to apply the remedial allocation method with respect to such an asset, then remedial allocations may be made with respect to that asset. Treas. Regs. §1.197-2(g)(4). Thus, unrealized appreciation in such an asset will generate tax deductions for the noncontributing partners as well as offsetting taxable income to the contributing partner.

PROBLEM

20-8. *J* and *K* form the *JK* general partnership, agreeing to be equal partners except as required by §704(c). *J* contributes cash of $24,000, and *K* contributes property with a fair market value of $24,000 and an adjusted basis of $8,000. This property is depreciable using the straight-line method over 10 years; at the time of its contribution by *K*, it has only four years remaining to its depreciable life. Compute the books of the partnership for its first 10 years of existence assuming (a) the partnership has no income or loss for any year other than depreciation from the contributed property; (b) the partnership has income of $2,000 each year in addition to its depreciation from the contributed property; and (c) the partnership has no income or deduction other than depreciation from the contributed property for its first two years and $1,000 of deduction each year thereafter. In each case, consider the traditional method, the traditional method with curative allocations, and the remedial allocation method.

2. *Reverse §704(c) Allocations to the Existing Partners*[7]

Suppose the *XY* partnership owns a single asset with an adjusted basis of $50,000 and fair market value of $80,000. If *Z* wants to join the partnership on an equal footing with *X* and *Y*, how much should *Z* be required to contribute to the partnership?

Prior to the admission of *Z*, each 50-percent interest in the partnership is worth $40,000. To avoid dilution of their interests, *X* and *Y* should insist that *Z* contribute an equal amount. Assuming *Z* contributes $40,000 to become a one-third partner, the partnership will have total assets worth $120,000, and each partner's interest will be worth $40,000. If the difference between the current fair market value and adjusted basis of the partnership's asset is entirely post-contribution appreciation, then *X* and *Y* should each have an outside basis and capital account of $25,000 immediately prior to the admission of *Z*.

If we simply admit *Z* and do not make any changes to the books, *Z*'s capital account will be $40,000 (the value of her contribution), while the capital accounts of *X* and *Y* will remain at $25,000. This is not right: After all, the three partners each have a one-third interest in the partnership.

The regulations provide that assets may be revalued and capital accounts may be restated to reflect fair market values upon the admission of a new partner to the partnership. Treas. Regs. §1.704-1(b)(2)(iv)(f). In other words, we increase *X*'s and *Y*'s capital accounts to their fair market value of $40,000 when we admit *Z*. However, we do *not* make any adjustment to their outside bases. The effect of the restatement, then, is to create a book/tax disparity for *X* and *Y* equal to the pre-admission appreciation in the partnership's assets. This book/tax disparity can be eliminated by allocating tax gain disproportionately to *X* and *Y*, or by allocating tax depreciation deductions disproportionately away from *X* and *Y* just as if the disparity were caused by the contribution of appreciated property. For example, the next $90,000 of partnership income could be allocated equally among *X*, *Y*, and *Z* for book purposes (i.e., $30,000 each) but divided between only *X* and *Y* for tax purposes (i.e., $45,000 each).

Note that we are *not* dealing with a true §704(c) problem because the book/tax disparity is not caused by the contribution of appreciated or loss property—the contribution of *any property* by the incoming partner causes the need to restate capital accounts. Thus, technically, we address the book/tax disparity with special allocations under §704(b) rather than with an allocation under §704(c)(1). Aside from this technicality, though, the issue is just the same as under §704(c), and the regulations under §704(b) incorporate the §704(c) analysis by reference. See Treas. Regs. §1.704-1(b)(4)(i). Allocations under Treas. Regs. §1.704-1(b)(4)(i) based on §704(c) principles are called "reverse §704(c) allocations." Treas. Regs. §1.704-3(e)(3)(i). See also Treas. Regs. §1.704-3(a)(6).

Note, though, that while application of §704(c)(1)(A) to any book/tax disparity in property contributed to the partnership is mandatory, restating partnership assets to fair market value upon the admission of a new partner (and then applying §704(c)(1)(A) principles to any resulting book/tax disparities) nominally is optional. See Treas. Regs. §1.704-(1)(b)(2)(iv)(f). Failure to revalue partnership assets in such circumstances (or to otherwise follow §704(c)(1)(A) principles,

7. See generally Howard E. Abrams, Reverse Allocations: More than Meets the Eye, 5 J. Passthrough Entities 35 (Sept.-Oct. 2002).

see Treas. Regs. §1.704-1(b)(5) (example 14(iv))), though, might be recharacterized as a gift or otherwise. See the final sentence of Treas. Regs. §1.704-1(b)(2)(iv)(f). It is unclear if a partnership may elect to revalue only some of its assets (presumably only those assets that have appreciated).[8]

If a partnership owns many assets having unrealized appreciation and loss, then properly tracking all reverse §704(c) allocations on an asset-by-asset basis can be expensive and time consuming. Nevertheless, the rules of §704(c) generally apply on an asset-by-asset basis. Treas. Regs. §1.704-3(a)(2). However, a "securities partnership" is permitted to aggregate unrealized gains and losses from "qualified financial assets" in making reverse §704(c) allocations. Treas. Regs. §1.704-3(e)(3). For the definition of a "securities partnership," see Treas. Regs. §1.704-3(e)(3)(iii). For the definition of "qualified financial assets," see Treas. Regs. §1.704-3(e)(3)(ii).

PROBLEMS

20-9. *A* and *B* are equal partners in the *AB* general partnership. Each partner has an outside basis and capital account of $40,000. The partnership owns Purpleacre with an adjusted basis of $80,000 and fair market value of $100,000. *C* is admitted to the partnership as a one-third partner, and *A* and *B* each reduce their interests from one-half to one-third. *C* contributes accounts receivable of $65,000 and accounts payable of $15,000 from her cash basis business in exchange for her partnership interest.

a. What are the outside bases and capital accounts once *C* is admitted?
b. How do the capital accounts and outside bases change if the partnership receives payment on the receivables, pays the payables, and sells Purpleacre for $160,000?

20-10. [*Highly computational*] Assume *X* and *Y* form the *XY* general partnership, with *X* contributing cash of $10,200 and *Y* contributing depreciable property with an adjusted basis of $6,000 and fair market value of $10,200. The property contributed by *Y* must be depreciated using the straight-line method and has five years remaining on its depreciation schedule; if newly placed in service, its basis would be recovered over seven years. Assume the partnership will allocate depreciation equally between the partners except as required by application of §704(c). The partnership elects to address the §704(c) book/tax disparity using the remedial allocation method. After one year, assume *Z* joins the partnership as a one-third partner, contributing cash of $9,615 for an interest worth the same amount. The partnership again elects to use the remedial allocation method.

E. FAILURE TO SATISFY THE ECONOMIC EFFECT TEST

What happens if some tax allocation fails to satisfy the general test as well as the alternate test for economic effect? As we have already seen, an allocation in the

8. For a discussion of some of the ambiguities and problems in the existing revaluation rules, see Howard E. Abrams, Partnership Book-Ups, 127 Tax Notes 435 (Apr. 26, 2010).

partnership agreement lacking substantial economic effect will be disregarded. However, Treas. Regs. §1.704-1(b)(2)(ii)(*i*) provides an "economic effect equivalence" test:

> Allocations made to a partner that do not otherwise have economic effect . . . shall nevertheless be deemed to have economic effect, provided that as of the end of each partnership taxable year a liquidation of the partnership at the end of such year or at the end of any future year would produce the same economic results to the partners as would occur if [the general or alternate tests] had been satisfied, regardless of the economic performance of the partnership.

As a first example, consider a two-person partnership in which it is agreed that all distributions, including liquidating distributions, will be made equally to each partner (who contributed equal value to the partnership). Regardless of any tax allocations in the partnership agreement (and subject to §704(c)), each partner's distributive share of all partnership tax items must be 50 percent. No other allocation would reflect the partners' economic sharing of benefits and burdens.

Consider next the *GL* partnership, in which *G* is the sole general partner, and *L* is the sole limited partner having no obligation to make further contributions to the partnership. Each partner contributes cash of $5,000, and the partnership agreement provides that capital accounts will be maintained properly for each partner and that liquidation proceeds will be distributed in accordance with final capital account balances. The general partner, *G*, has an unconditional obligation to restore any capital account deficit upon liquidation. *L* has no such obligation, but the partnership agreement provides that no allocation will be made to *L* that would drive *L*'s capital account below zero. Further, *L*'s capital account will be maintained in accordance with a look-ahead provision that reduces *L*'s account once it is reasonably foreseeable that some future event will result in a net capital account decrease to *L*.

This limited partnership agreement meets all requirements of the general test as to *G* and meets all the requirements of the alternate test as to *L except that* there is no qualified income offset provision in the partnership agreement. If in the first year there is a depreciation deduction of $1,000 allocated 50-50 under the partnership agreement, does this allocation satisfy the economic effect equivalence test as to *L*?

The allocation of $500 of loss to *L* reduces her capital account from its starting value of $5,000 down to $4,500. This allocation has economic effect in the sense that liquidation proceeds can be distributed in accordance with positive capital account balances in the current year. Indeed, so long as *L*'s capital account is not negative, economic effect is guaranteed.

However, we cannot say that a liquidation in any future year will have economic effect. Suppose, for example, that *L*'s capital account goes negative in some future year because of an unanticipated distribution of loan proceeds. Suppose further that there is sufficient income in that future year to bring *L*'s capital account up to zero but, under the partnership agreement, only half of the year's income is then allocated to *L*. Had there been a qualified income offset provision in the partnership agreement, *L* would have been allocated sufficient income to eliminate the capital account deficit. Without the qualified income offset provision, *L*'s capital account deficit is reduced but not fully eliminated. A liquidation at the end of this future year thus would leave *L* with a deficit capital account but no restoration obligation, and that situation would not have obtained had there been a qualified income offset provision in the partnership agreement.

To be sure, these hypothetical future facts are unlikely. Nonetheless, the economic equivalence test requires that "a liquidation of the partnership . . . at the end of any future year would produce the same economic results to the partners as would occur if [the general or alternate tests] had been satisfied, regardless of the economic performance of the partnership." Treas. Regs. §1.704-1(b)(2)(i). The "regardless of the economic performance" language presumably allows the Commissioner to test the partnership agreement annually against *any* hypothetical future events. If so, this agreement seems to fail not only the actual economic effect test but the economic equivalence test as well.

So what is each partner's distributive share of the depreciation? Under §704(b), distributive shares are determined "in accordance with the partner's interest in the partnership" if "the allocation to a partner under the agreement . . . does not have substantial economic effect." There once was a general presumption that all partners' interests in the partnership are equal (the pro rata presumption) in Treas. Regs. §1.704-1(b)(3)(i). Now, however, both the government and the taxpayer may look to the following nonexclusive factors that will be considered in determining a partner's "interest in the partnership," including (1) the partners' relative contributions to the partnership, (2) the interests of the partners in economic profits and losses, (3) the interests of the partners in cash flow and other nonliquidating distributions, and (4) the rights of the partners to distributions of capital upon liquidation. Treas. Regs. §1.704-1(b)(3)(ii). This regulation also states as a general principle that:

> a partner's interest in the partnership [means] the manner in which the partners have agreed to share the economic benefit or burden (if any) corresponding to the income, gain, loss, deduction, or credit . . . that is allocated. Treas. Regs. §1.704-1(b)(3)(i).

This statement in the regulations certainly invalidates, for example, an allocation of loss to a limited partner that drives the limited partner's capital account below the limited partner's obligation (if any) to make further contributions to the partnership. But what does this tell us with respect to the *GL* partnership lacking a qualified income offset provision? Because the allocation of depreciation to *L* reduces *L*'s capital account, *L* will bear the economic burden associated with the depreciation. Thus, the allocation to *L* should stand.

Does this mean that the qualified income offset requirement of the alternate test is unenforceable? Far from it. Should *L*'s capital account become negative because of some unforeseen distribution or similar event, an immediate liquidation would shift a loss to *G* although it had been allocated to *L*. Under the regulations, this possibility means that *L*'s share of all subsequent income must be increased to eliminate the problem as quickly as possible. Treas. Regs. §1.704-1(b)(3)(i). That is, the regulations impose a qualified income offset on the partnership even if the partnership agreement does not contain one.

NOTES

1. *Allocations lacking economic effect: in general.* Some tax items cannot be allocated in accordance with economic effect because the tax items do not have corresponding economic items. In such circumstances, the regulations provide rules that if followed will allow the allocations to be treated as if made in accordance with the partners' interest in the partnership. See, e.g., Treas. Regs. §1.704-1(b)(4)(ii) (tax credits). In other circumstances, the §704(b) rules governing tax substantial economic effect may not be controlling. See Treas. Regs. §1.704-1(b)(1)(iii). In still other circumstances, the §704(b) rules may fail to provide adequate guidance, in which case the partnership's allocations presumably should be consistent with the general principles of economic effect, see Treas. Regs. §1.704-1(b)(1)(i), or with the partners' interest in the partnership taking account of all facts and circumstances, see Treas. Regs. §1.704-1(b)(3). If, for example, the capital account maintenance rules fail to address a particular transaction, then the partnership must maintain the capital accounts so that they are "consistent with the underlying economic arrangement of the partners." Treas. Regs. §1.704-1(b)(2)(iv)(q).

2. *Tax credits.* The Code includes a number of tax credits, such as the general business credit in §38 and the low-income housing credit in §42. These tax credits often can be claimed by a partnership. How should tax credits be allocated under §704(b)? The regulations take the position that tax credits have no economic effect, and, therefore, allocations of tax credits can never satisfy the general or alternate tests for economic effect. Thus, the regulations conclude that tax credits must be allocated "in accordance with the partners' interests in the partnership as of the time the tax credit or credit recapture arises." Treas. Regs. §1.704-1(b)(4)(ii).

This conclusion is hardly inescapable. A tax credit is simply an alternative specification of tax-exempt income. See generally Yoseph Edrey & Howard Abrams, Equitable Implementation of Tax Expenditures, 9 Va. Tax Rev. 109 (1989). Accordingly, allocation of a tax credit might be seen as an allocation of exempt income coupled with a distribution of cash in the same amount. From this perspective, partners should have complete freedom to allocate tax credits. Nevertheless, the regulations adopt the opposite approach.

The regulations further provide that tax credits are not run through the partners' capital accounts. Treas. Regs. §1.704-1(b)(4)(ii). Accordingly, such allocations cannot have "economic effect." They further provide that:

> if a partnership expenditure (whether or not deductible) that gives rise to a tax credit in a partnership taxable year also gives rise to valid allocations of partnership loss or deduction (or other downward capital account adjustments) for such year, then the partners' interests in the partnership with respect to such credit (or the cost giving rise thereto) shall be in the same proportion as such partners' respective distributive shares of such loss or deduction (and adjustments). . . . Identical principles shall apply in determining the partners' interests in the partnership with respect to tax credits that arise from receipts of the partnership (whether or not taxable).

This rule thus requires, for example, that the research tax credit should be allocated consistently with the underlying research expenditures. See Treas. Regs. §1.41-7(a)(3)(i).

There is a special rule applicable to allocations of foreign tax credits arising under §901. Under this rule, the foreign tax credit must be allocated in proportion to the allocation of the partnership's net income generating the foreign tax liability rather than in proportion to the allocation of the tax liability itself. See Treas. Regs. §1.704-1T(b)(4)(xi). This requires that the allocation of the net income itself be valid under the "substantial economic effect" rules. *Id.* See also Treas. Regs. §1.704-1T(b)(5) (examples 25-28).

3. *Cumulative preferred returns.* Consider the following economic arrangement between partners *X* and *Y*. Each partner will contribute $100,000 to the *XY* partnership. *X* will be entitled to a cumulative preferred allocation equal to 10 percent of *X*'s contributed capital (that is, $10,000) annually, and the remainder of the partner's net income will be allocated 40 percent to *X* and 60 percent to *Y*. For example, if the partnership earns $25,000 each year, then $10,000 plus 40 percent of $15,000 (or $16,000 total) is allocated to *X* each year. If the partnership earns $40,000 each year, then *X*'s annual allocation will equal $10,000 plus 40 percent of $30,000 (or $22,000 total). The preferred return is cumulative so that if the partnership liquidates after, say, eight years, *X* should receive $80,000 plus 40 percent of the remainder of the partnership's net income. (The allocation of partnership losses is irrelevant for this discussion.)

What are the capital accounts after the second year if the partnership earns $15,000 in its first year and $5,000 in its second year? If the partnership sells its assets without realization of gain or loss and liquidates, how much cash should be distributed to each partner?

In the first year, the allocation should be $12,000 to *X* and $3,000 to *Y* to account for the preferential allocation and then for the 40/60 split. In the second year, the entire net profit of $5,000 must be allocated to *X*, and even so there is insufficient income to cover the preference. Accordingly, at the end of the second year the capital accounts equal $117,000 for *X* and $103,000 for *Y*. If the partnership now liquidates in accordance with capital account balances, its cash of $220,000 is distributed $117,000 to *X* and $103,000 to *Y*.

But that sharing does not reflect the agreement made by the partners: *X*'s preferential allocation was supposed to be a cumulative $10,000 per year. Here, the partnership earned exactly $20,000 in its two years of existence, and that means all of the profits should accrue to *X*. Giving $17,000 of the $20,000 profit to *X* is not what the partners agreed.

There is no way to solve this problem without reallocating year 1 income at the end of year 2 when the problem of too little net profit arises. But there is no direct authority for such a reallocation. If the partnership in fact sells its assets and distributes cash to the partners in liquidation of the venture at the conclusion of year 2, the problem will be solved by the recognition of gain (to *X*) and of loss (to *Y*) if the cash is distributed in accordance with their economic agreement. Because this means that liquidation proceeds in year 2 might not be distributed in accordance with final capital account balances, it jeopardizes the allocations made in year 1. But without knowing in advance what will happen in year 2, there simply is no way to fix the problem in year 1. (Consider the possibility that $30,000 is earned in year 1 and then nothing in years 2 and 3. Or $40,000 is earned in year 1 and nothing in years 2, 3, and 4. Must all net income be allocated to *X* in every year to cover future cumulative preference rights? If so, what happens when the partnership liquidates without any need to reallocate prior income?)

F. ALLOCATIONS OF DEDUCTIONS ATTRIBUTABLE TO NONRECOURSE DEBT

Ensuring that partnership allocations have economic effect requires no more than satisfying the general or alternate test of economic effect under the §704(b) regulations. See Treas. Regs. §1.704-1(b)(2)(ii). However, if the partnership has incurred any nonrecourse debt, then special rules under Treas. Regs. §1.704-2 can apply. In this section, we will examine those special rules to determine when they apply and how they apply. But before looking at these rules, it is helpful to master a few definitions. These definitions as well as the rules themselves can be found in Treas. Regs. §1.704-2.

1. *Definitions*

a. Nonrecourse Liability

A "nonrecourse" liability for purposes of §704(b) takes its meaning from two other regulations, Treas. Regs. §1.752-1(a)(2) and Treas. Regs. §1.752-7. See Treas. Regs. §1.704-2(b)(3). Under Treas. Regs. §1.752-1(a)(2), a nonrecourse liability is a partnership liability as to which no partner bears ultimate responsibility for repayment to any extent. In general, it is the partnership as an entity that is expected to repay partnership loans, with the funds coming from partnership activities or from capital contributions. But if the partnership is unable to make its loan payments as they come due, the lender may seek payment from the partners or may force a sale of partnership assets to satisfy the debt. Absent an agreement to the contrary, general partners bear ultimate responsibility for payment of all partnership obligations. That is, most partnership loans are recourse loans if the partnership has one or more general partners. But if the lender is willing, the loan agreement may provide that the lender will not seek repayment from any partner, and it is this contractual provision in a loan agreement that makes the loan nonrecourse. Equivalently, the entity (such as a limited liability company) might not have any partners generally liable for the entity's debts, making all of the entity's debts nonrecourse in this sense absent some special contractual agreement to the contrary.

Depending on the terms of the loan agreement, a lender may or may not have the right to proceed against all of the partnership's assets for repayment of the loan. If the lender has the right to go after all partnership assets without limitation, we sometimes say that the loan is "recourse as against the partnership." But for purposes of §704(b) and the regulations thereunder, the extent of the lender's rights against partnership assets is irrelevant. If the lender has rights against one or more partners, the loan is recourse. Treas. Regs. §1.752-1(a)(1). If the lender has rights only against partnership assets, the loan is nonrecourse. Thus, a partnership loan is a "nonrecourse liability" if and only if no partner bears ultimate responsibility for repayment, Treas. Regs. §1.752-1(a)(2), and the lender's rights against partnership assets are irrelevant.

b. Minimum Gain

Depreciation deductions reflect the possibility that property will waste in value over time, and the requirement of economic effect means that if a partner is allocated a share of a partnership's book depreciation, that partner must also bear the associated economic risk that the property will decline in value. But if the property is encumbered by a nonrecourse liability and the book value of the property is equal to or less than the amount of the nonrecourse debt, risk of diminution in value of the property is borne by the lender and not by any partner regardless of how the book depreciation deductions are allocated. Accordingly, allocation of depreciation deductions in such circumstances can never have economic effect, and so the regulations apply a different set of rules.

Recall that the Supreme Court in Commissioner v. Tufts, 461 U.S. 300 (1983), held that the amount realized from disposition of property includes the amount of any outstanding nonrecourse debt encumbering the property. Thus, even if the mortgage is foreclosed and the owner of the property receives nothing, the amount realized will be greater than zero because of the nonrecourse debt. Indeed, if the owner's adjusted basis is less than the outstanding nonrecourse debt, disposition of the property (by foreclosure or otherwise) will produce gain at least equal to the excess of the nonrecourse debt over the property's adjusted basis.

Because we are defining minimum gain for use in the definition of economic effect, and because economic effect is defined by reference to a capital account analysis, the regulations define minimum gain by reference to asset *book value* rather than by reference to adjusted basis. Treas. Regs. §1.704-2(d)(3). Accordingly, for any piece of partnership property encumbered by nonrecourse debt, the term "minimum gain" means the excess of the nonrecourse debt over the property's book value: disposition of the property will produce book gain at least equal to the "minimum gain" as defined in this way.

Total partnership minimum gain equals the aggregate of the minimum gain from all the partnership's property. Treas. Regs. §1.704-2(d)(1). Note that there is no such thing as negative gain or minimum loss: If the partnership's book value in a piece of property exceeds the outstanding nonrecourse encumbrance, then there simply is no minimum gain with respect to that property. In addition, minimum gain is computed property by property: There is no offset of gain by built-in loss unless debts are cross-collateralized. *Id.*; see also Treas. Regs. §1.704-2(d)(2).

Consider the following example: *X* and *Y* form the *XY* general partnership by contributing $50 apiece. The partnership acquires depreciable property for $1,000, paying $100 down and signing a nonrecourse note for the remaining $900, pledging the depreciable property as security for the debt. Assume that the property generates a depreciation deduction of $100 per year, and assume that the partnership's annual income is just sufficient to pay its annual expenses (including interest on its debt). If the partnership is not required to make any principal payments on the debt in the early years, then the partnership will have no cash flow and will report a taxable loss of $100 each year.

There is no minimum gain at the beginning of the first year because the partnership has a book value (and adjusted basis) of $1,000 in the property while the outstanding debt is only $900. At the end of the first year, there is still no minimum gain because the nonrecourse debt does not *exceed* the book value of the property: They are equal (and $900). But one year later, minimum gain appears because depreciation lowers the book value to $800 while the outstanding nonrecourse debt remains at $900. Accordingly, there is $100 of partnership minimum gain after the partnership's second year.

As this example demonstrates, partnership minimum gain can increase (and decrease) over time. As the partnership incurs nonrecourse debt, minimum gain will go up. Similarly, as the partnership repays its nonrecourse obligations, partnership minimum gain will go down. Increases in the partnership's book value of its assets (for example, if capital improvements are made) will decrease minimum gain while decreases in book value (for example, caused by depreciation allowed or allowable) will result in an increase in partnership minimum gain. The regulations require that each partnership compute its net increase or decrease in partnership minimum gain each year. Treas. Regs. §1.704-2(b)(4).

c. Nonrecourse Deductions

Whenever partnership minimum gain increases, we must identify those deductions causing the increase. Invariably, they will be depreciation deductions, although the regulations provide a set of rules for identifying the nonrecourse deductions when there is insufficient depreciation to cover the increase in minimum gain. See Treas. Regs. §1.704-2(c). These deductions, called "nonrecourse deductions" in the regulations, equal the increase (if any) in the partnership's minimum gain. See Treas. Regs. §1.704-2(c). All other deductions (including any additional depreciation deductions) are *not* "nonrecourse deductions." Thus, in the example above the depreciation deductions in year 2 (but not those in year 1) are nonrecourse deductions. The definition of nonrecourse deductions is important because it is these and only these deductions that are subject to the special rules of Treas. Regs. §1.704-2. Allocations of all other deductions and other partnership tax items are subject to the substantial economic effect rules we already have considered.

The key to understanding the rules governing the allocation of nonrecourse deductions lies in the Supreme Court's decision in Commissioner v. Tufts, 61 U.S. 300 (1983). Under *Tufts,* the amount realized from the disposition of property includes the amount of nonrecourse debt encumbering the property. And now you know why the nonrecourse regulations under §704(b) define "minimum gain" to mean the excess of encumbering debt over the encumbered property's book value: the "minimum gain" with respect to any piece of property is the book gain that would be recognized under *Tufts* if the property were immediately sold for no consideration other than satisfaction of the nonrecourse debt.

As explained above, nonrecourse deductions give rise to partnership minimum gain. Minimum gain gives rise to recognition of income upon disposition of the property. Even though nonrecourse deductions have no associated partnership *economic* burden (because it is the lender who bears risk of diminution in value of the property associated with nonrecourse deductions), there is a *tax* burden associated with nonrecourse deductions: minimum gain. That is, whenever nonrecourse deductions are claimed, minimum gain is created. The existence of minimum gain means that there will be income (but not necessarily any cash) upon disposition of the property. Recognition of, and paying tax on, the eventual recognition of minimum gain is the tax burden associated with nonrecourse deductions, and the regulations require that the partners who enjoy the nonrecourse deductions must also suffer the tax burden of the recognition of minimum gain. There is more to the nonrecourse regulations, but this aspect is the conceptual key.

It is helpful to have a term for partnership deductions *other than* nonrecourse deductions. One might call them "recourse" deductions but that is misleading because it suggests that such deductions only arise in connection with partnership borrowing on a recourse basis: in fact, of course, such deductions can arise in the absence of any partnership borrowing. The term "nonnonrecourse" deductions is possible but it seems a bit unwieldy. We will use the term "economic" deductions for all deductions other than nonrecourse deductions to remind ourselves that such deductions correspond with economic benefits and burdens and are subject to the economic effect tests.

2. *General Principles*

The touchstone of economic effect under the §704(b) regulations is that tax benefits and burdens must track economic benefits and burdens. Treas. Regs. §1.704-1(b)(2)(ii)(a). In the case of allocations of income, this requires that the partner who is allocated a dollar of income must eventually receive an equivalent dollar in distributions. And in the case of allocations of deductions, the partner who is allocated a dollar of loss must bear the economic risk of loss associated with that allocation. Properly maintaining partnership capital accounts and distributing liquidation proceeds in accordance with final capital account balances ensures that partnership allocations have economic effect within the meaning of these regulations. See generally Treas. Regs. §1.704-1(b)(2)(ii)(b).

The economic burden associated with depreciation deductions is risk of diminution in value of the depreciable asset. For example, suppose a partnership purchases depreciable equipment for $1,000. As depreciation is claimed by the partnership and allocated among the partners, asset book value goes down. If the asset actually declines in value as it was depreciated, there will be an economic loss (but not a book loss) realized when the property is sold. That economic loss has already been allocated among the partners in the form of the depreciation deductions: as each partner claimed her distributive share of depreciation, her capital account decreased. If the property is eventually sold for its book value (that is, if its economic value decreases as the depreciation is claimed), there will be no book gain or loss and so the sale will not affect partnership capital accounts. Thus, those partners who were allocated large percentages of the depreciation will have had their capital accounts significantly lowered, and they will receive pro tanto less at liquidation.

But what if the purchase was funded with nonrecourse debt? As the property declines in value, it is the lender and not the partnership that faces an economic loss: After all, the partnership can simply walk away from the investment. When property is secured by nonrecourse debt, the partnership's economic loss on the property is limited to the value of the property above the amount of the debt— that is, to the partnership's equity in the property. Once that equity is consumed (i.e., once the value of the property drops below the nonrecourse encumbrance), it is the lender who bears the risk of diminution of the property.

If it is the lender who bears the economic risk of diminution in value once the partnership's equity is gone, there is no economic risk borne by the partnership connected with depreciation deductions reducing adjusted basis below the amount of a nonrecourse encumbrance. Stated differently, allocations of depreciation deductions reducing book value below the amount of the nonrecourse encumbrance cannot have economic effect because there is no economic risk of loss (borne by the partnership) associated with such deductions. Treas. Regs. §1.704-2(b)(1).

Depreciation deductions reducing book value below the amount of a nonrecourse encumbrance are precisely the "nonrecourse deductions" defined above. There are special rules for the allocation of nonrecourse deductions because the standard rules cannot apply: allocations of nonrecourse deductions never have substantial economic effect because they never have economic effect at all. However, although there is no economic burden associated with nonrecourse deductions, there *is* a tax burden, and the nonrecourse rules require that the benefits of nonrecourse deductions be enjoyed by those partners who will also bear the associated tax burden.

What is this tax burden? Nonrecourse deductions by definition increase partnership minimum gain. Treas. Regs. §1.704-2(c). That means that these deductions will generate partnership book income upon disposition of the property. Treas. Regs. §1.704-2(b)(2). As these nonrecourse deductions are allocated among the partners, each partner's share of the partner's minimum gain increase pro tanto. Treas. Regs. §1.704-2(g)(1)(i). And as the partnership's minimum gain decreases (by disposition of the property, partial or full repayment of the nonrecourse loan, or otherwise), the partners must be allocated partnership income in proportion to their shares of the minimum gain. Treas. Regs. §1.704-2(b)(2). Such a "minimum gain chargeback" provision is required by the nonrecourse regulations. See Treas. Regs. §1.704-2(f). As you would expect, a minimum gain chargeback allocation is not required as to a partner who contributes capital to the partnership which is then used to pay down the nonrecourse debt, Treas. Regs. §1.704-2(f)(3), or if the partner becomes personally liable for some or all of the debt, Treas. Regs. §1.704-2(f)(2).

Technically, the nonrecourse regulations impose a three-part requirement on allocations of nonrecourse deductions. Treas. Regs. §1.704-2(e). First, the partnership agreement must satisfy the general or alternate economic effect test with respect to its allocations of tax items *other than* nonrecourse deductions. Treas. Regs. §1.704-2(e)(1). Second, allocations of nonrecourse deductions must be made "in a manner that is reasonably consistent with allocations that have substantial economic effect of some other significant partnership item attributable to the property securing the nonrecourse liabilities." Treas. Regs. §1.704-2(e)(2). Third, the partnership agreement must contain a "minimum gain chargeback provision." Treas. Regs. §1.704-2(e)(3).[9]

The apparent ambiguity of the "reasonably consistent" language is removed by one of the examples in the nonrecourse regulations. See Treas. Regs. §1.704-2(m)

9. If one partnership (the "upper tier" partnership) owns an interest in a second partnership (the "lower tier" partnership), then nonrecourse indebtedness of the lower tier partnership will create partnership minimum gain for the upper tier partnership and its partners. Treas. Regs. §1.704-2(k).

(example 1(ii)). Suppose *P* and *Q* form the *PQ* partnership to acquire and develop certain depreciable real estate. Suppose further that all income and loss will be allocated 90 percent to *P* and 10 percent to *Q* for the first five years, and all tax items will be allocated equally thereafter. The nonrecourse regulations provide that allocating 90 percent of the nonrecourse deductions to *P* satisfies the "reasonably consistent" requirement as does an allocation of 50 percent. Indeed, the regulations further provide that any percentage between 90 percent and 50 percent to *P* is satisfactory.

From this example, we see that a partnership's ability to allocate nonrecourse deductions can be quite broad. The nonrecourse deductions that can be allocated to any one partner can be as small as that partner's lowest share of economic deductions, and they can be as large as that partner's greatest share of economic deductions. Any share within this range should qualify as "reasonably consistent" with the allocation of some substantial tax item from the property.

The partnership agreement must also include a "minimum gain chargeback" provision. Treas. Regs. §1.704-2(e)(3). Such a provision must provide that "[i]f there is a net decrease in partnership minimum gain for a partnership taxable year . . . each partner must be allocated items of partnership income and gain for that year equal to that partner's share of the net decrease in partnership minimum gain." Treas. Regs. §1.704-2(f)(1). Upon disposition of the property, this provision will trigger recognition of income to each partner who was allocated nonrecourse deductions in an amount precisely equal to those deductions. Any additional gain can then be allocated among the partners however they wish, subject only to the familiar tests of substantial economic effect. See generally Treas. Regs. §1.704-1(b)(2)(ii).

Consider the following example: *G* and *L* form the *GL* limited partnership, with *G* (the general partner) contributing cash of $10,000 and *L* (the limited partner) contributing cash of $40,000. The *GL* partnership agreement specifically provides that *L* cannot be required to contribute additional funds to the enterprise.

On January 1, 2007, the partnership acquires an apartment building for $1,000,000, paying cash of $50,000 and signing a nonrecourse note for the remaining $950,000. Assume that the partnership (1) makes an interest payment of 10 percent of the outstanding loan balance each December 31, (2) pays deductible expenses of $15,000 each December 31, (3) makes a principal payment of $20,000 each January 1 (i.e., beginning the second year), and (4) receives rents each December 31 equal to its cash flow (that is, equal to its interest, expense, and principal payments). Assume also that the partnership is entitled to a depreciation deduction of $40,000 per year. Finally, assume that the *GL* partnership agreement provides that depreciation deductions will be allocated 90 percent to *L* and 10 percent to *G*, while all other items of income and deduction will be allocated 80 percent to *L* and 20 percent to *G*.

For 2007, these assumptions tell us that the partnership makes an interest payment of $95,000 and pays expenses of $15,000 out of its rent receipts of $110,000. Despite having a zero cash flow, the partnership shows a taxable loss of $40,000 for the year. This loss arises as follows: income equals $110,000 while deductions equal $95,000 [interest] + $15,000 [expenses] + $40,000 [depreciation], for $150,000 total deductions. Under the terms of the partnership agreement, these items of income and deduction affect the capital accounts as follows:

G	*L*	
$10,000	$40,000	Initial balance
22,000	88,000	Rent receipts
(19,000)	(76,000)	Interest
(3,000)	(12,000)	Expenses
(4,000)	(36,000)	Depreciation
$ 6,000	$ 4,000	Totals

As of the end of 2007, the partnership has an adjusted basis and book value in its apartment building of $960,000, and the property is subject to a nonrecourse debt of $950,000. Because this book value exceeds the amount of the outstanding debt, there is no partnership minimum gain. Accordingly, there are no nonrecourse deductions in 2007, so the validity of the partnership's allocations must be tested under the familiar general and alternate tests of economic effect. Assuming the partnership agreement provides that liquidating distributions will be made in accordance with ending capital account balances, these allocations should have economic effect. Note, though, that because *L* is a limited partner without any obligation to contribute additional funds to the partnership, the alternate test for economic effect will not permit *L*'s capital account to become negative.

Now consider 2008. Under our assumptions, *GL* makes its first principal payment of $20,000. That payment reduces the partnership's year-end interest payment to $93,000. Assuming the partnership's other expenses remain at $15,000, our assumption of zero cash flow means that the partnership receives rental income of $128,000. Putting these figures into the partnership's capital accounts produces:

G	*L*	
$ 6,000	$ 4,000	Initial balance
25,600	102,400	Rent receipts
(18,600)	(74,400)	Interest
(3,000)	(12,000)	Expenses
(4,000)	(36,000)	Depreciation
$ 6,000	($ 16,000)	Totals

At the close of 2008, the partnership's adjusted basis and book value in its property equals $920,000 while the amount of the outstanding debt is now $930,000. Accordingly, there is $10,000 of partnership minimum gain, and that means there is $10,000 of nonrecourse deductions for the current year. Under the nonrecourse regulations, the nonrecourse deductions for the current year are assumed to consist of $10,000 of the depreciation. The remaining $138,000 of deductions ($93,000 of interest, $15,000 of expenses, and the remaining $30,000 of depreciation) are not nonrecourse deductions and so must be tested by the usual economic effect tests.

To determine whether the partnership's allocations of the economic deductions have economic effect, we recompute the partner's capital accounts with the nonrecourse deductions removed. Eliminating $10,000 of the depreciation produces:

G	L	
$ 6,000	$ 4,000	Initial balance
25,600	102,400	Rent receipts
(18,600)	(74,400)	Interest
(3,000)	(12,000)	Expenses
(3,000)	(27,000)	Economic depreciation
$ 7,000	($ 7,000)	Totals

These ending capital account balances are inconsistent with the requirement of economic effect because *L*'s capital account is negative, and *L* has no unconditional obligation to restore a capital account deficit upon liquidation of her partnership interest. Accordingly, we must reallocate $7,000 of the deductions for the current year to *G* and away from *L*. Note that this reallocation has nothing to do with the partnership's nonrecourse deductions for the current year—we will turn to those in a moment.

Allocating an additional $7,000 of deductions to *G* produces the following capital accounts:

G	L	
$ 6,000	$ 4,000	Initial balance
25,600	102,400	Rent receipts
(18,600)	(74,400)	Interest
(3,000)	(12,000)	Expenses
(10,000)	(20,000)	Reallocated depreciation
$ 0	$ 0	Totals

These capital accounts ensure economic effect by keeping the limited partner's capital account nonnegative. Once we have established that the partnership's allocation of "economic" deductions satisfies the economic effect test, we determine whether the partnership's allocation of its nonrecourse deductions satisfies the nonrecourse regulations. There are $10,000 of nonrecourse deductions for the current year, and the partnership agreement allocates this amount $9,000 to *L* and $1,000 to *G*. Accordingly, the capital accounts become:

G	L	
$ 0	$ 0	Initial balance
(1,000)	(9,000)	Nonrecourse depreciation
($1,000)	($9,000)	Totals

It might seem that these ending capital account balances are invalid because *L*'s capital account is negative. However, the limitation that a partner's capital account cannot be more negative than the amount the partner can be required to contribute to the partnership is part of the economic effect requirement, while what causes *L*'s capital account to go negative here is the allocation of nonrecourse deductions. The nonrecourse regulations specifically provide that a limited partner's capital account may go negative not only by the maximum amount the partner can be forced to contribute to the partnership (if any) but also by the amount of the partner's share of the partnership's nonrecourse deductions. Treas. Regs. §1.704-2(g)(1). Here, *L*'s share of the partnership's nonrecourse deductions is $9,000, so *L*'s capital account deficit is allowed.

Recall the reason for the prohibition in the alternate test for economic effect on a limited partner's capital account becoming negative: If the partnership liquidates, each partner is supposed to receive her ending capital account balance or restore her ending capital account deficit. Treas. Regs. §1.704-1(b)(2)(ii)(b)(2). Because *L* cannot be required to restore a capital account deficit, the alternate test for economic effect seeks to avoid the creation of a deficit in the first place. See the "look ahead" requirement in Treas. Regs. §1.704-1(b)(2)(ii)(d)(4).

Here, *L*'s capital account deficit *necessarily* is temporary because *L*'s share of the partnership's minimum gain is $9,000. Therefore, upon disposition of the property, *L*'s capital account deficit will be eliminated by operation of the minimum gain chargeback. The nonrecourse regulations permit a limited partner to have a negative capital account balance up to, and only up to, the amount of the limited partner's share of minimum gain because a deficit of that amount is necessarily temporary. Treas. Regs. §1.704-2(g)(1).

It is worth saying this one more time. *A partner's capital account may go negative to the extent of the sum of (1) the maximum amount the partner can be required to contribute to the partnership to cover a capital account deficit upon liquidation of her partnership interest plus (2) the partner's share of the partnership's minimum gain.* A partner's share of partnership minimum gain equals the net amount of partnership nonrecourse deductions allocated to the partner.

Continue this example for one more year (that is, through 2009). Once again, the partnership makes a principal payment of $20,000, reducing the partnership's year-end interest payment to $91,000. With assumed expenses of $15,000 and depreciation of $40,000, our assumption of zero cash flow means that the partnership receives rental income of $126,000. In addition, the principal payment reduces the outstanding debt to $910,000, and the depreciation deduction reduces the partnership's book value and adjusted basis in its property down to $880,000. Accordingly, the partnership's minimum gain equals $30,000, an increase of $20,000 over the prior year.

We first check the validity of the partnership's allocations of the economic deductions by subtracting out the current year's nonrecourse deductions and then checking the partnership capital accounts. This produces:

G	*L*	
($ 1,000)	($ 9,000)	Initial balance
25,200	100,800	Rent receipts
(18,200)	(72,800)	Interest
(3,000)	(12,000)	Expenses
(2,000)	(18,000)	Depreciation
$ 1,000	($ 11,000)	Totals

Once again the partnership's allocation of its "economic" deductions fails to satisfy the economic effect test because *L*'s ending capital account is too negative. *L* has no obligation to contribute additional funds, and *L*'s share of the partnership's minimum gain (before taking into account the current year's increase) is $9,000.

Accordingly, *L*'s capital account is $2,000 below its minimum level so that $2,000 of the partnership's "economic" deductions must be reallocated to *G*. We thus replace the capital account analysis above with the following:

G	*L*	
($ 1,000)	($ 9,000)	Initial balance
25,200	100,800	Rent receipts
(18,200)	(72,800)	Interest
(3,000)	(12,000)	Expenses
(4,000)	(16,000)	Depreciation
($ 1,000)	($ 9,000)	Totals

We now put the current year's nonrecourse deductions into the partnership's capital accounts. The partnership agreement allocated depreciation 10 percent to *G* and 90 percent to *L*, so that the $20,000 of current nonrecourse deductions are allocated $2,000 to *G* and $18,000 to *L*. Putting these allocations into the capital accounts yields the following ending values:

G	*L*	
($1,000)	($ 9,000)	Initial balance
(2,000)	(18,000)	Nonrecourse depreciation
($3,000)	($27,000)	Totals

Total partnership minimum gain is $30,000, and of that amount, $27,000 is properly allocable to *L* ($9,000 from 2008 and $18,000 from 2009). Accordingly, if the partnership were to sell or otherwise dispose of the property immediately, the first $30,000 of gain would be allocated $3,000 to *G* and $27,000 to *L* under the partnership's minimum gain chargeback provision.

3. *Distribution of Refinancing Proceeds*

A partner's share of partnership minimum gain includes the amount of nonrecourse deductions that have been allocated to her. Treas. Regs. §1.704-2(g)(1). Allocating minimum gain in this way makes sense when the minimum gain arises from partnership deductions, usually depreciation. Recall that partnership minimum gain is the excess of the partnership's nonrecourse debts over the book value of the property securing those debts. Treas. Regs. §1.704-2(d)(1). In any one year, partnership minimum gain can increase in either of two ways. First, the partnership's book value of its assets may decline because of allowable depreciation deductions. Second, the debt may increase by reason of additional borrowing. If the partnership borrows on a nonrecourse basis and does not invest the proceeds in the security, the partnership's nonrecourse liabilities will increase without a concomitant increase in book value. Once again, partnership minimum gain will increase.

For example, suppose the *XY* partnership owns property with book value and adjusted basis of $100,000 and fair market value of $250,000. If the partnership borrows $120,000 against its property, the borrowing will create $20,000 of partnership minimum gain. If $20,000 of the loan proceeds is distributed to partner *X*, *X*'s capital account will decrease.

If the lender immediately forecloses on the partnership's property, there will be a taxable gain of $20,000 under the *Tufts* case. How should this taxable gain be allocated? The nonrecourse borrowing and foreclosure has the same effect as a sale of the property for $120,000, and that is precisely how the transaction is taxed. Who enjoyed the sale gain? *X* did when she was distributed the debt proceeds in excess of the partnership's adjusted basis. Accordingly, *X* should be allocated the gain from the foreclosure.

What this example demonstrates is that distribution of nonrecourse proceeds which causes an increase in partnership minimum gain should bring with it a dollar-for-dollar allocation of partnership minimum gain. Of course, if the partnership has cash in the bank when it incurs the nonrecourse debt, it will be impossible to determine the extent to which the subsequent distribution consists of nonrecourse proceeds as opposed to the bank funds. Under the nonrecourse regulations, "[a] partnership may use any reasonable method to determine whether a distribution by the partnership to one or more partners is allocable to proceeds of a nonrecourse liability." Treas. Regs. §1.704-2(h)(2).

4. *Book/Tax Disparities*

Recall that there can be a disparity between the adjusted basis of partnership property and its book value. Such a disparity will arise when property is contributed to the partnership having unrealized gain or loss. In addition, revaluations of partnership property—triggered, for example, by the admission of a partner or by the withdrawal of a partner—also can cause such book/tax disparities. The nonrecourse regulations provide for the computation of minimum gain in such circumstances by comparing the amount of the outstanding nonrecourse debt with the *book* value of the encumbered property. Because depreciation deductions attributable to partnership property having a book value different from its adjusted basis must be allocated in such a way as to take account of the property's book/tax disparity, adding nonrecourse debt to the partnership introduces a second layer of complexity beyond the scope of this discussion. The nonrecourse regulations provide an example of this difficult issue. See Treas. Regs. §1.704-2(m) (example 3). In addition, a special rule applies in the year partnership property is revalued to ensure that the revaluation does not trigger any immediate reallocation of income under the partnership's minimum gain chargeback provision. See Treas. Regs. §1.704-2(d)(4).

5. *Partner Nonrecourse Debt*

Recall that the regulations under §704 define a "nonrecourse" debt by reference to the definition in the §752 regulations. See Treas. Regs. §1.704-2(b)(3), §1.752-1(a)(2), and §1.752-7. Under the §752 regulations, there are only two types of partnership obligations, recourse and nonrecourse. But under the §704(b) regulations there is a third type of partnership obligation, a "partner nonrecourse" debt. Such an obligation is nonrecourse against the partnership (that is, the lender has rights against only specific partnership assets), but one or more partners (or persons related to a partner) is liable for repayment by means of a guarantee or otherwise. Such obligations are subject to a special set of rules. Treas. Regs. §1.704-2(j).

These rules provide that nonrecourse deductions arising from a partner nonrecourse liability must be allocated to the partner (or partners) who bear the risk of economic loss. Treas. Regs. §1.704-2(i)(1). Similarly, these rules provide that a net decrease in partner nonrecourse minimum gain must trigger a minimum gain chargeback provision allocating partnership income to the partner (or partners) having been allocated partner nonrecourse liability deductions. Treas. Regs. §1.704-2(i)(4). Finally, a distribution of the proceeds allocable to a partner nonrecourse liability must be treated in a manner consistent with the general rules governing the distribution of nonrecourse financing proceeds. See Treas. Regs. §1.704-2(i)(6).

PROBLEM

20-11. *L* and *G* form the *LG* limited partnership, with limited partner *L* contributing cash of $90,000 and general partner *G* contributing cash of $10,000. The partnership constructs an apartment building for $1,500,000, using its cash of $100,000 as well as $1,400,000 of the proceeds of a $1,500,000 nonrecourse loan. Under the terms of the partnership agreement, all losses and the first $200,000 of net profit will be allocated 90 percent to *L* and 10 percent to *G*. Net profits in excess of $200,000 will be allocated 50 percent to each partner. Assume (1) the apartments generate rents of $150,000 per year; (2) the property generates a depreciation deduction of $90,000 each year; and (3) the partnership makes an interest payment of $140,000 each year. Because the construction costs did not fully consume the loan, the partnership distributes $90,000 to *L* and $10,000 to *G* during its second year. After four years, *LG* sells the property for $2,000,000, pays off the outstanding loan of $1,500,000, and distributes its remaining cash to the partners in liquidation of their interests. Discuss the tax consequences for each of the years.

G. SUBSTANTIALITY UNDER §704(b)

Under §704(b), distributive shares are determined by the partnership agreement unless those shares lack "substantial economic effect." So far, we have looked only at the definition of "economic effect" under the regulations. However, substantial economic effect is a two-part test: "First, the allocation must have economic effect. . . . Second, the economic effect of the allocation must be substantial. . . ." Treas. Regs. §1.704-1(b)(2)(i). The regulations further provide that an allocation is substantial if

> there is a reasonable possibility that the allocation (or allocations) will affect substantially the dollar amounts to be received by the partners from the partnership, independent of tax consequences. Notwithstanding the preceding sentence, the economic effect of an allocation (or allocations) is not substantial if, at the time the allocation becomes part of the partnership agreement, (1) the after-tax economic consequences

> of at least one partner may, in present value terms, be enhanced compared to such consequences if the allocation (or allocations) were not contained in the partnership agreement, and (2) there is a strong likelihood that the after-tax economic consequences of no partner will, in present value terms, be substantially diminished compared to such consequences if the allocation (or allocations) was not contained in the partnership agreement.

Treas. Regs. §1.704-1(b)(2)(iii)(a).

Consider the following example: *P* and *Q* form the *PQ* general partnership by contributing $10,000 each, and they agree to allocate all tax items 50-50. The partnership invests in both taxable and tax-free securities. In a year in which *P* is in a low tax bracket and *Q* is in a high tax bracket, the partners amend the partnership agreement as follows:

Tax-exempt income is allocated to *Q* in an amount equal to the lesser of the partnership's tax-exempt income for the year and the partnership's taxable income for the year. Taxable income is allocated to *P* in an amount equal to the lesser of the partnership's tax-exempt income for the year and the partnership's taxable income for the year. Any remaining income (tax-exempt or taxable) not already allocated is divided equally between the partners.

Suppose the partnership has tax-exempt income of $10,000 and taxable income of $12,000. Under the partnership agreement, all $10,000 of the tax-exempt income is allocated to *Q* (the high-bracket partner), and an equal amount ($10,000) of taxable income is allocated to *P* (the low-bracket partner). The remaining $2,000 of taxable income is divided between the partners, so that each partner ends up with an allocation of $11,000 overall. The effect of the special agreements, in other words, is to continue the prior 50-50 in dollar terms but to allocate income by character to minimize the partners' collective tax liability.

Although these special allocations have economic effect (assuming capital accounts are maintained properly and liquidation proceeds will be distributed in accordance with final capital account balances), they will not be upheld because that economic effect is *insubstantial.* That is, the special allocations differ from the partners' general interests in the partnership only in a tax sense. Because the effect of the allocation is to allocate to each partner the same number of dollars as under the earlier, 50-50 sharing, the allocations lack substantiality because they will not affect the total number of dollars to be received by any partner. In the language of the regulations, these special allocations produce only *shifting* tax consequences. See Treas. Regs. §1.704-1(b)(2)(iii)(b).

While these special allocations probably ought not be upheld, it is surprisingly difficult to articulate a satisfactory basis for that result. It might be reasonable for the regulations to challenge all allocations by character (tax-exempt vs. taxable income, ordinary income vs. capital gain, etc.) as lacking economic effect. After all, dollars are fungible regardless of tax character. However, the regulations do not take such an all-encompassing approach.

For example, suppose the partnership agreement provided that all tax-exempt income would be allocable to *Q*, and all taxable income would be allocated to *P*. The regulations would seem to uphold these allocations so long as the relative amounts of taxable and tax-exempt income to be earned by the partnership are uncertain. See Treas. Regs. §1.704-1(b)(5) (example 7(i)). Is it reasonable for the regulations to distinguish between character allocations in which the dollar amounts are reasonably certain and those in which they are not?

On one hand, Congress has explicitly given its imprimatur to allocations made after the close of the taxable year in its definition of the "partnership agreement" in §761(c). Yet it is precisely such allocations (that is, allocations by character made with hindsight) that are rejected as "shifting" under the substantiality regulations. See Treas. Regs. §1.704-1(b)(5) (example 7(i)). Do these regulations define "substantial economic effect" in a way inconsistent with the flexibility of subchapter K? And if they do, are they invalid?

On the other hand, when allocations are made by character without knowing the precise amounts of income to be received by the partnership, the character of the partnership's income is being used as a measuring rod for allocating *amounts* of income. Once the partnership's income is known with relative certainty, however, allocations by character function only to control tax results: The same economic results could be obtained by allocating explicitly by amount.

For example, suppose the *XY* partnership invests in both taxable and tax-exempt securities. If the partners agree to allocate all taxable income to *X* and all tax-exempt income to *Y* at the beginning of the year before the partnership's income is known, the allocations will affect the dollar amounts to be received by the partners independent of tax consequences. That is, *X* may end up with a greater or lesser share of the partnership's income than *Y*.

Once it is known, say, that the partnership has $4,000 of taxable income and $6,000 of tax-exempt income, the same allocations to *X* and *Y* represent a complex method of making *X* and *Y* 40-60 partners. While there is nothing wrong with complex allocations per se, when the complexity is caused by using character allocations rather than percentages (i.e., 40 percent of all income to *X* and 60 percent of all income to *Y*), the complexity affects tax consequences without apparent justification. In such circumstances it seems appropriate to condemn the character allocations as having insufficient economic effect to support their legitimacy.

Also lacking substantiality are allocations characterized by the regulations as *transitory*. Treas. Regs. §1.704-1(b)(2)(iii)(c). For example, suppose one member of a partnership with an expiring loss carryforward is allocated a disproportionate share of partnership income on condition that an offsetting amount of partnership loss will be allocated to her in the future. Although the allocation of a disproportionate share of income has economic effect in the first year, that effect is negated by the subsequent allocation of loss. Thus, the combined allocations lack economic effect and are properly condemned in the regulations. See Treas. Regs. §1.704-1(b)(5) (example 8).

Is an allocation of depreciation transitory if combined with a gain chargeback? No: because it is uncertain if the gain chargeback will ever be triggered — the regulations adopt the peculiar (but pro-taxpayer) position that depreciable property actually declines in value as it is depreciated — there may be no gain at disposition. Treas. Regs. §1.704-1(b)(5) (example 1(xi)). Under the regulations, the economic effect of a set of allocations will be invalid as transitory only if there is a "strong likelihood" that one allocation will offset the other. Treas. Regs. §1.704-1(b)(2)(iii)(c).

When a depreciable capital asset is sold by a partnership, the depreciation recapture will be ordinary income under §1245 while the remainder of the gain will be capital. Whether the partnership agreement includes a gain chargeback or not, each partner must recognize ordinary income from the recapture in proportion to the depreciation deductions previously allocated to her, but in no event will any partner recognize more depreciation recapture than the amount of gain allocated to that partner from disposition of the property. See Treas. Regs. §1.1245-1(e).

NOTES

1. *The peculiar presumption as to fair market value.* In determining whether a set of potentially offsetting allocations lack substantiality as "transitory," Treas. Regs. §1.704-1(b)(2)(iii)(c)(2) provides that

> the adjusted tax basis of partnership property (or, if partnership property is properly reflected on the books of the partnership at a book value that differs from its adjusted tax basis, the book value of such property) will be presumed to be the fair market value of such property, and adjustments to the adjusted tax basis (or book value) of such property will be presumed to be matched by corresponding changes in such property's fair market value.

This presumption often is called the "value equals basis" presumption, another peculiarity because in fact it is a presumption that *fair market value* always equals *book* value.[10] This presumption represents an enormous opportunity for aggressive partners who seek to trade allocations across years. For example, if partner *X* is allocated an unusually large share of operating income in year 1 with an offsetting large allocation of operating income to partner *Y* in future years, the two allocations can be challenged as transitory if the partnership's future operating income is likely to occur within five years. But if the offsetting allocation to *Y* is made not out of operating income but rather out of unrealized appreciation in the partnership's assets, the allocations cannot be "transitory" because the unrealized appreciation conclusively is presumed not to occur as long as it is not reflected in the partners' capital accounts. See generally Howard E. Abrams, Revenue Ruling Suggests Strategic Partnership Failure to Book-up, 2000 The Tax Advisor 159 (March 2000).

2. *"Look-through" partners.* The government now believes that substantiality should be determined by taking a more sophisticated look at the pass-thru[11] of a partnership's tax attributes. In particular, if a partner is not itself a separate taxpayer but rather passes its tax item through to some other entity, then substantiality should be determined by looking at the ultimate taxpayer rather than at the nominal partner. The most compelling case for such an approach is when all of the partners are members of a consolidated group of corporations so that their distributive shares ultimately are combined on the group's tax return. Similar structures include partnerships owned by other partnerships, by S corporations, and by certain "controlled foreign corporations." See Treas. Regs. §1.704-1(b)(2)(iii)(d).

10. When Treas. Regs. §1.704-1(b) was promulgated, the primacy of book values in capital account maintenance was not yet appreciated. As a result, the regulations sometimes refer to the adjusted basis of partnership assets with a caveat that, when adjusted basis and book value differ, use book value. With such a caveat, adjusted basis becomes irrelevant and book value determinative.

11. For this spelling of "pass-through," see, e.g., §1(h)(10), §1366.

3. *Gain recognized under §1031(b).* When a taxpayer exchanges property in a transaction that would be described in §1031(a) except that the taxpayer receives boot in addition to the qualifying like-kind property, gain is recognized to the extent of the boot received. This rule applies as well when the exchanging party is a partnership. When the boot is used to fund the exit of one partner, the question arises whether the recognized gain should be allocated disproportionately to the exiting partner.

For example, suppose *X*, *Y*, and *Z* are equal partners in the *XYZ* partnership. The partnership owns Blackacre with an adjusted basis and book value of $120, although Blackacre has a fair market value of $270. *XYZ* transfers Blackacre to an unrelated party in exchange for cash of $90 along with Whiteacre having current value of $180. *Z* does not desire to continue in the venture after the exchange, and so *Z* will be distributed cash of $90 in liquidation of *Z*'s interest in the partnership. Immediately prior to the exchange, the books of the partnership should look as follows:

X		*Y*		*Z*	
CA	OB	CA	OB	CA	OB
$40	$40	$40	$40	$40	$40

Asset	Book Value	Adjusted Basis
Blackacre	$120	$120

On the exchange, the partnership realizes a gain of $150, of which $90 is recognized under §1031(b), and $60 is deferred. On the liquidating distribution, any unrealized appreciation in the partnership's assets should be booked into the partners' capital accounts. See Treas. Regs. §1.704-1(b)(2)(iv)(f)-(g). As a consequence, the partners' capital accounts should be increased in the aggregate by the full $150, and because they are equal partners that means each partner's capital account should be increased by $50 to $90. If we think of the aggregate book gain as composed of $90 of recognized gain and $60 of deferred gain, then one possible set of allocations is:

X		*Y*		*Z*	
CA	OB	CA	OB	CA	OB
$40	$40	$40	$40	$40	$40
30	30	30	30	30	30[1]
20	0	20	0	20	0[2]
$90	$70	$90	$70	$90	$70

Asset	Book Value	Adjusted Basis
Whiteacre	$180	$120
Cash	90	90
Totals	$270	$210

In this table, row [1] represents the allocation of the taxable gain equally among the three partners while row [2] represents the allocation of the deferred gain, again equally among the partners. Thus, each partner will report $30 of income from the

§1031(b) exchange, and then Z will report an additional $20 of gain on the liquidating distribution under §731(a).

But this scheme does not seem consistent with §1031(b), which provides that gain should be recognized to the extent property is cashed out but should be deferred if the ownership of property is continued in similar ("like-kind") form. As to *X* and *Y*, the transaction represents a continuation of their investment in largely unchanged form while as to Z the transaction is the equivalent of a complete sale. This suggests the allocations should be:

X		*Y*		*Z*	
CA	OB	CA	OB	CA	OB
$40	$40	$40	$40	$ 40	$ 40
0	0	0	0	90	90[1]
30	0	30	0	0	0[2]
$70	$40	$70	$40	$130	$130

Asset	Book Value	Adjusted Basis
Whiteacre	$180	$120
Cash	90	90
Totals	$270	$210

But this cannot be right because *Z*'s capital account must equal $90 (that is, one-third of the value of the partnership's assets) immediately prior to the liquidating distribution. That is, the economic relationship among the partners demands that the aggregate book increase of $150 be divided equally among the three partners. Within that constraint, however, it seems that the partnership ought to allocate the recognized gain as much as possible to *Z*. This gives:

X		*Y*		*Z*	
CA	OB	CA	OB	CA	OB
$40	$40	$40	$40	$40	$40
20	20	20	20	50	50[1]
30	0	30	0	0	0[2]
$90	$60	$90	$60	$90	$90

Asset	Book Value	Adjusted Basis
Whiteacre	$180	$120
Cash	90	90
Totals	$270	$210

This table reflects what seems a reasonable attempt to satisfy the rules of subchapter K as well as §1031(b): Taxable gain is allocated first to the partner cashing out his investment but in a manner that ensures the allocations have "economic effect" under the §704(b) regulations. Does that mean these allocations are proper? Not necessarily: As compared with the first set in which each partner was allocated one-third of the taxable gain and one-third of the deferred gain, these books reflect an allocation of a disproportionate amount of taxable gain to *Z* and a disproportionate amount of deferred gain away from *Z*. Allocations by character are subject to challenge under the "substantiality" rules of Treas. Regs. §1.704-1(b)(2)(iii). Note that regardless of the mix of recognized and deferred gain allocated to *Z*, *Z* ultimately will recognize $50 on the transaction because the liquidating cash distribution of $90 to *Z* will trigger whatever gain was avoided by *Z* on the exchange. Thus, the effect of allocating a disproportionate amount of taxable gain to *Z* has the effect of reducing the overall gain recognized by the partners in the current taxable year. Nonetheless, this set of allocations seems to best reflect the principles of §1031(b) and so should be valid under Treas. Regs. §1.704-1(b)(1)(iii) (recognizing that provisions beyond §704(b) may be relevant to partnership allocations so that "[t]he determination of a partner's distributive share . . . under section 704(b) . . . is not conclusive as to the tax treatment of a partner with respect to such distributive share").

PROBLEMS

20-12. *L* and *M* form the *LM* general partnership by contributing cash of $10,000 each. The partnership uses its $20,000 to purchase depreciable machinery. Assume the cost of this machinery is recoverable over five years using straight-line depreciation and the gain from the disposition of this machinery is subject to depreciation recapture under §1245. The partnership holds the machinery for two years and has operating income of $3,000 per year. After two years, the machinery is sold for $28,000. The partnership agreement provides that all income and loss is to be allocated equally between the partners except that all cost recovery deductions are allocated exclusively to *L*. In addition, the partnership agreement includes a gain chargeback provision, allocating gain from the disposition of the machinery entirely to *L* up to the amount of the prior depreciation.

a. What are the partners' capital accounts after sale of the machinery, and how much capital gain and ordinary income did each partner report from that sale?
b. What if the partnership agreement does *not* include a gain chargeback provision and the property is sold for only $22,000?
c. If acquisition of the machinery had entitled the partnership to a tax credit of $1,000 (which did not affect the partnership's basis in the machinery), how should that tax credit be allocated?

20-13. Read Rev. Rul. 99-43, 1999-2 C.B. 506, and then answer the following question. Why do the facts include the assumption that *A*, contributes additional cash of $500? (*Hint*: Treas. Regs. §1.704-1(b)(2)(iv)(f).)

H. PROHIBITIONS ON RETROACTIVE ALLOCATIONS

In §706(c)-(d), Congress has prohibited retroactive allocations. In this context, "retroactive" allocations do not refer to allocations made after the close of the taxable year (which are explicitly authorized by §761(c)) but rather allocations of items of partnership income and loss to persons who were not partners when the items accrued.

For example, suppose that individual *J* joins the *P* partnership on December 15 by contributing cash of $15,000. Suppose further that the partnership has an interest deduction for the year of $15,000. Can that entire interest deduction be allocated to *J*?

Under §706(d)(2), *J* can be allocated only so much of the interest deduction as accrues on or after December 15, the date of *J*'s admission to the partnership. Note that this rule applies regardless of the accounting method used by the partnership and is independent of when the interest is actually paid. In particular, if the interest is paid on December 20, and even if the partnership uses the cash receipts and disbursements method of accounting (so that none of the interest expense is recognized by the partnership prior to actual payment), *J* can be allocated no more than 1/24th (one-half of one month) of the interest expense.

The retroactive limitation in §706(c)-(d) predates the current version of §704(c)(1)(A). Regulations promulgated under §704(b) now allow partnership assets to be revalued upon the admission of a new partner, with any disparity between the fair market value and book value of partnership assets at the time of a revaluation allocated among the existing partners as they have agreed to share gain and loss from such assets. See Treas. Regs. §1.704-1(b)(2)(iv)(f)(5)(i). Further, accrued but unrecognized accounts payable are subject to this rule. Treas. Regs. §1.704-3(a)(4). Thus, application of §706(c)-(d) to unrealized cash basis items triggered by admission of a new partner should play a limited role given the current rules of §704(c)(1)(A).

Suppose that *J* had joined the partnership on July 1 as a 50-percent partner. While the partners could not allocate to *J* any of the interest expense accruing between January 1 and June 30, they are free under §704(b) to allocate much of the interest accruing on or after July 1 to *J*. For example, an allocation of all the interest accruing after June 30 would be valid even though the effect of such an allocation is the same as allocating half of the entire year's interest expense to *J*. Yet this latter allocation would run afoul of the rules in §706(d)(2). Astute lawyers, in other words, can accomplish by means of special allocations much of what seemingly is prohibited by the anti-retroactive rules.

Note that §706(c)(2)(B) and §706(d)(1) refer to a partner's changing interest in the partnership. For example, the admission of a new, equal partner to a two-person partnership reduces the interests of the continuing partners from one-half to one-third each. The anti-retroactive rules seem to require in such a situation that the continuing partners be allocated only one-third of the relevant "cash basis items" accruing after admission of the new partner (see §706(d)(2)(B)).

Yet you should understand by now that such a rule is premised on an overly naive conception of a partner's interest in a partnership under subchapter K. The two members of a partnership can be equal partners one year and unequal the next without running afoul of the §704(b) substantial economic effect test. Thus, to say that the continuing partners become one-third partners when a new member is admitted assumes (1) that the partners were each one-half partners prior to admission of the new partner, and (2) that the partners must continue to allocate all partnership items in accordance with some fixed percentage.

We know that it makes no sense to say that the continuing partners were each one-half partners for that part of the year prior to admission of the new partner because distributive shares are not determinable until the partnership agreement is no longer subject to modification — that is, until the "time prescribed by law for the filing of the partnership return for the taxable year." §761(c). Until that date, there simply *are no* distributive shares in any meaningful sense. If we could allocate as much or as little of any partnership tax item to one of the continuing partners had *J* not joined the partnership, then why should the admission of *J* restrict the partners' flexibility?

Can the anti-retroactive rules be applied in any coherent sense to partners who were members of the partnership during the period when the relevant tax items accrued to the partnership? No, although the Tax Court has written an opinion to the contrary. Lipke v. Commissioner, 81 T.C. 689 (1983), aff'd, 751 F.2d 369 (2d Cir. 1984). This opinion, like §706(c)-(d) that it interpreted, predates the current understanding of §704(c)(1)(A). Treasury has promulgated a proposed regulation requiring a partnership to account for varying interests in a partnership arising from the admission of new partners or attributable to the influx of new capital from existing partners. Prop. Treas. Regs. §1.706-4, REG-144689-04 (Apr. 13, 2009).

A partnership that amends its partnership agreement may be subject to the challenge that the nominal amendment actually reflects a prior agreement; that is, the government may argue that what purports to be a modification to the partnership agreement today in fact was agreed to and *effective* earlier. See Treas. Regs. §1.704-1(b)(4)(vi), providing that "the facts and circumstances surrounding the modification will be closely scrutinized to determine whether the purported modification was part of the original agreement."

PROBLEMS

20-14. The *ABC* partnership wishes to admit *D* as a new, one-quarter partner. *D* will be admitted with nine months remaining in the partnership's taxable year. Can *D* be allocated a full one-quarter of the partnership's income and deductions for the year?

20-15. The *PQRS* partnership has for many years owned a commercial office building. As of January 1, 2007, the building has an adjusted basis to the partnership of $240,000, is worth $800,000, and is subject to a recourse debt of $600,000. Each partner has an outside basis of $60,000 and a capital account of negative $90,000. Each month the building generates rents of $8,000 but costs $6,000 for utilities to run. On December 31, 2007, an interest payment of $60,000 will be due, and the partners have no more cash to contribute to the venture. Accordingly, the partnership on December 1, 2007, admits *T* as a new, 20-percent partner, and the existing partners each reduce their interests from 25 percent to 20 percent. In exchange for her partnership interest, *T* contributes cash of $50,000. Because *T*'s money is used to make the interest payment, the partners agree to specially allocate the interest deduction to *T*. Otherwise, *T* is to be allocated one-fifth of the partnership's income and deductions for the current year. Can they do this? How best can the partners accomplish their goal?

21

A Partner's Outside Basis

A. BASIC PRINCIPLES UNDER §705

A partner may acquire her partnership interest in at least any of four ways: (1) in exchange for property contributed to the partnership, (2) by purchase, (3) by gift, or (4) through the estate of a decedent.[1] If the interest is acquired by contribution, the partner's initial outside basis is the adjusted basis of the contributed property. §722. If the interest is acquired otherwise, §742 provides that usual rules apply: cost for purchases, §1012; carryover for gifts, §1015; and fair market value for devises and bequests, §1014. If multiple interests in a single partnership are acquired, either simultaneously or at different times, it is the Service's position that the partner has only a single, undifferentiated outside basis in all interests combined, Rev. Rul. 84-53, 1984-1 C.B. 159, which is consistent with the rule that a partner having multiple interests in a partnership has a single, unified capital account, Treas. Regs. §1.704-1(b)(2)(iv)(b).

The jargon term for a partner's adjusted basis in her partnership interest is "outside basis" to distinguish it from the partnership's "inside basis" in the partnership's assets. Regardless of the method of acquisition of the partnership interest, a partner's outside basis is adjusted under §705(a) for subsequent contributions, distributive share of income and loss, and distributions of cash and property. These adjustments generally ensure that partnership-level transactions affecting the entity's adjusted basis in its assets will be mirrored in adjustments to the partners' outside bases. Because aggregate inside basis and aggregate outside basis begin equal, see §722 and §723, as a general rule (subject to some notable exceptions to which §734(b) and §743(b) speak), aggregate inside and outside bases should remain equal throughout the life of the partnership.

There are a variety of situations when a taxpayer realizes income but is entitled to defer recognition of that income until some subsequent event occurs. For example, a taxpayer enjoys such deferral when it engages in a like-kind exchange

1. In addition, a corporate partner might acquire the partnership interest in a §351 transaction or as part of a corporate reorganization while a partnership that is itself a partner might receive the partnership interest in a §721 contribution. There are additional possibilities including distributions from corporate and partnership partners.

of appreciated property, contributes appreciated property to a corporation in a §351 transaction, or receives restricted property (within the meaning of §83) in connection with the performance of services. If it is not a taxpayer but instead a partnership that engages in such a transaction, should the partners increase their outside bases when the income is realized or only subsequently when the income is recognized?

The language of §705(a)(1)(A) referring to "taxable" income of the partnership makes clear that the basis adjustments must wait until the income is recognized. Indeed, if a basis adjustment were made for income realized but deferred, the plain language of §705(a)(1)(A) would mandate a second adjustment for the same income when the deferral ended. While the statutory language applicable to deferred deductions and losses of the partnership is less clear (note the absence of the word "taxable" in §705(a)(2)(A)), it hardly seems likely that Congress intended for there to be one rule for deferred income and a second rule for deferred deductions.

The reasoning must be quite different, though, if a partnership realizes income that is forever exempt from taxation. In such circumstances a basis adjustment must be made immediately because there is no subsequent opportunity to do so, and if no basis adjustment is made, the income nominally exempted from taxation will in fact be taxable to the partners when they sell their partnership interests. Thus, the statute makes clear, see §705(a)(1)(B), that a partner is entitled to increase outside basis for her distributive share of partnership-level exempt income and equivalently must reduce outside basis for her share of nondeductible, noncapitalizable expenditures (i.e., tax-exempt deductions) such as illegal bribes and kickbacks, §705(a)(2)(B).

For purposes of §705(a)(1)(B) and (a)(2)(B), the concept of tax-exempt income and deduction should be read broadly. For example, suppose a partnership receives property as a devise. The partnership will take such property without recognition of income under §102(a), and it will have a fair market value basis in such property under the general rule of §1014. Unless the partners share an equivalent outside basis adjustment under §705(a)(1)(B), the exemption provided by §102(a) and §1014 will be lost, with mere deferral substituted in its place. Accordingly, it seems clear that the partners should share an outside basis increase equal to the fair market value of the property pursuant to §705(a)(1)(B).

What if the property had been gifted to the partnership rather than devised? In such circumstances the partnership's basis in the property is not fair market value but rather is carried over from the donor. §1015. Assuming the donor's adjusted basis in the property was less than the property's fair market value, the effect of §102 and §1015 is to give the partnership exempt income as to the amount of the carry-over basis and deferral as to the amount of unrealized appreciation in the property. Following the reasoning used above, this means that the partners should share an outside basis increase under §705(a)(1)(B) equal only to the carry-over basis that the partnership takes in the gifted property.

Suppose that a partnership makes a contribution to a charity. Technically, a partnership is not entitled to claim a charitable deduction under §170. See §703(a)(2)(C). Instead, each partner's distributive share of the charitable contribution is reported directly by the partners (that is, the charitable deduction is a separately stated item, §702(a)(4)), subject to the various limitations applicable to charitable contributions generally. Even though the charitable deduction is not a deduction to the partnership, it must produce a downward outside basis adjustment else the partners will get a double benefit from the contribution, once as a separately stated item and again when the partnership interests are sold. The downward adjustment is mandated by §705(a)(2)(B) for nondeductible, noncapitalizable expenditures of the partnership. The amount of the adjustment should equal the partnership's adjusted basis in the gifted property. Rev. Rul. 96-11, 1996-1 C.B. 140. More generally, any transaction having a permanent downward adjustment on the partnership's asset basis should have an equivalent effect on the partners' aggregate outside bases. See Treas. Regs. §1.701-2(f) (example 2) (requiring §705(a)(2)(B) basis adjustment for stock basis reductions under §1059 from receipt of an extraordinary dividend).

B. PARTNERSHIP INDEBTEDNESS AND OUTSIDE BASIS

When a partnership borrows money (or incurs acquisition indebtedness), inside basis increases automatically. If the general equality between aggregate inside and outside bases is to be maintained, such partnership borrowing must also increase aggregate outside basis. This is accomplished by operation of §752(a), which treats an increase in a partner's share of partnership debt as a cash contribution by the partner. This rule, when coupled with §722, means that an increase in a partner's share of partnership debt results in a dollar for dollar increase in outside basis. Similarly, §752(b) provides that a decrease in a partner's share of partnership debt is treated as a cash distribution to the partner.

A §752(a) increase in outside basis is useful in two ways. First, it allows the partner to report a larger distributive share of partnership losses. To ensure that outside basis never becomes negative, §704(d) suspends a partner's distributive share of loss in excess of the partner's outside basis. For example, if a partner with an outside basis of $800 is allocated $1,000 of partnership loss, the partner will be entitled to report only $800 of that distributive share on her individual return. The remaining loss of $200 will be suspended until her outside basis is sufficiently positive to absorb it. Treas. Regs. §1.704-1(d)(1). By increasing a partner's outside basis by her share of the partnership's liabilities, §752(a) permits the partner to receive a greater allocation of deductions before triggering the loss suspension rule of §704(d).

Second, a §752(a) increase in outside basis allows the partner to receive a greater cash distribution without recognizing gain. Recall that §731(a)(1) provides that no gain is recognized on a partnership distribution except to the extent that any cash distributed exceeds the distributee partner's outside basis. Accordingly, a partner whose outside basis was increased by a share of partnership debt can receive more cash before triggering recognition of income under §731(a)(1).

You might think that a third benefit of a §752(a) increase in outside basis is a reduction of gain (or increase in loss) recognized on disposition of the partnership interest. However, because disposition of a partnership interest invariably involves a complete reduction in the partner's share of partnership liabilities, a selling partner obtains no benefit from the rule in §752(a). Indeed, the rule of Commissioner v. Tufts, 461 U.S. 300 (1983), applies to a selling partner, possibly forcing recognition of gain by reason of the release of a liability on disposition of the partnership interest.

1. *History and Basic Principles*

Traditionally, recourse partnership debt was allocated among the partners as they shared partnership losses, and nonrecourse partnership debt was shared according to profits interests. Treas. Regs. §1.752-1(e) (repealed 1989). While the regulations gave no justification for these rules, it was generally understood that recourse debt was allocated in proportion to loss interests because the partners would share repayment of the debt in that proportion if called upon to pay it. Nonrecourse debt, on the other hand, was allocated according to profits interests presumably on the theory that if the debt was to be repaid at all, repayment would come out of partnership profits.

These simple rules provided little guidance in allocating partnership indebtedness in complex transactions. For example, how should debt be allocated if it is nonrecourse by its terms but repayment is guaranteed by one of the partners? Because the guarantor partner would bear the entire burden of repayment if the partnership failed to meet its obligation, one might expect that the debt would be allocated entirely to the guarantor partner. However, the Claims Court in Raphan v. United States, 3 Cl. Ct. 457 (1983), aff'd in part, rev'd in part, 759 F.2d 879 (Fed. Cir. 1985), interpreted old regulation §1.752-1(e) as allocating partnership debt according to "the partners' rights and responsibilities *as partners*" (emphasis supplied), and so because the guarantee was not part of the partnership agreement, the court treated the liability as one for which no partner was liable.

In §79 of the Tax Reform Act of 1984, Pub. L. No. 98-369, §79, 98 Stat. 494, 597 (1984), Congress expressed its disapproval of this holding in *Raphan* and instructed the Treasury to issue new regulations "relating to liabilities including the treatment of guarantees, assumptions, indemnity agreements, and similar arrangements." The new regulations were to allocate partnership debt according to "the manner in which the partners . . . share the economic risk of loss with respect to [the] debt." H.R. Rep. No. 861, 98th Cong., 2d Sess. 868, 869 (1984). Although new regulations were not promulgated for five years, the courts followed the new congressional mandate immediately.

Abramson v. Commissioner

86 T.C. 360 (1986)

WHITAKER, Judge.

This consolidated case includes 10 different petitioners. . . . Each of the petitions includes, among other issues, the common issue of the tax consequences of the investment by the individual general partner and by all of the limited partners in a New Jersey limited partnership known as Surhill Company (Surhill). In the statutory notice, respondent disallowed each partner's share of the partnership losses, which included current expense and depreciation deductions. Issues related to this matter were severed and consolidated for the purposes of trial, briefing, and opinion. The issues arise out of the acquisition in 1976 and the exploitation of a movie originally entitled "Scandal" or "Scandello" and retitled "Submission" (Submission).

The issues as framed by respondent may be summarized as . . . whether petitioners may include in basis the amount of a nonrecourse note evidencing the unpaid portion of the purchase price due the seller of Submission. . . .

Findings of Fact

. . . Surhill was formed as a limited partnership under the laws of the State of New Jersey on December 10, 1976 by Edwin D. Abramson (Abramson). He and his wholly owned corporation, Creative Film Enterprises, Inc. (Creative), were the general partners of Surhill. The remaining petitioners were limited partners. . . . Surhill was organized for the purpose of purchasing the United States' rights to Submission. Creative was incorporated under the laws of the State of New Jersey by Abramson for the purpose of locating movies for acquisition by limited partnerships similar to Surhill and to become a general partner in such limited partnerships. The general partners together contributed $3,333 to Surhill and are entitled to 1 percent of the profit or loss. The limited partners together contributed the sum of $330,000 and are entitled to 99 percent of the profit or loss. . . .

In early 1976, Submission was brought to the attention of Joseph Brenner (Brenner) the principal officer of Joseph Brenner Associates, Inc. (Associates). . . . He negotiated with Walter Bedogni, an officer of Rizzoli Company, S.P.A., the owner of the film, which led to a proposal to contract with Associates for the distribution rights for an advance payment of $150,000 in cash plus a percentage of distributor film rentals. Negotiations ceased because the cash payment was more than Associates could afford to pay.

Thereafter, the film was presented to Abramson and Ziffer, with the information that Associates was interested in the distribution rights. . . .

The initial asking price for Submission was $1 million in cash plus a percentage of film rentals. The agreed upon price for the right to exploit Submission in the United States was $1,750,000, payable $225,000 in cash and $1,525,000 evidenced by a nonnegotiable nonrecourse promissory note with interest. The note was due in 10 years, but was also payable out of one-half of the revenues received by Surhill from the film's distribution. As discussed below, payment of the purchase price was guaranteed by the partners. . . .

The closing documents consisted of the purchase agreement between Surhill and the seller of Submission, the promissory note, a copy of which was attached to the purchase agreement, a security agreement, a copy of which was attached to the promissory note, and the guarantee agreements referred to in, and a copy attached to, the promissory note. . . .

The most critical document in this case is the so-called guarantee agreement[1] entered into by each of the limited partners and by the general partners. . . . The documents were drafted so as to respond to the requirements of the seller of the film that each partner would have personal liability for payment of a pro rata share of the

1. We have adopted petitioners' use of the terms "guarantee" and "guarantor," though neither term is used in its conventional sense. A guarantee is a collateral promise or undertaking by one person to answer for payment of some debt in case of default of another who is liable for such payment in the first instance. Thus, by right of subrogation, a guarantor has a remedy against the principal obligor to recover any amounts he has to pay to the creditor. See Brand v. Commissioner, 81 T.C. 821, 828 (1983).

As guarantors of an otherwise nonrecourse note, however, petitioners have incurred personal liability where the partnership has only limited liability. Therefore, petitioners and their assets are both primarily and ultimately liable to the sellers in the event of default. They are primarily liable because neither the partnership nor any of its assets (other than the film) is subject to the nonrecourse obligation. They are ultimately liable, because there is no primary obligor against whom they have a right of subrogation. See Smith v. Commissioner, 84 T.C. 889, 908 (1985). Thus, on these facts, we use the terms "guarantee" and "guarantor" as including both primary and ultimate liability.

note when due but to provide the limited partners with the benefit of limited partner status under New Jersey law and to preclude any partner, limited or general, from acquiring joint liability, that is, from being responsible to the seller of Submission for more than that partner's pro rata share of the promissory note. The pertinent part of the guarantee agreement reads as follows:

Guarantee Agreement

> The undersigned hereby guarantees and promises to pay to Transcontinental Films Anstalt that percentage of the unpaid balance due Transcontinental Films Anstalt pursuant to a certain Promissory Note of even date in the principal sum of $1,525,000 issued to it by Surhill Company, a New Jersey Limited Partnership, in the event of a default by Surhill Company in payment of such note, set forth opposite his name below. . . .
>
> Under no circumstances shall any of the undersigned persons have any liability under this guarantee or the Promissory Note issued to Transcontinental Films Anstalt in any amount greater than the percentage set forth opposite the undersigned's name above, multiplied by the outstanding balance due under the Promissory Note issued by Surhill Company to Transcontinental Films Anstalt at the time of default thereunder, after reduction for any amounts payable to Transcontinental Films Anstalt pursuant to the exercise of its rights under a certain Security Agreement of even date. Pertinent extracts from the subscription agreement, the promissory note, and the private placement memorandum are set forth in Appendix B attached hereto.

. . . The private placement memorandum fully summarizes the transaction, including the required execution of the guarantee agreement, a copy of which is attached together with copies of the other agreements requiring execution by the limited partners. The subscription agreement also emphasizes the personal liability to be assumed under the guarantee agreement. While the acquisition agreement describes the note as a "nonnegotiable, recourse promissory note," the note is actually a nonrecourse note in that it expressly provides that neither the general partners nor the limited partners will have any personal liability of any kind or nature on the note except as provided in the guarantee agreement. The so-called guarantee agreement, executed by each partner (general and limited) in his capacity as a partner, obligates each person to pay to the seller that percentage of the unpaid balance due the seller in the event of a default which is equal to the partner's percentage interest. A default occurs upon nonpayment of the balance due on the $1,525,000 on December 20, 1986. At that point, the seller must foreclose on the film and it may then look to each partner for that partner's share of the unpaid balance of the indebtedness. . . .

Opinion

. . . The next issue for decision is whether the petitioners may increase their bases in Surhill as a result of their guaranteeing the note given by Surhill to the seller of the film. . . .

As a result of the direct obligation undertaken by each petitioner qua partner to pay to the seller a portion of Surhill's debt pursuant to the so-called guarantee, each partner in Surhill increased his share of Surhill's liabilities. Thus, pursuant to sections 752(a) and 722, each partner's basis in Surhill is increased as a result of this additional personal obligation as to which each partner is ultimately liable. See Smith v. Commissioner, 84 T.C. 889, 908 (1985).

The guarantee of an otherwise nonrecourse note places each guaranteeing partner in an economic position indistinguishable from that of a general partner with liability under a recourse note — except that the guaranteeing partner's liability is limited to the amount guaranteed. While recognizing that under state law there may be differences between the obligations of a general partner and those of a limited partner guarantor, such differences should not be controlling for Federal tax purposes. Each is obligated to use his personal assets to satisfy pro rata the partnership liability. In effect, the limited partners are the equivalent of general partners to the extent of their pro rata guarantees especially since, as to this obligation, the liability of the general partners is limited. Economic reality dictates that they be treated equally, and we so hold. Consequently, both general and limited partners will be entitled to include such liabilities in their basis to the extent of their pro rata guarantees. The $1,525,000 liability is apportioned to them in accordance with their loss ratios under the partnership agreement.

This holding is consistent with, and foretold by, our decision in Smith v. Commissioner, supra. In the *Smith* case, one of the partners executed and contributed to the partnership an assumption agreement as to a nonrecourse partnership liability. We held that the partner's basis was increased by the amount of the debt assumed, saying:

> Where, as here, the partner becomes ultimately liable to pay the debt, it is irrelevant for purposes of section 752(a) that the partnership or its property remains liable to the mortgagee. . . . By taking on ultimate and unconditional liability, petitioner constructively contributed the amount of the indebtedness to the partnership, and was thus entitled to increase his basis.

Smith v. Commissioner, 84 T.C. at 980.

Our facts are different in that the property, i.e., Submission, was still liable for the indebtedness and Surhill was obligated to pay the seller of the film one-half of its film rentals. We do not believe that these differences alter the result. In this partnership transaction, each partner is directly and ultimately liable for a pro rata portion of the obligation. The fact that the obligation might be paid in part by application of film rentals to which each partner otherwise would be entitled does not preclude the acquisition of basis. . . .

Based upon the foregoing,

Appropriate orders will be issued.

Reviewed by the Court.

Sterrett, Goffe, Chabot, Parker, Shields, Cohen, Swift, Jacobs, Wright, Parr, and Williams, JJ., agree with the majority opinion.

Nims, Korner, and Hamblen, JJ., agree with the result only.

Simpson, Wilbur, and Gerber, JJ., did not participate in the consideration of this case.

Swift, J., concurring.

I agree with the result reached by the majority opinion but wish to comment on one aspect of the partnership's obligation under the loan. The majority correctly concludes that the $1,525,000 promissory note is nonrecourse as to the general and limited partners. Under the relevant loan documents, however, as I read them, it appears that the $1,525,000 promissory note is recourse as to the partnership itself (namely, Surhill). If so, the creditor, Rizzoli Company, is entitled to seek full recourse against all of Surhill's available assets if a default on the note occurs.

The apparent recourse nature of the promissory note as to Surhill, however, does not make the obligations of the general and limited partners secondary to Surhill's obligation. For Federal tax purposes, the fact that none of the partners has personal liability on the promissory note elevates the obligations of the partners under the guarantee agreements to primary obligations.

With the clarification that the promissory note appears to be recourse as to Surhill, I agree with the majority's conclusion that Brand v. Commissioner, 81 T.C. 821 (1983), is not applicable to the partners' obligations because the partners have no other person or partner to whom to look for reimbursement should they be required to make payments under the guarantee agreements.

[Dissenting opinion omitted.]

In Smith v. Commissioner, 84 T.C. 889 (1985), the Tax Court held that a partner who assumed a partnership's nonrecourse liability must be allocated that liability under §752. The Tax Court in *Abramson* similarly held that a partner who guaranteed part of a partnership's nonrecourse liability must be allocated the liability up to the amount of the guarantee. The court in *Abramson* distinguished an earlier loan guarantee case, Brand v. Commissioner, 81 T.C. 821 (1983). In that case, a partner had guaranteed a partnership's recourse liability, and the court determined that the guarantor did not bear the economic risk of nonpayment despite the guarantee. The court observed that when the liability is recourse as to the partnership, the guarantor partner has the right to seek reimbursement from the general partners if called upon to pay the debt. Ultimate liability for repayment, accordingly, remains with the general partners despite the guarantee. However, had the loan been nonrecourse as to the partnership, the guarantor partner would have no rights against the other partners if called upon to pay the debt. Thus, only in the case of a nonrecourse loan does a guarantee place ultimate risk of loss on the guarantor partner. When the loan is recourse as to the partnership, the guarantor partner's potential rights of subrogation leave ultimate risk of nonpayment on the partnership's general partners, and so the debt in this case should be allocated among those partners.

By the terms of the loan agreement in *Abramson,* the loan was recourse as to the partnership but the lender could not look through the partnership to its general partners for repayment. In effect, the court treated the loan under §752 as if it had been fully nonrecourse. In determining which partners bear ultimate liability for a partnership's debt, we must determine which partners will be called upon to pay the debt, assuming the partnership is unable to do so. If partner *A* can be forced to pay the lender but then has rights against partner *B,* there is no ultimate liability in *A.* However, if *A* has no rights against any partner, but *A* has rights against the partnership, *A does* have ultimate liability for the debt: In allocating debt among the partners, the court in *Abramson* recognized that rights of reimbursement against the *partnership* are irrelevant.

These principles can be extended to cover loans from partners to the partnership. For example, suppose limited partner *L* makes a loan to the *P* partnership, and assume that the loan is without recourse so that no partner can be forced to make good on the partnership's obligation. As with any *nonrecourse* loan, if the partnership is unable to repay the debt the economic loss will fall on the lender. Here, that lender is *L*, the limited partner. Accordingly, the debt should be allocated entirely to *L* because *L* bears the economic risk of repayment. To be sure, *L* bears this risk in her capacity as lender rather than as partner, but as Congress made clear when it disapproved of *Raphan*, partnership debts should be allocated among the partners in accordance with economic realities, taking account of all guarantees and other loss-allocation arrangements. Of course, partnership indebtedness as to which no partner is liable for repayment in any capacity must be allocated in some other manner. See Treas. Regs. §1.752-4.

The Treasury Department promulgated temporary regulations under §752 in 1989 and 1990, and final regulations were issued in 1991. These regulations are discussed in the next section. Prior to these regulations, the allocation of partnership debt was covered by the following brief language in Treas. Regs. §1.752-1(e):

> A partner's share of partnership liabilities shall be determined in accordance with his ratio for sharing losses under the partnership agreement. In the case of a limited partnership, a limited partner's share of partnership liabilities shall not exceed the difference between his actual contribution credited to him by the partnership and the total contribution which he is obligated to make under the limited partnership agreement. However, where none of the partners have any personal liability with respect to a partnership liability . . . then all partners, including limited partners, shall be considered as sharing such liability under §752(c) in the same proportion as they share the profits.

As you read the §752 regulations, ask yourself whether they better allocate partnership debt than did these simple rules as interpreted by *Abramson, Smith,* and *Brand.*

2. *Allocations under the Regulations*

The regulations continue to allocate recourse and nonrecourse liabilities according to different rules. A "recourse liability" is defined as "[any] partnership liability . . . to the extent that any partner or related person bears the economic risk of loss for th[e] liability. . . ." Treas. Regs. §1.752-1(a)(1). A "nonrecourse liability" is any partnership liability "to the extent that no partner or related person bears the economic risk of loss." Treas. Regs. §1.752-1(a)(2). For application of these definitions, a "related person" includes family members (but not brothers and sisters), controlled entities, and commonly controlled entities. See Treas. Regs. §1.752-4(b)(1) (incorporating definitions (with modifications) from §267(b) and §707(b)). Broadly speaking, the regulations continue the tradition of allocating recourse liabilities according to loss interests and nonrecourse liabilities according to profits interests.

For purposes of §752, a liability of the partnership includes any obligation to the extent that incurring the obligation created or increased the basis to the partnership of any of its assets, gave rise to an immediate deduction, or gave rise to a nondeductible, noncapitalizable expenditure. Treas. Regs. §1.752-1(a)(4). For example, a short sale of stock creates a liability for purposes of §752, Rev. Rul. 95-26, 1995-1 C.B. 131, although the contribution of an account payable by a cash basis partner does not constitute a liability for purposes of §752 but rather is treated as loss property under §704(c)(1)(A), Treas. Regs. §1.704-3(a)(4), thereby implicating §704(c).

NOTES

1. *Tiered partnerships.* If the owner of a partnership interest is itself a partnership, indebtedness of the lower-tier partnership will percolate through the upper-tier partnership into the outside basis of the upper-tier partners. For example, suppose individual *X* owns 10 percent of the capital, profits, and losses of the *P* partnership and that *P* owns 30 percent of the capital, profits, and losses of the *Q* partnership. If *P*'s indebtedness is allocated under §752 in proportion to capital, and *Q*'s indebtedness also is allocated in proportion to partnership capital, then *X*'s outside basis in *P* will be increased by 3 percent of the indebtedness of *Q*. See Treas. Regs. §1.752-4(a). Note that the lower-tier debt is allocated in two separate steps. For example, suppose on the facts above that no partner of *P* (the upper-tier partnership) is liable for *P*'s debts but that the partners in *Q* (the lower-tier partnership) are liable for *Q*'s debts. In that case, *Q*'s indebtedness will be allocated among its partners (including *P*) in accordance with the recourse debt rules while the upper-tier debt (including the debt passed through from *Q*) will be allocated among *P*'s partners in accordance with the nonrecourse rules.

2. *Obligations that are not "liabilities."* Recall the definition of a "liability" under Treas. Regs. §1.752-1(a)(4): an obligation is a liability to the extent that it increased the basis of any asset, gave rise to an immediate deduction, or gave rise to a nondeductible, noncapitalizable expenditure. There are many obligations that do not constitute a "liability" under this definition. For example, a taxpayer operating a nuclear power plant may be liable for substantial decommissioning costs once the plant is finally taken out of service, but those future costs are not "liabilities" under Treas. Regs. §1.752-1(a)(4), and the same would be true of most future environmental remediation expenses. The transfer of property subject to such obligations is covered by the complex rules in Treas. Regs. §1.752-7. This regulation also covers obligations whose face value exceeds net present value because of time value of money considerations. For example, if a partner transfers property subject to a "liability" with face value of $1,000 and having a present value of only $600 (because it bears below-market interest), then only $600 will be subject to the usual "liability" rules, and $400 of the obligation will be subject to the special rules of Treas. Regs. §1.752-7. If that obligation happens to be a deductible payable transferred by a cash basis partner, then the fair market value of the payable — that is, $600 of it — will be treated under the §704(c) rules applicable to contributed property having a variation between adjusted basis (in this case, $0) and fair market value at the time of contribution (in this case, negative $600). See Treas. Regs. §1.752-7(b)(6), §1.752-7(c)(1)(ii), §1.752-7(c)(2)

a. Recourse Liabilities

i. The Regulatory Scheme

Congress instructed the Treasury to issue regulations under §752 allocating partnership recourse liabilities in accordance with economic risk of loss, and that is what the regulations try to do. Under these regulations, a partner bears the economic risk of loss of a partnership liability to the extent the partner would be forced to make a payment to any person (including a contribution to the partnership) as the result of a constructive zero-value sale and liquidation of the partnership. See Treas. Regs. §1.752-2(b)(1). In this context a zero-value sale and liquidation means a liquidation of the partnership after all of its assets (including cash) have become worthless and are transferred for zero consideration in a fully taxable transaction. *Id.* The effect of a zero-value constructive liquidation is to determine how the capital account balances will stand if the partnership should lose all of its investments when the partnership's debts become due.

For example, suppose *A* contributes $600, and *B* contributes $400 to form the *AB* general partnership. The partnership agreement provides that capital accounts will be properly maintained for each partner, that liquidating proceeds will be distributed in accordance with final capital account balances, and that each partner has an obligation to restore a deficit capital account if one exists upon liquidation. In addition, assume that *A* is allocated 50 percent of partnership profits and 60 percent of partnership losses. *AB* borrows $9,000 on a fully recourse basis. The $10,000 cash is then used by the partnership to purchase Blackacre. How should the $9,000 indebtedness be allocated?

First, assume that all the partnership's assets (in this case, just Blackacre) become worthless and are sold for $0. This hypothetical sale is important because it means that the $10,000 hypothetical loss realized on Blackacre is recognized and adjusts the partners' capital accounts. Accordingly, after the hypothetical sale *A*'s capital account stands at minus $5,400 ($600 less 60% of $10,000) while *B*'s stands at minus $3,600 ($400 less 40% of $10,000). Thus, if the partnership liquidates immediately, *A* must contribute $5,400 while *B* must contribute $3,600. These final figures define the sharing ratios of the partnership liability: $5,400 to *A* and $3,600 to *B*. See examples 1 and 2 of Treas. Regs. §1.752-2(f).

One point worth making explicit is that we adjust the partners' capital accounts by the book (and not tax) loss realized on the hypothetical zero-value sale. This distinction will be important whenever a partnership owns an asset having a book value different from its tax basis. Such book/tax disparities can arise when appreciated or loss property is contributed to the partnership, see Treas. Regs. §1.704-1(b)(2)(iv)(d)(1), as well as when partnership assets are revalued for book purposes such as when new partners join an existing partnership owning appreciated or loss property, see Treas. Regs. §1.704-1(b)(2)(iv)(f)-(g).

This example demonstrates a point latent in the new definitions: Under the §752 regulations, recourse debt allocations are influenced not only by the way in which the partners share losses but also by existing capital accounts. Anything that affects capital account balances potentially affects debt sharing ratios as well. In particular, annual distributive shares of gain and loss will affect capital account balances each year, so that the regulations seemingly contemplate a reallocation of partnership debt at least annually even in the absence of a change in the partnership's debt. Also worth noting is the implicit incorporation of the §704(b) allocation rules via the hypothetical sale and liquidation.

Reconsider the example above but assume (1) that *B* is a limited partner who cannot be required to make additional contributions to the partnership and (2) that *B* gives the lender a personal guarantee for the $9,000 debt. Once again the hypothetical sale and liquidation produces a taxable loss of $10,000, but now that loss is allocated $9,600 to *A* and $400 to *B* because *B* has no obligation to restore a capital account deficit upon liquidation. Thus, the final capital accounts stand at minus $9,000 for *A* and $0 for *B*, and so the loan is allocated entirely to *A*.

But what if the lender enforces the guarantee by collecting $9,000 directly from *B*? If so, none of the $9,000 deficit in *A*'s capital account is needed to pay the lender. However, *B* as guarantor will be entitled to seek reimbursement from the partnership as principal debtor, and so *A* will still be required to contribute $9,000 to the partnership, although in this case for distribution to *B* rather than to the lender. In either event, *A* bears the ultimate economic liability associated with the debt despite *B*'s personal guarantee so it is proper that the debt be allocated entirely to *A*. See Treas. Regs. §1.752-2(b)(5); see also Treas. Regs. §1.752-2(f) (examples 3-4); Proesel v. Commissioner, 77 T.C. 992, 1004 (1981).

The outcome would be very different, though, if the loan had been nonrecourse with respect to the partnership. If the loan is nonrecourse (excluding *B*'s guarantee), the partnership's loss on the hypothetical sale will be only $1,000 because the amount of the outstanding debt, $9,000, is included in the partnership's amount realized under *Tufts* in computing loss on the hypothetical sale. Under the terms of the *AB* partnership agreement, this loss will be allocated $600 to *A* and $400 to *B*. Each partner's capital account ends up at zero, so that ending capital account balances cannot be used to allocate the debt.

This indeterminacy is appropriate because the loan is nonrecourse as to the partnership. The capital account analysis employed by the regulations determines the extent to which each partner is liable for partnership debt in his or her capacity as a partner. In this case, neither *A* nor *B* is liable as a partner.

However, *B* is liable for the debt as a result of the personal guarantee. Further, if *B* is forced to pay off the loan pursuant to the guarantee, *B* will have no rights against *A*: Because the loan is nonrecourse with respect to the principal debtor (the partnership), *B* (like the lender) has recourse only against the property securing the debt. Thus, *B* bears the ultimate burden of repayment of the loan, and so the loan is treated as a recourse loan to *B* as to this amount. *B* accordingly is allocated the entire $9,000 loan. Smith v. Commissioner, 84 T.C. 889, 908 n.18 (1985).

Other portions of the regulations worth noting include those governing persons related to a partner, Treas. Regs. §1.752-2(c), arrangements tantamount to a guarantee, Treas. Regs. §1.752-2(j)(2), and the general anti-abuse provision in Treas. Regs. §1.752-2(j).

NOTES

1. *The presumption of solvency.* Partnership recourse liabilities are, in general, allocated among the partners in proportion to capital account deficit restoration obligations arising after a zero-value sale and liquidation. It is possible that a partner would be unable to satisfy some or all of this obligation because of insufficient net worth. Treas. Regs. §1.752-2(b)(1). In general, this possibility is ignored: Under the *presumption of solvency* in Treas. Regs. §1.752-2(b)(8), all persons having obligations arising in connection with a zero-value sale and liquidation are assumed able to satisfy those obligations in full. However, this presumption of solvency can be rebutted in abusive situations. See Treas. Regs. §1.752-2(j). In Canal Corp. v. Commissioner, 135 T.C. 199 (2010), the Tax Court concluded that this anti-abuse rule should apply when credit-worthy partner *X* guarantees repayment of

an otherwise-nonrecourse liability, partner *Y* agrees to indemnify *X* if the guarantee is ever triggered, partner *Y* has insufficient assets to satisfy the full guarantee, and partner *Y* is under no contractual obligation to the lender or to *X* to maintain a minimum net worth.

PROBLEMS

21-1. *E* and *F* form the *EF* general partnership by contributing $20,000 apiece. The partnership purchases property for $100,000, paying $40,000 in cash and the remainder in the form of a $60,000 recourse note. Determine whether the debt is recourse and, if so, how it is allocated if

a. The partnership agreement provides that losses will be divided equally between the partners.
b. The partnership agreement provides that losses will be allocated 90 percent to *E* and 10 percent to *F*.
c. The partnership agreement allocates losses equally between the partners, but *F* is a limited partner who cannot be required to contribute more than an additional $10,000 to the partnership.
d. Both partners are general partners, losses are allocated equally between the partners, but *E* personally guarantees repayment of $60,000 of the debt.
e. Both partners are general partners, losses are all allocated equally between the partners, *E* personally guarantees the debt, and the debt is nonrecourse as to the partnership.

21-2. *A* and *B* form the *AB* general partnership by contributing $10,000 apiece. The partnership agreement provides that losses will be allocated equally between the partners. The partnership borrows $80,000 from *R*. Is the debt recourse and, if so, how is it debt allocated if

a. The debt is fully recourse, and *R* is a corporation wholly owned by *B*?
b. The debt is nonrecourse, and *R* is a corporation wholly owned by *B*?
c. The debt is nonrecourse, and *R* is a corporation owned 25 percent by *A* and 75 percent by *B*?

ii. Some Questions

Having seen how the regulations work, it is time to ask whether they work properly. Although the regulations have their supporters, it seems undeniable that they are fundamentally flawed. See generally Howard E. Abrams, Long-Awaited Regulations under Section 752 Provide Wrong Answers, 44 Tax L. Rev. 627 (1989). Consider example 1 of Regulation §1.752-2(f). *A* and *B* form the *AB* partnership by contributing $100 each. The partnership agreement provides that capital accounts will be maintained properly, that liquidating proceeds will be distributed in accordance with final account balances, and that any partner with a final capital account deficit will contribute the amount of the deficit to the partnership. In addition, losses are to be allocated 90 percent to *A* and 10 percent to *B*.

If the *AB* partnership borrows $800 on a fully recourse basis, the regulations conclude that the indebtedness is allocable entirely to *A*. Under the regulations, the constructive zero-value sale and liquidation will produce a taxable loss of $1,000, allocable under the partnership agreement $900 to *A* and $100 to *B*. Accordingly, final account balances will stand at negative $800 for *A* and zero for *B*. Thus, *A*'s deficit account restoration obligation is triggered, so that *A* must make a contribution to the partnership of $800 for distribution to the lender. Only *A* makes a net contribution as a result of the constructive liquidation and so the regulations allocate the entire $800 debt to *A*.

Yet the debt should be allocated partially to *A* and partially to *B*. Prior to the borrowing, a constructive zero-value sale and liquidation as defined in the regulations would produce a taxable loss of $200, allocable $180 to *A* and $20 to *B*. Such a liquidation would leave final capital accounts at negative $80 for *A* and positive $80 for *B*. Thus, *A* would be required to contribute $80 for distribution to *B*.

Comparing this constructive sale and liquidation with that of one occurring after the partnership borrowing, we see that the effect of the debt is to increase *A*'s net contribution by $720 (from $80 to $800) and to decrease *B*'s final capital account balance by $80 (from $80 to $0). Accordingly, the $800 debt potentially makes *A* worse off by $720 and *B* worse off by $80, and if it is to be allocated according to economic risk of loss (as mandated by Congress in the 1984 Tax Act), the debt should be allocated $720 to *A* and $80 to *B*.

The regulations err because of the tacit assumption that all net contributions following a constructive liquidation arise from partnership indebtedness. That simply is not true: If losses are allocated other than in proportion to capital account balances, a constructive liquidation can produce a net contribution that in part reflects the disparity between capital accounts and loss sharing ratios. For example, the first $80 of *A*'s $800 net contribution in example 1 is merely a payback of *B*'s initial capital contribution, an obligation that arose immediately upon formation of the partnership and not upon acquisition of the partnership debt.

It is no coincidence that the $800 debt in example 1 is properly allocable 90 percent to *A* and 10 percent to *B*—that is, according to their loss-sharing ratios. If the partners' loss-sharing ratios equal their capital account ratios (and assuming there are no §704(c) problems), a constructive liquidation under the regulations will reduce all capital account balances to zero (caused by assuming all assets become worthless) and then will produce capital account deficits to all partners in proportion to loss ratios (summing to the amount of the outstanding partnership debt). If loss sharing and capital account ratios differ from one another, ending capital deficits will not be in proportion to loss ratios, and that is precisely what causes the problem in the §752 regulations. In such circumstances, the difference between final capital account balances and loss ratios should *not* affect allocation of the debt.

b. Nonrecourse Liabilities

Under the regulations, partnership nonrecourse liabilities (that is, liabilities as to which no partner is liable, see Treas. Regs. §1.752-1(a)(2)) are allocated in three tiers. Treas. Regs. §1.752-3(a). Under the first tier, nonrecourse liabilities are allocated to each partner in an amount equal to each partner's share of partnership minimum gain (that is, in the same proportions as prior nonrecourse deductions were allocated). Treas. Regs. §1.752-3(a)(1). Under the second tier, the remaining nonrecourse liabilities are allocated to each partner in an amount equal to the partner's §704(c) gain (including reverse §704(c) gain arising from the revaluation of partnership property) that would be recognized if the property were sold *for the outstanding liability and no other consideration.* Treas. Regs. §1.752-3(a)(2). Finally, all remaining nonrecourse liabilities are allocated among the partners in proportion to their profits interests. Treas. Regs. §1.752-3(a)(3). Tier three allocations may be made in accordance with the partners' general profits interests, in a manner reasonably consistent with the allocation of some tax item having economic effect, in a manner that accounts for §704(c) gain not accounted for under tier 2, or in the manner in which the partners will share the nonrecourse deductions from the property. Treas. Regs. §1.752-3(a)(3).

While the three tiers may seem to speak to different concerns, in actuality all three seek to allocate the nonrecourse liabilities in accordance with profits interests. First consider tier one. Minimum gain is the least book gain that will be recognized by the partnership upon a disposition of the property, Treas. Regs. §1.704-2(d)(1), and minimum gain resulting from the disposition of property subject to a nonrecourse liability must be allocated to the partners as they were allocated the nonrecourse deductions, Treas. Regs. §1.704-2(f). Thus, by allocating partnership nonrecourse liabilities according to each partner's share of minimum gain, tier one simply allocates the liability according to partner profits interests over which the partners have no allocative discretion.

Now consider tier two. This tier allocates nonrecourse liabilities to each partner in an amount equal to the partner's share of §704(c) income. In determining the amount of §704(c) income allocable under tier two, you assume that the property is transferred in satisfaction of the nonrecourse debt and for no other consideration. Treas. Regs. §1.752-3(a)(2); see also Rev. Rul. 95-41, 1995-1 C.B. 132. Income arising under §704(c) is attributable to the excess (if any) of the value of contributed property over the adjusted basis of the property at the time of contribution. See Treas. Regs. §1.704-3(a)(3)(ii). Section 704(c)(1) requires that such pre-contribution appreciation be allocated to the contributing partner. Thus, tier two allocates partnership nonrecourse liabilities in accordance with partner profits interests over which the partners have no allocative discretion, just like tier one. Tier three then allocates the remainder of the nonrecourse liability in accordance with the allocation of gain over which the partners *do have* allocative discretion.

Consider how a partnership allocates gain from the disposition of an asset. If the asset is encumbered by a nonrecourse liability and the amount of that liability exceeds the partnership's book value, then there is partnership minimum gain that, under the §704(b) regulations, must be allocated to the partners as they shared the nonrecourse deductions. Treas. Regs. §1.704-2(f). The gain, in other words, must be allocated as was the liability under tier one.

Next, if the property's book value exceeds its adjusted basis, then the difference has been booked into one or more partners' capital accounts under §704(c) (or in accordance with §704(c) principles upon the revaluation of partnership assets under §704(b), see Treas. Regs. §1.704-1(b)(2)(iv)(f)(4)), and that difference must be allocated to those partners whose capital accounts include the excess book value. Treas. Regs. §1.704-3(a)(1). That is, the gain must be allocated as was the liability under tier two. Any remaining gain may be allocated as the partners agree (subject to the general limitation of substantial economic effect under §704(b)), and this is how the remainder of the liability is allocated under tier three.

As explained above, tier one allocates nonrecourse liabilities in accordance with the partners' profits interests properly considered. But it does more: Tier one backstops the provisions governing the allocation of nonrecourse deductions under §704(b) by ensuring that a partner properly allocated nonrecourse deductions will have sufficient outside basis to exploit them.

For example, assume *X* contributes $30,000, and *Y* contributes $10,000 to form the *XY* general partnership. The partnership then purchases depreciable property for $100,000, paying $40,000 in cash and signing a nonrecourse note for the remaining $60,000. Assume that the partnership agreement provides that all profits and losses will be divided equally between *X* and *Y* except that depreciation will be allocated 75 percent to *X* and 25 percent to *Y*.

If the partnership is entitled to claim a depreciation deduction each year of $10,000, the partners' equity will be fully consumed after four years (assuming the partnership has no other items of income or deduction, and assuming also that there are no distributions or further borrowings). After the fourth year, each partner's capital account should stand at zero. Because there has so far been no nonrecourse deductions and there is no §704(c) gain, the liability is allocated under tier three according to their profits interests (where the definition "profits interests" offers the partners some discretion, see Treas. Regs. §1.752-3(a)(3)). Accordingly, *X*'s outside basis should then equal $30,000, and *Y*'s outside basis should equal $30,000.

In year 5, the depreciation deduction of $10,000 is allocated $7,500 to *X* and $2,500 to *Y*. Assuming this allocation is deemed to satisfy the substantial economic effect test of §704(b), it lowers *X*'s capital account to negative $7,500 and lowers *Y*'s capital account to negative $2,500. The depreciation in year five is a nonrecourse deduction (because it lowers the book value of the property below that of the outstanding nonrecourse loan), and so it triggers a reallocation of the partnership debt. Under tier one, *X* must be allocated $7,500 of the debt, and *Y* must be allocated $2,500 of the debt. The remaining $50,000 continues to be allocated in accordance with partnership profits, or $25,000 to each partner. Thus, at the end of the fifth year each partner has an outside basis of $25,000, computed as follows: for *X*, prior year's outside basis of $30,000, less $7,500 distributable share of depreciation deduction, and plus $2,500 increase in share of debt; for *Y*, prior year's outside basis of $30,000, less $2,500 distributable share of depreciation deduction, and less $2,500 reduction in share of debt.

If we continue this analysis through the 10th year when the property is fully depreciated, we see that *X*'s capital account will stand at negative $45,000, and *Y*'s capital account will be negative $15,000. The entire debt now is allocated under tier one, so that it goes 75 percent (or $45,000) to *X* and 25 percent (or $15,000) to *Y*. Accordingly, *X*'s outside basis is zero (*X*'s share of the debt of $45,000 plus contributed capital of $30,000 less distributed share of depreciation of $75,000) as is *Y*'s outside basis. Thus, each partner had precisely enough outside basis to absorb the nonrecourse deductions. In essence, then, the rules governing the allocation of nonrecourse deductions under §752 ensure that they do not pose a second hurdle to the allocation of nonrecourse deductions. If the allocations of such deductions pass muster under §704(b), there should be adequate outside basis under §752 and §704(d) to use them on the partners' individual returns.

If property encumbered by a nonrecourse debt has a §704(c) or reverse §704(c) book/tax disparity, the analysis becomes more complicated. Consider the following example taken from Rev. Rul. 95-41: *A* and *B* form the *AB* general partnership, with *A* contributing depreciable property having an adjusted basis of $4,000, fair market value of $10,000, and subject to a nonrecourse liability of $6,000, while *B* contributes cash of $4,000. How is the liability initially allocated, assuming that *A* and *B* agree to divide profits and losses equally except as required by §704(c)?

A and *B* each begin with a capital account of $4,000, and ignoring any reallocation of the debt, each partner has an outside basis of $4,000 as well. To the extent any of the debt is allocated to *B*, *A*'s outside basis will decline and *B*'s outside basis will increase. In fact, if more than $4,000 of the debt is allocated to *B*, *A* will recognize income on the reallocation. Of course, reallocation of the debt has no effect on the partners' capital accounts.

Under tier one, the debt is allocated to the partners as they share minimum gain from the secured property, where minimum gain equals the excess of the debt over the book value of the property. Because the property was booked into the partnership at its current fair market value of $10,000, there is no minimum gain. Accordingly, there is no allocation of the debt under tier one.

Under tier two, the debt is allocated to the partners as they would share gain under §704(c)(1)(A) if the property were sold for the amount of the outstanding debt and for no other consideration. Here, that means we ask how much §704(c)(1)(A) gain there would be if the property were sold for $6,000. Because the adjusted basis of the property is $4,000, sale for $6,000 would yield a tax gain of $2,000 but a book loss of $4,000.

If the partners agree to use either the traditional method or the traditional method with curative allocations to address ceiling limitation problems, disposition of the property for $6,000 would produce a tax gain to *A* of $2,000 and no further tax allocations. Because this gain would be allocable to *A* under §704(c)(1), there is a $2,000 tier two allocation of the debt to *A* *if* the partnership uses the traditional method or the traditional method with curative allocations to address ceiling limitation issues arising under §704(c). Rev. Rul. 95-41 specifically provides that the possibility of curative allocations is ignored in determining the allocation of nonrecourse liabilities under tier two.

If the partnership uses the remedial allocation method to address ceiling limitation problems arising under §704(c)(1)(A), allocation of the debt under tier two is more complicated. Because a sale of the property for the amount of the debt (that is, a sale for $6,000) would yield a tax gain of $2,000 but a book loss of $4,000, the partnership would be required to make a remedial allocation of $2,000 of tax loss to *B* and an offsetting $2,000 remedial allocation of tax gain to *A*. Accordingly, the total allocation of tax gain to *A* from the hypothetical sale would be $4,000, and so this is the amount of the debt allocable to *A* under tier two *if* the partnership uses the remedial allocation method to address ceiling limitation problems.

Under tier three, the remainder of the debt is allocated between the partners as they share profits. Actually, the partners have four choices under this tier. First, they may agree to allocate the remainder of the debt in accordance with their general profits interest. Second, they may agree to allocate the remainder of the debt in any way that is reasonably consistent with some other allocation having economic effect. Third, they may allocate a portion of the debt as they share §704(c) gain (including reverse §704(c)) to the extent not accounted for under tier two. Fourth, they may agree to allocate the remainder of the debt in accordance with the way in which they will allocate the nonrecourse deductions from the property. Treas. Regs. §1.752-3(a)(3).

In summary, there is no allocation of the debt under tier one. If the partnership uses the traditional method or the traditional method with curative allocations to address ceiling problems arising from the property, the debt is allocated \$2,000 to *A* and \$0 to *B* under tier two; if the partners use the remedial allocation method, the tier two allocation is \$4,000 to *A* and \$0 to *B*. Finally, the remainder of the debt (which may be \$4,000 or \$2,000) is either divided equally between *A* and *B* or allocated entirely to *B* at the partnership's option.

PROBLEMS

21-3. *P* and *Q* form the *PQ* general partnership, agreeing that *P* will be allocated 40 percent and *Q* 60 percent of all tax items except that depreciation deductions will be divided equally. *P* contributes depreciable property subject to a nonrecourse liability of \$6,000, with an adjusted basis of \$4,000 and a fair market value of \$10,000. *Q* contributes \$6,000 cash.

a. What are the initial capital accounts and outside bases?
b. If the property contributed by *P* has five years remaining on its depreciable life (although a new depreciable life would be 10 years), what are the partners' capital accounts and outside bases after one year, assuming there is no other income or loss to the partnership and that the property is depreciated using the straight-line method?

21-4. *X* and *Y* are equal partners in the *XY* general partnership with capital accounts and outside basis of \$3,000 each. *Z* joins by contributing machinery to the partnership in exchange for a 25-percent interest in profits and losses. At the time of *Z*'s admission, the machinery has an adjusted basis to *Z* of \$15,000 and a fair market value of \$20,000, and it is encumbered by an \$18,000 nonrecourse debt. The partnership's only other asset is \$6,000 in cash. In the first taxable year after *Z* joins, the partnership is entitled to a \$6,000 depreciation deduction from the machinery. What are the partners' outside bases?

C. WHY §752?

Having examined how §752 does (and possibly should) operate, it is time to ask why partnership borrowing has any effect on outside basis. In fact, because there is no provision in subchapter S equivalent to §752, the possibility of using §752 to exploit entity-level borrowing can be one reason for using a partnership instead of an S corporation.

Consider first partnership recourse indebtedness. As we have seen, such debt is allocated among the partners as they share economic risk of repayment. An increase in outside basis provides tax advantages for the partners, so that if §752(a) did not provide the partners with a basis increase, they would seek to accomplish the same tax result some other way. Could they do it?

Yes. Rather than cause the partnership to incur the debt, the partners themselves could borrow the same amount and then contribute the borrowed proceeds to the partnership. Such actual contributions of cash would produce the outside basis increase under §722 as is obtained under §752(a) when the partnership incurs the debt directly. Similarly, if the partnership distributed cash to the partners so that they could pay off their debt, these actual distributions would have the same effect as a reduction of partnership debt has under §752(b). At least with respect to recourse debt, then, §752 can be justified as giving the partners directly what they could obtain indirectly.

From a more structural perspective, the effect of §752 is to continue the equality of aggregate inside and outside bases started by the double carry-over basis rules of §722 and §723 and continued by the basis adjustment rules of §705. When the partnership borrows funds, inside basis goes up by the amount of the debt, either implicitly in the form of cash or explicitly in the basis of the assets acquired with the loan proceeds. Under §752(a), aggregate outside basis increases by the same amount. Similarly, repayment by the partnership of the loan reduces inside basis by the amount of the repayment. By maintaining the equality of aggregate inside and outside bases, §752 helps minimize the disruptions caused by the entity model of partnership taxation: Inside basis and outside basis should simply be two different ways to dividing the partners' aggregate investment in the enterprise, either asset by asset (inside basis) or partner by partner (outside basis).

This last justification for §752 applies with equal force to nonrecourse partnership debt: Because nonrecourse debt increases inside basis, it should also increase outside basis if aggregate inside and outside bases are to remain equal. If an individual purchases property subject to a nonrecourse loan, the property's adjusted basis is increased by the amount of the debt. If partnership nonrecourse loans did not increase outside basis, the partners would stand in a worse tax position by reason of the partnership than they would if they owned the property directly.

D. HOLDING A PARTNERSHIP INTEREST THROUGH A DISREGARDED ENTITY

If a taxpayer interposes a disregarded entity ("DE") between himself and the partnership, the taxpayer will continue to be treated as the partner for all tax purposes although the DE will be treated as the partner for non-tax purposes. So, for example, it is the DE that should be named as the partner in the partnership agreement but it is the taxpayer's identification number ("TID") that should be placed by the partnership on the K-1 form.

While the taxpayer remains the partner for federal tax purposes, the impact of the DE under relevant non-tax law can affect the taxpayer. For example, suppose the partner is a member of a general partnership. The usual rule in such circumstances is that recourse debt of the entity will be allocated among the general partners in proportion to their loss-sharing ratios because that is how repayment of the debt will be shared if the entity is unable to satisfy its obligation with its own assets. However, as to a taxpayer who owns his interest through a disregarded entity, there is in fact no risk of repayment arising from the borrowing because the interposition of the DE eliminates all personal liability. Accordingly, as to this taxpayer the loan will be treated as nonrecourse under §752 because the creditor has, absent some additional contractual rights, no rights against the taxpayer who is the partner for tax purposes.

In such circumstances, the taxpayer may seek to acquire some of the entity's recourse debt in either of two ways: (1) by guaranteeing the debt or (2) by contributing assets to the DE, which then become available to the creditor for satisfaction of the entity's liability. Regulations address both ways of obtaining debt basis by a partner who owns a partnership interest through a disregarded entity.

1. *Guarantee of a Disregarded Entity's Partnership Obligation*

The law is clear that a partner who is liable for a share of the partnership's indebtedness by reason of a capital account deficit restoration obligation or otherwise will be allocated a portion of the debt by reason of that potential repayment obligation. Note, though, that a guarantee of partnership will debt will be effective to shift debt to the guarantor partner only if the guarantor partner has no right of subrogation against other partners if called upon to pay the entity's debt: Because debt is allocated in accordance with risk of repayment, a right of subrogation eliminates such a risk and so fails to shift debt.

For example, suppose that *DE* and *Y* are the two partners of the *XY* partnership, and *DE* is a disregarded entity owned by *X* having no assets other than its interest in the *XY* partnership. If the partnership borrows on a fully recourse basis, risk of repayment is borne by *Y* alone because the creditor cannot get past *DE* to seek repayment from *X*. Accordingly, all of the debt will be allocated to *Y* under the rules of §752. See Treas. Regs. §1.752-2(k)(1) (first sentence).

If *X* guarantees some or all of the debt and has the usual right of subrogation that comes with such a guarantee, the debt will continue to be allocated entirely to *Y*. To be sure, if the entity is unable to satisfy its obligation the creditor may seek repayment from *X* as guarantor. But if that happens *X* will be permitted to seek repayment from the principal obligor—that is, from the partnership—and through it from *Y*. And while ordinarily *Y* might have a right of contribution good against the other general partner, that right extends no further than *DE*. Thus, *X* will be able to shift the burden of the debt to *Y* without any ability of *Y* to shift it back to *X*.

In the absence of a right of subrogation, however, the economic risk of repayment of the liability will remain with *X* to the extent of the guarantee, and the effect of that is twofold. First, *X* will increase outside basis to the extent of the liability by reason of §752(a). Second, *X* will be treated as having a partial deficit restoration obligation and so allocations of loss and deduction can be made to *X* despite such allocations driving *X*'s capital account negative. That is, to the extent that a partner who holds his partnership interest through a disregarded entity is liable for debts of the partnership by reason of a guarantee or otherwise, the usual recourse debt rules of §752 apply. See Treas. Regs. §1.752-2(k)(1) (second sentence).

Consider the following example: *X* contributes cash of $1,000 to *DE*, and *DE* contributes that cash to *XY*. *Y* also contributes cash of $1,000 to *XY*, and for state law purposes *DE* and *Y* are equal general partners in *XY*. For tax purposes, the partners are *X* and *Y*, and *X* has no personal liability for the debts of the partnership except to the extent *X* specifically agrees to be liable for some or all of the obligations of *DE* or of the partnership directly.

Each partner starts the venture with a capital account and outside basis of $1,000. If the partnership were to spend $1,200 in the first year on deductible expenditures, no more than $1,000 of those deduction could be allocated to *X* under §704(b) because, under the alternate test for economic effect, no allocation of deduction can drive *X*'s capital account negative. Furthermore, even if additional deductions could be allocated to *X* under §704(b), such deductions could not in fact be claimed by *X* because of the outside basis limitation in §704(d).

Suppose that the partnership borrows $600 on a fully recourse basis. This indebtedness does not increase either partner's capital account (entity-level borrowing never does), and because the lender can seek repayment from *Y* but not from *X*, the borrowing is allocated to *Y* alone under §752. Thus, the debt does not increase the amount of deductions that can be allocated to *X* under §704(b), nor does it raise the outside basis limitation in §704(d).

But suppose *X* guarantees repayment of up to $200 of *DE*'s future obligations to the partnership, and suppose further that *X* relinquishes any right of subrogation or contribution that *X* might have against *Y*. Now, allocations of loss and deductions can drive *X*'s capital account negative by as much as $200 because, under state law, such a guarantee by *X* is treated as a capital account deficit restoration obligation. Further, because *X* bears a potential repayment obligation for the debt of up to $200, *X* is allocated $200 of the debt, and so *X*'s outside basis increases by that amount. Thus, the guarantee removes both the allocation and outside basis limitations.

What if *X* made this $200 guarantee despite having assets less than $200? There is a general presumption of solvency, and nothing in this rule limits its application to those who are partners for state law purposes. Thus, a guarantee should not be ineffective under §752 simply because the guarantor's potential exposure exceeds the net value of the guarantor's assets. However, there also is an anti-abuse rule in the §752 regulations, and application of this anti-abuse rule may modify the analysis.

Treas. Regs. §1.752-2(j)(1) provides in relevant part:

> An obligation of a partner or related person to make a payment may be disregarded or treated as an obligation of another person for purposes of this section if facts and circumstances indicate that a principal purpose of the arrangement between the parties is to eliminate the partner's economic risk of loss with respect to that obligation or create the appearance of the partner or related person bearing the economic risk of loss when, in fact, the substance of the arrangement is otherwise.

Suppose *X* Corp. owns *D* Corp., and *D* Corp. is the sole general partner in the *P* partnership. If *P* borrows on a recourse basis, the debt will be allocated to *D* unless the anti-abuse rule quoted above applies. If *D* has no assets other than its interest in *P*, this anti-abuse rule may apply. If *X* (*X* being a "related person" to *D*) guarantees a portion of *D*'s potential obligation to *P*, such a guarantee presumably will establish the lack of a tax avoidance motive. If so, the guarantee of *some* of the debt may suffice to ensure that *all* of the debt is allocated to *D* by defeating application of the anti-abuse rule. That is, if the anti-abuse does not apply, then the presumption of solvency should apply even though *D*'s net worth is less than its share of the partnership's indebtedness.

But suppose *D* is a disregarded entity. If *X* (now the partner for federal tax purposes) guarantees some of *D*'s potential obligation to *P*, then some of *P*'s debt will be allocated to *X* pro tanto. That is, *X* will be allocated only *so much* of *P*'s debt as *X*'s guarantees because of the "to the extent" language in Treas. Regs. §1.752-2(k)(2) (second sentence).

2. *The Impact of Assets Owned by the Disregarded Partner*

An alternative way for the owner ("*X*") of a disregarded entity ("*DE*") to get a share of partnership recourse indebtedness otherwise allocated to the disregarded entity is for the owner to contribute assets to the disregarded entity other than those contributed to the partnership. Such assets—treated as assets of *X* for federal tax law purposes—can be reached by creditors of the partnership (assuming that *DE* is a general partner under local law). Such assets are, in effect, treated as retained by *X* but pledged to secure the partnership's debt. Regulations under §752 have long provided that the pledge of assets by a partner will be treated as shifting the economic risk of the debt to the partner pledging the assets to the extent of the fair market value of the pledged assets. See Treas. Regs. §1.752-2(h). One might think that interposition of a disregarded entity between a partner and a partnership would be shoehorned into this pledged-asset rule. Alas, things are not so simple.

To be sure, regulations now provide that the owner of the disregarded entity will be treated as liable for the partnership indebtedness otherwise allocated to the disregarded entity to the extent of the net value of assets other than the partnership interest held by the disregarded entity. This leaves two important issues: (1) how to determine the "net value" of the disregarded entity and (2) when to make such a determination.

The "how to" question is answered by Treas. Regs. §1.752-2(k)(2)(i), providing that the net value of a disregarded entity equals the fair market value of its assets that are subject to the claims of creditors of the disregarded entity less all obligations of the disregarded entity. Note in particular that if a disregarded entity owns interests in two partnerships, the value of each partnership interest adds to the "net value" of the entity for purposes of allocating indebtedness of the other partnership. Treas. Regs. §1.752-2(k)(6) (example 4).

The "when to" question is more difficult to answer. The initial determination of the net value of a disregarded entity generally will be made at the close of the partnership's first taxable year in which the net value of the disregarded entity is relevant to the allocation of partnership indebtedness. Treas. Regs. §1.752-2(k)(2)(iv)(A). However, if the partnership for some other reason must compute the partners' share of debt earlier in that year, then valuation occurs at that time. *Id.*

The partnership's "net value" is redetermined upon the occurrence of various "valuation events." Such valuation events are (A) more than a de minimis contribution of property to the disregarded entity (excluding property immediately retransferred from the disregarded entity to the partnership); (B) more than a de minimis distribution of property from the disregarded entity (excluding property having just been received from the partnership); (C) a change in the legally enforceable obligation, if any, of the owner of the disregarded entity to make contributions to the disregarded entity; (D) the change of any obligation of the disregarded entity; and (E) the disposition of more than a de minimis amount of property by the disregarded entity, but then the revaluation equals the difference between the value received on the disposition as compared with the value of the property given up (as if the last valuation event). Treas. Regs. §1.752-2(k)(2)(iii).

So, for example, if *X* contributes Blackacre to *DE* with a value of $250,000, and Blackacre is retained by *DE* and is available to the creditors of the partnership to satisfy the partnership's liabilities, then $250,000 of the partnership's recourse liabilities will be allocated to *X* under this rule. Note, though, that it is the value of Blackacre as of the close of the partnership's taxable year that is used so that, for example, if Blackacre should decline from $250,000 to $175,000 during the year of contribution, the "net value" of *DE* will be only $175,000. Treas. Regs. §1.752-2(k)(6) (example 2(ii)).

The regulations fail to take advantage of valuations that exist for other purposes. Thus, if a disregarded entity receives rents of $15,000 from a tenant, there is no explicit support for increasing the "net value" of *DE* by the rent received. Perhaps the rents can be treated as contributed from *X* to *DE*. There is no support in the regulations for such a recharacterization, and such an approach would, under the regulations, trigger a revaluation of *all* the assets owned by *DE*.

There is one additional curiosity in the regulations worth mentioning. Appreciated assets contributed to a disregarded entity can shift recourse debt to the owner of the disregarded entity to the extent of the fair market value of the assets. This is consistent with the pledge rule in the §752 regulations as well as with the at-risk rules in §465. But if the property were actually contributed to the partnership rather than merely made available to the creditors of the partnership, basis would increase only by the adjusted basis of the contributed property. This preference for pledged property over contributed property exists in the at-risk rules as well, but it is especially hard to explain in the partnership context given the role of §704(c) forcing the allocation of pre-contribution appreciation in contributed property to the contributing partner just as gain from pledged property will be included to the owner.

E. BIFURCATED HOLDING PERIOD OF A PARTNERSHIP INTEREST

Despite the number of distinct interests in a single partnership that one partner may own, a partner has only one capital account, Treas. Regs. §1.704-1(b)(2)(iv)(b), and the Service has long maintained that a partner also has a single, unified outside basis, Rev. Rul. 84-53, 1984-1 C.B. 159. Nevertheless, a partner can have multiple holdings periods with respect to the partner's unified interest in the partnership. See generally Treas. Regs. §1.1223-3. A bifurcated holding period can arise either by contributing multiple properties to the partnership at one time or by making multiple contributions to the partnership over time. Treas. Regs. §1.1223-3(a). A partner having a bifurcated holding period can recognize both long- and short-term capital gain on the sale of her partnership interest or from a distribution of cash (including marketable securities treated as cash under §731(c)) in excess of outside basis. See Treas. Regs. §1.1223-3(c), -3(d)(2).

Suppose that *X* is a member of the *P* Partnership, and assume that *X* has a holding period in its partnership interest in excess of one year. If the fair market value of *X*'s interest equals $500, and *X* contributes additional cash of $250 to the partnership (increasing the value of *X*'s interest to $750), then *X* will be treated as having a short-term holding period in one-third of the partnership interest because of the cash contribution. So, for example, if *X* sells her partnership interest four months later, one-third of any gain or loss will be short-term. Note that this is true even though all of the appreciation in *X*'s partnership interest may have accrued many years earlier. Note also that this result would not change if *X* had contributed property rather than cash unless the property had been a capital asset in *X*'s hands immediately prior to the contribution and *X* had had a holding period in the contributed property in excess of eight months. See §1223(1) (tacking for substitute basis capital and §1231 assets).

As a general rule, distributions from a partnership do not affect the distributee partner's holding period in the partnership interest. Treas. Regs. §1.1223-3(d)(1). However, distributions of cash can reduce the short-term portion of a bifurcated holding period because only the net cash contributions made during any 12-month period create a bifurcated holding period for an otherwise long-term partnership interest. Treas. Regs. §1.1223-3(b)(2). For this purpose, deemed distributions arising from a decrease in a partner's share of partnership liabilities are ignored. Treas. Regs. §1.1223-3(b)(3). Deemed contributions arising from an increase in liability share equally are ignored. *Id.*

Suppose that *X* and *Y* are equal general partners in the *XY* partnership, and that *XY* owns unimproved real estate with an adjusted basis of $1,000,000 and fair market value of $5,000,000. Assume that *X* and *Y* each have an outside basis of $500,000, that each partner has held her partnership interest for more than one year, that the partnership has held the property for more than one year, and that *XY* has found a purchaser for its property. However, before the sale can be completed the partnership must invest an additional $500,000 in the transaction (to cover fees of lawyers and accountants and to make certain improvements to the property).

If each partner contributes additional cash of $250,000 and then the property is sold, the partnership's gain will be long term, and that gain will be includible by the partners. §702(a). As a result of that inclusion, the partners will increase their outside bases, §705(a)(1)(A), and so a subsequent distribution of the sale proceeds should be tax free. Thus, the contribution of cash will not affect the character of the gain recognized by the partnership.

However, if after the cash is contributed, the partners must sell their interests rather than the partnership sell its assets, a less favorable result would be obtained because the cash contribution would convert one-11th of the gain into short-term capital gain (for each partner, the cash contributed of $250,000 is one-10th of the pre-contribution $2,500,000 value of the partnership interest). If the transaction must be effected by the sale of partnership interests, then the partners should not have contributed the needed capital but rather should have caused the partnership to borrow it. So long as the form of the borrowing is respected, the borrowing will not affect the holding period of the property or of the partnership interests.

F. THE EFFECT OF INDEBTEDNESS ON PARTNERSHIP ALLOCATIONS

1. *Allocations under the Alternate Test for Economic Effect*

Consider first the limitation on allocations of deductions in the context of a debt-free partnership. For example, suppose *P* and *Q* form the *PQ* limited liability company by contributing cash of $100 each. In its first year of operations, *PQ* incurs deductible expenses of $120. What is the maximum deduction that can be allocated to *P* or to *Q*?

The answer is $100 because an allocation of deduction in excess of that amount to either partner will drive that partner's capital account negative. No allocation of deduction is valid to the extent it causes a capital account deficit in a member's capital account in excess of the amount, if any, that the member can be required to restore to the entity. Treas. Regs. §1.704-1(b)(2)(ii)(d). Here, neither member has a deficit restoration obligation, and so no capital account deficit can be created.

Now assume that in addition to equity contributions of $100 per member, the entity also borrows $60 from some third-party lender. Assuming that the assets of the entity are pledged against this debt, but that neither *P* nor *Q* provides a personal guarantee, this debt is treated as nonrecourse debt under the §752 regulations. Treas. Regs. §1.752-1(a). Accordingly, the debt will increase each member's outside basis by $30 (assuming profits from the activity will be allocated equally between *P* and *Q*). See generally Treas. Regs. §1.752-3.

Once again, the LLC incurs $120 of deductible expenses in its first year, and the question again is how much of that $120 can be allocated to either of the members? The answer, somewhat surprisingly, is that no more than $100 of the deductions can be allocated to either partner despite the existence of the debt. While the debt increases the members' outside bases, §752(a), it does not affect their capital accounts, Treas. Regs. §1.704-1(b)(2)(iv)(b), and without an increase in capital account or creation of a deficit restoration obligation, no allocation of deduction can create a capital account deficit.

To be sure: An allocation of nonrecourse deductions can create a capital account deficit (see Treas. Regs. §1.704-2(e)), but on the facts as presented there are no nonrecourse deductions (yet). A nonrecourse deduction is a deduction to the extent it increases the excess of the partnership nonrecourse indebtedness over the book value of the security. Treas. Regs. §1.704-2(c). Here, the debt started at $60, and the book value of the security started at $260 (because all of the partnership assets are pledged to secure the debt). The first year deductions reduce the book value of the security from $260 to $140, but that still exceeds the $60 of debt, so there are no nonrecourse deductions. That is, in year one it is the partners' equity that is being depreciated, and loss of equity cannot under the alternate test for economic effect create a capital account deficit without a deficit restoration obligation.

So assume now that *P* provided the lender with a personal guarantee of the debt. This converts the debt from nonrecourse to recourse because one of the members bears the economic risk of repayment. See Treas. Regs. §1.752-2(f) (example 5). Given this change, if *PQ* again incurs $120 of deductions in the first year, what is the maximum amount of that $120 that can be allocated to *P*? The answer, again, is only $100.

Now the debt is recourse as to *P*, which means that the entire debt adds to *P*'s outside basis. But it does not add to *P*'s capital account, and again no allocation of deduction can create a capital account deficit unless absent an unconditional deficit restoration obligation. Does the debt create such an obligation for *P*?

Without more it does not. To be sure, the effect of *P*'s guarantee is that *P* can be required to contribute additional funds to the venture. But that possible obligation is limited to satisfaction of the partnership's obligation to the lender; if *P*'s capital account is negative and there are sufficient funds to pay off the loan, *P* cannot be required to restore the capital account deficit. Indeed, after the partnership's first year there presumably are assets of $140, of which $60 could be used to repay the loan. The remaining $80 will go to *Q*, whose capital account balance stands at $100 if the entire $120 of deductions had been allocated to *P*. To ensure that each partner receives his capital account balance upon liquidation, *P* cannot be allocated more than $100 of the first year's deductions. See Rev. Rul. 97-38, 1997-2 C.B. 69.

2. *Property Encumbered by Multiple Indebtedness*

If a single piece of partnership property is encumbered by multiple debts at least one of which is "nonrecourse," the book value of the property must be allocated among the liabilities so that the amount of "minimum gain" with respect to each nonrecourse loan can be determined. Regulation §1.704-2(d)(2)(iii) provides

> If property is subject to two or more liabilities of equal priority, the property's adjusted [book value] is allocated among the liabilities in proportion to their outstanding balances. If property is subject to two or more liabilities of unequal priority, the [book value] is allocated first to the liability of the highest priority to the extent of its outstanding balance and then to each liability in descending order of priority to the extent of its outstanding balance, until fully allocated.

For example, suppose the *P* partnership owns Blackacre with book value of $100 and that Blackacre is encumbered by two debts, one nonrecourse and one recourse. Suppose further that the recourse debt is inferior to the nonrecourse debt—that is, if the partnership does not pay its debts as they come due, Blackacre will first be used to satisfy the nonrecourse debt and only after that debt is fully paid will any excess value from Blackacre be used to satisfy the recourse debt. Finally, suppose that the amount of the each debt equals $50.

On these facts, allocation of the first $50 of depreciation will be subject to the "substantial economic effect" test of Treas. Regs. §1.704-1(b) rather than to the special regime applicable to "nonrecourse deductions." In particular, such depreciation cannot be allocated to limited partners with $0 capital account balances except to the extent such partners can be forced to contribute some additional capital to the partnership.

This unfortunate result arises because the book value of the partnership is allocated to the superior debt prior to the inferior debt; here, that means that the book value is first allocated to the nonrecourse loan. As a result, so long as there is at least $50 of book value, there will be no partnership minimum gain because the book value of the property properly allocable to the nonrecourse debt will not exceed the amount of that debt. See Treas. Regs. §1.704-2(m) (example 1(v)).

3. *Partial Guarantees*

If one or more partners guarantees a portion of an otherwise nonrecourse loan, the loan will be bifurcated into recourse and nonrecourse portions. The book value of the encumbered assets must then be allocated between the two portions so that the partnership's minimum gain, if any, can be determined.

For example, suppose the *XY* limited liability company borrows $80 in order to purchase Blackacre for $100, with the remainder of the purchase price paid with the company's equity, equally contributed by *X* and by *Y*. If *X* (but not *Y*) guarantees repayment of $5 of the debt, what rules apply to allocation of the depreciation deductions?

Assuming neither partner has any obligation to contribute additional funds to the partnership, the first $10 of depreciation can be allocated however the partners desire, although the first $20 must be equally allocated between *X* and *Y*. This flexibility with respect to the first $10 of depreciation coupled with a complete lack of flexibility with respect to the next $10 of depreciation arises from application of the alternate test of economic effect: The depreciation may be allocated however the partners desire so long as no partner's capital account is driven negative.

However, once the partnership's equity has been fully depreciated, allocation of depreciation becomes subject to a different rule. If the depreciation is treated as coming out of the nonrecourse portion of the loan, then the depreciation is subject to the special nonrecourse deduction rules and so can be allocated between *X* and *Y*. But if the depreciation is treated as coming out of the recourse portion of the loan, then the depreciation is treated as a partner nonrecourse deduction and so can be allocated only to the partner liable for repayment of the loan (that is, to *X*). See generally Treas. Regs. §1.704-2(i) (definition and allocation of "partner nonrecourse deductions"). How the next dollar of depreciation is treated turns on the specifics of *X*'s guarantee.

a. Last Dollar Guarantee

Consider first an unqualified but limited dollar guarantee: That is, *X* guarantees repayment of the loan but cannot be required to contribute more than $5 on that guarantee. Thus, if the value of Blackacre drops below $80, *X* will be forced to make good on the guarantee, but as the value of Blackacre continues to fall below $75, the loss is borne entirely by the lender.

On these facts, depreciation deductions reducing the book value of Blackacre from $80 to $75 will be treated as partner nonrecourse deductions and so must be allocated entirely to *X*. To understand this result, assume that Blackacre is worth exactly $75 when the debts are foreclosed. Blackacre will be used to repay the nonrecourse portion of the loan, and the recourse portion will be paid not out of Blackacre but rather out of the guarantee. Thus, the nonrecourse portion of the debt has superiority with respect to Blackacre and so is allocated Blackacre's book value before any book value is allocated to the guaranteed portion of the debt. See Treas. Regs. §1.704-2(m) (example 1(vii)).

b. First Dollar Guarantee

Consider next a qualified and limited dollar guarantee: That is, *X* guarantees repayment of the loan only if and to the extent the value of the collateral drops below $5. Thus, the guarantee will not be triggered simply because the value of Blackacre falls below $80 but only if it falls below $5. This first dollar guarantee, in other words, represents substantially less economic risk than a last dollar guarantee.

On these facts, depreciation deductions reducing the book value of Blackacre from $80 to $5 will be treated as nonrecourse deductions and so can be allocated between *X* and *Y* in accordance with the nonrecourse deductions rule. Now, the recourse (guaranteed) portion of the debt is superior to the nonrecourse portion because the value of Blackacre, however small, will be used to satisfy the recourse portion of the debt before satisfying the nonrecourse portion. Accordingly, the recourse portion of the debt has superiority with respect to Blackacre and so is allocated Blackacre's book value before any book value is allocated to the guaranteed portion of the debt. See Treas. Regs. §1.704-2(m) (example 1(vii)).

Treating the first $75 of depreciation (after the partnership's equity is gone) as giving rise to nonrecourse deductions is consistent with the nonrecourse nature of the liability because neither partner has or is treated as having an obligation to restore any capital account deficit. Under Rev. Rul. 97-38, 1997-2 C.B. 69, a partner is treated as having a limited capital account deficit restoration obligation to the extent the partner would be called on to satisfy a partnership debt in favor of the lender were the security for the loan sold for book value. Here, so long as the security is sold for $5 or more, neither partner can be required to contribute additional funds to the partnership. Thus, no allocation of deductions subject to the substantial economic effect test could be made to either partner. Fortunately, as indicated above, these depreciation deductions are allocated not under the substantial economic effect test but rather under the special rules applicable to nonrecourse deductions.

22

Nonliquidating Distributions

A. DISTRIBUTIONS NOT SUBJECT TO §751(b)

1. Basic Taxation Rules

a. Recognition of Gain and Loss

The basic principle underlying the tax treatment of partnership distributions is that the distribution should be tax free to the partnership and to the distributee partner if possible. Under §731(a), loss is not recognized on a current distribution, and gain is recognized by the distributee partner only if and to the extent that the amount of cash distributed exceeds the distributee partner's pre-distribution outside basis, such gain being capital because of the final sentence in §731(a) combined with §741. This is consistent with the basic paradigm underlying subchapter K that transactions between a partner and the partnership should not be taxable; instead, taxation generally waits until the partnership or one of its partners engages in a transaction with someone outside the partnership. However, the relative simplicity of §731(a) can be overruled by application of §751(b).

b. Basis of Distributed Property and Outside Basis

Most distributions described in §731(a) are tax free, and those that are tax free have no net effect on the distributee partner's overall basis. In general, §732 provides that the distributee partner carries over the partnership's adjusted basis in the distributed assets, and whatever basis is allocated to the distributed property is subtracted from the distributee partner's outside basis under §733. Accordingly, the effect of a distribution tax free under §731 is to reallocate the distributee partner's pre-distribution outside basis between the distributed property and the partner's post-distribution outside basis. Of course, to the extent the distribution includes cash as well as property, the distributee partner's outside basis is first reduced by the amount of the cash distributed, §733(1).

When the distributee partner's pre-distribution outside basis is less than the partnership's basis in the distributed assets, asset basis cannot carry over without producing a negative outside basis. Because outside basis can never become less than zero, see §733, when the distributee partner's pre-distribution outside basis is less than the partnership's basis in the distributed assets, the partner's outside basis drops to zero as a result of the distribution, and the partner's entire pre-distribution outside basis is allocated to the distributed property, see §732(a)(2), with the shortfall allocated among the distributed assets in accordance with the rules of §732(c)(2). Once again, though, if the distribution includes cash as well as property, the partner's pre-distribution outside basis is first used to absorb the cash and only the excess is allocated to the distributed property.

Consider the following example. Individual *X* is a member of the *P* partnership. *P* distributes cash of $7,000, inventory with an adjusted basis of $6,000 and fair market value of $10,000, and a capital asset with an adjusted basis of $24,000 and fair market value of $29,000 to *X* in a transaction described in §731. At the time of the distribution, *X*'s outside basis equals $32,000.

Because the cash distributed does not exceed *X*'s pre-distribution outside basis, there is no gain on the distribution. §731(a)(1). Under §732(a)(2), *X*'s basis in the distributed assets equals $25,000, that being *X*'s pre-distribution outside basis of $32,000 less the $7,000 cash distributed. Of that $25,000 basis, $6,000 is first allocated to the inventory pursuant to §732(c)(1)(A)(i), and the remaining $19,000 is allocated to the capital asset under §732(c)(1)(B) and §732(c)(3)(B). *X*'s outside basis is reduced to $0 under §733(1)-(2).

Reconsider this example, assuming that instead of receiving inventory and a capital asset, *X* receives two capital assets, asset *A* having an adjusted basis to the partnership of $6,000 and fair market value of $10,000, and asset *B* having an adjusted basis to the partnership of $24,000 and fair market value of $29,000. Once again assume that *X* also receives cash of $7,000 and that *X*'s pre-distribution outside basis equals $32,000.

As before, *X* recognizes no gain because the cash distributed is less than *X*'s pre-distribution outside basis. Similarly, *X*'s basis in the distributed assets again totals $25,000. Because both assets are now assumed to be capital assets, there is no allocation under §732(c)(1)(A)(i). Instead, each capital asset is allocated under §732(c)(1)(B)(i) a carry-over basis taken from the partnership (that is, asset *A* is allocated a basis of $6,000, and asset *B* is allocated a basis of $24,000), but because the basis so allocated exceeds the $25,000 total provided by §732(a)(2), the basis of the capital assets is then decreased pursuant to §732(c)(1)(B)(ii) and §732(c)(3).

This decrease is computed in three steps. First, we must determine the total amount of the basis decrease. Here, that is $5,000 because giving each capital asset a carry-over basis yields a combined basis of $30,000 while the total basis to be allocated under §732(a)(2) equals only $25,000. Second, we allocate this $5,000 basis decrease to those capital assets having adjusted basis to the partnership in excess of fair market value (that is, to those distributed capital assets having unrealized loss). §732(c)(3)(A). In this example, there is no allocation under this second step because both capital assets are appreciated. Third, we allocate any remaining basis decrease to the distributed capital assets in proportion to their adjusted bases (as adjusted under step 2). §732(c)(3)(B). Thus, of the $5,000 basis decrease, $1,000 is allocated to capital asset *A*, and $4,000 is allocated to capital asset *B*.

Accordingly, *X* takes asset *A* with a basis of $5,000 and asset *B* with a basis of $20,000. *X*'s outside basis is reduced to $0 under §733(1)-(2).

Note that the way in which §732(c) is written ensures that ordinary income assets (that is, unrealized receivables and inventory) will be given a carry-over basis before any basis is given to capital assets, thereby minimizing the likelihood that a distribution will increase the amount of ordinary income recognized upon disposition of the distributed assets. Still, if a combined carry-over basis for the distributed ordinary income assets exceeds the distributee partner's pre-distribution outside basis (reduced by any cash received in the distribution), because outside basis cannot go negative, the ordinary income assets will have a basis in the hands of the distributee partner lower than the adjusted basis of those assets in the hands of the partnership.[1]

c. The Timing of Taxation

A loan from the partnership to a partner is not a distribution subject to §§731-733, at least unless and until the loan is forgiven by the partnership. This explains the rule that a draw against partnership share is not treated as a partnership distribution until the last day of the partnership taxable year, because until that day the partner's distributive share is uncertain and the partner may be required to repay some or all of the draw. See Treas. Regs. §1.731-1(a)(1)(ii).

At least one group of commentators interpreted this rule to mean that the tax consequences of all partnership distributions are determined as of the close of the partnership taxable year, thereby permitting the partners to use the current year's income to absorb distributed cash. 2 A. Willis, J. Pennell & P. Postlewaite, Partnership Taxation ¶13.02 (6th ed. 1997). Such a reading of Treas. Regs. §1.731-1(a)(1)(ii) seems inconsistent with the words of the statute and does not appear to be the Service's understanding of the issue. See, e.g., sources cited in 2 W. McKee, W. Nelson & R. Whitmire, Federal Taxation of Partnerships and Partners ¶19.03[2], at 19-26 n.87 (4th ed. 2007). Indeed, in Rev. Rul. 94-4, 1994-1 C.B. 195, the Service ruled that constructive distributions caused by a reduction in share of partnership liabilities are treated as draws until the close of the taxable year, but in so ruling the Service took pains to explain why treating constructive distributions as falling within Treas. Regs. §1.731-1(a)(1)(ii) was consistent with the statute. If all distributions fell within this regulation, the Service would have had no need to justify constructive distributions as a special case. While there is no published revenue ruling in which the Service has ruled that a distribution described in §731 is not a "draw or advance" within the meaning of Treas. Regs. §1.731-1(a)(1)(ii), at least one ruling expressly recognizes that the tax consequences of a distribution are determined by reference to the distributee partner's outside basis immediately prior to the distribution and that only "certain" distributions fall with the "draw or advance" exception. Rev. Rul. 92-97, 1992-2 C.B. 124.

1. Any asset basis lost because of the limitation in §732(a)(2) can be transferred to the remaining, undistributed assets of the partnership under §734(b)(1)(B), discussed infra in Chapter 27.

NOTES

1. *Partnership property.* Suppose a partnership purchases property and then immediately distributes that property to partner *Z*. Is this treated as a distribution of "property" even if the partnership acquired the property only to distribute it to *Z*? Presumably the partnership could have distributed the cash to *Z* who then could have used the cash to buy the property, but such a distribution would have been taxable to *Z* if the amount of cash exceeded *Z*'s outside basis. If *Z* in effect goes shopping with the partnership's money, will that be seen as an improper attempt to circumvent the gain recognition rule in §731(a)(1) applicable to distributions of excess cash? See ILM 200650014 (Sept. 16, 2006), concluding "Under the facts presented in this case, a carry-over basis is not appropriate for a unique parcel of residential property that apparently was selected by the distributee, acquired by the partnership immediately before the distribution, solely for the purpose of the distribution, and was unrelated to the partnership's business activities."

PROBLEMS

22-1. Individual *X* is a member of the *P* partnership. *P* distributes cash of $11,000, capital asset #1 with adjusted basis of $6,000 and fair market value of $9,000, and capital asset #2 with adjusted basis of $24,000 and fair market value of $18,000, to *X* in a transaction described in §731. At the time of the distribution, *X*'s outside basis equals $31,000. How much gain or loss does *X* recognize on the distribution, and what basis does *X* take in each of the distributed assets?

22-2. *A*'s outside basis and capital account is $22,000 prior to receiving a nonliquidating distribution consisting of the following:

	Adjusted Basis	*Fair Market Value*
Cash	$ 2,000	$ 2,000
Receivables	0	6,000
Inventory	2,000	5,000
Capital asset 1	8,000	7,000
Capital asset 2	14,000	21,000

Assuming §751 does not apply to this transaction, what are the tax consequences to *A* and what basis does *A* take in each of the distributed assets?

2. *Distributions and Capital Accounts*

a. Excess Cash

Distributions reduce the outside basis of the distributee partner. See §733. Because capital accounts and outside basis move up and down together (excluding the effect of partnership debt on outside basis), distributions of cash and property must also reduce capital accounts. That in fact is the rule, although the amount of the capital account adjustment under Treas. Regs. §1.704-1(b)(2)(iv)(e)(1) is somewhat different from the outside basis adjustment under §733.

Consider first a distribution of cash in an amount sufficient to trigger recognition of income under §731(a)(1). For example, suppose *P* receives a distribution of $10,000 from the *PQ* partnership when *P*'s outside basis and capital account are only $8,000. Under §731(a)(1), *P* recognizes income of $2,000 (which is capital gain under the last sentence of §731(a) combined with §741). In addition, *P* reduces her outside basis to $0 under §733(1). However, *P*'s capital account is reduced by the full amount of the distribution, leaving *P*'s capital account at negative $2,000.

This distribution is taxable to *P* because *P*'s outside basis is not large enough to absorb the distribution. Recall that for a distribution to be tax free, the distributee partner must allocate her pre-distribution outside basis between the distributed property and her continuing interest in the partnership. Because cash must always be allocated a basis equal to face value, a tax-free distribution to *P* of $10,000 would leave *P*'s outside basis at negative $2,000. To avoid this negative basis, *P* recognizes income of $2,000 and raises her outside basis to zero.

This trade-off of income recognition for outside basis is not possible with respect to *P*'s capital account. Capital accounts measure a partner's share of the partnership's book income. If a partner takes out of the partnership more than she has put in, her capital account must be negative. That she may have recognized income over the life of the partnership is irrelevant: Capital accounts reflect the partners' economic relationship and are unaffected by any partner's particular tax circumstances. Accordingly, *the distributee partner's capital account is reduced by the full amount of the distribution even if outside basis is reduced by less under the "not below zero" language of §733.* Treas. Regs. §1.704-1(b)(2)(iv)(b).

Whenever a distribution of cash forces the distributee partner to recognize income under §731(a)(1), the distribution will also cause a book/tax disparity for the distributee partner. To see this, note that the effect of the distribution will be to reduce the distributee partner's capital account by the amount of cash distributed while the partner's outside basis will, when gain is recognized on the distribution, be reduced by less. This book/tax disparity does not correspond to a book/tax disparity in some partnership asset and so will not be cured by a subsequent disposition of any partnership asset. Thus, it is not like a book/tax disparity caused by the contribution of appreciated or loss property (or like the book/tax disparity caused by revaluations of partnership property). In addition, because a distribution of excess cash does not create an offsetting book/tax disparity for some non-distributee partner, the distributee partner's book/tax disparity cannot be cured by curative allocations as described in Treas. Regs. §1.704-3(c) or by remedial allocations as described in Treas. Regs. §1.704-3(d). Accordingly, any book/tax disparity created by the distribution of excess cash is permanent and will be resolved only when the distributee partner's interest in the partnership is liquidated.

b. Appreciated and Loss Property

When property is distributed, the distributee partner's outside basis is reduced by whatever basis is allocated to the distributed property. §733(2). That amount usually is the pre-distribution adjusted basis of the property in the hands of the partnership, §732(a)(1), although if the distributee partner's outside basis is insufficient to absorb this amount, we use instead the partner's lesser, pre-distribution outside basis, §732(a)(2). This basis rule is consistent with the tax-free status of the distribution in that total basis to the distributee partner is neither raised nor lowered: Her pre-distribution outside basis is allocated between the distributed asset and her continuing interest in the partnership. Note, though, that a distribution of appreciated property can also trigger recognition of income under §737 if the distributee partner contributed appreciated property in the past.

How does a distribution of property affect the partnership capital accounts? Consistent with the treatment of booking-in contributed property at fair market value, Treas. Regs. §1.704-1(b)(2)(iv)(e)(1) provides,

> [A] partner's capital account [must] be decreased by the fair market value of property distributed by the partnership . . . to such partner. . . . To satisfy this requirement, the capital accounts of the partners first must be adjusted to reflect the manner in which the unrealized income, gain, loss and deduction inherent in such property (that has not been reflected in the capital accounts previously) would be allocated among the partners if there were a taxable disposition of such property . . . on the date of distribution.

For example, suppose *P* and *Q* are equal partners in the *PQ* partnership, each having a capital account and outside basis of $8,000. Assume that Blackacre is distributed to *P* when Blackacre has an adjusted basis and book value in the hands of the partnership of $6,000 and a current fair market value of $16,000. Assume further that the partners have agreed to allocate gain from the disposition of Blackacre 60 percent to *P* and 40 percent to *Q*. The effect of the distribution on the partners' capital accounts is

P	*Q*	
$ 8,000	$ 8,000	Initial balance
6,000	4,000	Unrealized book appreciation in Blackacre
(16,000)	0	Fair market value of Blackacre
($ 2,000)	$12,000	Totals

i. Pre-Distribution Book/Tax Disparities

Whenever a distributed asset is revalued incident to a distribution, it is the unrealized *book* gain or loss and not the unrealized *tax* gain or loss that must be allocated among the partners. Treas. Regs. §1.704-1(b)(2)(iv)(e). For example, suppose *X* and *Y* form the *XY* general partnership by *X* contributing cash of $10,000 and *Y* contributing nondepreciable property with adjusted basis of $7,000 and fair market value of $10,000. *X* and *Y* agree to allocate all gain and loss equally except as otherwise required under §704(c). If the property contributed by *Y* is subsequently distributed to *X* when it has a fair market value of $12,000 (and ignoring the impact of §704(c)(1)(B)), the capital accounts will be

X	*Y*	
$10,000	$10,000	Initial contributions
1,000	1,000	Book unrealized appreciation
(12,000)	0	Fair market value of property
($ 1,000)	$11,000	Totals

By allocating only the book unrealized appreciation between *X* and *Y* as a consequence of the distribution, we thereby ensure that the pre-contribution tax unrealized appreciation is not entered into the capital accounts twice: When the property was booked-in at $10,000, *Y*'s capital account was thereby credited with the $3,000 of pre-contribution appreciation. Accordingly, on the distribution we adjust the partners' capital accounts by the amount that their capital accounts would be adjusted had the property been sold for fair market value; that is, we adjust the capital accounts for any *book* unrealized appreciation or loss in the distributed property.

ii. Book/Tax Disparity Caused by Asset Revaluation

Reconsider the *PQ* example above. In that example, a capital asset having an adjusted basis and book value of $6,000 and fair market value of $16,000 was distributed to *P*. At the time of the distribution, each partner had a capital account and outside basis of $8,000, and the partners agreed to allocate gain from disposition of the distributed property 60 percent to *P* and 40 percent to *Q*. As a result of the distribution, the partnership's books become

P		*Q*		
CA	OB	CA	OB	
$ 8,000	$ 8,000	$ 8,000	$ 8,000	Formation
6,000	0	4,000	0	Revaluation
(16,000)	(6,000)	0	0	Distribution
($ 2,000)	$ 2,000	$ 12,000	$ 8,000	Totals

Does this result create a book/tax disparity for either of the partners? Consider first the non-distributee partner, *Q*. As a result of the distribution, *Q*'s capital account is booked up by *Q*'s share of the unrealized appreciation in Blackacre. However, the distribution works no change to *Q*'s outside basis. Accordingly, the distribution *does* create a book/tax disparity for the non-distributee partner (unless all unrealized appreciation in the distributed asset is allocated to the distributee partner).

And what of the distributee partner? The effect of the distribution on the distributee partner's capital account is twofold: There is an increase for the partner's share of the unrealized appreciation in the distributed asset and a decrease for the fair market value of the asset. Outside basis will, in general, be reduced by the partnership's pre-distribution adjusted basis in the asset. Only if the distributee partner is allocated the entire unrealized gain or loss in the asset will the capital asset adjustments equal the outside basis adjustment; otherwise, a book/tax disparity will be created for the distributee partner.

To see this, reconsider partner *P* above. *P*'s capital account is reduced from $8,000 to negative $2,000 by reason of the distribution, for a net reduction of $10,000. *P*'s outside basis, though, is reduced only from $8,000 to positive $2,000 under §733(2), so that the outside basis reduction is but $6,000, or $4,000 less than *P*'s capital account reduction. *Q* also has a $4,000 book/tax disparity because the distribution to *P* increases *Q*'s capital account by $4,000 yet leaves *Q*'s outside basis unchanged.

Suppose, though, that the partners had agreed that all the gain from disposition of the distributed asset was allocable to *P*. Now the distribution has no capital account *or* outside basis effect on *Q*. *P*, on the other hand, sees her capital account and outside basis decrease from $8,000 to positive $2,000, so that there is no book/tax disparity to *P* or to *Q* as a result of the distributions. What this boils down to is the following: Distribution of an appreciated or loss asset will create a book/tax disparity for both the distributee and non-distributee partners in equal but opposite amounts if any of the unrealized book appreciation or loss in the distributed property is allocable to the non-distributee partner. There is no net partnership book/tax disparity by reason of the distribution — the partners' book/tax disparities cancel each other out so that aggregate capital accounts continue to equal aggregate outside bases — but there is a book/tax disparity for each of the partners allocated some of the book unrealized appreciation in the distributed asset.

iii. Book/Tax Disparity Caused by Insufficient Outside Basis

The book/tax disparities caused by revaluations of distributed assets, like all book/tax disparities caused by revaluation of partnership assets, must under §704(b) be addressed in accordance with §704(c)(1)(A) principles. Treas. Regs. §1.704-1(b)(2)(iv)(g). However, some distributions of property can cause book/tax disparities unrelated to revaluations of partnership assets, and these book/tax disparities are permanent and cannot be cured by application of §704(c)(1)(A) principles.

Consider the distribution of an asset having an adjusted basis, book value, and fair market value of $10,000 to a partner having an outside basis of only $8,000. This distribution is tax-free under §731(a)(1), and under §732(a)(2), the distributee partner takes a basis in the distributed asset of $8,000. Finally, under §733(2), the distributee partner's outside basis is reduced to $0.

This distribution causes a book/tax disparity for the distributee partner because the outside basis reduction of $8,000 is not equal to the capital account reduction of $10,000. As when cash is distributed in an amount sufficient to trigger recognition of income, see §731(a)(1), the distribution of property with inside basis sufficiently high to implicate the basis limitation in §732(a)(2) causes a book/tax disparity that cannot be eliminated with curative or remedial allocations because there is no offsetting book/tax disparity for some other partner.

PROBLEM

22-3. Reconsider the facts of problem 22-2. If *A* had a one-third interest in the profits and losses of the partnership, what effect should this distribution have on *A*'s capital account assuming that each distributed asset has book value equal to inside basis? To what extent does this distribution create a book/tax disparity for *A*? Of that book/tax disparity, how much should be addressed by resort to §704(c) principles and how much is permanent and so cannot be eliminated by curative or remedial allocations?

3. *Distributions of Encumbered Property*

When encumbered property is distributed by a partnership, the debt allocation rules of §752 are triggered. As to the non-distributee partners, the effect is a constructive distribution equal to the share of debt eliminated. As to the distributee partner, though, the effect of the debt is twofold: The distributee loses her share of the debt *qua* partner but acquires the entire debt as an individual. These two effects are netted to produce a single, net increase in share of debt. See Treas. Regs. §1.752-1(f); Rev. Rul. 79-205, 1979-2 C.B. 255.

Rev. Rul. 79-205

1979-2 C.B. 255

. . . FACTS

A and *B* are general partners in *M*, a general partnership, which was formed for the purposes of owning and operating shopping centers.

On December 31, 1977, *M* made nonliquidating distributions in a single transaction of a portion of its property to *A* and *B*. *A* and *B* are equal partners in *M*. *M*, *A* and *B* are calendar year taxpayers. No assets of the type described in section 751(a) of the Internal Revenue Code of 1954 were distributed by *M* to either *A* or *B*.

Immediately prior to the distribution *A* had an adjusted basis for *A*'s interest in *M* of 1,000*x* dollars, and *B* had an adjusted basis for *B*'s interest in *M* of 1,500*x* dollars. The property distributed to *A* had an adjusted basis to *M* of 2,000*x* dollars, and was subject to liabilities of 1,600*x* dollars. The property distributed to *B* had an adjusted basis to *M* of 3,200*x* dollars and was subject to liabilities of 2,800*x* dollars. *A*'s individual liabilities increased by 1,600*x* dollars by reason of the distribution to *A*. *B*'s individual liabilities increased by 2,800*x* dollars by reason of the distribution to *B*. *A*'s share and *B*'s share of the liabilities of *M* each decreased by 2,200*x* dollars (1/2 of 1,600*x* + 1/2 of 2,800*x* dollars) by reason of the distributions. The basis and fair market value of the properties distributed were greater than the liabilities to which they were subject.

LAW

Section 705(a) of the Code provides, in part, that the adjusted basis of a partner's interest in a partnership shall be the basis of such interest determined under section 722 decreased (but not below zero) by partnership distributions as provided in section 733.

Section 722 of the Code provides, in part, that the basis of a partnership interest acquired by a contribution of money shall be the amount of such money.

Section 731(a)(1) of the Code provides that in the case of a distribution by a partnership to a partner gain shall not be recognized to such partner, except to the extent that any money distributed exceeds the adjusted basis of such partner's interest in the partnership immediately before the distribution.

Section 732(a)(1) of the Code provides that the basis of property (other than money) distributed by a partnership to a partner other than in liquidation of the partner's interest shall, except as provided in section 732(a)(2), be its adjusted basis to the partnership immediately before such distribution.

Section 732(a)(2) of the Code provides that the basis to the distributee partner of property to which section 732(a)(1) is applicable shall not exceed the adjusted basis of such partner's interest in the partnership reduced by any money distributed in the same transaction.

Section 733 of the Code provides that in the case of a distribution by a partnership to a partner other than in liquidation of a partner's interest, the adjusted basis to such partner of the interest in the partnership shall be reduced (but not below zero) by the amount of any money distributed to such partner and the amount of the basis to such partner of distributed property other than money, as determined under section 732.

Section 752(a) of the Code provides that any increase in a partner's share of the liabilities of a partnership, or any increase in a partner's individual liabilities by reason of the assumption by such partner of partnership liabilities, shall be considered as a contribution of money by such partner to the partnership.

Section 752(b) of the Code provides that any decrease in a partner's share of the liabilities of a partnership, or any decrease in a partner's individual liabilities by reason of the assumption by the partnership of such individual liabilities, shall be considered as a distribution of money to the partner by the partnership.

Section 752(c) of the Code provides that for purposes of section 752 a liability to which property is subject shall, to the extent of the fair market value of such property, be considered as a liability of the owner of the property.

Analysis and Holding

In general, partnership distributions are taxable under section 731(a)(1) of the Code only to the extent that the amount of money distributed exceeds the distributee partner's basis for the partner's partnership interest. This rule reflects the Congressional intent to limit narrowly the area in which gain or loss is recognized upon a distribution so as to remove deterrents to property being moved in and out of partnerships as business reasons dictate. See S. Rep. No. 1622, 83rd Cong., 2nd Sess., page 96 (1954). Here, since partner liabilities are both increasing and decreasing in the same transaction offsetting the increases and decreases tends to limit recognition of gain, thereby giving effect to the Congressional intent. Consequently, in a distribution of encumbered property, the resulting liability adjustments will be treated as occurring simultaneously, rather than occurring in a particular order. Therefore, on a distribution of encumbered property, the amount of money considered distributed to a partner for purposes of section 731(a)(1) is the amount (if any) by which the decrease in the partner's share of the liabilities of the partnership under section 752(b) exceeds the increase in the partner's individual liabilities under section 752(a). The amount of money considered contributed by a partner for purposes of section 722 is the amount (if any) by which the increase in the partner's individual liabilities under section 752(a) exceeds the decrease in the partner's share of the liabilities of the partnership under section 752(b). The increase in the partner's individual liabilities occurs by reason of the assumption by the partner of partnership liabilities, or by reason of a distribution of property subject to a liability, to the extent of the fair market value of such property.

Because the distribution was part of a single transaction, the two properties are treated as having been distributed simultaneously to *A* and *B*. Therefore, all resulting liability adjustments relating to the distribution of the two properties will be treated as occurring simultaneously, rather than occurring in a particular order.

Treatment of Partner *A*

A will be deemed to have received a net distribution of 600*x* dollars in money, that is, the amount by which the amount of money considered distributed to *A* (2,200*x* dollars) exceeds the amount of money considered contributed by *A* (1,600*x* dollars). Since 600*x* dollars does not exceed *A*'s basis for *A*'s interest in *M* immediately before the distribution (1,000*x* dollars), no gain is recognized to *A*.

Under section 732(a) of the Code, the basis of *A* of the property distributed to *A* is the lesser of (i) the adjusted basis of the property to the partnership (2,000*x* dollars), or (ii) the adjusted basis of *A*'s partnership interest (1,000*x* dollars) reduced by the amount of money deemed distributed to *A* (600*x* dollars). Therefore, the basis of the property in *A*'s hands is 400*x* dollars. Under section 733, the adjusted basis of *A*'s partnership interest (1,000*x* dollars) is reduced by the amount of money deemed distributed to *A* (600*x* dollars) and by the basis to *A* of the distributed property (400*x* dollars). The adjusted basis of *A*'s partnership interest is therefore reduced to zero.

Treatment of Partner *B*

B will be deemed to have made a net contribution of 600*x* dollars, that is, the amount by which the amount of money considered contributed by *B* (2,800*x* dollars) exceeds the amount of money considered distributed to *B* (2,200*x* dollars). In applying sections 732(a) and 733 of the Code to *B*, the adjustment to *B*'s basis in *B*'s partnership interest attributable to the liability adjustments resulting from the distributions will be treated as occurring first, and the distribution of property to *B* as occurring second. By so doing, *B*'s basis for the distributed property is increased and *B*'s basis in *B*'s partnership interest is decreased. This allocation gives greater effect to the general rule of section 732(a)(1), which provides for the partner to have the same basis in distributed property as the partnership had for that property.

Therefore, the first step is that *B*'s basis for *B*'s partnership interest (1,500*x* dollars) is increased under sections 722 and 705(a) by the amount of the net contribution deemed made by *B* (600*x* dollars), and is equal to 2,100*x* dollars. Next, under section 732(a) of the Code, the basis to *B* of the property distributed to *B* is the lesser of (i) the adjusted basis of the property to the partnership (3,200*x* dollars), or (ii) the adjusted basis of *B*'s partnership interest (2,100*x* dollars) reduced by the amount of money deemed distributed to *B* (zero). Therefore, the basis of the property in *B*'s hands is 2,100*x* dollars. Under section 733, the adjusted basis of *B*'s partnership interest (2,100*x* dollars) is reduced by the amount of money deemed distributed to *B* (zero) and by the basis to *B* of the distributed property (2,100x dollars). The adjusted basis of *B*'s partnership interest is therefore zero.

To make certain you understand this revenue ruling, consider the following example. Suppose *K* and *L* are equal members of the *KL* partnership, with each partner having a capital account of $10,000 and an outside basis of $13,000. Assume that the partnership has cash of $18,000 and Whiteacre with adjusted basis and fair market value of $8,000, subject to a debt of $6,000. What are the tax effects to *K* and to *L* if Whiteacre is distributed to *K*?

First, there is a change in partnership debt under §752. Prior to the distribution, each partner shared one-half of the partnership's $6,000 debt. After the distribution, the partnership debt is gone. However, the debt is now entirely allocable to *K* because *K* now owns the encumbered property. See §§752(a), 752(c). Accordingly, the distribution reduces *L*'s share of the liability from $3,000 to $0 and increases *K*'s share of the liability from $3,000 to $6,000. Applying §752(b) to *L* and §752(a) to *K*, we see that the effect of the liability shift is to decrease *L*'s outside basis by $3,000 (under §733(1)) and to increase *K*'s outside basis by the same amount (under §722). Of course, these changes in shares of partnership liabilities have no effect on the partners' capital accounts.

Second, there are the rules of §§731-733 with which to contend. Because this is a nonliquidating distribution of property, no gain or loss is recognized. §731(a). *K* takes the property with a carry-over basis of $8,000, §732(a)(1), and reduces her outside basis by the same amount, §733(2). Third, *K* reduces her capital account by the $2,000 fair market value of the property distributed net of liabilities. Treas. Regs. §1.704-1(b)(2)(iv)(b). To summarize: L recognizes no gain because the cash deemed received is less than L's outside basis, and K recognizes no gain because K receives no cash. The books of the venture become:

K		*L*		
CA	OB	CA	OB	
$10,000	$13,000	$10,000	$13,000	Start
0	3,000	0	(3,000)	§752
0	(8,000)	0	0	§733(2)
(2,000)	0	0	0	Net distribution
$ 8,000	$ 8,000	$10,000	$10,000	Ending balances

The distribution of Whiteacre was tax free, and the hallmark of a tax-free transaction is a carryover of basis without increase or reduction. Prior to the distribution, *K* and *L* each had outside bases of $13,000, for a total outside basis of $26,000. After the transaction, *K* has an outside basis of $8,000, and *L* has an outside basis of $10,000, for a total outside basis of $18,000. In addition, *K* now owns Whiteacre with a basis of $8,000 under §732(a)(1), so that total basis after the distribution is $26,000, the same as before the distribution.

As a second check, look at the partners' capital accounts. Prior to the distribution, each partner had a capital account of $10,000. The effect of the distribution is to give *K* $2,000 in value, so that *K*'s capital account should be reduced by $2,000, and *L*'s capital account should remain unchanged. And that is precisely how the ending capital account balances read.

NOTES

1. *The definition of "a distribution."* Suppose a partnership distributes an asset encumbered by a liability that exceeds the fair market value of the asset. For example, a partnership might distribute real estate having an adjusted basis of $400,000, fair market value of $900,000, and subject to a nonrecourse liability of $1,000,000. Is the distribution of this asset described in §731 even though no net value is transferred from the partnership to the partner?

Treasury regulations have long provided that the distribution of encumbered property from a corporate subsidiary to its corporate parent will not be treated as a tax-free distribution described in §332 if the encumbrance exceeds the value of the assets on the theory that some net value must be transferred to warrant tax-free treatment. Treas. Regs. §1.332-2(b). In 2005, this "net value" concept was extended to the contribution of encumbered property contributed to a corporation in a transaction otherwise described in §351, see Prop. Treas. Regs. §1.351-1(a)(iii), as well as to exchanges of stock and securities for stock and securities incident to a corporate reorganization, see Prop. Treas. Regs. §1.358-1(f). Should such a "net value" gloss be applied to partnership distributions otherwise described in §731?

The answer should be no. First, Treasury has not promulgated a "net value" limitation in any subchapter *K* context, suggesting that Treasury does not believe such a gloss is appropriate. After all, when Treasury believes that a "net value" requirement should be imposed, it knows how to draft an appropriate regulation. Second, the recently proposed extension of the "net value" concept to incorporations and corporate reorganizations is expressly based on the requirement of an "exchange" in §351 and §358, a requirement that is absent from the statutory language in §731. Third, Treasury has not attempted to extend the "net value" restriction to corporate distributions in §301, the closest corporate parallel to §731. Fourth, subchapter K includes mechanisms for dealing with encumbered property, both generally in §752 as well as specifically in connection with disguised sales, see Treas. Regs. §1.707-5. If §731 did not apply to over-encumbered property distributed by a partnership, then presumably the transaction would be recast as a disguised sale, and the absence of a "net value" requirement in rules as detailed as the disguised sale regulations strongly suggests no such restriction should be imputed.

PROBLEM

22-4. The *ABC* partnership owns ordinary income asset *X* and capital assets *Y* and *Z* with adjusted bases and fair market values as indicated:

	Adjusted basis	*Book value*	*Fair market value*
X	$10,000	$10,000	$30,000
Y	10,000	10,000	18,000
Z	25,000	25,000	15,000

C, a one-third partner, has an outside basis and capital account of $15,000. Assuming that §751 does not apply to the following distributions, what are the tax consequences to *C* if

a. she receives asset *X* in a nonliquidating distribution?
b. she receives asset *Z* in a nonliquidating distribution?
c. she receives asset *Z*, subject to the partnership's only debt (fully recourse) of $6,000, assuming *C*'s capital account immediately prior to the distribution was $13,000, and *C*'s share of the debt was $2,000?

4. *Distribution of Marketable Securities*

Under §731(c)(1), a distribution of marketable securities may be taxed as a distribution of cash rather than as a distribution of property, with the result that gain will be recognized if the value of the securities (plus any cash actually distributed) exceeds the distributee's pre-distribution outside basis. See §731(a)(1). The term "marketable securities" in this context includes stocks, bonds, other financial instruments broadly defined, §731(c)(2)(C), and other property whose value is determined substantially by reference to such securities, see §731(c)(2)(B), but only if such securities are actively traded, §731(c)(2)(A). However, even marketable securities generally will be treated as property if they were previously contributed to the partnership by the distributee partner. §731(c)(3)(A)(i).

The securities treated as cash rather than as property are reduced by the excess, if any, of (a) the distributee partner's distributive share of the unrealized appreciation in all marketable securities held by the partnership immediately prior to the distribution over (b) the distributee partner's share of the unrealized appreciation in the marketable securities held by the partnership immediately after the distribution. §731(c)(3)(B).[2] Thus, the greater the unrealized appreciation in the securities distributed, the less such securities will be treated as cash rather than as property. This rule reflects the recognition that appreciated securities are less like cash substitutes and more like other property.

Despite treating the securities as cash for purposes of recognition of income, they are treated as property for determining basis. Accordingly, the basis to the distributee of any marketable securities taxed as cash under §731(c) is determined under §732, increased by any gain recognized by the distributee by reason of treating the securities as cash. §731(c)(4). And the distributee's outside basis is adjusted under §733 as if no gain were recognized on the distribution. §731(c)(5).

These rules do not apply to most distributions from investment partnerships as defined in §731(c)(3)(C), see §731(c)(3)(A)(iii), §731(c)(3)(C)(iii). However, when these rules do apply, the marketable securities are taken into account at their fair market values. §731(c)(1)(B). A distribution of marketable securities can trigger taxation under §731(c), §704(c)(1)(B), and §737. For ordering rules, see Treas. Regs. §1.731-2(g).

2. The Code provides that this reduction is made separately by comparing securities of the same class and issuer, although the statute authorizes regulations allowing for an aggregate comparison (that is, treating all securities as being of the same class and issuer). The regulations now treat all securities as being of the same class and issuer. Treas. Regs. §1.731-2(b)(1).

PROBLEM

22-5. *X* and *Y* are each 50-percent partners in the *XY* general partnership, each having a capital account and outside basis of $6,500. *XY* owns cash of $7,000 along with marketable securities with an adjusted basis and book value of $6,000 and fair market value of $15,000. What are the tax consequences if *XY* distributes $9,000 of the securities (having inside basis of $3,600) to *X*? Assume that *XY* is not an "investment partnership" within the meaning of §731(c)(3)(A)(iii) and that none of the securities were contributed by either partner. How would your answer change if the distribution included cash of $1,000 in addition to the securities?

5. *Disposition of Distributed Assets*

Suppose individual *X* is a partner in the *P* partnership. The *P* partnership is a dealer in real estate and distributes Purpleacre, a piece of its real estate inventory, to *X*. Assume that *X*'s basis in Purpleacre becomes $10,000 under §732(a)(1). If *X* subsequently sells Purpleacre for $15,000, what are the tax consequences to *X*?

Under §1001(a), *X* realizes a gain of $5,000. Assuming no nonrecognition provision applies, *X* must recognize (i.e., report) this amount. But is it reportable as capital gain or ordinary income? Assuming that *X* is not a dealer in real estate, you would expect that the gain would be capital. However, that may not be the case.

As a general principle, the character of gain from the disposition of distributed property is determined by reference to the use of the property in the hands of the distributee. Because *X* is not a dealer in real estate, application of this principle means that *X*'s income of $5,000 would be capital gain. However, §735(a) provides that ordinary income assets of the partnership will produce ordinary income (or loss) to the distributee partner regardless of other considerations. Thus, *X*'s gain might be ordinary income by virtue of §735(a)(2).

The ordinary income assets of a partnership are divided into two groups: "unrealized receivables" and "inventory items." Although we will defer examining the definitions of unrealized receivables and inventory items until later, for now it suffices to think of unrealized receivables as including earned but uncollected fees for services and dispositions of noncapital assets, but only if the partnership uses the cash receipts and disbursements method of accounting. Inventory, for the most part, means those noncapital assets of the partnership described in §1221(a)(1). Note, though, that some partnership assets can be both unrealized receivables *and* inventory items. See §751(d)(2).

Section 735 treats unrealized receivables and inventory items differently. The ordinary income taint of §735(a) lasts forever as to unrealized receivables but only for five years as to inventory. Accordingly, distributed inventory can qualify for capital gain treatment if held by the distributee partner for more than five years. Of course, if the distributed inventory is not a capital asset in the hands of the distributee partner (for example, if it is also inventory within the meaning of §1221(a)(1) as to the distributee partner), then the §735(a) taint is redundant and disposition of the inventory will produce ordinary income to the distributee partner whenever sold. Finally, assets that are both unrealized receivables and inventory items will keep the §735(a) taint forever by the simultaneous application of §735(a)(1) and (2).

The operation of §735(a) can be summarized as follows: Property distributed by a partnership to a partner will produce ordinary income or loss upon disposition by the distributee partner if (1) the property is not a capital asset (or §1231 asset) in the hands of the distributee partner, (2) the property was an unrealized receivable to the partnership, or (3) the property was inventory to the partnership and the distributee partner sold or exchanged the property within five years of the distribution.

PROBLEM

22-6. The *P* partnership distributes assets to *X* in a nonliquidating distribution. Prior to the distribution, the assets have an adjusted basis to the partnership of $12,000 and a fair market value of $15,000. At the time of the distribution, *X*'s outside basis equals $12,000. What are the tax consequences to *X* if she sells the assets

a. for $20,000 three years later, and the assets were inventory to the partnership and are capital assets to her?
b. for $20,000 three years later, and the assets were capital assets to the partnership and are inventory to her?
c. for $10,000 three years later, and the assets were inventory to the partnership and are capital assets to her?
d. for $20,000 three years later, and the assets were unrealized receivables to the partnership and are capital assets to her?

B. DISTRIBUTIONS SUBJECT TO §751(b)

Under §751(b), distributions that rearrange the partners' interests in ordinary income assets may be taxed as a sale or exchange between the distributee partner and the partnership. As a result, either the partner or the partnership may recognize gain on the recharacterized transaction. Technically, §751(b) is triggered by a distribution that shifts interests in those ordinary income assets of the partnership falling within the definitions of "unrealized receivables" and "substantially appreciated inventory." Thus, before looking at the operation of §751(b), we need to consider the terms "unrealized receivables" and "substantially appreciated inventory." Note that cash is not §751 property. Treas. Regs. §1.751-1(e).

1. *The Definition of Unrealized Receivables*

The term "unrealized receivables" includes a variety of ordinary income assets including (but not limited to) uncollected receivables of a cash-method partnership for services performed or to be performed and dispositions of inventory and other noncapital assets. In addition, the second and third sentences of §751(c) have grown as Congress has carved more exceptions to the general definition of a capital asset in §1221. In particular, disposition of some assets—notably depreciable property subject to depreciation recapture under §1245 or §1250 and market discount bonds as defined in §1278—produce both capital gain and ordinary income, and the definition of unrealized receivables includes the ordinary income component of such assets. A partnership's unrealized receivables often are called its "hot assets," but as to these part capital, part noncapital assets, only the noncapital part constitutes a hot asset.[3]

For example, suppose a partnership owns some depreciable equipment. Assume that the partnership has an adjusted basis in equipment of $10,000, that the fair market value of the equipment is $60,000, and that the equipment is subject to depreciation recapture under §1245 of $15,000. Because the equipment is §1231 property, it is not (in general) §751 property. However, the depreciation recapture is included within the definition of unrealized receivables in §751(c). Accordingly, the equipment is treated as if it were two assets: non-§751 property with an adjusted basis of $10,000 and fair market value of $45,000 as well as an unrealized receivable with an adjusted basis of $0 and fair market value of $15,000.

Because of this expansive definition of the term "unrealized receivables," even accrual method partnerships can have §751(c) hot assets. Such partnerships will not have unrealized receivables in the common sense—because the partnership accrues its items of income as well as of expense, its business receivables should all be realized despite any lack of collection—but they can easily have *unaccrued* contract rights for services to be performed and goods to be delivered as well as the various ordinary income assets (and parts of assets) listed in the final sentences of §751(c).

2. *The Definition of Substantially Appreciated Inventory*

The ordinary income partnership assets to which §751(b) speaks include not only unrealized receivables but also "substantially appreciated inventory." As provided in §751(b)(3), the determination whether a partnership's inventory is "substantially appreciated" is made by looking at the inventory as a whole. If the inventory as a whole meets the definition of substantial appreciation, every item of the inventory is treated as substantially appreciated. On the other hand, if the inventory as a whole does not qualify as substantially appreciated, then no item of inventory is substantially appreciated. In particular, you *cannot* determine whether one item of the partnership's inventory is substantially appreciated without looking at the inventory as a group.

a. Partnership Inventory Items

The definition of inventory items in §751(d) includes not only what you would expect to be there (inventory as defined in §1221(a)(1)) but also "any other property of the partnership which, on sale or exchange by the partnership, would be considered property other than a capital asset and other than property described in

3. While these part capital, part noncapital assets are bifurcated under §751(b), they are treated as a single asset for all other provisions of the Internal Revenue Code. As a result, if the basis of the capital component is increased, that increase ultimately can reduce the amount of ordinary income that is recognized when the asset is sold by the partnership. Basis increases can arise under §734(b), §743(b), and §751(b).

§1231." This definition seems all-encompassing even to the point of swallowing up the unrealized receivables defined in §751(c). Could Congress really have intended that "inventory" be defined so broadly?

The regulations explicitly provide that inventory items include most unrealized receivables, Treas. Regs. §1.751-1(d)(2)(ii), as well as realized receivables, see Treas. Regs. §1.751-1(g) (example 2(b)). Despite this reading of §751(d), not all of a partnership's hot assets under §751(c) constitute inventory. For example, a capital asset subject to depreciation recapture under §1245 should not constitute inventory because the asset will produce capital gain (albeit not only capital gain) on disposition. Presumably, all unrealized receivables within the definition of §751(c) having both capital gain and ordinary income parts fall without even the most expansive definition of partnership inventory. Accordingly, it must be the case that "unrealized receivables" as used in the definition of "inventory" means "receivables" in the common, nontechnical sense.

b. Substantial Appreciation

A partnership's inventory items are "substantially appreciated" if the inventory's aggregate fair market value exceeds 120 percent of its aggregate adjusted basis. Because this test applies only to the inventory as a whole, either all inventory items will be treated as "substantially appreciated" or none of them will be. If the inventory is "substantially appreciated," then it will constitute §751 property along with the unrealized receivables (if any); if the inventory is not "substantially appreciated," then the inventory items are not §751 property except for those inventory items that also happen to be unrealized receivables.

For example, consider the *P* partnership owning the following assets:

	Adjusted basis	*Fair market value*
Cash	$60,000	$60,000
Receivables	0	30,000
Inventory	15,000	21,000
Land	30,000	45,000

The fair market value of the inventory items (which, for purposes of §751(b), includes the unrealized receivables) is $51,000, while the adjusted basis of the inventory items is $15,000. Because 120 percent of this adjusted basis figure is $18,000, the inventory items pass the appreciation test and so the partnership's inventory items are "substantially appreciated" within the meaning of §751(d). Thus, both the "inventory" and the "receivables" are §751 property.

Now reconsider this example but assume that the partnership uses an accrual method of accounting so that its receivables are realized:

	Adjusted basis	*Fair market value*
Cash	$60,000	$60,000
Receivables	30,000	30,000
Inventory	15,000	21,000
Land	30,000	45,000

Now that the receivables are realized, the aggregate basis of the partnership's inventory items (again including the receivables) is $45,000, and 120 percent of this amount is $54,000. The aggregate fair market value of the inventory items is only $51,000, so that the inventory items fail the appreciation test of §751(b)(3)(A) and are not considered to be substantially appreciated. Of course, the receivables also are *not* §751 property because they are fully realized.

Note that the inventory alone (that is, without the receivables) *would* satisfy the substantial appreciation test. The effect of including the partnership's receivables in this case is thus to allow the partnership to avoid characterizing its inventory as substantially appreciated. We can make the following generalization about including a partnership's receivables in the definition of inventory items: If unrealized, the receivables will make satisfaction of the appreciation test more likely, while if realized, the receivables will make satisfaction of the appreciation test less likely.

It is worthwhile making the following point explicit: Even if a partnership's inventory items are not substantially appreciated, the partnership's *unrealized* receivables are subject to §751(b) including those receivables classified as inventory items under the broad definition of that term in §751(d). That is, a partnership asset is classified as §751 property if it falls within the definition of an unrealized receivable or an inventory item (or both).

3. *Operation of §751(b)*

Detailed rules under §751(b) were promulgated in 1956 and have not been updated. See Treas. Regs. §1.751-1(b). The government recognizes that these rules no longer accommodate the changes to subchapter K that have been enacted in the last 50 years. In particular, the existing §751(b) rules do not incorporate the "substantial economic effect" requirement in §704(b) nor the principles promulgated under §704(c). In Notice 2006-14, the government identified some of the problems in the current §751(b) regime along with some possible solutions.

Notice 2006-14

2006-1 C.B. 498

Section 1. Purpose

This notice invites public comments on certain distributions treated as sales or exchanges under §751(b) of the Internal Revenue Code.

Section 2. Background

Section 751 was enacted to prevent the conversion of ordinary income into capital gain and the shifting of ordinary income among partners. . . . Section 751(a) provides for recharacterization of capital gain or loss when an interest in a partnership is sold or exchanged to the extent of the selling partner's share of unrealized receivables and inventory items of the partnership. Section 751(b) overrides the nonrecognition scheme of §731 for certain current and liquidating partnership distributions that alter a partner's share of unrealized receivables and substantially appreciated inventory items (disproportionate distributions). . . .

The current regulations under §751(b) require the identification of two classes of assets: (1) hot assets (unrealized receivables as defined in §751(c) and substantially appreciated inventory as defined in §751(b)(3) and (d)); and (2) cold assets (assets other than unrealized receivables and substantially appreciated inventory). In computing the distributee partner's income under §751(b), the current regulations provide that the distributee partner's share of the partnership's hot assets and cold assets before and after the distribution must be compared. For purposes of this comparison, each partner's share of the partnership's hot and cold assets is determined by reference to the gross value of the assets. If the distribution results in an exchange of all or a portion of the distributee partner's share of one class of assets (relinquished assets) for assets in the other class (acquired assets), it is necessary to construct a deemed exchange by identifying which relinquished assets are treated as exchanged for which acquired assets.

For example, if a partner receives more than the partner's share of the partnership's hot assets in a distribution, that partner is treated as exchanging a portion of the partner's interest in certain cold assets of the partnership for the other partners' shares of the acquired hot assets. In order to accomplish the exchange, the distributee partner is treated as (1) receiving the relinquished assets (the cold assets) in a nonliquidating distribution and (2) engaging in a taxable exchange (with the partnership) of those assets for the acquired assets (the hot assets). Both the distributee partner and the other partners may recognize income or loss on the exchange. The distributee partner and the partnership then hold the exchanged assets (or portions thereof) with a cost basis under §1012. The rest of the actual distribution (the part that is not subject to §751(b)) is characterized under the general rules for partnership distributions prescribed in §§731 through 736.

The current regulations under §751(b) were published in 1956 and have not been amended to reflect significant changes in subchapter K and in the operations of contemporary partnerships. Moreover, the current §751(b) regulations have been widely criticized as being extraordinarily complex and burdensome and as not achieving the objectives of the statute. As a result, a distribution may reduce a partner's pro rata share of the unrealized appreciation in the partnership's hot assets without triggering §751(b), and a distribution can trigger §751(b) even if the partner's pro rata share of the unrealized appreciation is not reduced.

The Treasury Department and the Service are considering several possible methods, discussed below, for addressing the issues associated with the current §751(b) regulations.

Section 3. Discussion

(A) Determining the Partners' Shares of Partnership Property

The current regulations under §751(b) provide little guidance on how each partner's share of partnership property is determined. Two economic rights are inherent in most partnership interests: a right to partnership capital, and a right to partnership profits and losses. A partner may have a different interest in each of these rights, and those interests may vary over time. Moreover, a partner's share of unrealized partnership items may be affected by both the economic arrangement of the partners and certain requirements of subchapter K, such as §704(c).

The legislative history of §751(b) emphasizes "income rights" of the partners and suggests that these rights may be treated as severable and subject to the same tax consequences as those of an individual entrepreneur. S. Rep. No. 1622, at 99. Consistent with this legislative history, in order to determine whether a distribution may be subject to §751(b), commentators have suggested that new regulations could require partnerships and their partners to compare the amounts of ordinary income that would be recognized by the partners if the partnership's hot assets (including distributed assets) were sold or exchanged for fair market value in a taxable transaction both before and after the distribution (hypothetical sale approach). If the amount of ordinary income that would be allocated to any partner (including the distributee) as a result of such a sale or exchange is reduced as a result of a distribution from the partnership, an analysis under §751(b) would be required. The hypothetical sale approach, combined with the application of §704(c) principles, could provide rules that achieve the objective of the statute in a less burdensome manner.

Under §704(c), if partnership property is sold or exchanged, the built-in gain or loss in contributed or revalued partnership property must be allocated to the contributing or appropriate historic partner (§704(c) principles). See §704(c)(1)(A) and §§1.704-1(b)(4)(i), 1.704-3(a)(2), and 1.704-3(a)(6). As a result of the application of §704(c) principles, there can be layers of appreciation in partnership assets (due to successive revaluations), each of which may be allocable separately. Moreover, distributed §704(c) property and §704(c) property with a substantial built-in loss must be analyzed separately to determine each partner's appropriate share of the unrealized gain or loss. See, e.g., §704(c)(1)(B) and (C). As a result, §704(c) generally operates to preserve each partner's share of the built-in appreciation and depreciation in partnership assets. If the regulations under §751(b) were amended to specify that §704(c) principles are taken into account for purposes of determining whether a partner's share of partnership hot assets has been altered by a distribution, significantly fewer distributions would trigger §751(b).

Example 1. Assume that *A, B,* and *C* each contribute $120 to partnership *ABC*. *ABC* purchases land for $210, which appreciates in value to $300. At a time when the partnership also has $90 of zero-basis unrealized receivables and cash of $150, *ABC* distributes $90 to *C*, reducing *C*'s interest in *ABC* from 1/3 to 1/5. If, immediately before the distribution, the partnership's assets are revalued and the partners' capital accounts are increased to reflect each partner's share of the unrealized appreciation in the partnership's assets, *C*'s entire pre-distribution share of the partnership's unrealized income in the accounts receivable (1/3 of $90, or $30) is preserved in *C*'s capital account after the distribution. *ABC* will have the following post-distribution balance sheet (before the application of section 751(b)):

Assets	*Basis*	*Value*	*Capital*	*Basis*	*Value*
Cash	$ 60	$ 60	*A*	$120	$180
Unrealized rec.	0	90	*B*	120	180
Land	210	300	*C*	30	90
Total	$270	$450		$270	$450

If §704(c) principles were applicable for purposes of §751(b), the distribution to *C* would not trigger §751(b), as *C*'s pre-distribution share of the unrealized income in the receivables ($30) is fully preserved in its capital account after the distribution. Section 704(c) principles would require the partnership to allocate that share of appreciation to *C* when it is recognized.

Special rules may be necessary to address distributions of hot assets to a partner where the adjusted basis of the distributed assets (and the unrealized appreciation in those assets) is different in the hands of the distributee partner than it was in the hands of the partnership. Under §§732(a)(2) and (b), the adjusted basis of distributed hot assets is reduced (and the unrealized appreciation in those hot assets is increased) if the distributee partner's basis in its partnership interest is insufficient to absorb the partnership's adjusted basis in the distributed hot asset. If the partnership has a §754 election in effect at the time of the distribution, §734(b)(1)(B) permits the partnership to increase the adjusted basis of the partnership's retained hot assets to the extent of the reduction in the basis of the distributed hot assets under §732(a)(2) or (b). Under these circumstances, the hot asset appreciation remaining in the partnership is reduced. As such, one of the issues raised by use of a hypothetical sale to measure changes in a partner's interest in hot asset appreciation is the extent to which basis adjustments under §§732 and 734(b) should be taken into account.

Moreover, a hypothetical sale at any one point in time does not take into account future allocations that are planned or expected. For example, a partner's allocations with respect to a particular asset may vary over time. Measuring income or loss on a hypothetical sale of that asset at a particular time may not accurately reflect that partner's income rights with respect to that asset over the life of the partnership.

Once it is determined that a partner's share of the income rights in the partnership's hot assets has been reduced by a distribution, the tax consequences of the distribution under §751(b) must be determined.

(B) DETERMINING THE TAX CONSEQUENCES OF DISPROPORTIONATE DISTRIBUTIONS

The current §751(b) regulations impose a complex deemed distribution/exchange approach for determining the tax consequences of a disproportionate distribution. One possible way to simplify this determination would be to treat a disproportionate distribution as triggering a taxable sale of the partners' shares of relinquished hot assets to the partnership immediately before the distribution (hot asset sale approach). The hot asset sale approach would apply §751(b) in a fully aggregate manner that is arguably consistent with its legislative history (under which each partner's tax treatment should be that of an individual entrepreneur).

This approach could be combined with the hypothetical sale approach. Thus, new regulations could provide that §751(b) applies if any partner's share of the net unrealized appreciation in hot assets of the partnership is reduced as a result of a distribution from the partnership. Under the hot asset sale approach, for any partner whose share of hot assets is reduced (selling partner), whether or not the selling partner is the distributee, the selling partner would be treated as receiving the relinquished hot assets in a deemed distribution and selling to the partnership the relinquished share of the hot assets immediately before the actual distribution.

The selling partner would recognize ordinary income from the deemed sale, and the partner's basis in the partnership interest and the partner's capital account would be adjusted to reflect the consideration treated as contributed to the partnership. The assets deemed sold to the partnership would have a cost basis under §1012. Under the hot asset sale approach there would be no deemed exchange for cold assets, thereby eliminating the need to identify cold assets to be exchanged and to construct a deemed distribution of those assets.

The hot asset sale approach can be straightforward if the distributee partner's share of hot asset appreciation is reduced by the distribution. In this situation, the partnership would be treated as distributing the relinquished share of hot assets to the distributee who sells the hot assets back to the partnership, recognizing ordinary income, with appropriate adjustments to the distributee partner's basis in the partnership interest and capital account. The asset deemed sold would take a cost basis, and the distribution would be governed by §§731 through 736.

Example 2. Assume *A, B* and *C* are each 1/3 partners in a partnership (*PRS*) that holds one hot asset and one cold asset, each with a basis of $0 and a fair market value of $150. *A, B,* and *C* each have an adjusted basis in the partnership interest of $0, and a $50 share of hot asset appreciation. *A* is fully redeemed by a distribution of 2/3 of the cold asset ($100). Immediately before the distribution, the partnership's assets are revalued and the partners' capital accounts are increased to $100 to reflect each partner's share of the unrealized appreciation in the partnership's assets. Because the entire $150 of hot asset appreciation remains in the partnership after the distribution, *A*'s share of that appreciation has been reduced by $50. Under the hot asset sale approach, *PRS* would be treated as distributing the relinquished share of the hot asset ($50) to *A* and then purchasing that share for $50. *A* would recognize income of $50 and would be treated as contributing the $50 to *PRS*. *A*'s basis in the partnership interest would increase to $50 and *A*'s capital account would be restored to $100. The portion of the hot asset deemed sold would take a cost basis, increasing the partnership's basis in the hot asset to $50.

In this example, because *A*'s basis in its partnership interest is $50, the basis of the distributed cold asset would be increased under §732(b) to $50 in *A*'s hands. The cold asset remaining in the partnership has a $0 basis and would not be subject to a basis reduction under §734(b) even if the partnership had a §754 election in effect. In these circumstances, $50 of capital gain is potentially eliminated from the system, however.

The hot asset sale approach also raises certain complications where the distributee partner has insufficient basis in its partnership interest to absorb the partnership's adjusted basis in the distributed hot assets. This can lead to results inconsistent with the intent of §751(b).

Example 3. Assume the same facts as Example 2, except that instead of distributing 2/3 of the cold asset to *A*, the partnership fully redeems *A* by a distribution of 2/3 of the hot asset ($100). Because only $50 of hot asset appreciation remains in the partnership after the distribution, *B*'s and *C*'s shares of that appreciation have been reduced by $25 each. Under the hot asset sale approach, *PRS* would be deemed to distribute the relinquished share of the hot asset ($50) equally to *B* and *C* and each would be treating as selling $25 worth of the hot asset to the partnership. *B* and *C* would each recognize $25 of ordinary income and would be treated as contributing $25 to the partnership. The portion of the hot asset deemed sold would take a cost basis, increasing the partnership's basis in the distributed portion of the distributed hot asset to $50. Because *A*'s basis in its partnership interest is $0, however, the basis of the distributed hot asset would be reduced under §732(b) to $0 in *A*'s hands. If the partnership had a §754 election in effect, the partnership would increase the basis of the retained hot asset under §734(b) by $50. After the distribution, *A*'s share of unrealized income in hot assets would still be $100, and *B* and *C*, who each recognized $25 of ordinary income, would recognize no additional ordinary income.

Commentators have suggested that, in these situations, it may be appropriate to permit or require the distributee partner to recognize capital gain to the extent the adjusted basis of the distributed hot assets exceeds that partner's basis in the partnership interest. In Example 3, *A* could elect, or be required, to recognize capital gain equal to the amount by which the adjusted basis of the distributed hot assets exceeds that partner's basis in the partnership interest ($50), thereby increasing *A*'s basis to $50. The distributed hot asset would take a $50 basis in *A*'s hands under §732(b), and no §734(b) adjustment would be made to the retained hot asset. If *A* recognizes capital gain on the distribution, future regulations could permit an equivalent increase to the basis of the partnership's retained cold assets.

. . .

C. DISTRIBUTIONS AND THE DYNAMIC NATURE OF RECOURSE DEBT[4]

We saw in Chapter 21 that the allocation of partnership recourse debt among the partners is dependent on the partners' relative capital accounts. Thus, anything that affects those capital accounts potentially affects debt sharing. In particular, because distributions described in §731 reduce the distributee partner's capital account, such distributions can rearrange debt sharing among the partners.

Debt reallocation caused by distributions can be surprising in its effects. The following examples all involve distributions of cash from general partnerships whose only asset consists of cash. No partnership will have any special allocations of income or deduction, and no §704(c) or reverse §704(c) problems will be present. In such circumstances one might expect the tax consequences of distributions to be simple. You be the judge.

Consider first the *PQ* general partnership in which *P* and *Q* each contribute $30 for a one-half interest in profits and losses. Because capital accounts and outside basis are credited with the amount of cash contributed by the partners to the partnership,[5] each partner's capital account and outside basis equals $30. The partnership then borrows $40 on a fully recourse basis, and under §752(a) this partnership-level borrowing must increase the partners' outside basis dollar for dollar. Thus, aggregate partnership outside basis increases from its pre-borrowing value of $60 to $100.

4. The materials in this section have been excerpted from Howard E. Abrams, Simple Distributions from Leveraged Partnerships, 1 Pitt. Tax L. Rev. 131 (2004).

5. For capital accounts, see Treas. Regs. §1.704-1(b)(2)(iv)(d)(1); for outside basis, see Treas. Regs. §1.722-1, §1.705-1(a)(2).

The regulations promulgated under §752 provide that this outside basis increase of $40 is apportioned between *P* and *Q* by reference to a hypothetical zero-value sale and liquidation. See Treas. Regs. §1.752-2(b). That is, the partnership is assumed to sell all its assets (including cash) for an assumed fair market value of $0, the losses incurred on this sale are booked into the partners' capital accounts, and then the partnership is liquidated, triggering capital account deficit restoration obligations for all partners having negative capital account balances. The point of this hypothetical sale and liquidation is to determine how the partners have agreed to share the partnership's repayment obligations if the partnership's assets are insufficient to satisfy its debts.

Applying this analysis to the facts of our *PQ* partnership, the zero-value sale produces a book loss of $100 (because both the contributed capital of $60 and the borrowed funds of $40 are assumed to decline in value to $0), allocated equally between *P* and *Q* under the terms of the partnership agreement. Thus, the hypothetical zero-value sale produces partnership books reading:

P		*Q*		
CA	OB	CA	OB	
$30	$30	$30	$30	Initial values
(50)	- - - -	(50)	- - - -	Zero-value sale
($20)	- - - -	($20)	- - - -	Ending values

Thus, if the partnership were to liquidate at this point, each partner would have an obligation to contribute $20 to the partnership for payment to its lender. Under the §752 regulations, the partnership's debt is allocated between *P* and *Q* in the same proportion as these potential contributions would arise, so that the debt is allocated equally between *P* and *Q*. That means the partnership books (remembering that the zero-value sale and liquidation were only hypothetical) stand after the borrowing as:

P		*Q*		
CA	OB	CA	OB	
$30	$50	$30	$50	Post-borrowing values

Suppose the partnership now distributes cash of $40 to partner *P* (presumably the allocation of future profits will be adjusted to reflect this distribution, but such an adjustment plays no role in the discussion that follows). The rules of §§731 and 733 are clear: No gain or loss is recognized by *P* or by *Q*, and *P* reduces her outside basis by the $40 distributed. The regulations providing for the maintenance of capital accounts are equally clear that *P* reduces her capital account by the same $40. Treas. Regs. §1.704-1(b)(2)(iv)(e)(1). Accordingly, application of these rules produces partnership books as follows:

P		*Q*		
CA	OB	CA	OB	
$30	$50	$30	$50	Current values
(40)	(40)	0	0	Distribution to *P*
($10)	$10	$30	$50	Ending values

However, we have not yet considered the possibility that the distribution reallocates the partnership's indebtedness between *P* and *Q*. Prior to the distribution, the debt was allocated equally between *P* and *Q*, or $20 each. To determine how the debt is allocated after the distribution, we again consider the effects of a hypothetical zero-value sale and liquidation.

A zero-value sale produces a book loss of $60 (because of the $100 formerly owned by the partnership, only $60 remains in its hands, the other $40 having been distributed), allocated equally between the partners under the terms of the partnership agreement. Thus, the effect of the zero-value sale is:

P		*Q*		
CA	OB	CA	OB	
($10)	$10	$30	$50	Current values
(30)	----	(30)	----	Zero-value sale
($40)	----	$ 0	----	Ending values

Because only *P* has a capital account deficit, the entire indebtedness of $40 is now allocated to *P*. That is an increase in *P*'s share of the debt of $20 (from $20 to $40) and a decrease in *Q*'s share of the same amount (from $20 to $0). A $20 increase in *P*'s share of the debt is treated as a contribution of $20 by *P* to the partnership, §752(a), Treas. Regs. §1.752-1(b), increasing *P*'s outside basis (but not her capital account) by that amount. Treas. Regs. §1.704-1(b)(2)(iv)(c). Similarly, the $20 decrease in *Q*'s share of the debt is treated as a distribution of cash to *Q*, §752(b), Treas. Regs. §1.752-1(c), decreasing *Q*'s outside basis (but not her capital account) by the same amount. Treas. Regs. §1.704-1(b)(2)(iv)(c). Thus, the books of the partnership agreement now read as follows:

P		*Q*		
CA	OB	CA	OB	
($10)	$10	$30	$50	Current values
0	20	0	(20)	Reallocation of debt
($10)	$30	$30	$30	Ending values

This example shows what should be a counterintuitive result: Even though the distribution was made only to partner *P* in an otherwise perfectly symmetrical partnership, the outside bases of the partners go down together and equally. Put another way, the debt reallocation following a distribution gives extra outside basis to the distributee partner and takes outside basis from the non-distributee partner. The following examples show that these consequences of the debt allocation rules can produce some surprising results.

Reconsider the *PQ* partnership's initial books, with capital accounts of $30 and outside basis of $50 per partner. How much cash can be distributed to one partner without the recognition of income? The rule of §731(a)(1) seems to specify the maximum amount as $50, and indeed that is the most that can be distributed *in a single distribution* without the recognition of income. But suppose we distribute more than that, say $52, to *P* in two separate distributions of $26 each. After the first distribution but before considering the possibility of a debt reallocation, the partnership books stand as follows:

P		*Q*		
CA	OB	CA	OB	
$30	$50	$30	$50	Current values
(26)	(26)	0	0	Distribution
$ 4	$24	$30	$50	Ending values

A zero-value sale will produce a book loss of $74, allocated equally between *P* and *Q* under the partnership agreement. Thus, after the hypothetical zero-value sale the books read:

P		*Q*		
CA	OB	CA	OB	
$ 4	$24	$30	$50	Current values
(37)	----	(37)	----	Distribution
($33)	----	($ 7)	----	Ending values

Because the capital account deficit balances have changed, the debt is reallocated. *P*'s share increases from $20 to $33, for an increase of $13. *Q*'s share of the debt decreases by the same amount, from $20 to $7. Therefore, the actual partnership books following the distribution and taking account of the debt reallocation are:

P		*Q*		
CA	OB	CA	OB	
$4	$24	$30	$50	Before debt reallocation
0	13	0	(13)	Debt reallocation
$4	$37	$30	$37	Ending values

It should be clear from these books that the second distribution of $26 to *P* will not exceed *P*'s pre-distribution outside basis and therefore will not force *P* to recognize income. In fact, the effect of the second distribution on the partnership books is:

P		*Q*		
CA	OB	CA	OB	
$ 4	$37	$30	$37	Current values
(26)	(26)	0	0	Distribution
0	7	0	(7)	Reallocation of debt
($22)	$18	$30	$30	Ending values

What is the maximum amount that can be distributed to *P* (in a series of distributions) without the imposition of any tax? Reconsider the starting books of the *PQ* partnership, and assume that *P* receives a series of distributions always equal in value to *P*'s pre-distribution outside basis. Thus, *P* first receives a distribution of $50, with the following consequences:

P		*Q*		
CA	OB	CA	OB	
$30	$50	$30	$50	Current values
(50)	(50)	0	0	Distribution
0	20	0	(20)	Reallocation of debt
($20)	$20	$30	$30	Ending values

Second, *P* receives a distribution of $20, and because the debt already is allocated entirely to *P*, this distribution works no reallocation of the debt, so that the partnership's books become:

P		*Q*		
CA	OB	CA	OB	
($20)	$20	$30	$30	Current values
(20)	(20)	0	0	Distribution
($40)	$ 0	$30	$30	Ending values

By this technique, *P* was able to receive his initial capital contribution of $30 as well as the entire debt of $40—that is, a total of $70—without recognizing income on the distributions. To be sure, a taxpayer who receives a series of distributions may face a Service challenge that the distributions should be taxed as a single transaction, but that is a fight most practitioners are well prepared to handle. Surely, though, no one involved in the drafting of the distributions rules of subchapter K possibly intended that two cash distributions of $50 and $20 should have a different combined tax consequence than a single distribution of $70, all other things being equal. Yet that is precisely the situation under current law. Or could a distributee argue that the outside basis increase arising from the debt shift occurs immediately prior to the tax consequences from the distribution? Does Rev. Rul. 79-205, supra, speak to this issue?

If one plays the preceding example backwards, it demonstrates an additional surprise for the ill-advised. Suppose you represent individual *P* whose capital account is negative $40 and whose outside basis is $0 as set forth above. If *P* contributes $20 in cash to the partnership, *P*'s capital account and outside basis will increase by the full amount of the cash contribution. But if *P* were to contribute not $20 but $70, her outside basis will increase only to $50: The $70 *P* contributes to the partnership will increase aggregate outside basis by that amount, but only $50 of the increase will be enjoyed by *P*, and the remaining $20 will increase the outside basis of partner *Q*. Accordingly, one must be very careful before advising a client on the tax consequences of even the simplest contributions to a partnership if there is any outstanding entity-level debt.

For an even more surprising outcome, assume that *X*, *Y*, and *Z* form the *XYZ* general partnership with *X* contributing cash of $10 and *Y* and *Z* contributing cash of $100. Each partner receives a one-third share of all profits and losses, and the partnership immediately borrows $60. Because a zero-value sale and liquidation allocates the entire debt to *X*,[6] the partnership books at this point are:

X		*Y*		*Z*		
CA	OB	CA	OB	CA	OB	
$10	$10	$100	$100	$100	$100	Initial capital
0	60	0	0	0	0	Debt allocation
$10	$70	$100	$100	$100	$100	Ending values

Assume that the partnership now distributes $70 to *X*. Because the debt was allocated entirely to *X* prior to this distribution, there is no debt reallocation.[7] Therefore, the books become:

X		*Y*		*Z*		
CA	OB	CA	OB	CA	OB	
$10	$70	$100	$100	$100	$100	Current values
(70)	(70)	0	0	0	0	Distribution to *X*
($60)	$ 0	$100	$100	$100	$100	Ending values

Now suppose that the partnership distributes $80 to *Y*. As a result of this distribution but prior to any debt reallocation, the books of the partnership become:

X		*Y*		*Z*		
CA	OB	CA	OB	CA	OB	
($60)	$0	$100	$100	$100	$100	Current values
0	0	(80)	(80)	0	0	Distribution to *Y*
($60)	$0	$20	$20	$100	$100	Ending values

To determine the effect of this distribution on the allocation of the partnership's debt, we consider the consequences of a hypothetical zero-value sale and liquidation. A zero-value sale will produce a book loss of $120, reducing *X*'s capital account to negative $100, *Y*'s capital account to negative $20, and *Z*'s capital account to positive $70. Thus, the distribution works a reallocation of the debt, with *Y*'s share increasing from $0 to $10 and *X*'s share decreasing from $60 to $50.[8] As a result, X *recognizes gain of $10,* and the partnership's books are:

6. A zero-value sale will produce a book loss of $270, allocated equally among the partners. Thus, *X*'s capital account will be reduced to negative $80 while the capital accounts of *Y* and *Z* will be reduced to positive $10 each.

7. That is, a zero-value sale and liquidation at this point will trigger a capital account deficit restoration obligation only as to *X*, and so the entire debt continues to be allocated to *X*.

8. The regulations do not explicitly provide for the allocation of partnership recourse indebtedness among the partners when a zero-value sale and liquidation yields capital account deficit restoration obligations exceeding the total outstanding debt, but presumably the debt in such circumstances should be allocated among the partners in proportion to the deficit restoration obligations, a rule that was explicit in the initial temporary regulations, Temp. Treas. Regs. §1.752-1T(d)(3)(i), but which inexplicably was removed from the final regulations.

X		*Y*		*Z*		
CA	OB	CA	OB	CA	OB	
($60)	$0	$100	$100	$100	$100	Current values
0	0	(80)	(80)	0	0	Distribution to *Y*
0	0	0	10	0	0	Debt reallocation
($60)	$0	$ 20	$ 30	$100	$100	Ending values

What should be surprising about this result is that the distribution *to* *Y* forced income recognition *to* *X*. The operation of §731 seems to impose gain recognition *only* when a partner removes from the partnership more than she has contributed. While we might argue about precisely how much *X* contributed (taking into account the partnership's debt), the taxable event to *X* was a distribution made entirely to *Y*; that is, *X* is taxed under application of §731 on a transaction in which it seems plain that *X* is removing nothing from the partnership. To be sure, complex arrangements can yield complex outcomes. But this partnership has no great complexity: All its assets are capital assets, and there are no special allocations. The simple rule of §731(a)(1) has somehow been twisted to produce what surely appears to be a bizarre outcome.

23

A Partner's Transactions with the Partnership

A. GUARANTEED AND SIMILAR PAYMENTS

Suppose partner *X* performs services for the *XYZ* partnership in exchange for a fixed salary. If the salary is treated as a distribution described in §731, there will be no gain or loss to the partnership or to *X* (assuming *X*'s outside basis can absorb the distribution) but rather a reduction in *X*'s outside basis. §733. If, though, the same payment had been made to a nonpartner, the recipient would have compensation income on the transaction and the partnership might be entitled to a business expense deduction under §162. Is it appropriate to allow *X* to defer recognition of what amounts to compensation income simply because of the happenstance that *X* is a partner in, as well as a service provider to, the *XYZ* partnership?

In §707(a)(1), Congress has provided that when a partner engages in a transaction with her partnership as would a nonpartner, the transaction should be taxed *as if* between the partnership and a nonpartner. In the example above, that means that *X* would have compensation income and the partnership likely would either deduct the expense under §162 or capitalize it under §263. Section 707(a)(1) also encompasses sales of property from a partner to the partnership and sales of property from the partnership to a partner.

Suppose the *XYZ* partnership agrees to pay $10,000 to partner *X* to manage the partnership. Such a payment might fall within §707(a)(1) if the compensation is equivalent to what a nonpartner would be paid for equivalent services. But what if the partnership agreement requires that the partnership be managed by a partner? In such circumstances it is hard to characterize *X* as acting other than in her capacity as a partner, and so §707(a)(1) arguably does not apply. Nevertheless, *X* should still have compensation income, and the partnership also should continue to enjoy a deduction, and those are precisely the effects of §707(c). Under §707(c), fixed payments (called "guaranteed" payments) made to a partner will be taxed as if made to a nonpartner even if the transaction does not fall within §707(a)(1). Accordingly, *X* will still be forced to recognize the distribution as compensation income, and the partnership should be entitled to claim an equivalent deduction (because management expenses are ordinary and necessary business expenses).

In Pratt v. Commissioner, 64 T.C. 203 (1975), aff'd in part, rev'd in part, 550 F.2d 1023 (5th Cir. 1977), the Tax Court narrowly construed §707(a)(1) and

§707(c). At issue were payments to a partner for ongoing management duties as well as interest payments on loans from a partner to the partnership. The management fees were set at a fixed percentage of the partnership's gross rental income, and the court held these fees were not described in §707(a)(1) or in §707(c).

The court rejected the §707(a)(1) characterization on two grounds. First, the court wrote that

> Section 707(a)[1] refers to "transactions" between a partner and a partnership and is susceptible of being interpreted as covering only those services rendered by a partner to the partnership in a specific transaction as distinguished from continuing services of the partner which would either fall within section 707(c) or be in effect a partner's withdrawal of partnership profits.

Second, the court felt that the partners were "to receive the management fees for performing services within the normal scope of their duties as general partners and pursuant to the partnership agreement." The court acknowledged that the fees were reasonable in amount and would have been paid to a third party if the general partner had not managed the partnership's rental activities. To the extent that the court's holding turned on the partnership agreement requiring the general partner to manage the partnership, perhaps the court was correct. To the extent that the court was saying that payments to a general partner for taking an interest in the partnership's affairs always fall outside of §707(a)(1), it seems to be reading §707(a)(1) for less than it is worth.

The court rejected the §707(c) characterization on the ground that payments based on the *gross income* of the partnership are not "determined without regard to the income of the partnership" within the meaning of §707(c). Yet the role of §707(c) (and §707(a)(1)) is to distinguish proprietary returns from compensatory payments. Because the management fees were not based on the *net* income of the partnership, they did not resemble the return of a proprietor. Indeed, the managing partner would be entitled to be paid even if the partnership reported a net loss for the year. Unfortunately, the court interpreted the language of §707(c) by resort to the dictionary rather than to the section's underlying purpose.

As to the interest payments, the court concluded that §707(c), not §707(a)(1), applied. Market interest on an enforceable debt would seem to be the paradigmatic §707(a)(1) payment. You should wonder, though, why it matters which section applies because both require the recipient partner to report the payment as income, and both allow the partnership to deduct the payment if it constitutes an ordinary and necessary business expense or other deductible expenditure (such as interest).

In *Pratt*, the partnership was an accrual taxpayer and the partners were cash basis individuals. Interest on the loan was accrued but not paid by the partnership. Ordinarily, an accrual basis taxpayer accrues deductions without regard to actual payment. Following this principle the partnership would deduct the interest under §163 during the current taxable year. The recipient partner, though, as a cash basis taxpayer, would not be required to include the interest in income until actually received. This timing whipsaw whereby the payment is deducted but not included is disallowed by §267(a)(2), a provision generally applicable to payments between related taxpayers.

When §267(a)(2) applies, an accrual payor of an otherwise deductible payment may not accrue the deduction until the recipient includes it in income. Section

267(a)(2) applies to a transaction whenever the payor and recipient are "related" within the meaning of §267(b). By reason of §267(e)(1)(B), each partner (owning a capital interest, a profits interest, or both) is treated as related to the partnership. Accordingly, the matching of income and deduction mandated by §267(a)(2) applies to payments described in §707(a)(1). In our example, this means that the partnership will not be entitled to accrue the interest deduction until the recipient partner includes it as income, and that, presumably, will occur in the year of payment. The effect of §267(a)(2), in other words, is to put the payor partnership on the same method of accounting as the recipient partner.

However, if the payment is described not by §707(a)(1) but rather by §707(c), a different matching rule applies. Under Treas. Regs. §1.707-1(c), a partner must report a guaranteed payment received from an accrual basis partnership in the year in which the partnership accrues it. That is, income and deduction once again are matched, but this time in accordance with the partnership's (i.e., the payor's) method of accounting. In *Pratt*, then, characterization under §707(c) required the recipient partner to include the interest income in the year in which it was due and payable even though actual receipt did not occur.

Why should a partnership care if a distribution is characterized as a §707(a)(1) (or §707(c)) payment as compared with a distribution described in §731? At least if the payment would be deductible, characterization under §707(a)(1) or as a guaranteed payment offers the partnership more flexibility than characterization as a distribution taxable under §§731-733. If the payment is taxed under §§731-733, there will be no tax consequences to the partnership, and the partner will defer recognition of income so long as her outside basis can absorb the distribution. That result is precisely the same as would be obtained under §707(a)(1) (or under §707(c)) if the deduction were allocated to the recipient partner. Thus, at least in the case of a deductible payment, the partnership can obtain the equivalent of §§731-733 treatment simply by specially allocating the deduction to the distributee partner. In addition, the partnership can allocate the deduction other ways, thus giving it added flexibility as compared with the §§731-733 route.

The interpretations given to §707(a)(1) and (c) by the Tax Court in *Pratt* seem erroneous, and the Service ultimately agreed. In two revenue rulings published in 1981, the Service gave back its *Pratt* victories. In Rev. Rul. 81-300, 1981-2 C.B. 143, the Service concluded that fees paid by a limited partnership to the general partner for managing a shopping mall owned by the partnership were described in §707(c) when computed as a percentage of the partnership's gross rental receipts. And in Rev. Rul. 81-301, 1981-2 C.B. 144, the Service ruled that payments made to a partner for investment advice on terms similar to those paid by third parties to the partner for similar services are described in what is now §707(a)(1). In the *coup de grace*, Congress determined that the transaction described in Rev. Rul. 81-300 should in fact fall within §707(a). 1 Committee on Finance, Committee Print on the Deficit Reduction Act of 1984, S. Prt. 169, at 226, 98th Cong., 2d Sess. (1984).

PROBLEMS

23-1. *A* and *B* each have a 50-percent interest in the profits and losses of *AB*, an accrual basis partnership. *A*, however, is entitled to an annual distribution of $10,000 in addition to his share of profits. This payment is for services rendered annually to the partnership, and the payment would be deductible to the partnership if paid to a third party.

a. If *AB* has taxable income (excluding any deduction arising out of its obligation to *A*) of $100,000, how are *A* and *B* taxed? What if the income is entirely long-term capital gain?
b. If *AB* has no taxable income or loss for the year (excluding any deduction arising out of its obligation to *A*), how are *A* and *B* taxed? What if the payment to *A* is not made until the middle of the following year?
c. In case (a), how do your answers change if the deduction arising out of *A*'s guaranteed payment is allocated solely to *A*?

23-2. *E* and *F* each contribute $60 to the *EF* partnership and agree to be equal partners. *EF* purchases a capital asset for $20. During the taxable year, the asset appreciates in value to $100 and then is distributed to *E* in satisfaction of a guaranteed payment obligation. The partnership has no income or loss and liquidates, distributing its cash of $100. How should that cash be divided between *E* and *F*, and what are the tax consequences to each partner? See Rev. Rul. 2007-40, 2007-1 C.B. 1426.

B. DISGUISED SALES

Two individuals agree to form a partnership for the purpose of constructing federally supported, low-cost housing. Individual *A* contributes real estate to the partnership having an adjusted basis of $40,000 and a fair market value of $100,000. Individual *B* makes only a nominal contribution of cash. The partners agree that they will divide all profits and losses equally. In addition, they agree that $100,000 will be distributed to *A* once the construction loan is obtained.

In effect, *A* has agreed to sell the real estate to the partnership, with the sale proceeds to come out of the partnership's debt. Had it been explicitly structured in that manner, *A* would recognize a gain on the transaction of $60,000, that being the excess of *A*'s amount realized for the real estate ($100,000) over *A*'s adjusted basis in the real estate ($40,000). If *A* takes the position that the contribution and subsequent distribution should be taxed as two separate transactions, the first described in §721 and the second described in §731, should *A* prevail over the Commissioner's §707(a)(1) challenge? In Otey v. Commissioner, 70 T.C. 312 (1978), aff'd per curiam, 800-2 U.S.T.C. ¶ 9816 (8th Cir. 1980), the Tax Court sustained the taxpayer's position. Unhappy with this result, Congress responded with §707(a)(2)(B).

Canal Corporation and Subsidiaries v. Commissioner

135 T.C. 199 (2010)

Kroupa, Judge.

Respondent determined a $183,458,981 deficiency in petitioner's (Chesapeake) Federal income tax for 1999, the year at issue. . . . We must determine whether Chesapeake's subsidiary's contribution of its assets and most of its liabilities to a newly formed limited liability company and the simultaneous receipt of a $755 million distribution should be characterized as a disguised sale, requiring Chesapeake to recognize a $524 million gain in 1999, the year of contribution and distribution. We hold that the transaction was a disguised sale, requiring Chesapeake to recognize the gain. . . .

Findings of Fact

. . .

Chesapeake is a Virginia corporation organized as a corrugated paper company in 1918. Chesapeake's business has expanded over time into several paper industry segments, including merchandising and specialty packaging, tissue, and forest and land development. Chesapeake eventually became a publicly traded company and served as the common parent of a group of subsidiary corporations filing consolidated Federal income tax returns. Each subsidiary managed its own assets and liabilities. Chesapeake received dividends from the subsidiaries and made loans to the subsidiaries as needed.

Chesapeake's largest subsidiary was Wisconsin Tissue Mills, Inc. (WISCO). Chesapeake purchased WISCO's stock from Philip Morris in 1985 in a leveraged buyout transaction. WISCO manufactured commercial tissue paper products, including napkins, table covers, towels, place mats, wipes, and facial and bathroom tissue. WISCO sold its products to commercial and industrial businesses such as restaurants, hotels, schools, offices, hospitals and airlines. WISCO accounted for 46 percent of Chesapeake's sales and 94 percent of Chesapeake's earnings before interest and tax for 1998. Chesapeake and WISCO shared most of the same executive officers.

. . .

Chesapeake, through WISCO and Chesapeake's Mexican subsidiary, Wisconsin Tissue de Mexico, S.A. de C.V. (WISMEX), was a second tier player in the tissue industry. Chesapeake sold its retail tissue business to the Fonda Group, Inc. in 1995. WISCO and WISMEX serviced only commercial accounts and lacked the large timber bases needed to support a retail business. Chesapeake had only two paper mills, one in Wisconsin and one in Arizona, and thus was at a significant logistical disadvantage in servicing the Southeast and Northeast.

. . .

Chesapeake considered selling WISCO to generate capital for Chesapeake's new specialty packaging business. Given Chesapeake's low tax basis in WISCO, however, the after-tax proceeds would have been low compared to the pre-tax proceeds. This tax differential caused Chesapeake to decide a direct sale of WISCO would not be advantageous.

Chesapeake thereafter engaged Salomon Smith Barney (Salomon) and PricewaterhouseCoopers (PWC) to explore strategic alternatives for the tissue business. Salomon recommended to Chesapeake's management that the best alternative for maximizing shareholder value would be a leveraged partnership structure with [Georgia Pacific ("GP")]. The leveraged partnership structure required WISCO to first transfer its tissue business assets to a joint venture. GP would then transfer its tissue business assets to the joint venture. Next, the joint venture would borrow funds from a third party and distribute the proceeds to Chesapeake (special distribution). Chesapeake would guarantee the third-party debt through a subsidiary. WISCO would hold a minority interest in the joint venture after the distribution, and GP would hold a majority interest. Salomon presented the leveraged partnership structure as tax advantageous to Chesapeake because it would allow Chesapeake to get cash out of the business yet still protect Chesapeake from recognizing a gain when the partnership distributed to Chesapeake the proceeds from the third-party loan.

Chesapeake's board liked the leveraged partnership idea and thought GP seemed like a good fit as a partner. Chesapeake made clear to PWC and Salomon that the asset transfer and special distribution had to be nontaxable for it to approve the transaction. Tax deferral enabled Chesapeake to accept a lower price.

GP's executives accepted the leveraged partnership structure to expand its tissue business. GP did not have any interest in Chesapeake receiving a tax deferral. GP recognized, however, that it was a necessary part of bridging the purchase price gap. Chesapeake agreed to a lower up-front valuation of WISCO, $775 million, because of the tax deferral benefit.

. . .

GP agreed to guarantee the joint venture's debt and did not require Chesapeake to execute an indemnity. Mr. Miller [a tax attorney] advised Chesapeake, however, that an indemnity was required to defer tax on the transaction. Chesapeake's executives wanted to make the indemnity an obligation of WISCO rather than Chesapeake to limit the economic risk to WISCO's assets, not the assets of Chesapeake. The parties to the transaction agreed that GP would guarantee the joint venture's debt and that WISCO would serve as the indemnitor of GP's guaranty.

WISCO attempted to limit the circumstances in which it would be called upon to pay the indemnity. First, the indemnity obligation covered only the principal of the joint venture's debt, due in 30 years, not interest. Next, Chesapeake and GP agreed that GP had to first proceed against the joint venture's assets before demanding indemnification from WISCO. The agreement also provided that WISCO would receive a proportionately increased interest in the joint venture if WISCO had to make a payment under the indemnity obligation.

No provision of the indemnity obligation mandated that WISCO maintain a certain net worth. Mr. Miller determined that WISCO had to maintain a net worth of $151 million to avoid taxation on the transaction. GP was aware that WISCO's assets other than its interest in the joint venture were limited. GP nonetheless accepted the deal and never invoked the indemnity obligation.

. . .

GP and WISCO formed Georgia-Pacific Tissue LLC (LLC) as the vehicle for the joint venture. GP and WISCO treated the LLC as a partnership for tax purposes. Both partners contributed the assets of their respective tissue businesses to the LLC. GP transferred to the LLC its tissue business assets with an agreed value of $376.4 million in exchange for a 95-percent interest in the LLC. WISCO contributed to the LLC all of the assets of its tissue business with an agreed value of $775 million in exchange for a 5-percent interest in the LLC. The LLC borrowed $755.2 million from Bank of America (BOA) on the same day it received the contributions from GP and WISCO. The LLC immediately transferred the loan proceeds to Chesapeake's bank account as a special cash distribution. GP guaranteed payment of the

BOA loan, and WISCO agreed to indemnify GP for any principal payments GP might have to make under its guaranty.

The LLC had approximately $400 million in net worth based on the parties' combined initial contribution of assets ($1.151 billion) less the BOA loan ($755.2 million), and it had a debt to equity ratio of around 2 to 1. The LLC assumed most of WISCO's liabilities. . . . Chesapeake and WISCO both indemnified GP and held it harmless for any costs and claims that it might incur with respect to any retained liabilities of WISCO. . . .

WISCO used a portion of the funds from the special distribution to repay an intercompany loan to Cary Street, Chesapeake's finance subsidiary. WISCO also used portions of the funds to pay a dividend to Chesapeake, repay amounts owed to Chesapeake and lend $151.05 million to Chesapeake in exchange for a note (intercompany note). The intercompany note was a 5-year note with an 8-percent interest rate. Chesapeake used the loan proceeds to repay debt, repurchase stock and purchase additional specialty packaging assets.

WISCO's assets following the transaction included the intercompany note with a face value of $151 million and a corporate jet worth approximately $6 million. WISCO had a net worth, excluding its LLC interest, of approximately $157 million. This represented 21 percent of its maximum exposure on the indemnity. . . .

. . .

Opinion

We are asked to decide whether the joint venture transaction constituted a taxable sale. Respondent argues that Chesapeake structured the transaction to defer $524 million of capital gain for a period of 30 years or more. Specifically, respondent contends that WISCO did not bear any economic risk of loss when it entered the joint venture agreement because the anti-abuse rule disregards WISCO's obligation to indemnify GP. See sec. 1.752-2(j), Income Tax Regs. Respondent concludes that the transaction should be treated as a taxable disguised sale.

Chesapeake asserts that the transaction should not be recast as a sale. Instead, Chesapeake argues that the anti-abuse rule does not disregard WISCO's indemnity and that the LLC's distribution of cash to WISCO comes within the exception for debt-financed transfers. We disagree and begin with the general rules on disguised sales.

I. Disguised Sale Transactions

The Code provides generally that partners may contribute capital to a partnership tax free and may receive a tax free return of previously taxed profits through distributions. See secs. 721, 731. These nonrecognition rules do not apply, however, where the transaction is found to be a disguised sale of property. See sec. 707(a)(2)(B).

A disguised sale may occur when a partner contributes property to a partnership and soon thereafter receives a distribution of money or other consideration from the partnership. *Id.* A transaction may be deemed a sale if, based on all the facts and circumstances, the partnership's distribution of money or other consideration to the partner would not have been made *but for* the partner's transfer of the property. Sec. 1.707-3(b)(1), Income Tax Regs. (emphasis added). Such contribution and distribution transactions that occur within two years of one another are presumed to effect a sale unless the facts and circumstances clearly establish otherwise (the 2-year presumption). Sec. 1.707-3(c)(1), Income Tax Regs.

Here, WISCO transferred its assets with an agreed value of $775 million to the LLC and simultaneously received a cash distribution of $755.2 million. After the transfer and distribution, WISCO had a 5-percent interest in the LLC. Its assets included only its interest in the LLC, the intercompany note and the jet. We therefore view the transactions together and presume a sale under the disguised sale rules unless the facts and circumstances dictate otherwise.

Chesapeake contends that the special distribution was not part of a disguised sale. Instead, it was a debt-financed transfer of consideration, an exception to the disguised sale rules. See sec. 1.707-5(b), Income Tax Regs. Chesapeake argues that the debt-financed transfer of consideration exception to the disguised sale rules limits the applicability of the disguised sale rules and the 2-year presumption in this case.

A. Debt-Financed Transfer of Consideration

We now turn to the debt-financed transfer of consideration exception to the disguised sale rules. The regulations except certain debt-financed distributions in determining whether a partner received "money or other consideration" for disguised sale purposes. See *id.* A distribution financed from the proceeds of a partnership liability may be taken into account for disguised sale purposes to the extent the distribution exceeds the distributee partner's allocable share of the partnership liability. See sec. 1.707-5(b)(1), Income Tax Regs. Respondent argues that the entire distribution from the LLC to WISCO should be taken into account for purposes of determining a disguised sale because WISCO did not bear any of the allocable share of the LLC's liability to finance the distribution. We turn now to whether WISCO had any allocable share of the LLC's liability to determine whether the transaction fits within the exception.

B. Partner's Allocable Share of Liability

In general a partner's share of a recourse partnership liability equals the portion of that liability, if any, for which the partner bears the economic risk of loss. See sec. 1.752-1 (a)(1), Income Tax Regs. A partner bears the economic risk of loss to the extent that the partner would be obligated to make an unreimbursable payment to any person (or contribute to the partnership) if the partnership were constructively liquidated and the liability became due and payable. Sec. 1.752-2(b)(1), Income Tax Regs.; see IPO II v. Commissioner, 122 T.C. 295, 300-301 (2004). Chesapeake contends that WISCO's indemnity of GP's guaranty imposes on WISCO the economic risk of loss for the LLC debt. Respondent concedes that an indemnity agreement generally is recognized as an obligation under the regulations. Respondent asserts, however, that WISCO's agreement should be disregarded under the anti-abuse rule for allocation of partnership debt.

C. Anti-Abuse Rule

Chesapeake counters that WISCO was legally obligated to indemnify GP under the indemnity agreement and therefore WISCO should be allocated the entire economic risk of loss of the LLC's liability. We assume that all partners having an obligation to make payments on a recourse debt actually perform those obligations, irrespective of net worth, to ascertain the economic risk of loss unless the facts and circumstances indicate a plan to circumvent or avoid the obligation. Sec. 1.752-2(b)(6), Income Tax Regs. The anti-abuse rule provides that a partner's obligation to make a payment may be disregarded if (1) the facts and circumstances indicate that a principal purpose of the arrangement between the parties is to eliminate the partner's risk of loss or to create a facade of the partner's bearing the economic risk of loss with respect to the obligation, or (2) the facts and circumstances of the transaction evidence a plan to circumvent or avoid the obligation. See sec. 1.752-2(j)(1), (3), Income Tax Regs. Given these two tests, we must review the facts and circumstances to determine whether WISCO's indemnity agreement may be disregarded as a guise to cloak WISCO with an obligation for which it bore no actual economic risk of loss. See IPO II v. Commissioner, supra at 300-301.

1. *Purpose of the Indemnity Agreement*

We first consider the indemnity agreement. The parties agreed that WISCO would indemnify GP in the event GP made payment on its guaranty of the LLC's $755.2 million debt. GP did not require the indemnity, and no provision of the indemnity mandated that WISCO maintain a certain net worth. WISCO was chosen as the indemnitor, rather than Chesapeake, after PWC advised Chesapeake's executives that WISCO's indemnity would not only allow Chesapeake to defer tax on the transaction, but would also cause the economic risk of loss to be borne only by WISCO's assets, not Chesapeake's. Moreover, the contractual provisions reduced the likelihood of GP invoking the indemnity against WISCO. The indemnity covered only the loan's principal, not interest. In addition, GP would first have to proceed against the LLC's assets before demanding indemnification from WISCO. In the unlikely event WISCO had to pay on the indemnity, WISCO would receive an increased interest in the LLC proportionate to any payment made under the indemnity. We find compelling that a Chesapeake executive represented to Moody's and Standard & Poor's that the only risk associated with the transaction was the tax risk. We are left with no other conclusion than that Chesapeake crafted the indemnity agreement to limit any potential liability to WISCO's assets.

2. *WISCO's Assets and Liabilities*

We now focus on whether WISCO had sufficient assets to cover the indemnity regardless of how remote the possibility it would have to pay. Chesapeake maintains that WISCO had sufficient assets to cover the indemnity agreement. WISCO contributed almost all of its assets to the LLC and received a special distribution and a 5-percent interest in the LLC. Moreover, Chesapeake contends that WISCO did not need to have a net worth covering the full amount of its obligations with respect to the LLC's debt. See sec. 1.752-2(b)(6), Income Tax Regs. WISCO's assets after the transfer to the LLC included the $151.05 million intercompany note and the $6 million jet. WISCO had a net worth, excluding its LLC interest, of approximately

$157 million or 21 percent of the maximum exposure on the indemnity. The value of WISCO's LLC interest would have been zero if the indemnity were exercised because the agreement required GP to proceed and exhaust its remedies against the LLC's assets before seeking indemnification from WISCO.

We may agree with Chesapeake that no Code or regulation provision requires WISCO to have assets covering the full indemnity amount. We note, however, that a partner's obligation may be disregarded if undertaken in an arrangement to create the appearance of the partner's bearing the economic risk of loss when the substance of the arrangement is in fact otherwise. See sec. 1.752-2(j)(1), Income Tax Regs. WISCO's principal asset after the transfer was the intercompany note. The indemnity agreement did not require WISCO to retain this note or any other asset. Further, Chesapeake and its management had full and absolute control of WISCO. Nothing restricted Chesapeake from canceling the note at its discretion at any time to reduce the asset level of WISCO to zero. In fact WISCO's board, which included many Chesapeake executives, did cancel the note and issued an intercompany dividend to Chesapeake in 2001. We find WISCO's intercompany note served to create merely the appearance, rather than the reality, of economic risk for a portion of the LLC debt.

. . .

We have carefully considered the facts and circumstances and find that the indemnity agreement should be disregarded because it created no more than a remote possibility that WISCO would actually be liable for payment. Chesapeake used the indemnity to create the appearance that WISCO bore the economic risk of loss for the LLC debt when in substance the risk was borne by GP. We find that WISCO had no economic risk of loss and should not be allocated any part of the debt incurred by the LLC.

[Discussion of penalty issues omitted.]

Decision will be entered for the respondent.

NOTES

1. *Basic principles.* A disguised sale within the meaning of §707(a)(2)(B) consists of the following: (1) a contribution of property or services to the partnership by a partner; (2) a distribution of cash or other property to that partner or some other partner; and (3) under circumstances such that the contribution and distribution properly should be characterized as constituting a single, integrated transaction. The most common situation in which a disguised sale will arise is a contribution of appreciated property to a partnership followed by either an actual distribution of cash to that contributing partner or a deemed distribution arising from a reallocation of partnership liabilities in connection with the contribution of encumbered property.

Note, though, that not all transfers of property from a partnership followed by a distribution to the contributing partner are taxed as sales under §707(a)(2)(B): Before the transaction is treated as a sale, the two transfers "when viewed together, [must] properly be characterized as a sale of property" under §707(a)(2)(B)(iii). What §707(a)(2)(B) leaves open, unfortunately, is determining when two transfers are properly viewed together as a sale.

Regulations provide that a transfer of property to a partnership by a partner followed by a distribution from the partnership to the partner will be treated as a disguised sale if the distribution to the partner would not have been made but for the partner's transfer of property and, if the two transactions are not simultaneous, the subsequent transaction is not dependent on the entrepreneurial risks of the partnership. Treas. Regs. §1.707-3(b)(1). This determination, so the regulations tell us, is made based on all the facts and circumstances in each case. Treas. Regs. §1.707-3(b)(2). However, these regulations also provide that if a transfer to the partnership and a distribution to the transferor partner are made within two years, the two transactions are presumed to constitute a sale. Treas. Regs. §1.707-3(c)(1). Conversely, contributions and distributions separated by more than two years are presumed not to constitute a sale. Treas. Regs. §1.707-3(d). In either situation, though, the particular facts and circumstances surrounding the transactions can overcome the presumption. Note though that distributions occurring within two years of a contribution and not treated by the taxpayer as a disguised sale must be disclosed to the Service unless one of the exceptions to the disguised sales rules (discussed below) applies to the distribution.

2. *Simultaneous contributions and distributions of unencumbered property.* In general, a contribution of money or property by a partner and a distribution of money or property to that partner will be treated as a single, disguised sale if the "transfer of money or other consideration [that is, the distribution to the partner] would not have been made but for the transfer of property [that is, but for the contribution]." Treas. Regs. §1.707-3(b)(1)(i). In the case of simultaneous contributions and distributions, this is the only test that must be satisfied for the contribution and distribution to be recharacterized as a single, integrated transaction. Furthermore, such simultaneous contributions and distributions are presumed to be related. Treas. Regs. §1.707-3(c)(1). Accordingly, unless one of the exceptions to the presumption applies, a simultaneous contribution and distribution invariably will be stepped together.

3. *Contributions of encumbered property.* If a partner contributes encumbered property to a partnership, the encumbrance is allocated among the partners. For determining the outside basis consequences of a liability shift, the rules of §752 are used. But for determining if a disguised sale has occurred, a subset of those rules (as discussed below) is used. See Treas. Regs. §1.707-5. The contribution may also affect the allocation of existing partnership liabilities among the partners. As a result, the contributing partner's net share of liabilities may remain unchanged, may decrease or even increase as a result of the contribution. However, with a single limited exception the contributing partner may not offset against the liability surrendered any portion of the partnership's existing liabilities now allocated to the contributing partner. See Treas. Regs. §1.707-5(a)(1). Thus, the netting of liabilities so familiar under the usual rules of §752 does not apply in the context of disguised sales.

For determining whether a contributing partner has engaged in a disguised sale as the result of a contribution of encumbered property, two special rules apply. First, many liabilities are ignored in determining whether the contributing partner is treated as having received a deemed distribution as a result of the contribution. Second, the rules for allocating nonrecourse liabilities under the disguised sales rules differs from the usual debt allocation rules.

4. *Which liabilities count?* In general, the contribution of encumbered property to a partnership will not result in a disguised sale even if some or all of the

encumbrance shifts to other partners if the encumbrance is a "qualified liability." Treas. Regs. §1.707-5(a)(5)(i). For this, purpose, a "qualified liability" must satisfy one of the following four tests: (1) The liability was incurred by the contributing partner more than two years prior to the transfer of the property to the partnership, and the liability has encumbered the contributed property continuously throughout the two-year period preceding the contribution; (2) the liability was not incurred in anticipation of the contribution of the property to a partnership and has encumbered the contributed property since the liability was incurred; (3) the liability is allocable under the rules of Treas. Regs. §1.163-8T to capital expenditures with respect to the contributed property; or (4) the liability was incurred in the ordinary course of the trade or business in which the contributed property was used, but only if all material assets related to the trade or business are transferred to the partnership. Treas. Regs. §1.707-5(a)(6)(i).

For example, suppose *X* joins the *P* partnership by contributing Blackacre when Blackacre has a fair market value of \$100,000 and is subject to a liability of \$60,000. Assume that *X* has an adjusted basis of \$35,000 in Blackacre at the time of contribution and that half of the liability shifts to other partners as a result of the contribution. If the liability is a "qualified liability" the contribution will be tax free to *X* and to the partnership, and *X* will take an initial capital account of \$40,000 and an initial outside basis of \$5,000. The partnership's inside basis in Blackacre will start at \$35,000.

If the liability is not a "qualified liability," then the transaction will be recharacterized as a disguised sale to the extent that the liability shifts away from *X* and to the other partner. In this case, *X* is treated as selling 30 percent of the property for its fair market value of \$30,000. *X*'s adjusted basis in that portion of the property is \$10,500, so that *X* recognizes a gain on the contribution of \$19,500. *X* also is treated as contributing 70 percent of the property to the partnership in a tax-free transaction, giving *X* an initial capital account of \$40,000 and an initial outside basis of \$24,500. The effect of the disguised sale is to tax *X* on a portion of the unrealized appreciation in Blackacre and to increase *X*'s outside basis by the amount of gain so recognized. The disguised sale has no effect on *X*'s capital account: capital accounts reflect the economic arrangement among the partners and so should be independent of the recognition and deferral pre-contribution gain.

As noted above, the analysis does not change if the partnership has existing liabilities when *X* joins the venture by contributing Blackacre. To be sure, *X* may be allocated some of those existing liabilities so that the net reduction in *X*'s share of liabilities is less than the amount treated as part of a disguised sale (indeed, *X*'s net share of liabilities may in fact increase as a result of the admission to *P* if the partnership's liabilities are substantial). Nonetheless, the disguised sale rules treat the liability shift away from *X* as part of a disguised sale without any offset for the liabilities shifted to *X* and away from the other partners.

However, if another partner (say, *Y*) contributes encumbered property (say, Whiteacre) to the partnership along with *X*'s contribution of Blackacre, *X* may be permitted to reduce the net liabilities picked up from Whiteacre against those from Blackacre and shifted to the other partners, with only the net reduction (if any) forming part of a disguised sale. This rule applies when the two contributions are part of a single plan and neither liability is transferred to the partnership with a principal purpose of reducing a partner's tax liability resulting from a disguised sale. Treas. Regs. §1.707-5(a)(4). In computing a contributing partner's net reduction in liability share under this rule, qualified liabilities contributed by any partner continue to be ignored. *Id.*

So, for example, if *P* and *Q* form the *PQ* partnership by contributing property encumbered by nonqualified liabilities, the liability shift will trigger disguised sale treatment to the partners only to the extent of any net reduction in liability share. There is no requirement that the liabilities each be recourse or each be nonrecourse, so that by appropriately tailoring the liabilities and their allocations, it may be possible to eliminate the disguised sale treatment to both partners. Note that if *P*'s liability is qualified while *Q*'s liability is not, no offsetting is permitted. In such circumstances it may be advisable to refreshen *P*'s liability.

5. *How are liabilities allocated?* In determining the extent to which the contribution of encumbered property is treated as a disguised sale, liabilities encumbering the contributed property are allocated under the usual debt allocation rules of §752 to the extent the liability is treated as "recourse" under the §752 rules. Treas. Regs. §1.707-5(a)(2)(i). Nonrecourse liabilities are allocated for this purpose, though, under a special rule.

For all purposes other than disguised sales, partnership nonrecourse liabilities are allocated under §752 in three tiers. Tier one of the debt is allocated among the partners as they share minimum gain from disposition of the property; in general, that means that this portion of the debt is allocated as the partners were allocated nonrecourse deductions from the property. Tier two of the debt is allocated as would gain from the property be allocated under §704(c)(1)(A) (including reverse allocations made under the principles of §704(c)(1)(A)) if the property were sold for the amount of the debt and for nothing else. This allocates debt as the partners would share gain that already has been allocated for book (i.e., capital account) purposes. The remainder of the debt is allocated under tier three in accordance with profits interests broadly defined. Treas. Regs. §1.752-3(a).

However, for disguised sale purposes, only the tier three rules (slightly modified) are used to allocate nonrecourse debt. Treas. Regs. §1.707-5(a)(2)(ii). For disguised sales, nonrecourse debt can be allocated by the partnership in accordance with shares of partnership profits, in a manner that is reasonably consistent with the allocation of some other significant item from the property (assuming that allocation has substantial economic effect), or in the manner in which it reasonably is expected that the deductions attributable to the nonrecourse liabilities will be allocated. Treas. Regs. §1.752-3(a)(3).

6. *Do reallocated debts count as distributions?* Sometime after a partner contributes property to a partnership, the debts of the partnership may be reallocated because of changes in the amount of the partnership's outstanding indebtedness, changes in relative capital account balances, or changes in the terms of the indebtedness. If the debt share of the partner declines, that decline is treated as a distribution of cash to the partner by reason of §752(b). Will such a deemed distribution be paired with an actual contribution of property to form a disguised sale?

In general, the answer should be no. It is unfortunate that the disguised sale of property rules do not directly address this issue, but the answer seems clear nonetheless. A partner's reduction in debt share does not place any cash or property in the hands of the partner and so there is no reason to treat the reduction as part of a disguised sale. To be sure, the contribution of encumbered property can be recharacterized as a disguised sale to the extent the encumbrance is shifted to other partners, but in this case the loan proceeds were retained by the contributing partner prior to the contribution. That is, the proceeds were and remain in the hands of the contributing partner. In the case of a deemed distribution under §752, no cash or property leaves the partnership nor ends up in the hands of a partner.

And while the regulations do not address this issue directly, they do address it by implication. When encumbered property is contributed by a partner to the partnership, a shifting of the debt to other partners can give rise to a disguised sale. That is, the contributing partner will be treated as receiving consideration in exchange for the contributed property to the extent of any reduction in the contributing partner's share of indebtedness secured by the property (excluding, of course, reduction in share of "qualified" liabilities). The regulations also provide in this circumstance that a subsequent reduction in the contributing partner's share of liabilities encumbering the contributed property will be treated as consideration for the transfer if "(i) [a]t the time that the partnership assumes or takes subject to a liability, it is anticipated that the transferring partner's share of the liability will be subsequently reduced; and (ii) [t]he reduction of the partner's share of the liability is part of a plan that has as one of its principal purposes minimizing the extent to which the assumption of or taking subject to the liability is treated as part of a sale under [Treas. Regs.] §1.707-3." Treas. Regs. §1.707-5(a)(3). Note that this rule applies only to a shift in contributed debt and then only if the shift is part of a plan to minimize the adverse tax consequences on the contribution. By implication, then, the mere shift of noncontributed debt, though constituting a deemed distribution under §752, does not constitute part of a disguised sale.

Further support for conclusion can be found in the (ultimately revoked) proposed regulations addressing the disguised sale of a partnership interest. These regulations provided that a contribution by one partner and a distribution to another partner can be treated as a single, unified transaction in which the contributing partner is treated as purchasing some or all of the partnership interest from the partner receiving the distribution. These proposed regulations were based on the disguised sale of property regulations discussed above, and these proposed regulations explicitly provided that deemed distributions under §752 do not constitute the distribution half of a disguised sale. See Prop. Treas. Regs. §1.707-7(j) (revoked by Ann. 2009-4, 2009-8 I.R.B. 597).

7. *Nonsimultaneous disguised sales: the two-year presumptions.* The regulations presume that transactions occurring within two years are part of a single, integrated transaction. See Treas. Regs. §1.707-3(c). For example, if appreciated property is contributed to a partnership on January 1, 2008, and a distribution is made to the contributing partner on January 1, 2009, the contribution and subsequent distribution will be treated as a disguised sale unless the facts and circumstances clearly establish that the transfers do not constitute a sale. Treas. Regs. §1.707-3(c)(1). The same analysis would apply if the transaction occurred in reverse order. *Id.*

In general, a contribution and subsequent distribution will constitute a disguised sale only if (1) the distribution would not have been made but for the prior contribution, and (2) the distribution is not dependent on the entrepreneurial risks of partnership operations. See Treas. Regs. §1.707-3(b)(1). The regulations specify several facts that tend to establish the existence of a sale.

> The timing and amount of the subsequent distribution is determinable with reasonable certainty;
>
> The partner has a legally enforceable right to the distribution;

> The partner's right to the distribution is secured in any manner;
>
> Any person has made or is legally obligated to make a contribution to fund the distribution;
>
> Any person has a legal obligation to make a loan to the partnership to fund the distribution;
>
> The partnership has incurred or is obligated to incur a debt to fund the distribution;
>
> The partnership has liquid assets beyond the reasonable needs of its business that could be used to fund the distribution;
>
> Partnership allocations and distributions have been used to effect an exchange of the economic benefits and burdens of ownership of partnership property;
>
> The distribution is disproportionately large in comparison with the partner's general interest in partnership profits; and
>
> The partner has no obligation to repay the distribution or any such obligation is likely to become due as such a distant point in the future that the present value of the obligation is small.

For example, suppose *C* transfers unimproved land having an adjusted basis of \$500,000 and fair market value of \$1,000,000 to the *CD* partnership in exchange for an interest in the partnership. The partnership intends to construct a building on this land, and the partnership agreement provides that upon completion of construction the partnership will distribute \$900,000 to *C*. If within two years of *C*'s transfer a distribution of \$900,000 is made, the contribution and distribution will be presumed to constitute a sale. However, if the partnership was able to fund the distribution out of construction loan proceeds that were available only because construction costs were significantly less than were reasonably projected, *C* may be able to rebut the presumption. See example 3 of Treas. Regs. §1.707-3(f).

If a contribution and subsequent distribution are determined to constitute a disguised sale, the sale is deemed to occur when the partnership becomes the owner of the property treated as being sold by the partner, Treas. Regs. §1.707-3(a)(2); that is, the disguised sale is treated as occurring when the contribution was made. For example, if a partner transfers property to a partnership on January 1, 2008, and the partnership distributes cash or property to the partner on January 1, 2009, and if these two transaction properly constitute a sale, then the sale is deemed to have occurred on January 1, 2008. As a result, some portion of the distribution may be recharacterized as an interest component under §483 or §1272. This recharacterization also affects the amount of the disguised sale that is deemed to occur. See example 2 of Treas. Regs. §1.707-3(f). Note that if the contribution and distribution are separated by more than two years, they are presumed to be unrelated. Treas. Regs. §1.707-3(d).

8. *Nonsimultaneous disguised sales: recomputing the sale price.* Suppose individual *X* contributes property to the *P* partnership when the property has an adjusted basis of \$10,000 and a fair market value of \$100,000. If a distribution is made to *X* within six months of the contribution in an amount equal to \$100,000, and if the contribution and distribution are treated as a single, disguised sale, then *X* is treated as selling the property rather than contributing it and *X* must recognize the \$90,000 appreciation in the property as taxable gain. Further, if this is a two-person partnership formed at the time of the contribution, there will in fact be no partnership formed (because a partnership requires two or more partners) until a later time. Treas. Regs. §1.703-3(a)(3). In such circumstances, the sale is treated as having been

made between *X* and the other nominal partner. *Id.* It is unclear whether the partnership could be treated as formed immediately after the disguised sale, with *X* treated as receiving a profits interest in the venture. Such a result does not seem inconsistent with the disguised sale rules and best preserves the economic arrangement of the parties.

Suppose that the $100,000 distribution to *X* is not made until one year after *X*'s contribution. If the transaction is still treated as a disguised sale, then because the payment to *X* was made more than six months after the partnership acquired the property, a portion of the $100,000 is treated as implicit interest in accordance with the rules of §1272. See Treas. Regs. §1.707-3(f) (example 2). *X* can report that gain on the installment method unless *X* elects otherwise or installment sale treatment is for some reason precluded. *Id.*

Assume that the appropriate discount under §1272 is 11 percent so that the deemed sale price is $90,000, and the remaining $10,000 is treated as interest paid by the partnership to *X*. Because the value of the property contributed by *X* was $100,000 while the deemed sale price was only $90,000, *X* is treated as selling only 90 percent of the property and contributing the remaining 10 percent. As a result, *X*'s gain on the disguised sale is only $81,000 (amount realized of $90,000 less $9,000 of allowable adjusted basis). Thus, *X*'s initial capital account begins at $10,000 (10 percent of the value of the property) while *X*'s outside basis begins at $1,000 (10 percent of the adjusted basis of the property). In addition, *X* must include $10,000 of interest received and the partnership likely will be entitled to claim a deduction for the $10,000 of interest deemed paid. For the proper allocation of this deduction, see the next note.

9. *Nonsimultaneous disguised sales: tax neutrality for the other partners.* The effect of the disguised sale of property rules is to characterize some or all of a contribution/distribution pair into a taxable sale of property. For the partners other than the contributing partner, the disguised sale rules have no direct impact. That makes sense: They are not taxed under these rules, and while the disguised sale rules affect the taxation of one of the partners, they should not affect the economic arrangement among the partners. Accordingly, application of these rules should affect neither the capital account balances of the partners nor the subsequent allocation of tax items.

If the contribution and distribution occur within six months, nothing need be done to ensure that the disguised sale recharacterization affects no one other than the contributing partner. However, if the contribution and distribution are separated in time, care must be taken in the allocation provisions to ensure this result. In particular, the partnership agreement should provide that any interest deemed paid by the partnership as a result of a disguised sale is allocated exclusively to the contributing partner.

For example, suppose *X* and *Y* form the *XY* partnership, with *X* contributing Blackacre having an adjusted basis of $60,000 and fair market value of $100,000 and *Y* contributing cash of $50,000. If the cash subsequently is distributed to *X*, and the contribution/distribution are not recharacterized as a disguised sale, then the books of the partnership will be:

X		*Y*	
CA	OB	CA	OB
$100,000	$60,000	$50,000	$50,000
(50,000)	(50,000)	0	0
$ 50,000	$10,000	$50,000	$50,000

If the transaction is recharacterized as a simultaneous disguised sale, then *X*'s contribution is bifurcated into a half contribution, half sale. On the sale portion, *X* recognizes a gain of $20,000 ($50,000 amount realized less $30,000 adjusted basis). *X* is treated as contributing half of the property to the partnership, yielding opening books of:

X		*Y*	
CA	OB	CA	OB
$50,000	$30,000	$50,000	$50,000

Note in particular that despite the disguised sale recharacterization, there is no change to *Y*'s capital account or outside basis, and there also is no change to *X*'s capital account. Thus, *Y* is unaffected by the disguised sale recharacterization, and the economic relationship between the partners is maintained.

Suppose, however, that the distribution to *X* is not made until one year after the partnership is formed. In such circumstances, the distribution of $50,000 will be treated as including both consideration for the contribution and an interest element for the delay in payment by the partnership. Assume that the interest component is $2,000 and that the consideration component is $48,000. As a result, *X* recognizes a gain on the disguised sale of $19,200 ($48,000 amount realized less $28,800 adjusted basis). Assuming that the partnership's interest deduction is allocated equally between the partners, the books will read:

X		*Y*	
CA	OB	CA	OB
$52,000	$31,200	$50,000	$50,000
(1,000)	(1,000)	(1,000)	(1,000)
$51,000	$30,200	$49,000	$49,000

These books likely do not reflect the economic agreement between the partners because they show that *X*'s share of the $100,000 value of the partnership's property is 51 percent while *Y*'s share is only 49 percent. To be sure, *Y* has received a $1,000 deduction so that *Y*'s economic loss is matched by a tax loss, but since the partnership has not lost any money, *Y* should take small consolation in that fact. While there is nothing wrong with these allocations if they reflect the partners' agreement, it is far more likely that a special allocation of the interest deduction entirely to *X* is what the parties expect. If that is done, the books become:

X		*Y*	
CA	OB	CA	OB
$52,000	$31,200	$50,000	$50,000
(2,000)	(2,000)	(0)	(0)
$50,000	$29,200	$50,000	$50,000

These books show that the disguised sale by *X* has no impact on the capital account or outside basis of *Y*. In particular, the capital account balances now show an equal ownership of the partnership by *X* and by *Y*.

10. *Effect on other provisions.* A transaction that is treated as a sale under §707(a)(2)(B) is treated as a sale for all tax purposes. Treas. Regs. §1.707-3(a)(2). Thus, a disguised sale might qualify for installment sale treatment under §453 or like-kind exchange treatment under §1031. The disguised sale provisions are applied before the other mixing bowl provisions in §704(c)(1)(B) and §737, and the disguised sale of interest rules defer to the disguised sale of property rules. Prop. Treas. Regs. §1.707-7(a)(6) (revoked by Ann. 2009-4, 2009-8 I.R.B. 597).

11. *The exceptions.* A reasonable guaranteed payment for the use of capital is not treated as part of a disguised sale. A "guaranteed payment" means a payment that is determined without regard to partnership income. §707(c). A guaranteed payment in this context will be presumed "reasonable" if it does not exceed the partner's unreturned capital for the year times 150 percent of the highest applicable federal rate (with preferred returns subject to the same safe harbor so that the sum of a partner's guaranteed payments for capital plus preferred returns on capital cannot be greater than 150 percent of unreturned capital for the safe harbor to apply). See Treas. Regs. §1.707-4(a)(1). Note that guaranteed payments for services are not expressly excluded from disguised sale treatment but should not, in fact, constitute part of a disguised sale for property if the connection to services can be proven.

A reasonable preferred return also is not treated as part of a disguised sale. A "preferred return" means a preferential distribution of partnership cash flow that will be matched, to the extent available, by an allocation of partnership income. Treas. Regs. §1.707-4(a)(3)(i). In this context a return is "reasonable" if it does not exceed the amount of the partner's unreturned capital times 150 percent of the highest applicable federal rate (with guaranteed payments added to the preferred returns). A preferred return can be cumulative without violating the "reasonable" requirement. See Treas. Regs. §1.707-4(a)(3)(ii).

Distributions of cash flow do not constitute part of a disguised sale unless the facts and circumstances clearly establish that the distribution is part of a sale. A distribution is treated as operating cash flow only to the extent that it does not exceed that partner's net share of the partnership's net cash flow. Treas. Regs. §1.707-4(b)(2). In determining the partner's "net share of partnership net cash flow," the regulations provide as a safe harbor the partner's smallest percentage interest in any material item of partnership income or gain that may be realized by the partnership in a three-year window. See Treas. Regs. §1.707-4(b).

A transfer of money or other property will not be treated as part of a disguised sale to the extent it represents reimbursement of capital expenditures that were incurred during the two-year period preceding the contribution. However, this exception is further limited: if the fair market value of the property exceeds 120 percent of adjusted basis, then the reimbursement will not be treated as part of a disguised sale only to the extent of 20 percent of the fair market value of the property. See Treas. Regs. §1.707-4(d). Note: This exception will also cover reimbursement of pre-formation organization and syndication expenses.

The "leveraged distribution" exception in Treas. Regs. §1.707-5(b) was at issue in the *Canal Corp.* case. This exception generally provides that a distribution from a partnership to a partner will not constitute part of a disguised sale if the distribution does not exceed the distributee partner's share of loan proceeds under the rules of Treas. Reg. §1.163-8T, a temporary regulation (promulgated in 1987) that provides rules for the tracing of cash. In *Canal Corp.*, WISCO, a subsidiary of Canal Corp., contributed appreciated property to a limited liability company taxable as a partnership, and then the limited liability company immediately borrowed cash almost equal in value to the contributed property and distributed the loan proceeds to WISCO. The noncontributing partner (Georgia Pacific) guaranteed the debt, and of course that guarantee would by itself cause all of the debt to be allocated to the guarantor partner, Treas. Regs. §1.752-2(b)(1), precisely the opposite of what the leveraged distribution exception requires. To move the debt back to the contributing partner, WISCO agreed to indemnify Georgia Pacific if the guarantee was ever enforced. Thus, ultimate liability for repayment of the debt rested on WISCO, and so the debt should be allocated entirely to WISCO under the §752 recourse rules. See Treas. Regs. §1.752-2(a) (allocation of recourse debt), §1.752-2(b)(3) (reimbursement rights).

The contributing partner (WISCO) had paid out the distributed loan proceeds to its parent corporation, Canal Corp., as a tax-free dividend. This distribution eliminated much of the value from WISCO so that its ability to make good on its indemnification was at best uncertain. Further, while WISCO owned a valuable intercompany note from its parent corporation, WISCO was under no legal obligation to maintain any minimum net worth, suggesting that the intercompany note might itself be eliminated through a dividend or similar transaction. While the debt allocation rules generally do not require that a taxpayer be able to prove an ability to satisfy the taxpayer's share of partnership-level debt, see Treas. Regs. §1.752-2(b)(6), the regulations contain an anti-abuse rule providing that an obligation to make a payment (such as WISCO's potential indemnity obligation) can be ignored "if the facts and circumstances indicate that a principal purpose of the arrangement between the parties is to eliminate [a] partner's economic risk of loss . . . when, in fact, the substance of the arrangement is otherwise." Treas. Regs. §1.752-2(j)(1). In effect, the court concluded that the lender looked to the credit of Georgia Pacific rather than to WISCO in making the loan.

12. *The disclosure rules.* If a contribution and a distribution occur within two years, and the partner does not treat them as constituting a disguised sale, then the partner is required to disclose the transaction to the Service on Form 8275. Treas. Regs. §1.707-3(c)(2). This disclosure must include a caption identifying the statement as a disclosure under §707, it must identify the transactions subject to the disclosure, it must include the amounts of each relevant transaction, and it must include a statement of the facts relevant to the application of §707. Treas. Regs. §1.707-8(b). A similar disclosure obligation is imposed if contributed property is encumbered by a liability, and the liability is treated as "qualified" within the meaning of Treas. Regs. §1.707-5(a)(6). See Treas. Regs. §1.707-5(a)(7)(ii).

However, three distributions are exempted from the disclosure rules. Treas. Regs. §1.707-3(2)(iii). They are (1) distributions presumed to constitute reasonable guaranteed payments for capital; (2) distributions presumed to be reasonable preferred returns; and (3) distributions of operating cash flow. Note that reimbursement of preformation expenditures as well as debt-financed distributions are not excepted from the disclosure rules.

In connection with the promulgation of proposed regulations governing the disguised sale of a partnership interest, the disclosure requirement was to be extended to distributions and contributions separated by not more than seven years. Note that it remains the case that contributions and distributions separated by more than two years continue to benefit from a presumption that they do not constitute a disguised sale. These proposed regulations were revoked without ever becoming final.

PROBLEMS

23-3. Individual *Z* joins the *XY* general partnership by contributing property with a fair market value of $100,000 and an adjusted basis of $40,000 to the partnership. One day later, the partnership distributes cash of $50,000 to *Z*.

a. What are the tax consequences to *Z* of these events, and what are *Z*'s outside basis and capital account? What is the partnership's adjusted basis in the property contributed by *Z*?
b. Without doing any calculations, what differences would arise if the distribution were made one year after *Z*'s admission to the partnership?

23-4. *P* and *Q* form the *PQ* limited liability company, with *P* contributing cash of $800,000 and *Q* contributing property with a fair market value of $1,600,000, an adjusted basis of $900,000, and subject to a debt of $800,000. *P* and *Q* agree to be equal partners for all items of income, deduction, credit, and loss, and neither partner is liable for repayment of the debt. What are the partners' initial capital accounts and outside bases?

23-5. Individual *X* owns unimproved real estate with an adjusted basis of $400,000 and fair market value of $2,000,000. Prior to contributing this property to a partnership, *X* improves the property by constructing a building at a cost of $2,500,000, increasing the value of the property to $5,000,000.

a. What is the maximum reimbursement for construction costs that can be made to *X* without triggering a disguised sale?
b. How might *X* have structured the transaction to permit a greater reimbursement without incurring an immediate tax liability?

C. DISTRIBUTIONS OF CONTRIBUTED PROPERTY: §704(c)(1)(B)

When appreciated property is contributed to a partnership in exchange for an equity interest in the venture, the appreciation is not taxed at the time of the exchange. §721(a). However, the cost of that nonrecognition is not only a lower inside and outside basis, §722, §723, but also the requirement that when the gain is recognized by the partnership, it will be allocated to the contributing partner, §704(c)(1)(A). How might a partnership try to avoid that requirement?

Three ways come to mind. First, the partnership might exchange the contributed property for other property and then claim that the gain from the new property can be allocated under the rules of §704(b) rather than §704(c)(1)(A). This strategy will not work because the regulations long have provided that if contributed property is exchanged for other property in a nonrecognition exchange, the replacement property is treated as the contributed property for purposes of §704(c)(1)(A). Treas. Regs. §1.704-3(a)(8). This rule captures post-contribution like-kind exchanges of contributed property as well as contributions of contributed property to corporations under §351 and to lower-tier partnerships under §721.[1]

A second possibility is to distribute the contributed property to one of the noncontributing partners. Such a distribution is tax free without the receipt of a replacement property by the partnership, effectively eliminating the possibility of transferring the §704(c)(1)(A) taint to other property. And because the contributed property is owned outside of the partnership once the distribution is made, a subsequent sale of the property shifts the pre-contribution gain to the distributee partner because it is the distributee partner who owns the property at the time of sale. Once, such a strategy avoided the requirement of §704(c)(1)(A), but now many distributions of contributed property will be captured and taxed under §704(c)(1)(B).

Section 704(c)(1)(B) provides that if contributed property is distributed by the partnership within seven years of the contribution, gain or loss must be recognized by the contributing partner in an amount equal to the gain or loss that would be allocable to the contributing partner under §704(c)(1)(A) (that is, excluding any gain or loss allocable under §704(b)) if the property were sold to a third party for its current fair market value. For example, assume that *X* and *Y* form a partnership with *X* contributing Blackacre with a fair market value of $50,000 and adjusted basis of $40,000 and *Y* contributing cash of $100,000. Within seven years of formation, the partnership distributes Blackacre (still worth $50,000) to *Y*. This distribution triggers recognition to *X* of a $10,000 gain under §704(c)(1)(B). Note that, because of the parenthetical in §704(c)(1)(B), the rule of §704(c)(1)(B) does not apply if the property is distributed back to the contributing partner (in our example, §704(c)(1)(B) does not apply if Blackacre is distributed to *X*). In addition, §704(c)(1)(B) does not apply if the transaction has the effect of a like-kind exchange. §704(c)(2).

Consistent with treating the distribution to *Y* as an implicit sale by *X*, appropriate basis adjustments are made to outside bases and to *Y*'s post-distribution basis in Blackacre. §704(c)(1)(B)(iii). That is, immediately before applying §731, §732 and §733 to the distribution, we recompute *X*'s contribution as if *X* had recognized gain on the contribution, and then we recompute the distribution to *Y* based on the first recomputation. Thus, *X* takes an initial outside basis of $50,000, and the partnership takes an inside basis in Blackacre of the same amount. Accordingly, when Blackacre is distributed to *Y*, *Y* takes a basis in Blackacre of $50,000 under §732(a)(1) and reduces her outside basis by that amount to $50,000 under §733(2). For the relationship of §731(c) to §704(c)(1)(B), see Treas. Regs. §1.731-2(g)(1).

PROBLEM

23-6. *P* and *Q* form the *PQ* general partnership, with *P* contributing depreciable property having an adjusted basis of $6,000 and fair market value of $10,000

1. For the rules applicable to contribution of contributed property to lower-tier partnerships, see Treas. Regs. §1.704-3(a)(9).

and *Q* contributing cash of $10,000. *P* and *Q* are equal partners except as required by §704(c). Assume that the basis of the property contributed by *P* is recovered ratably over five years and that the partnership elects not to use remedial allocations. What are the tax consequences if the partnership distributes the property to *Q* after one year when the property has a fair market value of $10,000? Explain why there is a book/tax disparity for each partner. What if the property is worth $12,000 at the time of distribution? What if it is worth $4,000?

D. SWAP TRANSACTIONS UNDER §737

Reconsider the possible ways a partnership might try to avoid allocating pre-contribution gain to the contributing partner, that is, avoiding the requirement of §704(c)(1)(A). We already have seen that transferring the contributed property in some nonrecognition exchange will not avoid §704(c)(1)(A) and the distribution of the contributed property will work only if the distribution occurs more than seven years after the contribution. But consider the possibility of distributing partnership property to the contributing partner in a liquidating distribution. Once the contributing partner exits the venture, the contributed property can be sold and the gain must be allocated under §704 among only the remaining partners. And because most distributions of property—even liquidating distributions—are tax free to the distributee, this technique would allow the contributing partner to avoid recognition of the pre-contribution gain.

Congress has ensured that partnerships cannot be used in this way. Section 737 is triggered by the distribution of property to a partner who contributed appreciated property in the past. In such circumstances, the distributee will recognize gain equal to the *lesser* of (1) the excess of the fair market value of the property distributed over the distributee's outside basis immediately prior to the distribution (but reduced by any cash received in the distribution (§737(a)(1))) or (2) the net amount of the pre-contribution appreciation in all property *contributed* by the distributee within the past seven years §737(a).

For example, suppose individual *X* contributes Blackacre with an adjusted basis of $60 and a fair market value of $100 to the *P* partnership in exchange for a partnership interest. Within seven years of that contribution, the partnership distributes other property having an adjusted basis and a fair market value of $100 to *X*. If only §§731-733 applied to the transaction, the distribution would be tax free to *X*, and *X* would take the distributed property with a basis of $60. Of course, *X* would also reduce her outside basis to $0 under §733(2).

However, application of §737 to the transaction means that *X* will recognize a gain of $40 on the distribution, gain that is treated as realized from the sale or exchange of the contributed property. §737(a) (final sentence). Consistent with taxing *X* on the appreciation in the contributed asset, §737(c) provides for a basis increase to the partner's outside basis as well as to the partnership's inside basis in the contributed asset. This basis provision plays the same role as that in §704(c)(1)(B)(iii).

Section 737 will not force the recognition of income on a distribution of cash because the amount defined in §737(a)(1) will equal zero. Recall that a distribution of cash triggers recognition of income under §731(a)(1) to the extent the cash distributed exceeds the distributee's outside basis. Thus, application of §737 would be redundant because the measure of recognition in §731(a)(1) is the same measure employed by §737(a)(1) (with cash substituting for property).

A partner's "net precontribution gain" is defined in §737(b) to include only the pre-contribution appreciation (net of pre-contribution loss) remaining in property contributed by the partner within the last seven years and still held by the partnership. This seven-year limitation presumably is based on the notion that if the contribution and distribution are separated by more than seven years, it is inappropriate to treat them as related. The limitation that the property continue to be owned by the partnership coordinates §737 with §704(c)(1). Under §704(c)(1)(A), the pre-contribution gain will be allocated to the contributing partner upon disposition of the asset. Under §704(c)(1)(B), the pre-contribution gain will be taxed to the contributing partner upon distribution of the asset to some other partner. Thus, the pre-contribution appreciation will already have been taxed to the contributing partner except in the case when the contributed asset is still held by the partnership. And this last situation is precisely when §737 applies.

Section 737 explicitly limits its application to the amount of pre-contribution appreciation that would be taxed to the contributing partner if the property were distributed to some other partner. See §737(b). That is, §737 cannot tax a partner more harshly than would §704(c)(1)(B). In particular, the effect of §737 will be mitigated or eliminated entirely if the contributing partner has managed to eliminate the prior §704(c) book/tax disparity by some means. For example, if the contributed property is depreciable by the partnership, the §704(c) book/tax disparity may be eliminated over time by differing allocations of book and tax depreciation. See, e.g., Treas. Regs. §1.704-3(b)(2) (example 1(ii)).

Section 737 provides an exception for property distributed to the partner who originally contributed the property to the partnership. §737(d)(1). And by referencing §704(c)(1)(B) in the definition of "net precontribution gain," §737 implicitly includes an exception for swap transactions that have the effect of a like-kind exchange. See §704(c)(2). Note also that the gain recognized under §737 is in addition to any gain recognized under §731(a)(1) if the distribution consists of cash as well as of property and that application of §737 defers to the application of §751(b) should they both apply to the same transaction. §737(a). In addition, if distributed marketable securities are treated as cash under §731(c), then they are treated as cash for purposes of §737. Treas. Regs. §1.731-2(g)(1)(iii)(A).

NOTES

1. *The temporary need for outside basis.* Consider *T*, who has an outside basis of $0 and will receive a nonliquidating distribution of partnership property ("Blackacre") having an inside basis of $0 and fair market value of $10,000. Assume that *T*'s "net precontribution gain" at the time of the distribution equals or exceeds $10,000. This distribution will trigger taxation under §737 unless *T* can increase her outside basis prior to the distribution.

Such an outside basis increase can be accomplished in at least two separate ways. First, *T* might contribute additional cash or property to the partnership. Second, the partnership might incur additional debt that is allocable to *T* under the rules of §752. If either of these routes are taken and *T*'s outside basis can be increased to at least $10,000, taxation of *T* under §737 is avoided.

Note that once the distribution is made, the basis increase can be unwound. For example, if *T* contributes cash of $10,000, that cash can be distributed to *T* after the distribution of Blackacre without triggering income recognition under §731(a)(1). That is, while *T* needed a basis increase to avoid taxation under §737, the distribution otherwise implicating §737 did not actually consume that basis increase (although, if Blackacre had had an inside basis greater than $0, some or all of the basis increase would in fact have been consumed).

Contributing cash or property to avoid triggering taxation under §737, if quickly followed by a distribution of the contributed cash or property, is sometimes referred to as "doing the hokey-pokey." Does it accomplish the taxpayer's goal? See the anti-abuse rule in Treas. Regs. §1.737-4 and examples 1 and 2 in Treas. Regs. §1.737-4(b). But read carefully example 2(ii) of Treas. Regs. §1.737-4 in which an allocation of debt is made to a partner "[w]ith a principal purpose of avoiding . . . gain" under §737, and yet the regulation concludes that the avowedly tax-avoidance transaction succeeds. In addition, note that if property is contributed and distributed within a two-year period, the contribution and distribution might be treated as a single disguised sale because the disguised sale rules do not include an exception for distributions of previously contributed property. It is hard to see, though, how a taxpayer can be treated as exchanging a piece of property for the very same property.

2. *The peculiarities of §737.* As discussed in the note above, it is difficult to explain why the gain recognized under §737 is limited to the lesser of (i) the contributing partner's pre-contribution gain and (ii) the excess of the value of the property distributed over the partner's outside basis. But this second limitation might be explained by the application of §737 to nonliquidating distributions: It would be peculiar if recognition of all of the partner's pre-contribution gain were triggered by the distribution of a very small amount of property.

Why is §737 applicable to nonliquidating distributions? After all, if the contributing partner remains a partner after the distribution, then §704(c)(1)(A) is not avoided by the distribution because, when the contributed property is sold, the pre-contribution gain can be allocated to the contributing partner. While there is no clear explanation for the extension of §737 to nonliquidating distributions, one answer might be the limitation of §704(c)(1)(B) to distributions within seven years of the contribution. Because of this limitation, a partner seeking to avoid §704(c)(1)(A) might receive a distribution of property (not the contributed property) sufficient to reduce the value of her partnership interest to a very small amount. Once that is accomplished, it would be easy for the partner to remain a member of the partnership until the seven-year period has expired, at which point the contributed property can be distributed to some other partner. That is, the over-reach of §737 might be explained by the under-reach of §704(c)(1)(B).

PROBLEM

23-7. *P* and *Q* form the *PQ* general partnership, with *P* contributing depreciable property having an adjusted basis of $6,000 and fair market value of $10,000 and *Q* contributing unimproved real estate with an adjusted basis of $2,000 and fair market value of $10,000. *P* and *Q* are equal partners except as required by §704(c). Assume that the basis of the property contributed by *P* is recovered ratably over five years and that the partnership elects not to use remedial allocations.

a. How would *Q* be taxed under §737 if the partnership distributes the depreciable property to *Q* after one year when the property has a fair market value of $10,000?
b. What if the property contributed by *Q* had an adjusted basis of $9,000 rather than $2,000?

E. CAPITALIZATION AVOIDANCE AND §707(a)(2)(A)

Sections 707(a)(2)(A) and 707(a)(2)(B) are similar in that both are triggered by a transfer to the partnership and a related distribution from the partnership to a partner. What distinguishes §707(a)(2)(A) from §707(a)(2)(B) is the requirement in §707(a)(2)(A)(ii) that the contributing/distributee partner receive *an allocation of income* to go along with the distribution of money or property. By reason of this allocation requirement, the contributing/distributee partner will recognize income on the transaction, and so transactions described in §707(a)(2)(A) cannot represent attempts to reduce the tax burden imposed on the contributing/distributee partner. Rather, such transactions may represent an attempt by the partnership to avoid the capitalization requirement of §263.

For example, suppose the *P* partnership constructs a commercial office building. The architect, whose normal fee is $40,000, contributes cash for a 25-percent interest in the partnership and receives in addition a gross income allocation of $20,000 per year for the first two years of the partnership. Further, the partnership agreement provides that the architect will be distributed $20,000 of cash in each of the first two years in addition to her 25-percent share as partner. For ease of illustration, assume that the partnership generates rental income each year of $120,000.

This gross income allocation and distribution produces the same tax consequences to the architect as a salary of $40,000: The architect must report $40,000 of income over the first two years in addition to her 25-percent distributive share, and the architect's outside basis and capital account each enjoy a net increase equal to her general 25-percent interest in the partnership. That is, after two years the architect will have included $40,000 by reason of the special gross income allocation as well as $50,000 (25 percent of the remaining $100,000 in each of the two years) as distributive share of partnership taxable income. In addition, the architect's outside basis will have increased by $90,000 by reason of the special allocations and one-quarter distributive shares and will have decreased by $40,000 by reason of the distributions, for a net increase of $50,000.

But consider the effect of the gross income allocation on the partnership generally. Had the architect been paid a straight salary, that salary would have been capitalizable as part of the cost of the building. Treas. Regs. §1.263(a)-2(d). As a result, each year the architect would have reported $20,000 of compensation income and the partnership would have had $120,000 of income to be allocated among its partners (of which $30,000 would have been the architect's distributive share). Because the architect was compensated indirectly with the special gross income allocation and distribution, though, the partnership has only $100,000 per year remaining after the gross income allocation to allocate among its members. The money used to pay the architect's fee thus is not reported by the partners in their distributive shares, and that is the equivalent of including those funds and then deducting the fee. *In other words, allocating income to one partner and thus away from the others is equivalent to paying the same amount of income as a deductible expense.*

Of course, not all allocations are subject to recharacterization under §707(a)(2)(A). The legislative history of §707(a)(2)(A) indicates that a partner is acting as a third party to the extent that the partner's profit from a transaction is assured without regard to the success or failure of the joint undertaking. An allocation of *net* partnership income ordinarily should not fall within the scope of §707(a)(2)(A) because net income is dependent on the economic success of the partnership venture. Allocations of *gross* partnership income do not share this element of entrepreneurial risk and so are more liable to challenge under §707(a)(2)(A). Indeed, from this perspective the effect of §707(a)(2)(A) is to identify those allocations and distributions that together constitute disguised guaranteed payments.

Congress identified several specific factors that should be considered under §707(a)(2)(A). S. Rep. No. 169, 98th Cong., 2d Sess. at 227-228 (1984). The most important factor is the extent to which the distribution is subject to appreciable risk. Even an allocation of net income can be virtually risk free as to both fact of payment and amount if the partnership's income stream is assured. For example, if the partnership owns property rented on a long-term lease to a credit-worthy lessee, an allocation of a fixed percentage of the partnership's net income might be tantamount to a risk-free allocation of a specific dollar sum. Capped allocations (that is, allocations equal to the lesser of a percentage of the partnership's net income or a fixed annual sum) should easily be classified as falling within §707(a)(2)(A).

The second factor to be considered is the duration of the distributee partner's status as a partner. If the distributee's status as a partner is transitory, the allocation and distribution are more likely to be recharacterized as a fee for services or for property. Even if the distributee's status as a partner is not transitory, if the distributee's continuing interest in the partnership is small as compared with the special allocation and distribution, the transaction is likely to fall within §707(a)(2)(A). Indeed, the legislative history indicates that this factor is particularly important if the special allocation lasts for only a short period of time. Thus, a special allocation of $25,000 for one year is ripe for recharacterization if the value of the partner's continuing profits interest is substantially less than $25,000 annually. Of course, no recharacterization is possible unless there is a related transfer of property or services to the partnership, payment for which would be capitalizable in full or in part.

Other factors identified by the legislative history include the proximity in time of the contribution of services or property and the distribution, the effect of the transaction on providing tax benefits to the partnership, and whether the contribution was booked in at less than fair market value.

PROBLEM

23-8. *X* Corp. owns a business worth between $10,000,000 and $12,000,000. *Y* Corp. is willing to invest cash of $12,000,000 for a 50-percent interest in a partnership to be formed with *X*. The parties agree to credit *X* with a $10,000,000 initial capital account. While each partner will have a 50-percent interests in profits and losses, the partnership agreement provides for a gross income allocation to *X* of up to $1,000,000 in each of the first two years if the partnership attains certain profitability goals. Is this gross income allocation valid? If *X* anticipates exiting from the partnership after a few years, what net effect will this gross income allocation have had on *X* and on *Y*?

F. LIMITATIONS APPLICABLE TO CONTROLLED PARTNERSHIPS

Section 707(b) imposes two limits on a controlling partner's ability to exploit her position in the partnership for tax advantages. In this context, a controlling partner is one who owns (directly or indirectly) more than 50 percent of the capital or profits of the partnership. While determining a partner's share of capital should be purely mechanical, determining a partner's share of profits is more problematic in any complex partnership that specially allocates some profit items. This aspect of §707(b) is one more example of how some parts of subchapter K reflect a surprising ignorance of the workings of partnership taxation. Be sure to note that a partner's share of both capital and profits include the capital and profits interests of all related parties, where related parties are defined in §267(c). See §707(b)(3).

1. *Disallowed Losses*

The loss disallowance rule in §707(b)(1) can apply to sales of property from partnerships *to* a related party as well as to sales of property to partnerships *from* a related party. Consider first the sale of loss property from a partnership to a related party.

The *AB* general partnership has two partners, *A* and *B*. Partner *A* has a capital account and outside basis of $25,000 while partner *B* has a capital account and outside basis of $75,000; assume the partnership agreement allocates all tax items 25 percent to *A* and 75 percent to *B*, and the partnership owns Blackacre with an adjusted basis and book value of $40,000 as well as cash of $60,000. If the partnership sells Blackacre to *B* for its current fair market value of $30,000, what are the tax consequences to the partners?

The sale produces a book loss to the partnership of $10,000, and under the partnership agreement that loss is allocated $2,500 to *A* and $7,500 to *B*. Accordingly, *A*'s capital account is reduced to $22,500, and *B*'s capital account is reduced to $67,500. While the partnership realizes a tax loss of $10,000 on the sale, that loss is disallowed by application of §707(b)(1) because the purchaser (*B*) is in control of the selling partnership.

Despite the absence of a recognized tax loss, the partners must reduce their outside bases by their shares of the realized but unrecognized tax loss. Because the operation of §707(b)(1) is not to defer the loss but instead to disallow it entirely, the loss is properly treated as falling within §705(a)(2)(B) as a nondeductible, noncapitalizable expenditure. Or, in the words of Rev. Rul. 96-10, 1996-1 C.B. 138, this item falls within §705(a)(2)(B) because it "has a permanent effect on the partnership's basis in its assets, without a corresponding current or future effect on its taxable income." Thus, *A*'s outside basis is reduced to $22,500, and *B*'s outside basis is reduced to $67,500.

B's basis in Blackacre is its cost to *B* of $30,000. However, if *B* subsequently sells Blackacre at a gain, *B* may use the loss disallowed to the partnership to offset any gain realized on the sale. Cf. §267(d). For example, if *B* eventually sells Blackacre for $45,000, *B*'s recognized gain will be only $5,000. The effect of this rule is to permit *B* to use not only that part of the loss denied to *B* under §707(b)(1) but also to use the remaining portion of the loss denied to *A* under that section as well.

Now consider the reverse transaction in which a controlling partner sells loss property to the partnership. For example, suppose partner *B* in the example above sells Whiteacre to the partnership for its fair market value of $8,000 when Whiteacre has an adjusted basis of $10,000 in *B*'s hands. Assume that at the time of the sale *A*'s outside basis and capital account equal $22,500 while *B*'s outside basis and capital account equal $67,500.

By virtue of §707(b)(1), the loss of $2,000 realized by *B* on the sale goes unrecognized, and the partnership takes a cost basis of $8,000 in Whiteacre. As before, if Whiteacre is subsequently sold at a gain, only so much of the gain as exceeds the disallowed loss must be recognized. Thus, if the partnership subsequently sells Whiteacre to a third party for its then fair market value of $14,000, the partnership realizes a book gain of $6,000 over its acquisition cost of $8,000. However, the partnership recognizes only $4,000 of tax gain by virtue of the penultimate sentence in §707(b)(1). How should this gain be allocated among the partners?

In the absence of any special allocation, *B* will be allocated 75 percent of the $4,000 tax gain, or $3,000. However, the partnership's tax gain is only $4,000 rather than $6,000 because of the prior tax loss that *B* sustained but was not allowed to deduct. Accordingly, when that disallowed loss reappears in the form of an income offset to the partnership, arguably it should benefit the partner who generated it; in other words, it should benefit *B*. Thus, *B* should be taxed on her share of the book gain (that is, on 75 percent of $6,000, or $4,500) less that $2,000 income offset, for a net share of $2,500. The remaining $1,500 tax gain recognized by the partnership would then be allocable to *A*. Note that the effect of this approach is to tax *A* as she would be taxed had *B*'s loss not been disallowed: The $1,500 tax gain allocated to *A* is precisely 25 percent of the partnership's book gain on the subsequent sale.

Put another way, the disposition of Whiteacre by the partnership for $14,000 produces book income of $6,000, taxable gain of $4,000, and tax-exempt income of $2,000. Should the partners be permitted (perhaps even required) to allocate all the exempt income to *B* because it was *B*'s disallowed loss that generated it? Assuming the partners in fact agree to allocate all the exempt income as well as $2,500 of the taxable income to *B* and the remaining $1,500 of taxable income to *A*, do these allocations lack substantiality because they do not affect the actual dollars either partner will receive but only affect the partners' tax positions? While there is no direct authority on this point, it would seem that allocating to *B* the tax benefit of the income offset generated by *B*'s prior disallowed loss should be permissible.

NOTES

1. *From "partner" to "person."* Until 1986, §707(b)(1)(A) and (B) applied to transactions between a partnership and "partner" who owns more than 50 percent

of the capital and profits of the partnership. Now, these provisions apply to transactions between a partnership and a controlling "person." This change from "partner" to "person" ensures that these provisions can apply to persons who do not directly own an interest in the partnership but who are related to a partner. Until this statutory change was made, a sale of loss property between a nonpartner and a partnership could not be covered by §707(b)(1) but could be covered by §267(a)(1).

Section 267(a)(1) applied to partnership transactions on a partner-by-partner basis. So, for example, if *T* sold loss property to the *P* partnership, and *T* was related to partner *X* but not to partner *Y*, then that portion of *T*'s loss allocable to *X* would be disallowed, but that portion of *T*'s loss allocable to *Y* would pass §267(a)(1) unscathed. See Treas. Regs. §1.267(b)-1(b). This rule is harsher than the rule in §707(b)(1)(A) with respect to persons constructively owning a minority interest in the partnership (because some of the loss is disallowed) but more favorable with respect to persons constructively owning a majority interest (because some of the loss may be allowed).

Now that §707(b)(1)(B) has been extended to include nonpartners related to partners, no loss is allowed on the sale of property by a nonpartner to the partnership if the selling taxpayer is related to one or more partners who together own a majority of the capital and profits of the partnership. But what of nonpartners related to partners who own less of the partnership? The regulation cited above, though promulgated under prior law, remains in effect. If it continues to apply, then a nonpartner who sells loss property to a partnership and is related to one or more partners recognizes none of the loss if the related partners own more than 50 percent of the partnership's profits and capital or recognizes only a portion of the loss if the related partners own less of the partnership. A court might reasonably conclude, however, that the statutory change in language renders Treas. Regs. §1.267(b)-1(b) obsolete.

2. *Capital Gains*

Under §707(b)(2), gains from sales and exchanges between a partnership and its controlling partner (or between commonly controlled partnerships) are taxable as ordinary income if the transferred property is not a capital asset in the hands of the transferee. The same result obtains if the property is depreciable in the hands of the transferee by reason of the more general rule in §1239(a), see §1239(c)(1)(B). These two provisions deny capital gains benefits to dispositions that work little actual change in control over the transferred asset. Note that these rules apply only to gains and not to losses, so they will never operate to convert a capital loss into an ordinary deduction.

PROBLEMS

23-9. *M* has an 80-percent interest in the capital, profits, and losses of the *MNOP* partnership. *M* sells unimproved real estate to *MNOP* for its fair market value of $16,000 although *M* has an adjusted basis in the real estate of $20,000 at the time of the transaction. *MNOP* subsequently sells the real estate for $18,000.

a. How much gain or loss should the partnership report on this sale, and of that gain or loss, how much should be allocated to *M*?
b. What is the net effect on *M*'s capital account and outside basis as a result of these transactions?
c. How would your answers to part (a) change if the subsequent sale were for $30,000 instead of $18,000?

23-10. *H* has a 40-percent interest in the capital and profits of the *P* partnership. *H* sells Blackacre to *P* for its current fair market value of $10,000 while *H*'s adjusted basis in Blackacre is $12,000.

a. What part of *H*'s loss may be recognized? What if *H*'s interest in the partnership had been 60 percent?
b. For each possibility in part (a), what are the tax consequences to the partnership if it subsequently sells Blackacre for $15,000? For $9,000? For $11,000?
c. Do your answers to part (a) change if the sale is made by *W*, *H*'s spouse?

24

Acquisitions of Partnership Interests

A. CONTRIBUTIONS OF PROPERTY

Partnership interests may be acquired in different ways and at different times. At formation of the partnership, each of the partners will contribute property (possibly including cash) or services to the partnership in exchange for a partnership interest. Subsequently, new partners may be admitted in exchange for additional contributions, existing partners may make further contributions, or a nonpartner may join the enterprise by buying a partnership interest, receiving a partnership interest as a gift, or receiving a partnership interest through the estate of a decedent. Unless otherwise indicated in this chapter, assume all debts are "qualified liabilities" within the meaning of the disguised sales rules.

1. *Basic Principles*

In general, no gain or loss is recognized by the partnership or by any partner (including the contributing partner). §721(a). The contributing partner's adjusted basis in the property is carried over into the hands of the partnership, §723, as well as into the contributing partner's partnership interest, §722. We also have seen that the contributing partner's capital account is credited with the *fair market value* of the contributed property. Treas. Regs. §1.704-1(b)(2)(iv)(d)(1).

Capital accounts, more so than outside bases, reflect the partners' share of the partnership's value. When property is contributed to a partnership in exchange for a partnership interest, presumably the interest so created reflects the fair market value of the contributed property at the time of contribution. Crediting the contributing partner's capital account with the fair market value of the contributed property ensures that whatever value is acknowledged by the partners also is reflected in the capital accounts.

The partnership interest received by the contributing partner should reflect the fair market value of the contributed property as compared with the fair market value of the partnership's current assets. For example, suppose the *AB* partnership owns assets worth \$100. If *C* is admitted to the partnership in exchange for a contribution of property worth \$50, *C*'s capital account will properly reflect a one-third interest only if *C*'s interest is set equal to $50 (as it is) *and* the capital accounts of *A* and *B* total $100. That is, the capital accounts of *A* and *B* must reflect asset values as of the admission of the new partner, *C*. Accordingly, if we are to reflect all aspects of the contribution in the capital accounts, we should adjust each capital account by taking into account the current value of all partnership assets. The regulations specifically permit a partnership to revalue its assets and adjust capital accounts when property is contributed by a new (or continuing) partner. Treas. Regs. §1.704-1(b)(2)(iv)(f)(5)(i).

As a second example, suppose the *XY* partnership owns a single asset with a book value and adjusted basis of $100 and a fair market value of $140 when *Z* is admitted as a one-third partner in exchange for a cash contribution of $70. Assuming *X* and *Y* were equal partners prior to the admission of *Z*, we should increase the capital accounts of *X* and *Y* from $50 to $70 to reflect the value of the partnership as of the admission of *Z*. Thus, each one-third partner will have a capital account of $70 after the admission of *Z*. The $40 of unrealized appreciation in the partnership's asset should be allocable only to *X* and *Y* under principles similar to those applicable to §704(c) transactions. Treas. Regs. §1.704-1(b)(2)(iv)(d)(3).

These rules apply to contributions of "property," where property includes cash but does not include services. See Treas. Regs. §1.721-1(b)(1). Some kinds of property, notably copyrights and patents, have a strong service flavor, yet the courts have been willing to treat such property as falling within the ambit of §721. There is a similar "property" limitation applicable to the formation of a corporation, see §351(a), and courts will look to cases in that context for guidance under §721.

For example, in United States v. Stafford, 727 F.2d 1043 (11th Cir. 1984), a taxpayer contributed a letter of intent to a partnership in exchange for a 5-percent partnership interest. This letter of intent recited that the taxpayer and an insurance company had begun negotiations to finance and construct a hotel, with the insurance company providing a favorable loan and ground lease. The taxpayer contributed the letter of intent to the partnership and agreed to continue negotiations. Relying heavily on §351 cases and rulings, the court held that the letter of intent was "property" within the meaning of §721 even though it gave no enforceable rights to the partnership. The court likened the letter of intent to the goodwill of a sole proprietorship. See also Rev. Rul. 64-56, 1964-1 C.B. (pt. 1) 133, and Rev. Rul. 71-564, 1971-2 C.B. 179, for guidelines distinguishing between industrial know-how and services.

The rules in §721 and §722 apply not only when a partnership is formed but also subsequently if property is transferred to the partnership in exchange for a partnership interest. Treas. Regs. §1.721-1. In fact, they also apply to transfers of property by an existing partner even if nothing is received in return. Rev. Rul. 78-357, 1978-2 C.B. 227. However, the Treasury has been instructed to promulgate regulations providing that nonrecognition under §721 will not be available if application of §721 would permit income to escape taxation by shifting it offshore.

2. *Encumbered Property*

When encumbered property is contributed to a partnership in exchange for a partnership interest, the partnership debt rules of §752 are implicated. As to the contributing partner, the effect of the transaction is a reduction of share of the debt from 100 percent (prior to the contribution) to a lesser percentage based on the debt allocation rules provided in the §752 regulations. With respect to the noncontributing partners, the effect is precisely the opposite. Accordingly, the contributing partner will be treated as receiving a distribution of cash under §752(b) while the noncontributing partners will be treated as making contributions of cash under §752(a).

For example, suppose that the *XY* partnership owns one asset with fair market value and adjusted basis of $200, and assume also that the partnership has no debt. *X* has a 75-percent interest in the profits and losses of the partnership while *Y* has the remaining 25-percent interest. Assume that the partnership's books stand as follows:

X		*Y*	
CA	OB	CA	OB
$150	$150	$50	$50

Z is admitted as a new partner in exchange for a contribution of Blackacre. *Z*'s adjusted basis in Blackacre is $50. Blackacre is worth $160 and is encumbered by a debt of $60, which the partnership agrees to assume. After the admission of *Z*, *X*'s interest in the partnership drops to one-half, *Y*'s interest drops to one-sixth, and *Z*'s interest becomes one-third. The partnership's books after the admission of *Z* are as follows:

X		*Y*		*Z*	
CA	OB	CA	OB	CA	OB
$150	$180	$50	$60	$100	$10

To understand this table, look first at the capital accounts. The capital accounts of the noncontributing partners (i.e., of *X* and *Y*) remain unchanged. Technically, the partnership assets could be revalued as a result of the admission of *Z*, and the capital accounts of *X* and *Y* should be adjusted to reflect any unrealized appreciation or loss in the partnership's assets. Treas. Regs. §1.704-1(b)(2)(iv)(f). However, because there was no unrealized appreciation or loss in the partnership's assets, no adjustments to the noncontributing partners' capital accounts are made. *Z*'s capital account is equal to the value of Blackacre, net of its encumbrance. Because Blackacre is worth $160 and is subject to a debt of $60, its net value is $100, and that is the amount of *Z*'s initial capital account. Treas. Regs. §1.704-1(b)(2)(iv)(b).

The ending outside bases are best understood via a two-step process. In step one, Blackacre is contributed without regard for the possible debt reallocation under §752. Under §722, *Z* takes an initial outside basis of $50 because that was *Z*'s adjusted basis in Blackacre. *X* and *Y* continue their outside bases of $150 and $50 because nothing has occurred to warrant a change.

In step 2, we consider the effects of §752. Prior to the contribution of Blackacre, *Z*'s share of the $60 debt was the entire $60. After the contribution, *Z*'s interest in the debt must be determined by reference to a hypothetical zero-value sale and liquidation. Treas. Regs. §1.752-2(b)(1). A zero-value liquidation would produce a book loss of $360, allocable $180 to *X*, $60 to *Y*, and $120 to *Z*. Accordingly, final capital account balances will be negative $30 for *X*, negative $10 for *Y*, and negative $20 for *Z*. Each partner will be required to contribute her final capital account deficit to the partnership for distribution to the lender, and so these final capital account deficits determine the allocation of the debt: $30 for *X*, $10 for *Y*, and $20 for *Z*. Treas. Regs. §1.752-2(b)(1).

Thus, as a result of *Z*'s admission to the partnership, *Z*'s interest in the debt drops from $60 to $20. Accordingly, *Z* is deemed to receive a cash distribution of $40 under §752(b). Under §731, this deemed distribution does not produce any gain to *Z* because *Z*'s outside basis is able to absorb it, and under §733(1), *Z* reduces her outside basis by $40 from $50 to $10.

As to *X* and *Y*, they are treated under §752(a) as making cash contributions equal to their increases in their shares of the partnership's debt. Prior to the admission of *Z*, there was no partnership debt so that each partner's share was zero. After the admission of *Z*, the partnership's debt equals $60, see §752(c), and *X* and *Y* are allocated $30 and $10 of that amount. Accordingly, *X* increases her outside basis by $30 and *Y* increases her outside basis by $10, in each case under §722.

Reconsider this example but assume Blackacre has a fair market value of $220 and is encumbered by a debt of $120. Once again *Z*'s net contribution is $100, so the capital accounts will end up as before. However, there will be a difference in outside bases because of the greater debt. Once *Z* transfers Blackacre to the partnership, *Z*'s share of the debt decreases from $120 to $40 while *X*'s share increases from $0 to $60, and *Y*'s increases from $0 to $20.

As to *Z*, there is a deemed distribution of $80 under §752(b), which means that *Z* recognizes $30 of income under §731(a)(1) and takes an initial outside basis of $0. *X* enjoys an increase in outside basis of $60 pursuant to §752(a) and §722, while *Y*'s outside basis enjoys a similar increase of $20. Accordingly, the partnership books will read:

X		*Y*		*Z*	
CA	OB	CA	OB	CA	OB
$150	$210	$50	$70	$100	$0

Consider one more variation on this theme. Assume again that Blackacre has a fair market value of $220 and is encumbered by a debt of $120, but assume this time that the debt is fully nonrecourse. As a result, the debt will be allocated among *X*, *Y*, and *Z* in three tiers: (1) first, in proportion to partnership minimum gain; (2) second, as the partners would share gain under §704(c)(1)(A), assuming the property were sold for the amount of the liability and for no other consideration; and (3) third, according to profits interests. Treas. Regs. §1.752-3(a).

There is no partnership minimum gain because the book value of Blackacre ($220) exceeds the debt ($120), Treas. Regs. §1.704-2(d)(1), so there is no tier one allocation. Treas. Regs. §1.752-3(a)(1). Under tier two, *Z* is allocated up to $70 of the debt, assuming the partners agree to address ceiling limitations with respect to the property contributed by *Z* by using the traditional method or the traditional method with curative allocations. Treas. Regs. §1.752-3(a)(2). The $50 remainder of the debt is allocated among the partners as they will share profits,[1] so *X*'s share is $25, *Y*'s share is $8.33, and *Z*'s share under tier three is $16.67. Treas. Regs. §1.752-3(a)(3). Accordingly, *Z*'s total share of the debt is $86.67, which means that *Z* is treated as receiving a deemed distribution of $33.33, *X* is treated as contributing cash of $25, and *Y* is treated as contributing cash of $8.33. Thus, rounding all capital accounts to whole dollar amounts, the partnership books will read:

1. If the partnership elects, *Z* can be allocated a greater proportion of the debt under tier 3 pursuant to Treas. Regs. §1.752-3(a)(3) (see the sentence beginning with "additionally").

X		*Y*		*Z*	
CA	OB	CA	OB	CA	OB
\$150	\$175	\$50	\$58	\$100	\$17

PROBLEM

24-1. *A* and *B* agree to form the *AB* general partnership. *A* will have a 25-percent interest in profits and losses while *B* will have a 75-percent interest in profits and losses. *A* agrees to contribute Whiteacre with adjusted basis of \$60, fair market value of \$120, and subject to a recourse debt of \$20. *B* agrees to contribute Blackacre with adjusted basis of \$25, fair market value of \$260, and subject to a recourse debt of \$160. What are the partners' initial capital accounts and outside bases?

3. *Payables and Receivables*

When an ongoing business is transferred to a partnership, it is inevitable that the transfer will include accounts payable as well as accounts receivable. Receipt of the receivables presents no unusual problems. If the transferor is a cash basis taxpayer, the receivables will have a zero basis and will trigger application of §704(c), while if the transferor had accrued the receivables, they enter the partnership as unappreciated property.

Payables are more difficult. Unaccrued accounts payable contributed to a partnership by a cash basis transferor do not fall within the scope of §752. Rather, such payables are to be treated in accordance with §704(c) principles. Treas. Regs. §1.704-3(a)(4). To simplify the discussion as much as possible, consider the contribution of nothing but cash and accounts payable by a cash basis partner.

Assume that *C* joins the *AB* partnership by contributing cash of \$150 and payables of \$50. The net value of *C*'s contribution is \$100, and so that becomes the initial value of *C*'s capital account. *C*'s outside basis, on the other hand, begins at \$150 under §722.

When the partnership pays the payables, the resulting deduction should be allocable to *C* under §704(c). This allocation will reduce *C*'s outside basis by \$50 pursuant to §705(a)(2)(A). No reduction should be made to *C*'s capital account, though, because the (negative) value of the payables was taken into account when *C* was admitted to the partnership and given an initial capital account of only \$100.

If the payables had been accrued by *C* prior to the transfer, the analysis would be slightly different. Accrued payables are treated as liabilities of the partnership and are accounted for under §752. Accordingly, *C*'s initial basis will start at \$150 less the amount of the payables properly allocable to *A* and *B*. When the payables are subsequently paid by the partnership, each partner will have a deemed distribution under §752(b). Because the payables are treated as liabilities of the partnership, no §704(c) problem is created when they are transferred to the partnership.

PROBLEM

24-2. *X*, *Y*, and *Z* form the *XYZ* general partnership. *X*, a cash basis taxpayer, contributes accounts receivable of \$150 (with adjusted basis of \$0) and accounts payable of \$50 in exchange for a 25-percent interest in profits and losses. *Y* contributes unimproved real estate with an adjusted basis of \$120 and fair market value of \$100 in exchange for a 25-percent interest in profits and losses. *Z* contributes investment property with an adjusted basis of \$40, a fair market value of \$300, and encumbered by a debt of \$100, in exchange for a 50-percent interest in profits and losses.

a. Assuming both the contributed real estate and investment property are capital assets in the hands of the partnership, what are the outside bases and capital accounts of the partners if the receivables are collected, the payables are paid, and all the property is sold for its fair market value?
b. What is the character of the partnership's income and loss?
c. Was the partnership entitled to tack the contributing partner's holding period to its own with respect to the real estate and *Z*'s inventory?
d. How do your answers to part (a) change if *X* and *Y* each have a 20-percent interest in the profits and losses of the partnership, and *Z* has the remaining 60-percent interest?

4. *Promissory Notes*

If a taxpayer contributes her own promissory note (other than a readily tradeable one) to a partnership, her capital account is not increased until there is a taxable disposition of the note by the partnership or as principal payments are made by the partner on the note. Treas. Regs. §1.704-1(b)(2)(ii)(d). However, because such a note represents a promise by the partner to contribute additional funds to the partnership, contribution of such a note by a limited partner will permit that partner's capital account to go negative by the amount remaining unpaid on the note. See Treas. Regs. §1.704-1(b)(2)(ii)(d). A partner's outside basis is not increased by the contribution of such a note, Oden v. Commissioner, T.C. Memo 1981-184, aff'd in unpublished opinion, 679 F.2d 885 (4th Cir. 1982), although any plausible rationale for that result is lacking.

5. *Holding Periods*

Section 1223 provides various tacking rules applicable to tax-free exchanges. For example, §1223(2) provides that the holding period of property acquired in a carryover basis transaction includes the holding period of the transferor. Under this rule, the holding period of property acquired by a partnership in exchange for a partnership interest includes the holding period of the transferor partner. Thus, if property is held for more than one year before it is contributed to a partnership and then is disposed of immediately by the partnership, any capital gain or loss on the disposition will be long term to the partnership by reason of §1223(2).

The tacking rule applicable to the contributing partner is found in §1223(1), and it is slightly more complex. Under §1223(1), the contributing partner may tack her holding period of the contributed property onto that of her partnership interest if the contributed property was a capital or §1231 asset. As a result, tacking is not available if the contributed property was an ordinary income asset in the hands of the contributing partner. Note that it is irrelevant for application of §1223(1) whether the contributed property is a capital asset in the hands of the partnership once contributed.

But what if a partner contributes multiple properties, each with its own (tackable) holding period? Or what if a partner contributes property long after joining the partnership? While one answer would be to treat a partner as owning multiple partnership interests, each with its own holding period, the government has resolved the problem differently. Despite the number of distinct interests in a single partnership that one partner may own, a partner has one capital account, Treas. Regs. §1.704-1(b)(2)(iv)(b), and the Service has long maintained that a partner also has a single, unified outside basis, Rev. Rul. 84-53, 1984-1 C.B. 159. Nevertheless, a partner can have multiple holdings periods with respect to the partner's unified interest in the partnership. See generally Treas. Regs. §1.1223-3. A bifurcated holding period can arise either by contributing multiple properties to the partnership at one time or by making multiple contributions to the partnership over time. Treas. Regs. §1.1223-3(a). A partner having a bifurcated holding period can recognize both long- and short-term capital gain on the sale of her partnership interest or from a distribution of cash (including marketable securities treated as cash under §731(c)) in excess of outside basis. See Treas. Regs. §1.1223-3(c), -3(d)(2).

Suppose that *X* is a member of the *P* partnership, and assume that *X* has a holding period in its partnership interest in excess of one year. If the fair market value of *X*'s interest equals $500, and *X* contributes additional cash of $250 to the partnership (increasing the value of *X*'s interest to $750), then *X* will be treated as having a short-term holding period in one-third of the partnership interest because of the cash contribution. So, for example, if *X* sells her partnership interest six months later, one-third of any gain or loss will be short term. Note that this is true even though all of the appreciation in *X*'s partnership interest may have accrued many years earlier. Note also that this result would not change if *X* had contributed property rather than cash unless the property had been a capital asset in *X*'s hands immediately prior to the contribution and *X* had had a holding period in the contributed property in excess of six months. See §1223(1) (tacking for substitute basis capital assets).

6. *Disposition of Contributed Property*

Ordinary income assets distributed by a partnership to a partner will be subject to an ordinary income taint under §735(a). Section 724 provides a similar rule for property contributed to a partnership. However, §724 is broader than §735(a) in that it speaks not only to the conversion of ordinary income into capital gain but also to the conversion of capital loss into ordinary loss. Furthermore, this aspect of §724 operates in a more complex manner than do the ordinary income provisions of §724 and §735(a).

Under §724(a), disposition of contributed property by a partnership will produce ordinary income if the property was an unrealized receivable in the hands of the contributing partner. Under §724(b), a similar result obtains if the property was an inventory item in the hands of the contributing partner, but only if the disposition by the partnership occurs within five years of contribution of the property to the partnership. As under §735(a), the definitions of "unrealized receivables" and "inventory items" are found in §751(c)-(d). See §724(d).

Under §724(c), the contribution of capital loss property will taint subsequent loss on disposition by the partnership up to the amount of the built-in loss at contribution if the loss is recognized within five years of the contribution. For example, suppose partner *P* contributes property to the partnership having a fair market value of $100 and an adjusted basis of $120, and assume further that the property is a capital asset in the hands of *P* but constitutes an inventory item in the hands of the partnership. If the partnership subsequently sells the property for $75, it will recognize a loss of $45 on the sale. Of this loss, $20 will be capital under §724(c).

What if the property had been sold by the partnership for $105? In this case, the loss recognized by the partnership is only $15, and the entire amount of that loss is capital under §724(c). Section 724(c), in other words, does not affect the amount of the loss but only its character as ordinary or capital.

As a last example, what if the property were sold by the partnership for $150? In this case, there is a gain to the partnership of $30. Because the property is sold at a gain, §724(c) does not apply. Because the property was a capital asset to the contributing partner, §724(a)-(b) does not apply. Accordingly, no special recharacterization rules apply to this sale so that the gain of $30 is ordinary to the partnership because the property is an ordinary income asset in the hands of the partnership.

PROBLEM

24-3. The chart below describes various property contributed to the *P* partnership by its partners. For each piece of property, determine the tax consequences to the partnership if the property is sold for the indicated price.

Basis to partner	*Value at contribution*	*Sale price*	*Character to partner*	*Character to partnership*
$6,000	$8,000	$10,000	Inventory	Capital
6,000	8,000	7,500	Inventory	Capital
6,000	4,000	7,000	Inventory	Capital
6,000	4,000	7,000	Capital	Inventory
6,000	4,000	3,000	Capital	Inventory
6,000	8,000	5,000	Capital	Inventory

7. *Contributions to Investment Companies*

The general rule of nonrecognition for transfers of property to a partnership in exchange for a partnership interest does not apply if the partnership would be treated as an investment company were it incorporated. §721(b). This rule largely parallels the rule for transfers to corporations, see §351(e)(1), and both are intended to deny the benefits of deferral to business entities offering little more than diversification to its investors. See Treas. Regs. §1.351-1(c)(1). Note, however, that if property is transferred to an investment partnership, *gain but not loss* can be recognized. For the definition of "diversification" in this context, see Treas. Regs. §1.351-1(c)(5).

The broad definition of investment company assets in §351(e)(1) can produce some surprising results. Suppose five partners each contribute $100 in cash to a newly formed partnership while a fifth individual contributes land with value of $100 and an adjusted basis of $15. This partnership formation will be taxable to the contributor of the land because more than 80 percent of the partnership's assets consist of money, and money is treated as "stock and securities" for determining whether a partnership (or a corporation) is an investment company. While it is hard to imagine that this result was intended when the definition of investment company assets was expanded to include most financial assets, the statutory language does not seem to admit any other reading. The regulations, though, contain the following: "The determination of whether a corporation is an investment company shall ordinarily be made by reference to the circumstances in existence immediately after the transfer in question. However, where circumstances change thereafter pursuant to a plan in existence at the time of the transfer, this determination shall be made by reference to the later circumstances." Treas. Regs. §1.351-1(c)(2). Perhaps when it is anticipated that contributed cash will be invested quickly in nonmarketable assets, the cash will not count toward investment company status.

B. CONTRIBUTIONS OF SERVICES

A partner might be admitted to a partnership in exchange for future or past services. Does §721 apply to such an exchange? By its terms, §721 only applies to a contribution of "property." A longstanding regulation provides that

> To the extent that any of the partners gives up any part of his right to be repaid his contributions (as distinguished from a share in partnership profits) in favor of another partner as compensation for services . . . section 721 does not apply. The value of an interest in such partnership capital so transferred to a partner as compensation for services constitutes income to the partner under section 61. Treas. Regs. §1.721-1(b)(1). See also Prop. Treas. Regs. §1.721-1(b)(1) (proposed June 3, 1971).

This regulation apparently draws a distinction between a service partner who receives an interest in the current value of the partnership (i.e., a "capital" interest) and one who receives an interest only in future profits (i.e., a "profits" interest). Does it make sense to distinguish between a capital interest and a profits interest? A capital interest presumably is easier to value: The service partner receiving an interest in the current value of the partnership presumably should be taxed on the value of the capital interest acquired, measured by the current liquidation value of that partnership interest.

Valuing a profits interest is more difficult. If the partnership liquidated immediately after the service partner was given her profits interest, presumably the service partner would receive nothing. That the immediate liquidation value of the profits interest is zero does not, however, indicate that the profits interest has no value.

For example, suppose the *XY* partnership owns a single asset rented out to a credit-worthy lessee on a long-term lease. If *Z* performs services for the partnership in exchange for an interest in future profits — that is, in exchange for a share of future rent receipts — surely the profits interest has an immediate value equal to *Z*'s percentage interest in the discounted value of the expected rental income stream. While in the typical case the partnership's income stream will be more difficult to value than this one, it remains true that the right to share in a partnership's future profits has an immediate nonzero value.

And what of the partnership? Recall that §721 provides nonrecognition for both the contributing partner and for the partnership. If §721 does not cover a contribution of services, should the partnership recognize gain or loss on the transaction? If we follow an aggregate model of taxation, presumably the partnership should be treated as if it transferred a percentage of its assets to the service partner in a taxable exchange. On the other hand, if we follow an entity model of taxation, we might characterize the exchange as services for an unappreciated partnership interest akin to the taxation of corporations issuing stock for services under §1032.

1. *Taxation of the Contributing Partner*

Until 1971, most commentators assumed that the contribution of services to a partnership in exchange for a partnership interest was taxable only if the service partner received an immediate interest in partnership capital. That assumption was shattered in Diamond v. Commissioner, 492 F.2d 286 (7th Cir. 1974), aff'g 56 T.C. 530 (1971), where it was held that the fair market value of a partnership interest received in exchange for past services is taxable compensation. *Diamond* presented unusually simple facts because the service partner sold his partnership interest almost immediately after receipt, enabling the Commissioner to use the subsequent sale price to value the partnership interest. Indeed, all that was at issue in *Diamond* was whether the partner's income should be taxable as ordinary income (as compensation) or as short-term capital gain (from the sale of a partnership interest). Despite winning the *Diamond* case, the government eventually decided to give back most of its victory.

Revenue Procedure 93-27

1993-27 C.B. 343

Section 1. Purpose

This revenue procedure provides guidance on the treatment of the receipt of a partnership profits interest for services provided to or for the benefit of the partnership.

Section 2. Definitions

The following definitions apply for purposes of this revenue procedure.

.01 A capital interest is an interest that would give the holder a share of the proceeds if the partnership's assets were sold at fair market value and then the proceeds were distributed in a complete liquidation of the partnership. This determination generally is made at the time of receipt of the partnership interest.

.02 A profits interest is a partnership interest other than a capital interest.

Section 3. Background

Under section 1.721-1(b)(1) of the Income Tax Regulations, the receipt of a partnership capital interest for services provided to or for the benefit of the partnership is taxable as compensation. On the other hand, the issue of whether the receipt of a partnership profits interest for services is taxable has been the subject of litigation. Most recently, in *Campbell v. Commissioner*, 943 F.2d 815 (8th Cir. 1991), the Eighth Circuit in dictum suggested that the taxpayer's receipt of a partnership profits interest received for services was not taxable, but decided the case on valuation. Other courts have determined that in certain circumstances the receipt of a partnership profits interest for services is a taxable event under section 83 of the Internal Revenue Code. See, e.g., Campbell v. Commissioner, T.C. Memo 1990-236, *rev'd*, 943 F.2d 815 (8th Cir. 1991); St. John v. United States, No. 82-1134 (C.D. Ill. Nov. 16, 1983). The courts have also found that typically the profits interest received has speculative or no determinable value at the time of receipt. See *Campbell*, 943 F.2d at 823; *St. John*. In Diamond v. Commissioner, 56 T.C. 530 (1971), *aff'd*, 492 F.2d 286 (7th Cir. 1974), however, the court assumed that the interest received by the taxpayer was a partnership profits interest and found the value of the interest was readily determinable. In that case, the interest was sold soon after receipt.

Section 4. Application

.01 Other than as provided below, if a person receives a profits interest for the provision of services to or for the benefit of a partnership in a partner capacity or in anticipation of being a partner, the Internal Revenue Service will not treat the receipt of such an interest as a taxable event for the partner or the partnership.

.02 This revenue procedure does not apply:

(1) If the profits interest relates to a substantially certain and predictable stream of income from partnership assets, such as income from high-quality debt securities or a high-quality net lease;
(2) If within two years of receipt, the partner disposes of the profits interest; or
(3) If the profits interest is a limited partnership interest in a "publicly traded partnership" within the meaning of section 7704(b) of the Internal Revenue Code.

NOTES

1. *Unvested partnership interests.* The relief provided by Rev. Proc. 93-27 was extended to the receipt of a nonvested partnership profits interest in Rev. Proc. 2001-43, 2001-2 C.B. 191. Indeed, this latter revenue procedure made clear that there is no income to a partner receiving a nonvested partnership profits interest

in exchange for the contribution of services even upon the vesting of the interest. Thus, the Service seems to have concluded that §83's generally applicable rules for taxing the receipt of property in connection with the performance of services should not be applied in the partnership context.

Both Rev. Proc. 93-27 and Rev. Proc. 2001-43 are limited in application to receipt of a "profits" interest, where a profits interest is an interest in the partnership that does not give the holder the right to a share of the proceeds if the partnership were to immediately sell all of its assets for fair market value and distribute the proceeds in complete liquidation of the partnership. To satisfy this requirement, a partnership can elect to revalue its assets and restate the capital accounts immediately prior to the admission of the service partner. Such a revaluation and restatement is expressly authorized in the capital account maintenance rules. Treas. Regs. §1.704-1(b)(2)(iv)(f)(5)(iii).

2. *The* Campbell *case.* In Campbell v. Commissioner, 943 F.2d 815 (8th Cir. 1991), the Eighth Circuit concluded that the contribution of services for a partnership profits interest was not taxable to the service partner on the fact-specific (yet still dubious) grounds that the profits interest "had only speculative, if any value." See also United States v. Pacheco, 912 F.2d 297 (9th Cir. 1990). However, the *Campbell* court also advanced a novel theory that the decision in *Diamond* was inconsistent with application of §707. The court wrote,

> [Section 707(a)(2)(A)] was enacted to prevent partnerships from using direct allocations of income to individuals, disguised as service partners, to avoid the requirement that certain expenses be capitalized. However, it was not intended to apply when a service provider acts within his capacity as a partner. See §707(a)(2)(A)(iii). Arguably, section 707(a) would be unnecessary if compensatory transfers of profits interests were taxable upon receipt because, if so, every transfer would be taxed without this section.

This reasoning is faulty for two reasons. First, while §707 does speak in part to transfers of property to a partner in exchange for services, it is unlikely that a partnership interest was intended to be "property" within the meaning of §707: Nothing in the legislative history of that section supports the *Campbell* court's reading. In addition, §707(a)(2)(A) should only apply to services the cost of which must be capitalized and in return for which the service partner is given a nonproprietary return; that is, by its explicit terms §707(a) is about transactions between a partnership and a partner *acting as a nonpartner,* and the contribution of services for a bona fide partnership interest simply has nothing to do with any part §707(a).

In the two decades between *Diamond* and *Campbell,* the law applying to service partners was relatively settled, if only because the Service did not seek to enforce its victory in *Diamond.* With the Circuit Court's conflicting opinion in *Campbell,* the law became unsettled. Rather than resolve this conflict in the courts, the Service in 1993 repudiated most of its victory in *Diamond.* In Rev. Proc. 93-27, the Service announced that it will not attempt to tax the contribution of services in exchange for a profits interest in most circumstances.

Is it appropriate for the Service to provide such relief? In its *Diamond* opinion, the Seventh Circuit held that the statute requires immediate taxation of a partner contributing services to a partnership in exchange for a partnership interest. Is Rev. Proc. 93-27 good law in the Seventh Circuit? Might the Service be estopped from arguing contrary to its published position?

3. *The proposed regulations.* Section 83, enacted largely to rationalize the taxation of restricted stock provided by a corporation in exchange for services, applies broadly whenever property is received "in connection with the performance of services." §83(a). While neither Rev. Proc. 93-27 nor Rev. Proc. 2001-43 mention §83, proposed regulations have been promulgated under §704 that apply the rules of §83 to a partnership interest received in connection with the performance of services. Prop. Treas. Regs. §1.83-3(e), §1.721-1(b)(1). In general, §83(a) provides that the excess of the fair market value of property over the price paid by the service provider is includible in the service provider's gross income when the property first becomes vested, where vested means no longer subject to a substantial risk of forfeiture.[2] In this context, a "substantial risk of forfeiture" includes a requirement that service be provided in the future. §83(c)(1). Thus, a service partner who must perform future services can defer recognition of income that would otherwise be immediately includible under *Diamond.*

There is, though, a cost for this deferral: When the partnership interest becomes transferable or is no longer conditioned on the performance of future services, the service partner must include the then-current fair market value of the interest as ordinary income. Treas. Regs. §1.83-1(a)(1). Thus, if the partnership interest appreciates, the entire appreciation eventually will be taxed as ordinary income.

Property covered by §83(a) is not treated as transferred until the recipient is taxed. Prop. Treas. Regs. §1.761-1(b); see generally Treas. Regs. §1.83-1(a)(1). Thus, while the interest remains unvested, the service partner cannot be treated as a partner unless the service partner owns an additional partnership interest. That means, in particular, that no allocations of partnership-level items can be made to the service partner with respect to the unvested interest. Once the interest vests, the service partner is taxed, §83(a), the partnership is entitled to a deduction if payment to the service partner would have been deductible under §162 or §212, §83(h), and the service partner is treated as contributing property to the partnership equal to the amount includible under §83(a), Prop. Treas. Regs. §1.704-1(b)(2)(iv)(l).

This result can be avoided if the service partner files an election under §83(b) within 30 days of receiving the interest. If such an election is filed, the service partner must immediately recognize as ordinary income the excess of the value of the partnership interest over the amount (if any) paid for the interest. §83(b)(1). For determining the value of the interest, any risk of forfeiture is ignored. §83(b)(1)(A). If a partner files an election under §83(b) with respect to an unvested partnership interest received in connection with the contribution of services and the interest subsequently is forfeited, the service partner is *not* entitled to a deduction despite the prior inclusion. §83(b)(1) (final flush language).

The regime created by the proposed regulations appears at first blush to be quite different from that provided by Rev. Proc. 93-27 and Rev. Proc. 2001-43. However, the proposed regulations allow a service partner and the partnership to elect into a system of taxation much like that described in these revenue procedures. See Prop. Treas. Regs. §1.83-3(l). If a service partner receives a vested interest,

2. Technically, property becomes vested for purposes of §83(a) when it no longer is subject to a substantial risk of forfeiture or is transferable. However, property is not vested under §83(a) even if transferable if the substantial risk of forfeiture continues in the hands of the transferee. §83(c)(2); Treas. Regs. §1.83-3(d).

receives an unvested interest and files an election under §83(b), or receives an unvested interest that eventually vests, the income recognized by the service partner can be based on the initial liquidation value of the interest. See Notice 2005-43, 2005-1 C.B. 1221. As a result, if the service partner receives only a profits interest, there is no income to the service partner. This election is not permitted with respect to an interest (a) in a publicly traded partnership, (b) that is transferred to the service partner in anticipation of a subsequent disposition by the service partner, or (c) if the interest is related to a substantially certain and predictable stream of income.

If an unvested interest is received by a service partner and an election is filed by the service partner under §83(b), a subsequent forfeiture of the interest will trigger a set of "forfeiture" allocations to back-out prior allocations to the service partner. See Prop. Treas. Regs. §1.704-(1)(b)(4)(xii)(c), §1.706-3(b). Note that the partnership must include in income any amount deducted upon the grant of the unvested interest if that interest ultimately is forfeited. Treas. Regs. §1.83-6(c).

4. *Proposed §710.*[3] In 2007 and again in 2008, Congress proposed but ultimately did not enact an amendment to subchapter K that would have radically changed the taxation of service partners. The basic thrust of this proposed §710 is that distributive share of partnership income should be treated as compensation income to the extent it is attributable to the contribution of a "substantial quantity" of investment activity services to the partnership. The crucial term "investment services partnership interest" is defined in proposed §710(c)(1) to mean a partnership interest if the partner provides to the partnership any of the following services: (1) advising as to the advisability of investing in, purchasing, or selling any "specified asset"; (2) managing, acquiring, or disposing of any "specified asset"; or (3) arranging financing with respect to acquiring "specified assets." In this context, a "specified asset" includes securities, commodities, and real estate.

Under the general rule of proposed §710(a)(1), the net income with respect to an "investment services partnership interest" must be treated by the partner as ordinary income without regard to the character of the partnership's activity. If, for example, the partnership owns an apartment complex, then this rule would have little impact on the partner's distributive share of rental income (because it would be ordinary income even in the absence of proposed §710) but would convert distributive share from disposition of the real estate into ordinary income from capital gain. Further, even as to the rental income, proposed §710 would have an impact because proposed §710 specifically provides that the net income allocated to the owner of an "investment services partnership interest" is treated as compensation for purposes of §1402(a).

However, proposed §710 does not recharacterize as compensation that portion of a partner's distributive share reasonably allocated by the partnership to the "invested capital" of the partner owning an "investment services partnership interest." For this purpose an allocation will not be considered as reasonable if it results in an allocation of income to the "invested capital" of a partner providing investment services in excess of the amount that is allocated to the same amount of "invested capital" of any other partner not providing investment services. "Invested

3. See Howard E. Abrams, A Close Look at the Carried Interest Legislation, 117 Tax Notes 961 (Dec. 3, 2007); Howard E. Abrams, The Carried Interest Catastrophe, 128 Tax Notes 523 (Aug. 2, 2010); see also the comments of the ABA Tax Section, Doc. 2007-25289, 2007 TNT 220-25 (Nov. 14, 2007).

capital" includes the amount of cash contributed by a partner as well as the fair market value of other property contributed by the partner (measured as of the date of contribution of the property).

"Invested capital" of a partner owning an "investment services partnership interest" does not include any funds loaned by the partner to the partnership (because it includes only the value of cash and property "contributed" to the partnership). In addition, it does not include any amount contributed by such a partner to the extent "attributable to the proceeds of any loan or other advance made or guaranteed, directly or indirectly, by any partner or [by] the partnership." Application of this rule does not turn on whether the loan is with or without recourse, whether the owner of the "investment services partnership interest" is credit worthy, or to whom the creditor will look for repayment. In the most extreme case, funds could be borrowed by a credit-worthy service partner ("*G*") on a fully recourse basis and then contributed to the partnership. But if the partnership's assets are pledged to secure the loan, the loan will not count as "invested capital" of *G* even though *G* is fully liable to the lender and, if the partnership's assets eventually are used to repay some or all of the debt, *G* is fully liable to the partnership and to the other partners. Further, in computing a "reasonable" allocation on the investment services partner's "invested capital" as compared with the "invested capital" of partners who have not contributed services to the venture, [loans made or guaranteed by a nonservice partner are] treated as "invested capital" of that nonservice partner.

Gain recognized on the disposition of an "investment services partnership interest" is recharacterized as compensation while loss recognized on such a sale are treated as ordinary only to the extent that the aggregate net income for all prior years allocated to that interest exceeds the aggregate net loss for all prior years. However, this recharacterization does not apply to the extent a reasonable allocation of the gain or loss is made to account for the "invested capital" of the partner. An "investment services partnership interest" is treated as an inventory item when held by a partnership.

If appreciated property is distributed to a partner with respect to an "investment services partnership interest," the property is treated as sold by the partnership. As a result, gain will be recognized to the partnership and allocated among the partners in accordance with the usual rules of §704(b) and (c), with that portion of the gain allocated to the owner of an "investment services partnership interest" subject to recharacterization as compensation under proposed §710(a) to the extent not attributable to the partner's "invested capital."

Will proposed §710 become law? Perhaps not: It has too many technical flaws and too few conceptual underpinnings. Most significantly, the allocation of distributive share between a partner's contribution of services and contribution of capital will be surprisingly difficult to draw. Even for a partner who contributes nothing but services, such an allocation will be necessary after the first year unless that partner's entire distributive share is in fact distributed because, if the service partner has undistributed distributive share, she has a positive capital account balance. In effect, the undistributed distributive share should be treated as distributed to the service partner and then recontributed to the partnership, and that deemed recontribution should allow the service partner to be recognized for tax purposes as the owner of a partnership interest received in exchange for contributed capital. This same problem arises ab initio if the service partner also contributes cash or property to the venture. Yet such an apportionment may be extraordinarily difficult to compute.

For example, assume the *XY* partnership is formed by *X* contributing cash of $96 and *Y* contributing cash of $4, and assume that *Y* also agrees to contribute future services. Assume further that under the partnership agreement, net profit from the venture will be allocated 80 percent to *X* and 20 percent to *Y*. On these facts and assuming the partnership has a single class of capital, §710 should not apply to *Y*'s distributive share to the extent of *Y*'s contributed capital (that is, as to 4 percent) while the remainder (16 percent) of the allocation to *Y* should be treated as compensation under §83 or proposed §710. For example, assume the partnership earns a taxable profit of $50 in year 1 and that this income is allocated 80 percent (that is, $40) to *X* and 20 percent (that is, $10) to *Y*. Under the analysis presented above, of the $10 allocated to *Y*, $2 will be treated as attributable to *Y*'s capital, and $8 will be treated as compensation to *Y*. If the partnership retains its $50 profit, it now has aggregate capital of $150, of which $100 was contributed and $50 was earned.

How should *Y*'s distributive share be characterized in the following year? If there again is taxable income of $50 and *Y*'s share remains at $10, then substantially more than $2 of *Y*'s distributive share should be treated as a return on *Y*'s capital interest. To see this, note that while *Y*'s contributed capital remains at $4, *Y*'s share of the contributed *and accumulated* capital now equals $14 or almost 10 percent of the venture's aggregate capital ($14 of $150). Accordingly, almost $5 of the partnership's income in year 2 should be treated as a return on *Y*'s capital. That is, as the partnership allocates profit to *Y* in excess of *Y*'s relative share of contributed capital, *Y*'s share of the aggregate capital increases. To be sure, if the first year's profit had been distributed in the same proportion as it was allocated (that is, $40 to *X* and $10 to *Y*), there would have been be no change in shares of aggregate capital. But to the extent the earnings remain undistributed, the maximum allowable allocation on *Y*'s capital should increase to reflect the prior taxable inclusion by *Y*.

Indeed, if *X* enjoys a preferential right to distributions, this problem is exacerbated: first for *Y*'s undistributed but allocated share of the venture's profit and a second time for *X*'s return of contributed capital. Nothing in the existing rules of §83 nor in proposed §710 accounts for such factors or the myriad other complications that will arise.

PROBLEM

24-4. *A* and *B* are equal partners in the *AB* general partnership. The partnership's only asset is a racehorse with an adjusted basis of $80,000 to the partnership. When the horse is worth $160,000, *C* is admitted to the partnership, receiving one-fourth of all future profits in exchange for training the horse for the next two years. At the time of *C*'s admission to the partnership, *A* and *B* each have an outside basis and capital account of $40,000, and the partnership is free of debt.

a. What are the tax consequences to all parties of *C*'s admission to the partnership?
b. How would your answer change if *C* had contributed cash of $15,000 as well as future services?
c. In either case, should *C* make an election under §83(b)?

d. Reconsider the questions above, assuming that *C* is given a one-quarter interest in partnership profits and capital immediately upon her admission to the partnership.

2. *Taxation of the Partnership*

If a partner contributes services to a partnership in exchange for an interest in partnership capital, the partner is taxed on the transaction. Treas. Regs. §1.721-1(b)(1). Should the partnership be taxed as well? At first blush the answer seems to be that it should. After all, taxation of the service partner presumably is justified on the theory that services and a partnership interest are so dissimilar that the exchange should not be tax free. And if that is true for the service partner, it ought to be equally true for the partnership.

Under this theory, we would tax the partnership as if it exchanged a pro rata portion of its assets to the service partner in exchange for the services, and the partnership would be taxed on the unrealized appreciation or loss in that portion of its assets. These assets would then be deemed recontributed back to the partnership in exchange for the service partner's partnership interest. Thus, the partnership's adjusted basis in its assets would be increased by the gain (or decreased by the loss) it recognizes on the admission of the service partner.

At closer examination, however, the argument for taxing the partnership cannot hold up. Although the partnership should be taxed if it exchanges its assets for dissimilar property, no such exchange has occurred by reason of the admission of the service partner. The service partner has *not* received an interest in the partnership's assets. Rather, the service partner has received an interest in the business venture, and as to that exchange §1001 cannot apply because a business enterprise cannot have a basis in itself.

A corporation does not realize income when it exchanges its own stock for money, other property, or for services. That result is mandated by §1032, which provides an absolute bar to recognition of income or loss on the exchange. No similar provision exists in subchapter K, and the lack of a partnership analog to §1032 sometimes is used to suggest that the contribution of property or services to a partnership is taxable to the partnership except to the extent that some section (i.e., §721) provides otherwise.

That suggestion is misguided, however, because it misappreciates the role of §1032. Prior to enactment of §1032, corporations issued stock for property without the recognition of income or loss because the Service conceded that the basis concept could not be applied to newly issued stock. However, the Service took the position that if a corporation acquired some of its own stock in the market, held it in treasury, and then reissued it for property, the corporation would be taxed on the reissuance on an amount equal to the excess of the value of the property received over the corporation's cost basis in the stock.

As you might expect, treating the reissuance of treasury stock as taxable while exempting the issuance of fresh stock caused corporations to reissue treasury stock only when the transaction would produce a taxable loss to the corporation—if the value of the property received would exceed the corporation's cost basis in its treasury stock, fresh stock would be used. Section 1032 was enacted to put treasury stock on a par with unissued stock.

Partnerships have no need of a provision akin to §1032 because a partnership interest cannot be held in treasury. Accordingly, issuance of a partnership interest, like issuance of unissued stock, cannot be taxable under §1001 because the basis concept cannot be applied to the exchange. Section 1032 is simply irrelevant to the problem.

Further, if a partnership *were* taxed on the issuance of a partnership interest in exchange for services, presumably that taxation could be avoided whenever desired by the partnership. All the partnership need do is pay the service partner in cash for the services rendered, and then the service partner can recontribute the cash for her partnership interest. (Quaere whether the Service could then argue that the circular flow of cash should be ignored.) If the partnership does not have available cash, it easily could be borrowed and the loan can be repaid the following day once the cash is recontributed to the partnership by the service partner.

Having determined that a partnership should not be taxed on issuance of a partnership interest in exchange for services, are there any tax consequences of the transaction to the partnership? If the partnership had purchased the services for cash, the partnership would either deduct the expense or capitalize it depending on whether the expense was ordinary and necessary. This should be equally true if the services are acquired for a partnership interest: Either the nonservice partners should be entitled to a deduction or some partnership asset (possibly including goodwill) should show an increase in adjusted basis. Of course, this assumes that the partner is taxed on the contribution either because it involves a capital shift or falls outside the bounds of Rev. Proc. 93-27.

This rule preserves the equality of aggregate inside and outside bases. When the service partner is admitted to the partnership in a taxable transaction, her outside basis should equal the fair market value of her partnership interest. Because no new assets are added to the partnership by reason of admission of the service partner, aggregate outside basis will rise above aggregate inside basis unless the admission of the service partner either reduces the nonservice partners' outside basis or increases the inside basis of some asset. Giving the partnership a deduction reduces the nonservice partners' outside bases while capitalizing the value of the services raises aggregate inside basis. Thus the overall equality of aggregate inside and outside bases is preserved.

The Service now agrees that a partnership should not be taxed on the issuance of a partnership interest in exchange for services rendered to the partnership, neither when the interest is issued nor when it vests. Prop. Treas. Regs. §1.721-1(b)(2). Note, however, that this proposed regulation is effective only when promulgated in final form.

C. NONCONTRIBUTION ACQUISITIONS

Partnership interests can be acquired in ways other than by contribution. Like other property, partnership interests can be bought, received as a gift, or received from the estate of a decedent. In each case the initial outside basis of the transferee is determined by the usual, non–subchapter K rules, see §742, as modified by §752 to account for partnership debt. Vis-à-vis the partnership, though, the transferee steps into the shoes of the transferor. In particular, the transferee assumes the capital account of the transferor, Treas. Regs. §1.704-1(b)(2)(iv)(l), and the capital accounts are *not* adjusted to reflect the current value of the partnership's assets, see Treas. Regs. §1.704-1(b)(2)(iv)(f).

This last rule, that the partnership's assets are not revalued for book purposes, seems to be a flaw in the regulations. Had the transferor's interest been liquidated and then the transferee admitted as a new partner, the partnership assets would be revalued. See Treas. Regs. §1.704-1(b)(2)(iv)(f). This regulation seems to be based on the notion that partnership assets should be booked to fair market value whenever some transaction dependent on the value of the assets has occurred. Surely by this standard the sale or exchange of a partnership interest ought to trigger an asset revaluation because the price that the transferee is willing to pay is dependent on the current value of the partnership's assets.

Suppose *N* sells her limited partnership interest in the *LMN* partnership to *O* for $10,000. At the time of the sale, the partnership owns a single asset with an adjusted basis of $21,000 and fair market value of $30,000, and assume *N* had a one-third interest in the capital and profits of the partnership. Assuming *N* had an outside basis and capital account of $7,000 at the time of the sale, *N* will recognize a gain of $3,000, and *O* will start with *N*'s capital account of $7,000.

Because *O* has acquired a limited partnership interest, *O* cannot be allocated deductions in excess of her positive capital account balance. Treas. Regs. §1.704-1(b)(2)(ii)(d). Accordingly, *O* cannot be allocated more than $7,000 of partnership losses. But *O*'s investment in the partnership is $10,000, and there is no obvious reason why an allocation of loss to *O* in excess of $7,000 but not exceeding $10,000 should be improper. Had *O*'s capital account been booked to fair market value, this problem would not arise.

PROBLEM

24-5. *D* has a 10-percent interest in the profits and losses of the *P* partnership. *D*'s outside basis equals $25,000, and her capital account stands at negative $10,000. In order to acquire her partnership interest, *D* borrowed $20,000 from the *B* bank, and *D* pledged her partnership interest as security for this loan. *D* defaults on the loan, and the *B* bank forecloses on the partnership interest.

a. What is the bank's basis in the partnership interest?
b. What is the bank's capital account in the partnership?

25

Dispositions of Partnership Interests

Like any other asset, a partnership interest may be sold, exchanged, gifted, or devised. In addition, a partnership interest can be retired in exchange for a liquidating distribution. While the taxation of liquidating distributions is subject to specific and highly unusual rules of subchapter K, sales, exchanges, and other dispositions of a partnership interest are taxed, in general, under the usual nonpartnership rules that cover sales and exchanges of property. For example, the sale or exchange of a partnership interest will produce gain or loss to the transferor while the gift or devise of a partnership interest will not. Furthermore, §742 specifically provides that the basis of a transferred interest in the hands of the transferee is determined under the familiar basis rules (§§1011 et seq.) generally applicable to transfers of property. This chapter will focus on those rules specially applicable to the transfer of partnership interests with the understanding that such rules apply against the backdrop of the more general disposition of property rules.

A. DISTRIBUTIONS IN LIQUIDATION OF A PARTNERSHIP INTEREST

Payments made in liquidation of a partner's interest are taxed pursuant to §736, see §731(c), where §761(d) defines "liquidation of a partner's interest" to be "the termination of a partner's entire interest in a partnership by means of a distribution, or a series of distributions, to the partner by the partnership." Note that this definition of a liquidation includes not only distributions to all partners when the full partnership is dissolved but also distributions to one or more retiring partners from a continuing partnership. However, a distribution in retirement of one partnership interest (for example, an interest as a limited partner) is not considered a liquidating distribution under §761(d) if the distributee continues to hold a separate partnership interest (for example, a continuing interest as a general partner). See Treas. Regs. §1.761-1(d).

Although the logical starting point for an analysis of a liquidating distribution is §736, we will begin with the taxation of liquidating distributions under §§731-732. Section 736 is not itself a taxing provision. Rather, it provides that some distributions are to be taxed under the usual distribution rule of §§731-732 (see §736(b)) while other distributions are taxed under §704 or §707 (see §736(a)). The actual rules of taxation are found only in these other provisions of subchapter K. The application of §§731-732 to liquidating distributions can be very different from their application to nonliquidating distributions, and we turn first to these familiar code sections to discover their unfamiliar and unusual rules governing distributions in liquidation of a partnership interest.

1. *A Note on §§731-732*

The basic provisions covering the taxation of all partnership distributions are §731, §732, and §733. Section 731 specifies when and to what extent a distribution is taxable to the distributee partner. (A distribution under §731 is never taxable to the distributing partnership, §731(b), except to the extent that §751(b) may apply to the transaction, §731(c).) Sections 732 and 733 are basis provisions, with §732 addressing the basis of distributed property in the hands of the distributee partner, while §733 speaks to the effect, if any, on the distributee partner's outside basis. In the context of liquidating distributions, §733 plays no role because the distributee partner necessarily has no outside basis (because she has no partnership interest) after the transaction.

Most nonliquidating distributions are nontaxable because gain is not recognized unless the amount of cash distributed exceeds the distributee partner's pre-distribution outside basis. §731(a). Because the hallmark of a tax-free transaction is a continuation of basis, when a nonliquidating distribution is nontaxable there can be no net change in the tax basis available to the distributee partner. Accordingly, the basis effect of a nontaxable nonliquidating distribution is to divide the distributee partner's pre-distribution outside basis between her post-distribution outside basis and the distributed property. See §§732-733. This basic scheme is continued in the context of liquidating distributions with the added wrinkle that the distributee partner's post-distribution outside basis always is zero, so that the distributee partner's pre-distribution outside basis must be allocated entirely to the distributed property. §732(b).

Consider the following example. *P* receives a distribution of Blackacre in retirement of her partnership interest. At the time of the distribution, *P*'s outside basis was $10,000. Blackacre had an inside basis to the partnership of $8,000 and was worth $13,000 at the time of its distribution. Under §732(b) and (c)(1)(B)(i), we see that *P* takes a basis of $10,000 in Blackacre, for no net change in *P*'s overall basis. Consistent with this basis result, the distribution is tax free to *P* under §731. Indeed, no net change in basis invariably is coupled with a tax-free transaction; basis increase results from recognition of income, while basis decrease comes from a recognition of loss (or other deduction).

In this example, *P realizes* a gain of $3,000 under §1001(a) because that is the excess of the amount realized (the fair market value of Blackacre, or $13,000) over *P*'s adjusted basis in her partnership interest (i.e., her outside basis, or $10,000). No gain is *recognized* by virtue of §731(a), and the basis rule of §732(b) ensures that this unrecognized gain is deferred rather than exempted: Because Blackacre takes a basis in *P*'s hands of $3,000 less than fair market value, the realized but unrecognized gain will reappear upon disposition of Blackacre by *P*.

To appreciate why all liquidating distributions cannot be taxed so simply, reconsider the example but assume that *P* receives cash of $13,000 in lieu of Blackacre. In this circumstance we cannot defer recognition of *P*'s income without giving *P* a low basis in the cash received. Because cash always takes an implicit basis equal to face value, the effect of the transaction is to increase *P*'s tax basis from $10,000 (in the form of *P*'s pre-distribution outside basis) to $13,000 (in the form of *P*'s post-distribution cash), for a net increase of $3,000. Accordingly, it must be the case that *P* recognizes $3,000 of income, and that is precisely the rule of §731(a)(1): As in the context of nonliquidating distributions, a liquidating distribution of cash in excess of the distributee partner's outside basis produces gain equal to that excess. Here, that excess is $3,000.

But what if the amount of the cash distribution had been only $7,500? Once again, cash must take an implicit basis equal to face value so that the effect of the transaction is a net reduction of $2,500 in *P*'s tax basis. Accordingly, *P* should be able to report a loss on the transaction of $2,500, and that is the rule of §731(a)(2). See also Treas. Regs. §1.732-1(c)(3). Indeed, note that the amount of loss allowed in §731(a)(2) is defined, as it should be, by reference to the distributee partner's pre-distribution outside basis as compared with the distributee partner's post-distribution basis in distributed property (see §731(a)(2)(B)) plus the basis implicit in any cash distributed (see §731(a)(2)(A)).

There is but one last wrinkle to the taxation of liquidating distributions under §§731-732, and it concerns distributions consisting *only* of ordinary income assets and cash. Consider once again a liquidating distribution to *P*, but assume now that *P* receives inventory of the partnership having inside basis of $8,000 and fair market value of $13,000. *If* we treated the inventory just like we treated Blackacre, the distribution would be tax free to *P*, and *P* would take the inventory with a basis of $10,000.

Note, though, that prior to the distribution there was ordinary income of $5,000 to be had from disposition of the inventory because the partnership's pre-distribution basis in the inventory was $8,000 while fair market value was $13,000. If we followed the rule of §732(b) and allowed *P* to inject her entire outside basis into the inventory, there would be ordinary income of only $3,000 when *P* sells the inventory. While there is nothing inherently wrong with this approach, Congress is unwilling to allow a partnership distribution to reduce the amount of ordinary income to be recognized. Accordingly, ordinary income assets can take a basis no higher than carryover when received in a partnership distribution. See §732(c)(1)(A)(i). In particular, note that the allocation of additional basis under §732(c)(2) applies only to nonordinary income assets because it applies by its express language only to increases mandated by application of §732(c)(1)(B).

If the liquidating distribution includes one or more capital assets as well as ordinary income assets and cash, excess outside basis can be allocated to the nonordinary income assets pursuant to §732(c)(2). For example, suppose *P* with an outside basis of $10,000 receives a liquidating distribution consisting of cash of $5,000, inventory with an inside basis of $1,000 and fair market value of $6,000, and a capital asset with an inside basis and fair market value of $2,000. If this distribution is tax free to *P*, *P* must carry over her outside basis into the assets distributed. §732(b). The cash takes an implicit basis of $5,000, the inventory can take a basis of no more than $1,000 under §732(c)(1)(A)(i), and that leaves $4,000 for the capital asset. Under §732(b)-(c), this is exactly how *P*'s outside basis is allocated among the distributed assets. In particular, *P*'s basis in the capital asset can exceed the partnership's former adjusted basis in that asset, §732(c)(2)(A), and can even exceed the asset's fair market value, §732(c)(2)(B).

But what if there had been no capital asset? For example, reconsider the possibility that the inventory has an adjusted basis of $8,000 and a fair market value of $13,000, and the liquidating distribution consists only of this inventory. Section 732(b) certainly seems to say that *P*'s pre-distribution outside basis of $10,000 goes into the basis of the property distributed. However, §732(c)(1)(A) specifies that the inventory may take a basis of no more than carryover; that is, of no more than $8,000. If we have $10,000 of basis to allocate under §732(b) but only $8,000 of that basis is allocated under §732(c), where does the remaining $2,000 of basis go? Note that §732(c)(2) is not applicable because there is no basis increase "required under paragraph §732(c)(1)(B)."

Surprisingly, the additional $2,000 of basis goes nowhere! Although §732(b) purports to specify the amount of basis to be allocated among the distributed properties, in reality it specifies only the *maximum* amount of basis to be allocated. If less basis is allocated under §732(c)(1)(A)(i), *and if there are no non-§751 assets to be allocated basis under §732(c)(2)*, then the basis rule of §732(b)—although unconditional on its face—is ignored. In such circumstances, the important basis rule is contained in §732(c)(1)(A)(i), with §732(b) defining only the maximum possible basis of the ordinary income assets.

Can this be true? If basis is lost by *P*, it must be the case that *P* recognizes a loss on the transaction. That in fact is what happens under §731(a)(2) where loss can be recognized only on a liquidating distribution consisting entirely of cash and §751 property. In such cases there is no property that can absorb basis in excess of carryover. Accordingly, in such circumstances the distributee partner loses tax basis and a loss is recognized precisely equal to the amount of the basis so lost.

We can summarize the rule covering the taxation of liquidating distributions under §§731-732 as follows: (1) Gain is recognized only if the amount of cash distributed exceeds the distributee partner's outside basis; (2) loss is recognized only if the distribution consists of no assets other than cash and §751 assets, and the inside basis of the distributed property, plus the amount of the distributed cash, is less than the distributee partner's outside basis; (3) if no loss is recognized on the distribution, the distributee partner's outside basis, less the amount of cash received, will be allocated among the properties distributed (first to the §751 properties by reason of §732(c)(1)(A)); and (4) if loss is recognized on the distribution, the distributee partner will take a basis in each distributed asset equal to its pre-distribution basis in the hands of the partnership. In each of the three following examples, assume that *Q* receives a liquidating distribution taxable under §§731-732, and assume that *Q*'s outside basis immediately prior to the distribution equals $20,000.

Example 1: Suppose *Q* receives cash of $10,000 plus inventory with an adjusted basis and fair market value of $8,000. No gain is recognized by *Q* because the amount of the cash distributed does not exceed *Q*'s outside basis. To determine whether *Q* recognizes a loss, we must first determine *Q*'s basis in the distributed inventory. Under §732(b), the maximum amount of basis to be allocated under §732(c) equals $10,000. Under §732(c)(1)(A)(i), $8,000 of that amount is allocated to the inventory. Furthermore, because only cash and §751 assets were distributed to *Q*, the remainder of *Q*'s outside basis goes unallocated. Then, under §731(a)(2),

Q recognizes a loss of $2,000, a loss that is capital by reason of the final sentence in §731(a) coupled with §741.

Example 2: Suppose once again that *Q* receives cash of $10,000 plus inventory with an adjusted basis of $8,000, but now assume that the inventory has a fair market value of $15,000. Once again, gain is not recognized because the amount of the cash distributed does not exceed *Q*'s outside basis. Also once again, *Q* takes a basis in the inventory of $8,000 under §732(c)(1). Thus, there is once again a capital loss of $2,000 under §731(a)(2). The tax consequences to *Q* in example two are precisely the same as in example 1.

But notice what is different about example 2. In example 1, *Q* realized (and recognized) a loss on the distribution of $2,000, where that realized loss, computed under §1001, is the excess of *Q*'s outside basis over the value of the property (and cash) distributed. In example 2, however, *Q* realizes a gain on the distribution yet recognizes a loss! That is correct: *Recognition* of a loss under §731(a)(2) is independent of any gain or loss *realized* on the transaction. Indeed, if you go back and look closely at the rules governing liquidating distributions in §731 and §732, you will see that the *value* of the distributed property plays no role in determining the extent to which the distributee partner recognizes gain or loss on the liquidating distribution. To be sure, the *inside basis* of distributed property can be important (under §732(c)(1)), but its value—so important in calculating realized gains and losses under §1001—is simply irrelevant. Accordingly, in a liquidating distribution taxable under §731 and §732, the distributee partner can recognize a loss even though she realizes a gain.

Example 3: *Q* receives a liquidating distribution consisting of cash of $11,000, inventory with an adjusted basis of $8,000 and fair market value of $12,000, and an unrealized receivable with an adjusted basis of $4,000 and fair market value of $10,000. Under §732(b), there is a maximum basis of $9,000 to be allocated between the inventory and the receivable. Under §732(c)(1)(A)(i), the inventory is allocated a carry-over basis of $8,000, and the receivable is allocated a carry-over basis of $4,000. However, because these basis allocations total more than the $9,000 maximum as specified by §732(b), we adjust these bases downward pursuant to §732(c)(1)(ii) and (c)(3). In particular, under §732(c)(3)(B) there is a total negative adjustment of $3,000, of which $2,000 is allocated to the inventory and $1,000 is allocated to the receivable. Thus, the inventory takes an adjusted basis of $6,000 and the receivable takes an adjusted basis of $3,000.

NOTES

1. *Allocation of basis under §732(c)(1).* The exiting partner's basis in assets received in a liquidating distribution is determined under §732(c). The aggregate amount to be allocated will, in general, equal the exiting partner's outside basis less any money received in the distribution. §732(b). Basis is first tentatively allocated to distributed ordinary income assets in an amount equal to the basis of those assets in the hands of the partnership immediately before the distribution. §732(c)(1)(A)(i). If the aggregate tentative bases in the distributed ordinary income assets exceeds the total amount available to be allocated, then the tentative bases are decreased in accordance with the rules of §732(c)(3). See §732(c)(1)(A)(ii). In such

circumstances, the distributee will take a zero basis in every distributed capital and §1231 asset.

If the amount to be allocated exceeds the partnership's inside basis in the distributed ordinary income assets, then a tentative carry-over basis is allocated to the distributed capital and §1231 assets. §732(c)(1)(B)(i). If this tentative carry-over basis exceeds the amount to be allocated, then the excess reduces the tentative carry-over bases of the distributed capital and §1231 assets in accordance with the rules of §732(c)(3). Conversely, if this tentative carry-over basis is less than the amount to be allocated, then the remainder is allocated to the distributed capital and §1231 assets in accordance with the rules of §732(c)(2). Note that the basis of distributed ordinary income assets under §732(c) can never exceed the partnership's adjusted basis immediately prior to the distribution.

2. *Allocation of a basis increase under §732(c)(2).* Any basis increase allocated to capital and §1231 assets under §732(c)(2) is allocated first to appreciated capital and §1231 assets in proportion to unrealized appreciation and then among all the capital and §1231 assets in proportion to relative fair market values. For example, assume that after allocation of basis to distributed ordinary income assets there is $36,000 to be allocated to the capital and §1231 assets, and assume that the exiting partner receives capital asset #1 with a pre-distribution inside basis of $4,000 and fair market value of $6,000 as well as capital asset #2 with a pre-distribution inside basis of $15,000 and fair market value of $12,000. Asset #1 takes a tentative basis of $4,000 and asset #2 takes a tentative basis of $15,000, leaving $17,000 still to be allocated. Of that $17,000, $2,000 is first allocated to asset #1 and then the remaining $15,000 is allocated $5,000 to asset #1 and $10,000 to asset #2. As a result, the exiting partner takes a basis of $11,000 in asset #1 and of $25,000 in asset #2.

3. *Allocation of a basis decrease under §732(c)(3).* Any basis decrease allocated to a class of assets under §732(c)(3) is allocated first to loss assets in proportion to unrealized loss and then among all the assets within the class in proportion to relative adjusted bases (as adjusted in the first step). For example, assume that after allocation of basis to distributed ordinary income assets there is $12,000 to be allocated to the capital and §1231 assets, and assume that the exiting partner receives capital asset #1 with a pre-distribution inside basis of $4,000 and fair market value of $6,000 as well as capital asset #2 with a pre-distribution inside basis of $15,000 and fair market value of $12,000. Asset #1 takes a tentative basis of $4,000, asset #2 takes a tentative basis of $15,000, and that total of $19,000 exceeds the amount to be allocated by $7,000. Accordingly, a $3,000 decrease is first allocated to asset #2, and then the remaining $4,000 decrease is allocated $1,000 to asset #1 and $3,000 to asset #2. As a result, the exiting partner takes a basis of $3,000 in asset #1 and of $9,000 in asset #2. Be sure to note that when a decrease is allocated among a class of assets in proportion to relative adjusted bases, it is relative adjusted bases *after reductions for unrealized losses have been made.*

2. *Application of §736*

a. A First Note on the Application of §736

In the absence of §736, the taxation of liquidating distributions would be controlled by §§731-732, discussed above, as well as by §751(b), a provision that can overrule the application of §731, see §731(c). Like §751(b), §736 also trumps the application of §731 by virtue of an explicit statement in §731(c). Accordingly, we need to determine precisely when §736 applies.

By its terms, §736(a) applies to "payments" made in liquidation of a partnership interest. A liquidating distribution of cash certainly falls within the scope of §736, but does a distribution of non-cash partnership property also fall within it? Arguably, the term "payment" is narrower than the term "distribution" to which §731 and §732 apply.

Does §736 apply to non-cash distributions? Surprisingly, there is no definitive answer. The regulations under §736 do not speak to this issue, and every example in those regulations considers only cash distributions. The leading commentators quite clearly assume that §736 can apply to non-cash distributions, but they give no indication of having considered any alternative.

Look closely at §736(b)(1). Under certain conditions, a "payment" to which §736 speaks "shall be considered a distribution by the partnership and not as a distributive share or guaranteed payment." If the term "payment" was intended to be synonymous with "distribution," then this section would be saying that a distribution shall be considered as a distribution. While it is not impossible that is what Congress intended (the Code is full of truisms), surely it is at least possible that what was intended was something more informative.

The regulations promulgated under §751 cast a murky light on this problem. In example 2 of Treas. Regs. §1.751-1(g), a liquidating distribution of non-cash property is explicitly assumed to be taxed under §736. However, because the partnership has no unrealized receivables and no goodwill, the entire distribution is taxed under §736(b) and through it to §731 and §732. Thus, §736 has no impact, and that might help explain why the application of §736 goes unexplained.

In example 6 of that same regulation, another liquidating distribution of non–cash property is considered. Here, though, the partnership owns unrealized receivables so that application of §736 to the liquidating distribution is germane. Unfortunately, no mention of §736 is to be found, and the analysis presented by the regulations seems to tacitly assume that the distribution is taxed directly under §731 and §732 (except to the extent that §751(b) overrules §731). No explanation for the inconsistency between examples (2) and (6) is offered.

Fortunately, this issue is largely irrelevant because most liquidating distributions will be taxed the same whether §736 applies or not. However, that is not always the case, and at the end of this section we will return to this issue to pinpoint its implications.

b. Classification of Payments under §736

All payments made in liquidation of a partnership interest are divided into two groups: the §736(a) payments and the §736(b) payments. Payments made in exchange for a partner's interest in "partnership property" are classified as §736(b) payments, and all other payments are classified as §736(a) payments. In general, all payments are treated as payments for "partnership property," see §736(b)(2), (b)(3). However, when the liquidating distribution is made to a general partner and capital is not a material income producing factor in the partnership (that is, the distribution is made to a general partner by a service-oriented partnership), a special rule applies. In this case, §736(b)(2) provides that "partnership property" does not include unrealized receivables.[1] Accordingly, liquidating distributions from a service partnership to a general partner made in exchange for the partner's share of unrealized receivables are classified as §736(a) payments. In addition, if this partner receives payments for her share of the partnership's goodwill, these payments also are taxed as §736(a) payments. However, under §736(b)(2)(B), the partnership agreement may elect to have payments for partnership goodwill taxed under §736(b) instead. Thus, there is an elective component to §736 that applies only to payments for partnership goodwill. Of course, none of this is relevant unless capital is not a material income-producing factor in the partnership *and* the liquidating distribution is made to a general partner.

If a liquidating distribution can contain a §736(a) component because capital is not a material income-producing factor in the partnership and the distribution is in liquidation of a general partnership interest, determining the current value of partnership goodwill can be important. For example, suppose general partner *P* receives a liquidating payment of $20,000 in exchange for her one-fourth interest in the service-oriented *PQRS* partnership. If the partnership owns only receivables with aggregate fair market value of $80,000, then the entire payment is classified as a §736(a) payment because it is received by *P* in exchange for her share of the receivables. But what if the partnership's receivables are not worth $80,000, so that some of the $20,000 distributed to *P* is for *P*'s share of the partnership's goodwill. If the partnership agreement provides that liquidating payments for goodwill are taxable under §736(b), then that portion of the $20,000 properly allocable to partnership goodwill is taxable under §736(b) and, through it, under §731 and §732. The regulations provide: "Generally, the valuation placed by the partners upon a partner's interest in partnership property in an arm's length agreement will be regarded as correct." Treas. Regs. §1.736-1(b)(1).

When a liquidating distribution is made to a general partner from a service-oriented partnership, two details must be kept in mind. First, if the partnership agreement is silent as to the taxation of liquidating distributions received in exchange for goodwill, then such payments fall within §736(a). Smith v. Commissioner, 313 F.2d 16, 21 (10th Cir. 1962). In addition, to the extent partnership goodwill appears on the partnership books with a positive basis (as in the case of purchased goodwill), this goodwill is treated as "partnership property," and payments to a retiring partner for her share of such purchased goodwill are taxed under §736(b). See Treas. Regs. §1.736-1(b)(3).

An entity can be taxed as a partnership even though it is not a "partnership" under relevant state law. For example, the members of a limited liability company usually can elect partnership or corporate taxation. If the members of a service-oriented limited liability company elect to be taxed as partners, will payments made to a retiring member in exchange for a share of the entity's unrealized receivables be described in §736(a)? Recall that §736(a) usually applies only to payments made to *general* partners. While a member of a limited liability company may have rights to participate in the management of the entity similar to those of a general partner, the member lacks the general liability for entity obligations associated with general

1. For purposes of §736, the term "unrealized receivable" includes only traditional receivables as defined in §751(c)(1)-(2) (parenthetical in the flush language following §736(c)(2)).

partner status. Assuming the retiring member performed substantial services for the entity (recall that it must be a service-oriented entity for §736(a) to apply), presumably the member will be treated as a "general" partner for purposes of §736(a).

c. Taxation of Payments in Liquidation of a General Partnership Interest When Capital Is Not a Material Income-Producing Factor

Those payments classified as §736(a) payments (which can only include payments for unrealized receivables and, unless the partnership agreement provides otherwise, payments for goodwill) must be further divided into two groups: (1) those §736(a) payments taxed as the distributee partner's distributive share and (2) those §736(a) payments taxed to the distributee partner as a guaranteed payment. Under §736(a), payments are taxed as distributive share if determined *with regard* to the income of the partnership. If the amount of a §736(a) payment is determined *without regard* to the income of the partnership, it is taxed as a guaranteed payment.

For example, suppose *Q* is a one-third general partner in the service-oriented *PQR* partnership. Suppose further that *PQR* owns cash of $30,000 plus receivables worth $60,000. If *Q* receives a liquidating distribution of $30,000 in cash, one-third of the distribution (i.e., $10,000) will be taxed under §736(b) and the remaining two-thirds (i.e., $20,000) will be characterized as a §736(a) payment. If the partnership also agrees to distribute 5 percent of its net income to *Q* during each of the next three years, these additional payments will be characterized as §736(a) payments unless the partnership agreement provides to the contrary. Assuming these additional payments fall within §736(a), they will be taxed as distributive share to *Q* because they are determined with regard to the partnership's income. If, though, *Q* were to receive a fixed amount each year instead of the 5 percent of income, the additional payments would be taxed as guaranteed payments.

Saying that *Q*'s additional payments are taxed as distributive share means that (1) *Q* must report the amount in her gross income, as all partners must do with respect to distributive share, and (2) the character of that income to *Q* is dependent on its character to the partnership. If the payments were taxed as guaranteed payments, they would be includible to *Q* as ordinary income: guaranteed payments always are includible as ordinary income. Treas. Regs. §1.707-1(c); see also Treas. Regs. §1.736-1(a)(4). Furthermore, the regulations provide that any §736(a) payment taxed to the recipient as a guaranteed payment is deductible to the partnership. Treas. Regs. §1.736-1(a)(4).

Is there a significant difference between those §736(a) payments taxed as distributive share and those taxed as guaranteed payments? Not much: While the guaranteed payments can be deducted by the partnership, taxing income as a distributive share to the retiring partner has the effect of excluding the income from all other partners. Similarly, the distributee partner must include the payment regardless of the characterization. Thus, only the character of the income is affected: Distributive share can be capital gain or exempt income while guaranteed payments always are ordinary.

A distribution in liquidation of a general partnership interest from a service partnership can include both §736(a) and §736(b) components. However, the §736(b) component represents that portion of the liquidating distribution received in exchange for partnership property (excluding unrealized receivables), and since there can be *no* §736(a) component unless capital is not a material income-producing factor,[2] it is unlikely that the §736(b) component will be substantial. Nonetheless, even a service partnership can own some assets and certainly can have zero-basis goodwill.

Consider the following example: Individual *D* is a one-quarter partner in the *ABCD* general partnership. The partnership owns capital assets with an adjusted basis of $12,000 and fair market value of $16,000, as well as unrealized receivables of $80,000, and self-generated goodwill with an adjusted basis of $0 and fair market value of $20,000. If $29,000 is distributed to *D* in liquidation of her partnership interest (assume the distributed cash represents loan proceeds obtained to liquidate *D*'s partnership interest), $20,000 will be taxable under §736(a)(2) as a guaranteed payment, $4,000 will be taxable under §736(b) in exchange for partnership property, and $5,000 will be taxable under §736(a)(2) or §736(b) depending on what the partnership agreement says concerning partnership goodwill. Assuming *D*'s outside basis at the time of the distribution equals $3,000 and that the partnership agreement says nothing about partnership goodwill, *D* will have ordinary income of $25,000 under §736(a)(2) and a capital gain of $1,000 under §736(b)(1) and §731(a)(1).

There is one more complexity to taxation under §736(a). As discussed above, liquidating distributions made to a general partner from a partnership in which capital is not a material income-producing factor will be classified as §736(a) payments if made for the distributee partner's share of unrealized receivables. For application of §736, the definition of an "unrealized receivable" is narrower than usual. See the parenthetical in the first sentence of §751(c) following subsection (2).

d. Taxation of Payments under §751(b)

Most liquidating payments made by a partnership, including all partnerships in which capital *is* a material income-producing factor as well as all liquidating distributions to *limited* partners, are classified as §736(b) payments, and such payments are then taxed under §731, §732, and §751(b). Formally, application of §751(b) to liquidating distributions is the same as for nonliquidating distributions. However, if the distribution consists exclusively of cash, it necessarily is the case that the distributee partner's post-distribution share of the partner's §751 assets is zero, and so the distribution has the effect of exchanging the partner's share of §751 assets for cash, and so §751(b) is triggered.

2. If the amount of the payments to the retiring partner exceeds the fair market value of the retiring partner's interest in the venture, then that excess might be described in §736(a). However, the regulations promulgated under §704(b) require the partnership agreement to provide that a retiring partner will receive only the positive balance, if any, of her capital account. Treas. Regs. §1.704-1(b)(2)(ii)(b)(2). Accordingly, there should be no such excess.

For example, suppose *A* is a one-quarter partner in the *ABCD* partnership when the partnership books stand as follows:

Assets

	Adjusted basis	*Fair market value*
Capital asset	$12,000	$20,000
Receivables	0	12,000
Inventory	8,000	16,000
Cash	20,000	20,000

Liabilities and Capital

	Adjusted basis	*Fair market value*
A	$10,000	$17,000
B	10,000	17,000
C	10,000	17,000
D	10,000	17,000

If *A* receives cash of $17,000 in liquidation of her partnership interest, what are the tax consequences to *A* and to the partnership? Because capital is a material income-producing factor in this partnership, the entire $17,000 received by *A* in liquidation of her partnership interest is treated as a §736(b) payment, see §736(b)(2), and under §736(b)(1), taxation is determined under §§731 and 751. Prior to the liquidating distribution, *A*'s share of the partnership's §751 property was $3,000 of the receivables with $0 adjusted basis and $4,000 of the inventory with $2,000 adjusted basis. Accordingly, the effect of the liquidating distribution is to reduce *A*'s interest in the §751 assets from $7,000 to $0.

Under §751(b), there is a hypothetical nonliquidating distribution of *A*'s share of the §751 property, see generally Treas. Regs. §1.751-1(b)(3), so that *A* is deemed to receive $3,000 of the receivables with a basis of $0 and $4,000 of the receivables with a basis of $2,000, see §732(a), and no gain or loss is recognized, §731. Under §733(2), *A* reduces her outside basis by $2,000, down to $8,000. Next, *A* is treated as selling both the receivables and the inventory back to the partnership, producing ordinary income to *A* of $3,000 on the receivables and $2,000 on the inventory. Because the partnership takes a cost basis in the property it is treated as buying from *A*, the partnership's adjusted basis in the receivables becomes $3,000 and its adjusted basis in the inventory becomes $10,000.

Finally, *A* is treated as receiving the remainder of the cash ($17,000 less $7,000, or $10,000) in a liquidating distribution taxable under §731. This produces a capital gain of $2,000. Thus, *A* has recognized total income of $7,000, of which $5,000 is ordinary and $2,000 is capital. The partnership increases its basis in its ordinary income assets by $5,000.

In this example, *A* recognizes income of $7,000 whether or not §751(b) applies. The effect of §751(b) is to convert part of that gain (in this case, $5,000 of the gain) into ordinary income. *A*'s recognition of ordinary income reflects her share of the appreciation in the partnership's inventory and unrealized receivables: Prior to the distribution, the partnership owned inventory and unrealized receivables with adjusted basis of $8,000 and value of $28,000, so that *A*'s one-quarter share of the appreciation was $5,000. After the transaction the partnership's basis in the inventory and receivables is increased by the ordinary income recognized by *A*. This makes sense because *A*'s share of the appreciation has already been taxed; the basis increase to the partnership ensures that *A*'s share of the appreciation will not be taxed again.

e. Deferred Payments under §736

Payments made to a retiring partner in liquidation of her partnership interest can be made over time. For example, the partnership might agree to pay a fixed amount of money or a fixed percent of its profits each year for some fixed number of years. In such circumstances, the tax consequences of the §736 payments spread out over several years. Regulations under §736 give substantial flexibility in allocating the partner's outside basis to the §736(b) payments received over time, and, in the rare occasion when the deferred payments include both §736(a) and §736(b) components, similar flexibility in allocating each payment between §736(a) and §736(b) (although the total amount allocated to each section over all years must reflect the value of the retiring partner's interest in the various assets of the partnership). Treas. Regs. §1.736-1(b)(4)-(7).

Consider the following example. *X* retires from the *XYZ* partnership when the partnership books stand as follows. In liquidation of her partnership interest, *X* receives cash of $10,000 and will receive four additional annual distributions in the same amount.

Assets

	Adjusted basis	*Fair market value*
Cash	$45,000	$45,000
Receivables	0	45,000
Capital asset	12,000	15,000
Goodwill	0	45,000

Liabilities and Capital

	Adjusted basis	*Fair market value*
X	$19,000	$50,000
Y	19,000	50,000
Z	19,000	50,000

Because capital is a material income-producing factor in the partnership, the entire $50,000 to be distributed to *X* is described in §736(b) and so is taxable under §§731 and 751(b). Prior to the distribution, *X*'s interest in the partnership's §751(b) assets consisted of $15,000 of the receivables with adjusted basis of $0. Putting the timing issue aside, *X* is treated as receiving a nonliquidating distribution of $15,000 of the receivables, tax free under §731 and with a carry-over basis of $0 under §732. Because the receivables take a $0 basis in *X*'s hands, there is no reduction to *X*'s outside basis under §733(2).

X is then treated as selling these receivables back to the partnership, producing ordinary income to *X* of $15,000 and the partnership takes a cost basis in the receivables deemed purchased, so the partnership increases its adjusted basis in its receivables to $15,000. Finally, the remainder of the cash, namely $35,000, is taxed to *X* under §731, yielding a capital gain of $16,000. Thus, *X* recognizes ordinary income of $15,000 and capital gain of $16,000 on the liquidating distribution, and the partnership can increase the basis of its receivables by $15,000.

Taking the installment nature of the payments into account, we first observe under Treas. Regs. §1.736-1(b)(5) that there is no §736(a) component to any of the payments. The regulation further seems to provide that *X* may elect to treat the payments as a recovery of basis first or under the installment method. If *X* makes no election to the contrary, the first payment will be tax free and the second will be taxable only to the extent of $1,000, while the third, fourth, and fifth payments will be taxable in full. To the extent any payment is taxable, presumably *X* will recognize 15/31 of the income as ordinary and 16/31 as capital.

X may elect to recognize a portion of the $31,000 income with each payment. If *X* so elects, 31/50 of each payment will be taxable, while 19/50 of each payment will be treated as a recovery of basis. Thus, *X* will have income of $6,200 from each payment. Of that $6,200, presumably 15/31 (or $3,000) will be ordinary, while 16/31 (or $3,200) will be capital. Certainly it is possible that the Service will seek to require *X* to report the ordinary income first and the capital gain last.

f. Section 736, Partnership Goodwill, and the §704(b) Regulations

Payments in liquidation of a general partnership interest when capital is not a material income-producing factor can be divided into three groups: (1) payments for the distributee's share of unrealized receivables, taxed under §736(a); (2) payments for the distributee's share of all other partnership property, taxed under §736(b); and (3) payments for goodwill, taxed under §736(a) or under §736(b) depending on the partnership's election, see §736(b)(2)(B). Under longstanding regulations, goodwill of the partnership in this context includes "an arrangement among the partners in the nature of mutual insurance." Treas. Regs. §1.736-1(a)(2). Is this broad interpretation of "goodwill" consistent with the §704(b) regulations?

In general, the goodwill of a business means its value as a going concern in excess of its asset value; that is, a business has goodwill to the extent that its reputation is valuable. Investments in advertising, quality control, customer service and other intangibles all help to increase the value of a company's goodwill. Goodwill within the meaning of §736(b)(2)(B) certainly includes this traditional concept of the term, but in this sense the goodwill is like any other asset of the business.

Recall that allocations of partnership income, deduction, credit, and loss will be allowed only if they have substantial economic effect within the meaning of §704(b)(2). Under the §704(b) regulations, a partnership will fail the substantial economic effect test if liquidating distributions are made other than in accordance with final capital account balances after adjustment is made for all unrealized appreciation and loss in partnership assets. Treas. Regs. §1.704-1(b)(2)(ii)(b)(2). Partnership goodwill in the traditional sense will be reflected in such adjusted capital account balances, so that distributions in liquidation of a partnership interest may (indeed, must) include amounts for the distributee's share of partnership goodwill *in the traditional sense.*

But what of the "arrangement[s] among the partners in the nature of mutual insurance" allowed by the §736 regulations. Such arrangements reflect a shifting of value from the remaining partners to the retiring partner (or to the beneficiaries of a deceased partner) unrelated to any economic event of the partnership. Accordingly, payments in the nature of mutual insurance are unrelated to the partners' capital accounts and so fail to meet the standards of the §704(b) regulations. Treas. Regs. §1.704-1(b)(2)(ii)(b)(2). These regulations do not, of course, prohibit partnerships from providing for liquidating distributions in the nature of mutual insurance—such a prohibition would go well beyond the authority of §704—but they do seem to say that the tax allocations of such a partnership are subject to challenge. Treas. Regs. §1.704-1(b)(1)(i). If you write a partnership agreement that provides for some mutual insurance among the partners, be sure to think carefully if the risks are worth it and, even more importantly, be certain to explain the risks to your clients.

Suppose partner *X* is offered the opportunity to sell the partnership interest for an amount in excess of *X*'s capital account balance even adjusted for all unrealized gain and loss in the partnership's assets. If *X* reports this opportunity to the partnership and the partnership proposes to acquire *X*'s interest for the same price as *X* was offered, does such an offer violate the requirement of economic effect that liquidating distributions will at all times equal the value of the exiting partner's capital account?

Surprisingly, the answer is that such an agreement does *not* violate the requirement of economic effect. Treas. Regs. §1.704-1(b)(2)(ii)(b)(3) validates this and similar transactions, providing that the requirement of economic effect is not violated if

> all or part of the partnership interest of one or more partners is purchased (other than in connection with the liquidation of the partnership) by the partnership or by one or more partners . . . pursuant to an agreement negotiated at arm's length by persons who at the time such agreement is entered into have materially adverse interests and if a principal purpose of such purchase and sale is not to avoid the principles of [the requirement of economic effect].

In such circumstances, the liquidating distribution could include an amount in excess of the exiting partner's share of the partnership's property, and that amount (if the exiting partner is a general partner and if the partnership is a service partnership) could therefore be described in §736(a).

g. A Final Note on the Application of §736

As discussed above, §736 unambiguously applies to liquidating distributions of cash, but its application to distributions of property is less than clear. If §736 does *not* apply to distributions of property, then such distributions will be taxable directly under §731 and §732. These same provisions apply even if §736 *is* applicable, at least as to distributions in exchange for the partner's share of partnership property as defined in §736(b). Application of §736, therefore, can make a difference only as to distributions *not* in exchange for the partner's interest in partnership property—that is, to distributions for a general partner's share of partnership unrealized receivables and goodwill from a partnership in which capital is not a material income-producing factor.

Let us first focus on non-§751 property received by the retiring partner in exchange for her share of the partnership's receivables. Under §736(a), the retiring partner will recognize ordinary income equal to the value of this property, assuming §736 can apply to such distributions. If §736 does not apply, then the distribution will be taxed under §§731-732 and §751(b), and precisely the same result will obtain under §751(b) because unrealized receivables have a zero basis to the partnership, so long as the retiring partner's share of the receivables drops to zero. Thus, if the distributed property does not include any §751 property, the possible application of §736 is irrelevant to the retiring partner. As to the partnership, application of §736 will provide a deduction, while application of §751(b) will produce a basis increase in the receivables. Thus, all else being equal the continuing partners would prefer that §736 apply.

However, if the liquidating distribution includes some §751 property, possible application of §736 becomes even more important. If §736 applies to the distribution, the retiring partner recognizes income under §707(c) (or as distributive share) and the partnership enjoys a corresponding deduction (or exclusion). Treas. Regs. §1.736-1(a)(4). However, if §736 does not apply, the retiring partner might avoid recognition of income because the distribution might have little or no effect on the partner's interest in §751 property: There will be a rearrangement of interests in §751 property to which §751(b) speaks *only if* the distribution contains less than the retiring partner's full share of §751 property. Treas. Regs. §1.751-1(b)(1)(ii). As to the remaining partners, to the extent that the retiring partner avoids recognition of income, the partnership receives no deduction or inside basis increase.

For example, suppose the service-oriented *MNOP* general partnership owns unrealized receivables with an adjusted basis of $0 and fair market value of $20,000, and assume that each partner has an outside basis of $0. If the partnership liquidates by distributing one-quarter of the receivables to each partner, what are the tax consequences to the partners? If the distributions are not subject to §736 because they are not "payments," then each partner takes a carry-over basis of $0 in the receivables under §732(b) and there is no gain or loss under §731(a) and §751(b). If, though, §736 applies to these distributions, each partner has a guaranteed payment of $5,000 under §736(a)(2), producing $5,000 of income to each partner under §707(c), as well as $20,000 of income (under §1001(a)), and a $20,000 deduction (under Treas. Regs. §1.736-1(a)(4)) to the partnership.

Application of §736 to liquidating distributions of property again can be important with respect to partnership goodwill. If §736 applies to distributions of property, election by the partnership under §736(b)(2)(B) to treat payments for goodwill under §736(b) causes such payments to be taxed under §§731-732. In such circumstances, the possible application of §736 is irrelevant because the same sections—§731-732 and §751(b)—apply to the distribution. However, if no election under §736(b)(2)(B) is made, taxation under §736 produces ordinary income to the partner and a deduction (under §736(a)(1)) to the partnership, while taxation under §§731-732 produces no income to the partner and no deduction to the partnership.

PROBLEM

25-1. *A* retires from the *ABC* partnership when the partnership books stand as indicated below. *A* receives a cash payment of $40,000 and will receive four additional payments in the same amount.

Assets

	Adjusted basis	*Fair market value*
Capital asset	$30,000	$ 60,000
Receivables	0	240,000
Inventory	30,000	90,000
Cash	90,000	90,000
Goodwill	0	120,000

Liabilities and Capital

	Adjusted basis	*Fair market value*
A	$50,000	$200,000
B	50,000	200,000
C	50,000	200,000

Assuming that each partner's capital account equals that partner's outside basis, how is *A* taxed?

B. DISPOSITION OF A PARTNERSHIP INTEREST

We now turn to the transfer of a partnership interest *other than* in exchange for a liquidating distribution. When *any* asset is transferred, certain questions should leap to mind. First, is the transferor taxable on the transaction? Second, if gain or loss is recognized, how is the asset's holding period computed and, more generally, is any gain or loss characterized as ordinary or capital? Third and finally, how does the transferee compute her basis in the newly acquired asset? With respect to the transfer of a partnership interest, the difficult issues usually arise in connection with the second question.

1. Basic Rules

Under §741, the sale or exchange of a partnership interest produces gain or loss to the transferor. The amount of the gain or loss is determined simply by comparing the transferor partner's amount realized on the transaction with her outside basis in her partnership interest. Note that, except as modified by §751(a), this gain or loss is taxable as capital gain or loss. §741.

While computing the amount of gain or loss on the disposition of a partnership interest is not difficult, one aspect of the computation is easy to forget. Under §752(d), the amount realized in exchange for a partnership interest includes the transferor partner's share of the partnership's liabilities. For example, if *P* is a one-half partner in the *PQ* partnership that owns Blackacre worth $1,000,000 and subject to a debt of $600,000, *P*'s amount realized should she sell her partnership interest will include not only what she actually receives for her interest (presumably $200,000) but also an additional $300,000 as her one-half share of the partnership's liability. See Treas. Regs. §§1.752-1(h), 1.1001-2(a). Including the transferor's share of partnership liabilities in amount realized makes sense for the same reason that liabilities contribute to amount realized in a nonpartnership setting: What goes into basis must be reflected either in an out-of-pocket expenditure or in an adjustment to amount realized. Commissioner v. Tufts, 461 U.S. 300 (1983).

The general capital gain (or loss) rule in §741 is modified by application of §751(a). Under §751(a), we divide the gain or loss realized on the sale into ordinary income and capital gain components. Note, though, that the following rule always holds true: *The net gain (or loss) recognized by the transferor partner under §751(a) will always equal the gain or loss computed under §741 without regard to §751(a).* That is, the effect of §751(a) is only to bifurcate the overall gain or loss between ordinary and capital components. It may be the case, however, that one of the components is positive (an ordinary or capital gain) while the other is negative (an ordinary or capital loss).

2. *Application of §751(a)*

Application of §751(a) is computed in three steps. Treas. Regs. §1.751-1(a)(2). In step 1, the selling partner determines how much ordinary income or loss would be includible as distributive share if, instead of selling her partnership interest, the partnership sold all of its assets for fair market value. This first step is computed by taking into account all provisions that affect the selling partner's distributive share including curative and remedial allocations under §704(c)(1)(A) principles in connection with reverse §704(c) adjustments. This is the amount of ordinary income (or loss) the selling partner reports under §751(a). In step 2, the partner determines the gain or loss that is realized on the sale of her partnership interest, computed by ignoring the application of §751(a). This is the selling partner's net income or loss from the sale. And in step 3, the selling partner determines the capital gain or loss from the sale by subtracting from the net income or loss as determined in step 2 the amount of ordinary income computed in step 1.

Consider the following example. *X* is a one-third partner in the *XYZ* general partnership with partnership books as follows:

Assets

	Adjusted basis	*Fair market value*
Inventory	$7,500	$ 9,000
Receivables	0	18,000
Land	9,000	12,000

Liabilities and Capital

	Adjusted basis	*Fair market value*
X	$5,500	$13,000
Y	5,500	13,000
Z	5,500	13,000

If partner *X* sells her partnership interest for its fair market value of $13,000, *X* will recognize ordinary income of $6,500 because that is the amount of ordinary income that *X* would report if the partnership sold all its assets for their current fair market values. Because the gain realized on the sale is $7,500 (computed as amount realized of $13,000 less adjusted basis of $5,500), the capital gain on the sale is $7,500 less $6,500, or $1,000. Note that in this case the amount of capital gain recognized on the sale equals *X*'s share of the unrealized appreciation in the partnership's capital asset.

Reconsider this example but assume that *X*'s outside basis is $8,000 rather than $5,500 (perhaps because *X* acquired her partnership interest by purchase at a time when the partnership owned additional appreciated assets). If *X* again sells her one-third interest in the partnership for $13,000, *X* again reports ordinary income of $6,500 because that figure is determined by the fair market value of the partnership's assets as compared with the partnership's basis in those assets: The selling partner's outside basis has no relevance to the computation of the ordinary income component under §751(a). Now, though, the net income realized on the sale is only $5,000 (amount realized of $13,000 less outside basis of $8,000), and so *X* recognizes a capital loss of $1,500 on the sale ($5,000 total income less $6,500 ordinary income).

As this second example demonstrates, the capital gain or loss component on the sale of a partnership interest will not necessarily equal the selling partner's share of the unrealized gain or loss in the partnership's capital and §1231 assets. In this example, *X* reports a capital loss even though all the partnership's assets are appreciated. Note also that in computing the ordinary income component of the sale, all aspects of the selling partner's distributive share are relevant, including if the partnership owns assets with an adjusted basis more or less than book value, §704(c) considerations.

PROBLEMS

25-2. Reconsider the facts of problem 25-1 above. How would *A* be taxed if she sold her partnership interest to *B* and *C*?

25-3. *G* has a 50-percent interest in the losses of the *GH* partnership and a 75-percent interest in its profits. What are the tax consequences to *G* if she sells her partnership interest for $98,000 when the partnership books stand as follows?

Assets

	Adjusted basis	*Fair market value*
Capital asset	$30,000	$50,000
Receivables	0	40,000
Inventory	60,000	64,000
Cash	10,000	10,000

Liabilities and Capital

	Adjusted basis	*Fair market value*
G	$50,000	$98,000
H	50,000	66,000

25-4. *XYZ*, an accrual partnership, has the following assets:

Assets

	Adjusted basis	*Fair market value*
Capital asset	$30,000	$45,000
Receivables	30,000	30,000
Inventory	15,000	21,000
Cash	60,000	60,000

X, a one-third partner in *XYZ* for the past five years, would like to exit the partnership. *X*, *Y*, and *Z* decide to adopt one of the three following plans. Plan A is for *X* to receive cash of $52,000 in liquidation of her partnership interest. Plan B is for *X* to receive a liquidating distribution consisting of an undivided one-third interest in all partnership assets, followed by a sale of that undivided interest to *Y* and *Z* for $52,000. Plan C is for *X* to sell *X*'s partnership interest for its fair market value of $52,000. *X*'s adjusted basis in her partnership interest equals $45,000. Determine the tax consequences of each plan to *X*, *Y*, *Z*, and the partnership.

25-5. How do your answers in problem 25-4 above change if the partnership uses the cash receipts and disbursements method of accounting so that the partnership books stand as follows and *X*'s outside basis equals $35,000?

Assets

	Adjusted basis	*Fair market value*
Capital asset	$30,000	$45,000
Receivables	0	30,000
Inventory	15,000	21,000
Cash	60,000	60,000

25-6. Reconsider your answers to problem 25-4 above, assuming that the capital asset is subject to a liability of $12,000 so that each partnership interest is worth only $48,000. Now, plan A is for *X* to receive cash of $48,000, while plan B is for *X* to receive an unencumbered one-third interest in each non-cash asset and $4,000 less cash, followed by a sale to *Y* and *Z* for $48,000. Plan C has *X* selling the partnership interest for $48,000.

25-7. *P* and *Q* form the *PQ* general partnership by contributing cash of $800,000 apiece. The partnership uses its cash of $1,600,000 to purchase depreciable equipment. The partnership leases this equipment to a third party and gives that third party the right to purchase the equipment for the partnership's adjusted basis any time after the fifth year of the lease. Assume that this option is exercised when the partnership has an adjusted basis in the property of $1,000,000, and the property is worth $1,400,000. How will the partners be taxed if they

a. sell the asset to the third party for $1,000,000?
b. sell their partnership interests to the third party for $500,000 each?

Recall that depreciable property is subject to depreciation recapture under §1245.

3. *Taxation of the Capital Gain Portion*

a. Holding Period

Despite the number of distinct interests in a single partnership that one partner may own, a partner has a single capital account, Treas. Regs. §1.704-1(b)(2)(iv)(b), and the Service has long maintained that a partner also has a single, unified outside basis, Rev. Rul. 84-53, 1984-1 C.B. 159. Nevertheless, a partner can have multiple holding periods with respect to the partner's unified interest in the partnership. See generally Treas. Regs. §1.1223-3. A bifurcated holding period can arise either by contributing multiple properties to the partnership at one time or by making multiple contributions to the partnership over time. Treas. Regs. §1.1223-3(a). A partner having a bifurcated holding period can recognize both long- and short-term capital gain on the sale of her partnership interest or from a distribution of cash (including marketable securities treated as cash under §731(c)) in excess of outside basis. See Treas. Regs. §1.1223-3(c), -3(d)(2).

Suppose that *X* is a member of the *P* partnership, and assume that *X* has a holding period in its partnership interest in excess of one year. If the fair market value of *X*'s interest equals $500 and *X* contributes additional cash of $250 to the partnership (increasing the value of *X*'s interest to $750), then *X* will be treated as having a short-term holding period in one-third of the partnership interest because of the cash contribution. So, for example, if *X* sells her partnership interest six months later, one-third of any gain or loss will be short term. Note that this is true even though all of the appreciation in *X*'s partnership interest may have accrued many years earlier. Note also that this result would not change if *X* had contributed property rather than cash unless the property had been a capital or §1231 asset in *X*'s hands immediately prior to the contribution and *X* had had a holding period in the contributed property in excess of six months. See §1223(1) (tacking for substitute basis capital or §1231 assets).

As a general rule, distributions from a partnership do not affect the distributee partner's holding period in the partnership interest. Treas. Regs. §1.1223-3(d)(1). However, distributions of cash can reduce the short-term portion of a bifurcated holding period because only the *net* cash contribution made during any 12-month period creates a bifurcated holding period for an otherwise long-term partnership interest. Treas. Regs. §1.1223-3(b)(2). For this purpose, deemed distributions arising from a decrease in a partner's share of partnership liabilities are ignored. Treas. Regs. §1.1223-3(b)(3). Deemed contributions arising from an increase in liability share equally are ignored. *Id.*

Suppose that *X* and *Y* are equal general partners in the *XY* partnership and that *XY* owns unimproved real estate with an adjusted basis of $1,000,000 and fair market value of $5,000,000. Assume that *X* and *Y* each have an outside basis of $500,000, that each partner has held her partnership interest for more than one year, that the partnership has held the property for more than one year, and that *XY* has found a purchaser for its property. However, before the sale can be completed the partnership must invest an additional $500,000 in the transaction (to cover fees of lawyers and accountants and to make certain improvements to the property).

If each partner contributes additional cash of $250,000 and then the property is sold, the partnership's gain will be long-term and that gain will be includible by the partners. §702(a). As a result of that inclusion, the partners will increase their outside bases, §705(a)(1)(A), and so a subsequent distribution of the sale proceeds should be tax free. Thus, the contribution of cash will not affect the character of the gain recognized by the partnership.

However, if after the cash is contributed it is determined that the partners must sell their interests rather than cause the partnership to sell its assets, a less favorable result would be obtained because the cash contribution would convert one-11th of the gain into short-term capital gain (for each partner, the cash contributed of $250,000 is one-10th of the pre-contribution $2,500,000 value of the partnership interest). If the transaction must be effected by the sale of partnership interests, then the partners should not have contributed the needed capital but rather should have caused the partnership to borrow it. So long as the form of the borrowing is respected, the borrowing will not affect the holding period of the property or of the partnership interests and the loan can be repaid out of the sale proceeds without tax consequences.

b. Capital Gain Rate

Section 751(a) effectively looks through a partnership interest to any ordinary income assets owned by the partnership. Sections 1(h)(5)(B) and 1(h)(9) play the same role as to collectibles gain (generally taxed at 28 percent) and unrecaptured §1250 gain (generally taxed at 25 percent). See generally Treas. Regs. §1.1(h)-1(b). *Note that there is no equivalent look-though rule applicable to taxable distributions from a partnership to a partner.* Treas. Regs. §1.1(h)-1(b)(2)(ii) (final sentence), -1(b)(3)(ii) (final sentence).

4. *Non-Sale Dispositions*

If a partnership interest is exchanged for other property, the transaction is taxed as a sale. §1001(a). This is true even if the other property is itself a partnership interest because an exchange of partnership interests cannot qualify for like-kind treatment under §1031. See §1031(a)(2)(D). If a partnership interest is abandoned, the loss will be ordinary because of the lack of sale or exchange unless the abandonment works a reduction in the partner's share of partnership debt; in such a case, reduction of debt is treated as a constructive distribution under §731, and so there is capital gain or loss except to the extent that §751(b) applies to the transaction. Rev. Rul. 93-80, 1993-2 C.B. 239.

5. *Closing of the Taxable Year*

In general, a partnership's taxable year does not close as a result of the disposition of a partner's interest. §706(c)(1). However, the partnership's taxable year *does* terminate with respect to the exiting partner. §706(c)(2)(A). Thus, the exiting partner will report her distributive share of the partnership's income and deduction up to the time of her exit. The partnership may close its books as of the date of the partner's exit (called an interim closing of the books) or it can wait until the close of its taxable year and then apportion year-end totals to the periods before and after the partner's exit. See Treas. Regs. §1.706-1(c)(2)(ii). It is worth noting that the partnership year closes with respect to a partner who dies as well as to an exiting partner, whether the partner exits by selling her interest or by having the interest liquidated. §706(c)(2)(A).

A cash basis partnership is forced to accrue most deductions under §706(d) whenever partnership interests change during the year. See §706(d)(2). Thus, when a partner exits the partnership during the partnership's taxable year, the exiting partner will include her distributive share of accrued partnership deductions regardless of the partnership's method of accounting. However, the exiting partner will not include accrued but unreceived income of the partnership unless the partnership uses an accrual method of accounting or the partnership apportions year-end totals in lieu of an interim closing of the books.

6. *Termination of the Partnership*

If a partnership terminates, there is a liquidating distribution to all the partners. Under §708(b)(1), a partnership can terminate in either of two ways. First, a partnership terminates if "no part of any business . . . continues to be carried on by any of its partners in a partnership." §708(b)(1)(A). Second, a partnership terminates if "within a 12-month period there is a sale or exchange of 50 percent or more of the total interest in partnership capital and profits." §708(b)(1)(B). Only sales and exchanges of partnership interests are relevant to termination under §708(b)(1)(B), so that transfers by gift and devise are ignored, as are liquidations of partnership interests. See Treas. Regs. §1.708-1(b)(1)(ii). This second type of partnership termination often is called a "technical termination."

When a partnership terminates, its taxable year ends and a liquidating distribution is made to its partners. In the case of a technical termination triggered by the sale of a partnership interest, the liquidating distribution is made to the continuing partners and to the *purchasing* partner. That is, the liquidation is deemed to occur immediately *after* the sale triggering the termination. Treas. Regs. §1.708-1(b)(1)(iv). Technically, the terminating partnership is deemed to contribute all of its assets to a new partnership in exchange for all of the interests in this new partnership, and then the terminating partnership is deemed to distribute those interests in the new partnership to its members in liquidation of the terminating partnership. Treas. Regs. §1.708-1(b)(1)(iv).

Although an actual partnership termination and reformation would affect the partners' capital accounts and introduce new §704(c)(1) problems, no such complexity results from a technical termination under §708(b)(1)(B) because a technical termination does not affect the partners' capital accounts. Treas. Regs. §1.704-1(b)(2)(iv)(l). In addition, a technical termination does not trigger recognition of income under §704(c)(1)(B), Treas. Regs. §1.704-4(c)(3), or under §737, Treas. Regs. §1.737-2(a). And while property in the newly formed partnership will be treated as §704(c) property only if it was §704(c) property in the hands of the predecessor partnership, Treas. Regs. §1.704-3(a)(3)(i), the newly formed partnership is *not* required to use the same method for addressing ceiling limitations as did the predecessor partnership, Treas. Regs. §1.704-3(a)(2). See Treas. Regs. §1.708-

1(b)(1)(iv) for additional guidance. The most significant drawback of a technical termination is that any depreciable property owned by the partnership must be treated as newly placed in service, see §168(i)(7)(B) (final sentence), thereby lengthening the period over which the partnership will recover its remaining basis in its property.

A ceasing to conduct business termination can arise not only if the partnership goes out of business but also if all but one of the partners quits the partnership. The definition of a "partnership" in §761(a) includes only groups of investors, so that a partnership cannot exist with but a single partner. As a consequence, a two-person partnership necessarily terminates if one partner buys out the other or if one partner's interest in the partnership is liquidated. See Treas. Regs. §1.708-1(b)(1)(i).

If all but one of the partners dispose of their interests in the venture, the partnership will terminate because a partnership requires at least two partners. Treas. Regs. §301.7701-3(a). Transfer of the business into the hands of the sole remaining member can be accomplished in different ways, and the particular form selected can affect the tax consequences of the transaction.

For example, suppose individuals *X*, *Y*, and *Z* are equal one-third partners in the *XYZ* general partnership having outside bases and capital accounts of $14,000. Assume that the partnership's assets consists of cash of $24,000 as well as inventory with an adjusted basis to the partnership of $18,000 and fair market value of $12,000, so that each partner's interest in the venture is worth $12,000. The partnership could terminate, distributing the inventory to *X* and $12,000 of cash to *Y* and *Z*. Equivalently, *X* could purchase the interests of *Y* and *Z* for cash of $12,000 each, and then the partnership would terminate automatically, distributing its cash and the inventory to *X* in a liquidating distribution. Whichever route is taken, *X* ends up with the inventory, and *Y* and *Z* each get $12,000 in cash.

If the first route is taken, the distribution will produce a loss of $2,000 to *Y* and to *Z*, capital under §731(a) (final sentence) and §741 except to the extent recharacterized under §751(b). On these facts, though, §751(b) will not apply because the inventory has declined in value and application of §751(b) is limited to "substantially appreciated" inventory. *X* will receive the inventory tax free under §731 and will take a $14,000 basis in the $12,000 worth of inventory, see §732(b), so that if *X* sells the inventory there will be a loss of $2,000, ordinary under §735(a)(2) if the sale is made within five years of the liquidating distribution. Thus, of the $6,000 loss on the inventory, only *X*'s share will qualify for ordinary loss treatment, with *Y* and *Z* saddled with $2,000 of capital loss apiece.

But if the second route is taken, *Y* and *Z* will each recognize a loss of $2,000 on the sale of her partnership interest to *X*. That sale will be subject to §751(a), and so the loss will be ordinary because §751(a), unlike §751(b), applies to all partnership inventory whether substantially appreciated or not. The liquidating distribution will again give *X* a $14,000 basis in the inventory worth $12,000, so as before *X* can enjoy an ordinary loss by selling the inventory within five years. Thus, by taking the second route rather than the first, the partners have preserved the entire ordinary loss in the partnership's inventory.

Next consider the two-person *PQ* general partnership holding an appreciated capital asset with an adjusted basis of $50,000 and fair market value of $80,000. Assume that each partner has a capital account and outside basis of $25,000 and that the partnership has held its asset and the partners have held their partnership interests for more than a year. Thus, there is unrealized appreciation of $30,000 in the partnership, and that unrealized appreciation and any subsequent appreciation should eventually produce a long-term capital gain.

If *P* wants to buy *Q*'s interest in the property, *P* might simply pay cash of $40,000 to *Q* for *Q*'s partnership interest. This would produce a capital gain of $15,000 to *Q*, and then the partnership would liquidate, distributing the asset to *P* in a liquidating distribution. *P*'s outside basis in her partnership interest immediately prior to the distribution would be $65,000 ($25,000 in half the partnership and cost of $40,000 in the other half), so that *P*'s basis in the distributed property would be $65,000 under §732(b). Suppose *P* subsequently sells the property for $90,000. *P* clearly recognizes a capital gain of $25,000 under §1001(a), but is all of that gain long term?

Under §735(b), a partner's holding period in distributed property includes the holding period of the distributing partnership. Thus, on these facts the statute clearly says that *P*'s holding period exceeds one year immediately after the distribution because *P* is entitled to tack the partnership's holding period to her own. As a result, the gain should be entirely long term.

In McCauslen v. Commissioner, 45 T.C. 588 (1966), the Tax Court held that some of the gain (here, $5,000 of the gain) would be short term because *P* may not tack the partnership's holding period to that portion of the asset attributable to the partnership interest purchased from *Q*. In effect, the court rewrote §735(b) to tack not the partnership's holding period in the distributed asset but rather the partner's holding period in her partnership interest. The court's holding in *McCauslen* was essentially unreasoned and quite clearly indefensible; no court ever followed it (though no court ever expressly disavowed it, either).

McCauslen was one of those cases consigned to the junk-heap of history until January of 1999, at which time the Service issued a revenue ruling expressly following the peculiar holding of *McCauslen*, Rev. Rul. 99-6, 1999-1 C.B. 432. This ruling concludes that a sale by one partner in a two-person partnership of her interest in the venture to the other partner is taxable to the selling partner under §741, but that for determining the purchasing partner's holding period in distributed assets, the transaction should be recast as if the partnership made a liquidating distribution to the two partners, followed by a sale of half the assets from one partner to the other. By recasting the transaction in this way, the purchasing partner loses the tacking benefit of §735(b) because half the assets are deemed acquired by purchase and not by distribution.

This ruling makes little sense. First, it is internally inconsistent: the same transaction is treated as a sale to the selling partner yet as a presale distribution to the purchasing partner. Second, it is inconsistent with the structure of subchapter K: A capital asset held by a partnership for more than one year will produce long-term capital gain to all the partners without regard for the length of period these partners have held their partnership interests. See, e.g., Podell v. Commissioner, 55 T.C. 429 (1970); Madison Gas & Elec. Co. v. Commissioner, 72 T.C. 521 (1979); Treas. Regs. §1.702-1(a)(2). There is no reason why the benefit of long-term capital gain treatment should be lost simply because the partnership distributes its assets in liquidation of the partnership. After all, such a distribution generally is tax free, and the partners essentially step into the shoes of the partnership. See §731(a), §732(b), §735(b). Hopefully this ruling will be dismissed by the courts; its long-term effect on the credibility of the Service cannot help but be negative.

NOTES

1. *Conversion into new form of entity.* Under some circumstances, partners may wish to convert their partnership into a different but related form. For example, the partners may wish to convert a general partnership into a limited partnership or convert a limited or general partnership into a limited liability company (electing to be taxable as a partnership). Such a conversion is not treated as a liquidation of the partnership nor as a sale or exchange of the partnership interests. Accordingly, the only tax consequences of such a conversion would be deemed contributions and deemed distributions under §752(a)-(b) if the conversion worked a change in the partners' shares of partnership debt. See Rev. Rul. 95-37, 1995-1 C.B. 130; Rev. Rul. 84-52, 1984-1 C.B. 157. If the partnership elects to be taxable as a corporation, see Treas. Regs. §301.7701-3(g)(1).

2. *Treatment of partnership amortizable §197 intangibles.* While all depreciable property is treated as newly placed in service following a technical termination of the partnership, the same is not true as to amortizable §197 intangibles held by the partnership. See §197(f)(2) (and recall that on the technical termination of a partnership, all assets of the terminated partnership are treated as contributed to a new partnership in a transaction described in §721). This is an extremely peculiar result because, for all other purposes, amortizable §197 intangibles are treated as depreciable property. §197(f)(7). While impossible to explain, this distinction in treatment can be important for those partnerships whose assets consist of intellectual property such as trademarks and goodwill: for such partnerships, there are no significant negative consequences resulting from a technical termination.

3. *Transfer of an interest in a disregarded entity.* Suppose individual *X* owns disregarded entity *DE*, and *X* sells half of *DE* to *Y*. We know that *DE* becomes a partnership as a result of the transaction, Treas. Regs. §301.7701-3(a), but how is that treated as occurring? In Rev. Rul. 99-5, 1999-1 C.B. 434 (situation 1), the Service recharacterized such a transaction as a sale of half of the underlying assets from *X* to *Y* followed by the joint formation by *X* and *Y* of a new partnership. As a result, *X* will recognize gain or loss on the transaction and the partnership will take a fair market value basis in the assets deemed sold to *Y*.

The recharacterization would be different if *Y*, instead of buying a membership interest in *DE* from *X*, had contributed property directly to *DE* in exchange for a newly issued membership interest. Rev. Rul. 99-5 (situation 2) provides in that case that *X* and *Y* are treated as jointly forming a partnership, with *X* contributing the pre-transaction assets of *DE* simultaneously with *Y*'s contribution. Thus, neither *X* nor *Y* should recognize gain or loss on the transaction.

PROBLEMS

25-8. *A*, *B*, and *C* are each one-third partners in the *ABC* partnership. On February 1, 2013, *C* sells her partnership interest to *D*. On March 1, 2013, *D* sells her partnership interest to *E*. On April 1, 2013, *A* sells her interest to *F*. On May 1, 2013, *B* sells her interest to *G*. When does the partnership terminate and to whom are liquidating distributions made?

25-9. *P* and *Q* intend to form a joint venture in which each will have an equal stake. The partnership will own depreciable property, and *Q* may be forced to sell her interest in the venture within two or three years of formation.

a. Will the following structure avoid the possible technical termination otherwise triggered by *Q*'s exit? *P* and *Q* form the *PQ* partnership, with *P* owning 60 percent of *PQ* and *Q* owning 40 percent. *P*, *Q*, and *PQ* then form the *PQ* operating partnership, with *P* owning 14 percent of *PQ*-Operating, *PQ* owning 60 percent of *PQ*-Operating, and *Q* owning 26 percent of *PQ*-Operating. Be sure to consider the tiered partnership rules in Treas. Regs. §1.708-1(b)(2).
b. Could this structure be extended to give *Q* an overall 60-percent interest in the operating partnership without triggering a technical termination if *Q* sells her interest in the venture?

7. *Death of a Partner*

In general, property received from the estate of a decedent takes a fair market value basis in the hands of the transferee. §1014. However, this basis rule does not apply to income in respect of a decedent ("IRD") as defined in §691. In general, IRD within the meaning of §691 includes those items of income that would have been includible to the decedent had the decedent been an accrual taxpayer. In other words, IRD includes all accrued but unrealized items of income received by the estate or the decedent's successor.

If a partner dies, does the partnership interest qualify for a full step-up in basis under §1014 regardless of the assets held by the partnership? In a related context, the Tax Court has held that no basis step-up is appropriate with respect to the decedent partner's share of partnership unrealized receivables on the theory that if such receivables had been held directly by the decedent they would constitute IRD. Quick Trust v. Commissioner, 54 T.C. 1336 (1970), aff'd per curiam, 444 F.2d 90 (8th Cir. 1971); see also Woodhall v. Commissioner, 454 F.2d 226 (9th Cir. 1972). Such an approach is overbroad, however, because much of what constitutes an unrealized receivable under §751(c) (such as depreciation recapture) does not constitute IRD if held directly. See §691(a)(1). Note that §736(a) payments received by a decedent's successor always are treated as IRD by reason of §753.

C. PARTIAL DISPOSITIONS

A partner might sell some but not all of her interest in a partnership. There is surprisingly little authority on the proper computation of such a partial disposition, but the basics are clear. Gain or loss is determined by comparing the amount realized by the selling partner with the selling partner's adjusted basis in the interest sold. §1001(a).

The selling partner's adjusted basis in the interest sold is a portion of her total outside basis, with that total outside basis "equitably apportioned" between the interest sold and the interest retained. Treas. Regs. §1.61-6(a). Note that while no statutory provision or regulations expressly says so, it is the government's position that a partner has a single outside basis even if the partner owns multiple partnership interests in the same partnership. Rev. Rul. 84-53, 1984-1 C.B. 159. This position is consistent with the rule that a partner has a single capital account in a partnership even if the partners own multiple interests of different classes (such as a general partnership interest and a limited partnership interest). Treas. Regs. §1.704-1(b)(2)(iv)(b). After the sale, the capital account of the selling partner that is attributable to the transferred interest carries over to the transferee partner. Treas. Regs. §1.704-1(b)(2)(iv)(l).

1. *No Partnership Liabilities*

a. Partial Sale of a Single Interest

If a partner owns a single partnership interest and sells a portion of that interest, the portion of the selling partner's adjusted basis allocable to the interest sold should be the same proportion of the total outside basis as the value the sold interest bears to the selling partner's total interest. So, for example, if a partner owning a partnership interest worth $15,000 sells a portion of that interest for $5,000, the selling partner should allocate one-third of her outside basis to the sale. If the selling partner's outside basis immediately before the sale equaled $12,000, then the selling partner should recognize gain on the sale of $1,000.

b. Sale of One Interest Out of Many

Suppose *T* joins the *P* partnership by contributing cash of $5,000 in exchange for a general interest in the partnership. Sometime later, *T* contributes additional cash of $7,000 in exchange for a limited interest in the venture. Sometime later (after income and loss has been earned by the partnership and allocated among the partners and distributions have been made) when *T*'s outside basis again equals $12,000, *T* sells her limited interest for $5,000. Assume that at the time of sale, the combined value of *T*'s interests in the partnership equals $15,000.

As in the example immediately above, *T* should recognize gain on the sale of $1,000 because *T*'s outside basis should be allocated between the interest sold and the interest retained based on relative fair market values. It might seem as if *T* should somehow track her separate basis in the two interests, accounting for distributive shares of each interest and distributions on each interest. Most commentators do not agree with this approach, though, and the Service requires that the partner's unitary basis be allocated in proportion to relative values. Rev. Rul. 84-53, 1984-1 C.B. 159.

2. *Partnership Liabilities Are Present*

If the partnership has leveraged its assets, then the selling partner must account for this inside debt in computing gain from the sale of the partial interest. Again, there are no special statutory rules, suggesting that the debt implications of the sale will work out simply by applying the rules of §752. Alas, it is much more complicated than that.

The regulations provide that a reduction in a partner's share of partnership liabilities arising from the sale or exchange of an interest in the partnership is treated as an "amount realized" on the sale or exchange. Treas. Regs. §1.752-1(h). Thus, rather than treat such a reduction as a deemed distribution of cash, we treat the reduction as cash received on the sale. But are there any tax implications arising from a partner's share of the debt that is not reduced?

Consider the following. *X* and *Y* each own half of the *XY* partnership. *XY* owns Blackacre with inside basis of $400, fair market value of $500, and subject to a debt of $380. Each partner has an outside basis of $200. *Y* sells one-half of his interest (that is, 25 percent of the partnership) to *Z* for $30. Assume that one-quarter of the debt moves to *Z* as a result of the sale. *Y*'s gain on the sale equals $25, computed as follows: amount realized of $30 (for the cash) + $95 (for the debt) less allocable basis of $100 = $25. Since the property has a built-in gain of $100, and *Y* has in effect sold a quarter interest in the property, the $25 gain to *Y* on the sale is correct.

But suppose none of the debt shifts to *Z*. For example, the debt might be nonrecourse to the partnership with guarantees by *X* and *Y*, and *Z* might purchase half of *Y*'s interest in the venture but be unwilling to guarantee repayment of the debt. Now, how is *Y*'s sale gain computed? If we simply apply the rule of §1001 as before but remove the debt shift from *Y*'s amount realized, then we get the peculiar result that *Y* recognizes a loss of $70 (amount realized is reduced to $30 while *Y*'s allocable adjusted basis remains $100). But the partnership's asset has appreciated!

The Service has taken the position that when an existing partner sells a portion of its partnership interest, the selling partner must exclude from basis her share of entity-level debt that does not shift as a result of the sale. Rev. Rul. 84-53, 1984-1 C.B. 159.[3] While this ruling spoke to a partner who owned both a general partnership interest and a limited partnership interest, in one Field Service Advice this approach was extended to all partial sales of partnership interests. 1997 FSA Lexis 416 (October 15, 1997). On the facts above, this would mean that *Y*'s amount realized is $30, and *Y*'s adjusted basis is $5 (one-half of outside basis reduced by debt share), yielding a taxable gain of $25. While this surely is the correct result, it is hard to find any statutory or regulatory authority for the computation.

Y's outside basis (that is, *Y*'s adjusted basis in his partnership interest) unambiguously equals $200 because it includes *Y*'s $190 debt share. Longstanding regulations provide that "when a part of a part of larger property is sold, the cost or other basis of the entire property shall be equitably apportioned among the several parts." Treas. Regs. §1.61-6(a). Rev. Rul. 84-53 does not so much apportion the taxpayer's outside basis as defer its use. To see this, note that if the taxpayer had sold the other half of the partnership interest, the tax result would be the same. That is, the revenue ruling in effect allocates all of the taxpayer's debt basis to whatever portion of the partnership interest is retained rather than sold. This does not seem like an equitable apportionment, but it does produce the correct result in this case.[4]

3. This rule is modified if the selling partner's outside basis is less than her share of the partnership's liabilities to avoid the possibility of a negative basis in the interest sold.

4. It may not produce correct results in all cases. See Howard E. Abrams, Partnership COD Income and Other Debt Issues, 126 Tax Notes 845 (Feb. 15, 2010); Howard E. Abrams, Now You See It, Now You Don't: Exiting a Partnership and Making Gain Disappear, 50 Tax Mgmt. Mem. 75 (2009).

26

Loss Limitations

Under §702(a) (especially §702(a)(8)), a partner includes her distributive share of partnership tax items in her individual gross income. Each partner's distributive share is determined under §704, and through it (usually) by the partnership agreement. Thus, partnership items of income, deduction, credit, and loss are claimed by a partner to the extent of her distributive share of each item.

Does that mean a partner reports all items of distributive share on her individual return? Absolutely not! With respect to distributive share of partnership loss, a variety of limitations must be overcome before the tax benefit of such losses can flow through to the partner's return. For example, capital losses cannot, in general, offset ordinary income. See §1211(b). In this chapter we will look at four similar loss limitations: the first, §704(d), applies exclusively to distributive share of partnership loss, while the others, §465, §469, and §163(d), apply to all losses including but not limited to partnership distributive shares.

A. SECTION 704(d): THE OUTSIDE BASIS LIMITATION

Under §704(d), a partner's distributive share of partnership loss can be claimed on the partner's individual tax return only to the extent of the partner's outside basis. Although neither the Code nor the regulations promulgated under §704(d) specifically say so, the term "loss" in this context includes all partnership deductions.[1] The limitation of §704(d) only arises at the conclusion of each partnership taxable year (because that is when distributive share is determined), and in applying the §704(d) limitation, the regulations specifically provide that the partner's outside basis is first adjusted upward for distributive share of partnership income. Treas. Regs. §1.704-1(d)(2). The partner's outside basis is also adjusted downward for distributions deemed made on the last day of the taxable year (see Treas. Regs.

1. See, e.g., Rev. Rul. 77-401, 1977-2 C.B. 215; Rev. Rul. 77-311, 1977-2 C.B. 218.

§1.731-1(a)(1)(ii)) and distributive share of nondeductible, noncapitalizable partnership expenses (such as illegal bribes and kickbacks).[2]

Losses disallowed under §704(d) are not lost forever. Rather, they are deferred until the partner's year-end outside basis is able to absorb them. For example, suppose partner *X* has an outside basis of $60 and a distributive share of partnership loss equal to $100. By reason of §704(d), *X* will be allowed to claim only $60 of the partnership's loss on her individual return. The remainder of the loss will be suspended. If *X*'s outside basis the following year exceeds next year's distributive share of loss by $40 or more, all of the suspended loss will be allowed at that time. If, though, *X*'s outside basis next year is $50 while her share of distributive loss is $40, only $10 of the suspended loss will be allowed then and the remaining $30 will continue to be suspended to the following year, or later.

Although §704(d) seems to suspend a loss until additional funds are contributed to the partnership (note the use of the word "repaid" in the final sentence of §704(d)), the regulations make clear that any year-end positive outside basis can revive a suspended loss. Treas. Regs. §1.704-1(d)(1), §1.704-1(d)(4) (example 1). Accordingly, not only contributions but also distributive share of partnership income as well as allocations of partnership debt can trigger recognition of a suspended loss.

Note that if §704(d) suspends a partner's loss in any year but the partner is allocated more than one type of loss, the partner suspends a proportionate amount of each loss. See Treas. Regs. §1.704-1(d)(2). For example, if *X* has an $8,000 outside basis and is allocated a $15,000 capital loss and a $5,000 ordinary loss, $12,000 of the aggregate loss is suspended under §704(d). Thus, three-fifths ($12,000/$20,000) of each loss is suspended, that being $9,000 of the capital loss and $3,000 of the ordinary loss.

A partner's capital account, like outside basis, is adjusted downward to reflect the partner's distributive share of partnership loss. If some of the partner's distributive share is disallowed by reason of §704(d), should the partner's capital account be adjusted only for that portion of the loss allowed? Recall that capital accounts reflect the economic relationships among the partners. Capital accounts are not, therefore, adjusted for tax aspects of partnership transactions per se. Distributive shares of partnership income and loss affect capital accounts not because such shares are includible on the partners' individual income tax returns but because such shares correspond to how the partners have agreed to allocate economic gain and loss. For example, distributive shares of tax-exempt income increase capital accounts just as do distributive shares of taxable income even though tax-exempt income has no effect on the partners' individual tax returns. Accordingly, distributive share of partnership loss reduces capital accounts without regard to the impact, if any, of §704(d).

1. The Relation of §704(d) to §704(c)

Consider the following example: *A* and *B* form the *AB* general partnership as equal partners, with *A* contributing cash of $500 and *B* contributing property worth $500

2. A more common nondeductible, noncapitalizable item is the 50 percent of meals and entertainment expenses disallowed by §274(n).

but having an adjusted basis of $100. In its first year of operation, the partnership sustains a taxable loss of $300. As equal partners, *A* and *B* are each allocated half of the partnership's loss. But for application of §704(d), each partner would report a loss of $150 on her individual return as her distributive share. Because of §704(d), though, *B* can report only $100 of that loss, with the remaining $50 of loss suspended until *B*'s year-end outside basis is sufficient to absorb it.

B's distributive share of partnership loss is disallowed presumably because it is inappropriate for *B* to recognize a loss from the partnership's activity in excess of *B*'s after-tax investment in the partnership. *B*'s book share of the loss equals $150 because *B*'s capital account was credited with the *value* of the property *B* contributed to the venture. But until the pre-contribution unrealized appreciation in that property is taxed, *B*'s investment has consisted primarily of pretax dollars.

In general, only after-tax investments can generate deductions. For example, suppose individual *C* owns property (outside of a partnership) with a value of $500 and an adjusted basis of $100. If the entire investment is lost, *C*'s deduction cannot exceed $100: losing the $400 of unrealized appreciation cannot produce a deduction because it is the loss of basis, not of value, that produces a tax deduction. Recall the definition of "loss" in §1001(a).

Further, allowing a partner to recognize distributive share of loss in excess of outside basis would force the partner to take a negative basis in her partnership interest. As we have seen, recognition of distributive share of partnership loss must be coupled with an outside basis decrease if the loss is not to be recognized twice, once as distributive share and a second time upon disposition of the partnership interest.

There is, of course, a way to increase investment basis without making a contribution of after-tax dollars: promise to make an after-tax contribution in the future. In the case of a nonpartnership investment, this means borrowing and incorporating the debt proceeds in the investment. In a partnership context, debt could be introduced in either of two ways: (1) have the partner borrow directly (outside debt) or (2) have the partnership borrow and attribute the debt to the partner under §752 (inside debt). We will consider the impact of debt on the application of §704(d) in Section C below.

2. *Transfers of Partnership Interests*

Suppose *P* transfers her partnership interest after some prior distributive share of partnership loss had been suspended under §704(d). Should *P* be entitled to claim the suspended loss upon disposition of the interest? Should the suspended loss be available to the transferee of *P*'s partnership interest? Under §704(d), a suspended loss is never available to a transferee, although the loss may be available to the transferor if the transfer of the partnership interest is a taxable disposition.

Reconsider the *AB* general partnership in which *A* contributed cash of $500, and *B* contributed property with value of $500 and an adjusted basis of $100. As discussed above, if the partnership sustains a taxable loss of $300, allocable equally to *A* and *B*, only $100 of *B*'s share will be allowable, and the remaining $50 of distributive share of loss will be suspended under §704(d). If *B* sells her partnership interest for $400 in the middle of the next year, can *B* claim any of the suspended $50 of loss?

It depends. Disposition of a partnership interest closes the partnership's taxable year with respect to the transferor partner. §706(c)(2)(A). Accordingly, the sale forces *B* to recognize her share of the partnership's income and loss as of the date of sale, computed either by an interim closing of the partnership's books or by apportionment of the partnership's year-end totals. See Treas. Regs. §1.706-1(c)(2)(ii). If *B*'s distributive share of partnership income for this short partnership year exceeds *B*'s distributive share of loss, then *B*'s year-end outside basis will be positive, and *B* will be entitled to reclaim some or all of the suspended loss. For example, if *B*'s share of income for the short partnership taxable year equals $140, and *B*'s share of loss equals $100, *B* will be entitled to claim $40 of the $50 suspended loss. Of course, if *B* made a contribution to the partnership during this same period, the outside basis increase resulting from such a contribution also would allow *B* to claim some or all of the suspended loss, depending on the extent of the outside basis increase resulting from the contribution. In either case, if the suspended loss were gone forever, how would that affect *B*?

If, in the example above, only $40 of *B*'s suspended loss is allowable to *B* as a result of *B*'s sale of her partnership interest, what happens to the remaining $10 of suspended loss? It is lost forever, and that is the appropriate result. Recall that §704(d) requires a partner to trade loss recognition for outside basis: In the absence of §704(d), excess distributive share of loss would be recognized but outside basis would become negative. When a partner sells her partnership interest, the §704(d) suspended loss is gone forever but the dispositional gain on sale of the interest is computed with reference to a zero (not negative) outside basis. The transferee is not entitled to the suspended loss because the transferor in effect used it on disposition of the partnership interest by reporting less gain.

Note that §704(d) is a *timing* provision: a loss is suspended until outside basis can absorb it or until a taxable disposition has, in effect, consumed it. But what if a partner with a suspended §704(d) loss transfers the partnership interest in a tax-free transaction? Should the suspended loss be available to the transferee if her year-end outside basis can absorb it?

The transferee should be able to reclaim the suspended loss of her transferor when her year-end outside basis becomes positive. Of course, the issue still is one of timing: If the transferee can claim the suspended loss, her outside basis will decrease pro tanto and so there will be more gain (or less loss) upon disposition of her partnership interest. Nonetheless, since the partnership sustained a loss in the past that was not, by reason of §704(d), claimed on any partner's individual tax return, it seems appropriate for the transferee to claim the transferor's suspended loss if the transfer was, for example, by gift. Unfortunately, there appears to be no authority for the transfer of a §704(d) suspended loss to a transferee.

PROBLEM

26-1. *J* is a partner in the *JKL* partnership and has a 10 percent interest in profits and losses. Both *J* and the partnership use the calendar year as their taxable year and each uses the cash receipts and disbursements method of accounting. As of December 30, 2013, *J* has an outside basis and capital account of $10,000. For the year ending December 31, 2013, the partnership reports a net loss of $250,000. On June 30, 2014, *J* sells her partnership interest to Buyer for $15,000. Between

January 1, 2014, and June 30, 2014, the partnership incurs $300,000 in losses. Between July 1, 2014, and December 31, 2014, the partnership recognizes $400,000 of income in excess of deductions.

a. How much of the 2013 loss can *J* claim?
b. How much of the 2014 loss can *J* claim, assuming the partnership uses an interim closing of the books to determine *J*'s distributive share for 2014? How does your answer change if the partnership allocates its year-end totals ratably over the year?
c. *J* makes a payment to the partnership in December of 2014 equal to her closing capital account deficit. Does this payment allow *J* to claim an additional share of partnership losses? If not, what are the tax consequences of the payment?

B. SECTION 465: THE AT-RISK LIMITATION

1. *An Overview of §465*

Section 465 disallows deductions from an activity to the extent such deductions exceed the investor's "at-risk" investment in the activity, with such disallowed deductions deferred until that time, if ever, when the taxpayer's at-risk investment increases. Section 465 thus is similar to §704(d), with the taxpayer's at-risk investment in §465 standing in for outside basis in §704(d). Section 465, though, is broader in scope than §704(d) in that §465 can apply to any investment activity whether conducted in a partnership or otherwise. However, §465 applies primarily to individuals (including individuals who invest in an activity as partners or S corporation shareholders), although it also applies to certain closely held C corporations. See §465(a)(1).

The general rule of disallowance of §465 is contained in §465(a)(1). By reason of §465(a)(2), losses disallowed under §465(a)(1) are suspended only until the taxpayer's at-risk investment in the activity increases or income from the activity is includible by the taxpayer. In general, this will occur no later than when the taxpayer disposes of her interest in the activity in a taxable transaction. An example will help make this clear, but before we can understand an example we must look at some of the defined terms in §465.

A taxpayer's amount "at-risk" in an activity is defined in §465(b) to include all cash invested, the adjusted basis of all property contributed, and most borrowed amounts as to which the taxpayer is personally responsible for repayment. Thus, a taxpayer's amount at risk in an investment is similar to the taxpayer's adjusted basis in the property with the major difference being that nonrecourse loans can add to basis but will not, in general, increase a taxpayer's amount at risk. However, some nonrecourse loans are treated as at-risk contributions in real estate investments, see §465(b)(6), while some fully recourse loans are excluded, see §465(b)(3). We will return to these details in the definition of "at-risk" later.

Section 465(a)(1) broadly disallows "loss[es]" in excess of at-risk investment, and "loss" is defined in §465(d) to include "the excess of the deductions . . . allocable to an activity . . . over the income . . . from such activity." Thus, the term "loss" is given a much greater scope than is usual under §1001(a). Under §465(d), *all* deductions including ordinary and necessary business expenses and depreciation can be losses subject to the loss limitation rule of §465(a)(1). On the other hand, no deduction is a §465 "loss" except to the extent it exceeds the taxpayer's income from the activity. Thus, the loss limitation rule of §465(a)(1) applies only to deductions from an activity in excess of the taxpayer's income from the activity, and so the at-risk limitation of §465 is an anti-shelter rule just like §704(d), the passive activity loss rules of §469, and the investment interest limitation of §163(d).

Section 465(a)(1) by its terms only applies to certain specified activities. This was once an important constraint on the application of §465 because only the investment activities specified in §465(c)(1) were covered. However, §465 has applied to all investment activities since 1979, see §465(c)(3). Section 465(c)(3) by its language includes any activity engaged in by the taxpayer in carrying on a trade or business or for the production of income.

One thing that has not changed since §465 was first enacted in 1976 is that it generally applies on an activity-by-activity basis. See §465(a)(1) (final flush language). Multiple activities may be aggregated only under two circumstances. First, aggregation is allowed if the activities constitute a single trade or business and the taxpayer actively participates in management of that trade or business. §465(c)(3)(B)(i). Second, aggregation is allowed if the activities constitute a trade or business carried on by a partnership or S corporation and 65 percent of the losses for the taxable year are allocable to persons who actively participate in the management of the trade or business. If neither situation exists, the activities are treated separately. §465(c)(3)(B)(ii).

This is an important aspect of §465 because, as an anti-shelter provision, §465 only limits losses in excess of income. Application on an activity-by-activity basis means that income from one venture cannot be offset by a loss (in excess of amounts at risk) from another. In contradistinction, §704(d) applies to all investments of a single partnership and the passive-loss rules of §469 allow income from one passive investment to be offset by a loss from almost any other passive investment.

It is time to consider an example. Individual *X* purchases an apartment complex for $1,000,000, paying $100,000 down and signing a nonrecourse note for the remaining $900,000. Assume that the apartments generate income of $30,000, deductible expenses of $20,000, and a depreciation deduction of $50,000 per year. Finally, assume that the special rule in §465(b)(6) applicable to certain real estate financing does not apply.

We know that *X* must include the $30,000 in income, but may *X* also claim the deductions of $70,000? The first $30,000 of deductions are not subject to limitation under §465 because of the definition of "loss" in §465(d): Only deductions *in excess of* the investment's income are losses under §465. As to the remaining $40,000 of deductions, they are losses under §465 (and thus are subject to §465), but in the first year they are not disallowed by §465(a) because *X*'s amount at risk equals $100,000. Remember that losses under §465(d) are disallowed only to the extent that they exceed the taxpayer's amount at risk.

After this first year, *X*'s deduction of $40,000 of §465 "losses" will have caused *X*'s amount at risk to decrease from $100,000 down to $60,000, and *X*'s adjusted basis in the property will have declined from $1,000,000 to $950,000 (because of the depreciation deduction of $50,000). Year 2 mirrors year 1, with *X* including $30,000 and deducting $70,000 (of which $50,000 is depreciation), so *X*'s amount at risk will further decline to $20,000, and X's adjusted basis in the property will drop to $900,000.

Year 3 of the investment triggers §465(a). In year 3, there is $30,000 of income and $70,000 of deduction. Once again, the first $30,000 of deductions are not subject to §465 because they do not exceed the activity's income and so are not "losses" under §465(d). The remaining $40,000 of deductions are subject to §465, and because the taxpayer's amount at risk equals only $20,000, only $20,000 of deductions are allowable. The remaining $20,000 are disallowed under §465(a)(1), and these deductions will be treated as deductions in the next year pursuant to §465(a)(2).

Before considering year 4 of the investment, we must determine X's adjusted basis in the property. Prior to year 3, X's adjusted basis in the property was $900,000. In year 3, the property generated $50,000 of depreciation. Thus, in the absence of §465 X's adjusted basis in the property would be $850,000.

That analysis does not change in the presence of §465: The basis of the property becomes $850,000 after year 3 even though some of the depreciation deduction was disallowed by reason of §465(a)(1). This rule may seem peculiar to you: why should basis go down if the depreciation deduction was disallowed? The answer is that the depreciation deduction was not disallowed but merely suspended: Under §465(a)(2), the deduction will reappear in some subsequent year. Follow the example two more years and everything will become clear.

In the next year there again is income of $30,000, all of which is taxable to X. In addition, there are $90,000 of deductions, $70,000 arising this year and $20,000 carried forward from the prior year under §465(a)(2). Of these deductions, $30,000 are not "losses" under §465 and so are allowable, and the remaining $60,000 of deductions are disallowed under §465(a)(1). Note that if there had been rental income of $90,000 or more, all the deductions would have been allowable because they would not be "losses" within the meaning of §465(d). Furthermore, the deductions would have been allowable even without additional investment income had X made an additional at-risk investment.

At the end of year 4, X's adjusted basis in the property is $800,000, X's at-risk investment is $0, and $60,000 of deductions have been suspended. Suppose X now defaults on the mortgage and loses the property. As a result of the foreclosure, X realizes income of $100,000 under the *Tufts* doctrine.[3] The suspended deductions are now allowable because the dispositional gain ensures that the suspended deductions do not exceed the investment's income for the year. That is, in the year of disposition the suspended deductions will not be §465(d) "losses" because they do not exceed the dispositional income. And because they are not §465(d) losses, they are not disallowed by operation of §465(a)(1).

2. *The §465 Proposed Regulations*

Proposed in 1979, the regulations under §465 have yet to be either adopted in final form or withdrawn. Consequently, their status is uncertain. Nevertheless, they can help develop an understanding of the more subtle applications of §465. For example, loss that exceeds the taxpayer's amount at risk cannot drive the amount

3. Commissioner v. Tufts, 461 U.S. 300 (1983); Treas. Regs. §1.1001-2(a).

at risk negative but instead must be suspended. Proposed regulation §1.465-3(b), however, explains that amount at risk may be reduced below zero in some cases. This can occur when a taxpayer receives a distribution from an activity in excess of the taxpayer's amount at risk. For example, if a taxpayer's amount at risk in an activity is $90 and the taxpayer is distributed $110 from the activity, the taxpayer's amount at risk is reduced to negative $20. Similarly, if a recourse loan of $110 is converted to nonrecourse the amount at risk will also be reduced to negative $20.

Another aspect of the proposed regulations is the treatment of repayments based on the occurrence of a contingency. The nature of the contingent liability determines the effect on the taxpayer's amount at risk. If the likelihood of the contingency occurring is such that the taxpayer is effectively protected against loss then the amount is not treated as being at-risk. Conversely, amounts will be considered at-risk where the likelihood of the contingency occurring is not such that the taxpayer is effectively protected from risk or the protection does not cover all likely possibilities. Specifically, the regulations contemplate the purchasing of hazard insurance protection for contributed assets. Hazard insurance protection will not cause a taxpayer to be considered "not at risk." See Prop. Treas. Regs. §1.465-4(c).

The proposed regulations also illustrate an instance in which a taxpayer's amount at risk will be increased even though the taxpayer is not personally liable for a borrowed amount. Where an amount used in an activity covered by §465 is secured by property not used in the activity, the net fair market value of the secured property will equal the increase in amount at risk. See Prop. Treas. Regs. §1.465-25(a)(1).[4] If the net fair market value of the secured property changes, the amount at risk in the activity will be adjusted to reflect the change in net fair market value. Note, though, that revaluation of the pledged security is severely constrained. Prop. Treas. Regs. §1.465-25(a)(4). Note also that any amounts paid on the loan must first be applied to that portion of the loan, if any, that exceeds the net fair market value of the secured property. Consequently, those amounts will not increase amount at risk but will be considered repayment of a nonrecourse loan secured by property used in the activity. See Prop. Treas. Regs. §1.465-25(a)(2). If the property used as security is later contributed to the activity, the amount at risk attributed to the property will be adjusted as if the net fair market value of the property was reduced to zero. Prop. Treas. Regs. §1.465-25(a)(3).

3. *Application of §465 to Partners and Partnerships*

Section 465 does not apply to partnerships but only to their partners.[5] Because §465 applies on an activity-by-activity basis, a partner's distributive share of losses otherwise allowable can be claimed on a partner's individual return only to the

4. This rule has the counterintuitive implication that a taxpayer holding appreciated property will have a greater amount at risk if the property is pledged rather than contributed to the activity. A similar rule applies in the partnership context with respect to the allocation of recourse debt. See Treas. Regs. §1.752-2(h)(1).

5. If one partnership (the "upper-tier partnership") owns an interest in a second partnership (the "lower-tier partnership"), the application of §465 to partners in the upper-tier partnership will require (1) a computation of at-risk amounts in the lower-tier partnership, (2) an allocation of those amounts to its partners including the upper-tier partnership, and (3) an analysis of the at-risk amounts of the upper-tier partnership including the pass-thru of at-risk amounts from the lower-tier partnership.

extent of the partner's distributive share of income plus the partner's at-risk investment in the partnership. Because §704(d) is applied before §465, deductions in excess of a partner's outside basis will never reach the disallowance rule of §465(a)(1). Accordingly, the impact of §465 is limited to distributive share of partnership loss *less than* a partner's outside basis but *more than* the partner's at-risk investment in the partnership.

How can such a situation arise? Because contributions to the partnership of cash and property increase outside basis and at-risk investment equally, only deductions in excess of the adjusted basis of contributed property can be subject to §465. Contributed appreciated property and partnership debt—more specifically, nonrecourse partnership debt that increases outside basis but that does not qualify as an at-risk amount—is what presents the possibility of application of §465(a)(1).

For example, suppose *A* and *B* form the *AB* general partnership as equal partners by contributing cash of $500 each. If the partnership then purchases a computer for $10,000 by paying $1,000 down and signing a nonrecourse note for $9,000, each partner's outside basis will equal $5,000. However, because borrowed funds only constitute at-risk funds to the extent the partners are personally liable for repayment, §465(b)(2)(A), each partner's at-risk investment remains at $500. Accordingly, neither *A* nor *B* will be entitled to claim a distributive share of partnership loss in excess of $500 unless further contributions are made, partnership income is recognized but not distributed, or the loan is converted to a recourse obligation. Note if a loan starts out as recourse and then is converted to a nonrecourse obligation, the conversion may trigger income recognition under §465(e).

A second way in which §465 can apply to a partnership investment is by outside nonrecourse borrowing. Suppose individual *X* borrows $10,000 to contribute to partnership *P*, and suppose further that this loan is nonrecourse and secured only by *P*'s partnership interest. While *P* will have an outside basis of $10,000 under §722, *P* should have no at-risk investment because *P* is not personally liable for repayment of the loan.

Not all nonrecourse partnership borrowing is disqualified under §465(b)(2). The real estate industry successfully lobbied for §465(b)(6) providing that nonrecourse borrowing against a real estate investment *is* treated as an at-risk amount so long as the lender is a government instrumentality, see §465(b)(6)(B)(ii), or is a qualified person as defined in §465(b)(6)(D).[6] Combining the rules of §§752, 704(d), and 465, we see that only nonrecourse funding of a real estate investment can provide limited partners with deductions in excess of contributions: recourse financing will not provide *limited* partners with outside basis while nonrecourse financing will not provide an at-risk increase except as to real estate investments.

Just as real estate provides the one exception to the rule that nonrecourse financing will not satisfy §465, there is also one situation in which fully recourse financing will not qualify as at-risk. Under §§465(b)(3) and 465(c)(3)(D), borrowed funds will not be treated as at-risk even if the borrower is fully liable for repayment if the lender is "any person who has an interest in [the] activity," where the definition of an "interest in [the] activity" is left undefined except that being only a creditor is *not* a tainted interest. See §465(b)(3)(B)(i). The legislative history of §465 fails to explain why a fully recourse loan should be treated as nonrecourse if made from one

6. See generally Howard E. Abrams, New Changes to the At-Risk Rules, 6 J. Passthrough Taxation 37 (Sept.-Oct. 2003).

involved in the activity, but presumably Congress was afraid that loans between involved parties are easy to fabricate and often unenforced. This aspect of §465 finds a surprising resonance in the application of §704(d). See below.

Suppose a partner guarantees a nonrecourse loan of the partnership. For allocating the debt under §752, the debt is treated as recourse because the guarantor-partner has no ability to seek reimbursement from any other partner. Should such a guarantee also increase the guarantor-partner's "at-risk" amount? Clearly it should, although the regulations seem to take the opposite view. See Prop. Treas. Regs. §1.465-6(d). For a cogent analysis of this regulation and its failings, see Richard W. Harris & Louis H. Moran, Guaranteed LLC Debt: Does the Guarantor-Member Receive At-Risk Basis, 91 J. Taxation 16 (1999).

PROBLEM

26-2. Individual *K* invests $10,000 in the *KLM* partnership. The partnership purchases real estate from an unrelated third-party for $1,000,000, paying $100,000 in cash and signing a recourse note for the remaining $900,000. Assume that *K*'s share of the debt is $25,000 under §752. If *K*'s distributive share of loss for each of the first two years is $20,000 (and *K* has no distributive share of income during those years), how much partnership loss can *K* claim on her individual return for the first two years, and what is *K*'s outside basis at the end of the second year? If *K* has a $40,000 distributive share of income for the partnership's third year, what does *K* put on her individual return from the partnership's activities?

C. A REEXAMINATION OF §704(d) AND ITS RELATION TO §704(b)

1. *Misallocation of Loss*

Consider the following example: *X* and *Y* form the *XY* general partnership by contributing cash of $10,000 each. The partnership incurs no debt, and it generates deductions of $12,000 in its first year. What are the tax consequences to *X* and *Y* if this entire deduction is allocated to *X*?

So long as the partnership maintains proper capital accounts and provides that liquidating proceeds will be distributed in accordance with final capital account balances, and each partner has a deficit restoration obligation, this allocation is valid under §704(b) because it has substantial economic effect. To be sure, the allocation drives *X*'s capital account negative, but that is irrelevant in light of *X*'s deficit restoration obligation. The only relevance of *X*'s negative capital account is that if *X*'s partnership interest is liquidated before *X*'s capital account becomes positive, *X* will be obligated to restore the amount of her capital account deficit to the partnership for distribution to creditors or to *Y*. For example, if the partnership liquidates immediately after its first year, *X* will be required to contribute $2,000 for distribution to *Y*.

Even though the allocation of the partnership's $12,000 deduction to *X* satisfies the substantial economic effect test of §704(b), *X* will not be entitled to claim the full $12,000 deduction on her individual return because of §704(d). Prior to the allocation, *X*'s outside basis totals $10,000. Under §704(d), distributive share of loss is suspended to the extent it exceeds outside basis. Accordingly, *X* may claim only $10,000 of her $12,000 distributive share of loss.

Why? The problem is *not* that *X* will bear the economic burden of the loss only to the extent of $10,000: Satisfaction of the substantial economic effect test ensures that the economic benefits and burdens associated with tax allocations follow the allocations. Treas. Regs. §1.704-1(b)(2)(ii)(a). Section 704(d) plainly is about something *other than* economic effect, but it is less than obvious just what that might be.

In this example, the §704(d) problem could have been avoided by allocating no more than $10,000 of the loss to *X* so that the remaining loss could be absorbed by *Y*'s outside basis. In general, §704(d) problems always can be avoided in this way because the aggregate of all partners' outside bases should be sufficient to cover their partnership's total loss. A partnership's total loss (deductible and nondeductible combined) should never exceed its total inside basis — recovery of basis, after all, is what a loss (or other deduction) represents. Further, the aggregate outside basis will almost always equal aggregate inside basis. Thus, if total partnership loss will not exceed aggregate inside basis, it generally will not exceed aggregate outside basis, and that means that all losses can be claimed without implicating §704(d) if the losses are allocated properly.

In one sense, then, §704(d) is not about excess deductions but about misallocation of deductions. Except in very limited circumstances, a partnership can avoid triggering §704(d) by reallocating its losses. Of course, the substantiality requirement of §704(b) imposes some limitations on the partnership's ability to manipulate subsequent allocations of income and loss to offset earlier allocations. Still, suspended losses under §704(d) should be avoidable by careful planning and tailored allocations.

That §704(d) often can be avoided does not explain why we have §704(d). To answer that question, note that if the partnership has no §704(c) problems, and putting aside the possibility of partnership debt, outside bases should equal capital accounts. A distributive loss that would implicate §704(d) — that is, a distributive share of loss in excess of outside basis — also would drive the partner's capital account negative. Negative capital accounts present no difficulties (as to general partners) under the substantial economic effect test of §704(b), but §704(d) is not satisfied. Why?

The reason that general partners can have negative capital accounts without violating the economic effect test is that they are subject to a capital account deficit restoration obligation. Reconsider the *XY* example above, with *X* being allocated the entire $12,000 first year loss. This allocation reduces *X*'s capital account to negative $2,000, so that if the partnership were to liquidate immediately, *X* would owe $2,000 to *Y*.

In effect, *X* has borrowed $2,000 from *Y*. Twelve thousand dollars of the partners' capital was lost in the first year, which means that if the entire loss is allocated to *X*, we are treating *X* as losing everything she contributed to the partnership plus

$2,000 more. This additional $2,000 came from *Y*, and *X*'s capital account deficit restoration obligation ensures that *X* cannot leave the partnership without repaying the debt. That is, in the absence of partnership indebtedness a deficit capital account means that one partner has borrowed from another.

Indeed, partners *X* and *Y* could have avoided the §704(d) problem entirely by making their borrowing explicit. Suppose that *Y* had loaned *X* $2,000, and then the partnership had been formed by *X* contributing cash of $12,000 (her original $10,000 plus the borrowed $2,000) and *Y* contributing cash of $8,000. Again there is $20,000 invested in the partnership, but now the first year's loss of $12,000 can be allocated to *X* without implicating §704(d) because *X*'s outside basis can absorb the entire $12,000 distributive share of loss. By substituting explicit borrowing outside the partnership for the implicit borrowing within the partnership created by a negative capital account, *X* and *Y* can avoid the limitation of §704(d).

But *X* still cannot claim more than $10,000 of partnership loss on her individual return! Having escaped the clutches of §704(d), the partners have landed squarely within the confines of §465 because *X*'s amount at risk is only $10,000. To be sure, *X* has contributed a full $12,000 to the partnership, but of that amount, $2,000 was borrowed. Further, although *X* is fully responsible for repayment of her debt to *Y*, the borrowed proceeds are not treated as "at-risk" because *X*'s lender (that is, *Y*) has an interest in the partnership. Recall that even fully recourse loans do not contribute to a taxpayer's at-risk amount if the lender "has an interest in [the] activity" other than as a creditor. See §465(b)(3).

At least in the context of a partnership without debt (and assuming no §704(c) problems), the effect of §704(d) is to ensure that the partners cannot avoid the related party rules of §465 by implicitly borrowing within the partnership. This cannot have been the rationale for enactment of §704(d) — §704(d) was enacted decades before §465 — but it does provide some support for §704(d) as part of the current Code.

Now let us add some partnership borrowing to the example. Once again, suppose *X* and *Y* each contribute $10,000 to the *XY* general partnership. Once again, assume that the partnership loses $12,000 during its first year. We will again try to allocate the entire loss to partner *X*, but now assume that the partnership has borrowed $10,000 from some third-party lender on a fully recourse basis. Can *X* now claim the entire $12,000 loss?

X can claim the entire loss without limitation under §704(d) because *X*'s outside basis is increased to $15,000 under §752(a) by reason of the partnership debt. In the absence of the partnership's borrowing, *X* cannot claim more than $10,000 of partnership loss on her individual return because of §704(d). Existence of the debt, though, allows *X* to claim up to $15,000 of losses because partnership indebtedness increases outside basis. This miraculous effect of the partnership debt on *X*'s ability to claim distributive share of loss in excess of actual contributions should cause you pause, though, because the partnership debt has had no real effect on *X*'s economic position. Recall that, even in the absence of any partnership borrowing, *X*'s distributive share of loss in excess of her capital contribution (implicitly) resulted in a loan from *X* to *Y* of $2,000. Whether the partnership incurs any liability or not, the excess allocation of loss to *X* imposes a repayment obligation on *X*. Why should the happenstance of a third-party lender be relevant?

Once again, recall §465. Under that section, borrowed funds contribute to a taxpayer's amount at risk so long as the taxpayer is responsible for repayment of the loan *and* the lender does not have an interest in the investment activity. Sections 752(a) and 704(d) seem to echo this rule by increasing outside basis for a partner's share of partnership debt but not for inside borrowing implicitly occurring whenever one partner's capital account goes negative.

However, the existence of third-party debt ought to be irrelevant to the application of §704(d). Once again, reconsider the *XY* example, and look at the partnership books following the partners' contributions and the borrowing by the partnership of $10,000. The partnership has $30,000 of cash, each partner has an initial capital account of $10,000, and the partnership owes $10,000. Once $12,000 is lost, the partnership's assets have declined to $18,000, and *X*'s capital account has dropped to negative $2,000; *Y*'s capital account remains at $10,000.

If the partnership liquidates immediately, *X* will be required to contribute $2,000 to the partnership by reason of her capital account deficit restoration obligation. That $2,000 will not, though, be distributed to the third-party lender: The partnership's indebtedness is only $10,000, and the partnership has assets of $18,000 even without *X*'s contribution arising from her capital account deficit restoration obligation. The $2,000 that *X* must contribute is for distribution to *Y*, and the existence of the third-party loan is an economic irrelevancy. Because the third-party lender must be paid before *Y* is entitled to receive her partnership capital, *X*'s negative capital account represents a loan from *Y* and not from the third-party lender.

If §704(d) were to backstop §465 properly, distributive share of partnership loss would be disallowed only to the extent it reflects an implicit loan from one partner to another. Such an implicit loan arises whenever one partner's distributive share of loss forces that partner's capital account negative while the aggregate of all capital accounts remains positive. Distributive share of loss causing a negative capital account should not be disallowed when the sum of all partners' capital accounts is negative, for it is at that point that the capital account deficit restoration obligations reflect obligations to third-party lenders and not to other partners.

PROBLEM

26-3. *X*, *Y*, and *Z* form the *XYZ* general partnership, with *X* contributing cash of $10 and *Y* and *Z* contributing cash of $100 each. The partnership borrows $60, and profits and losses are generally allocated one-third to each partner except as follows. In year 1, the partnership loses $70, and this loss is allocated entirely to *X*. In year 2, the partnership loses $80, and this loss is allocated entirely to *Y*. What are the tax consequences of these transactions, and how do the partnership books stand at the close of year 2?

2. *Contributions of Notes*

Suppose a taxpayer joins a partnership by contributing a promise to pay a sum certain, plus fair interest, in exchange for a partnership interest. That is, suppose the partner contributes her own note to the partnership. What are the tax consequences of the contribution, and what happens when the note is paid?

Outside of the partnership context, we know that acquisition indebtedness generally is treated like cash. That is, a taxpayer who purchases a building for $1,000,000 takes a basis in the building equal to the full cost whether she pays with cash, a note, or cash plus a note. In essence, all taxpayers accrue their debt obligations, even those otherwise using the cash method of accounting. Consistent with this approach, payment of the note has no tax consequences and release of the debt without payment yields income (*Kirby Lumber* or *Tufts* income) to the debtor.

Should a rule for the purchase of a partnership interest be any different? Surprisingly, the courts have said that it should be. In Oden v. Commissioner,[7] the Tax Court held that a taxpayer transferring his own note to a partnership in exchange for a partnership interest acquired a zero basis in his partnership interest under §722. According to the court, the taxpayer's basis in the note was zero because the taxpayer paid nothing for it. Thus, the court reasoned, the substitute basis rule of §722 gives the taxpayer the same zero basis in the partnership interest.

What little merit this overly technical interpretation of §722 possesses[8] is more than outweighed by the disastrous implications of giving the contributing partner a zero outside basis. If the court is correct that the taxpayer takes an initial outside basis of zero under §722, then it must be the case that the partnership takes a zero basis in the note under §723. Accordingly, if the partnership sells the note, it will recognize income equal to the entire amount realized on the sale. Yet had the partner simply borrowed the same amount from a third party and then contributed the cash to the partnership ab initio, the partnership would have the cash and the third-party lender would own the note without there being any income to the partnership.

In fact, if the partnership takes a zero basis in the note, does it have income when the contributing partner makes principal payments? That result would seem to follow from the *Oden* decision, but it plainly makes no sense. Is the contributing partner entitled to claim a deduction as payments are made, or do such payments result in outside basis when, and as, made? Consider the possibility that the principal payments on the note might be made after the contributing partner withdraws from the partnership.

As we know, contributed property is booked into capital accounts at fair market value rather than at adjusted basis. Presumably, a partner who contributes her own note should then increase her capital account by the value of the note. Not so: The regulations specifically (and surprisingly) provide that the contributing partner's capital account is increased only when principal payments are made on the note or the note is transferred by the partnership in a taxable disposition. Treas. Regs. §1.704-1(b)(2)(iv)(d)(2). However, to ensure that the contributing partner is properly credited for the value of the note upon liquidation, the same regulation provides that the note will be deemed satisfied to the extent of its fair market value upon liquidation of the contributing partner's partnership interest.

This zero basis problem also arises in the context of subchapter C when a taxpayer contributes her own note to a corporation in exchange for stock in a transaction to which §351(a) applies. See the discussion of *Peracchi* above.[9]

7. T.C. Memo 1981-184, aff'd in unpublished opinion, 679 F.2d 885 (4th Cir. 1982).

8. Indeed, the Court's conclusion that the taxpayer has a zero basis in his own note because he paid nothing for it is inaccurate. If a taxpayer's basis in property is the value the taxpayer can receive in exchange for the property tax free, see §1001(a), then a taxpayer's basis in his own note is fair market value (i.e., face value if the note pays fair interest).

9. See page 43 supra.

D. SECTION 469: THE PASSIVE LOSS LIMITATIONS

The passive loss limitation of §469 represent the most recent and most successful attack on tax shelters. Section 469 reflects a congressional concern that excess deductions from investments have allowed taxpayers to shelter unrelated taxable income. Somewhat surprisingly, the congressional response was not to reduce or eliminate the deductions felt to be excessive. Instead, §469 prevents losses from most investments from offsetting unrelated income. Thus, §469 does not eliminate the tax advantages of investments that produce economic profit without the recognition of current income such as can be obtained by exploiting generous deductions for research, §174, machinery, §168, and farming, e.g., §180.

Under §469(a), net deductions and credits from a taxpayer's passive activities are disallowed and carried over to the following year. Like the at-risk rules of §465, the passive loss limitations of §469 disallow *excess* deductions: Passive losses may offset passive income without limitation under §469. Any losses suspended by operation of §469(a) are allowable when the taxpayer disposes of her investment in the passive activity in a fully taxable transaction. See §469(g). However, §469 generally applies only to the aggregate of all passive losses over all passive income, thereby allowing losses from one passive activity to offset income from an unrelated passive activity. See §469(d)(1). The at-risk rules, in contradistinction, generally operate on an activity-by-activity basis. §465(c)(2).

The definition of "passive activity" in §469 is surprising. Under §469(c), a passive activity is any activity "which involves the conduct of any trade or business, and in which the taxpayer does not materially participate." This definition requires that the activity be an active trade or business for some taxpayer but not for the particular taxpayer in question. See §469(c)(6), §469(h). Under this definition, holding stocks and bonds is *not* a passive activity because the holding of financial assets by one taxpayer is not a trade or business for some other taxpayer. Portfolio income,[10] such as interest and dividends, accordingly cannot be offset by passive losses. See §469(e)(1)(A)(i).

Section 469 specifically provides that all rental activity is passive. §469(c)(2). However, special rules apply to the rental of real estate. For taxpayers who "actively participate" in renting real estate (and "active participation" is less than material participation, compare §469(i)(6) with §469(h)), the first $25,000 of net loss is not treated as passive and so can offset active income (such as salary) and portfolio income. §469(i). However, this $25,000 advantage for rental real estate is phased out for taxpayers with adjusted gross income in excess of $100,000. §469(i)(3).

Two special rules apply only to partners. First, owning a limited partnership interest never constitutes material participation in the partnership's activity. §469(h)(2). This rule ensures that distributive income and loss of a limited partner is passive if the partnership actively conducts a trade or business. Second, passive loss from publicly traded partnerships (as defined in §469(k)(2)) cannot offset passive income from any other activity. See §469(k)(1). In essence, then, income from publicly traded partnerships is treated as portfolio income while loss is treated as passive, the worst of both worlds.

10. While the term "portfolio income" often is used to describe interest and dividends, for purposes of §469 such portfolio income is generally treated the same as active income such as compensation.

It might seem that there is some redundancy between §465 and §469 since both are tax shelter provisions and §465 has such broad application. However, they speak to different issues: §469 will disallow "losses" from activities even if the taxpayer has substantial funds at risk while §465 can disallow "losses" even if the taxpayer actively participates in the activity. Thus, most losses must pass both hurdles. Nevertheless, many tax scholars agree that with the enactment of §469, §465 should either be eliminated entirely or limited to seller-financed debt.

Section 469 applies, with respect to post-enactment taxable years, even to investments acquired prior to its enactment.[11] For many taxpayers, enactment of §469 rendered worthless and nonmarketable many of their prior investments because §469 eliminated the tax benefit of excess losses produced by their tax shelters. For such taxpayers, what was needed were new investment vehicles producing passive income. Such investments could then be purchased and the income they produce would be sheltered by the taxpayer's existing tax shelter vehicles. Such investments—affectionately called PIGs (for passive income generators)—are highly desirable under current law.

E. SECTION 163(d): THE INVESTMENT INTEREST LIMITATION

The investment interest limitation of §163(d) is one congressional response to the deferral opportunities presented by the realization doctrine. As you know, while the realization doctrine nominally defers recognition of both gains and losses, in practice it defers only gains because taxpayers are free to sell their loss properties while holding on to their appreciating assets. Indeed, it is precisely this potential manipulation of the realization doctrine that explains §1211 limiting a taxpayer's recognition of capital losses to the extent of realized capital gains (plus up to $3,000 for noncorporate taxpayers).

Just as a taxpayer might try to accelerate recognition of capital losses while deferring recognition of capital gains, a taxpayer might try to accelerate recognition of interest expenses while deferring the recognition of appreciation in an asset purchased with borrowed funds. For example, consider a taxpayer who can invest in young wine at an initial cost of $1,000,000. Assume that the wine increases in value as it ages; in fact, assume that it increases in value at a rate of 10 percent per year. What is the taxpayer's net return on the investment if she borrows the entire purchase price of $1,000,000 at an interest rate of 10 percent per annum, assuming the taxpayer holds the wine for three years?

It is obvious that the taxpayer has no pretax gain or loss from the investment: Borrowing at 10 percent to invest at 10 percent is a wash transaction. However, if the interest is paid annually and is deductible against other income as paid, the investment produces a positive after-tax return. Let us assume the taxpayer is in the 40-percent tax bracket and compute the taxpayer's after-tax gain.

11. For an excellent discussion of such retroactive effects of seemingly prospective-only legislation, see Michael Graetz, Legal Transitions: The Case of Retroactivity in Income Tax Revision, 126 U. Pa. L. Rev. 47 (1977).

The cost of the investment includes three interest payments of $100,000 apiece as well as a principal payment of $1,000,000. Assuming interest is deductible as paid, the after-tax cost of each interest payment is $60,000. To compute the present value of the cost of the investment, we discount each payment for the time value of money until the payment is due. Using an after-tax discount rate of 6 percent (which corresponds to a pretax interest rate of 10 percent, the same rate at which the wine investment appreciates), the present cost of the investment is $1,000,000.00.

We compare that present cost to the present value of the expected return. The taxpayer will receive $1,331,000 in three years. Of that amount, $331,000 will be taxable, producing a tax liability of $132,400. Accordingly, the net after-tax return to the taxpayer will be $1,198,600, and the present value of that return is $1,006,367.67, for an after-tax profit of $6,367.67. By deducting the interest currently but reporting the appreciation only at the end of the investment, the taxpayer is able to turn a profit without making any real investment. Application of §163(d), though, would defer the interest deduction until the taxpayer sold the wine, reducing the taxpayer's after-tax profit to $0. Of course, interest expenses often fall within the reach of the passive loss limitation in §469, diminishing the importance of §163(d).

PROBLEMS

26-4. Reconsider problem 26-2 taking the possible application of §469 into account.

26-5. The partnership agreement of the *XYZ* partnership provides that each of 10 limited partners must contribute $100,000 initially and an additional $25,000 per year for four years. Individual *X* is one such limited partner, and after two years in the partnership, *X* resigns and receives the amount she has contributed ($150,000) in liquidation of her partnership interest. Assuming *X*'s capital account and outside basis equaled $150,000 as of the date *X*'s interest was liquidated, does *X* have any tax consequences as a result of the liquidation? In particular, must *X* report any income from the cancellation of indebtedness because she no longer is obligated to contribute to the partnership $25,000 per year for two more years?

26-6. Individual *C* invests $10,000 to acquire a 10-percent limited interest in the *P* partnership. During each of its first two taxable years, the partnership recognizes $20,000 of taxable interest income as well as a loss of $100,000 from its ownership of a professional football team. How much of *C*'s distributive share of loss may *C* claim on her individual return? How do your answers change if *C* also invested $5,000 to acquire a 5-percent general partnership interest as well as the limited interest?

27

Inside Basis Adjustments

Aggregate outside basis equals aggregate inside basis when a partnership is formed. §§722-723. Because outside basis is adjusted for inside recognition of income and loss as well as for inside borrowing, §705, §752, aggregate outside basis should remain equal to aggregate inside basis throughout the life of the partnership. Similarly, the double basis adjustments in §704(c)(1)(B)(iii) and §737(c) further ensure that aggregate inside and outside bases remain equal.

However, some partnership distributions and most dispositions of partnership interests can disturb this equality of inside and outside bases. Yet, it is the equality of aggregate inside and outside bases that supports the fundamental transparency metaphor underlying subchapter K: So long as total inside basis equals total outside basis, the partners essentially are treated as an aggregate of co-owners. If this equality is broken, existence of the partnership can produce timing disparities for the partners. Positive inside basis adjustments generally will be desired by the partners but will only be allowed if an election under §754 is made or is in effect from a prior year. Negative inside basis adjustments generally are undesirable and, except in certain de minimis situations, must be made even if no §754 election is in effect.

Note that while there are *two* basis adjustment provisions, §734(b) (which applies to distributions) and §743(b) (which applies to dispositions of partnership interests), there is only a *single* election, §754. This one election applies to both §734(b) and to §743(b), so that a partnership must elect to take both or neither: there is no way to elect the §734(b) adjustment without the §743(b) adjustment, or vice versa. Treas. Regs. §1.754-1(a). In addition, there is no provision for revoking a §754 election without the consent of the government. Treas. Regs. §1.754-1(c).

Until 2004 even the negative inside basis adjustments in §734(b) and §743(b) were entirely optional, and considerable strategy informed the decision whether to make an election under §754 or not. Consider the following fact pattern. *A*, *B*, and *C* each contribute $100,000 to the *ABC* partnership, and the partnership purchases a capital asset for $300,000. When the property is worth only $180,000, *C* sells her partnership interest to *D* for its fair market value of $60,000, and *C* recognizes an immediate capital loss of $40,000. Thereafter, the partnership sells the property for $180,000, and the partnership recognizes a capital loss on that sale of $120,000, allocable equally among the partners. In particular, *D*'s distributive share includes one-third of that loss (i.e., $40,000) even though *C* already recognized that loss when *C* exited the partnership.[1]

While the basis adjustments of §734(b) and §743(b) are similar, they have their differences. The basis adjustment under §734(b) arises upon the occurrence of certain partnership distributions (note that §734 immediately follows the provisions governing the taxation of partnership distributions, §§731-733). The basis adjustment under §743(b) arises upon the taxable disposition of a partnership interest or upon the death of a partner (taxation of dispositions of partnership interests are covered by §§741-742). The most significant difference between the operation of §734(b) and §743(b) is that the inside basis adjustment under §734(b) applies to all partners equally while the inside basis adjustment under §743(b) applies only to the transferee partner.

A. THE INSIDE BASIS ADJUSTMENT UNDER §734(b)

1. *Distributions Triggering the Inside Basis Adjustment*

a. Nonliquidating Distributions of Excess Cash

Suppose cash is distributed to a partner in a nonliquidating distribution covered by §731. The effect of this distribution on the partnership's inside basis is to reduce that inside basis by the amount of cash distributed: When *any* property is distributed by a partnership, the partnership's inside basis is reduced by the amount of the partnership's basis in the distributed property for the simple reason that the partnership no longer owns the property. Because cash always has an implicit basis equal to face value, a distribution of cash reduces inside basis by the amount of cash distributed.

What is the effect of this distribution on the partners' aggregate outside basis? It depends on whether the distributee partner recognizes income under §731 by reason of the distribution. For example, suppose the distributee partner has an outside basis of $10,000 immediately before the distribution. If the distribution consists of $7,000, the distributee takes the cash tax free and reduces her outside basis to $3,000 under the rules of §731(a)(1) and §733(1). Outside basis thus is reduced by the amount of cash distributed, so that the effect of the distribution is to reduce aggregate inside and outside bases equivalently. That is, a distribution of cash fully absorbed by the distributee partner's outside basis preserves the equality of inside and outside bases.

But what if the distribution consists of $12,000? In this case the distributee partner must recognize a $2,000 gain because her outside basis is insufficient to

1. Because *D*'s cost basis in her partnership interest was $60,000, her outside basis drops to $20,000 once the partnership sells its capital asset and she includes a distributive share of $40,000 of loss. At that point, *D* owns a partnership interest worth $60,000, so that if she exits the partnership in exchange for a liquidating distribution of cash or by selling her partnership interest, she will have $40,000 of income that fully offsets the prior distributive share of loss. Thus, *C*'s exit followed by the partnership's sale of the asset did not duplicate *C*'s share of the loss permanently but only created a temporarily duplicative loss. But cf. §1014.

absorb the entire distribution. §731(a)(1). By reason of the parenthetical language in §733, she reduces her outside basis by $10,000. Accordingly, the distribution reduces aggregate outside basis by only $10,000 while aggregate inside basis is reduced by the full $12,000 (because the $12,000 is no longer owned by the partnership). This distribution breaks the equality of aggregate inside and outside bases: aggregate inside basis will be lower than aggregate outside basis after the distribution. Further, the amount of the disparity is precisely equal to the gain recognized by the distributee partner on the distribution. If an election under §754 is in effect, the partnership is entitled to a positive inside basis adjustment equal to the amount of gain recognized by the distributee. §734(b)(1)(A).

b. Nonliquidating Distributions of High-Basis Property

A nonliquidating distribution of property is tax free to the distributee under §731. The inside basis effect of such a distribution is clear: Once the property is distributed, aggregate inside basis is reduced by the partnership's adjusted basis in the distributed property because it no longer owns the property. As with distributions of cash, the distribution of property *may* disturb the equality of aggregate inside and outside bases depending on the pre-distribution outside basis of the distributee partner.

For example, suppose the partnership distributes Blackacre to partner *X* having an outside basis of $10,000. Assume the partnership has an inside basis in Blackacre of $7,000 immediately prior to the distribution. Assuming §751(b) does not apply to this distribution, the outside basis consequences to *X* are determined by application of §§732-733.

Under §732(a)(1), *X* takes Blackacre with a carry-over basis of $7,000. Under §733(2), *X* reduces her outside basis by that same $7,000. Accordingly, the effect of the distribution in this case is to reduce both aggregate inside basis and aggregate outside basis by the partnership's pre-distribution adjusted basis in the property distributed. The distribution therefore does not disturb the equality of aggregate inside and outside bases.

But now reconsider the distribution, assuming the property has a pre-distribution adjusted basis to the partnership of $12,000. The distribution remains tax free to *X* under §731, but now *X*'s basis in Blackacre is *not* carried over from the partnership. Instead, *X* takes a basis of only $10,000 in Blackacre under the limitation of §732(a)(2). And under §733(2), *X* reduces her outside basis to zero (the parenthetical language of §733 is not implicated in this case). Accordingly, aggregate outside basis is reduced only by $10,000 although inside basis is reduced by the full $12,000. More generally, whenever a nonliquidating distribution of property triggers the basis limitation rule of §732(a)(2), the distribution will reduce inside basis more than outside basis, with the difference equal to the excess of the partnership's pre-distribution adjusted basis in the distributed property over the distributee partner's pre-distribution outside basis. A distribution of high-basis property, like a distribution of excess cash, will thus cause aggregate inside basis to be low relative to aggregate outside basis. In such circumstances, the partnership will be entitled to an inside basis adjustment if an election under §754 is in effect. §734(b)(1)(B).

c. Liquidating Distributions

When a partnership makes a liquidating distribution, inside basis is lost because partnership property is removed from the partnership and outside basis is reduced because the distributec ceases to be a member of the partnership. While both aggregate inside basis and aggregate outside basis are thus reduced, the amount of the reductions will not be equal unless the pre-distribution inside basis of the property distributed (including any cash distributed) happens to equal the distributee partner's pre-distribution outside basis. In the absence of such a coincidence, the equality of aggregate inside basis and outside basis will be broken, and without knowing more, we cannot predict which will be greater.

For example, suppose individual *X* is a partner in the *XYZ* partnership, and assume the partnership distributes capital asset Blackacre, with an adjusted basis of \$7,000 to the partnership, to *X* in complete liquidation of *X*'s partnership interest. Assuming this distribution is taxed to *X* under §§731-732, *X* will not recognize any gain or loss on the transaction. If *X* had an outside basis of \$10,000 immediately before the distribution, the effect of the distribution is to reduce aggregate inside basis by \$7,000 (because the partnership no longer owns Blackacre) and to reduce aggregate outside basis by \$10,000 (because *X* no longer is a partner). Thus, aggregate inside basis will now exceed aggregate outside basis by the \$3,000 difference. In such circumstances, a downward inside basis adjustment will be required under §734(b)(2)(B) and §734(d) if the adjustment exceeds \$250,000; if the downward adjustment is less than or equal to \$250,000, it will be made only if an election under §754 is in effect.

But suppose that the partnership had a \$12,000 adjusted basis in Blackacre prior to the distribution. *X* still recognizes no gain or loss, but now aggregate inside basis is reduced by \$12,000 while aggregate outside basis is reduced by only \$10,000. Thus, aggregate inside basis will now be less than aggregate outside basis by \$2,000. In short, a distribution in liquidation of a partner's interest in the partnership can cause the post-distribution aggregate inside basis to be greater than or less than the post-distribution aggregate outside basis. See §734(b)(1)(B), §734(b)(2)(B). Liquidating distributions producing taxable gain or loss to the exiting partner under §731(a) also can affect inside and outside basis unequally. See §734(b)(1)(A), §734(b)(2)(A).

2. *The Amount of the Adjustment under §734(b)*

If a partnership has a §754 election in effect, no distribution can disturb the equality between aggregate inside and aggregate outside bases. More accurately, no distribution can affect the relationship between aggregate inside and aggregate outside bases: if they were equal prior to the distribution, they will be equal afterward. If they were unequal before, they will continue to be unequal in the same amount after.

How could aggregate outside and aggregate inside bases be unequal? Because the §734(b) and §743(b) basis adjustments are optional in many circumstances, a partnership can operate without them. If such a partnership makes a distribution that breaks the equality, or if a partner disposes of her partnership interest in a manner that breaks the equality, a subsequent §754 election will ensure that future distributions preserve the discontinuity caused by the pre-election distribution or disposition. That is, the effect of the inside basis adjustment in §734(b) is to preserve the absolute difference between aggregate inside basis and aggregate outside basis. If that absolute difference is zero when the election is made (i.e., if they are equal), it will remain zero. If that difference is positive, it will remain positive.

Consider the following example: *A* and *B* form the *AB* general partnership by contributing cash of $10,000 each. During its first year, the partnership distributes $15,000 to *A*. During its second year, the partnership distributes an additional $1,000 to *A*. Assume that the partnership has no taxable income at any point and that it incurs no indebtedness. Finally, assume that a §754 election is filed by the partnership effective on the first day of the partnership's second taxable year.

The effect of the first distribution on *A* is to reduce her outside basis to zero, see §733(1), and to cause her to recognize $5,000 of income, see §731(a)(1). As a result of the distribution, aggregate inside basis decreases to $5,000 and aggregate outside basis drops to $10,000. Because no §754 election is in effect when the distribution occurs, a disparity between aggregate inside and aggregate outside bases arises.

When the second distribution is made, *A* recognizes an additional $1,000 of income under §731(a)(1). Because *A*'s outside basis is zero, the distribution does not reduce *A*'s outside basis. Thus, the effect of the distribution is to decrease aggregate inside basis to $4,000 while leaving aggregate outside basis at $10,000.

However, because a §754 election is now in place, the distribution triggers a basis adjustment under §734(b)(1)(A) of $1,000. This is a positive inside basis adjustment, increasing aggregate inside basis back to $5,000. Accordingly, the second distribution does not change the relationship between aggregate inside and outside bases: Aggregate outside basis exceeds aggregate inside basis by $5,000 both before and after the distribution.

Under some circumstances, the basis adjustments mandated by §734(b) are deferred. See Treas. Regs. §1.755-1(c)(4), discussed below. When such deferral occurs, the relationship between aggregate inside and outside bases will be upset by the amount of the deferred adjustment. Once the deferral terminates, the proper relationship will be restored.

3. *Allocating the §734(b) Adjustment under §755*

While §734(b) and §743(b) specify the *net amount* of the optional basis adjustments, the actual allocation of those amounts to specific partnership assets is governed by §755. Regulations promulgated in January of 1998 have significantly overhauled the §755 basis adjustments. One feature of these regulations is that they provide one set of rules for basis adjustments arising under §734(b) and a separate set of rules for basis adjustments arising under §743(b).

Before allocating a §734(b) basis adjustment to the partnership's remaining assets, those assets must be divided into *two classes*: One class consists of the partnership's ordinary income assets, while the other class consists of the partnership's cash, capital assets, and assets described in §1231. If a §734(b) basis adjustment is triggered by the distribution of an ordinary income asset, the basis adjustment may be made only to any remaining ordinary income assets of the partnership. Treas.

Regs. §1.755-1(c)(1)(i). Similarly, if the distribution consists of cash, capital assets, or assets described in §1231, any resulting §734(b) adjustment will be limited to the partnership's remaining capital and §1231 assets. Treas. Regs. §1.755-1(c)(1)(i)-(ii). If an adjustment arising from application of §734(b) cannot be made because the partnership lacks assets of the appropriate class (ordinary or capital), then the adjustment is deferred until the partnership acquires property of the appropriate class. Treas. Regs. §1.755-1(c)(4).

a. Allocation of Positive §734(b) Adjustments

Assuming a partnership owns assets of the proper class, a *positive* adjustment under §734(b) is allocated among those *appreciated* assets of the proper class in proportion to their unrealized appreciation. If the amount of the increase exceeds the total unrealized appreciation in the assets of the proper class, the excess of the adjustment is then allocated among all assets of the proper class in proportion to their fair market values. Treas. Regs. §1.755-1(c)(2)(i).

Consider the following problem. The *ABC* partnership owns ordinary income asset *W* and capital assets *X*, *Y*, and *Z* with adjusted bases and fair market values as follows:

Asset	*Adjusted basis*	*Fair market value*
Ordinary asset *W*	$ 4,000	$30,000
Capital asset *X*	30,000	24,000
Capital asset *Y*	15,000	24,000
Capital asset *Z*	50,000	12,000

C, a one-third partner, receives asset *Z* in a nonliquidating distribution. At the time of this distribution, *C* has an outside basis and a capital account of $33,000. Assume that §751(b) does not apply to this transaction.

Because this is a nonliquidating distribution of property, *C* recognizes no gain or loss. See §731. Because the adjusted basis of the distributed property in the hands of the partnership exceeds *C*'s pre-distribution outside basis, *C* does not take a carry-over basis in the asset. Instead, *C* transfers her entire outside basis into asset *Z* and reduces her outside basis to zero. See §732(a)(2), §733(2). Assuming the partnership has a §754 election in effect, the partnership is entitled to an optional basis adjustment of positive $17,000 pursuant to §734(b).

Because the distributed property was a capital asset, the §734(b) adjustment can be made only to the remaining capital assets of the partnership—that is, to assets *X* and *Y*. Because the basis adjustment is positive, it is made first to asset *Y* to the extent of the unrealized appreciation in that asset. Thus, of the $17,000 basis adjustment, $9,000 is first made to asset *Y*.

The remaining $8,000 of basis adjustment is allocated to all partnership capital assets (that is, to assets *X* and *Y*) in proportion to relative fair market values. Treas. Regs. §1.755-1(c)(2)(i). Because assets *X* and *Y* have equal fair market values, the remaining $8,000 of basis adjustment is divided equally between them, leaving the post-adjustment books of the partnership as follows:

Asset	*Adjusted basis*	*Fair market value*
Ordinary asset *W*	$ 4,000	$30,000
Capital asset *X*	34,000	24,000
Capital asset *Y*	28,000	24,000

Strategic distribution of a high-basis asset in anticipation of a sale of some low-basis asset can effect a *basis strip*. Consider the case of a partnership owning two capital assets, one high-basis and the other low-basis. For example, suppose that asset *X* has an inside basis of $0 while asset *Y* has an inside basis of $100, with each asset having a fair market value of $100. What are the tax consequences of a non-liquidating distribution of asset *Y* to a partner having a zero outside basis in her partnership interest immediately prior to the distribution?

The partner recognizes no gain or loss by reason of the distribution, and the distributee partner takes a basis in asset *Y* of $0 under §732(a)(2). Assuming the partnership has an election under §754 in effect at the time of the election, the distribution triggers an upward basis adjustment under §734(b) of $100, allocable to asset *X*. That is, the effect of the distribution is to strip basis from asset *Y* and transfer it to asset *X*. Assuming the partnership anticipates selling asset *X* in the near future and the distributee partner anticipates holding asset *Y* for some time, this shifting of inside basis allows the partners to defer recognition of $100 of income.

b. Allocation of Negative §734(b) Adjustments

If the §734(b) basis adjustment is *negative*, the adjustment is allocated a little differently. It remains true that the basis adjustment must be made only to assets of the proper class, and when the adjustment is negative, it is allocated first to partnership assets of the proper class having unrealized loss, to the extent of such loss. Any additional negative basis adjustment is made to assets of the proper class in proportion to their adjusted bases (taking into account any adjustments made with respect to unrealized loss), Treas. Regs. §1.755-1(c)(2)(ii), but in no event is any basis reduced below zero, Treas. Regs. §1.755-1(c)(3). If the partnership does not have assets of the proper class with sufficient adjusted basis to absorb a negative §734(b) basis adjustment, the unallocated portion of the adjustment is suspended until the partnership acquires assets of the proper class that can absorb the negative basis adjustment. Treas. Regs. §1.755-1(c)(4).

For example, suppose partner *N* has an outside basis of $30,000 and receives a liquidating distribution consisting of $20,000 in cash when the books of the partnership read:

Asset	*Adjusted basis*	*Fair market value*
Cash	$30,000	$30,000
Ordinary asset *W*	51,000	21,000
Capital asset *X*	7,000	4,000
Capital asset *Y*	2,000	5,000

The amount of the basis adjustment is $10,000 under §734(b)(2)(A), allocable only to partnership capital assets because the distribution consisted only of cash.

See Treas. Regs. §1.755-1(c)(1)(ii). Of the $10,000 total adjustment, $3,000 is first allocated to asset *X* because that asset has an unrealized loss to the partnership of that amount. Of the remaining $7,000, $4,000 is allocated to asset *X*, and $2,000 is allocated to asset *Y*, reducing the basis of each asset to zero. Because the partnership now has no capital asset with a positive adjusted basis, the remaining $1,000 of negative basis adjustment must be suspended until the partnership acquires a capital asset having a positive adjusted basis.

c. Allocation of §734(b) Adjustments to Depreciable Property

When a §734(b) basis adjustment is made to depreciable property, there is an additional issue: Should the basis adjustment be recovered over the remaining recovery period of the depreciable property or over a new (and therefore longer), fresh recovery period? The partners generally would prefer that upward adjustments be recovered over the existing property's remaining recovery period (that is, over a relatively short period) and that downward adjustments be recovered over some longer period.

But the regulations adopt just the reverse approach. Treas. Regs. §1.734-1(e). For example, if a positive §734(b) basis adjustment of $55,000 is allocable to some residential real estate (such as an apartment complex) having a statutory recovery period of 27.5 years, see §168(c)(1), that adjustment will produce additional depreciation of $2,000 per year for 27.5 years[2] even if the underlying property has been depreciated for many years.[3] Conversely, if the adjustment is negative $55,000, that adjustment will reduce the partnership's depreciation over the remaining recovery term of the underlying property. Thus, if the real estate has only 11 years remaining to its depreciable life, then the depreciation will be reduced by $5,000 for each of those years.

NOTES

1. *The mandatory substantial basis adjustment.* While all positive basis adjustments under §734(b) are optional, most negative §734(b) adjustments are mandatory and so must be made even in the absence of an effective election under §754. More specifically, a negative §734(b) adjustment must be made if the adjustment exceeds $250,000 in amount. Note that the same rules apply for allocating mandatory and optional basis adjustments; the only significance of a "substantial basis adjustment" under §734(d) is that such an adjustment must be made even if no §754 election is in effect.

2. *Securitization partnerships.* Under §734(e), a "securitization partnership" is not subject to the mandatory inside basis adjustment even if the adjustment would constitute a "substantial basis adjustment" within the meaning of §734(d). A "securitization partnership" is defined in §743(f) to mean a partnership holding

2. Assuming the depreciation must be taken using the straight-line method, see §168(b)(3), and ignoring the mid-month convention, see §168(d)(2).

3. Treating a basis increase as newly placed in service is consistent with the more general rule in §168(i)(7). This same rule applies to any basis increase allocable to an amortizable §197 intangible held by the partnership. Treas. Regs. §1.197-2(g)(3).

only financial assets the cash flow from which will be used by the partnership to retire its outstanding interests (constituting securities) over a finite period of time.

PROBLEMS

27-1. The *ABC* partnership owns assets as set forth in the chart below:

Asset	*Adjusted basis*	*Fair market value*
Inventory	$33,000	$45,000
Receivable #1	0	15,000
Receivable #2	0	45,000
Land	9,000	6,000
Building	9,000	18,000
Securities	30,000	6,000

A, B, and *C* are one-third partners having a capital account and outside basis of $27,000. *Ignoring the possible impact of §751(b),* what basis adjustments are appropriate under §§734(b) and 755 if the partnership has an election under §754 in effect and

a. *C* receives the inventory in a nonliquidating distribution?
b. *C* receives the securities in a nonliquidating distribution?
c. *C* receives receivable #2 in a liquidating distribution?

27-2. Suppose in problem 27-1(b) that the partnership sells the building after the distribution. How much income does each partner report?

4. *The Flaw in the §734(b) Inside Basis Adjustment*[4]

Suppose that *P* and *Q* form the *PQ* partnership by contributing cash of $100 each. The partnership uses $60 of its cash to purchase nondepreciable Blackacre, and after Blackacre has increased in value to $340, cash of $120 is distributed to *P* in a nonliquidating distribution. After the distribution, the books of the partnership read (assuming the partnership elects to book its undistributed assets to current fair market value):

P		*Q*		
CA	OB	CA	OB	
$100	$100	$100	$100	Formation
140	0	140	0	Book-up of Blackacre
(120)	(100)	0	0	Distribution of cash
$120	$ 0	$240	$100	Totals

4. The material in this section is excerpted from Howard E. Abrams, The Section 734(b) Basis Adjustment Needs Repair, 57 Tax Lawyer 343 (2004).

Assets	*Book value*	*Adjusted basis*	*Fair market value*
Cash	$ 20	$20	$ 20
Blackacre	340	60	340

The partnership's only asset has appreciated from its cost of $60 to its current value of $340. If the asset is now sold, there will be a tax gain of $280, allocable equally between the partners. Thus, each partner must include gain of $140 on his individual return, and the books will become:

P		*Q*		
CA	*OB*	*CA*	*OB*	
$100	$100	$100	$100	Formation
140	0	140	0	Book-up of Blackacre
(120)	(100)	0	0	Distribution of cash
0	140	0	140	Sale of Blackacre
$120	$140	$240	$240	Totals

Assets	*Book value*	*Adjusted basis*	*Fair market value*
Cash	$360	$360	$360

If the partnership now liquidates, it will distribute cash of $120 to *P* and $240 to *Q*, giving them each a total return of $240. Since each partner invested $100, each should be taxed on $140, and for *Q* that is exactly what happened: The only taxable event was the sale of Blackacre, and *Q* reported a gain of $140 as a result. Thus, the liquidation is tax free to *Q*, as it should be.

But for *P* the analysis is more complex. The initial distribution of $120 was taxable to the extent of $20 because, at the time of the distribution, *P*'s outside basis was only $100; distributed cash is taxable to the extent that it cannot be absorbed by the distributee's outside basis. Thus, although the partnership had not yet earned any income, *P* was forced to report $20 of income on his individual return.

When the partnership subsequently sold Blackacre, *P* was allocated half of the tax gain from that sale, or $140. Thus, *P* will have included at this point a total of $160 from partnership activities, which is in fact $20 more than *P*'s 50-percent share of the partnership's total income. However, when the partnership distributes cash of $120 to *P* in a liquidating distribution, *P* will be entitled to claim a loss of $20 at that time because *P*'s final outside basis is not the $120 received but $140 as shown in the chart above.

Thus, each partner reports aggregate income of $140, as is proper. But while *Q*'s income recognition occurs when Blackacre is sold by the partnership, *P* in fact recognizes excess income during the life of the partnership with an offsetting loss upon liquidation. This timing mismatch disadvantages *P* without helping *Q* in any way, and the optional basis under §734(b) eliminates it. Or at least it should.

There is no doubt that the cash distribution triggers, if elected, the optional basis adjustment provided by §734(b) equal to a positive $20. But what is surprising—what is really unfathomable—is that this adjustment is made not for the benefit of

P alone but rather is made to the common basis of the partnership's assets (here, Blackacre) for the benefit of both *P* and *Q*.

If the basis adjustment were allocable only to *P*, then the sale of Blackacre by the partnership would generate taxable income of $140 to *Q* but only $120 to *P*. Thus, *P*'s share of gain from Blackacre would be reduced for the prior gain recognized by *P* on the earlier cash distribution. This allocation of the basis adjustment ensures that there is no timing mismatch once Blackacre is sold, and so neither partner recognizes gain or loss on a liquidation of his partnership interest.

But under current law the basis adjustment reduces not *P*'s gain alone but rather the overall gain to the partnership. Thus, the effect of the basis adjustment is to reduce the aggregate gain from $280 to $260 and so reduces each partner's share of that gain from $140 to $130. As a result, the books become:

P		*Q*		
CA	OB	CA	OB	
$100	$100	$100	$100	Formation
140	0	140	0	Book-up of Blackacre
(120)	(100)	0	0	Distribution of cash
0	130	0	130	Sale of Blackacre
$120	$130	$240	$230	Totals

Assets	*Book value*	*Adjusted basis*	*Fair market value*
Cash	$360	$360	$360

Now, when the partnership is liquidated, *P* has a $10 loss on the distribution of $120, and *Q* has an equivalent $10 gain on the distribution of $240. By allocating the basis adjustment to the partnership's common basis, we have permitted *Q* to defer recognition of income (reporting only $130 rather than $140 on the sale of Blackacre) while forcing *P* to overstate gross income ($20 from the cash distribution plus $130 from the sale of Blackacre) until each partner exits the partnership.

This result is wrong for *P*, wrong for *Q*, and, as is always the case when some rule misallocates income, wrong for the Treasury. Suppose *P* is a low-bracket taxpayer (such as an exempt organization or an offshore corporation) while *Q* is a high-bracket domestic taxpayer. Now, the early income recognition to *P* is irrelevant while the deferral to *Q* is a revenue leak. Of course, if the relative tax brackets are reversed, there is a revenue gain. But because the transaction is wholly within the partnership's control (if excess cash is not distributed to *P* prior to the sale of Blackacre, this issue never arises), the revenue gain should never occur for well-advised taxpayers.

It should not be surprising that the current common basis adjustment provided by §734(b) fails in this example: the adjustment arises only because income is recognized by *P* on the cash distribution, and since it is *P* who recognizes that income, it should be *P* who enjoys the basis increase. The distribution had no effect on either the economics of the venture or the tax position of the non-distributee partner, *Q*. Thus, changing the amount of gain that *Q* recognizes on the sale of Blackacre when sold by the partnership violates one of the most important rules of taxation: A taxpayer's tax results should be determined by what happens to him and not to others, a rule occasionally breached and always to bad effect.

PROBLEM

27-3. *A* and *B* each contribute \$100 to the *AB* partnership as equal partners. The partnership purchases two assets, Blackacre for \$60 and Whiteacre for \$140. When Blackacre increases in value to \$300, and Whiteacre increases in value to \$200, Whiteacre is distributed to *A* in a nonliquidating distribution. Assume the partnership elects to restate its undistributed assets (Blackacre) on the distribution of Whiteacre. What inside basis adjustment is triggered by the distribution of Whiteacre, and how *should* that basis adjustment be allocated to ensure that the distribution does not produce any inappropriate tax deferral or acceleration? What other tax consequences *should* result from the distribution?

B. THE INSIDE BASIS ADJUSTMENT UNDER §743(b)

When a partnership interest is sold in a taxable transaction, the purchaser takes a cost basis in the acquired partnership interest under §1012(a). This means that if the purchaser should sell that partnership interest before the assets of the partnership have changed in value, there will be no gain or loss on this resale. But in the absence of an adjustment under §743, if the partnership should sell some or all of its assets immediately after the purchaser acquires the partnership interest, there can be gain or loss that is passed through to and includible by the purchaser even if the assets have not changed in value since acquisition of the partnership interest. That is, while §1012 gives the purchaser a cost basis in the partnership interest, it does not push that cost basis into the underlying assets of the partnership.

For example, suppose *P*, *Q*, and *R* are equal partners in the successful *PQR* general partnership. Assume each partner has an outside basis and capital account of \$10,000, and assume also that the partnership owns assets with an aggregate adjusted basis of \$30,000 and aggregate fair market value of \$90,000. If the partnership has no outstanding debt, each partner's interest should be worth \$30,000.

Suppose *R* wishes to sell her partnership interest to *S* for its current value of \$30,000. *R* will realize and recognize a taxable gain of \$20,000 on the sale, and depending on the make-up of the partnership's assets, some or all of that gain may be ordinary income under §751(a). Of course, *S* will take an initial outside basis equal to her cost of \$30,000. §742 and §1012. However, *S* acquires *R*'s capital account without regard to the amount paid by *S* for the partnership interest. Treas. Regs. §1.704-1(b)(2)(iv)(l).

If no §754 election is in place when *S* buys into the partnership, a sale by the partnership of its assets for \$90,000 forces the partnership to recognize a gain of \$60,000. This gain will be allocated among the partners in accordance with the partnership agreement, which presumably means that each partner will recognize gain of \$20,000. Indeed, *P* and *Q* should be unaffected by *R*'s sale to *S*, so recognition of \$20,000 apiece for *P* and *Q* is appropriate. Because the partnership recognizes a total gain of $60,000 on the sale of its assets, that leaves $20,000 of gain for *S* (the same amount of gain that would have been allocated to *R* if *R* had never sold her interest).

Thus, *S* must report $20,000 of income even though *S*'s partnership interest has not increased in value. This phantom income will be offset by a phantom loss when *S* sells her partnership interest, because *S*'s outside basis is increased to $50,000 under §705(a)(1)(A) while its value remains at $30,000 (a one-third interest in $90,000 of cash). In effect, *R*'s share of the unrealized appreciation is taxed twice: once to *R* on the sale of her interest and a second time when the partnership sells its assets and *R*'s share of the gain is includible by *S*. Because *S*'s cost basis in her outside basis did not flow through the partnership into the partnership's assets, *S* reports phantom income during the life of the partnership and an offsetting phantom loss at its end. In addition, if the partnership owns ordinary income assets, the phantom income will include an ordinary income component without any guarantee that the dispositional loss will include a similar amount of noncapital loss. Typically, not a good deal for *S*.

The basis adjustment provided by §743(b) solves this problem. When such an adjustment is made, it permits the transferee of a partnership interest to push her outside basis into the inside basis of the assets. If the transferee pays neither more nor less than fair market value for the partnership interest, then the effect of §743(b) is to give the purchasing partner the equivalent of a cost basis in each partnership asset. As a result, if any partnership asset is sold without a change in its value, the purchasing partner's share of the taxable gain or loss from the asset sale, after accounting for the §743(b) basis adjustment, will be exactly $0. In the example above, *S* would be entitled to an adjustment of $20,000, and that adjustment will precisely offset *S*'s distributable share of income from the sale by the partnership of its asset.

One would think that this rule could be embodied in relatively simple regulations. Unfortunately, that is not the case: the §743(b) basis adjustment regulations are among the most complex regulations in all of subchapter K. These regulations in fact yield what seems to be the right mathematical answer in all cases, but they still seem far more complex than necessary to arrive at such answers. As you read the following material covering these regulations, ask yourself whether the complexity of the regulations could have been eliminated without changing the substantive outcomes.

The transfer of a partnership interest by sale or exchange can trigger a basis adjustment under §743(b), as can the death of a partner. Surprisingly, even a tax-free exchange of a partnership interest can trigger §743(b) even though the transferee takes the transferor's outside basis. In particular, the transfer of a partnership interest to a corporation under §351 as well as the transfer of a partnership interest to another partnership under §721 will trigger any applicable §743(b) basis adjustment. In addition, the distribution under §731 of an interest in a lower-tier partnership by an upper-tier partnership is treated as an exchange of the distributed partnership interest. §761(e)(2).

If the sale or exchange triggering the §743(b) adjustment is a substituted basis transaction, the rules outlined above and described below do not apply. Treas. Regs. §1.755-1(b)(1). Instead, the rules generally applicable to §734(b) adjustments apply. Treas. Regs. §1.755-1(b)(5). However, adjustments can be made to both classes of property (the class of ordinary income assets and the class of capital assets and §1231 assets). See Treas. Regs. §1.755-1(b)(5)(ii)-(iii).

1. *Two-Way Adjustments under §743(b)*

In general, the effect of a §743(b) adjustment is to give the purchasing partner a cost basis in her share of the each of the partnership's assets. While that result ensures that the purchasing partner will not be allocated any phantom income or deductions from operation of the partnership, it can require that a single §743(b) adjustment give rise to both positive and negative basis adjustments, a result finding precious little support in the statute.

For example, suppose the *LMNO* partnership owns two assets, inventory with an adjusted basis of $800 and fair market value of $1,000, as well as a capital asset with an adjusted basis of $1,600 and fair market value of $1,400. Assume each partner has an outside basis and capital account of $600 and that each partner's interest is worth the same amount. Thus, the books of the partnership are

Asset	*Book value*	*Inside basis*	*Fair market value*
Inventory	$ 800	$ 800	$1,000
Capital asset	1,600	1,600	1,400
	$2,400	$2,400	$2,400

	Capital account	*Outside basis*	*Fair market value*
L	$ 600	$ 600	$ 600
M	600	600	600
N	600	600	600
O	600	600	600
	$2,400	$2,400	$2,400

If partner *L* sells her partnership interest for $600, it is clear that the amount of the §743(b) basis adjustment is $0, and the regulations come to that conclusion. See Treas. Regs. §1.743-1(b). However, the §755 regulations mandate not zero but two basis adjustments: a positive basis adjustment of $50 to the purchasing partner's share of the inventory as well as a negative $50 basis adjustment to the purchasing partner's share of the capital asset. These two basis adjustments always net to the amount defined by §743(b) (here, they net to $0), but as this example demonstrates either can in magnitude exceed that amount.

For a fair market value purchase, the §743(b) basis adjustment in favor of the purchasing partner can be computed using the following three steps:

(i) The partnership computes the gain or loss that it would recognize if it had sold its assets in a fair market value sale immediately after the purchase;

(ii) The partnership determines the portion of the gain or loss it would allocate to the purchased interest for each asset; and

(iii) The purchasing partner has a *positive* basis adjustment for an asset equal to any allocated tax gain or a *negative* basis adjustment for an asset equal to any allocated tax loss.

If the partnership later sells an asset, it computes gain or loss on the sale before taking §743(b) basis adjustments into account. A partner's distributive share of gain or loss from the asset sale equals (a) her allocable share of the partnership gain or loss computed without regard to any §743(b) adjustments, minus (b) the partner's positive §743(b) basis adjustment, if any, for the asset, plus (c) the partner's negative §743(b) basis adjustment, if any, for the asset. Thus, a partner's positive basis adjustment for an asset will decrease the partner's gain (or increase her loss) on the asset while the partner's negative basis adjustment for an asset will do the opposite.

Technically, the regulations provide that the net amount of a §743(b) basis adjustment is equal to the difference between (1) the transferee's outside basis immediately after the transfer and (2) the transferee's share of the adjusted basis of the partnership's property. The first of these two values is easy to determine: When a partnership interest is sold or exchanged, the transferee's outside basis will be the purchasing partner's cost of the partnership interest, while if the partnership interest is transferred as a result of the death of a partner, the transferee's outside basis generally will be fair market value as of the date of death. In each case, the regulations make clear that the transferee's outside basis includes the transferee's share, if any, of partnership indebtedness as provided for under §752.

The second of the two values—the transferee's share of the adjusted basis of the partnership's property—is more complex. The regulations provide that the transferee's "share of the partnership's adjusted basis in the partnership's assets" is equal to the sum of (1) the transferee's share of "previously taxed capital" plus (2) the transferee's share of partnership liabilities. The transferee's share of "previously taxed capital" is then defined to equal the amount of cash that the transferee would receive if the partnership immediately sold all its assets and then liquidated, but increased by the transferee's distributive share of tax loss from that hypothetical sale of assets and decreased by the transferee's distributive share of tax gain. Note that this computation provides for an *increase* for distributive share of tax loss and a *decrease* for distributive share of tax gain, adjustments that might at first glance seem reversed.

Consider the following example. *A* and *B* each have a 25-percent interest in the capital, profits, and losses of the *ABC* general partnership, and *C* has the remaining 50-percent interest. When the partnership's books stand as follows, *A* sells her partnership interest to *D* for its current fair market value of $7,000.

Asset	*Book value*	*Inside basis*	*Fair market value*
Capital asset X	$10,000	$10,000	$18,000
Capital asset Y	6,000	6,000	10,000
	$16,000	$16,000	$28,000

	Capital account	*Outside basis*	*Fair market value*
A	$ 4,000	$ 4,000	$ 7,000
B	4,000	4,000	7,000
C	8,000	8,000	14,000
	$16,000	$16,000	$28,000

On the sale from *A* to *D*, *A* realizes a gain of $3,000. Absent an election under §754, the effect of the sale would be to increase aggregate outside basis from $16,000 to $19,000 without any offsetting effect on aggregate inside basis. §743(a). If, though, such an election has been filed, then the partnership is entitled to adjust the inside basis of its assets by $3,000 under §743(b) (benefiting only *D*), computed as follows.

When *D* purchases *A*'s partnership interest, *D* assumes *A*'s capital account without adjustment. Treas. Regs. §1.704-1(b)(2)(iv)(*l*). If all the assets of the partnership were sold in a fully taxable transaction, *D* would be allocated one-quarter of the $12,000 gain, increasing *D*'s capital account from $4,000 to $7,000. Thus, if the partnership were immediately liquidated, *D* would be entitled to receive $7,000 in cash.

D's share of the partnership's previously taxed capital thus equals $7,000 less the $3,000 gain allocated to *D* on the final sale, or $4,000. Because *D*'s outside basis is *D*'s cost of $7,000, the §743(b) adjustment equals $7,000 minus $4,000, or $3,000. Note that this adjustment to the partnership's basis in its assets restores the equality of aggregate inside and outside bases broken by the sale of *A*'s partnership interest.

Reconsider this example, but assume that capital asset *Y* has a book value and an adjusted basis to the partnership of $10,000 but is subject to a recourse liability of $4,000. Now, taking into account the liability under §752, the partnership's books become:

Asset	*Book value*	*Inside basis*	*Fair market value*
Capital asset *X*	$10,000	$10,000	$18,000
Capital asset *Y*	10,000	10,000	10,000
	$20,000	$20,000	$28,000

	Capital account	*Outside basis*	*Fair market value*
Liability	$ 4,000	$	$ 4,000
A	4,000	5,000	6,000
B	4,000	5,000	6,000
C	8,000	10,000	12,000
	$20,000	$20,000	$28,000

If partner *A* now sells her partnership interest to *D* for its current fair market value of $6,000 while an election under §754 is in effect, there is an inside basis adjustment of $2,000 under §743(b), computed as follows: *D*'s share of the partnership's previously taxed capital remains at $4,000,[5] but now *D*'s share of the liabilities equals $1,000. Accordingly, *D*'s "proportionate share of the adjusted basis of the partnership's property" equals $5,000, and because *D*'s initial outside basis equals $7,000 (purchase price of $6,000 plus *D*'s $1,000 share of the partnership's liabilities), the adjustment equals $7,000 less $5,000, or $2,000. Note once again that this adjustment to the partnership's basis in its assets restores the equality of aggregate inside and outside bases broken by the sale of *A*'s partnership interest.

It can be the case that a partner's share of the partnership's inside basis as defined by the regulations is negative, although there is no evidence that the drafters of the §743 regulations appreciated this possibility. For example, suppose

5. Final capital account balance of $5,000 less $1,000 distributive share of gain equals $4,000.

X and *Y* form the *XY* general partnership, with *X* contributing cash of $300 in exchange for a 75-percent interest in profits and losses and *Y* contributing a capital asset with adjusted basis and fair market value of $100 in exchange for the remaining 25-percent interest in profits and losses. When an election under §754 is not in effect, the partnership distributes $200 in cash to *Y*. This distribution forces *Y* to recognize income of $100 under §731(a)(1) and reduces *Y*'s outside basis to $0 under §733(2). Assume that the capital asset appreciates to $900, so that the books of the partnership stand as follows:

Asset	*Book value*	*Inside basis*	*Fair market value*
Cash	$100	$100	$ 100
Capital asset	100	100	900
	$200	$200	$1,000

	Capital account	*Outside basis*	*Fair market value*
X	$ 300	$300	$ 900
Y	(100)	0	100
	$ 200	$300	$1,000

Because no election under §754 was in effect when the distribution of cash was made to *Y*, the distribution did not result in an adjustment to the partnership's inside basis. §734(a). Thus, one effect of the distribution was to break the equality between aggregate inside basis (now equal to $200) and aggregate outside basis (now equal to $300). If *Y* sells her partnership interest to *Z* for its current value of $100, the §743(b) adjustment equals $200. This value arises by comparing *Z*'s cost basis of $100 with *Z*'s share of inside basis as defined in the regulations. Under that definition, *Z*'s share of inside basis equals negative $100 (current capital account balance) plus $200 (capital account increase if all partnership assets sold) less $200 (distributive share of gain from hypothetical sale of assets), for a net value of negative $100! Note that this produces a §743(b) basis adjustment of $200, and that basis adjustment will precisely offset *Z*'s distributive share of gain if the capital asset is sold for its current value of $900.

Suppose that it is *X* rather than *Y* who sells her partnership interest, this time for its current value of $900. Now, the §743(b) basis adjustment equals $600. This adjustment equals the excess of the price paid by *Z* for the partnership interest (that is, $900) over *Z*'s share of the partnership's inside basis. *Z*'s share of inside basis equals the amount of cash *Z* would receive in liquidation of the partnership if all the assets were sold in a fully taxable transaction, or $900, less distributive share of tax gain on the hypothetical sale of asset, or $600, for a net value of $300. Note that under this definition *Z*'s share of the partnership's inside basis ($300) exceeds the partnership's *total* inside basis ($200). The §743(b) adjustment is then $900 less $300, or $600.

To help understand the convoluted definition of a partner's share of "previously taxed capital," consider the following two examples. The *CDE* partnership owns three assets: *X*, a capital asset; *Y*, a capital asset; and *Z*, inventory. *C*, a one-third partner in capital, profits, and losses, has a capital account and outside basis of $700.

C sells her interest in *CDE* for $1,000 while the partnership has a §754 election in effect and the partnership books stand as follows:

Asset	*Book value*	*Inside basis*	*Fair market value*
X	$ 600	$ 600	$1,500
Y	900	900	600
Z	600	600	900
	$2,100	$2,100	$3,000

	Capital account	*Outside basis*	*Fair market value*
Purchaser	$ 700	$1,000	$1,000
D	700	700	1,000
E	700	700	1,000
	$2,100	$2,400	$3,000

The purchaser's outside basis immediately after the purchase equals cost of $1,000 because there are no partnership liabilities. The purchaser's share of previously taxed capital equals $700 because a fair market value sale of all the partnership assets would produce a gain of $1,200 (on assets *X* and *Z*) and a loss of $300 (on asset *Y*). Thus, the result of this hypothetical sale is to increase the purchaser's capital account from $700 (taken from *C*) to $1,000 (one-third of the book gain [or $400] less one-third of the book loss [or $100], for a net distributive share of positive $300). From this, the purchaser's share of previously taxed capital equals $1,000 (final capital account balance) less $400 (distributive share of tax gain from the hypothetical sale) plus $100 (distributive share of tax loss from the hypothetical sale), for a net total of $700. From these two computations we can determine that the amount of the §743(b) adjustment is $300, that being the excess of the purchaser's initial outside basis of $1,000 over the purchaser's share of previously taxed capital of $700. This inside basis adjustment of $300 will cause aggregate outside basis to equal aggregate inside basis, restoring the equality that existed prior to the sale by *C*.

In this example, the transferee's share of previously taxed capital equals the transferee's capital account. The reason that the definition of a partner's share of previously taxed capital (sometimes called the partner's share of inside basis) is more complex can be explained by the need to account for §704(c)(1)(A) and reverse §704(c) allocations — that is, by tax allocations accounting for a variance between the book value of an asset and its adjusted basis to the partnership. If there are no such variations, then a partner's share of inside basis equals her capital account plus her share of the partnership's liabilities. If, though, the partner's capital account has been increased for appreciation that has not yet been recognized by the partnership, then the partner's capital account must be reduced by that appreciation to properly measure the partner's share of *previously* taxed capital. Similarly, if a partner's capital account has been reduced by some element of unrealized loss in partnership assets, then that partner's capital account must be increased by that unrealized loss to equal the partner's share of *previously* taxed capital.

For example, reconsider the example above but assume that partner *C* initially contributed asset *X* to the partnership when it had an adjusted basis of only $300 and a fair market value of $600. Making this change, once *C* sells her interest the books of the partnership will read:

Asset	*Book value*	*Inside basis*	*Fair market value*
X	$ 600	$ 300	$1,500
Y	900	900	600
Z	600	600	900
	$2,100	$1,800	$3,000

	Capital account	*Outside basis*	*Fair market value*
Purchaser	$ 700	$1,000	$1,000
D	700	700	1,000
E	700	700	1,000
	$2,100	$2,400	$3,000

Once again the purchaser's initial outside basis equals $1,000, but the purchaser's share of inside basis is only $400. This figure is computed as follows: If the partnership sold its assets for fair market value, the purchaser's distributive share of book gain would be $400 ($300 from asset *X* and $100 from asset *Z*) as well as distributive share of book loss of $100 (from asset *Y*). That net book gain of $300 would increase the purchaser's capital account, so the purchaser's final capital account balance would be $1,000. We subtract from that figure the purchaser's distributive share of *tax* gain (i.e., $700) and add to that the purchaser's distributive share of *tax* loss (i.e., $100), for a net reduction of $600, making the purchaser's share of the partnership's inside basis $1000 – $600, or $400. Accordingly, the §743(b) adjustment is $1,000 less $400, or $600. In short, a partner's share of "previously taxed capital" is defined the way it is to take into account the possibility that a sale of the partnership's assets would affect capital accounts by one set of numbers (book gain and loss) and outside bases by another set of numbers (tax gain and loss).

The crucial definition in the §743(b) regulations is that of "previously taxed capital." Under these regulations, that definition is the liquidation value of the transferee's partnership interest less distributive share of taxable gain plus distributive share of taxable loss allocable to the transferee on a hypothetical sale by the partnership of all its assets. Another way to say this is that previously taxed capital equals the liquidation value of the transeferee's partnership interest plus (and minus) unrealized taxable gain (and loss) in the partnership's assets.

But what is the "liquidation value of the transferee's partnership interest"? It is the amount of cash the transferee would receive if the partnership sold all of its assets for fair market value and then liquidated. And as we know, upon liquidation of a partnership, each partner must receive her final capital account balance. Thus, the liquidation value of the transferee's partnership interest equals the current value of the transferee partner's interest plus (and minus) her share of the unrealized *book* gain (and loss) in the partnership's assets. Putting all this together, we get:

Share of Previously Taxed Capital = Current Capital Account + (Unrealized Book Gain – Unrealized Tax Gain) – (Unrealized Book Loss – Unrealized Tax Loss)

In the absence of any forward or reverse §704(c) layer allocable to the transferee, unrealized book gain and loss will equal unrealized tax gain and loss. This means that if the transferee partner does not take on any forward or reverse §704(c) layer from the transferor partner, then "previously taxed capital" is equal to the transferee's initial capital account (carried over from the transferor partner). And if there are forward or reverse §704(c) layers, then "previously taxed capital" equals that same initial capital account minus any §704(c) gain and plus any §704(c) loss.

2. *Allocating the §743(b) Adjustment under §755*

a. Basic Rules

When a partnership interest is sold, is exchanged, or passed through the estate of a decedent, the transferee will take what amounts to a fair market value basis in the partnership interest (unless the purchaser pays a premium or receives a discount). If an election under §754 is in effect at the time of the transaction, regulations provide, in general, that an optional basis adjustment will be made to each partnership asset in an amount that reflects the transferee's share of the unrealized appreciation or loss in that asset. In contradistinction to the basis adjustment arising from distributions under §734(b), this basis adjustment triggered by application of §743(b) affects the transferee partner only and so has no effect on the partnership's common basis.

Because optional basis adjustments under §743(b) affect the transferee partner only, the partnership must now keep two sets of partnership books, one unadjusted by §743(b) for the entire partnership and one reflecting the §743(b) adjustment for the transferee partner. Indeed, once an election under §754 is filed, the partnership must open an additional set of books every time a partnership interest is sold or exchanged, or when a partner dies.

Technically, a §743(b) adjustment is computed under §755 in two steps. In step one, the adjustment for each class of property is determined, where one class consists of the partnership's ordinary income assets and the other class consists of the partnership's capital assets, §1231 assets, and cash. In step two, the basis adjustment for each class is allocated among the partnership's assets within each class.

Consider the following example. The *ABC* partnership owns ordinary income asset *W* and capital assets *X*, *Y*, and *Z* with adjusted bases and fair market values as follows:

Asset	*Adjusted basis*	*Fair market value*
W (ordinary)	$ 3,000	$30,000
X (capital)	30,000	24,000
Y (capital)	15,000	24,000
Z (capital)	51,000	12,000

C, a one-third partner with a capital account and outside basis of $33,000 sells her interest to *D* for its fair market value of $30,000 when an election under §754 is in effect. Under §743(b), the amount of the adjustment equals negative $3,000, that being the excess of *D*'s purchase price over *D*'s share of the "previously taxed capital" of the partnership. The partnership's class of ordinary income assets consists of asset *W* alone while the class of capital assets includes assets *X*, *Y*, and *Z*.

The §743(b) basis adjustment is divided between the two classes as follows. First, it must be determined what *D*'s share of the partnership's ordinary income would be if the partnership sold it assets for fair market value. Here, that would be a sale of asset *W* for $30,000, producing a taxable gain to the partnership of $27,000 of which *D*'s share as a one-third partner would be $9,000. Thus, the §743(b) basis adjustment to the class of ordinary income assets (that is, to asset *W* in this example) is $9,000. Treas. Regs. §1.755-1(b)(2)(i). The §743(b) basis adjustment allocated to the class of capital assets (that is, to assets *X*, *Y*, and *Z* in this example) is that amount which, when added to the adjustment allocated to the ordinary income assets, yields the total adjustment as defined by §743(b). Because the total §743(b) adjustment is negative $3,000, the §743(b) adjustment allocated to the class of capital assets is negative $12,000. Treas. Regs. §1.755-1(b)(2)(i)(A)-(B).

The negative $12,000 basis adjustment allocated to the class of capital assets must then be divided into adjustments for each capital asset; here, that means the negative $12,000 basis adjustment must be allocated among assets *X*, *Y*, and *Z* in proportion to *D*'s share of the unrealized appreciation or loss in each asset. Accordingly, the negative $12,000 basis adjustment is allocated as follows: negative $2,000 to asset *X*, positive $3,000 to asset *Y*, and negative $13,000 to asset *Z*.[6] In tabular form:

Asset	*Adjusted basis*	*Fair market value*	*Adjustment*
W (ordinary)	$ 3,000	$30,000	$ 9,000
X (capital)	30,000	24,000	(2,000)
Y (capital)	15,000	24,000	3,000
Z (capital)	51,000	12,000	(13,000)

b. Allocation of §743(b) Adjustments to Depreciable Property

If an adjustment is made to depreciable property, the proper recovery applicable to the adjustment must be determined. As in the case of adjustments arising under §734(b), the general rule here is the negative basis adjustments are recovered over the remaining depreciable life of the asset while positive basis adjustments are recovered over a new depreciable life as if the asset were newly placed in service. Treas. Regs. §1.743-1(j)(4)(B)(1).

However, if there is a §743(b) positive basis adjustment allocable to property having §704(c)(1)(A) built-in gain, then there is an exception to this general rule *if* the partnership has elected to use the remedial allocation method with respect to the appreciated property. In such circumstances, any positive §743(b) basis adjustment is recovered over the remaining recovery period applicable to the built-in gain, Treas. Regs. §1.743-1(j)(4)(B)(2), that being a useful life determined not by reference to the depreciable life of the property in the hands of the partner who contributed the property but a new depreciable life as of the date of the property's contribution to the partnership. See Treas. Regs. §1.704-3(d)(2) (final sentence).

6. If *D*'s share of the net unrealized appreciation or loss in the capital assets did not exactly equal *D*'s basis adjustment allocable to the class of capital assets, then the adjustment to each capital asset must be adjusted for the difference. See Treas. Regs. §1.755-1(b)(3)(ii)(B).

Presumably, the same rule applies to use of the remedial allocation method in connection with reverse §704(c) allocations.

c. Partnership Disposition of Adjusted Property

Reconsider the problem immediately above. The chart set forth below shows the partnership's common basis for each of its assets as well as the §743(b) adjustment allocable to partner *D* who purchased a one-third interest in the partnership for $30,000 when an election under §755 was in effect.

Asset	*Adjusted basis*	*Fair market value*	*Adjustment*
W (ordinary)	$ 3,000	$30,000	$ 9,000
X (capital)	30,000	24,000	(2,000)
Y (capital)	15,000	24,000	3,000
Z (capital)	51,000	12,000	(13,000)

If the partnership should subsequently sell asset *W* for $27,000, how will partner *D* be taxed? The regulations make clear that the partnership first determines *D*'s distributive share of gain or loss by reference to the partnership's common basis in the property and then that amount is decreased by any positive adjustment or increased by any negative adjustment allocable to the property. Thus, when asset *W* is sold for $27,000, the partnership recognizes a taxable gain of $24,000, of which $8,000 (i.e., one-third) is allocable to *D*. Because *D*'s §743(b) basis adjustment is positive $9,000, *D* reports her $8,000 distributive share of income less her $9,000 basis adjustment—that is, *D* recognizes a $1,000 loss.

It is worth mentioning that a substantial part of what someone pays for a partnership interest might represent the value of the partnership's goodwill. Goodwill, like any other partnership asset, can be allocated inside basis under §§743(b) and 755. Note that inside basis allocated to partnership goodwill can be amortized over 180 months under the rules of §197. See Treas. Regs. §1.197-2(g)(3).

3. *Distribution of Property Subject to a §743(b) Basis Adjustment*

If a partnership distributes property subject to a basis adjustment under §743(b), the partner who is entitled to benefit from the adjustment will lose that benefit. If the distribution happens to be to that partner, we can give her an equivalent benefit by increasing her basis in the distributed property. That is, we can add the basis adjustment benefiting the distributee partner to the asset's inside basis and then follow the standard rules governing the distribution of property in §§731-733.

For example, once again reconsider the problem discussed on page 827, the solution to which is reproduced below. This chart sets forth the partnership's common basis for each of its assets as well as the §743(b) adjustment allocable to partner *D* who purchased a one-third interest in the partnership for $30,000 when an election under §755 was in effect.

Asset	*Adjusted basis*	*Fair market value*	*Adjustment*
W (ordinary)	$ 3,000	$30,000	$9,000
X (capital)	30,000	24,000	(2,000)
Y (capital)	15,000	24,000	3,000
Z (capital)	51,000	12,000	(13,000)

If asset *Y* is distributed to partner *D* in a nonliquidating distribution, *D*'s adjusted basis in the property under §732(a)(1) will not be the partnership's common basis of $15,000 but rather the partnership's common basis as adjusted by *D*'s §743(b) basis adjustment, or $15,000 plus $3,000 for a total of $18,000. Treas. Regs. §1.743-1(g)(1)(i). As a consequence, *D* must reduce her outside basis by that same amount, leaving *D* with an outside basis of $12,000.

Note that the basis adjustment given to asset *Y* is, in effect, taken away from the distributee partner's outside basis under §733(2). This should not be surprising: By adjusting only *inside* basis, the optional basis adjustments affect only timing of income, not ultimate amount of income. Giving additional basis to the distributed asset and taking it from the distributee partner's outside basis changes the timing of recognition of income: Less income is recognized when the asset is sold while more will be recognized when the partnership interest is sold. If the optional basis adjustment were given to the asset *without* taking it from outside basis, an inside adjustment affecting timing would be converted into an outside adjustment affecting the total amount of income to be recognized.

If the asset is distributed to some partner *other than* the purchasing partner, we can preserve the optional basis adjustment only by reallocating it to some other asset of the partnership. Treas. Regs. §1.743-1(g)(2)(ii). For example, if asset *Y* above were distributed to partner *A* or *B*, we would reallocate *D*'s $3,000 §743(b) basis adjustment formerly allocated to asset *Y* to some other partnership asset. The regulations provide that such an adjustment should be made to the remaining partnership assets pursuant to the rules generally applicable to §734(b) adjustments. *Id.* This means that the $3,000 basis adjustment must be reallocated only to the partnership's remaining capital assets in proportion to their relative fair market values. As a result, *D* will no longer have a basis adjustment with respect to asset *X* and *D*'s basis adjustment with respect to asset *Z* will become negative $12,000. See Treas. Regs. §1.755-1(c).

If a partnership terminates because of sales or exchanges of interests totaling more than 50 percent of partnership profits and capital, see §708(b)(1)(B), the partnership is deemed to transfer all of its assets to a new partnership in exchange for all interests in that new partnership, and then these interests in the new partnership are deemed distributed by the terminating partnership to its members, Treas. Regs. §1.708-1(b)(1)(iv). The basis to the new partnership will include any optional basis adjustment to partnership property arising under §743(b). Treas. Regs. §1.743-1(h)(1); see Treas. Regs. §1.708-1(b)(1)(v); cf. Treas. Regs. §1.743-1(h)(2)(i) (applicable to transfers to corporations).

NOTES

1. *The mandatory negative adjustment for a substantial built-in loss.* For most partnerships, a negative inside basis adjustment must be made under §743(b) even if no

election under §754 is in effect if the partnership has a "substantial built-in loss" when a partnership interest is sold or exchanged. §743(a). In this context, a partnership has a "substantial built-in loss" if the aggregate inside basis of the partnership's assets exceeds the fair market value of its assets by more than $250,000. §743(d)(1).

For example, suppose partnership *ABC* owns a single asset with an inside basis of $500,000 and fair market value of $200,000. Suppose further that *C* sells his 10-percent interest in the venture to *D* for its fair market value of $20,000. Because the partnership's inside basis of $500,000 exceeds its fair market value of $200,000 by more than $250,000, the partnership must make a §743(b) basis adjustment on the transfer. That adjustment presumably will equal $30,000 (one-10th of the built-in loss of $300,000, assuming there are no forward or reverse §704(c) layers in the property). Note that this mandatory basis adjustment is substantially less than $250,000. That is, the $250,000 threshold in §743(d) applies to the loss within the partnership and not to the basis adjustment that must be made with respect to the new partner.

2. *Exceptions to the mandatory negative adjustment.* There are two exceptions to the basic §743(b) rule mandating negative adjustments triggered by the transfer of an interest in a partnership having a "substantial built-in loss": neither an "electing investment partnership" nor a "securitization partnership" is subject to §743(d). See §743(e)(1), (f)(1). However, as to an "electing investment partnership," §743(e)(2) provides for the equivalent of a negative inside basis adjustment as to the transferee partner. An "electing investment partnership" is defined in §743(e)(6). A "securitization partnership" is defined in §743(f)(2).

PROBLEMS

27-4. Suppose on the facts of problem 27-1 that no distribution is made but instead *C* sells her partnership interest to *D* for its fair market value of $45,000.

a. What basis adjustments are appropriate under §743 and §755?
b. How does this affect the partnership's computation of depreciation from the building?
c. If the partnership then sells all of its assets, how much gain or loss does each partner report and what is each partner's capital account?

27-5. *P* and *Q* form the *PQ* partnership, with *P* contributing cash of $10,000 and *Q* contributing depreciable property having an adjusted basis of $6,000 and fair market value of $10,000. Assume that the property contributed by *Q* has five years remaining to its depreciable life and that it is depreciated using the straight-line method. Assume further that the partnership elects to use the traditional method to account for the variation between the book value and the adjusted basis of the property contributed by *Q*. In its first year, the partnership has no activity other than depreciation from the property contributed by *Q*. On the first day of the partnership's second taxable year, *Q* sells one-half of her partnership interest to *R* for $4,600 (assume that the property contributed by *Q* is now worth $8,400). Assuming that an election under §754 is made by the partnership, what is the amount of the basis adjustment under §743(b) triggered by the sale by *Q*?

27-6. Ignoring the possible application of §751(b),

a. using the facts of problem 27-4(a), what basis adjustments must be made if the partnership distributes receivable #1 to partner *A*?
b. using the facts of problem 27-4(a), what is *D*'s basis in receivable #2 if that receivable is distributed to *D* in complete liquidation of her partnership interest?

C. MECHANICS OF THE ELECTION

An election under §754 must be filed by the partnership (not by each partner separately), and it must be filed along with the partnership's tax return. Under some circumstances, a partnership is not required to file a partnership return. Nonetheless, if such a partnership wishes to file a §754 election, it must file a return and attach the §754 election to it.

Does it make sense for a partnership to file a §754 election? In general, basis adjustments under §734(b) are much less common than adjustments under §743(b), so the issue boils down to this: Who profits and who loses when a §743(b) basis adjustment is generated? Since most partners anticipate that the partnership will make rather than lose money, most partners anticipate eventually selling their interests at a gain. Recall that disposition of a partnership interest for more than the selling partner's outside basis results in a *positive* basis adjustment under §743(b).

A positive basis adjustment under §743(b) will benefit the purchaser of a partnership interest by allowing the purchaser to recognize less gain when the partnership sells its appreciated assets, albeit at the cost of additional gain (or less loss) upon a subsequent disposition of the partnership interest. Thus, the *nominal* beneficiary of the optional basis adjustment is a prospective purchaser of a partnership interest. Accordingly, the purchaser should be willing to pay more for an appreciated partnership interest if there is an election under §754 in effect, so that some of the value of the §754 election should be captured by the selling partner in the form of a higher sale price. Because the selling partner will profit from the election and the other partners seemingly are unaffected by it, one might think that §754 elections are commonplace and noncontroversial.

Nothing could be further from the truth. Because an adjustment under §743(b) affects only the purchasing partner, each transfer of a partnership interest forces the partnership to open a new set of books reflecting the inside basis of all partnership assets as adjusted under §743(b) and §755. Opening and maintaining a new set of books increases the partnership's accounting costs, accounting costs that will be borne for the indefinite future by every partner *other than* the selling partner. That is, the benefit of the §743(b) basis adjustment flows to one partner and its costs remain with the others. As you can imagine, the propriety of filing a §754 election can be controversial within a partnership.

In the case of a publicly held partnership, the costs associated with repeated sales of small partnership interests by hundreds or even thousands of partners far exceed the benefits of the optional basis adjustments, and so the partnership agreements for such partnerships invariably provide that no §754 election will be filed unless a statute or regulation (such as an SEC rule) requires. For smaller partnerships, the costs associated with a §754 election are lower, and so the election might be worth its costs. But these smaller partnerships should follow the teachings of their larger brethren in at least one respect: *The mechanism for determining whether a §754 election will be made should be spelled out in the partnership agreement.*

For example, the partnership agreement could provide that any partner holding more than 30 percent (or 50 percent, or 12 percent, or any other percentage) has an absolute right to insist that a §754 election be filed by the partnership. Conversely, the partnership agreement could provide that no election will be filed unless every partner agrees, or unless three-quarters of the partners agree. What is important is that the partners' rights to force or veto a prospective §754 election be defined in the partnership agreement well *before* a conflict arises. There are a variety of tax elections that a partnership must make, and a well-drafted partnership agreement should specify how these elections will be made or, alternatively, who will decide when the time arises.

NOTES

1. *The §743(b) notification requirement.* A partnership is unable to compute the amount of a basis adjustment under §743(b) without knowing the fair market value of the interest transferred. In general, this will be the price paid by the transferee partner. Under Treas. Regs. §1.743-1(k)(2)(i), the transferee is required to notify the partnership within 30 days of the transfer of the price paid for the partnership interest. Upon the death of a partner, the transferee has one year in which to notify the partnership of the transfer. Treas. Regs. §1.743-1(k)(2)(ii). Until the partnership learns of a transfer triggering an adjustment under §743(b), it is not required to make the inside basis adjustment. Treas. Regs. §1.743-1(k)(4). See also Treas. Regs. §1.743-1(k)(5) for the filing requirements imposed on a partnership when it discovers the transfer despite the absence of timely notice.

D. OPTIONAL BASIS ADJUSTMENTS AND CAPITAL ACCOUNTS

The regulations promulgated under §704(b) provide specific rules governing the effects of the basis adjustments on partners' capital accounts. Treas. Regs. §1.704-1(b)(2)(iv)(m). Despite the statutory similarity of the §734(b) and §743(b) basis adjustments, the capital account consequences of these two basis adjustments differ substantially. Under these rules, the optional basis adjustment under §734(b) triggered by the distribution of property produces capital account adjustments to all the partners while the §743(b) adjustment arising upon the taxable disposition of a partnership interest produces no capital account adjustment to the purchaser or to any other partner.

As we know, the basis adjustment under §734(b) affects the partnership's common basis in its assets; that is, the basis adjustment benefits all the partners in the partnership by reducing the gain (or increasing the loss) recognized by the partnership upon disposition of the adjusted property. Under the regulations, a §734(b) basis adjustment affects the partners' capital accounts precisely the same as the basis adjustment from the adjusted property is shared. Treas. Regs. §1.704-1(b)(2)(iv)(m)(4).

For example, suppose *A* has a 25-percent interest in the profits of the *AB* partnership while *B* owns the remaining 75-percent interest. If a distribution to one of the partners triggers an optional basis adjustment of $1,000 to some partnership asset, then *A* should receive a $250 capital account increase, and *B* should receive a $750 capital account increase. Note, however, that the capital account adjustment is made when the basis adjustment is made. Therefore, if the basis adjustment is suspended because the partnership does not own property that can absorb the basis adjustment, the capital account adjustment is likewise suspended en passant. Treas. Regs. §1.704-1(b)(2)(iv)(m)(5).

Surprisingly, the basis adjustment under §743(b) does not yield a similar rule. The regulations make clear that, in general, no capital account adjustment is allowed when partnership assets are adjusted under §743(b). Treas. Regs. §1.704-1(b)(2)(iv)(m)(2); see Treas. Regs. §1.704-1(b)(5) (example 13(iii)). Recall that the basis adjustment under §743(b) affects the purchasing partner only, so one might suspect that a §743(b) basis adjustment would produce a capital account adjustment for the incoming partner only. But that is not the case, and this rule can lead to some surprises.

For example, suppose *Z* purchases *Y*'s limited partnership interest in the *XY* limited partnership. Assume that *Y*'s capital account balance at the time of the sale was $10,000, and assume also that because partnership assets have appreciated, *Z* pays $15,000 for the partnership interest. Even if the partnership has a §754 election in effect at the time of the sale, *Z* takes *Y*'s capital account without an increase for the premium paid by *Z* to *Y*. As a consequence, unless *Z* can be required to make additional contributions to the partnership (which is uncommon for limited partners), *Z* cannot be allocated more than $10,000 of partnership deductions for the current year even though *Z* has sufficient basis to absorb up to $15,000 of losses.

E. BASIS ADJUSTMENTS UNDER §732(d)

Even if an election under §754 is not filed by a partnership, the distribution of property can trigger the equivalent of a §743(b) basis adjustment. If a partner acquires her partnership interest by purchase, taxable exchange, or devise and no §754 election is in effect at the time the partnership interest is acquired, then this partner may elect to have the equivalent of a §743(b) basis adjustment applied to any property distributed by the partnership to her within two years of the acquisition of her partnership interest. §732(d).

The effect of a §732(d) basis adjustment should be a basis swap between the distributed property and the distributee partner's outside basis. For example, consider the case of the *ABC* general partnership owning cash of $300 and property with an adjusted basis of $1,500 and fair market value of $2,100. Individuals *A*, *B*, and *C* are each one-third partners in *ABC*. Assume that partner *C* sells her partnership interest to *D* for its fair market value of $800 when an election under §754 is not in effect. At the time of the sale, *C*'s outside basis and capital account equal $600.

Because no §754 election is in effect when *D* purchases *C*'s partnership interest, this purchase has no effect on the partnership's inside basis. §743(a). If the partnership then distributes one-sixth of the property to *D* in a nonliquidating distribution (that is, one half of D's share of the property), *D* will recognize no gain or loss on the distribution and, absent a basis adjustment under §732(d), *D* will take a carryover basis in the distributed property of $250. §732(a)(1). *D*'s outside basis will decline from $800 to $550. §733(2).

If *D* elects to have an optional basis adjustment under §732(d), then we recompute the basis consequences of the distribution as if the distributed property had been subject to a basis adjustment under §743(b) when *D* purchased an interest in the partnership. Such a basis adjustment would have resulted in a $200 total basis increase in the property, benefiting only *D*. As a consequence, *D*'s basis in the distributed portion of the property is now $350, §732(a)(1), and *D*'s outside basis is reduced to $450, §733(1). As compared with the same transaction lacking a §732(d) basis adjustment, we see that the effect of the election is to shift $100 of basis from *D*'s partnership interest into the distributed property. Accordingly, a §732(d) basis adjustment can be a strategic tool with respect to property the partnership holds and intends to sell: Gain from the sale can be reduced by distributing to new partners their share of the property that they (rather than the partnership) will then sell.

This optional application of §732(d) has three requirements: (1) No §754 election was in effect when the distributee acquired her partnership interest; (2) property is distributed within two years of acquisition of the partnership interest; and (3) the distributee partner files an appropriate election. Under some circumstances, even if the distribution occurs more than two years following the distributee partner's acquisition of her partnership interest, the basis adjustment provided by §732(d) is mandatory. Under Treas. Regs. §1.732-1(d)(4), the basis adjustment under §732(d) is mandatory if (1) a partner acquires her partnership interest by purchase, taxable exchange, or devise when a §754 election is not in effect; (2) at the time of acquisition, the fair market value of all partnership property (excluding money) exceeds 110 percent of the partnership's adjusted basis in its property; (3) if the acquiring partner's interest in the partnership were liquidated immediately after the acquisition, the effect of the basis allocation rules in §732(c) would be to shift basis from nondepreciable property to depreciable property; and (4) the effect of applying §732(d) would be to avoid such a basis shift.

In general, the basis allocation rules of §732(c) prevent a distribution of property from shifting basis of capital assets (sometimes called "cold" assets) into the basis of ordinary income assets (often called "hot" assets). Such a basis shift is not permitted because Congress is unwilling to exchange taxation of ordinary income for taxation of capital gain. If depreciable capital assets are not quite "hot," they are also not quite "cold": Additional basis given to a depreciable capital asset likely will produce an increase in the distributee partner's depreciation deductions, deductions that will offset ordinary income. Thus, it might be fair to classify depreciable capital assets as "lukewarm": hotter than nondepreciable capital assets yet cooler than unrealized receivables and inventory. The mandatory operation of §732(d) was designed to ensure that a strategic failure to file a §754 election cannot be used to move basis from cold assets to lukewarm ones. See, e.g., Rudd v. Commissioner, 79 T.C. 225 (1982).

As part of the Taxpayer Relief Act of 1997, the basis allocation rules of §732(c) were modified. While these modifications responded to criticisms having little to do with §732(d), see generally William D. Andrews, Inside Basis Adjustments and Hot Asset Exchanges in Partnership Distributions, 47 Tax L. Rev. 3 (1991); Noël B. Cunningham, Needed Reform: Tending the Sick Rose, 47 Tax L. Rev. 77 (1991), one effect is to reduce substantially the circumstances triggering a mandatory application of §732(d).

28

Partnership-Level Issues

A. CLASSIFICATION AS A PARTNERSHIP

"Partnership" is a defined term; in fact, it is *twice* defined. Under §761(a), a partnership is any profit-seeking (i.e., business) organization other than a corporation, trust, or estate. A similar definition is provided in §7701(a)(2). Because each of these definitions define the term "partnership" by exclusion (that is, as everything *other than* corporations, trusts, and estates), it really is the definition of "corporation" in §7701(a)(3) that sets the contours of the partnership definition. Note, though, that §761(a) specifically limits partnerships to unincorporated entities: If an organization is incorporated under applicable state law, it cannot be taxed as a partnership. In addition, the statute plainly contemplates the existence of certain noncorporate "associations" taxable as corporations.

Not all organizations are *business* organizations. See Treas. Regs. §301.7701-2(a). A joint undertaking to share expenses (say, by a group of homeowners agreeing to care for common property) does not constitute a partnership under subchapter K. Treas. Regs. §301.7701-1(a)(2). In Madison Gas & Elec. Co. v. Commissioner, 72 T.C. 521 (1979), aff'd, 633 F.2d 512 (5th Cir. 1980), a group of power companies joined together to construct a nuclear power plant that would deliver power to the joint venturers for resale. At issue was the deductibility of various construction expenses: The power companies argued that these costs were ordinary and necessary expenses incurred in their existing business while the Service argued that they were nondeductible start-up costs of a newly formed partnership, see §195. The taxpayer argued that the arrangement among the power companies was no more than an agreement to share expenses without any profit-seeking motive, but the court held that the in-kind distribution of electricity constituted a sharing of economic profit sufficient to support partnership status.

As to those organizations that are undoubtedly business organizations, for several decades the regulations tried to distinguish entities taxable as partnerships from associations taxable as corporations by reference to certain supposed "corporate characteristics" such as continuity of life, centralization of management, limited liability, and free transferability of interests. Treas. Regs. §301.7701-2(a)(1) (repealed 1996). While these regulations were not by their terms elective, taxpayers usually could structure their unincorporated business organizations to be taxed as partnerships or as corporations as they preferred by manipulating relatively insignificant aspects of the organization.

In the late 1980s and early 1990s, most states enacted limited liability company statutes, thereby permitting businesses to have all the non-tax characteristics of corporations (including limited liability for all investors) while technically not being corporations. Thus, the organizer of a limited liability company files articles of organization and an operating agreement instead of articles of incorporation and corporate bylaws, investors contribute cash or property to the limited liability company and receive membership certificates instead of shares, and these investors are called "members" instead of "shareholders." Somewhat surprisingly, courts and the Service were willing to treat such corporate look-alikes as unincorporated entities, and so limited liability companies could then qualify for taxation as partnerships by manipulating their various "corporate characteristics."

As the efficacy of the old association regulations was declining, Congress enacted §7704 providing that publicly traded partnerships (including limited liability companies and similar business organizations otherwise taxable as partnerships) must be taxed as corporations if their interests are traded on an established securities market or for which there is a secondary market making the interests readily tradeable. These two factors—the increasing failure of the meaningless "corporate characteristics" in the association regulations and the more objective standard imposed by §7704—ultimately convinced the Treasury to repeal the old association regulations and replace them with an explicitly elective regime for distinguishing entities taxable as partnerships from associations taxable as corporations. However, because the statutory term "partnership" explicitly excludes all corporations, the regulations continue to provide that incorporated entities may not be taxed as partnerships. See Treas. Regs. §301.7701-2(b)(1).

1. *Elective Classification*

Under Treas. Regs. §301.7701-2(b)(1)-(8) (excluding (2)), a variety of business organizations are denied elective classification and must instead be taxed as corporations. These entities include all incorporated entities, heavily regulated entities such as insurance companies and banks, entities wholly owned by a state or municipality, and a variety of foreign business entities traditionally treated as corporations under domestic and foreign laws. All other business organizations are classified as "eligible" entities, see Treas. Regs. §301.7701-3(a), and a multiple-owner organization can elect to be taxed as a partnership or as a corporation, with the default rule generally favoring partnership treatment. See Treas. Regs. §301.7701-3(b)(1)(i). However, if an eligible entity has a single owner and elects not to be taxed as a corporation, the electing entity is ignored for tax purposes and so will be treated as a division if its owner is a corporation or a partnership or as a sole proprietorship if its owner is an individual.[1] Treas. Regs. §301.7701-3(b)(1)(ii). An eligible entity may change its tax classification at any time after its initial election, Treas. Regs. §301.7701-3(c)(1)(iv), but once a change is made, another change

1. See generally Howard E. Abrams & Fred T. Witt, Disregarded Entities, 704-2nd T.M. (Bloomberg/BNA 2012).

cannot be made for 60 months. *Id.* Thereafter, the entity need only file a new election if it is changing its status. Treas. Regs. §301.7701-3(c)(1)(i).

An entity with only one owner that is treated as a disregarded entity is disregarded for all substantive tax provisions although recognition of the entity under state law can be important for application of the federal tax laws. For example, if an individual owns a general partnership interest through a disregarded entity, the individual will be treated as having no liability for the debts of the entity absent a personal guaranty or a contribution of additional property to the disregarded entity that can be reached by creditors of the partnership. See Treas. Regs. §1.752-2(k).

Most foreign business organizations are not eligible entities. See Treas. Regs. §301.7701-2(b)(8). For example, a Naamloze Vennootschap (NV) formed in the Netherlands is always taxable as a corporation. Treas. Regs. §301.7701-2(b)(8)(i). If in response to our current elective classification regime the Netherlands creates a new form of business organization (say, an NNV) with all the attributes of an NV but with a new name, will such an entity be eligible for elective classification or will the Treasury amend its list of ineligible foreign entities? If we have truly moved to elective classification, then presumably foreign governments will be able to exploit elective classification by creating their own versions of limited liability companies.

NOTES

1. *Change in ownership structure: from disregarded entity to partnership.* An automatic classification change occurs when an entity's ownership changes in such a way that it no longer is eligible to retain its prior tax classification status. The most common way this can occur is for a single member entity classified as a disregarded entity to change to a multimember entity (and so become a partnership) or for a partnership to become a single member entity (and so become a disregarded entity.) Such an automatic classification change is not treated as an elective change, so the 60-month waiting period is not triggered or restarted. Treas. Regs. §301.7701-3(f)(3). Thus, if a disregarded entity is formed and subsequently becomes classified as a partnership because its owner transfers some but not all of the ownership interests in the entity, the partnership can elect to be classified as a corporation at any time because there has never been an elective classification change of the entity. Note that the transfer of the entire ownership of a disregarded entity from one owner to another does not change the classification status of the transferred disregarded entity. Rev. Rul. 2004-85 (situation 3), 2004-2 C.B. 189.

An eligible entity will be treated as a disregarded entity only if it is not taxed as a corporation and it has a single owner. If some but not all of the interests in such an entity are transferred to another person, the disregarded entity will become a regarded partnership. In Rev. Rul. 99-5, the Service considered the tax implications of automatic changes arising both from a transfer of a partial interest from the existing owner and of a transfer of interest directly from the entity in exchange for a contribution of property.

In Situation 1 of Rev. Rul. 99-5, 1991-1 C.B. 434, *B* purchases 50 percent of *A*'s ownership in a limited liability company when *A* is the sole owner of the entity and the entity has elected to be classified as a disregarded entity. Because the entity is disregarded for tax purposes until the transfer, the ruling concludes that the transaction should be recharacterized as (1) the sale from *A* to *B* of an undivided

50-percent interest in each of the entity's assets followed by (2) a joint contribution by *A* and *B* to a newly formed partnership entity.

For example, suppose *A* owns all 100 outstanding membership interests of the *DE* limited liability company, and that *DE* properly is disregarded for tax purposes. Suppose further that *DE* owns real estate with adjusted basis of $100 and fair market value of $500. If *A* sells 50 of the membership interests in *DE* to *B* for $250, this transaction will be treated as if *A* sold half the real estate to *B*, and then *A* and *B* each contributed their interest in the real estate to a newly formed partnership in a tax-free transaction described in §721. As a result, A recognizes gain of $200 on the deemed asset sale to *B*, *A* has an initial outside basis of $50, and *B* has an initial outside basis of $250. Consistent with this characterization, the partnership holds the real estate with an inside basis of $300. Note that the character of the gain recognized by *A* is determined by reference to *DE*'s assets in the hands of *A* because the transaction is treated as an asset transfer by *A*.

2. *Change in ownership structure: from partnership to disregarded entity.* If all but one of the partners of the *P* partnership sell their partnership interests to the remaining partner, the partnership will liquidate for tax purposes because it cannot continue with only a single partner. This transaction is treated as a sale of partnership interests for the selling partners but as an asset purchase for the purchasing partner. Rev. Rul. 99-6, 1999-1 C.B. 432. If *P* remains in existence under applicable local law, it will be treated as a disregarded entity owned by the purchasing partner.

For example, suppose *X*, *Y*, and *Z* are the three owners of the *P* partnership, and *X* and *Y* sell their partnership interests to *Z*. *X* and *Y* will treat the transaction as the sale of their partnership interests, implicating §§741 and 751(a) on the transaction. Treas. Regs. §1.741-1(b). It is the Service's position, though, that for *Z* the transaction will be taxed as if the partnership distributed its assets to the three partners, and then *Z* purchased the distributed assets from *X* and from *Y*. Rev. Rul. 99-6 (situation 1), 1999-1 C.B. 432; see also McCauslen v. Commissioner, 45 T.C. 588 (1966). If the form of the transaction were respected, *Z* would be treated as acquiring partnership interests from *X* and *Y* and the partnership would be deemed to liquidate, with *Z* tacking the partnership's holding periods in its assets and determining her basis in partnership assets under §732. But the Service's recharacterization prevents *Z* from tacking the partnership's holding period, a result otherwise mandated by application of §735(b). Note that this recharacterization should not implicate the anti-mixing bowl provisions of §§704(c)(1)(B) and 737 because the transaction is recharacterized as an asset sale only with respect to the purchaser.

Essentially the same recharacterization applies if all the partners sell their interests to a single buyer: (1) The selling partners are treated as selling their interests in the partnership, (2) the buyer is treated as purchasing assets, and (3) the entity is treated as liquidating (and so becomes a disregarded entity). Rev. Rul. 99-6 (situation 2), 1999-1 C.B. 432. If all of the partnership interests are contributed to a corporation, the partnership is treated as liquidating into the corporate transferee. Rev. Rul. 84-111, 1984-2 C.B. 88.

3. *Elective classification changes.* If an entity elects a change in tax classification, the tax consequences are determined under all relevant provisions of the Internal Revenue Code. Note that if the tax consequences of a classification change are undesirable, the entity can change its classification through a structural modification rather than by means of an election. So, for example, to go from an entity classified as a partnership to a corporation, a new corporation could be formed and

the partnership could transfer all of its assets to the new corporation in a transaction described in §351. Equivalently, the partners could transfer their partnership interests to a new or existing corporation. Such a structural modification could also be advantageous when an elective classification is not available because a change was made more recently than 60 months prior.

When an eligible entity having multiple owners elects to change its tax status from an association taxable as a corporation to a partnership, the change in tax status should be treated as a corporate liquidation followed by a partnership formation. The deemed liquidation should be treated as the equivalent of an actual liquidation for all tax purposes. For example, if the assets of the entity were used in a trade or business, then the liquidation will be treated as the sale of business assets for purposes of determining whether any gain recognized by the liquidating corporation on the liquidation constitutes subpart F income. Similarly, the deemed liquidation is a sufficiently "identifiable event" to support for its owners a worthless security deduction under §165(g)(3) if the entity is insolvent at the time of the classification change. Rev. Rul. 2003-125, 2003-2 C.B. 1243.

4. *Entity owned by husband and wife.* If an eligible entity is owned solely by a husband and wife in a jurisdiction that classifies ownership of the entity as community property, the owners may elect to treat the entity as a partnership with two owners or as a disregarded entity with a single owner (assuming no election is made to treat the entity as a corporation). Surprisingly, the ability to treat the entity as disregarded is not conditioned on the husband and wife filing a joint return. A change in reporting position is treated as a conversion of the entity. Rev. Proc. 2002-69, 2002-2 C.B. 831.

PROBLEMS

28-1. LLC-1 is a disregarded entity owned by *X* Corp. LLC-1 owns LLC-2 and LLC-3, two disregarded entities. LLC-2 and LLC-3 form *P*, a partnership under relevant state law. Can *P* be classified as a partnership for tax purposes?

28-2. Individual *X* owns LLC-*B*, a disregarded entity whose only asset is real estate (Blackacre). Individuals *Y* and *Z* each own half of LLC-*W*, a partnership whose only asset is real estate (Whiteacre). *X* transfers half of the ownership of LLC-*B* to *Y* and half to *Z* in exchange for all of the ownership interests of LLC-*W*. Assuming Blackacre and Whiteacre are like-kind within the meaning of §1031, what are the tax consequences of this exchange of ownership interests in the two limited liability companies.

2. *Publicly Traded Partnerships*

In §7704(a), Congress has provided that certain publicly traded partnerships will be taxed as corporations. For this purpose, a "publicly traded partnership" is one whose partnership interests (1) are traded on an established securities market or (2) are readily traded on a secondary market. §7704(b). This provision was enacted as part of the Revenue Act of 1987 in response to the growth of "master limited partnerships," huge entities having thousands of partners and assets worth tens (or hundreds) of millions of dollars.

Note, though, that if a partnership's income in a taxable year consists of 90 percent or more of investment income as defined in §7704(d), the partnership will avoid the clutches of §7704(a) for that year. The legislative history of this provision explains that no corporate-level tax need be imposed because a corporate-level tax was imposed on the underlying income-producing investment. The definition of "qualifying income" in §7704(d), however, imposes no requirement that the passive-type income come from a corporate taxpayer. In recent years, the government has adopted a very broad view of what constitutes qualifying income under §7704(d). See, e.g., Priv. Ltr. Rul. 200845035 (Nov. 7, 2008) (transportation and storage of natural gas); Priv. Ltr. Rul. 200909006 (Feb. 27, 2009) (acquiring and licensing land and marine seismic data).

3. Recognizing Partner Status

a. General Principles

In Commissioner v. Culbertson, 337 U.S. 733 (1949), the Supreme Court held that a partnership consists of two or more persons who have proprietary interests in the profits of their joint venture. An agreement to divide profits is strong evidence that an arrangement is a partnership and that the parties are partners. On the other hand, one whose compensation from the organization is fixed in amount or otherwise independent of the success of the venture (e.g., one whose compensation is based on net receipts) is likely to be treated as an employee or independent contractor.

Whether someone is recognized for tax purposes as a partner turns on the application of federal law, although a court might conclude that in this area federal law should be informed by state law definitions of partnership status. Yet the Service has on occasion ignored state definitions to take an expansive view of partnership status. In Rev. Rul. 77-137, 1977-1 C.B. 178, the Service ruled that an assignee of a partnership interest will be taxed as a partner if she acquires substantially all dominion and control over a limited partnership interest even if the assignee fails to satisfy conditions imposed by the partnership agreement. And in Rev. Rul. 77-332, 1977-2 C.B. 484, the Service ruled that non-CPA members of a CPA firm with the rights and liabilities of partners must be taxed as partners despite local law prohibiting them from being partners because they were not CPAs.

b. Family Partnerships

As you know, the existence of progressive tax rates encourages taxpayers to structure their affairs so that taxable income is reported by low-bracket taxpayers. In Lucas v. Earl, 281 U.S. 111 (1930), the Supreme Court held that earned income is taxable to the income earner without regard to contractual assignments of the right to receive the income. On the other hand, in Blair v. Commissioner, 300 U.S. 5 (1937), the Court held that the incidence of taxation on income from property can be shifted by an assignment of the property (but not by assignment of only the income from the property) from one taxpayer to another.

You can imagine that a partnership might offer substantial assignment of income opportunities to an aggressive taxpayer. For example, a highly compensated professional might form a partnership with her child, with the child contributing little of value in exchange for a substantial partnership share. The parent could then enter into an employer/employee relationship with the partnership, and the partnership will report as its net income the excess of what it receives for the parent's services from third parties over what it pays the parent as salary. Accordingly, if the salary paid to the parent is small, the partnership will have large earnings. These earnings will then be passed through to the partners in accordance with their distributive shares, allowing the child to report (at low tax rates) what amounts to some of the parent's income. An extreme example of taxpayer initiative is Tinkoff v. Commissioner, 120 F.2d 564 (7th Cir. 1941), where an accountant took his son into his accounting firm on the day the son was born.

Congress has in §704(e) attempted to address the assignment of income possibilities consistent with the two-pronged assignment of income doctrine articulated in *Earl* and *Blair.* Under §704(e)(1), the donee of a partnership interest will be recognized as the true owner *if* capital is a material income-producing factor in the partnership. If capital is *not* a material income-producing factor in the partnership, then presumably the partnership's income is attributable to the labor of its partners, and the incidence of taxation on income from labor cannot be shifted under *Earl.* On the other hand, if capital *is* a material income-producing factor, the *Blair* prong of the assignment of income doctrine militates in favor of recognizing the donee as a partner for tax purposes.

Consider, though, the case of a partnership in which both labor and capital are material income-producing factors. If one partner received her partnership interest as a gift from another partner, there remains the possibility of an impermissible assignment of earned income if the donor partner receives an inadequate salary. To combat this possibility, §704(e)(2) provides that the donee partner will be treated as the true owner of her interest only if the donor partner received reasonable compensation for services rendered to the partnership.

In addition, §704(e)(2) speaks to attempted assignments of income lacking a full transfer of the underlying income-producing property. For example, suppose the donor partner transfers one-10th of the partnership's capital to the donee partner but the partnership agreement allocates one-half of all partnership income to the donee. While such an allocation should pass the substantial economic effect test of §704(b), it fails to satisfy the *Blair* prong of the assignment of income doctrine that taxation of income from property income can be shifted only by a transfer of the income-producing property. See, e.g., Helvering v. Horst, 311 U.S. 112 (1940). In this example, the donor has transferred one-10th of the property yet seeks to shift one-half of the taxation.

Under §704(e)(2), special allocations of income to a donee partner are invalid to the extent they allocate disproportionately more income to the donee partner than to the donor partner, as measured by relative capital shares. Note that for this section as well as for §704(e)(1), a donee partner includes any partner who acquires a partnership interest from a family member (as defined in the final sentence of §704(e)(3)) even if the acquisition was fully paid. For purposes of §704(e), in other words, even sales of partnership interests between family members are considered gifts.

In Carriage Square, Inc. v. Commissioner, 69 T.C. 119 (1977), Arthur Condiotti was the president and controlling shareholder of Carriage Square, Inc. That corporation and several trusts each benefiting an immediate member of Condiotti's family formed a limited partnership, and at issue was the extent to which the interests of the trusts in the partnership should be respected for tax purposes. The partnership engaged in the business of developing real estate, and each partner made a minor capital contribution to the venture. In fact, substantially all of the funds used in the enterprise came as borrowed funds from a third-party lender, and Condiotti guaranteed repayment of the loans to permit the partnership to obtain favorable interest rates.

In a reviewed opinion, the Tax Court held that the trusts' interests in the partnership had to be ignored despite §704(e)(1) because capital was not a "material income producing factor" in the partnership within the meaning of §704(e)(1). While it seems plain that all of the partnership's profits came from capital and not from labor, the court held that for purposes of §704(e)(1), only capital contributed by the partners can be considered, relying on language in Treas. Regs. §1.704-1(e)(1)(i).

The majority opinion held that capital was not a material income-producing factor in the partnership's business because the business assets were purchased with borrowed capital. Yet §704(e)(1) limits its application to partnerships in which capital is a material income-producing factor to preserve the *Earl* prong of the assignment of income doctrine, namely that the incidence of taxation on income from labor cannot be shifted. Certainly it cannot be said that the partnership's business was primarily a service business; after all, the partnership was in the business of developing real estate. Dissenting in part and concurring in part, Judge Tannenwald observed that the regulations under §704(e) emphasize the function capital serves for the partnership, not the source from which it is obtained.

How can a business lacking any significant capital investment turn a profit? In *Carriage Square*, the partnership entered into a risky enterprise, with the prospect of high returns compensating for the significant risk of partial or even total loss. The activity was funded by a commercial bank that accepted a more certain and more limited return on its investment. What allowed the partnership to make a profit in this case was the willingness of Carriage Square, Inc., as general partner (and of the sole shareholder of the general partner in the capacity as guarantor) to accept a risk of loss in exchange for the possibility of gain.

What motivated the bank to fund the partnership's activity was its substantial certainty of repayment, a certainty based upon the capital of the partnership's general partner as well as that of Condiotti, its sole shareholder (in his capacity as guarantor). Judge Tannenwald imputed Condiotti's capital to his corporation and then relied on §704(e)(2) and its emphasis on the relative partnership capital of donor and donee to allocate most of the income to Carriage Square, Inc. But should Candiotti's capital be imputed to his corporation?

If the motivation for the guarantee was to benefit Condiotti by increasing his corporation's net worth, then imputation of Condiotti's capital to the corporation should be appropriate. But recall the circumstances of the partnership's formation: The sole general partner was a corporation controlled by Condiotti, and each of the limited partners was a trust created for the benefit of Condiotti or one of his near relatives. In guaranteeing the partnership's debt, Condiotti presumably was intending to benefit himself and his loved ones. The intended beneficiary of the guarantee most likely was Condiotti's family rather than his corporation. If so, who should have won the case?

Under the unearned income prong of the assignment of income doctrine, the incidence of taxation on income from capital can be shifted only by a transfer of the underlying capital; a mere assignment of the income unaccompanied by the capital will not suffice. Helvering v. Horst, 311 U.S. 112 (1940). By guaranteeing the partnership's debt, Condiotti sought to generate income for the trusts without an actual transfer of significant capital. This attempt should fail, not because of §704(e) but because of the more general assignment of income doctrine. To the extent the partnership's income was generated by its ability to borrow at an interest rate lower than it could have obtained without the guarantee, the income should be taxable to Condiotti as guarantor. However, the courts to date have been unable to articulate a consistent approach to the taxation of gratuitous guarantees, both for the income tax and for the transfer (gift, estate, and generation-skipping) taxes. *Carriage Square* was one more opportunity forgone.

PROBLEM

28-3. *X* and *Y* form the *XY* general partnership, with *X* contributing cash of $100,000 and *Y* contributing unimproved real estate with adjusted basis of $20,000 and fair market value of $100,000. *X* and *Y* agree to be equal partners. One year after *XY* is formed, the partnership distributes $100,000 to *Y*. Assume that this distribution is treated as a disguised sale under §707(a)(2)(B). Is there a partnership? When was it formed?

B. PARTNERSHIP ELECTIONS

Any taxpayer can be faced with a variety of elections: taxable year, methods of accounting (including installment method treatment), and depreciation methods for depreciable assets, just to name a few. A partnership is faced with these same elections as well as some special ones such as the optional basis election under §754. Specifying who has the authority to make these elections is an important part of any partnership agreement.

1. *Taxable Year*

Under §706, a partnership's taxable year is determined by reference to the taxable years of its partners. To understand why this is important, we must recall how and when partnership income is includible on each partner's individual tax return.

Under §706(a), a partner's distributive share of partnership income and deduction is includible "for any taxable year of the partnership ending within or with the taxable year of the partner." In effect, this means that the partner's distributive share is recognized by the partner on the last day of the *partnership's* taxable year.

For example, consider the case of a partnership using a fiscal year ending January 31 of each year and an individual partner using the calendar year as her taxable year.

Each January 31, the partner includes her distributive share of the partnership's income for the prior 12 months. In particular, on January 31, 2013, she includes her share of the partnership's activities from February 1, 2012, through January 31, 2013. Because this partner uses the calendar year as her taxable year, her tax return for 2013 will be due on April 15, 2014. Although 11/12ths of the partnership's activity was conducted in 2012, the partner will owe no tax on it until April 2014, producing deferral up to 26 ½ months (from February of 2012 until April 15, 2014). Outside of the partnership context, maximum deferral should be no more than 15½ months (from January of one year until April 15 of the following year). The mismatch of partner and partnership taxable years, in other words, produced added deferral of 11 months.

Now suppose that the partnership's taxable year ended November 30 instead of January 31. Now, the partner's individual return for 2013 (due April 15, 2014) will include her distributive share for the partnership's activities from December 1, 2012, through November 30, 2013. Maximum deferral is reduced to 16½ months, only one month more than that available to all taxpayers under our system of annual accounting. If the partnership's taxable year had coincided with the partner's taxable year, there would be no additional deferral.

The rules of §706(b) seek to minimize the deferral by limiting the mismatch between the partnership's taxable year and that of its partners. Section 706(b) creates three rules for determining a partnership's taxable year. Under rule 1, if any group of partners having a combined interest in partnership capital and profits exceeding 50 percent share a common taxable year, then the partnership must adopt that common taxable year (called the "majority interest taxable year" in §706(b)(1)(B)(i)) as its taxable year.

If no group satisfies this test, then under rule 2 the partnership must adopt the taxable year shared by its "principal" partners, if they in fact share a common taxable year. §706(b)(1)(B)(ii). For this purpose, a "principal" partner is any partner owning 5 percent or more of partnership capital or profits. §706(b)(3). If the principal partners do not share a common taxable year (or if there are no principal partners), then under rule 3 the partnership must adopt the calendar year as its taxable year or another taxable year prescribed by regulations. §706(b)(1)(B)(iii). Regulations now require partnerships whose taxable years are not determined under rules 1 and 2 to adopt that taxable year that results in the least aggregate deferral of income to the partners, Treas. Regs. §1.706-1(b)(2)(C), taking into account each partner's particular taxable year and the partners' relative interests in the partnership, Treas. Regs. §1.706-1(b)(3).

Consider the following example. The *P* partnership is formed by *X* corporation and 90 calendar year individuals. *X* corporation has a 10-percent interest in the capital and profits of *P* and uses a fiscal year ending March 31 as its taxable year. Each individual owns 1 percent of *P*'s capital and profits and uses the calendar year as her taxable year. The partnership must adopt the calendar year as its taxable year under rule 1: Any 51 of the individual partners hold more than 50 percent of the partnership's capital and profits, and they share the calendar year as their taxable year. Under §706(b)(1)(B)(i), the partnership must adopt that common year as its taxable year.

Suppose, however, that the 1-percent interests were held by 90 separate corporations all using different fiscal years as their taxable years. *P* would now be required to use *X*'s fiscal year as its taxable year because there is no "majority interest taxable year" under rule 1, and *X* is the only "principal" partner for purposes of rule 2. And if *X*'s interest amounted to only 4 percent of the partnership (with six additional 1-percent owners), the partnership would be required to follow the regulations in determining its taxable year under rule 3.

There are two exceptions to these rules. A partnership may adopt any taxable year without regard to the rules of §706(b)(1) *if* it can convince the government that it has an adequate business purpose for its selection. §706(b)(1)(C). Also, a partnership may adopt a taxable year beginning up to three months *earlier* than the required taxable year as determined under the rules of §706(b) (i.e., one producing up to three months deferral) simply by electing to do so under §444. However, any partnership electing to take advantage of §444 is required to pre-pay to the Treasury the value of the deferral so obtained. See §7519.

PROBLEMS

28-4. Consider the following situations:

a. Corporations *X* and *Y* form a general partnership, with *X* and *Y* each having a 50-percent interest in partnership capital, profits, and losses of the venture. *X* uses a fiscal year ending January 31, and *Y* uses a fiscal year ending June 31. What taxable year must the partnership adopt?
b. If *Z* subsequently joins the partnership as a 20-percent partner (reducing *X*'s and *Y*'s shares to 40 percent each), what taxable year must the partnership use, assuming *Z* is a calendar year taxpayer?

28-5. Consider the following situations:

a. Using the facts of problem 28-4(b) above, suppose *X* and *Z* form the *XZ* partnership, with *X* owning two-thirds and *Z* owning one-third of the partnership. *XZ* and *Y* then form the *XYZ* partnership, with *XZ* owning 60 percent of this lower-tier partnership and *Y* owning the remaining 40 percent. What is the taxable year of the *XYZ* partnership?
b. How does your answer change if *Y* and *Z* form the *YZ* partnership (with *Y* owning two-thirds and *Z* owning one-third), and then *YZ* joins with *X* to form the *XYZ* lower-tier partnership, with *YZ* owning 60 percent and *X* owning 40 percent of *XYZ*?

2. *Method of Accounting*

A partnership, like any taxpayer, must adopt a method of accounting. Under §446(a), a taxpayer's method of accounting for tax purposes must be kept using the same method used for financial purposes. Under §446(b), a taxpayer's method of accounting must clearly reflect the taxpayer's income. Subject to these two limitations, a taxpayer generally is free to use the cash receipts and disbursements method of accounting, an accrual method of accounting, or any other method allowed by regulations. §446(c). In addition, a taxpayer having two or more businesses may use separate methods of accounting for each business. §446(d).

Most businesses use an accrual method of accounting. The cash method is unavailable to most corporations and to most partnerships having a corporate taxpayer, see §448(a), and any business involved in the production, purchase, or sale of merchandise must use an inventory method of accounting. See Treas. Regs. §1.446-1(a)(4)(i).

Under §179, each taxpayer may elect to expense the cost of its newly acquired tangible business property in lieu of depreciation, up to a certain dollar amount and subject to certain income limitations, see §179(b)(2), (3), both of which Congress changes regularly. While it is the partnership that makes the §179 election, §703(b), the dollar limitation applies at both the partnership *and* the partner level. §179(d)(8); Treas. Regs. §1.179-1(f)(2). For example, if the maximum amount allowable under §179 is $500,000, then a partnership may file a §179 election with respect to no more than $500,000 of partnership property without regard to the number of partners in the partnership and no partner may claim more than $500,000 of deduction under §179 including any distributive share of the partnership's §179 deduction.

C. SPECIAL ISSUES

1. *The Anti-Abuse Rules*

Various provisions in subchapter K respond to congressionally perceived abuses of the more structural aspects of partnership taxation. For example, the possibility that contributions and distributions can be used to achieve inappropriate deferral led to enactment of the disguised sale provision in §707(a)(2)(B) as well as the anti-mixing bowl provisions of §§704(c)(1)(B) and 737. Similarly, that allocations of gross income might be used to convert capital expenses into the equivalent of deductible expenditures led to §707(a)(2)(A). In contrast to these targeted anti-abuse provisions enacted by Congress, the Department of Treasury has promulgated two broad anti-abuse rules under §701 that potentially apply to *all* partnership transactions. While these rules seek to prevent taxpayers from using the partnership form to reduce income taxes, the rules explicitly have no relevance to partnerships used to minimize the estate, gift, or generation-skipping taxes. Treas. Regs. §1.701-2(i).

a. The General Anti-Abuse Rule

Under the general anti-abuse rule of Treas. Regs. §1.701-2(b), any inappropriate use of the rules of partnership taxation can lead to the following remedies: (1) The partnership will not be treated as a separate entity; (2) one or more of the partners will not be treated as a partner; (3) the method of accounting used by the partnership will be adjusted to more clearly reflect income; (4) partnership-level items of income, gain, loss, deduction, or credit will be reallocated; and (5) the claimed tax treatment will be adjusted or modified. In this context, inappropriate use of the rules of partnership taxation means that "a partnership is formed or availed of in connection with a transaction a principal purpose of which is to reduce substantially the present value of the partners' aggregate federal tax liability in a manner that is inconsistent with the intent of subchapter K, in light of the applicable statutory and regulatory provisions and the pertinent facts and circumstances." Treas. Regs. §1.701-2(b).

This regulation is troublesome because of its reference to the "intent of subchapter K." A definition of the intent of subchapter K is provided in Treas. Regs. §1.701-2(a). According to this regulation, the purpose of subchapter K is to allow "taxpayers to conduct joint business activities through a flexible economic arrangement without incurring an entity-level tax." However, the regulation further provides that three requirements are encompassed within this definition: (1) A partnership must be bona fide, and all transactions must have a substantial business purpose; (2) the form of transactions must be respected under substance over form principles; and (3) tax consequences under subchapter K must be an accurate reflection of economic reality unless a contrary result is clearly contemplated by the provision being utilized.

Suppose a transaction complies with all the requirements of subchapter K yet produces significant tax advantages to the participants. For example, suppose appreciated property is contributed to a partnership and then distributed to some other partner more than seven years after the contribution. Such a distribution does not trigger income to the contributing partner under §704(c)(1)(B) because that provision has only a seven-year reach. In such circumstances, can the Service invoke the general anti-abuse rule, effectively extending application of §704(c)(1)(B)?

Or consider the following: A partnership is formed and the partners deliberately do not file an election under §754, thereby eschewing the optional basis adjustments of §§734(b) and 743(b). Because these optional basis adjustments are not made, aggregate inside basis eventually exceeds aggregate outside basis, thereby permitting the partners to enjoy some deferral of income until they exit the partnership. Can the Service invoke the general anti-abuse rule to treat the partners as if a §754 election had been filed, even though such an election is expressly optional? Surprisingly, the Treasury believes that such administrative discretion is allowable. See Treas. Regs. §1.701-2(d) (example 8).

Application of the general anti-abuse rule has two threshold requirements: (1) a principal purpose of reducing tax liability (2) in a manner inconsistent with the intent of subchapter K. The first requirement may be the most troubling aspect of the general anti-abuse provision because it appears to require that the subjective intentions of the partners' entering into a questionable transaction be carefully examined. If a transaction is otherwise unchallengeable, why should the motives of the taxpayer affect the tax consequences? Conversely, if a transaction is otherwise questionable, can a taxpayer avoid application of the general anti-abuse rule by proving that her motives were pure?

In the example in the regulations involving the alleged improper failure to make an optional basis adjustment, the regulations provide: "On these facts, any purported business purpose for the transaction is insignificant in comparison to the tax benefits that would result if the transaction were respected for federal tax purposes." Treas. Regs. §1.701-2(d) (example 8). This example suggests that taxpayer motivation is a one-way street: Improper motive may condemn an otherwise legitimate transaction but pure motives cannot save an overly beneficial one.

The New York State Bar Association, in a report on the general anti-abuse regulation prior to its final adoption, stated its opinion that the regulations should make clear that the general anti-abuse rule does not apply to transactions that have passed muster under more specific anti-abuse rules found in subchapter K. New York State Bar Association Tax Section, *Report on the Proposed Partnership Antiabuse Rule,* TAX NOTES TODAY, July 11, 1994, at 233-252. For example, if a transaction is not characterized as a disguised sale under §707(a)(2)(B) (say, because there was more than two years between the transfers), it should not be recharacterized under the general anti-abuse rule in Treas. Regs. §1.701-2(b). That is, if Treas. Regs. §1.707-3(d) provides for a presumption that a transfer made after more than two years is not a sale, should not a taxpayer be entitled to that presumption? Unfortunately, no such statement was included in the final regulations.

PROBLEM

28-6. *X* Corp., a publicly traded corporation, would like to obtain the assets of individual *A* in a tax-free manner, but a direct transfer of assets to *A* would not be tax free because (i) *A* will not be "in control" of *X* Corp. immediately after the transaction, and (ii) the assets that will be transferred by *A* are encumbered by liabilities in excess of adjusted basis. Accordingly, *X* Corp. and *A* form the *XA* partnership, with *X* Corp, contributing some of its assets and *A* contributing *A*'s assets. Under the terms of the partnership agreement, all items of income, gain, loss, and deduction will be allocated between *X* and *A* in proportion to contributed capital. *A* has the right at any time to convert some or all of *A*'s partnership interest into stock of *X* Corp. Will the partnership be recognized for federal income tax purposes? Will it be recharacterized as a corporation?

b. The Abuse of Entity Rule

Treasury Regulations §1.701-2(e) provides a separate "abuse of entity" rule. This rule provides that "[t]he Commissioner can treat a partnership as an aggregate of its partners in whole or in part as appropriate to carry out the purpose of any provision of the Internal Revenue Code or the regulations promulgated thereunder." However, this rule exempts provisions that clearly contemplate entity treatment of a partnership, as long as the tax results of the transaction are explicitly contemplated by the provision in question.

The abuse of entity rule seems to be directed at little more than one type of violation of the more general anti-abuse rule, albeit without imposing on the Service any obligation to find that a principal purpose of the transaction was tax avoidance. For example, suppose two corporations are engaged in legitimate business activities through a partnership. The partnership issues a certain type of high-yield discount obligations to a third party. Section 163(e)(5) limits the interest deductions that a corporation may take on this type of obligation. In this circumstance, the regulations provide that the partnership must be treated as an aggregate of its partners to give effect to §163(e)(5). Treas. Regs. §1.701-2(d) (example 1). Compare this supposedly abusive use of the partnership form with a partnership formed by an S corporation and a nonresident alien (who could not own stock in the S corporation directly without terminating the corporation's subchapter S status). Here, the regulations provide that no abuse exists. Treas. Regs. §1.701-2(d) (example 2).

2. *Treatment of Organization and Syndication Expenses*

A partnership often is formed by an individual as a device to raise needed capital. For example, *D* may own unimproved real estate that could be improved by constructing apartments or an office building. To raise the needed capital, *D* proposes to form a partnership with *D* as the sole general partner and 35 limited partners. *D* will contribute the real estate in exchange for her general partnership interest and each limited partner will be required to contribute cash of $30,000. If the development needs an equity investment of about $1,000,000, this partnership will provide adequate funding if and only if all the limited partnership interests can be sold.

D will have a lawyer draft the proposed partnership agreement as well as documents explaining the venture to prospective investors. These documents are usually referred to as the prospectus or offering statement for the investment. Depending on the anticipated financial sophistication and number of prospective investors, these documents might have to be filed with federal or state regulators.

D will then try to sell the project to various investors. Because the project cannot succeed unless all limited partnership interests are purchased, the partnership agreement will include a provision specifying that capital contributions of limited partners will be placed in a special escrow account. If all limited interests have been sold by a specified date, the escrowed funds will be distributed to the partnership and the activity will begin. If some interests remain unsold, the escrowed accounts will be returned to the investors and the partnership will never form.

The process of selling interests to investors is called syndication, and it can be an expensive process. Lawyer's fees will be incurred in drafting the prospectus, and most likely accountant's fees will arise as well. The promoter of the investment might be entitled to reimbursement of some filing fees, registration fees, and even selling costs, all depending on the terms of the partnership agreement.

Under §709(a), a partnership is forbidden from deducting organization and syndication expenses. However, if an election is made by the partnership under §709(b)(1), up to $5,000 of organization (but not syndication) expenses can be deducted, with any remaining organization expenses deducted ratable over the next 180 months. For application of §709(b)(1), "organization expenses" are defined in §709(b)(3).

Syndication expenses cannot be deducted by reason of §709(a) and cannot be amortized under §709(b); syndication expenses, in other words, will never be recovered at the entity level. While these nonamortizable syndication costs are treated as capital expenditures for accounting purposes, for proper maintenance of capital accounts the regulations surprisingly treat syndication costs as nondeductible, noncapitalizable expenses under §705(a)(2)(B) so that syndication costs must reduce the partners' capital accounts (but not outside bases) when incurred. Treas. Regs. §1.704-1(b)(2)(iv)(i)(2).

PROBLEM

28-7. *R*, an individual, owns unimproved real estate worth $100,000. In order to develop this property, *R* forms *R* Group, a limited partnership comprised of *R* and 10 investors. *R* spends $10,000 on legal and accounting fees developing the *R* Group offering circular; $5,000 in legal fees to ensure that the *R* Group is properly formed and registered with the state; $1,000 in transfer fees to transfer title to the property from *R* to the partnership; and $2,500 in miscellaneous expenses such as the cost of opening the partnership checking account and purchasing liability insurance for the partnership's officers. The partnership reimburses *R* for these costs. What are the tax consequences to *R* and to the partnership of the payment by *R* of these expenses and of *R*'s reimbursement?

3. Cancellation of Indebtedness Income and §108

If a partnership acquires its outstanding debt for less than the debt's principal amount, the partnership will realize cancellation of indebtedness income just as any other taxpayer would in the same circumstances. See §108(e)(8). Such income is subject to the relief provisions in §108, but that section has a peculiar application to partners and partnerships. Although income resulting from a discharge of a partnership debt is partnership-level income, §108(d)(6) specifically provides that the basic relief provisions of §§108 (i.e., 108(a), (b), and (g)) apply only at the partner level.

Section 108(a) allows a taxpayer to exclude cancellation of indebtedness (COI) income if the taxpayer is involved in a bankruptcy proceeding, §108(a)(1)(a), or, even in the absence of a formal bankruptcy proceeding, to the extent that the taxpayer is insolvent, §§108(a)(1)(B), 108(a)(3). Because these sections apply only at the partner level, §108(d)(6), partnership COI income is includible in each partner's distributive share without regard to partnership bankruptcy or insolvency. The exclusion provided by §108(a) can apply to such income, but only to the extent that an individual partner is involved in a bankruptcy proceeding or is insolvent. In short, partnership COI income is includible to the partnership without regard to the possible application of §108.

Because only §108(a), (b), and (g) are explicitly made applicable at the partner level, an implication arises that the other parts of §108 are applicable at the entity level. In particular, it seems that application of §108(e)(5) is limited to the entity level. And that can cause a problem.

Section 108(e)(5) codifies the purchase-price reduction exception to the *Kirby Lumber* rules: No COI income results from the mere reduction in price (paid over time) of property purchased by the taxpayer. Because of the limited scope of §108(d)(6), this provision applies when the *partnership* enjoys a price reduction on property it purchased. That makes sense: if the partnership purchases property and the price is then reduced, there should be no COI income to the partnership or to any partner. Thus, limiting application of §108(e)(5) to the entity level seems to work.

However, by its terms the purchase-price reduction exception in §108(e)(5) is limited to cases *other than* when the purchaser is in bankruptcy or is insolvent. This limitation seems to be no more than an ordering rule: If the taxpayer is bankrupt, exclusion under §108(a) will be available even in a purchase-price reduction situation, while if the taxpayer is solvent, exclusion under §108(e)(5) still obtains. Consider, though, the case of a partnership that is insolvent while its partners are financially sound. For example, suppose the *X* partnership was formed to operate an apartment complex, and *X* is owned by doctors, lawyers, and other professionals. If real estate prices fall, the partnership's property might fall in value to less than the amount of its outstanding mortgage on the property. If so, the partnership is insolvent.

Now consider the tax consequences if the seller of the property, holding the mortgage on the partnership's property, agrees outside of a bankruptcy proceeding to reduce the outstanding debt down to the current value of the property. Such an extra-judicial debt reorganization often is called a nonbankruptcy "workout."

Reduction of the debt triggers COI income to the partnership. Can this COI income be excluded under §108? For any other taxpayer, the answer is clearly yes. But for the partnership and its partners, a technical reading of §108 gives a surprising no.

To see this, note first that §108(a) cannot apply here because its application is limited to bankrupt and insolvent taxpayers and, because it applies only at the partner level, the various partners rather than the partnership would have to be in financial difficulty. Does §108(e)(5) exclude the COI income? It cannot apply at the partnership level because by its terms it only applies when the debt reduction occurs *other than* in connection with a Title 11 bankruptcy case or insolvency of *the purchaser*. Since the purchaser (that is, the partnership) is insolvent, §108(e)(5) should not apply.

Can §108(e)(5) apply to protect each individual partner? Presumably not, because it seems to be the case that §108(e)(5) applies only at the entity level. Recall that §108(d)(6) specifies which parts of §108 apply at the partner level, and §108(e)(5) is not in that list. Thus, there seems to be no exclusion of COI income resulting from a price reduction of partnership property when the partnership itself is involved in a bankruptcy proceeding or is insolvent. There is no indication that Congress intended this result, but the statute apparently demands it. Fortunately, the Service has ruled that in such circumstances each partner may apply §108(e)(5) at the partner level despite the lack of statutory support for its application. Rev. Proc. 92-92, 1992-2 C.B. 505. No statutory authority for this largesse is given.

Table of Cases

Italics indicate principal cases.

Table of Revenue Rulings and Procedures and Other Miscellaneous IRS Pronouncements

Principal rulings are in italics.

Revenue Rulings

Private Letter Rulings

Index

SUSTAINABLE FORESTRY INITIATIVE
Certified Sourcing
www.sfiprogram.org
SFI-01234
SFI label applies to the text stock